Fodor's

THE COMPLETE GUIDE TO EUROPEAN CRUISES

1ST EDITION

A Cruise Lover's Guide to Selecting the Right Trip, with All the Best Ports of Call

Fodor's Travel Publications   New York, Toronto, London, Sydney, Auckland
www.fodors.com

FODOR'S THE COMPLETE GUIDE TO EUROPEAN CRUISES

Editors: Douglas Stallings, Vincent Penge

Editorial Production: Evangelos Vasilakis
Editorial Contributors: Linda Coffman, Lindsay Bennett, Ralph Grizzle
Maps & Illustrations: David Lindroth, *cartographer*; Bob Blake and Rebecca Baer, *map editors*
Design: Fabrizio LaRocca, *creative director*; Siobhan O'Hare, *art director*; Tina Malaney, *designer*; Melanie Marin, *senior picture editor;* Moon Sun Kim, *cover designer*
Cover Photo (Santorini): Daryl Benson/Masterfile
Production/Manufacturing: Angela McLean

1st Edition

ISBN 978–1–4000–1924–3

ISSN 1939–9936

SPECIAL SALES

This book is available at special discounts for bulk purchases for sales promotions or premiums. Special editions, including personalized covers, excerpts of existing books, and corporate imprints, can be created in large quantities for special needs. For more information, write to Special Markets/ Premium Sales, 1745 Broadway, MD 6-2, New York, New York 10019, or e-mail specialmarkets@ randomhouse.com.

AN IMPORTANT TIP & AN INVITATION

Although all prices, opening times, and other details in this book are based on information supplied to us at press time, changes occur all the time in the travel world, and Fodor's cannot accept responsibility for facts that become outdated or for inadvertent errors or omissions. So **always confirm information when it matters,** especially if you're making a detour to visit a specific place. Your experiences—positive and negative—matter to us. If we have missed or misstated something, **please write to us.** We follow up on all suggestions. Contact the THE COMPLETE GUIDE TO EUROPEAN CRUISES editor at editors@fodors.com or c/o Fodor's at 1745 Broadway, New York, NY 10019.

PRINTED IN THE UNITED STATES OF AMERICA
10 9 8 7 6 5 4 3 2 1

Be a Fodor's Correspondent

Your opinion matters. It matters to us. It matters to your fellow Fodor's travelers, too. And we'd like to hear it. In fact, we need to hear it.

When you share your experiences and opinions, you become an active member of the Fodor's community. That means we'll not only use your feedback to make our books better, but we'll publish your names and comments whenever possible. Throughout our guides, look for "Word of Mouth," excerpts of your unvarnished feedback.

Here's how you can help improve Fodor's for all of us.

Tell us when we're right. We rely on local writers to give you an insider's perspective. But our writers and staff editors—who are the best in the business—depend on you. Your positive feedback is a vote to renew our recommendations for the next edition.

Tell us when we're wrong. We're proud that we update most of our guides every year. But we're not perfect. Things change. Hotels cut services. Museums change hours. Charming cafés lose charm. If our writer didn't quite capture the essence of a place, tell us how you'd do it differently. If any of our descriptions are inaccurate or inadequate, we'll incorporate your changes in the next edition and will correct factual errors at fodors.com immediately.

Tell us what to include. You probably have had fantastic travel experiences that aren't yet in Fodor's. Why not share them with a community of like-minded travelers? Maybe you chanced upon a beach or bistro or B&B that you don't want to keep to yourself. Tell us why we should include it. And share your discoveries and experiences with everyone directly at fodors.com. Your input may lead us to add a new listing or highlight a place we cover with a "Highly Recommended" star or with our highest rating, "Fodor's Choice."

Give us your opinion instantly at our feedback center at www.fodors.com/feedback. You may also e-mail editors@fodors.com with the subject line "THE COMPLETE GUIDE TO EUROPEAN CRUISES Editor." Or send your nominations, comments, and complaints by mail to THE COMPLETE GUIDE TO EUROPEAN CRUISES Editor, Fodor's, 1745 Broadway, New York, NY 10019.

You and travelers like you are the heart of the Fodor's community. Make our community richer by sharing your experiences. Be a Fodor's correspondent.

Happy Traveling!

Tim Jarrell, Publisher

CONTENTS

CONTENTS

THE BEST OF CRUISING

Best Suites at Sea

If you want the best accommodations at sea, then look for the plushest suites. The highest-category cabins on today's cruise ships are stocked with extra amenities and services, offering much more room than the typical cruise-ship cabin. While the prices are high, you certainly get what you pay for when you book the best.

■ **Cunard Lines' *Queen Mary 2.*** Fit for a queen, or anyone who wants to be treated like one, two Grand Duplex apartments each cover 2,250 square feet. Each main level is connected to an upstairs bedroom and bath by a gently curving staircase. Make a grand entrance while the butler serves your guests predinner cocktails.

■ **Norwegian Cruise Line's *Norwegian Jewel-class* ships.** High atop each ship, two Garden Villas are the ultimate seagoing digs. More apartments than suites, they have bedrooms and bathrooms offering all the comforts of home—if your home is posh—and the private decks are idyllic retreats.

■ **Oceania Cruises' *Regatta.*** Aft-facing with huge verandas, Owner's Suites are decorated in an English-country style suitable for a prince or princess. Even the bed is royal, with a draped half-canopy and heavenly Egyptian cotton linens. A butler will serve breakfast there if you choose.

■ **Silversea Cruises' *Silver Whisper* and *Silver Shadow.*** Owner's suites aren't the largest suites on board, but they have an ideal midship location, stylish furnishings, and plenty of room to entertain guests for cocktails or a complete dinner party.

Best Regular Cabins

Cruise-ship accommodations are not created equal; however, you don't have to book the highest-price cabin to have a comfortable cruise. The following cruise lines offer something a bit above the ordinary for the kind of prices the typical cruiser can afford to pay.

■ **Carnival Cruise Line.** Consistently larger than industry standard and with plenty of storage space, Carnival cabins are spacious for two and surprisingly roomy for families. A basket of sample-size goodies in the bathroom often includes new products, such as cinnamon-flavored toothpaste.

■ **Holland America Line.** Comfort is key, and all cabins have the types of conveniences we take for granted at home. DVD and CD players, flat-screen televisions, lighted magnifying makeup mirrors, and baskets of fresh fruit are unexpected bonuses in all categories.

■ **Windstar Cruises.** The nautical feel and nautical efficiency of Windstar cabins get our nod. From the view through the portholes to the lockers to stow our gear, these quarters are "ship-y" and ultimately ship-shape.

Best Bathrooms Afloat

Let's face it: cruise-ship bathrooms aren't usually noted for their roominess or luxury. However, there are exceptions. Here's a rundown of our favorite bathrooms on the high seas.

■ **Regent Seven Seas Cruises.** Without a doubt, the marble bathrooms with separate shower and full-size tub on *Seven Seas Voyager* and *Seven Seas Navigator* are totally pampering.

■ **Seabourn Cruises.** Although not the biggest shipboard bathrooms, Seabourn's bath amenities are nonetheless deluxe. Just ask, and your stewardess will draw your bath using luxury products of your choice from the Pure Pampering menu.

- **Silversea Cruises.** Double vanities, marble-clad showers, separate tubs, and fluffy, oversize towels are luxurious appointments, even in standard suites. Top suites add whirlpool jets to the tub for total bathing decadence.

Best Ships for Romantics

There's something about being on the open ocean under a blanket of thousands of stars that gets your heart racing. Whether you're planning your honeymoon or just a quiet getaway for two, these are the ships you should consider above all others.

- **Regent Seven Seas Cruises' *Seven Seas Mariner* & *Seven Seas Voyager*.** Every single suite on these distinctive ships has its own private veranda. The Cordon Bleu restaurants are elegant and the cuisine sublime—perfect for a quiet dinner for two.

- **SeaDream Yacht Club's *SeaDream I* & *II*.** Luxurious, intimate settings include snug alcoves for private dining alfresco and the feel of being a guest on a private yacht. Suites feature Belgian bed linens, and bathrooms have a to-die-for shower large enough for two with multijet massaging showerheads.

- **Windstar Cruises' *Wind Surf* & *Wind Spirit*.** For sheer enchantment, you can't beat billowing white sails overhead and the thrill of skimming across the sea. Windstar ships are cozy and inviting, with warm, unobtrusive service and coed saunas.

Best Cruise Lines for Families

A cruise vacation is ideal for families with children. With a safe environment and enough facilities and activities to keep everyone amused, parents can relax, and kids can have fun. Put these cruise lines at the top of your list when you want to bring the kids along.

- **Carnival Cruise Line.** Kid- and teen-friendly spaces packed with toys, games, and activities—combined with nonstop adult action—offer families a casual, laid-back vacation with something for everyone.

- **Norwegian Cruise Line.** Facilities for teens and tots on the newest ships have to be seen to be believed. Pools, playrooms, and discos are elaborate, and even picky kids should find the active programs enticing.

- **Ocean Village.** There's a lot of family fun to share, yet when parents are ready for an evening alone, babysitting is complimentary from 6 PM until midnight and available (for an hourly charge) until 3 AM.

- **Royal Caribbean International.** Well-conceived areas for children and teens, plus sports facilities that invite active family members to play together, are bonuses for parents who want to spend quality family time with the kids.

Best Spas Afloat

Some cruisers are more interested in a hot stone massage or a luxurious facial than a midnight buffet. Happily, gone are the days when the most you could expect was a new bouffant hairdo. Today's ships offer better equipped spas with more services than at any time in the history of cruising. Our favorite spas can go head to head with the best of the landlocked variety.

- **Celebrity Cruise Line Spas.** Attractive, tranquil decor and a full complement of wraps, massages, and deluxe treatments are features of all AquaSpas; however, only Millennium-class ships also feature complimentary bubbly saltwater thalassotherapy pools to melt away tension.

- **Costa Concordia & Costa Serena.** Each features Samsara Spa, some of the largest spas at sea (more than 23,000 square feet). Ninety-nine Samsara staterooms, including 12 suites, have direct spa access and exclusive use of Ristorante Samsara, which features a wellness menu.

- **Norwegian Cruise Line.** Massages and facials take a back seat to the elaborate pleasures of long, long indoor lap pools, soothing whirlpools, and indoor relaxation areas worthy of a fine European spa resort.

THE BEST OF CRUISING

■ *Queen Mary 2.* Canyon Ranch operates this utterly decadent, plush spa on board Cunard Line's flagship. In addition to offering a wide range of massages and spa treatments, the Aqua Therapy Center facilities are simply the finest afloat. For a daily fee, you have access to the huge therapy pool, reflexology basins, herbal or Finnish saunas, steam room, and sensory showers.

Best Sports & Fitness Centers

If you'd rather lift more than a mai tai or play something more strenuous than shuffleboard, then consider booking a cruise on a ship with a full-service health club. Once, a shipboard gym meant a treadmill and some dumbells in a small room deep in the hull. These days, some shipborne fitness centers are as well-outfitted as your gym at home, and they probably come with much better views. We can especially recommend the following.

■ **Carnival Cruise Line.** Gyms afford a view of the sea from nearly every stair-stepper, treadmill, and exercise cycle. After your individual workout or aerobics class, a therapy pool, saunas, and steam rooms offer relaxation with equally good sea views.

■ **Princess Cruises' Grand Class.** Stationary bicycles, treadmills, and step, rowing, and weight machines are positioned for wide-open views of sea and sky during cardiovascular workouts. Laps in the waterfall-generated, swim-against-the-current pool also provide a stimulating workout.

■ **Royal Caribbean's Voyager Class & Freedom Class.** Huge and well-equipped gyms and exercise classes almost take a back seat to full-size outdoor basketball courts, rock-climbing walls, and the unique experience of ice-skating at sea. The addition of full-size Everlast boxing rings to Freedom Class gyms gives new meaning to "working up a sweat."

Best Entertainment at Sea

The quality of cruise-ship entertainment is higher these days than it has ever been. You're likely to find a Las Vegas–quality revue or Broadway-quality show on most cruise ships. Still, some lines stand out with their offerings. These are our favorites.

■ **Carnival Cruise Lines.** Flash, dazzle, and special effects worthy of Las Vegas are backdrops for the talented teams of entertainers in Carnival production shows.

■ **Ocean Village.** Aerial deck shows feature a company of international circus artists, dancers, singers, and stilt-walkers. Set on and under unique top-deck aerial structures—with a grand-finale laser-and-light show—there is like nothing else like it at sea.

■ **Royal Caribbean Cruise Line.** In addition to lavish production shows and guest entertainers fleetwide, only Royal Caribbean's megasize ships feature world-class ice-skating performances.

Best Specialty Restaurants

Virtually every cruise line now offers reservations-only specialty restaurants, which prepare restaurant-quality meals for a special cover charge. Many of these tables are hard to come by, a testament to the restaurants' quality and imaginative cuisine. Here are the lines that stand apart, with specialty restaurants that are well worth planning ahead for.

■ **Carnival Cruise Lines.** When Carnival introduced supper clubs, the line took shipboard dining to a new level with a sophisticated ambience and the ingredients for outstanding meals at sea. Anyone familiar with big-city steak houses will recognize the presentation of a tray displaying the evening's entrées.

- **Celebrity Millennium-class ships.** Decorated with authentic ocean-liner artifacts and the actual paneling from the White Star liner *Olympic,* these restaurants feature table-side food preparation, classical music, and food that is described in hushed, reverent tones.

- **Crystal Cruises.** Asian-theme restaurants on Crystal ships receive rave reviews for the beautifully prepared dishes, including ultrafresh sushi. Presentation is as beautiful as the divine food. If you aren't adept with chopsticks, no one will raise an eyebrow if you use a fork.

- **Cunard Line's *Queen Mary 2.*** Cuisine in Todd English Restaurant, named for the award-winning chef and restaurateur, is as other-worldly as the exotic Moroccan surroundings in which it is served. The small cover charge for lunch or dinner wouldn't be sufficient for a tip at his Olives restaurants on land and you won't have to wait months for a reservation at sea.

Best Regular Dining Room Cuisine

With more than 2,000 passengers, today's large cruise ships simply can't offer elegant, restaurant-quality food on such a vast scale. However, most cruise lines do manage to provide good food to their passengers. A few do even better, and you may be surprised to find that they aren't always the most luxurious lines.

- **Carnival Cruise Line.** Yes, Carnival! The line offers what is possibly the most-improved dining experience at sea. The waiters still take time out to dance and sing, but, with the added touch of chef George Blanc's Signature Selections (offered since 2006), the food is tastier, more sensibly portioned, and nicely presented.

- **Celebrity Cruises.** Celebrity made its mark with food and service that was decidedly a cut above the average and hasn't wavered over the years. While serving hundreds of diners at set mealtimes, the waiters manage the illusion that yours is the most important meal being presented.

- **Regent Seven Seas Cruises.** Creative dishes spiced just so and wines chosen to complement all menus are a hallmark of Radisson ships. Service is attentive, but not hovering or intrusive.

- **SeaDream Yacht Club.** A true gourmet meal is hard to come by on land, let alone at sea, but SeaDream chefs accomplish just such a feat. With only 110 passengers on board, every meal is individually prepared.

Best Access for Travelers with Disabilities

The U.S. Supreme Court ruled in 2005 that all cruise lines that call on U.S. ports must make some effort to make their ships more accessible to travelers with disabilities. While it's unlikely that every nook and cranny of every ship will ever be fully accommodating to passengers with mobility problems, some lines have made great strides in the right direction and have even influenced their European counterparts.

- **Holland America Line.** At the forefront of accessible cruise travel, Holland America offers a variety of services to passengers with mobility, sight, and breathing impairments. Shore tenders are equipped with wheelchair-accessible platforms that simplify transferring wheelchairs and scooters.

- **Princess Cruises.** Not only are accessible staterooms and suites available in a wide range of categories, Princess takes care to also provide shoreside wheelchair access to appropriate tours on vehicles equipped with lifts.

THE BEST OF CRUISING

■ **Silversea Cruises.** While suites designed for accessibility are limited, the ships are small and easy to navigate with wide, wide passageways and elevators that reach all decks. Public rooms with broad entryways are clustered together aft, and the distance between them is small.

Best Shops on Board

The need to shop doesn't fade away with the receding coastline, and many cruise lines have now made the experience of onboard shopping a more pleasant one. The best have taken things a step further.

■ **Carnival Cruise Line.** You'll find a great selection of popular logo souvenirs, many of them priced under $10, as well as low-price liquor and sundries and sales on some nifty high-end baubles and trinkets.

■ **Crystal Cruises.** Signature apparel, sportswear, formal wear, and luxury cosmetics are all available in thousands of square feet of exclusive boutiques. A favorite is the Crystal Home Collection, featuring the Bistro's Guy Buffet porcelain tableware.

■ **Princess Cruise Line.** Should you have the misfortune of lost or delayed luggage, you're in luck. Princess shipboard boutiques are stocked with nearly everything you need to carry on in style.

Best Service

When you go away on a relaxing cruise vacation, you want to be pampered and waited on. While service in all ships is pretty good these days, it's a given that with more than 2,000 passengers, large ships just can't give the kind of personalized service as a smaller ship. So it shouldn't be surprising that the best service at sea is on cruise lines that operate smaller ships.

■ **SeaDream Yacht Club.** A Corona with no lime, extra juice in your rum punch: whatever your preference, it will be remembered by all servers on board. They seem to network behind the scenes to ensure perfection.

■ **Silversea Cruises.** The mostly European staff don't seem to understand the word "no." Every attempt is made to satisfy even the most unusual request, even if it means buying a bottle of guava juice in the next port of call.

■ **Windstar Cruises.** Graduates of Holland America's training school in Indonesia, Windstar's Filipino and Indonesian stewards and servers go out of their way to provide gracious service with a sincere smile and genuine warmth.

Best Fun & Funky Activities

Being on vacation means having fun. While you may be able to amuse yourself, your fellow passengers sometimes need a little push. The best activities get passengers involved in the fun and give them an opportunity to let loose a bit. We don't claim these are always the most sophisticated activities at sea, but they will make you smile.

■ **Carnival contests.** As wacky to watch as they are to participate in, the knobby knees, hairy chest, and men's nightgown contests are something of a throwback, but you have to love the enthusiasm.

■ **The Costa toga party.** Do as the Romans did—dress up in a toga (supplies and accessories provided on board) and join in the Bacchanal. Peel a grape for your significant other.

■ **Ocean Village.** If you've always longed to run away with the circus, now you can. Join a circus workshop and learn how to juggle or fly through the air on the trapeze.

Best Enrichment Programs

All travel is enlightening, but if you wish to return home with more than souvenir photos and a suntan, you might want to explore the variety of enrichment programs currently offered by cruise lines. As outlined on the cruise lines' Web sites, most curricula are available year-round, but the specific courses and lecturers may change. These are the ones we've found most inspirational as well as entertaining.

- **Crystal Cruises.** Discover your inner artist by learning to play piano in the Crystal Cruises Creative Learning Institute. Expert instruction and lectures can be found in the areas of Arts & Entertainment, Business & Technology, Lifestyle, Wellness, and Wine & Food. Consistently popular is the Computer University@Sea program, which teaches computer basics as well as advanced techniques.

- **Cunard Line.** After a trip through the heavens in the only planetarium at sea, on board *Queen Mary 2* you can attend lectures presented by Oxford University luminaries and other guest speakers on topics from diplomacy to interior design, delve into classes ranging from computers to wine appreciation, foreign languages to photography, and even study acting with graduates of the Royal Academy of Dramatic Art.

- **Holland America Line.** The Explorations Speaker Series features lecturers whose topics may cover the wildlife, history, and culture of worldwide destinations; other subjects of interest might include astronomy, ocean liner history, wellness, and personal finance. For hands-on cooking classes, gourmet food presentations, and tasting events, each ship features a Culinary Arts Center.

Best Beds

A good night's sleep is important to a feeling of well-being, so why would anyone want to sleep on a lumpy mattress outfitted with pancake-thin pillows and scratchy sheets? No one does. Since Westin introduced their "Heavenly Bed" to travelers, hotels have been in the process of offering upgraded beds and bedding for years. Cruise lines have joined the wave and these are our favorites.

- **Carnival Cruise Lines.** The Carnival Comfort Bed features an 8-inch spring mattress, a downlike nonallergenic pillow, high-quality sheets and pillowcases, and a 100% hypoallergenic down duvet covered by an ultrafine, ring-spun, satin-striped cotton blend duvet cover.

- **Holland America Line.** The Mariner's Dream bed is a Sealy 9-inch innerspring mattress with a pillow top layer of fibers and foams and additional plush foam comfort layers. Hypoallergenic poly or goose-down pillows and cuddly down blanket are covered in 300-thread-count sheeting with a one-inch woven stripe pattern and a soft sateen finish.

- **Oceania Cruises.** Inaugurating the "bed wars" afloat with their "Tranquility Bed," Oceania has outfitted all accommodations with high-quality mattresses, 350-thread-count Egyptian cotton linens, silk-cut duvets, and goose-down pillows.

- **Royal Caribbean Line.** A 9-inch spring mattress with 2-inch microfiber pillow top sets the stage for 220-thread-count long-staple cotton blend sheets and cushy microfiber pillows. It's all topped with a 23-ounce synthetic blend duvet with a cotton blend cover.

THE BEST OF CRUISING

Best Ports for Strolling

The real draw of a European cruise is that it gives you the opportunity to visit more places in a single vacation than you might have been able to get to on your own. But you don't always have to travel miles and miles to find something interesting to see and do. These are our favorite ports to explore on foot.

- **Amsterdam, The Netherlands.** Here's a city that's made for walking. Stroll along the canals, visit Anne Frank's house, see the works of the Dutch Masters, have coffee at a sidewalk café. You can easily jump on a tram if your feet are weary, but the real pleasure of Amsterdam is streetside.

- **Dubrovnik, Croatia.** Damaged heavily by Serbian shelling in 1991–92, Dubrovnik's structures have been lovingly restored and the city is once again a favored port stop on Adriatic itineraries. Surrounded by medieval ramparts, the ancient streets, stone houses, and historic buildings are a trip back to the 13th century. Explore the city center (the Placa), cobbled side streets, and the pathway atop the Old Town's walls the old fashioned way—by walking.

- **Ephesus, Kusadasi, Turkey.** Although it requires a quick, 15-minute bus ride from the cruise terminal, the only way to see this spectacular archaeological site is on foot. Walk along the marble road that Mark Antony's and Cleopatra's chariots once passed over to reach the Great Theater, where St. Paul addressed the Ephesians and gladiatorial contests entertained up to 24,000 spectators.

Excursions Worth the Trip

The best things to see in Europe aren't always right by the port; sometimes you have to jump on a bus, train, or even a rental car to see the best a region has to offer. Here are our favorite places that are worth the trip from your ship, even if it requires a couple of hours to reach them.

- **The Alhambra, Granada, Spain.** Yes, it's a 90-minute trip, but if your ship calls at Málaga, this is one excursion you should consider carefully. The oldest and best-preserved of the 14th-century Moorish palaces, the Alhambra is a feast for the senses, with intricate tile mosaics, carved wood ceilings, elaborate pools, and lush gardens.

- **Le Havre, France.** There's little to see in Le Havre itself, but while you could make the two-plus-hour trip into Paris, your time ashore might be better spent exploring a bit of Normandy, which is much closer. You can choose Bayeux for its remarkable tapestry, Honfleur for its picturesque, cobbled streets, or the historic (and sobering) D-Day beaches.

- **Rome, Italy.** Rome wasn't built in a day and it's impossible to see *everything* in a day ashore there either. First, your ship will dock in Civitavecchia, about a 90-minute drive by bus (the train is quicker). A comprehensive tour that includes stops at the city's highlights, with a bit of free time for independent sightseeing or shopping, is a good bet for the first-time visitor. Shore excursions may include the Colosseum and Vatican, as well as driving past such monuments as the Arch of Constantine and ruins of the Roman Forum.

New For 2008

While some European-bound ships scheduled for launch in 2008 are new vessels that are almost identical to existing ships (Royal Caribbean's *Independence of the Seas*, a Freedom-class ship) or brand-new designs (Holland America Line's *Eurodam*). A few "new" ships are actually refurbished older ships—*Royal Princess, Azamara Journey,* and *Azamara Quest—are from the defunct Renaissance Cruises.* Fred. Olsen Cruises' *Balmoral was once* NCL's Norwegian Crown. Britain's Swan Hellenic is relaunching with one of its original ships in May 2008, the popular 394-passenger *Minerva.*

CARNIVAL SPLENDOR

The first ship in a new class—at 112,000 tons and 3,006 passenger capacity (double occupancy)—Carnival Splendor will incorporate some unique features for the Carnival line. A retractable dome over the mid-ship pool will be a Carnival first. It will also have the largest spa aboard any Carnival vessel, the line's first thalassotherapy pool, and the largest Camp Carnival facilities with a play area featuring Water Wars, the popular water-balloon attraction.

CELEBRITY SOLSTICE

At 118,000 tons, *Celebrity Solstice* will be a 2,850-guest vessel measuring 1,033 feet in length and 121 feet in width, and will have larger standard staterooms, 90% of which will be outside (85% of which will be balcony cabins), and an exceptional range of guest-inspired services and amenities. Look for all the trademark elements of the Millennium-class ships and a few surprises as well.

EASYCRUISE LIFE

This addition to the easyCruise fleet has ramped up the space (500 passengers) and added amenities like the FushionOn6 bar and restaurant, an Apivita spa, and a range of cabins that even extend to suite-like accommodations.

EURODAM

Eurodam, which is due in summer 2008, marks Holland America Line's next class of vessels. At 86,000 tons, it's the largest ever constructed for the line. The 2,044-passenger ship features 86% outside staterooms, of which 67% have balconies. An Explorer's Lounge Bar, a new Italian restaurant, a new atrium bar area, an enhanced and reconfigured show lounge with theater-style seating, a Pan-Asian restaurant and lounge, and a new photographic and imaging center are some of the highlights.

MSC FANTASIA

This brand-new ship class is MSC's biggest to date. At 133,500 tons, *MSC Fantasia* will have 3,300 lower berths, with a full capacity of 3,887 passengers and 1,600 crew members. Outside cabins will make up 80% of accommodations, nearly all of which have balconies. A 3-D cinema, 161,000 square-foot spa, interactive sports bar, and a 24-hour Tex-Mex restaurant are new features. MSC's new La Dolce Vita concept will offer a concierge, private swimming pool, solarium, lounge, butler service, and a dedicated spa entrance for 100 balcony cabins.

VENTURA

P&O Cruises' *Ventura* promises to be a truly inspirational cruise ship. With 15 decks and 881 balcony cabins, she will be 951 feet in length and showcase more than 7,000 works of contemporary art as well as feature a trendy circus school where passengers can learn to swing on a trapeze. A giant Scalextric race car track will provide excitement for all ages. Chef Marco Pierre White is creating Ventura's unique fine-dining venue, the White Room, plus a number of her other menus.

ABOUT THIS BOOK

Our Ratings

Sometimes you find terrific travel experiences and sometimes they just find you. But usually the burden is on you to select the right combination of experiences. That's where our ratings come in.

As travelers we've all discovered a place so wonderful that its worthiness is obvious. And sometimes that place is so experiential that superlatives don't do it justice: you just have to be there to know. These sights, properties, and experiences get our highest rating, **Fodor's Choice.**

By default, there's another category: any ship, experience, or establishment we include in this book is by definition worth your time, unless we say otherwise. And we will.

Disagree with any of our choices? Care to nominate a ship or suggest that we rate one more highly? Visit our feedback center at www.fodors.com/feedback.

Budget Well

Hotel and restaurant price categories from ¢ to $$$$ are defined in the opening pages of each chapter. For attractions, we always give standard adult admission fees; reductions are usually available for children, students, and senior citizens. Want to pay with plastic? **AE, D, DC, MC, V** following restaurant and hotel listings indicate if American Express, Discover, Diners Club, MasterCard, and Visa are accepted.

Restaurants

Unless we state otherwise, restaurants are open for lunch and dinner daily. We mention dress only when there's a specific requirement and reservations only when they're essential or not accepted—it's always best to book ahead.

Hotels

Hotels have private bath, phone, TV, and air-conditioning and operate on the European Plan (aka EP, meaning without meals), unless we specify that they use the Continental Plan (CP, with a continental breakfast), Breakfast Plan (BP, with a full breakfast), or Modified American Plan (MAP, with breakfast and dinner) or are all-inclusive (including all meals and most activities). We always list facilities but not whether you'll be charged an extra fee to use them, so when pricing accommodations, find out what's included.

Many Listings
- ★ Fodor's Choice
- ★ Highly recommended
- ⊠ Physical address
- ♦ Directions
- ⌂ Mailing address
- ☎ Telephone
- 🖷 Fax
- ⊕ On the Web
- ✉ E-mail
- 🎫 Admission fee
- ⊙ Open/closed times
- Ⓜ Metro stations
- ▭ Credit cards

Hotels & Restaurants
- 🏨 Hotel
- 🛏 Number of rooms
- ♿ Facilities
- ℗ Meal plans
- ✕ Restaurant
- ⟲ Reservations
- ⚲ Smoking
- BYOB
- ✕🏨 Hotel with restaurant that warrants a visit

Outdoors
- ⛳ Golf
- ⛺ Camping

Other
- ☺ Family-friendly
- ⇨ See also
- ⊠ Branch address
- ☞ Take note

Planning a European Cruise

Canal in Amsterdam

WORD OF MOUTH

"We based our decision [about which European cruise to take] on where the cruise went. We wanted to see Athens, so we chose [a] cruise that included Athens. . . . You can explore most ports on your own. That way you can do what you want and spend as much time on shore as you want. Research is the key."

—BarbAnn

www.fodors.com/forums

Updated by
Linda Coffman

"IN FOURTEEN HUNDRED NINETY-TWO, COLUMBUS sailed the ocean blue. He had three ships and left from Spain; he sailed through sunshine, wind and rain."—Columbus Day song taught to generations of schoolchildren.

Columbus may not have technically "discovered" America, as suggested by that ditty; however, his journey marked the discovery of the New World and could be considered the first-ever Caribbean cruise.

Today, the tide has turned as modern-day explorers are discovering Europe on ships that would astound Columbus and his small crew. Unprecedented waves of cruisers are journeying through the Old World and, as one top cruise-line executive puts it, they are doing it aboard "the Carnival Nina, the Pinta of the Seas, and the MSC Santa Maria."

With a wealth of art, architecture, and culture drawing them, it's easy to understand why Europe is the world's second-most-popular cruising region (only the Caribbean surpasses it). On a single cruise it's possible to visit a different country each day and explore a variety of important destinations, either right alongside the sea or not far from port.

The allure of a sea cruise is its ability to appeal to a wide range of vacationers as a safe and convenient way to travel. This is particularly true in Europe, where differences in language and culture can appear as insurmountable hurdles to the first-time visitor. And on a cruise, meals and accommodations are paid for in advance, so there's no worry about fluctuating euros to spoil your budget. And, while your ship follows the same sea routes as early mariners and traders, you don't have to hassle with transportation from country to country.

Major cruise lines that are familiar to most North Americans position some of their most exciting ships in Europe on a seasonal basis. Passengers are primarily Americans, the U.S. dollar prevails on board, and English is the dominant language. On cruise lines based in the United Kingdom, English is also the primary language, but you'll pay for onboard purchases in British pounds, which will be a distinct disadvantage to Americans since the dollar is particularly weak against the pound at this writing. The option of European-based cruise lines is also available. On those, you will find a more international flavor, multiple languages are spoken, and the currency is the euro.

CHOOSING YOUR CRUISE

Are you intrigued by the glory that is Rome or the antiquities of Greece? Do you want to venture behind the former Iron Curtain and unlock the mysteries of Russia? Unlike the "if it's Tuesday, this must be St. Thomas" nature of predictable Caribbean sailings, European itineraries come in shapes and sizes to suit a variety of interests. One voyage might emphasize the highlights of Baltic capital cities, while another focuses on classic Mediterranean cultures and cuisine. Equally rewarding, they nonetheless offer different experiences. Where to go to satisfy your inner explorer is a highly personal decision and one of the first you must make.

After giving some thought to your itinerary and where in Europe you might wish to go, the ship you select is the most vital factor in your cruise vacation. Big ships offer stability and a huge variety of activities and facilities. Small ships feel more intimate—more like a private club. For every big-ship fan there is someone who would never set foot aboard a "floating resort." Examine your lifestyle to see which kind of ship best meets your needs. But realize also that the size of your ship will also impact which ports you visit as well as how you see them. Big ships visit major ports of call such as Barcelona, Civitavecchia (for Rome), Amsterdam, and Venice; when they call at smaller, shallower ports, passengers must disembark aboard shore tenders (small boats that ferry dozens of passengers to shore at a time). Or they may skip these smaller ports entirely. Small and midsize ships can visit smaller ports, such as Monte Carlo, Monaco, more easily; passengers are often able to disembark directly onto the pier without having to wait for tenders to bring them ashore.

ITINERARIES

Ship size and cruise length have the greatest impact on the number of ports you can visit, but the itinerary type and embarkation port will also impact the number and variety of ports. **One-way cruises** are much more prevalent in European sailings than in the Caribbean and will allow you to visit a wider variety of ports and travel farther from your port of embarkation. **Loop cruises** begin and end at the same point and often visit ports in relatively close proximity to one another. After deciding where to go, take a hard look at the number of hours your preferred itinerary spends in individual ports. You don't want to be frustrated by a lack of time ashore to do what you've come so far to accomplish. A late departure or overnight stay may be attractive if you wish to enjoy the local nightlife in a particular port.

NORTHERN EUROPE & BALTIC ITINERARIES

Typical one-week to 12-night cruises include a day or two at sea, but ships on these itineraries spend as much time as possible docked in Baltic capitals and major cities. Departing from such ports as Dover (U.K.), Amsterdam, Copenhagen, or Stockholm, highlights of Baltic itineraries may include Amsterdam, Oslo, Helsinki, Tallin (Estonia), and St. Petersburg (Russia); ships calling on St. Petersburg often dock for two or three nights there. Some itineraries may focus on a theme or specific region, such as cruises around the British Isles or Norwegian fjords and North Cape.

WESTERN MEDITERRANEAN ITINERARIES

Some of the most popular Mediterranean itineraries, especially for first-time cruisers to Europe, are one-week sailings that embark in Barcelona and stop in southern European ports that range from Nice to Civitavecchia (Rome) and may include more exotic off-the-beaten-path destinations like Malta and Corsica. A sea day might include a cruise through the narrow Strait of Messina or sailing past the volcanic island of Stromboli. Longer, one-way itineraries can even start in Lisbon and end as far away as Venice, while possibly calling at not only Gibraltar, the French Riviera, and Sicily, but Dubrovnik (Croatia) as well.

EUROPEAN CRUISE SHIPS AND ITINERARIES

CRUISE LINE	SHIP NAME	ITINERARY/REGION
Azamara Cruises	Azamara Journey	W Mediterranean, Adriatic, Baltic, British Isles
	Azamara Quest	W or E Mediterranean
Carnival Cruise Lines	Carnival Freedom	W or E Mediterranean
	Carnival Splendor	W Mediterranean, Baltic
Celebrity Cruises	Celebrity Century	W Mediterranean, Baltic, British Isles
	Celebrity Constellation	Baltic, British Isles
	Celebrity Galaxy	E Mediterranean
	Celebrity Summit	W Mediterranean
Costa Cruises	Costa Atlantica	W Mediterranean, Baltic
	Costa Classica	W or E Mediterranean
	Costa Concordia	W or E Mediterranean
	Costa Europa	W or E Mediterranean
	Costa Fortuna	E Mediterranean
	Costa Magica	W Mediterranean
	Costa Mediterranea	W Mediterranean, Baltic
	Costa Romantica	W or E Mediterranean
	Costa Serena	E Mediterranean
	Costa Victoria	W Mediterranean, Baltic
Crystal Cruises	Crystal Serenity	W or E Mediterranean, Adriatic
	Crystal Symphony	W Mediterranean, Baltic
Cunard Line	Queen Elizabeth 2	W Mediterranean, Baltic
	Queen Mary 2	W Mediterranean
	Queen Victoria	W or E Mediterranean, Greek Isles, Baltic
easyCruise	easyCruise One	E Mediterranean, Greek Isles, Baltic
Fred. Olsen Cruises	Balmoral	W or E Mediterranean, Baltic
	Black Prince	W Mediterranean, Adriatic, Baltic
	Black Watch	W or E Mediterranean, Baltic
	Boudica	W or E Mediterranean, Baltic
	Braemer	W or E Mediterranean, Adriatic, Baltic
Holland America Line	Eurodam	Baltic
	Maasdam	Baltic
	Noordam	W or E Mediterranean
	Prinsendam	Baltic, British Isles
	Rotterdam	W or E Mediterranean, Baltic
	Zuiderdam	W or E Mediterranean
Hurtigruten	Finnmarken	Norwegian coast

EUROPEAN CRUISE SHIPS AND ITINERARIES

Hurtigruten (continued)	Fram	Antarctica, Greenland
	Kong Harald	Norwegian coast
	Midnastol	Norwegian coast
	Nordkapp	Norwegian coast
	Nordnorge	Norwegian coast
	Nordlys	Norwegian coast
	Polarlys	Norwegian coast
	Richard With	Norwegian Coast
	Trollfjord	Norwegian Coast
Lindblad Expeditions	National Geographic Endeavour	W Mediterranean, Baltic
	Sea Cloud II	Danube River
MSC Cruises	MSC Armonia	E Mediterranean, Baltic
	MSC Lirica	W Mediterranean, Baltic
	MSC Melody	W Mediterranean
	MSC Musica	E Mediterranean
	MSC Opera	Greek Isles
	MSC Orchestra	W or E Mediterranean
	MSC Poesia	E Mediterranean
	MSC Rhapsody	W Mediterranean
	MSC Sinfonia	W Mediterranean
Norwegian Cruise Line	Norwegian Gem	W Mediterranean
	Norwegian Jade	W or E Mediterranean, Baltic, British Isles
	Norwegian Jewel	Baltic
Oceania Cruises	Insignia	W or E Mediterranean, Greek Isles
	Nautica	W or E Mediterranean, Greek Isles
	Regatta	W Mediterranean, Baltic
Ocean Village	Ocean Village 1	E Mediterranean, Greek Isles
	Ocean Village 2	W Mediterranean
P&O Cruises	Arcadia	W or E Mediterranean, Baltic
	Artemis	E Mediterranean, Baltic
	Aurora	W or E Mediterranean, Baltic
	Oceana	W Mediterranean, Baltic
	Oriana	W or E Mediterranean, Baltic
	Ventura	W or E Mediterranean, Baltic
Princess Cruises	Crown Princess	Baltic
	Emerald Princess	E Mediterranean, Greek Isles
	Grand Princess	W or E Mediterranean, Greek Isles, British Isles
	Pacific Princess	W or E Mediterranean

EUROPEAN CRUISE SHIPS AND ITINERARIES

Princess Cruises (continued)	Royal Princess	W Mediterranean, Baltic
	Sea Princess	W Mediterranean, Baltic
Regent Seven Seas Cruises	Seven Seas Navigator	W or E Mediterranean
	Seven Seas Voyager	W or E Mediterranean, Baltic
Royal Caribbean Intl	Brilliance of the Seas	W Mediterranean, Greek Isles
	Independence of the Seas	W Mediterranean, British Isles
	Jewel of the Seas	Baltic, British Isles
	Legend of the Seas	W or E Mediterranean, Greek Isles
	Navigator of the Seas	W or E Mediterranean
	Splendour of the Seas	W or E Mediterranean, Greek Isles
	Voyager of the Seas	W Mediterranean
Saga Cruises	Saga Rose	W or E Mediterranean, Baltic, British Isles
	Saga Ruby	W or E Mediterranean, Baltic, British Isles
Seabourn Cruise Line	Seabourn Legend	W Mediterranean
	Seabourn Pride	W Mediterranean, Baltic, British Isles
	Seabourn Spirit	E Mediterranean, Greek Isles
SeaDream Yacht Club	SeaDream I	W or E Mediterranean, Greek Isles
	SeaDream II	W or E Mediterranean, Greek Isles
Silversea Cruises	Silver Cloud	W or E Mediterranean, Greek Isles, Baltic
	Silver Whisper	W or E Mediterranean, Greek Isles
	Silver Wind	W or E Mediterranean, Greek Isles, Baltic, British Isles
Star Clippers	Royal Clipper	W Mediterranean
	Star Clipper	E Mediterranean, Greek Isles
Windstar Cruises	Wind Spirit	W or E Mediterranean, Greek Isles
	Wind Star	W or E Mediterranean, Greek Isles
	Wind Surf	W Mediterranean

EASTERN MEDITERRANEAN & GREEK ISLES ITINERARIES

The most exotic and port-intensive cruises are those embarking in Venice, Athens, and Istanbul. Often one-way voyages, these cruises visit coastal centers of antiquity such as Kusadasi (Ephesus) in Turkey and Katakolon (Olympia) in Greece, but also the Roman outposts of Dubrovnik and Korčula, Croatia. For a transit through Greece's historic Corinth Canal, you'll have to select an itinerary on one of the high-end, small cruise ships, such as Seabourn or SeaDream cruise lines' yacht-size vessels. A sea day might be spent cruising past the grandeur of Mount Athos after leaving Istanbul or along the coastline in the Adriatic Sea. Best explored by small ship—preferably one with sails that add to the allure—Greek Island itineraries that include Santorini, Corfu, Rhodes, and Mykonos are popular with honeymooners and couples for the romantic ambience of sun-splashed beaches and leisurely alfresco meals accompanied by local wines and breathtaking sea views, but these ports are also visited by the larger ships, which must usually tender their passengers ashore.

WHEN TO GO

Baltic cruises are scheduled from May through September, with midsummer being high season, when the weather is predictably more pleasant. Temperatures throughout the Baltic are somewhat unpredictable but can range from balmy mid- to high-70s F on sunny days to chilly 50s F in the evening, even if the sun doesn't set until well into the night. Mediterranean cruises are available year-round, with high season from late April through October when temperatures range from the upper 70s to mid-90s F, depending on your ports of call. Early spring and late fall aren't the best times to cruise in the Mediterranean if your plans include spending time on the beaches, yet the cooler temperatures are ideal for touring. Weather can be unpredictable and damp in fall and winter, but days often warm up when the sun is shining.

CRUISE COSTS

Average cruise fares vary considerably by itinerary and season, as well as by the category of accommodations you select. Published rates are highest for the most unique and desirable itineraries, as well as for cruises during peak summer months, when most North Americans plan for vacations in Europe. Europeans are known to prefer late-summer holidays, with August being the busiest month. Typical daily per diems on a luxury line such as Silversea or Seabourn can be as much as three times or more the cost of a cruise on a mainstream line such as Royal Caribbean or even a premium Celebrity Cruises ship. It goes without saying that longer cruises are naturally more expensive.

Solo travelers should be aware that single cabins have virtually disappeared from cruise ships. Taking a double cabin can cost up to twice the advertised per-person rates (which are based on double occupancy). Some cruise lines will find same-sex roommates for singles; each then pays the per-person, double-occupancy rate.

While the overall price you pay for your cruise is always a consideration, don't think of the bottom line in terms of the fare alone. You also have to figure in the cost of other shipboard charges beyond the basic fare. However, the ultimate cost isn't computed only in dollars spent; it is in what you get for your money. The real bottom line is value. Many cruise passengers don't mind spending a bit more to get the vacation they really want.

TIPS

One of the most delicate—yet frequently debated—topics of conversation among cruise passengers involves the matter of tipping. Who do you tip? How much? What's "customary" and "recommended?" Should parents tip the full amount for children or is just half adequate? Why do you have to tip at all?

Saving Money on Your Cruise Fare

You can save on your cruise fare in several ways. Obviously, you should shop around. Some travel agents will discount cruise prices, though this is becoming a thing of the past. One thing never changes—do not ever, under any circumstances, pay brochure rate. You can do better, often as much as half off published fares. These are a few simple strategies you can follow:

■ **Book early**: Cruise lines discount their cruises if you book early, particularly during the annual "Wave" season between January and March.

■ **Cruise during the off-season**: If you take a cruise during the very early spring or late fall (especially in March, October, and November) or the period between Thanksgiving and Christmas, you'll often find specials.

■ **Book late**: Sometimes you can book a last-minute cruise at substantial savings if the ship hasn't filled all its cabins.

■ **Choose accommodations with care**: Cabins are usually standardized and location determines the fare. Selecting a lower category can result in savings while giving up nothing in terms of cabin size and features.

■ **Book a "guarantee"**: You won't be able to select your own cabin because the cruise line will assign you one in the category you book, but a "guarantee" fare can be substantially lower than a regular fare.

■ **Cruise with friends and family**: Book a minimum number of cabins, and your group can generally receive a special discounted fare.

■ **Reveal your age and affiliations**: Fare savings may be available for seniors and members of certain organizations, and for cruise line stockholders.

■ **Cruise often**: Frequent cruisers usually get discounts from their preferred cruise lines.

When transfers to and from your ship are a part of your air-and-sea program, gratuities are generally included for luggage handling. In that case, do not worry about the interim tipping. However, if you take a taxi to the pier and hand over your bags to a stevedore, be sure to tip him. Treat him with respect and pass along the equivalent of at least $5.

During your cruise, room service waiters generally receive a cash tip of $1 to $3 per delivery. A 15% to 18% gratuity will automatically be added to each bar bill during the cruise. If you use salon and spa services, a similar percentage might be added to the bills there as well. If you dine in a specialty restaurant, you may be asked to provide a one-time gratuity for the service staff.

There will be a "disembarkation talk" on the last day of the cruise that explains tipping procedures. If you are expected to tip in cash, small white "tip" envelopes will appear in your stateroom that day. If you tip in cash, you usually give the tip envelope directly to each person on the last night of the cruise. Tips generally add up to about $10 to $12 per person per day. You tip the same amount for each person who shares the cabin, including children, unless otherwise indicated.

Most cruise lines now either automatically add gratuities to passengers' onboard charge accounts or offer the option. If that suits you, then do nothing further. However, you are certainly free to adjust the amounts up or down to more appropriate levels or ask that the charge be removed altogether if you prefer distributing cash gratuities.

Recommended Gratuities by Cruise Line

1

Each cruise line has a different tipping policy. Some allow you to add tips to your shipboard account, others expect you to dole out the dollars in cash on the last night of the cruise. Here are the suggested tipping amounts for each line covered in this book. Gratuity recommendations are often higher if you're staying in a suite with extra services, such as a butler. *The individual ship profiles in Chapter 2 give you the details:*

Azamara Cruises $12.25 per person per day

Carnival Cruise Line $10 per person per day

Celebrity Cruises $10.50 per person per day

Costa Cruises €4.50–€6 per person per day, depending on cruise length

Crystal Cruises $11 per person per day

Cunard Line $11–$13 per person per day

easyCruise Tipping is up to your discretion

Fred. Olsen Cruise Lines £2 per person per day

Holland American Line $10 per person per day

Hurtigruten Tipping is up to your discretion

Lindblad Expeditions $12–$14 per person per day

MSC Cruises €6 per person per day

Norwegian Cruise Line $10 per person per day

Oceania Cruises $11.50 per person per day

Ocean Village Included in fare

P&O Cruises £3.75 per person per day

Princess Cruises $10 per person per day

Regent Seven Seas Cruises No tipping expected

Royal Caribbean International $9.75 per person per day

Saga Cruises Included in fare

Seabourn Cruises No tipping expected

SeaDream Yacht Club No tipping expected

Silversea Cruises No tipping expected

Star Clippers €8 per person per day

Windstar Cruises $11 per person per day

EXTRAS

In addition to the cost of your cruise there are further expenses to consider, such as airfare to the port city. These days, virtually all cruise lines offer air add-ons, which are sometimes—but not always—less expensive than the lowest available airline fare. Airfares to Europe can be considerably more expensive from May through September than during the rest of year.

Shore excursions can also be a substantial expense; the best shore excursions are not cheap. But if you skimp too much on your excursion budget you'll deprive yourself of an important part of the European cruising experience. European shore excursions can be as simple as a stroll through Copenhagen's fanciful Tivoli Gardens or as splendid as tours through the imperial residences of the Czars in St. Petersburg. You can inspect the architecture of Gaudí in Barcelona, take an all-day guided tour of Rome with a stop at Vatican City, and climb to the top of the Acropolis in Athens. One of the most popular excursions is from the port of Kusadasi (Turkey) to the ancient excavated city of Ephesus. You will walk along the marble road that Mark Antony's and Cleopatra's chariots once passed over to reach the Great Theater, where gladiatorial contests entertained up to 24,000 spectators and where St. Paul addressed the Ephesians. If you want to take a ship-sponsored shore excursion, prebooking is highly recommended as they can sell out weeks before you reach the ship.

But you don't necessarily have to take the tour offered by your ship. Although there's a distinct advantage these days to having your shore excursions priced in dollars rather than euros, you can still have a high-quality (though perhaps not cheaper) experience by banding together with a group of like-minded travelers to arrange a private tour rather than relying on the ship's big-bus experience. Or if you are more intrepid, you can simply hop in a taxi or onto public transportation and do some independent exploring. Whether you choose to take ship-sponsored tours or go it alone, you do need to budget for off-ship touring since that's the reason you came to Europe in the first place.

Finally, there will be many extras added to your shipboard account during the cruise, including drinks (both alcoholic and nonalcoholic), activity fees (you pay to use that golf simulator), dining in specialty restaurants, spa services, gratuities, and even cappuccino and espresso on most ships.

CABINS

In years gone by, cabins were almost an afterthought. The general attitude of both passengers and the cruise lines used to be that a cabin is a cabin and is used only for changing clothes and sleeping. That's why the cabins on most older cruise ships are skimpy in size and short on amenities.

Until you actually get on board you may not realize that nearly every cabin on your ship is identical. These days, cruise ships are built in sections and, except for some luxury suites, the cabins are prefabricated and dropped into place with everything all ready to hook up, even the plumbing. There are some variations in size, but the main difference between cabins in the myriad price categories is location: higher or lower decks, forward or aft, inside or outside.

Cabins high on the ship with a commanding view fetch higher fares. But you should know that they are also more susceptible to side-to-side movement; in rough seas you could find yourself tossed right out of bed. On lower decks, you'll pay less and find more stability, particularly in the middle of the ship.

Forward cabins have a tendency to be oddly shaped, as they follow the contour of the bow. They are also likely to be noisy; when the ship's anchor drops, you won't need a wake-up call. In rough seas, you can feel the ship's pitch (its upward and downward motion) more in the front.

Should you go for the stern location instead? You're more likely to hear engine and machinery noise there, as well as feel the pitch and possibly some vibration. However, many passengers feel the view of the ship's wake (the ripples it leaves behind as its massive engines move it forward) is worth any noise or vibration they might encounter there.

Above all, don't be confused by all the categories listed in cruise line brochures—the categories more accurately reflect price levels based on location than any physical differences in the cabins themselves (keep repeating: prefabricated). Shipboard accommodations fall into four basic configurations: inside cabins, outside cabins, balcony cabins, and suites.

INSIDE CABINS

An inside cabin has no window or porthole. These are always the least expensive cabins and are ideal for passengers who would rather spend their vacation funds on excursions or other incidentals than on upgraded accommodations. Inside cabins are generally just as spacious as outside cabins, and decor and amenities are similar. Many ships locate triple and quad cabins (accommodating three or more passengers) on the inside. Essentially, they look just like a standard double cabin but have bunk beds that either fold down from the wall or disappear into the ceiling. Parents sometimes book an inside cabin for their older children and teens, while their own cabin is an outside across the hall with a window or balcony.

OUTSIDE CABINS

A standard outside cabin has either a picture window or porthole. To give the illusion of more space, these cabins might also rely on the generous use of mirrors for an even airier feeling. In addition to the usual amenities, outside staterooms often have a small refrigerator and a sitting area. Two twin beds can be joined together to create one large bed. Going one step further, standard and larger outside staterooms on modern ships are often outfitted with a small sofa or loveseat with a cocktail table or small side table. Floor-to-ceiling curtains that can be drawn from wall to wall to create a private sleeping space are a nice touch in some outside cabins with sitting areas. Some larger cabins may have a combination bathtub–shower instead of just a shower.

BALCONY CABINS

A balcony—or veranda—cabin is an outside cabin with floor-to-ceiling glass doors that open onto a private deck. Although the cabin may have large expanses of glass, the balcony is sometimes cut out of the cabin's square footage (depending on the ship). Balconies are usually furnished with two chairs and a table for lounging and casual dining outdoors. However, you should be aware that balconies are not always completely private; sometimes your balcony is visible both from balconies next door and also from balconies above, particularly when you are in an aft-facing cabin on the back of a ship with tiered balconies. The furnishings and amenities of balcony cabins are otherwise much like those in standard outside cabins.

SUITES

Suites are the most lavish accommodations afloat, and although suites are always larger than regular cabins, they do not always have separate rooms for sleeping. Some luxury ships designate all accommodations as suites. The most expansive (and expensive) have large living rooms and separate bedrooms and may also have huge private outdoor sundecks equipped with hot tubs and dining areas. Even smaller suites (often termed minisuites) and penthouses are generous in size.

Suites almost always have amenities that standard cabins do not have. True suites have separate living and sleeping areas, but these areas are still occasionally separated only by a curtain. Depending on the cruise line, you may find a small refrigerator or minibar stocked with complimentary soft drinks, bottled water, and the alcoholic beverages of your choice. Top suites on some ships include the luxurious touch of complimentary

DECIPHERING YOUR DECK PLAN

LIDO DECK

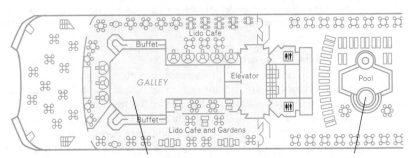

The Lido Deck is a potential source of noise—deck chairs are set out early in the morning and put away late at night; the sound of chairs scraping on the floor of the Lido buffet can be an annoyance.

Music performances by poolside bands can often be heard on upper-deck balconies located immediately below.

UPPER DECK AFT

Take note of where lifeboats are located—views from some outside cabins can be partially, or entirely, obstructed by the boats.

Upper-deck cabins, as well as those far forward and far aft, are usually more susceptible to motion than those in the middle of the ship on a low deck.

Cabins near elevators or stairs are a double-edged sword. Being close by is a convenience; however, although the elevators aren't necessarily noisy, the traffic they attract can be. •

Balcony cabins are indicated by a rectangle split into two sections. The small box is the balcony.

MAIN PUBLIC DECK

Cabins immediately below restaurants and dining rooms can be noisy. Late sleepers might be bothered by early breakfast noise, early sleepers by late diners.

Theaters and dining rooms are often located on middle or lower decks.

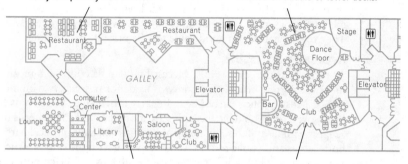

The ship's galley isn't usually labeled on deck plans, but you can figure out where it is by locating a large blank space near the dining room. Cabins beneath it can be very noisy.

Locate the ship's show lounge, disco, children's playroom, and teen center and avoid booking a cabin directly above or below them for obvious reasons.

LOWER DECK AFT

Cabins designated for passengers with disabilities are often situated near elevators.

Interior cabins have no windows and are the least expensive on board.

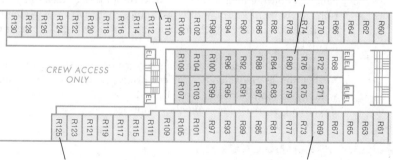

Lower-deck cabins, particularly those far aft, can be plagued by mechanical noises and vibration.

Ocean-view cabins are generally located on lower decks.

laundry service, in-cabin Internet connections, and complex entertainment centers with big-screen plasma TVs, VCR/DVD players, and CD stereo systems. An added bonus to the suite life is the extra level of services many ships offer. Little extras might include afternoon tea and evening canapés delivered to you and served by a white-gloved butler.

Although minisuites on most contemporary ships have separate sitting areas with a sofa, chair, and a cocktail table, don't let the marketing skill of the cruise lines fool you: so-called minisuites are usually little more than slightly larger versions of standard balcony cabins and don't often include extra services and elaborate amenities you can get in regular suites. They're still generally a good value for the price if space matters.

ACCESSIBILITY ISSUES

As recently as the early 1990s, "accessibility" on a cruise ship meant little more than a few inside staterooms set aside for passengers with mobility issues. Most public restrooms and nearly all en suite bathrooms had a "step-over" threshold. Newer ships are more sensitive to the needs of passengers with disabilities, but many older ships still have physical barriers in both cabins and public rooms. And once you get off the ship—particularly in ports with cobblestone streets—your problems will be compounded.

All cruise lines offer a limited number of staterooms designed to be wheelchair- and scooter-accessible. Booking a newer vessel will generally assure more choices. On newer ships, public rooms are generally more accessible, and more facilities have been planned with wheelchair users in mind. Auxiliary aids, such as flashers for the hearing impaired and buzzers for visually impaired passengers, as well as lifts for swimming pools and hot tubs, are available. However, more than the usual amount of preplanning is necessary for smooth sailing if you have special needs.

For example, when a ship is unable to dock—as is the case in Villefranche or Santorini, for instance—passengers are taken ashore on tenders that are sometimes problematic even for the able-bodied to negotiate under adverse conditions. Some people with limited mobility may find it difficult to embark or disembark the ship when docked due to the steep angle of gangways during high or low tide at certain times of day. In some situations, crew members may offer assistance that involves carrying guests, but if the sea is choppy when tendering is a necessity, that might not be an option.

Passengers who require continuous oxygen or have service animals have further hurdles to overcome. You can bring both aboard a cruise ship, but your service animal may not be allowed to go ashore with you if the port has strict laws regarding animal quarantines.

BOOKING YOUR CRUISE

Charting your cruising course doesn't have to be difficult, but it isn't as simple as booking airplane seats or reserving a hotel room. Even after you've settled on a cruise line and cruise ship that's right for you, there will still be many questions to answer and details to get right. First-time cruisers, who may want and need some additional insight and advice, may wish to stick to a traditional travel agent who is close at hand. Of course, if you've taken numerous cruises and are more concerned with the price—and if you're willing to go to bat for yourself if something goes wrong—a Web-based agency might be the way to go.

USING A TRAVEL AGENT

Whether it is your first or 50th sailing, your best friend in booking a cruise is a knowledgeable travel agent. The last thing you want when considering a costly cruise vacation is an agent who has never been on a cruise, calls a cruise ship "the boat," or—worse still—quotes brochure rates. The most important steps in cruise travel planning are research, research, and more research; your partner in this process is an experienced travel agent. Booking a cruise is a complex process, and it's seldom wise to try to go it alone, particularly the first time. But how do you find a cruise travel agent you can trust?

The most experienced and reliable agent will be certified as an Accredited Cruise Counselor (ACC), Master Cruise Counselor (MCC), or Elite Cruise Counselor (ECC) by CLIA (the Cruise Lines International Association). These agents have completed demanding training programs, including touring or sailing on a specific number of ships. Your agent should also belong to a professional trade organization. In North America, membership in the American Society of Travel Agents (ASTA) indicates an agency has pledged to follow the code of ethics set forth by the world's largest association for travel professionals. In the best of all worlds, your travel agent is affiliated with both ASTA and CLIA.

Some agencies have preferred-supplier relationships with specific cruise lines and prominently display only their products. If you have done your homework and know what cruise line sounds most appealing to you, be alert if an agent tries to change your mind without very specific reasons.

When you've found a jewel of an agent, then what? Ask many questions. Above all else, be honest about your expectations and budget. Seldom can a travel agent who doesn't know you well guess what your interests are and how much you can afford to spend. Don't be shy. If you have champagne taste and a beer budget, say so. Do not hesitate to interview prospective agents and be wary if they do not interview you right back.

Contrary to what conventional wisdom might suggest, cutting out the travel agent and booking directly with a cruise line won't necessarily get you the lowest price. More than 90% of all cruise bookings are still handled through travel agents. In fact, cruise-line reservation systems simply are not capable of dealing with tens of thousands of direct calls from potential passengers. Without an agent working on your behalf, you're on your own. Do not rely solely on Internet message boards for authoritative responses to your questions—that is a service more accurately provided by your travel agent.

Travel Agent Professional Organizations **American Society of Travel Agents** (*ASTA* ☎ *703/739-2782, 800/965-2782 24-hr hotline* 🖨 *703/684-8319* ⊕ *www.travelsense.org*). Cruise Line Organizations **Cruise Lines International Association** (*CLIA* ☎ *754/224-2200* ⊕ *www.cruising.org*). Recommended Travel Agents **AAA** (☎ *800/222-6953* ⊕ *www.csaa.com*) isn't just for car travel. The company has a searchable database to locate member agencies by zip code.

10 Questions to Answer Before Visiting a Travel Agent

If you've decided to use a travel agent, congratulations. You'll have someone on your side to make your booking and to intercede if something goes wrong. Ask yourself these 10 simple questions, and you'll be better prepared to help the agent do his or her job:

1. Who will be going on the cruise?

2. What can you afford to spend for the entire trip?

3. Where would you like to go?

4. How much vacation time do you have?

5. When can you get away?

6. What are your interests?

7. Do you prefer a casual or structured vacation?

8. What kind of accommodations do you want?

9. What are your dining preferences?

10. How will you get to the embarkation port?

American Express Travel (☎ *800/297–5627* ⊕ *travel.americanexpress.com*) offers options for online booking or a searchable database of local American Express travel offices.

Cruise Brothers (☎ *800/827–7779 or 401/941–3999* ⊕ *www.cruisebrothers.com*), in business since the mid-1970s, is one of the largest family-owned, cruises-only agencies in the United States.

Cruise Connections Canada (☎ *800/661–9283* ⊕ *www.cruise-connections.com*) is Canada's leading cruise retailer and one of the largest cruise retailers in North America.

Cruise Master Travel (☎ *800/603–5755* ⊕ *www.cruisemaster.com*) specializes in groups and honeymoons.

Cruise One (⊕ *www.cruiseone.com*) is affiliated with Boston-based NLG, the world's largest cruise retailer, and offers a satisfaction guarantee. The company has more than 400 member agencies nationwide, and its Web site has a searchable database of member cruise specialists.

Cruise Planners, Inc. (☎ *800/683–0206* ⊕ *www.cruiseplanners.com*) is a network of home-based agent franchises. The Web site offers a searchable database to locate member agencies.

Cruises Inc. (☎ *888/218–4228 or 800/854–0500* ⊕ *www.cruisesinc.com*) is an affiliate of Boston-based NLG, the world's largest cruise retailer, and offers a satisfaction guarantee. The company has more than 450 member agencies nationwide, and its Web site has a searchable database of member cruise specialists.

Cruises Only (☎ *800/278–4737* ⊕ *www.cruisesonly.com*) is affiliated with NLG, the world's largest cruise retailer, and offers a lowest-price guarantee as well as a money-back satisfaction guarantee. Agents are available to assist clients around the clock.

Ensemble Travel (☎ *866/350–7460* ⊕ *www.ensembletravel.com*) is an international network of 1,100 expert travel agencies. Call to be connected to the nearest member agency.

Hartford Holidays (☎ *800/828–4813 or 516/746–6670* ⊕ *www.hartfordholidays.com*) has been family-owned and -operated for 30 years.

Lighthouse Travel (☎ *800/719–9917 or 805/566–3905* ⊕ *www.lighthousetravel.com*) specializes in cruises.

Northstar Cruises (☎ *800/249–9360 or 973/228–5005* ⊕ *www.northstarcruises.com*) is a top producer for most major cruise lines.

Skyscraper Tours, Inc. (☎ *888/278–9648* ⊕ *www.skyscrapertours.com*) offers several annual hosted group cruises.

Uniglobe International (⊕ *www.uniglobetravel.com*) has more than 700 franchise locations worldwide; the Internet Web site has a searchable database of member cruise agencies.

Vacation.com (☎ *800/843–0733* ⊕ *www.vacation.com*) is a network of more than 5,700 travel agency locations across the United States and Canada.

Virtuoso (☎ *866/401–7974 or 817/870–0300*) is the world's most exclusive association of upscale travel agencies. Call to locate members specializing in cruises.

BOOKING YOUR CRUISE ONLINE

In addition to local travel agencies, there are many hard-working, dedicated travel professionals working for Web sites. Both big-name travel sellers and mom-and-pop agencies compete for the attention of cyber-savvy clients, and it never hurts to compare prices from a variety of these sources. Some cruise lines even allow you to book directly with them through their Web sites.

As a rule, Web-based and toll-free brokers will do a decent job for you. They often offer discounted fares, though not always the lowest, so it pays to check around. If you know precisely what you want and how much you should pay to get a real bargain—and you don't mind dealing with an anonymous voice on the phone—by all means make your reservations when the price is right. Just don't expect the personal service you get from an agent you know. Also, be prepared to spend a lot of time and effort on the phone if something goes wrong.

Online Agencies Cruise.com (⊕ *www.cruise.com* ☎ *888/333–3116*) lays claim to being the largest Web site specializing in discounted cruises on the Internet and offers a lowest-price guarantee.

Cruise Compete (⊕ *www.cruisecompete.com* ☎ *800/764–4410*) allows you to get competing bids from top travel agencies, who respond to your request for bids with their best rates for your trip.

Cruise Direct (⊕ *www.cruisedirect.com* ☎ *888/407–2784*) allows customers to book their own travel arrangements through the Web site and a toll-free number.

Cruise411.com (⊕ *www.cruise411.com* ☎ *800/553–7090*) has a booking engine online that allows you to book directly or temporarily hold most cruise reservations without deposit or payment if you prefer to call in your booking.

Expedia (⊕ *www.expedia.com* ☎ *800/397–3342*) is a full-service online travel seller that books cruises, too.

iCruise.com (⊕ *www.icruise.com* ☎ *866/389–9219*) charges a pretty hefty cancellation fee, so be sure you know what you want before using their booking engine.

jetBlue (⊕ *www.jetblue.com* ☎ *800/538–2583*) now allows you to book cruises on its Web site.

Moment's Notice (⊕ *www.moments-notice.com* ☎ *888/241–3366*) offers a searchable database for last-minute deals; call toll-free for reservations.

Orbitz (⊕ *www.orbitz.com* ☎ *888/656–4546*) is a full-service online travel seller that books cruises.

7 Blue Seas (⊕ *www.7blueseas.com* ☎ *800/242–1781*) offers a comprehensive online cruise information Web site; bookings are made through the toll-free call center.

Travelocity (⊕ *www.travelocity.com* ☎ *877/815–5446*) is a full-service online travel seller with a 24-hour help desk for service issues.

BEFORE YOU GO

To expedite your preboarding paperwork, some cruise lines have convenient forms on their Web sites. As long as you have your reservation number, you can provide the required immigration information (usually your
citizenship information and passport number), prereserve shore excursions, and even indicate any special requests from the comfort of your
home. Less-wired cruise lines might mail preboarding paperwork to you
or your travel agent for completion after you make your final payment
and request that you return the forms by mail or fax. No matter how you
submit them, be sure to make hard copies of any forms you fill out and
bring them with you to the pier to smooth the embarkation process.

DOCUMENTS

It is every passenger's responsibility to have proper identification. If you
arrive at the airport without it, you will not be allowed to board your
plane. Should that happen, the cruise line will not issue a fare refund.
Most travel agents know the requirements and can guide you to the proper
agency to obtain what you need if you don't have it.

Everyone must have a valid passport to travel to Europe. Additionally,
some countries to which cruise ships call require visas, though it's also true
that tourist visas are sometimes not required for cruise passengers, even if
they are generally required to visit a particular country. For instance, a visa
is not necessary in Russia if you book all your shore excursions through
your cruise line, but a visa is required if you tour independently. If your
itinerary requires a visa of *all* passengers prior to boarding, you should
receive an information letter from your cruise line with instructions and,
possibly, application forms. It is your responsibility to obtain all necessary
visas. Visa information and applications may also be obtained through
the local embassy or consulate of the country you will be visiting. Visas
can be obtained through embassies and consulates, but while you can do
it yourself, a more hassle-free route is to use a visa service that specializes
in the process. **Zierer Visa Service** (⊕*www.zvs.com*) and **Travisa** (⊕*www.
travisa.com*) are two such services.

Children under the age of 18—when they are not traveling with *both*
parents—almost always require a letter of permission from the absent
parent(s). Airlines, cruise lines, and immigration agents can deny children
initial boarding or entry to foreign countries without proper proof of identification and citizenship *and* a notarized permission letter from absent or
noncustodial parents. Your travel agent or cruise line can help with the
wording of such a letter.

GETTING OR RENEWING A PASSPORT

In light of changing government regulations, you should apply for a passport as far in advance of your cruise as possible. In normal times, the process usually takes at least six weeks, but it can take as long as 12 weeks
during very busy periods. You can expedite your passport application if
you are traveling within two weeks by paying an additional fee of $60 (in
addition to the regular passport fee) and appearing in person at a regional
passport office. Also, several passport expediting services will handle your

SAMPLE PERMISSION LETTER

Here's the text you might use for a typical letter of permission. You should type this up yourself, putting in all the specific details of your trip in place of the blanks.

CONSENT FOR MINOR CHILDREN TO TRAVEL

Date:

I (we): _____

authorize my/our minor child(ren): _____

to travel to: _____ on _____

aboard Airline/Flight Number: _____

and/or Cruise Ship: _____

with _____

Their expected date of return is: _____

In addition, I (we) authorize: _____ to consent to any necessary routine or emergency medical treatment during the aforementioned trip.

Signed: _____ (Parent)

Signed: _____ (Parent)

Address: _____

_____

_____

Telephone: _____

Sworn to and signed before me, a Notary Public,

this _____ day of _____, 20_____

_____ _____

Notary Public Signature and Seal

application for you (for a hefty fee, of course) and can get you a passport in as few as 48 hours. You can read all about the passport application process at the Web site of the **U.S. Department of State** (⊕*travel.state.gov/passport*). A passport costs $97 if you are 16 or older and is valid for 10 years, $82 if you are under 16, when it is only valid for 5 years. **A. Briggs Passport & Visa Expeditors** (☎*800/806–0581 or 202/464–3000* ⊕*www.abriggs.com*) is a passport expediting service.

MONEY

On board your ship you won't have any worries about money, but you will need cash while ashore. If you have not arranged for transfers from the airport to the ship, you will need taxi fare in the local currency, which is the euro for most embarkation cities and the British pound in Great Britain. The Scandinavian countries Denmark, Norway, and Sweden also have their own currencies.

Currency exchange can be more costly in your home country than at your foreign destination, but many banks, as well as the American Automobile Association (AAA), American Express, and Travelex bureaus offer the service. In addition, you may find a currency exchange booth in the international terminal at your departure airport. However, the simplest, and usually least expensive, method of obtaining local currency is from an ATM. VISA and MasterCard debit and credit cards are widely accepted at ATMs throughout the world; however, some banks impose a fee for international withdrawals. Before leaving home, make sure you have a PIN (personal identification number) for your card and understand any fees associated with its use. You might also be wise to notify the credit card company that you will be using your card overseas so they don't refuse your charges when they notice its repeated use in foreign locales.

For days in port you will also want some cash on hand for beverages, snacks, and small souvenir purchases. Your cruise ship may offer a foreign currency exchange service onboard, but, like hotels, the exchange rate is not always the most favorable. We suggest, instead of carrying large amounts of cash when ashore, using a credit card for major purchases.

Resources **American Automobile Association** (*AAA* ☎*315/797–5000* ⊕*www.aaa. com*) **American Express** (☎*888/412–6945 in U.S., 801/945–9450 collect outside of U.S. to add value or speak to customer service* ⊕*www.americanexpress.com*). **Travelex** (⊕*www.travelex.com*).

WHAT TO PACK

As far as clothing goes, cruise wear falls into three categories: casual, informal, and formal. Cruise documents should include information indicating how many evenings fall into each category. You will know when to wear what by reading your ship's daily newsletter—each evening's dress code will be prominently announced.

For days on board, you'll need **casual** wear. When your ship has a covered swimming pool or is sailing to warm-weather Mediterranean cruises, you'll typically need swimwear, a cover-up, and sandals for the pool. Time spent ashore touring and shopping calls for comfortable clothing and good walking shoes. At some point, you'll be confronted with cobblestones. While locals seem to navigate them with ease, even in Italian designer shoes, they can be tricky and even slippery.

Conservative is a rule to dress by in Europe, and mix-and-match will save room in your suitcase. Keep in mind that respectful attire is required when visiting cathedrals, mosques, synagogues, and even some museums. Shorts, and even short skirts, are frowned upon or banned outright, and women's arms are expected to be covered. On the other hand, beach resorts in the Med are more relaxed and resort clothing is entirely appropriate; in fact, be prepared to see topless and even nude sun-worshippers on some of the more permissive beaches along the French Riviera. Leave clothing adorned with slogans or logos and clunky white athletic shoes on the ship unless you want to stand out as an American tourist.

Back aboard your ship, evening casual means khakis and nice polo or sport shirts for men. Ladies' outfits are dresses, skirts and tops, or pants outfits. By sticking to two or three complementary colors and a few accessories, you can mix up tops and bottoms for a different look every night.

Informal attire is a little trickier. It applies only to evening wear and can mean different things depending on the cruise line. Informal for women is a dressier dress or pants outfit; for men it almost always includes a sport coat and sometimes a tie. Check your documents carefully.

Formal night means dressing up, but these days even that is a relative notion. You will see women in everything from simple cocktail dresses to elaborate glittering gowns. A tuxedo (either all black or with white dinner jacket) or dark suit is required for gentlemen. If you have been a mother-of-the-bride lately, chances are your outfit for the wedding is just perfect for formal night. For children, Sunday-best is entirely appropriate.

Men can usually rent their formal attire from the cruise line, and if they do so, it will be waiting when they board. Be sure to make these arrangements in advance; your travel agent can get the details from the cruise line. But if you are renting a tux, buy your own studs: a surefire way to spot a rented tuxedo is by the inexpensive studs that come with it. Also, many men with a little girth consider a vest more comfortable than a cummerbund.

An absolute essential for women is a shawl or light sweater. Aggressive air-conditioning can make public rooms uncomfortable, particularly if you are sunburned from a day at the beach. Put things you can't do without—such as prescription medication, spare eyeglasses, toiletries, a swimsuit, and change of clothes for the first day—in your carry-on. Most cruise ships provide soap, shampoo, and conditioner, so you probably won't need those. And plan carefully. In fact, we'd strongly advise you to make a list so you don't forget anything.

LUGGAGE

You know the days of massive steamer trunks are history, but is there a maximum amount of luggage that you can bring on a cruise ship? Yes, there really is a limit of sorts. Although some cruise lines state that each passenger is allowed 200 pounds of personal luggage, you're unlikely to see anyone's bags actually being weighed. However, it's not the cruise-line restrictions that passengers need to worry about.

Cruisers arriving at their embarkation port by air should be aware of airline baggage restrictions. Most major airlines enforce luggage size and weight policies, resulting in a rude (and expensive) surprise to some travelers with large, heavy suitcases. In the United States you may be charged extra for checked bags weighing more than 50 pounds. Abroad, some airlines don't allow you to check bags over 60 to 70 pounds. While most airlines and airports require that you check your luggage onto your flight at least 30 minutes before scheduled departure time, some now require 45 minutes or more. Check-in time for international flights can be at least an hour before departure (and often longer). Also note that some flights between cities within Europe limit the total weight of checked baggage to 20 kilos, which is only 44 pounds, per passenger and allow fewer carry-on items. Check with your air carrier for the latest guidelines and restrictions.

If your luggage goes astray, make sure that you leave all the information regarding your ship's itinerary with the airline baggage desk before you leave the airport, and make sure the cruise line's representative knows as well. Ask about any compensation you may be entitled to; in some cases, the airline will give you cash to purchase your immediate necessities. If you booked an air-and-sea package with your cruise line, the cruise line may give you an onboard credit to purchase necessary items if your bags are delayed. With luck, your bags will catch up to you before your ship departs; if that doesn't happen, they will be forwarded to the next port of call by your airline. In the interim, you will have to borrow or purchase clothing and personal items; you may be offered the use of formal wear by the cruise line. Save the receipts for all purchases to request reimbursement by the airline, or your insurance company, if you have baggage delay coverage.

INSURANCE

It's a good idea to purchase travel insurance, which covers a variety of possible hazards and mishaps, when you book a cruise. One important concern for cruise passengers is being delayed en route to the port of embarkation and missing the ship. Another major consideration is lost luggage (*for more information on lost luggage, see* ⇨ *Luggage, above*)— or even the delay of luggage. Both of these possibilities should be covered by your policy. You may miss the first day or two of your cruise, but all will not be lost financially. A travel policy will ensure you can replace delayed necessities secure in the knowledge that you will be reimbursed for those unexpected expenditures. Save your receipts for all out-of-pocket expenses to file your claim and be sure to get an incident report from the airline at fault.

No one wants their cruise vacation spoiled by a broken arm, heart attack, or worse, but if one of life's tragedies occurs, you want to be covered. The medical insurance program you depend on at home might not extend coverage beyond the borders of the United States. Medicare assuredly will not cover you if you are hurt or sick while abroad. It is worth noting that all ships of foreign registry are considered to be "outside the United States" by Medicare. If there is any question in your mind, check your cruise-ship's registry—with very few exceptions, it will *not* be the United States. Without basic coverage, travelers should be prepared to pay for

Duct Tape—the Essential Travel Tool

So, your bags are packed and you're ready to cruise? Not quite yet if you skipped the duct tape. You don't want to leave your home port without one of a traveler's handiest necessities. Duct tape no longer belongs only in the garage. Some of its more mundane uses are luggage repair (fix a broken hinge with ease) and security (baggage handlers won't tamper with duct tape, it's too much trouble). Wrapped in duct tape, your luggage is easy to spot in terminals as well. For individuality, duct tape comes in colors, as well as the traditional silver. For even higher suitcase visibility, there are snazzy neon colors. It's water resistant (an important feature for ocean travelers) and can serve as an indestructible luggage tag as well as a strap—just write your name and address on the tape. Best of all, duct tape is easy to tear by hand and you don't need scissors to cut it.

There are literally thousands of uses for duct tape. Every homeowner knows that when something is supposed to stick together and it doesn't, nothing holds like duct tape. What about at sea? Is the bottom ready to fall out of your cabin's vanity drawer? Tape it until the carpenter arrives. You're a late sleeper and the drapes don't quite close? Keep the sun at bay by taping them together. Everyone has had the stitching in a hem unravel at the last minute. Duct tape to the rescue! There are bottle lids to secure, rattles to silence, drawers that won't stay shut when the ship is rolling, and other little things that happen when you least expect them.

One of duct tape's most creative uses is as a replacement for an uplifting foundation garment. Under low-cut or backless dresses—or when a brassiere just won't work with a gown—create your own Wonder Duct Bra. Duct tape sticks well for hours and peels off without pain. Best of all, the variety of colors means more coordinating choices and even less chance of a sliver of silver tape peeping from a black décolleté neckline.

any care they require, either by credit card or wire transfer of funds to the provider.

Some independent insurers such as Travel Guard, Access America, or CSA offer very comprehensive policies at attractive rates. Nearly all cruise lines offer their own line of insurance. Compare the coverage and rates to determine which is best for you. Keep in mind that insurance purchased from an independent carrier is more likely to include coverage if the cruise line goes out of business before or during your cruise. Although it is a rare and unlikely occurrence, you do want to be insured in the event that it happens.

U.S. Travel Insurers Access America (☎ 800/729-6021 ⊕ www.accessamerica.com). **CSA Travel Protection** (☎ 800/873-9855 ⊕ www.csatravelprotection.com). **HTH Worldwide** (☎ 610/254-8700 or 888/243-2358 ⊕ www.hthworldwide.com). **Travelex Insurance** (☎ 800/228-9792 ⊕ www.travelex-insurance.com). **Travel Guard International** (☎ 715/345-0505 or 800/826-4919 ⊕ www.travelguard.com). **Travel Insured International** (☎ 800/243-3174 ⊕ www.travelinsured.com).

ARRIVING & EMBARKING

Most cruise-ship passengers fly to the port of embarkation, even if their cruise is a transatlantic crossing to Europe. If you book your cruise far enough in advance, you'll be given the opportunity to purchase an air-and-sea package, which may—or may not—save you money on your flight. You might get a lower fare by booking your air independently, so it's a good idea to check for the best fare available. Independent air arrangements might save you enough to cover the cost of a hotel room in your embarkation port so you can arrive early. It's not a bad idea to arrive a day early to overcome inevitable jet lag and avoid the possibility of delayed flights.

If you buy an air-and-sea package from your cruise line, a uniformed cruise line agent will meet you at baggage claim to smooth your way from airport to pier. You will need to claim your own bags and give them to the transfer driver so they can be loaded on the bus. Upon arrival at the pier, luggage is automatically transferred to the ship for delivery to your cabin. The cruise line ground transfer system can also be available to independent fliers. However, be sure to ask your travel agent how much it costs; you may find that a taxi or shuttle service is less expensive and more convenient.

BOARDING

Once the planning, packing, and anticipation are behind them, veteran cruise passengers sometimes view embarkation day as anticlimactic. However, for first-time cruise travelers, embarking on their first ship can be more than exhilarating—it can be downright intimidating. What exactly can you expect?

Once inside the cruise terminal, you'll see a check-in line. Actual boarding time is often scheduled for noon or later, but some cruise lines will begin processing early arrivals and then direct them to a holding area. During check-in, you will be asked to produce your documents and any forms you were sent to complete ahead of time, plus your passport and a credit card (to cover onboard charges). You are issued a boarding card that often also doubles as your stateroom key card and shipboard charge card. At some point—either before you enter the check-in area or before proceeding to the ship—you and your hand luggage will pass through a security procedure similar to those at airports.

Don't be alarmed if your passport is retained at check-in. The purser holds passports to expedite the process of "clearing" the ship when entering each country for the first time. To clear the ship, immigration officials board and check the ship's manifest and passengers'—as well as crewmembers'— passports before anyone can go ashore. However, you may find that some banks and currency exchanges require identification to exchange money and, for that purpose, it's a good idea to make a color copy of your passport's photo page to carry ashore in lieu of the actual passport itself. Should you be required to carry your actual passport ashore—when visiting Russia, for instance—it will be returned to you for the day.

The lines for check-in can be long, particularly at peak times. If check-in starts at noon but continues to 4 PM, you can expect lines to trail off as the boarding deadline approaches. Everyone is anxious to get on board and begin their vacation, so if you arrive at one of the busy periods, keep in mind that this is not the time to get cranky if you have to wait.

Once boarding begins, you will inevitably have your first experience with the ship's photographer and be asked to pose for an embarkation picture. It only takes a second, so smile. You are under no obligation to purchase any photos taken of you during the cruise, but they are nice souvenirs. Further procedures vary somewhat once you are greeted by staff members lined up just inside the ship's hull; however, you'll have to produce your boarding card and, possibly, a picture ID for the security officer. At some point, either at the check-in desk or when boarding the ship for the first time, you may be photographed for security purposes—your image will display when your boarding card is swiped into a computer as you leave and reboard the ship in ports of call. Depending on the cruise line, you will be directed to your cabin, or a steward will relieve you of your carry-on luggage and accompany you. Stewards on high-end cruise lines not only show you the way, but hand you a glass of champagne as a welcome-aboard gesture. However, if you board early, don't be surprised if you are told cabins are not ready for occupancy—passageways to accommodations may even be roped off. In that case you can explore the ship, sample the luncheon buffet, or simply relax until an announcement is made that you can go to your cabin.

ON BOARD

Check out your cabin to make sure that everything is in order. Try the plumbing and set the thermostat to the temperature you prefer. Your cabin may feel warm while docked but will cool off when the ship is underway. You should find a copy of the ship's daily schedule in the cabin. Take a few moments to look it over—you will want to know what time the lifeboat (or muster) drill takes place (a placard on the back of your cabin door will indicate directions to your emergency station), as well as meal hours and the schedule for various activities and entertainments.

Rented tuxedoes are either hanging in the closet or will be delivered some-time during the afternoon; bon voyage gifts sent by your friends or travel agent usually appear as well. Be patient if you are expecting deliveries, particularly on megaships. Cabin stewards participate in the ship's turn-around and are extremely busy, although yours will no doubt introduce himself at the first available opportunity. It will also be a while before your checked luggage arrives, so your initial order of business is usually the buffet, if you haven't already had lunch. Bring along the daily schedule to check over while you eat.

While making your way to the Lido buffet, no doubt you'll notice bar waiters offering trays of colorful bon voyage drinks, often in souvenir glasses that you can keep. Beware—they are not complimentary! If you choose one, you will be asked to sign for it. Again, like the photos, you are under no obligation to purchase.

Do your plans for the cruise include booking shore excursions and indulg-ing in spa treatments? The most popular tours sometimes sell out, and spas can be very busy during sea days, so your next stops should be the Shore Excursion Desk to book tours and the spa to make appointments if you didn't already book your spa visits and excursions in advance.

Dining room seating arrangements are another matter for consider-ation. If you aren't happy with your assigned dinner seating, speak to the maitre d'. The daily schedule will indicate where and when to meet with him. If you plan to dine in the ship's specialty restaurant, make those reservations as soon as possible to avoid disappointment.

PAYING FOR THINGS ON BOARD

Let's step back a moment and take a look at what happened when you checked in at the pier. Because a cashless society prevails on cruise ships, an imprint was made of your credit card, or you had to place a cash deposit for use against your onboard charges. Then you were issued a charge card that usually doubles as your stateroom key card. Most onboard expenditures are charged to your shipboard account with your signature as verification, with the possible exception of casino gaming—even so, you can often get cash withdrawals from your account from the casino cashier.

An itemized bill is provided at the end of the voyage listing your purchases. In order to avoid surprises, it is a good idea to set aside your charge slips and request an interim printout of your bill from the purser to ensure accuracy. Should you change your mind about charging onboard purchases, you can always inform the purser and pay in cash or traveler's checks instead. If your cash deposit was more than you spent, you will receive a refund.

DINING

All food, all the time? Not quite, but it is possible to literally eat away the day and most of the night on a cruise. A popular cruise directors' joke is, "You came on as passengers, and you will be leaving as cargo." Although it is meant in fun, it does contain a ring of truth. Food—tasty and plentiful—is available 24 hours a day on most cruise ships, and the dining experience at sea has reached almost mythical proportions. Perhaps it has something to do with legendary midnight buffets and the absence of menu prices, or maybe it's the vast selection and availability.

RESTAURANTS

Every ship has at least one main restaurant and a Lido, or casual buffet alternative. Increasingly important are specialty restaurants. Meals in the primary and buffet restaurants are included in the cruise fare, as are round-the-clock room service, midday tea and snacks, and late-night buffets. Most mainstream cruise lines levy a surcharge for dining in alternative restaurants that may, or may not, also include a gratuity, although there generally is no additional charge on luxury cruise lines.

You may also find a pizzeria or a specialty coffee bar on your ship—increasingly popular favorites cropping up on ships old and new. Although pizza is complimentary, expect an additional charge for specialty coffees at the coffee bar and, quite likely, in the dining room as well. You will also likely be charged for sodas and drinks during meals other than iced tea, regular coffee, tap water, and fruit juice.

There is often a direct relationship between the cost of a cruise and the quality of its cuisine. The food is very sophisticated on some (mostly expensive) lines, among them Crystal, Cunard, Regent Seven Seas, Seabourn, and Silversea. In the more moderate price range, Celebrity Cruises has always been known for its fine cuisine. The trend toward featuring specialty dishes and even entire menus designed by acclaimed chefs has spread throughout the cruise industry; however, on most mainstream cruise lines, the food is the quality that you would find in any good hotel banquet—perfectly acceptable but certainly not great.

DINNER SEATINGS

If your cruise ship has traditional seatings for dinner, the one decision that may set the tone for your entire cruise is your dinner seating. Which is best? Early dinner seating is generally scheduled between 6 and 6:30 PM, while late seating can begin from 8:15 to 8:45 PM. European cruise lines generally ahere to the custom of dining later and schedule restaurant hours accordingly. Even cruise lines that cater to Americans may adjust dining hours when in Europe. So the "best" seating depends on you, your lifestyle, and your personal preference.

Families with young children and older passengers often choose an early seating. Early seating diners are encouraged not to linger too long over dessert and coffee because the dining room has to be readied for late seating. Late seating is viewed by some passengers as more romantic and less rushed.

Cruise lines understand that strict schedules no longer satisfy the desires of all modern cruise passengers. Many cruise lines now include alternatives to the set schedules in the dining room, including casual dinner menus in their buffet facilities where more flexibility is allowed in dress and meal-times. Open seating is primarily associated with more upscale lines; it allows passengers the flexibility to dine any time during restaurant hours and be seated with whomever they please.

Led by Norwegian Cruise Line and Princess Cruises, more contemporary and premium cruise lines are exploring adaptations of open seating to offer variety and a more personalized experience for their passengers. Carnival Cruise Lines has added a twist with four seating times instead of the usual two, plus casual evening dining in the Lido buffet.

SPECIALTY RESTAURANTS

A growing trend in shipboard dining is the emergence of sophisticated specialty restaurants that require reservations and frequently charge a fee. From as little as $15 per person for a complete steak dinner to $200 per person for an elaborate gourmet meal including vintage wines paired with each course, specialty restaurants offer a refined dining option that cannot be duplicated in your ship's main restaurants. If you anticipate dining in your ship's intimate specialty restaurant, make reservations as soon as possible to avoid disappointment.

SPECIAL DIETS

Cruise lines make every possible attempt to ensure dining satisfaction. If you have special dietary considerations—such as low-salt, kosher, or food allergies—be sure to indicate them well ahead of time and check to be certain your needs are known by your waiter once on board. In addition to the usual menu items, so-called "spa," low-calorie, low-carbohydrate, or low-fat selections, as well as children's menus, are usually available. Requests for dishes not featured on the menu can often be granted if you ask in advance.

SPECIALTY RESTAURANTS

CRUISE LINE	SHIP	CUISINE TYPE	CHARGE (PER PERSON)
Azamara Cruises	Azamara Journey & Quest	Steak house	$25
		Mediterranean	$20
Carnival	Spirit-class & Conquest-class	Steaks & seafood	$30
Celebrity	Millennium-class & Century	Continental	$30
Costa	Costa Fortuna & Mediterranea	Italian/Tuscan steak house	$23 (comp. dinner for two for suite occupants)
Crystal	Crystal Symphony	Italian, Asian	No charge/$6 tip suggested
	Crystal Serenity	Italian, Asian, Sushi	No charge/$6 tip suggested
	All ships	International with wine pairings	$180
Cunard	Queen Mary 2, Queen Victoria	Mediterranean	$30 dinner, $20 lunch
		International	No charge
Disney	Disney Magic & Wonder	Northern Italian	$10 dinner, $10 Champagne brunch, $5 High Tea
Holland America	All ships	Steaks & seafood	$30 dinner, $15 lunch
Norwegian	Dawn-/Jewel-class	Asian	$13/$10
		Sushi	à la carte or $12.50
		Teppanyaki	à la carte or $20
		Shabu-shabu (Pearl & Gem only)	$12.50
		French Mediterranean	$15/$10
		Steak house	$20/$15
		Italian	No charge
	Sun	Steak house	$20
		Sushi	$13
Norwegian (continued)	Sun (continued)	Teppanyaki	à la carte
		French Mediterranean	$15
		Italian	$13
	Majesty	French Mediterranean	$15
		Italian	No charge
Oceania	Regatta	Italian	No charge
		Steak house	No charge
Princess	Sun-class	Steak house	$15
	Coral-class	Steak house	$15
		Italian	$20
	Grand-class	Steak house	$15

SPECIALTY RESTAURANTS

		Italian	$20 dinner, $20 brunch (sea days only)
	Crown Princess	Steaks & seafood	$25
		Italian	$20
Regent Seven Seas	Navigator	Italian	No charge
	Mariner, Voyager	French	No charge
		Asian	No charge
Royal Caribbean	Freedom-, Radiance-class and Mariner & Navigator of the Seas	Steak house	$20
		Italian	$20
	Other Voyager-class and Empress of the Seas	Italian	$20
	Enchantment of the Seas	Steak house	$20
	Freedom-class, Voyager-class and Sovereign of the Seas	Johnny Rockets diner	$3.95
Seabourn	Legend & Pride	International & steak house	No charge
Silversea	All ships	International with wine pairings	$150
		Italian	No charge

ALCOHOL

On all but the most upscale lines, you pay for alcohol aboard the ship, including wine with dinner. Wine typically costs about what you would expect to pay at a nice lounge or restaurant in a resort or in a major city. Wine by the bottle is a more economical choice at dinner than ordering it by the glass. Any wine you don't finish will be kept for you and served the next night. Gifts of wine or champagne ordered from the cruise line (either by you, a friend, or your travel agent) can be taken to the dining room. Wine from any other source will incur a corkage fee of approximately $10 to $15 per bottle.

ENTERTAINMENT

It's hard to imagine, but in the early years of cruise travel, shipboard entertainment consisted of little more than poetry readings and passenger talent shows. Those days are long gone. These days, seven-night cruises usually include two original production shows. One of these might be a Las Vegas–style extravaganza and the other a best-of-Broadway show featuring old and new favorites from the Great White Way. Other shows highlight the talents of individual singers, dancers, magicians, comedians, and even acrobats.

Real treats are the folkloric shows or other entertainments arranged to take place while cruise ships are in port. Local performers come aboard, usually shortly before the ship sails, to present their country's songs and dances. It's an excellent way to get a glimpse of the cultural history of their performing arts.

CLOSE UP

Drinking & Gambling Ages

Many underage passengers have learned to their chagrin that the rules that apply on land are also adhered to at sea. On most mainstream cruise ships you must be 21 to imbibe alcoholic beverages. There are exceptions—for instance, on cruises departing from countries where the legal drinking age is typically lower than 21. By and large, if you haven't achieved the magic age of 21, your shipboard charge card will be coded as booze-free, and bartenders won't risk their jobs to sell you alcohol.

Gambling is a bit looser, and 18-year-olds can try their luck on cruise lines such as Carnival, Celebrity, Holland America, Silversea, Norwegian, and Royal Caribbean; most other cruise lines adhere to the age-21 minimum. Casinos are trickier to patrol than bars, though, and minors who look old enough may get away with dropping a few coins in an out-of-the-way slot machine before being spotted on a hidden security camera. If you hit a big jackpot, you may have a lot of explaining to do to your parents.

Most ships also have movie nights, or in-cabin movies, or you may be able to rent or borrow movies to watch on your in-cabin VCR or DVD player. The latest twist in video programming can be found on some Princess, Costa, and Carnival ships—huge outdoor LED screens where movies, music video concerts, news channels, and even the ship's activities are broadcast for passengers lounging poolside.

Enrichment programs have also become a popular pastime at sea. It may come as a surprise that port lecturers on many large contemporary cruise ships offer more information on shore tours and shopping than insight into the ports of call. If more cerebral presentations are important to you, consider a cruise on a line that features stimulating enrichment programs and seminars at sea. Speakers can include destination-oriented historians, popular authors, business leaders, radio or television personalities, and even movie stars.

LOUNGES & NIGHTCLUBS

You'll often find live entertainment in the ship lounges after dinner (and even sometimes before dinner). If you want to unleash your inner-American Idol, look for karaoke. Singing along in a lively piano bar is another shipboard favorite for would-be crooners. Some passengers even take the place of the ship's pianist during breaks to demonstrate their skill.

Other lounges might feature easy-listening or jazz performances or live music for pre- and postdinner social dancing. Later in the evening, lounges pick up the pace with music from the 1950s and '60s; clubs aimed at a younger crowd usually have more contemporary dance music during the late-night hours.

CASINOS

On most ships, lavish casinos pulsate with activity. On ships that feature them, the rationale for locating casinos where most passengers must pass either through or alongside them is obvious—the unspoken allure of winning. In addition to slot machines in a variety of denominations, cruise ship casinos usually have table games. Casino hours vary based on the itinerary or location of the ship; most are required to close while in port, while others may be able to offer 24-hour slot machines and simply close

1

table games. Every casino has a cashier, and you may be able to charge a cash advance to your onboard account, for a fee.

SPORTS & FITNESS

Onboard sports facilities might include a court for basketball, volleyball, tennis—or all three—a jogging track, or even an in-line skating track. Some ships are even offering innovative and unexpected features, such as rock-climbing walls, bungee trampolines, and surfing pools on some Royal Caribbean ships. For the less adventurous, there's always table tennis and shuffleboard. Golf is a perennial seagoing favorite of players who want to take their games to the next level and include Europe's most challenging courses on their scorecards. Shipboard programs can include clinics, use of full-motion golf cages, and even individual instruction from resident pros using state-of-the-art computer analysis. Golf excursions will take you shoreside.

Naturally, you will find at least one swimming pool and, possibly, several. Cruise-ship pools are generally on the small side—more appropriate for cooling off than doing laps—and the majority contain filtered salt water. But some are elaborate affairs, with waterslides and interactive water play areas for family fun. Princess Grand-class ships have challenging, freshwater "swim against the current" pools for swimming enthusiasts who want to get their low-impact exercise while on board.

Shipboard fitness centers have become ever more elaborate, offering state-of-the-art exercise machines, treadmills, and stair steppers, not to mention weights and weight machines. As a bonus, many fitness centers with floor-to-ceiling windows have the world's most inspiring sea views. Most ships also offer complimentary fitness classes, but you might find classes in Pilates, spinning, or yoga (usually for a fee). Personal trainers are usually on board to get you off on the right foot, also for a fee.

SPAS

With all the usual pampering and service in luxurious surroundings, simply being on a cruise can be a stress-reducing experience. Add to that the menu of spa and salon services at your fingertips and you have a recipe for total sensory pleasure. Spas have also become among the most popular of shipboard areas. Steiner Leisure is the largest spa and salon operator at sea (the company also operates the Mandara and the Greenhouse spa brands), with facilities on more than 100 cruise ships worldwide.

In addition to facials, manicures, pedicures, massages, and sensual body treatments, other hallmarks of Steiner Leisure are salon services and products for hair and skin. Founded in 1901 by Henry Steiner of London, a single salon prospered when Steiner's son joined the business in 1926 and was granted a Royal Warrant as hairdresser to Her Majesty Queen Mary in 1937. In 1956 Steiner won its first cruise-ship contract to operate the salon on board the ships of the Cunard Line. By the mid-1990s Steiner Leisure began taking an active role in creating shipboard spas offering a wide variety of wellness therapies and beauty programs for both women and men.

CLOSE UP

Safety at Sea

Safety begins with you, the passenger. Once settled into your cabin, locate your life vests and review the posted emergency instructions. Make sure the vests are in good condition and learn to secure them properly. Make certain the ship's purser knows if you have a physical infirmity that may hamper a speedy exit from your cabin so that in an emergency he or she can quickly dispatch a crew member to assist you. If you're traveling with children, be sure that child-size life jackets are placed in your cabin.

Within 24 hours of embarkation, you'll be asked to attend a mandatory lifeboat drill. Do so and listen carefully. If you're unsure about how to use your vest, now is the time to ask. Only in the most extreme circumstances will you need to abandon ship—but it has happened. The time you spend learning the procedure may serve you well in a mishap.

In actuality, the greatest danger facing cruise-ship passengers is fire. All cruise lines must meet international standards for fire safety, which require sprinkler systems, smoke detectors, and other safety features. Fires on cruise ships are not common, but they do happen, and these rules have made ships much safer. You can do you part by *not* using an iron in your cabin and taking care to properly extinguish smoking materials. Never throw a lit cigarette overboard—it could be blown back into an opening in the ship and start a fire.

OTHER SHIPBOARD SERVICES

COMMUNICATIONS

Just because you are out to sea does not mean you have to be out of touch. However, ship-to-shore telephone calls can cost $5 to $15 a minute, so it makes more economic sense to use e-mail to remain in contact with your home or office. Most ships have basic computer systems, while some newer vessels offer more high-tech connectivity—even in-cabin hookups or wireless connections for either your own laptop computer or one you can rent on board. Expect charges in the 50¢- to $1-per-minute range for the use of these Internet services. Ships usually offer some kind of package so that you get a reduced per-minute price if you pay a fee up front.

The ability to use your own mobile phone from the high seas is a relatively new alternative that is gaining popularity. It's usually cheaper than using a cabin phone if your ship offers the service; however, it can still cost up to $4 or $5 a minute. A rather ingenious concept, the ship acts as a cell "tower" in international waters—you use your own cell phone and your own number when roaming at sea. Before leaving home, ask your cell phone service provider to activate international roaming on your account. When in port, depending on the type of cell phone you own and the agreements your mobile service-provider has established, you may be able to connect to local networks. Most GSM phones that use SIM cards are also usable in Europe. Rates for using the maritime service, as well as any roaming charges from European ports, are established by your mobile service carrier and are worth checking into before your trip.

LAUNDRY & DRY CLEANING

Most cruise ships offer valet laundry and pressing (and some also offer dry-cleaning) service. Expenses can add up fast, especially for laundry, since charges are per item and the rates are similar to those charged in hotels. If doing laundry is important to you and you do not want to send

Crime on Ships

Crime aboard cruise ships has occasionally become headline news, thanks in large part to a few well-publicized cases. Most people never have any type of problem, but you should exercise the same precautions aboard ship that you would at home. Keep your valuables out of sight—on big ships virtually every cabin has a small safe. Don't carry too much cash ashore, use your credit card whenever possible, and keep your money in a secure place, such as a front pocket that's harder to pick. Single women traveling with friends should stick together, especially when returning to their cabins late at night. When assaults occur, it often

comes to light that excessive drinking of alcohol is a factor. Be careful about whom you befriend, as you would anywhere, whether it's a fellow passenger or a member of the crew. Don't be paranoid, but do be prudent.

Your cruise is a wonderful opportunity to leave everyday responsibilities behind, but don't neglect to pack your common sense. After a few drinks it might seem like a good idea to sit on a railing or lean over the rail to get a better view of the ship's wake. Passengers have been known to fall. "Man overboard" is more likely to be the result of carelessness than criminal intent.

it out to be done, many cruise ships have a self-service laundry room (which usually features an iron and ironing board in addition to washer and dryer). If you book one of the top-dollar suites, laundry service may be included for no additional cost. Upscale ships, such as those in the

Regent Seven Seas Cruises, Silversea Cruises, and Seabourn fleets, have complimentary self-service launderettes. On other cruise lines, such as Princess Cruises, Oceania Cruises, Carnival Cruise Lines, and Holland America Line (except Vista-class ships), you can do your own laundry for about $3 or less per load. Norwegian Cruise Line's Jewel-class ships have complimentary self-service laundry rooms, but there is a nominal fee for the detergent. None of the vessels in the Royal Caribbean or Celebrity Cruises fleets has self-service laundry facilities.

DISEMBARKATION

All cruises come to an end eventually, and the disembarkation process actually begins the day before you arrive at your ship's final port. During that day your cabin steward delivers special luggage tags to your stateroom, along with customs forms and instructions.

The night before you disembark, you'll need to set aside clothing to wear the next morning when you leave the ship. Many people dress in whatever casual outfits they wear for the final dinner on board, or change into travel clothes after dinner. Also, do not forget to put your passport or other proof of citizenship, airline tickets, and medications in your hand luggage. The luggage tags go onto your larger bags, which are placed outside your stateroom door for pickup during the hours indicated.

A statement itemizing your onboard charges is delivered before you arise on disembarkation morning. Plan to get up early enough to check it over for accuracy, finish packing your personal belongings, and vacate your stateroom by the appointed hour. Any discrepancies in your onboard account should be taken care of before leaving the ship, usually at the purser's desk. Breakfast is served in the main restaurant as well as the buffet on the last morning, but room service isn't available. Disembarkation procedures vary by cruise line, but you'll probably have to wait in a lounge or on deck for your tag color or number to be called.

Then you take a taxi, bus, or other transportation to your post-cruise hotel or to the airport for your flight home. If you are flying out the day your cruise ends, leave plenty of time to go through the usual check-in, passport control/immigration, and security procedures at the airport. You may also want to do some duty-free shopping at the airport; some airports, particularly Amsterdam's Schiphol Airport, are bursting with last-minute opportunities for retail therapy. However, you need to be aware the EU does not allow you to do any duty-free shopping in an airport unless that airport is your last stop in the EU zone. Thus, if you leave from Athens but connect in Paris, you'll have to do your shopping in Paris rather than Athens. Unless you are flying from a non-EU country to an EU country, you probably won't go through Immigration or Customs until you reenter the United States, always at your first point of reentry; if you are continuing on a U.S. domestic flight to your final destination, you have to recheck your bags as you leave Customs.

CUSTOMS & DUTIES

TAXES

If you make any purchases while in Europe, you should ask for a V.A.T. refund form and find out whether the merchant gives refunds—not all stores do, nor are they required to. Have the form stamped like any customs form by customs officials when you leave the country or, if you're visiting several European Union countries, when you leave the EU. This has to be done at the airport on the day you are flying home. After you're through passport control, take the form to a refund-service counter for an on-the-spot refund (which is usually the quickest and easiest option), or mail it to the address on the form (or the envelope with it) after you arrive home. You receive the total refund stated on the form, but the processing time can be long, especially if you request a credit-card adjustment.

Global Refund is a Europe-wide service with 225,000 affiliated stores and more than 700 refund counters at major airports and border crossings. Its refund form, called a Tax Free Check, is the most common across the European continent. The service issues refunds in the form of cash, check, or credit-card adjustment.

V.A.T. Refunds **Global Refund** (☎ 800/566–9828 ⊕ www.globalrefund.com).

U.S. CUSTOMS

Each individual or family returning to the United States must fill out a customs declaration form, which will be provided before your plane lands. If you owe any duties, you will have to pay them directly to the customs inspector, with cash or check. Be sure to keep receipts for all purchases; and you may be asked to show officials what you've bought. If your cruise is a transatlantic crossing, U.S. Customs clears ships sailing into arrival ports. After showing your passport to immigration officials, you must collect your luggage from the dock, then stand in line to pass through the inspection point. This can take up to an hour.

ALLOWANCES   You're always allowed to bring goods of a certain value back home without having to pay any duty or import tax. But there's a limit on the amount of tobacco and liquor you can bring back duty-free. The values of so-called "duty-free" goods are included in these amounts. When you shop abroad, save all your receipts, as customs inspectors may ask to see them as well as the items you purchased. If the total value of your goods is more than the duty-free limit, you'll have to pay a tax (most often a flat percentage) on the value of everything beyond that limit. For U.S. citizens who have been in Europe for at least 48 hours, the duty-free exemption is $800. But the duty-free exemption includes only 200 cigarettes, 100 cigars, and 1 liter of alcohol (this includes wine); above these limits, you have to pay duties, even if you didn't spend more than the $800 limit.

U.S. Information **U.S. Customs and Border Protection** (⊕ *www.cbp.gov*).

SENDING   Although you probably won't want to spend your time looking for a post
PACKAGES   office, you can send packages home duty-free, with a limit of one parcel
HOME   per addressee per day (except alcohol or tobacco products or perfume worth more than $5). You can mail up to $200 worth of goods to yourself, or $100 worth of goods to a friend or relative; label the package "personal use" or "unsolicited gift" (depending on which is the case) and attach a list of the contents and their retail value. If the package contains your used personal belongings, mark it "personal goods returned" to avoid paying duty on your laundry. You do not need to declare items that were sent home on your declaration forms for U.S. Customs.

FODOR'S CRUISE PREPARATION TIMELINE

4 MONTHS BEFORE SAILING

■ A passport *will* be required for travel to Europe. Gather the necessary identification you need. If you must replace a lost birth certificate, apply for a new passport, or renew one that's about to expire, start the paperwork now. Doing it at the last minute is stressful and often costly.

60 TO 75 DAYS BEFORE SAILING

■ Make the final payment on your cruise fare. Though the dates vary, your travel agent should remind you when the payment date draws near. Failure to submit the balance on time can result in the cancellation of your reservation.

■ Make a packing list for each person you'll be packing for.

■ Begin your wardrobe planning now. Try things on to make sure they fit and are in good repair (it's amazing how stains can magically appear months after something has been dry cleaned). Set things aside in your closet.

■ If you need to shop, get started so you have time to find just the right thing (and perhaps to return or exchange just the right thing). You may also need to allow time for alterations. Start early—last-minute shopping for just the right thing can be hazardous to your nerves.

■ Make kennel reservations for your pets. (If you're traveling during a holiday period, you may need to do this even earlier.)

■ Arrange for a house sitter.

■ If you're cruising, but your kids are staying home:

■ Make child-care arrangements.

■ Go over children's schedules to make sure they'll have everything they need while you're gone (gift for a birthday party, supplies for a school project, permission slip for a field trip).

■ If you have small children, you may want to put together a small bag of treats for them to open while you're gone—make a tape of yourself reading a favorite bedtime story or singing a lullaby (as long as it's you, it will sound fantastic to them).

30 DAYS BEFORE SAILING

■ If you purchased an Air & Sea package, call your travel agent for the details of your airline schedule. Request seat assignments and any special airline meals.

■ If your children are sailing with you, check their wardrobes now (do it too early, and the really little kids may actually grow out of garments).

■ Make appointments for any personal services you wish to have prior to your cruise. For example, a haircut, manicure, or a pedicure.

■ Get out your luggage and check the locks and zippers. Check for anything that might have spilled inside on a previous trip.

■ If you need new luggage or want an extra piece to bring home your souvenirs, purchase it now.

■ If your new passport has not yet arrived, call the U.S. Passport Office hotline to track it; alert your Congressional representative's office if you need help in getting your passport expedited.

2 TO 4 WEEKS BEFORE SAILING

■ Receive your cruise documents through the travel agent.

■ Examine the documents for accuracy (correct cabin number, sailing date, and dining arrangements) and make sure names are spelled correctly. If there's something you do not understand, ask your travel agent or the cruise line now.

■ Read all the literature in your document package for suggestions specific to your cruise. Most cruise lines include helpful information.

■ Pay any routine bills that may be due while you're gone.

■ Go over your personalized packing list again. Finish shopping.

1 WEEK BEFORE SAILING

■ Finalize your packing list and continue organizing everything in one area.

■ Buy film or memory cards and check the batteries in your camera.

■ Refill prescription medications with an adequate supply (and bring along a copy

1

of the written prescription if this is critical medication).

■ Make two photocopies of your passport or ID and credit cards. Leave one copy with a friend, and carry the other copy separately from the originals.

■ Get cash and/or traveler's checks at the bank. If you use traveler's checks, keep a separate record of the serial numbers. Get a supply of one dollar bills for tipping baggage handlers (at the airport, hotel, pier, etc.).

■ You may also want to put valuables and jewelry that you won't be taking with you in the safety deposit box while you're at the bank. (See "1 Day Before Sailing"—you may want to put some of the contents of your wallet in the safety deposit box as well.)

■ Arrange to have your mail held at the post office or ask a neighbor to pick it up.

■ Stop newspaper delivery or ask a neighbor to bring it in for you.

■ Arrange for lawn and houseplant care or snow removal during your absence (if necessary).

■ Leave your itinerary, the ship's telephone number (plus the name of your ship and your stateroom number), and a house key with a relative or friend. If the ship's telephone number is not included in your documents, your travel agent can get the number for you.

■ If traveling with small children, purchase small games or toys to keep them occupied while en route to your embarkation port.

3 DAYS BEFORE SAILING

■ Confirm your airline flights; departure times are sometimes subject to change.

■ Put a card with your name, address, telephone number, and itinerary inside each suitcase.

■ Fill out the luggage tags that came with your document packet, and follow the instructions regarding when and how to attach them.

■ Complete any other paperwork that the cruise line included with your documents (foreign customs and immigration forms, onboard charge application, etc). Do not wait until you're standing in the pier check-in line to fill them in!

■ Do last-minute laundry and tidy up the house.

■ Pull out the luggage and begin packing.

THE DAY BEFORE SAILING

■ Take pets to the kennel.

■ Water houseplants and lawn (if necessary).

■ Dispose of any perishable food in the refrigerator.

■ Mail any last-minute bills.

■ Set timers for indoor lights.

■ Reorganize your wallet. Remove anything you will not need (check cashing cards, department store, or gas credit cards, etc.), put these in an envelope, and leave in a secure place.

■ Finish packing and lock your suitcases.

DEPARTURE DAY

■ Adjust the thermostat and double-check the door locks.

■ Turn off the water if there's danger of frozen pipes while you're away.

■ Arrange to be at the airport a minimum of two hours before your departure time (follow the airline's instructions).

■ Have photo ID and passport ready for airport check-in.

■ Slip your car keys, parking claim checks, and airline tickets in your carry-on luggage. Never pack these items in checked luggage.

■ Breathe a sigh of relief . . . you're on your way.

■ To expedite your preboarding paperwork, some cruise lines have convenient forms on their Web sites. As long as you have your reservation (or booking) number, you can provide the required immigration information, reserve shore excursions, and even indicate any special requests from the comfort of your home. Be sure to print a copy of the form to present at the pier.

Cruise Lines & Cruise Ships

Costa Classica

WORD OF MOUTH

"I personally prefer the smaller, more intimate, service-oriented ships. Regent is our favorite line, and it's nice that it's all-inclusive (even liquor and tips). Some prefer the large ships, so it's a personal preference. You will be very port intensive in the Med but to me, the ship itself is one of the destinations."

—petlover

Linda Coffman

SECOND ONLY TO THE CARIBBEAN in popularity with cruise passengers, Europe has it all—beautifully preserved castles, romantic gardens, fabulous art treasures, antiquities, and some of the world's most breathtaking scenery. Great cities flourished along all the coasts of the Continent, which makes it possible to explore many of Europe's richest treasures by ship.

Every year major North American cruise lines satisfy the seasonal demand for what amounts to an old-fashioned Grand Tour afloat by repositioning a large portion of their Caribbean fleets to Europe. They join European-based ships that are ported in the Baltic for the summer and the Mediterranean year-round. The largest vessels generally stick to predictable routes that include major cities along the coasts such as Amsterdam, Venice, Barcelona, and Athens, or those, like Rome, close enough to visit during a port call. Small to midsize ships offer the advantage of visiting ports off the beaten path of the large ships and can call at intriguing destinations like the less-visited Greek Isles and jet-set favorite Ibiza without the necessity of tendering passengers ashore.

CRUISE LINES

Seated in an airplane after a week of enjoying an exceptionally nice cruise, I overheard the couple behind me discussing their "dreadful" cruise vacation. What a surprise when they mentioned the ship's name. It was the one I'd just spent a glorious week on. I never missed a meal. They hated the food. My cabin was comfortable and cheery, if not large. Their identical accommodations resembled a "cave." One size definitely does not fit all in cruising. What's appealing to one passenger may be unacceptable to another. Ultimately, most cruise complaints arise from passengers whose expectations were not met. The couple I eavesdropped on were on the wrong cruise line and ship for them.

I enjoy cruises. Some have suited me more than others, but I've never sailed on a cruise that was completely without merit. Make no mistake about it: cruise lines have distinct personalities. Lines appeal to different demographics and offer different levels of comfort and service. We have divided the cruise lines in this book into three main categories: Mainstream, Premium, and Luxury, but some defy easy categorization. And when you are cruising in Europe, there are also the European cruise lines to consider. While they cater to a more international mix of travelers, they also offer the more European experience favored by many Americans when traveling abroad. Just as cruise lines differ, the ships of the line may also differ, although they will share many basic similarities. Most lines try to standardize the overall experience throughout their fleets, which is why you'll find a waterslide on every Carnival ship. But you won't find an ice-skating rink on any but the largest Royal Caribbean ships.

So, which cruise line is best? Only you can determine which is best for you. You won't find ratings by Fodor's—either quality stars or value scores. Why? Think of those people seated behind me on the airplane. They assuredly would rate their experience differently than I did. Instead of rating and ranking lines and ships based on the reviewer's opinion, we've tried to give more objective overviews. Your responsibility is to select the right cruise for you—no one knows your expectations better than you do yourself. The short wait for a table might not bother you because you would prefer a casual atmosphere with open seating; however, some people want the security of a set time at an assigned table served by a waiter who gets to know their preferences. You know what you are willing to trade off in order to get what you want.

MAINSTREAM CRUISE LINES

The mainstream lines are the ones most often associated with modern cruising. They offer the advantage of something for everyone and nearly every available sports facility imaginable. Some ships even have ice-skating rinks, 18-hole miniature golf courses, bowling alleys, and rock-climbing walls.

Generally speaking, the mainstream lines have two basic ship sizes—large cruise ships and megaships—in their fleets. These vessels have plentiful outdoor deck space, and many have a wraparound outdoor promenade deck that allows you to stroll or jog the ship's perimeter. In the newest vessels, traditional meets trendy. You'll find atrium lobbies and expansive sun and sports decks, picture windows instead of portholes, and cabins that open onto private verandas. For all their resort-style innovations, they still feature cruise-ship classics—afternoon tea, complimentary room service, and lavish pampering. The smallest ships carry 1,000 passengers or fewer, while the largest accommodate more than 3,000 passengers and are filled with diversions.

These ships tend to be big and boxy. Picture windows are standard equipment, and cabins in the top categories have private verandas. From their casinos and discos to their fitness centers, everything is bigger and more extravagant than on other ships. You'll pay for many extras on the mainstream ships, from drinks at the bar, to that cup of cappucino, to spa treatments, to a game of bowling, to dinner in a specialty restaurant. You may want to rethink a cruise aboard one of these ships if you want a little downtime, since you'll be joined by 1,500 to 3,000 fellow passengers.

PREMIUM CRUISE LINES

Premium cruise lines have a lot in common with the mainstream cruise lines, but with a little more of everything. The atmosphere is more refined, surroundings more gracious, and service more polished and attentive. There are still activities like pool games, although they aren't quite the high jinks typical of mainstream ships. In addition to traditional cruise activities, onboard lectures are common. Production shows are somewhat more sophisticated than on mainstream lines.

Ships tend to be newer midsize to large vessels that carry fewer passengers than mainstream ships and have a more spacious feel. Decor is usually more glamorous and subtle, with toned-down colors and extensive original art. Staterooms range from inside cabins for three or four to outside cabins with or without balconies to suites with numerous amenities, including butlers on some lines.

Most premium ships offer traditional assigned seatings for dinner. High marks are afforded the quality cuisine and presentation. Many ships have upscale bistros or specialty restaurants, which usually require reservations and command an additional charge. Although premium lines usually have as many extra charges as mainstream lines, the overall quality of what you receive is higher.

LUXURY CRUISE LINES

Comprising only 5% of the market, the exclusive luxury cruise lines, such as Crystal, Cunard, Regent Seven Seas, Seabourn, SeaDream, and Silversea offer high staff-to-guest ratios for personal service, superior cuisine in a single open seating (except Crystal, with two assigned seatings and Cunard, with dual-class dining assignments), and a highly inclusive product with few onboard charges. These small and midsize ships offer much more space per passenger than you will find on the mainstream lines' vessels. Lines differ in what they emphasize, with some touting luxurious accommodations and entertainment and others focusing on exotic destinations and onboard enrichment.

If you consider travel a necessity rather than a luxury and frequent posh resorts, then you will appreciate the extra attention and the higher level of comfort that luxury cruise lines offer. Itineraries on these ships often include the marquee ports, but luxury ships also visit some of the more uncommon destinations. With an intimate size, the smaller luxury ships can visit such ports as Marbella, Spain, and Korçula, Croatia.

OTHER CRUISE LINES

A few small cruise lines sail through Europe and offer boutique to nearly bed-and-breakfast experiences. Notably, Star Clippers and relative newcomer easyCruise appeal to passengers who eschew mainstream cruises. Most of these niche vessels accommodate 200 or fewer passengers, and their focus is on soft adventure. Cruising between nearby ports and anchoring out so passengers can swim and snorkel directly from the ship, as offered by Star Clippers, they have itineraries that usually leave plenty of time for exploring and other activities on- or offshore. Many of these cruises schedule casual enrichment talks that often continue on decks, at meals, and during trips ashore.

EUROPEAN CRUISE LINES

With more similarities to American-owned cruise lines than differences, these European-owned and -operated cruise lines compare favorably to the mainstream cruise lines of a decade ago. Although some lines have embarked upon shipbuilding programs that rival the most ambitious in the cruise industry, most European fleets consist of older, yet well-maintained vessels. While they cater to Europeans—announcements may be broadcast in as many as five languages—and Americans are generally in the minority, English is widely spoken.

RIVER CRUISES

River boats and barges present an entirely different persepective on European cruising. Smaller than even the smallest ocean cruise ships, they offer a convenient alternative to bus tours—you only unpack once—while navigating the rivers and canals to reach legendary inland cities. Just as on cruise ships, accommodations and meals are included. Some shore excursions might be part of the package as well. These cruises are covered in Chapter 3.

ABOUT THESE REVIEWS

The following Cruise Line Profiles offer a general idea of what you can expect in terms of overall experience, quality, and service. For each cruise line described, we list the ships (grouped by class or similar configurations) that regularly cruise in Europe. However, not all ships spend the entire year in Europe; for example, some go to the Caribbean during winter months, while others spend part of the year in Asia or the South Pacific. We've excluded entirely those that have no regular itineraries in Europe as of this writing. Thus, not all ships owned by the cruise lines we cover are described.

When two or more ships belong to the same class—or are substantially similar—they are listed together in the subhead under the name of the class; the year each was introduced is also given in the same order in the statistics section. Passenger-capacity figures are given on the basis of two people sharing a cabin; however, many of the larger ships have three- and four-berth cabins, which can increase the total number of passengers tremendously when all berths are occupied. When total occupancy figures differ from double occupancy, we give them in parentheses.

Because cruise ships can float off to far-flung (and not always warm) regions, many are designed with an eye to less-than-perfect weather. For that reason, you're likely to find indoor swimming pools featured on their deck plans. Except in rare cases, these are usually dual-purpose pools that can be covered when necessary by a sliding roof or magrodome to create an indoor swimming environment. Our reviews indicate the total number of swiming pools found on each ship, with permanently and/or temporarily covered pools included in the total and also noted as "# indoors" in parentheses. We also indicate whether there is a dedicated children's pool.

Unlike other guidebooks, we describe not only the features, but the cabin dimensions for each accommodation category available on the ships reviewed. Dimensions should be considered approximate and used for comparison purposes only as they sometimes vary depending on location. For instance, while staterooms are largely prefabricated in the same size and design with all electrical and plumbing fixtures preinstalled, those located at the front of some ships may by necessity be oddly curved to conform to the shape of the bow.

Demand is high and cruise ships are sailing at full capacity, so someone is satisfied by every ship. When you're armed with all the right information, we're sure you'll be able to find one that not only fits your style, but offers you the service and value you expect.

AZAMARA CRUISES

In something of a surprise move, parent company Royal Caribbean International announced the formation of an all-new, deluxe cruise line in 2007. Two vessels originally slated for service in the Celebrity Cruises fleet, which were built for now-defunct Renaissance Cruises and acquired with the purchase of

Azamara Journey at sea

Spanish cruise line Pullmantur, are the basis for the new line, Azamura Cruises. Designed to offer exotic destination–driven itineraries, Azamara Cruises are set to present a more intimate onboard experience, while allowing access to the less-traveled ports of call experienced travelers want to visit.

AZAMARA CRUISES
1050 Caribbean Way
Miami, FL 33132
877/999-9553
www.azamaracruises.com

Cruise Style: Premium

One distinguishing aspect of Azamara is a wide range of enrichment programs to accompany the destination-rich itineraries. Popular enrichment programs include guest speakers and experts on a wide variety of topics, including destinations, technology, cultural explorations, art, music, and design. Lectures might include how to get the best photos from your digital camera or the proper way to pair wine and food, as taught by resident sommeliers. An onboard "excursion expert" can not only help you select shore excursions based on your personal interests, but also will serve as a destination guide, offering information about the culture and history of each port of call. Entertainment, on the other hand, leans toward cabaret-size production shows and variety entertainers in the main lounge. Diverse musical offerings throughout the ships range from upbeat dance bands to intimate piano bar entertainers.

CHOOSE A CRUISE ON AZAMARA CRUISES IF...

1 Your taste leans toward luxury, but your budget doesn't.

2 You prefer leisurely, open seating dining in casual attire to the stiffness of assigned tablemates and waiters.

3 The manner in which you "get there" is as important to you as your destination.

Food

Expect dinner favorites to have an upscale twist, such as gulf shrimp with cognac and garlic, or a filet mignon with black truffle sauce. Specialty restaurants include the Mediterranean-influenced Aqualina and the stylish steak and seafood restaurant Prime C. Guests in suites receive two nights of complimentary dining in the two specialty restaurants, while guests in staterooms receive one. Daily in-cabin afternoon tea service and delivery of canapés is available to all passengers who want them.

Fitness & Recreation

In addition to a well-equipped gym and an outdoor jogging track, features of Azamara's fitness program include yoga at sunset, Pilates, and access to an onboard wellness consultant. Both ships offer a full menu of spa treatments, an outdoor spa relaxation lounge, and an aesthetics suite featuring acupuncture, laser hair removal, and microdermabrasion.

Your Shipmates

Azamara is designed to appeal to discerning travelers, primarily American couples of any age who appreciate a high level of service in a nonstructured atmosphere. The ships have no facilities or programs for children.

Dress Code

All evenings are designated resort casual; there are no scheduled formal nights. However, passengers who choose to wear formal attire are welcome to do so.

Service

Gracious and polished service throughout the ships affords everyone an exclusive experience. Azamara offers butler service in every stateroom and suite.

Tipping

Gratuities are automatically charged to onboard accounts at the daily rate of $12.25 per person, which covers all restaurant and stateroom service personnel. Amounts may be adjusted according to the level of service received. A standard 15% is added to beverage charges.

Noteworthy

■ Since Azamara is a subsidiary of Celebrity Cruises, repeat cruisers will be members of Celebrity's Captain's Club.

■ Initially, you may bring two bottles of wine per stateroom aboard, but you will pay a $25 corkage fee if you bring it to one of the dining rooms.

■ Smokers are restricted to one lounge and a small section on the pool deck; all other public and private areas are no-smoking.

AZAMARA CRUISES

2

Grand Lobby on *Azamara Journey*

DON'T CHOOSE A CRUISE ON AZAMARA CRUISES IF...

❶ You want an all-inclusive cruise; alcoholic beverages and soft drinks are not included.

❷ The services of a butler would make you uncomfortable.

❸ You insist upon smoking whenever and wherever you want to.

AZAMARA JOURNEY, AZAMARA QUEST

2000, 2001	ENTERED SERVICE
710	PASSENGER CAPACITY
390	CREW MEMBERS
355	NUMBER OF CABINS
30,277	GROSS TONS
593 feet	LENGTH
95 feet	WIDTH

700 ft.

500 ft.

300 ft.

Public Areas & Facilities

At 30,277 tons, *Azamara Quest* and *Azamara Journey* are medium-size ships are well suited for the somewhat more exotic itineraries for which they are deployed, whether in Europe or South America. The ships initially entered service for Renaissance Cruises and served in Spain under the Pullmantur flag until 2007. With their entry into the brand-new Azamara Cruises fleet, a new option is available to passengers who prefer the boutique-hotel atmosphere of a smaller ship without the luxury-class price tag.

After separate one-month drydocks, the ships now have a variety of signature features, including the Martini Bar in Casino Luxe, the casual Mosaic Café, the distinctive Astral Spa with an acupuncture suite and expansive relaxation deck and therapy pool. Each ship has two specialty restaurants. The exclusive experience includes butler service and concierge amenities in all categories of accommodations.

WOW Factor

The most photographed spot on board is certainly the dramatic grand staircase, reminiscent of those found on grand, transatlantic ocean liners.

Top: Open seating dining
Bottom: Balcony stateroom

Restaurants

Some details were still being developed at this writing, but the formal restaurant serves evening meals in one open seating and is supplemented by a casual Lido buffet and two upscale alternative restaurants (which require reservations and a cover charge). A luncheon grill, pizzeria, Mosaic Café patisserie, and 24-hour room service augment dining choices.

What Works & What Doesn't

In the smaller space of midsize ships, these vessels offer a lot of big-ship features, despite being built to another cruise line's specifications. Expect to have a comfortably sophisticated experience in an intimate environment. One staff member for every two passengers and the attention of a butler for each stateroom ensures unparalleled service at this level. Upscale amenities make up for the lack of bathroom space in standard staterooms.

Accommodations

Layout: Designed for lengthy cruises, all staterooms have ample closet and storage space, and even standard cabins have at least a small sitting area, although bathrooms in lower categories are somewhat tight. Wood cabinetry adds warmth to the decor. In keeping with the trend for more balconies, 73% of all outside cabins and suites have them.

Amenities: Amenities include plush beds and bedding that were installed during the ships' makeovers. Bath toiletries, a hair dryer, TV, personal safe, and robes for use during the cruise are all included, but you must move up to a suite to have a bathtub since lower-category cabins have shower only.

Suites: Full suites are particularly luxurious, with living/dining rooms, entertainment centers, minibars, two TVs, separate bedrooms, whirlpool bathtubs, guest powder rooms, and very large balconies overlooking either the bow or stern. Thirty-two Sky Suites newly incorporated into each ship have a queen size bed, minibar, television, whirlpool, personal safe, and hair dryer.

Worth Noting: Six staterooms are designated as wheelchair accessible.

Cabin Type	Size (sq. ft.)
Penthouse/Royal Suites	560/440–501
Sky Suites/Sunset Veranda	266/175
Oceanview Balcony	175
Oceanview	175
Inside	151

Fast Facts

- 9 passenger decks
- 2 specialty restaurants, dining room, buffet, pizzeria
- Wi-Fi, in-cabin safes, some in-cabin minibars, in-cabin refrigerators, some in-cabin DVDs
- 1 pool
- Fitness classes, gym, hair salon, 2 hot tubs, spa, steam room
- 8 bars, casino, dance club, library, showroom
- Dry cleaning, laundry service
- Computer room

In the Know

Forward-facing Royal Suite balconies offer remarkable views, but depending on the force of the wind when the ship is under way, they can be virtually unusable. Also, it's best to keep the suite balcony doors locked when at sea as they tend to slide open if the ship rolls from side to side.

Favorites

Best Balcony Cabins: Aft-facing Sunset Verandas on decks six and seven are simply standard balcony cabins sandwiched between suites. However, they have much larger balconies than other similar accommodations and terrific views of the ship's wake as well as evening sunsets.

Best Place to Warm Up the Evening: The sophisticated Martini Bar in Casino Luxe offers popular variations of this famous cocktail, and the bartenders are willing to follow your instructions to mix your favorite even if it's not on the menu.

Our Favorite Spot for a Nightcap: We like the quiet sounds of a grand piano and deep, welcoming seating that add to the ambience of the Drawing Room.

Best Splurge: Sure there's an extra charge, but we just can't pass up the aromatic specialty coffees and divine pastries in Mosaic Café. The "Best Unexpected Treat" on board is that certain pastries in Mosaic Café are complimentary throughout the day, and tapas are available in the evening.

Casual dining

2

AZAMARA CRUISES

CARNIVAL CRUISE LINES

The world's largest cruise line originated the Fun Ship concept in 1972
with the relaunch of an aging ocean
liner, which got stuck on a sandbar
during its maiden voyage. In true
entrepreneurial spirit, founder Ted
Arison shrugged off an inauspi-
cious beginning to introduce super-
liners only a decade later. Sporting

Lobby Bar onboard *Fantasy*

red-white-and-blue flared funnels, which are easily recognized from afar, new
ships are continuously added to the fleet and rarely deviate from a successful
pattern. If you find something you like on one vessel, you're likely to find something similar on another.

CARNIVAL CRUISE LINES
3655 N.W. 87 Avenue
Miami, FL 33178-2428
305/599-2600 or
800/227-6482
www.carnival.com

Cruise Style: Mainstream

Even the decor is fun; each vessel features themed public
rooms, ranging from ancient Egypt to futuristic motifs.
More high-energy than cerebral, the entertainment consists of lavish Las Vegas–style revues presented in main
show lounges by a company of singers and dancers. Other
performers might include comedians, magicians, jugglers,
acrobats, and even passengers taking part in the talent
show or stepping up to the karaoke microphone. Live
bands play a wide range of musical styles for dancing and
listening in smaller lounges, and each ship has a disco.

Arrive early to get a seat for bingo and art auctions. Adult
activities, particularly the competitive ones, tend to be
silly and hilarious and play to full houses. Relaxing poolside can be difficult when bands crank up the volume
or the cruise director selects volunteers for pool games;
fortunately, it's always in fun and mostly entertaining.
There's generally a quieter, second pool to retreat to.

Carnival is so sure passengers will be satisfied with their
cruise experience that they are the only cruise line to offer
a "Vacation Guarantee." Just notify them before arriving at the first port of call if you're unhappy for any reason. Should you choose to disembark at the ship's first
non-U.S. port, Carnival will refund the unused portion

of your cruise fare and pay for your flight back to your embarkation port. It's a generous offer for which they get very few takers.

Food

Carnival ships have both flexible dining options and casual alternative restaurants. A staggered dining room schedule, which includes a selection of four set meal times on all but the Spirit-class ships (5:45 or 6:15 PM for early dining and 8 or 8:30 PM for late dining), means the ships' galleys serve fewer meals at any one time. The result is better service and higher-quality food preparation. Carnival's less harried restaurant staff deliver a more satisfying dining experience for passengers because they have fewer passengers to cook for and to serve at any given time.

Choices are numerous, and the addition of "George Blanc Signature Selections," created by the French master chef, have elevated Carnival's menus to an unexpected level. While the waiters still sing and dance, the good-to-excellent dining-room food appeals to American tastes and includes second helpings if you want. Upscale supper clubs on certain ships serve cuisine comparable to the best high-end steak houses and seafood restaurants ashore.

Carnival serves the best food of the mainstream cruise lines. In addition to the regular menu, vegetarian, low-calorie, low-carbohydrate, low-salt, and no-sugar selections are available. A children's menu includes such favorites as macaroni and cheese, chicken fingers, and peanut butter-and-jelly sandwiches. If you don't feel like dressing up for dinner, the Lido buffet serves full meals and excellent pizza.

Fitness & Recreation

Manned by staff members trained to keep passengers in ship-shape form, Carnival's trademark spas and fitness centers are some of the largest and best equipped at sea. Spas and salons are operated by Steiner, and treatments include a variety of massages, body wraps, and facials; the latest in hair and nail services are offered in the salons. Tooth-whitening is a recent addition to the roster. State-of-the-art cardiovascular and strength-training equipment, a jogging track, and basic exercise classes are available at no charge in the fitness centers. There's a fee for personal training, body composition analysis, and specialized classes such as yoga and Pilates.

Your Shipmates

Carnival's passengers are predominantly active Americans, mostly couples in their mid-30s to mid-50s. Many families enjoy Carnival cruises in the Caribbean year-round. Holi-

Top: *Carnival Victory* dining room
Bottom: *Carnival Legend* waterslide

Top: *Carnival Triumph* walking & jogging track
Middle: *Carnival Elation* at sea
Bottom: *Carnival Destiny* penthouse suite

days and school vacation periods are very popular with families, and you'll see a lot of kids in summer.

Dress Code

Two formal nights are standard on seven-night cruises; one formal night is the norm on shorter sailings. Although men are encouraged to wear tuxedos, dark suits or sport coats and ties are more prevalent. All other evenings are casual, although jeans are discouraged in restaurants. All ships request that no shorts be worn in public areas after 6 PM, but that policy is often ignored.

Junior Cruisers

"Camp Carnival" earns high marks for keeping young cruisers busy and content. Run year-round by professionals, dedicated children's areas include great playrooms with separate splash pools. Toddlers from two to five years are treated to puppet shows, sponge painting, face painting, coloring, drawing, and crafts. As long as diapers and supplies are provided, toddlers do not have to be toilet trained to participate. Activities for ages six to eight include arts and crafts, pizza parties, computer time, T-shirt painting, a talent show, and fitness programs. Nine-to 11-year-olds can play Ping-Pong, take dance lessons, play video games, and participate in swim parties, scavenger hunts, and sports. Teens 12 to 15 particularly appreciate social events, parties, contests, and sports. Every night they have access to the ships' discos from 9:30 until 10:45 PM, followed by late-night movies, karaoke, or pizza.

"Club O2" is geared toward teens from 15 to 17. Program directors play host at the spacious teen clubs, where kicking back is the order of the day between scheduled activities and nonalcoholic parties. The fleetwide "Y-Spa" program for older teens offers a high level of pampering. Staff members also accompany teens on shore excursions designed just for them.

Daytime group babysitting for infants two and under allows parents the freedom to explore ports of call without the kids from port arrival until noon. Parents can also pursue leisurely adults-only evenings from 10 PM to 3 AM, when slumber party–style group babysitting is available for children from ages 4 months to 11 years. Babysitting

CHOOSE A CRUISE ON CARNIVAL CRUISE LINES IF...

❶ You want an action-packed casino with a choice of table games and rows upon rows of clanging slot machines.

❷ You don't mind standing in line—these are big ships with a lot of passengers, and lines are not uncommon.

❸ You don't mind hearing announcements over the public-address system reminding you of what's next on the schedule.

fees are $6 an hour for one child and $4 an hour for each additional child in the same family.

Service

Service on Carnival ships is friendly but not polished. Stateroom attendants are not only recognized for their attention to cleanliness, but also for their expertise in creating towel animals—cute critters fashioned from bath towels that appear during nightly turndown service. They've become so popular that Carnival publishes an instruction book on how to create them yourself.

Tipping

A gratuity of $10 per passenger, per day is automatically added to passenger accounts, and gratuities are distributed to stewards and waitstaff. Passengers may adjust the amount based on the level of service experienced. All beverage tabs at bars get an automatic 15% addition.

Past Passengers

After sailing on one Carnival cruise, you'll receive a complimentary two-year subscription to *Currents*, the company magazine, and access to your past sailing history on the Carnival Web site. You are recognized on subsequent cruises with color-coded key cards—Gold (starting with second cruise) or Platinum (starting with your 10th cruise)—which serve as your entrée to the by-invitation-only repeat passengers' cocktail reception. You're also eligible for exclusive discounts on future cruises, not only on Carnival but on all the cruise lines owned by Carnival Corporation.

In addition, Platinum members are eligible for "Concierge Club" benefits, including priority embarkation and debarkation, guaranteed dining assignments, supper club and spa reservations, logo items, and complimentary laundry service.

Good to Know

If you've never sailed on a Carnival ship, or haven't sailed on one in recent years, you may not understand how Carnival cruises have evolved. The shipboard atmosphere is still bright, noisy, and fun, but the beer-drinking contests and bawdy, anything-goes image are history. Unfortunately, much like Casual Friday has evolved from no tie in the office to jeans and a polo shirt, it isn't unusual to see Carnival passengers dressed very casually after dinner, even on formal nights. You may be surprised at how quickly some passengers can swap their black ties and gowns for T-shirts and shorts between the dining room and show lounge. The fun of a Carnival cruise can begin before you leave home if you log on to the Carnival Web site at www.carnivalconnections.com, where you will find planning tips, cruise reviews, and a message board.

2

CARNIVAL CRUISE LINES

DON'T CHOOSE A CRUISE ON CARNIVAL CRUISE LINES IF...

1 You want an intimate, sedate atmosphere. Carnival's ships are big and bold.

2 You want elaborate accommodations. Carnival suites are spacious but not as feature-filled as the term "suite" suggests.

3 You're turned off by men in tank tops. Casual on these ships means casual indeed.

CONQUEST CLASS
Carnival Conquest, Glory, Valor, Liberty, Freedom

Public Areas & Facilities

Taking Fun Ships to new lengths and widths, Conquest-class ships are the largest in the Carnival fleet. They're basically larger and more feature-filled versions of earlier Destiny-class vessels. More space translates into additional decks, an upscale Supper Club, and even more bars and lounges; however, well-proportioned public areas belie the ships' massive size. You'll hardly notice that there's slightly less space per passenger after you take a thrilling trip down the spiral waterslide.

Public rooms flow forward and aft from stunning central atriums. Just off each ship's main boulevard is an array of specialty bars, dance lounges, discos, piano bars, and show lounges, plus seating areas along the indoor promenades. The promenade can get crowded between dinner seatings and show lounge performances, but with so many different places to spend time, you're sure to find one with plenty of room and an atmosphere to suit your taste.

ENTERED SERVICE	2002, 2003, 2004, 2005, 2007
PASSENGER CAPACITY	2,974 (3,700 max)
CREW MEMBERS	1,160
NUMBER OF CABINS	1,487
GROSS TONS	110,000
LENGTH	952 feet
WIDTH	116 feet

WOW Factor

If the atrium doesn't grab your attention immediately, you're in too much of a hurry. Plan to sit down and soak up the details.

Restaurants

Two formal restaurants serve open-seating breakfast and lunch; dinner is served in four assigned seatings. The casual Lido buffet's food stations offer a variety of choices (including different daily regional cuisines). At night it is the Seaview Bistro for casual dinner. The ship also has a supper club, pizzeria, outdoor grills, a patisserie, a sushi bar, and 24-hour room service.

Top: *Carnival Glory* at sea
Bottom: *Conquest*-class balcony cabin

What Works & What Doesn't

No one got short-changed in the design of these ships. The teen clubs-discos and video arcades are huge and a huge improvement. With appealing spaces dedicated to them, teens tend to get into less mischief. For sybarites, the saunas and steam rooms in the spa have glass walls and ocean views.

A seat at the wine bar should be serene; instead, the volume from adjacent lounges creates the sensation of being surrounded by dueling musicians. Ultracomfortable massage loungers are strategically placed along the indoor promenade; unfortunately, you have to pay to get the effect.

Accommodations

Cabins: As on all Carnival ships, cabins are roomy and generally larger than industry standard. More than 60% have an ocean view and, of those, 60% have balconies. For those suites and ocean-view cabins that have them, private balconies outfitted with chairs and tables add additional living space; extended balconies are 50% larger than standard ones. Every cabin has adequate closet and drawer-shelf storage, as well as bathroom shelves. High thread-count linens and plush pillows and duvets are a luxurious touch in all accommodations. Suites have a whirlpool tub, VCR, and walk-in closet.

Decor: Light-wood cabinetry, pastel colors, mirrored accents, a small refrigerator, a personal safe, a hair dryer in the top vanity-desk drawer, and a sitting area with sofa, chair, and table are typical Conquest-class amenities.

Bathrooms: Shampoo and bath gel are provided in shower-mounted dispensers; you also get an array of sample toiletries, as well as fluffy towels and a wall-mounted magnifying mirror. Bathrobes for use during the cruise are provided for all.

Other Features: A plus for families are a number of connecting staterooms in a variety of ocean-view and interior categories. Balcony dividers can be unlocked to provide connecting access in upper categories. Twenty-five staterooms are designed for wheelchair accessibility.

Cabin Type	Size (sq. ft.)
Penthouse Suite	345
Suite	230
Ocean View	185
Interior	185

Fast Facts

- 13 passenger decks
- Specialty restaurant, 2 dining rooms, buffet, ice-cream parlor, pizzeria
- Wi-Fi, in-cabin safes, in-cabin refrigerators, some in-cabin VCRs
- 3 pools (1 indoor), children's pool
- Fitness classes, gym, hair salon, 7 hot tubs, sauna, spa, steam room
- 9 bars, casino, dance club, library, showroom, video game room
- Children's programs (ages 2–15)
- Laundry facilities, laundry service
- Computer room

In the Know

The children's playroom has the best view on the ship—looking forward from high over the bow. If your little ones balk at joining Camp Carnival, point out that they're seeing the same thing as the captain; that news seems to captivate kids, even if there's nothing on the horizon.

Shooting hoops on
Carnival Valor

Favorites

Best Place to Escape the Crowds: Look for a deck chair in a quiet area of the deck above the aft Lido pool. Most sunbathers there are simply seeking a peaceful and quiet place to read or snooze in the sunshine.

Best Splurge: New York–style supper clubs on these ships are some of the best restaurants—and specialty dining bargains—at sea. Not only is the food outstanding (escargot, Russian caviar, lobster bisque, Alaskan king crab claws, grilled lamp chops, lobster, and several cuts of beef from 9 to 24 ounces), but the presentation is sophisticated and the atmosphere sublime.

Our Favorite Spot for a Nightcap: The grand bar serves up jazz and cigars as well as brandy and cordials and has some comfortable nooks and crannies for privacy. The Internet center is steps away, just in case checking e-mail is important before bedtime.

Best Lunch Choice: Tucked away on the Lido buffet's second floor, an unassuming fish-and-chips counter serves outstanding bouillabaisse.

CARNIVAL CRUISE LINES

2

CELEBRITY CRUISES

The Chandris Group, owners of budget Fantasy Cruises, founded Celebrity in 1989. Initially utilizing an unlovely, refurbished former ocean liner from the Fantasy fleet, Celebrity gained a reputation for fine food and professional service despite the shabby-chic vessel where it was elegantly served. The

Celebrity Galaxy at sea

cruise line eventually built premium, sophisticated cruise ships. Signature amenities followed, including a martini bar, large standard staterooms with generous storage, fully equipped spas, and butler service for top suites. Valuable art collections grace the fleet, which merged with Royal Caribbean International in 1997.

CELEBRITY CRUISES
1050 Caribbean Way
Miami, FL 33132
800/647-2251
www.celebritycruises.com

Cruise Style: Premium

Even as *Constellation* and *Summit* passengers have been treated to 30-minute performances of "A Taste of Cirque du Soleil," a unique concept at sea, entertainment has never been a primary focus; a lineup of lavish, although somewhat uninspired, revues is presented in the main show lounges by production companies of singers and dancers. In addition to shows featuring comedians, magicians, and jugglers, bands play a wide range of musical styles for dancing and listening in smaller lounges. Cirque du Soleil performers add an interactive element to the custom-built Bar at the Edge of the Earth on *Constellation*.

Two to five guest lecturers participate in the Enrichment Series program on every Celebrity cruise. Presentations may range from financial strategies, astronomy, wine appreciation, photography tips, and politics to the food, history, and culture of ports of call. Culinary demonstrations, bingo, and art auctions are additional diversions throughout the fleet. There are plenty of activities, although you'll have to read the daily program of events to find out about them. There are no public address announcements for bingo or hawking of gold-by-the-inch sales. You can still play and buy, but you won't be reminded repeatedly.

While spacious accommodations in every category are a Celebrity standard, the addition of ConciergeClass, an upscale element on all ships, makes certain premium ocean-view and balcony staterooms almost the equivalent of suites in terms of service. A ConciergeClass stateroom includes numerous extras such as chilled champagne, fresh fruit, and flowers upon arrival, exclusive room-service menus, evening canapés, luxury bedding, pillows, and linens, upgraded balcony furnishings, priority boarding and luggage service, and other VIP perks. At the touch of a single telephone button, a ConciergeClass desk representative is at hand to offer assistance. Suites are still the ultimate, though, and include the services of a butler to assist with unpacking, booking spa services and dining reservations, shining shoes, and even replacing a popped button.

Food

Aside from the sophisticated ambience of its restaurants, the cuisine designed by master chef Michel Roux was always reason enough to cruise on a Celebrity ship. However, in early 2007, Celebrity and Roux ended their affiliation, though his legacy promises to shine into the future. His hands-on involvement—personally creating menus and overseeing all aspects of dining operations—was integral in helping the line achieve the reputation it enjoys today. Happily, every ship in the fleet has a highly experienced team headed by executive chefs and food and beverage managers, who have developed their skills in some of the world's finest restaurants and hotels.

Alternative restaurants on the Millennium-class ships and *Century* offer fine dining and table-side food preparation amid classic ocean liner and Venetian splendor. A less formal evening alternative is offered fleetwide in the Casual Dining Boulevard, where you'll find a sushi bar, pizza and baked pasta, healthy spa items, and an area where you can order from the dining room menu. Reservations are required, but there are no long waits, and reserving a table is usually not a problem. Cova Café serves specialty coffees and pastries in surroundings inspired by the original in Milan; some offerings carry on additional charge. Gourmet Bites, the late-night treats served by white-gloved waiters in public rooms throughout the ships, can include mini–beef Wellingtons and crispy tempura.

To further complement the food, in 2004 Celebrity introduced a proprietary Cellarmaster Selection of wines, which initially included a Russian River Valley chardonnay and a Sonoma County cabernet sauvignon.

Noteworthy

■ Cova Café di Milano on each ship serves genuine coffee and chocolates from Milan.

■ The letter X on the ships' funnels is the Greek letter for C and stands for Chandris, the line's founding family.

■ Fresh-baked pizzas can be delivered to your stateroom in an insulated carrier.

Top: The *Millennium* AquaSpa
Bottom: Millennium-class cinema & conference center

2

CELEBRITY CRUISES

Top: *Century* Rendezvous Lounge
Middle: Lunch on deck
Bottom: Lounging on deck

Fitness & Recreation

Celebrity's AquaSpa by Elemis and fitness centers are some of the most tranquil and nicely equipped at sea with thalassotherapy pools on all but *Century* (complimentary on Millennium-class ships; a fee is assessed on Century-class). Spa services are operated by Steiner Leisure, and treatments include a variety of massages, body wraps, and facials. Trendy and traditional hair and nail services are offered in the salons.

State-of-the-art exercise equipment, a jogging track, and basic fitness classes are available at no charge. There's a fee for personal training, body composition analysis, and specialized classes such as yoga and Pilates. Golf pros offer hands-on instruction, and game simulators allow passengers to play world-famous courses. Each ship also has an "Acupuncture at Sea" treatment area staffed by licensed practitioners of Oriental Medicine.

Your Shipmates

Celebrity caters to American cruise passengers, primarily couples from their mid-30s to mid-50s. Many families enjoy cruising on Celebrity's fleet during summer months and holiday periods, particularly in the Caribbean. Lengthier cruises and exotic itineraries attract passengers in the over-60 age group.

Dress Code

Two formal nights are standard on seven-night cruises. Men are encouraged to wear tuxedos, but dark suits or sport coats and ties are more prevalent. Two evenings are designated informal, and other evenings are casual, although jeans are discouraged in restaurants. The line requests that no shorts be worn in public areas after 6 PM, and most people observe the dress code of the evening, unlike on some other cruise lines.

Junior Cruisers

Each Celebrity vessel has a dedicated playroom and offers a four-tier program of age-appropriate games and activities designed for children aged 3 to 6, 7 to 9, 10 to 12, and 13 to 17. Younger children must be toilet-trained to participate in the programs and use the facilities; however, families are welcome to borrow toys for their untoilet-

CHOOSE A CRUISE ON CELEBRITY CRUISE LINE IF...

❶ You want an upscale atmosphere at a really reasonable fare.

❷ You want piping-hot late-night pizza delivered to your cabin in pizzeria fashion.

❸ You want to dine amid elegant surroundings in some of the best restaurants at sea.

trained kids. A nominal fee may be assessed for participation in children's dinner parties, the Late-Night Slumber Party, and Afternoon Get-Togethers while parents are ashore in ports of call. Evening in-cabin babysitting can be arranged for a fee. Millennium-class and Century-class ships have teen centers, where teenagers can hang out and attend Coke-tail and pizza parties.

Service

Service on Celebrity ships is unobtrusive and polished. ConciergeClass adds an unexpected level of service and amenities that are usually reserved for luxury ships or passengers in top-category suites on other premium cruise lines.

Tipping

Gratuities (in cash) are personally distributed by passengers on the last night of the cruise. Suggested guidelines are per person, per day: waiter $3.50; assistant waiter $2; maitre d' 75¢; cabin steward $3.50; cabin attendant in ConciergeClass $4; assistant chief housekeeper 75¢; and, for suite occupants only, butler $3.50. Passengers may adjust the amount based on the level of service experienced. For children under 12 who accompany adults as third or fourth occupants of a stateroom, half the suggested amount is recommended. An automatic gratuity of 15% is added to all beverage tabs.

Past Passengers

Once you've sailed with Celebrity, you become a member of the Captain's Club and receive benefits commensurate with the number of cruises you've taken, including free upgrades, the chance to make dining reservations before sailing, and other benefits. Classic members have been on at least one Celebrity cruise. Select members have sailed at least six cruises and get more perks, including an invitation to a senior officer's cocktail party. After 10 cruises, you become an Elite member, and can take advantage of a private departure lounge. Royal Caribbean International, the parent company of Celebrity Cruises, also extends the corresponding levels of their Crown & Anchor program to Celebrity Captain's Club members.

Good to Know

Small refinements add touches of luxury to a Celebrity cruise. White-gloved stewards are present at the gangway upon embarkation to greet weary passengers with the offer of assistance.

Waiters will happily carry your trays from the buffet line to your table in the casual restaurant. Just ask the bartender for the recipe if a specialty martini or other cocktail appeals to you so you can re-create it at home.

CELEBRITY CRUISE LINE

2

DON'T CHOOSE A CRUISE ON CELEBRITY CRUISE LINE IF...

1 You need to be reminded of when activities are scheduled. Announcements are kept to a minimum.

2 You look forward to boisterous pool games and wacky contests. These cruises are fairly quiet and adult-centered.

3 You think funky avant-garde art is weird. Abstract modernism abounds in the art collections.

MILLENNIUM CLASS
Millennium, Summit, Infinity, Constellation

Public Areas & Facilities

Millennium-class ships are the largest, newest, and most feature-filled in the Celebrity fleet. Innovations include the Conservatory, a unique botanical environment; show lounges reminiscent of splendid opera houses; and alternative restaurants where diners find themselves in the midst of authentic ocean liner decor and memorabilia. The spas simply have to be seen to be believed—they occupy nearly as much space inside as is devoted to the adjacent outdoor Lido deck pool area. Although the spas offer just about any treatment you can think of—and some you probably haven't—they also house a complimentary hydrotherapy pool and spa café. These ships also have the most to offer for families, with the largest children's facilities in the Celebrity fleet.

Rich fabrics in jewel tones mix elegantly with the abundant use of marble and wood accents throughout public areas. The atmosphere is not unlike a luxurious European hotel filled with grand spaces that flow nicely from one to the other.

700 ft.	**2000, 2001,2001, 2002**
	ENTERED SERVICE
	1,950 (2,450)
	PASSENGER CAPACITY
	999
	CREW MEMBERS
	975
	NUMBER OF CABINS
500 ft.	**91,000**
	GROSS TONS
	965 feet
	LENGTH
300 ft.	**105 feet**
	WIDTH

WOW Factor

In lieu of atriums, Grand Foyers on these ships are stylishly appointed, multideck lobbies, with sweeping staircases crying out for grand entrances.

Top: *Millennium* Cova Café
Bottom: *Millennium* Ocean Grill

Restaurants

The formal two-deck restaurant serves evening meals in two assigned seatings and is supplemented by a casual Lido buffet and upscale alternative restaurant that houses a demonstration kitchen and wine cellar (and also requires reservations and a per-person cover charge). A luncheon grill, Cova Café patisserie, and 24-hour room service augment dining choices.

What Works & What Doesn't

There are just too many passengers to expect that your every wish will be granted on ships this size, but crew members try extremely hard to make everyone feel special. Although you'd expect to pay far more for a comparable meal ashore, wines suggested to complement alternative restaurant meals are probably a bit too rich for most passengers' pocketbooks.

The real gems are the Aquaspa Café, which serves light and healthy cuisine from breakfast until early evening, and the Sushi Café, where masters of the Japanese culinary art prepare the colorful treats.

Accommodations

Cabins: As on all Celebrity ships, cabins are thoughtfully designed with ample closet and drawer-shelf storage, as well as bathroom shelves in all standard inside and outside categories. Some ocean-view cabins and suites have private balconies. Penthouse suites have guest powder rooms.

Amenities: Wood cabinetry, mirrored accents, a small refrigerator, a personal safe, a hair dryer, and a sitting area with sofa, chair, and table are typical standard amenities. Extras include bathroom toiletries (shampoo, soaps, and lotion) and bathrobes for use during the cruise. Suite luxuries vary, but most include a whirlpool tub, VCR, Internet station, and walk-in closet, while all have butler service, personalized stationery, and a logo tote bag. For pure pleasure, Penthouse and Royal suites have outdoor whirlpool tubs on the balconies.

Worth Noting: Most staterooms and suites have convertible sofa beds, and many categories are capable of accommodating third and fourth occupants. Connecting staterooms are available in numerous categories, including the Celebrity suites. Family staterooms feature huge balconies and some have not one, but two sofa beds. Twenty-six staterooms are designed for wheelchair accessibility.

Cabin Type	Size (sq. ft.)
Penthouse Suite	1,432
Royal Suite/Celebrity Suite	538/467
Sky Suite/Family Ocean View	251/271
Concierge Class	191
Ocean View/Interior	170

Fast Facts

- 11 passenger decks
- Specialty restaurant, dining room, buffet, ice-cream parlor, pizzeria
- In-cabin broadband (*Constellation*), Wi-Fi, in-cabin safes, in-cabin refrigerators, some in-cabin VCRs, some in-cabin DVDs
- 3 pools (1 indoor), children's pool
- Fitness classes, gym, hair salon, 6 hot tubs, sauna, spa, steam room
- 7 bars, casino, cinema, dance club, library, showroom, video game room
- Children's programs (ages 3–17)
- Dry cleaning, laundry service
- Computer room

In the Know

Enhance your personal outdoor space by booking cabins 6035, 6030, or any of the seven cabins forward of those two on deck six. You can't tell from the deck plan, but your balcony will be extra deep, and you won't be looking down into a lifeboat.

Favorites

Best Added Value: There's no charge for use of the thalassotherapy pool in the huge Aqua Spa, a facility that rivals the fanciest ashore.

Best Splurge: There isn't much difference in size between an Ocean-view Stateroom with a balcony and ConciergeClass Stateroom, but if you plan to spend a lot of time in your quarters, the upgrade to ConciergeClass is well worth the extra expense, especially if you're planning your cruise as a honeymoon or other special occasion.

Our Favorite Spot for a Nightcap: Be daring, and alternate between the Martini and Champagne Bar's specialties. With no traffic flowing through the area after the last straggler leaves the dining room, it's a quiet retreat.

Best Way to Curb Your Appetite: The AquaSpa Café serves light and healthy selections for breakfast, lunch, and dinner, as well as fresh fruit smoothies.

Unexpected Freebie: You'll find a logo tote bag in your cabin.

Millennium-class conservatory

CELEBRITY CRUISE LINE

2

CENTURY CLASS

Century, Galaxy, Mercury

Public Areas & Facilities

Not quite identical, these sister ships nevertheless have essentially the same layout, though they differ dramatically in decor. *Century* has an eclectic air, while *Galaxy* and *Mercury* are more traditional in design and quietly elegant. All display fine collections of modern and classical art. With an additional 50 feet in length, *Galaxy* and *Mercury* have room for children's pools as well as a third swimming pool with a sliding roof for cover in inclement weather. A 2006 rejuvenation of *Century* added 14 suites and 10 staterooms (both inside and outside), not to mention 314 verandas, the most ever added to an existing cruise ship).

Each vessel has facilities for children and teens, but on *Galaxy* and *Mercury* they seem almost an afterthought. Adults fare better with spectacular spas and sophisticated lounges dedicated to a variety of tastes. The dining rooms are nothing short of gorgeous. Overall, the first impression is that these are fine resort hotels that just happen to float.

1995, 1996, 1997	ENTERED SERVICE
1,750 (2,150)/1,870 (2,681)/1,886 (2,681)	PASSENGER CAPACITY
858/909/909	CREW MEMBERS
875/935/943	NUMBER OF CABINS
70,606/77,713/77,713	GROSS TONS
815/865/866 feet	LENGTH
105 feet	WIDTH

700 ft.
500 ft.
300 ft.

WOW Factor

Descend to dine in the tradition of great ocean liners. Both ships have stunning double-height dining rooms with soaring columns and window walls.

Restaurants

The formal two-deck restaurant serves evening meals in two assigned seatings and is supplemented by a casual Lido restaurant serving buffet-style breakfast and lunch. (By night, the Lido restaurant is a reservations-only restaurant and Sushi café.) *Century* has both a spa café and an upscale, reservations-only restaurant that has an extra cover charge.

What Works & What Doesn't

The atmosphere throughout is decidedly upscale, despite some over-the-edge art pieces on *Century*. For sheer tranquillity, head for the heavenly AquaSpa. Be forewarned, though, the posh and soothing surroundings translate into dollars; unless you're occupying a suite or have booked a massage or other treatment from the spa menu, plan to pay a fee for relaxing in the huge thalasso-therapy saltwater pool on *Galaxy* and *Mercury*. Murano, *Century*'s deluxe extra-charge restaurant, has striking Murano-glass chandeliers. Underfoot, jewel-granite resembles the paving of an Italian piazza.

Top: Formal dining on *Century*
Bottom: *Century* Shipmates Fun Factory

Accommodations

Layout: As on all Celebrity ships, cabins are thoughtfully designed with ample closet and drawer-shelf storage and bathroom shelves. Some ocean-view cabins and suites have balconies with chairs and tables. Penthouse and Royal suites have a whirlpool bathtub and separate shower as well as a walk-in closet; Penthouse suites have a guest powder room. Although Royal and Sky suites are bigger on *Galaxy*, most other cabins are slightly smaller than on *Century*.

Amenities: Light-wood cabinetry, mirrored accents, a refrigerator, a personal safe, a hair dryer, and a sitting area with sofa, chair, and table are typical standard amenities. Extras include bathroom toiletries (shampoo, soaps, and lotion) and bathrobes for use during the cruise. Penthouse and Royal suites have elaborate entertainment centers with large TVs, while all suites include butler service, personalized stationery, VCR or DVD, and a tote bag.

Worth Noting: On *Galaxy* and *Mercury*, spacious family ocean-view staterooms have a double bed, sofa bed, and upper berth; *Century* has slightly smaller Family Veranda Staterooms.

Cabin Type	Size (sq. ft.)
Penthouse Suite	1,101
Royal Suite/Sky Suite	522/245
Standard Suite/ Family Ocean View*	220/210
Concierge & Ocean View	175/172
Interior	174/171

Cabins sizes are averages.
*Only *Century* has regular suites.

In the Know

While the rest of the industry was rushing to add affordable balconies to a high percentage of staterooms, Celebrity was somewhat slower to get on the bandwagon. When Century *emerged from her dry-dock revitalization in June 2006 with 314 new verandas, the tide had turned.*

Favorites

Best Dessert: Just about any selection from the rolling tea cart on the day Elegant Tea is offered.

Best Splurge: Cova Café di Milano is somewhat loosely styled after its Italian namesake, which opened in 1817 next to Milan's La Scala Opera House. Featuring Cova liqueurs, chocolates, and fresh pastries, it's a delightful sidewalk café-style spot to order up the best coffee on board while you polish your people-watching skills. There's a charge for the specialty coffee and Cova treats, but complimentary croissants and pastries are available in the morning and late afternoon.

Our Favorite Spot for a Nightcap: The stogie craze has all but died, and the air has cleared in Michael's Clubs, the lounges formerly devoted to cigar smoking. Now billed as piano bars, they remain quiet spaces for after-dinner cordials.

Unexpected Luxury: Penthouse suites have outdoor whirlpool tubs on their balconies.

Fast Facts

- 10 passenger decks
- Specialty restaurant (*Century* only), dining room, buffet, ice-cream parlor, pizzeria
- Wi-Fi, in-cabin safes, in-cabin refrigerators, some in-cabin VCRs, some in-cabin DVDs
- 2 pools (*Century* only), 3 pools (1 indoor on *Galaxy* & *Mercury*), children's pool (*Galaxy* & *Mercury*)
- Fitness classes, gym, hair salon, 5 hot tubs, sauna, spa, steam room (*Galaxy* & *Mercury*)
- 7 bars (8 on *Galaxy* & *Mercury*), casino, cinema, dance club, library, showroom, video game room
- Children's programs (ages 3–17)
- Dry cleaning, laundry service
- Computer room

Galaxy oasis pool

COSTA CRUISES

Europe's number-one cruise line combines a Continental experience, enticing itineraries, and Italy's classical design and style with relaxing days and romantic nights at sea. Genoa-based Costa Crociere, parent company of Costa Cruise Lines, had been in the shipping business for more than 100 years and in the

Dining alfresco

passenger business for almost 50 years when it was bought by Airtours and Carnival Corporation in 1997. In 2000 Carnival completed a buyout of the Costa line and began expanding the fleet with larger and more dynamic ships.

COSTA CRUISES
200 S. Park Road, Suite 200
Hollywood, FL 33021-8541
954/266-5600 or
800/462-6782
www.costacruise.com

Cruise Style: Mainstream

Italian-style cruising is a mixture of Mediterranean flair and American comfort, beginning with a *buon viaggio* celebration and topped off by a signature Roman Bacchanal Parade and zany toga party. The supercharged social staff works overtime to get everyone in the mood and encourages everyone to be a part of the action.

Festive shipboard activities include some of Italy's favorite pastimes, such as playing games of boccie, dancing the tarantella, and tossing pizza dough during the Festa Italiana, an Italian street festival at sea. Other nights are themed as well—a welcome-aboard celebration or Benvenuto A Bordo, hosted by the captain on the first formal night, and Notte Tropical, a tropical deck party with a Mediterranean twist that culminates with the presentation of an alfresco midnight buffet.

There's also a nod to the traditional cruise-ship entertainment expected by North American passengers. Pool games, trivia, bingo, and sophisticated production shows blend nicely with classical concerts in lounges where a wide range of musical styles invite dancing or listening. The enrichment series might include topics such as personal finance as well as the usual health and beauty sessions. Italian language and cooking classes are extremely popular. Every ship has a small chapel suitable for intimate weddings, and Catholic Mass is celebrated most days.

Acknowledging changing habits (even among Europeans), Costa Cruises has eliminated smoking entirely in dining rooms and show lounges. However, smokers are permitted to light up in designated areas in other public rooms, as well as on the pool deck.

A new vessel-building program has brought Costa ships into the 21st century with innovative large-ship designs that reflect their Italian heritage and style without overlooking the amenities expected by modern cruisers.

Food

Costa is noted for themed dinner menus and retractable backdrops that convey the evening's mood. Dining features regional Italian cuisines: a variety of pastas, chicken, beef, and seafood dishes, as well as authentic pizza. European Wchefs and culinary school graduates, who are members of Chaîne des Rôtisseurs, provide a dining experience that's notable for a delicious, properly prepared pasta course, if not exactly living up to gourmet standards. Vegetarian and healthy diet choices are also offered, as are selections for children. Alternative dining is by reservation only in the upscale supper clubs, which serve choice steaks and seafood from a Tuscan steakhouse menu as well as traditional Italian specialties.

While there is normally a per-person charge for the specialty restaurants, suite passengers receive one complimentary dinner for two.

Costa ships also retain the tradition of lavish nightly midnight buffets, a feature that is beginning to disappear on other mainstream lines.

Fitness & Recreation

Taking a cue from the ancient Romans, Costa places continuing emphasis on wellness and sensual pleasures. Spas and salons are operated by Steiner Leisure, and treatments include a variety of massages, body wraps, and facials that can be scheduled à la carte or combined in packages to enjoy during one afternoon or throughout the entire cruise. Hair and nail services are available in the salons.

State-of-the-art exercise equipment in the terraced gym, a jogging track, and basic fitness classes for all levels of ability are available. Costa ships offer a Golf Academy at Sea, with PGA clinics on the ship and golf excursions in some ports.

Noteworthy

■ The cuisine of Italian chef Gualtiero Marchesi is served on Versace tableware in Costa's alternative restaurants.

■ Original works of art, including sculptures, paintings, and hand-crafted furnishings, are created for all Costa ships.

■ For dessert, Costa chefs tempt you with tiramisu, crème brûlée, cannoli, Sambuca sundaes, and gelato.

Top: Showtime on *Costa*
Bottom: Casino action

2

COSTA CRUISES

Top: Costa chefs
Middle: Jogging on deck
Bottom: Las Vegas—style
entertainment

Your Shipmates

Couples in the 35- to 55-year-old range are attracted to Costa Cruises; on most itineraries, up to 80% of passengers are Europeans, and many of them are Italian. An international air prevails on board and announcements are often made in a variety of languages. The vibe on Costa's newest megaships is most likely to appeal to satisfy American tastes and expectations.

Dress Code

Two formal nights are standard on seven-night cruises. Men are encouraged to wear tuxedos, but dark suits or sport coats and ties are appropriate and more common than black tie. All other evenings are resort casual, although jeans are discouraged in restaurants. It's requested that no shorts be worn in public areas after 6 PM.

Junior Cruisers

Caribbean sailings feature age-specific youth programs that include such daily activities as costume parties, board games, junior aerobics, and even Italian-language lessons for children in four age groups: ages 3 (toilet trained) to 6; ages 7 to 11; junior teens ages 12 to 14; and teens ages 15 to 17. The actual age groupings may be influenced by the number of children on board. Special counselors oversee activities, and specific rooms are designed for children and teens, depending on the ship. Children under three years old can use the playroom facilities if accompanied and supervised by their parents.

Organized sessions for all children between the ages of 3 and 17 are available every day, even when in port, from 9 to noon and 3 to 6, as well as from 9 to 11:30 in the evening. Parents can enjoy at least a couple of evenings alone by taking advantage of two complimentary Parents Nights Out while their children dine at a supervised buffet or pizza party and take part in evening and nighttime activities. Nighttime group babysitting for children ages 3 to 11 is complimentary in the children's area until 1:30 AM. Unfortunately, no late-night babysitting service is offered for children under 3, nor is there in-cabin babysitting.

CHOOSE A CRUISE ON COSTA CRUISES IF...

❶ You're a satisfied Carnival past passenger and want a similar experience with an Italian flavor.

❷ You want pizza hot out of the oven whenever you get a craving for it.

❸ You're a joiner: there are many opportunities to be in the center of the action.

Service

Service in dining areas can be spotty and rushed but is adequate, if not always overly friendly.

Tipping

A standard gratuity of $8.50 per passenger, per day ($4.25 for children) is automatically added to shipboard accounts and is distributed as follows: $3 to cabin stewards; $3 to waiters; $1.50 to assistant waiters; and $1 to headwaiters. Passengers may adjust the amount based on the level of service experienced. An automatic 15% gratuity is added to all beverage tabs, as well as to checks for spa treatments and salon services.

Past Passengers

The Costa Club has three levels of membership: Aquamarine (2,000 points), Coral (2,001 to 5,000 points) and Pearl (5,001 or more points). Points are assigned for the number of cruising days (100 points per day) and the amount of money spent aboard (40 points for 52 euros).

Membership privileges vary and can include discounts on selected cruises, fruit baskets, and bottles of Spumante delivered to your cabin, discounts on boutique merchandise and beauty treatments, or a complimentary dinner in a specialty restaurant.

Good to Know

Mama Mia! Connoisseurs of classical Italian art and design may feel they've died and gone to Caesars Palace. Costa's newest ships try to convey what Americans think of as Roman: gilt surfaces, marble columns, and all. Overlook the gaudiness and pay particular attention to the best details: the Murano glass chandeliers and lighting fixtures are simply superb. And when you're packing don't forget to toss something in the suitcase to wear beneath your toga; while sheets and accessories are provided, it's considered bad form to flash fellow passengers during the revelry.

While 24-hour room service is available fleet-wide, there is a charge for certain items, as is the custom among European cruise lines.

2

COSTA CRUISES

DON'T CHOOSE A CRUISE ON COSTA CRUISES IF...

❶ You find announcements in a variety of languages annoying.

❷ You want an authentic Italian cruise. The crew has grown more international than Italian as the line has expanded.

❸ You prefer sedate splendor in a formal atmosphere. The Caribbean-based ships are almost Fellini-esque in style.

COSTA CONCORDIA/ SERENA

2006/2007	ENTERED SERVICE
3,000	PASSENGER CAPACITY
1,068	CREW MEMBERS
1,500	NUMBER OF CABINS
112,000	GROSS TONS
951 feet	LENGTH
116 feet	WIDTH

Public Areas & Facilities

The largest ships built for an Italian cruise line, *Costa Concordia* and *Costa Serena* are larger versions of identical sister ships *Costa Magica* and *Costa Fortuna*, which were derived from parent Carnival Cruise Lines' *Carnival Triumph*. But Costa has pulled out all the stops with these two vessels.

The Samsara Spas are far from ho-hum, both in facilities and amenities. The largest at sea, they span 20,500 square feet. A first for Costa passengers are luxurious, Samsara staterooms and suites, located adjacent to and one deck below the spa itself. A health-conscious Samsara Restaurant is reserved for their dining pleasure on Deck 3. Other cool features are two swimming pools with retractable roofs (the largest such pools on any ship), a huge outdoor movie screen, and a Grand Prix racing simulator—just like the ones Formula One race car drivers use for training.

WOW Factor

La dolce vita—the sweet life—is celebrated on board vessels designed to pay homage to the romance and vitality of Italy through art, music, and food.

Restaurants

Two restaurants serve open-seating breakfast and lunch; dinner is in two assigned seatings. An upscale alternative, reservations-only restaurant carries a service charge—a perk for suite passengers is a complimentary dinner for two there. The Lido buffet, pizzeria, and 24-hour room service are alternatives. Costa ships retain the tradition of lavish nightly midnight buffets.

What Works & What Doesn't

Top: *Concordia* at sea
Bottom: *Concordia* Samsara minisuite

Designed by Carnival's Joe Farcus, both ships feature bright themed interiors and original works of art. *Costa Concordia*'s design draws inspiration from a variety of European architectural styles and *Costa Serena* reflects Roman and Greek mythology.

Couples counting on *amore* will want to check bed configurations carefully. A handful of outside cabins have one lower bed and a single sofa bed.

In European style, dinner seatings are later than is customary in North America and coffee isn't routinely offered with dessert.

The lack of Wi-Fi is disappointing.

Accommodations

Cabins: Accommodations generally follow the outline of recently introduced fleet mates. More than 60% of outside staterooms have a balcony with chairs and a table. Every cabin has adequate closet and drawer/shelf storage, as well as bathroom shelves; suites have generous walk-in closets and come with the services of a butler. Connecting staterooms are somewhat scarce but can be found in ocean-view categories. Light wood cabinetry, soft pastel decor, mirrored accents, Murano glass lighting fixtures, and a small sitting area are typical in all categories; all accommodations have a small refrigerator, personal safe, and hair dryer. Some outside cabins have only a lower twin bed and a sofa bed.

Bathrooms: Bathroom extras include shampoo and bath gel in shower-mounted dispensers. Additionally, suites feature a whirlpool tub and double sinks.

Good to Know: Popular Samsara Spa accommodations were increased in number from a total of 67 on *Costa Concordia* to 99 on *Costa Serena*. Passengers who reserve Samsara suites and staterooms adjacent to the spa facility have direct access to the spa and exclusive access to Samsara Restaurant. Twenty-seven staterooms are designed for accessibility.

Cabin Type	Size (sq. ft.)
Grand Suite	650
Suite	360
Minisuite	300
Ocean View with Balcony	210
Ocean View/Interior	175/160

Dimensions for accommodations with balconies include the balcony square footage.

Fast Facts

- 13 passenger decks
- Specialty restaurant, 2 dining rooms, buffet, pizzeria
- In-cabin safes, in-cabin refrigerators
- 3 pools (2 indoor), children's pool
- Fitness classes, gym, hair salon, 5 hot tubs, sauna, spa, steam room
- 13 bars, casino, 2 dance clubs, showroom, library, video game room
- Children's programs (ages 3–17)
- Laundry service
- Computer room

In the Know

Look carefully at the mural near the entrance of Costa Concordia's *Gran Bar Berlino—seated alongside such great European architects as Antoni Gaudí of Spain is Joe Farcus, the genius behind the designs of Costa Cruises' latest ships.*

Favorites

May I Have This Dance: While the discos are certainly lively, we prefer the nightly live music and lower-key energy level of the ships' Grand Bar ballrooms for dancing.

Our Favorite Spot for a Nightcap: We like to kick back under the stars in lounge chairs on the pool deck, where we can catch a late-night movie on the big screen.

Best Snack Food Choices: What would an Italian cruise ship be without pizza and gelato? We love all the pizza varieties and the authentic frozen treats.

Most Civilized Custom: Unlike North Americans, Europeans are accustomed to enjoying their after-dinner coffee in a café. It's a relaxing time for quiet conversation and serious people-watching, so when in Rome, do as the Romans do and join us at the coffee bar for an espresso. Avoid ordering cappuccino, though. That's considered a breakfast drink in Italy.

Ceres restaurant, *Serena*

COSTA FORTUNA/ MAGICA

2003, 2004	ENTERED SERVICE
2,720 (3,470 max)	PASSENGER CAPACITY
1,068	CREW MEMBERS
1,360	NUMBER OF CABINS
105,000	GROSS TONS
890 feet	LENGTH
124 feet	WIDTH

Public Areas & Facilities

With a bit of interior alteration, *Costa Fortuna* and *Costa Magica* are essentially Euro-clones of parent company Carnival Cruise Line's *Carnival Triumph* and *Carnival Victory*. The mix and size of public rooms was determined to appeal to European as well as North American passengers sailing on itineraries that include the Mediterranean Sea.

Like Carnival ships designed by Joe Farcus, these Costa beauties have a theme running throughout—the decor is inspired by the grand Italian steamships of the past. Incorporated into the design of these ships, scale models of historic liners grace nearly every public area. A "fleet" of 26 former ships of the Costa fleet boldly "sail" upside down across the ceiling of the atrium. Ceilings in the formal, two-deck dining rooms are also decorated; Michelangelo Restaurant features reproductions of the master's frescoes, while Raffeallo Restaurant displays its namesake's Vatican artwork. Art deco touches add grace to all the public spaces.

WOW Factor

Art, art, and even more art! Millions of dollars were invested in original paintings, sculptures, wall hangings, and specially designed artisan furnishings.

Top: Romantic dinner
Bottom: *Costa Magica* Grand Suite

Restaurants

Two restaurants, each spanning two decks, serve open-seating breakfast and lunch; dinner is served in two assigned seatings. Club Grand Conte, a reservation-only restaurant and upscale alternative, features a Tuscan steakhouse menu of steaks and seafood dishes in addition to Italian specialties. Casual meals and pizza are available in the Lido buffet.

What Works & What Doesn't

Group participation is a major component of a Costa cruise, and Costa Magica's energetic social staff gets the ball rolling by encouraging everyone on board to join in for their signature activities and parties. Surprisingly, even the most hesitant often succumb to the coaxing and take part in the antics. Afterward, they may sheepishly reveal they enjoyed wearing a toga. With all this constant activity, though, you may feel that you need a vacation when your cruise is finished. The Internet Café is placed adjacent to the disco, not a spot conducive to peaceful Internet surfing.

2

Accommodations

Layout: Cabins on *Costa Fortuna* and *Costa Magica* generally follow the outline of their Carnival counterparts, with the notable addition of a Grand Suite category. More than 60% of accommodations have an ocean view and, of those, 60% have balconies. Balconies have chairs and tables, and dividers can be unlocked to connect some cabins. Every cabin has adequate closet and drawer-shelf storage, as well as bathroom shelves. Suites have a generous walk-in closet.

Amenities: Light-wood cabinetry, soft pastel decor, mirrored accents, Murano glass lighting fixtures, a small refrigerator, a personal safe, a hair dryer, and a sitting area with a sofa, chair, and table are typical for ocean-view cabins and suites. Inside cabins have ample room, but sitting areas consist only of a small table and chairs.

Bathrooms: Bathroom extras include shampoo and bath gel in shower-mounted dispensers. Additional features in the suites on *Costa Magica* include a whirlpool tub and double sink. Suite passengers also enjoy an enhanced room-service menu.

Worth Noting: Well-designed lifeboat placement ensures unobstructed sea views from all outside cabin windows. Eight staterooms are designed for wheelchair accessibility.

Cabin Type	Size (sq. ft.)
Grand Suites	650
Suites	360
Minisuites	300
Ocean View	175
Interior	160

Fast Facts

- 13 passenger decks
- Specialty restaurant, 2 dining rooms, buffet, pizzeria
- In-cabin safes, in-cabin refrigerators
- 3 pools (1 indoor), children's pool
- Fitness classes, gym, hair salon, 6 hot tubs, sauna, spa, steam room
- 7 bars, casino, 2 dance clubs, 2 show-rooms, library, video game room
- Children's programs (ages 3–17)
- Laundry service
- Computer room

In the Know

Costa Fortuna and Costa Magica *share many of the same attributes as their Carnival cousins, but make no mistake, these are Costa vessels. In the style that Europeans favor, the casino is much smaller to make room for the huge Conte Di Savoia Grand Bar that houses a suitably large dance floor.*

Favorites

Best Place to Escape the Crowds: The library doesn't have a large collection of books, but it does contain some nifty wraparound cabanalike chairs that envelope the occupants in privacy.

Best Added Value: With floor-to-ceiling glass walls, the saunas and steam rooms for men and women (not coed) are bright and cheery. Better still,

they're so huge that they're seldom crowded, and you don't have to book a spa treatment or pay a fee to use them.

Our Favorite Spot for a Nightcap: The Classico Roma Bar is a hideaway with a nautical flavor and a faux fireplace. The clean lines of the mid-century modern style seating belie how comfortable the late-night watering

hole is for savoring a cognac or cigar.

Best Splurge: Dinner in the reservations-only Club Grand Conte is well worth the extra charge of $23 per person for the intimate, candlelit atmosphere.

Deck games

COSTA ATLANTICA, COSTA MEDITERRANEA

	2000, 2003
	ENTERED SERVICE
	2,114 (2,682 max)
	PASSENGER CAPACITY
700 ft.	**920**
	CREW MEMBERS
	1,057
	NUMBER OF CABINS
500 ft.	**86,000**
	GROSS TONS
	960 feet
	LENGTH
300 ft.	**106 feet**
	WIDTH

Public Areas & Facilities

The basic layout of this contemporary ship is nearly identical to parent Carnival Cruise Line's Spirit-class vessels. Interiors were designed by Carnival's ship architect Joe Farcus, whose abundant use of marble reflects Costa's Italian heritage. Artwork commissioned specifically for each ship was created by contemporary artists and includes intricate sculptures in silver and glass. Don't overlook the lighting fixtures, which were created especially for the ship, most of them crafted by the artisans in Venice's Murano glass factories.

The nice flow between public lounges is broken only by piazzas, where you can practice the Italian custom of *passeggiata* (seeing and being seen). And there's plenty to see; these are visually stimulating interiors, with vivid colors and decor elements to arouse a sense of discovery. One of the most elegant spaces on board is the least Italian in appearance—inspired by the Palazzo Roero Di Guarene, the Roero Bar contains cases to display artifacts from four ancient Chinese dynasties.

WOW Factor

As one passenger put it, if earlier Costa ships were Armani (clean, cool, and serene), then this one is Versace (glittering, sexy, and slightly outrageous).

Top: *Costa Mediterranea* at sea
Bottom: European service

Restaurants

A single two-deck-high formal restaurant serves Italian-accented cuisine in two traditional assigned seatings. An upscale, reservations-only alternative restaurant features a Tuscan steak-house menu of steaks and seafood dishes in addition to Italian specialties. The Lido buffet, pizzeria, and 24-hour room service are alternatives to dining room meals.

What Works & What Doesn't

As a nod to the spirit of La Dolce Vita, much socializing takes place during the Italian Bacchanal. However, there's a not-so-subtle current of Americanization underlying the overall experience. Thankfully, that hasn't extended to the lavish midnight buffets and utterly wacky toga party. A quirk, however, is the strange double use of the balcony in the specialty restaurant, which becomes a cigar lounge after regular dinner hours; don't linger over your coffee if you find that offensive. As long as you leave before 10 PM, nothing should distract you from the romantic, candlelit atmosphere.

Accommodations

Layout: *Costa Mediterranea* cabins generally follow the outline of their Carnival counterparts, with the distinctive addition of a Grand Suite category. Nearly 80% of the suites and staterooms have an ocean view, and of those, more than 80% have balconies. Every cabin has adequate closet and drawer-shelf storage, as well as bathroom shelves; suites have a walk-in closet.

Amenities: Light-wood cabinetry, pastel decor, Murano glass lighting fixtures, mirrored accents, a small refrigerator, a personal safe, a hair dryer, and a sitting area with sofa, chair, and table are typical for ocean-view cabins and suites. Inside cabins have somewhat smaller sitting areas for lounging. Suites have VCRs.

Bathroom: Extras include shampoo and bath gel in shower-mounted dispensers. Suites have a whirlpool bathtub.

Worth Noting: Although connecting staterooms are somewhat scarce throughout the ships, balcony dividers can be unlocked to provide connecting access in upper-category staterooms. Eight staterooms are designed for wheelchair accessibility.

Cabin Type	Size (sq. ft.)
Grand Suites	650
Suites	360
Ocean View*	185
Interior	160

*Extended balcony cabins have balconies at least 50% larger than average.

Fast Facts

- 12 passenger decks
- Specialty restaurant, dining room, buffet, pizzeria
- In-cabin broadband, in-cabin safes, in-cabin refrigerators, some in-cabin VCRs
- 3 pools (1 indoor), children's pool
- Fitness classes, gym, hair salon, 4 hot tubs, sauna, spa, steam room
- 6 bars, casino, cinema, 2 dance clubs, 2 showrooms, video game room
- Children's programs (ages 3–17)
- Laundry service
- Computer room

2

COSTA CRUISES

In the Know

Tucked away far forward is a stunning chapel with an altar, wood pews, stained-glass panels, and religious icons. Unlike other ships' generic wedding chapels, this is a tiny house of worship afloat.

Workout with a sea view

Favorites

Best Place to Escape the Crowds: Forward on the outdoor promenade decks are serene retreats in the form of enclosed terraces, which might have been termed winter gardens on ocean liners.

Best Splurge: Italians consider cappuccino a breakfast beverage, so don't order it in the dining room following dinner—specialty coffees are not available there

anyway. Instead, follow the Roman custom of going out for coffee and head to the Oriental Café, where traditional espresso and cappuccino are served.

Our Favorite Spot for a Nightcap: It may sound unusual, but the lobby bar and the area just aft of the atrium are rather nice places to end the evening. While everyone is busy in the

dance clubs, casino, or show lounges, the lounge-y lobby areas can be almost restful.

Best Retail Therapy: Duty-free boutiques offer enough Italian designer items to satisfy the most addicted shopaholics.

COSTA CLASSICA/ ROMANTICA

Public Areas & Facilities

These two sisterships were designed to bring the Costa fleet up to speed with other cruise lines in the 1990s, and the effort has paid off. Public areas clustered on four upper decks are filled with marble and furnished with sleek, contemporary furnishings and modern Italian artworks. The effect is vibrant, chic, and surprisingly restful. Lounges and bars are sweeping and grand; however, the areas set aside for children are pretty skimpy by today's family-friendly standards. A large forward-facing spa and fitness center on *Costa Classica* was displaced for additional high-end suites on *Costa Romantica*, which accounts for the difference in passenger capacity. Neither ship has a true promenade deck, but the Lido areas for sunning and swimming are expansive.

Midsize and intimate, each ship retains a like-new luster from regular refurbishments. Unfortunately, they lack the large number of balconies that are becoming as popular with Europeans as North Americans.

1992/1993	Entered Service
1,308/1,356	Passenger Capacity
650/610	Crew Members
654/678	Number of Cabins
53,000	Gross Tons
722 feet	Length
102 feet	Width

700 ft.
500 ft.
300 ft.

WOW Factor

The round, almost futuristic structure at the forward top deck is a lounge that does double duty. By day, it's an observation lounge and by night a swinging disco.

Restaurants

The single restaurant serves open-seating breakfast and lunch, and dinner in two assigned seatings. Breakfast and lunch are also available at the Lido buffet, with seating indoor or out. Dinner buffets are scheduled for certain nights during the cruise, as are traditional midnight buffets. There's both a pizzeria and a patisserie, and 24-hour room service is available.

What Works & What Doesn't

Upgrades and renovations over the years haven't spoiled the classic overall feel of these two traditional ships. Originally designed to appeal to the tastes of Europeans, they also incorporate the comforts Americans expect.

Carefully check the deck plan before booking. Plenty of cabins sleep three and four, but they can be tight for families traveling together. Cabins with connecting doors are preferable, but scarce.

Following European preference, dinner seatings are later than is customary in North America, and coffee isn't routinely offered after meals.

Top: *Classica* at sea
Bottom: Tivoli restaurant on *Classica*

Accommodations

Cabins: Liberally paneled in light cherrywood, cabins are fairly spacious and have ample storage. Ocean-view staterooms feature large porthole-style windows. Suites are generous in size with large sitting areas; they also have butler service. Designed when the balcony craze was just taking off, each ship has only 10 suites with balconies; *Costa Romantica* has six forward-facing suites without balconies as well as an added category—18 minisuites that have the same amenities as the suites but are not as large.

Decor: All accommodations have soft-color fabrics in a minimalist style and have a personal safe, TV, and hair dryer. The combination desk and dressing table has a large mirror; a small sitting area with a table and two chairs are typical furnishings.

Bathrooms: Bathrooms are tight in ocean-view and inside cabins, even by modern cruise-ship standards. The usual bath amenities include the basic soap and shampoo. Suites have the added luxury of a whirlpool bathtub and double sinks.

Good to Know: Six staterooms are wheelchair accessible.

Cabin Type	Size (sq. ft.)
Suite	580
Minisuite**	340
Ocean View	200
Interior	175
**CostaRomantica only	

Fast Facts

- 10 passenger decks
- Dining room, buffet, pizzeria
- In-cabin safes, some in-cabin refrigerators
- 2 pools
- Fitness classes, gym, hair salon, 4 hot tubs, sauna, spa
- 7 bars, casino, 2 dance clubs, library, showroom, video game room
- Children's programs (ages 3–17)
- Dry cleaning, laundry service
- Computer room

In the Know

Passengers barely needed to bother checking the daily schedule of a Costa ship in the past because announcements were made frequently—too frequently—throughout the day in at least five languages. The announcements, still tedious, are much less intrusive these days.

Favorites

What's That You Said?: We like being exposed to different cultures and opinions, so the international mix of travelers on this ship is a plus. The minus is that people may seem rude or aloof because they assume fellow passengers will not understand them. As a result, they tend to not speak in passing and not apologize when appropriate.

Our Favorite Spot for a Nightcap: We like the cosmopolitan atmosphere of the Piazza Grand Bar in the heart of each ship.

Best Smoking Advancement: Europeans like to smoke, and the habit may have seemed out of control in years past. The best news is that smoking is no longer allowed in dining rooms or at the bars, but there are designated smoking areas in each lounge. While still present, cigarette smoke is no longer as intolerable as it once was.

Best Splurge: Duty-free shops on board feature stylish Italian designer goods as well as a variety of quality souvenirs.

Main pool, *Romantica*

COSTA VICTORIA

History

Costa's first large ship is a stunning contemporary, sun-filled vessel. In addition to a seven-deck atrium with an overhead skylight and panoramic elevators at the ship's center, a unique four-deck-high observation lounge has floor-to-ceiling windows overlooking the ship's bow. *Costa Victoria* has all the bells and whistles expected on contemporary ships, including large entertainment lounges and cozy spaces for cocktails and conversation. All public spaces reflect a chic Italian flair with marble-accented floors and walls.

Restaurants

Two restaurants serve open-seating breakfast and lunch; dinner is served in two assigned seatings. An upscale alternative, reservations-only restaurant carries a service charge—a perk for suite pas-sengers is a complimentary dinner for two here. The Lido buffet, pizzeria, poolside grill, and room service are alternatives to dining room meals. Lavish midnight buffets are offered nightly.

	1996
	ENTERED SERVICE
	1,928
	PASSENGER CAPACITY
700 ft.	**766**
	CREW MEMBERS
	964
	NUMBER OF CABINS
500 ft.	**76,000**
	GROSS TONS
	828 feet
	LENGTH
300 ft.	**106 feet**
	WIDTH

Accommodations

Light-wood cabinetry, soft pastel decor, and a small sitting area are typical of all cabins, which have a small refrigerator, personal safe, and hair dryer. Floor space is tight in standard categories, bit every cabin has adequate closet and storage space. Suites also have a whirlpool tub, double sink, and generous closet. Passengers in suites and minisuites enjoy butler service. While the ship had no balconies at all when it was launched, 246 were later added to four minisuites and 242 standard outside cabins. Six cabins are wheelchair accessible.

Cabin Sizes (in sq. ft.): Suites 430; minisuites 310; ocean view with balconies 175; standard outside 150; and inside 120–150.

Top: Festival Theater
Bottom: Oceanview stateroom

In the Know

To beat the heat, stake out a lounge chair on the Solarium Deck, where misting stations spray chilled water on sun-worshippers at regular intervals. The aft-facing Tavernetta Lounge is one of the most tranquil spots on board.

Fast Facts

- 10 passenger decks
- 3 restaurants
- Safes, refrigerators, 3 pools, gym, spa, casino, children's programs (ages 3–17), laundry service, computer room

COSTA EUROPA

1986	ENTERED SERVICE
1,494	PASSENGER CAPACITY
636	CREW MEMBERS
747	NUMBER OF CABINS
54,000	GROSS TONS
798 feet	LENGTH
101 feet	WIDTH

700 ft.
500 ft.
300 ft.

History

A ship with history, *CostaEuropa* was built in 1986 as the *Homeric* for defunct Homes Lines. She was acquired by Holland America Line, renamed *Westerdam*, and "stretched" in 1990. Look closely, and you can tell where a center section was added to lengthen the ship—windows and portholes are larger in that area. *Westerdam* was rechristened *Costa Europa* in 2002. A change of interior decor has brightened her up, but she retains classic touches of elegance such as the teak wrap-around promenade deck lined with wooden steamer chairs.

Restaurants

A single restaurant serves open-seating breakfast and lunch, with two assigned seatings for dinner. Breakfast and lunch are also available at two buffet restaurants, with seating indoors or outside. Dinner buffets are scheduled, as are traditional midnight buffets. An outdoor grill serves fast foods and, befitting an Italian ship, pizza is a staple. Room service is available.

Accommodations

As on other ships of her vintage, *Costa Europa* has few balconies; only six suites on this ship have balconies, and these were additions during the refit (replacing a former cinema). All cabins have a small sitting area, TV, hair dryer, and a personal safe. Storage is adequate, and most outside cabins have bathtubs. Single-occupancy cabins exist, but supplements are assessed anyway. All suites have whirlpool bathtubs and enjoy butler service. Four cabins are wheelchair accessible.

Cabin Sizes (in sq. ft.): Suites 414; ocean view 189; inside 153

Top: *Costa Europa* at anchor
Bottom: Lerna Casino

In the Know

Think *Costa Europa* looks vaguely familiar? It could be because she starred in *Out to Sea* with Walter Matthau and Jack Lemmon. If you are planning on romance during your cruise, cabin selection requires special care—some twin beds cannot be combined to form a queen.

Fast Facts

- 9 passenger decks
- 3 restaurants
- Safes, refrigerators, 3 pools, gym, spa, casino, children's programs (ages 3–17), laundry facilities, laundry service, computer room

CRYSTAL CRUISES

Winner of accolades and too many hospitality industry awards to count, Crystal Cruises offers a taste of the grandeur of the past along with all the modern touches discerning passengers demand these days. Founded in 1990 and owned by Nippon Yusen Kaisha (NYK) in Japan, Crystal ships, unlike other

Crystal Serenity wraparound promenade

luxury vessels, are large, carrying upward of 900 passengers. What makes them distinctive are superior service, a variety of dining options, spacious accommodations, and some of the highest ratios of space per passenger of any cruise ship.

CRYSTAL CRUISES
2049 Century Park E,
Suite 1400
Los Angeles, CA 90067
888/799-4625 or
310/785-9300
www.crystalcruises.com

Cruise Style: Luxury

Beginning with ship designs based on the principles of feng shui, the Eastern art of arranging your surroundings to attract positive energy, no detail is overlooked to provide passengers with the best imaginable experience. Just mention a preference for a certain food or beverage, and your waiter will have it available whenever you request it.

The complete roster of entertainment and activities includes Broadway-style production shows, and bingo, but where Crystal really shines is in the variety of enrichment and educational programs. Passengers can participate in the hands-on Computer University@Sea, interactive Creative Learning Institute classes, or attend lectures featuring top experts in their fields: keyboard lessons with Yamaha, language classes by Berlitz, wellness lectures with the Cleveland Clinic, and an introduction to tai chi with the Tai Chi Cultural Center. Professional ACBL Bridge instructors are on every cruise, and dance instructors offer lessons in contemporary and social dance styles.

An added highlight for women traveling solo is the Ambassador Host Program, which brings cultured gentlemen on each cruise to dine, socialize, and dance with unaccompanied ladies.

Somewhat unique among cruise lines, Crystal Cruises' casinos offer complimentary cocktails to players at the tables and slot machines.

A delightful daily event is afternoon tea in the Palm Court. You're greeted by staff members in 18th-century Viennese brocade and velvet costumes for Mozart Tea; traditional scones and clotted cream are served during English Colonial Tea; and American Tea is a summertime classic created by Crystal culinary artists.

Food

The food alone is a good enough reason to book a Crystal cruise. Dining in the main restaurants is an event starring a Continental-inspired menu of dishes served by European-trained waiters. Off-menu item requests are honored when possible, and special dietary considerations are handled with ease. Full-course vegetarian menus are among the best at sea. Casual poolside dining beneath the stars is offered on some evenings in a relaxed, no-reservations option. A variety of hot-and-cold hors d'oeuvres are served in bars and lounges every evening before dinner and again during the wee hours.

But the specialty restaurants really shine. Jade Garden on *Crystal Symphony* serves traditional Japanese dishes as well as offerings from the menu of Wolfgang Puck's Chinois. Contemporary Asian cuisine is served in *Crystal Serenity*'s Silk Road. The Sushi Bar offers the signature dishes of Nobu Matsuhisa. Both ships have Prego, which serves regional Italian cuisine by Piero Selvaggio, owner of Valentino in Los Angeles and Las Vegas.

Exclusive Wine & Champagne Makers dinners are hosted in the Vintage Room. On select evenings, casual poolside theme dinners are served under the stars.

Crystal has an extensive wine list, including its own proprietary label called C Wines, which are produced in California. Unfortunately, there are no complimentary wines with dinner, as is common on other luxury cruise lines. However, you won't pay extra for bottled water, soft drinks, and specialty coffees; all are included in your basic fare.

Fitness & Recreation

Large spas offer innovative pampering therapies, body wraps, and exotic Asian-inspired treatments by Steiner Leisure. Feng shui principles were scrupulously adhered to in their creation to assure the spas and salons remain havens of tranquillity. Fitness centers have a range of

Noteworthy

- Before sailing, each passenger receives a personal e-mail address.
- Ambassador Hosts on Crystal cruises are cultured, well-traveled gentlemen, who are accomplished dancers and interact with female passengers.
- Complimentary self-service laundry rooms as well as complete laundry, dry-cleaning, and valet services are available.

Top: *Crystal Serenity* fitness center
Bottom: Crystal casino entrance

Top: Spa treatment
Middle: Keyboard lessons
Bottom: *Crystal Symphony* Crystal
Penthouse

exercise and weight-training equipment and workout areas for aerobics classes, plus complimentary yoga and Pilates instruction. In addition, golfers enjoy extensive shipboard facilities, including a driving range practice cage and putting green. Passengers can leave their bags at home and rent top-quality Callaway clubs for use ashore. The line's resident golf pros offer complimentary lessons and group clinics.

Your Shipmates

Affluent, well-traveled couples, from their late-30s and up, are attracted to Crystal's destination-rich itineraries, shipboard enrichment programs, and elegant ambience. The average age of passengers is noticeably higher on longer itineraries.

Dress Code

Formal attire is required on at least two designated evenings, depending on the length of the cruise. Men are encouraged to wear tuxedos, and many do, although dark suits are also acceptable. Other evenings are informal or resort casual; the number of each is based on the number of sea days. The line requests that dress codes be observed in public areas after 6 PM, and few, if any, passengers disregard the suggestion. Most, in fact, dress up just a notch from guidelines.

Junior Cruisers

Although these ships are decidedly adult-oriented, Crystal welcomes children but limits the number of children under age three on any given cruise. Children under six months are not allowed.

Dedicated facilities for children and teens from ages 3 to 17 are staffed by counselors during holiday periods, select summer sailings, and when warranted by the number of children booked. Activities—including games, computer time, scavenger hunts, and arts and crafts—usually have an eye toward the educational. Teenagers can play complimentary video games to their heart's content in Waves, the arcade dedicated for their use. Babysitting can be arranged with staff members for a fee. Baby food, high chairs, and booster seats are available upon request.

CHOOSE A CRUISE ON CRYSTAL CRUISES IF...

1 You crave peace and quiet. Announcements are kept to a bare minimum, and the ambience is sedate.

2 You prefer to plan ahead. You can make spa, restaurant, shore excursion, and class reservations when you book your cruise.

3 You love sushi and other Asian delights; Crystal ships serve some of the best at sea.

2

Service

Crystal's European-trained staff members provide gracious service in an unobtrusive manner.

Tipping

Tips may be distributed personally by passengers on the last night of the cruise or charged to shipboard accounts. Suggested gratuity guidelines per person, per day are: waiter $4; assistant waiter $2.50; cabin stewardess $4; and, for suite occupants only, butler $4. Passengers may adjust the amount based on the level of service experienced. All beverage tabs include an automatic 15% gratuity, as do spa and salon services. A minimum of $6 per person, per dinner is suggested for the servers in specialty restaurants.

Past Passengers

You're automatically enrolled in the Crystal Society upon completion of your first Crystal cruise and are entitled to special savings and member-only events. Membership benefits increase with each completed Crystal cruise and include such perks as stateroom upgrades, shipboard spending credits, special events, gifts, air upgrades, and even free cruises. Society members also receive Crystal Cruises' complimentary quarterly magazine, which shares up-to-date information on itineraries, destinations, special offers, and Society news.

Good to Know

While two assigned dining room seatings are advertised as an advantage that offers flexibility, the reality is that open-seating is the true mark of choice and the most preferred option at this level of luxury cruising. If you haven't done so in advance, on embarkation day you can reserve a table to dine one night in each specialty restaurant, but don't dawdle until the last minute; if you wait, you may find a line has developed—one of the few lines you'll encounter on board—and all the choice dining times are already booked. You may also be able to reserve additional nights after the cruise is under way, depending on how busy the restaurants are.

DON'T CHOOSE A CRUISE ON CRYSTAL CRUISES IF...

1 You don't want to follow the dress code. Everyone does, and you'll stand out–and not in a good way–if you rebel.

2 You want total freedom. Unlike other luxury cruise lines, Crystal assigns you a seating and a table for dinner.

3 You want a less structured cruise. With set dining times, Crystal is a bit more regimented than other luxury lines.

CRYSTAL SERENITY

2003	ENTERED SERVICE
1,080	PASSENGER CAPACITY
635	CREW MEMBERS
540	NUMBER OF CABINS
68,000	GROSS TONS
820 feet	LENGTH
106 feet	WIDTH

700 ft.
500 ft.
300 ft.

Public Areas & Facilities

Crystal Serenity is Crystal Cruises' long-awaited third ship, the first to be introduced since 1995. Although more than a third larger than Crystal's earlier ships, it's similar in layout and follows the line's successful formula of creating intimate spaces in understated, yet sophisticated surroundings.

Stylish public rooms are uncrowded and uncluttered, yet clubby, in the tradition of elegantly proportioned drawing rooms (even the main show lounge is on a single level). Muted colors and warm woods create a soft atmosphere conducive to socializing in the refined environment. The Palm Court could be mistaken for the kind of British colonial-era lounge you might have seen in Hong Kong or India in the 19th century.

A thoughtful touch is an entirely separate room for scrutinizing the art pieces available for auction. The understatement even continues into the casino, although it contains plenty of slot machines and gaming tables.

WOW Factor

It's what you don't see that creates a sensation. The Asian restaurants and enrichment programs are unsurpassed on any other cruise line.

Restaurants

The formal restaurant serves international cuisine in two assigned evening seatings. There's no additional charge for the intimate Asian and Italian specialty restaurants, but reservations are required, and a gratuity is suggested for the servers. Daytime dining choices include a Lido buffet, poolside grill, a patisserie, and an ice-cream bar.

What Works & What Doesn't

Top: *Crystal Serenity* at sea
Bottom: Sushi bar

Crystal Serenity is aptly named. A few anxious moments may pass until dining reservations are secured for the specialty restaurants, but those nerves are nothing compared to what you'd feel trying to get a table at the chef's shoreside counterparts. A West Coast lifestyle prevails, which can be somewhat off-putting to people from fly-over country until they relax and go with the flow. Upscale and tasteful, this ship offers kid-centric spaces, but it isn't a particularly family-friendly cruise experience.

Great for walkers, a wide teak promenade deck encircles the ship.

Accommodations

Layout: As you'd expect on a luxury vessel, *Crystal Serenity* has no inside cabins; however, although suites are generous in size, lesser categories are somewhat smaller than industry standard at this level. All accommodations are designed with ample closet and drawer-shelf storage, as well as bathroom shelves and twin sinks. An impressive 85% of all cabins have private balconies furnished with chairs and tables. Most suites and penthouses have walk-in closets. Crystal Penthouse suites have private workout areas, pantries, and guest powder rooms.

Amenities: Rich wood cabinetry, soft colors, a small refrigerator with complimentary bottled water and soft drinks, a personal safe, a hair dryer, broadband connection for laptop computer, a television with a DVD player, and a sitting area with sofa, chair, and table are typical standard amenities. Most suites and penthouses also have CD players;

all have flat-screen TVs, butler service, personalized stationery, and a fully stocked minibar.

Good to Know: Few staterooms have interior interconnecting doors. Eight staterooms are designed for wheelchair accessibility.

Cabin Type	Size (sq. ft.)
Crystal Penthouse	1,345
Penthouse Suites	538
Regular Penthouses	403
Deluxe Ocean View (w/balcony)	269
Deluxe Ocean View (regular)	226

All dimensions except for regular Deluxe staterooms (the only category that does not have a veranda) include the balcony square footage.

In the Know

A common occurrence on cruise ships is last-night syndrome (when you return to your cabin after that last dinner to find that certain amenities have vanished). Gone are fruit baskets, minibar beverages, and even unwrapped bars of soap. On Crystal that is not the case; the last night is just like the first.

Favorites

Best Splurge: You don't have to swipe the logo china used in the Bistro to impress your friends back home. It's for sale in one of the boutiques.

Best Added Value: A splendid selection of alternative restaurants is yours to enjoy at no additional cost. You may get the urge to drop at least $20 on the table after dessert—the food and service are that

good—but the suggested gratuity is a mere $6.

Our Favorite Spot for a Nightcap: The Avenue Saloon is dark and inviting, just the right spot to duck into following an after-dinner cigar and brandy in the adjacent Connoisseur Club.

Best Bath News: Every bathroom has a full-size tub, Aveda toiletries, plush towels, and bathrobes are provided for

use during the cruise. Most suites and penthouses have whirlpool tub and separate shower.

Best Way to Curb Your Aggression: Take a stone sculpting class (part of the Masterpieces of Art program).

Fast Facts

- 9 passenger decks
- 3 specialty restaurants, dining room, buffet, ice-cream parlor
- In-cabin broadband, Wi-Fi, in-cabin safes, some in-cabin minibars, in-cabin refrigerators, in-cabin DVDs
- 2 pools (1 indoor)
- Fitness classes, gym, hair salon, 2 hot tubs, sauna, spa, steam room
- 6 bars, casino, cinema, 2 dance clubs, library, showroom, video game room
- Children's programs (ages 3–17)
- Dry cleaning, laundry facilities, laundry service
- Computer room
- No kids under 6 months

Crystal spa

CRYSTAL SYMPHONY

	1995
	ENTERED SERVICE
	940 (1,010 max)
	PASSENGER CAPACITY
700 ft.	**545**
	CREW MEMBERS
	470
	NUMBER OF CABINS
500 ft.	**51,044**
	GROSS TONS
	781 feet
	LENGTH
300 ft.	**99 feet**
	WIDTH

Public Areas & Facilities

Crystal Symphony, despite being a relatively large ship with some big-ship features, is noteworthy in the luxury market for creating intimate spaces in understated, yet sophisticated surroundings. Generous per-passenger space ratios have become a Crystal trademark, along with forward-facing observation decks, a Palm Court lounge, and a wide teak promenade encircling the ship. A complete makeover in 2006 refreshed the Bistro Café and shops, reconstructed the casino and Starlite Lounge, and added a new nightclub called Luxe. The extensive refurbishment infused all staterooms and bathrooms with a chic, boutique-style freshness.

Accented by a lovely waterfall, the focal point of the central two-deck atrium is a sculpture of two ballet dancers created especially for the space. Crystal Cove, the lobby lounge, is the spot to meet for cocktails as you make your way to the nearby dining room. Throughout the ship, public rooms shine with low-key contemporary style and flow easily from one to the next.

WOW Factor

The refined and gracious atmosphere without a hint of unnecessary glitter is immediately apparent, but it's the professionalism of the staff that adds sparkle.

Top: Casino gaming
Bottom: Computer University@Sea

Restaurants

The formal restaurant serves international cuisine in two assigned evening seatings. There's no additional charge for the intimate Asian and Italian specialty restaurants, but a gratuity is suggested and reservations required. Daytime dining choices include the Lido buffet, an outdoor grill, ice-cream bar, and the Bistro patisserie.

What Works & What Doesn't

Dedicated areas for children and teens take a backseat to what's offered for adults—the Creative Learning Institute enrichment programs, complimentary Computer University@Sea instruction, and a full roster of distinguished guest speakers barely scratch the surface of what's at hand. Crystal began including complimentary bottled water and soft drinks when *Crystal Serenity* was introduced and also extended the perk to *Crystal Symphony.* Unlike other top-end luxury cruise lines, wine is not included with dinner.

Accommodations

Layout: There are no inside cabins on *Crystal Symphony*. Still, relatively small stateroom sizes are cozy and chic with boutique-hotel style decor; however, all cabins have ample closet and drawer-shelf storage, as well as bathroom shelves. Many have private balconies furnished with chairs and tables. Most suites and penthouses have a walk-in closet. Crystal Penthouse suites have guest powder rooms.

Amenities: Rich wood cabinetry, soft pastel fabrics, a small refrigerator filled with complimentary bottled water and soft drinks, a personal safe, a hair dryer, a television with a DVD player, and a sitting area with sofa, chair, and table are typical standard features in all cabins. Suite and penthouse extras vary, but many have a flat-screen television and CD player. All have butler service, personalized stationery, and stocked minibars with wine, beer, and choice of liquor.

Bathrooms: Every bathroom has oval glass sinks, granite counters, a full-size tub, Aveda toiletries, plush towels, and bathrobes for use during the cruise. Many suites and penthouses have a whirlpool tub and separate shower.

Good to Know: Seven staterooms are wheelchair-accessible.

Cabin Type	Size (sq. ft.)
Crystal Penthouse	982
Penthouse Suites	491
Regular Penthouses	367
Deluxe Ocean View (w/balcony)	246
Deluxe Ocean View (regular)	202

All dimensions except for regular Deluxe staterooms (the only category that does not have a veranda) include the balcony square footage

In the Know

Steam rooms and saunas are completely complimentary, and no spa treatments or other purchases are required before using them. Simply go in anytime you please. In addition, bathrobes and disposable slippers are provided for use in the men's and women's locker rooms.

Favorites

Best Added Value: If you feel the need to pack light and do laundry during your cruise or return home with clean clothing in your suitcases, passenger launderettes are complimentary.

Best Way to Take in a Film: The large theater seats almost as many movie buffs as an average multiplex ashore and serves free popcorn.

Screenings alternate between recent releases and classic favorites.

Our Favorite Spot for a Nightcap: Happily, Crystal doesn't mess with a good thing. Just as on *Crystal Serenity*, the Avenue Saloon and its Connoisseur Club annex are winners for a quiet drink before bed.

Best Place to Relax: With no aft-facing passenger accommodations,

Crystal Symphony's stern retains the traditional styling of open decks with plenty of lounge chairs, so you can relax and watch the ship's wake. For a bit more privacy, a canopy-covered sun deck is behind the spa.

Most Difficult Choice: Which one of the proprietary wines will you order with dinner?

Fast Facts

- 8 passenger decks
- 2 specialty restaurants, dining room, buffet, ice-cream parlor
- Wi-Fi, in-cabin safes, in-cabin refrigerators, some in-cabin minibars, in-cabin DVDs
- 2 pools (1 indoor)
- Fitness classes, gym, hair salon, 2 hot tubs, sauna, spa, steam room
- 5 bars, casino, cinema, dance club, library, showroom, video game room
- Children's programs (ages 3–17)
- Dry cleaning, laundry facilities, laundry service
- Computer room
- No kids under 6 months

Library

CUNARD LINE

One of the world's most distinguished names in ocean travel since 1840, Cunard Line's history of deluxe transatlantic crossings and worldwide cruising is legendary for comfortable accommodations, excellent cuisine, and personal service. After a series of owners tried with little success to revive the com-

Romantic sunset at sea

pany's flagging passenger shipping business after the advent of the jet age, Carnival Corporation saved the day in 1998 with an infusion of ready cash and the know-how to turn the cruise line around. The result is the heralded *Queen Mary 2* and newly launched *Queen Victoria*.

CUNARD LINE
24303 Town Center Drive
Valencia, CA 91355
661/753-1000 or
800/728-6273
www.cunard.com

Cruise Style: Luxury

Entertainment has a decidedly English flavor with nightly production shows or cabaret-style performances and even plays starring Great Britain's Royal Academy of Dramatic Arts alumni. An authentic pub gives the liner an even more British air, while a wide variety of musical styles can be found for dancing and listening in other bars and lounges. In the first-ever shipboard planetarium, high-tech presentations and virtual-reality shows dramatize the origins of the universe and the history of the galaxies on a virtual ride through space.

Cunard's fine enrichment programs include lectures by experts in their fields. Classes vary by cruise and include a wide assortment of topics taught by top designers, master chefs, and artists. Even seamanship and navigation courses are offered to novice mariners. Passengers can plan their activities prior to departure by consulting the syllabus of courses available online at Cunard Line's Web site.

Delightful daily events are afternoon tea and the maritime tradition of sounding the ship's bell at noon. *Queen Elizabeth 2* continues the tradition of North Atlantic crossings and sails on lengthy worldwide cruises, but she no longer does regularly scheduled cruises in the Caribbean; *Queen*

Mary 2 also offers North Atlantic crossings and seasonal shorter cruises, including Caribbean itineraries.

Food

In the tradition of multiclass ocean liners, dining room assignments are made according to the accommodation category booked. You can get as much luxury as you are willing to pay for on *Cunard liners,* where passengers in Junior Suites are assigned to the single-seating Princess Grill; the posh Queen's Grill serves passengers booked in duplex apartments and the most lavish suites. All other passengers are assigned to one of two seatings in the dramatic, three-deck-high Britannia Restaurant.

Almost lost in the specialty restaurant hype is acclaimed chef Daniel Boulud, who designed the menus in *Queen Mary 2*'s main restaurants. Although fare in Britannia is reasonably traditional and often outstanding, off-menu requests by Grill passengers are commonly granted—provided the galley has the ingredients. Menus also include vegetarian and low-calorie selections.

Quite possibly the world's most coveted table reservations are those in the restaurant named for Todd English, the celebrity American chef and restaurateur noted for his innovative Mediterranean cuisine and sumptuous desserts. Dinner (for a $35 per-person cover charge) was so popular that lunch was added (for $20 per person) so more passengers would have the opportunity to dine in the intimate restaurant.

The Chef's Galley is another small reservations-required restaurant, where diners look on as their food is prepared in an open galley setting; the only charge here is for wine. The King's Court buffet is transformed each evening into three no-charge casual alternative dining spots: the Carvery specializes in carved meats; La Piazza is dedicated to pasta, pizza, and Italian dishes; and Lotus offers Asian regional specialties.

Fitness & Recreation

Swimming pools, golf driving ranges, table tennis, paddle tennis court, shuffleboard, and jogging tracks barely scratch the surface of shipboard facilities dedicated to recreation. Top-quality fitness centers offer high-tech workout equipment, a separate weight room, and classes ranging from aerobics to healthy living workshops.

Queen Mary 2's Canyon Ranch Spa Club is a one-of-a-kind facility at sea offering salon services for women and men and a menu of more than 60 treatments, including the famous land-based spa's signature 80-minute Canyon Stone Massage. The focal point of the facility is a

Noteworthy

■ *Queen Mary 2* uses an Arabic 2 rather than the Roman numeral used by monarchs because it's a sequel to the original ship.

■ The captain steers the *Queen Mary 2* with a single lever or joystick on the bridge.

■ The sound of *Queen Mary 2*'s whistle carries for 10 mi but doesn't disturb passengers on deck.

Top: Cunard White Star service
Bottom: Illluminations planetarium

Top: Fine dining
Middle: Royal Court Theater
Bottom: Junior suite

30- by 15-foot thalassotherapy pool featuring a deluge waterfall, air tub, massage-jet benches, neck fountains, and air-bed recliner lounges. To further achieve the therapeutic benefits of water and heat, you may want to try the thermal suite with its herbal sauna, Finnish sauna, aromatic steam room, and reflexology basins. Use of these special features is complimentary if you purchase a massage or other body treatment; otherwise, there's a per-day charge.

The daily SpaClub Passport costs $35 and includes use of the fitness center, thermal suite, aqua therapy center, locker rooms, and a choice of fitness classes. Robes, sandals, and complimentary beverages are also available for spa goers and SpaClub Passport holders in the relaxation lounge.

Your Shipmates

Discerning, well-traveled American and British couples from their late-30s to retirees are drawn to Cunard's traditional style and the notion of a cruise aboard an ocean liner. The availability of spacious accommodations and complimentary self-service laundry facilities make Cunard liners a good option for families, although there may be fewer children on board than you might expect.

Dress Code

Glamorous evenings are typical of Cunard cruises, and specified attire includes formal, informal, and casual. Although resort casual clothing prevails throughout the day, Cunard vessels are ocean liners at heart and, as expected, are dressier than most cruise ships at night. To maintain their high standards, the cruise line requests passengers to dress as they would for dining in fine restaurants.

Junior Cruisers

The kid-friendly Kid Zone has both a dedicated play area and a splash pool for children ages one to six. Separate programs are reserved for older children ages 7 to 12 and teens. Toys and activities range from simple games to more educational computer classes. Children can practice their social graces when they're served their own afternoon teatime goodies. Toddlers are supervised by English nannies. Facilities are only operated until midnight; however, group babysitting is complimentary. Infants under

CHOOSE A CRUISE ON CUNARD LINE IF...

❶ You want to boast that you have sailed on the world's largest ocean liner, though larger ships are already on the way.

❷ You enjoy a brisk walk. *Queen Mary 2* is massive, and you'll find yourself walking a great deal.

❸ A posh English pub is your ideal of the perfect place to hang out.

one year are not allowed; children from ages one to two sail free (except for government fees).

Service
Although most crew members are international rather than British, service is formal and sophisticated.

Tipping
Suggested gratuities of $13 per person per day (for Grill Restaurant accommodations) or $11 per person per day (all other accommodations) are automatically charged to shipboard accounts for distribution to stewards and waitstaff. An automatic 15% gratuity is added to beverage tabs for bar service. Passengers can still tip individual crew members directly in cash for any special services.

Past Passengers
After one sailing aboard a Cunard liner, passengers are automatically enrolled as members of Cunard World Club; they are accorded Silver status on their second cruise. Silver-level members receive discounts of up to 50% off Early Booking Savings on all sailings, access to the shipboard World Club Representative and World Club Desk, and a quarterly newsletter, *The Cunarder*.

After completing two Cunard cruises or 20 days on board, members are accorded Gold status and are additionally invited to shipboard World Club cocktail receptions, two hours of Internet service, and receive a Gold Cunarder pin. Passengers who complete seven sailings, or who have completed a Cunard voyage of 48 consecutive days or more, achieve the Platinum status. Additional benefits to Platinum members include a shipboard World Club cocktail reception, priority check-in and boarding in certain embarkation ports, an invitation to the Senior Officers' party, four hours of Internet service, and a Platinum Cunarder pin.

Diamond membership is for guests who have completed 15 voyages or 150 days on board. In addition to the above, they receive priority luggage delivery, complimentary lunch in Todd English, eight hours of Internet service, and a Diamond Cunarder pin.

Good to Know

The idea of a multiple-class ship offends some people's sense of democracy, and Cunard ships are ocean liners that adhere in not-so-subtle fashion to the tradition of class distinctions. This is the 21st century, though, so you won't find steerage class, and even regular folks in the cheaper cabins will enjoy the superior surroundings. However, certain areas, including the Queen's Grill Lounge, a private sun terrace, and even a private elevator, are reserved for occupants of privileged accommodations. So luxury on a Cunard ship is a relative experience and certainly more luxurious for some.

CUNARD LINE

DON'T CHOOSE A CRUISE ON CUNARD LINE IF...

1 You prefer informality, especially in the Caribbean. *Queen Mary 2* is a traditional formal liner.

2 You want real luxury with no add-on costs.

3 Your sense of direction is really bad. Nearly everyone gets lost on board at least once.

QUEEN VICTORIA

Public Areas & Facilities

Designers of Cunard's newest vessel drew upon the rich history of previous Cunard ocean liners. From the ship's double- and triple-height spaces—design features of grand liners of the past—to rooms imbued with an elegant yet understated British charm, the overall effect is both contemporary and historically classic.

Queen Victoria herself might very well feel at home upon entering the double-height Queens Room, a loggia-style venue designed in the manner of the grand ballrooms found in large English country houses, such as Her Majesty's own Osborne House. Reminiscent of QE2, the ballroom has cantilevered balconies overlooking an inlaid wooden dance floor; the staircase is detailed with classically ornate, curved railings.

In addition to the intimate dining spaces and a lounge reserved for occupants of Queens and Princess Grill accommodations, an outdoor terrace is devoted to their exclusive use. All other public rooms are accessible to everyone on board.

	2007
	ENTERED SERVICE
	1,970
	PASSENGER CAPACITY
700 ft.	**900**
	CREW MEMBERS
	985
	NUMBER OF CABINS
500 ft.	**90,000**
	GROSS TONS
	965 feet
	LENGTH
300 ft.	**106 feet**
	WIDTH

WOW Factor

The impact of the dramatic Grand Lobby's triple-height ceiling, sweeping staircase, and sculpted balconies is immediate and unmistakable.

Top: Main pool
Bottom: Queens grill suite

Restaurants

The Britannia Restaurant serves dinner in two assigned seatings for most passengers, while those in Princess and Queens Grill-classes dine single seatings. Todd English, the alternative restaurant, requires reservations and has a fee. The Lido buffet and Golden Lion Pub offer relaxed dining options, while specialty teas, coffees, and pastries are featured in Café Carinthia. A proper English tea is served daily and room service is always available.

What Works & What Doesn't

Queen Victoria offers the best of Cunard's heritage and traditions, along with modern-day luxuries and exciting innovations. Included are the first private boxes in the Royal Court Theatre, the first Cunardia museum exhibit at sea (housing Cunard artifacts and memorabilia), and the first two-deck library at sea, featuring nearly 6,000 titles, warm mahogany wood paneling, leather sofas, and an elegant spiral staircase. Highlighted by a glass roof that opens to admit warm sea breezes, the Winter Garden is a more pleasing conservatory than the similar space found on Queen Mary 2.

2

CUNARD LINE

Accommodations

Layout: While there are more than two-dozen stateroom and suite categories from which to choose, cabins really fall into eight configurations. At the top are the Queens Grill suite categories, which have the most luxurious amenities; next are the Princess Grill sutes; finally come the standard staterooms (some with a balcony) as well as inside cabins, whose passengers dine in the Britannia Restaurant. The majority of the cabins fall into the standard categories. More than 86% of staterooms on the ship are outside and 76% have private balconies. All are designed with ample closet and storage spaces, and even the least expensive outside categories have a small sitting area. Private balconies are furnished with chairs, table, and some have loungers.

Amenities: All passengers are greeted upon embarkation with sparkling wine or champagne and will find a refrigerator, safe, hair dryer, fresh fruit basket, bath toiletries, slippers, and a bathrobe for use during the cruise. Butlers are on hand to attend to Queens Grill occupants, whose bars are stocked with spirits, wines, and soft drinks.

Good to Know: Fourteen cabins are wheelchair accessible.

Cabin Type	Size (sq. ft.)
Grand Suite/Master Suite	1,918–2,131/1,100
Penthouse Suite/ Queen Suite	520–707/508–771
Princess Suite	335–513
Ocean View with Balcony	242–472
Ocean View/Interior	180–201/152–243

All dimensions include the square footage for balconies

Fast Facts

- 12 passenger decks
- Specialty restaurant, 3 dining rooms, buffet, ice-cream parlor, pizzeria
- Wi-Fi, in-cabin safes, in-cabin refrigerators, some in-cabin minibars, some in-cabin DVDs
- 2 pools (1 indoor)
- Fitness classes, gym, hair salon, 4 hot tubs, sauna, spa, steam room
- 10 bars, casino, 2 dance clubs, library, showroom
- Children's programs (ages 1–17)
- Dry cleaning, laundry facilities, laundry service
- Computer room

In the Know

Check the deck plan carefully when selecting balcony accommodations—on decks 4 through 7 there are "jogs" in the interior passageways where you'll find more than a dozen balcony cabins in a variety of categories that are larger than average. Aft-facing balconies are the most spacious of all.

Favorites

Best Place for a Power Walk: The promenade deck encircles the ship and is ideal for a casual stroll or serious jogging.

Best Retail Therapy: Inspired by London's Burlington and Royal Arcades, these shops invite us to shop amid the wood paneling, wrought iron, green marble, and white-stone accents.

Our Favorite Spot for a Nightcap: We naturally choose the heavenly Commodore Club for a nightcap, or cocktails anytime. Martinis—shaken not stirred—simply taste better with the panoramic view.

Most Fun & Almost Funky: A dramatic chandelier challenges the starlight twinkling through the glass-domed roof for your attention

in the stunning, contemporary Hemispheres nightclub. Dance styles alternate between classic big-band sounds and up-to-the-minute tunes spun by the DJ.

Brittania stateroom

QUEEN MARY 2

Public Areas & Facilities

With the clever use of design elements, *Queen Mary 2*, one of the largest passenger liners ever built, bears a striking external resemblance to the smaller, older *Queen Elizabeth 2*. The world's grandest and most expensive liner is something of a transitional ship, incorporating classic ocean-liner features—sweeping staircases, soaring public rooms, a 360-degree promenade deck, and a grand ballroom—all comfortably within a hull that also includes a trendy Canyon Ranch Spa and a full-scale planetarium.

Interior spaces blend the traditional style of early-20th-century liners with all the conveniences 21st-century passengers expect. Public rooms are mainly located on two decks low in the ship—remember, this is a liner designed for North Atlantic crossings. Befitting a queen, the grand lobby is palatial with broad, curving staircases and stately columns. Wide passageways lead to a variety of lounges, shops, a casino, showroom, and planetarium. The Queen's room is especially regal.

700 ft.	**2004**
	ENTERED SERVICE
	2,620 (3,090 max)
	PASSENGER CAPACITY
	1,253
	CREW MEMBERS
	1,310
	NUMBER OF CABINS
500 ft.	**151,400**
	GROSS TONS
	1,132 feet
	LENGTH
300 ft.	**135 feet**
	WIDTH

WOW Factor

Anyone who claims they aren't impressed just seeing Queen Mary 2 *waiting alongside the dock is probably faking their lack of enthusiasm.*

Restaurants

Queen Mary 2 offers different levels of dining assignment that correspond to accommodation category booked. The Britannia Restaurant serves dinner in two seatings to most passengers; those in junior suites and above dine in the single-seating Grill restaurants; those in AA Britannia Club Balcony Cabins dine in the single-seating Britannia Club Dining Room.

What Works & What Doesn't

The full majesty of yesteryear's grand liners is re-created within *Queen Mary 2*'s hull—she appears to be a throwback to the days of opulence and celebrity sightings. Although it's certainly exciting to sail on such an impressive ship, no one harbors the illusion that booking an inside cabin results in the same level of pampering and attention received by occupants of a Penthouse or Royal Suite. So the illusion of total luxury falls short in reality.

On the other hand, proper afternoon tea and great, pub-style fare in the Golden Lion suggest that Britannia still rules the waves.

Top: Intimate lounges
Bottom: Grand duplex suite

Accommodations

Layout: Selecting a stateroom or suite on *Queen Mary 2* is a complex endeavor due to the many variations. As expected on the world's most luxurious liner, an impressive 78% of her accommodations are outside cabins and more than 86% of these feature spacious private balconies. There are fewer than 300 inside cabins; however, a dozen insides have an atrium view. All accommodations are designed with ample closet, drawer-shelf storage, and bathroom shelves. Private balconies are furnished with chairs, loungers, and tables. Duplex apartment and suite luxuries vary, but most have a whirlpool tub, dressing area, entertainment center, and dining area; all have private balconies. In addition, duplex apartments and most suites feature guest powder rooms and whirlpool tubs; some have his-and-hers dressing rooms.

Amenities: Warm-wood cabinetry, quality fabrics, a small refrigerator, a personal safe, a hair dryer, broadband computer hookup, interactive television, and a sitting area with sofa or chairs and dual-height table are typical standard amenities. Toiletries, slippers, and bathrobes for use during the cruise are standard.

Good to Know: Thirty cabins are wheelchair-accessible.

Cabin Type	Size (sq. ft.)
Grand Duplex/Duplex	2,249/1,194
Royal Suite/Penthouse	796/758
Suite/Jr. Suite	506/381
Deluxe/Premium Balcony	248/249
Standard Ocean View/ Inside	194

In the Know

Yes, you read the deck plan correctly: there's a kennel on Queen Mary 2. But, no, sadly you can't bring Fido or Fluffy along on a Caribbean cruise. Kennel use is restricted to transatlantic crossings, although service animals can avail themselves of the fire hydrant during cruises.

Favorites

Share the Captain's Viewpoint: For a glimpse into all things nautical, visit the bridge observation area. Through glass windows directly behind the main console, you'll have a view of both the long-range and short-range radar. Open on most sea days, access the area by using the "A" stairwell or elevators and stay as long as you like.

Shall We Dance?: The Queen's Room is a true ballroom with the largest ballroom dance floor at sea. Spanning the width of the ship beneath a high, arched ceiling and crystal chandelier, it's a majestic space where you'll want to waltz the night away.

Our Favorite Spot for a Nightcap: So many bars, so little time . . . for the atmosphere of an ocean crossing, the Chart Room wins out. For a nightclub vibe, we prefer the Commodore Club.

Best Splurge: Dine in Todd English, which bears the name of the celebrity chef who designed the menu; his innovative Mediterranean cuisine is the best thing going on the *QM2*.

Fast Facts

- 14 passenger decks
- 2 specialty restaurants, 3 dining rooms, buffet, ice-cream parlor, pizzeria
- In-cabin broadband, Wi-Fi, in-cabin safes, in-cabin refrigerators, some in-cabin minibars, some in-cabin DVDs
- 5 pools (2 indoor), 2 children's pools
- Fitness classes, gym, hair salon, 7 hot tubs, sauna, spa, steam room
- 11 bars, casino, cinema, 2 dance clubs, library, showroom, video game room
- Children's programs (ages 1–17)
- Dry cleaning, laundry facilities, laundry service
- Computer room
- No kids under age 1

Pool deck

QUEEN ELIZABETH 2

Public Areas & Facilities

Built on land, *Queen Elizabeth 2*, the ship, was "launched" into the water in 1967 by Queen Elizabeth II, the monarch. Two years later, the ship entered service with a minicruise to the Canary Islands, followed by her first transatlantic crossing. In subsequent years, she's served as ocean liner, cruise liner, and even troop ship. Compared to a city at sea, *Queen Elizabeth 2* has onboard "neighborhoods"—she was constructed as a two-class liner—and, like major cities, has undergone urban renewal over the decades. Only a vestige of her multiple-class days remains in the form of dining room assignments, which are still made according to the category of accommodations selected. The only area off-limits to everyone but Grill-class passengers is the Queens Grill Lounge. The grand ship is scheduled to sail her last cruise in November 2008, after which she will become a floating hotel in Dubai.

1969	ENTERED SERVICE
1,791	PASSENGER CAPACITY
921	CREW MEMBERS
950	NUMBER OF CABINS
70,327	GROSS TONS
963 feet	LENGTH
105 feet	WIDTH

700 ft.

500 ft.

300 ft.

WOW Factor

It's impossible to miss QE 2's massive red and black funnel. Gracefully balanced by her long and sleek hull, her distinctive funnel towers like a skyscraper on the horizon.

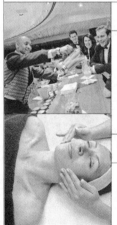

Restaurants

Queens Grill, Princess Grill, Britannia Grill, and Caronia Restaurant all have a single assigned dinner seating, while the larger Mauretania Restaurant has two assigned seatings; breakfast and lunch are open seating. The Lido Restaurant is the more casual buffet; the Pavilion is a poolside grill; there's also the Golden Lion Pub. Afternoon tea is offered in the Queens Room, and room service is available around the clock.

What Works & What Doesn't

Top: Have a perfect cocktail
Bottom: Pampered pleasures in Cunard Royal Spa

QE 2 is one of the world's most glamorous and formal ships in service today. She retains a certain level of class separation due to the dining arrangements. Proving that old isn't always classic, *QE2* has undergone so many makeovers through the years that her interiors are presently superior to the original, somewhat plastic, 1960s designs. Her decor has evolved into a more traditional and warmer look with richer woods and fabrics. With the majority of staterooms outside, it's possible to book accommodations with an ocean view without breaking the budget. For solo travelers, 118 single cabins are available.

2

CUNARD LINE

Accommodations

Layout: Most staterooms are spacious, but some inside cabins are quite small, especially those designated Inside Singles. As on most older ships, even accommodations within the same category have layouts and amenities that vary. Outside cabins comprise 70% of all accommodations, but only some in top categories have balconies. Cabins should be selected carefully; fortunately, the ship's deck plan is very detailed.

Amenities: Mauretania staterooms, whether inside or outside, feature ample storage, hair dryers, personal safes, TVs, and bathrooms with shower and/or bathtub. Similarly furnished and slightly larger, Caronia accommodations are all outside; some have small sitting areas. Princess and Britannia Grill accommodations include Deluxe and Ultra Deluxe outside staterooms with sitting areas, walk-in closets, and bathrobes provided for use during the cruise.

Suites: Princess and Queens Grill accommodations, which range from Ultra Deluxe staterooms to Grand Suites, typically have a sitting area, refrigerator, personalized stationery, and bathrobes provided for use during the cruise; some have a VCR and private balcony.

Good to Know: For solo travelers, 118 cabins are available for single occupancy. Eight staterooms are wheelchair-accessible.

Cabin Type	Size (sq. ft.)
Grand Suite	1,184
Suites	575–777
Duplex Suites/Deluxe Outside	241–355
Outside	121–195
Inside	115–121

Fast Facts

- 12 passenger decks
- 5 dining rooms, buffet
- Wi-Fi, in-cabin safes, some in-cabin minibars, some in-cabin refrigerators, some in-cabin VCRs
- 2 pools (1 indoor)
- Fitness classes, gym, hair salon, 2 hot tubs, sauna, spa, steam room
- 6 bars, casino, cinema, library, showroom, video game room
- Children's programs (ages 1–17)
- Dry cleaning, laundry facilities, laundry service
- Computer room

In the Know

While she's quite regal, Queen Elizabeth 2 *is not named after Her Majesty Queen Elizabeth II. The "2" indicates she is the second ship to bear the name. Therefore, the Arabic number 2 is used in the ship's name, not the Roman numeral II, which denotes the monarch.*

Favorites

Best Place to Use Binoculars: We like a seat at the Sun Deck Bar for an unobstructed view of the horizon.

Best Splurge: A Q-grade stateroom is worth the big bucks to dine in the Queens Grill, where selections include à la carte menu items and complimentary caviar, and where special requests are honored whenever possible.

Our Favorite Spot for a Nightcap: We like the Yacht Club for its proximity to one of the aft decks, where we can see the ship's wake sparkle in the moonlight.

Most Surprising Passenger: You might think someone who witnessed the sinking of an ocean liner from a lifeboat in the North Atlantic would never want to embark on another ship, but Milvina

Dean did. Ms. Dean, a *Titanic* survivor, sailed on the *QE 2.*

Best Added Value: Parents love the no-charge evening babysitting service as much as their children enjoy the Children's Playroom.

Service Fit for a Queen: Queens Grill cabins also command butler service.

Formal dining on *QE2*

EASYCRUISE

Introduced in Europe with great fanfare in 2005 by Stelios (like many celebrities, he goes by one name), the business model for easyCruise was easily the quirkiest endeavor to hit the cruise industry. Stelios, known as a "serial" entrepreneur and the guiding force behind low-fare air carrier easyJet,

easyCruise One at anchor

has designed a cross between a traditional cruise ship and a ferry. Rather than book an entire voyage, independent-minded passengers are offered the flexibility to book as few as three nights, embarking and departing in any scheduled port along the way.

easyCruise (UK) Ltd.
The Rotunda
42/43 Gloucester Crescent,
London, UK NW1 7DL
(30)211/211-6211
www.easycruise.com.

Cruise Style: Mainstream

Aimed at youthful travelers interested in island-hopping and sampling the local nightlife, itineraries are scheduled to arrive in port mid-morning, stay until the partying winds down, and then move on to the next destination. However, a hint that easyCruise may be heading along a more traditional path is that fares are now available in packages consisting of 3, 4, and 7 nights. EasyCruise is still able to offer rock-bottom pricing by eliminating all onboard frills and nearly all necessities. Passengers are encouraged to dine ashore since no meals are included in the cruise fare and onboard meal service is limited. You'll also pay for all cabin services, including cleaning, fresh towels, and bed linens. Fellow passengers on easyCruise don't seem to mind making their own beds.

CHOOSE A CRUISE ON EASYCRUISE IF...

❶ You've never considered a traditional cruise but find the idea of sampling a different destination every day appealing.

❷ You don't mind paying extra for anything and everything on board in exchange for a very low up-front fare.

❸ Your expectations and your budget are low.

Food

The best dining is still found ashore when in port. On board, an upgraded restaurant supplements the diner-quality snacks, sandwiches, and dessert items that have always been available. But the quality of the food is more like Starbucks or Ruby Tuesday. The best offerings are often found at breakfast. You pay for all food on board; there are no meal plans, and, although menus are priced in dollars, the individual items are on the pricey side for what you get. There are few options for passengers with special dietary needs, but numerous choices are suitable for vegetarians.

Fitness & Recreation

A small gym has exercise equipment, but you will be more likely to burn off calories walking in ports and swimming when you head for the beach. There's no pool on easy-Cruise One, but there is a popular hot tub.

Your Shipmates

The plan was to appeal to active adults in their 20s and 30s. In reality, depending on the season and itinerary, passenger ages might lean toward the 40-something and older set. Most passengers hail from Great Britain or North America, with Brits usually in the majority.

Dress Code

This is as informal as cruising can get. The only provision is that you wear clothing.

Service

While it's adequate for food and beverages, you'll have to carry your own bags and make your bed yourself. You can pay for maid service, as well as clean sheets and towels.

Tipping

Tip for dining and drinks as you would at any shoreside bar or restaurant. Other gratuities are completely up to you, but since there is little service, you'll have few opportunities to tip.

Noteworthy

- An easyCruise is pay-as-you-go cruising. While a low fare gets you on board, virtually nothing else is included.
- *EasyCruise1* was rebuilt to cram in nearly twice as many passengers as it was designed for. Space and privacy are at a premium.
- Be prepared to entertain yourself, though there is a nightly DJ and an occasional passenger participation game.

Top: Tropical drinks from the bar
Bottom: Relaxation in the sauna

DON'T CHOOSE A CRUISE ON EASYCRUISE IF...

1. You have a high-maintenance wardrobe and tend to over-pack. Only "suites" have close-to-adequate storage.

2. Your expectations are for pampering attention and over-the-top services with facilities to match.

3. You can't take care of yourself and make your own good times without a rigid schedule of activities.

EASYCRUISE ONE

Public Areas & Facilities

From a small upmarket vessel designed to carry 100 passengers in comfort and luxury, *easyCruiseOne* was transformed by gutting the interiors and replacing them with spartan, modular cabins that sleep nearly twice as many passengers when fully booked. While the bright neon-orange hull emblazoned with "easycruise.com" acted in the past as a beacon to late-night revelers returning from shoreside restaurants and clubs, the garish look has undergone a transformation. A new graphite-gray paint job with discreet orange trim gives the ship a more refined appearance but shouldn't hamper the party spirit of its passengers. Even in its new livery, *easyCruiseOne* is easy to spot late at night—it's likely to be the only ship at the pier.

The ship's public spaces have also been redecorated and now have more of the look of a boutique hotel. While the ship now has a sauna, small spa, and Internet café, the list of what isn't on board is still longer than the list of what is. There's still no swimming pool, casino, library, or even entertainment.

1990	
ENTERED SERVICE	
170	
PASSENGER CAPACITY	
700 ft.	**54**
	CREW MEMBERS
	86
	NUMBER OF CABINS
500 ft.	**4,077**
	GROSS TONS
	290 feet
	LENGTH
300 ft.	**50 feet**
	WIDTH

WOW Factor

Budget-conscious cruisers feel the WOW factor in their wallets—even without all the "extras" that are not included, the bottom line on an easyCruise is easy to handle.

Top: New menu options
Bottom: Spa pampering

Restaurants

Meals are served on a come-when-you-want and pay-as-you-go basis. The main restaurant, Fusion on 4, serves all day long. Sun&Moon, the combination bar and café, serves a laundry list of snacks, sandwiches, coffee, and tea. Outdoor seating is available for alfresco dining.

What Works & What Doesn't

For its free-spirited and independent passengers, easyCruise has been a rousing success, particularly in the Caribbean, where the ship not only remains until the party ashore winds down but also arrives early enough so that passengers can enjoy a full day at the beach or sightseeing.

Passengers don't miss the lack of daytime entertainment on the ship because there are no sea days on easy-Cruise itineraries. With little nighttime entertainment, most cruisers enjoy the easy camaraderie, both on and off the ship.

Accommodations

Layout: Cabin decor has been toned down and is no longer quite so orange. Standard twin cabins for two are tiny, inside cabins tinier; quadruple cabins have two sets of bunk beds. Futon beds set on platforms are standard. Some doubles have windows that resemble square portholes, but all quads are inside. Bathrooms have surprisingly chic, if minimalist, glass basins, but there's no barrier between the shower and the rest of the bathroom, so the floor will likely be soaked. Storage consists of a few hooks and open shelves, so pack light. Toiletries, other than soap in a dispenser, are not provided. With no in-cabin telephones, TVs, or safes, you may wish to leave your valuables at home and pack a travel alarm clock instead. Bring your own hair dryer and beach towels as well. Happily for Americans, electrical outlets deliver 110-volt current with U.S.-style plugs.

Suites: Four suites have small sofas and balconies (as well as more space) but otherwise are similar to regular cabins with the same small bathrooms and platform futon-style beds. Storage in suites is a bit better but is nothing like what you'd get in even the smallest regular cruise-ship cabin.

Good to Know: New, small windows have been cut through to create an ocean view for about 60 cabins on Deck 3. Bring earplugs; soundproofing seems to have been overlooked. One stateroom is designed to be wheelchair-accessible.

Cabin Type	Size (sq. ft.)
Suite	258
Inside/Outside Double	108/129
Quadruple	162

Fast Facts

- 5 passenger decks
- 1 restaurant, 1 café
- Gym, 1 hot tub, sauna, spa
- 2 bars
- Computer room, no kids under 14

In the Know

Don't look for nightly turn-down service or a chocolate on your pillow. In do-it-yourself fashion, cabin service is not automatic, but is available as an option. You don't have to make your own bed if you are willing to pay the add-on price. Just sign up at the reception desk.

Favorites

Best Place to Wind Down: With happy-hour cocktails in hand, a soak in the hot tub is a relaxing interlude before dressing to head ashore for dinner.

Best Splurge: For more personal space, fares are so low that couples might want to consider booking a quad cabin, but the suites are both much larger and more expensive.

Best Onboard Dining: Breakfast items, available all day in the Fusion on 4 restaurant, are top menu selections among passengers who choose to eat on board.

Best Spot to Get Away From It All: There are a small number of lounge chairs for sunning on Deck 6.

Our Favorite Spot for a Nightcap: With a view over the stern and the stars overhead, we like the new seating area around the hot tub on Deck 5.

Dining alfresco

FRED. OLSEN CRUISE LINES

Family-owned Fred. Olsen Cruise Lines proudly boasts a Norwegian heritage of seamanship and a fleet of small ships that offer an intimate cruising experience. While the fleet doesn't consist of new vessels, all were well constructed originally and have been refitted since 2001. Two sister ships from the defunct luxury Royal Viking Line, *Royal Viking Star* and *Royal Viking Sky,* have reunited under the Fred. Olsen house flag and now sail as *Black Watch* and *Boudicca.* And while the line is destination-focused—itineraries are seldom repeated within any cruise season—itinerary planning is versatile.

Shuffleboard action

FRED. OLSEN CRUISE LINES
Fred. Olsen House,
Whitehouse Road, Ipswich,
UK 1P1 5LL
01/473/742–424
www.fredolsencruises.com.

Cruise Style: Mainstream

Shipboard ambience is friendly, relaxed, and unabashedly British. As Fred. Olsen Cruise Lines expands, the line takes pride in maintaining the consistency their passengers prefer and expect, both on board and ashore. Activities and entertainment are traditional cruise-ship fare with a laid-back tempo, though on a much smaller scale than you find on the typical American megaship. Ballroom dancers outnumber the late-night disco set, and shows are more cabaret than Vegas. Particular favorites with most passengers are theme nights and the crew show. Cruises range from four-night "mini-breaks" to lengthier 7- to 78-night sailings. British pounds are used for all transactions on board.

CHOOSE A CRUISE ON FRED. OLSEN CRUISE LINES IF...

1 You are partial to British traditions and food and especially like a proper afternoon tea service.

2 You don't like cigarette smoke. Smoking is strictly limited on board all ships and banned in *Boudicca* cabins.

3 You don't like taxis. The line always provides a shuttle (small fee) to beaches and town centers more than 15 minutes away by foot.

Food

Attractively presented and above-average in quality, a wide variety of menu options are available in the dining rooms and buffets. Vegetarian selections are always available, and other special dietary considerations can be fulfilled with three to four weeks' advance notice. The line's Norwegian ownership is clearly evident in the high quality of seafood and fish dishes offered. A fairly extensive and quite affordable wine list enhances the cuisine.

Fitness & Recreation

Spas, beauty salons, and fitness centers are featured throughout the fleet. Spas and salons offer a full menu of services, including some spa treatments clearly designed for older passengers, such as an "Arthritic Body & Retention Fluid" procedure. There is no fee to use fitness equipment in the gyms, but there is a charge for some specialized exercise classes, like yoga and kickboxing. Golfers can sign up for tee times for rounds ashore with the resident PGA pro, who freely offers tips and advice during play.

Your Shipmates

Well-traveled, mature British passengers who enjoy the time-honored shipboard environment with a formal style make up the majority on board Fred. Olsen sailings. However, it's not unusual to find several generations of families all cruising together during summer months and school holiday breaks, when children's activity programs are offered to please grandparents who wish to spend quality time with their extended families.

Dress Code

Requested attire is appropriately casual during the day and consists of three types of traditional shipboard evening dress—formal, informal, and casual.

Service

The mostly Filipino staff provides good service with warmth and friendliness, but not a lot of polish.

Tipping

Recommended gratuities are £2 passenger per day for your cabin steward and the same amount for your dining room waiter.

Noteworthy

■ Theme nights, such as British Night, 1960s Night, and Tropical Night are festive occasions when passengers dress up and participate in related activities.

■ Special-interest cruises may bring aboard experts in specialized fields such as music, gardening, or painting.

■ To complement the number of single-occupancy cabins, Gentlemen Hosts are on hand to dance with unaccompanied ladies.

Top: A day at sea
Bottom: Winning casino play

2

FRED. OLSEN CRUISE LINES

DON'T CHOOSE A CRUISE ON FRED. OLSEN CRUISE LINES IF...

❶ You want to drink your own duty-free liquor aboard. Everything is collected as you board and returned at the end of the cruise.

❷ You like extravagant entertainment. Smallish showrooms comfortably stage only small reviews and stand-up comedians.

❸ You must have instant access to your e-mail. Computer rooms are small, and there's no Wi-Fi on these ships.

BLACK PRINCE

History

Originally a passenger and cargo ferry, diminutive *Black Prince* has been retrofitted over the years, drawing a loyal following devoted to her small size and coziness. The Marina Outdoor Leisure Center—a drop-down water-sports deck—is a feature usually found only on luxury ships. Entertainment is cabaret-style, or you can just have a quiet drink in a lounge. The bars and casino are open late. *Black Prince* is favored by passengers who don't miss the lack of cabin telephones or Internet access.

700 ft.	**1966**
	ENTERED SERVICE
	412
	PASSENGER CAPACITY
	220
	CREW MEMBERS
	241
	NUMBER OF CABINS
500 ft.	**11,209**
	GROSS TONS
	470 feet
	LENGTH
300 ft.	**67 feet**
	WIDTH

Restaurants

Breakfast in the two main dining rooms is generally open seating while lunch and dinner are in two assigned seatings. The Balblom Restaurant, with indoor and outdoor seating, is a casual buffet option for meals, late-night snacks, and the occasional specialty dinner, which requires a reservation. Light meals from room service are available from 10 AM to 10 PM; beverages can be ordered around the clock.

Accommodations

Cabins can be tiny. Although they have a TV and hair dryer, cabins do not have a safe or even a phone. Many categories are furnished with a twin bed and a Pullman bed affixed to the floor and can be made into a sofa during the day—the twin and Pullman cannot be pushed together. Junior Suites and Family Outsides have refrigerators. Two cabins are wheelchair-accessible.

Cabin Size (in sq. ft.): Junior Suites 220; Superior Outsides 170; Family Outsides (sleep 3) 225; Standard Outside 90–130; Inside 80–120; and Single 70–90.

Top: Deck chess
Bottom: Relax after a day ashore

In the Know

Voltage on *Black Prince* is 230 volts and requires a Continental-style two-pin plug. There is no laundry room, but there is an ironing room. Elevators don't service the Sauna Deck, and you'll need to negotiate a rather steep stairway to reach the indoor swimming pool.

Fast Facts

- 6 passenger decks
- 2 dining rooms
- Some refrigerators, 2 pools, gym, spa, casino, laundry service, computer room

BLACK WATCH

History

Launched in 1972, the former *Royal Viking Star* was built for the luxurious, long-distance cruises for which Royal Viking Line was known. Today's *Black Watch* retains much of her inherent grace. Passengers have plenty of space, both on deck and inside, including two swimming pools and a large fitness center and spa—unusual for a ship of this vintage. Piper's Bar and Lido Lounge are popular spots for a leisurely drink and conversation, while the Observatory, a spacious lounge high atop the ship, has the best views.

	1972
	ENTERED SERVICE
	807
	PASSENGER CAPACITY
700 ft.	350
	CREW MEMBERS
	421
	NUMBER OF CABINS
500 ft.	28,338
	GROSS TONS
	674 feet
	LENGTH
300 ft.	83 feet
	WIDTH

Restaurants

Breakfast in the main dining room—and in a smaller annex off to the side—is generally open seating, while lunch and dinner are in two assigned seatings. The Garden Café is a casual buffet option for meals and late-night snacks. Casual snacking options are offered near the pools. Light meals from room service are complimentary during limited hours.

Accommodations

Black Watch has spacious cabins and suites. Designed for long-distance voyages, all are equipped with a TV, telephone, lockable drawer, and hair dryer; many have a bathtub/shower combination. Suites have balconies, sitting areas, and refrigerators. The top two suite categories have VCRs or DVD players, welcome-aboard champagne, flowers, fruit basket, and bathrobes for use during the cruise. Numerous cabins are outfitted for single occupancy. Four cabins are designed for wheelchair accessibility.

Cabin Size (in sq. ft.): Owner's Suite 625; Suites 260–550; Junior Suites 240; Outside cabins 160–200, Inside cabins 140; and Singles 150.

Top: *Black Watch*
Bottom: Romantic sea vistas

In the Know

Voltage on *Black Watch* is 110 volts (U.S.-style two-pin plugs) as well as 220 volts (requires a Continental-style two-pin plug). Smokers are restricted to lighting up in the Pipers Bar and the Cove, a cigar- and pipe-smoking room—the only two indoor locations on board where smoking is allowed.

Fast Facts

- 8 passenger decks
- 2 dining rooms
- Some refrigerators, some DVDs, 2 pools, gym, spa, casino, laundry facilities, laundry service, computer room

BOUDICCA

History

Built for luxurious, long-distance cruises, *Boudicca* retains much of her grace and style. As on sister ship *Black Watch*, passengers have plenty of space on deck and inside, as well as two swimming pools, and a large fitness center and spa. Like her sister ship, she has an Observatory lounge high atop the ship to supplement the art deco Lido Lounge, a popular spot for leisurely drinks, conversation, and dancing. Budding artists enjoy the Crafts Room where hands-on activity sessions are held.

1973	ENTERED SERVICE
839	PASSENGER CAPACITY
320	CREW MEMBERS
437	NUMBER OF CABINS
28,388	GROSS TONS
674 feet	LENGTH
83 feet	WIDTH

700 ft.

500 ft.

300 ft.

Restaurants

Breakfast in the two main dining rooms is generally open seating, while lunch and dinner are in two assigned seatings. A casual buffet option is available for meals, late-night snacks, and occasional evening buffets. For casual snacks near the pools, there is the Poolside Buffet and Marquee Pool Bar. Light meals from room service are complimentary during limited hours.

Accommodations

Boudicca's spacious cabins and suites are bigger than on many ships of this size. All have a television, telephone; a lockable drawer, and hair dryer; many categories have a bathtub/shower combination. Suites have balconies, sitting areas, and refrigerators. The top two suite categories feature minibars, CD/DVD players, bathrobes for use during the cruise and receive welcome-aboard champagne, flowers, and a fruit basket. Numerous cabins are outfitted for single occupancy. Four cabins are designed for wheelchair accessibility.

Cabin Size (in sq. ft.): Owner's Suite 625; Suites 215–550; Junior Suites 240; Outside cabins 160–200, Inside cabins 140; Single cabins 150.

Top: *Boudicca* at Sea
Bottom: Tastefully appointed contemporary lounges

In the Know

Voltage on *Boudicca* is 110 volts (U.S.-style two-pin plugs) as well as 220 volts (requires a Continental-style two-pin plug). Coffee and tea are always available in the Secret Garden Café, which is just aft of the main dining rooms.

Fast Facts

- 8 passenger decks
- 3 dining rooms
- Some refrigerators, some DVDs, 2 pools, gym, spa, casino, laundry facilities, laundry service, computer room

BRAEMAR

History

Fred. Olsen's newest ship, formerly the *Crown Dynasty*, is more modern in design and layout than her fleet mates, with a light-filled atrium and a swimming pool surrounded by sunning space on the top deck. *Braemar* primarily sails one- to two-week itineraries and shorter minicruises for which she is well-suited. Public rooms on the Lounge Deck are surrounded by a wraparound promenade lined with cushioned deck chairs. *Braemar*'s atrium is off-center, opening up to public rooms on two successive decks above the Lounge Deck.

	1993
	ENTERED SERVICE
	727
	PASSENGER CAPACITY
700 ft.	320
	CREW MEMBERS
	376
	NUMBER OF CABINS
500 ft.	19,089
	GROSS TONS
	537 feet
	LENGTH
300 ft.	74 feet
	WIDTH

Restaurants

Breakfast and lunch in the main dining room are generally open seating, while dinner is served in two assigned seatings. A casual buffet option for meals and late-night snacks features panoramic views from within and also has some outdoor seating. A grill is on the pool deck for dining poolside. Light meals from room service are complimentary.

Accommodations

Not large by today's standards, *Braemar*'s cabins are attractively furnished, but have limited storage space. They are equipped with a TV, telephone, personal safe, and hair dryer; all categories have only showers. Suites have a balcony, sitting area, VCR, and refrigerator. Some categories also receive welcome-aboard gifts and bathrobes for use during the cruise. Numerous cabins are outfitted for single occupancy. Four cabins are designed for wheelchair accessibility.

Cabin Size (in sq. ft.): Suites 220–300; Superior Outside cabins 150; Inside and Outside cabins 130–140.

Top: *Braemar* Gym
Bottom: Dancing in the Coral Club

In the Know

Voltage on *Braemar* is 110 and 220–240 volts (U.S. and Continental-style two-pin plugs). Adapters can be rented or purchased on board. Take care when selecting a seat in public areas—the typical passenger mix might include many who smoke, and it may be difficult to steer clear of them.

Fast Facts

- 7 passenger decks
- Dining room
- Safes, some refrigerators, some VCRs, pool, gym, spa, casino, laundry service, computer room

HOLLAND AMERICA LINE

Holland America Line has enjoyed a distinguished record of traditional cruises, world exploration, and transatlantic crossings since 1873—all facets of its history that are reflected in the fleet's multimillion dollar shipboard art and antiques collections. Even the ships' names follow a pattern set long ago: all end in the suffix "dam" and are either derived from the names of various dams that cross Holland's rivers, important Dutch landmarks, or points of the compass. The names are even recycled when vessels are retired, and some are in their fifth and sixth generation of use.

A day on the Lido Deck

HOLLAND AMERICA LINE
300 Elliott Avenue W
Seattle, WA 98119
206/281-3535 or
800/577-1728
www.hollandamerica.com

Cruise Style: Premium Deluxe

Noted for focusing on passenger comfort, Holland America Line cruises are classic in design and style; however, with an infusion of younger adults and families on board, they remain refined without being stuffy or stodgy. Following a basic design theme, returning passengers feel as at home on the newest Holland America vessels as they do on older ones.

Entertainment tends to be more Broadway-stylish than Las Vegas–brash. Colorful revues are presented in main show lounges by the ships' companies of singers and dancers. Other performances might include a range of cabaret acts: comedians, magicians, jugglers, and acrobats. Live bands play a wide range of musical styles for dancing and listening in smaller lounges and piano bars. Movies are shown daily in cinemas that double as the Culinary Arts Centers.

Holland America Line may never be considered cutting edge, but the Signature of Excellence concept introduced in 2003 sets them apart from other premium cruise lines. An interactive Culinary Arts Center offers cooking demonstrations and wine-tasting sessions; Explorations Café (powered by *the New York Times*) is a coffeehouse-style library and Internet center; and the Explorations Guest

Speakers Series is supported by in-cabin televised programming on flat-screen TVs in all cabins; the traditional Crow's Nest observation lounge has a new nightclub-disco layout, video wall, and sound-and-light systems; and facilities for children and teens have been greatly expanded. Signature of Excellence upgrades were completed on the entire Holland America fleet in 2006.

Food

Holland America Line chefs, members of the Confrerie de la Chaîne des Rôtisseurs gourmet society, utilize more than 500 different food items on a typical weeklong cruise to create the modern Continental cuisine and traditional favorites served to their passengers. Vegetarian options as well as healthy Inbalance Spa Cuisine by Jeanne Jones are available, and special dietary requests can be handled with advance notice. Holland America's passengers used to skew older than they do now, so the sometimes bland dishes were no surprise; however, the food quality, taste, and selection have greatly improved in recent years. A case in point is the reservations-required Pinnacle Grill alternative restaurants, where fresh seafood and premium cuts of Sterling Silver beef are used to prepare creative specialty dishes. The $30 per person charge for dinner would be worth it for the Dungeness crab cakes starter and dessert alone. Other delicious traditions are afternoon tea, a Dutch Chocolate Extravaganza, and Holland America Line's signature bread pudding.

Flexible scheduling allows for early (5:45) or late (8:15) seatings in the two-deck, formal restaurants. "As You Wish" open seating from 5 to 9 is being introduced fleet-wide.

Fitness & Recreation

Well-equipped and fully staffed fitness facilities contain state-of-the-art exercise equipment; basic fitness classes are available at no charge. There's a fee for personal training, body composition analysis, and specialized classes such as yoga and Pilates.

Treatments in the Greenhouse Spa include a variety of massages, body wraps, and facials. Hair styling and nail services are offered in the salons. All ships have a jogging track, multiple swimming pools, and sports courts. Some have hydrotherapy pools and soothing thermal suites.

Your Shipmates

No longer just your grandparents' cruise line, today's Holland America Caribbean sailings attract families and discerning couples, mostly from their late-30s on up. Holidays and summer months are peak periods when you'll find more children in the mix. Comfortable retirees are

Noteworthy

■ Trays of mints, dried fruits, and candied ginger can be found outside the dining rooms.

■ Passengers are presented with a complimentary cotton canvas carryall bag imprinted with the line's logo.

■ Each ship has a wrap-around promenade deck for walking, jogging, or stretching out in the shade on a padded steamer chair.

Top: Casino action
Bottom: Stay fit afloat

HOLLAND AMERICA LINE

2

Top: Wine tasting
Middle: Production showtime
Bottom: Spa relaxation

often still in the majority, particularly on longer cruises. Families cruising together who book five or more cabins receive a fountain-soda package for each family member, Club HAL T-shirts for children who participate in the youth program, a family photo for each stateroom, and either dinner for the entire family in the upscale Pinnacle Grill or complimentary water toys at Half Moon Cay (for Caribbean itineraries that call at the private island). If the group is larger—10 cabins or more—the Head-of-Family is recognized with an upgrade from outside stateroom to a veranda cabin. It's the best family deal at sea, and there's no extra charge.

Dress Code

Evenings on Holland America Line cruises fall into three categories: casual, informal, and formal. Ties are optional, but men are asked to wear a sport coat on one informal night. For the two formal nights standard on seven-night cruises, men are encouraged to wear tuxedos, but dark suits or sport coats and ties are acceptable, and you'll certainly see them. Other nights are casual. It's requested that no T-shirts, jeans, swimsuits, tank tops, or shorts be worn in public areas after 6 PM.

Junior Cruisers

Club HAL is Holland America Line's professionally staffed youth and teen program. Age-appropriate activities planned for children ages three to seven include storytelling, arts and crafts, ice-cream or pizza parties, and games; for children ages 8 to 12 there are arcade games, Sony PlayStations, theme parties, on-deck sports events, and scavenger hunts. Club HAL After Hours offers late-night activities from 10 PM until midnight for an hourly fee. Baby food, diapers, cribs, high chairs, and booster seats may be requested in advance of boarding. Private in-cabin babysitting is sometimes available if a staff member is willing.

Teens aged 13 to 17 have their own lounge with activities including dance contests, arcade games, sports tournaments, movies, and an exclusive sun deck on some ships. Select itineraries offer water park-type facilities and kid-

CHOOSE A CRUISE ON HOLLAND AMERICA IF...

1 You crave relaxation. Grab a padded steamer chair on the teak promenade deck and watch the sea pass by.

2 You like to go to the movies, especially when the popcorn is free.

3 You want to bring the kids—areas designed exclusively for children and teens are hot new features on all ships.

friendly shore excursions to Half Moon Cay, Holland America Line's private island in the Bahamas.

Service

Professional, unobtrusive service by the Indonesian and Filipino staff is a fleetwide standard on Holland America Line. It isn't uncommon for a steward or server to remember the names of returning passengers from a cruise taken years before. Crew members are trained in Indonesia at a custom-built facility called the ms *Nieuw Jakarta*, where employees polish their English-language skills and learn housekeeping in mock cabins.

Tipping

$10 per passenger, per day is automatically added to shipboard accounts, and gratuities are distributed to stewards and waitstaff. Passengers may adjust the amount based on the level of service experienced. Room-service tips are usually given in cash (it's the passenger's discretion here). An automatic 15% gratuity is added to bar-service tabs.

Past Passengers

All passengers who sail with Holland America Line are automatically enrolled in the Mariner Society and receive special offers on upcoming cruises as well as insider information concerning new ships and product enhancements. Mariner Society benefits also include preferred pricing on many cruises; Mariner baggage tags, and buttons that identify you as a member during embarkation; an invitation to the Mariner Society champagne reception and awards party hosted by the captain; lapel pins and medallions acknowledging your history of Holland America sailings; a special collectible gift delivered to your cabin; and a subscription to *Mariner,* the full-color magazine featuring news and Mariner Society savings. Once you complete your first cruise, your Mariner identification number will be assigned and available for lookup online.

Good to Know

The sound of delicate chimes still alerts Holland America Line passengers that it's mealtime. Artful flower arrangements never seem to wilt. A bowl of candied ginger is near the dining room entrance if you need a little something to settle your stomach. These simple, but nonetheless meaningful, touches are what make Holland America Line stand out from the crowd.

HOLLAND AMERICA LINE

2

DON'T CHOOSE A CRUISE ON HOLLAND AMERICA LINE IF...

1 You want to party hard. Most of the action on these ships ends relatively early.

2 Dressing for dinner isn't your thing. Passengers tend to ramp up the dress code most evenings.

3 You have an aversion to extending tips. The line's "tipping not required" policy has been amended.

VISTA CLASS

Zuiderdam, Oosterdam, Westerdam, Noordam

Public Areas & Facilities

Ships for the 21st century, Vista-class vessels successfully integrate new youthful and family-friendly elements into Holland America Line's classic fleet. Exquisite Waterford crystal sculptures adorn triple-deck atriums and reflect vivid, almost daring color schemes throughout. Although all the public rooms carry the traditional Holland America names (Ocean Bar, Explorer's Lounge, Crow's Nest) and aren't much different in atmosphere, their louder decor (toned down a bit since the introduction of the *Zuiderdam*) may make them unfamiliar to returning passengers.

Only two decks are termed "promenade," and the exterior teak promenade encircles public rooms, not cabins. As a result, numerous outside accommodations have views of the sea restricted by lifeboats on the Upper Promenade Deck. Veterans of cruises on older Holland America ships will find the layout of public spaces somewhat different; however, everyone's favorite Crow's Nest lounges still offer those commanding views.

2002, 2003, 2004, 2006	ENTERED SERVICE
1,848 (2,272 max)	PASSENGER CAPACITY
800	CREW MEMBERS
924	NUMBER OF CABINS
82,000	GROSS TONS
950 feet	LENGTH
106 feet	WIDTH

700 ft.
500 ft.
300 ft.

WOW Factor

Keep your sunglasses on. The color palette is not only bright and bold, but some of the furniture approaches the edge of funkiness.

Top: *Oosterdam* hydro pool
Bottom: Vista-class oceanview stateroom

Restaurants

The formal dining room offers two dinner seatings and open seating; alternatives are Pinnacle Grill, which requires reservations and has a cover charge, and the casual Lido café that also serves buffet breakfast and lunch. Terrace Grill serves lunch poolside. The extra-charge Explorations Café offers specialty coffees and pastries. Room service is available 24 hours.

What Works & What Doesn't

Adjacent to the Crow's Nest, outdoor seating areas covered in canvas are wonderful, quiet hideaways during the day as well as at night when the interior is transformed into a dance club—a better choice for dancing than the disco. Missing from the Vista-class ships are self-service laundry rooms, a serious omission for families with youngsters and anyone sailing on back-to-back Caribbean itineraries or cruises of more than a week. The murals in Pinnacle Grill restaurants are strangely chintzy looking, especially considering the priceless art throughout the rest of the ships' interiors.

Accommodations

Layout: Comfortable and roomy, 85% of all Vista-class accommodations have an ocean view, and almost 80% of those also have the luxury of a private balcony furnished with chairs, loungers, and tables. Every cabin has adequate closet and drawer-shelf storage, as well as bathroom shelves. Some suites have a whirlpool tub, powder room, and walk-in closet.

Amenities: All staterooms and suites are appointed with Euro-top mattresses, 250-thread-count cotton bed linens, magnifying halogen-lighted makeup mirrors, hair dryers, a fruit basket, flat-panel TVs, and DVD players. Bathroom extras include Egyptian cotton towels, shampoo, body lotion, and bath gel, plus deluxe bathrobes to use during the cruise.

Suites: Suite luxuries include duvets on beds, a fully stocked minibar; some also have a whirlpool tub, powder room, and walk-in closet. Penthouse

Verandah and Deluxe Verandah suites have exclusive use of the private Neptune Lounge, personal concierge service, canapés before dinner, and complimentary laundry, pressing, and dry-cleaning services.

Good to Know: Twenty-eight state-rooms are wheelchair-accessible.

Cabin Type	Size (sq. ft.)
Penthouse Suites	1,000
Deluxe Verandah Suite	380
Superior Verandah Suite	298
Deluxe Ocean View	200
Standard Ocean View/ Inside	194/185

Fast Facts

- 11 passenger decks
- Specialty restaurant, dining room, buffet, pizzeria
- In-cabin broadband, Wi-Fi, in-cabin safes, in-cabin refrigerators, in-cabin DVDs
- 2 pools (1 indoor)
- Fitness classes, gym, hair salon, 5 hot tubs, sauna, spa, steam room
- 9 bars, casino, cinema, 2 dance clubs, library, showroom, video game room
- Children's programs (ages 3–17)
- Dry cleaning, laundry service
- Computer room

In the Know

If you want complete privacy on your balcony, choose your location carefully. Take a close look at the deck plans for the ones alongside the exterior panoramic elevators. Riders have views of adjacent balconies as well as the seascape.

Favorites

Most Unusual: Tables in the Pinnacle Grill specialty restaurant are set with Frette linens, Riedel stemware, and Bulgari china by Rosenthal, but traditional appointments stop at the table top. The chair design is based on organic forms and resembles delicate, silvery tree branches. Some may require seating assistance, though—in reality, the chairs are cast aluminum and so

heavy that they don't budge without a great deal of effort.

Moving with the View: Take a good look at the etched-glass doors of the four outside scenic elevators—they mirror the 1920s motif of the 10 interior elevator doors, which are done in cast aluminum. The design effect may look vaguely familiar because it was modeled after the

art deco Chrysler building in New York City.

Our Favorite Spot for a Nightcap: The canvas-covered areas outside the Crow's Nest narrowly edge out second choice—a seat by the faux fireplace in the Oak Room.

Westerdam at sea

ROTTERDAM, AMSTERDAM

Public Areas & Facilities

Amsterdam is a sister ship to *Rotterdam,* which sails on world cruises and extended voyages, and both share Holland America Line flagship status. The most traditional ships in the fleet, their interiors display abundant wood appointments in the public areas on Promenade and Lower Promenade decks and priceless works of art throughout.

The Ocean Bar, Explorer's Lounge, Wajang Theater, and Crow's Nest are familiar lounges to longtime Holland American passengers. Newer additions are a thermal suite in the spa, a culinary-arts demonstration center in the theater, Explorations Café, and expansive areas for children and teens.

Multimillion-dollar collections of art and artifacts are showcased throughout both vessels. In addition to works commissioned specifically for each ship, Holland America Line celebrates its heritage by featuring antiques and artworks that reflect the theme of worldwide Dutch seafaring history.

1997, 2000	ENTERED SERVICE
1,316/1,380 (1,792 max)	PASSENGER CAPACITY
644/647	CREW MEMBERS
658/680	NUMBER OF CABINS
59,652/61,000	GROSS TONS
780 feet	LENGTH
106 feet	WIDTH

700 ft.

500 ft.

300 ft.

WOW Factor

The astrolabe (Amsterdam) *and clock tower* (Rotterdam) *rising above the marble floor of each ship's central atrium are finely detailed sculptures as well as timepieces.*

Restaurants

The formal dining room offers both open and assigned seating. Alternatives are the upscale specialty restaurant Pinnacle Grill, which requires reservations and a cover charge, and the casual Lido café that also serves buffet breakfast and lunch. Terrace Grill serves lunch poolside. The extra-charge Explorations Café offers specialty coffees and pastries. Room service is available 24 hours.

What Works & What Doesn't

Top: Pinnacle Grill dining
Bottom: *Rotterdam* at sea

The Crow's Nest is the center of late-night activity. Lounges on the Promenade and Upper Promenade decks are lively before and after dinner, but passengers tend to call it a night early after either taking in a movie or one of the production shows. Although outside cabins on the Lower Promenade deck are ideally situated for easy access to fresh air, occupants should heed the warning that the so-called one-way window glass does not offer complete privacy—passersby who get up close can see in, especially after dark, when interior lights are on.

Accommodations

Layout: Staterooms are spacious and comfortable, although fewer have private balconies than newer fleetmates. Every cabin has adequate closet and drawer-shelf storage, as well as bathroom shelves. Some suites also have a whirlpool tub, powder room, and walk-in closet.

Amenities: All staterooms and suites are appointed with Euro-top mattresses, 250-thread-count cotton bed linens, magnifying halo-lighted mirrors, hair dryers, a fruit basket, flat-panel TVs, and DVD players. Bathrooms have Egyptian cotton towels, shampoo, body lotion, and bath gel, plus deluxe bathrobes to use during the cruise.

Suites: Extras include duvets on beds, a fully stocked minibar, and personalized stationery. Penthouse Verandah and Deluxe Verandah suites have exclusive use of the private Neptune Lounge, personal concierge service, canapés before dinner on request, binoculars and umbrellas for use during the cruise, an invitation to a VIP party with the captain, and complimentary laundry, pressing, and dry-cleaning services.

Good to Know: Connecting cabins are available in a range of categories. Although there are a number of triple cabins to choose from, there are not as many that accommodate four. Twenty-one staterooms are designed for wheelchair accessibility.

Cabin Type	Size (sq. ft.)
Penthouse Suite	973
Deluxe Verandah Suite	374
Verandah Suite	225
Ocean View	197
Inside	182

Fast Facts

- 9 passenger decks
- Specialty restaurant, dining room, buffet
- Wi-Fi, in-cabin safes, in-cabin refrigerators, some in-cabin mini-bars, in-cabin DVDs
- 2 pools (1 indoor), 2 children's pools
- Fitness classes, gym, hair salon, 2 hot tubs, sauna, spa, steam room
- 6 bars, casino, cinema, dance club, library, showroom, video game room
- Children's programs (ages 3–17)
- Dry cleaning, laundry facilities, laundry service
- Computer room

2

HOLLAND AMERICA LINE

In the Know

The creation of the expansive floral stained-glass ceiling that provides a focal point for Amsterdam's *formal dining room required the use of some state-of-the-art technology that was developed especially for the ship. Traditional stained-glass in leaded frames wouldn't have been safe on a moving ship.*

Favorites

Best Place to Escape the Crowds: When there are few children on the ship, adults like to take over the Oasis, which is normally reserved for teenage cruisers.

From Classic to Wacky: On *Amsterdam*, four very special art deco pieces are mounted on the landing just outside the Crow's Nest. The gold-plated *Four Seasons* first graced the *Nieuw Amsterdam* of 1938, and Holland America Line was able to purchase them from a collector. At the polar opposite of the artistic spectrum, realistic landscapes with surreal touches accent the dining alcoves in the Pinnacle Grill (look closely and you'll notice a Swiss Army knife strutting through a tranquil garden scene).

Our Favorite Spot for a Nightcap: The Ocean Bar is the ideal spot not only for sipping a brandy, but also for a bird's-eye view of the astrolabe. When it's quiet, you can hear the carillon bells play a melody on the hour.

Don't-Miss Munchies: Servers circulate throughout lounges before and after dinner with canapés.

A brisk walk starts the day

STATENDAM CLASS

Statendam, Maasdam, Ryndam, Veendam

1993, 1993, 1994, 1996	ENTERED SERVICE
1,258 (1,627 max)	PASSENGER CAPACITY
602	CREW MEMBERS
629	NUMBER OF CABINS
55, 451	GROSS TONS
720 feet	LENGTH
101 feet	WIDTH

700 ft.

500 ft.

300 ft.

Public Areas & Facilities

The sister ships included in the S- or Statendam-class retain the most classic and traditional characteristics of Holland America Line vessels. Routinely updated with innovative features, they combine all the advantages of intimate, midsize vessels with high-tech and stylish details.

At the heart of the ships, triple-deck atriums graced by suspended glass sculptures open onto three so-called promenade decks; the lowest contains staterooms encircled by a wide, teak outdoor deck furnished with padded steamer chairs, while interior art-filled passageways flow past lounges and public rooms on the two decks above. It's easy to find just about any area on board, with the possible exception of the main level of the dining room. Either reach the lower dining room floor via the aft elevator, or enter one deck above and make a grand entrance down the sweeping staircase.

WOW Factor

Carefully chosen antiques and works of art are arranged in passageways, stairwells, and niches all over these ships.

Top: Select from an extensive wine list
Bottom: Deluxe veranda suite

Restaurants

The formal dining room offers both open and assigned seating. Alternatives are Pinnacle Grill, which requires reservations and a cover charge, and the casual Lido café that also serves buffet breakfast and lunch. Terrace Grill serves lunch poolside. The extra-charge Explorations Café offers specialty coffees and pastries. Room service is available 24 hours.

What Works & What Doesn't

After dark there's a bit more action in public areas; however, you'll find it rather subdued in lounges along the promenade decks. The livelier Crow's Nest is the center of late-night activity. Try to make it to the production shows in time to grab seats on the lower level of the main show lounges—railings on the balcony level obstruct the view from all rows behind the first two or three. Escalators between decks in the lower atrium areas seem out of place; they appear to be more of a curiosity than a real convenience.

Accommodations

Layout: Staterooms are spacious and comfortable, although fewer of them have private balconies than on newer fleetmates. Every cabin has adequate closet and drawer-shelf storage, as well as bathroom shelves. Some suites have a whirlpool tub, powder room, and walk-in closet.

Amenities: Gone are the flowery chintz curtains and bedspreads of yesteryear—all staterooms and suites are now appointed with Euro-top mattresses, 250-thread-count cotton bed linens, magnifying lighted mirrors, hair dryers, a fruit basket, flat-panel TVs, and DVD players. Bathroom extras include Egyptian cotton towels, shampoo, body lotion, and bath gel, plus deluxe bathrobes to use during the cruise.

Suites: Suites have duvets on beds, a fully stocked minibar, and personalized stationery. Penthouse Verandah and Deluxe Verandah suites have exclusive use of the private Neptune Lounge,
personal concierge service, canapés before dinner on request, binoculars and umbrellas for use during the cruise, an invitation to a VIP party with the captain, and complimentary laundry, pressing, and dry-cleaning services.

Good to Know: Connecting cabins are featured in a range of categories. Six staterooms are wheelchair-accessible; nine are modified with ramps although doors are standard width.

Cabin Type	Size (sq. ft.)
Penthouse Suite	946
Deluxe Verandah Suite	385
Verandah Suite	230
Ocean View	196
Inside	186

Fast Facts

- 10 passenger decks
- Specialty restaurant, dining room, buffet
- Wi-Fi, in-cabin safes, in-cabin minibars, in-cabin refrigerators, in-cabin DVDs
- 2 pools (1 indoor), 2 children's pools
- Fitness classes, gym, hair salon, 2 hot tubs, sauna, spa, steam room
- 9 bars, casino, cinema, dance club, library, showroom, video game room
- Children's programs (ages 3–17)
- Dry cleaning, laundry facilities, laundry service
- Computer room

In the Know

Do you recognize the portraits etched into the glass doors to the main show lounges? They are the likenesses of great Dutch artists for whom the spaces are named.

Favorites

Best Place to Escape the Crowds: A padded steamer chair on the teak promenade deck is our favorite cocoon. You'll never want to leave.

Best Dessert: It just might be the best in the world—Holland America Line's signature bread-and-butter pudding with a creamy sauce. Ask for the recipe.

Our Favorite Spot for a Nightcap: Popular with the after-dinner crowd, yet quiet enough for conversation, the Ocean Bar hits just the right balance for late-night socializing.

Best Extra Touches: As you board, you are serenaded by musicians and escorted to your cabin, where you'll find a signature HAL-logo canvas tote bag.

Other deluxe touches include complimentary shoeshine service and terry fingertip towels in public restrooms.

Our Choice for Outdoor Dining: Weather permitting, an evening poolside barbecue buffet is usually scheduled during every cruise.

Share a sunset

PRINSENDAM

Public Areas & Facilities

Alongside her newer fleet mates, *Prinsendam* appears positively diminutive. Launched in 1988 and originally christened *Royal Viking Sun* for the now-defunct Royal Viking Line, the luxury ship subsequently sailed as Seabourn Cruise Line's *Seabourn Sun* before joining Holland America Line in 2002. Extensive renovations added signature Holland America Line features to the boutique-style *Prinsendam*. Artwork, antiques, and Signature of Excellence elements such as a Culinary Arts Center and upgraded cabin amenities have now made their way on board.

Originally designed for lengthy worldwide cruising, Holland America has dubbed *Prinsendam* the "Elegant Explorer" and filled her interiors with classic and comfortable public rooms. The nautically appointed Ocean Bar and Explorer's Lounge are favorite gathering spots for predinner drinks, live music, and dancing. A traditional 360-degree promenade deck floored in teak and lined with cushioned deck chairs encircles Lower Promenade Deck.

1988	ENTERED SERVICE
794	PASSENGER CAPACITY
443	CREW MEMBERS
398	NUMBER OF CABINS
38,000	GROSS TONS
669 feet	LENGTH
106 feet	WIDTH

700 ft.
500 ft.
300 ft.

WOW Factor

A tall cylinder of Bolae glass, which is lighted from within by fiber optics so that etched dolphins and sea turtles seem to swim up the center, pierces the compact atrium.

Restaurants

The formal dining room has two dinner seatings. Alternatives are Pinnacle Grill, the elegant specialty restaurant, and the casual Lido Restaurant with indoor and outdoor seating. The Lido buffet and poolside grill also serve breakfast and lunch, and the dining room offers open seating for those meals. Afternoon tea is a daily event and room service is available around the clock.

Top: Holland America Line's "Elegant Explorer"
Bottom: Yoga

What Works & What Doesn't

Longer itineraries to far-flung destinations attract older passengers with enough time and disposable income for extended travel. As a result, you will usually find very few children aboard *Prinsendam*. A supervised Club HAL children's program is offered on most sailings, but this isn't the best ship for families. Unfortunately, the ship's library is quite small and doesn't incorporate the popular Explorations Café concept in the rest of the fleet. Fortunately, there is the nearby Java Bar for coffee and quiet alcoves for reading in the adjacent Explorer's Lounge and Oak Room.

Accommodations

Layout: Staterooms are spacious, but furniture placement and amenities within each category can vary. Only a handful of cabins are inside, but a mere 38% of outside cabins and suites have private balconies. Every stateroom has adequate storage for long cruises, and most have walk-in closets. Some cabins near the bow have portholes instead of large windows. Cabin selection must be made carefully; fortunately, the ship's deck plan is very detailed.

Amenities: All staterooms and suites are appointed with Euro-top mattresses, 250-thread-count cotton bed linens, magnifying lighted mirror, hair dryer, fruit basket, flat-panel TV, and DVD player. Bathroom extras include Egyptian cotton towels, shampoo, body lotion, and bath gel, plus bathrobes to use during the cruise. Balcony cabins have refrigerators.

Suites: Suites have a stocked minibar, and personalized stationery. Occupants have the use of the private Neptune Lounge, concierge service, predinner canapés, binoculars, and umbrellas for use during the cruise, an invitation to a VIP party, and complimentary laundry, pressing, and dry-cleaning service.

Good to Know: Eight staterooms are wheelchair-accessible.

Cabin Type	Size (sq. ft.)
Penthouse Suite	577
Verandah Suites	251–391
Deluxe Verandah Outside	177–187
Ocean View	181–191
Inside	128–138

Fast Facts

- 8 passenger decks
- Specialty restaurant, dining room, buffet
- Wi-Fi, in-cabin safes, some in-cabin minibars, some in-cabin refrigerators, in-cabin DVDs
- 2 pools
- Fitness classes, gym, hair salon, 4 hot tubs, sauna, spa, steam room
- 6 bars, casino, cinema, library, showroom
- Children's programs (ages 3–17)
- Dry cleaning, laundry facilities, laundry service
- Computer room

In the Know

Former Holland America captain Stephen Card commemorates his love for ships and the sea by creating technically accurate paintings of Holland America Line ships. Ask at reception for a "Self-Guided Artwork Tour" list, and look for five of Captain Card's paintings on display aboard Prinsendam.

Favorites

Smoke on the Water: One of the most charming places at sea to smoke cigars and enjoy an after-dinner brandy or port is *Prinsendam*'s Oak Room, with its clubby atmosphere and faux fireplace.

Best Place to See the Sea: We enjoy seeing where we are going, so we love the view from the Crow's Nest observation lounge, a Holland America trademark. Any of the outside forward-facing decks provides a tempting spot to watch the horizon.

Favorite Spot for a Nightcap: For quiet conversation with a little night music in the background, we head for the Ocean Bar or Explorer's Lounge.

Just for Golfers: Bring your game up a notch and hone your strokes between courses in port. *Prinsendam* has a nifty golf simulator.

Best Place to Get Wet: Ten staterooms aft of the public rooms on Promenade Deck are just steps from a nearly private hot tub with a view of the ship's wake.

Formal dining

HURTIGRUTEN

Originally intended as a communications and travel link between the villages on Norway's western coast, Hurtigruten (formerly known in the U.S. as Norwegian Coastal Voyage) provides an up-close look at the fascinatingly intricate fjords, mountains, and villages that not too

Cruising the fjords of Norway

long ago were isolated and difficult to navigate. Sailing with comfortable cruise ships that still do double-duty transferring cargo and the occasional village-to-village passenger, the Hurtigruten itineraries are often described as "the world's most beautiful voyage," as they provide access to some of the most stunning scenery and the unique cultures of Norway, many of them above the Arctic Circle.

HURTIGRUTEN
405 Park Avenue, Suite 904
New York, NY 10022
800/323-7436
www.hurtigruten.us

Cruise Style: Small-ship

Eleven Hurtigruten ships are committed year-round to Norwegian coastal itineraries, known in Norway as "Hurtigruten," the word from which the cruise line's name is derived. Options include six-night northbound, five-night southbound, or 11-night round-trip sailings, calling at 34 ports in each one-way segment. During the summer, the Millennium, Contemporary, and Mid-Generation ships follow this route; in the winter, *Nordnorge* and *Nordkapp* reposition, joining the company's newest ship, MS *Fram*, in the southern hemisphere to sail Antarctic and Chilean Fjord itineraries, replaced in Norway by *Lofoten* and *Nordstjernen*. The *Polar Star* and *Nordstjernen* make summer voyages to Spitsbergen, an island midway between Norway and the North Pole. The MS *Fram* makes summer expeditions to Greenland as well as a 67-day longitudinal world cruise in the fall.

CHOOSE A CRUISE ON HURTIGRUTEN IF...

1 You wish to sail past some of the most beautiful scenery in the world, including such exotic spots as Antarctica and Greenland.

2 You will be comfortable aboard the small, modern Hurtigruten ships that visit the quaint but welcoming coastal villages of Norway.

3 You are a confident traveler, and you are comfortable controlling your daily activities.

Food

The itinerary is the primary point of emphasis on these cruises, and dining takes a far less prominent role than on cruises for the American market. There are two dinner seatings, and the three-course dinners allow no individual selection—everyone on a given evening will have the same appetizer, entrée, and dessert. There is a 24-hour café, but it is not a free amenity; passengers must pay for their meals there. Liquor, wine and beer, priced in Norwegian *kroner*, are expensive, but the line allows guests to bring their own alcohol on board.

Fitness & Recreation

There is no organized nightly entertainment, so this is the type of cruise for the person who prefers watching the Midnight Sun (mid-May through late July) or Northern Lights (during the winter months). Mother Nature is the entertainer. The cruise can be extremely social, however. Passengers often spend time together in the panoramic lounge after dinner, chatting over cocktails.

Your Shipmates

Americans are usually in the minority on these sailings. Travelers who find this kind of cruising attractive are usually sophisticated yet unpretentious individuals who can be comfortable in an internationally diverse group. They tend to be independent folks who are comfortable controlling their vacation experiences and are perfectly content enjoying spectacular scenery and visiting picturesque communities, mostly on their own.

Dress Code

Hurtigruten ships are truly casual, with no dress-up nights.

Service

Service can be splendid but also subtle, without a lot of flourishes.

Tipping

There is a "no tipping required" policy, and the mostly Norwegian crew does not expect gratuities. If you want to tip a crewmember for exceptional service, however, it is at your discretion.

Noteworthy

- Dizzying views of dramatic landscapes and the deep emerald waters of the fjords make this a "must-do" destination.

- Bergen is the departure port for Hurtigruten's 11-night round-trip Norwegian cruises (one-way cruises also are available) to Kirkenes, near Norway's border with Russia.

- Hurtigruten vessels have cash registers in the dining room since some passengers hop on and sail for a couple of days, paying for everything à la carte.

Top: *Polarlys* underway
Bottom: Majestic scenery awaits

2

HURTIGRUTEN

DON'T CHOOSE A CRUISE ON HURTIGRUTEN IF...

1 You require the large-scale entertainment activities found on big cruise ships; you will probably be happier elsewhere.

2 You want to work out. A couple of the Hurtigruten ships have gyms, but the smaller ones do not.

3 You can't keep up. Ships call at dozens of villages, where passengers can stroll, shop, and visit. The activity can be vigorous.

FINNMARKEN

History

One of the Millennium ships that Hurtigruten introduced in 2002 and 2003, *Finnmarken* is a beautifully appointed ship, decorated in art nouveau style reminiscent of the first Coastal Voyage ships in old-world elegance. Eleven Norwegian artists have put the finishing touches on the interior with drawings, watercolors, oil paintings, charcoal drawings, lithographs, and sculptures. The fitness center with saunas and a massage room is located on Deck 7, as are the hair salon and the Internet café; the outdoor swimming pool is on Deck 6.

Restaurants

One main dining room, the no-smoking Finnmarken Restaurant, hosts three meals daily. Breakfast and lunch, which feature the famous Norwegian koldtbord (cold buffet) are self-serve, but the three-course dinner is served in two seatings. Other dining and bar venues include the Morestuen Bistro and Babette's Café.

700 ft.	2002
	ENTERED SERVICE
	643
	PASSENGER CAPACITY
	75
	CREW MEMBERS
	282
	NUMBER OF CABINS
500 ft.	15,000
	GROSS TONS
	545.4
	LENGTH
300 ft.	70.5
	WIDTH

Accommodations

Ten cabin grades are available. Double beds are available in only in the 32 suites (14 of which have balconies). All the other cabins have fixed twin beds and berths. Some cabins also have a third upper berth. A number of cabins are available for single occupancy at a premium. Only 55 cabins are inside, and the remaining 195 are ocean-view (no balconies, however). Three are wheelchair accessible. Suites have TVs and minibars. The 220-volt outlets require adapters for U.S. appliances.

Cabin Size (in sq. ft.): Suites 194–398; Outside cabins 118–140; Inside 86–108.

Top: MS *Finnmarken*
Bottom: Balcony suite

In the Know

The views are the thing on this itinerary, and even the glass elevators and saunas have them. Hurtigruten allows passengers to bring their own alcohol aboard; you should consider taking advantage of that policy. Alcoholic drinks on board are very expensive, even more so because all prices are in Norwegian kroner.

Fast Facts

- 8 decks
- 1 dining room, café
- Some in-cabin minibars, no TV in some cabins, gym, hot tub, sauna, bar, library, laundry facilities, computer room

FRAM

History

The first cruise ship built exclusively for sailing in Greenland, *MS Fram* was named after the polar ship built by Fridtjof Nansen, who explored Greenland in the late 1800s. Artists from Greenland were commissioned to create the ship's original artwork, which complements *MS Fram*'s Nordic ambience. Interior design is characterized by extensive use of wool, leather, and oak. The ship's glass-enclosed observation salon offers panoramic views of the scenic destinations. The ship also has a full wellness center.

2007	ENTERED SERVICE
318	PASSENGER CAPACITY
50	CREW MEMBERS
136	NUMBER OF CABINS
12,700	GROSS TONS
374	LENGTH
66	WIDTH

700 ft.

500 ft.

300 ft.

Restaurants

One main dining room, the no-smoking Restaurant Imaq, an Inuit word meaning "sea," hosts three meals daily. Breakfast and lunch, which feature the famous Norwegian koldtbord (cold buffet) are self-serve, but the three-course dinner is served in two seatings. A separate dining area, the Bistro, offers snacks and drinks for purchase.

Accommodations

Eight cabin grades are available. *Fram* features more suites and minisuites than any other ship in Hurtigruten's fleet. Suites include one grand suite, seven standard suites, and 31 minisuites. All the full suites have queen-size beds, minibars, and separate sitting areas (the grand suite comprises two rooms), and some have private balconies. Additionally, there are 95 standard cabins (24 inside), two of which are wheelchair-accessible. All accommodations feature TVs and refrigerators.

Cabin Size (in sq. ft.): Suites 183–420; Outside cabins 118–140; Inside cabins 118–140.

Top: MS *Fram* on expedition
Bottom: Balcony suite on *Fram*

In the Know

With its ice-hardened hull, MS *Fram* was built specifically for operations in Arctic waters. Regular cabins are adequate, if a little spartan. Minisuites, on the other hand, come equipped with all the comforts you would expect to find in a cruise-ship cabin today, quite a luxury for a true expedition ship.

Fast Facts

- 8 decks
- 1 dining room, 1 café
- Some in-cabin refrigerators, gym, hot tub, sauna, bar, library, computer room

KONG HARALD

History

The *Kong Harald,* which is one of six contemporary ships that Hurtigruten brought on line between 1993 and 1997, is a small but comfortable cruise ship with a modest array of public rooms and facilities. Although this ship is formally named after the King of Norway, you'll find other famous Norwegian names on board: the bar is named after Nobel Peace laureate Fridtjof Nansen, the café after explorer Roald Amundsen. True to Hurtigruten tradition, many well-known artists have put their own individual stamps on this exquisite ship.

1993	Entered Service
490	Passenger Capacity
70	Crew Members
227	Number of Cabins
11,200	Gross Tons
399.6	Length
62.9	Width

700 ft.
500 ft.
300 ft.

Restaurants

One main dining room, the no-smoking Martha Salen Restaurant, hosts three meals daily. Breakfast and lunch, which feature the famous Norwegian koldtbord (cold buffet) are self-serve, but the three-course dinner is served in two seatings. The 24-hour Roald Amundsen Café has snacks and light meals available for purchase.

Accommodations

Seven cabin grades are available. Double beds are available in only the suites (with no balconies), and all the other cabins have fixed twin beds and berths. Some cabins also have a third upper berth. A number of cabins are available for single occupancy at a premium. Only 44 cabins are inside, and the remaining 181 are ocean-view. Suites and some ocean-view cabin categories have TVs and minibars. The 220-volt outlets require adapters for U.S. appliances. Three cabins are wheelchair-accessible.

Cabin Size (in sq. ft.): Suites 301; outside cabins 86–108; inside 86.

Top: Regular outside double
Bottom: Coast Arcade

In the Know

When the weather gets rough, the *Kong Harald* rocks with the waves; it has no stabilizers to prevent movement, so beware if you become seasick easily. Because prices on board are in Norwegian kroner, already-expensive alcoholic drinks are even more dear; take advantage of Hurtigruten's policy that allows passengers to bring their own alcohol aboard.

Fast Facts

- 7 decks
- 1 dining room, café
- Some in-cabin minibars, no TV in some cabins, gym, sauna, library, laundry facilities, computer room

MIDNASTOL

History

The *Midnastol* is one of three Millennium ships that Hurtigruten introduced in 2002 and 2003. The modern design employs natural materials extensively. The ship is named for the midnight sun, and the decor is a celebration of the extended summer solstice enjoyed in Norway. Large glass expanses allow outside light to enter, along with extraordinary views. She has a large two-story panoramic lounge on the two upper decks and a top deck with saunas, a gym, a bar, and a large sun deck with a small swimming pool and Jacuzzi.

Restaurants

One main dining room, the no-smoking Midnastol Restaurant, hosts three meals daily. Breakfast and lunch, which feature the famous Norwegian koldtbord (cold buffet) are self-serve, but the three-course dinner is served in two seatings. Other dining and bar venues include the Hamsund Cognac Lounge, Mysteriet Bar, Paradis Snack Bar, and Midtsommer Market Café.

2003	ENTERED SERVICE
674	PASSENGER CAPACITY
75	CREW MEMBERS
300	NUMBER OF CABINS
15,000	GROSS TONS
445.2	LENGTH
70.5	WIDTH

700 ft.

500 ft.

300 ft.

Accommodations

Eleven grades of cabin are available. Double beds are available in only in the 23 suites (five of which have balconies); all the other cabins have fixed twin beds and berths. Some cabins also have a third upper berth. A number of cabins are available for single occupancy at a premium. Only 89 cabins are inside, and the remaining 188 are ocean-view (no balconies). Four are wheelchair-accessible. Suites and some other cabin categories have TVs and minibars. The 220-volt outlets require adapters for U.S. appliances.

Cabin Size (in sq. ft.): Suites 194–484; outside cabins 118–140; inside 86–108.

Top: *Midnastol* underway
Bottom: *Midnastol* suite

In the Know

The *Midnastol*'s entire journey can be done in seven days northbound or six days southbound, like all Hurtigruten itineraries. Because prices on board are in Norwegian kroner, already-expensive alcoholic drinks are even more dear; take advantage of Hurtigruten's policy that allows passengers to bring their own alcohol aboard.

Fast Facts

- 9 decks
- 1 dining room, café, snack bar
- Some minibars, no TV in some cabins, pool, gym, hot tub, sauna, 2 bars, laundry facilities, computer room

HURTIGRUTEN

2

NORDKAPP

History

Beautiful art and sublime scenery distinguish the *Nordkapp*. The dramatic themes from coastal culture in the paintings by renowned Norwegian artist Karl Erik Harr make the ship a floating art gallery. To take advantage of the beautiful natural surroundings, the ship offers fantastic views from all the panoramic lounges. The *Nordkapp* is one of six contemporary ships that Hurtigruten brought on line from 1993 to 1997. She has since been upgraded with four additional Junior Suites, Jacuzzis, and an Internet café.

1996	ENTERED SERVICE
490	PASSENGER CAPACITY
70	CREW MEMBERS
222	NUMBER OF CABINS
11,386	GROSS TONS
399.6	LENGTH
62.9	WIDTH

700 ft.
500 ft.
300 ft.

Restaurants

One main dining room, the no-smoking Nessekongen Restaurant, serves three meals daily. Breakfast and lunch, which features the famous Norwegian koldtbord (cold buffet) are self-serve, but the three-course dinner is served in two seatings. The 24-hour Ut-Rost Café has snacks and light meals available for purchase. The panoramic lounges have bars.

Accommodations

Eight grades of cabin are available. Double beds are available in only in the 10 suites; all the other cabins have fixed twin beds and berths. Some cabins also have a third upper berth. A number of cabins are available for single occupancy at a premium. Only 36 cabins are inside, and the remaining 172 are outside. Three cabins are wheelchair-accessible. Suites have TVs and minibars. The 220-volt outlets require adapters for U.S. appliances.

Cabin Size (in sq. ft.): Suites 194–301; outside cabins 86–108; inside 86.

Top: *Nordkapp* underway
Bottom: A suite aboard
Nordkapp

In the Know

When the weather gets rough, the *Nordkapp* rocks with the waves; it has no stabilizers to prevent movement, so beware if you become seasick easily. Because prices on board are in Norwegian kroner, already-expensive alcoholic drinks are even more dear; take advantage of Hurtigruten's policy that allows passengers to bring their own alcohol aboard.

Fast Facts

- 7 decks
- 1 dining room, 1 café
- Some in-cabin minibars, no TV in some cabins, gym, sauna, 2 bars, library, laundry facilities, computer room

NORDNORGE

History

The *Nordnorge* is distinguished by the magnificent settings through which it travels. The dramatic themes of coastal culture are reinforced by the abundant artwork on display throughout the ship. To take advantage of the beautiful natural surroundings, the ship offers fantastic views from its panoramic lounges. This is one of six contemporary ships that Hurtigruten brought online from 1993 to 1997. Two outdoor Jacuzzis were added in 2005.

1996	ENTERED SERVICE
490	PASSENGER CAPACITY
70	CREW MEMBERS
222	NUMBER OF CABINS
11,386	GROSS TONS
399.6	LENGTH
62.9	WIDTH

700 ft.

500 ft.

300 ft.

Restaurants

One main dining room, the no-smoking Halogaland Restaurant, offers three meals daily. Breakfast and lunch, which features the famous Norwegian koldtbord (cold buffet) are self-serve, but the three-course dinner is served in two assigned seatings. The 24-hour Vagar Café has snacks and light meals available for purchase.

Accommodations

Nine grades of cabin are available. Double beds are available only in the 14 suites (none of which has a balcony); all the other cabins have fixed twin beds and berths. Some cabins also have a third upper berth. A number of cabins are available for single occupancy at a premium. Only 32 cabins are inside, and the remaining 157 are ocean-view (no balconies); three of these are wheelchair-accessible. Suites have TVs and minibars. The 220-volt outlets require adapters for U.S. appliances.

Cabin Size (in sq. ft.): Suites 194–301; outside cabins 86–108; inside 86.

Top: Observation lounge
Bottom: *Nordnorge* regular double cabin

In the Know

The *Nordnorge* has no stabilizers to prevent rocking, so when the weather gets rough, the ship rocks with the waves; beware if you become seasick easily. Because prices on board are in Norwegian kroner, already-expensive alcoholic drinks are even more dear; take advantage of Hurtigruten's policy that allows passengers to bring their own alcohol aboard.

Fast Facts

- 7 decks
- 1 restaurant, 1 café
- Some minibars, no TV in some cabins, gym, sauna, steam room, bar, library, laundry facilities, computer room

NORDLYS

History

One of six contemporary ships that Hurtigruten brought on line from 1993 to 1997, the *Nordlys* is a small-scale cruise ship with a modest array of public rooms and facilities. The ship's art, decor, and colors were inspired by the namesake Northern Lights ("Nordlys"). Public areas are comfortable, though not lavish. As on other Hurtigruten ships, the original artworks that decorate walls of public spaces were provided by Norwegian artists from the country's coastal regions.

Restaurants

One main dining room, the no-smoking St. Jernesalen Restaurant, serves three meals daily. Breakfast and lunch, which features the famous Norwegian koldtbord (cold buffet) are self-serve, but the three-course dinner is served in two seatings. The 24-hour Aurora Café has snacks and light meals available for purchase.

1994	ENTERED SERVICE
482	PASSENGER CAPACITY
70	CREW MEMBERS
226	NUMBER OF CABINS
11,200	GROSS TONS
399	LENGTH
62.9	WIDTH

700 ft.
500 ft.
300 ft.

Accommodations

Eight grades of cabin are available. Double beds are found in only the six suites (none of which has a balcony), and all the other cabins have fixed twin beds and berths. Some cabins also have a third upper berth. A number of cabins are available for single occupancy at a premium. Only 30 cabins are inside, and the remaining 190 are ocean-view (no balconies); three of these are wheelchair-accessible. Suites have TVs and minibars. The 220-volt outlets require adapters for U.S. appliances.

Cabin Size (in sq. ft.): Suites 194–301; outside cabins 86–108; inside 86.

Top: *Nordlys* underway
Bottom: Salon/Bar on *Nordlys*

In the Know

Nordlys hits only 30 coastal ports instead of the 34 on most other 13-day itineraries. It also has no stabilizers, so you will feel the ship's movement in rough weather. Because prices on board are in Norwegian kro- ner, already-expensive alcoholic drinks are even more dear; take advantage of Hurtigruten's policy that allows passengers to bring their own alcohol aboard.

Fast Facts

- 7 decks
- 1 dining room, café
- Some in-cabin mini-bars, no TV in some cabins, gym, sauna, bar, laundry facilities

POLARLYS

History

One of six contemporary ships that Hurtigruten brought on line from 1993 to 1997, the *Polarlys* is a small-scale cruise ship with a modest array of public rooms and facilities. Although relatively small and simple, it's still a stylish ship, furnished with mahogany paneling, polished brass, and a choice selection of Norwegian contemporary art, including sculptures, carvings, paintings, and glass art. And of course, Mother Nature, the ship's entertainer, provides an unparalleled view from every quarter of the ship.

700 ft.	**2002** ENTERED SERVICE
	643 PASSENGER CAPACITY
	75 CREW MEMBERS
	282 NUMBER OF CABINS
500 ft.	**15,000** GROSS TONS
	545.4 LENGTH
300 ft.	**70.5** WIDTH

Restaurants

One main dining room, the no-smoking Polarlys Restaurant, serves three meals daily. Breakfast and lunch, which features the famous Norwegian koldtbord (cold buffet) are self-serve, but the three-course dinner is served in two seatings. The 24-hour Fjorden Café has snacks and light meals available for purchase.

Accommodations

Eight grades of cabin are available. Double beds are available in only in the six suites (no balconies), and all the other cabins have fixed beds and berths. Some cabins also have a third upper berth. A number of cabins are available for single occupancy at a premium. Only 44 cabins are inside, and the remaining 172 are ocean-view (no balconies); three are wheelchair-accessible. Suites have TVs and minibar. The 220-volt outlets require adapters for U.S. appliances.

Cabin Size (in sq. ft.): Suites 194–301; outside cabins 86–108; inside 86.

Top: *Polarlys*
Bottom: Panoramic lounge

In the Know

Ports visited during the day on the northbound voyage are visited at night on the south-bound voyage, so pick an itinerary based on what you want to see. Because prices on board are in Norwegian kro-ner, already-expensive alcoholic drinks are even more dear; take advantage of Hurtigruten's policy that allows passengers to bring their own alcohol aboard.

Fast Facts

- 7 decks
- 1 dining room, 2 cafés
- Some in-cabin mini-bars, no TV in some cabins, gym, sauna, 2 bars, laundry facilities

RICHARD WITH

History

Richard With, the namesake of this ship, was the founder of the Coastal fleet, which had as its original mission to provide regular communications and transit between the remote villages of Norway's west coast. As on all Hurtigruten ships, the art is by local artists, in this case by Eva, Karl Erik, and Jan Harr. This is one of six contemporary ships Hurtigruten brought online between 1993 and 1997. Eight Junior Suites and Jacuzzis and an Internet café were added during a renovation in 2006.

Restaurants

One main dining room, the no-smoking Polar Restaurant, serves three meals daily. Breakfast and lunch, which features the famous Norwegian koldtbord (cold buffet) are self-serve, but the three- course dinner is served in two assigned seatings. The 24-hour Los Holtes Café has snacks and light meals available for purchase. The panoramic lounges Horisont and Syvstjernen have bars.

1993	ENTERED SERVICE
490	PASSENGER CAPACITY
70	CREW MEMBERS
227	NUMBER OF CABINS
11,205	GROSS TONS
399.6	LENGTH
62.9	WIDTH

700 ft.
500 ft.
300 ft.

Accommodations

Eight grades of cabin are available. Double beds are available in only 10 suites; all the other cabins have fixed twin beds and berths. Some cabins also have a third upper berth. A number of cabins are available for single occupancy at a premium. Only 36 cabins are inside, and the remaining 173 are outside; three cabins are wheelchair-accessible. Suites have TVs and minibars. The 220-volt outlets require adapters for U.S. appliances.

Cabin Size (in sq. ft.): Suites 194–301; outside cabins 86–108; inside 86.

Top: *Richard With*
Bottom: Coffee break in the salon

In the Know

When the weather gets rough, the *Richard With* rocks with the waves; it has no stabilizers to prevent movement, so beware if you become seasick easily. Because prices on board are in Norwegian kroner, already-expensive alcoholic drinks are even more dear; take advantage of Hurtigruten's policy that allows passengers to bring their own alcohol aboard.

Fast Facts

- 7 decks
- 1 dining room, café
- Some in-cabin minibars, no TV in some cabins, gym, sauna, bar, library, laundry facilities, computer room

TROLLFJORD

2002	ENTERED SERVICE
674	PASSENGER CAPACITY
75	CREW MEMBERS
298	NUMBER OF CABINS
15,000	GROSS TONS
445.2	LENGTH
70.5	WIDTH

700 ft.

500 ft.

300 ft.

History

The *Trollfjord* is one of three Millennium ships that Hurtigruten introduced in 2002 and 2003. A beautifully appointed small ship, its decor has a winter theme and a modern design; particularly noteworthy are the wood and stone (all from Norway) that are used throughout the ship. Large panoramic windows let in both light and scenery; like all Hurtigruten ships, the original artwork is from local Norwegian artists. The sauna, gym, pool, and Jacuzzi are on the top deck, where there is also an enclosed observation lounge.

Restaurants

The main dining room, Saga Hall Restaurant, hosts three meals daily. Breakfast and lunch, which feature the famous Norwegian koldtbord (cold buffet) are self-serve, but the three-course dinner is served in two assigned seatings. Other dining venues include the Saga Snack Bar, Café Viking Safari, and Café Viking Saga. Three bars and shops round out the roster of food and beverage outlets.

Accommodations

Eleven grades of cabin are available. Double beds are available only in the 23 suites (five of which have balconies); all the other cabins have fixed twin beds and berths. Some cabins also have a third upper berth. A number of cabins are available for single occupancy at a premium. Only 89 cabins are inside, and the remaining 188 are ocean-view (no balconies). Four are wheelchair-accessible. Suites and inside cabins have TVs. The 220-volt outlets require adapters for U.S. appliances.

Cabin Size (in sq. ft.): Suites 194–484; outside cabins 118–140; inside 86–108.

Top: *Trollfjord*
Bottom: Main bar

In the Know

Even saunas and glass elevators have views of the scenery, in addition to the two main panoramic lounges, which are popular spots for viewing the fjords and coastline. Because prices on board are in Norwegian kroner, already-expensive alcoholic drinks are even more dear; take advantage of Hurtigruten's policy that allows passengers to bring their own alcohol aboard.

Fast Facts

- 9 decks
- 1 dining room, 2 cafés, 1 snack bar
- No TV in some cabins, pool, gym, 2 saunas, hot tub, 3 bars, library, laundry facilities, computer room

LINDBLAD EXPEDITIONS

Founded by Sven-Olof Lindblad in 1979, Lindblad Expeditions has earned a reputation for creating eye-opening expeditions to out-of-the-way places, always emphasizing responsible tourism. Operating a fleet of small expedition ships that nose into ports where large cruise ships cannot go, the company

Excercising on deck, *Sea Cloud II*

prides itself on providing adventurous travelers with original and authentic experiences. Important components to all of Lindblad's cruises, the company's onboard expedition leaders and naturalists (all experts in their field), have a passion for helping travelers uncover—and interpret—the mysteries of nature and history.

LINDBLAD EXPEDITIONS
96 Morton Street
New York, NY 10014
800/397-3348
www.expeditions.com

Cruise Style: Expedition Cruising

The company's underlying mission is to introduce "curious and intrepid travelers" to the "international capitals of wildness." The far-flung reaches of Alaska, Antarctica, Baja, Central America, and Galapagos serve up what the company calls "the most fascinating, unspoiled, and life-enhancing destinations on the planet." That's not to say that Lindblad ignores traditional destinations, because its ships also sail in the British Isles, the Mediterranean, and the Baltic—even in the Caribbean—but the emphasis is always on active exploration, learning, and sustainable tourism.

Lindblad offers active vacations, and if there were icons for the cruise line, they might well be the kayak and the Zodiac. All ships offer opportunities to launch from small ships to even smaller vessels for exploration of the marine world.

CHOOSE A CRUISE ON LINDBLAD EXPEDITIONS IF...

1 You prefer learning over relaxing on your vacations. The typical Lindblad shore excursion doesn't include shopping or beach-going.

2 You want an active vacation in out-of-the-way destinations. Think Galapagos, not St. Maarten or the French Riviera.

3 You desire to travel with like-minded people who want to learn more about the world they live in.

Shore excursions are included in the cruise fare. Lindblad's cruises, in fact, are nearly all-inclusive. About the only thing you'll need to dip into your wallet for is alcohol.

Food
Breakfast and lunch are typically served buffet-style, although you may order eggs and omelets from the kitchen. Afternoon tea features sandwiches and sweets, and hors d'oeuvres are served during cocktail hour. Dinner typically consists of two entrées—meat or fish—as well as several always-available items such as steak and chicken breast. All meals are served in a single open seating.

Fitness & Recreation
Fitness areas are small but well-appointed, with stationary bicycles, treadmills, light weights, yoga mats, a sauna, and massage-treatment rooms. Stretching and movement classes are offered.

Your Shipmates
Lindblad's passengers—who tend to be aged 55-plus—are likely to be fit for the many activities that the cruise line offers, including hiking, snorkeling, and kayaking. Some cruises are aimed specifically at families with children.

Dress Code
The dress on these cruises is informal, leaning toward expedition-style clothing and gear. There's absolutely no need for jackets or evening gowns.

Service
Like everything on these ships, service is professional but without pretense.

Tipping
Recommended gratuities for the ship's crew is $10 per day per passenger.

Noteworthy

■ Lindblad's *National Geographic Endeavour* is equipped with a fleet of Zodiac landing craft, kayaks, a glass-bottom boat, and high-tech underwater video equipment.

■ One of Lindblad's founders, Lars-Eric Lindblad, led the first nonscientific expeditions to the Galapagos in 1967. Today, the company has two ships based in the Galapagos year-round, offering weekly departures.

■ Lars-Eric Lindblad also operated the first cruise to Antarctica.

Top: Relaxing on *Sea Cloud II*
Bottom: Conversation on *National Geographic Endeavour*

2

LINDBLAD EXPEDITIONS

DON'T CHOOSE A CRUISE ON LINDBLAD EXPEDITIONS IF...

❶ You require the large-scale entertainment found on big cruise ships; you won't find Las Vegas reviews on these ships.

❷ You require big-ship amenities. Lindblad's ships have small gyms and spas, but the focus is on what you can see off the ship.

❸ You could care less for learning about nature or the natural environment; these are Lindblad's main goals.

NATIONAL GEOGRAPHIC ENDEAVOUR

History

Built in 1996 as a fishing trawler for the North Sea, *National Geographic Endeavour* was converted into a cruise ship in 1984, when she operated as the *North Star*, then *Caledonian Star*. She was reburbished in 1999 and given her present name in 2001. Lindblad's partnership with the National Geographic Society began in 2005. The comfortable expedition vessel carries Zodiac landing craft, kayaks, scuba gear (on select itineraries), snorkeling gear, and apparatus for viewing underwater marine life and the ocean environment.

Restaurants

All meals are served in one main dining room, on deck, and sometimes even on shore—perhaps at a remote beach. Full buffet breakfasts are offered each morning. The single dinner seating is at unassigned tables so that passengers may meet and mingle. There is no dress code. The menu is international, primarily European, high-quality, and with a local flair.

700 ft.	**1966**
	ENTERED SERVICE
	124
	PASSENGER CAPACITY
	64
	CREW MEMBERS
	62
	NUMBER OF CABINS
500 ft.	**3,132**
	GROSS TONS
	292.6
	LENGTH
300 ft.	**45.9**
	WIDTH

Accommodations

Five categories of cabins are available. The two suites on Upper Deck feature separate sleeping and living rooms as well as a convertible sofa for a third person. The four remaining categories all have lower single beds, with some that can convert to queen-size beds, and portholes. Some nonsuite categories can sleep three. All cabins feature a minibar-fridge and VCR.

Cabin Size (in sq. ft.): 191–269.

Top: *National Geographic Endeavour*
Bottom: Dining in style

In the Know

Photo Expeditions and Workshops, developed in collaboration with National Geographic Society photographers, allows passengers to learn from some of the most respected names in nature and travel photography. An experienced naturalist is always on board to offer enrichment lectures and to lead shore excursions.

Fast Facts

- 6 decks
- 1 dining room
- In-cabin refrigerators, in-cabin safes, in-cabin DVD, pool, gym, sauna, library, laundry service, computer room

SEA CLOUD II

History

A modern three-masted sailing ship, *Sea Cloud II* was built by devoted travelers who love the romance of sailing. The hand-sailed square-rigger was constructed in traditional style but with fine amenities and modern navigation and safety features. *Sea Cloud II* slices silently through the waters when the engines are turned off. When there's not enough wind to sustain sufficient speed, up to two diesel engines can kick in. *Sea Cloud II* features spacious deck areas, elegant public rooms, and fine accommodations.

	2001
	ENTERED SERVICE
	86
	PASSENGER CAPACITY
700 ft.	60
	CREW MEMBERS
	46
	NUMBER OF CABINS
500 ft.	3,849
	GROSS TONS
	383.8
	LENGTH
300 ft.	52.9
	WIDTH

Restaurants

All meals are served in a single seating with unassigned tables, so passengers may meet and mingle. An early-riser breakfast is offered on the Lido Deck. The menu features nouvelle cuisine, enhanced by regional specialties depending on where the ship is sailing. Complimentary fine wines and beers are served with lunch and dinner. Sunset cocktail hours are held nightly at the Lido Bar.

Accommodations

Four categories of cabins are available. The two Owner's Suites on Lido Deck feature separate living and sleeping areas, panoramic windows, king-size canopy bed (using two side-by-side mattresses), decorative fireplace, and a tub with a separate shower. The remaining categories have queen-size beds (all use two mattresses). Sixteen junior suites are distinguished by panoramic windows and larger living spaces than the remaining cabins, which have only portholes. All cabins have a minibar, TV with VCR, bathroom with gold-plated fixtures, and a marble sink.

Cabin Size (in sq. ft.): 215–323.

Top: *Sea Cloud II* at sea
Bottom: Time to relax and read

In the Know

As a traditional sailing ship, *Sea Cloud II* offers passengers opportunities to learn navigational and nautical skills—from knot-tying to the use of a sextant. Passengers can visit the bridge during the day, with the captain's permission.

Fast Facts

- 4 decks
- 1 dining room
- In-cabin refrigerator, in-cabin VCR, gym, sauna, laundry service, computer room

MSC CRUISES

More widely known as one of the world's largest cargo shipping companies, MSC has operated cruises with an eclectic fleet since the late 1980s. Since introducing two graceful, medium-size ships in 2003 and 2004, MSC's expansion plans include operating newer and larger vessels with a growing

Pool deck after dark

variety of European itineraries. MSC's ships sail the Mediterranean year-round and now offer seasonal Baltic cruises as well. New ships are being added to the fleet on a fairly regular basis, as the demand for cruises rises in popularity with travelers to Europe.

MSC CRUISES

6750 N. Andrews Avenue

Fort Lauderdale, FL 33309

954/662-6262 or

800/666-9333

www.msccruises.com

Cruise Style: Premium

The MSC Cruises fleet can almost be described as three fleets in one. First, there are budget-priced "classic" cruise ships, which aren't normally marketed in North America; these include the *MSC Melody* and *MSC Rhapsody*. Second are the acquired ships, the relatively new *MSC Armonia* and *MSC Sinfonia,* which were acquired when the defunct First European/Festival Cruises ceased operations. Third are the new ships that have been built specifically for MSC's expanding fleet—*MSC Lirica* (launched in 2003) and *MSC Opera* (which followed a year later). The success of those stylish, modern vessels prompted MSC Cruises to commission a new series of even larger and more elaborate cruise ships with a higher percentage of cabins with private balconies.

MSC Cruises blankets the Mediterranean nearly year-round with a dizzying selection of cruise itineraries that allow a lot of time in ports of call and include few, if any, sea days. In summer months, several ships sail off to northern Europe to ply the Baltic. Itineraries planned for repositioning sailings visit some intriguing, off-the-beaten-track ports of call that other cruise lines pass by.

No glitz, no clutter—just elegant simplicity—is the standard of MSC's seaworthy interior decor. Extensive use of marble, brass, and wood reflects the best of Italian styling and design; clean lines and bold colors set their modern sophisticated tone.

MSC has adopted some activities that appeal to American passengers without abandoning those preferred by Europeans (you should be prepared for announcements in Italian as well as English while on board). In addition to the guest lecturers, computer classes, and cooking lessons featured in the enrichment programs, Italian-language classes are a popular option. Nightly shows accentuate the cruise line's Mediterranean heritage; there might be a flamenco show in the main showroom and live music for listening and dancing in the smaller lounges, while the disco is a happening late-night spot.

The MSC entertainment staff shine off-stage as well as in front of the spotlight. They seek out passengers traveling solo, who might be looking for activity or dance partners, so that they feel fully included in the cruise.

In addition to some of the most reasonable fares in the premium cruise market, MSC doesn't nickel-and-dime passengers during their cruises. Cocktails and wines are sensibly priced. Although it may not last, it's been a long time since Dom Perignon by the bottle has been listed for less than $100 on most other cruise ships.

Regardless of the intinerary, be prepared for a very Italian-influenced experience. Also expect to hear announcements in several languages.

Food

Dinner on MSC ships is a traditional seven-course event centered on authentic Italian fare. Menus list Mediterranean regional specialties and classic favorites prepared from scratch the old-fashioned way. Some favorites include lamb and mushroom quiche, a Tuscan dish, and veal scaloppini with tomatoes and mozzarella, a recipe from Sorrento in Campania. In its ongoing efforts to appeal to American passengers, although food is still prepared the Italian way. In a nod to American tastes, broiled chicken breast, grilled salmon, and Caesar salad are additions to the dinner menu and are always available. Healthy Choice and vegetarian items are offered as well as tempting sugar-free desserts. A highlight is the bread-of-the-day, freshly baked on board. The nightly midnight buffet is a retro food feast missing from most of today's cruises. Room service is always available, though the options are somewhat limited, and there is a charge.

Noteworthy

■ Sleek lines and plenty of open deck space are hallmarks of MSC ship design.

■ Traditional midnight buffets are supplemented by late-night snacks offered throughout the lounges by strolling waiters.

■ MSC has adapted some of their Italian style and menus for North Americans, but not to the extent of becoming fully Americanized.

Top: Miniature golf is family fun
Bottom: *MSC Lirica*

Top: Thermal Suite
Middle: Expansive pool deck
Bottom: *MSC Lirica* suite with
balcony

Fitness & Recreation

Up-to-date exercise equipment, a jogging track, and basic fitness classes for all levels are available in the fitness centers.

Spa treatments include a variety of massages, body wraps, and facials that can be scheduled à la carte or combined in packages to encompass an afternoon or the entire cruise. The hottest hair-styling techniques and nail services are offered in the salons. Unlike most cruise lines, MSC Cruises operates its own spas.

Your Shipmates

Most passengers are couples in the 35- to 55-year-old range, as well as some family groups who prefer the international atmosphere prevalent on board. While as many as half the passengers on Caribbean itineraries may be American, expect a more international mix on Mediterranean cruises, with North Americans in the minority.

Dress Code

Two formal nights are standard on seven-night cruises, and three are scheduled on 11-night cruises. Men are encouraged to wear dark suits, but sport coats and ties are appropriate. All other evenings are casual, although jeans are discouraged in restaurants. It's requested that no shorts be worn in public areas after 6 PM.

Junior Cruisers

Children from ages 3 to 17 are welcome to participate in age-appropriate youth programs. The Mini Club is for ages 3 to 8, Junior Club for ages 9 to 12, and Teenage Club for youths 13 years and older. Counselors organize daily group activities such as arts and crafts, painting, treasure hunts, games, a mini-Olympics, and shows. Children under age three may use the playroom if accompanied at all times by an adult. Babysitting can be arranged for a fee once you're on board.

Service

Service can be inconsistent, yet it's more than acceptable, even if it's not overly gracious. The mainly Italian staff can seem befuddled by American habits and expectations. Ongoing training and improved English proficiency

CHOOSE A CRUISE ON MSC CRUISES IF...

1 You appreciate authentic Italian cooking. This is the real thing, not an Olive Garden clone.

2 You want your ship to look like a ship. MSC's vessels are very nautical in appearance.

3 You want the Continental flair of a premium cruise at a fair price.

for staff are top priorities for MSC, and these weaknesses are showing improvement.

Tipping

Passengers may reward staff members with a gratuity for exceptional service should they choose to do so; however, tipping is not obligatory. Customary gratuities are added to your shipboard account. Guidelines are similar to those on other lines (suggested amounts are per person, per day): waiter $3.50–$5; maître d' $1–$2; stateroom attendant $3.50–$5. You can always adjust these amounts at the reception desk or even pay in cash, if you prefer. Automatic 15% gratuities are incorporated into all bar purchases.

Past Passengers

After sailing on MSC Cruises once, you are eligible to join the MSC Club by completing the registration form found in your cabin or by writing to the club through the line's Web site. Membership benefits include discounts on your cruise fare for the best itineraries, travel cancellation insurance, shore excursions, and even onboard purchases. You will also receive *MSC Club News* magazine.

Membership levels are achieved on a point system determined by the number of cruises taken. Classic members have up to 21 points; Silver, between 22 and 42 points; Gold, 43 points and over. Silver and Gold members receive pins to commemorate their status.

Good to Know

MSC Cruises has catered almost exclusively to Europeans since the company's founding, and the style and habits favored by North Americans can still seem somewhat foreign to them. For example, Europeans prefer to go out for coffee after dinner; Americans want to be served coffee with their dessert. Unfortunately, this culture clash can cause misunderstandings and some contentiousness. Little things like too-small water glasses and no iced tea can make Americans cranky. To eliminate these issues and broaden their appeal, staff members on board embrace cultural differences, and they try hard to please everyone.

DON'T CHOOSE A CRUISE ON MSC CRUISES IF...

1 Announcements in more than one language get on your nerves.

2 You aren't able to accept things that are not always done the American way.

3 Myriad dining choices and casual attire are imperatives. MSC cruises have assigned seating and observe a dress code.

MSC LIRICA/OPERA

Public Areas & Facilities

Though these two sleek, medium-size ships are exactly the same dimensions and differ only slightly in basic layout, *Opera* holds almost 200 more passengers typically and has almost 100 extra cabins. Light and bright by day, intimate and sophisticated by night, the contemporary design may not measure up to the sizzle expected by those North American passengers who don't understand more understated European tastes.

Public rooms are spacious and uniformly elegant with grand touches of marble, brass accents, and lots of wood. The refreshing lack of glitz is more than compensated for by the sparkle of glass and a mixture of primary and neutral colors. With most public areas on the lower two passenger decks, getting acclimated is a breeze. Conveniently located elevator and stairway lobbies make even vertical movement less challenging.

Space around the Lido pools feels particularly lavish, with two swimming pools and hot tubs.

2003, 2004	ENTERED SERVICE
1,560 (2,065 max)*	PASSENGER CAPACITY
700*	CREW MEMBERS
765*	NUMBER OF CABINS
58,600	GROSS TONS
763 feet	LENGTH
84 feet	WIDTH

700 ft.
500 ft.
300 ft.

*Opera has 850 cabins and holds 740 crew and 1,700 passengers (2,199 maximum)

WOW Factor

Who knew marble contains so many rich colors? It's everywhere you look on these ships.

Restaurants

Two formal restaurants serve Mediterranean and Italian-accented cuisine in traditional early and late assigned seatings. The Lido buffet, poolside grill, coffee bar, and pizzeria offer casual daytime options.

Although there are no true alternative dining restaurants, La Pergola and Il Patio restaurants have outdoor tables protected from the elements by overhead canvas.

Top: L'Approdo Restaurant
Bottom: *MSC Opera* stateroom with balcony

What Works & What Doesn't

Oddly, only the forward and aft elevators and stairwells reach all decks; the central ones don't even go as high as the top deck of staterooms. However, this seeming design flaw results in an uninterrupted expanse of

wide-open space on the pool deck, so perhaps it wasn't such a bad choice after all.

Encircling the Lido Deck from above is additional sunning space where well-placed glass screens cut the wind.

Lounge chairs are plentiful, and you shouldn't have trouble finding one, even during peak sunning hours.

Accommodations

Layout: There are nearly a dozen stateroom price categories; however, they fall into three basic configurations: suite with balcony, ocean view, and inside. The addition of a fourth category on *MSC Opera* (ocean-view cabin with balcony instead of some of the larger suites) increased the number of balconies available, but the size of these new balcony cabins is identical to that of the ocean-view cabins with only windows. Inside cabins were added to nearly an entire deck on MSC Opera as well, which accounts for the higher double-occupancy rate.

Amenities: All cabins are comfortably decorated in primary colors and have a vanity-desk, side chair, television, small minibar refrigerator, personal safe, and a hair dryer. Bathrooms are supplied with MSC Cruises' own brand of shampoo, bath gel, and soaps, plus a handy sewing repair kit. Suites also have a computer connection.

Suites: Suites (which would be more accurately described as minisuites) have a sitting area and a bathroom with bathtub; all but two forward-facing suites on each ship (which are designated family-size suites on *MSC Opera*) have a balcony as well.

Good to Know: Four interior cabins on *MSC Lirica* and five on *MSC Opera* are wheelchair-accessible.

Cabin Type	Size (sq. ft.)
Suite with Balcony	247
Suite without Balcony	236
Ocean View with Balcony	140
Ocean View without Balcony	140

Fast Facts

- 12 passenger decks
- 2 dining rooms, buffet, pizzeria
- Some in-cabin broadband, Wi-Fi, in-cabin safes, in-cabin minibars
- 2 pools, fitness classes, gym, hair salon, 2 hot tubs, sauna, spa, steam room
- 8 bars, casino, dance club, library, showroom, video game room
- Children's programs (ages 3–17)
- Laundry service
- Computer room

In the Know

Prepare for a treat the first time you use a bath towel. Instead of skimpy standard towels, they are thick bath sheets. The hand towels aren't much smaller than most standard bath towels; they're easily large enough for a woman to wrap her hair in. Beware, though—shower stalls are miniscule.

MSC Lirica sauna

Favorites

Best Places to Get Away From It All: Head outside behind the disco, where there's an open deck furnished with covered tables and chairs. Because there are no aft-facing cabins, most passenger decks have a small covered area at the stern where you'll find lounge chairs. These are perfect spots for reading or watching the ships' wake disappear behind you, and many people don't discover them.

Best Splurge: Specialty coffees, cocktails, wine, and other alcoholic beverages are some of the most reasonably priced at sea.

Best Added Value: Midnight buffets of the kind rarely seen on cruise ships anymore are an extravaganza worthy of attending even if you aren't hungry. Be sure to bring a camera.

Our Favorite Spot for a Nightcap: High above the stern, cozy seating areas create an intimate atmosphere in the discos, which don't really crank up into high gear (and volume) until quite late. If it's a bit noisy, there's that seating outside.

MSC MUSICA/
ORCHESTRA/POESIA

History

MSC Cruises took a giant leap with the introduction of this large and entirely new ship class. A highlight of *MSC Musica*'s design is a three-deck waterfall in the central foyer, where a piano is suspended on a transparent floor above a pool of water. Interiors are a blend of art deco and art nouveau themes as well as the authentic Italian designs for which other MSC Cruises ships are known. In addition to its soothing Zen garden and Oriental music, the Sushi Bar is a bonus to the dining experience.

Restaurants

Two formal restaurants serve open-seating breakfast and lunch; dinner is served in two traditional assigned seatings. The à la carte specialty restaurant requires reservations and carries an additional charge.

Reservations are not required for the Sushi Bar, which serves extra-charge sushi and other Asian foods. The buffet is a casual dining option. There is a charge for room service.

700 ft.	2006/2007/2008 ENTERED SERVICE
	2,550 PASSENGER CAPACITY
	987 CREW MEMBERS
	1,275 NUMBER OF CABINS
500 ft.	89,600 GROSS TONS
	964 feet LENGTH
300 ft.	105 feet WIDTH

Accommodations

A whopping 80% of staterooms have an ocean view and 65% have balconies. Decorated in jewel-toned colors, all are comfortable yet somewhat smaller than the average new-ship cabin. All cabins have a vanity-desk, TV, adequate closet and storage space, small refrigerator, and hair dryer. Suites have a broadband connection for a laptop, a tub in the bathroom, plenty of storage, and a sitting area. Bathrooms have basic toiletries. Seventeen cabins are wheelchair-accessible.

Cabin Size (in sq. ft.): Suite with balcony 269; ocean-view stateroom with balcony 166–192; outside cabin 183; inside cabin 151.

Top: *Orchestra* at sea
Bottom: *Musica* Theater

In the Know

Wi-Fi means you can use your laptop throughout the ship; cell-phone service allows you to stay connected by phone (albeit for a hefty surcharge). While there's a walking track high atop the ship, a better bet on windy or wet days is the little-used promenade on Deck 7— while it doesn't encircle the ship, it is covered.

Fast Facts

- 13 passenger decks
- 4 restaurants
- Wi-Fi, safes, refrigerators, 3 pools, gym, spa, casino, children's programs (ages 3–17), laundry service, computer room

MSC ARMONIA/MSC SINFONIA

History

These sleek sister ships were originally built for the now-defunct First European (Festival) Cruises and entered MSC Cruises fleet in 2004. Art deco forms are apparent in *MSC Armonia's* lobby, but beyond that the interior decor could be termed minimalist modern with some funky chairs and colors ranging from bland to bright. While *MSC Sinfonia* was said to draw inspiration from the music of several great European symphonies, it's hard to see the connection. However, it's easy to see that this ship holds the decorative edge.

Restaurants

Two formal restaurants serve open-seating breakfast and lunch; dinner is served in two traditional seatings with assigned tables and tablemates. The buffet is a casual dining option, and a grill and ice-cream parlor near the swimming pools are also popular casual spots. The coffee bar serves pastries and sweets. Room service is available for a charge.

2001/2002	Entered Service
1,566	Passenger Capacity
700	Crew Members
783	Number of Cabins
58,625	Gross Tons
824 feet	Length
94 feet	Width

700 ft.
500 ft.
300 ft.

Accommodations

Cabins are comfortable yet quite small by modern cruise-ship standards. All cabins have a vanity-desk, TV, adequate closet and storage space, a small refrigerator, and a hair dryer. Bathrooms are supplied with basic toiletries. Suites have a tub in the bathroom, balconies, extra storage space, a sitting area, and in-cabin broadband connection for a laptop computer. Four cabins are wheelchair-accessible.

Cabin Size (in sq. ft.): Suites with balconies 286 on *Armonia*, 237 on *Sinfonia*; family suites 286 on *Armonia*, 237 on *Sinfonia*; oceanview and inside staterooms 140.

Top: MSC *Armonia* recreation room
Bottom: MSC *Armonia* sports deck

In the Know

Coffee is not served with dessert in the American way since Europeans—and especially Italians—prefer to go to the specialty coffee bar after dinner. Multilingual travelers will be very much at home on these ships, while those who dread announcements in several languages will be pleased to find they are kept to a minimum. The exception is the boat drill, which can seem endless.

Fast Facts

- 9 passenger decks
- 2 dining rooms
- Safes, refrigerators, 2 pools, gym, sauna, spa, 8 bars, casino, children's programs (ages 3–17), laundry service, computer room

MSC MELODY

History

Originally built for now-defunct Homes Lines, this ship sailed for Premier Cruise Line as a "Big Red Boat" before that cruise line declared bankruptcy; she joined MSC in 1997 and is the largest ship in the line's "classic" Italian fleet. The lifeboats lining the highest reaches of her superstructure give away her age. Interiors fare somewhat better with lively color combinations. The main dining room is located low in the ship, but other public rooms are on the uppermost decks and are bright and cheerful.

	1982
	ENTERED SERVICE
	1,064
	PASSENGER CAPACITY
700 ft.	**535**
	CREW MEMBERS
	532
	NUMBER OF CABINS
500 ft.	**35,143**
	GROSS TONS
	671 feet
	LENGTH
300 ft.	**98 feet**
	WIDTH

Restaurants

The formal restaurant serves breakfast and lunch in open seating; dinner is served in two traditional seatings with assigned tables and tablemates. The buffet is a casual dining choice with indoor and outside seating. The coffee bar serves pastries and sweets. Room service is available for a charge.

Top: Galaxy Restaurant on *MSC Melody*
Bottom: Lucky Star Casino

Accommodations

Decorated with punches of color, all accommodations are comfortable yet are quite small by modern cruise-ship standards. All cabin categories have a vanity-desk, TV, closet and storage space, and a hair dryer. Bathrooms are supplied with basic toiletries. Suites have a bathtub in the bathroom, adequate storage space, small refrigerator, a personal safe, and a surprisingly roomy sitting area. Four staterooms are wheelchair-accessible.

Cabin Size (in sq. ft.): Suites 366; standard ocean-view and inside cabins 118.

In the Know

Despite her age, *MSC Melody* has a retractable, transparent roof over one swimming pool, a feature that not even some new ships have. The space that would normally be an observation lounge on a newer ship houses indoor seating for the casual buffet restaurant. A great spot to begin the day, it's appropriately named Sunrise Terrace.

Fast Facts

- 8 passenger decks
- Dining room
- Some safes, some refrigerators, 3 pools, gym, sauna, spa, 5 bars, casino, children's programs (ages 3–17), laundry service

MSC RHAPSODY

History

Launched to sail the Caribbean for Cunard Line as *Cunard Princess* in 1977, this small ship has sailed as *MSC Rhapsody* since 1995. Well suited for warm-weather voyages, the outdoor spaces are more than adequate. Interiors are cozy and comfortable with some multipurpose lounges—the Top Sail Lounge is both a piano bar and casino; the disco/nightclub has both an indoor and outdoor dance floor. While there is no wraparound promenade deck, a track for walking and jogging encircles the pool area.

700 ft.	1977
	ENTERED SERVICE
	764
	PASSENGER CAPACITY
	370
	CREW MEMBERS
	382
	NUMBER OF CABINS
500 ft.	17.095
	GROSS TONS
	534 feet
	LENGTH
300 ft.	76 feet
	WIDTH

Restaurants

The formal restaurant serves open-seating breakfast and lunch; dinner is served in two traditional seatings with assigned tables and tablemates. The buffet is a casual dining choice for breakfast and lunch, sometimes even dinner (depending on the itinerary), with indoor and outside seating. Adjacent to the buffet restaurant are a coffee bar and grill. Room service is available for a charge.

Accommodations

Decorated in primary colors, all cabins are comfortable, yet they are all quite small by comparison to most modern cruise ships. All accommodation categories have a vanity-desk, TV, closet and storage space, and a hair dryer. Bathrooms are supplied with basic toiletries. Suites have a bathtub in the bathroom, adequate storage space, a small refrigerator, a personal safe, and a sitting area. There are no wheelchair-accessible cabins on this ship.

Cabin Size (in sq. ft.): Suites 215; ocean-view and inside cabins 129.

Top: Dining on deck
Bottom: Rhapsody restaurant

In the Know

Passengers accustomed to ships with all the bells and whistles may be disappointed, but this ship is a gem for a relaxing in the sun and dancing under the stars. As on most ships of this vintage, the hair salon is not located adjacent to the spa. You'll find it on a lower deck.

Fast Facts

- 7 passenger decks
- Dining room
- Some safes, some refrigerators, 2 pools, gym, sauna, spa, 7 bars, casino, children's programs (ages 3–17), laundry service

NORWEGIAN CRUISE LINE

Norwegian Cruise Line (NCL) set sail in 1966 with an entirely new concept: regularly scheduled Caribbean cruises from the then obscure port of Miami. Good food and friendly service combined with value fares established NCL as a winner for active adults and families. With the introduction of the

Le Cirque-style extravaganza on Norwegian Cruise Line

now-retired SS *Norway* in 1979, NCL ushered in the era of cruises on mega-size ships. Innovative and forward-looking, NCL has been a cruise-industry leader for four decades and is as much at home in Europe as it is in the Caribbean.

NORWEGIAN CRUISE LINE
7665 Corporate Center Drive
Miami, FL 33126
305/436-4000 or
800/327-7030
www.ncl.com

Cruise Style: Mainstream

When the pent-up demand in North America for European cruises reached a fever pitch, Norwegian Cruise Line rose to the challenge by deploying three of its newest and most feature-filled "Freestyle Cruising" vessels to the Mediterranean and Baltic seas. *Norwegian Jewel, Norwegian Jade,* and *Norwegian Gem*—all launched since 2005—make up the NCL European fleet for 2008. With some of the largest suites at sea, and an abundance of interconnecting staterooms in most categories, these ships are particularly attractive for family groups. With the hassle of set dining times removed, it's possible to spend more time ashore without the worry of missing dinner.

Noted for top-quality, high-energy entertainment and emphasis on fitness facilities and programs, NCL combines action, activities, and a variety of dining options in a casual, free-flowing atmosphere. Freestyle cruising was born when Asian shipping giant Star Cruises acquired NCL—the new owners were confounded that Americans meekly conformed to rigid dining schedules and dress codes. All that changed with NCL's introduction of a host of flexible dining options that allow passengers to choose open seating in the main dining rooms or dine in any of a number of à la carte and specialty restaurants at any time and with whom they please.

More high jinks than high-brow, entertainment after dark features extravagant Broadway and Las Vegas–style revues presented in main show lounges by lavishly costumed singers and dancers—some of the most talented and professional at sea. Other performers might include comedians, magicians, jugglers, and acrobats. Passengers can get into the act by taking part in talent shows or step up to the karaoke microphone. Live bands play for dancing and listening passengers in smaller lounges, and each ship has a lively disco. Passengers on some ships are treated to performances and improvisation workshops featuring players from Chicago's world-famous Second City company, training ground for some of the most gifted comedians in movies and stars of *Saturday Night Live*.

Casinos, bingo sessions, and art auctions are well attended. Adult games, particularly the competitive ones, are fun to participate in and provide laughs for audience members. Goofy pool games are an NCL staple, and the ships' bands crank up the volume during afternoon and evening deck parties. It's lively and enjoyable, even if you just watch the action from a lounge chair.

From a distance, most cruise ships look so similar that it's often difficult to tell them apart, but NCL's largest, modern ships stand out with their distinctive use of hull art. Each new ship is distinguished by murals extending from bow to mid-ship.

Food

Main dining rooms serve what is traditionally deemed Continental fare, although it's about what you would expect at a really good hotel banquet. Health-conscious menu selections are nicely prepared from *Cooking Light* magazine's recipes, and vegetarian choices are always available.

Where NCL really shines is the specialty restaurants, especially the French-Mediterranean Le Bistro (on all ships), the pan-Asian restaurants, and steak houses (on the newer ships). As a rule of thumb, the newer the ship, the wider the variety since new ships were purpose-built with as many as 10 or more places to eat. You may find Spanish tapas, an Italian trattoria, a steak house, and a pan-Asian restaurant complete with a sushi and sashimi bar and teppanyaki room. Some, but not all, carry a cover charge or are priced à la carte and require reservations. An NCL staple, the late-night Chocoholic Buffet continues to be a favorite event.

Noteworthy

- Numerous connecting staterooms and suites can be combined to create multicabin family accommodations.
- Freestyle Cruising offers the flexibility of dining with anyone you choose and when you actually wish to eat.
- The newest ships in the NCL fleet sport hull art—huge murals that make them easily recognizable from afar.

Top: Casual freestyle dining
Bottom: *Norwegian Jewel* spa relaxation suite

NORWEGIAN CRUISE LINE

2

Top: Casino play
Middle: Stay connected to the Internet
Bottom: *Norwegian Dream* superior Ocean View stateroom

Fitness & Recreation

Mandara Spa offers unique and exotic spa treatments fleetwide on NCL, although facilities vary widely. Spa treatments include a long menu of massages, body wraps, and facials and the latest trends in hair and nail services are offered in the salons.

State-of-the-art exercise equipment, jogging tracks, and basic fitness classes are available at no charge. There's a nominal fee for personal training, body composition analysis, and specialized classes such as yoga and Pilates.

Your Shipmates

NCL's mostly American cruise passengers are active couples ranging from their mid-30s to mid-50s. Many families enjoy cruising on NCL ships during holidays and summer months. Longer cruises and more exotic itineraries attract passengers in the over-55 age group.

Dress Code

Resort casual attire is appropriate at all times; however, the option of one formal evening is available on all cruises of seven nights and longer. Most passengers actually raise the casual dress code a notch to what could be called casual chic attire.

Junior Cruisers

For children and teens, each NCL vessel offers Kid's Crew program of supervised entertainment for young cruisers ages 2 to 17. Younger children are split into three groups, ages 2 to 5, 6 to 9, and 10 to 12; activities range from storytelling, games, and arts and crafts to dinner with counselors, pajama parties, and treasure hunts.

Evening group "Port Play" is available in the children's area to accommodate parents booked on shore excursions. Babysitting services are available for a fee. Parents whose children are not toilet trained are issued a beeper to alert them when diaper changing is necessary. Children under age two cruise free with their parents, and there's no minimum age for infants.

For teens age 13 to 17, options include sports, pool parties, teen disco, movies, and video games. Some ships

CHOOSE A CRUISE ON NORWEGIAN CRUISE LINE IF...

❶ Doing your own thing is your idea of a real vacation. You could almost remove your watch and just go with the flow.

❷ You want to leave your formal dress-up wardrobe at home.

❸ You're competitive. There's always a pick-up game in progress on the sports courts.

2

have their own cool clubs where teens hang out in adult-free zones.

Service

Somewhat inconsistent, service is nonetheless congenial. Although crew members tended to be outgoing Caribbean islanders in the past, they have largely been replaced by Asians who are well-trained, yet are inclined to be more reserved.

Tipping

A fixed service charge of $10 per person, per day is added to shipboard accounts. For children ages 3 to 12, a $5 per-person, per-day charge is added; there's no charge for children under age three. An automatic 15% gratuity is added to bar tabs. Staff members are encouraged to go the extra mile for passengers and are permitted to accept cash gratuities. Passengers in suites who have access to concierge and butler services are asked to offer a cash gratuity at their own discretion.

Past Passengers

Upon completion of your first NCL cruise you're automatically enrolled in Latitudes, the club for repeat passengers. Membership benefits accrue based on the number of cruises completed: Bronze (1–4); Silver (5–8); Gold (9–13); and Platinum (14 or more). Everyone receives "Latitudes," NCL's quarterly magazine, Latitudes pricing, Latitudes check-in at the pier, a ship pin, access to a special customer service desk and liaison on board, and a members-only cocktail party hosted by the captain. Higher tiers receive a welcome basket, an invitation to the captain's cocktail party and dinner in Le Bistro, and priority for check-in, tender tickets, and disembarkation.

Good to Know

When considering an NCL cruise, keep in mind that the ships weren't cut from a cookie-cutter mold, and they differ widely in size and detail. Although all are brightly appointed and attempt to offer a comparable experience, the older ships just don't have the panache or the numerous Freestyle dining selections found on the newer, purpose-built ships. On the plus side, the newest vessels have many options for families, including large numbers of interconnecting staterooms that make them ideal for even super-size clans. By 2009 NCL will have one of the newest fleets at sea following the introduction of two large, new vessels; older midsize ships are being transferred to parent Star Cruises in Asia.

DON'T CHOOSE A CRUISE ON NORWEGIAN CRUISE LINE IF...

1 You don't like to pay extra for food on a ship. The best specialty restaurants have extra charges.

2 You don't want to stand in line. There are lines for nearly everything.

3 You don't want to hear announcements. They're frequent on these ships—and loud.

JEWEL CLASS

Norwegian Jewel, Norwegian Jade, Norwegian Pearl, Norwegian Gem

Public Areas & Facilities

Jewel-Class ships are the next step in the continuing evolution of Freestyle ship design: the interior location of some public rooms and restaurants has been tweaked since the introduction of "Freestyle" cruising vessels, and new categories of deluxe accommodations have been added.

These ships have more than a dozen dining options, a variety of entertainment options, enormous spas with thermal suites (for which there is a charge), and expansive areas reserved for children and teens. Pools have water slides and a plethora of lounge chairs, although when your ship is full it can be difficult to find one in a prime location. *Norwegian Pearl* and *Norwegian Gem* introduced the line's first rock-climbing walls as well as Bliss Lounge, which has trendy South Beach decor and the first full-size 10-pin bowling alleys on modern cruise ships.

2005/2006/2006/2007	ENTERED SERVICE
2,376/2,466/2,394/2,394	PASSENGER CAPACITY
700 ft. **1,154**	CREW MEMBERS
1,188/1,233/1,197/1,197	NUMBER OF CABINS
500 ft. **92,100/93,500/93,530/93,530**	GROSS TONS
965 feet	LENGTH
300 ft. **106/106/125/125 feet**	WIDTH

Statistics for Norwegian Jewel are offered first, followed by those for Norwegian Jade, Pearl, and Gem.

WOW Factor

From the moment you step aboard, you begin to feel a special ambience. The bright colors and fun surroundings set just the right tone for casual cruising.

Top: *Norwegian Jewel's* Azura restaurant
Bottom: Hydropool in the spa

Restaurants

Continental and specialty dining is offered in a dozen dining rooms and ethnic restaurants with open seating and flexible hours. Main dining rooms are complimentary, but most of the specialty restaurants, including NCL's signature Le Bistro, carry a cover charge and require reservations. The Italian restaurant is still complimentary. Casual choices are the Lido Buffet, Blue Lagoon, and poolside grill.

What Works & What Doesn't

The thermal suites in the spa have large whirlpools, saunas, steam rooms, and a relaxation area with loungers facing the sea. While there is an additional charge to use the facility, you can purchase a cruise-long pass for a discount off the daily charge. Freestyle dining doesn't mean you can get a table in the main dining rooms at precisely the moment you want; however, waiting times can be reduced if you time your arrival at nonpeak periods. Screens located throughout the ship estimate the waiting time you can expect for each restaurant.

Accommodations

Layout: NCL ships are not noted for large staterooms, but all have a small sitting area with sofa, chair, and table. Every cabin has adequate closet and drawer-shelf storage, as well as limited bathroom storage. Suites have walk-in closets.

Amenities: A small refrigerator, tea/coffeemaker, personal safe, Ethernet connection, duvets on beds, a wall-mounted hair dryer, and bathrobes are standard. Bathrooms have a shampoo/bath gel dispenser on the shower wall and a magnifying mirror. Suites have whirlpool tubs, entertainment centers with CD/DVD players, and concierge and butler service.

Garden & Courtyard Villas: Garden Villas, with three bedrooms, a living-dining room, and private deck garden with a spa tub, are among the largest suites at sea. Courtyard Villas—not as large as Garden Villas—nevertheless have an exclusive concierge lounge and a shared private courtyard with pool, hot tub, sundeck, and small gym.

Good to Know: Some staterooms interconnect in most categories. Twenty-seven staterooms are wheelchair accessible.w

Cabin Type	Size (sq. ft.)
Garden Villa/Courtyard Villa	4,390/574
Owner's Suites	823–928*
Penthouse Suite/Minisuite	575/284
Ocean View with Balcony	205–243
Ocean View/Inside	161/143

*Deluxe Owner's Suites on *Norwegian Pearl* and *Norwegian Gem* only.

Fast Facts

2

NORWEGIAN CRUISE LINE

- 15 passenger decks
- 7 restaurants, 2 dining rooms, buffet, ice-cream parlor, pizzeria
- In-cabin broadband, Wi-Fi, in-cabin safes, in-cabin refrigerators, some in-cabin DVDs
- 2 pools, children's pool
- Fitness classes, gym, hair salon, 6 hot tubs, spa, steam room
- 9 bars, casino, cinema, dance club, library, showroom, video game room
- Children's programs (ages 2–17)
- Dry cleaning, laundry facilities, laundry service
- Computer room

In the Know

You may feel you've slipped into wonderland when you first encounter some of the fanciful furniture in the lounges aboard each ship and in Bliss Ultra Lounge on Norwegian Pearl *and* Norwegian Gem. *Some are covered in wildly colorful velvets and are designed as thrones and even lounging beds.*

Favorites

Best Place to Escape the Crowds: Try the ship's tranquil library, which is also a good spot to gaze at the sea if your book proves to be less than compelling.

Best Splurge: Courtyard Villas, which are smaller than the pricier Garden Villas, are a good bet for all the privacy and creature comforts you might crave. With access to the courtyard's pool, hot tub, steam room, exercise area, and private sun deck, it's like a ship within a ship.

Our Favorite Spot for a Nightcap: The dimly lighted Star Bar overlooking the pool reminds us of a favorite piano bar with its comfortable seating and sophisticated atmosphere.

Best Split-Your-Sides Show: Performances by Second City, Chicago's famous improvisation artists are scheduled in the theater as well as in more intimate nightclub settings. Passengers can even get a behind-the-scenes look at the shows during an improv workshop.

Best Beer Bar: Try Maltings for the most comprehensive beer (and whiskey) menu at sea.

The sports deck

OCEANIA CRUISES

This distinctive cruise line was founded by Frank Del Rio and Joe Watters, cruise-industry veterans with the know-how to satisfy the wants of inquisitive passengers. By offering itineraries to interesting ports of call and upscale touches— all for fares much lower than you would expect—they are succeed-

Oceana's *Regatta*

ing quite nicely. Oceania Cruises set sail in 2003 to carve a unique, almost boutique niche in the cruise industry by obtaining midsize R-class ships that formerly made up the popular Renaissance Cruises fleet. The line is now owned by Apollo Management, a private equity company.

OCEANIA CRUISES
8120 N.W. 53rd Street,
Suite 100
Miami, FL 33166
305/514-2300 or
800/531-5658
www.oceaniacruises.com

Cruise Style: Premium

Intimate and cozy public spaces reflect the importance of socializing on Oceania ships. Indoor lounges feature numerous conversation areas, and even the pool deck is a social center. The Patio is a shaded slice of deck adjacent to the pool and hot tubs. Defined by billowing drapes and carpeting underfoot, it is furnished with plush sofas and chairs ideal for relaxation. Evening entertainment leans toward light cabaret, solo artists, music for danc-ing, and conversation with fellow passengers; however, you'll find lively karaoke sessions on the schedule as well. The sophisticated, adult atmosphere on days at sea is enhanced by a combo performing jazz or easy-listening melodies poolside.

While thickly padded single and double loungers are arranged around the pool, if more privacy appeals to you, eight private cabanas are available for rent on Deck 11. Each one has a double chaise longue with a view of the sea; overhead drapery can be drawn back for sunbathing, and the side panels can be left open or closed. Waiters are on standby to offer chilled towels or serve occupants with beverages or snacks. In port, this luxury will set you back $50, but at sea it is $100 per day. In addition, you can request a spa service in your cabana.

Varied, destination-rich itineraries are an important characteristic of Oceania Cruises, and most sailings are in the 10- to 12-night range. Before arrival in ports of call, lectures are presented on the historical background, culture, and traditions of the islands.

Culinary demonstrations by guest presenters and Oceania's own executive chefs are extremely popular. Lectures on varied topics, computer courses, hands-on arts and crafts classes, and wine or champagne seminars round out the popular enrichment series on board.

Food

Several top cruise-industry chefs were lured away from other cruise lines to ensure that the artistry of world-renowned master chef Jacques Pépin, who crafted five-star menus for Oceania, is properly carried out. The results are sure to please the most discriminating palate. Oceania simply serves some of the best food at sea, particularly impressive for a cruise line that charges far less than luxury rates. The main restaurant offers trendy, French-Continental cuisine with an always-on-the-menu steak, seafood, or poultry choice and vegetarian option.

Intimate specialty restaurants require reservations, but there's no additional charge for Toscana, the Italian restaurant, or Polo Grill, the steak house. A fourth dinner option is Tapas on the Terrace, alfresco dining at the Terrace Café (the daytime Lido deck buffet). Although service is from the buffet, outdoor seating on the aft deck is transformed into a charming Spanish courtyard with Catalonian-style candleholders and starched linens.

The Terrace Café also serves breakfast and lunch buffet-style and has a small pizzeria window that operates during the day. At an outdoor poolside grill you can order up burgers, hot dogs, and sandwiches for lunch and then take a seat; waiters are at hand to serve you either at a nearby table or your lounge chair by the pool. Afternoon tea is a decadent spread of finger foods and includes a rolling dessert cart, which has to be seen to be believed.

Fitness & Recreation

Although small, the spa, salon, and well-equipped fitness center are adequate for the number of passengers on board. In addition to individual body-toning machines and complimentary exercise classes, there's a walking-jogging track circling the top of the ship. A personal trainer is available for individual instruction for an additional charge. The spa menu lists massages, body wraps, and facials, while a full range of hair and beauty services are available for women and men in the salon. Just forward of the locker rooms you can find a large therapy pool and

Noteworthy

■ The Oceania signature Tranquility Bed has a firm mattress, 350-thread count linens, goose-down pillows, and a silk-cut duvet.

■ Instead of on easels cluttering passageways, artworks for auction are displayed on stairwell landings and in lounges.

■ Pool decks are outfitted with attractive wood tables and chairs, market umbrellas, and couples lounge chairs with cushy pads and colorful bolsters.

Top: Penthouse suite
Bottom: Toscana Restaurant

Top: Cocktails before dinner
Middle: Veranda stateroom
Bottom: Martini's Lounge

quiet deck for relaxation and sunning on padded wooden steamer chaises. Locker rooms contain good-size steam rooms and rain showers, but no saunas.

Your Shipmates

Oceania Cruises appeal to singles and couples from their late-30s to well-traveled retirees, who have the time for and prefer longer cruises. Most are American couples attracted to the casually sophisticated atmosphere, creative cuisine, and high level of service. Many are past passengers of the now-defunct Renaissance Cruises who are loyal to their favorite ships, which now offer a variety of destination-rich itineraries.

Dress Code

Leave the formal wear at home—attire on Oceania ships is country-club casual every evening, although some guests can't help dressing up to dine in the beautifully appointed restaurants. A jacket and tie are never required for dinner, but many men wear sport jackets, as they would to dine in an upscale restaurant ashore. Jeans, shorts, T-shirts, and tennis shoes are discouraged after 6 PM in public rooms.

Junior Cruisers

Oceania Cruises are adult-oriented and not a good choice for families, particularly those traveling with infants and toddlers. No dedicated children's facilities are available, and parents are completely responsible for the behavior and entertainment. Teenagers with sophisticated tastes (and who don't mind the absence of a video arcade) might enjoy the intriguing ports of call.

Service

Highly personalized service by a mostly European staff is crisp and efficient without being intrusive. Butlers are on hand to fulfill the requests of suite guests and will even assist with packing and unpacking when asked.

Tipping

Gratuities of $11.50 per person, per day are added to shipboard accounts for distribution to stewards and waitstaff; an additional $3.50 per person, per day is added for occupants of suites with butler service. Passengers may adjust the amount based on the level of service experi-

CHOOSE A CRUISE ON OCEANA CRUISES IF...

1 Socializing plays a more important role in your lifestyle than boogying the night away.

2 You love to read. These ships have extensive libraries that are ideal for curling up with a good book.

3 You have a bad back. You're sure to love the Tranquility Beds.

enced. An automatic 18% gratuity is added to all bar tabs for bartenders and drink servers.

Past Passengers

After you take one Oceania cruise, you'll receive several benefits along with a free subscription to *The Oceania Club Journal*. Shipboard Club parties hosted by the captain and senior officers, complimentary amenities or exclusive privileges on select sailings, an Oceania Club membership recognition pin after 5, 10, 15, and 20 cruises, and special pricing and mailings about upcoming promotions are some of the benefits. Members further qualify for elite-level status based on the number of sailings aboard Oceania Cruises. Starting with your fifth cruise, you begin to accrue more valuable benefits on every cruise you take, beginning with a $200 shipboard credit per stateroom on cruises five through nine. On your 10th cruise, you will receive a $400 shipboard credit per stateroom plus complimentary gratuities on cruises 10 through 14. Once you take your 20th cruise, you get a free cruise as well as complimentary spa treatments, shore excursions, and gratuities on all future cruises.

Good to Know

When these ships were operated by Renaissance, they were entirely smoke-free, and many people booked cruises because of that. Now, two very small areas are set aside for smokers, one near the pool bar and the other set in a portside corner of the Horizons Lounge. Staterooms and balconies continue to be no-smoking zones, and if you light up in either spot, you could find yourself put ashore in the next port.

2

OCEANIA CRUISES

DON'T CHOOSE A CRUISE ON OCEANIA CRUISES IF...

1 You like the action in a huge casino. Oceania casinos are small, and seats at a poker table can be difficult to get.

2 You won't take a cruise without your children. Most passengers book with Oceania anticipating a kid-free atmosphere.

3 Glitzy production shows are your thing. Oceania's showrooms are decidedly low-key.

REGATTA, INSIGNIA, NAUTICA

	1998, 1998, 2000 ENTERED SERVICE
	684 (824 max) PASSENGER CAPACITY
700 ft.	**400** CREW MEMBERS
	342 NUMBER OF CABINS
500 ft.	**30,200** GROSS TONS
	594 feet LENGTH
300 ft.	**84 feet** WIDTH

Public Areas & Facilities

Carefully furnished to impart the atmosphere of a private English country manor, these mid-size ships are casual yet elegant, with sweeping central staircases and abundant flower arrangements. Brocade and toile fabrics cover the windows, overstuffed sofas, and wing chairs to create a feeling throughout that is warm and intimate. The entire effect is that of a weekend retreat in the English countryside.

Authentic-looking faux fireplaces are inviting elements adjacent to cozy seating areas in the Grand Bar, near the Martini Bar's grand piano, and in the beautiful libraries—some of the best at sea with an enormous selection of best sellers, nonfiction, and travel books. The casinos are quite small and can feel cramped, nor do they allow smoking. There might be a wait for a seat at a poker table; however, there are enough slot machines to go around.

Other than decorative trompe l'oeil paintings in several public areas, the artwork is ordinary.

WOW Factor

Everyone has to have a photograph taken on the lobby staircase—it's practically a twin of the one in the movie Titanic.

Restaurants

Oceania passengers enjoy the flexibility of four open-seating restaurants: the Grand Dining Room; Toscana and Polo Grill, the reservations-required alternative restaurants; and Terraces, the buffet restaurant, which transforms into Tapas after dark for a relaxed atmosphere and alfresco dining. All dining venues have nearby bars, and there's no additional cover charge.

Top: Teatime in Horizons
Bottom: Breakfast in bed

What Works & What Doesn't

A relaxed, social atmosphere pervades all areas on board, particularly during sea days. Passengers mix easily and create their own entertainment, depending very little on organized activities.

Shipboard charges can add up fast since drink prices and even Internet services are above the average charged by most cruise lines. The one miniuscule self-serve laundry room can get steamy, particularly when there's a wait for the machines. The absence of a sauna in the spa is an unfortunate oversight, although you'll be happy to find a rain shower and nifty tiled steam room in the changing areas.

Accommodations

Layout: Private balconies outfitted with chairs and tables add additional living space to nearly 75% of all outside accommodations. All cabins have a vanity-desk and a sitting area with sofa, chair, and table. Every cabin has generous closet and drawer-shelf storage and bathroom shelves. Owner's and Vista suites have a separate living-dining room as well as a separate powder room.

Amenities: Dark-wood cabinetry, soothing blue decor, mirrored accents, personal safe, Tranquility Beds, 350-thread-count linens, goose-down pillows, silk-cut duvets are typical stateroom features. Bathrooms have a hair dryer, shampoo, lotion, and bath gel, plus robes.

Suites: Owner's and Vista Suites have an entertainment center with a DVD and CD player, a small refrigerator, and a second TV in the bedroom; the main bathroom has a combination shower-whirlpool tub. Penthouse suites also have refrigerators and bathtubs. Butlers are on hand to coordinate reservations and serve evening canapés and dinner ordered from any of the ship's restaurants.

Good to Know: Several cabins accommodate third and fourth passengers, but few have connecting doors. Three staterooms are designed for wheelchair accessibility.

Cabin Type	Size (sq. ft.)
Owner's/Vista Suite	962/786
Penthouse Suite	322
Concierge Ocean View	216
Deluxe/Standard Ocean View	165/150–165
Inside	160

Fast Facts

- 9 passenger decks
- 2 specialty restaurants, dining room, buffet, pizzeria
- In-cabin broadband, Wi-Fi, in-cabin safes, some in-cabin refrigerators, some in-cabin DVDs
- Pool
- Fitness classes, gym, hair salon, 3 hot tubs, spa, steam room
- 4 bars, casino, dance club, library, showroom
- Dry cleaning, laundry facilities, laundry service
- Computer room
- No-smoking cabins

In the Know

Don't plot to take the divine linens home with you—it's been tried with embarrassing consequences. Take heart, though. You can purchase the luxurious sheets, pillow slips, and duvet covers on the cruise line's Web site, and the prices are reasonable.

Favorites

Best Place to Get Away From It All: Passengers don't always discover the teak deck just forward of the spa and fitness center. Padded wood steamer chairs surrounding a large saltwater therapy pool are the ideal spot to sunbathe and watch the ship's bow slice through the water.

Best Dessert: Choose anything chocolate from the dessert cart at teatime.

Our Favorite Spot for a Nightcap: Despite its location adjacent to the casino, Martini's feels more like a living room with its cushy seating and fireplace. With a pianist playing softly in the background, you'll be disturbed only if some lucky player hits a jackpot.

Best Splurge: Certain staterooms on decks 7 and 8 receive an extra level of service and amenities, such as chilled champagne on embarkation, an in-cabin refrigerator, 20-inch TV, DVD player, cashmere throw, plush robes and slippers, a complimentary tote bag, and updated bathroom amenities.

Regatta at sea

OCEAN VILLAGE

This small division of the Carnival Corporation is just about as hip as a cruise line can get and still be considered a cruise line. Headquartered and marketed in the U.K., the line's motto promises to be "the cruise for people who don't do cruises." Quite simply, Ocean Village cruises are flexible and

An Ocean Village fleet rendezvous

relatively unstructured, although the company does follow the typical British holiday scheme of being a total package deal (including airfare to the port of embarkation), if that's what you desire.

OCEAN VILLAGE
Richmond House,
Terminus Terrace
Southampton, UK SO14 3PN
0845/358-5000
www.oceanvillageholidays.
co.uk
Cruise Style: Mainstream

While the two vessels in the current Ocean Village fleet aren't brand-new, they have been extensively refurbished and have many of the amenities typical of much newer ships. They're also very family-friendly, with many supervised activities for children and teens. Upbeat and trendy, Ocean Village places stress on informal island-hopping and itineraries that include sunny, beach-centric destinations along with major city ports of call. Most cruises range in length from one to three weeks.

Food

Dining is buffet-style for the most part, and dishes lean heavily toward British favorites with a sprinkling of Mediterranean- and Asian-influenced items for variety. Vegetarian options can also be found. Alternative dining spots with waiter service include menus inspired by British celeb-

CHOOSE A CRUISE ON OCEAN VILLAGE IF...

❶ An unconventional cruise appeals to your inner nonconformist.

❷ You need evening childcare—babysitting is complimentary from 6 PM until midnight and available.

❸ You're most comfortable with knowing everything is taken care of for you in an entire package vacation–both cruise and airfare.

rity chef James Martin; these restaurants carry an extra charge. A popular children's tea is served every afternoon, and baby food can be provided upon advance request. There is a charge for items ordered from room service, but every cabin has its own tea- and coffeemaker.

Fitness & Recreation

Each ship has swimming pools, a well-equipped gym, exercise classes—some complimentary, others for a small fee—as well as deck spaces designated for joggers. Spas offer a typical menu of massages, facials, and exotic treatments. There is a fee for the use of saunas and steam rooms. Mountain bikes can be rented for trips ashore. In a unique twist on activities, you can learn to juggle or fly on a trapeze in circus workshops.

Your Shipmates

Ocean Village cruises draw mostly active British singles and couples from their 30s to 50s, Many consider themselves unconventional in a don't-tell-us-what-we-want-to-do manner. This relaxed style of cruising is ideal for families of all ages and particularly for multigenerational family groups.

Dress Code

Quite simply, the only requirement is that you wear something. Ocean Village cruises are very casual, and there is never a need for formal attire, although you are free to dress up if you choose. Most passengers opt for the ultra-casual route unless they are celebrating a special occasion by dining in an alternative restaurant. In that case, they might ramp up their attire a notch.

Service

Service is friendly and accommodating, adequate but not overwhelming.

Tipping

Basic gratuities are included in the fare, but additional tips are cheerfully accepted if a crew member performs a special service for you. There are no suggested tipping guidelines.

Noteworthy

■ To offer peace of mind for parents, children's play areas are netted for safety, as are private balconies.

■ With buffet dining offered around the clock, no set meal times, no dress code, and no assigned tables, you can tailor your cruise vacation to your preferred schedule, not someone else's.

■ When you book online, Ocean Village offers a savings of 5% in addition to the best possible discounted fare.

Top: Catamaran excursion
Bottom: Balcony stateroom

DON'T CHOOSE A CRUISE ON OCEAN VILLAGE IF...

❶ Dining mostly at buffets leaves you cold. There is an extra charge for sit-down restaurants with waiter service.

❷ You are extremely traditional and look forward to dressing to the nines for the formal events usually associated with a cruise.

❸ You are class-conscious. Ocean Village cruises are definitely British, but very trendy in style.

OCEAN VILLAGE ONE

History

The line's namesake ship was originally designed to be Sitmar's *Fair Majesty* but became *Star Princess* when Princess Cruise Line acquired Sitmar. Before joining Ocean Village in 2003, it was redesigned to appeal to the young, trendy British market, which tends to be a bit nonconventional. Interiors are bright and cheerful, and there's no stuffiness in the decor of the public spaces or the cabins. The pool area is particularly interesting, with structures devoted to contemporary circus performances.

700 ft.	**1987** ENTERED SERVICE
	1,578 (1,856 max) PASSENGER CAPACITY
	574 CREW MEMBERS
500 ft.	**801** NUMBER OF CABINS
	63,500 GROSS TONS
	811 feet LENGTH
300 ft.	**105 feet** WIDTH

Restaurants

Two buffet restaurants serve breakfast, lunch, and dinner, and one is open 24 hours. A poolside restaurant serves lunch by day and morphs into a reservations-required, extra-charge specialty restaurant for dinner. The Bistro is an extra-charge, reservations-required restaurant with menus conceived by celebrity chef James Martin. Afternoon tea, including children's tea, is served daily.

Accommodations

Bright and cheerful, all cabins have plenty of closet and drawer storage, plus a vanity–writing desk, personal safe, small refrigerator, tea- and coffeemaker, hair dryer, and a sitting area with either a sofa or easy chair. Suites and upper-category cabins have balconies. Every suite also has a walk-in closet, trouser press, iron and ironing board, and combination shower-bathtub. Eight cabins are wheelchair-accessible. Check the deck plan carefully before booking—cabin views in category II on C Deck are blocked by safety equipment.

Cabin Size (in sq. ft.): Suite 328–372; balcony cabin 228; outside and inside cabin 146–188.

Top: *Ocean Village One*
Bottom: Cycling in the surf

In the Know

Some staterooms (including categories II on C Deck and NN insides on D Deck) have twin beds that don't convert to a single larger bed. While there's a gym adjacent to the spa, a somewhat quirky area with more fitness equipment is also located alongside the observation lounge and functions as a late-night disco.

Fast Facts

- 11 passenger decks
- 4 restaurants
- Safes, refrigerators, 3 pools, gym, spa, casino, children's programs (ages 2–17), laundry service, laundry facilities, computer room

OCEAN VILLAGE TWO

	1990
	ENTERED SERVICE
	1,708 (1,912 max)
	PASSENGER CAPACITY
700 ft.	**619**
	CREW MEMBERS
	832
	NUMBER OF CABINS
500 ft.	**70,000**
	GROSS TONS
	804 feet
	LENGTH
300 ft.	**105 feet**
	WIDTH

History

Famed—and controversial—Italian architect Renzo Piano designed this ship for Princess Cruises. Christened *Crown Princess*, she was the flagship of the Princess fleet and one of the largest cruise ships in 1990. She was rechristened *Ocean Village Two* in 2006 after spending a stint with a German cruise line as the *AIDAblu*. Her unusual profile is capped by a dome forward on the top deck; originally a massive casino and entertainment complex, it now houses a spa, fitness center, and teen center.

Restaurants

Two buffet restaurants serve breakfast, lunch, and dinner; one buffet is open 24 hours. A poolside restaurant serves lunch by day and is transformed into a reservations-required, extra-charge specialty restaurant for dinner. For special nights out, the Bistro is an extra-charge, reservations-required restaurant with menus conceived by celebrity chef James Martin. Afternoon tea is served daily. There is a charge for room service.

Accommodations

Each relatively spacious cabin has plenty of closet and drawer storage, a vanity/writing desk, personal safe, small refrigerator, tea- and coffeemaker, walk-in closet, hair dryer, and a small sitting area with a sofa or easy chair. In addition, suites and upper-category cabins have balconies, which increase personal space with outdoor chairs and a table and fresh ocean air. Suites also feature a combination shower-bathtub. Numerous cabins are family-friendly, with third and fourth berths. Ten cabins are wheelchair-accessible.

Cabin Size (in sq. ft.): Suite 375; balcony cabin 180–187; standard outside and inside cabin 150–187.

Top: *Ocean Village Two*
Bottom: Sauna with a sea view

In the Know

Don't assume all balconies are created equal. Deck 10 balconies are solid steel beneath the railing, which obstructs views and makes them stuffy when the ship isn't moving. Was that Rod Stewart, Neil Diamond, Madonna, Lionel Richie, or Elton John that you saw? Not exactly. Tribute acts are some of the most popular performances on board *Ocean Village Two* cruises.

Fast Facts

- 11 passenger decks
- 4 restaurants
- Safes, refrigerators, 3 pools, gym, spa, casino, children's programs (ages 2–17), laundry service, laundry facilities, computer room

P&O CRUISES

P&O Cruises (originally the Peninsular & Oriental Steam Navigation Company), boasts an illustrious history in passenger shipping since 1837. While the company's suggestion that they invented cruising may not be entirely accurate, P&O is assuredly a pioneer of modern cruising. Having set aside such

Oceana in Portfino

throwbacks as passenger classes, the company acquired Princess Cruises in 1974. P&O then purchased Sitmar Cruises and merged it with Princess in 1988, and the passenger-cruise business—known as P&O Princess—was spun off in 2000.

P&O CRUISES
Richmond House,
Terminus Terrace
Southampton, UK SO15 3BF
0845/678-0014
www.pocruises.com

Cruise Style: Mainstream

P&O Cruises remains Britain's leading cruise line, sailing the U.K.'s largest and most modern fleet. The ships are equipped with every modern facility you could think of, from swimming pools to stylish restaurants, spas, bars, casinos, theaters, and showrooms. An abundance of balcony and outside cabins ensures that a view to the sea is never far away. P&O ships, with accommodation from inside cabins to lavish suites, cater to a wide cross-section of budgets and tastes.

To offer passengers a variety of choices, P&O has adapted their fleet to match their preferences. While most of the fleet caters to families as well as couples and singles of all ages, *Arcadia* and *Artemis* are adults-only ships.

CHOOSE A CRUISE ON P&O CRUISES IF...

1 You are British or an aficionado of all things British. The vast majority of P&O passengers hail from the U.K.

2 You like to do things your way—P&O allows more flexible dining options than most other European cruise lines.

3 You like theme cruises: P&O has a wide range of them.

Food

P&O has jumped on the choice bandwagon in dining and offers a somewhat dizzying number of options, although actual menu offerings vary quite a bit across the fleet. Club Dining, with assigned seating, is available on all ships; Select Dining in specialty restaurants requires reservations and carries a small charge; Freedom Dining is an open-seating dinner offered in certain restaurants on *Arcadia* and *Oceana*. Meals are tailored to British tastes, so you will see a lot of curries on the menu. Requests for special diets such as diabetic, fat-free, vegetarian, and gluten-free can be satisfied with advance notice. A children's menu is available, and baby food can be provided upon request. Afternoon tea is served daily. There is a charge for items ordered from room service, but every cabin has tea- and coffeemakers.

Fitness & Recreation

Each ship has a well-equipped gym and exercise classes as well as deck spaces designated for joggers. Deck quoits, an informal shipboard form of ring toss (rope rings are thrown alternately by players at round targets on the deck), is popular with passengers, and areas are set aside for the game.

Your Shipmates

Count on fellow passengers to be predominantly British singles, couples, and families, although you may find Scandinavians, Americans, and Australians aboard for some sailings. *Arcadia* and *Artemis* are all-adult ships, and passengers must be 18 or older to sail aboard them.

Dress Code

Daytime attire is appropriately casual; evening wear falls into three traditional categories: formal, informal, and smart casual. Both formal and informal generally require men to wear a jacket to dinner.

Service

You should expect friendly, yet proper, service throughout the fleet.

Tipping

The recommended gratuity is £3.75 per passenger (age 12 and older) per day.

Noteworthy

■ P&O ships are up-to-date but still somewhat traditional. Afternoon tea is still an occasion, and passengers dress formally for dinner on designated nights.

■ With both child-friendly and all-adult ships, you'll find a ship that caters to your preference.

■ Tailored to British passengers, P&O cruise holidays combine high standards of service and comfort with attention to detail.

Top: Family fun on *Aurora*
Bottom: Flexible dining on P&O

DON'T CHOOSE A CRUISE ON P&O CRUISES IF...

1 Formality isn't your thing. Passengers generally expect their fellow travelers to adhere to dress codes.

2 You are looking for the latest cruising trends. The fleet is modern, but the experience is more traditional than trendy.

3 You need to bring your laptop to the pool to do some work. There is no Wi-Fi on these ships.

ARCADIA

Public Areas & Facilities

Designed for adults only, *Arcadia* is sophisticated and fresh. Her understated elegance is highlighted by an extensive art collection that showcases modern British artists.

P&O's first new ship in a decade, *Arcadia* was built on Holland America Line's Vista-class platform (indeed, she was destined to be a Holland America Ship until Carnival Corporation aquired P&O in 2003), but the new owners made modifications to suit British tastes. A refined yet lively British Victorian–style pub hosts karaoke, talent shows, dancing, and sports viewing.

Arcadian Rhodes, the extra-charge specialty restaurant, is the creation of Gary Rhodes, one of Britain's most popular contemporary chefs.

700 ft.	**2005** ENTERED SERVICE
	1948 PASSENGER CAPACITY
	880 CREW MEMBERS
	998 NUMBER OF CABINS
500 ft.	**83,000 tons** GROSS TONS
	936 feet LENGTH
300 ft.	**105 feet** WIDTH

WOW Factor

We tip our hats to P&O for dedicating a contemporary ship to adults-only cruises, a concept that is almost unheard of in today's family-focused cruise industry.

Restaurants

In the main dining room, breakfast and lunch are open seating; dinner two assigned seatings. Two specialty restaurants serve dinner nightly and lunch on sea days (reservations only, extra charge). The buffet restaurant is open 24 hours a day; an outdoor grill is another option for lunches and light snacks. Outdoor barbeques are offered on certain days. There is a charge for room service.

What Works & What Doesn't

There's plenty of sunning and swimming space outside and a lavish spa, which has a large thalassotherapy pool and thermal suite as well as gently heated loungers facing floor-to-ceiling windows.

It wouldn't be a British ship without a pub, which isn't too authentic, but nevertheless serves up favorite ales and bitters. Other interiors are a mix of contemporary and traditional style—a library with writing desks, cozy bars for evening cocktails, a huge showroom for production shows, a cinema, and the Crow's Nest observation lounge with views forward and to both sides.

Accommodations

Cabins: Accommodations in all categories have adequate storage space in closets and drawers and feature a vanity-desk, flat-screen TV, personal safe, hair dryer, refrigerator, coffee- and tea-maker, and telephone, but standard cabins are slightly smaller than the corresponding categories on the HAL Vista class, the platform on which this ship was based. Outside cabins with balconies and some of the larger standard inside and nonbalcony outside cabins also have a small seating area with a sofa.

Decor: All cabins and suites are tastefully decorated in light woods and pastel tones. Although the colors throughout tend to be somewhat bland, they are soothing retreats. The balconies in suites and mini-suites are generous enough in size to have tables and chairs suitable for dining.

Suites: Minisuites and suites have larger sitting areas and balconies than regular outside cabins. In addition, they have a trouser press, ironing board, DVD player, whirlpool tub, and a separate shower. Full-suite bathrooms feature dual sinks and a dressing area, which is a nice touch. Suite occupants enjoy the added services of a butler.

Other Features: Thirty cabins are wheelchair-accessible.

Cabin Type	Size (sq. ft.)
Suite	516
Minisuite	384
Ocean View with Balcony	254
Ocean View	170
Interior	170

Dimensions for accommodations with balconies include the balcony square footage

Fast Facts

- 11 passenger decks
- 2 specialty restaurants, dining room, buffet
- In-cabin safes, in-cabin refrigerators, some in-cabin DVDs
- 2 pools (1 indoor)
- Fitness classes, gym, hair salon, 5 hot tubs, sauna, spa, steam room
- 14 bars, casino, cinema, dance club, library, showroom
- Dry cleaning, laundry facilities, laundry service
- Computer room
- No kids under 18

In the Know

Feel free to dress to the nines and beyond for formal nights on board. One-upping the competition is a chic and ladylike sport often practiced by very proper British women who aggressively over pack their entire wardrobe for even the shortest cruises.

Romantic stroll at sunset

Favorites

Best Splurge: A lifestyles program features talks on such topics as gardening, interior design, and health, after which in-depth workshops are available for a small fee.

Favorite Place to Escape the Crowds: With our fellow passengers all at least 18 years old, we don't often find the need to get away from it all for peace and quiet, but we like the wraparound promenade deck, where there are plenty of padded chairs to relax with a book or take an afternoon snooze.

Our Favorite Sport for a Nightcap: We like the intimacy of the snug seating areas on either side of the Crow's Nest. Whether port or starboard, we are far enough away to enjoy the music and close enough to reach the dance floor if the mood hits.

Quirkiest Name for a Pub: Despite its name— The Rising Sun— this is a real pub where you can find a lively game of darts and a pint of your preferred brew.

AURORA

History

Aurora is a bit more formal than her fleet mates *Arcadia* and *Oceana* but has superb facilities for children. Adjacent to the playroom and teen center, parents and kids have a dedicated area at the ship's stern with its own pool, hot tub, and table tennis setup. There's even a bar nearby and waiter service for when you're thirsty. Not merely kid stuff, *Aurora* has a lot to like for adults. Interiors are designed in such a way that an open feel prevails, even though public rooms are quite distinct.

700 ft.	**2000** ENTERED SERVICE
	1,870 PASSENGER CAPACITY
	850 CREW MEMBERS
	934 NUMBER OF CABINS
500 ft.	**76,000 tons** GROSS TONS
	886 feet LENGTH
300 ft.	**106 feet** WIDTH

Restaurants

Breakfast and lunch are open seating in two dining rooms; for dinner, two traditional seatings, known as Club Dining, are at assigned tables. Two specialty restaurants require dinner reservations and there is a charge. The buffet restaurant serves breakfast, lunch, and afternoon tea. An outdoor café serves fast-food snacks and pizza; a bistro-style café is open 24 hours. There is a charge for room service.

Accommodations

All accommodations are tastefully decorated and have adequate storage space, a vanity-desk, TV, personal safe, hair dryer, refrigerator, coffee- and tea-maker, and a small seating area. Minisuites and suites have a spacious sitting area, balcony, trouser press and ironing board, VCR player, and whirlpool bathtub. In addition, full suite and penthouse suite bathrooms have dual sinks. Twenty-two cabins are wheelchair-accessible.

Cabin Size (in sq. ft.): Pentouse Suite 937; suite 520; mini-suite 382; balcony cabin 211–246; standard outside or inside 150. Dimensions for cabins with balconies include the balcony square footage.

Top: Family games on *Aurora*
Bottom: An elegant evening out

In the Know

All balconies are not created equal. Balconies for A104 and A105 are completely shaded; A106 and A107 are partially shaded: and C104 and C107 are smaller than suite balconies. The centerpiece of Aurora's impressive four-deck-high atrium is a sculptural Lalique-inspired waterfall.

Fast Facts

- 9 passenger decks
- 4 restaurants
- Safes, refrigerators, 4 pools, gym, spa, casino, kids programs (2–17), laundry facilities, laundry service, computer room

OCEANA

History

Oceana was originally *Ocean Princess* but was transferred to P&O in 2003. While she retains her original layout and fixtures, the decor has been refined to suit the tastes of British passengers. The delicate circular staircase in the four-deck-high atrium seems to float. Easy on the eyes and the senses, indoor decor is pleasant, with intimate spaces creating the illusion of a much smaller ship. Main public rooms are situated on a vertical arrangement on four lower decks, with cabins located forward and aft.

Restaurants

Breakfast and lunch are open seating in two main dining rooms. For dinner, one dining room offers two traditional assigned seatings, while the other has open seating. Two extra-charge specialty restaurants require dinner reservations. The buffet is open 24 hours; an outdoor grill is a lunch option; and a 24-hour café serves breakfast, snacks, and pizza. There is a charge for room service.

2000	ENTERED SERVICE
2,016	PASSENGER CAPACITY
870	CREW MEMBERS
975	NUMBER OF CABINS
77,000 tons	GROSS TONS
857 feet	LENGTH
106 feet	WIDTH

700 ft.

500 ft.

300 ft.

Accommodations

Cabins and suites are tastefully decorated and cozy. All have adequate storage in closets and drawers. Each cabin has a vanity-desk, TV, personal safe, hair dryer, refrigerator, and coffee- and tea-maker. More than 40% of cabins and suites have balconies. Minisuites and suites have a sitting area, balcony, walk-in closet, trouser press, VCR, whirlpool tub, and separate shower. Full-suite bathrooms have two sinks. Thirty cabins are wheelchair-accessible.

Cabin Size (in sq. ft.): Suite 538; minisuites 375; standard balcony 178; standard outside 155; inside 135; dimension for balcony cabins include the balcony square footage.

Top: *Oceana* cruising
Bottom: Freedom dining

In the Know

In a nice twist, the casino is somewhat isolated, and you aren't forced to use it as a passageway to reach dining rooms or the main show lounge. If you love to dance, you'll be pleased to find several proper wooden dance floors and plenty of music on the entertainment schedule.

Fast Facts

- 10 passenger decks
- 4 restaurants
- Safes, refrigerators, 4 pools, gym, spa, casino, kid's programs (2–17), laundry facilities, laundry service, computer room

ORIANA

History

The first contemporary ship to be built specifically for the British market, *Oriana* introduced several features that are shared by her larger fleet mate *Aurora,* including a range of facilities for families with children. Adjacent to the playroom and teen center, parents and kids have a dedicated area with a pool, hot tub, table tennis set. The four-deck-high atrium has an impressive Tiffany glass dome overhead. With no balcony accommodations cluttering her aft decks, *Oriana* has wide-open spaces overlooking her wake.

1995	ENTERED SERVICE
1,822	PASSENGER CAPACITY
800	CREW MEMBERS
914	NUMBER OF CABINS
69,000 tons	GROSS TONS
853 feet	LENGTH
106 feet	WIDTH

700 ft.

500 ft.

300 ft.

Restaurants

Breakfast and lunch are open seating in two dining rooms; dinner is served in two seatings at assigned tables. Two specialty restaurants require dinner reservations and carry a charge. The buffet restaurant serves breakfast, lunch, and afternoon tea; a café near the Lido serves snacks and pizza, while a bistro-style café is open 24 hours. There is a charge for room service.

Accommodations

All cabins have adequate storage space, a vanity-desk, sitting area with small sofa, TV, personal safe, hair dryer, refrigerator, coffee- and tea-maker, and telephone. Minisuites and suites have a spacious sitting area, balcony, a trouser press, ironing board, VCR, and whirlpool tub. Suites also have a walk-in dressing area and guest powder room as well as butler service. Eight cabins are wheelchair accessible.

Cabin Size (in sq. ft.): Suite 497; minisuite 368; balcony cabin 250; standard outside and inside 150; dimensions for balcony cabins include the balcony square footage.

Top: Club Dining in the Oriental Restaurant
Bottom: Lounging on deck

In the Know

In cabins that have them, lower twin beds cannot be made up into a double bed when upper berths are in use. Some single cabins have a reduced supplement (40%–80%). A galley "walkthrough" (a tour for those of us in North America) is usually combined with the popular chocaholic's buffet.

Fast Facts

- 9 passenger decks
- 4 restaurants
- Safes, refrigerators, 4 pools, gym, spa, casino, kid's programs (2–17), laundry facilities, laundry service, computer room

ARTEMIS

History

Artemis was launched as *Royal Princess* in 1984. Her god-mother, Princess Diana, added an air of grace and style during her christening that remains undiminished. The ship was a trail blazer—the first mainstream ship to feature only outside cabins. A sea view is never far from sight; not only do all cabins have a large window or balcony, there are windows in all public spaces. One of the most drastic changes the ship has undergone since joining the P&O fleet is that it is now an adults-only vessel.

Restaurants

Breakfast and lunch are open seating in the main dining room. For dinner, two traditional seatings are at assigned tables, known as Club Dining. A specialty restaurant that requires reservations and assesses a charge serves dinner nightly. The buffet restaurant serves breakfast, lunch, and afternoon tea. There is no casual dinner option, and there is a charge for room service.

1984	ENTERED SERVICE
1,188	PASSENGER CAPACITY
537	CREW MEMBERS
600	NUMBER OF CABINS
45,000	GROSS TONS
755 feet	LENGTH
96 feet	WIDTH

700 ft.

500 ft.

300 ft.

Accommodations

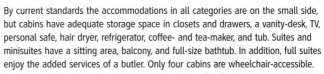

By current standards the accommodations in all categories are on the small side, but cabins have adequate storage space in closets and drawers, a vanity-desk, TV, personal safe, hair dryer, refrigerator, coffee- and tea-maker, and tub. Suites and minisuites have a sitting area, balcony, and full-size bathtub. In addition, full suites enjoy the added services of a butler. Only four cabins are wheelchair-accessible.

Cabin Size (in sq. ft.): Suite 425; outside with balcony 302; twin with balcony 215; standard outside twin 168. Dimension for all balcony cabins include balcony square footage.

Top: Crystal pool
Bottom: Sunset at sea

In the Know

Twin cabins appear more spacious by day when one bed is folded up flat to the wall; it's possible—but awkward—to push the beds together. Lectures, workshops, and classes in the New Horizons series offer the opportunity to expand your knowledge of such topics as history, art, architecture, literature, and classical music.

Fast Facts

- 8 passenger decks
- 2 restuarants
- Safes, refrigerators, 3 pools, gym, spa, casino, no children under age 18, laundry facilities, laundry service, computer room

PRINCESS CRUISES

Princess Cruises may be best known for introducing cruise travel to millions of viewers, when its flagship became the setting for *The Love Boat* television series in 1977. Since that heady time of small-screen stardom, the Princess fleet has grown both in the number and size of ships plying European waters. Although

Splash around in the family pool

most are large in scale, Princess vessels manage to create the illusion of intimacy through the use of color and decor in understated yet lovely public rooms graced by multimillion-dollar art collections.

PRINCESS CRUISES
24305 Town Center Drive
Santa Clarita, CA 91355-4999
661/753-0000 or
800/774-6237
www.princess.com

Cruise Style: Premium

Princess has also become more flexible lately; Personal Choice Cruising offers alternatives for open-seating dining (when you wish and with whom you please) and entertainment options as diverse as those found in resorts ashore.

Welcome additions to Princess's roster of adult activities, which still include standbys like bingo and art auctions, are ScholarShip@Sea enrichment programs featuring guest lecturers, cooking classes, wine-tasting seminars, pottery workshops, and computer and digital photography classes. Nighttime production shows tend toward Broadway-style revues presented in the main show lounge, and performers might include comedians, magicians, jugglers, and acrobats. Live bands play a wide range of musical styles for dancing and listening in smaller lounges throughout the ships and each ship has a disco.

On Pub Night the cruise director's staff leads a rollicking evening of fun with passenger participation. At the conclusion of the second formal night, champagne trickles down over a champagne waterfall, painstakingly created by the arrangement of champagne glasses in a pyramid shape. It's a great photo-op when several women are invited to join the maître d' atop the platform to assist in the pouring.

Lovely chapels or the wide-open decks are equally roman-tic settings for weddings at sea. Princess Cruises explode the myth that just any captain of any ship can marry starry-eyed couples. Legally, ceremonies with the captain officiat-ing can only be performed on certain Grand-class Princess vessels. It's an option not offered by any other cruise.

Food

Personal choices regarding where and what to eat abound, but there's no getting around the fact that Prin-cess ships are large and carry a great many passengers. Unless you opt for traditional assigned seating, you could experience a brief wait for a table in one of the open-seating dining rooms.

Menus are varied and extensive in the main dining rooms, and the results are good to excellent considering how much work is going on in the galleys. Vegetarian and healthy lifestyle options are always on the menu, as well as steak, fish, or chicken. A special menu is designed espe-cially for children.

Alternative restaurants are a staple throughout the fleet, but vary by ship class. Grand-class ships have upscale steak houses and Sabatini's for Italian food; both require reservations and carry an extra cover charge. Sun-class ships offer complimentary sit-down dining in the pizzeria and a similar steak-house option, although it's in a sec-tioned-off area of the buffet restaurant. On *Caribbean, Crown,* and *Emerald Princess,* a casual evening alterna-tive to the dining rooms and usual buffet is Café Caribe—adjacent to the Lido buffet restaurant, it serves cuisine with a Caribbean flair. With a few breaks in service, Lido buffets on all ships are almost always open, and a pizzeria and grill offer casual daytime snack choices. The fleet's patisseries and ice-cream bars charge for specialty coffee, some pastries, and premium ice cream.

An utterly posh dining opportunity for passengers who have balconies and want to celebrate a special occasion is Ultimate Balcony Dining. Breakfast is $30 per couple, dinner $50 per person. A server is on duty throughout the four-course dinner, and a photographer also stops by to capture the romantic evening.

Fitness & Recreation

Spa rituals include a variety of massages, body wraps, and facials; numerous hair and nail services are offeredin the salons. Both the salon and spa are operated by Steiner Leisure, and the menu of spa services includes special pampering treatments designed specifically for men and teens as well as couples.

Noteworthy

■ The traditional gala cham-pagne waterfall on formal night is a not-to-be-missed event.

■ Bathrobes are provided for use during your cruise—all you have to do is ask the room steward to deliver them.

■ Wheelchair-accessible state-rooms with 33-inch wide entry and bathroom doorways, plus bathrooms fitted to ADA stan-dards, are available in an array of categories.

Top: Place a bet in the casino
Bottom: Disco into the night

PRINCESS CRUISES

2

Modern exercise equipment, a jogging track, and basic fitness classes are available at no charge. There's a nominal fee for personal training, body composition analysis, and specialized classes such as yoga and Pilates. Grand-class ships have a resistance pool so you can get your laps in effortlessly.

Your Shipmates

Princess Cruises attract mostly American passengers, ranging from their mid-30s to mid-50s. Families enjoy cruising together on the Princess fleet, particularly during holiday seasons and summer months, when many children are on board. Longer cruises appeal to well-traveled retirees and couples who have the time.

Dress Code

Two formal nights are standard on seven-night cruises; an additional formal night may be scheduled on longer sailings. Men are encouraged to wear tuxedos, but dark suits are appropriate. All other evenings are casual, although jeans are discouraged in restaurants, and it's requested that no shorts be worn in public areas after 6 PM.

Top: Sunset at sea
Middle: Morning stretch
Bottom: Freshwater Jacuzzis

Junior Cruisers

For young passengers ages 3 to 17, each Princess vessel has a playroom, teen center, and programs of supervised activities designed for different age groups: ages 3 to 7, 8 to 12, and 13 to 17. Activities to engage youngsters include arts and crafts, pool games, scavenger hunts, deck parties, backstage and galley tours, games, and videos. Events such as dance parties in their own disco, theme parties, athletic contests, karaoke, pizza parties, and movie fests occupy teenage passengers. With a nod toward science and educational entertainment, children also participate in learning programs focused on the environment and wildlife in areas where the ships sail.

Afford parents independent time ashore, youth centers operate as usual during port days, including lunch with counselors. For a nominal charge, group babysitting is available nightly from 10 PM until 1 AM. Family-friendly conveniences include self-service laundry facilities and two-way family radios that are available for rent at the Purser's Desk. Infants under six months are not permit-

CHOOSE A CRUISE ON PRINCESS CRUISES IF...

1 You're a traveler with a disability. Princess ships are some of the most accessible at sea.

2 You'd like to gamble but hate a smoke-filled casino. Princess casinos are well-ventilated and spacious.

3 You want a balcony. Princess ships feature them in abundance at affordable rates.

ted; private in-cabin babysitting is not available on any Princess vessel. Children under age three are welcome in the playrooms if supervised by a parent.

Service
Professional service by an international staff is efficient and friendly. It's not uncommon to be greeted in passageways by smiling stewards who know your name.

Tipping
A gratuity of $10 per person, per day is added to shipboard accounts for distribution to stewards and waitstaff. Passengers may adjust the amount based on the level of service experienced. An automatic 15% is added to all bar tabs for bartenders and drink servers; gratuities to other staff members may be extended at passengers' discretion.

Past Passengers
Membership in the Captain's Circle is automatic following your first Princess cruise. All members receive a free subscription to *Captain's Circle News*, a quarterly newsletter, as well as discounts on selected cruises.

Perks are determined by the number of cruises completed: Gold (2 through 5), Platinum (6 through 15), and Elite (16 and above). While Gold members only receive the magazine, an invitation to an onboard event, and the services of the Circle Host on the ship, benefits really begin to accrue once you've completed five cruises. Platinum members receive upgraded insurance (when purchasing the standard policy), expedited check-in, a debarkation lounge to wait in on the ship, and, best of all, limited free Internet access during the cruise. Elite benefits are even more lavish, with many complimentary services.

Good to Know
Some people like the time-honored tradition of assigned seating for dinner, so they can get to know their table companions and their servers; others prefer to choose with whom they dine as well as when. Princess lets you have things your way or both ways. If you're unsure whether Personal Choice is for you, select Traditional dining when you reserve your cruise. You can easily make the switch to anytime dining once on board; however, it can be impossible to change from Personal Choice to Traditional.

DON'T CHOOSE A CRUISE ON PRINCESS CRUISES IF...

1 You have a poor sense of direction. The ships, especially the Grand-class ships, are very large.

2 You want to meet *The Love Boat* cast. That was just a TV show, and it was more than three decades ago.

3 You're too impatient to stand in line or wait. Debarkation from these large ships can be a nightmare.

CARIBBEAN, CROWN, EMERALD, RUBY PRINCESS

2004, 2006, 2007, 2008	ENTERED SERVICE
3,100	PASSENGER CAPACITY
1,200	CREW MEMBERS
1,550	NUMBER OF CABINS
113,000	GROSS TONS
951 feet	LENGTH
206 feet	WIDTH

Public Areas & Facilities

With dramatic atriums and Skywalker's Disco (the spoiler hovering 150 feet above the stern), *Caribbean Princess* is a supersize version of the older Grand-class vessels with an extra deck of passenger accommodations.

Not quite identical to *Caribbean Princess, Crown, Emerald,* and *Ruby Princess* have introduced more dining options. Several signature public spaces have been redesigned or relocated on both ships as well—the atrium on *Crown, Emerald,* and *Ruby Princess* resembles an open piazza and sidewalk café; Sabatini's Italian Trattoria is found on a top deck with views on three sides and adjacent space for alfresco dining; and Skywalker's Disco is forward near the funnel (where it's topped with a sports court).

Inside spaces on all three vessels are quietly neutral, with touches of glamour in the sweeping staircases and marble-floor atriums. Surprising intimacy is achieved by the number of public rooms and restaurants that swallow up passengers.

WOW Factor

Visible from afar, the huge screen for Movies Under the Stars proved to be such a WOW that other cruise lines have installed them.

Top: Sailing at sunset
Bottom: Broadway-style revue

Restaurants

Passengers have the choice between two traditional dinner seating times in an assigned dining room or open seating in the ships' other two formal dining rooms. Alternative dinner options include reservations-only Sabatini's and Sterling Steakhouse or Crown Grill (with a supplement), as well as Café Caribe, a Caribbean buffet with linen-dressed tables and limited waiter service.

What Works & What Doesn't

Movies Under the Stars on the huge poolside screen may have seemed like a gimmick, but the clever programming and interactive party atmosphere have proven to be a big hit. Popcorn is free, but other movie snacks aren't. Passengers who opt for Personal Choice dining may encounter a short wait for a table unless they're willing to join other diners. Personal Choice is all about flexibility, and it's no big deal to just go to a different dining room that might not be as busy. *Crown Princess* introduces pub snacks to the trademark Wheelhouse Bar.

Accommodations

Layout: On these ships 80% of the outside staterooms have balconies. The typical stateroom has a sitting area with a chair and table; even the cheapest categories have ample storage. Minisuites have a separate sitting area, walk-in closet, combination shower-tub, and a balcony, as well as two TVs. Grand Suites have a separate sitting room and dining room, as well as a walk-in closet. Owner's, Penthouse, Premium, and Vista suites have a separate sitting room with a sofa bed and desk, as well as a walk-in closet.

Amenities: Decorated in attractive pastel hues, all cabins have refrigerators, hair dryers, a personal safe, and bathrobes to use during the cruise. Bathrooms have shampoo, lotion, and bath gel.

Good to Know: Two family suites are interconnecting staterooms with a balcony that each sleep up to eight people (D105/D101 and D106/D102). State-rooms in a variety of categories will accommodate three and four people, and some adjacent cabins can be interconnected through interior doors or by unlocking doors in the balcony dividers. Twenty-five staterooms are designed for wheelchair accessibility and range in size from 234 to 396 square feet, depending upon the category.

Cabin Type	Size (sq. ft)
Grand Suite	1,279
Other Suites	461–689
Family Suite/Minisuite	607/324
Ocean view Balcony/ Standard Balcony	233–285/ 158–182
Inside	163

All dimensions include the square footage for balconies.

In the Know

These ships are marginally larger than Grand-class with the addition of the extra passenger deck, but do they seem crowded with the extra passengers on board? Not necessarily, although when booked to maximum capacity, lines can form with more frequency than on their smaller fleetmates.

Favorites

Best Place to Escape the Crowds: The terrace overlooking the aft swimming pool is a little-used spot after dark, but bring your own refreshments if you plan to stay a while because the adjacent bar may close early.

Best Dessert: Any soufflé is scrumptious, and a scoop of ice cream on the side is a special treat. Try them all!

Our Favorite Spot for a Nightcap: The dimly lighted Wheelhouse Bar has oversize comfy chairs and a clubby feel.

Best Splurge: Book a suite to get two TVs, a wet bar, and a separate shower and tub (whirlpool tub in Grand Suites). An extended room-service menu is also available for suite passengers, as are priority dining reservations and all the amenities extended to Elite Captain's Circle members.

Best Place to De-Stress: Only on *Crown* and *Emerald Princess*, it's the adults-only Sanctuary, a private, partially shaded deck with posh loungers, waiter service for snacks and drinks, and a small fee to keep capacity down.

Fast Facts

- 15 passenger decks
- 2 specialty restaurants, 3 dining rooms, buffet, ice-cream parlor, pizzeria
- Wi-Fi, in-cabin safes, in-cabin refrigerators
- 4 pools (1 indoor), children's pool
- Fitness classes, gym, hair salon, 7 hot tubs, sauna, spa, steam room
- 9 bars, casino, cinema, 2 dance clubs, library, 2 showrooms, video game room
- Children's programs (ages 3–17)
- Dry cleaning, laundry facilities, laundry service
- Computer room
- No kids under 6 months

Movies Under the Stars

GRAND CLASS
Grand Princess, Golden Princess, Star Princess

Public Areas & Facilities

When *Grand Princess* was introduced as the world's largest cruise ship in 1998, she also boasted one of the most distinctive profiles. Not only did the Skywalker's Disco appear futuristic, hovering approximately 150 feet above the water line, but Grand-class vessels also advanced the idea of floating resort to an entirely new level with more than 700 staterooms that included private balconies.

Like their predecessors, the interiors of Grand-class ships feature soothing pastel tones with splashy glamour in the sweeping staircases and marble-floor atriums. Surprisingly intimate for such large ships, human scale in public lounges is achieved by judicious placement of furniture as unobtrusive room dividers.

The 300-square-foot Times Square–style LED screen that hovers over *Grand Princess*'s Terrace Pool shows up to seven movies or events daily.

	1998, 2001, 2002
	ENTERED SERVICE
	2,600
	PASSENGER CAPACITY
700 ft.	**1,100/1,100/1,200**
	CREW MEMBERS
	1,300
	NUMBER OF CABINS
500 ft.	**109,000**
	GROSS TONS
	951 feet
	LENGTH
300 ft.	**201 feet**
	WIDTH

WOW Factor

When Grand Princess *was introduced in Europe, she was affectionately dubbed the* Shopping Cart *because her stern spoiler reminded Europeans of a grocery cart.*

Top: *Star Princess* at sea
Bottom: Grand-class balcony stateroom

Restaurants

Passengers choose between two traditional dinner seatings in an assigned dining room or open-seating in the ships' other two formal dining rooms. Alternative evening dining options include reserva-tions-only Sabatini's Italian Trattoria and Sterling Steakhouse specialty restaurants (both with a cover charge). The Horizon Court buffet is a casual option.

What Works & What Doesn't

Four pools, each with a distinctive personality, ensure it's nearly always possible to find a sun lounger—either in the midst of the action or a quiet corner. Sports bars get jam-packed and lively when important games are televised; however, they're also the only indoor bars where cigar smoking is allowed and can become stuffy and close. The Wheel-house Bar has a combo for predinner dancing and easy listening during the cocktail hour. There is a charge for frozen treats at the ice-cream bar, but they are still free in the dining room.

Accommodations

Layout: On these ships, 80% of the outside staterooms have balconies. The typical stateroom has a sitting area with a chair and table; even the cheapest categories have ample storage. Minisuites have a separate sitting area, walk-in closet, combination shower-tub, and a balcony, as well as two TVs. Grand Suites have a separate sitting room and dining room, as well as a walk-in closet. Owner's, Penthouse, Premium, and Vista suites have a separate sitting room with a sofa bed and desk, as well as a walk-in closet.

Amenities: Decorated in attractive pastel hues, all cabins have refrigerators, hair dryers, a personal safe, and bathrobes to use during the cruise. Bathrooms have shampoo, lotion, and bath gel.

Good to Know: Two family suites are interconnecting staterooms with a balcony that each sleep up to eight people (D105/D101 and D106/D102).

Staterooms in a variety of categories will accommodate three and four people, and some adjacent cabins can be interconnected through interior doors or by unlocking doors in the balcony dividers. Twenty-eight staterooms are wheelchair-accessible.

Cabin Type	Size (sq. ft.)
Grand Suite	730/1,314*
Other Suites	468–591
Family Suite/Minisuite	607/323
Ocean View Balcony/Standard	232–274/168
Inside	160

All dimensions include the square footage for balconies. *Grand Princess* dimensions followed by *Golden* and *Star Princess*

Fast Facts

- 14 passenger decks
- 2 specialty restaurants, 3 dining rooms, buffet, ice-cream parlor, pizzeria
- Wi-Fi, in-cabin safes, in-cabin refrigerators
- 4 pools (1 indoor), children's pool
- Fitness classes, gym, hair salon, 9 hot tubs, sauna, spa, steam room
- 9 bars, casino, outdoor cinema, 2 dance clubs, library, 2 showrooms, video game room
- Children's programs (ages 3–17)
- Dry cleaning, laundry facilities, laundry service
- Computer room
- No kids under 6 months

In the Know

Port and starboard balconies are stepped out from the ships' hulls in wedding-cake fashion. That means, depending on location, yours will likely be exposed a bit—or a lot—to passengers on higher decks. Exceptions are balconies on Emerald deck, which are covered.

Golden Princess grand plaza atrium

Favorites

Best Place to Escape the Crowds: Skywalker's Disco has comfy semi-private alcoves facing port and starboard and is virtually deserted during the day. It's the ideal spot to read or just watch the sea. The bar isn't open, though, so bring your own refreshments if you plan to stay awhile.

Best Added Value: For a few dollars you can wash and dry a load

of dirty clothing in the convenient self-service passenger laundry rooms. You'll also find irons there to touch up garments wrinkled from packing.

Our Favorite Spot for a Nightcap: The Wheelhouse Bar, with soft lighting, comfortable leather chairs, shining brass accents, ship paintings, and nautical memorabilia, has become a Princess tradition.

Best Balcony Cabins: Nearly famous for the huge size of their balconies are minisuites E728 and E729. Both spaces are great for relaxing and entertaining, but both cabins can be noisy.

SUN CLASS
Sun Princess, Dawn Princess, Sea Princess

	1995, 1997, 1998
	ENTERED SERVICE
	1,950
	PASSENGER CAPACITY
700 ft.	**900**
	CREW MEMBERS
	975
	NUMBER OF CABINS
500 ft.	**77,000**
	GROSS TONS
	856 feet
	LENGTH
300 ft.	**106 feet**
	WIDTH

Public Areas & Facilities

Refined and graceful, Sun-class ships offer the choices attributed to larger Grand-class ships without sacrificing the smaller-ship atmosphere for which they're noted. The four-story atrium with a circular marble floor, stained-glass dome, and magnificent floating staircase are ideal settings for relaxation, people-watching, and making a grand entrance.

Onboard decor is a combination of neutrals and pastels, which is easy on the eyes after a sunny day ashore. The main public rooms are situated in a vertical arrangement on four lower decks and, with the exception of Promenade Deck, cabins are located forward and aft. In a nice design twist, the casino is somewhat isolated, and passengers aren't forced to use it as a passageway to reach dining rooms or the art deco main show lounge.

Sea Princess also has an outdoor Movies Under the Stars LED screen.

WOW Factor

From the marble floor at its base to the stained-glass dome atop the atrium, a delicate circular staircase seems to float higher and higher between decks.

Top: *Sea Princess* at sea
Bottom: Sun-class ocean-view stateroom

Restaurants

Sun-class ships have one dining room with two traditional assigned dinner seatings and one open-seating dining room for Personal Choice cruisers. Alternatives are the reservations-only Sterling

Steakhouse specialty restaurant (a section of the buffet that's dressed up for the evening and for which there's a charge) and the complimentary pizzeria.

What Works & What Doesn't

Horizon Court Lido buffet restaurants occupy one of the most prestigious spots on these ships—far forward, with a true view of the horizon. There's nothing about the interior decor that'll knock your socks off—some areas still have echoes of *The Love Boat* television series sets—but the cool palette enhanced by marble accents showcases impressive original artwork and murals. These are large ships, but not large enough to overcome the invasive nature of regularly scheduled art auctions. Why, oh why, do the auction displays have to intrude on the carefully selected artworks that are chosen to enhance the decor?

Accommodations

Layout: Princess Cruises' trademark is an abundance of staterooms with private balconies, yet even the least expensive inside categories have ample storage and a small sitting area with a chair and table. Suites have two TVs, a separate sitting area, dining-height table with chairs, walk-in closets, double-sink vanities, and a separate shower and whirlpool tub. Minisuites have a separate sitting area, two TVs, walk-in closet, and separate shower and whirlpool tub.

Amenities: Decorated in pastel colors, staterooms typically have mirrored accents, a personal safe, a refrigerator, a hair dryer, and bathrobes for use during the cruise. Bathrooms have shampoo, lotion, and bath gel.

Good to Know: Cabins that sleep third and fourth passengers aren't as numerous as on other Princess ships, and no staterooms have interconnecting interior doors. Adjacent cabins with balconies can be interconnected by unlocking doors in the balcony dividers. Nineteen staterooms are designed for wheelchair accessibility and range in size from 213 to 305 square feet, depending upon category.

Cabin Type	Size (sq. ft.)
Suite	538–695
Minisuite	370–536
Ocean View Balcony/ Deluxe	179/173
Ocean View Standard	135–155
Interior	135–148
All dimensions include the square footage for balconies.	

In the Know

Check and double-check your bed configurations when booking an outside quad cabin for your family. There are balcony cabins with three and four berths, but some have two lower twin-size beds that cannot be pushed together to form a queen.

Favorites

Best Place to Escape the Crowds: You can always escape to the cozy, wood-panel reading room, where each oversize chair faces its own bay window.

Best Dessert: As on other Princess ships, the soufflés can't be beat. It doesn't matter what flavor is on the menu; they're all divine, but chocolate with a warm berry sauce is truly to die for.

Best Splurge: Treat yourself by day to specialty coffees and fresh pastries at the patisserie. In the evening, a flute of bubbly champagne and a caviar snack are indulgent pleasures at the wine and caviar bar.

Our Favorite Spot for a Nightcap: For after-dinner drinks and a late-night rendezvous, the elegant Rendez-Vous Lounge gets our nod.

Best Value: There's no charge to dine at night in the pizzeria, which offers traditional Italian dishes in a trattoria-style setting.

Fast Facts

- 10 passenger decks
- 2 dining rooms, buffet, ice-cream parlor, pizzeria
- Wi-Fi, in-cabin safes, in-cabin refrigerators
- 3 pools (1 indoor), children's pool
- Fitness classes, gym, hair salon, 5 hot tubs, sauna, spa, steam room
- 7 bars, casino, 2 dance clubs, library, 2 showrooms, video game room
- Children's programs (ages 3–17)
- Dry cleaning, laundry facilities, laundry service
- Computer room
- No kids under 6 months

Riviera pool

PACIFIC/TAHITIAN/ ROYAL PRINCESS

Public Areas & Facilities

At 30,277 tons, these ships appear positively tiny beside their megaship fleet mates. In reality, they are medium-size ships that entered service for the now-defunct Renaissance Cruises. With their entry into the Princess line-up, real choice is available to Princess passengers—a true alternative for passengers who prefer the clubby atmosphere of a smaller "boutique"-style ship, yet one that has big-ship features galore.

This trio has cozy public spaces, a stunning observation lounge—where the view is visible through floor-to-ceiling windows on three sides— and the loveliest libraries at sea, with their domed trompe l'oeil–painted ceilings, faux fireplaces, comfortable seating areas, and (most importantly) well-stocked bookshelves. Although the main showroom isn't particularly suited for glitzy production company performances, it is ideal for cabaret shows.

	1999/1999/2001
	ENTERED SERVICE
	670
	PASSENGER CAPACITY
700 ft.	373
	CREW MEMBERS
	335
	NUMBER OF CABINS
500 ft.	30,277
	GROSS TONS
	592 feet
	LENGTH
300 ft.	84 feet
	WIDTH

WOW Factor

The most photographed spot on board is the dramatic grand staircase, reminiscent of those found on transatlantic liners at the height of the Gilded Age.

Top: *Royal Princess*
Bottom: *Pacific Princess*
Grand Lobby

Restaurants

The only disappointment is the lack of a Personal Choice dining room. Breakfast and lunch are open seating; dinner is in two assigned seatings. Sabatini's Italian Trattoria and Sterling Steakhouse specialty restaurants are reservations-required and extra charge dinner alternatives. The Lido buffet and room service are available 24 hours at no charge, and there's a pizzeria and poolside grill.

What Works & What Doesn't

These three ships offer many Princess Cruises' trademark big-ship features, despite the fact they are smaller and were built to another cruise line's specifications. Personal Choice dining is limited, but meals and snacks are available any time day or night. The spa doesn't have saunas, but the steam rooms are spacious, and a nice therapy pool overlooks the ships' bow. Fitness rooms are more than adequate. Lounges have the comfortable intimacy that is so appealing on the largest ships in the fleet. There are even a plethora of private balconies, a signature feature of Princess Cruises.

Accommodations

Layout: Designed for longer cruises, all staterooms have ample closet and storage space, although bathrooms in lower-priced categories are somewhat tight. Dark-wood cabinetry adds warmth to the pastel decor. In keeping with the rest of the fleet, 73% of all outside cabins and suites have a balcony, and interiors are similar in size to those you'll find on other Princess ships.

Amenities: Amenities in standard cabins are a bit spartan compared to other Princess ships, yet all have at least a small sitting area. Bath toiletries, a hair dryer, personal safe, and robes for use during the cruise are all included, but you must move up to a minisuite or suite to have a real bathtub.

Suites: Full suites are particularly nice, with living/dining rooms, entertainment centers, separate bedrooms, whirlpool bathtubs, a guest powder room, and large balconies overlooking the bow or stern.

Good to Know: Five staterooms are wheelchair accessible on *Pacific Princess*, while there are four on *Tahitian* and *Royal Princess*.

Cabin Type	Size (sq. ft.)
Suites	786–962
Minisuites	322
Ocean-View Balcony	216
Ocean View	165
Inside	158

All dimensions include the square footage for balconies.

Fast Facts

- 9 passenger decks
- 2 specialty restaurants, dining room, buffet, pizzeria
- Wi-Fi, in-cabin safes, some in-cabin minibars, some in-cabin refrigerators, in-cabin DVDs
- 1 pool
- Fitness classes, gym, hair salon, 3 hot tubs, spa, steam room
- 8 bars, casino, dance club, library, showroom
- Children's programs (ages 3–17)
- Dry cleaning, laundry facilities, laundry service
- Computer room
- No kids under 6 months

In the Know

The view from forward-facing suites is stupendous, but if you are a late sleeper you might want to check the itinerary for the number of ports where the ship will anchor instead of docking. A wake-up call is unnecessary when the anchor is lowered.

Pacific Princess card room

Favorites

Best Balcony Cabins: Location, location, location: on decks six and seven there are two aft-facing standard balcony cabins sandwiched between suites. They have terrific views of the wake, and the balconies are larger than other similar cabins.

Our Favorite Spot for a Nightcap: We like the selection of cozy antique-style chairs near the faux fireplace in the Casino Bar, where the piano drowns out the clanging of slot machines.

Kid Stuff: There are no dedicated children's facilities on these ships, but when the numbers warrant it, counselors conduct a limited kid's program in a variety of public rooms.

Best Added Value: You might consider it a spa amenity, but there is no charge for the peace and tranquillity you'll find on the private forward deck, where the thalassotherapy pool is located.

Best Splurge: Ultimate Balcony Dining for breakfast or dinner is available in all balcony cabins.

REGENT SEVEN SEAS CRUISES

The December 1994 merger of Radisson Diamond Cruises and Seven Seas Cruise Line launched Radisson Seven Seas Cruises with an eclectic fleet of vessels that offered a nearly all-inclusive cruise experience in sumptuous, contemporary surroundings. The line was

The end of a perfect day

rebranded as Regent Seven Seas Cruises in 2006 and purchased by Apollo Management, a private equity company, in 2008. Even more inclusive than in the past, the line has maintained its traditional tried-and-true formula—delightful ships offering exquisite service, generous staterooms with abundant amenities, a variety of dining options, and superior lecture and enrichment programs.

REGENT SEVEN SEAS
CRUISES
1000 Corporate Drive,
Suite 500
Fort Lauderdale, FL 33334
954/776-6123 or
877/505-5370
www.rssc.com

Cruise Style: Luxury

Guests are greeted with champagne upon boarding and find an all-inclusive beverage policy that offers not only soft drinks and bottled water, but also cocktails and select wines at all bars and restaurants throughout the ships.

The cruises are destination-focused, and most sailings host guest lecturers—historians, anthropologists, naturalists, and diplomats. Spotlight cruises center around popular pastimes and themes, such as food and wine, photography, history, archaeology, literature, performing arts, design and cultures, active exploration and wellness, antiques, jewelry and shopping, the environment, and marine life. Passengers need no urging to participate in discussions and workshops led by celebrated experts. All passengers have access to these unique experiences on board and on shore.

Activities and entertainment are tailored for each of the line's distinctive ships with the tastes of sophisticated passengers in mind. Don't expect napkin-folding demonstrations or nonstop action. Production revues, cabaret acts, concert-style piano performances, solo performers, and comedians may be featured in show lounges, with combos playing for listening and dancing in lounges and bars throughout the ships. Casinos are more akin to Monaco than Las Vegas. All ships display tasteful and varied art collections, including pieces that are for sale.

Food

Menus may appear to include the usual beef Wellington and Maine lobster, but in the hands of Regent Seven Seas chefs, the results are some of the most outstanding meals at sea. Specialty dining varies within the fleet, but the newest ships, *Seven Seas Voyager* and *Seven Seas Mariner*, have the edge with the sophisticated Signatures, which features the cuisine of Le Cordon Bleu of Paris, and Latitudes, offering a set "tasting" menu inspired by Indochine cooking. The authentic fare is prepared using French cooking techniques and served in traditional family style by Asian waiters. In addition, Mediterranean-influenced bistro dinners that need no reservations are served in La Veranda, the venue that is the daytime casual Lido buffet restaurant.

Evening alternative dining in *Seven Seas Navigator*'s Portofino is a lively affair that focuses on food and wines from four major regions of Italy and requires reservations.

Held in a tranquil setting, Wine Connoisseurs Dinners bring together people with an interest in wine and food. Each of five courses on the degustation menu is complemented by a fine wine pairing. Participation begins at $120 per person, and the dinners can be scheduled as many times as demand warrants.

Room service menus are fairly extensive, and you can also order directly from the restaurant menus during regular serving hours.

Although special dietary requirements should be relayed to the cruise line before sailing, general considerations such as vegetarian, low-salt, or low-cholesterol food requests can be satisfied on board the ships simply by speaking with the dining room staff. Wines chosen to complement dinner menus are freely poured each evening.

Fitness & Recreation

Although gyms and exercise areas are well-equipped, these are not large ships, so the facilities tend to be on the small size. Each ship has a jogging track, and the larger ones feature a variety of sports courts.

Exclusive to Regent Seven Seas, the spa and salon are operated by high-end Carita of Paris. The extensive range of beauty treatments offered follow the Carita approach of tailoring services to the unique needs of the individual for maximum results. Facials are on the pricey side, but massage treatments are quite reasonable when compared to those in other cruise-ship spas.

Noteworthy

■ Passengers enjoy open-seating dining with complimentary wines of the world in the elegant restaurants.

■ Italian fare with flair is an alternate dinner option on each Regent ship.

■ Regent's ship photographers are most unobtrusive. You may have to ask for your picture to be taken—a far cry from most cruise ships.

Top: Sunrise job
Bottom: *Seven Seas Navigator*

Top: Fitness center
Middle: Pool decks are never crowded
Bottom: Pampering in the Carita of Paris spa

Your Shipmates

Regent Seven Seas Cruises are inviting to active, affluent, well-traveled couples ranging from their late-30s to retirees who enjoy the ships' chic ambience and destination-rich itineraries. Longer cruises attract veteran passengers in the over-60 age group.

Dress Code

Formal attire is required on designated evenings. Men are encouraged to wear tuxedos, and many do so, although dark suits are acceptable. Cruises of 7 to 10 nights usually have one or two formal nights; longer cruises may have three. Other evenings are informal or resort casual; the number of each is based on the number of sea days. It's requested that dress codes be observed in public areas after 6 PM.

Junior Cruisers

Regent Seven Seas' vessels are adult-oriented and do not have dedicated children's facilities. However, a Club Mariner youth program for children from ages 6 to 11 and 12 to 17 is offered on selected sailings, both during summer months and during school holiday periods. Supervised by counselors, the organized, educational activities focus on nature and the heritage of destinations the ship will visit. Activities, including games, craft projects, movies, and food fun, are organized to ensure that every child has a memorable experience. Teens are encouraged to help counselors select the activities they prefer.

Service

The efforts of a polished European staff go almost unnoticed, yet special requests are handled with ease. Butlers provide an additional layer of personal service to guests in the top-category suites.

Tipping

Gratuities are included in the fare, and none are expected. To show their appreciation, passengers may elect to make a contribution to a crew welfare fund that benefits the ship's staff.

CHOOSE A CRUISE ON REGENT SEVEN SEAS IF...

1 You want to learn the secrets of cooking like a Cordon Bleu chef (for a charge, of course).

2 You want to stay connected. Regent Seven Seas Internet packages are reasonably priced by the hour.

3 A really high-end spa experience is on your agenda.

2

Past Passengers

Membership in the Seven Seas Society is automatic upon completion of a Regent Seven Seas cruise. Members receive 5%–10% cruise fare savings on select sailings; exclusive shipboard and shoreside special events on select sailings; a Seven Seas Society recognition cocktail party on every sailing; and *Inspirations* newsletter highlighting special events, sailings, and destination- and travel-related information. The tiered program offers rewards based on the number of nights you have sailed with RSSC. The more you sail, the more you accrue. Basic benefits are offered to members with less than 20 nights; from 21 through 74 nights, Silver members also receive complimentary Internet access on board, free pressing, and an hour of free phone time; from 75 through 199 nights, Gold members are awarded priority disembarkation at some ports, another hour of complimentary phone time, more complimentary pressing, an exclusive Gold & Platinum activity aboard or ashore on every sailing, and priority reservations at restaurants and spas; from 200 through 399, Platinum members can add complimentary air deviation services (one time per sailing), six hours of complimentary phone use, and unlimited free pressing and laundry services; Titanium members who have sailed 400 or more nights get free dry cleaning and free transfers.

Good to Know

So why did Carlson Hospitality change the name from Radisson to Regent Seven Seas? It probably seemed logical in the beginning to give their new cruise line a recognizable name—Radisson. However, the name wasn't recognizable for the right reasons. Radisson Seven Seas Cruises aspired to be recognized as upscale (which it was), while the Radisson hotel chain is a decidedly middle-of-the-road. The hotel name turned off some potential passengers who didn't perceive the cruise line as being luxurious or exclusive. It just so happened that Carlson Hospitality's small, but growing, Regent chain of hotels is more in tune with today's definition of luxury and a better fit to co-brand with a top-of-the-line cruising experience. Voila! Early in 2006, a "fleet christening" accomplished the renaming and, best of all, the cruise line's initials didn't change and neither did its Web site address.

DON'T CHOOSE A CRUISE ON REGENT SEVEN SEAS IF...

❶ Connecting cabins are a must. Very few are available, and only the priciest cabins connect.

❷ You can't imagine a Caribbean cruise without the hoopla of pool games and steel bands.

❸ You think dressing up for dinner is too much trouble. Most passengers look forward to the ritual

SEVEN SEAS VOYAGER

Public Areas & Facilities

The world's second all-balcony, all-suite ship continues the Regent Seven Seas tradition of offering posh accommodations on a vessel with generous space for every passenger.

Lounges are predominantly decorated in soothing neutrals and cool marine blues with splashes of color, soft leather, and glass-and-marble accents. Even areas that can accommodate all (or nearly all) passengers at once, including the formal dining room and show lounge, appear intimate; good design elements don't hint at their size and indoor spaces seem smaller than they actually are. With so much room, public areas are seldom crowded, and you won't have to hunt for a deck chair by the swimming pool.

The two-tiered Constellation Theater is a state-of-the-art show room with a full-size proscenium stage, where Broadway-inspired shows created by renowned producer Peter Grey Terhune are staged.

2003	ENTERED SERVICE
700	PASSENGER CAPACITY
447	CREW MEMBERS
350	NUMBER OF CABINS
46,000	GROSS TONS
670 feet	LENGTH
95 feet	WIDTH

700 ft.

500 ft.

300 ft.

WOW Factor

After an effortless check-in and warm greeting, can it get any better? Yes, when you're offered a flute of champagne to sustain you as you are escorted to your suite.

Restaurants

Four restaurants function on an open-seating basis. In addition to Compass Rose, the main dining room, choices include Signatures, Le Cordon Bleu restaurant, and Latitudes, which features Indochine cuisine prepared in an open galley (reservations required); and La Veranda, the daytime buffet, which is a Mediterranean bistro by night.

Top: Afternoon tea in Horizon Lounge
Bottom: *Seven Seas Voyager*

What Works & What Doesn't

In a successful, if somewhat unorthodox, blending of indoor and outdoor spaces, Horizon Lounge treats passengers to a variety of diversions, from afternoon tea to a piano duet at night followed by dancing, either inside or just outside under the stars. With private balconies for all and a 360-degree jogging track encircling the deck above the pool, there's no real necessity for a lengthy promenade deck, and most passengers probably won't miss it. Should you choose to dine in your suite, dinner can be ordered from the full dining-room menu and served course by course.

Accommodations

Layout: Rich-textured fabrics and warm-wood finishes add a touch of coziness to the larger-than-usual suite accommodations in all categories. Every suite has a vanity-desk, walk-in closet, and sitting area with sofa, chairs, and table. Marble bathrooms have a separate tub and shower. Most balconies are approximately 50 square feet in size.

Amenities: All suites have an entertainment center with CD/DVD player, stocked refrigerator, stocked bar, personal safe, hair dryer, and fine linens and duvets on the bed. Bathrooms have robes for use during the cruise and toiletries including shampoo, lotion, and bath gel.

Top-Category Suites: The top three suite categories feature Bose Wave Music Systems. Butler service is available for passengers in Master, Grand, Navigator, and Penthouse Suites. The top-category Master Suites have a separate sitting-dining room, two bedrooms (each has its own TV), a powder room as well as two full bathrooms (the master bath has dual vanities, a bidet, separate shower, and whirlpool tub). Some of the other high-end suites do not have the powder room or whirlpool tubs.

Good to Know: Four suites are designed for wheelchair accessibility and are equipped with showers only.

Cabin Type	Size (sq. ft.)
Master Suite	1,152–1,216
Grand Suite	753
Seven Seas Suite	441–495
Penthouse Suite	320
Deluxe Suite	306

Fast Facts

- 9 passenger decks
- 2 specialty restaurants, dining room, buffet
- Wi-Fi, in-cabin safes, in-cabin refrigerators, in-cabin DVDs
- Pool
- Fitness classes, gym, hair salon, 2 hot tubs, sauna, spa, steam room
- 5 bars, casino, dance club, library, showroom
- Children's programs (ages 6–17)
- Dry cleaning, laundry facilities, laundry service
- Computer room

In the Know

Regent combined the best features from their other ships when planning the Seven Seas Voyager, *and the result is an elegant vessel with a lot of room per passenger, more easily navigable layout of public rooms, and arguably some of the best bathrooms at sea, even in entry-level suites.*

Favorites

Best Splurge: Shopping in the well-stocked boutiques is always a pleasure.

Best Added Value: The self-service passenger launderettes with ironing stations on every accommodations deck are complimentary. Plan carefully, or you may have a slight wait because they get a lot of use.

Our Favorite Spot for a Nightcap: Every suite has a balcony, and there's no better spot for sharing quiet conversation and a libation before retiring.

Best Suite Locations: The dimensions of the upper-category suites can vary depending on where they are on the ship. Seven Seas Suites located aft are larger than those located mid-ship and have enormous balconies that measure 215 square feet. Also facing aft, Horizon View suites are simply standard Deluxe Suites, but with balconies that range in size from 105 to 180 square feet, depending on deck location.

Attentive butler service

SEVEN SEAS MARINER

Public Areas & Facilities

The world's first all-balcony, all-suite ship introduced the innovative Regent Seven Seas concept of luxury while retaining the tradition of stylish accommodations on a vessel with exceptionally generous space per passenger throughout.

Modern by design, traditional lounges feature comfortable furnishings with large expanses of glass to bring the sea views inside and fill interiors with sunlight. Mariner Lounge serves as a piano bar and a delightful spot to meet for predinner cocktails and conversation. Paneled walls separating the bar from the groupings of deep navy chairs and love seats contain niches with classical bronze sculptures.

A spiral staircase provides a grand entrance from the casino to Stars Nightclub, a late-night dance club, where wood paneling, granite-color wall coverings, and contrasting blue tub chairs and square high-back chairs in paler shades create an interesting and eclectic mix of styles. The room's centerpiece is the unusual staircase.

2001	ENTERED SERVICE
700	PASSENGER CAPACITY
445	CREW MEMBERS
350	NUMBER OF CABINS
50,000	GROSS TONS
709 feet	LENGTH
93 feet	WIDTH

700 ft.
500 ft.
300 ft.

WOW Factor

From the atrium, three glass elevators climb skyward past remarkable human shadow sculptures mounted on the opposite wall.

Top: Atrium
Bottom: *Seven Seas Mariner*

Restaurants

Four restaurants function on an open-seating basis with no dining assignments. In addition to Compass Rose, the main dining room, choices include Signatures, Le Cordon Bleu restaurant (reservations required); Latitudes, which serves Indochine cuisine (reservations required); and La Veranda, the daytime buffet that's converted to an evening bistro serving Mediterranean cuisine.

What Works & What Doesn't

There's no getting around the appeal of balconies for all suites and the abundance of space per passenger, but those appealing features have a small downside as well. The beautifully appointed lounges appear almost deserted at times, and you may wonder where everyone is. Dedicated to after-dinner brandy and cigars, Connoisseur Club is the one lounge that is disappointing; although the very masculine setting has oversize buttery soft leather chairs, huge cigar proportioned ashtrays, and even a faux fireplace, it looks sterile and isn't very inviting.

Accommodations

Layout: Rich, textured fabrics and warm-wood finishes add a touch of coziness to the larger-than-usual suite accommodations in all categories. Every suite has a vanity-desk, walk-in closet, and sitting area with sofa, chairs, and table. Marble bathrooms have a combination tub-shower. Master suites have two bedrooms (each with a TV) and a separate sitting-dining room, as well as a guest powder room and two full baths (with dual vanities, bidet, separate shower, and whirlpool tub in the master bedroom), not to mention two balconies (one for each bedroom). Other suites have but a single bedroom; forward Penthouse, Horizon, and Seven Seas suites do not have the guest powder room or whirlpool tub.

Amenities: Every suite has an entertainment center with CD/DVD player, stocked refrigerator, stocked bar, personal safe, hair dryer, and beds dressed with fine linens and duvets. Bathrooms have robes for use during the cruise; toiletries include shampoo, lotion, and bath gel.

Top-Category Suites: The top three suite categories have Bose Wave Music Systems; butler service is available for passengers in Master, Grand, Navigator, Penthouse, and Horizon suites.

Good to Know: Six suites are wheelchair-accessible and are equipped with showers only.

Cabin Type	Size (sq. ft.)
Master Suite	1,204
Grand/Mariner Suite	903/650
Seven Seas Suite	505–561
Horizon/Penthouse Suite	359/376
Deluxe Suite	252

Fast Facts

- 8 passenger decks
- 2 specialty restaurants, dining room, buffet
- Wi-Fi, in-cabin safes, in-cabin refrigerators, in-cabin DVDs
- Pool
- Fitness classes, gym, hair salon, 2 hot tubs, sauna, spa, steam room
- 5 bars, casino, dance club, library, showroom
- Children's programs (ages 6–17)
- Dry cleaning, laundry facilities, laundry service
- Computer room

In the Know

You might find the standard combination bathtub-shower a tight fit if you're over 6 feet tall. The ceiling isn't too low—it's the bathtub height that can cause a problem. The solution is booking a minimum of a Mariner Suite for a separate shower stall.

Favorites

Best Splurge: Individually tailored services in the upscale Carita of Paris spa are a divine indulgence. Don't be concerned about a hard sell since the staff focuses on pampering, not pressure.

Best Added Value: The specialty restaurants, with superb food and service, are fine dining at its finest—and at no additional cost.

Best Seat in the House: It doesn't matter where you sit—the view is unobstructed from every seat in the show lounge.

Our Favorite Spot for a Nightcap: Chairs and tables provide a peaceful aft-facing retreat for stargazing just outside the Horizon Lounge.

Best Bathroom News: In a rather nifty move, bathrooms in 47 suites were rebuilt in 2005 to include rain showers with tiled seats. Accommodations that have them are scattered throughout categories ranging from Deluxe Suites to Horizon Suites.

Perfect your swing

SEVEN SEAS NAVIGATOR

Public Areas & Facilities

The first ship outfitted uniquely to Regent Seven Seas' specifications, the *Seven Seas Navigator* is a particular favorite of returning passengers for its small-ship intimacy, big-ship features, and comfortable, well-designed cabins.

The generous use of wood and the addition of deep-tone accents to the predominantly blue color palette give even the larger lounges an inviting feel. Artwork and elaborate flower arrangements add a bit of sparkle and interest to the somewhat angular modern decor.

Due to the aft location of the two-deck-high main showroom, the only lounges that afford sweeping seascapes are Galileo's—typically the most popular public space, with nightly entertainment—and the Vista Lounge. Although views from the Vista Lounge are spectacular, there's no permanent bar, and it's primarily a quiet spot for reading when there are no lectures or activities scheduled there.

1999	ENTERED SERVICE
490	PASSENGER CAPACITY
340	CREW MEMBERS
245	NUMBER OF CABINS
33,000	GROSS TONS
560 feet	LENGTH
81 feet	WIDTH

700 ft.
500 ft.
300 ft.

WOW Factor

There are no massive atriums on ships this size, but with staircases that seem to float in mid-air, Seven Seas Navigator's *modest atrium is nonetheless impressive.*

Top: Casino
Bottom: *Navigator* suite

Restaurants

Two restaurants, including Compass Rose, the main dining room, function on an open-seating basis, so there are no set dining assignments. For alternative dining, Portofino Grill, the daytime buffet, is converted to a reservations-only evening trattoria serving Mediterranean cuisine accompanied by spirited Italian-style entertainment. A poolside grill serves casual daytime meals.

What Works & What Doesn't

Navigating the *Navigator* is a relatively simple matter with most public rooms and the formal Compass Rose Restaurant clustered aft on three decks adjacent to the atrium. Aft-facing outdoor tables adjoining Portofino Grill are extremely popular for alfresco dining on sunny days; unfortunately, seating is somewhat limited. Internet use can be heavy on sea days, and the lines that form in the computer area can add a bit of congestion—and inevitable noise—to the adjacent library, a space that should be a quiet haven.

Accommodations

Layout: Attractive textured fabrics and honeyed wood finishes add a touch of coziness to the larger-than-usual suites in all categories, 90% of which have balconies. All have a vanity-desk, walk-in closet, and sitting area with a sofa, chairs, and table. Marble bathrooms have a separate tub and shower. Master Suites have a separate sitting-dining room, a separate bedroom, and a powder room; only Grand Suites also have a powder room.

Amenities: Every suite has an entertainment center with CD/DVD player, stocked refrigerator, stocked bar, personal safe, hair dryer, and beds dressed with fine linens and duvets. Bath toiletries include shampoo, lotion, and bath gel.

Suites: Master Suites have a second TV in the bedroom, butler service, and whirlpool tub in the master bathroom. Grand and Navigator Suites are similarly outfitted. The top three suite categories feature Bose Wave Music Systems. Penthouse suites, which include butler service, are only distinguished from Deluxe suites by location and do not have a whirlpool bathtub.

Good to Know: Very few suites have the capacity to accommodate three people, and only 10 far-forward suites adjoin with those adjacent to them. Four suites are wheelchair-accessible.

Cabin Type	Size (sq. ft.)
Master Suite	1,067
Grand Suite	539
Navigator Suite	448
Penthouse/Balcony Suite	301
Window Suite	301*
*Except for Suite 600, which measures 516	

2

REGENT SEVEN SEAS CRUISES

Fast Facts

- 8 passenger decks
- Specialty restaurant, dining room, buffet
- Wi-Fi, in-cabin safes, in-cabin refrigerators, in-cabin DVDs
- Pool
- Fitness classes, gym, hair salon, hot tub, sauna, spa, steam room
- 4 bars, casino, dance club, showroom
- Children's programs (ages 6–17)
- Dry cleaning, laundry facilities, laundry service
- Computer room

In the Know

From Russia, With Love: Regent Seven Seas took over an unfinished hull that was originally destined to be a Soviet spy ship and redesigned it to create the Seven Seas Navigator. *They did such a good job completing the interiors that even James Bond would feel right at home.*

Favorites

Best Added Value: The library contains hundreds of novels, best-sellers, and travel books, as well as newspapers, movies for in-suite viewing, and even a selection of board games.

Best Dance Floor: Galileo's smallish dance floor may seem somewhat cramped, but when the doors are opened to the adjacent stern-facing deck, it becomes a magical spot to dance beneath the stars.

Our Favorite Spot for a Nightcap: The Navigator Lounge is just about as cozy a space as anyone could want for a late-night chat before retiring.

Best Balconies: Grand Suites on Deck 8 have considerably larger wraparound balconies than those with only side-facing balconies on Deck 7.

Most Fun with Food: Loyal passengers mourned the sale of the *Radisson Diamond* and the loss of its lively Italian trattoria experience known as Don Vito's. Happily, the singing waiters and festivities have reappeared aboard *Navigator.*

Casual poolside dining

ROYAL CARIBBEAN INTERNATIONAL

Big, bigger, biggest! More than a decade ago, Royal Caribbean launched *Sovereign of the Seas,* the first of the modern megacruise liners, which continues to be an all-around favorite of passengers who enjoy traditional cruising ambience with a touch of daring and whimsy tossed in. Plunging into the 21st

Adventure of the Seas solarium

century, each ship in the current fleet carries more passengers than the entire Royal Caribbean fleet of the 1970s and has features—such as new surfing pools—that were unheard of in the past.

ROYAL CARIBBEAN INTERNATIONAL
1050 Royal Caribbean Way
Miami, FL 33132-2096
305/539-6000 or
800/327-6700
www.royalcaribbean.com

Cruise Style: Mainstream

All Royal Caribbean ships are topped by the company's distinctive signature Viking Crown Lounge. These lofty perches allow passengers to contemplate the passing seascape by day and dance away the night in a heavenly space high above the water. Expansive multideck atriums and the generous use of brass and floor-to-ceiling glass windows give each vessel a sense of spaciousness and style.

A variety of lounges and high-energy stage shows draw passengers of all ages out to mingle and dance the night away. Production extravaganzas showcase singers and dancers in lavish costumes. Comedians, acrobats, magicians, jugglers, and solo entertainers fill show lounges on nights when the ships' companies aren't performing. Professional ice shows are a highlight of cruises on Voyager- and Ultra Voyager-class ships—the only ships at sea with ice-skating rinks.

The action is nonstop in casinos and dance clubs after dark, while daytime hours are filled with poolside games and traditional cruise activities. Port talks tend to lean heavily on shopping recommendations and the sale of shore excursions.

Food

Dining is an international experience with nightly changing themes and cuisines from around the world. Passenger preference for casual attire and a resortlike atmosphere has prompted the cruise line to add laid-back alternatives to the formal dining rooms in the Windjammer Café and, on certain ships, the fun and retro Johnny Rockets Diner; Seaview Café evokes the ambience of an island beachside stand.

Room service is available 24 hours, but choices are limited. Only certain dishes that travel well can be ordered from the restaurant menu during dinner hours.

Royal Caribbean doesn't place emphasis on celebrity chefs or specialty alternative restaurants, although they have introduced a more upscale and intimate dinner experience in the form of Portofino, an Italian-specialty restaurant, and/or Chops Grille, a steak house, on Radiance- and Voyager-class ships, as well as the Freedom-class ships.

Fitness & Recreation

Royal Caribbean has pioneered such new and previously unheard of features as rock-climbing walls, ice-skating rinks, bungee trampolines, and even the first self-leveling pool tables on a cruise ship. Interactive parks, boxing rings, surfing simulators, and cantilevered whirlpools suspended 112 feet above the ocean made their debuts on the Freedom-class ships.

Facilities vary by ship class, but all Royal Caribbean ships have state-of-the-art exercise equipment, jogging tracks, and rock-climbing walls; passengers can work out independently or in classes guaranteed to sweat off extra calories. Most exercise classes are included in the fare, but there's a fee for specialized spinning, yoga, and Pilates classes, as well as the services of a personal trainer. Spas and salons are top-notch, with full menus of day spa-style treatments and services for pampering and relaxation for adults and teens.

Your Shipmates

Royal Caribbean cruises have a broad appeal for active couples and singles, mostly in their 30s to 50s. Families are partial to the newer vessels that have larger staterooms, huge facilities for children and teens, and seemingly endless choices of activities and dining options.

Noteworthy

■ Each ship's Schooner Bar features nautically inspired decor, right down to a unique scent.

■ The signature Viking Crown Lounge found on every RCI ship was originally inspired by the Seattle World's Fair Space Needle.

■ Hot tubs and certain swimming pools are designated for adults only on Royal Caribbean ships.

Top: Adventure Beach for kids
Bottom: Voyager-class Interior Stateroom

Top: Miniature golf
Middle: *Adventure of the Seas*
Bottom: *Serenade of the Seas*
rock-climbing wall

Dress Code

Two formal nights are standard on seven-night cruises; one formal night is the norm on shorter sailings. Men are encouraged to wear tuxedos, but dark suits or sport coats and ties are more prevalent. All other evenings are casual, although jeans are discouraged in restaurants. It's requested that no shorts be worn in public areas after 6 PM, although there are passengers who can't wait to change into them after dinner.

Junior Cruisers

Supervised age-appropriate activities are designed for children ages 3 through 17; babysitting services are available as well (either group sitting or in-stateroom babysitting, but sitters will not change diapers). Children are assigned to the Adventure Ocean youth program by age. They must be at least three years old and toilet trained to participate (children who are in diapers and pull-ups or who are not toilet trained are also not allowed in swimming pools or whirlpools). Youngsters who wish to join a different age group must participate in one daytime and one night activity session with their proper age group first; the manager will then make the decision based on their maturity level. All participants earn credits for activities which they can trade for prizes at the end of the cruise.

In partnership with toy maker Fisher-Price, Royal Caribbean offers interactive 45-minute Aqua Babies and Aqua Tots play sessions for children from 6 months to 36 months of age. The playgroup classes, which are hosted by youth staff members, were designed by early childhood development experts for parents and their babies and toddlers, and teach life skills through playtime activities.

A teen center with a disco is an adult-free gathering spot that will satisfy even the pickiest teenagers. A flat-rate soda card program is a bonus for family budgets—children can have all the fountain soft drinks they desire for a single charge. Pluses are family-size staterooms on certain ships; drawbacks are the small standard cabins in the older vessels and the lack of self-service laundry facilities.

CHOOSE ROYAL CARIBBEAN INTERNATIONAL IF...

1 You want to see the sea from atop a rock wall—it's one of the few activities on these ships that's free.

2 You're active and adventurous. Even if your traveling companion isn't, there's an energetic staff on board to cheer you on.

3 You want your space. There's plenty of room to roam; quiet nooks and crannies are there if you look.

Service

Service on Royal Caribbean ships is friendly, but not consistent. Assigned meal seatings assure that most passengers get to know the waiters and their assistants, who in turn get to know the passengers' likes and dislikes; however, that can lead to a level of familiarity that is uncomfortable to some people. Some ships have a concierge lounge for the use of suite occupants and top-level past passengers.

Tipping

Tips can be prepaid when the cruise is booked, added on to shipboard accounts, or given in cash on the last night of the cruise. Suggested gratuities per passenger, per day are: $3.50 for the cabin steward; $3.50 for the waiter; $2 for the assistant waiter; and $0.75 for the headwaiter. Passengers may adjust the amounts based on the level of service experienced. An automatic 15% gratuity is automatically added to all bar tabs.

Past Passengers

After one cruise, you can enroll in the Crown & Anchor Society. All members receive the *Crown & Anchor* magazine and have access to the member section on the Royal Caribbean Web site. All members receive an Ultimate Value Booklet, an invitation to a complimentary wine tasting, a welcome back party, and commemorative gift. Platinum members (after five cruises) also have the use of a private departure lounge and receive priority check-in (where available), the onboard use of robes during the cruise, an invitation to an exclusive onboard event, and complimentary custom air arrangements.

Diamond members (after 10 cruises) also receive consideration on a priority wait list for sold-out shore excursions and spa services, concierge service on select ships, priority departure from the ship, complimentary custom air fee, special rates on balcony and suite accommodations, and a priority wait list for dining room seating. When you achieve Diamond Plus status (after 24 cruises), you're offered behind-the-scenes tours and preferred seating in main dining rooms.

Good to Know

Royal Caribbean ships are truly resorts afloat with an emphasis on recreation and family enjoyment. You could spend a week on board the huge Voyager-class and Freedom-class ships and never leave. You would also be hard-pressed to try to do everything at hand, so it's important to pace yourself by setting priorities and budgeting your time. A good idea is to try new things that you may not be able to do at home—climb a rock wall and learn to snorkel, for example.

If you're a Crown & Anchor member, your status level is the same whenever you sail on Royal Caribbean's sister cruise line, Celebrity Cruises.

2

ROYAL CARIBBEAN INTERNATIONAL

DON'T CHOOSE ROYAL CARIBBEAN INTERNATIONAL IF...

❶ Patience is not one of your virtues. Lines are not uncommon.

❷ You want to do your own laundry. There are no self-service facilities on any Royal Caribbean ships.

❸ You don't want to hear announcements, especially in your cabin. There are a lot on these cruises.

FREEDOM CLASS
Freedom, Liberty, Independence of the Seas

Public Areas & Facilities

The world's largest cruise ships (for now) live up to Royal Caribbean's reputation for imaginative thinking that results in features to stir the imagination and provide a resortlike atmosphere at sea. Whether you are hanging 10 in the surf simulator, going a few rounds in the boxing ring, or strolling the Royal Promenade entertainment boulevard, there's almost no reason to go ashore.

The layout is more intuitive than you might expect on such a gigantic ship. Freedom-class vessels have a familiar mall-like Promenade lined with shops and bistros, an ice-skating rink/theater, numerous lounges, and dining options but are not simply enlarged Voyager-class ships. With plenty of room, even the most intimate spaces do not feel crowded. A good fit for extended families, these ships have expansive areas devoted to children and teens and enough adults-only spaces to satisfy everyone.

2006, 2007, 2008	ENTERED SERVICE
3,634	PASSENGER CAPACITY
1,360	CREW MEMBERS
160,000	NUMBER OF CABINS
160,000	GROSS TONS
1,112 feet	LENGTH
185 feet	WIDTH

700 ft.

500 ft.

300 ft.

WOW Factor

Surf's Up! The FlowRider surfing simulator is such an exciting attraction that bleacher seating on threes sides of the deck is often full of spectators.

Restaurants

Triple-deck-high formal dining rooms serve meals in two evening seatings and are supplemented by two specialty restaurants, Portofino and Chops Grille, which charge a supplement and are open by reservation only. The casual Lido buffet offers service nearly around the clock, and Johnny Rockets is a popular option, though it too has a separate charge, albeit a modest one.

What Works & What Doesn't

"Of the Seas" takes on new meaning with a combination of pools that encompass 43% more space than Voyager-class ships. The H2O Zone waterpark with interactive fountains is the ideal play area for kids; a sports pool accommodates water volleyball, basketball, and golf; and a Solarium contains a tranquil pool for adults, as well as hammocks for relaxation and two huge hot tubs cantilevered 12 feet from the sides of the ship. The self-serve frozen yogurt bar is a cool treat, but its location near the kids' pool means that it often ends up messy.

Top: Dining is fun in Johnny Rockets
Bottom: Hang ten on the surf simulator

Accommodations

Layout: As on other Royal Caribbean ships, cabins are bright and cheerful. Although 60% are outside cabins—and a whopping 78% of those have private balconies—bargain inside cabins, including some that are uniquely configured with a bowed window for a view overlooking the action-packed promenade, are plentiful. Cabins in every category have adequate closet and drawer-shelf storage, as well as bathroom shelves. Family ocean-view cabins with a window sleep up to six people with two twin beds (convertible to queen-size), bunk beds in a separate area, a sitting room with a sofa bed, a vanity area, and a shower-only bathroom. At 1,215 square feet, the Presidential Suite sleeps 14 people and has an 810-square-foot veranda with a hot tub and bar.

Amenities: Wood cabinetry, a small refrigerator/minibar, Ethernet connection, vanity-desk, flat-panel TV, personal safe, a hair dryer, and a sitting area with sofa, chair, and table are typical features in all categories. Bathrooms have shampoo and bath gel. Premium beds and bedding complete the comfortable package.

Good to Know: Thirty-two staterooms are wheelchair accessible.

Cabin Type	Size (sq. ft.)
Royal/Presidential	1,406/1,215Suite
Owner's/Grand Suite	614/387
Junior Suite/Family Stateroom	287/293
Balcony Stateroom	177–189
Oceanview/Inside	161–214/149–152

Fast Facts

- 15 passenger decks
- 2 specialty restaurants, dining room, buffet, ice cream parlor, pizzeria
- In-cabin broadband, Wi-Fi, in-cabin safes, some in-cabin minibars, in-cabin refrigerators, some in-cabin DVDs
- 3 pools, children's pool
- Fitness classes, gym, hair salon, 7 hot tubs, sauna, spa, steam room
- 14 bars, casino, cinema, 2 dance clubs, library, 3 showrooms, video game room
- Children's programs (ages 3–17)
- Dry cleaning, laundry service
- Computer room

In the Know

Shipboard personnel expressed concern upon realizing the posteriors of the cows atop Ben & Jerry's marquee were aimed at the bay window of atrium-view stateroom 6305. They suggested the occupants be offered free ice cream during their cruise, so the ships now have a Ben & Jerry's "Sweet."

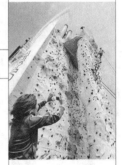

Climb the wall

Favorites

Best Splurge: Burgers, onion rings, and all the trimmings in Johnny Rockets diner are a deal at only $3.95 (the malts are extra).

Our Favorite Spot for a Nightcap: Soft lights, hot music, and drinks with the best view on board—the jazz club in the Viking Crown Lounge has it all.

Grown-up Stuff: Kids, don't even think of trying to crash Twenty Nightclub, a late-night adult dance party that takes place in the open-air Solarium. You won't get past the doorman who guards the entry.

Float With the Flow: Full of bright and whimsical "family" figures—including a puppy—the H2O Zone is a fun place to beat the heat beneath a waterfall, fountain sprays, and in a lazy river (where the fountain sculptures mist everyone who floats by). Parents can join in or watch the kids from adjacent shaded hot tubs or convenient deck chairs.

Best Photo Op: Pose seated beside the Morgan car on *Freedom of the Sea*'s Royal Promenade.

2

ROYAL CARIBBEAN INTERNATIONAL

VOYAGER CLASS
Voyager, Explorer, Adventure, Navigator, Mariner of the Seas

Public Areas & Facilities

A truly massive building program introduced one of these gigantic Voyager-class ships per year over a five-year period. With their rock-climbing walls, ice-skating rinks, in-line skating tracks, miniature golf, and multiple dining venues, they are destinations in their own right. Sports enthusiasts will be thrilled with nonstop daytime action.

Only the unique horizontal, multiple-deck promenade-atriums on Voyager-class vessels can stage some of the pageantry for which Royal Caribbean is noted. Fringed with boutiques, bars, and even coffee shops, the mall-like expanses set the stage for evening parades and events, as well as simply spots to kick back for some people-watching.

Other public rooms are equally dramatic. Though it's considered to be three separate dining rooms, the triple-deck height of the single space is stunning. These ships not only carry a lot of people, but carry them well. Space is abundant, and crowding is seldom an issue.

1999, 2000, 2001, 2002, 2003	
	ENTERED SERVICE
3,114 (3,835 max)	
	PASSENGER CAPACITY
700 ft.	1,185
	CREW MEMBERS
	1,557
	NUMBER OF CABINS
500 ft.	142,000
	GROSS TONS
	1,020 feet
	LENGTH
300 ft.	158 feet
	WIDTH

WOW Factor

A lot of things on these ships is impressive, but the Royal Promenade, particularly when a parade or other event is center stage, may elicit the biggest "Wow!"

Top: Rock-climbing wall
Bottom: Fitness class

Restaurants

Triple-decker formal dining rooms serve meals in two evening seatings and are supplemented by Portofino, a reservations-only Italian restaurant that charges a supplement. Additionally, *Mariner of the Seas* and *Navigator of the Seas* also feature Chops Grille. The casual Lido buffet offers an Island Grill for casual dinners and does not require reservations.

What Works & What Doesn't

Active families will surely find something to keep everyone busy—rock climbing, ice-skating, full-size basketball courts, in-line skating, miniature golf. The good news is that equipment to participate in all those sports activities is provided at no additional charge. The bad news is that, with the exception of the gym and some fitness classes, nearly everything else on board—including soft drinks, specialty coffees, meals in the alternative dining venues, spa services, bingo, and alcoholic beverages—carries a price tag. More good news is that snacks and pizza in Café Promenade are free.

Accommodations

Layout: As on other Royal Caribbean ships, cabins are bright and cheerful. Although more than 60% are outside—and a hefty 75% of those have private verandas—there are still plenty of bargain inside cabins, some with a bowed window for a view overlooking the action-packed promenade. Cabins in every category have adequate closet and drawer-shelf storage and bathroom shelves. Junior Suites have a sitting area, vanity area, and bathroom with bathtub. Family ocean-view cabins with a window sleep up to six people and can accommodate a roll-away bed and/or crib, have two twin beds (convertible to a queen), and additional bunk beds in a separate area, a separate sitting area with a sofa bed, vanity area, and a private bathroom with shower.

Amenities: Wood cabinetry, a small refrigerator-minibar, computer connection, vanity-desk, TV, personal safe, a hair dryer, and a sitting area with sofa, chair, and table are typical Voyager-class features in all categories. Bathrooms have shampoo and bath gel.

Good to Know: Twenty-six staterooms are designed for wheelchair accessibility. 14 passenger decks

Cabin Type	Size (sq. ft.)
Royal Suite	1,188–1,325
Other Suites	*277–610
Superior/Deluxe/Family Ocean View**	173–328
Large/Standard Ocean View	211/161–180
Interior	153–167

*Owner's (506–618 sq. ft.), Grand (381–390 sq. ft.), Royal Family (512–610 sq. ft.), Jr. (277–299 sq. ft).

**Superior (202–206 sq. ft.), Deluxe (173–184 sq. ft.), Family (265–328 sq. ft.).

In the Know

Long queues can form at security and check-in counters before the boarding process begins because many passengers arrive early and clog the terminal before the scheduled boarding time. Avoid the hassle by arriving a bit later to breeze through and start your cruise relaxed.

Favorites

Best Place to Escape the Crowds: The clubby and quiet cigar bars are comfortable retreats day and night. Even nonsmokers can't fail to be impressed with a ventilation system that eliminates any lingering scent.

Fun & Funky: In the sports bars, at the ships' rail, and around the pools, colorful sculptures add a touch of whimsy.

Best Added Value: Although you could spend extra for specialty coffee and ice cream, it's possible to grab a complimentary snack instead in the Café Promenade.

Our Favorite Spot for a Nightcap: Music and drinks with a view gets our vote—the jazz clubs in the Viking Crown Lounge have it all.

Suite Stuff: Full suites and family suites have concierge service, balconies, and sitting areas. All suites are furnished with a DVD/VCR player and stereo; bathrooms with a tub and double sinks; and (in many) walk-in closets. Top-category suites have flat-screen TVs, whirlpool tubs, dining rooms, multiple bedrooms, and even hot tubs on balconies.

Fast Facts

- Specialty restaurant (2 on *Mariner* and *Voyager*), dining room, buffet, ice-cream parlor, pizzeria
- In-cabin broadband, Wi-Fi, in-cabin safes, in-cabin refrigerators, some in-cabin VCRs, some in-cabin DVDs
- 3 pools, children's pool (only *Voyager, Explorer,* and *Adventure*)
- Fitness classes, gym, hair salon, 7 hot tubs, sauna, spa, steam room
- 12 bars, casino, cinema, 2 dance clubs, library, 3 showrooms, video game room
- Children's programs (ages 3–17)
- Dry cleaning, laundry service
- Computer room

Relax poolside

RADIANCE CLASS

Radiance, Brilliance, Serenade, Jewel of the Seas

	2001, 2002, 2003, 2004
	ENTERED SERVICE
	2,112 (2,501 max)
	PASSENGER CAPACITY
700 ft.	**857**
	CREW MEMBERS
	1,056
	NUMBER OF CABINS
500 ft.	**90,090**
	GROSS TONS
	962 feet
	LENGTH
300 ft.	**106 feet**
	WIDTH

Public Areas & Facilities

Considered by many people to be the most beautiful vessels in the Royal Caribbean fleet, Radiance-class ships are large but sleek and swift, with sun-filled interiors and panoramic elevators that span 10 decks along the ships' exteriors.

High-energy and glamorous spaces are abundant throughout these sister ships. From the rock-climbing wall, children's pool with waterslide, and golf area to the columned dining room, sweeping staircases, and the tropical garden of the solarium, these ships hold appeal for a wide cross section of interests and tastes.

The ships are packed with multiple dining venues, including the casual Windjammer, which has both indoor and outdoor seating, and the Latte-Tudes patisserie, which sells specialty coffees, pastries, and ice-cream treats.

WOW Factor

Vast expanses of glass bring the outdoors inside, so there's no excuse to miss a sunset, even if you're on an elevator.

Top: Pool deck
Bottom: Sports courts

Restaurants

The double-deck formal dining room serves meals in two evening seatings and is supplemented by Portofino Italian restaurant and Chops Grill steak house, each of which requires reservations. The casual Lido buffet serves three meals a day, and the Seaview Café is open for quick lunches and dinners. A pizzeria serves pizza by the slice.

What Works & What Doesn't

Radiance-class ships take the concept of expanses of glass in a new direction, with panoramic elevators allowing sea views while you move vertically through the ship. Aft on Deck 6, four distinct lounges and the billiard room form a clubby adult entertainment center furnished in rich colors and accented by warm woods. With the traditional and nautical-leaning decor on these otherwise classy ships, the weird freeform atrium sculptures are a jarring throwback to earlier design elements.

2

Accommodations

Layout: With the line's highest percentage of outside cabins, standard staterooms are bright and cheery as well as roomy. Nearly three-quarters of the outside cabins have private balconies. Every cabin has adequate closet and drawer-shelf storage, as well as bathroom shelves.

Amenities: Light-wood cabinetry, small refrigerator-minibar, computer connection, vanity-desk, TV, personal safe, hair dryer, and a sitting area with sofa, chair, and table are typical Radiance-class features in all categories. Bathroom extras include shampoo and bath gel.

Suites: All full suites and family suites have private balconies and include concierge service. Top-category suites have wet bars, separate living/dining areas, multiple bathrooms, entertainment centers with flat-screen TVs, VCRs, and stereos. Some bathrooms have twin sinks, steam showers, and whirlpool tubs.

Junior suites have a sitting area, vanity area, and bathroom with a tub.

Good to Know: Nineteen staterooms are wheelchair-accessible.

Cabin Type	Size (sq. ft.)
Royal/Owner's Suite	1,001/512
Other Suites*	277–610
Superior/Deluxe Ocean View	204/179
Large/Family Ocean View	170/319
Interior	165

Fast Facts

■ 12 passenger decks

■ 2 specialty restaurants, dining room, buffet, pizzeria

■ In-cabin broadband, Wi-Fi, in-cabin data ports, in-cabin safes, in-cabin refrigerators, some in-cabin VCRs

■ 2 pools (1 indoor), children's pool

■ Fitness classes, gym, hair salon, 3 hot tubs, sauna, spa, steam room

■ 11 bars, casino, cinema, dance club, library, showroom, video game room

■ Children's programs (ages 3–17)

■ Dry cleaning, laundry service

■ Computer room

In the Know

Other cruise ships may have rollicking sports bars (and these do as well), but only on the Radiance-class Royal Caribbean vessels will you find self-leveling pool tables.

Favorites

Best Place to Escape the Crowds: Not everyone discovers the out-of-the way Seaview Cafés, making them a favored casual dining spot for those passengers who take the time to locate them.

Our Favorite Spot for a Nightcap: In a setting overlooking the atriums, yet with intimate seating arrangements, the Champagne Bars offer

privacy at the heart of the action.

Best Family Quarters: Particularly spacious, family ocean-view cabins, which sleep up to six people and can accommodate a roll-away bed and/or a crib, have two twin beds (convertible into one queen-size), additional bunk beds in a separate area, a separate sitting area with a sofa

bed, a vanity area, and a bathroom with a shower.

Go Local: A sincere attempt is made to pair the onboard experience with your cruising region. Tapas may be offered when sailing in the Mediterranean.

Shared moments on your personal balcony

VISION CLASS

Legend, Splendour, Grandeur, Rhapsody,
Vision of the Seas

Public Areas & Facilities

The first Royal Caribbean ships to offer private balconies in a number of categories, these Vision-class vessels, named for sister ship *Vision of the Seas* (which does not sail in the Mediterranean), have acres of glass skylights that allow sunlight to flood in and windows that offer wide sea vistas. The soaring central atrium at the heart of each ship is anchored by champagne bars and fills with music after dark.

Built in pairs, the ships follow the same general layout but are different in overall size and the total number of passengers on board. Cabin sizes also vary somewhat; as the total size of the ships increased from *Legend* and *Splendour* at 69,130 tons (1,800 passengers) to *Grandeur* at 74,140 tons (1,950 passengers), and finally, *Rhapsody* and *Vision* at 78,491 tons (2,000 passengers), so did the size of the accommodations. In some categories, it's only a matter of a few feet, so don't look for huge—or even noticeable—differences.

1995, 1996, 1996, 1997, 1998	ENTERED SERVICE
1,800-2,000 (2,076-2,435 max)	PASSENGER CAPACITY
720, 760, 765	CREW MEMBERS
900; 975; 1,000	NUMBER OF CABINS
69,130-78,491	GROSS TONS
867; 916; 915 feet	LENGTH
106 feet	WIDTH

700 ft.
500 ft.
300 ft.

Legend and *Splendour* are the smallest, followed by *Grandeur*, then *Rhapsody* and *Vision*

WOW Factor

Lots and lots of wide-open space everywhere and a bit more glitter than other Royal Caribbean ships give the Vision-class vessels a distinctive look and feel.

Restaurants

The double-deck-high formal dining room serves meals in two assigned evening seatings. Lunch in the dining room is open seating. Windjammer, the casual Lido buffet, serves three meals a day, including a laid-back dinner. Room service is available 24 hours a day, and a poolside grill serves burgers in the solarium. Sadly, there are no specialty restaurants on these ships.

What Works & What Doesn't

Top: Viking Crown lounge overlooks the pool deck
Bottom: *Splendour of the Seas*

Open, light-filled public areas offer sea views from almost every angle on these ships. Each vessel features double-deck-height dining rooms with sweeping staircases that are a huge improvement over previous ship designs. Some lounges, particularly the popular Schooner Bars, serve as a thoroughfare and suffer from continuous traffic flow before and after performances in the ships' main show lounges. These ships were the first in the fleet to include indoor/outdoor solarium pools with expansive adjacent fitness centers and spas. Legend and Splendour have miniature golf courses for tuning your short game.

Accommodations

Layout: Cabins are airy and comfortable, but the smaller categories are a tight squeeze for more than two adults. Every cabin has adequate closet and drawer-shelf storage.

Amenities: Light woods, pastel colors, vanity-desk, TV, personal safe, a hair dryer, and a sitting area with sofa, chair, and table are typical Vision-class features in all categories. Bathrooms have shampoo and bath gel.

Suites: All full suites and family suites have private balconies and a small minibar; full suites also include concierge service. Royal Suites have a living room, wet bar, separate dining area, entertainment center with TV, stereo, and VCR, separate bedroom, and a bathroom (twin sinks, whirlpool tub, separate steam shower, bidet) and separate powder room. Owner's Suites have a separate living area, minibar, entertainment center with TV, stereo, and VCR, dinette area, and one bath-room (twin sinks, bathtub, separate shower, bidet). Grand Suites have similar amenities on a smaller scale.

Good to Know: On *Legend* and *Splendour*, 17 cabins are wheelchair-accessible; on *Grandeur*, *Vision*, and *Rhapsody*, 14 cabins are wheelchair-accessible.

Cabin Type	Size (sq. ft.)
Royal Suite	1,074
Owner's/Grand Suite	523/355
Royal Family/Jr. Suite	512/240
Superior/Large Ocean View*	193/154
Interior	135–174

All cabin sizes are averages of the 5 ships since cabins vary somewhat in size among the Vision-class ships (all *Legend* and *Splendour* cabins are the same size). *Rhapsody* has Family Ocean View cabins at 237 sq. ft.

Fast Facts

- 11 passenger decks
- Dining room, buffet, ice-cream parlor, pizzeria
- Wi-Fi, in-cabin safes, some in-cabin refrigerators, some in-cabin VCRs
- 2 pools (1 indoor)
- Fitness classes, gym, hair salon, 6 hot tubs, sauna, spa
- 6 bars, casino, dance club, library, showroom, video game room
- Children's programs (ages 3–17)
- Dry cleaning, laundry service
- Computer room

In the Know

All suites on Vision-class ships are not created equal. A Royal Family Suite is a roomy choice for parents with younger children, but goodies that other suites receive—including bathrobes to use on board, welcome-aboard champagne, evening canapés, and concierge service—aren't included.

Favorites

Best Added Value: With no real specialty restaurants, it's an advantage to be able to order some items from the dining room menu through room service. Only those dishes that travel well are offered, but there are plenty from which to choose for a private dinner or balcony picnic.

Best Dance Spot: The Viking Crown Lounge is a rocking late-night dance

club where the DJ spins pop tunes until well into the early hours of the morning. You can probably count on hearing *YMCA* at least once.

Our Favorite Spot for a Nightcap: Tucked into an atrium nook, the Champagne Bar on each ship is not only an elegant spot for predinner drinks and dancing, but also for quiet after-

dinner or after-the-show drinks and conversation.

Best Small Splurge: While regular coffee and ice cream are complimentary, you can kick it up a notch and indulges in a Ben & Jerry's cone or a specialty coffee in Latte-tudes Café.

Vision-class Owner's Suite

SAGA CRUISES

Saga Holidays, the U.K.-based tour company founded in 1951 and designed to offer vacation packages to mature travelers, started its cruise program in 1975 with charter sailings. After building a 20-year reputation for comfortable cruise travel, Saga purchased its first ship in 1996, the venerable

Saga Rose enters port

Sagafjord, and renamed it *Saga Rose.* Following the success of *Saga Rose,* her former sister ship *Vistafjord* was acquired in 2004 and sails as *Saga Ruby.* Itineraries brim with longer sailings to far-flung corners of the globe, making Saga voyages destination oriented.

SAGA CRUISES
The Sage Building
Folkestone, Kent, UK
CT20 3SE
1303/771-111
www.sagacruises.com

Cruise Style: Premium

Classic cruisers in every sense of the word, Saga's passengers are travelers who expect inspiring itineraries coupled with traditional onboard amenities and comfortable surroundings. In the style of Saga Holidays' land-based tours, Saga Cruises takes care of the details that discerning passengers don't wish to leave to chance—from providing insurance and arranging visas to placing fruit and water in every cabin.

Activities and entertainment range from dance lessons to presentations of West End–style productions, from computer software lessons to lectures on wide-ranging topics. Wine-tasting, deck game competitions, classical concerts, and even Bingo are found on the daily programs. Both ships have card rooms, but you won't find casinos.

With numerous accommodations designed for solo cruisers, Saga Cruises are particularly friendly for senior

CHOOSE A CRUISE ON SAGA CRUISES IF...

❶ You are over 50 and want to sail on an all-adult cruise; the demographic on these cruises is primarily 60-plus.

❷ You prefer a classic cruise on a gracious, older ship. None of Saga's ships is new, but all are well-kept.

❸ You like the idea of dressing up on occasion for dinner. These are not all-casual cruises.

singles. Especially convenient on lengthy sailings, each ship features complimentary self-service launderettes and ironing facilities.

Food
In addition to offering a wide selection of dishes to appeal to a variety of discriminating tastes, many British favorites find their way onto menus in the main restaurants. Ingredients are high in quality, well-prepared, and served in a single leisurely seating. Vegetarian, sugar-free, and healthy selections are always alternatives. A traditional English tea is served every afternoon, and midnight buffets are set up in the Lido restaurants. While alcoholic beverages and wine are not included in the fare, prices from the bar and wine lists are quite affordable.

Fitness & Recreation
Gentle exercise classes tailored to different levels of ability and fully equipped gyms are available for active seniors, and each ship has two swimming pools, one outdoors and one indoors. Passengers can work on their golf swing at the practice nets, jog on deck, or book a fitness session with a personal trainer. Each ship has a hair salon, as well as a full-service spa with a broad menu of massages, facials, and aromatherapy treatments, including procedures tailored especially for mature cruisers.

Your Shipmates
Saga Cruises are exclusively for passengers age 50 and older; the minimum age for traveling companions is 40. The overwhelming majority of passengers are from Great Britain, with a sprinkling of North Americans in the mix.

Dress Code
Requested attire on board is generally casual during the day. At night, there are three dress codes—formal, informal, and smart casual.

Service
The warm and friendly service staff provides polished, yet unobtrusive, service.

Tipping
Gratuities are included in the fare, and additional tipping is not expected.

Noteworthy
- Prices on board are in British pounds, but Saga ships operate under a cashless system for shipboard charges.
- Voltage on board is 110 volts. Sockets may be either recessed European or American-type.
- Mealtimes may vary daily depending on arrival times in port, departure times for shore excursions, or sometimes even the schedule of shipboard activities.

Top: *Saga Ruby* South Cape Bar
Bottom: *Saga Rose* Lido Pool

DON'T CHOOSE A CRUISE ON SAGA CRUISES IF...
1. You want to bring the entire family (unless they are all adults over 40).
2. Casino gaming is a big part of your cruise experience; there are no casinos on Saga ships.
3. You prefer independent travel and feel smothered when you aren't in total control of your arrangements.

SAGA ROSE

History

Saga Rose began sailing for Norwegian American Line in 1965 as *Sagafjord* and, despite being a bit long in the tooth, she is beloved for her sleek appearance and comfortable interiors. Well-built and beautifully maintained, she is a classic ship with many of the attributes of a true ocean liner—a teak wraparound promenade deck, thickly padded deck chairs, and an indoor swimming pool deep within the hull. In addition to a genuine ballroom, *Saga Rose* also has a cinema-theater and lounges for cocktails, dancing, and quiet conversation.

700 ft.	1965 ENTERED SERVICE
	587 PASSENGER CAPACITY
	350 CREW MEMBERS
	322 NUMBER OF CABINS
500 ft.	24,474 GROSS TONS
	620 feet LENGTH
300 ft.	80 feet WIDTH

Restaurants

The main dining room is large enough to accommodate all passengers in one sitting at assigned tables. For casual meals, the Lido Café is the ship's buffet restaurant for breakfast and lunch as well as midnight buffets. When the weather cooperates, outdoor seating is available for alfresco dining. Afternoon tea is served daily, and 24-hour room service is available.

Accommodations

Each cabin has a generous closet and adequate storage, a vanity-desk, TV, and hair dryer. Most have a small sitting area and a bathtub. Robes are provided for use during the cruise, as are bathroom toiletries. All cabins have lower berths, although some twin beds cannot be pushed together; some cabins have a balcony or refrigerator. Two suites offer commanding views over the ship's bow. There are also several single staterooms. Two cabins are wheelchair-accessible.

Cabin Size (in sq. ft.): Cabin sizes vary even within the same category. Those at the front of the ship follow the curvature of the ship's hull and are generally roomier.

Top: *Saga Rose*
Bottom: *Saga Rose* dining

In the Know

Couples celebrating a wedding anniversary ending in a five or zero—from 5 to 60 years of marriage—are feted with flowers, champagne, a framed photograph, and a crystal gift on certain cruises. After-noon tea is arguably the most popular daily event. Don't arrive late, or you may miss out on the scones and genuine clotted cream.

Fast Facts

- 7 passenger decks
- Dining room, buffet
- Safes, some refrigerators, 2 pools, gym, spa, laundry facilities, laundry service, computer room, no children under age 18

SAGA RUBY

1973	ENTERED SERVICE
655	PASSENGER CAPACITY
380	CREW MEMBERS
376	NUMBER OF CABINS
25,000	GROSS TONS
627 feet	LENGTH
82 feet	WIDTH

700 ft.

500 ft.

300 ft.

History

While not a twin to *Saga Rose*, *Saga Ruby* is the perfect sister ship. Originally christened *Vistafjord* in 1973, she sailed alongside her present Saga fleet mate in the now-defunct Norwegian American Line. Their differences were subtle then and remain barely discernible from afar. With her interiors fine-tuned in 2005, *Saga Ruby* has modern furnishings, a brand-new spa, and a top-deck fitness center. She also has a ballroom and cinema, a card room, and library, where DVDs and computers with Internet access can be found in addition to books.

Restaurants

The main dining room accommodates all passengers in one sitting at assigned tables. View is the intimate specialty restaurant that requires reservations but charges no additional fee. For casual meals, the Lido

Café is the ship's buffet restaurant for breakfast and lunch as well as midnight buffets. Afternoon tea is served daily and 24-hour room service is available.

Accommodations

Each cabin has generous storage, a vanity-desk, flat-screen TV, DVD player, and hair dryer. Most have a bathtub and shower. All cabins have lower berths, although some twin beds cannot be pushed together; some have a balcony or refrigerator. Two duplex suites have two balconies (one with a hot tub), a whirlpool tub, private sauna, and exercise equipment. There are also single staterooms. Six cabins are wheelchair-accessible.

Cabin size (in square feet): Cabin sizes vary, even within the same category. Those at the front of the ship are generally roomier.

Top: *Saga Ruby*
Bottom: View restaurant

In the Know

In addition to an annual World Cruise, *Saga Ruby* is noted for a variety of theme cruises devoted to music, history, the arts, and food and wine. "View," the intimate specialty restaurant, has only a dozen tables, so

reservations go fast. Book your table as soon as you board to avoid disappointment.

Fast Facts

■ 8 passenger decks
■ 2 restaurants, buffet
■ Safes, some refrigerators, DVDs, 2 pools, gym, spa, laundry facilities, laundry service, computer room, no children under age 18

SEABOURN CRUISE LINE

Seabourn was founded on the principle that dedication to personal service in elegant surroundings would appeal to sophisticated, independent-minded passengers whose lifestyles demand the best. Lovingly maintained since their introduction in 1987—and routinely updated with new features—the megayachts

Make memories to last a lifetime

of Seabourn have proved to be a smashing success over the years. They remain favorites with people who can take care of themselves but would rather do so aboard a ship that caters to their individual preferences.

SEABOURN CRUISE LINE
6100 Blue Lagoon Drive,
Suite 400
Miami, FL 33126
305/463-3000 or
800/929-9391
www.seabourn.com

Cruise Style: Luxury

Recognized as a leader in small-ship, luxury cruising, Seabourn delivers all the expected extras—complimentary wines and spirits, a stocked minibar in all suites, and elegant amenities. Expect the unexpected as well—from travel document portfolios and luggage tags by Tumi to the pleasure of a complimentary minimassage while lounging at the pool. If you don't want to lift a finger, Seabourn will even arrange to have your luggage picked up at home and delivered directly to your suite—for a price.

Dining and evening socializing are generally more stimulating to Seabourn passengers than splashy song-and-dance revues; however, proportionately scaled production shows and cabarets are presented in the main showroom and smaller lounge. Movies Under the Stars are shown on the wind-protected sun deck at least one evening on virtually all cruises as long as the weather permits. The library stocks not only books, but also movies for those who prefer to watch them in the privacy of their suites—popcorn will naturally be delivered with a call to room service.

The Dress Circle Series enrichment program features guest appearances by luminaries in the arts and world affairs. Due to the size of Seabourn ships, passengers have the opportunity to mingle with presenters and interact one-on-one.

Peace and tranquillity reign on these ships, so the daily roster of events is somewhat thin. Wine-tastings, lectures, and other quiet pursuits might be scheduled, but most passengers are pleased to simply do what pleases them.

One don't-miss activity is the daily team trivia contest. Prizes are unimportant: it's the bragging rights that most guests seek.

Food
Exceptional cuisine created by celebrity chef Charlie Palmer is prepared *à la minute* and served in open-seating dining rooms. Upscale menu offerings include foie gras, quail, fresh seafood, and jasmine crème brûlée. Dishes low in cholesterol, salt, and fat, as well as vegetarian selections, are prepared with the same attention to detail and artful presentation. Wines are chosen to complement each day's luncheon and dinner menus, and caviar is always available. A background of classical music sets the tone for afternoon tea. The weekly Gala Tea features crêpes Suzette.

A casual dinner alternative is "Tastings @ 2," serving innovative cuisine in multiple courses nightly in the Veranda Café, where outdoor tables enhance the romantic atmosphere. Evening attire in the Veranda Café is specified as casual or elegant casual—when men are asked to wear a jacket but no tie. A second, and even more laid back, dinner alternative is offered on select occasions in the open-air Sky Bar, where grilled seafood and steaks are served. "Sky Grill" dinners are scheduled on a couple of nights during each cruise, weather permitting. Both Tastings @ 2 and Sky Grill require reservations, but happily there is no additional charge for either.

Room service is always available. Dinner can even be served course by course in your suite during restaurant hours.

Fitness & Recreation
A full array of exercise equipment, free weights, and basic fitness classes are available in the small gym, while some specialized fitness sessions are offered for a fee.

Many passengers are drawn to the pampering spa treatments, including a variety of massages, body wraps, and facials. Hair and nail services are offered in the salon. Both spa and salon are operated by Steiner Leisure. The water sports marina at the stern is popular with active passengers who want to Jet Ski, windsurf, kayak, or

Noteworthy

■ Dinner can always be served in your suite, served course by course from the regular menu.

■ Nearly half the suites on Seabourn ships have minibalconies with doors that open to admit fresh sea breezes.

■ Complimentary shore experiences can range from a beach barbecue to an evening of classical music amid the ancient ruins of Ephesus.

Top: A good book and breakfast in bed
Bottom: The Club

Top: French balcony
Middle: Dining by candlelight in
The Restaurant
Bottom: Relax on deck

swim in the integrated salt-water pool while anchored in calm waters.

Your Shipmates

Seabourn's yachtlike vessels appeal to well-traveled, affluent couples of all ages who enjoy destination-intense itineraries, a subdued atmosphere, and exclusive service. Passengers tend to be 50-plus and retired couples who are accustomed to evening formality.

Dress Code

Two formal nights are standard on seven-night cruises and three to four nights, depending on the itinerary, on two-week cruises. Men are required to wear tuxedos or dark suits after 6 PM, and the majority prefer black tie. All other evenings are elegant casual, and slacks with a jacket over a sweater or shirt for men and sundresses, skirts, or pants with a sweater or blouse for women are suggested.

Junior Cruisers

Seabourn Cruise Line is adult-oriented and unable to accommodate children under one year. A limited number of suites are available for triple-occupancy; anyone two years of age and older traveling as the third passenger in a suite pays 50% of the Category A brochure fare. No dedicated children's facilities are present on these ships, so parents are responsible for the behavior and entertainment of their children.

Service

Personal service and attention by the professional staff are the orders of the day. Your preferences are noted and fulfilled without the necessity of reminders. It's a mystery how nearly every staff member knows your name within hours, if not minutes, after you board.

Tipping

Tipping is neither required nor expected.

Past Passengers

Once you have completed your first Seabourn cruise, you are automatically enrolled in the Seabourn Club for past guests. Benefits include up to a 50% discount on selected cruises (not combinable with Early Booking Savings); the

CHOOSE A CRUISE ON SEABOURN CRUISE LINE IF...

1 You consider fine dining the highlight of your vacation.

2 You own your own tuxedo. These ships are dressy, and most men wear them on formal evenings.

3 You feel it's annoying to sign drink tabs; everything is included on these ships.

Seabourn Club newsletters and periodic mailings featuring destinations, special programs, and exclusive savings; and an exclusive online e-mail contact point to the Club Desk through the membership page on the Seabourn Web site.

On the ships, Club members receive a 5% discount on future bookings; special recognition for frequent cruisers; and a Club party hosted by the captain. Passengers who sail 140 days aboard Seabourn are awarded a complimentary cruise of up to 14 days.

Good to Know

Shore excursions often include privileged access to historic and cultural sites when they are not open to the general public. A highlight of Seabourn's warm-weather cruises is a picnic on a private beach when the uniformed captain and crew members wade into the surf to serve champagne and caviar to guests enjoying a refreshing dip in the sea.

2

SEABOURN CRUISE LINE

DON'T CHOOSE A CRUISE ON SEABOURN CRUISE LINE IF...

❶ Dressing down is on your agenda.

❷ You absolutely must have a spacious private balcony; they are limited in number and book fast.

❸ You need to be stimulated by constant activity.

SEABOURN LEGEND, PRIDE, SPIRIT

Public Areas & Facilities

The height of absolute luxury, *Seabourn Legend* and *Seabourn Pride* surround passengers in comfort and understated style punctuated by polished brass accents and etched-glass panels. Public rooms are intimate, but that isn't to say cramped, although predinner cocktail gatherings tend to strain the room available in the popular Club bar.

The relative amount of ship-wide space devoted to passengers is among the highest in the cruise industry, and the public areas and deck spaces were designed so that no one aboard feels crowded. Fresh flower arrangements add a gracious touch to the classic decor of every public room.

After an ambitious program of extensive refurbishment, which was completed in 2008, each of Seabourn's yacht-like vessels emerged from drydock in ship-shape.

	1992, 1988, 1989
	ENTERED SERVICE
	208
	PASSENGER CAPACITY
700 ft.	**160**
	CREW MEMBERS
	104
	NUMBER OF CABINS
500 ft.	**10,000**
	GROSS TONS
	439 feet
	LENGTH
300 ft.	**63 feet**
	WIDTH

WOW Factor

As the high crew member-to-guest ratio suggests, service is nonstop. If you're the slightest bit indecisive, the staff seems to anticipate your wishes.

Top: Sky Bar
Bottom: Balcony Suite

Restaurants

The formal restaurant offers open seating during scheduled hours. For a more laid-back setting, the Veranda Café has indoor and outdoor seating for breakfast and lunch, plus reservations-required tasting dinners in a smart-casual atmosphere every evening, including formal nights. The grill serves outdoors when weather permits.

What Works & What Doesn't

Everything on board is in keeping with the ship's small scale, including entertainment, which leans toward pianists or singers accompanied by a small combo for dancing. Repeat passengers can't keep the secret whirlpool on the ship's bow from being discovered—it's a preferred spot for watching the sun set. A single outdoor swimming pool is deep, but not long enough for serious laps. Art, or the absence of it, is noteworthy on a ship of this style. Some well-chosen, colorful pieces would add vibrancy to the otherwise predominantly blue and neutral color schemes.

Accommodations

Layout: All suites are on three mid-level decks and none are aft, which can be noisy on a ship with a water-sports marina. The roomy accommodations are truly of suite proportion: large walk-in closets, a spacious sitting area with coffee table that converts to a dining table for meals, a vanity-desk, and a marble bathroom with a separate shower and tub (in most suites). Owner's, Classic, and Double suites actually have a dining table and chairs; Owner's suites have a guest bathroom. Both Owner's and Classic suites have fully furnished balconies.

Amenities: Amenities are also befitting a true luxury suite: flat-screen TV with DVD player, Bose Wave CD stereo, a personal safe, and hair dryer. Other amenities include a stocked minibar, fresh fruit and flowers, a world atlas, personalized stationery, shampoo, conditioner, designer soap and lotion, Egyptian cotton towels and robes, slippers, umbrellas, and beds dressed with silky, high thread-count linens. The only apparent difference between the sister ships is that *Seabourn Pride* has twin sinks in the bathrooms, while *Seabourn Legend* bathrooms have but one.

Good to Know: Four suites are designed for wheelchair accessibility.

Cabin Type	Size (sq. ft.)
Owner's Suite	530–575
Classic Suite	400
Double Suite	554
Balcony Suite*	277
Ocean View Suite	277
*The balcony isn't functional.	

Fast Facts

- 6 passenger decks
- Specialty restaurant, dining room, buffet
- Wi-Fi, in-cabin safes, in-cabin refrigerators, in-cabin DVDs
- Pool
- Fitness classes, gym, hair salon, 3 hot tubs, sauna, spa, steam room
- 3 bars, casino, dance club, library, showroom
- Dry cleaning, laundry facilities, laundry service
- Computer room

2

SEABOURN CRUISE LINE

In the Know

Brush up on obscure facts before boarding if you plan to participate in Team Trivia: the hotly contested competition can be brutal. Bridge is another serious pastime on Seabourn cruises, and you're sure to find a foursome. Decks and score pads are provided on board, so leave your cards at home.

Favorites

Floating Pleasure: For pure indulgence, make a selection from the aromatherapy bath menu before a soak in the tub. Your cabin attendant will even draw it for you, although you'll have to wash your own back and dry yourself off afterward.

Best Added Value: Complimentary Massage Moments on deck are soothing tension tamers and an antidote to travel weariness.

Our Favorite Spot for a Nightcap: The deck surrounding the whirlpool on Deck 5 is usually deserted after dark and terribly romantic on a starry night.

Make It a Double: Double suites consist of two standard suites combined, with one half furnished as a living-dining room and two full bathrooms. They're the ultimate indulgence if you have the money.

Suite-est Indulgence: A limited number of mini-balconies are available in standard suites; however, they're simply for fresh air, as there's no room to stand outside on them. Go this route if you want a taste of the sea air but can't upgrade to a full balcony.

At anchor in Santorini

SEADREAM YACHT CLUB

SeaDream yachts began sailing in 1984 beneath the Sea Goddess banner and, after a couple of changes of ownership and total renovation in 2002, they have evolved into the ultimate boutique ships. A voyage on one of these sleek mega-yachts is all about personal choice.

Sea Dream I

Passengers enjoy an unstructured holiday at sea doing what they please, making it easy to imagine the diminutive vessel really is a private yacht. The ambience is refined and elegantly casual.

SEADREAM YACHT CLUB
2601 S. Bayshore Drive,
Penthouse 1B
Coconut Grove, FL 33133
305/856-5622 or
800/707-4911
www.seadreamyachtclub.com

Cruise Style: Luxury

Fine dining and socializing with fellow passengers and the ships' captains and officers are preferred yachting pastimes. Other than a pianist in the tiny piano bar, a small casino, and movies in the main lounge, there's no roster of activities. The late-night place to be is the Top of the Yacht Bar, where passengers gather to share the day's experiences and kick their shoes off to dance on the teak deck. The captain hosts welcome aboard and farewell cocktail receptions in the Main Salon each week. Otherwise, you're on your own to do as you please.

A well-stocked library has books and movies for those who prefer quiet pursuits in the privacy of their staterooms. In addition, MP3 jukeboxes stocked with all types of music—enough to play for a complete sailing without repeating a selection—are available for personal use at no charge.

The weekly picnic on a private beach is considered by many passengers as their most memorable experience ashore during a SeaDream cruise. It begins with refreshing drinks served during a wet landing from Zodiacs and is followed by SeaDream's signature champagne and caviar splash served to passengers from a surfboard bar in the crystal-clear water. On voyages where it isn't possible to host the champagne and caviar splash ashore, it is celebrated poolside.

SeaDream yachts are often chartered by families, corporations, and other affinity groups, but the company does not charter both ships at the same time. If your chosen sailing is closed to you because of a charter, the other yacht will be available.

Food

Every meal is prepared-to-order using the freshest seafood and U.S. Prime cuts of beef. Menus include vegetarian alternatives and Asian wellness cuisine for the health-conscious. Cheeses, petits fours, and chocolate truffles are offered after dinner with coffee, and the Grand Marnier soufflé is to die for. A weekly dining event, the Chef's Menu Gustation, features an interesting medley of dishes planned by the executive chef for their variety and flavor; portions are sensibly sized, enabling diners to enjoy each course.

Weather permitting, daily breakfast, lunch, and special dinners are served alfresco in the canopied Topsider Restaurant. Wines are chosen to complement each luncheon and dinner menu from shipboard cellars that stock 3,500 bottles on each ship. Sommeliers are more than happy to discuss the attributes of each vintage and steam off the labels if you want to search for them at home. Snacks, from caviar to popcorn, are always available and delivered wherever you might be when hunger strikes, although there is a charge for caviar.

Room service is always available, but not just in your suite; you can dine anywhere you wish on deck.

Fitness & Recreation

Small gyms on each ship are equipped with treadmills, elliptical machines, recumbent bikes, and free weights. A personal trainer is available for consultation, and tai chi, yoga and aerobics classes are offered on deck as requested by passengers.

The yachts' unique SeaDream Spa facilities are also on the small side, yet offer a full menu of individualized, gentle Asian pampering treatments including massages, facials, and body wraps utilizing Eastern techniques. Hair and nail services are offered in the salon. SeaDream Spa is a member of the Thai Spa Association; products utilized for spa and salon services are among the best available from around the world. Massages are also available in cabanas ashore during the private beach party. It's recommended that passengers schedule time for use of the sauna, as its size limits the number of people who can comfortably use it at once.

Noteworthy

■ You may use an MP3 jukebox stocked with all types of music at no charge during your cruise.

■ The bar is always open with a wide selection, but an additional fee applies to certain wines and premium liquor brands.

■ Activities directors conduct informal talks prior to each port of call to help you orient yourself ashore.

Top: Relax on a Balinese dream bed
Bottom: Fitness classes

Top: Dining at Topside Restaurant
Middle: SeaDream Spa
Bottom: The Top of the Yacht bar

The water-sports marina is popular with active passengers who want to water-ski, kayak, windsurf, or take a Jet Ski for a whirl while anchored in calm waters. Mountain bikes are available for use ashore, and a Segway people-mover can be rented for a unique spin around the pier. On board, the state-of-the-art golf simulator offers play on 30 worldwide championship golf courses.

Your Shipmates

SeaDream yachts attract energetic, affluent travelers of all ages, as well as groups. Passengers tend to be couples in their mid-40s up to retirees who enjoy the unstructured informality, subdued ambience, and utterly exclusive service.

These ships are not recommended for passengers who use wheelchairs. Although there's one stateroom considered accessible, public facilities have thresholds and the elevator doesn't reach the uppermost deck. Tide conditions can cause the gangway to be steep when docked, and negotiating shore tenders would be impossible.

Dress Code

Leave the formal duds at home—every night is yacht casual on SeaDream. Men wear open-collar shirts and slacks; sport coats are preferred but not required. A tie is never necessary. For women, sundresses, dressy casual skirts and sweaters, or pants and tops are the norm.

Junior Cruisers

SeaDream yachts are adult-oriented. High chairs and booster seats are available for the youngsters occasionally on board, but no children's facilities or organized activities are available. Parents are responsible for the behavior and entertainment of their children. Additionally, children under the age of one are not allowed.

Service

Personal service and attention to detail are amazing; everyone will greet you by name within minutes of boarding. Passenger preferences are shared among staff members, who all work hard to assist one another. You seldom, if ever, have to repeat a request. Waiting in line for anything is unthinkable.

CHOOSE A CRUISE ON SEADREAM YACHT CLUB IF...

❶ You enjoy dining as an event, as courses are presented with a flourish and wines flow freely.

❷ You don't like to hear the word "no."

❸ You have good sea legs. In rough seas, the SeaDream yachts tend to bob up and down.

Tipping
Tipping is neither required nor expected.

Past Passengers
The SeaDream Club was designed to extend appreciation to past passengers, who are automatically enrolled in the club upon completion of one sailing. Members receive the *SeaDreamer* newsletter, which is published three times a year and features news and photos from the SeaDream yachts, profiles of the yachts' captains and other onboard personalities, profiles of various ports of call, news of special sailings, and other information of interest.

Other SeaDream Club benefits include advance notice of new itineraries, an annual club-members cruise, perks for introducing new passengers to SeaDream, a priority wait list on sold-out cruises, the ability to reserve spa appointments and shore excursions online, 5% savings when booking a future cruise while on board, an onboard club member cocktail party, and special savings in the ships' Boutique and Asian Spa.

Good to Know
Don't miss cocktails before dinner, when the activities director gives a brief overview of the next day's port of call and other happenings. There's a daily schedule, but you'll miss a lot of fun and camaraderie if you skip the cocktail hour. You may also miss a last-minute decision by the captain to extend a port call or even change the order of ports if there's something interesting going on ashore.

DON'T CHOOSE A CRUISE ON SEADREAM YACHT CLUB IF...

❶ You like to dress up. While you could wear a sport coat to dinner, no one ever wears a tie on these ships.

❷ You must have a balcony: there are none on any of Seadream's yachtlike vessels.

❸ You need structured activities: you'll have to plan your own.

SEADREAM I, SEADREAM II

Public Areas & Facilities

Although these vessels are not huge, the public rooms are quite spacious; the Main Salon and Dining Salon are large enough to comfortably seat all passengers at once. Decor is elegant in its simplicity and surprisingly non-nautical. Instead, it's modern and sleek, utilizing the hues of the sea, sky, and sandy beaches. Oriental rugs cover polished teak floors in the reception area, and in the large, sun-splashed library, where you'll find more than 1,000 books from which to select as well as computers to access the Internet. The library also lends movies to watch on the flat-screen TV/DVD player in your suite.

Balinese dream beds are the ideal spot to relax by day, either for sunbathing or reading beneath an umbrella. A telescope mounted at each ship's stern is handy for spotting land and other vessels at sea.

	1984, 1985
	ENTERED SERVICE
	110
	PASSENGER CAPACITY
700 ft.	**90**
	CREW MEMBERS
	55
	NUMBER OF CABINS
500 ft.	**4,300**
	GROSS TONS
	344 feet
	LENGTH
300 ft.	**47 feet**
	WIDTH

WOW Factor

Every passenger is treated like the most important guest on board. Crew members take all requests very seriously.

Restaurants

The formal restaurant offers open-seating dining during scheduled hours. For a more casual setting, the Topside restaurant has outdoor seating for breakfast and lunch—either with table service or from a small buffet—plus scheduled dinners alfresco (the indoor restaurant is also open for those who do not wish to dine outside). Room service is always available.

What Works & What Doesn't

Exceptional food and service in a comfortable, yet sophisticated yachting atmosphere are the allure of these diminutive ships. No smoking is allowed indoors, which is either refreshing or an annoyance, depending on your point of view (and habits).

Cocktail glasses (and even a corkscrew) are provided in suite cabinets; however, there's a charge for wines and spirits ordered for your suite. This is some-what odd considering the open-bar policy throughout the ships and the complimentary soft drinks, bottled water, and beer that are provided in passengers' mini-refrigerators.

Top: The Top of the Yacht bar
Bottom: Casino play

2

Accommodations

Layout: Every stateroom is outside with an ocean view; every cabin has a sitting area, and there's plenty of drawer space for storage. A curtain can be drawn between the bed and sitting area for privacy. Bathrooms are marble-clad and have large, glass-enclosed showers with twin shower heads that make up for the tiny overall size of the bathrooms.

Amenities: All cabins contain an entertainment center with a large, flat-screen TV, CD, and DVD system, broadband Internet connection, personalized stationery, and a wet bar stocked with complimentary beer, soft drinks, and bottled water. A lighted, magnifying mirror and hair dryer are at a vanity table. Beds are dressed with Belgian linens and your choice of synthetic or down pillows and a duvet or woolen blankets. Bathrooms are stocked with deluxe Bulgari shampoo, shower gel, soap, and lotion. Turkish cotton bath-robes and slippers are provided for use during the cruise.

Good to Know: The single Owner's suite has a living room, dining area, separate bedroom, a bathroom with a sea view (as well as a separate tub and shower), and a guest bathroom. Commodore Club staterooms are basically double staterooms with one side configured as a sitting-dining area room; they feature two identical bathrooms with showers. One stateroom is designed for wheelchair accessibility.

Cabin Type	Size (sq. ft.)
Owner's Suite	450
Commodore Club	390
Yacht Club*	195

*16 of the Yacht Club staterooms are convertible to 8 Commodore staterooms, giving a variable passenger capacity.

Fast Facts

- 5 passenger decks
- Dining room, buffet
- In-cabin safes, in-cabin refrigerators, in-cabin broadband, in-cabin DVDs
- Pool
- Fitness classes, gym, hair salon, hot tub, sauna, spa
- 3 bars, casino, library, showroom
- Dry cleaning, laundry service
- Computer room
- No-smoking cabins

In the Know

The Balinese sun beds adjacent to the Top of the Yacht Bar have such thick, comfortable pads that passengers occasionally choose to spend the night there after everyone else has gone below deck to their quarters.

Favorites

How'd They Do That?: The weekly barbeque held on a deserted stretch of beach would be a highlight even if it didn't include champagne and caviar. Servers are somehow able to do forward flips in the surf while gripping champagne bottles and never spill a drop.

It's Your Yacht: There's a good selection of music CDs at the Top of the Yacht Bar, but feel free to bring some from home if you have favorites for listening and dancing.

Best Added Value: The single stateroom (215) that is designed for accessibility has a huge bathroom and can be booked by anyone unless it's required by a person with mobility challenges.

Our Favorite Spot for a Nightcap: The Top of the Yacht Bar is the sociable choice; however, for a bit of privacy, take your brandy to one of the secluded alcoves on either side of the open-air Topsiders Restaurant.

Best Eye Opener: Coffee and pastries are set out at Top of the Yacht Bar for early risers.

Pool deck

SILVERSEA CRUISES

Silversea Cruises was launched in 1994 by the former owners of Sitmar Cruises, the Lefebvre family of Rome, whose concept for the new cruise line was to build and sail the highest-quality luxury ships at sea. Intimate ships, paired with exclusive amenities and unparalleled hospitality are the hallmarks of Sil-

The most captivating view on board

versea cruises. All-inclusive air-and-sea fares can be customized to include not just round-trip airfare, but all transfers, porterage, and deluxe precruise accommodations as well.

SILVERSEA CRUISES
110 E. Broward Boulevard
Fort Lauderdale, FL 33301
954/522-4477 or
800/722-9955
www.silversea.com

Cruise Style: Luxury

Personalization is a Silversea maxim. Although their ships offer more activities than other comparably sized luxury vessels, you can either take part in those that interest you or opt instead for a good book and any number of quiet spots to read or snooze in the shade.

Guest lecturers are featured on nearly every cruise; language, dance, and culinary lessons and excellent wine appreciation sessions are always on the schedule of events. Silversea also schedules culinary arts cruises and a series of wine-focused voyages that feature award-winning authors, international wine experts, winemakers, and acclaimed chefs from the world's top restaurants. During afternoon tea, ladies gather for conversation over needlepoint, and the ranks of highly competitive trivia teams increase every successive afternoon.

After dark, the Bar is a predinner gathering spot and the late-night place for dancing to a live band. A multitiered show lounge is the setting for talented singers and musicians, classical concerts, magic shows, big-screen movies, and folkloric entertainers from ashore. A small casino offers slot machines and gaming tables.

2

Food

Dishes from the galleys of Silversea's Master Chefs are complemented by those of La Collection du Monde, created by Silversea's culinary partner, the world-class chefs of Relais & Châteaux. Menus include hot-and-cold appetizers, at least four entrée selections, a vegetarian alternative, and Cruiselite cuisine (low in cholesterol, sodium, and fat). Special off-menu orders are prepared whenever possible, provided that the ingredients are available on board. In the event that they aren't, you may find after a day in port that a trip to the market was made in order to fulfill your request.

Chef Marco Betti, the owner of Antica Pasta restaurants in Florence, Italy, and Atlanta, Georgia, has designed a new menu for La Terrazza that focuses on one of the most luxurious food trends, the "slow food" movement. The goal of the movement is to preserve the gastronomic traditions of Italy through the use of fresh, traditional foods, and it's spread throughout the world. At La Terrazza (by day the Terrace Café, a casual buffet) the menu showcases the finest in Italian cooking, from classic favorites to Tuscan fare. The restaurant carries no surcharge; however, seating is limited, so reservations are a must to ensure a table. It's one reservation you'll be glad you took the time to book.

An intimate dining experience aboard each vessel is the Wine Restaurant by Relais & Châteaux—Le Champagne (*Silver Shadow, Silver Whisper*) or La Saletta (*Silver Wind, Silver Wind, Silver Cloud*). Adding a dimension to dining, the exquisite cuisine is designed to celebrate the wines served—a different celebrated vintage is served with each course. Menus and wines are chosen by Relais & Châteaux sommeliers to reflect regions of the world noted for their rich wine heritage.

An evening poolside barbeque is a weekly dinner event, weather permitting. A highlight of every cruise is the Galley Brunch, when passengers are invited into the galley to select from a feast decorated with imaginative ice and vegetable sculptures. Even when meals are served buffet-style in the Terrace Café, you will seldom have to carry your own plate as waiters are at hand to assist you to your table. Wines are chosen to complement each day's luncheon and dinner menus.

Grilled foods, sandwiches, and an array of fruits and salads are served daily for lunch at the poolside Grill. Always available are extensive selections from the room-service menu. The full restaurant menu may also be used for room service orders, which can be served course by course in your suite during regular dining hours.

Noteworthy

■ Prior to departure, Silversea provides a list of port addresses, to which your mail can be forwarded throughout your voyage.

■ Gentlemen are no longer required to wear a tie with their jackets on informal evenings.

■ Silversea does not utilize the services of photographers aboard their ships.

Top: Stylish entertainment
Bottom: Terrace Café alfresco dining

Top: Table tennis
Middle: Caring, personal service
Bottom: Veranda Suite

Fitness & Recreation

The rather small gym is equipped with cardiovascular and weight-training equipment, and fitness classes are held in the mirror-lined, but somewhat confining, exercise room.

South Pacific–inspired Mandara Spa offers numerous treatments including exotic sounding massages, facials, and body wraps. Hair and nail services are available in the busy salon. A plus is that appointments for spa and beauty salon treatments can be made online from 60 days until 48 hours prior to sailing.

Golfers can sign up with the pro on board for individual lessons utilizing a high-tech swing analyzer and attend complimentary golf clinics or participate in a putting contest.

Your Shipmates

Silversea Cruises appeal to sophisticated, affluent couples who enjoy the country-clublike atmosphere, exquisite cuisine, and polished service on board, not to mention the exotic ports and unique experiences ashore.

Dress Code

Two formal nights are standard on seven-night cruises and three to four nights, depending on the itinerary, on longer sailings. Men are required to wear tuxedos or dark suits after 6 PM. All other evenings are either informal, when a jacket is called for (a tie is optional, but most men wear them), or casual, when slacks with a jacket over an open-collar shirt for men and sporty dresses or skirts or pants with a sweater or blouse for women are suggested.

Junior Cruisers

Silversea Cruises is adult-oriented and unable to accommodate children less than one year of age, and the cruise line limits the number of children under the age of three on board. No dedicated children's facilities are available, so parents are responsible for the behavior and entertainment of their children.

Service

Personalized service is exacting and hospitable, yet discreet; the staff strive for perfection and often achieve

CHOOSE A CRUISE ON SILVERSEA CRUISES IF...

❶ Your taste leans toward learning and exploration.

❷ You enjoy socializing as well as the option of live entertainment, just not too much of it.

❸ You like to plan ahead. You can reserve shore tours, salon services, and spa treatments online.

it. The attitude is decidedly European and begins with a welcome-aboard flute of champagne, then continues throughout as personal preferences are remembered and satisfied. The word "no" doesn't seem to be in the staff vocabulary in any language. Guests in top-category suites are pampered by butlers who are certified by the Guild of Professional Butlers.

Tipping

Tipping is neither required nor expected.

Past Passengers

Membership in the Venetian Society is automatic upon completion of one Silversea cruise. Members begin accruing Venetian Society cruise days and are eligible for discounts on select voyages; onboard recognition and private parties; milestone rewards; exclusive gifts; the *Venetian Society Newsletter*; ship visitation privileges; complimentary early embarkation or late debarkation at certain milestones; members-only benefits at select Leading Hotels of the World and Relais & Châteaux hotels and resorts; and select offers through Silversea's preferred partners.

Through the Friends of Society programs, members can double their accumulated cruise days and receive a shipboard spending credit by inviting friends or family members to sail on select Venetian Society sailings. Friends or family will enjoy the same Venetian Society savings as members for those cruises, a really nice perk.

Good to Know

You might expect a bit of stodginess to creep in at this level of ultraluxury, but you wouldn't necessarily be correct. Socializing isn't quite as easy-going as on smaller ships, and some passengers can come off as a bit standoffish. However, you will encounter like-minded fellow passengers if you make the effort to participate in group activities, particularly the highly competitive afternoon-trivia sessions. With an increasingly younger crowd on board, you are more likely to encounter partyers at late-night disco sessions than couples waltzing between courses during dinner.

DON'T CHOOSE A CRUISE ON SILVERSEA CRUISES IF...

❶ You want to dress informally at all times on your cruise. Passengers on these cruises tend to dress up.

❷ You need highly structured activities and have to be reminded of them.

❸ You prefer the glitter and stimulation of Las Vegas to the understated glamour of Monaco.

SILVER SHADOW, SILVER WHISPER

Public Areas & Facilities

The logical layout of these sister ships, with suites located in the forward two-thirds of the ship and public rooms aft, makes orientation simple. The clean, modern decor that defines public areas and lounges might almost seem stark, but it places the main emphasis on large expanses of glass for sunshine and sea views as well as passenger comfort.

Silversea ships boast unbeatable libraries stocked with best-sellers, travel books, classics, and movies for in-suite viewing. Extremely wide passageways in public areas are lined with glass-front display cabinets full of interesting and unusual artifacts from the places the ships visit.

The Humidor by Davidoff is a clubby cigar smoking room with overstuffed leather seating and a ventilation system that even nonsmokers can appreciate.

700 ft.	**2000, 2001** ENTERED SERVICE
	382 PASSENGER CAPACITY
	295 CREW MEMBERS
500 ft.	**191** NUMBER OF CABINS
	28,258 GROSS TONS
	610 feet LENGTH
300 ft.	**82 feet** WIDTH

WOW Factor

Pommery champagne on ice welcomes you to your suite. And the champagne flows freely throughout your cruise.

Restaurants

The formal restaurant offers open-seating during scheduled hours. Specialty dining is offered by reservation in Le Champagne (extra charge) and La Terrazza. For a more casual meal, the Terrace Café has indoor and outdoor seating for buffet-style breakfast and lunch. The poolside Grill offers an ultracasual lunch option.

What Works & What Doesn't

Sailing on a Silversea ship is like spending time as a pampered guest at a home in the Hamptons. Everything is at your fingertips, and if it isn't, all you have to do is ask. Silversea is so all-inclusive that you'll find your room key-charge card is seldom used for anything but opening your suite door. Room service is prompt, and orders arrive with crystal, china, and even a linen tablecloth for a complete dining room-style setup in your suite. In an odd contrast to the contents of display cases and lovely flower arrangements, artwork on the walls is fairly ho-hum and not at all memorable.

Top: The Casino
Bottom: *Silver Shadow* at sea

Accommodations

Layout: Every suite is outside with an ocean view, and more than 80% have a private teak-floor balcony. Standard suites have a sitting area that can be curtained off from the bed for more privacy. Marble bathrooms have double sinks and a separate, glass-enclosed shower as well as a tub. All suites have generous walk-in closets.

Amenities: Standard suites have an entertainment center with a TV and DVD or VCR, personalized stationery, a cocktail cabinet, personal safe, and a refrigerator stocked with complimentary beer, soft drinks, and bottled water. A hair dryer is provided at a vanity table, and you can request a magnifying mirror. Beds are dressed with high-quality linens, duvets, or blankets, and your choice of synthetic or down pillows. Bathrooms have huge towels and terry bathrobes for use during the cruise as well as designer shampoo, soaps, and lotion.

Top Suites: In addition to much more space, top-category suites have all the standard amenities plus dining areas, separate bedrooms, and CD players. Silver suites and above have whirlpool tubs. The top three categories have separate powder rooms.

Good to Know: Two suites are designed for wheelchair accessibility.

Cabin Type	Size (sq. ft.)
Grand Suite	1,286–1,435
Royal Suite	1,312–1,352
Owner's Suite	1,208
Silver/Medallion Suite	701/521
Verandah/Vista Suite	345/287

In the Know

Nine Vista suites on deck five have doors to the outside that access a common, semiprivate veranda area. Even though the area is not furnished, it's like having a balcony without paying a higher fare.

The Poolside Grille: lunch and light snacks

Favorites

Best Added Value: The spas' complimentary saunas and steam rooms are tiny treasures. Although small, they are adequate and seldom occupied.

Most Appreciated Freebie: Also on the small side are the totally free laundry rooms (even the soap is included). Perfectly adequate for ships this size, they are frequently in use. Just about the only line you're likely to encounter on a Silversea ship is the one to use a washing machine.

Best Nightly Treat: Other cruise lines leave a chocolate on your pillow to wish you sweet dreams. Silversea's little gold boxes of Godiva chocolates are distinctively a cut above the usual.

Our Favorite Spot for a Nightcap: We love to sink into a cushy leather seat in the candlelighted cigar lounge to end a full evening of dinner and dancing.

Mama Mia: Our favorite pasta is prepared using Isabella Rossellini's own receipe.

SILVER CLOUD, SILVER WIND

Public Areas & Facilities

These two yachtlike gems are all about style, understatement, and personal choice, so if you want to snuggle into a book in the well-stocked library, no one will lift an eyebrow. While there simply isn't room on these ships for huge rooms, the public spaces are more than adequate and designed to function well. These ships served as the models for their larger sisters, *Silver Shadow* and *Silver Whisper*, which expanded on the smaller ships' concept of locating all passenger accommodations forward and public rooms aft.

The Restaurant is one of the loveliest dining rooms at sea with a domed ceiling and musicians to provide dance music between courses. Either the Bar or Panorama Lounge are comfortable spots to socialize, dance, or enjoy cocktails before or after the evening entertainment, which might include a classical concert or smallish production show in the showroom or Moonlight Movies, feature films shown outside on the Pool Deck.

1994, 1995	ENTERED SERVICE
296	PASSENGER CAPACITY
212	CREW MEMBERS
148	NUMBER OF CABINS
16,800	GROSS TONS
514 feet	LENGTH
71 feet	WIDTH

700 ft.

500 ft.

300 ft.

WOW Factor

Cold towels and chilled fruit poolside and a fridge stocked with chilled water in the fitness area don't go unnoticed by appreciative passengers.

Restaurants

Top: The bar
Bottom: Royal Suite

The Restaurant has open seating for all meals. Saletta has a special tasting menu with wine pairings for an extra charge. La Terrazza is the indoor-outdoor buffet; on most evenings it serves as an alternative restaurant. The Pool Grill offers casual fare. Room service is available 24 hours a day, and items from The Restaurant menu can be served course-by-course.

What Works & What Doesn't

Silversea is one of the most all-inclusive cruise lines, and the ambience on board is comfortably upscale, heightened by never having to sign a bar ticket. Wine is poured freely at lunch and dinner, and no one has to cringe when ordering a round of drinks for new friends, which reinforces camaraderie between passengers. While the minimalist modern decor is accented by beautiful flower arrangements throughout the ship, the artwork is somewhat uninspired. However, whatever might be lacking in terms of decorative art is more than made up for by the excellent enrichment programs.

Accommodations

Layout: All accommodations are considered suites; all are outside and have at least an ocean view; an outstanding 80% also have private balconies. Suite interiors are enhanced with appealing artwork, flowers, sitting areas, and bedding topped with plush duvets and choice of pillow style. A writing desk, refrigerator, TV with DVD player, dressing table with lighted mirror and hair dryer, walk-in closet, and personal safe are all standard. The marbled bathrooms have full-size bathtubs.

Amenities: Champagne on ice awaits the arrival of all passengers, and it is replenished as desired; the beverage cabinet is stocked daily on request with individual selections of wines, spirits, and beverages. A fruit basket is replenished daily. Bathrooms are stocked with European toiletries, and slippers and bathrobes are provided for use during the cruise.

Good to Know: Teak-floored balconies have patio furniture and floor-to-ceiling glass doors. Two suites are wheelchair-accessible.

Cabin Type	Size (sq. ft.)
Grand and Rossellini Suite	1,314
Royal Suite	1,031
Owner's Suite	827
Silver Suite	541
Veranda Suite/Vista Suite	295/240

Cabin sizes include the square footage of any balcony.

Fast Facts

- 6 passenger decks
- 2 specialty restaurants, dining room, buffet
- WiFi, in-cabin safes, some in-cabin minibars, some in-cabin refrigerators, in-cabin DVDs
- 1 pool
- Fitness classes, gym, hair salon, 1 hot tub, sauna, spa, steam room
- 3 bars, casino, dance club, library, showroom
- Dry cleaning, laundry facilities, laundry service
- Computer room

In the Know

Silversea's spokesperson Isabella Rossellini is the personification of the line's standard of glamour and sophistication. Rossellini makes her home away from home aboard each Silversea ship in a suite she has personally selected, customized, and renamed.

Favorites

Our Favorite Spot for a Nightcap: Le Champagne, the wine and cigar room on Deck Eight, is a cozy retreat with sumptuous leather chairs. It's just naturally a haven for a rare port after dinner or a nightcap accompanied by a fine cigar.

Best Place to Get Away: Practice yoga, train with the latest Pilates program, or work out utilizing state-of-the-art fitness equipment while drawing inspiration from the breathtaking, panoramic views of the ocean from the Fitness Center.

Best Way to Expand Your Mind: Every cruise features regionally specific lectures by noted historians, ambassadors, state leaders, authors and geographers—all experts and each sharing special insights into areas of the world they know intimately. Guest chefs and wine experts also join special Culinary Arts and Wine Series Voyages.

Best Added Value: Silversea is so all-inclusive that you seldom need to reach for your charge card, but what we appreciate most is feeling like a valued guest in a gracious retreat.

The pool deck

STAR CLIPPERS

In 1991 Star Clippers unveiled a new tall-ship alternative to sophisticated travelers, whose desires included having an adventure at sea but not on board a conventional cruise ship. Star Clippers vessels are four- and five-masted sailing beauties—the world's largest barquentine and full-rigged sailing ships.

Sun yourself on the bow netting

Filled with modern, high-tech equipment as well as the amenities of private yachts, the ships rely on sail power while at sea unless conditions require the assistance of the engines. Minimal heeling, usually less than 6%, is achieved through judicious control of the sails.

STAR CLIPPERS
7200 N.W. 19th Street,
Suite 206
Miami, FL 33126
305/442-0550 or
800/442-0551
www.starclippers.com

Cruise Style: Sailing Ship

A boyhood dream became a cruise-line reality when Swedish entrepreneur Mikael Krafft launched his fleet of authentic re-creations of classic 19th-century clipper ships. The day officially begins when the captain holds an informative daily briefing on deck with a bit of storytelling tossed in. Star Clippers are not cruise ships in the ordinary sense with strict agendas and pages of activities. You're free to do what you please day and night, but many passengers join the crew members topside when the sails or raised or for some of the lighthearted events like crab-racing contests, scavenger hunts, and a talent night. The informality of singing around the piano bar typifies an evening on one of these ships, although in certain ports local performers come on board to spice up the action with an authentic taste of the local music and arts.

The lack of rigid scheduling is one of Star Clippers' most appealing attractions. The bridge is always open, and passengers are welcome to peer over the captain's shoulder as he plots the ship's course. Crew members are happy to demonstrate how to splice a line, reef a sail, or tie a proper knot.

As attractive as the ships' interiors are, the focal point of Star Clippers cruises is the outdoors. Plan to spend a lot of time on deck soaking in the sun, sea, and sky. It doesn't get any better than that. Consider also that each ship has at least two swimming pools. Granted, they are tiny, but they are a refreshing feature uncommon on true sailing ships and all but the most lavish yachts.

Although the Star Clippers ships are motorized, their engines are shut down whenever crews unfurl the sails (36,000 square feet on *Star Clipper* and 56,000 square feet on *Royal Clipper*) to capture the wind. On a typical cruise, the ships rely exclusively on sail power anytime favorable conditions prevail.

As the haunting strains of Vangelis's symphony "1492: Conquest of Paradise" are piped over the PA system and the first of the sails are unfurled, the only thing you'll hear on deck is the sound of the music and the calls of the line handlers until every sail is in place. While the feeling of the wind powering large ships through the water is spine-tingling, you will miss the wondrous sight of your ship under sail unless the captain can schedule a photo opportunity utilizing one of the tenders. It's one of the most memorable sights you'll see if this opportunity avails itself. However, when necessary, the ships will cruise under motor power to meet the requirements of their itineraries.

Food

Not noted for gourmet fare, the international cuisine is what you would expect from a trendy shoreside bistro, albeit an elegant one. All meals are open-seating in the formal dining room during scheduled hours; breakfast and lunch—an impressive spread of seafood, salads, and grilled items—are served buffet-style, while dinners are leisurely affairs served in the European manner. Hint: If you want your salad *before* your main course, just ask; the French style is to serve it after the main course. Menus, created in consultation with chef Jean Marie Meulien (who has been awarded Michelin stars throughout his career), include appetizers, soups, pasta, a sorbet course, at least three choices of entrees, salad, cheese, and, of course, dessert. Mediterreanan-inspired entrées, vegetarian, and light dishes are featured. A maître d' is present at the more formal evening meals to seat passengers, but it isn't uncommon on these small ships for them to arrange their own groups of dinner company.

Early risers on each ship find a continental breakfast offered at the Tropical Bar, and coffee and fresh fruit are always available in the Piano Bar. Should you want to remain in your swimsuit, casual buffets are set up adjacent to the Tropical Bar at noon (the "Deck Snack Buffet") and at

Noteworthy

■ Don't ask for connecting staterooms on Star Clippers ships—there are none.

■ Look for secret hideaways on one of the hidden balconies on either side of *Royal Clipper's* bow.

■ You are free to dine when and with whomever you wish on Star Clippers ships, including with the officers, who join passengers in the dining room most nights.

Top: Cooling off in one of the pools
Bottom: *Royal Clipper* Deluxe Suite

Top: View from the bow
Middle: *Royal Clipper* piano bar
Bottom: *Royal Clipper* spa

5 PM (the "Afternoon Snack"). Some of the "snacks" are themed and quite popular—a Neptune seafood luncheon, snacks with waffles or crepes, and a taco bar. On select itineraries, an outdoor barbecue is served on shore.

With the exception of occupants of Owner's Suites and Deluxe Suites on *Royal Clipper,* there is no room service available unless you are sick and can't make it to the dining room for meals.

Fitness & Recreation

Formal exercise sessions take a backseat to water sports, although aerobics classes and swimming are featured on all ships. Only *Royal Clipper* has a marina platform that can be lowered in calm waters to access water sports and diving; however, the smaller ships replicate the experience by using motorized launches to reach reefs for snorkeling. A gym-spa with an array of exercise equipment, free weights, spa treatments and unisex hair services are also found only on *Royal Clipper.* Despite the lack of a formal fitness center on *Star Clipper,* morning aerobics or yoga classes are usually held on deck for active passengers. Massages, manicures, and pedicures can be arranged as well.

Your Shipmates

Star Clippers cruises draw active, upscale American and European couples from their 30s on up, who enjoy sailing but in a casually sophisticated atmosphere with modern conveniences. Many sailings are equally divided between North Americans and Europeans, so announcements are made in several languages accordingly.

This is not a cruise line for the physically challenged; there are no elevators or ramps, nor are staterooms or bathrooms wheelchair-accessible. Gangways and shore launches can also be difficult to negotiate.

Dress Code

All evenings are elegant casual, so slacks with an open-collar shirt are fine for men, and sundresses, skirts, or pants with a sweater or blouse suggested for women. Coats and ties are never required. Shorts and T-shirts are not allowed in the dining room at dinner.

CHOOSE A CRUISE ON STAR CLIPPERS IF...

1 You wouldn't consider a vacation on a traditional cruise ship but are a sailing enthusiast.

2 You love water sports, particularly snorkeling and scuba diving.

3 You want to anchor in secluded coves and visit islands that are off the beaten path.

Junior Cruisers

Star Clippers ships are adult-oriented. Although children are welcome and may participate in shipboard activities suited to their ability, there are no dedicated youth facilities. Parents are responsible for the behavior and entertainment of their children. Mature teens who can live without video games and a lot of other teens are the best young sailors.

Service

Service is friendly and gracious, similar to what you would find in a boutique hotel or restaurant. You may find that you have to flag down a waiter for a second cup of coffee, though.

Tipping

Gratuities are not included in the cruise fare and are extended at the sole discretion of passengers. The recommended amount is 8 euros per person per day. Tips are pooled and shared; individual tipping is discouraged. You can either put cash in the tip envelope that will be provided to you and drop it at the purser's office or charge gratuities to your shipboard account. An automatic 15% gratuity is added to each passenger's bar bill.

Past Passengers

Top Gallant is the loyalty club for past passengers. No specific fare discount is offered to members; however, they receive a newsletter and special offers on fare reductions from time to time. Nearly 60% of all passengers choose to make a repeat voyage on Star Clippers ships.

Funds

Note that while fares are quoted in U.S. dollars, all shipboard charges are in euros. Accounts can be settled with cash, traveler's checks, or credit cards on the final day of your cruise.

Good to Know

Fresh air is prevalent inside as well as on deck. Smoking is restricted to limited public rooms and not permitted in cabins. For the ultimate in fresh air, an unparalleled treat is the climb to a lookout station at the first yardarm on each of *Royal Clipper*'s masts where you can relax on a teak settee and take in the view.

DON'T CHOOSE A CRUISE ON STAR CLIPPERS IF...

1. You have a preexisting or potentially serious medical condition. There's no physician on board.

2. You must have a private balcony—there are a few, but only in top accommodation categories.

3. You can't live without room service. Only *Royal Clipper* has it, and only in a few high-end suites.

ROYAL CLIPPER

Public Areas & Facilities

Royal Clipper is the first five-masted, full-rigged sailing ship built since 1902. As the largest true sailing clipper ship in the world today, she carries 42 sails with a total area of 56,000 square feet.

Unusual for a sailing ship, a three-deck atrium graces the heart of the vessel.

Her interior is decorated in Edwardian-era style with abundant gleaming woods, brass fixtures, and nautical touches. Light filters into the piano bar, three-deck high atrium, and the dining room through the glass bottom and portholes of the main swimming pool located overhead.

The rarely used Observation Lounge is located forward of the deluxe suites and affords great sea views. It is also the location of the computer station for all Internet access.

700 ft.	**2000**
	ENTERED SERVICE
	227
	PASSENGER CAPACITY
	106
	CREW MEMBERS
	114
	NUMBER OF CABINS
500 ft.	**5,000**
	GROSS TONS
	439 feet
	LENGTH
300 ft.	**54 feet**
	WIDTH

WOW Factor

Expanses of teak, neatly coiled rope, and honest-to-goodness speed under sail: Royal Clipper *can crank out 20 knots without the engines.*

Restaurants

The multilevel dining room serves a single, open-seating breakfast, lunch, and dinner. For early-risers, a continental breakfast is set up in the piano bar, and a buffet lunch is sometimes offered in the Tropical Bar, as are late-afternoon snacks and predinner canapés. Room service is only available to occupants of the Owner's Suites and Deluxe Suites.

What Works & What Doesn't

The feeling of the wind powering this large vessel through the water is spine-tingling. Unfortunately, you will miss the glorious sight of her under way unless the captain can schedule a photo-op via one of the tenders. Always lively and the center of most of the action day and night, the Tropical Bar on the main deck is where the evening entertainment happens. Outdoors, on the teak deck, is the place to be. The library, with its cushy seating and faux fireplace, is a cozy place to read or play board games; it also offers a surprisingly good selection of books.

Top: *Royal Clipper* dining room
Bottom: Sighting land

2

STAR CLIPPERS

Accommodations

Layout-Amenities: Think yacht, and the cabin sizes make sense. Although efficiently laid out with tasteful, sea-going appointments and prints of clipper ships and sailing yachts on the walls, cabins are small by comparison to most cruise ships. All have a TV, personal safe, desk-vanity, small settee, hair dryer, and marble bathroom with standard toiletries. Closet space is compact, and bureau drawers are narrow, but an under-the-bed drawer is a useful nautical touch for extra storage.

Suites: Owner's Suites, Deluxe Suites, and Category 1 cabins have a sitting area, minibar, whirlpool tub-shower combinations, and bathrobes to use during the cruise. Deluxe Suites also feature a private veranda. Category 1 cabins have doors that open onto a semiprivate area on the outside deck. Only the two Owner's Suites have connecting doors.

Good to Know: Cabins are equipped with 220-volt electrical outlets and a 110-volt outlet suitable only for electric shavers. For 110-volt appliances, you'll need to bring a transformer; for dual-voltage appliances, pack a plug converter. None of the staterooms is designed for wheelchair accessibility, nor are there any elevators. Only the two Owner's Suites have interconnecting doors.

Cabin Type	Size (sq. ft.)
Owner's Suite	355
Deluxe Suite & Cat. 1 Ocean View	204
Standard Ocean View	150
Cat. 5 Ocean View	118
Inside	107

Fast Facts

- 5 passenger decks
- Dining room
- In-cabin safes, some in-cabin refrigerators, some in-cabin DVDs
- 3 pools
- Fitness classes, gym, hair salon, spa, steam room
- 3 bars, library
- Dry cleaning, laundry service
- Computer room
- No-smoking cabins

In the Know

Most cabin showers have only a 1-inch marble lip, so water tends to spread across the bathroom floor in bumpy seas. While there's a second drain outside the shower, anything left on the floor will get soaked. A rolled-up beach towel outside the shower will help contain the flood.

Favorites

Heads Up: In Category 3 cabins forward, you'll notice a definite slant to the floor, due to the location near the bow. You may also feel a bit more motion forward than aft and should also remember that creaking sounds are common on sailing ships.

Best Splurge: Massages in the spa are no-nonsense and reasonably priced.

Best Place to Escape the Crowds: Lookout stations at the first yardarm on each mast are the most private spaces on board and afford the best views—provided that you aren't bothered by heights.

Our Favorite Spot for a Nightcap: Almost anywhere outside at the rail is about perfect on a moonlit night.

Best Snack Spot: Coffee and fresh fruit are always available in the Piano Bar.

Best Underwater View: Peek-a-boo submarine portholes are adjacent to the gym and spa in the Captain Nemo Lounge, where underwater marine life can be spotted when the ship is at anchor.

Royal Clipper under sail

STAR CLIPPER

Public Areas & Facilities

With its bright, brass fixtures, teak-and-mahogany paneling and rails, and antique prints and paintings of famous sailing vessels, *Star Clipper*'s interior decor reflects the heritage of grand sailing ships.

Lighted from overhead by porthole-shape skylights, an atrium-like effect is created by the central opening in the piano bar, which leads to a graceful staircase and the dining room one deck below. The centerpiece of the vaguely Edwardian-style library is a belle epoque–period fireplace.

The Piano Bar is noted for being intimate and cozy. The Tropical Bar, one of the most popular areas on board, is the center of social activity, for predinner cocktails and late-night socializing and dancing. It's the covered outdoor lounge adjacent to the open deck space, where local entertainers often perform.

1992	Entered Service
170	Passenger Capacity
72	Crew Members
85	Number of Cabins
3,000	Gross Tons
360 feet	Length
50 feet	Width

700 ft.

500 ft.

300 ft.

WOW Factor

You can't help but appreciate the silence and harmony with the sea when the engines are turned off and the ship is under sail.

Restaurants

The mahogany-paneled dining room serves a single open-seating breakfast, lunch, and dinner. For early-risers, a continental breakfast is set up in the piano bar, and a buffet lunch is sometimes served on deck. Late-night canapés are offered in the piano bar. There's no room service unless you're sick and can't make it out to meals.

Top: Dining on *Star Clipper*
Bottom: Friendly, efficient service

What Works & What Doesn't

If the sheer beauty of real sailing isn't enough to satisfy your inner pirate, creature comforts are only as far away as your fingertips. However, the bathroom taps can be frustrating until you are accustomed to the regulated water flow. To conserve water, the flow shuts off with annoying regularity, and you have to press a button to restart it. The beds in four Category 5 cabins aft are raised several feet off the floor, and most passengers require the ladder to climb into them. That could be a problem after a long day and a bit too much rum punch.

2

STAR CLIPPERS

Accommodations

Layout-Amenities: Traditional, yachty, and efficiently designed, *Star Clipper*'s cabins are adequate but far from spacious by modern standards. All cabins have a personal safe, desk-vanity, small settee, hair dryer, TV (except Category 6 inside), and marble bathroom with standard toiletries. As would normally be expected on a sailing vessel, staterooms forward and aft are more susceptible to motion than those amidship. There is also a noticeable slant to the floor in cabins near the bow. Unless you are particularly agile, you will want to avoid the inside cabins on Commodore Deck, where beds are strictly upper and lower berths. Some cabins are outfitted with a third, pull-down berth, but most passengers will find the space too cramped for three occupants.

Top-Category Cabins: The Owner's Cabin and Category 1 cabins have a minibar, whirlpool tub-shower combination, and the use of bathrobes during the cruise. Category 1 cabin doors open onto the outside deck, and the Owner's Cabin has a sitting room.

Good to Know: All cabins are equipped with 110-volt electrical outlets and a 110-volt outlet in the bathroom that is suitable only for electric shavers. None of the staterooms are designed for wheelchair accessibility, nor do any staterooms have connecting doors.

Cabin Type	Size (sq. ft.)
Owner's Suite	266
Cat. 1 Ocean View	150
Cat. 2 Ocean View	129
Standard Ocean View	118
Inside	97

Fast Facts

- 4 passenger decks
- Dining room
- In-cabin safes
- 2 pools
- Fitness classes
- 2 bars, library, laundry service
- Computer room
- No-smoking cabins

In the Know

For tranquillity and ample sunbathing space, head to the stern or the bowsprit net. The sails block less sunlight on the deck around the aft pool, and it tends to be quieter, but crawling onto the netting at the bowsprit is even better.

Favorites

Best Place to Escape the Crowds: On a ship this size there aren't too many spots to get away from fellow passengers. Fortunately, there aren't that many passengers, and there's seldom what anyone would consider a crowd.

Our Favorite Spot for a Nightcap: The banquettes that line the piano bar provide a suitably cozy spot to end your evening.

Best Meet-and-Mingle Spot: It's the dining room. Booths and tables that seat six to eight are designed to maximize socializing. There are no tables for two, and few passengers seem to mind.

Best Place to Get Caffeinated: Stop by the Piano Bar anytime for a jolt of java. Complimentary coffee and tea are available there around the clock. Specialty coffee beverages (for which there is a charge) are served only during bar hours.

Star Clipper under sail

WINDSTAR CRUISES

Are they cruise ships with sails or sailing ships designed for cruises? Since 1986, these masted sailing yachts have filled an upscale niche. They often visit ports of call inaccessible to huge, traditional cruise ships and offer a unique perspective of any cruising region. However, Windstar ships seldom depend on

Windstar in the Greek Isles

wind alone to sail. Nevertheless, if you're fortunate and conditions are perfect, as they sometimes are, the complete silence of pure sailing is heavenly. Stabilizers and computer-controlled ballast systems ensure no more than a mere few degrees of lean, making the ships reliably stable in heavy sea conditions.

WINDSTAR CRUISES
2101 Fourth Avenue
Suite 1150
Seattle, WA 98119
206/292-9606 or
800/258-7245
www.windstarcruises.com

Cruise Style: Luxury

When you can tear yourself away from the sight of thousands of yards of Dacron sail overhead, it doesn't take long to read the daily schedule of activities on a typical Windstar cruise. Simply put, there are very few scheduled activities. Diversions are for the most part social, laid-back, and impromptu. You can choose to take part in the short list of daily activities, borrow a book, game, or DVD from the library or do nothing at all. There's never pressure to join in or participate if you simply prefer relaxing with a fully loaded iPod, which you can check out on board.

Evening entertainment is informal, with a small dance combo playing in the main lounges. Compact casinos offer games of chance and slot machines, but don't look for bingo or other organized contests. A weekly show by the crew is delightful; attired in the traditional costumes of their homelands, they present music and dance highlighting their cultures. You may also find occasional movies in the main lounges, which are outfitted with state-of-the-art video and sound equipment. Most passengers prefer socializing, either in the main lounge or an outdoor bar where Cigars Under the Stars attracts not only cigar aficionados, but stargazers as well.

Welcome aboard and farewell parties are hosted by the captain, and most passengers attend those as well as the nightly informational sessions regarding ports of call and activities that are presented by the activities staff during predinner cocktails.

A multimillion-dollar "Degrees of Difference" initiative enhanced each ship from stern to stern in 2006–07. The Yacht Club, which replaces the library on *Wind Surf*, is envisioned to be the social hub of the ship, with computer stations, a coffee bar, and a more expansive feel than the room it replaced. You will be able to join other passengers in comfortable seating around a large flat-screen TV to cheer on your favorite team during sporting events. In addition, all accommodations and bathrooms have been remodeled with updated materials; new weights and televisions were added to the gym; a couples massage room enhances the *Wind Surf* spa; the casual Veranda was expanded; the decks now have Balinese sun beds, and cooling mist sprayers are near the pools. Updates to *Wind Spirit* were not completed at this writing but are expected to be similiar to those on other ships.

Food

Since 1994, Windstar menus have featured Signature Cuisine, a collection of dishes originated by trendy West Coast chef and restaurateur Joachim Splichal and his Patina Group of bistro-style restaurants. Splichal integrates new recipes into the menus regularly in Windstar Cruises' main restaurants and also at Degrees, the alternative restaurant on *Wind Surf*. Splichal and his culinary team spend time aboard each ship with Windstar's executive chefs perfecting the menus and recipes.

In a nod to healthy dining, low-calorie and low-fat Sail Lite spa cuisine alternatives created by chef and cookbook author Jeanne Jones are prepared to American Heart Association guidelines. Additional choices are offered from the vegetarian menu.

Alcoholic beverages and soft drinks are not included in your cruise fare. Neither are the contents of the stocked minibar in your cabin.

A mid-cruise deck barbeque featuring grilled seafood and other favorites is fine dining in an elegantly casual alfresco setting. Desserts are uniformly delightful, and you'll want to try the bread pudding, a Windstar tradition available at the luncheon buffet. With daily tea and hot-and-cold hors d'oeuvres served several times during the afternoon and evening, no one goes hungry. Room service is always available, and you can place your order for dinner from the restaurant's menu during scheduled dining hours.

Noteworthy

■ The shipboard computers that monitor wind velocity and direction also control heeling of the ships to less than six degrees.

■ Evening entertainment on Windstar usually includes a trio for dancing, a small casino, and stargazing.

■ Windstar ships have hot tubs and saltwater swimming pools in addition to retractable stern-mounted water-sports marinas.

Top: Cuisine devised by Chef Charlie Palmer
Bottom: Compass Rose Bar on *Wind Surf*

2

WINDSTAR CRUISES

Top: Backgammon on deck
Middle: Friendly service
Bottom: *Wind Surf* stateroom

Fitness & Recreation

Most of the line's massage and exercise facilities are quite small, as would be expected on a ship that carries fewer than 150 passengers; however, *Wind Surf*'s WindSpa and fitness areas are unexpectedly huge. An array of exercise equipment, free weights, and basic fitness classes are available in the gym and Nautilus room. There is an extra charge for Pilates and yoga classes. A wide variety of massages, body wraps, and facial treatments are offered in the spa, while hair and nail services are available for women and men in the salon. Both spa and salon are operated by Steiner Leisure.

Stern-mounted water-sports marinas are popular with active passengers who want to kayak, windsurf, and water ski. Watery activities are free, including the use of snorkel gear that can be checked out for the entire cruise. The only charge is for diving; PADI-certified instructors offer a two-hour course for noncertified divers who want to try scuba and are also available to lead experienced certified divers on underwater expeditions. The dive teams take care of everything, even prepping and washing down the gear. If you prefer exploring on solid ground, sports coordinators are often at hand to lead an early-morning guided walk in port.

Your Shipmates

Windstar Cruises appeal to upscale professional couples in their late-30s to 60s and on up to retirees, who enjoy the unpretentious, yet casually sophisticated atmosphere, creative cuisine, and refined service.

Windstar's ships were not designed for accessibility, and are not a good choice for the physically challenged. Although every attempt is made to accommodate passengers with disabilities, *Wind Surf* has only two elevators, and the smaller ships have none. There are no staterooms or bathrooms with wheelchair accessibility, and gangways can be difficult to navigate, depending on the tide and angle of ascent. Service animals are permitted to sail if arrangements were made at the time of booking.

CHOOSE A CRUISE ON WINDSTAR CRUISES IF...

❶ You want a high-end experience, yet prefer to dress casually every night on your vacation.

❷ You love water sports, particularly scuba diving, kayaking, and wind surfing.

❸ You're a romantic: tables for two are plentiful in the dining rooms.

Dress Code

All evenings are country-club casual, and slacks with a jacket over a sweater or shirt for men and sundresses, skirts or pants with a sweater or blouse for women are suggested. Coats and ties for men are not necessary, but some male passengers prefer to wear a jacket with open-collar shirt to dinner.

Junior Cruisers

Windstar Cruises' unregimented atmosphere is adult-oriented, and children are not encouraged. Children less than two years of age are not allowed at all; older children traveling as the third passenger in a stateroom with their parents incur the applicable third person fare. No dedicated children's facilities are available, so parents are responsible for the behavior and entertainment of their children.

Service

Personal service and attention by the professional staff is the order of the day. Your preferences are noted and fulfilled without the necessity of reminders. Expect to be addressed by name within a short time of embarking.

Tipping

For many years, Windstar sailed under a "tipping not required" policy. Windstar has now changed that policy. A service charge of $11 per guest, per day (including children) is now added to each shipboard account. A 15% service charge is now added to all bar bills. All these proceeds are paid directly to the crew.

Past Passengers

Windstar guests who cruise once with the line are automatically enrolled in the complimentary Foremast Club. Member benefits include savings on many sailings in addition to the Advance Savings Advantage Program discounts, Internet specials, and a free subscription to the Foremast Club magazine.

Good to Know

Don't offer to help hoist the sails. They're operated by computer from the bridge and unfurl at the touch of a button in only two minutes. If you're interested in how everything works, take advantage of the open bridge policy and drop in for a chat with the captain.

WINDSTAR CRUISES

DON'T CHOOSE A CRUISE ON WINDSTAR CRUISES IF...

❶ You must have a spacious private balcony; there are none.

❷ You're bored unless surrounded by constant stimulation; activities are purposely low-key.

❸ You have mobility problems; these ships are simply not very good for passengers in wheelchairs.

WIND SURF

Public Areas & Facilities

To make finding your way around simple, remember that all dining and entertainment areas are located on the top three decks, with restaurants located forward and indoor-outdoor bars facing aft. The main lounge and casino are midship on Main Deck, as is the library. The fitness center is one deck higher. Most public areas have expansive sea views, although an exception is the WindSpa, which is tucked away aft on Deck 2 just forward of the water-sports platform and large sauna. Stairways are rather steep, but forward and aft elevators assure that moving about is relatively easy.

Don't expect nautical kitsch to predominate *Wind Surf*'s decor. Although the main lounge has an understated sailing-flag motif, all other public areas are simply designed for comfort, with deep seats and an abundance of polished teak. Fresh flower arrangements and sailing-related artwork are lovely touches shipwide.

700 ft.	**1990**
	ENTERED SERVICE
	312
	PASSENGER CAPACITY
	190
	CREW MEMBERS
	156
	NUMBER OF CABINS
500 ft.	**14,745**
	GROSS TONS
	617 feet
	LENGTH
300 ft.	**66 feet**
	WIDTH

WOW Factor

The sight of crisp white sails being raised against a clear, blue Caribbean sky is positively breathtaking.

Top: Sea views at the rail
Bottom: *Wind Surf* at sea

Restaurants

The formal restaurant has open-seating dining and is large enough to serve all passengers at once. For a more casual setting, the Veranda Café has indoor and outdoor seating for breakfast and lunch. An adjacent grill whips up cooked-to-order breakfast items and serves barbeque selections outdoors when weather permits. Degrees is a reservations-only, casual alternative.

What Works & What Doesn't

Superb service is delivered with a smile by waiters and stewards who greet you by name from almost the moment you board. Utter contentment is assured with such a high ratio of staff members to pamper passengers. The open bridge policy means you can stop by when you wish for a chat with the captain or his navigation staff; however, don't count on a warm reception at all times. They may be busier than they appear to be. Keep in mind that tightened security measures also might prevent you from stopping in for a visit.

Accommodations

Layout-Amenities: *Wind Surf*'s ocean-view staterooms are a study in efficiency and clever design. Hanging lockers ("closets" to nonsailors) are generous. A small enclosed cabinet conceals a personal safe and an entertainment center features a flat-screen TV and DVD and CD players. The combination vanity-desk and bedside table have drawers for ample storage. A few standard cabins have upper fold-down Pullman berths for a third passenger.

Suites: Double the size of standard staterooms, suites were created by reconfiguring two standard cabins to create accommodations with twice as much storage, two bathrooms, and a generous sitting area with a sofa bed to offer a berth for a third passenger. The bedroom and sitting room can be separated by drawing a curtain for privacy. Two super-size bridge suites have living and dining areas, a separate bedroom, walk-in closet, and bathroom with a whirlpool tub and separate shower.

Good to Know: Special touches in each stateroom and suite are fresh flowers, terry robes for use during the voyage, and bath toiletries. Teak-floor bathrooms are sensibly laid out and spacious enough for two people to actually share the space. All staterooms and suites are equipped with barware, a minibar, and hair dryer. Voltage is 220, so converters are needed for most small appliances. There are no cabins configured for wheelchair accessibility.

Cabin Type	Size (sq. ft.)
Suite	376
Ocean View	188
Bridge Suite	500

Fast Facts

- 6 passenger decks
- Specialty restaurant, dining room, buffet
- Wi-Fi, in-cabin safes, in-cabin refrigerators, in-cabin DVDs
- 2 pools
- Fitness classes, gym, hair salon, 2 hot tubs, sauna, spa
- 3 bars, casino, dance club, library
- Laundry service
- Computer room

2

WINDSTAR CRUISES

In the Know

Don't be alarmed if you go below deck and find the passageways blocked. Those watertight doors are normally tucked out of sight but must be closed when Wind Surf *is departing from (or arriving in) port.*

Favorites

Don't Miss: Teatime at the Compass Rose, where sweets are served in addition to the finger foods and a duo performs easy-listening tunes, is a highlight every afternoon.

Best Added Value: All cabins are outside and none have obstructed views.

Best Dessert: Handsdown, the best dessert is the signature bread pudding. Look for it daily at the lunch buffet.

Our Favorite Spot for a Nightcap: The deck behind the Compass Rose Bar is close enough to enjoy good service and music and yet far enough away for privacy.

Closest Thing to a Sports Bar: Smoke your cigars under the stars outside the Terrace Bar, which has a high-tech humidor and a flat-screen TV.

Most Cuddle-Worthy Hangouts: A hammock for two or a Balinese sun bed offer opportunities for relaxing with your loved one.

Unwind with a soothing massage

WIND SPIRIT, WIND STAR

Public Areas & Facilities

Comfort is the key element that ties *Wind Spirit*'s interiors together. Blue and cream, echoing hues of the sea and sandy beaches, predominate in the formal restaurant and cozy main lounge, where you'll find a tiny casino tucked into a corner. With its large windows and a skylight, the lounge is flooded with natural light during daytime hours.

Public spaces are proportionately small on such a diminutive vessel and feature yachtlike touches of polished wood, columns wrapped in rope, and nautical artwork shipwide as well as abundant fresh flower arrangements. The library contains books, movies to play in your cabin, and a computer for sending or receiving e-mail (although there's no Internet access at this writing).

Passenger accommodations and public areas are all found in the aft two-thirds of the ship, with dining and entertainment located on the top two decks.

700 ft.	**1988** ENTERED SERVICE
	148 PASSENGER CAPACITY
	90 CREW MEMBERS
	74 NUMBER OF CABINS
500 ft.	**5,350** GROSS TONS
	440 feet LENGTH
300 ft.	**52 feet** WIDTH

WOW Factor

No question, it's the sails that take your breath away—their first appearance is beguiling.

Top: Elegant dining in a casual atmosphere
Bottom: A sunny day at the pool

Restaurants

The formal restaurant offers open seating during scheduled hours and is large enough to serve all passengers at once. For a more casual setting, the Veranda Café has indoor and outdoor seating for breakfast and lunch. A grill whips up cooked-to-order breakfast items, and an outdoor barbeque when weather permits.

What Works & What Doesn't

Water babies, no matter what their age, naturally gravitate to the water-sports platform when the ship is at anchor in calm water. Water toys and activities, including sail boats, sailboards, and kayaks—as well as water skiing and banana boat rides—are plentiful, and there's seldom a wait. In contrast, with so much time spent outside, the aft pool and hot tub are popular relaxation spots and apt to feel crowded. The pool bar has a permanent food station for continental breakfast, afternoon tea, desserts, and evening canapés.

Accommodations

Layout-Amenities: *Wind Spirit*'s ocean-view staterooms are ingeniously designed for efficiency. Hanging lockers (closets) are generous and contain shoe racks and shelves for gear. A small enclosed cabinet conceals a personal safe, and an entertainment center includes a flat-screen TV and DVD and CD players. The combination vanity-desk and bedside table have drawers for ample storage.

Suites: A single Owner's Suite, the only premium accommodation on board, has a sitting area with a sofa bed to offer a berth for a third passenger.

Good to Know: Special touches in each stateroom are fresh flowers, terry robes for use during the voyage, and bath toiletries. The teak-floor bathrooms are big enough for two. All staterooms and suites are equipped with barware, a minibar, and hair dryer (voltage is standard 110 AC); portholes have deadheads, which can be closed in high seas. Ten staterooms have adjoining doors, and a limited number of standard cabins have upper fold-down Pullman berths for a third passenger. There are no cabins configured for wheelchair accessibility.

Cabin Type	Size (sq. ft.)
Suite	220
Ocean View	188

Fast Facts

- 5 passenger decks
- Dining room, buffet
- Wi-Fi, in-cabin safes, in-cabin refrigerators, in-cabin DVDs
- Pool
- Fitness classes, gym, hair salon, hot tub, sauna
- 2 bars, casino, dance club, library
- Laundry service
- Computer room

In the Know

Slide out the ingenious hidden table in your stateroom cabinetry, and pull up a chair for relaxed room-service dining.

Favorites

Best Splurge: A scuba-diving adventure—the dive team rigs and maintains the gear so just sign up and be ready—allows even novices to participate after they complete a two-hour course.

Best Added Value: Each evening before dinner, most passengers gather in the lounge for really informative port talks while hot-and-cold appetizers are served by roaming waiters.

Our Favorite Spot for a Nightcap: Deck chairs by the pool, especially on a starry night when the sails are raised, are the best place to sit for a quiet drink.

Best Thoughtful Touch: Select a movie from the extensive DVD collection to watch in the privacy of your stateroom, and don't forget the popcorn. Just call room service.

Best Way to Beat the Heat: Mist sprayers near the pool offer a refreshing way to keep cool.

Tune In: All cabins have an entertainment center with an iPod dock. Use your own, or borrow one from the ship.

Wind Spirit at sea

Barge & River Cruises

3

Canal barging in France

WORD OF MOUTH

"Some may feel that the river cruises are very expensive. They usually include all the shore excursions, unlike the ocean cruises. There is also always beautiful scenery to watch as you cruise. There are no casinos, not much in the way of entertainment—local groups brought on board are usually very good. There are fewer passengers—an opportunity to really get to know your fellow passengers. We have taken 5 cruises. . . . They are so relaxing."

—momc

Ralph Grizzle

IN 1992, EUROPE'S AGE-OLD MARI-
TIME landscape changed dramatically when the Main–Danube Canal
opened, connecting the Continent's
main arteries—and along with them,
all of Europe. The completion of the
canal made grand cruise itineraries
from Amsterdam to Budapest—and
beyond—possible for the first time.
An engineering marvel, the 106-mi

> **AN UPLIFTING EXPERIENCE**
>
> A series of 16 locks lifts river cruisers nearly 1,400 feet above sea level as they transit the Main–Danube Canal to cross the Swabian Alps, south of Nürnberg and Europe's Continental Divide.

Main–Danube Canal permits modern-day vessels to travel from the North
Sea to the Black Sea, opening up more than 2,200 mi of rivers and expos-
ing today's travelers to life along the banks.

Tributaries and smaller rivers that flow into the Main and Danube rivers
provide additional opportunities to reach not only deep into the heart of
the Continent but also to explore some of its more remote regions. The
opening of the canal also meant that no longer would travelers need to sit
with their noses pressed against the windows of buses as they moved from
one destination to the next. Instead, travelers can now admire the scenery
from the ship's sundeck as they are transported *along with* their accommodations. Nor do travelers have to obligingly put out their luggage by
7 AM (or earlier) to be loaded onto the motorcoach before it sets off to the
next destination. River travelers unpack only once during the course of
their cruise as they move from one city to the next.

THE APPEAL OF RIVER CRUISING

River cruising was an entirely new concept to Europe when it was introduced in the mid-1970s: a floating hotel that journeys between destinations. In its simplest form, a river cruiser is nothing more than a barge with
a hotel on top. For many travelers, the slow chug along the river is just
the right pace for getting the lay of the land. Sitting on the top deck of a
ship under brilliant blue skies, you gaze on fabled landscapes dotted with
castles, villages, and vineyards. A flight of stairs down you have all the
amenities of a modern hotel—restaurants, bars, lounges, fitness facilities,
spas, Internet access, and comfortable staterooms.

River cruises offer opportunities to step ashore in fairy-tale towns and
major European capitals that can't be reached on a traditional cruise ship.
Most river cruisers take these trips to immerse themselves in Europe's contemporary culture in a way they can't when traveling between a different
Mediterranean port every day and to learn something about the history
of the towns along the Continent's greatest rivers.

The onboard ambience spans such a range that there are ships to suit most
travel preferences and lifestyles. While some vessels emphasize elegance,
others are much more casual. Travelers can find river cruisers that rival
Europe's finest boutique hotels at one end of the spectrum while at the
other, it's possible to cruise Europe's rivers much like an independent traveler who opts only for basic accommodations and dining.

The main river-cruising season begins in March and continues through the end of December, beginning with "tulip time" cruises in the Benelux countries and ending with "Christmas market" cruises in Hungary, Austria, and Germany. The majority of itineraries are seven nights, though longer cruises are

available. For popular itineraries, you may need to book your cruise up to a year in advance, but if you can't deal with so much advance planning, consider cruising from March through May or from September through December, when the crowds are thinner and airfares may be more reasonably priced than during peak periods.

River cruising is perfect for those who want a relaxed grand tour of Europe and for cruisers who want to explore Europe beyond the coastline. River cruising presents the grandeur and charm of Europe as well as the indelible landscapes that inspired Europe's great artists. Few things in life can beat the views of Europe over the ripples of its rivers.

WHY RIVER CRUISING IS NOT FOR EVERYONE

With more than 100 barges and ships plying Europe's rivers, river cruising is an exceptionally satisfying experience for many people. Still, river cruising is not be for everyone. Nonsmokers, in particular, should beware since few river ships ban smoking completely. On some vessels smoking is allowed in all public areas or at least a part of the lounge, and sensitive travelers still may be offended by the prevalence of cigarette smoke. Be sure to ask whether smoking is permitted on the ship, and if so, where. If smoking is permitted in the lounge, the social hub on many ships, you may want to consider looking at other river cruise companies or consider other forms of vacation.

Families with infants or small children may find river cruising to be less than ideal when compared to other forms of cruise travel. While ocean-going ships often have babysitting services and children's programs, river cruisers typically do not. That said, barges are popular options for families, as the smaller vessels typically carry family-size loads, from 6 to 24 passengers.

The physically challenged will want to look for vessels with easy access from ship to shore and elevators; not all river vessels have them.

If you're the type who dreads the thought of dining with others each evening, then river cruising may not be for you. Few, if any, river vessels offer room service, and even fewer have alternative dining venues as is the norm on the big cruise ships. That said, some ships now offer tables for two. And it's also possible to use the vessel only as a floating hotel, skipping the dinners on board and dining ashore instead, though you will probably not get a refund for uneaten meals.

If you're accustomed to ocean cruising and require all of the big-ship trappings, then you may find river cruising a bit boring. River cruisers are smaller and have fewer facilities. Entertainment is on a much smaller scale, if it exists at all. You won't find expansive gyms and spas, though they are sometimes offered on the larger ships.

One aspect of river cruising that is not so different from ocean cruising is that single travelers will usually have to pay a hefty supplement if they choose to occupy a double cabin alone. There are few single cabins, just as on regular cruise ships.

SPECIAL-INTEREST CRUISING

Increasingly, river-cruise lines are seeking to appeal a wider range of interests. Some river vessels offer theme cruises focusing on such activities as gardening, golf, and history. Many river cruisers carry bicycles on board so that active travelers may cycle once ashore.

HOW RIVER CRUISES & BARGE CRUISES DIFFER

The opening of the Main–Danube Canal in 1992 not only spawned river cruising as we know it today but also spawned the contemporary river-cruise vessel. There are more than 100 river cruisers operating on Europe's rivers. A building boom since 2000 has seen the introduction of more than 50 new ships. But on a smaller scale, barge cruising has also become more popular. While large river ships generally offer more bells and whistles, a barge is more intimate and less elaborate. Smaller barges may even be chartered by a small group of friends or family members who prefer to do it themeslves.

WHAT RIVER CRUISES OFFER

Designed specifically to transit the canal's locks, modern river cruisers are long and narrow, as are the locks themselves, which may be 600 feet long but are only about 40 feet wide. These dimensions, particularly the width of the locks, continue to pose challenges for designers of river vessels. Though some river cruisers feature balcony staterooms, many retain the real estate that would be allocated for balconies to create more expansive interior space. Some river cruisers do have balcony staterooms, where you can sit and watch the landscape pass, but take solace if your stateroom does not have a balcony: nearly all vessels have a broad expanse of sundeck only a deck or two up.

The typical river cruiser has four decks, including an upper sundeck, with two to three decks below it containing a series of staterooms on each side of the ship. Staterooms typically have a queen-size bed that can be reconfigured to two single beds, a TV, storage space, and a small, though often well-appointed, bathroom with shower and usually no tub.

Public rooms typically include restaurant, lounge, spa, and fitness center. While other features vary, some cruisers offer Wi-Fi service, bicycles for use on shore, a whirlpool tub, and sauna. At least two river cruisers in operation today have swimming pools.

River cruisers are essentially barges with an integrated hotel above and typically carry 100 or more passengers. Some river cruiser are à la carte, but some are nearly all-inclusive, meaning that wine and beer are served at lunch and dinner (one cruise line offers beer one morning of each cruise at breakfast), and that some form of shore excursions, such as guided city walks, are included for each port.

Cruises are competitively priced, and you should expect to pay from $200 per person per day to $400 per person per day depending on the ship, itinerary, and level of accommodations.

> **TIGHT SQUEEZE**
>
> One of the unique features of river cruisers is that the top decks on some vessels are designed to lower so that the top deck is flat, allowing them to pass under the many bridges that cross Europe's rivers. Railings are hinged, and the wheelhouse is built on a mechanism that allows it to submerge beneath the deck. Some wheelhouses feature a cutout in the top so that the captain may poke his head out to navigate under the bridge.

WHAT BARGE CRUISES OFFER

Barges typically are smaller and have fewer frills and amenities than river cruisers. Whereas river cruisers may carry more than 100 passengers, barges range from a few passengers to few dozen.

One of the big differences between a river cruise and a barge cruise is the amount of territory you're able to cover. Barge cruises usually span six days and travel fewer than 50 mi of river in a week, while river cruisers may travel few hundred miles. Transiting the locks can be time-consuming, and passengers often prefer to walk or bicycle along the canal's banks (often outpacing the barge). Activities such as hot-air ballooning, horseback riding, guided tours, tennis, and golf are offered by most barges, usually for additional costs.

A barge normally cruises within one region of one country (usually France) while a river cruiser can travel through several countries and on several rivers during the span of one sailing. Barges typically have only one deck, smaller staterooms, and a combination dining room and lounge. Barge staterooms almost always have private facilities.

Barges are usually all-inclusive, including drinks, fine wine and champagne; gourmet cuisine (using fresh, local ingredients and cooked to order); pickup and drop-off from local airports, train stations, and hotels; shore excursions and all entrance fees included in the cruise fare. Bicycles are often available for use on shore. Some barges even have a whirlpool tub, pool, and exercise equipment.

Although barge cruises are offered in Belgium, Germany, and Holland, France is the most popular destination. While you may think of a river ship as a floating hotel, a barge is more reminiscent of a country manor house.

Though most barges are staffed, there are self-drive barges. Small groups, such as family or friends, may book the entire barge, or barges may be booked by individuals, preferably liked-minded people who don't mind sharing space in a small setting.

Barge cruises are more expensive than river cruises and can range from $350 per person per day to more than $1,000 per person per day. These are for six-day weeks, because one day is reserved to prepare the barge for the next group of people. Whole barges can be chartered from $15,000 to more than $50,000.

WHERE CRUISES GO: EUROPE'S RIVERS

Europe has more navigable rivers than any other region in the world, and arguably more diverse cultures along its river banks than almost any other region. Cruising the entire length of the Rhine and Danube rivers alone—made possible thanks to the Main–Danube Canal—exposes travelers to 10 countries in Central and Western Europe. Along the way are charming villages, storied capital cities, fairy-tale castles, vineyards, and more—all accessible from your floating hotel.

THE DANUBE

The most popular region for river cruising in continental Europe—and a good choice for first-time river cruisers—is the Danube. Immortalized in Strauss's waltz *The Blue Danube*, the river winds from Germany's Black Forest through Austria into the Balkans before dumping into the Black Sea.

Most Danube river cruises span 7 to 10 nights and allow sufficient time to explore the major cities along the river. The Danube flows through six countries and meanders for nearly 1,800 mi. Some of Europe's most fabled cities—Regensburg, Passau, Linz, Vienna, Bratislava, Budapest—are situated on the banks of the Danube. Some vessels operate round-trip from Passau; some operate one-way between Regensburg and Budapest; and others cruise between Vienna or Budapest to Nürnberg, which includes transiting a section of the Main–Danube Canal over Europe's Continental Divide in the Franconian Alps. Cruises that begin on the Main River may begin in Würzburg but more frequently begin or end in Nürnberg, which was virtually destroyed during World War II but has been restored.

And while most river cruises take place during the spring, summer, and fall, **Nürnberg** hosts the world's largest Christmas market (*Christkindlesmarkt* in German), featured on so-called Christmas-market cruises during the month of December.

Dating back to Roman times, **Regensburg** was practically untouched during World War II. The city is the oldest on the Danube, tracing its history back nearly 2,000 years. Still standing are the Roman gates, Porta Pretoria, built in AD 179. Regensburg also lays claim to Germany's oldest surviving bridge and its oldest restaurant, Alte Wurstküche, a small sausage kitchen and dining room situated right on the river and within walking distance of where most river vessels dock.

From **Passau** (in Germany) and **Linz** (in Austria), excursions can be made to Salzburg (about two hours away), the birthplace of Mozart and the setting for the acclaimed musical *The Sound of Music*.

Vienna was home to the Habsburgs, one of Europe's principal sovereign dynasties from the 15th to the 20th centuries. Just outside the inner city is Schonbrunn Palace, the imperial summer palace of the Habsburgs.

Vienna is characterized by beautiful parks, legendary coffee houses, and baroque palaces. One of the city's most famous landmarks, Stephansdom (St. Stephen's Cathedral) is also one of Europe's most impressive Gothic churches. The musically inclined will appreciate that Mozart, Beethoven, and Strauss composed their greatest operas and symphonies in Austria's capital city. The composer Schubert was born here.

Slovakia's capital, **Bratislava** was a capital in exile for Hungary's kings and archbishops during Turkey's occupation of Hungary and most of the middle Danube basin from 1526 to 1784. Bratislava is dominated by an enormous castle that stands sentinel over the river. Though the castle dates back to the 9th century, it was razed in 1811 and rebuilt.

On opposite sides of the Danube, Buda and Pest were united in the 19th century to form the Hungarian capital **Budapest.** The beginning or ending point for most Danube cruises, Budapest was once referred to as the "Queen of the Danube" because of the city's cultural significance at a time when Hungary was three times the size it is today. On one side of the Danube, hilly Buda retains much of its Middle Ages charm. Its cobbled streets and Gothic buildings have been well preserved. On the other side of the river, Pest is the thriving city center.

Because Danube cruises are typically seven days in length and visit larger, more familiar destinations, many travelers may wish to begin river-cruising here and then move onto the Rhine and its tributaries for future cruises.

THE RHINE & ITS TRIBUTARIES

The Rhine flows 820 mi through four countries—Switzerland, France, Germany, and the Netherlands–from the Swiss Alps to the North Sea. Although some cruises operate between Basel, Switzerland, and Amsterdam, in the Netherlands, or Dusseldorf, Germany, the most popular section of the Rhine for cruising is between Mainz, at the confluence of the Main and Rhine, and Cologne.

Mainz is the birthplace of Johannes Gutenberg and home to the Gutenberg Museum, which presents the history of printing. It's not long before riverboats departing Mainz reach Rüdesheim, perhaps one of the Rhine's most charming villages.

Rüdesheim is in the heart of the Rheingau wine-producing region, and the wine taverns along the narrow and lively pedestrian street known as Drosselgasse are packed with locals and tourists enjoying glasses of Riesling, sparking Sekt, or local brandy.

Heading north from Rüdesheim, river cruisers pass half a dozen or more castles on both banks as well as the storied **Lorelei**, immortalized by poet Heinrich Heine, who wrote about a mysterious nymph who distracted sailors and lured their boats onto the rocks to their deaths.

Ships continue along this section of the Rhine, certainly the most "castled" section of river in Europe, before reaching **Koblenz,** at the confluence of the Rhine and Mosel rivers. Some cruises continue to follow the Mosel from Koblenz.

Cruises that continue along the Rhine pass more castles before reaching West Germany's former capital, **Bonn**, and **Cologne**, with its famous cathedral, a World Heritage Site and one of Germany's best-known architectural monuments. These cruises conclude (or begin) farther along the river at Düsseldorf or Amsterdam.

THE RHINE TRIBUTARIES

The Rhine has many tributaries, the most important for cruisers being the Main, Mosel, and Neckar rivers.

THE MAIN

The Main is one of the Rhine's most significant tributaries. It, along with the Main–Danube Canal, connects the North Sea with the Black Sea. The Main has 34 locks and becomes navigable at **Bamberg**, Germany, at the northern end of the Main–Danube Canal. Some river cruise companies offer itineraries along the Main between **Nürnberg**, which is about midway on the Main–Danube Canal, to **Trier**, on the Mosel, which branches off the Rhine.

THE MOSEL

The Mosel is regarded as the most beautiful—and perhaps the most romantic—of the navigable European rivers. The distance from its headwaters in the Vogesen Mountains to where it joins the Rhine at Koblenz, the Mosel is only about 175 mi long as the crow flies. But the actual length of the winding river is a little more than 335 mi, making it the Rhine's longest tributary. The Mosel weaves its way through the vertical slopes of the Schiefergebirge mountains into Luxembourg and northeastern France. Cities and towns along the river are of fairy-tale charm: picturesque **Cochem**, settled by the Celts and later by Romans before being granted a town charter in 1332; **Bernkastel-Kues**, with its castle ruin overlooking the city center of half-timbered buildings and cobblestone streets; and the Romanesque **Trier**, Germany's oldest city and also one that claims to be 1,300 years older than Rome itself. Trier's Porta Nigra (Black Gate) dates from the 2nd century, when Trier was a Roman city.

The Mosel is known for its (mostly) white wines, such as Riesling and Piesporter, and indeed much of the pleasure of a Mosel cruise can be found in sampling the wines along the way.

THE NECKAR

This tributary of the Rhine flows 228 mi from the Black Forest through some of Germany's most beautiful countryside. The primary attraction for many travelers is **Heidelberg**, Germany's oldest university town and the cradle of the German Romantic movement.

OTHER GERMANIC RIVERS

THE ELBE

The Elbe runs 725 mi from the Czech Republic to the North Sea. Most weeklong Elbe itineraries are between Berlin and Prague and include hotel stays at one or both ends of the cruise. Other ports often include Potsdam, Magdeburg, Wittenberg, Meissen, Dresden, and Konigstein.

The German poet Goethe called **Prague** "the prettiest gem in the stone crown of the world," and indeed the capital of the Czech Republic is remarkable. The city's rich architectural heritage reflects an urban life extending back more than 1,000 years. Prague's highlight is the Charles Bridge, which crosses the Vltava River. On one side is Prague Castle, dominating the Mala Strana.

Konigstein and its dramatic fortress, 1,180 feet above the river, provide a scenic backdrop for brief visits, while farther along, **Dresden** is known as the "Florence of the Elbe," for its art treasures.

> ### TULIP-TIME CRUISES
>
> Other popular river cruises include so-called "tulip-and-windmill" cruises, which take place during the spring in the Netherlands and Belgium. Cruises typically begin and end in Amsterdam, overnighting in the Dutch city so that you have time to explore. Leaving Amsterdam, you will cruise past Holland's annual floral splendor to visit two of Belgium's most beautifully preserved medieval cities—Brussels and Brugge.

Meissen is known for its porcelain, while **Wittenberg** marks the birthplace of the Protestant Reformation. In 1517, Martin Luther, an Augustine monk and university lecturer, nailed his 95 theses on the door of the Palace Church.

Magdeburg is situated midway on the Elbe. Nearly destroyed during World War II, the rebuilt city is an example of a traditional German town.

Ships usually moor in Potsdam for transfers to and from **Berlin** at the beginning or end of each cruise. Berlin once symbolized Germany's partition—East Berlin being part of the German Democratic Republic (East Germany) and West Berlin being part of the Federal Republic of Germany (West Germany). The Berlin Wall, which separated Germany, fell in 1989, and today Berlin has heralded itself into a historically and culturally prominent European city.

FRENCH RIVERS

THE SEINE, RHÔNE & SAÔNE

Also popular for barge cruises, the rivers of France course through the vineyard-canopied hillsides of Burgundy to the lavender fields of Provence. Positioned in between is the City of Lights, Paris, with its broad boulevards, charming cafés, and world-renowned museums.

Coursing 505 mi, the **Rhône** is the only major European river flowing south into the Mediterranean. Most river cruises operate from Lyon on the Rhône, traveling as far south in Provence as Arles and the Côte d'Azur. The same stretch of river is also popular with barge cruises.

Other river cruises combine the Rhône and **Saône** rivers for itineraries from Chalon-sur-Saône to Avignon. Along the way, passengers enjoy Avignon's Papal Palace; the early Roman ruins in Vienne and Arles; wine tours of Beaune, Burgundy's acclaimed wine capital; the history and beauty of Lyon and Vienna; and the Middle Age charm of Viviers.

Seine cruises include at least one night in Paris before traveling northwest toward Honfleur and the English Channel. Major stops include Giverny, home of the artist Claude Monet and one of France's most-visited destinations; and Rouen, known as the "City of 100 Spires," for its many churches and cathedrals.

The Seine is practically synonymous with Paris; thus, the City of Lights is one of the main attractions on Seine cruises. The river has been used for sightseeing within Paris since the 19th century.

BARGING ON FRENCH CANALS

With more than 5,000 mi of canals, France is a major barging destination. The country's most popular canals for barging are the **Canal de la Marne au Rhin,** which links the Rhein with the Marne, and operates between Strasboug and Lagarde; the **Burgundy Canal,** which links the Saône and Yonne between Dijon and Migennes; the **Doubs River,** which empties into the Saône; **Canal Latéral a la Marne,** a canal that follows the course of the Marne River, passing through the heart of Champagne; and **Canal Latéral a la Loire,** which follows the course of the upper Loire. (*Latéral* indicates that the waterway parallels the course of the river; some rivers, including the upper Loire, are not navigable, hence the necessity for a latéral.)

Transiting these canals takes lots of time; your barge may take 20 minutes to pass through a single lock. But barge cruising is meant to be relaxing, and if you get bored, just hop on a bike or walk to meet the barge at another lock upstream.

CONTACTS & RESOURCES

Most of the companies we recommend below operate their own barges and/or river cruisers, and since many companies offer both kinds of cruises, we have not separated them into "barge" and "river cruising" companies.

Abercrombie & Kent. Founded in 1953 as a safari-tour operator, the upscale travel company known as A&K offers barge cruises on vessels that carry no more than 22 passengers—and some that carry as few as six. Areas of operation in Continental Europe include France, Germany, and the Netherlands. A&K also owns and operates two of its own river vessels, the 90-passenger *River Cloud* and the 88-passenger *River Cloud II*, on the Rhine, Main, and Danube rivers. ⌂*1520 Kensington Rd., Suite 212, Oak Brook, IL 60523-2156* ☎*800/554–7016* ⊕*www.abercrombiekent.com.*

Amadeus Waterways. Amadeus Waterways' Austrian founder was involved with several of the other major river cruise companies before launching his own line in 2002. Since then, the company has introduced four new ships: *Amadagio, Amalegro, Amacello,* and *Amadante,* the latter two launched in 2008. These ships, the newest among the river cruisers operating today, were designed exclusively for the English-speaking market and have staterooms equipped with flat-screen TVs and Internet access; French balconies on the top two decks, an elevator, a whirlpool, and bicycles for exploration ashore. Amadeus Waterways operates a wide range of itineraries in Europe on the Rhine, Main, Danube and Mosel rivers. A fifth ship, *Amadeus Pearl,* operates cruises on the rivers of France. The company also offers Christmas-market cruises from late November through December. ⌂*21625 Prairie St., Chatsworth, CA 91311-5833* ☎*800/626–0126* ⊕*www.amadeuswaterways.com.*

Avalon Waterways. Group Voyagers has been a leader in escorted tours of Europe for more than 75 years—under well-known brands such as Globus, Cosmos, and Brennan Vacations—but it was not until 2003 that the company launched Avalon Waterways and its fleet of small river cruisers. Avalon Waterways now operates six ships in Europe: *Artistry, Imagery, Poetry, Tapestry, Tranquility,* and *Scenery,* the latter launched in 2008. All offer such big-ship amenities as accommodations with hotel-quality beds, satellite TV, floor-to-ceiling sliding glass doors in most staterooms, and even some private balconies. Ships also have Internet access and fitness equipment. Avalon Waterways operates on the Rhine, Main, Danube, Mosel, and Rhône rivers. The company also offers French wine country cruises on the Saône and Rhône rivers, as well as Christmas-market cruises from late November through December. ⌂*5301 S. Federal Circle, Littleton, CO80123* ☎*877/797–8791* ⊕*www.avalonwaterways.com.*

The Barge Lady. Founded in 1986, this Chicago-based booking agency is operated by Ellen Sack, who not only boasts first-hand knowledge of barge vacations but takes pride in the fact that she always answers the phone herself. In continental Europe, the Barge Lady offers barge vacations in France, Holland, and Germany. ⌂*101 W. Grand Ave., Suite 200, Chicago, IL 60610* ☎*800/880–0071* ⊕*www.bargelady.com.*

GoBarging/European Waterways. Based in England, GoBarging/European Waterways works with the English-speaking market worldwide. In continental Europe, the company operates 13 luxury barges, ranging in capacity from 4 to 12 people. Countries of operation include France, Belgium, Holland, Germany, the Czech Republic, and Italy (the company also operates barge cruises in the United Kingdom). ⌂*35 Wharf Rd., Wraysbury, Middlesex, U.K. TW19 5JQ* ☎*800/394–8630* ⊕*www.gobarging.com.*

Grand Circle Travel. Grand Circle Travel got its start in 1958 as the touring arm of the American Association of Retired Persons (AARP). In 1985, Alan Lewis purchased Grand Circle Travel and moved its offices from New York to Boston (not far from his office is his brother's office, Vantage Travel, another river-cruise-vacation contender). Grand Circle now operates 12 ships in Europe. The vessels range in capacity from 50 passengers to 164 passengers, with the majority capable of carrying 140 passengers. All ships were launched between 1998 and 2003.

Designed for the Rhine, Main, and Danube rivers are *River Symphony, River Harmony, River Melody, River Rhapsody,* and *River Concerto.* All have a capacity of 140 and are equipped with elevators. Some upper-deck cabins have balconies. Limited primarily to wider sections of the Danube are the company's largest river cruisers, the *River Aria* and *River Adagio,* each with a capacity of 164. On smaller rivers, the company operates the 120-passenger *River Debussy, River Ravel,* and *River Bizet.* Smaller still, for cruise programs in France, are the 50-passenger *River Chardonnay* and *River Provence.* These ships have no elevators and only two main decks. ⌂*347 Congress St., Boston, MA 02210* ☎*800/992–3008* ⊕*www.gct.com.*

Le Boat. Founded in 1979, Le Boat specializes in self-drive barge vacations (the company also markets barges for GoBarging/European Waterways and other operators). Self-drive barges, ranging in capacity from just a couple of people to 10, operate in Germany, Belgium, Holland, France, and Italy. ⌂*980 Awald Rd., Suite 302, Annapolis, MD 21403* ☎*800/394–8630* ⊕*www.leboat.com.*

Peter Deilmann River Cruises. Based in the Baltic town of Neustadt in Holstein, the eponymous Peter Deilmann was the first company to build river cruisers that reflected the style and amenities of oceangoing cruise ships. The privately owned German company, which also offers ocean cruises, was founded in 1968 and has an office in the U.S.

The entrepreneur Deilmann launched his river-cruise fleet in 1987 with the now-retired *Danube Princess.* The company's first newly built river cruisers followed in 1991 and 1992. Deilmann died in 2003, and his two daughters, Gisa and Hedda Deilmann, now operate the company. Deilmann's ships are extremely upscale, resembling fine boutique hotels, and are arguably the most luxurious in Europe. The company recently revised its no-smoking policies to exclude smoking in all areas inside of its eight vessels. The company's ships sail on more European rivers than almost any other operator: the Rhine, Mosel, Main–Danube Canal, Danube, Neckar, Rhône, Saône, Seine, Vitava, Havel, and Elbe, as well as Dutch and Belgian canals.

Mozart is the largest of the Deilmann ships, carrying 200 passengers. *Princess de Provence* is next-largest, accommodating 148 passengers. *Heidelberg* holds 110, *Dresden* 106, *Cezanne* 100, *Casanova* 96, and the smallest—*Frederic Chopin* and *Katharina von Bora*—each carry 79. ⌂*1800 Diagonal Rd., Suite 170, Alexandria, VA 22314* ☎*800/438–8287* ⊕*www.deilmann-cruises.com.*

Tauck World Discovery. Though Tauck Tours was founded in 1925, its river-cruise division is one of the new kids on the block. Christened into service in 2006, Tauck World Discovery now operates three ships: the 118-passenger *Swiss Emerald* and *Swiss Sapphire,* sister ships launched in 2006 and 2008 respectively; and the *Swiss Diamond,* originally built in 1996 and renovated in 2006. In addition to standard staterooms, *Swiss Emerald* and *Swiss Sapphire* each have 14 suites measuring 300 square feet with floor-to-ceiling windows, walk-in closets, and marble baths with full-size tubs. The two newest ships also have Wi-Fi access throughout. All cabins have a flat-screen TV, minibar, radio, safe, and L'Occitane toiletries. The company's ships cruise the Danube, Rhine, Mosel, and Main rivers, as well as the scenic canals of the Netherlands and Belgium in spring. ⌂*10 Norden Pl., Norwalk, CT 06855* ☎*800/468–2825* ⊕*www.tauck.com.*

Uniworld Grand River Cruises. Uniworld was founded in 1976 by a Yugoslavian entrepreneur. Currently California-based, the company began offering European river cruises in 1994. Operating nine ships in Europe, Uniworld offers itineraries from 7 to 28 days on the Rhône, Mosel, Danube, Seine, and Saône rivers, as well as in the Netherlands and Belgium. It is one of the few river-cruise companies to offer cruises in Portugal and Spain on the Douro River, from Lisbon to Porto. (Uniworld charters the 130-passenger *Douro Queen,* launched in 2005, for these itineraries.) The company launched its first ship (as opposed to chartering ships during the company's inception), the 128-passenger *River Ambassador,* in 1996, followed by a sister ship, *River Baroness,* in 1997. Both ships underwent major remodeling in 2006 and in 2005, respectively; neither has an elevator. The 132-passenger *River Queen* came in 1999 and was refurbished in 2006.

In 2001, Uniworld introduced a new series of ships—each carrying 132 to 134 passengers in 151-square-foot standard cabins (as well as four 214-square-foot suites)—*River Princess* (2001), *River Empress* (2002), and *River Countess* and *River Duchess* (2003). Uniworld built the 132-passenger *River Royale* in 2006 primarily for cruises in France (*River Baroness* and *River Royale* also operate in France). ⌂ *17323 Ventura Blvd., Los Angeles, CA 91316* ☎ *800/733–7820* ⊕ *www.uniworld.com.*

Vantage Deluxe World Travel. Founded in 1994, Vantage World Deluxe Travel is a close relative of Grand Circle Travel, Vantage's president being the brother of Grand Circle's chairman. Vantage operates four river cruisers: the 166-passenger *River Discovery,* which entered service in 2007; the 170-passenger *River Explorer* (2001); the 170-passenger *River Odyssey* (2003); and the 140-passenger *River Navigator* (2000).

While standard cabins have TVs (some flat-screen), bath with shower, and a safe, junior suites add a French balcony, DVD player, minibar, and coffee- and tea-maker. *River Discovery* also has a 300-square-foot Owner's Suite with two French balconies, a Jacuzzi, and a separate bedroom and sitting area. Additionally, *River Discovery* is wired throughout for Wi-Fi. Cruises operate on the Rhine, Main, Danube, and Mosel rivers. The company also offers Christmas-market cruises. ⌂ *90 Canal St., Boston, MA 02114-2031* ☎ *800/322–6677* ⊕ *www.vantagetravel.com.*

Viking River Cruises. Established in 1997, the company merged with KD River Cruises in 2000. The California-based company now operates 11 ships. The founding chairman is Norwegian and of Viking descent, hence the Viking moniker extending to the names of all its ships, the newest and largest of which is the 198-passenger *Viking Sun,* built in 2004. Next-largest are the 154-passenger ships *Viking Seine* and *Viking Burgundy;* both entered service in 2000.

The company operates six 150-passenger river cruisers: *Viking Danube* and *Viking Sky,* both built in 1999; *Viking Europe, Viking Neptune, Viking Pride* and *Viking Spirit,* all built in 2001. Finally, there are two, 124-passenger vessels, *Viking Fontane* and *Viking Schumann* dating from 1991 and refurbished since. Cruises are offered on the Rhine, Main, Danube, Elbe, Saône, Seine, and Rhône rivers, as well as the canals of the Netherlands and Belgium. ⌂ *5700 Canoga Ave., Suite 200, Woodland Hills, CA 91367* ☎ *877/668–4546* ⊕ *www.vikingrivers.com.*

Western Mediterranean

PORTS IN FRANCE, ITALY, MALTA, PORTUGAL, & SPAIN

Gondolas, Venice

WORD OF MOUTH

"My wife and I are are going on a trip of a lifetime next June—
12-day Mediterranean/Greece cruise starting [in] Rome and ending
in Venice. . . . Probably our biggest dilemma is in Naples. With only
one day, do you go to Isle of Capri, try to see Pompeii and Mount
Vesuvius, or see the Amalfi Coast?"

—MurrayMartin

www.fodors.com/forums

Lindsay Bennett   **IF YOU'RE A FIRST-TIME CRUISER** in Europe and want to stop at some of the most popular destinations in Europe, a Western Mediterranean itinerary might be ideal for you. Western Mediterranean itineraries often begin in either Barcelona or Civitavecchia (for Rome) and may be one-way or round-trip cruises. One-week cruises in Europe tend to be one-way cruises, while those of 10 days or more are sometimes loop cruises. A few of these itineraries may take you as far as Venice, though that city is a more popular jumping-off point for cruises through the Adriatic and Aegean. While some of the ports included in this chapter (such as Venice or Bari in Italy) are more likely to be on Eastern Mediterranean itineraries, others (such as Le Havre or Bordeaux in France) may be a part of some Northern European cruise routes. We've kept all the ports in Italy and France together in this chapter to make them easier to find. Larger ships will be limited in the ports at which they can call, but smaller ships may hit some of the lesser-visited spots on the French or Italian Riviera.

ABOUT THE RESTAURANTS

All the restaurants we recommend serve lunch, and many also serve dinner. If your cruise ship stays late in port, you may choose to dine off the ship. While the cuisine in Europe is varied, one thing is constant across the continent: Europeans tend to eat a leisurely meal at lunch. In most ports there are quicker and simpler alternatives for those who just want to grab a quick bite before returning to the ship.

WHAT IT COSTS IN EUROS					
	$$$$	$$$	$$	$	¢
RESTAURANTS	over €30	€23–€30	€17–€23	€11–€17	under €11

Restaurant prices are per person for a main course, including tax.

A CORUÑA, SPAIN (FOR SANTIAGO DE COMPOSTELA)

One of Spain's busiest ports, A Coruña (La Coruña in Castilian) prides itself on being the most progressive city in the region. The weather can be fierce, wet, and windy—hence the glass-enclosed, white-pane galleries on the houses lining the harbor. This is one of two main ports at which cruise ships call so they can offer an overland trek to the pilgrimage city of Santiago de Compostela; the other is Vigo (⇨ *Vigo, below, for information on Santiago de Compostela, including a map*), though at 57 km (35 mi) to the north, A Coruña is marginally closer. Occasionally, a cruise ship will offer an overland excursion beginning in one port and ending in the other.

ESSENTIALS

CURRENCY   The euro (€1 to US$1.46 at this writing); U.S. currency is generally not accepted in Europe, but ATMs are common and credit cards are widely accepted.

HOURS   Museums are generally open from 9 until 7 or 8, many are closed on Monday and some close in the afternoon. Most stores are open Monday through Saturday 9 to 1:30 and 5 to 8, but tourist shops may open in the afternoon and also on Sunday between May and September.

INTERNET **Estrella Park Street** ⊠*Estrella 12A Coruña* ☎*981/229070.*

TELEPHONES Most tri- and quad-band GSM phones work in Spain, which has a 3G-compatible network. Public kiosks accept phone cards that support international calls (cards sold in press shops, bars, and telecom shops). Major companies include Vodafone.

COMING ASHORE

Ships dock at Liners Quay in the interior of the port. There are few services at the port itself, but from the port entrance you can explore the town on foot.

Bus 1 runs from the port to the main bus station every 20 minutes for €0.96. There is at least one train per hour to Santiago de Compostela. Journey time is 50 minutes, and tickets cost approximately €9 return.

A tourist tram operates around the town of A Coruña throughout the year (weekends only October through June). Tickets cost €1. Taxis wait at the port entrance and can be hired by the day for tourist itineraries. Renting a car would allow you to explore Santiago de Compostela plus the rugged countryside of the wild corner of Spain, but prices are expensive. Expect to pay €93 per day for a manual economy vehicle.

EXPLORING A CORUÑA

Castillo de San Antón. At the northeastern tip of the old town is St. Anthony's Castle, a 16th-century fort. Inside is A Coruña's **Museum of Archaeology,** with remnants of the prehistoric Celtic culture that once thrived in these parts. ☎*981/189850* ⊡€2 ⊙*July and Aug., Tues.–Sat. 10–8:30, Sun. 10–2:30; Sept.–June, Tues.–Sat. 10–7, Sun. 10–2.*

Church of Santiago. The 12th-century church is the oldest church in A Coruña and was the first stop on the *camino inglés* (English route) toward Santiago de Compostela. Originally Romanesque, it's now a hodgepodge, with Gothic arches, a baroque altarpiece, and two 18th-century rose windows. ⊠*Pl. de la Constitución s/n.*

Colegiata de Santa María. This Romanesque beauty from the mid-13th century is often called Santa María del Campo (St. Mary of the Field) because it was once outside the city walls. A quirk of this church is that, because of an architectural miscalculation, the roof is too heavy for its supports, so the columns inside lean outward, and the buttresses outside have been thickened. ⊠*Pl. de Santa María.*

Dársena de la Marina. To see why sailors once nicknamed A Coruña *la ciudad de cristal* (the glass city), stroll what is said to be the longest seaside promenade in Europe. Although the congregation of boats is charming, the real sight is across the street: a long, gracefully curved row of houses. Built by fishermen in the 18th century, the houses actually face *away* from the sea. Nets were hung from the porches to dry, and fish was sold on the street below. The **glass galleries** ultimately spread across the harbor and eventually throughout Galicia.

Domus/Casa del Hombre. The slate-covered Museum of Mankind was designed by Japanese architect Arata Isozaki. In the shape of a ship's sail, this museum is dedicated to the study of the human being, and particularly the human body. ⊠*C. Santa Teresa 1* ☎*981/189840* ⊕*www. casaciencias.org* ⊠*Museum €2, IMAX €1* ⊙*July and Aug., daily 11–9; Sept.–June, daily 10–7.*

Museo de Bellas Artes. The Museum of Fine Arts, housed in a converted convent on the edge of the old town, has French, Spanish, and Italian paintings, and a curious collection of etchings by Goya. ⊠*C. Zalaeta s/n* ☎*981/223723* ⊠*Free* ⊙*Tues.–Fri. 10–8, Sat. 10–2 and 4:30–8, Sun. 10–2.*

Plaza de María Pita. The focal point of the *ciudad vieja* (old town) is this expansive plaza. Its north side is given over to the neoclassical **Palacio Municipal,** or city hall, built 1908–12. The **monument** in the center, built in 1998, depicts the heroine herself, Maior (María) Pita, holding her lance. When England's notorious Sir Francis Drake arrived to sack A Coruña in 1589, the locals were only half finished building the defensive Castillo de San Antón, and a 13-day battle ensued. When María Pita's husband died, she took up his lance, slew the Briton who tried to plant the Union Jack here, and revived the exhausted Coruñesos.

Torre de Hercules. Much of A Coruña sits on a peninsula, on the tip of which is the oldest still-functioning lighthouse in the world. Originally built during the reign of Trajan, the Roman emperor born in Spain in AD 98, the lighthouse was rebuilt in the 18th century and looks strikingly modern; all that remains from Roman times are inscribed foundation stones. Scale the 245 steps for superb views of the city and coastline. ⊠*Ctra. de la Torre s/n* ☎*981/223730* ⊠*€2* ⊙*Sept.–June, daily 10–6; July and Aug., Sun.–Thurs. 10–6, Fri. and Sat. 10–11:45* PM.

SHOPPING

The main shopping streets at A Coruña are Calle Canzones, Calle San Andres, and Calle Real.

Alfares de Buño (⊠*Plazuela de los Angeles 6, A Coruña* ☎*No phone*) sells glazed terra-cotta ceramics from Bunho, 40 km (25 mi) west of A Coruña. These crafts are prized by aficionados.

Authentic Galician *zuecos* (hand-painted wooden clogs) are still worn in some villages to navigate mud; the cobbler **José López Rama** (⊠*Rúa do Muiño 7, Carballo* ☎*981/701068*) has a workshop 15 minutes south of A Coruña in the village of Carballo.

For hats and Galician folk clothing, stop into **Sastrería Iglesias** (⊠*Rego do Auga 14, A Coruña* ☎*981/221634*)—founded 1864—where artisan José Luis Iglesias Rodrígues sells his textiles.

AJACCIO, CORSICA

Guy de Maupassant called Corsica "the mountain in the sea." This vertical granite world, plopped down in the Mediterranean between Provence and Tuscany, Corsica's gifts of artistic and archaeological treasures, crystalline waters, granite peaks, and pine forests add up to one of France's most unspoiled sanctuaries. Mountain people born and bred, true Corsicans are highland spirits, at home in the all-sustaining chestnut forest, the Laricio pines, or the dense undergrowth of the *maquis*, a variety of wild and aromatic plants that gave Corsica one of its sobriquets, "the perfumed isle." Its strategic location 168 km (105 mi) south of Monaco and 81 km (50 mi) west of Italy made Corsica a prize hotly contested by a succession of Mediterranean powers. Their vestiges remain in impressive citadels, churches, bridges, and medieval watchtowers. The Italian influence is also apparent in the Corsican language, which is a combination of Italian, Tuscan dialect, and Latin.

ESSENTIALS

CURRENCY The euro (€1 to US$1.46 at this writing); U.S. currency is generally not accepted in Europe, but ATMs are common.

HOURS Stores are open Monday–Saturday 9–7, but many close at lunchtime (usually noon–2 or 3), and some open later and on Sunday during July and August. Museums are open 10–5 but most are closed on either Monday or Tuesday.

TELEPHONES Tri-band GSM phones work in France. You can buy prepaid phone cards at telecom shops, news-vendors and tobacconists in all towns and cities. Phone cards can be used for local or international calls. France Telecom and Orange are leading telecom companies.

COMING ASHORE

Ships dock in Ajaccio port, from where it is a short walk into the town of Ajaccio. Cafés and shops can be found immediately outside the port gates.

The local bus network is geared to residents, who take it to school and work. At least two buses a day connect all the southern towns with Ajaccio, but timetables may not coincide with your ship's departure time, so check carefully.

Renting a vehicle would allow you to explore several towns and surrounding attractions during your stay on the island; however, be aware that travel times may be longer than map distances suggest as the mountain roads can be narrow and winding. Vehicle rental costs approximately €50 per day for an economy manual car. Delivery to the port will be an additional charge. Hertz serves the entire island; its 18 offices are at all airports and harbors and in the major towns. Be sure to reserve at least two weeks in advance in July and August.

EXPLORING CORSICA

Numbers in the margin correspond to points of interest on the Corsica map.

AJACCIO

Ajaccio, Napoléon's birthplace and Corsica's modern capital, is a busy, French-flavored town with a bustling port and ancient streets. The city has a long history dating back to its founding in 1492, and some of the original buildings can still be seen on rue Roie-de-Rome, near the Musée du Capitellu.

❻ **Cathédrale.** The 16th-century baroque cathedral where Napoléon was baptized is at the end of rue St-Charles. The interior is covered with trompe-l'oeil frescoes, and the high altar, from a church in Lucca, Italy, was

278 <

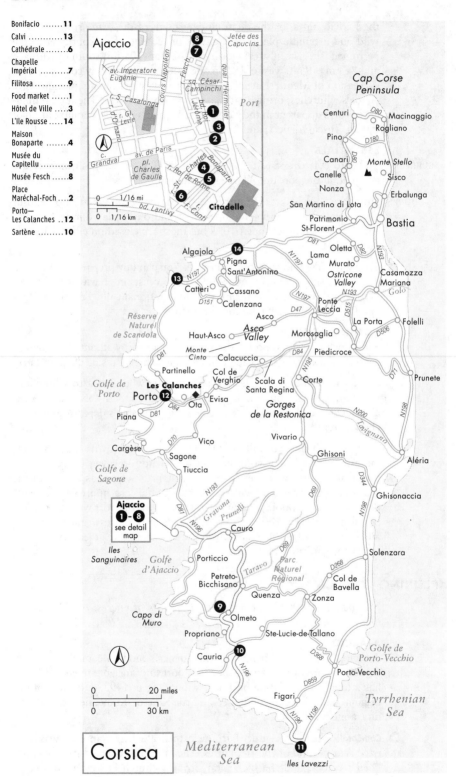

Ajaccio

av. Imperatore Eugénie
cours Napoléon
r. S. Casalonga
c. d'Ornano
c. Grandval
r. Gl. Levie
r. Jérôme
Fesch
sq. César Campinchi
quai l'Hermnier
Jetée des Capucins
Port
av. de Paris
r. Charles Bonaparte
pl. Charles de Gaulle
r. Roi de Rome
r. Charles Bonaparte
r. F. Conti
bd. Lantivy
Citadelle

0   1/16 mi
0   1/16 km

Corsica

Cap Corse Peninsula

Centuri
Macinaggio
Rogliano
Pino
Canari
Monte Stello
Canelle
Sisco
Nonza
Erbalunga
San Martino di Lota
Patrimonio
St-Florent
Bastia
Oletta
Lama
Murato
Casamozza
Ostricone Valley
Mariana
Golo
Algajola
Pigna
Sant'Antonino
Ponte Leccia
Catteri
Cassano
La Porta
Folelli
Calenzana
Asco
Morosaglia
Réserve Naturel de Scandola
Haut-Asco
Asco Valley
Piedicroce
Monte Cinto
Calacuccia
Scala di Santa Regina
Corte
Prunete
Partinello
Col de Verghio
Golfe de Porto
Les Calanches
Porto
Ota
Evisa
Gorges de la Restonica
Piana
Vico
Vivario
Aléria
Cargèse
Sagone
Ghisoni
Golfe de Sagone
Tiuccia
Ghisonaccia
Ajaccio
1 - 8
see detail map
Cauro
Iles Sanguinaires
Golfe d'Ajaccio
Porticcio
Solenzara
Petreto-Bicchisano
Col de Bavella
Quenza
Zonza
Capo di Muro
Olmeto
Ste-Lucie-di-Tallano
Propriano
Golfe de Porto-Vecchio
Cauria
Porto-Vecchio
Figari
Tyrrhenian Sea
Iles Lavezzi
Mediterranean Sea

0   20 miles
0   30 km

donated by Napoléon's sister Eliza after he made her princess of Tuscany. Eugène Delacroix's *Virgin of Sacré Coeur* hangs above the altar. ⊠*Rue F.-Conti.*

❼ Chapelle Impérial *(Imperial Chapel).* This Renaissance-style chapel was built in 1857 by Napoléon's nephew, Napoléon III, to accommodate the tombs of the Bonaparte family (Napoléon Bonaparte himself is buried in the Hôtel des Invalides in Paris). The Coptic crucifix over the altar was taken from Egypt during the general's 1798 campaign. ⊠*50 rue Fesch* 🎫*€1.50* ⊙*Tues.–Sat. 10–12:30 and 3–7.*

CORSICA BEST BETS

Bonifacio. Rising seemingly out of the living rock, this medieval stronghold is now a maze of tourist-friendly cafés and shops.

Calvi. A picture perfect little town topped by a walled citadel, Calvi also offers some of the finest beaches on the island.

The Calanques de Piana. Russet red inlets of jagged rocks lapped by azure waters, this vista, which you can see if you drive between Ajaccio and Calvi, is truly breathtaking.

❶ Food market. A spectacular food market is held every morning except Monday in place Campinchi, across the quay from the ferry port, an opportunity to admire an enticing parade of Corsican cheeses, pastries, sausages, and everything from traditional chestnut-flour beignets to prehistoric *rascasse* (red scorpion fish), at the fish market tucked in under the Hôtel de Ville.

❸ Hôtel de Ville. Ajaccio's town hall is home to **Le musée Napoléonien.** Here, in
★ an Empire-style grand salon, you'll find portraits of a long line of Bonapartes. Also note the fine bust of Letizia, Napoléon's formidable mother; a bronze death mask of the emperor himself; and a frescoed ceiling depicting Napoléon's meteoric rise. ⊠*Pl. Maréchal-Foch* 🕾*04–95–51–52–62* 🎫*€2.50* ⊙*Weekdays 9–noon and 2:30–5:30.*

❹ Maison Bonaparte *(Bonaparte House).* Here Napoléon was born on August
Fodor'sChoice 15, 1769. Today this large (once middle-class) house contains a museum
★ with portraits of the entire Bonaparte clan. Most of the salons are 20th-century redos and homages to the emperor's favored Empire neoclassical style. Fans of the man—and connoisseurs of *le style empire à la ajaccienne*—will find this very worthwhile. ⊠*Rue St-Charles* 🕾*04–95–21–43–89* ⊕*www.musee-maisonbonaparte.fr* 🎫*€5* ⊙*Oct.–Mar. Tues.–Sun. 10–noon and 2–5, Apr.–Sept., Tues.–Sun. 10–noon and 2–6.*

❺ Musée du Capitellu. At the corner of rue St-Charles and rue Roie-de-Rome, this museum traces the history of Ajaccio through the career of a single family. It's on this street that you'll also find some of the city's oldest houses, opposite the tiny church of St-Jean Baptiste; most of these buildings were built shortly after the town was founded in 1492. If you walk east down rue Roie-de-Rome from the museum, you can get a good look at Ajaccio's Citadelle. ⊠*18 bd. Danielle Casanova* 🕾*04–95–21–50–57* 🎫*€4* ⊙*Mon.–Sat. 10–noon and 2–6, Sun. 10–noon.*

❽ Musée Fesch. Adjacent to the Chapelle Impérial, the museum houses a fine
★ collection of Italian masters, ranging from Botticelli and Canaletto to De Tura—part of a massive collection of 30,000 paintings bought at bargain prices by Napoléon's uncle, Cardinal Fesch, archbishop of Lyon, follow-

ing the French Revolution. Thanks to his nephew's military conquests, the cardinal was able to amass (steal, some would say) many celebrated Old Master paintings, the most famous of which are now in the Louvre. ⊠*50 rue Fesch* ☎*04–95–21–48–17* ⊕*www.musee-fesch.com* ⊠*€5.50* ⊙*Apr., June, Sept., and Oct., Wed.–Mon. 9:30–noon and 3–6:30; July and Aug., Tues.–Sat. 3–9:30, Sun. and Mon. 9:30–noon and 3–6:30; Nov.–Mar., Wed.–Mon. 9:30–noon and 2:30–6.*

❷ **Place Maréchal-Foch.** Rows of stately palm trees lead up to a marble statue of Napoléon on the city's main square."

FILITOSA

❾ *71 km (43 mi) southeast of Ajaccio off N196.*

★ Filitosa is the site of Corsica's largest grouping of megalithic menhir statues. Bizarre, life-size stone figures of ancient warriors rise up mysteriously from the undulating terrain, many of them have human faces whose features have been flattened over time by erosion. A small museum on the site houses archaeological finds, including the menhir known as *Scalsa Murta*, whose delicately carved spine and rib cage are surprisingly contemporary for a work dating from some 5,000 years ago. ⊠*Centre Préhistorique Filitosa* ☎*04–95–74–00–91* ⊠*Guided tours in English €5* ⊙*June–Aug., daily 8–7.*

SARTÈNE

❿ *27 km (16 mi) southeast of Filitosa on N196.*

Described as the "most Corsican of all Corsican towns" by French novelist Prosper Mérimée, Sartène, first founded in the 16th century, has survived pirate raids and bloody feuding among the town's families. The word "vendetta" is believed to have originated here as the result of a 19th-century family feud so serious that French troops were brought in to serve as a peacekeeping buffer force.

Vieux Sartène (Old Sartène), surrounded by ancient ramparts, begins at place de la Libération, the main square. To one side is the **Hôtel de Ville** (Town Hall), in the former Genoese governor's palace. Slip into the Middle Ages through the tunnel under the Town Hall to place du Maggiu and the ancient **Santa Anna** quarter, a warren of narrow, cobbled streets lined with granite houses. Scarcely 100 yards from the Hôtel de Ville, down a steep and winding street, is a 12th-century *tour de guet* (watchtower).

Housed in a magnificently perched stone-castle redoubt, some of the island's best prehistoric relics are at the **Musée Départemental de Préhistoire Corse** *(Regional Museum of Corsican Prehistory)*. In fact, this was the town's former prison, a building as stark and forbidding as the rest of this village. ⊠*Rue Croce* ☎*04–95–77–01–09* ⊕*www.toute-la-corse.com* ⊠*€4* ⊙*Mon.–Sat. 10–noon and 2–6.*

BONIFACIO

⓫ *52 km (31 mi) southeast of Sartène via N196.*

Fodor'sChoice The ancient fortress town of Bonifacio occupies a spectacular cliff-top
★ aerie above a harbor carved from limestone cliffs. It's 13 km (8 mi) from Sardinia, and the local speech is heavily influenced by the accent and idiom of that nearby Italian island. Established in the 12th century as Genoa's

first Corsican stronghold, Bonifacio remained Genoese through centuries of battles and sieges. As you wander the narrow streets of the **Haute Ville** (Upper Village), inside the walls of the citadel, think of Homer's *Odyssey*. It's here, in the harbor, that scholars place the catastrophic encounter (Book X) between Ulysses's fleet and the Laestrygonians, who hurled lethal boulders down from the cliffs.

From place d'Armes at the city gate, enter the **Bastion de l'Étendard** *(Bastion of the Standard)*; you can still see the system of weights and levers used to pull up the drawbridge. The former garrison now houses life-size dioramas of Bonifacio's history. €2 *Mid-June–mid-Sept., daily 9–7.*

In the center of the maze of cobbled streets that makes up the citadel is the 12th-century church of **Ste-Marie-Majeure,** with buttresses attaching it to surrounding houses. Inside the church, note the Renaissance baptismal font, carved in bas-relief, and the 3rd-century white-marble Roman sarcophagus. Walk around the back to see the loggia, which is built above a huge cistern that stored water for use in times of siege, as did the circular stone silos seen throughout the town.

PORTO–LES CALANCHES
12 *140 km (87 mi) north of Ajaccio.*

The flashy resort town of Porto doesn't have much character, but its setting on the crystalline **Golfe de Porto** (Gulf of Porto), surrounded by massive pink-granite mountains, is superb. Activity focuses on the small port, where there is a boardwalk with restaurants and hotels. A short hike from the boardwalk will bring you to a 16th-century Genoese tower that overlooks the bay. Boat excursions leave daily for the **Réserve Naturel de Scandola.**

Detour south of Porto on D81 to get to **Les Calanches,** jagged outcroppings of red rock considered among the most extraordinary natural sites in France. Look for arches and stelae, standing rock formations shaped like animals and phantasmagoric human faces.

CALVI
13 *30 km (19 mi) north of Porto, 159 km (100 mi) north of Ajaccio.*

Calvi, Corsica's slice of the Riviera, grew rich by supplying products to Genoa; its citizens remained loyal supporters of Genoa long after the rest of the island declared independence. Calvi also claims to be the birthplace of Christopher Columbus. During the 18th century the town endured assaults from Corsican nationalists, including celebrated patriot Pasquale Paoli. Today Calvi sees a summertime invasion of tourists, drawn to the 6-km (4-mi) stretch of sandy white beach, the citadel, and the buzzing nightlife.

The Genoese **Citadelle,** perched on a rocky promontory at the tip of the bay, competes with the beach as a major attraction. An inscription above the drawbridge—CIVITAS CALVI SEMPER FIDELIS (The citizens of Calvi always faithful)—reflects the town's unswerving allegiance to Genoa. At the welcome center, just inside the gates, you can see a video on the city's history and arrange to take a guided tour given in English (three times a day) or a self-guided walking tour. *Up the hill off av. de l'Uruguay* 04–95–65–

36–74 ⊕*www.nordsud-calvi.com/visite.htm* ✉*Guided tour and video show €9* ⊙*Tours Easter–early Oct., daily at 10, 4:30, and 6:30.*

L'ILE ROUSSE

⓮ *10 km (6 mi) northeast of Algajola, 37 km (22 mi) southwest of St-Florent.*

L'Ile Rousse, famous for its market and named for the island of reddish rock now connected to the town by a causeway, is a favorite for vacationers who come to bask in its Riviera-like mise-en-scène. A small two-car train runs along the coast to Calvi, delivering sun-worshippers to beaches not accessible by road.

SHOPPING

Traditional handicrafts are found in abundance in the shopping streets of the major towns. Until the middle of the 20th century, most Corsicans had to be relatively self-sufficient, and this has led to all manner of crafts from knifes and walking sticks to warm winter sweaters. Look for pottery, for which the island is known. Corsican knives are a specialty item, and the finest examples have exquisite blades and handles. Also look for items carved from wood and bone, some practical, some ornate. Because food had to be put back for the winter, preserved foods became very important parts of the Corsican diet and are now well-known; the charcuterie is excellent—in addition to a range of hams and salamis, you'll find aromatic dried herbs, numerous cheeses, plus fragrant jams and honey. Don't forget to sample a bottle of Corsican wine.

The citadel of Bonifacio has excellent boutiques set in historic stone cottages and cellars. Both Ajaccio and L'Isle Rousse have excellent markets and in Calvi the major shopping streets are rue Clemenceau and boulevard Wilson.

Paese Nostru (✉*Passage GuinguettaAjaccio*) sells Corsican crafts of all kinds. **U Tilaghju** (✉*Rue Forcioli ContiAjaccio*), one of several artisanal shops near the cathedral, has an impressive collection of ceramics.

SPORTS & ACTIVITIES

The area around Bonifacio is ideal for water sports, including windsurfing and sea kayaking. The island also has several golf courses for those who can't bear to be away from the greens. In summer, sailing is a major pastime with wealthy French and Italians plying a course to the chic harbors and the secluded rocky coves. Well-being is also taken very seriously, with several excellent spas.

For water sports, contact **Club Atoll** (✉*Rte. de Porto-Vecchio* ☎*04–95–73–02–83*).

The best golf course on Corsica (and one of the best in the Mediterranean), a 20,106-foot, par-72 gem designed by Robert Trent Jones, is at **Sperone** (✉*Domaine de Sperone* ☎*04–95–73–17–13*), just east of Bonifacio.

Institut de Thalassothérapie (Institute of Thalassotherapy), on the Punta di Porticcio, in the *grand luxe* Le Maquis hotel is notable for its seawater cures. ⊠*D55, Porticcio* ☎*04–95–25–05–55* ⊕*www.lemaquis.com.*

BEACHES

There are fine Riviera-like strands north of Calvi reached by a little train service that runs around the bay to L'Isle Rousse. These do get very busy between late July and the end of August but can be delightfully peaceful early or late in the season. During the summer there are numerous cafés and restaurants for refreshment. Note that topless sunbathing is acceptable here, and you will find bare breasts at every beach. **Plage d'Ostriconi** (⊠*20 km [13 mi] north of L'Isle Rousse*) is at the mouth of the Ostriconi River. A wilder beach that is frequented by nudists is **Plage Saleccia**, which was used as a location for the 1960s film *The Longest Day.*

WHERE TO EAT

¢–$$ ✕**20123.** This well-loved Ajaccio restaurant is known for its traditional cuisine, fresh fish from the nearby market and, in season, game specials such as *civet de sanglier* (wild boar stew) with *trompettes de la mort* (wild mushrooms) served in a bubbling earthenware casserole. ⊠*2 rue Roi-de-Rome, Ajaccio* ☎*04–95–21–50–05* ⊕*www.20123.fr* ▭*MC, V* ⊙*Closed Mon., Tues., and Jan. 15–Feb. 15. No lunch June 15–Sept. 15.*

¢–$$ ✕**Le Voilier.** This popular year-round restaurant in the port serves carefully
★ selected and prepared fish and seafood, along with fine Corsican sausage and traditional cuisine from *soupe corse* to *fiadone* (cheesecake). ⊠*Quai Comparetti, Bonifacio* ☎*04–95–73–07–06* ⊕*www.levoilier.fr* ▭*AE, DC, MC, V* ⊙*Closed Mon. No dinner Sun.*

BARCELONA, SPAIN

Capital of Catalonia, 2,000-year-old Barcelona commanded a vast Mediterranean empire when Madrid was still a dusty Moorish outpost on the Spanish steppe. Relegated to second-city status only in 1561, Barcelona has long rivaled and often surpassed Madrid's supremacy. Catalans jealously guard their language and their culture. Barcelona has long had a frenetically active cultural life. It was the home of architect Antoni Gaudí, and the painters Joan Miró and Salvador Dalí. Pablo Picasso also spent his formative years in Barcelona. Native musicians include cellist Pablo (Pau, in Catalan) Casals, opera singers Montserrat Caballé and José (Josep) Carreras, and early music master Jordi Savall. One of Europe's most visually stunning cities, Barcelona balances its many elements, from the medieval intimacy of its Gothic Quarter to the grace of the wide boulevards in the Moderniste Eixample. In the 21st century, innovative structures, such as the Ricardo Bofill *Vela* (sail) hotel, demonstrate Barcelona's insatiable appetite for novelty and progress.

ESSENTIALS

CURRENCY The euro (€1 to US$1.46 at this writing); U.S. currency is generally not accepted in Europe, but ATMs are common and credit cards are widely accepted.

HOURS Museums are generally open from 9 until 7 or 8; many are closed on Monday and some close in the afternoon. Most stores are open Monday through Saturday 9 to 1:30 and 5 to 8, but a few remain open all afternoon. Virtually all close on Sunday.

INTERNET **easyInternetcafé** ⊠*La Rambla 21* ☏*93/301–7507.*

TELEPHONES Spain has good land and mobile services. Public kiosks accept phone cards that support international calls (cards sold in press shops, bars and telecom shops). Mobile services are GSM and 3G compatible. Major companies include Vodafone.

COMING ASHORE

Barcelona is one of Europe's busiest cruise ports. Vessels dock at the Port Vell facility, which has seven terminals catering to cruise-ship traffic. All terminals are equipped with duty-free shops, telephones, bar/restaurants, information desks, and currency exchange booths. The ships docking closest to the terminal entrance are a 10-minute walk from the southern end of Las Ramblas (The Rambla), but those docked at the farthest end have a long walk or must catch a shuttle bus to the port entrance. The shuttle, which runs every 20 minutes, links all terminals with the public square at the bottom of The Rambla. If you walk up Las Ramblas, after about 10 minutes you'll reach Drassanes metro station for onward public transport around the city. A metro or bus single ticket price is €1.25; a day ticket is €5.25.

If you intend to explore Barcelona, a vehicle is not practical. Public transportation or a taxi are by far the most sensible options. City buses run daily from 5:30 AM to 11:30 PM. The fare is €1.30. For multiple journeys purchase a Targeta T10, (€7), valid for metro or bus. The FCG (Ferrocarril de la Generalitat) train is a comfortable commuter train that gets you to within walking distance of nearly everything in Barcelona. Changes to the regular city metro are free. The Barcelona Tourist Bus is another excellent way to tour the city. Three routes (Roman, Modernisme, and Gausi) cover just about every place you might want to visit, and you can hop on and off whenever you want. A one-day ticket is €19; you can buy online at ⊕*www.tmb.net.*

If you plan to explore the Spanish coast or countryside, a vehicle would be beneficial, but even an economy car (manual transmission) is expensive at approximately €93 per day.

EXPLORING BARCELONA

Barcelona's Old City includes **El Barri Gòtic** (the Gothic Quarter). Although this section of the city is being cleaned up, bag-snatching is common here, so keep your wits about you, and if at all possible, carry nothing in your hands. Nearby is Sant Pere, which was once Barcelona's old textile neighborhood.

Barcelona's best-known promenade, **La Rambla,** is a constant and colorful flood of humanity with flower stalls, bird vendors, mimes, musicians, and outdoor cafés. Federico García Lorca called this street the only one in the world that he wished would never end; traffic plays second fiddle to the endless *paseo* (stroll) of locals and travelers alike. The whole avenue is referred to as Las Ramblas (Les Rambles, in Catalan) or La Rambla, but each section has its own name: Rambla Santa Monica is at the southeastern, or port, end; Rambla de les Flors in the middle; and Rambla dels Estudis at the top, near Plaça de Catalunya.

North of Plaça de Catalunya is the checkerboard known as the **Eixample.** With the dismantling of the city walls in 1860, Barcelona embarked upon an expansion scheme. The street grid was the work of urban planner Ildefons Cerdà; much of the building here was done at the height of Modernisme. The Eixample's principal thoroughfares are Rambla de Catalunya and Passeig de Gràcia, where the city's most elegant shops vie for space among its best art nouveau buildings.

Once Barcelona's pungent fishing port, **Barceloneta** retains much of its maritime flavor. Nearby is **La Ciutadella,** once a fortress but now the city's main downtown park. **Montjuïc,** a hill to the south of town, may have been named for the Jewish cemetery that was once on its slopes.

WHAT TO SEE
Numbers in the margin correspond to points of interest on the Barcelona map.

❹ Boqueria. Barcelona's most spectacular food market, also known as the Mercat de Sant Josep, is an explosion of life and color sprinkled with delicious little bar-restaurants. ⊠ *La Rambla 91, Rambla ⊕ www.boqueria. info ⊗ Mon.–Sat. 8–8* Ⓜ *Liceu.*

FodorśChoice
★

❽ Fundació Miró. The Miró Foundation was a gift from the artist Joan Miró to his native city and is one of Barcelona's most exciting showcases of contemporary art. The late-20th-century building makes a perfect canvas for Miró's unmistakably playful and colorful style. ⊠ *Av. Miramar 71, Montjuïc* ☎ *93/443–9470* ⊕ *www.bcn.fjmiro.es* 💷*€8 ⊗ Tues., Wed., Fri., and Sat. 10–7, Thurs. 10–9:30, Sun. 10–2:30.*

★

❼ Manzana de la Discòrdia. On this city block you can find three main Moderniste masterpieces. **Casa Lleó Morera** (No. 35) has a facade is covered with ornamentation and sculptures of female figures using the modern inventions of the age: the telephone, the telegraph, the photographic camera, and the Victrola. The pseudo-Flemish **Casa Amatller** (No. 41) was built by Josep Puig i Cadafalch in 1900 with decorative elements by Eusebi Arnau.

FodorśChoice
★

At No. 43, the colorful and bizarre **Casa Batlló** is Gaudí at his most spectacular, with its mottled facade resembling anything from an abstract pointillist painting to rainbow sprinkles on an ice-cream cone. Nationalist symbolism is at work here: the motifs are allusions to Catalonia's Middle Ages, with its codes of chivalry and religious fervor. ⊠ *Passeig de Gràcia 43, between Consell de Cent and Aragó, Eixample* ☎ *93/216–0306* ⊕ *www.casabatllo.es* 💷 *€17 ⊗ Daily 9–8* Ⓜ *Passeig de Gràcia.* "

❶ Museu d'Història de Catalunya. Built into what used to be a port warehouse, this state-of-the-art museum traces 3,000 years of Catalan history. The rooftop cafeteria, open to the general public, has excellent views over the harbor. ⊠ *Pl. Pau Vila 3, Barceloneta* ☎ *93/225–4700* ⊕ *www.mhcat.net* 💷 *€4; free 1st Sun. of month ⊗ Tues. and Thurs.–Sat. 10–7, Wed. 10–8, Sun. 10–2:30* Ⓜ *Barceloneta.*

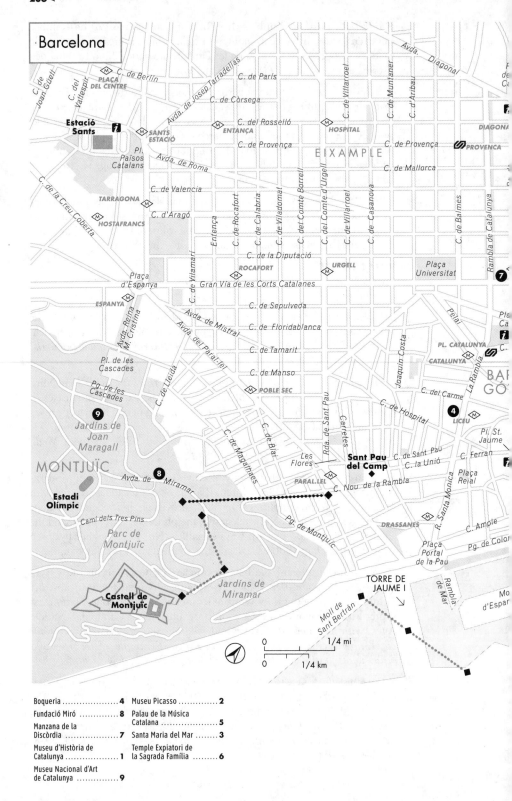

Barcelona

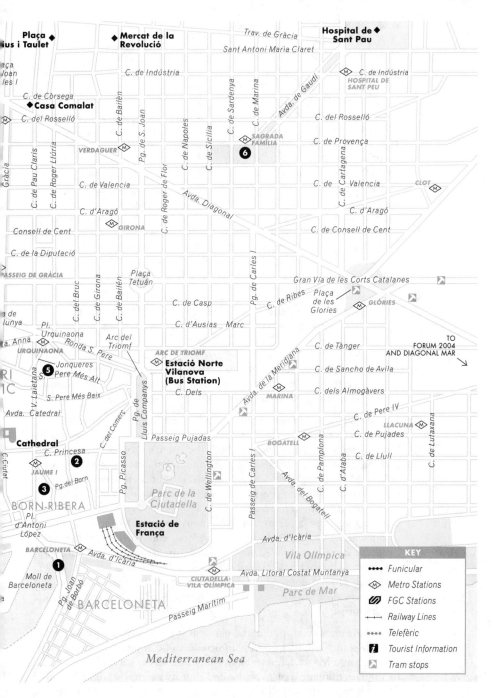

Plaça
ius i Taulet ◆

◆ Mercat de la
Revolució

Trav. de Gràcia

Hospital de ◆
Sant Pau

Sant Antoni Marìa Claret

aça
Joan
les I

C. de Indústria

C. de Indústria
HOSPITAL DE
SANT PEU

C. de Còrsega
◆ Casa Comalat

C. del Rosselló

C. de Bailèn

Pg. de S. Joan

C. de Sardenya

C. de Marina

C. de Gaudí

C. del Rosselló

C. de Sicília

VERDAGUER

C. de Napoles

SAGRADA
FAMÍLIA

C. de Provença

6

C. de Cartagena

Gràcia

C. de Pau Claris

C. de Roger Llúria

C. de Valencia

C. de Roger de Flor

Avda. Diagonal

C. de Valencia

CLOT

C. d'Aragó

C. d'Aragó

Consell de Cent

C. de Consell de Cent

C. de la Diputació

>
PASSEIG DE GRÀCIA

C. del Bruc

C. de Girona

C. de Bailèn

Plaça
Tetuán

Pg. de Carles I

Gran Vía de les Corts Catalanes

a de
lunya

ta. Anna

Pl.
Urquinaona

Ronda S. Pere

Arc del
Triomf

C. de Casp

C. d'Ausias   Marc

C. de Ribes

Plaça
de les
Glories

GLÓRIES

URQUINAONA

Jonqueres

5 Pere Més Alt

V. Laietana

ARC DE TRIOMF

Estació Norte
Vilanova
(Bus Station)

Avda. de la Meridiana

C. de Tànger

C. de Sancho de Avila

TO
FORUM 2004
AND DIAGONAL MAR

RI
IC

S. Pere Més Baix

Pg. de
Lluis Companys

C. Dels

MARINA

C. dels Almogàvers

Avda. Catedral

C. del Comerç

Passeig Pujadas

BOGATELL

C. de Pere IV

LLACUNA

C. de Lutxana

Cathedral

C. Princesa

2

Pg. Picasso

C. de Wellington

Passeig de Carles I

C. de Pamplona

C. de Pujades

C. d'Alaba

C. de Llull

JAUME I

C. Ciutat

3 Pg. del Born

BORN-RIBERA

Pl.
d'Antoni
López

Pg. Picasso

Avda. del Bogatell

Parc de la
Ciutadella

Estació de
França

Avda. d'Icària

BARCELONETA

Avda. d'Icària

Vila Olímpica

Moll de
Barceloneta

1

Pg. Joan
de Borbó

CIUTADELLA-
VILA OLÍMPICA

Avda. Litoral Costat Muntanya

Parc de Mar

BARCELONETA

Passeig Marítim

Mediterranean Sea

	KEY
•••••	Funicular
◈	Metro Stations
🚇	FGC Stations
⊢—⊣	Railway Lines
•••••	Telefèric
ℹ	Tourist Information
↗	Tram stops

4

9 **Museu Nacional d'Art de Catalunya**

Fodor's Choice
★

(MNAC; Catalonian National Museum of Art). Housed in the imposing **Palau Nacional,** built in 1929 as the centerpiece of the World's Fair, this superb museum was renovated in 1995 by Gae Aulenti, architect of the Musée d'Orsay in Paris. The eclectic collection spans the Romanesque period to the 20th century and includes works by Rubens, Tintoretto, and Velázquez. Pride of place, however, goes to the Romanesque exhibition, the world's finest collection of Romanesque frescoes, altarpieces, and wood carvings. ✉*Mirador del Palau 6, Montjuïc* ☎*93/622–0375* ⊕*www.mnac.es* 🎫*€9* ⊙*Tues.–Sat. 10–7, Sun. 10–2:30.*

2 **Museu Picasso.** Picasso spent key formative years (1895–1904) in Barcelona,

Fodor's Choice
★

and this 3,600-work permanent collection is strong on his early production. Displays include childhood and adolescent sketches, works from Picasso's Blue and Rose periods, and the famous 44 cubist studies based on Velázquez's *Las Meninas.* ✉*Carrer Montcada 15–23, Born-Ribera* ☎*93/319–6310* ⊕*www.museupicasso.bcn.es* 🎫*Permanent collection €7, temporary exhibits €6, combined ticket €9.50; free 1st Sun. of month* ⊙*Tues.–Sat. 10–8, Sun. 10–3* Ⓜ*Catalunya, Liceu, Jaume I.*

5 **Palau de la Música Catalana.** A riot of color and form, Barcelona's Music

Fodor's Choice
★

Palace is the flagship of the city's Moderniste architecture. Designed by Lluís Domènech i Montaner in 1908, the Palau's exterior is remarkable in itself, but the interior is an uproar. Wagnerian cavalry erupts from the right side of the stage over a heavy-browed bust of Beethoven, and Catalonia's popular music is represented by the flowing maidens of Lluís Millet's song *Flors de Maig (Flowers of May)* on the left. Overhead, an inverted stained-glass cupola seems to offer the divine manna of music; painted rosettes and giant peacock feathers explode from the tops of the walls. Even the stage is populated with muselike art nouveau musicians, each half bust, half mosaic. ✉ *Ticket office, Sant Francesc de Paula 2, off Via Laietana, around corner from hall, Sant Pere* ☎*902/442–882* ⊕*www. palaumusica.org* 🎫*Tour €8* ⊙*Tours daily 10–3:30, 10–7 July and Aug.* Ⓜ*Catalunya.*

3 **Santa Maria del Mar.** This pure and classical space enclosed by soaring col-

Fodor's Choice
★

umns is something of an oddity in ornate and complex Moderniste Barcelona. Santa Maria del Mar (Saint Mary of the Sea) was built from 1329 to 1383, in fulfillment of a vow made a century earlier by Jaume I to build a church to watch over all Catalan seafarers. The architect, Montagut de Berenguer, designed a bare-bones basilica that is now considered the finest existing example of Catalan (or Mediterranean) Gothic architecture. ✉*Pl. de Santa Maria, Born-Ribera* ☎*93/310–2390* ⊙*Daily 9–1:30 and 4:30–8* Ⓜ*Catalunya, Jaume I.*

6 **Temple Expiatori de la Sagrada Família.** Barcelona's most unforgettable landmark, Antoni Gaudí's Sagrada Família was conceived as nothing short of a Bible in stone. The cathedral is comprised of a series of magnificent monumental tableau drawing inspiration from the long tradition of medieval allegory in church design and decoration yet standing firmly in the Modernist era in its delivery. This landmark is one of the most important architectural creations of the 19th to 21st centuries but remained unfinished at the time of Gaudí's death. Controversy surrounds subsequent work to complete the structure. ⊠*Mallorca 401, Eixample* ☎*93/207–3031* ⊕*www.sagradafamilia.org* ⊠*€10, bell tower elevator €2* ☉*Oct.–Mar., daily 9–6; Apr.–Sept., daily 9–8* Ⓜ*Sagrada Família.*

Fodor'sChoice
★

4

SHOPPING

Between the surging fashion scene, a host of young clothing designers, clever home furnishings, delicious foodstuffs including wine and olive oil, and ceramics, art, and antiques, Barcelona is the best place in Spain to unload extra ballast from your wallet.

Barcelona's prime shopping districts are the Passeig de Gràcia, Rambla de Catalunya, Plaça de Catalunya, Porta de l'Àngel, and Avinguda Diagonal up to Carrer Ganduxer. For high fashion, browse along Passeig de Gràcia and the Diagonal between Plaça Joan Carles I and Plaça Francesc Macià. There are two-dozen antiques shops in the Gothic Quarter, another 70 shops off Passeig de Gràcia on Bulevard dels Antiquaris, and still more in Gràcia and Sarrià. For old-fashioned Spanish shops, prowl the Gothic Quarter, especially **Carrer Ferran**. The area around the church of Santa Maria del Mar, an artisans' quarter since medieval times, is full of cheerful design stores and art galleries. The area surrounding **Plaça del Pi**, from the Boqueria to Carrer Portaferrissa and Carrer de la Canuda, is thick with boutiques and jewelry and design shops. The **Barri de la Ribera**, around Santa Maria del Mar, especially El Born area, has a cluster of design, fashion, and and food shops. Design, jewelry, and knickknack shops cluster on Carrer Banys Vells and Carrer Flassaders, near Carrer Montcada.

Galeria Joan Prats (⊠*La Rambla de Catalunya 54, Eixample*) is a veteran, known for the quality of its artists' works. **Art Escudellers** (⊠*C. Escudellers 23–25, Barri Gòtic*) has ceramics from all over Spain, with more than 200 different artisans represented and maps showing where the work is from. The Eixample's **Centre d'Antiquaris** (⊠*Passeig de Gràcia 55, Eixample*) contains 75 antiques stores.

BEACHES

Five kilometers (3 mi) of beaches now run from the Platja (beach) de Sant Sebastià, a nudist enclave, northward through the Barceloneta, Port Olímpic, Nova Icària, Bogatell, Mar Bella, Nova Mar Bella, and Novíssima Mar Bella beaches to the Fòrum complex and the rocky Illa Pangea swimming area. Next to the mouth of the Besòs River is Platja Nova. Topless bathing is common. The beaches immediately north of Barcelona include Montgat, Ocata, Vilasar de Mar, Arenys de Mar, Canet, and Sant Pol de Mar, all accessible by train from the RENFE station in Plaça de Catalunya. Especially worthy is **Sant Pol** (⊠*Passeig Maritim 59* ☎*93/665–1347*), with clean sand and a handsome old part of town and Carme Ruscalleda's famous **Sant Pau,** one of the top three restaurants in Catalonia.

WHERE TO EAT

$–$$ ✕**El Foro.** This hot spot near the Born is always full to the rafters with lively young and young-at-heart people. Painting and photographic exhibits line the walls, and the menu is dominated by pizzas, salads, and meat cooked over coals. Flamenco and jazz performances downstairs are a good post-dinner option. ⊠*Princesa 53, Born-Ribera* ☎*93/310–1020* ▤*AE, DC, MC, V* ⊘*Closed Mon.* Ⓜ*Jaume I.*

$ **Cal Pep.** A two-minute walk east from Santa Maria del Mar toward the Fodor'sChoice   Estació de França, Pep's has Barcelona's best and freshest selection of ★   tapas, cooked and served piping hot in this boisterous space. ⊠*Pl. de les Olles 8, Born-Ribera* ☎*93/319–6183* ⊘*Tues.–Sat. 1–4 and 8–midnight, Mon. 8 PM–midnight* Ⓜ*Jaume I.*

BARI, ITALY

Puglia is one of three regions making up the heel and toe of Italy's boot and informally known collectively as the *mezzogiorno,* a name that translates literally as "midday." It's a curiously telling nickname because midday is when it's quietest here. This is Italy's deep south, where whitewashed buildings stand silently over the turquoise Mediterranean, castles guard medieval alleyways, and grandmothers dry their handmade orecchiette pasta in the mid-afternoon heat. At every turn, Puglia boasts unspoiled scenery, a wonderful country food tradition, and an openness to outsiders. Beyond the cities, seaside resorts, and the few major sights, there's a sparsely populated countryside with expanses of silvery olive trees, vineyards of *primitivo* and *aglianico* grapes, and giant prickly pear cacti. Puglia still doesn't make it onto the itineraries of most visitors to Italy. This translates into an unusual opportunity to engage with a rich culture and landscape virtually untouched by mass tourism. Bari is at the top of the boot; it's the biggest city in the mezzogiorno, a lively, quirky, and sometimes seamy port city on the Adriatic coast.

ESSENTIALS

CURRENCY   The euro (€1 to US$1.46 at this writing); U.S. currency is generally not accepted in Europe, but ATMs are common and credit cards are widely accepted.

HOURS   Shops are generally open from 8 AM until noon or 1 PM, then again from 3 or 4 until 8, perhaps opening later in summer. Most shops are closed on Sunday. Most museums and attractions open throughout the day, though some, particularly churches, close in the afternoon.

INTERNET   **The Netkiosk** (⊠*Via Guiseppe Pellegrini 31, Bari* ☎*080/5429667*) is open from Monday to Saturday but closes in the afternoons.

TELEPHONES   Tri-band GSM phones work in Italy. You can buy prepaid phone cards at telecom shops, news-vendors and tobacconists in all towns and cities. Phone cards can be used for local or international calls.

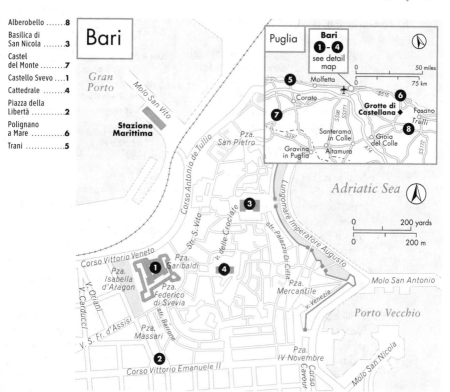

COMING ASHORE

Bari is a large port and has a dedicated cruise terminal; ships dock, giving passengers only a short walk to the port entrance. From here, it is a further short walk into the city, where you can explore on foot.

Bari is linked by rail to all the major towns in the region. Trani can be reached in 34 to 50 minutes; there are two trains per hour and the single fare is €2.60. Polignano a Mare is less than 30 minutes from Bari by train; there is one service per hour and single fare costs €5.10. Alberobello is a journey time of 80 to 100 minutes. All train tickets can be bought online at www.trenilatia.com and retrieved from machines in Bari station. Renting a vehicle would allow you to explore the Puglia countryside at your own pace. An economy manual vehicle costs approximately €54 per day, but delivery to the port may cost more.

EXPLORING BARI & PUGLIA

Numbers in the margin correspond to points of interest on the Bari map.

BARI

The biggest city in the mezzogiorno, Bari is a major port and a transit point for travelers catching ferries across the Adriatic to Greece, but it's also a cosmopolitan city with one of the most interesting historic centers in the region. Most of Bari is set out in a logical, 19th-century grid, following the designs of Joachim Murat (1767–1815), Napoléon's brother-in-law and King of the Two Sicilies. By day, explore the old town's winding alleyways, where Bari's open-door policy offers a glimpse into the daily routine of southern Italy—matrons hand-rolling pasta with their grandchildren home from school for the midday meal, and handymen perched on rickety ladders, patching up centuries-old arches and doorways.

❷ **Piazza della Libertà.** The heart of the modern town is this central piazza, but just beyond it, across Corso Vittorio Emanuele, is the *città vecchia* (old town), a maze of narrow streets on the promontory that juts out between Bari's old and new ports, circumscribed by Via Venezia, offering elevated views of the Adriatic in every direction. Stop for an outdoor drink at **Greta** (⊠ *Via Venezia 24*) for a commanding view of the port and sea.

BARI BEST BETS

Soaking in the atmosphere in Bari's old town. The dramas of life in Italy's deep south is not a show put on for tourists but a fascinating daily performance for lovers of people-watching.

Exploring Polignano a Mare. This whitewashed village's roots are well in sync with the Mediterranean heartbeat.

Touring Trulli country. These unique humble stone buildings surrounded by vines are one of Italy's most unusual architectural treasures.

---

❸ **Basilica di San Nicola.** In the città vecchia, overlooking the sea and just off Via Venezia, is the church that was built in the 11th century to house the bones of St. Nicholas, also known as St. Nick, or Santa Claus. His remains, buried in the crypt, are said to have been stolen by Bari sailors from Myra, where St. Nicholas was bishop, in what is now Turkey. The basilica, of solid and powerful construction, was the only building to survive the otherwise wholesale destruction of Bari by the Normans in 1152. ⊠ *Piazza San Nicola* ☎ *080/5737111* ⊗ *Daily 9–1 and 4–7.*

❹ **Cattedrale.** Bari's 12th-century cathedral is the seat of the local bishop and was the scene of many significant political marriages between important families in the Middle Ages. The cathedral's solid architecture reflects the Romanesque style favored by the Normans of that period. ⊠ *Piazza dell'Odegitria* ☎ *080/5288215* 🎫 *Free* ⊗ *Daily 9–1 and 4–7.*

❶ **Castello Svevo.** Looming over Bari's cathedral is this huge fortress. The current building dates from the time of Holy Roman Emperor Frederick II (1194–1250), who rebuilt an existing Norman-Byzantine castle to his own exacting specifications. Designed more for power than beauty, it looks out beyond the cathedral to the small Porto Vecchio (Old Port). Inside a haphazard collection of medieval Puglian art is frequently enlivened by changing exhibitions featuring local, national, and international artists. Hours and admission are subject to change depending on the current exhibiton. ⊠ *Piazza Federico II di Svevia* ☎ *080/5286218* 🎫 *€2* ⊗ *Daily 9:30–7:30; last entrance at 6:30.*

TRANI
❺ *43 km (27 mi) northwest of Bari.*

Smaller than the other ports along this coast, Trani has a quaint old town with polished stone streets and buildings, medieval churches, and a harbor filled with fishing boats. Trani is also justly famous for its sweet dessert wine, Moscato di Trani.

The stunning, pinkish-white-hue 11th-century **Duomo** (⊠ *Piazza Duomo* ⊙ *Daily 8–noon and 3:30–7*), considered one of the finest in Puglia, is built on a spit of land jutting into the sea.

The boxy, well-preserved **Castle** (☏ *0883/506603* ⊙ *Daily 8:30–7:30; last entrance at 7* PM) was built by Frederick II in 1233.

The Jewish community flourished here in medieval times, and on **Via Sinagoga** *(Synagogue Street)* two of the four synagogues still exist: **Santa Maria Scolanova** and **Santa Anna**, both built in the 13th century; the latter still bears a Hebrew inscription.

POLIGNANO A MARE

6 *40 km (24 mi) southeast of Bari.*

With a well-preserved whitewashed old town perched on limestone cliffs overlooking the Adriatic, Polignano a Mare makes an atmospheric base for exploring the surrounding area. Bari is only a half-hour train ride up the coast. The town is virtually lifeless all winter, but becomes something of a weekend hot spot for city dwellers in summer.

CASTEL DEL MONTE

7 *56 km (35 mi) southwest of Bari.*

★ Built by Frederick II in the first half of the 13th century on an isolated hill, Castel del Monte is an imposing octagonal castle with eight austere towers. Very little is known about the structure, since virtually no records exist: the gift shop has many books that explore its mysterious past and posit fascinating theories based on its dimensions and Federico II's love of mathematics. It has none of the usual defense features associated with medieval castles, so it probably had little military significance. Some theories suggest it might have been built as a hunting lodge or may have served as an astronomical observatory, or even as a stop for pilgrims on their quest for the Holy Grail. ⊠ *On signposted minor road 18 km (11 mi) south of Andria* ☏ *0883/569997 tour reservations, 339/1146908* ⊕ *www.castellipuglia.org* ⊠ *€3* ⊙ *Daily 9–6:30. Optional guided tours in English and Italian available daily at 10:30, 11:30, 3:30, and 4:30; call to reserve.*

ALBEROBELLO

8 *59 km (37 mi) southeast of Bari.*

Although Alberobello is something of a tourist trap, the amalgamation of more than 1,000 *trulli* (beehive-shape homes) huddled together along steep, narrow streets is nonetheless an unusual sight (as well as a national monument and a UNESCO World Heritage Site). The origins of the beehive-shape trulli go back to the 13th century and maybe further. The trulli, found nowhere else in the world, are built of local limestone, without mortar, and with a hole in the top for escaping smoke. As one of the most popular tourist destinations in Puglia, Alberobello has spawned some excellent restaurants (and some not-so-excellent trinket shops).

Alberobello's largest trullo, the **Trullo Sovrano,** is up the hill through the trulli zone (head up Corso Vittorio Emanuele past the obelisk and the basilica). Though you can go inside, where you'll find a fairly conventional domestic dwelling, the real interest is the structure itself.

The trulli in Alberobello itself are impressive, but the most beautiful concentration of trulli are along **Via Alberobello–Martina Franca**. Numerous conical homes and buildings stand along a stretch of about 15 km (9 mi) between those two towns. Amid expanses of vineyards, you'll see delightfully amusing examples of trulli put to use in every which way—as wineries, for instance.

SHOPPING

Puglia is Italy's second most productive wine region, so taste a few including the famed dessert wine Moscato di Trani, and buy some bottles of your favorite. Olives are grown in great abundance, too. The virgin olive oil pressed here is of excellent quality. Other souvenirs include ceramics in a range of styles from practical terracotta to beautiful glazed ornaments. Miniature trulli take on many forms, from faithfully finished stone copies to kitsch plastic fridge magnets. Italian styling is very much in evidence in the streets of Bari.

The main shopping streets in Bari are Via Argiro and Via Sparano. Souvenir shops are numerous in the narrow streets of the old town. Alberobello has many trulli that have been converted into souvenir shops. **Louis Vuitton** (⊠ *Via Sparano 127Bari* ☎ *080/5245499*) has a full range of original fashion items and accessories.

WHERE TO EAT

$$$$ ✕ **Ristorante al Pescatore.** This is one of Bari's best fish restaurants, in the old town opposite the castle and just around the corner from the cathedral. Summer cooking is done outside, where you can sit amid a cheerful clamor of quaffing and dining. Try a whole grilled local fish, accompanied by crisp salad and a carafe of invigorating local wine. Reservations are essential in July and August. ⊠ *Piazza Federico II di Svevia 6, Bari* ☎ *080/5237039* ▤ *AE, MC, V.*

$$$ ✕ **La Regia.** This small hotel-restaurant occupies a 17th-century palazzo
★   superbly positioned in front of the Duomo, on a swath of land jutting out into the sea. Don't expect grand or spacious rooms, though they are perfectly adequate. The restaurant has attractive stonework, vaulted ceilings, and a terra-cotta-tile floor. Regional specialties are presented imaginatively: try the baked crêpes (similar to cannelloni) or grilled fish. Reservations are essential for Sunday lunch and for dinner on summer weekends. ⊠ *Piazza Mons. Addazi 2, Trani* ☎ *0883/584444* ▤ *MC, V* ☾ *Closed Mon.* ⑩ *BP.*

BORDEAUX, FRANCE

Bordeaux as a whole, rather than any particular points within it, is what you'll want to visit in order to understand why Victor Hugo described it as Versailles plus Antwerp, and why, when he was exiled from his native Spain, the painter Francisco de Goya chose it as his last home (he died here in 1828). The capital of southwest France and the region's largest city, Bordeaux remains synonymous with the wine trade, and wine shippers have long maintained their headquarters along the banks of the River

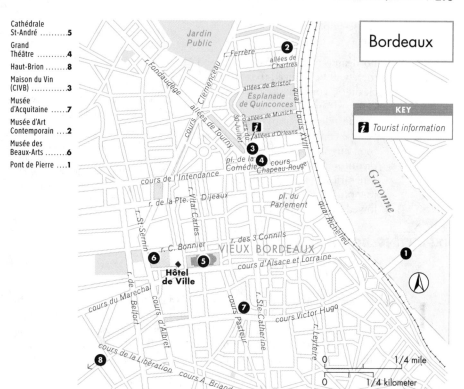

Garonne at the heart of town. As a whole, Bordeaux is a less exuberant city than many others in France. The profits generated by centuries of fine vintages have been carefully invested in fine yet understated architecture and an aura of 18th-century elegance permeates the downtown core. Conservative and refined, the city rewards visitors with its museums, shopping, and restaurants.

ESSENTIALS

CURRENCY The euro (€1 to US$1.46 at this writing); U.S. currency is generally not accepted in Europe, but ATMs are common.

HOURS Museums are open 10–5, but most close on Monday or Tuesday. Stores are open Monday–Saturday 9–7, but some close for lunch (usually noon–2).

INTERNET **Art Obas** (⌧*7 rue Maucoudinat* ☎*05–56–44–26–30*). **Cyberstation** (⌧*23 cours Pasteur south of cathedral* ☎*05–56–01–15–15*). **Net Tel Com** (⌧*26 cours de la Marne* ☎*05–56–31–94–08*).

TELEPHONES Tri-band GSM phones work in France. You can buy prepaid phone cards at telecom shops, news-vendors, and tobacconists in all towns and cities. Phone cards can be used for local or international calls. France Telecom and Orange are leading telecom companies.

COMING ASHORE

Cruise ships sail up the Gironde River and dock directly on the city waterfront within walking distance of all the major city attractions. Because of its proximity to the downtown core, there are no facilities specifically for cruise-ship passengers at the dock site.

Bordeaux is a compact city, and there will be no need to rent a vehicle unless you want to tour the many vineyards in the surrounding countryside independently. Cost of rental is approximately €70 per day for an economy manual vehicle. Taxis are plentiful and can provide tourist itineraries. For single journeys tariffs, rates are €2.30 for pick up followed by €0.69 per km.

BORDEAUX BEST BETS

Opening a bottle of a fine wine. Bordeaux is famed more for its wines than anything else, so indulge your olfactory sense and your taste buds with a vintage from an excellent château.

Touring the vineyards. Not only is it wonderful to watch the grapes maturing on the vines, but to tour the historic château and their extensive cellars is to understand the understated essence of this small region of France.

EXPLORING BORDEAUX

Numbers in the margin correspond to points of interest on the Bordeaux map.

5 **Cathédrale St-André.** This hefty edifice isn't one of France's finer Gothic cathedrals, but the intricate 14th-century chancel makes an interesting contrast with the earlier nave. Excellent stone carvings adorn the facade. You can climb the 15th-century, 160-foot **Tour Pey-Berland** for a stunning view of the city. ⊠*Pl. Pey-Berland*⊗*Tower, Tues.–Sun. 10–12:30 and 2–5:30* 🎟 *Tower €5*

4 **Grand Théâtre.** The city's leading 18th-century monument was designed by Victor Louis and built between 1773 and 1780. It's the pride of the city, with an elegant exterior ringed by graceful Corinthian columns and a dazzling foyer with a two-winged staircase and a cupola. The theater hall has a frescoed ceiling with a shimmering chandelier composed of 14,000 Bohemian crystals. ⊠*Pl. de la Comédie* ☎*05–56–00–85–95* ⊕*www.opera-bordeaux.com* 🎟*€5* ☞*Contact tourist office for guided tours.*

8 **Haut-Brion.** One of the region's most famous wine-producing châteaux is actually within the city limits: follow N250 southwest from central Bordeaux for 3 km (2 mi) to the district of Pessac, home to Haut-Brion, producer of the only non-Médoc wine to be ranked a *premier cru* (the most elite wine classification). It is claimed the very buildings surrounding the vineyards create their own microclimate, protecting the precious grapes and allowing them to ripen earlier. The white château looks out over the celebrated pebbly soil. The wines produced at **La Mission–Haut Brion (Domaine Clarence Dillon)**, across the road, are almost as sought-after. ⊠*133 av. Jean-Jaurès, Pessac* ☎*05–56–00–29–30* ⊕*www.haut-brion.com* 🎟*Free 1-hr visits by appointment, weekdays only, with tasting* ⊗*Closed mid-July–mid-Aug.*

3 **Maison du Vin.** Run by the CIVB (Conseil Interprofessionnel des Vins de Bordeaux), the headquarters of the Bordeaux wine trade (the city tourist office is just across the street from here) is right in the heart of Bordeaux. Before you set out to explore the regional wine country, stop at the Maison to gain clues from the (English-speaking) person at the Tourisme de Viticole desk, who has helpful guides on all the various wine regions.

More important, tasting a red (like Pauillac or St-Émilion), a dry white (like an Entre-Deux-Mers, Graves, or Côtes de Blaye), and a sweet white (like Sauternes or Loupiac) will help you decide which of the 57 wine appellations (areas) to explore. You can also make purchases at the **Vinothèque** opposite. ⊠*8 cours du XXX-Juillet* ☎*05–56–52–32–05* ⊕*www.la-vinotheque.com* ✉*Free* ⊙*Mon.–Sat. 10–7:30.*

❼ **Musée d'Aquitaine.** This excellent museum takes you on a trip through Bordeaux's history, with emphases on Roman, medieval, Renaissance, port-harbor, colonial, and 20th-century daily life. Aquitaine is the region in which Bordeaux sits, so there are many artifacts from the surrounding countryside. The detailed prehistoric section almost saves you a trip to the Lascaux II, as the magnificent ancient cave paintings found there are reproduced here in part. The collection of religious objects from Africa and the Middle East forms an interesting contrast to the more parochial galleries. ⊠*20 cours Pasteur* ☎*05–56–01–51–00* ✉*Free* ⊙*Tues.–Sun. 11–6.*

❷ **Musée d'Art Contemporain** *(Contemporary Art Center).* Imaginatively housed in a converted 19th-century spice warehouse, the Entrepôt Lainé, this museum is just north of the sprawling Esplanade des Quinconce. Many shows here showcase cutting-edge artists who invariably festoon the huge expanse of the place with hanging ropes, ladders, and large video screens. ⊠*7 rue Ferrère* ☎*05–56–00–81–50* ✉*Free* ⊙*Tues. and Thurs.–Sun. 11–6, Wed. 11–8.*

❻ **Musée des Beaux-Arts.** Across tidy gardens behind the ornate Hôtel de Ville (town hall), Bordeaux's biggest art museum has a collection of works spanning the 15th to 21st centuries, with important paintings by Paolo Veronese (*St. Dorothy*), Camille Corot (*Bath of Diana*), and Odilon Redon (*Apollo's Chariot*), and sculptures by Auguste Rodin. The museum has one of the largest collections of Dutch and Flemish paintings outside their native region including works by Rubens, Van Dyck, and Ruysdael. ⊠*20 cours d'Albret* ☎*05–56–10–20–56* ✉*Free* ⊙*Wed.–Mon. 11–6.*

❶ **Pont de Pierre.** For a view of the picturesque quayside, stroll across the Garonne on this bridge that was built on the orders of Napoléon between 1810 and 1821 and until 1965 the only bridge across the river.

SHOPPING

Between the cathedral and the Grand Théâtre are numerous pedestrian streets where stylish shops and clothing boutiques abound—Bordeaux may favor understatement but there's no lack of elegance. Couture is well in evidence here for both women and men. Wines are of course a must if you haven't bought direct from the château, or indulge in France's other culinary obsession—cheese (perhaps for a picnic lunch).

For an exceptional selection of cheeses, go to **Jean d'Alos Fromager-Affineur** (⊠*4 rue Montesquieu* ☎*05–56–44–29–66*). The **Vinothèque** (⊠*8 cours du XXX-Juillet* ☎*05–56–52–32–05*) sells top-ranked Bordeaux wines. **La Maison des Millésimes** (⊠*37 rue Esprit-des-Lois* ☎*05–56–44–03–92*) has a wide range of great wines and will deliver to anywhere in the world.

WHERE TO EAT

If you are looking for just a small bite to eat or a refreshment stop, the trendy **Museum Café** ✉*ww* next to the art library on the top floor of the Musée d'Art Contemporain, offers a good choice of beverages and snacks, and fine views over the Bordeaux skyline. It's open Tuesday through Sunday, 11 until 6.

$–$$ ✗**Café Français.** For more than 30 years, Madame Jouhanneau has presided over this venerable bistro in the heart of the Vieille Ville hard by the Cathédrale St-André. The interior, with large mirrors and plush curtains, is sober, the mood busy. But it's the food, solidly based on fresh regional specialties, that counts, and, for solid sustenance at reasonable prices, it's hard to beat. Try for a table on the terrace: the view over Place Pey-Berland is never less than diverting. ✉*5–6 pl. Pey-Berland* ☎*05–56–52–96–69* ▤*AE, DC, MC, V.*

CÁDIZ, SPAIN (FOR SEVILLE & JEREZ)

Gypsies, bulls, flamenco, horses—Andalusia is the Spain of story and song, the one Washington Irving romanticized in the 18th century. Andalusia is, moreover, at once the least and most surprising part of Spain: least surprising because it lives up to the hype and stereotype that long confused all of Spain with the Andalusian version, and most surprising because it is, at the same time, so much more. All the romantic images of Andalusia, and Spain in general, spring vividly to life in Seville. Spain's fourth-largest city is an olé cliché of matadors, flamenco, tapas bars, gypsies, geraniums, and strolling guitarists. The smaller cities of Cádiz—the Western world's oldest metropolis, founded by Phoenicians more than 3,000 years ago—and Jerez, with its sherry cellars and purebred horses, have much to explore as well.

ESSENTIALS

CURRENCY The euro (€1 to US$1.46 at this writing); U.S. currency is generally not accepted in Europe, but ATMs are common and credit cards are widely accepted.

HOURS Museums generally open 9 until 7 or 8, many are closed on Monday and some close in the afternoon. Most stores are open Monday through Saturday 9 to 1:30 and 5 to 8, but a few in the afternoon. Virtually all close on Sunday.

INTERNET **Enrada2** ✉*Calle Sacramento 36* ☎*95/680–8181.*

TELEPHONES Spain has good land and mobile services. Public kiosks accept phone cards that support international calls (cards sold in press shops, bars, and telecom shops). Mobile services support most tri-band GSM phones and are 3G compatible. Major companies include Vodafone.

COMING ASHORE

Vessels dock at the Alfonso XIII quay in the Cádiz Port, which is in the heart of the city. The passenger terminal has a restaurant, press outlet, phones, and taxi kiosk. From the port, the sights of downtown Cádiz are all within walking distance.

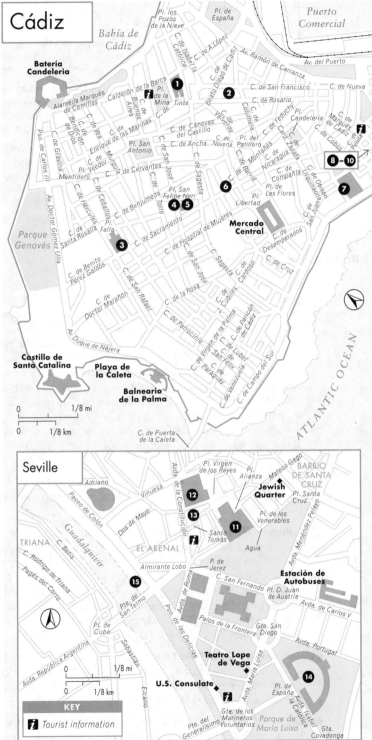

If you wish to travel independently, there is one train per hour from Cádiz to Seville. The journey takes between 1 ½ hours and 2 hours. Tickets cost €9.40 single. Taxi fare from Cádiz to Seville is currently €92 each way—a vehicle takes four people. There is also one train per hour to Jerez. The journey takes 45 minutes, and the ticket price is €3.40 one way. A car rental would open up much of the region to you, but parking and navigation in the cities is difficult. The price for an economy manual vehicle is approximately €60 per day.

CÁDIZ BEST BETS

Explore Seville's Alcázar. One of Spain's finest historic palaces was built to symbolize victory over the Moors.

Be awe-inspired by Seville Cathedral. The largest Gothic building in the world and the third-largest church, this is a building of superlatives.

Sip a glass of fine sherry in a sidewalk café accompanied by tasty tapas. Your tastebuds will tingle, and you can watch the languorous life of southern Spain happen around your table.

EXPLORING CÁDIZ, SEVILLE & JEREZ

CÁDIZ

Founded as Gadir by Phoenician traders in 1100 BC, Cádiz claims to be the oldest continuously inhabited city in the Western world. Hannibal lived in Cádiz for a time, Julius Caesar first held public office here, and Columbus set out from here on his second voyage, after which the city became the home base of the Spanish fleet. During the 18th century, Cádiz monopolized New World trade and became the wealthiest port in Western Europe. Most of its buildings—including the cathedral, built in part with gold and silver from the New World—date from this period. Today, the old city is African in appearance and immensely intriguing—a cluster of narrow streets opening onto charming small squares. The golden cupola of the cathedral looms above low white houses, and the whole place has a charming if slightly dilapidated air.

⑨ Ayuntamiento. Cadiz's impressive city hall overlooks the Plaza San Juan de Diós, one of Cádiz's liveliest hubs. Built in two parts, in 1799 and 1861, the building is attractively illuminated at night.

⑦ Cathedral. Five blocks southeast of the Torre Tavira is Cádiz's cathedral, with its gold dome and baroque facade. Construction of the cathedral began in 1722, when the city was at the height of its power. The cathedral **museum,** on Calle Acero, displays gold, silver, and jewels from the New World, as well as Enrique de Arfe's processional cross, which is carried in the annual Corpus Christi parades. The entrance price includes the crypt, museum, and church of Santa Cruz. ⊠ *Pl. Catedral* ☎ *956/259812* 🎫 *€4* ⊙ *Mass Sun. at noon; museum Tues.–Fri. 10–2 and 4:30–7:30, Sat. 10–1.*

③ Gran Teatro Manuel de Falla. Four blocks west of Santa Inés is the Plaza Manuel de Falla, overlooked by an amazing neo-Mudejar redbrick theater. The classic interior is impressive as well; try to attend a performance. ⊠ *Pl. Manuel de Falla* ☎ *956/220828.*

① Museo de Cádiz. A good place to begin your explorations of Cádiz is the Plaza de Mina, a large, leafy square with palm trees and plenty of benches.

On the east side of the Plaza de Mina, is the *provincial museum*. Notable pieces include works by Murillo and Alonso Cano as well as the *Four Evangelists* and set of saints by Zurbarán, which have much in common with his masterpieces at Guadalupe, in Extremadura. The archaeological section contains Phoenician sarcophagi from the time of this ancient city's birth. ✉ *Pl. de Mina* ☎ *956/212281* 💶 *€1.50, free for EU citizens* ⏰ *Tues. 2:30–8, Wed.–Sat. 9–8, Sun. 9–2.*

5 **Museo de las Cortes.** Next door to the Oratorio de San Felipe Neri, this small but pleasant museum has a 19th-century mural depicting the establishment of the Constitution of 1812. Its real showpiece, however, is a 1779 ivory-and-mahogany model of Cádiz, with all of the city's streets and buildings in minute detail, looking much as they do now. ✉ *Santa Inés 9* ☎ *956/221788* 💶 *Free* ⏰ *Oct.–May, Tues.–Fri. 9–1 and 4–7, weekends 9–1; June–Sept., Tues.–Fri. 9–1 and 5–8, weekends 9–1.*

2 A few blocks east of the Plaza de Mina, next door to the Iglesia del Rosario, is the **Oratorio de la Santa Cueva**, an oval 18th-century chapel with three frescoes by Goya. ✉ *C. Rosario 10* ☎ *956/222262* 💶 *€2.50* ⏰ *Tues.–Fri. 10–1 and 4:30–7:30, weekends 10–1.*

4 **Oratorio de San Felipe Neri.** Heading up Calle San José from the Plaza de la Mina, you see the church in which Spain's first liberal constitution was declared in 1812. ✉ *Santa Inés 38* ☎ *956/211612* 💶 *€2.50* ⏰ *Mon.–Sat. 10–1:30.*

10 **Plaza San Francisco.** This plaza near the ayuntamiento is a pretty square surrounded by white-and-yellow houses and filled with orange trees and elegant street lamps. It's especially lively during the evening *paseo* (promenade).

8 **Roman Theater.** Next door to the church of Santa Cruz are the remains of a 1st-century BC Roman amphitheater that was discovered by chance in 1982; the theater is still under excavation. ✉ *C. Rosario* 💶 *Free* ⏰ *Daily 10–2.*

6 **Torre Tavira.** At 150 feet, this tower, attached to an 18th-century palace that's now a conservatory of music, is the highest point in the old city. ✉ *Marqués del Real Tesoro 10* ☎ *956/212910* 💶 *€4* ⏰ *Mid-June–mid-Sept., daily 10–8; mid-Sept.–mid-June, daily 10–6.*

SEVILLE

149 km (93 mi) northeast of Cádiz.

Seville's whitewashed houses, bright with bougainvillea, its ocher-color palaces, and its baroque facades have long enchanted both Sevillanos and travelers. Lord Byron's well-known line, "Seville is a pleasant city famous for oranges and women," may be true, but is far too tame. Seville's color and vivacity is legendary but best seen during one of the traditional *fiestas,* when modern dress is swapped for vivid ruffled costume, and the streets come alive with song and dance.

11 **Alcázar.** This palace was built by Pedro I (1350–69) on the site of Seville's former Moorish *alcázar* (fortress). Don't mistake the Alcázar for a genuine Moorish palace, like Granada's Alhambra—it may look like one, but it was commissioned and paid for by a Christian king more than 100 years after the reconquest of Seville. In its construction, Pedro the Cruel incorporated stones and capitals he pillaged from Valencia, from Córdoba's Medina Azahara, and from Seville itself. The palace serves as the official Seville residence of the king and queen. If the king and queen are not in residence, it is possible to visit their apartments by a guided tour (separate ticket from the Alcázar, mornings only). ⊠ *Pl. del Triunfo, Santa Cruz* ☎ *95/450–2323* ⊕ *www.patronato-alcazarsevilla.es* ⊡ *€7* ⊙ *Tues.–Sat. 9:30–7, Sun. 9:30–5.*

⓭ **Archivo de las Indias** *(Archives of the Indies).* This dignified Renaissance building holds archives of more than 40,000 documents, including drawings, trade documents, plans of South American towns, even the autographs of Columbus, Magellan, and Cortés. ⊠ *Av. de la Constitución, Santa Cruz* ☎ *95/421–1234* ⊡ *Free* ⊙ *Mon.–Sat. 10–4, Sun. 10–2.*

⓬ **Cathedral.** After Ferdinand III captured Seville from the Moors in 1248, the great mosque begun by Yusuf II in 1171 was reconsecrated and used as a Christian cathedral. But in 1401 the people of Seville decided to erect a new cathedral, one that would equal the glory of their great city. Today, it is still the world's third-largest church, after St. Peter's in Rome and St. Paul's in London. The magnificent *retablo* (altarpiece) in the main chapel is the largest in Christendom (65 feet by 43 feet). It depicts some 36 scenes from the life of Christ, with pillars carved with more than 200 figures. Scientific studies have proved that the **monument to Christopher Columbus** houses some earthly remains of the great explorer, though not enough to be a complete skeleton. You can climb to the top of the **Giralda,** which dominates Seville's skyline. Once the minaret of Seville's great mosque, it was built between 1184 and 1196, and the Christians incorporated it into their new cathedral. ⊠ *Pl. Virgen de los Reyes, Santa Cruz* ☎ *95/421– 4971* ⊡ *Cathedral and Giralda €7.50* ⊙ *Cathedral Mon.–Sat. 11–5, Sun. 2:30–6, and for mass.*

⓮ **Plaza de España.** This grandiose half-moon of buildings Spain's centerpiece pavilion at the 1929 Exhibition. The brightly colored azulejo pictures represent the 50 provinces of Spain, while the four bridges symbolize the medieval kingdoms of the Iberian Peninsula. You can rent small boats for rowing along the arc-shape canal.

⓯ **Torre de Oro.** A 12-sided tower built by the Moors in 1220 to complete the city's ramparts, it served to close off the harbor when a chain was stretched across the river from its base to another tower on the opposite bank. In 1248 Admiral Ramón de Bonifaz broke through this barrier, and thus did Ferdinand III capture Seville. The tower now houses a small naval museum. ⊠ *Paseo Alcalde Marqués de Contadero s/n, El Arenal* ☎ *95/422–2419* ⊡ *€1* ⊙ *Tues.–Fri. 10–2, weekends 11–2.*

JEREZ DE LA FRONTERA
52 km (34 mi) northeast of Cádiz.

Jerez, world headquarters for sherry, is surrounded by vineyards of chalky soil, whose Palomino grapes have funded a host of churches and noble mansions. Names such as González Byass, Domecq, Harvey, and Sandeman are inextricably linked with Jerez. At any given time, more than half a million barrels of sherry are maturing in Jerez's vast aboveground wine cellars.

If you have time for only one bodega, tour the **González Byass** (☎*956/357000* ⊕*www.gonzalezbyass.com*), home of the famous Tío Pepe. This tour is well organized and includes La Concha, an open-air aging cellar designed by Gustave Eiffel. Your guide will explain the *solera* method of blending old wine with new, and the importance of the *flor* (a sort of yeast that forms on the surface of the wine as it ages) in determining the kind of sherry. You'll be invited to sample generous amounts of pale, dry fino; nutty *amontillado*; or rich, deep *oloroso*, and, of course, to purchase a few bottles.

The **Museo Arqueológico** is one of Andalusia's best archaeological museums. The collection is strongest on the pre-Roman period. The star item, found near Jerez, is a Greek helmet dating from the 7th century BC. ✉*Pl. del Mercado s/n* ☎*956/341350* 🎫*€2* 🕐*Sept.–mid-June, Tues.–Fri. 10–2 and 4–7, weekends 10–2:30; mid-June–Aug., Tues.–Sun. 10–2:30.*

🕐 The **Real Escuela Andaluza del Arte Ecuestre** *(Royal Andalusian School of Eques-trian Art)* operates on the grounds of the Recreo de las Cadenas, a 19th-century palace. You can visit the stables and tack room of this prestigious school and watch the horses being put through their paces. Every Thursday the horses and skilled riders demonstrate intricate dressage techniques and jumping in the spectacular show "Cómo Bailan los Caballos Andaluces." (🎫*€8* 🕐*Mon.–Wed. and Thurs. 10–1)* for the show. Reservations are essential. ✉*Av. Duque de Abrantes s/n* ☎*956/319635* ⊕*www.realescuela.org* 🎫*€17–€25* 🕐*Nov.–Feb., Thurs. at noon; Mar.–July 14, Tues. and Thurs. at noon; July 15–Oct., Fri. at midday; in Mar.*

Fodor'sChoice
★

SHOPPING

The region abounds with colorful souvenirs including fine flamenco costumes, classical guitars, ornate fans traditional to Andalusia. Look out also for copious choices in ceramics, porcelain, and textiles, including beautiful hand-stitched embroidery (be aware that machine-embroidered items have flooded the market). Don't forget a bottle or two of excellent Jerez sherry, or Spanish olives and olive oil to augment your larders back home.

Seville is the region's main shopping area and the place for archetypal Andalusian souvenirs, most of which are sold in the Barrio de Santa Cruz and around the cathedral and Giralda, especially on Calle Alemanes. The main shopping street for Sevillanos themselves is Calle Sierpes, along with its neighboring streets Cuna, Tetuan, Velázquez, Plaza Magdalena, and Plaza Duque—boutiques abound here. The streets of old Cádiz are the place to browse and buy.

Casa Rubio (✉*Sierpes 56, Centro, Seville* ☎*95/422–6872)* is Seville's premier fan store, no mean distinction, with both traditional and contemporary designs. You can find all kinds of blankets, shawls, and embroidered tablecloths woven by local artisans at the three shops of **Artesanía Textil** (✉*Sierpes 70, Centro, Seville* ☎*95/422–0125)*, but the Centro branch is the most central option. La Cartuja china, originally crafted at La Cartuja Monastery but now made outside Seville, is sold at **La Alacena** (✉*Alfonso XII 25, San Vicente, Seville* ☎*95/422–8021)*

WHERE TO EAT

¢–$ ✕ **Casa Manteca.** Cádiz's most quintessentially Andalusian tavern is just down the street from El Faro restaurant and a little deeper into the La Viña barrio (named for the vineyard that once grew here). *Chacina* (Iberian ham or sausage), served on waxed paper, and Manzanilla (sherry from Sanlúcar de Barrameda) are standard fare at this low wooden counter that has served bullfighters and flamenco singers, as well as dignitaries from around the world since 1953. ✉*Corralón de los Carros 66, Cádiz* ☎*956/213603* ⊟*AE, DC, MC, V* ⊗*Closed Mon. No lunch Sun.*

¢–$$ ✕ **El Corral del Agua.** Abutting the outer walls of the Alcázar on a narrow pedestrian street in the Santa Cruz neighborhood is a restored 18th-century palace, with a patio filled with geraniums and a central fountain. Andalusian specialties, such as *cola de toro al estilo de Sevilla* (Seville-style bull's tail), are prepared with contemporary flair. ✉*Callejón del Agua 6, Santa Cruz, Seville* ☎*95/422–4841* ⊟*AE, DC, MC, V* ⊗*Closed Sun. and Jan. and Feb.*

CANNES, FRANCE (WITH THE ILES DE LÉRINS & ANTIBES)

A tasteful and expensive breeding ground for the upscale, Cannes is a sybaritic heaven for those who believe that life is short and sin has something to do with the absence of a tan. Backed by gentle hills and flanked to the southwest by the Estérel, warmed by dependable sun but kept bearable in summer by the cool Mediterranean breeze, Cannes is pampered with the luxurious climate that has made it one of the most popular and glamorous resorts in Europe. The cynosure of sun worshippers since the 1860s, it has been further glamorized by the modern success of its film festival. If you're a culture-lover into art of the noncelluloid type you should look elsewhere. Come to Cannes for incomparable Continental panache and as a stepping stone to attractions a little farther afield.

ESSENTIALS

CURRENCY The euro (€1 to US$1.46 at this writing); U.S. currency is generally not accepted in Europe, but ATMs are common.

HOURS Most stores are open Monday–Saturday 9–7 but many close at lunchtime (usually noon–2 or 3) and some will open later and on Sunday during July and August. Museums are open 10–5, but most are closed on either Monday or Tuesday.

INTERNET **Pl@net Center** (✉*10 rue Joseph Barthélemy* ☎*04–92–97–10–10*) sits just off the seafront boulevard.

TELEPHONES Tri-band GSM phones work in France. You can buy prepaid phone cards at telecom shops, news-vendors and tobacconists in all towns and cities. Phone cards can be used for local or international calls. France Telecom and Orange are leading telecom companies.

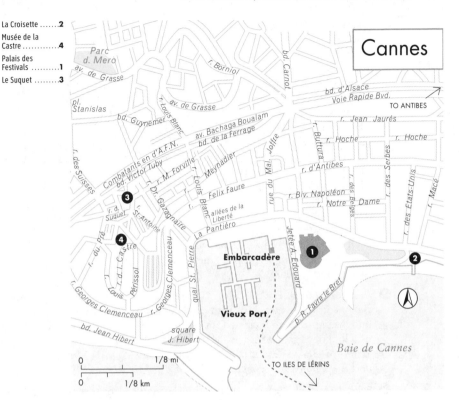

4

COMING ASHORE

Cruise vessels anchor offshore in Cannes, and passengers are tendered shore to the old port. For there it is walking distance to all the city attractions. Taxis are on hand, and it's a five-minute ride to the train or bus station.

There will be no need to rent a vehicle unless you want to tour the surrounding Provençal countryside. The rental cost is approximately €70 per day for an economy manual vehicle. Taxis are plentiful and can provide tourist itineraries. For single journeys tariffs are €2.30 at flag fall, then €0.69 per km.

Local trains are frequent; you can reach Nice in 20 minutes (€4), Antibes in 10 minutes (€3) and almost all other coastal towns can also be reached on a local train in less than an hour. Both RCA and TAM bus lines have frequent service (RCA's 200 bus between Cannes and Antibes runs every 20 minutes).

EXPLORING CANNES

CANNES

Numbers in the margin correspond to points of interest on the Cannes map.

2 La Croisette. The most delightful thing to do in Cannes is to head to the famous mile-long waterfront promenade that starts at the western end by the Palais des Festivals and the town port, and allow the *esprit de*

Cannes to take over. This is precisely the sort of place for which the verb *flâner* (to dawdle, saunter) was invented, so stroll among the palm trees and flowers and crowds of poseurs (fur coats in tropical weather, cell phones and Rollerblades, sunglasses at night). Head east past the broad expanse of private beaches, glamorous shops, and luxurious hotels (such as the wedding-cake Carlton, famed for its see-and-be-seen terrace-level brasserie). The beaches along here are almost all private, though open for a fee— each beach is marked with from one to four little life buoys, rating their quality and expense.

❹ **Musée de la Castre.** The hill called "Le Suquet," for which the neighborhood is named, is crowned by an 11th-century château that houses this museum and the imposing four-sided **Tour du Suquet** (Suquet Tower), built in 1385 as a lookout against Saracen-led invasions. ⊠ *Pl. de la Castre, Le Suquet* ☎ *04–93–38–55–26* ⊡ *€3* ⊗ *Apr.–June, Tues.–Sun. 10–1 and 2–6; July and Aug., daily 10–7; Sept., Tues.–Sun. 10–1 and 2–6.*

❶ **Palais des Festivals.** Pick up a map at the tourist office, the scene of the famous Festival International du Film, otherwise known as the Cannes Film Festival. As you leave the information center, follow the Palais to your right to see the red-carpeted stairs where the stars ascend every year. Set into the surrounding pavement, the **Allée des Etoiles** (Stars' Walk) enshrines some 300 autographed imprints of film stars' hands—of Dépardieu, Streep, and Stallone, among others.

❸ **Le Suquet.** Climb up Rue St-Antoine into the picturesque Vieille Ville neighborhood known as Le Suquet on the site of the original Roman *castrum*. Shops proffer Provençal goods, and the atmospheric cafés give you a chance to catch your breath; the pretty pastel shutters, Gothic stonework, and narrow passageways are lovely distractions.

ÎLES LÉRINS
15–20 minutes by ferry off the coast of Cannes.

When you're glutted on glamour, you may want to make a day trip to the peaceful Iles de Lérins (Lérins Islands); boats depart from Cannes's Vieux Port. Allow at least a half day to enjoy either of the islands; you can fit both in only if you get an early start. Access to the ferry is across the large parking in front of the Sofitel hotel, southwest from the Palais des Festivals. You have two ferry options.

Compangie Planaria (⊠ *Quai Lauboeuf, port of Cannes La Croisette, Cannes* ☎ *04–92–98–71–38*) goes to Ile St-Honorat.

Trans Cote D'Azur (⊠ *Quai Lauboeuf, port of Cannes, La Croisette, Cannes* ☎ *04–92–98–71–30*) goes to Isle St. Margueritte.

Ile Ste-Marguerite is a 15-minute trip from Cannes that costs €11 round-trip (summer) or €5 round-trip (winter). Its **Fort Royal,** built by Richelieu and improved by Vauban, offers views over the ramparts to the rocky island coast and the open sea.

Behind the prison buildings is the **Musée de la Mer** *(Marine Museum),* with a Roman boat dating from the 1st century BC and a collection of amphorae and pottery recovered from ancient shipwrecks. It is more famous, however, for reputedly being the prison of the Man in the Iron Mask. Inside you can see his cell and hear his story, and although the truth of his captivity is not certain, it is true that many Huguenots were confined here during Louis XIV's religious scourges. ☎*04–93–43–18–17* 📷*€3* ⊙*Oct.– Mar., Tues.–Sun. 10:30–1:15 and 2:15–4:45; Apr.–mid-June, Tues.–Sun. 10:30–1:15 and 2:15–5:45; mid-June–mid-Sept., daily 10:30–5:45, mid-Sept.–late-Sept., Tues.–Sun. 10:30–1:15 and 2:15–5:45.*

Ile St-Honorat can be reached in 20 minutes (€11 round-trip) from the Vieux Port. Smaller and wilder than Ste-Marguerite, it is home to an active monastery and the ruins of its 11th-century predecessor. Oddly enough, the monks are more famous in the region for their nonreligious activity: manufacturing and selling a rather strong liqueur called Lerina.

ANTIBES
11 km (7 mi) northeast of Cannes, 15 km (9 mi) southeast of Nice.

★ No wonder Picasso once called this home—Antibes (pronounced Awnteeb) is a stunner. With its broad stone ramparts scalloping in and out over the waves and backed by blunt medieval towers and a skew of tile roofs, it remains one of the most romantic old towns on the Mediterranean coast. As gateway to the Cap d'Antibes, Antibes's Port Vauban harbor has some of the largest yachts in the world tied up at its berths—their millionaire owners won't find a more dramatic spot to anchor, with the tableau of the snowy Alps looming in the distance and the formidable medieval block towers of the Fort Carré guarding entry to the port. Stroll Promenade Amiral-de-Grasse along the crest of Vauban's sea walls, and you'll understand why the views inspired Picasso to paint on a panoramic scale. Yet a few steps inland you'll enter a souklike maze of old streets that are relentlessly picturesque and joyously beautiful.

To visit Old Antibes, pass through the **Porte Marine,** an arched gateway in the rampart wall. Follow Rue Aubernon to **Cours Masséna,** where the little sheltered market sells lemons, olives, and hand-stuffed sausages, and the vendors take breaks in the shoebox cafés flanking one side.

★ From Cours Masséna head up to the **Église de l'Immaculée-Conception** (⊠*Pl. de la Cathédrale*). The church's 18th-century facade, a marvelously Latin mix of classical symmetry and fantasy, has been restored in shades of ocher and cream. Its stout medieval watchtower was built in the 11th century with stones "mined" from Roman structures. Inside is a baroque altarpiece painted by the Niçois artist Louis Bréa in 1515.

★ Next door to the cathedral, the medieval **Château Grimaldi** rises high over the water on a Roman foundation. Famed as rulers of Monaco, the Grimaldi family lived here until the Revolution, but this fine old castle was little more than a monument until in 1946 its curator offered use of its vast chambers to Picasso, at a time when that extraordinary genius was enjoying a period of intense creative energy. The result is now housed in the **Musée Picasso,** a bounty of exhilarating paintings, ceramics, and lithographs inspired by the sea and by Greek mythology—all very Mediterranean. Even those who are not great Picasso fans should enjoy his vast paintings on wood, canvas, paper, and walls, alive with nymphs, fauns, and centaurs. The museum houses more than 300 works by the artist, as well as pieces by Miró, Calder, and Léger. At this writing, the museum is closed for renovations, with plans to reopen in winter 2008. ⊠*Pl. du Château* ☎*04–92–90–54–20* ⌑*€6 (may change)* ☉*June–Sept., Tues.–Sun. 10–6; Oct.–May, Tues.–Sun. 10–noon and 2–6 (may change).*

Fodor's Choice ★ A few blocks south of the Château Grimaldi is the **Commune Libre du Safranier** *(Free Commune of Safranier)* , a magical little 'hood with a character all its own. Here, not far off the seaside promenade and focused around the Place du Safranier, tiny houses hang heavy with flowers and vines and neighbors carry on conversations from window to window across the stone-stepped Rue du Bas-Castelet. It is said that Place du Safranier was once a tiny fishing port; now it's the scene of this sub-village's festivals.

The Bastion St-André, a squat Vauban fortress, now contains the **Musée Archéologique** *(Archaeology Museum)*. Its collection focuses on Antibes's classical history, displaying amphorae and sculptures found in local digs as well as salvaged from shipwrecks from the harbor. ⊠*Av. Général-Maizières* ☎*04–92–90–54–35* ⌑*€3* ☉*Oct.–May, Tues.–Sun. 10–noon and 2–6; June–Sept., Tues.–Sun. 10–noon and 2–8.*

SHOPPING

Cannes caters to the upmarket crowd with a wealth of designer boutiques such as Chanel and Dior, and high-class jewelers. But if you don't want to max out your credit cards there's a wealth of choice of less expensive ready to wear fashion. Boutiques also sell colorful crafts from the Provence region including basketware, bright fabrics, olive wood items, plus delicious olives, olive oils, honey, dried herbs, and quaffable local wines. Film buffs may also want to stock up on official Cannes Film Festival merchandise.

Rue d'Antibes, running parallel with the Croisette but two blocks inland, is Cannes's main high-end shopping street. At its western end is **Rue Meynadier,** packed tight with trendy clothing boutiques and fine food shops. Not far away is the covered **Marché Forville,** the scene of the animated morning food market. The narrow alleyways of **Le Suquet,** are also a great place to browse. Film Festival merchandise can be bought at the **Palais du Festivals,** but the official Film Festival shop is found on La Croisette, close to the Majestic Hotel.

Vieil Antibes has an excellent shopping, though you'll find far fewer designer boutiques than in Cannes. Small shops sell an excellent range of local crafts and foodstuffs and there are several galleries selling work by local artists.

BEACHES

The pebble beach that fronts the full length of La Croisette has a chic atmosphere in summer. Most sections have been privatized and are owned by hotels and/or restaurants that rent out chaise longues, mats, and umbrellas to the public and hotel guests (who also have to pay). Public beaches are between the color-coordinated private beach umbrellas and offer simple open showers and basic toilets. The restaurants here are some of the best places for lunch or refreshment, though you do pay extra for the location.

WHERE TO EAT

$-$$$ ✗**Le Petit Lardon.** Popular and unpretentious, this tiny bistro is feisty and fun. Watch for a great mix of seasonal Provençal and Burgundian flavors: escargot served with butter and garlic, roast rabbit *au jus* stuffed with raisins, and melt-in-your-mouth lavender crème brûlée. Busy, bustling and friendly, it is ideal for a casual meal, but it is tiny, so reserve well in advance. ⊠*Rue de Batéguier, La Croisette* ☎*04–93–39–06–28* ▭*AE, MC, V* ⊘*Closed Sun.*

¢-$$$ ✗**La Pizza.** Sprawling up over two floors and right in front of the old port, this busy Italian restaurant serves steaks, fish, and salads, but go there for what they're famous for: gloriously good right-out-of-the-wood-fire-oven pizza in hungry-man-size portions. There is an outpost in Nice as well. ⊠*3 quai St-Pierre, La Croisette* ☎*04–93–39–22–56* ▭*AE, MC, V.*

CIVITAVECCHIA, ITALY (FOR ROME)

Rome is a heady blend of artistic and architectural masterpieces, classical ruins, and extravagant baroque churches and piazzas. The city's 2,700-year-old history is on display wherever you look; the ancient rubs shoulders with the medieval, the modern runs into the Renaissance, and the result is a bustling open-air museum. Julius Caesar and Nero, the Vandals and the Popes, Raphael and Caravaggio, Napoléon and Mussolini—these and countless other luminaries have left their mark on the city. Today Rome's formidable legacy is kept alive by its people, their history knit into the fabric of their everyday lives. Raphaelesque teenage girls zip through traffic on their *motorini*; priests in flowing robes stride through medieval piazzas talking on cell phones. Modern Rome has one foot in the past, one in the present—a fascinating stance that allows you to tip back an espresso in a square designed by Bernini, then hop on the metro to your next attraction.

ESSENTIALS

CURRENCY The euro (€1 to US$1.46 at this writing); U.S. currency is generally not accepted in Europe, but ATMs are common and credit cards are widely accepted.

HOURS Stores are generally open from 9 or 9:30 to 1 and from 3:30 or 4 to 7 or 7:30. There's a tendency for shops in central districts to stay open all day. Many places close Sunday, and some also close Monday morning from September to mid-June and Saturday afternoon from mid-June through August.

INTERNET   Internet cafés are relatively common in Rome. There are several centrally located spots near Piazza Navona and Campo dei Fiori.

TELEPHONES   Tri-band GSM phones work in Italy. You can buy prepaid phone cards at telecom shops, news-vendors, and tobacconists in all towns and cities. Phone cards can be used for local or international calls.

COMING ASHORE

Civitavecchia is a large port, and you will be bused from the ship to the terminal area. There are passenger facilities such as cafés and information offices, but these are shared with commercial ferry traffic and can be crowded. A shuttle will take you to the railway station, from where you can catch trains to Rome, or you can walk along the harborfront to the station in less than 10 minutes. Taxis charge around €20 for the journey to the train station. Train tickets to Rome cost approximately €9 round-trip. If you prebook on the Trenitalia Web site ⊕ *www.trenitalia.com*, you can print your tickets out at the station. There are three trains per hour, and the journey time is 1 hour 15 minutes. The cost for a private car with driver to Rome is approximately €130 one-way.

Taxis charge approximately €2.33 initially, then €0.78 per km (½-mi) with an increment of €0.11 per 140 meters (260 feet) when the taxi travels at less than 20 kph (12 mph). You shouldn't rent a car if you want to explore only Rome because both traffic and parking are difficult; however, if you want to explore the countryside around Civitavecchia a car would be useful. Rental costs are approximately €45 per day for a compact manual vehicle.

Rome's metro (subway) is somewhat limited, but it's a quick if you are headed somewhere that it goes. The public bus and tram system is slow. Taking the compact electric buses of Lines 117 and 119 through the center of Rome can save a lot of walking. A ticket valid for 75 minutes on any combination of buses and trams and one entrance to the metro costs €1. Tickets for the public transit system are sold at tobacconists, newsstands, some coffee bars; you can also buy them in the green machines positioned in Metro stations and some bus stops. A BIG ticket, valid for one day on all public transport, costs €4.

EXPLORING ROME

Numbers in the margin correspond to points of interest on the Rome map.

❿ **Colosseo** *(Colosseum)*. The most spectacular extant edifice of ancient Rome,

Fodor's Choice
★

this sports arena was designed to hold more than 50,000 spectators for gory entertainments such as combats between wild beasts and gladiators. Designed by order of the Flavian emperor Vespasian in AD 72, the arena has a circumference of 573 yards. Among the stadium's many wonders was a *velarium,* an ingenious system of sail-like awnings rigged on ropes and maneuvered by sailors from the imperial fleet, who would unfurl them to protect the arena's occupants from sun or rain.

Some experts maintain that it was in Rome's circuses, and not here, that thousands of early Christians were martyred. Still, tradition has reserved a special place for the Colosseum in the story of Christianity, and it was

Pope Benedict XIV who stopped the use of the building as a quarry when, in 1749, he declared it sanctified by the blood of the martyrs. ✉ *Piazza del Colosseo* ☎ *06/39967700* ⊕ *www.pierreci.it* 🎫 *€8* 🕓 *Daily 9–1 hr before sunset.*

③ Basilica di San Pietro. The largest church in the world, built over the tomb of
★ St. Peter, is also the most imposing and breathtaking architectural achievement of the Renaissance (although much of the lavish interior dates to the baroque). The physical statistics are impressive: it covers 18,000 square yards, runs 212 yards in length, and carries a dome that rises 435 feet and measures 138 feet across its base. Its history is equally impressive: no less than five of Italy's greatest artists—Bramante, Raphael, Peruzzi, Antonio Sangallo the Younger, and Michelangelo—died while striving to erect this new St. Peter's.

The history of the original St. Peter's goes back to AD 349, when the emperor Constantine completed a basilica over the site of the tomb of St. Peter, the Church's first pope. In 1452 a reconstruction job was authorized, but it wasn't until 1626 that the basilica was completed and consecrated.

The basilica is filled with innumerable masterpieces, and the visit is free, but you must pay to enter the **Museo Storico** or to take in the view from the **roof**. The **Grotte Vaticane** (containing the tombs of the popes) has a separate line, but the exit is outside the church; it's best to leave this for last, after you've visited the basilica (though it's often possible to reenter the basilica by going directly up the steps). Be aware that you will have to pass through metal detectors and go through a bag-check before admission. This means that lines can form well into St. Peter's Square, but they tend to move fairly quickly. Free one-hour English-language tours of the basilica depart Monday–Saturday at 10 and 3, Sunday at 2:30 (sign up at the little desk under the portico). St. Peter's is closed during ceremonies in the piazza (such as the Pope's weekly audience on Wednesday mornings). ✉ *Piazza San Pietro* ⊕ *www.vatican.va* 🎫 *Basilica free; Museo Storico €9; elevator to roof €7, stairs to roof €4* 🕓 *Apr.–Sept., daily 7–7; Oct.– Mar., daily 7–6.*

① Musei Vaticani *(The Vatican Museums).* Other than the pope and his papal court, the occupants of the Vatican are some of the most famous art works in the world, a collection so rich that you will only be able to skim the surface.

Fodor's Choice
★

The gems of the Vatican's sculpture collection are in the **Pio-Clementino Museum,** with items rescued from ancient piazzas and palaces from around the city. In the **Octagonal Courtyard,** is the *Laocoön* group, held to be possibly the single most important antique sculpture group in terms of its influence on Renaissance artists.

Rivaling the Sistine Chapel for artistic interest are the **Stanze di Raffaello** (Raphael Rooms). When people talk about the Italian High Renaissance, it's Raphael's frescoes they're probably thinking about. The **Segnatura Room** was painted almost entirely by Raphael himself. All the revolutionary characteristics of High Renaissance art are here: naturalism; humanism; and a profound interest in the ancient world, the result of the 15th-century rediscovery of archaeology and classical antiquity.

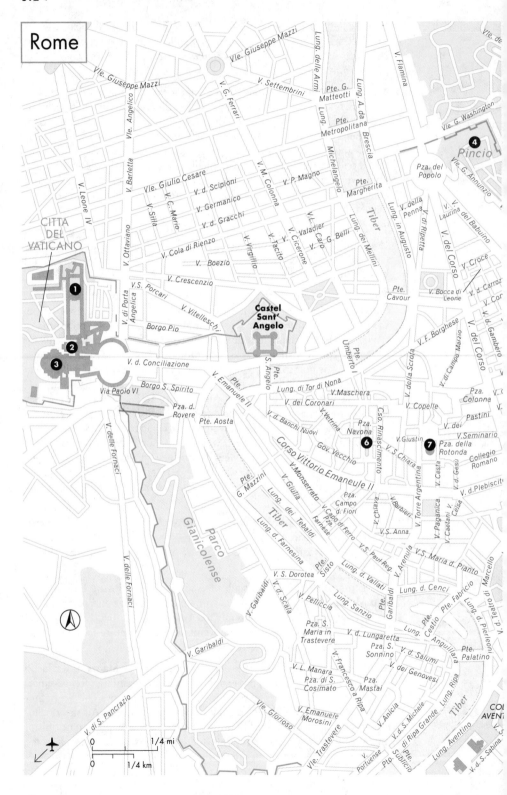

Rome

CITTA
DEL
VATICANO

Castel
Sant'
Angelo

Pincio

Parco
Gianicolense

Tiber

Vle. Giuseppe Mazzi
Vle. Giuseppe Mazzi
V. Settembrini
V. G. Ferrari
Lung. delle Armi
Pte. G. Matteotti
Lung.
Pte. Metropolitana
V. Flamina
V. della Penna
Vle. G. Washington
Pza. del Popolo
Vle. G. Annunzio

V. Leone IV
V. Angelico
V. Barletta
Vle. Giulio Cesare
V. d. Scipioni
V. Germanico
V. d. Gracchi
V. C. Mario
V. Stilla
V. Ottaviano
V. M. Colonna
V. P. Magno
Michelangelo
Brescia
Pte. Margherita
Lung. in Augusto
Lung. di Ripetta
V. della Penna
V. Laurina
V. di Babuino
V. Croce
V. del Corso
V. Bocca di Leone
V. d. Carrozze
V. Cor

V. Cola di Rienzo
V. Valadier
V. Caro
V. G. Belli
V. Cicerone
V. Virgilio
V. Tacito
Lung. dei Mellini
V. Boezio
V. Crescenzio
V.S. Porcari
V. d. Porta Angelica
V. Vitelleschi
Borgo Pio
V. d. Conciliazione
Borgo S. Spirito
Via Paolo VI
Pza. d. Rovere
Pte. Aosta

Tiber
Pte. Cavour
Pte. Umberto I
Pte. S. Angelo
Pte. Emanuele II

V. F. Borghese
V. della Scrofa
V. di Campo Marzio
V. del Corso
V. del Gambero
Pza. Colonna
Pastini
V. dei
V. Seminario
Pza. della Rotonda
Collegio Romano
V. d. Plebiscito

Lung. di Tor di Nona
V. Maschera
V. Copelle
V. dei Coronari
V. Vetrina
Pza. Navona
Cso. Rinascimento
V.S. Chiara
V. Giustin
V. Cesta
V. d. Banchi Nuovi
Gov. Vecchio
V. Torre Argentina

Corso Vittorio Emaneule II
V. Monserrato
V. Giulia
Lung. dei Tebaldi
Lung. d. Farnesina
Pte. G. Mazzini
Pza. Campo d. Fiori
V. Capo d. Ferro
Pza. Farnese
V.S. Anna
V. Chiavari
V. Barbieri
V. Caetani
V. Celsa
V. Paganica
V.S. Maria d. Pianto
Marcello

V. delle Fornaci
V. delle Fornaci

V. S. Dorotea
Pte. Sisto
Lung. d. Vallati
Lung. d. Sanzio
Pte. Garibaldi
Lung. Garibaldi
Lung. d. Cenci
Pte. Fabricio
Lung. d. Pierleoni
COL
AVEN

V. di S. Pancrazio
V. Garibaldi
V. d. Scala
V. Pelliccia
Pza. S. Maria in Trastevere
V. d. Lungaretta
Pza. S. Sonnino
V. d. Salumi
Pte. Palatino
V. L. Manara
Pza. di S. Cosimato
Pza. Mastai
V. dei Genovesi
V. Anicia
V. d. S. Michele
Lung. Ripa
Tiber

V. Garibaldi
Vle. Glorioso
V. Emanuele Morosini
V. Francesco a Ripa
Vle. Trastevere
V. Portuense
Ptp. Sublicio
Pte. Cestio
Pte. Anguillara
Lung. Aventino
V. d. S. Sabina

0   1/4 mi

0   1/4 km

4

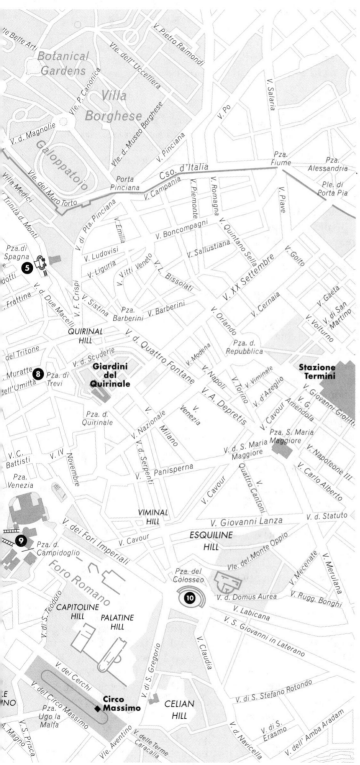

It's generally believed that Cesare Borgia murdered his sister Lucrezia's husband, Alphonse of Aragon, in the Room of the Sibyl in the **Borgia apartments**. Other highly ornate rooms have religious scenes featuring many Borgia family members.

The paintings in the **Pinacoteca** (Picture Gallery) are almost exclusively of religious subjects and are arranged in chronological order, beginning with works of the 11th and 12th centuries. Highlights include a Giotto triptych, and Madonnas by the Florentine 15th-century painters Fra Angelico and Filippo Lippi along with further Raphael masterpieces.

> **ROME BEST BETS**
>
> **The Colosseum.** Although jam-packed with tourists, this is still one of ancient Rome's most iconic relics and was the scene of some of its bloodiest contests.
>
> **Basilica di San Pietro.** The mother church for all Catholics is redolent with spirit and filled with artistic masterpieces. Just remember that the Sistine Chapel can only be visited if you go to the Vatican Museums.
>
> **Join the throng at Piazza Navona.** Visit this large square with its three fountains and immerse yourself in the energy that is modern Rome.

2 In 1508, the redoubtable Pope Julius II commissioned Michelangelo to
Fodor'sChoice fresco more than 10,000 square feet of the ceiling of the **Cappella Sistina**
★ *(Sistine Chapel).* The task took four years. The result was a masterpiece. Before the chapel was consecrated in 1483, its lower walls had been decorated by a group of artists including Botticelli, Ghirlandaio, Perugino, Signorelli, and Pinturicchio. More than 20 years later, Michelangelo was called on again, this time by the Farnese Pope Paul III, to add to the chapel's decoration by painting the *Last Judgment* on the wall over the altar. *Vatican Museums* ⊠ *Viale Vaticano* ☎ *06/69883332* ⊕ *www.vatican.va* ✆ *€12* ⊘ *Mid-Mar.–Oct., weekdays 8:45–4:45, Sat. 8:45–2:45, last Sun. of month 8:45–1:45; Nov.–mid-Mar., Mon.–Sat. and last Sun. of month 8:45–1:45* ☞ *Note: ushers at entrance of St. Peter's and Vatican Museums will bar entry to people with bare knees or bare shoulders.*

8 **Fontana di Trevi** *(Trevi Fountain).* Alive with rushing waters and marble sea
Fodor'sChoice creatures commanded by an imperious Oceanus, this aquatic marvel is one
★ of the city's most exciting sights. The work of Nicola Salvi—though it's thought that Bernini may have been responsible for parts of the design—was completed in 1762 and is a perfect example of the rococo taste for dramatic theatrical effects. Usually thickly fringed with tourists tossing coins into the basin to ensure their return to Rome (the fountain grosses about €120,000 a year, most of it donated to charity). ⊠ *Piazza di Trevi.*

9 **Musei Capitolini.** If you have time for just one museum in Rome other than
★ the Vatican Museums, make it this one. This immense collection, housed in the twin Palazzi del Museo Capitolino and Palazzo dei Conservatori buildings, which flank Michelangelo's piazza, is a greatest hits collection of Roman art through the ages, from the ancients to the baroque. After your tour of the museum, you can stroll through the Foro Romana (free) all the way up to the Colosseo. ⊠ *Piazza del Campidoglio* ☎ *06/39967800 or 06/67102475* ⊕ *www.pierreci.it* ⊘ *Tues.–Sun. 9–8.*

6 **Piazza Navona.** Here everything that makes Rome unique is compressed
Fodor'sChoice into one beautiful baroque piazza. It has antiquity, Bernini sculptures,
★

three gorgeous fountains, a magnificently baroque church (Sant'Agnese in Agone) and, above all, the excitement of people out to enjoy themselves—strolling, café-loafing, seeing, and being seen. The piazza's most famous work of art is the **Fontana dei Quattro Fiumi**, created for Innocent X by Bernini in 1651. ✉*Junction of Via della Cuccagna, Corsia Agonale, Via di Sant'Agnese, and Via Agonale.*

❺ **Piazza di Spagna** *(Spanish Steps).* Those icons of postcard Rome, the Spanish Steps, and the piazza from which they ascend both get their names from the Spanish Embassy to the Vatican on the piazza, in spite of the fact that the staircase was built with French funds in 1723. For centuries, the steps welcomed tourists: among them Stendhal, Honoré de Balzac, William Makepeace Thackeray, and Byron.

❼ **Pantheon.** This onetime pagan temple, a marvel of architectural harmony and proportion, is the best-preserved monument of imperial Rome. Dating from around AD 120, the most striking thing about the Pantheon is the remarkable unity of the building. You don't have to look far to find the reason for this harmony: the diameter described by the dome is exactly equal to its height. It's the use of such simple mathematical balance that gives classical architecture its characteristic sense of proportion and its nobility and timeless appeal. The great opening at the apex of the dome, the oculus, is nearly 30 feet in diameter and was the temple's only source of light. It was intended to symbolize the "all-seeing eye of heaven."

✉*Piazza della Rotonda* ☎*06/68300230* ✉*Free* ⊙*Mon.–Sat. 9–7:30, Sun. 9–5:30.*

❹ **Pincio.** The Pincio gardens have always been a favorite spot for strolling. Even a pope or two would head here to see and be seen among the beau monde of Rome. From the balustraded Pincio terrace you can look down at Piazza del Popolo and beyond, surveying much of Rome. ✉*Piazzale Napoleone I and Viale dell'Obelisco, Villa Borghese.*

SHOPPING

Italian style is everywhere in Rome, from couture clothing to fashion accessories by all the best names. Specialties of the city include excellent silks, linens, lace, and other fabrics. Edibles include wines, olive oils, pasta, and sweet biscotti, small hard biscuits.

★ The city's most famous shopping district, **Piazza di Spagna,** is a galaxy of boutiques selling gorgeous wares with glamorous labels. **Via del Corso,** a main shopping avenue, has more than a mile of clothing, shoes, leather goods, and home furnishings from classic to cutting-edge. **Via Cola di Rienzo** is block after block of boutiques, shoe stores, department stores, and mid-level chain stores, as well as street stalls and upscale food shops. **Via dei Coronari** has quirky antiques and home furnishings. Via Giulia and other surrounding streets are good bets for decorative arts. Should your gift list include religious souvenirs, shop between Piazza San Pietro and **Borgo Pio.** Liturgical vestments and statues of saints make for good window-shopping on **Via dei Cestari. Frette** (✉*Piazza di Spagna 11* ☎*06/6790673*) is a Roman institution for luxurious linens. **Federico Polidori** (✉*Via Pie di Marmo 7, near Pantheon* ☎*06/6797191*) crafts custom-made leather bags and briefcases complete with monograms. **Fratelli Bassetti** (✉*Corso Vittorio Emanuele II*

FodorśChoice
★

FodorśChoice
★

4

73, near Campo de' Fiori ✆06/6892326) has a vast selection of world-famous Italian silks and fashion fabrics in a rambling palazzo.

WHERE TO EAT

$$-$$$$ ✕**Dal Bolognese.** The classic Dal Bolognese is both a convenient shopping-spree lunch spot and the tables on the expansive pedestrian piazza are prime people-watching real estate. Choose from delicious fresh pastas in creamy sauces, and steaming trays of boiled meats. ✉*Piazza del Popolo 1, near Piazza di Spagna* ✆*06/3611426* ☰*AE, DC, MC, V* ⊗*Closed Mon. and Aug.*

$-$$$ ✕**Alle Fratte.** Here staple Roman trattoria fare shares the menu with dishes
Fodor'sChoice   that have a southern Italian slant. Boisterous owner Francesco, his Ameri-
★   can relatives, and their trusted waiter Peppe make you feel at home. ✉*Via delle Fratte di Trastevere 49/50* ✆*06/5835775* ⊕*www.allefratteditrastevere.com* ☰*AE, DC, MC, V* ⊗*Closed Wed. and 2 wks in Aug.*

GENOA, ITALY

Genoa (Genova, in Italian) claims that it was the birthplace of Christopher Columbus (one of several places that claim the explorer), but the city's proud history predates that explorer by several hundred years. Genoa was already an important trading station by the 3rd century BC, when the Romans conquered Liguria. Known as *La Superba* (The Proud), Genoa was a great maritime power in the 13th century, rivaling Venice and Pisa. But its luster eventually diminished, and the city was outshined by these and other formidable cities. By the 17th century it was no longer a great sea power. It has, however, continued to be a profitable port. Genoa is now a busy, sprawling, and cosmopolitan city. But with more than two millennia of history under its belt, magnificent palaces and museums, the largest medieval city center in Europe, and an elaborate network of ancient hilltop fortresses, Genoa may be just the dose of culture you are looking for. Portofino can be visited on a day-trip from Venice if your ship doesn't call there directly (⇨*Portofino*).

ESSENTIALS

CURRENCY   The euro (€1 to US$1.46 at this writing); U.S. currency is generally not accepted in Europe, but ATMs are common and credit cards are widely accepted.

HOURS   Stores are generally open from 9 or 9:30 to 1 and from 3:30 or 4 to 7 or 7:30. Many shops close Sunday, though this is changing, too, especially in the city center. Many national museums are closed on Monday and may have shorter hours on Sunday.

INTERNET   There is passenger Internet access in the port terminal.

TELEPHONES   Tri-band GSM phones work in Italy. You can buy prepaid phone cards at telecom shops, news-vendors, and tobacconists in all towns and cities. Phone cards can be used for local or international calls.

COMING ASHORE

Genoa is a massive port, and cruise ships usually dock at one of two terminals, the Ponte dei Mille Maritime Station and Ponte Andrea Dora Maritime Station. Ponte dei Mille is a magnificent 1930s building (renovated 2001) with good passenger facilities that include shops, restaurants, an information center, and a bank. Neighboring Ponte Andrea Dora was refurbished in 2007 with similar facilities but on a slightly smaller scale. From here, it's a few minutes walk to the port entrance, from which you can also walk into the city; however, the streets around the port are workaday and gritty, so you may want to take a taxi rather than walk into the city proper.

With the occasional assistance of public transportation, the only way to visit Genoa is on foot. Many of the more interesting districts are either entirely closed to traffic, have roads so narrow that no car could fit, or are, even at the best of times, blocked by gridlock. A vehicle might be useful if you want to explore the Ligurian countryside and coastline around Genoa. Rental costs are approximately €45 per day for a compact manual vehicle.

Within Liguria local trains make innumerable stops. Regular service operates from Genoa's two stations: departures from Stazione Principe travel to points west and Stazione Brignole to points east and south. All the coastal resorts are on this line. If you buy tickets though Trenitalia's (Italian Railway's) Web site (⊕ *www.trenitalia.com*), you can print them out at self-service machines in Genoa station.

EXPLORING GENOA

Numbers in the margin correspond to points of interest on the Genoa map.

THE MEDIEVAL CORE

The medieval center of Genoa, threaded with tiny streets flanked by 11th-century portals, is roughly the area between the port and Piazza de Ferrari. This mazelike pedestrian zone is officially called the Caruggi District, but the Genovese, in their matter-of-fact way, simply refer to the area as the place of the *vicoli* (narrow alleys). In this warren of narrow, cobbled streets extending north from Piazza Caricamento, the city's oldest churches sit among tiny shops selling antique furniture, coffee, cheese, rifles, wine, gilt picture frames, camping gear, and even live fish. The 500-year-old apartment buildings lean so precariously that penthouse balconies nearly touch those across the street, blocking what little sunlight would have shone down onto the cobblestones. Wealthy Genovese built their homes in this quarter in the 16th century, and prosperous guilds, such as the goldsmiths for whom Vico degli Indoratori and Via degli Orefici were named, set up shop here.

❸ **Galleria Nazionale.** This gallery, housed in the richly adorned **Palazzo Spinola** north of Piazza Soziglia, contains masterpieces by Luca Giordano and Guido Reni. The *Ecce Homo,* by Antonello da Messina, is a hauntingly beautiful painting, of historical interest because it was the Sicilian da Messina who first brought Flemish oil paints and techniques to Italy from his sojourns in the Low Countries. ⊠*Piazza Pellicceria 1, Maddalena*

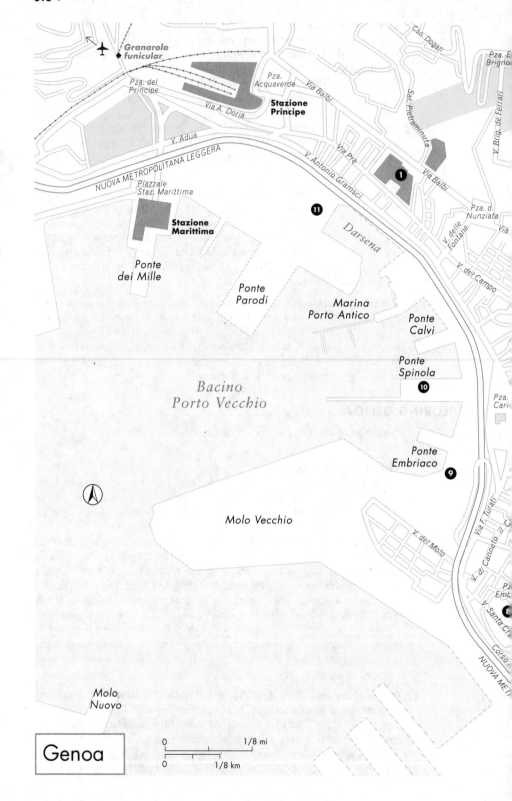

Genoa

Granarolo funicular

Pza. del Principe

Pza. Acquaverde

Via Balbi

Via A. Doria

Stazione Principe

Cso. Dogali

Pza. E. Brigno

Sal. Pietraminuta

V. Brig. de Terrari

Via Balbi

V. Adua

NUOVA METROPOLITANA LEGGERA

Via Pre

Via Antonio Gramsci

Pza. d. Nunziata

Via

V. delle Fontane

Piazzale Staz. Marittima

Stazione Marittima

11

Darsena

V. del Campo

Ponte dei Mille

Ponte Parodi

Marina Porto Antico

Ponte Calvi

Ponte Spinola

10

Pza. Cari

Bacino Porto Vecchio

Ponte Embriaco

9

Molo Vecchio

V. del Molo

V. F. Turati

V. di Canneto il C

Pza Emb

V. Santa Cr

8

Molo Nuovo

Corso

NUOVA ME

| 0 | | 1/8 mi |
| 0 | | 1/8 km |

4

☎010/2705300 ⊕*www.palaz-zospinola.it* ✉*€4, €6.50 including Palazzo Reale* ⊙*Tues.–Sat. 8:30–7:30, Sun. 1:30–7:30.*

⑤ **Palazzo Bianco.** It's difficult to miss the splendid white facade of this town palace as you walk down Via Garibaldi, once one of Genoa's most important streets. The building houses a fine collection of 17th-century art, with the Spanish and Flemish schools well represented. ⊠*Via Garibaldi 11, Maddalena* ☎010/2759185 ⊕*www.museopalazzobianco.it* ✉*€7, includes Palazzo Rosso and Palazzo Doria Tursi* ⊙*Tues.–Fri. 9–7, weekends 10–7.*

Fodor'sChoice
★

① **Palazzo Reale.** Lavish rococo rooms provide sumptuous display space for paintings, sculptures, tapestries, and Asian ceramics. The 17th-century palace—also known as Palazzo Balbi Durazzo—was built by the Balbi family, enormously wealthy Genovese merchants. Its regal pretensions were not lost on the Savoy, who bought the palace and turned it into a royal residence in the early 19th century. The gallery of mirrors and the ballroom on the upper floor are particularly decadent. Look for works by Sir Anthony Van Dyck, who lived in Genoa for six years, beginning in 1621, and painted many portraits of the Genovese nobility. The formal gardens, which you can visit for €1, provide a welcome respite from the bustle of the city beyond the palace walls, as well as great views of the harbor. ⊠*Via Balbi 10, Pré* ☎010/27101 ⊕*www.palazzorealegenova.it* ✉*€4, €6 including Galleria Nazionale* ⊙*Tues. and Wed. 9–1:30, Thurs.–Sun. 9–7.*

④ **Palazzo Rosso.** This 17th-century baroque palace was named for the red stone used in its construction. It now contains, apart from a number of lavishly frescoed suites, works by Titian, Veronese, Reni, and Van Dyck. ⊠*Via Garibaldi 18, Maddalena* ☎010/2759185 ⊕*www.museopalazzorosso.it* ✉*€7, includes Palazzo Bianco and Palazzo Doria Tursi* ⊙*Tues.–Fri. 9–7, weekends 10–7.*

② **Zecca-Righi funicular.** This is a seven-stop commuter funicular beginning at Piazza della Nunziata and ending at a high lookout on the fortified gates in the 17th-century city walls. Ringed around the circumference of the city are a number of huge fortresses; this gate was part of the city's system of defenses. From Righi you can undertake scenic all-day hikes from one fortress to the next. ⊠*Piazza della Nunziata, Pré* ☎010/5582414 ⊕*www.amt.genova.it* ✉*€1.20, free with bus ticket* ⊙*Daily 6 AM–11:45 PM.*

SOUTHERN DISTRICTS & THE AQUARIUM

Inhabited since the 6th century BC, the oldest section of Genoa lies on a hill to the southwest of the Caruggi District. Today, apart from a section of 9th-century wall near Porta Soprana, there is little to show that an imposing castle once stood here. Though the neighborhood is considerably rundown, some of Genoa's oldest churches make it a worthwhile excursion. No visit to Genoa is complete, however, without at least a stroll along the harborfront. The port was given a complete overhaul during Genoa's preparations for the Columbus quincentennial celebrations of 1992, and additional restorations in 2003 and 2004 have done much to revitalize the waterfront.

🔟 **Acquario di Genova.** Europe's biggest aquarium, second in the world only to Osaka's in Japan, is the third-most-visited museum in Italy and a must for children. Fifty tanks of marine species, including sea turtles, dolphins, seals, eels, penguins, and sharks, share space with educational displays and re-creations of marine ecosystems, including a tank of coral from the Red Sea. Timed tickets permit entrance every half-hour. ⊠*Ponte Spinola, Porto Vecchio* ☎*0101/23451* ⊕*www.acquario.ge.it* 🎫*€14* ⊙*July and Aug., daily 9 AM–11 PM; Sept.–June, Mon.–Wed. and Fri. 9:30–7:30, Thurs. 9:30 AM–10 PM, weekends 9:30–8:30; last entrance 1½ hrs before closing.*

⓫ **Galata Museo del Mare.** Devoted entirely to the city's seafaring history, this museum is probably the best way, at least on dry land, to get an idea of the changing shape of Genoa's busy port. Highlighting the displays is a full-size replica of a 17th-century Genovese galleon. ⊠*Calata de Mari 1, Ponte dei Mille* ☎*010/2345655* ⊕*www.galatamuseodelmare.it* 🎫*€10* ⊙*Mar.–Oct., daily 10–7:30; Nov.–Feb., Tues.–Fri. 10–6, weekends 10– 7:30; last entrance 1½ hrs before closing.*

❻ **San Lorenzo.** Contrasting black slate and white marble, so common in Liguria, embellished the cathedral at the heart of medieval Genoa—inside and out. Consecrated in 1118, the church honors St. Lawrence, who passed through the city on his way to Rome in the 3rd century. For hundreds of years the building was used for religious and state purposes such as civic elections. Note the 13th-century Gothic portal, fascinating twisted barbershop columns, and the 15th- to 17th-century frescoes inside. The last campanile dates from the early 16th century. The **Museo del Tesoro di San Lorenzo** (San Lorenzo Treasury Museum) housed inside has some stunning pieces from medieval goldsmiths and silversmiths, for which medieval Genoa was renowned. ⊠*Piazza San Lorenzo, Molo* ☎*010/2471831* 🎫*Cathedral free, museum €5.50* ⊙*Cathedral daily 8–11:45 and 3–6:45. Museum Mon.–Sat. 9–11:30 and 3–5:30.*

❼ **Sant'Agostino.** This 13th-century Gothic church was damaged during World War II, but it still has a fine campanile and two well-preserved cloisters that house an excellent museum displaying pieces of medieval architecture and fresco paintings. Highlighting the collection are the enigmatic fragments of a tomb sculpture by Giovanni Pisano (circa 1250–circa 1315). ⊠*Piazza Sarzano 35/r, Molo* ☎*010/2511263* ⊕*www.museosantagostino.it* 🎫*€4* ⊙*Tues.–Fri. 9–7, weekends 10–7.*

❽ **Santa Maria di Castello.** One of Genoa's most significant religious buildings, an early Christian church, was rebuilt in the 12th century and finally completed in 1513. You can visit the adjacent cloisters and see the fine artwork contained in the museum. Museum hours vary during religious services. ⊠*Salita di Santa Maria di Castello 15, Molo* ☎*010/2549511* 🎫*Free* ⊙*Daily 9–noon and 3:30–6.*

❾ **Il Bigo.** The bizarre white structure erected in 1992 to celebrate the Columbus quincentennial looks like either a radioactive spider or an overgrown potato spore, depending on your point of view. Its most redeeming feature is the **Ascensore Panoramico Bigo** (Bigo Panoramic Elevator), from which you can take in the harbor, city, and sea. Next to the elevator, in an area covered by sail-like awnings, there's an ice-skating rink in winter. ⊠*Ponte Spinola, Porto Vecchio* ☎*010/23451, 347/4860524 ice-skating* ✉*Elevator €3.30, skating rink €7.50* ☉*Elevator Feb. and Nov., weekends 10–5; June–Aug., Tues., Wed., and Sun. 10–8, Thurs.–Sat. 10 AM–11 PM; Mar.– May and Sept., Tues.–Sun. 10–6; Oct., Tues.–Sun. 10–5; Dec. 26–Jan. 6, daily 10–5. Skating rink Nov. or Dec.–Mar., weekdays 8 AM–9:30 PM, Sat. 10 AM–2 AM, Sun. 10 AM–midnight.*

SHOPPING

In addition to the Italian reputation for fine leather and haute couture, Liguria is famous for its fine lace, silver-and-gold filigree work, and ceramics. Look also for bargains in velvet, macramé, olive wood, and marble. Genoa is the best spot to find all these specialties. Don't forget the excellent wines, cheeses, dried meats, and olive oils.

In the heart of the medieval quarter, Via Soziglia is lined with shops selling handicrafts and tempting foods. Via XX Settembre is famous for its exclusive shops. High-end shops line Via Luccoli. The best shopping area for trendy-but-inexpensive Italian clothing is near San Siro, on Via San Luca. At **Vinoteca Sola** (⊠*Piazza Colombo 13–15/r, near Stazione Brignole, Foce* ☎*010/594513*) you can purchase the best Ligurian wines and have them shipped home. You can even buy futures for vintages to come. **Pescetto** (⊠*Via Scurreria 8, Molo* ☎*010/2473433*) sells designer clothes, perfumes, and gifts at its fancy shop.

WHERE TO EAT

$$$–$$$$ ✕**Da Domenico.** Don't be dismayed by the labyrinth of rooms and wood passages that lead to your table at this restaurant in a quiet square near Piazza Dante—you've found one of those hidden corners that only the Genovese know. Traditional seafood and meat dishes make up most of the menu. ⊠*Piazza Leonardo 3, Molo* ☎*010/540289* ⚐*Reservations essential* ▤*AE, DC, MC, V* ☉*Closed Mon.*

¢–$ ✕**Exultate.** When the weather permits, umbrella-shaded tables spread out from this tiny eatery into the nearby square. Its selection popular with locals, the restaurant's inexpensive daily menu is presented on a chalkboard for all to see, with elaborate salads and homemade desserts highlighting the list. ⊠*Piazza Lavagna 15/r, Maddalena* ☎*010/2512605* ▤*MC, V* ☉*Closed Sun.*

GIBRALTAR

The tiny British colony of Gibraltar—nicknamed Gib, or simply The Rock—whose impressive silhouette dominates the strait between Spain and Morocco, was one of the two Pillars of Hercules in ancient times, marking the western limits of the known world and in an ace position commanding the narrow pathway between the Mediterranean Sea and the Atlantic Ocean. Today, the Rock is like Britain with a suntan. There are double-decker buses, policemen in helmets, and bright red mailboxes. Gibraltar was ceded to Great Britain in 1713 by the Treaty of Utrecht, and Spain has been trying to get it back ever since. Recently, Britain and Spain have been talking about joint Anglo-Spanish sovereignty, much to the ire of the majority of Gibraltarians, who remain fiercely patriotic to the crown. Millions of dollars have been spent in developing the Rock's tourist potential, and Gibraltar's economy is further boosted by its important status as an offshore financial center.

ESSENTIALS

CURRENCY Gibraltar uses the Pound Sterling (£1 to $2.07 at present exchange rate). Euros can also be used in most of the shops, but the exchange rate may be unfavorable; U.S. currency is generally not accepted, but ATMs are common and credit cards are widely accepted.

HOURS Shops are open weekdays from 9:30 to 7:30 PM, Saturday from 10 to 1. Some shops open Sunday when a ship is in port. Attractions have varied hours, but these are generally weekdays from 10 to 5, and some may open weekends.

TELEPHONES Mobile services are single band and there is no 3G service. GibTel is the main service provider.

COMING ASHORE

There is a dedicated cruise terminal within Gibraltar commercial port. The passenger terminal has a range of facilities, including a bar-café, souvenir shop, tourist information center, bank and currency exchange facilities, and an exhibition area. From here it is an easy walk into Gibraltar itself from where all the sites of town can be accessed on foot (or where you can take a bus to the attractions that are farther afield). You can also take a taxi; fares are £2.40 for pick up and £0.15 per 200 meters or per minute of travel.

The town of Gibraltar is compact, and it's easy to walk around. Vehicles rented in Gibraltar can be taken over the border into Spain, so you could explore some of the southern Spanish coastline from here in a day. Vehicles are only rented to people between the ages of 23 and 70. The Official Rock Tour—conducted either by minibus or, at a greater cost, taxi—takes about 90 minutes and includes all the major sights, allowing you to choose which places to come back to and linger at later.

The cable car to the top of the rock costs €9 per round-trip.

EXPLORING GIBRALTAR

The colorful, congested library is where the dignified Regency architecture of Great Britain blends well with the shutters, balconies, and patios of southern Spain. Shops, restaurants, and pubs beckon on busy Main Street; at the Governor's Residence, the ceremonial Changing of the Guard takes place six times a year and the Ceremony of the Keys takes place twice a year. Also make sure you see the Law Courts,; the Anglican Cathedral of the Holy Trinity; and the Catholic Cathedral of St. Mary the Crowned.

Numbers in the margin correspond to points of interest on the Gibraltar map.

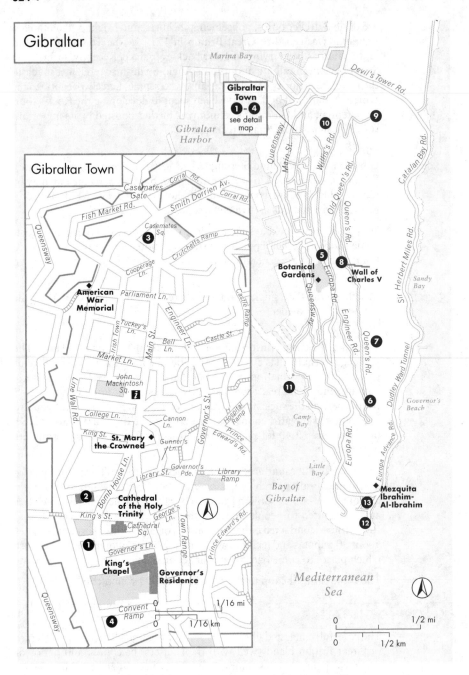

Gibraltar

Marina Bay

Gibraltar Harbor

Gibraltar Town ❶ - ❹ see detail map

Devil's Tower Rd.

Queensway

Main St.

Willis's Rd.

Old Queen's Rd.

Queen's Rd.

Catalan Bay Rd.

Sir Herbert Miles Rd.

❿

❾

Gibraltar Town

Corral Rd.

Casemates Gate

Fish Market Rd.

Smith Dorrien Av.

Corral Rd.

Casemates Sq.

❸

Cooperage Ln.

Crutchett's Ramp

Castle Ramp

Queensway

American War Memorial

Parliament Ln.

Tuckey's Ln.

Engineer Ln.

Bell Ln.

Castle St.

Main St.

Irish Town

Market Ln.

Line Wall Rd.

John Mackintosh Sq.

College Ln.

Cannon Ln.

King St.

St. Mary the Crowned

Gunner's Ln.

Governor's St.

Hospital Ramp

Prince Edward's Rd.

Library St.

Governor's Pde.

Library Ramp

❷

Cathedral of the Holy Trinity

King's St.

Bomb House Ln.

Cathedral Sq.

George's Ln.

Town Range

❶

Governor's Ln.

King's Chapel

Governor's Residence

Prince Edward's Rd.

Queensway

Convent Ramp

❹

0   1/16 mi
0   1/16 km

Botanical Gardens

❺ ❽ Wall of Charles V

Europa Rd.

Queensway

Engineer Rd.

Queen's Rd.

Sandy Bay

Sir Herbert Miles Rd.

Dudley Ward Tunnel

❼

Governor's Beach

❻

❿

Camp Bay

Little Bay

Bay of Gibraltar

Europa Rd.

Europa Advance Rd.

◆ Mezquita Ibrahim-Al-Ibrahim

❶❸

❶❷

Mediterranean Sea

0   1/2 mi
0   1/2 km

❶ Main Tourist Office. Gibraltar's main tourist office is on Cathedral Square. ✉ *Duke of Kent House, Cathedral Sq.* ☎ *9567/45000* ⊘ *Weekdays 9–5:30.*

❽ Apes' Den. The famous Barbary Apes are a breed of cinnamon-color, tailless monkeys native to Morocco's Atlas Mountains. Legend holds that as long as the apes remain in Gibraltar, the British will keep the Rock; Winston Churchill went so far as to issue an order for their preservation when the apes' numbers began to dwindle during World War II. They are publicly fed twice daily, at 8 and 4, at a rocky area down Old Queens Road and near the Wall of Charles V. Among the apes' mischievous talents are grabbing food, purses, and cameras.

> **GIBRALTAR BEST BETS**
>
> **The town of Gibraltar.** Immerse yourself in a little piece of Britain far south of the white cliffs of Dover.
>
> **Take in the panorama from the top of the Rock.** Look south to the northern coast of Africa and north to the southern coastal plains of Spain.
>
> **Make friends with a Barbary ape.** These cheeky primates inhabit the slopes of the Rock. They have a penchant for steeling bags and sunglasses—so you have been warned!

❺ Cable Car. You can reach St. Michael's Cave—or ride all the way to the top
★ of Gibraltar—on this cable car. The car doesn't go high off the ground, but the views of Spain and Africa from the Rock's pinnacle are superb. It leaves from a station at the southern end of Main Street. 🎫 *Cable car £8 round-trip* ⊘ *Daily 9:30–5:45.*

❸ Casemates Square. This square in the northern part of town is Gibraltar's social hub and has been pedestrianized. There are now plenty of places to sit out with a drink and watch the world go by. In the square is a branch of the **tourist office** (☎ *9567/50762* ⊘ *Weekdays 9–5:30, weekends 10–4*).

⓬ Europa Point. From here, have a look across the straits to Morocco, 23 km (14 mi) away. You're now standing on one of the two ancient Pillars of Hercules. In front of you, the lighthouse has dominated the meeting place of the Atlantic and the Mediterranean since 1841; sailors can see its light from a distance of 27 km (17 mi). ✉ *Continue along the coast road to the Rock's southern tip.*

❷ Gibraltar Museum. Housing a beautiful 14th-century Moorish bathhouse and an 1865 model of the Rock, Gibraltar's museum has displays that evoke the Great Siege and the Battle of Trafalgar. There's also a reproduction of the "Gibraltar Woman," the Neanderthal skull discovered here in 1848. ✉ *Bomb House La.* ☎ *9567/74289* 🎫 *£2* ⊘ *Weekdays 10–6, Sat. 10–2.*

❾ Great Siege Tunnels. The tunnels, formerly known as the Upper Galleries, were carved out during the Great Siege of 1779–82. You can plainly see the openings from whence the guns were pointed at the Spanish invaders. These tunnels form part of what is arguably the most impressive defense system anywhere in the world.

❿ Moorish Castle. Built by the descendants of Tariq, who conquered the Rock in 711, the present Tower of Homage dates from 1333, and its besieged walls bear the scars of stones from medieval catapults (and, later, cannonballs). Admiral George Rooke hoisted the British flag from its summit when he captured the Rock in 1704, and it has flown here ever since. The castle is on Willis's Road.

4 **Nefusot Yehudada Synagogue.** The 18th-century synagogue on Line Wall Road is one of the oldest synagogues on the Iberian Peninsula, dating back to 1724. There are guided tours twice a day at 12:30 PM and 2:30 PM, accompanied by a short history of the Gibraltar Jewish community.

11 **Rosia Bay.** For a fine view, drive high above the bay to which Nelson's flagship, HMS *Victory*, was towed after the Battle of Trafalgar in 1805. On board were the dead, who were buried in Trafalgar Cemetery on the southern edge of town—except for Admiral Nelson, whose body was returned to England preserved in a barrel of rum. ⊠*From Europa Flats, follow Europa Rd. back along the Rock's western slopes.*

13 **Shrine of Our Lady of Europe.** This shrine has been venerated by seafarers since 1462. Once a mosque, the small Catholic chapel has a little museum with a 1462 statue of the Virgin and some documents. ⊠*Just west of Europa Point and lighthouse, along Rock's southern tip* 🖼*Free* ⊗ *Weekdays 10–7.*

7 **St. Michael's Cave.** The largest of Gibraltar's 150 caves is a series of underground chambers hung with stalactites and stalagmites. It's an ideal performing-arts venue. Sound-and-light shows are held here most days at 11 AM and 4 PM. St. Michael's is on Queens Road.

6 The **Upper Rock Nature Preserve.** Accessible from Jews' Gate, the preserve includes St. Michael's Cave, the Apes' Den, the Great Siege Tunnels, the Moorish Castle, and the Military Heritage Center, which chronicles the British regiments who have served on the Rock. ⊠*From Rosia Bay, drive along Europa Rd. as far as Casino, above Alameda Gardens. Make a sharp right here up Engineer Rd. to Jews' Gate, a lookout over docks and the Bay of Gibraltar toward Algeciras.* 🖼*£8, includes all attractions, plus £1.50 per vehicle* ⊗ *Daily 9:30–6:30.*

SHOPPING

The quintessential Britishness of Gibraltar is reflected in its shopping. Many British high street names can be found here, including Marks and Spencer, so you can stock up on marmalades, biscuits, and Cheddar cheese. Fine English china and glassware also make an appearance along with oodles of Royal memorabilia. Inexpensive items include Union Jack motifs and red double-decker buses printed on everything from T-shirts to coffee mugs. The islands are tax-friendly so prices are cheaper than in Spain or the U.K.

Gibraltar Crystal (⊠*Grand Casemates* 🕾*350/50136* ⊕*www.gibraltarcrystal.com*) produces a range of brightly colored glass pieces from its factory on the island. **Marks and Spencer** (⊠*215 Main St.* 🕾*350/75857*) has all things British, from clothing to food.

WHERE TO EAT

$$–$$$ ✕ **Terrace Restaurant.** Upstairs from the casino, this is one of the best restaurants for sea views. Tarifa's colorful kite-surfers and Africa's Atlas mountains are visible on a clear day. The menu here is comfortably traditional and as good as the black bow-tie service. Dishes include beef Wellington, chicken Roquefort, and lobster thermidor. Afterward, choose from the diet-defying dessert trolley with classic English desserts, such as trifle, and fresh fruit tarts. ✉ *7 Europa Rd.* ☎ *9567/76666* ✍ *Reservations essential* ▭ *AE, DC, MC, V* ⊘ *Closed Sun. No lunch.*

$ ✕ **Sacarello's.** Right off Main Street, this place is as well known for its excellent coffee and cakes as it is for its adjacent restaurant. There's a daily lavish salad buffet, as well as filled baked potatoes; panfried noodles with broccoli, mussels, and chicken; and rack of lamb with wine and fine herbs. Top your meal off with a specialty coffee with cream and vanilla. The restaurant has several rooms warmly decorated in English-pub style, with cozy corners, dark-wood furnishings, and low ceilings. ✉ *57 Irish Town* ☎ *9567/70625* ▭ *MC, V* ⊘ *No dinner Sun.*

IBIZA, SPAIN

Sleepy from November to May, the capital of Ibiza is transformed in summer into Party Central for retro hippies and nonstop clubbers, but the town and the island have so much more to offer. Dalt Vila, the medieval quarter on the hill overlooking Ibiza Town, is a UNESCO World Heritage site with narrow alleyways brimming with atmosphere. While around the coastline the island has 50 sandy beaches. Ibiza was discovered by sun-seeking hippies in the late 1960s, eventually emerging as an icon of counter-culture chic. In the late 1980s and 1990s, club culture took over. Young ravers flocked here from all over the world, to dance all night and pack the sands of beach resorts all day. That Ibiza is still alive and well, but emblematic of the island's future are its growing numbers of luxury hotels, spas, and gourmet restaurants. Ibiza is toning down and scaling up.

ESSENTIALS

CURRENCY The euro (€1 to US$1.46 at this writing); U.S. currency is generally not accepted in Europe, but ATMs are common and credit cards are widely accepted.

HOURS Museums generally open 9 until 7 or 8, many are closed on Monday and some close in the afternoon. Most stores are open Monday through Saturday 9 to 1:30 and 5 to 8, but tourist shops may open in the afternoon and also on Sundays between May and September.

INTERNET **Cibermatic** (✉ *Cayetano Soler 3, Ibiza Town* ☎ *971303382*) is open from Monday to Saturday but closes from 1:30 to 5 in the afternoon.

TELEPHONES Tri-band GSM phones should work in Spain, and mobile services are 3G compatible. Public kiosks accept phone cards that support international calls (cards sold in press shops, bars and telecom shops). Major companies include Vodafone.

COMING ASHORE

Boats dock on the town pier at the edge of town. From here, you can walk into the capital without problem, and for this reason, facilities at the terminal are limited. You won't need transport to enjoy Ibiza Town, however if you rent a car, you can explore much of this small but fascinating island in a day. An economy rental car for one day is €87. There are 25 buses a day between Ibiza Town, Sant Rafael, and San Antonio, several per day between Ibiza, Sant Jordi, Salinas, Cala Tarida, and Sant Eulalia. Fares start at €1.10 and all are under €5.

Taxis are also numerous and are metered. They can undertake tourist tours. Fares start at €0.90 per minute (min €3.01) and waiting time of €16.24 per hour. There is a small supplement for port pick-up.

EXPLORING IBIZA

Numbers in the margin correspond to points of interest on the Ibiza map.

IBIZA TOWN (EIVISSA)

Hedonistic and historical, Eivissa (Ibiza, in Catalan) is a city jam-packed with cafés and nightspots and trendy shops; looming over it are the massive stone walls of **Dalt Vila**—the medieval city was declared a UNESCO World Heritage site in 1999—and its Gothic cathedral. Squeezed between the north walls of the old city and the harbor is **Sa Penya,** a long labyrinth of narrow stone-paved streets that offer the city's best exploring. What would the fishermen who used to live in this quarter have thought, to see so many of their little whitewashed houses transformed into bars and offbeat restaurants and boutiques with names like the Kabul Sutra Tantra Shop, and Good Times Jewelry, and Bitch?

One enters the Dalt Vila via a ramp through the **Portal de ses Taules,** the old city's main gate. On each side stands a statue, Roman in origin and now headless: Juno on the right, an armless male on the left. Keep going up until you reach the sights.

② **Bastió de Santa Llúcia.** Uphill from the contemporary art museum is a sculpture of a priest sitting on one of the stone seats in the gardens. On the left, the wide Bastion of St. Lucia has a panoramic view.

⑥ **Bastió de Sant Bernat.** Behind the cathedral, from the Bastion of St. Bernard, a promenade with sea views runs west to the bastions of Sant Jordi and Sant Jaume, past the **Castell**—a fortress formerly used as an army barracks, turned over to the city of Ibiza in 1973, and left to fall apart until 2006, when work began to transform it into a 70-room luxury parador. The promenade ends at the steps to the **Portal Nou** (New Gate).

④ **Cathedral.** From the church of San Domingo, follow any of the streets or steps leading uphill to Carrer Obispo Torres (Carrer Major). The cathedral is on the site of religious structures from each of the cultures that have ruled Ibiza since the Phoenicians. Built in the 13th and 14th centuries and renovated in the 18th century, the cathedral has a Gothic tower and a baroque nave. ⊠ *Carrer Major* ☎ *971/312774* ⊗ *Weekdays 10–1, Sun. 10:30–noon.*

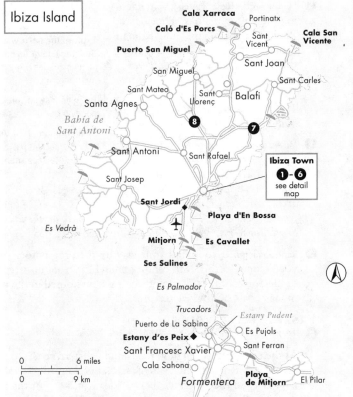

Ibiza Island

Cala Xarraca
Portinatx
Caló d'Es Porcs
Sant Vicent
Cala San Vicente
Puerto San Miguel
Sant Joan
San Miguel
Sant Carles
Sant Mateo
Sant Llorenç
Balafi
Santa Agnes
*Bahía de
Sant Antoni*
8
7
Sant Antoni
Sant Rafael
Ibiza Town
1-**6**
see detail map
Sant Josep
Es Vedrà
Sant Jordi
Playa d'En Bossa
Mitjorn
Es Cavallet
Ses Salines
Es Palmador
Trucadors
Estany Pudent
Puerto de La Sabina
Es Pujols
Estany d'es Peix
Sant Ferran
Sant Francesc Xavier
Cala Sahona
Playa de Mitjorn
El Pilar
Formentera
Cabo de Berbería

0 ____ 6 miles
0 ____ 9 km

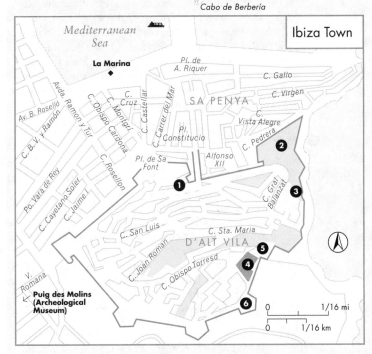

Mediterranean Sea

Ibiza Town

La Marina

Pl. de A. Riquer
C. Gallo
Avda. Ramon y Tur
C. Virgen
C. Montgri
C. Castellar
C. Cruz
C. Carrer del Mar
C. Obispo Cardona
SA PENYA
C. Vista Alegre
Av. B. Roselló
Pl. Constitucio
C. Pedrera
C. B. V. y Ramón
2
C. Rosellon
Pl. de Sa Font
Alfonso XII
C. Gral Balanzat
1
3
Po. Vara de Rey
C. Cayetano Soler
C. Jaime I
C. San Luis
C. Sta. Maria
D'ALT VILA
5
C. Joan Roman
4
C. Obispo Torresd
V. Romana
Puig des Molins
(Archeological Museum)
6

0 ____ 1/16 mi
0 ____ 1/16 km

4

⑤ Museu Arqueològic. Eivissa's archaeological museum has Phoenician, Punic (Carthaginian), and Roman artifacts. It's across the plaza from the cathedral. ✉ *Plaça Catedral 3* ☎ *971/301231* 🎫 *€2.40, Sun. free* ⊙ *Oct.–Mar., Tues.–Sat. 9–3, Sun. 10–2; Apr.–Oct., Tues.–Sat. 10–2 and 6–8, Sun. 10–2.*

IBIZA BEST BETS

Explore the narrow alleyways of Sa Penya. Ibiza Town's most atmospheric quarter is great for browsing and shopping.

Bring your swim suit. Spend an afternoon on one of Ibiza's trendy beaches.

Stroll uphill in Dalt Vila. The quarter's architecture has been designated a World Heritage site.

① Museu d'Art Contemporani. A little way up Sa Carroza, a sign on the left points back toward the museum, which is housed in the gateway arch. ✉ *Ronda Pintor Narcis Putget s/n* ☎ *971/302723* 🎫 *€1.20, Sun. free* ⊙ *Oct.–Apr., Tues.–Fri. 10–1:30 and 4–6, weekends 10–1:30; May–Sept., Tues.–Fri. 10–1:30 and 5–8, weekends 10–1:30.*

③ Sant Domingo. If you wind your way up the promontory of Santa Llúcia, you'll come to this 16th-century church, its roof an irregular landscape of tile domes. Eivissa's city offices are now housed in the church's former monastery. ✉ *Carrer de Balanzat.*

SANTA EULÀRIA DES RIU
❼ *15 km (9 mi) northeast of Eivissa.*

At the edge of this town on the island's eastern coast, to the right below the road, a Roman bridge crosses what is claimed to be the only permanent river in the Balearics (hence "des Riu," or "of the river"). Ahead, on the hilltop, are the cubes and domes of the church—to reach it, look for a narrow lane to the left, signed PUIG DE MISSA, itself so named for the hill where regular mass was once held. A stoutly arched, cryptlike covered area guards the entrance; inside are a fine gold reredos and blue-tile stations of the cross. Santa Eurària itself follows the curve of a long sandy beach, a few blocks deep with restaurants, shops, and holiday apartments. From here it's a 10-minute drive to **Sant Carles** and the open-air **hippie market** held there every Saturday morning.

SANTA GERTRUDIS DE FRUITERA
❽ *15 km (9 mi) north of Eivissa.*

Blink and you miss it: that's true of most of the small towns in the island's interior—and especially so of Santa Gertrudis, not much more than a bend in the road from Eivissa to the north coast. But don't blink: Santa Gertrudis is strategic, and it's cute. From here, you are only a few minutes' drive from some of the island's flat-out best resort hotels and spas. You are minutes from the most beautiful secluded north coves and beaches: **S'Illa des Bosc, Benirrás** (where they have drum circles to salute the setting sun), **S'Illot des Renclí, Portinatx, Caló d'En Serra.** Santa Gertrudis itself has offbeat shops, and laid-back sidewalk cafés, and good food. Artists and expats like it here: they've given it an appeal that now makes for listings of half a million dollars for a modest three-bedroom flat.

SHOPPING

In the late 1960s and '70s, Ibiza built a reputation for extremes of fashion. Little of this phenomenon survives, though the softer designs of Smilja Mihailovich (under the Ad Lib label) still prosper. Clothing and beachwear plus fashion accessories of all kinds are the major buys here, including excellent leather goods, but there is also a community of artists working in glass, ceramics, and bronze. Along Carrer d'Enmig is an eclectic collection of shops and stalls selling fashion and crafts. Although the Sa Penya area of Eivissa still has a few designer boutiques, much of the area is now called the Mercat dels Hippies (hippie market), with more than 80 stalls of overpriced tourist ephemera.

For trendy casual gear, sandals, belts, and bags, try **Ibiza Republic** (⊠*Antoni Mar 15, Eivissa* ☎*971/314175*).

For leather wear, belts, bags, and shoes, go to **Heltor** (⊠*Madrid 12, Eivissa* ☎*971/391225*).

BEACHES

Immediately south of Ibiza Town is a long, sandy beach, the nearly 3-km (2-mi) **Playa d'en Bossa**. Farther on, a left turn at Sant Jordi on the way to the airport leads across the salt pans to **Es Cavallet** and **Ses Salines**, two of the best beaches on the island. Topless bathing is accepted all over Ibiza, but Es Cavallet is the official nudist beach. The remaining beaches on this part of the island are accessible from the Ibiza–Sant Josep–Sant Antoni highway, down side roads that often end in rough tracks. North of Sant Antoni, there are no easily accessible beaches until you reach **Puerto San Miguel,** an almost rectangular cove with relatively restrained development. Next along the north coast, accessible via San Juan, is Portinatx, a series of small coves with sandy beaches, of which the first and last, **Cala Xarraca** and **Caló d'Es Porcs**, are the best. East of San Juan is the long, curved cove beach of **Cala San Vicente**. Popular with families, it has a more leisurely pace than Ibiza's other resorts. The beaches on the east coast have been developed, but **Santa Eulalia** remains attractive. The resort has a narrow, sloping beach in front of a pedestrian promenade that is much less frenetic than Sant Antoni.

WHERE TO EAT

¢–$$ ✕**Mezzanotte**. Opened in 2006, this charming little portside restaurant is a branch of the popular Mezzanotte in Eivissa. There are 12 tables inside, softly lighted with candles and track lights; in summer, seating expands to an interior patio and tables on the sidewalk. The kitchen prides itself on hard-to-find fresh ingredients flown in from Italy. The linguini with jumbo shrimp, saffron, and zucchini—or with *bottarga* (dried and salted mullet roe from Sardinia)—is wonderful. Value for price here is excellent; the €15 prix-fixe lunch menu is an absolute bargain. ⊠*Paseo de s'Alamera 22, Santa Eulària* ☎*971/319498* ▭*MC, V* ⊗*Closed Jan. and Mon.*

¢–$ ✕**Can Caus**. Ibiza might pride itself—justly—on its seafood, but there comes a time for meat and potatoes. When that time comes, take the 20-minute drive from Eivissa to the outskirts of Santa Gertrudis, to this informal, family-style roadside restaurant, and feast on skewers of barbe-cued *sobrasada* (soft pork sausage), goat chops, lamb kebabs, or grilled sweetbreads with red peppers, onions, and eggplant. For starters, there's fried goat cheese with garden salad, and a great crusty bread with garlic mayonnaise. Most people eat at the long wooden tables on the terrace. ✉*Ctra. Sant Miquel, Km. 3.5Santa Gertrudis* ☎*971/197516* 🖃*AE, MC, V* ⊘*Closed Mon.*

LE HAVRE, FRANCE (FOR NORMANDY & PARIS)

Le Havre, France's second-largest port (after Marseille), was destroyed in World War II. You may find the rebuilt city bleak and uninviting; on the other hand, you may admire Auguste Perret's audacious modern architecture, which earned the city UNESCO World Heritage status in 2005. The city is the perfect starting point for some of the highlights of Normandy, the French region of rolling verdant farmland and long, sandy beaches. Tiny fishing villages dot the coves around the city, a world away from the gritty urban feel of Le Havre itself. Normandy was also the location of the D-Day invasion of Europe by Allied forces during WWII, the largest wartime seaborne invasion of all time. You can visit the beach landing sites and evocative museums about the battle. From Le Havre it's also possible to visit Paris, one of the world's most famous cities.

ESSENTIALS

CURRENCY
The euro (€1 to US$1.46 at this writing); U.S. currency is generally not accepted in Europe, but ATMs are common.

HOURS
Stores are generally open Monday through Saturday 9–7, but many close at lunchtime (usually noon–2 or 3) and some will open later and on Sunday during July and August. Museums open 10–5, but most are closed on either Monday or Tuesday.

INTERNET
Cyber Metro (✉*21 Cours de la Republique* ☎*02–35–53–11–15*), a games room at the Hotel de Bourgogne, has 32 computers and Wi-Fi access.

TELEPHONES
Tri-band GSM phones work in France. You can buy prepaid phone cards at telecom shops, news-vendors, and tobacconists in all towns and cities. Phone cards can be used for local or international calls. France Telecom and Orange are leading telecom companies.

COMING ASHORE

Le Havre a very large port with vast amounts of freight traffic in addition to cruise ships. Disembarking passengers will find a small Welcome Center with practical information and multilingual staff, a small shop, plus taxi and tour services, including a shuttle service into the city, which stops at the railway station. If you intend to spend the day in Le Havre, it is only a few minutes walk from the port entrance to the downtown area.

Le Havre is the main cruise port for visits to Paris; however, the city is a two- to two-and-a-half-hour journey time away depending on the service chosen. From the railway station there are hourly trains to Paris terminating at Gare St-Lazare. SNCF (⊕*www.sncf.com*), the French railway company, is reliable and efficient. Prices are cheaper if you buy tickets in advance, but a same-day second-class round-trip should be around €28 if purchased on the day of travel.

We would advise against renting a car just to make the trip into Paris (traffic and parking are both very difficult); however, a rental car is an ideal way to explore the rolling countryside of Normandy. An economy manual car costs around €70 per day. Taxis wait outside the port gates and can provide tourist itineraries. For single journeys, ares are €2.30 at pick-up, then €0.69 per km.

EXPLORING NORMANDY & PARIS

LE HAVRE

1 *Numbers in the margin correspond to points of interest on the Paris map.*

4

The **Musée André-Malraux,** the city art museum, is an innovative 1960s glass-and-metal structure surrounded by a moat, and includes an attractive sea-view café. Two local artists who gorgeously immortalized the Normandy coast are showcased here—Raoul Dufy (1877–1953), through a remarkable collection of his brightly colored oils, watercolors, and sketches; and Eugène Boudin (1824–98), a forerunner of impressionism, whose compelling beach scenes and landscapes tellingly evoke the Normandy sea and skyline. ✉ *2 bd. Clemenceau* ☎ *02–35–19–62–62* 💶 *€5* ⏰ *Wed.–Mon. 11–6.*

Cite Perret. The postwar reconstruction of the city designed by architect Auguste Perret is a tour de force of moderism. Called the "poet of concrete," Perret's new town gained UNESCO World Heritage status for its unique and coherent whole. The style produces very different reactions in people; you either love or hate it. The tourist office in Le Havre organizes 90-minute walking tours of the area, and these can be booked from the cruise terminal welcome center.

HONFLEUR

2 *24 km (15 mi) southeast of Le Havre via A131 and the Pont de Normandie.*

Fodor's Choice ★ The town of Honfleur, full of half-timber houses and cobbled streets, was once an important departure point for maritime expeditions, including the first voyages to Canada in the 15th and 16th centuries. The 17th-century harbor is fronted on one side by two-story stone houses with low, sloping roofs and on the other by tall, narrow houses whose wooden facades are topped by slate roofs. Note that parking can be a problem. Your best bet is the parking lot just beyond the Vieux-Bassin (old harbor) on the left as you approach from the land side.

★ Soak up the seafaring atmosphere by strolling around the old harbor and paying a visit to the ravishing wooden church of **Ste-Catherine,** which dominates a tumbling square. The church and ramshackle belfry across the way were built by townspeople to show their gratitude for the departure of the English at the end of the Hundred Years' War, in 1453. ✉ *Rue des Logettes* ☎ *02–31–89–11–83.*

BAYEUX

3 *10 km (6 mi) southwest of Arromanches via D516, 28 km (17 mi) northwest of Caen.*

Bayeux, the first town to be liberated during the Battle of Normandy, was already steeped in history—as home to a Norman Gothic cathedral and

Paris

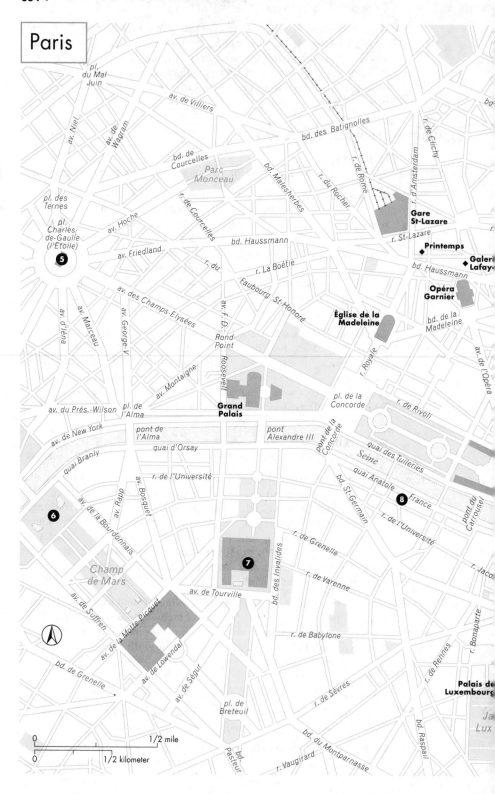

pl.
du Mal
Juin

av. de Villiers

bd. des Batignolles

r. de Clichy

bd. de
Courcelles

r. du Rocher

r. d'Amsterdam

bd. Malesherbes

Parc
Monceau

r. de Rome

r. de Courcelles

Gare
St-Lazare

pl. des
Ternes

av. Hoche

r. St-Lazare

pl.
Charles
de-Gaulle
(l'Étoile)

5

bd. Haussmann

Printemps

av. Friedland

r. du

r. La Boétie

bd. Haussmann

Galeri
Lafay

av. Niel

av. de Wagram

Faubourg St-Honoré

Opéra
Garnier

av. des Champs-Elysées

av. F.-D.-

Église de la
Madeleine

bd. de la
Madeleine

av. d'Iéna

av. Marceau

av. George-V

Rond
Point

Roosevelt

r. Royale

av. de l'Opéra

av. Montaigne

Grand
Palais

pl. de la
Concorde

r. de Rivoli

av. du Prés.-Wilson

pl. de
l'Alma

pont de
l'Alma

pont
Alexandre III

pont de la
Concorde

quai des Tuileries

av. de New York

quai d'Orsay

Seine

quai Branly

r. de l'Université

quai Anatole

pont du
Carrousel

av. Rapp

av. Bosquet

bd. St-Germain

8

France

r. de l'Université

6

av. de la Bourdonnais

r. de Grenelle

r. Jaco

Champ
de Mars

7

bd. des Invalides

r. de Varenne

r. Bonaparte

av. de Suffren

av. de Tourville

r. de Babylone

r. de Rennes

av. de la Motte-Picquet

av. de Lowendal

r. de Sèvres

Palais d
Luxembourg

bd. de Grenelle

av. de Ségur

pl. de
Breteuil

Ja
Lux

bd. Raspail

0   1/2 mile

0   1/2 kilometer

bd. du Montparnasse

bd.
Pasteur

r. Vaugirard

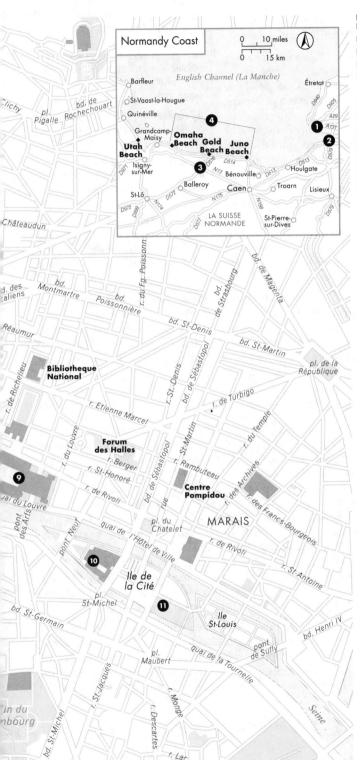

Normandy Coast

0   10 miles
0   15 km

English Channel (La Manche)

Barfleur
Étretat
St-Vaast-la-Hougue
Quinéville
Grandcamp-
Maisy
Omaha
Beach Gold   Juno
Utah   Beach Beach
Beach
Isigny-
sur-Mer
Bénouville
Houlgate
Balleroy
Caen
Troarn
Lisieux
St-Lô
LA SUISSE
NORMANDE
St-Pierre-
sur-Dives

4

the world's most celebrated piece of needlework: the Bayeux Tapestry.

Fodor's Choice ★ The **Bayeux Tapestry** *(Tapestry Museum)*, known in French as the *Tapisserie de la Reine Mathilde* (Queen Matilda's Tapestry), depicts, in 58 comic strip–type scenes, the epic story of William of Normandy's conquest of England in 1066, culminating in the Battle of Hastings on October 14, 1066. The tapestry was probably commissioned from Saxon embroiderers by the count of Kent.

It's showcased in the **Musée de la Tapisserie**; headphones are provided free for you to listen to an English commentary about the tapestry, scene by scene. ⊠ *Centre Guillaume-le-Conquérant, 13 bis rue de Nesmond* ☎ *02–31–51–25–50* ⊠ *€7.70, joint ticket with Musée Baron-Gérard* ⊗ *May–Aug., daily 9–7; Sept.–Apr., daily 9:30–12:30 and 2–6.*

Bayeux's mightiest edifice, the **Cathédrale Notre-Dame** is a harmonious mixture of Norman and Gothic architecture. Note the portal on the south side of the transept that depicts the assassination of English archbishop Thomas à Becket in Canterbury Cathedral in 1170, following his courageous opposition to King Henry II's attempts to control the church. ⊠ *Rue du Bienvenu* ☎ *02–31–92–01–85* ⊗ *Daily 8:30–6.*

THE D-DAY BEACHES

❹ *Omaha Beach is 16 km (10 mi) northwest of Bayeux.*

History focused its sights along the coasts of Normandy at 6:30 AM on June 6, 1944, as the 135,000 men and 20,000 vehicles of the Allied troops made land in their first incursion in Europe in World War II. The entire operation on this "Longest Day" was called Operation Overlord—the code name for the invasion of Normandy. You won't be disappointed by the rugged terrain and windswept sand of **Omaha Beach** (⊠ *16 km [10 mi] northwest of Bayeux*). Here you'll find the **Monument du Débarquement** (Monument to the Normandy Landings) and nearby, in Vierville-sur-Mer, the **U.S. National Guard Monument.** The hilltop American Cemetery and Memorial (⊠ *Colleville-sur-Mer*), designed by the landscape architect Markley Stevenson, is a moving tribute to the fallen, with its Wall of the Missing (in the form of a semicircular colonnade), drumlike chapel, and avenues of holly oaks trimmed to resemble open parachutes.

In **La Madeleine** (⊠ *Plage de La Madeleine* ☎ *02–33–71–53–35*) inspect the glitteringly modern **Utah Beach Landing Museum** (⊠ *Ste-Marie-du-Mont* ☎ *02–33–71–53–35*), whose exhibits include a W5 Utah scale model detailing the German defenses; it's open April–June, September, and October, daily 9:30–noon and 2–6, and July and August, daily 9:30–6:30.

PARIS

A day trip to Paris of just a few hours can barely scratch the surface of what one of the world's greatest city can offer, but that doesn't mean you won't find those few hours really worthwhile. Below are the highlights of the highlights.

⑤ Arc de Triomphe. Set on Place Charles-de-Gaulle—known to Parisians as
★ L'Étoile, or the Star (a reference to the streets that fan out from it)—the colossal, 164-foot Arc de Triomphe arch was planned by Napoléon but not finished until 1836, 20 years after the end of his rule. A small museum halfway up the arch is devoted to its history. France's Unknown Soldier is buried beneath the archway. ✉ *Pl. Charles-de-Gaulle, Champs-Élysées* ☎ *01–55–37–73–77* ⊕ *www.monum.fr* 🎟 *€8* ⊙ *Apr.–Sept., daily 10 AM– 11 PM; Oct.–Mar., daily 10 AM–10:30 PM* Ⓜ *Métro or RER: Étoile.*

⑦ Les Invalides. Famed as the final resting place of Napoléon, the Hôtel des
★ Invalides, to use its official name, is an outstanding monumental baroque ensemble, designed by Libéral Bruand in the 1670s at the behest of Louis XIV to house wounded, or invalid, soldiers. The 17th-century **Église St-Louis des Invalides** is the Invalides's original church. More impressive is Jules Hardouin-Mansart's **Église du Dôme**, which includes **Napoléon's Tomb.** ✉ *Pl. des Invalides, Trocadéro/Tour Eiffel* ☎ *01–44–42–37–72 Army and Model museums* ⊕ *www.invalides.org* 🎟 *€7* ⊙ *Église du Dôme and museums Apr.–Sept., daily 10–6; Oct.–Mar., daily 10–5. Closed 1st Mon. of every month* Ⓜ *La Tour-Maubourg.*

⑨ Louvre. This is the world's greatest art museum—and the largest. The num-
Fodor's Choice ber one attraction—ever more so, since Dan Brown's *The Da Vinci Code*
★ took over best-seller lists the world over—is The Most Famous Painting in the World: Leonardo da Vinci's enigmatic *Mona Lisa* (*La Joconde,* to the French), painted in 1503–06. However, The Louvre is packed with legendary collections, which are divided into seven sections: Asian antiquities; Egyptian antiquities; Greek and Roman antiquities; sculpture; paintings, prints, and drawings; furniture; and objets d'art. ✉ *Palais du Louvre, Louvre/Tuileries* ☎ *01–40–20–53–17* ⊕ *www.louvre.fr* 🎟 *€8.50, €6 after 6 PM Wed. and Fri. Free 1st Sun. of month; €8.50 for Napoléon Hall exhibitions* ⊙ *Mon., Thurs., and weekends, 9–6, Wed. and Fri. 9 AM–10 PM* Ⓜ *Palais-Royal.*

⑧ Musée d'Orsay. In a spectacularly converted belle epoque train station, the
★ Orsay Museum—devoted to the arts (mainly French) spanning the period 1848–1914—is one of the city's most popular, thanks to the presence of the world's greatest collection of impressionist and postimpressionist paintings. There is a dazzling rainbow of masterpieces by Renoir, Sisley, Pissarro, and Monet. Cézanne, van Gogh, Gauguin, and Toulouse-Lautrec, Degas and Matisse, to name just a few.

✉ *1 rue de la Légion d'Honneur, St-Germain-des-Prés* ☎ *01–40–49–48– 14* ⊕ *www.musee-orsay.fr* 🎟 *€7.50, €5.50 Sun.* ⊙ *Tues., Wed., Fri., and Sat. 10–6, Thurs. 10–9:45, Sun. 9–6* Ⓜ *Solférino; RER: Musée d'Orsay.*

⑪ Notre-Dame. Looming above the large, pedestrian Place du Parvis is la cathé-
Fodor's Choice drale de Notre-Dame, the most enduring symbol of Paris. Begun in 1163,
★ completed in 1345, and restored by Viollet-le-Duc in the 19th century,

4

Notre-Dame may not be France's oldest or largest cathedral, but in terms of beauty and architectural harmony, it has few peers. The 387-step climb to the top of the towers is worth the effort for a close-up of the famous gargoyles—most added in the 19th century by Viollet-le-Duc. The spectacular cathedral interior, with its vast proportions, soaring nave, and soft multicolor light dimly filtering through the stained-glass windows, inspires awe. ⊠*Pl. du Parvis, Ile de la Cité* ☏*01–53–10–07–00* ⊕*www.monum. fr* 🎟*Cathedral free, towers €7, crypt €3.30, treasury €2.50, museum €2.50* ⊙*Cathedral daily 8–7. Towers Apr.–June and Sept., daily 9:30– 7:30; July and Aug., weekdays 9–7:30, weekends 9 AM–11 PM; Oct.–Mar., daily 10–5:30. Towers close early when overcrowded. Treasury Mon.–Sat. 9:30–11:30 and 1–5:30. Crypt Tues.–Sun. 10–6. Museum Wed. and weekends 2:30–6* Ⓜ*Cité.*

⑩ Sainte-Chapelle *(Holy Chapel).* Not to be missed and one of the most magical sights in European medieval art, this Gothic chapel was built by Louis IX (1226–70; later canonized as St. Louis) in the 1240s to house what he believed to be Christ's Crown of Thorns, purchased from Emperor Baldwin of Constantinople. A dark lower chapel is a gloomy prelude to the shimmering upper one. Here the famous beauty of Sainte-Chapelle comes alive: instead of walls, all you see are 6,458 square feet of stained glass, delicately supported by painted stonework that seems to disappear in the colorful light streaming through the windows. It's an easy walk here from Notre Dame. ⊠*4 bd. du Palais, Ile de la Cité* ☏*01–53–73– 78–51* ⊕*www.monum.fr* 🎟*€6.10, joint ticket with Conciergerie €10.40* ⊙*Daily 9:30–6, entry closes at 5:30, or 4:30 Nov.–Feb.* Ⓜ*Cité.*

*Fodor's*Choice
★

⑥ Tour Eiffel *(Eiffel Tower).* Known to the French as La Tour Eiffel (pronounced ef-*el*), Paris's most famous landmark was built by Gustave Eiffel for the World Exhibition of 1889. At first many Parisians hated the structure, but now the largest Tinkertoy in the world is the beloved symbol of Paris. If you're full of energy, stride up the stairs as far as the third deck. If you want to go to the top, you'll have to take the elevator. ⊠*Quai Branly, Trocadéro/Tour Eiffel* ☏*01–44–11–23–23* ⊕*www.tour-eiffel.fr* 🎟*By elevator: 2nd fl. €4.10, 3rd fl. €7.50, 4th fl. €10.70. Climbing: 2nd and 3rd fl. only, €3.80* ⊙*June–Aug., daily 9 AM–midnight; Sept.–May, daily 9 AM–11 PM, stairs close at dusk in winter* Ⓜ*Bir-Hakeim; RER: Champ de Mars.*

SHOPPING

The French practically created ready-to-wear fashion—think Cartier, Chanel, and Lacroix. The French love quality and style—and are willing to pay for it—so prices aren't cheap. The vast department stores **Galeries Lafayette** and **Printemps** on Boulevard Haussmann stock a vast range of clothing. The districts on the Left Bank and the Marais offer excellent boutiques selling one-of-a-kind accessories for the body and the home.

Normandy specialties include heavy cotton sailor's smocks, blue-and-white striped T-shirts, and chunky knits; popular choices in this traditional seafaring region. Calvados (distilled apple liqueur) is unique to the area, but other food-stuffs (pure butter and creamy cheeses) aren't really suitable to take home.

Honfleur has a huge choice of art galleries, craft shops, and boutiques with one-of-a-kind items. **Galerie Arthur Boudin** (⊠*6 pl. de l'Hôtel de VilleHonfleur* ☎*02–31–89–06–66*) displays fine range of original paintings, specializing in Normandy landscapes. **Galerie Dassonvalle** (⊠*16 quai Ste CatherineHonfleur* ☎*02–31–89–94–67*) offers prints and limited editions.

WHERE TO EAT

$ ╳**Casino.** You can't get closer to the action. This handsome, postwar, triangular-gabled stone hotel, run by the same family since it was built in the 1950s, looks directly onto Omaha Beach. The bar is made from an old lifeboat, and it's no surprise that fish, seafood, and regional cuisine with creamy sauces predominate in Bruno Clemençon's airy sea-view restaurant. ⊠*Rue de la Percée, Vierville-sur-Mer* ☎*02–31–22–41–02* ▭*AE, MC, V* ⊘*Closed mid-Nov.–late Mar.*

¢–$ ╳**L'Ancrage.** Massive seafood platters top the bill at this bustling restaurant in a two-story 17th-century building overlooking the harbor. The cuisine is authentically Norman—simple but good. If you want a change, try the succulent calf sweetbreads. ⊠*16 rue Montpensier, Honfleur* ☎*02–31–89–00–70* ▭*MC, V* ⊘*Closed Wed. and last 2 wks in Mar. No dinner Tues. Sept.–June.*

LEIXÕES, PORTUGAL (FOR PORTO)

Lining the river that made it a trading center ever since pre-Roman times, vibrant and cosmopolitan Porto centers itself some 5 km (3 mi) inland from the Atlantic Ocean. The Moors never had the same strong foothold here that they did farther south, nor was the city substantially affected by the great earthquake of 1755; as a result, Porto's architecture shows off a baroque finery little seen in the south of Portugal. Its grandiose granite buildings were financed by the trade that made the city wealthy: wine from the upper valley of the Rio Douro (Douro River, or River of Gold) was transported to Porto, from where it was then exported around the world. Industrious Porto considers itself the north's capital and, more contentiously, the country's economic center. In the shopping centers, the stately stock exchange building, and the affluent port-wine industry, Porto oozes confidence though the fashionable commercial heart of the city contrasts with the gritty workaday atmosphere in the old town.

ESSENTIALS

CURRENCY The euro (€1 to US$1.46 at this writing); U.S. currency is generally not accepted in Europe, but ATMs are common and credit cards are widely accepted.

HOURS Most shops are open weekdays 9–1 and 3–7 and Saturday 9–1; malls and supermarkets often remain open until at least 10. Some are also open on Sunday. Note that most museums are closed Monday, and that churches generally close for a couple of hours in the middle of the day.

INTERNET Check your e-mail at **Cybercafe** ⊠*Rua Martires da Libertad, Porto* ☎*22/008–263.*

TELEPHONES Most quad- or tri-band GSM phones work in Portugal, which has a well-organized 3G compatible mobile network. You can buy prepaid phone cards at telecom shops, news vendors and tobacconists in all towns and cities. Phone cards can be used for local or international calls. Major companies include Vodafone and Optimus.

COMING ASHORE

Vessels dock at the quays of Leixões port, just north of the mouth of the River Douro. It's a two-minute walk or a short shuttle trip to the passenger terminal (depending on the exact quay), which has few facilities, but the restaurants and shops of Leixões town are within walking distance. Taxis wait at the port entrance.

From the port, it is another 10-minute walk to the Matosinhos district, where the state-of-the-art metro will transfer you to central Porto in 30 minutes. Single tickets cost between €0.85 and €1.85. A 24-hour card is €7 for all zones (which you'll need for the trip to the port). Bus 76, which has a stop just outside the port, will also take you into Porto, but the journey time is longer.

If you intend to explore Porto on your day in port, the best option by far is to take the metro into the city. For exploration of the vineyards of the Douro River, a vehicle would be useful. Prices are approximately €65 per day for a manual economy car.

EXPLORING PORTO

Numbers in the margin correspond to points of interest on the Porto map.

② Avenida dos Aliados. This imposing boulevard is lined with bright flower beds and grand buildings and is essentially the heart of the central business district. In addition to corporate businesses and banks, you'll find clothing and shoe stores, plus restaurants and coffeehouses. At one end of it is the broad Câmara Municipal (town hall). A tall bell tower sprouts from the roof of this palacelike, early-20th-century building, inside of which an impressive Portuguese wall tapestry is displayed. Praça da Liberdade—the hub from which Porto radiates—is at the other end of the avenue. Two statues adorn the square: a cast of Dom Pedro IV sitting on a horse and a modern statue of the great 19th-century Portuguese poet and novelist Almeida Garrett.

⑥ Cais da Ribeira. A string of fish restaurants and *tascas* (taverns) are built
Fodor's Choice into the street-level arcade of timeworn buildings along this pier. In the
★ Praça da Ribeira, people sit and chat around an odd, modern, cubelike sculpture; farther on, steps lead to a walkway above the river that's backed by tall houses. The pier also provides the easiest access to the lower level of the middle bridge across the Douro. Boats docked at Cais da Ribeira offer various cruises around the bridges and up the river to Peso da Régua and Pinhão.

⑤ Casa-Museu de Guerra Junqueiro. This 18th-century white mansion, another of the city's buildings attributed by some to a pupil of Italian painter and architect Nicolau Nasoni and by others to Nasoni himself, was home to the poet Guerra Junqueiro (1850–1923). Although furnishings, sculptures, and paintings are labeled in Portuguese, English, and French (and there are brochures in English), the short tour of the elegant interior is less than enlightening if you don't speak Portuguese. ⊠ *Rua de Dom Hugo*

Porto

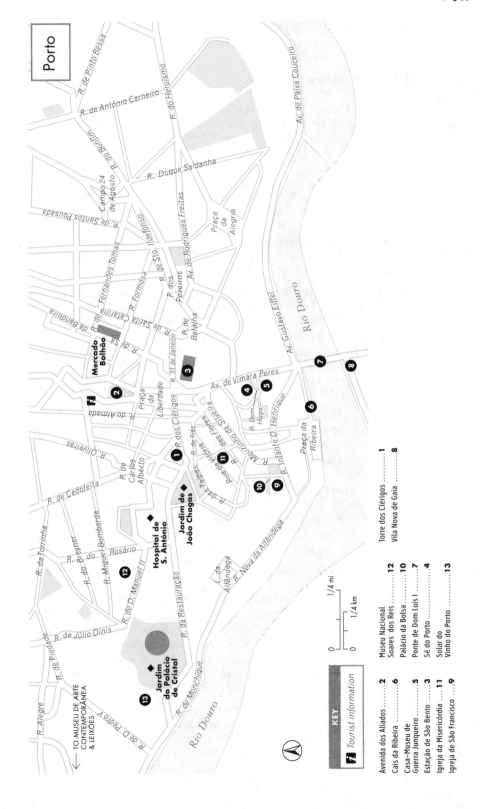

0 ———— 1/4 mi
0 ———— 1/4 km

TO MUSEU DE ARTE
CONTEMPORÂNEA
& LEIXÕES

32 ☎*22/200–3689* 🎫*Tues.–Fri.* €*1, free weekends* ☉*Tues.–Sat. 10–12:30 and 2–5:30, Sun. 2–5:30.*

❸ **Estação de São Bento.** This train station

Fodor'sChoice   was built in the early 20th century

★   (King D. Carlos I laid the first brick himself in 1900) and inaugurated in 1915, precisely where the Convent of S. Bento de Avé-Maria was located. Therefore it inherited the convent's name—Saint Bento. The atrium is covered with 20,000 azulejos painted by Jorge Colaço (1916) depicting scenes of Portugal's history as well as ethnographic images.

✉*Praça Almeida Garret* ☎*22/205–1714* ☎*808/208208 national call center* ⊕*www.cp.pt.*

⓫ **Igreja da Misericórdia.** Today's building represents a compromise between the church first built during the late 16th century and its reconstruction between 1749 and 1755 Nicolau Nasoni. At the church museum next door you can see *Fons Vitae* (Fountain of Life), a vibrant, anonymous, Renaissance painting, depicting the founder of the church, Dom Manuel I, his queen, and their eight children kneeling before a crucified Christ. ✉*Rua das Flores 5* ☎*22/207–4710* ⊕*www.scmp.pt* 🎫*Church free, museum* €*1.50* ☉*Church Tues.–Fri. 8–12:30 and 2–5:30, museum weekdays 9:30–12:30 and 2–5:30.*

❾ **Igreja de São Francisco.** During the last days of Porto's siege by the absolutist army (the *miguelistas*) in July 1842, there was gunfire by the nearby São Francisco Convent. These shootings caused a fire that destroyed most parts of the convent, sparing only this church. The church is an undistinguished, late-14th-century Gothic building on the outside, but inside is an astounding interior: gilded carving—added in the mid-18th century—runs up the pillars, over the altar, and across the ceiling. ✉*Rua do Infante Dom Henrique 93* ☎*22/206–2100* 🎫€*3* ☉*Nov.–Mar., daily 9–5; Apr.–Oct., daily 9–6; May–Sept., daily 9–7.*

⓬ **Museu Nacional Soares dos Reis.** This art museum was the first in Portugal,

★   founded in 1833 by King D. Pedro IV. In 1911 it was renamed after the 19th-century Portuguese sculptor whose works are contained within it. In 1940 it moved to this late-19th-century home, the Palácio dos Carrancas, which was once home to the royal family. The large art collection includes several Portuguese primitive works of the 16th century as well as superb collections of silver, ceramics, glassware, and costumes. ✉*Palácio dos Carrancas, Rua de Dom Manuel II* ☎*22/339–3770* ⊕*www.ipmuseus.pt* 🎫*Tues.–Sat.* €*3, free Sun.* ☉*Tues. 2–6, Wed.–Sun. 10–12:30 and 2–6.*

❿ **Palácio da Bolsa.** Porto's 19th-century, neoclassical stock exchange takes

Fodor'sChoice   up much of the site of the former Franciscan convent at the Igreja de São

★   Francisco. Guided tours are the only way to see the interior of this masterpiece of 19th-century Portuguese architecture. The Arab-style ballroom, in particular, is one of the most admired chambers and was designed by civil engineer Gustavo Adolfo Gonçalves e Sousa. ⊠*Rua Ferreira Borges* ☎*22/339–9013* ⊕*www.palaciodabolsa.pt* 🎫*Tours €5* ⊙*Apr.–Oct., daily 9–7; Nov.–Mar., daily 9–1 and 2–6.*

❼ Ponte de Dom Luís I. This two-tier bridge, completed in 1886, leads directly to the city of Vila Nova de Gaia. Designed by Teófilo Seyrig it affords the magnificent vistas of downtown Porto. A jumble of red-tile roofs on pastel-color buildings mixes with gray-and-white Gothic and baroque church towers, and all is reflected in the majestic Douro River; if the sun is shining just right, everything appears to be washed in gold.

❹ Sé do Porto. Originally constructed in the 12th century by the parents of Afonso Henriques (Portugal's first king), Porto's granite cathedral has been rebuilt twice: first in the late 13th century and again in the 18th century, Nicolau Nasoni, was among those commissioned to work on its expansion. Despite the renovations, it remains a fortresslike structure—an uncompromising testament to medieval wealth and power. Notice a low relief on the northern tower, depicting a 14th-century vessel and symbolizing the city's nautical vocation. Size is the only exceptional thing about the interior; when you enter the two-story, 14th-century cloisters, however, the building comes to life. Decorated with gleaming azulejos, a staircase added by Nasoni leads to the second level and into a richly furnished chapter house, from which there are fine views through narrow windows. ⊠*Terreiro da Sé* ☎*22/205–9028* 🎫*Cathedral free; cloisters €2 per person if group is fewer than 10 people, €1.25 per person for groups of 10 or more* ⊙*Mon.–Sat. 9–12:30 and 2:30–6, Sun. 2:30–6.*

⓭ Solar do Vinho do Porto. Located in a 19th-century country house called the
★ Quinta da Macierinha, the institute offers relaxed tastings of Porto's famous wine. Tasting prices start at around €0.80 per glass. The Quinta da Macierinha is home to the **Museu Romântico da Quinta da Macierinha** (Romantic Museum), with displays of period furniture. ⊠*Quinta da Macierinha, Rua de Entre Quintas 220* ☎*22/609–4749 Port Wine Institute, 22/605–7033 museum, 22/606–6207 for guided tours* ✏solarporto@ivp.pt ⊕*www.ivp. pt* 🎫*Port Wine Institute free, tasting prices vary, museum €1* ⊙*Port Wine Institute Mon.–Sat. 2–midnight; museum Tues.–Sat. 10–12:30 and 2–5:30, Sun. 2–6.*

❶ Torre dos Clérigos. Designed by Italian architect Nicolau Nasoni and begun in 1754, the tower of the church Igreja dos Clérigos reaches an impressive height of 249 feet. There are 225 steep stone steps to the belfry, and the considerable effort required to climb them is rewarded by stunning views of the old town, the river, and beyond to the mouth of the Douro. The church itself, also built by Nasoni, predates the tower and is an elaborate example of Italianate baroque architecture. ⊠*Rua S. Filipe Nery* ☎*22/200–1729* 🎫*Tower €1.50* ⊙*Tower Sept.–May, daily 10–noon and 2–5; June and July, daily 9:30–1 and 2–7; Aug., daily 10–7. Church Mon.–Thurs. and Sat. 9–noon and 3:30–7:30, Sun. 10–1 and 8:30–10:30.*

❽ Vila Nova de Gaia. A city across the Rio Douro from central Porto, Vila Nova de Gaia has been the headquarters of the port-wine trade since the late 17th century, when import bans on French wine led British merchants to look for alternative sources. By the 18th century, the British had established companies and a regulatory association in Porto. The wine was transported from vineyards on the upper Douro to port-wine caves at Vila Nova de Gaia, where it was allowed to mature before being exported. Very little has changed in the relationship between Porto and the Douro since those days, as wine is still transported to the city, matured in the warehouses, and bottled. Instead of traveling down the river on *barcos rabelos* (flat-bottom boats), however, the wine is now carried by truck. A couple of the traditional boats are moored at the quayside on the Vila Nova de Gaia side. *For more on the port companies here, see Shopping, below.*

SHOPPING

The Portuguese specialize in a range of handicrafts collectively known as *artesanato*. The term includes bright *azulejos* (blue-and-white-glaze tiles), pottery and ceramics, colorful textiles, olive wood, cork items and basket wear. Gold and plated filigree is also a regional specialty, and the shoe trade is well established. You'll see port on sale throughout the city. But first taste the wine at either the Solar do Vinho do Porto or the caves at Vila Nova de Gaia. You may want to buy a bottle of the more unusual white port, drunk as an aperitif, as it's not commonly sold in North America.

The best shopping streets are those off the Praça da Liberdade, particularly Rua 31 de Janeiro, Rua dos Clérigos, Rua de Santa Catarina, Rua Sá da Bandeira, Rua Cedofeita, and Rua das Flores. Traditionally, Rua das Flores has been the street for silversmiths found along the same street and along Rua de Santa Catarina. Rua 31 de Janeiro you'll find goldsmiths working.

Fodor's Choice ★ The **Artesanato Centro Regional de Artes Tradicionais** (*Center for Traditional Arts* ⊠*Rua da Reboleira 37* ☎*22/332–0201*) has an excellent selection of regional arts and crafts. **Livraria Lello e Irmão** (⊠*Rua das Carmelitas 144* ☎*22/200–2880*) is one of the most special and important bookshops in Portugal. It opened in 1906, and shelters more than 60,000 books. It is also famous for its neo-Gothic design and two-story interior with intricate wood-carved details.

WHERE TO EAT

¢–$ ✗**Chez Lapin.** At this Cais da Ribeira restaurant overlooking the river, the
Fodor's Choice ★ service may be slow and the folksy decor may be overdone, but the food is excellent, and the outdoor terrace is attractive. The menu has such traditional but sometimes uncommon Porto dishes as bacalhau *e polvo assado no forno* (baked and with octopus) and *caldeirada de peixe* (fish stew), all served in generous portions. ⊠*Rua Canastreiros 40–42* ☎*22/200–6418 or 22/208–0677* ⚱*Reservations essential* ⊟*AE, DC, MC, V.*

¢–$ ✗**Majestic Café.** Opened in 1921, this is one of Porto's grand old coffee-
★ houses, and it serves double duty as a reasonably priced grill-restaurant. Sit amid the sculpted wood, carved nymphs, and mirrors and choose from a fair list of omelets, sandwiches, salads, burgers, and steaks. Or just have coffee and a pastry. ⊠*Rua de Santa Catarina 112* ☎*22/200–3887* ⊟*AE, DC, MC, V* ⊗*Closed Sun.*

LISBON, PORTUGAL

Lisbon bears the mark of an incredible heritage with laid-back pride. Spread over a string of seven hills north of the Rio Tejo (Tagus River) estuary, the city also presents an intriguing variety of faces to those who negotiate its switchback streets. In the oldest neighborhoods, stepped alleys are lined with pastel-color houses and crossed by laundry hung out to dry; here and there *miradouros* (vantage points) afford spectacular river or city views. In the grand 18th-century center, black-and-white mosaic cobblestone sidewalks border wide boulevards. *Elétricos* (trams) clank through the streets, and blue-and-white azulejos (painted and glazed ceramic tiles) adorn churches, restaurants, and fountains. Some modernization has improved the city. To prepare for its role as host of the World Exposition in 1998, Lisbon spruced up its public buildings, overhauled its metro system, and completed an impressive bridge across the Rio Tejo, but Lisbon's intrinsic, slightly disorganized, one-of-a-kind charm hasn't vanished in the contemporary mix.

ESSENTIALS

CURRENCY The euro (€1 to US$1.46 at this writing); U.S. currency is generally not accepted in Europe, but ATMs are common and credit cards are widely accepted.

HOURS Most shops are open weekdays 9–1 and 3–7 and Saturday 9–1; malls and supermarkets often remain open until at least 10. Some are also open on Sunday. Note that most museums are closed Monday, and that churches generally close for a couple of hours in the middle of the day.

INTERNET **Pavilhão do Conhecimento** (⊠*Parque das Nações* ☎*21/891–9898*) has a cybercafé with free Internet access. It's open Tuesday–Friday 10–6, weekends and holidays 11–7.

TELEPHONES You can use most tri- and quad-band GSM phones in Portugal, which has a well-organized 3G-compatible mobile network. You can buy prepaid phone cards at telecom shops, news-vendors, and tobacconists in all towns and cities. Phone cards can be used for local or international calls. Major companies include Vodafone and Optimus.

COMING ASHORE

Vessels dock at one of three quays along the River Tagus in a port area rebuilt for Expo '98 (the 1998 World's Fair). The main cruise port is the Cais de Alcántara, which has a a terminal with shops, taxi ranks, and restrooms, Cais da Rocha Conde Óbidos also has a terminal with the same facilities. From both these terminals there are public transit routes into the city by bus (Buses 28, 201, 714, 727, 729, 751) or tram (Tram 15E). A suburban train also runs alongside the cruise terminal, and the Alcántara Mar station is the place to get on; the trip to Lisbon's main railway station takes about 10 minutes. Fares for all these options are €1.30 per journey. The walk into town from the cruise port takes around an hour but is not unpleasant if you have the time.

Some small and midsize ships call at a smaller terminal in Santa Apolónia, which is closer to the center of the city and from where it's possible to walk to Alfalma and central Lisbon.

Lisbon

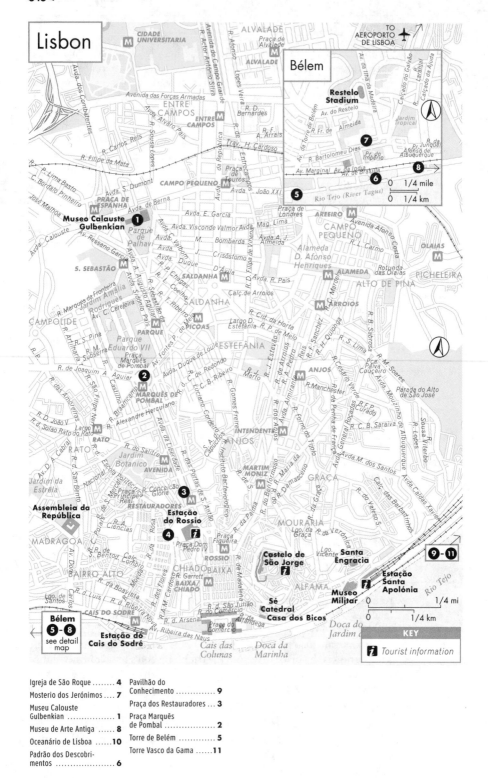

Bélem

KEY

i Tourist information

There are many companies running tours of the city. Don't rent a car if you are staying in Lisbon, where navigation and parking are almost impossible, but if you want to explore the countryside, you'll need one. An economy manual vehicle is about €72 per day.

EXPLORING LISBON

Numbers in the margin correspond to points of interest on the Lisbon map.

The center of Lisbon stretches north from the spacious Praça do Comércio—one of Europe's largest riverside squares—to the Rossío, a smaller square lined with shops and cafés. The district in between is known as the Baixa (lower town), an attractive grid of parallel streets built after the 1755 earthquake and tidal wave. The Alfama, the old Moorish quarter that survived the earthquake, lies east of the Baixa. In this part of town are the Sé (the city's cathedral) and, on the hill above, the Castelo de São Jorge (St. George's Castle).

West of the Baixa, sprawled across another of Lisbon's hills, is the Bairro Alto (upper town), an area of intricate 17th-century streets, peeling houses, and churches. Five kilometers (3 mi) farther west is Belém. A similar distance to the northeast is Lisbon's post modernist Parque das Nações.

The modern city begins at Praça dos Restauradores, adjacent to the Rossío. From here the main Avenida da Liberdade stretches northwest to the landmark Praça Marquês de Pombal, dominated by a column and a towering statue of the man himself. The praça is bordered by the green expanse of the Parque Eduardo VII, named in honor of King Edward VII of Great Britain, who visited Lisbon in 1902.

❹ Igreja de São Roque. Filippo Terzi, the architect who designed São Vicente on the outskirts of the Alfama, was also responsible for this Renaissance church. He was commissioned by Jesuits and completed the church in 1574. Curb your impatience with its plain facade and venture inside. Its eight side chapels have statuary and art dating from the early 17th century. The last chapel on the left before the altar is the extraordinary 18th-century Capela de São João Baptista (Chapel of St. John the Baptist): designed and built in Rome, with rare stones and mosaics that resemble oil paintings, the chapel was taken apart, shipped to Lisbon, and reassembled here in 1747. ⌂*Largo Trindade Coelho, Bairro Alto* ☎*21/323–5381* ✆*Church free; museum €1.50 Mon.–Sat., free Sun.* ☉*Church weekdays 8:30–5, weekends 9:30–5; museum daily 10–5* Ⓜ*Baixa-Chiado.*

FodorsChoice ★

❼ Mosteiro dos Jerónimos. Conceived and commissioned by Dom Manuel I, who petitioned the Holy See for permission to build it in 1496, Belém's

FodorsChoice ★

> ### LISBON BEST BETS
>
> **Take time to enjoy the exquisite decoration at the Mosteiro dos Jerónimos.** Paid for with the profits from the sale of treasures from New World colonies.
>
> **Enjoy the first-class artifacts on display at Museu Calouste Gulbenkian.** The collection reflects the personal taste of Gulbenkian himself.
>
> **Stroll the avenues of the Biaxa district.** An architectural whole built after the devastating earthquake of 1755 is Lisbon's most attractive neoclassical neighborhood.

famous Jerónimos Monastery was financed largely by treasures brought back from Africa, Asia, and South America. Construction began in 1502. The monastery is a supreme example of the Manueline style of building (named after King Dom Manuel I), which represented a marked departure from the prevailing Gothic. Much of it is characterized by elaborate sculptural details. Inside, the remarkably spacious interior contrasts with the riot of decoration on the six nave columns, which disappear into a complex latticework ceiling. ⊠*Praça do Império, Belém* ☎*21/362–0034* ⊕*www.mosteirojeronimos.pt* 🖃*Cloister €4.50, free Sun.* ☉*May–Sept., Tues.–Sun. 10–6:30; Oct.–Apr., Tues.–Sun. 10–5.*

❶ Museu Calouste Gulbenkian. On its own lush grounds, the museum of the celebrated Fundação Calouste Gulbenkian (Calouste Gulbenkian Foundation), a cultural trust, houses treasures collected by Armenian oil magnate Calouste Gulbenkian (1869–1955) and donated to the people of Portugal in return for tax concessions. The collection is split in two: one part is devoted to Egyptian, Greek, Roman, Islamic, and Asian art and the other to European acquisitions. Both holdings are relatively small, but the quality of the pieces on display is magnificent.

Fodor's Choice
★

One of the highlights in the astounding Egyptian Room is a haunting gold mummy mask. Greek and Roman coins and statuary, Chinese porcelain, Japanese prints, and a set of rich 16th- and 17th-century Persian tapestries follow. The European art section has pieces from all the major schools from the 15th through the 20th century. ⊠*Av. de Berna 45, São Sebastião* ☎*21/782–3000* ⊕*www.museu.gulbenkian.pt* 🖃*€3, combined ticket with Modern Art Center €5; free Sun.* ☉*Tues.–Sun. 10–5:45* Ⓜ*São Sebastião or Praça de Espanha.*

❽ Museu de Arte Antiga. The only museum in Lisbon to approach the status of the Gulbenkian is the Ancient Art Museum, founded in 1884. It was the first large public museum dedicated to the arts in Portugal. In a 17th-century palace, once owned by the Counts of Alvor, and vastly enlarged in 1940 when it took over the Convent of St. Albert, it has a beautifully displayed collection of Portuguese art—mainly from the 15th through 19th century. Of all the holdings, the religious works of the Portuguese school of artists (characterized by fine portraiture with a distinct Flemish influence) stand out, especially the acknowledged masterpiece of Nuno Gonçalves, the *St. Vincent Altarpiece.* ⊠*Rua das Janelas Verdes, Lapa* ☎*21/396–2825 or 21/396–4151* ⊕*www.mnarteantiga-ipmuseus. pt* 🖃*€3* ☉*Tues. 2–6, Wed.–Sun. 10–6.*

Fodor's Choice
★

❿ Oceanário de Lisboa. With 25,000 fish, seabirds, and mammals, this is Europe's largest aquarium and the first ever to incorporate several ocean habitats (North Atlantic, Pacific, Antarctic, and Indian) in one place. ⊠*Esplanada D. Carlos I (Doca dos Olivais), Parque das Nações* ☎*21/891–7002 or 21/891–7006* ⊕*www.oceanario.pt* 🖃*€10.50* ☉*Apr.–Oct., daily 10–8, last admission 7; Nov.–Mar., daily 10–7, last admission 6.*

❻ Padrão dos Descobrimentos. The white, monolithic Monument of the Discoveries was erected in 1960 to commemorate the 500th anniversary of the death of Prince Henry the Navigator. It was built on what was the departure point for many voyages of discovery, including those of Vasco da Gama for India and—during Spain's occupation of Portugal—of the Spanish Armada for England in 1588. Henry is at the prow of the monument, facing the water; lined up behind him are the Portuguese explorers of Brazil and Asia, as well as other national heroes. On the ground adjacent to the monument an inlaid map shows the extent of the explorations undertaken by the 15th- and 16th-century Portuguese sailors. ⊠*Av. de Brasília, Belém* ☎*21/303–1950* ☷*€2.50; 15-min movie €2, 30-min movie €3* ☉*Tues.–Sun. 10–7.*

❾ **Pavilhão do Conhecimento.** The white, angular, structure designed by architect Carrilho de Graça for the expo seems the perfect place to house the Knowledge Pavilion, or Living Science Centre, as it's also known. All of the permanent and temporary exhibits here are related to math, science, and technology. ⊠*Parque das Nações* ☎*21/891–9898* ⊕*www. pavconhecimento.pt* ☷*€6* ☉*Tues.–Fri. 10–6, weekends and holidays 11–7.*

❷ **Praça Marquês de Pombal.** Dominating the center of Marquês de Pombal Square is a statue of the marquês himself, the man responsible for the design of the "new" Lisbon that emerged from the ruins of the 1755 earthquake. On the statue's base are representations of both the earthquake and the tidal wave that engulfed the city; a female figure with outstretched arms signifies the joy at the emergence of the refashioned city.

❸ **Praça dos Restauradores.** Although this square, which is adjacent to Rossío train station, marks the beginning of modern Lisbon, it's technically part of the Baixa district. Here the broad, tree-lined Avenida da Liberdade starts its northwesterly ascent. *Restauradores* means "restoration," and the square commemorates the 1640 uprising against Spanish rule that restored Portuguese independence. An obelisk (raised in 1886) commemorates the event. Note the elegant 18th-century Palácio Foz, on the square's west side. Today it houses a tourist office. The only building to rival the palace is the restored Eden building, just to the south.

❺ **Torre de Belém.** The openwork balconies and domed turrets of the fanciful
★ Belém Tower make it perhaps the country's purest Manueline structure. It was built between 1514 and 1520 on an island in the middle of the Rio Tejo, and dedicated to St. Vincent, the patron saint of Lisbon. Today the chalk-white tower stands near what has become the north bank—evidence of the river's changing course. It was originally constructed to defend the port entrance, but it has also served as a customs control point, a telegraph station, a lighthouse, and even a prison from the late-16th through the 19th centuries. ⊠*Av. de Brasília, Belém* ☎*21/362– 0034* ☷*€3* ☉*Wed.–Sun. 10–6.*

⓫ **Torre Vasco da Gama.** Rising 480 feet, the graceful, white Vasco da Gama Tower is Portugal's tallest structure. Three glass elevators whisk you up 345 feet to the observation deck. In addition to taking in vistas across Lisbon and the Atlantic Ocean, you'll feel as if you're eye to eye with the 18-km (11-mi) Ponte Vasco da Gama (Vasco da Gama Bridge). ⊠*Av. Pinto Ribeiro, Parque das Nações* ☎*21/893–9550* ☷*€2.49* ☉*Daily 10–6.*

SHOPPING

Although fire destroyed much of Chiado, Lisbon's smartest shopping district, in 1988, a good portion of the area has been restored. The neighborhood has a large new shopping complex as well as many small stores with considerable cachet, particularly on and around Rua Garrett. The Baixa's grid of streets from the Rossío to the Rio Tejo have many small shops selling jewelry, shoes, clothing, and foodstuffs. The Bairro Alto is full of little crafts shops with stylish, contemporary goods. Excellent stores continue to open in the residential districts north of the city, at Praça de Londres and Avenida de Roma. Most of Lisbon's antiques shops are in the Rato and Bairro Alto districts along one long street, which changes its name four times as it runs southward from Largo do Rato: Rua Escola Politécnica, Rua Dom Pedro V, Rua da Misericórdia, and Rua do Alecrim.

Handmade goods, such as leather handbags, shoes, gloves, embroidery, ceramics, linens and basketwork, are sold throughout the city. Apart from top designer fashions and high-end antiques, prices are moderate.

Antiquália (⊠ *Praça Luís de Camões 37, Chiado* ☎ *21/342–3260)* is packed with furniture, chandeliers, and porcelain. The **Atelier** (⊠ *Rua dos Bacalhoeiros 12-A, Alfama* ☎ *21/886–5563* ⊕ *www.loja-descobrimentos.com*), specializes in hand-painted tiles. You can often see an artist at work here. What's more, they ship worldwide and you can even order online. Portugal's most famous porcelain producer, **Vista Alegre** (⊠ *Largo do Chiado 18, Chiado* ☎ *21/346–1401*), established its factory in 1824.

WHERE TO EAT

¢–$$ ✕ **Andorra.** On the renowned Baixa street of fish restaurants, the Andorra is a perfect place for a simple lunch; from the terrace you can people-watch and smell the charcoal-grilled sardines. The friendly staff serves plates of well-cooked Portuguese favorites, and you can choose from a short wine list that caters to most tastes. ⊠ *Rua Portas de Santo Antão 82, Restauradores* ☎ *21/342–6047* ▭ *MC, V.*

¢–$ ✕ **Solar dos Bicos.** As the name implies, this charming restaurant with stone arches and beautiful azulejos offers typical Portuguese cuisine at very reasonable prices. ⊠ *Rua dos Bacalhoeiros, 8-A, Alfama* ☎ *21/886–9447* ⊕ *www.solardosbicos.com* ▭ *MC, V.*

LIVORNO, ITALY (FOR FLORENCE & PISA)

One of the biggest and grittiest ports on the northwestern Italian coast, Livorno has little to attract visitors in itself. Nevertheless, the city is one of the most popular cruise ports of call in the western Mediterranean as the gateway to some of Italy's finest attractions, the cities of Florence and Pisa, not to mention the delightful landscapes of Tuscany. Florence, the city of the lily, gave birth to the Renaissance and changed the way we see the world. For centuries it has captured the imagination of travelers, who have come seeking rooms with views and phenomenal art. Pisa is famous for one of the world's most quirky historical attractions: its leaning tower, but this structure is one part of a triumvirate that offers one of the most dramatic architectural vista's in the country. It's unlikely you'll have time to see everything during this port stop, so plan your time wisely.

ESSENTIALS

CURRENCY The euro (€1 to US$1.46 at this writing); U.S. currency is generally not accepted in Europe, but ATMs are common.

HOURS   Shops are generally open 9 to 1 and 3:30 to 7:30 and are closed Sunday and Monday morning most of the year. Summer (June to September) hours are usually 9 to 1 and 4 to 8, and some shops close Saturday afternoon instead of Monday morning.

INTERNET   **Internet Train** (⊠ *Borgo San Jacappo 30/r, Florence* ☎ *055/2657935*) has views of the Ponte Vecchio, so you can sightsee and surf at the same time.

TELEPHONES   Tri-band GSM phones work in Italy. You can buy prepaid phone cards at telecom shops, news-vendors, and tobacconists in all towns and cities. Phone cards can be used for local or international calls.

COMING ASHORE

The port of Livorno has good cruise facilities, including car rental offices, ticket and information offices, a bar, and a garden. It is near the heart of the town, just a few blocks from Livorno's central area. The railway station is 3 km (2 mi) from the port, but there is no good public transport option there, so take a taxi at a cost of about €20.

Trains from Livorno to Florence currently run once per hour throughout the day. The journey time is about 90 minutes. Prices are about €12 round-trip. From Livorno, it is just a 15-minute train journey to Pisa at a price of about €1.70; from Pisa Central Station take a train to San Rossore, from where it is a 5-minute walk to the leaning tower area. If you buy tickets on Trenitalia's (Italian railways') Web site (⊕ *www.trenitalia.com*), you can print them out at self-service machines in Livorno station.

Taxis charge approximately €2.33 initially, then €0.78 per km (½-mi) with an additional €0.11 per 140 meters (260 feet) when the taxi travels at less than 20 kph (12 mph). Car rental would give you greater flexibility to explore Tuscany, but if you are going only to Florence, then a train will be better since parking is difficult in Florence. Rentals are approximately €45 per day for a compact manual vehicle.

EXPLORING FLORENCE & PISA

FLORENCE
95 km (60 mi) east of Livorno, 82 km (51 mi) east of Pisa.

The heart of Florence, stretching from the Piazza del Duomo south to the Arno, is as dense with artistic treasures as anyplace in the world. The churches, medieval towers, Renaissance palaces, and world-class museums and galleries contain some of the most outstanding aesthetic achievements of Western history.

Numbers in the margin correspond to points of interest on the Florence map.

❺ **Bargello.** During the Renaissance, this building was headquarters for the *podestà*, or chief magistrate. Today it houses the **Museo Nazionale,** home ★ to what is probably the finest collection of Renaissance sculpture in Italy. For Renaissance-art lovers, the Bargello is to sculpture what the Uffizi is to painting. ⊠ *Via del Proconsolo 4, Bargello* ☎ *055/2388606* ⊕ *www. polomuseale.firenze.it* ☞ €4 ⊙ *Daily 8:15–6; closed 2nd and 4th Mon. of month and 1st, 3rd, and 5th Sun. of month.*

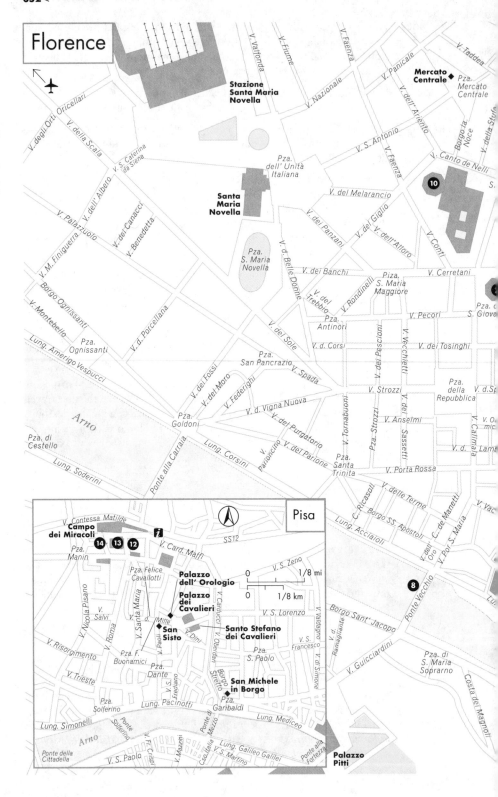

Florence

Stazione
Santa Maria
Novella

Mercato
Centrale

Pza.
Mercato
Centrale

V. Valfonda
V. Fiume
V. Faenza
V. Panicale
V. Taddea
V. della Stufa
V. Nazionale
V. S. Antonio
V. Faenza
V. dell' Ariento
Borgo la Noce
V. Canto de Nelli

V. degli Orti Oricellari
V. della Scala
V. S. Caterina da Siena
V. Palazzuolo
V. dell' Albero
V. dei Canacci
V. Benedetta

Pza.
dell' Unità
Italiana

Santa
Maria
Novella

10

V. del Melarancio
V. dei Panzani
V. del Giglio
V. dell' Alloro
V. Conti

Pza.
S. Maria
Novella

V. M. Finiguerra
Borgo Ognissanti
V. Montebello
Lung. Amerigo Vespucci

V. d. Porcellana
V. d. Belle Donne
V. del Trebbio
V. dei Banchi
V. Rondinelli
Piza. S. Maria Maggiore
V. Cerretani
S. Giova

Pza.
Ognissanti

Pza.
Antinori

V. Pecori

Pza. d.
S. Giova

Arno

V. dei Fossi
V. del Moro
V. del Sole
V. d. Corsi
V. dei Pesciolini
V. Vecchietti
V. dei Tosinghi

Pza.
San Pancrazio
V. Spada

Pza. di
Cestello

V. Federighi
V. d. Vigna Nuova
V. Strozzi
V. dei Sassetti
Pza. della Repubblica
V. d. Sp

Pza.
Goldoni

V. del Purgatorio
V. del Parione
V. Tornabuoni
V. Anselmi
V. O.
mic

Lung. Soderini

Ponte alla Carraia
Lung. Corsini
V. Parioncino
Pza.
Santa
Trinita

V. Porta Rossa
V. d. Lamt
V. d. Calimala

Lung. Acciaioli
V. delle Terme
C. Ricasoli
Borgo SS. Apostoli
C. de Maretti
V. Vac

Pisa

Campo
dei Miracoli

14 13 12

Pza.
Manin

V. Contessa Matilde
V. Card. Maffi
SS12

Pza. Felice
Cavallotti

Palazzo
dell' Orologio

Palazzo
dei
Cavalieri

V. S. Zeno

0   1/8 mi

0   1/8 km

V. Nicola Pisano
V. Salvi
V. Santa Maria
V. Roma
V. d.
Mille
V. Paoli
V. d. Dini

San
Sisto

Santo Stefano
dei Cavalieri

V. Carducci
V. Oberdan
V. S. Lorenzo

V. Risorgimento
Pza. F.
Buonamici
Pza.
Dante

V. S. Frediano

V. S.
Francesco
Pza.
S. Paolo

V. di Simone

8

V. Trieste

Borgo
Stretto

San Michele
in Borgo

Borgo Sant' Jacopo

Ponte Vecchio

Pza. di
S. Maria
Soprarno

Pza.
Solferino

Lung. Pacinotti

Pza.
Garibaldi

Lung. Mediceo

V. Guicciardini

Costa dei Magnoli

Lung. Simonelli

Ponte
Solferino

Ponte
di
Mezzo

Arno

Ponte della
Cittadella

V. F. C. Crispi
V. Mazzini
C. S. d'Italia
V. S. Martino
Lung. Galileo Galilei

Ponte alla
Fortezza

Palazzo
Pitti

V. S. Paolo

TO CHIOSTRO
DELLA SCALZA

**Santissima
Annunziata**

V. Guella

V. C. Battisti

V. Gino Capponi

V. San Gallo

V. Cavour

V. de Ginori

11

Pza. della
SS. Annunziata

V. della
Colonna

V. Laura

V. Ricasoli

**Palazzo
Medici-
Riccardi**

V. Martelli

V. Pucci

V. dei Servi

V. d. Castellaccio

V. degli Alfani

enzo

V. Bufalini

V. della Pergola

V. Nuova
dei Caccini

1

3 Pza.
del Duomo

4

V. S. Egidio

Borgo Pinti

V. d. Calzaivoli

V. d.Oche

V. d. Studio

V. del Proconsolo

V. Fiesolana

Pza.
San Pier
Maggiore

Pza.
Salvemini

V. del Corso

Borgo degli Albizi

V. d.
Tavolini

V. Dante Alighieri

V. dei Pandolfini

V. San Pier
Maggiore

V. dell' Ulivo

V. dei Cimatori

V. dei Magazzini

V. Matteo Palmieri

V. dell' Agnolo

V. della Condotta

5

V. Ghibellina

Pza.
S. Firenze

V. della Vigna Vecchia

V. Giuseppe Verdi

V. Verrazzano

V. Ghibellina

Pza. della
Signoria

V. d.Gondi

V. dell'Acqua

V. d. Burella

V. Anguillara

V. Torta

6

Borgo dei Greci

Pza.
Santa
Croce

ccia

V. Leoni

V. d. Corno

V. Vinegia

V. d. Parlascio

V. dei Neri

V. d. Magalotti

V. d. Rustici

V. de' Benci

V. di
S. Giuseppe

7

Pza.
dei
Giudici

i

9

chibusteri

V. Antonio Magliabechi

Borgo S. Croce

V. d. Vagelli

V. V. Malenchini

Corso Tintori

Lung. Diaz

no

Lung. d. Grazie

V. Tripoli

Lung. d.
Zecca Vecchia

Ponte alle Grazie

Arno

Lung. Torrigiani

V. dei Bardi

Scarpuccia

Pza.
dei Mozzi

Lung. Serristori

KEY

i *Tourist information*

0 ———— 1/4 mi

0 ———— 1/4 km

4

② **Battistero** *(Baptistery)*. The octagonal Baptistery across from the Duomo is one of the supreme monuments of the Italian Romanesque style and one of Florence's oldest structures. The interior dome mosaics from the beginning of the 14th century are justly renowned, but—glittering beauties though they are—they could never outshine the building's famed bronze Renaissance doors decorated with panels crafted by Lorenzo Ghiberti. The doors—or at least copies of them (the originals are in the Museo dell'Opera del Duomo—are on the north and east sides of the Baptistery, and the Gothic panels on the south door were designed by Andrea Pisano (circa 1290–1348) in 1330. ⊠ *Piazza del Duomo* ☎ *055/2302885* ⊕ *www.operaduomo. firenze.it* 🎫 *€3* ⊗ *Mon.–Sat. noon–7, Sun. 8:30–2.*

> **LIVORNO BEST BETS**
>
> **The Uffizi.** This huge gallery is basically the mother lode of Renaissance art, with priceless examples by artists including Michelangelo, Botticelli, and Raphael.
>
> **Galleria dell'Accademia.** The number one draw in this museum is the original Michelangelo's *David*, a sculpture that has captured human imagination, but don't miss the rest of the collection.
>
> **Torre Pendente.** Completed in 1173 Pisa's famous tower began to subside almost immediately. Intervention in the 1990s saved it from collapse and stabilized the structure.

③ **Campanile.** The Gothic bell tower designed by Giotto (circa 1266–1337) is a soaring structure of multicolor marble originally decorated with reliefs that are now in the Museo dell'Opera del Duomo. A climb of 414 steps rewards you with a sweeping view of the city. ⊠ *Piazza del Duomo* ☎ *055/2302885* ⊕ *www.operaduomo.firenze.it* 🎫 *€6* ⊗ *Daily 8:30–7:30.*

❿ **Cappelle Medicee** *(Medici Chapels)*. This magnificent complex includes the
★ **Cappella dei Principi,** the Medici chapel and mausoleum that was begun in 1605 and kept marble workers busy for several hundred years, and the **Sagrestia Nuova** (New Sacristy), designed by Michelangelo and so called to distinguish it from Brunelleschi's Sagrestia Vecchia (Old Sacristy) in San Lorenzo. ⊠ *Piazza di Madonna degli Aldobrandini, San Lorenzo* ☎ *055/294883* 🎫 *€6* ⊗ *Daily 8:15–5. Closed 1st, 3rd, and 5th Mon. and 2nd and 4th Sun. of month.*

❶ **Duomo** *(Cattedrale di Santa Maria del Fiore)*. In 1296 Arnolfo di Cam-
★ bio (circa 1245–circa 1310) was commissioned to build "the loftiest, most sumptuous edifice human invention could devise." The immense Duomo was not completed until 1436. The imposing facade dates only from the 19th century; its neo-Gothic style complements Giotto's genuine Gothic 14th-century campanile. The real glory of the Duomo, however, is Filippo Brunelleschi's dome, presiding over the cathedral with a dignity and grace that few domes to this day can match. Brunelleschi's **cupola** was an ingenious engineering feat, and today the Duomo has come to symbolize Florence in the same way that the Eiffel Tower symbolizes Paris. ⊠ *Piazza del Duomo* ☎ *055/2302885* ⊕ *www.operaduomo.firenze. it* 🎫 *Church free, crypt €3, cupola €6* ⊗ *Church Mon.–Wed. and Fri. 10–5, Thurs. 10–4:30, Sat. 10–4:45, Sun. 1:30–4:45, 1st Sat. of month 10–3:30. Crypt Mon.–Wed. and Fri. 10–5, Thurs. 10–3:30, Sat. 10–5:45,*

1st Sat. of month 10–3:30. Cupola weekdays 8:30–7, Sat. 8:30–5:40, 1st Sat. of month 8:30–4.

⑦ Galleria degli Uffizi. The venerable Uffizi Gallery occupies the top floor of the U-shaped **Palazzo degli Uffizi** (Uffizi Palace), designed by Giorgio Vasari (1511–74) in 1560 to hold the administrative offices of the Medici grand duke Cosimo I (1519–74). Later, the Medici installed their art collections here. It's probably the greatest collection of Renaissance paintings in the world. Lines can be long, and you may wish to consider buying your tickets in advance or going on a ship-sponsored shore excursion to avoid them. A bar inside the gallery is a good place for a coffee break; for a close-up view of the Palazzo Vecchio, step out onto the terrace. ✉*Piazzale degli Uffizi 6, Piazza Signoria* ☎*055/2388651 advance tickets* ✉*Consorzio ITA, Piazza Pitti 1, 50121* ☎*055/294883* ⊕*www.uffizi.firenze.it* 🎟*€6.50, reservation fee €3* ⊗*Tues.–Sun. 8:15–6:50.*

FodorśChoice ★

⑪ Galleria dell'Accademia *(Accademia Gallery).* The collection of Florentine paintings, dating from the 13th to the 18th centuries, is largely unremarkable, but the sculptures by Michelangelo are worth the price of admission. The unfinished *Slaves,* fighting their way out of their marble prisons, were meant for the tomb of Michelangelo's overly demanding patron Pope Julius II (1443–1513). But the focal point is the original *David,* moved here from Piazza della Signoria in 1873. ✉*Via Ricasoli 60, San Marco* ☎*055/294883 reservations, 055/2388609 gallery* 🎟*€6.50, reservation fee €3* ⊗*Tues.–Sun. 8:15–6:50.*

④ Museo dell'Opera del Duomo *(Cathedral Museum).* Ghiberti's original Baptistery door panels and the *cantorie* (choir loft) reliefs by Donatello and Luca della Robbia (1400–82) keep company with Donatello's *Mary Magdalen* and Michelangelo's *Pietà* (not to be confused with his more famous *Pietà* in St. Peter's in Rome). Renaissance sculpture is in part defined by its revolutionary realism, but in its palpable suffering Donatello's *Magdalen* goes beyond realism. ✉*Piazza del Duomo 9* ☎*055/2302885* ⊕*www.operaduomo.firenze.it* 🎟*€6* ⊗*Mon.–Sat. 9–7:30, Sun. 9–1:45.*

⑥ Palazzo Vecchio *(Old Palace).* Florence's forbidding, fortresslike city hall was begun in 1299 and its massive bulk and towering campanile dominate the Piazza della Signoria. The interior courtyard is a good deal less severe, having been remodeled by Michelozzo (1396–1472) in 1453; a copy of Verrocchio's bronze *puttino* (little infant boy), topping the central fountain, softens the space. The main attraction is on the second floor: two adjoining rooms that supply one of the most startling contrasts in Florence. The first is the vast **Sala dei Cinquecento,** which contains Michelangelo's *Victory* group. The second room is the little **Studiolo,** to the right of the sala's entrance, designed by Vasari and decorated by Vasari and Bronzino (1503–72); it's intimate, civilized, and filled with complex, questioning, allegorical art. ✉*Piazza della Signoria* ☎*055/2768465* 🎟*€6* ⊗*Mon.–Wed., Fri. and Sat. 9–7, Thurs. 9–2, Sun. 9–7.*

⑧ Ponte Vecchio *(Old Bridge).*This charmingly simple bridge is to Florence what the Tower Bridge is to London. It was built in 1345 and the shops along the bridge housed first butchers, then grocers, blacksmiths, and other merchants. But in 1593 the Medici grand duke Ferdinand I (1549–1609), whose private corridor linking the Medici palace (Palazzo Pitti) with the

Medici offices (the Uffizi) crossed the bridge atop the shops, decided that all this plebeian commerce under his feet was unseemly. So he threw out the butchers and blacksmiths and installed 41 goldsmiths and 8 jewelers. The bridge has been devoted solely to these two trades ever since.

9 Santa Croce. Like the Duomo, this church is Gothic, with a facade dating from the 19th century. As a burial place, the church probably contains more skeletons of Renaissance celebrities than any other in Italy including those of Michelangelo, Galileo, Machiavelli, and the composer Gioacchino Rossini, as well as a memorial for Dante Alighieri. The collection of art within the complex is by far the most important of any church in Florence. ⊠*Piazza Santa Croce 16* ☎*055/2466105* 💶*€5 combined admission to church and museum* ◷*Mon.–Sat. 9:30–5:30, Sun. 1–5.*

FodorsChoice ★

PISA
22 km (14 mi) north of Livorno, 82 km (51 mi) west of Florence.

All of Pisa's treasures date from a short period between the 11th and the 13th centuries, when Pisa was a leading power in the region. The three buildings set on Pisa's grassy Field of Miracles form one of the finest Romanesque ensembles in Italy.

Numbers in the margin correspond to points of interest on the Pisa map.

12 Torre Pendente. Probably one of the most recognizable tourist attractions in the world, this funny little tower refuses to fall down. We've all seen the pictures, but nothing can prepare you for seeing it for real; it's kooky, but it's also very beautiful. The tower leans because 14.5 thousand tons of marble press down on badly formed foundations. The tower settled at an incline of 5.5 degrees to the vertical, the top being displaced by 15 feet from the base. Visitor numbers are limited to 40 per group at 30-minute intervals throughout the day. Buy a ticket as soon as you arrive at the site or book online. ⊠*Piazza del Duomo* ☎*050/560547* ⊕*www.opapisa.it* 💶*€15 for all three Pisa sites* ◷*Daily 8:30–8:30 in summer, 8:30–sunset rest of year.*

13 Duomo. The magnificent black-and-white decoration of the exterior of the Duomo ushered in the Pisan style. The foundation was laid in 1063, a century before the tower was completed. Sadly, a fire in 1595 destroyed much of the interior decoration, though not the ornate font (1310) by Giovanni Pisaro. The bronze doors at **Portale di San Renieri,** the main entrance, are also original (1180). ⊠*Piazza del Duomo* 💶*€15 for all three Pisa sites* ◷*Daily 8:30–8:30.*

14 Battistero. This smaller baptistery building completes the collection of Pisa's top sights. Remarkable for its ornate exterior, the interior is almost devoid of adornment. ⊠*Piazza del Duomo* 💶*€15 for all three Pisa sites* ◷*Daily 8:30–8:30 in summer, 8:30–sunset rest of year.*

SHOPPING

Window-shopping in Florence is like visiting an enormous contemporary-art gallery. Many of today's greatest Italian artists are fashion designers—Prada, Gucci, Versace, to name but a few—and most keep shops in Florence. Italian leather is famed for its quality and fashioned into clothing, shoes, and accessories, True art makes also makes a big impact on the souvenir market, with many street artists around the town and smarter galleries in the historic center. Terra-cotta pottery, straw goods, and handmade paper are all traditional handicrafts. Excellent olive oils and wines are also worthwhile buys in Florence.

The fanciest designer shops are mainly on **Via Tornabuoni** and **Via della Vigna Nuova**. The city's largest concentrations of antiques shops are on **Borgo Ognissanti** and the Oltrarno's **Via Maggio**. The **Ponte Vecchio** houses reputable but very expensive jewelry shops, as it has since the 16th century. The area near **Santa Croce** is the heart of the leather merchants' district.

Pollini (⊠ *Via Calimala 12/r, Piazza della Repubblica, Florence* ☎*055/ 214738*) has beautifully crafted shoes and leather accessories for those willing to pay that little bit extra. **Sbigoli Terrecotte** (⊠ *Via Sant'Egidio 4/r, Santa Croce, Florence* ☎*055/2479713*) carries traditional Tuscan terracotta and ceramic vases, pots, and cups and saucers.

WHERE TO EAT

$$–$$$$ ✗**Frescobaldi Wine Bar.** Frescobaldi Wine Bar serves lunch and dinner in a swank setting. The food is typically Tuscan with twists of fantasy, including *acciughe marinate* (marinated anchovies) and *affettati misti* (a selection of sliced, cured meats). There's a separate wine bar within the restaurant called Frescobaldino. ⊠ *Via de'Magazzini 2–4/r, near Piazza della Signoria* ☎*055/284724* ▭*MC, V* ⊙*Closed Sun. No lunch Mon.*

$$$ ✗**Il Latini.** It may be the noisiest, most crowded trattoria in Florence, but it's also one of the most fun. The genial host, Torello ("little bull") Latini, presides over his four big dining rooms, and somehow it feels as if you're dining in his home. Ample portions of *ribollita*, the traditional Tuscan vegetable and bread soup, prepare the palate for the hearty meat dishes that follow. Both Florentines and tourists alike tuck into the *agnello fritto* (fried lamb) with aplomb. Though reservations are advised, there's always a wait anyway. ⊠ *Via dei Palchetti 6/r, Santa Maria Novella* ☎*055/210916* ▭*AE, DC, MC, V* ⊙*Closed Mon. and 15 days at Christmas.*

MÁLAGA, SPAIN (WITH MARBELLA, NERJA & GRANADA)

The city of Málaga and the surrounding region of eastern Andalusia creates the kind of contrast that makes travel in Spain so tantalizing. A Moorish legacy is a unifying theme and offers some of its most interesting and visually stunning historical attractions. Since the birth of mass tourism, Europeans have flocked here to the Costa del Sol or Sunshine Coast, a 70-km (43-mi) sprawl of hotels, vacation villas, golf courses, marinas, and nightclubs west of Málaga. Since the late 1950s this area has mushroomed from a group of impoverished fishing villages into an overdeveloped seaside playground and retirement haven. Despite the hubbub, you *can* unwind here. Málaga itself is a vibrant Spanish city, virtually untainted by tourism, and inland are quiet whitewashed villages just waiting to be explored.

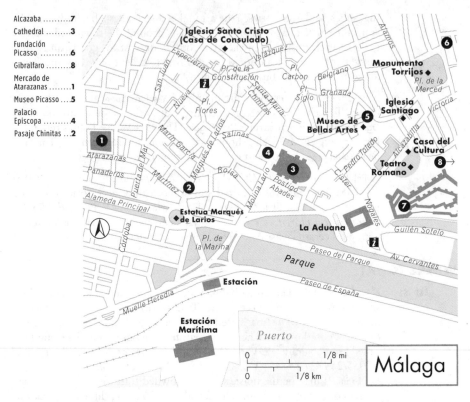

ESSENTIALS

CURRENCY The euro (€1 to US$1.46 at this writing); U.S. currency is generally not accepted in Europe, but ATMs are common and credit cards are widely accepted.

HOURS Museums generally open 9 until 7 or 8, many are closed on Monday and some close in the afternoon. Most stores are open Monday through Saturday 9 to 1:30 and 5 to 8, but a few tourist shops open in the afternoon and on Sunday.

INTERNET **Navegaweb** ⊠*Calle Molina Lario 11, Málaga* ☎*952/352300.*

TELEPHONES Most tri-band and quad-band GSM phones work in Spain, where mobile services are 3G-compatible. Public kiosks accept phone cards that support international calls (cards sold in press shops, bars, and telecom shops). Major companies include Vodafone.

COMING ASHORE

The cruise port at Málaga is coming to the end of a vast regeneration; its two new passenger terminals were expected at this writing to open before the end of 2007. The port area will have attractions, including an aquarium, shopping, eateries, and parks. Málaga is a large port with several berths and shuttle buses carry passengers to the terminal areas, and passenger facilities will be extensive once the program is complete.

The city of Málaga awaits just beyond the gates of the port, and you can explore the old town on foot. Granada is 1½ hours away to the north by road. Bus services are frequent, and buses are modern and air-conditioned; the fare at this writing is €9.11. The main bus station is next to the railway station in the city. Taking a taxi from the cruise port is the quickest and simplest transfer. Rail travel from Málaga to Granada is a much slower option, at 3 hours, and with few trains each day this is not a realistic option for passengers in town for just a day. Renting a car would allow you to visit Granada or explore some of the resorts ot countryside surrounding Málaga. The price for an economy manual vehicle is approximately €85 per day.

> **MÁLAGA BEST BETS**
>
> **Climb the parapets of the Alcazaba.** Málaga's Moorish fortress is the city's greatest monument.
>
> **Take a hike in the Parque Natural del Torcal de Antequera.** Walk through a surreal wind-sculpted landscape of pink granite.
>
> **Strolling through the Alhambra.** The Moorish palace in Granada is about 90 minutes from Málaga and well worth the trip.

EXPLORING MÁLAGA & VICINITY

MÁLAGA

Numbers in the margin correspond to points of interest on the Málaga map

7 Alcazaba. Just beyond the ruins of a Roman theater on Calle Alcazabilla, this Moorish fortress Málaga's greatest monument. It was begun in the 8th century, when Málaga was the principal port of the Moorish kingdom, though most of the present structure dates from the 11th century. The inner palace was built between 1057 and 1063, when the Moorish emirs took up residence; and Ferdinand and Isabella lived here for a while after conquering Málaga in 1487. ✉*Entrance on Calle Alcazabilla* 💶*€1.90, €3.15 combined entry with Gibralfaro* 🕐*Nov.–Mar., Tues.–Sun. 8.30–7; Apr.–Oct., Tues.–Sun. 9:30–8.*

3 Cathedral. Málaga's main cathedral, built between 1528 and 1782, is a triumph. Because it lacks one of its two towers, the building is nicknamed *La Manquita* (The One-Armed Lady). The enclosed choir, which miraculously survived the burnings of the civil war, is the work of 17th-century artist Pedro de Mena. A walk around the cathedral on Calle Cister will take you to the magnificent Gothic Puerta del Sagrario. ✉*C. de Molina Larios* ☎*952/215917* 💶*€3.50* 🕐*Mon.–Sat. 10–6:45.*

6 Fundación Picasso. The childhood home of Málaga's most famous native son, Pablo Picasso, has been painted and furnished in the style of the era and houses a permanent exhibition of Picasso's early sketches and sculptures, as well as memorabilia, including the artist's christening robe and family photographs. ✉*Pl. de la Merced 15* ☎*952/600215* 💶*€1* 🕐*Mon.–Sat. 10–8, Sun. 10–2.*

8 Gibralfaro. Magnificent vistas beckon at this fort. The fortifications were built for Yusuf I in the 14th century; the Moors called them Jebelfaro, from the Arab word for "mount" and the Greek word for "lighthouse," after a beacon that stood here to guide ships into the harbor and warn of pirates. ✉*Gibralfaro Mountain* ☎*952/220043* 💶*€1.90, €3.15 com-*

bined entry with Alcazaba ⊗Nov.–Mar., daily 9–5:45; Apr.–Oct., daily 9–7:45.

❶ Mercado de Atarazanas. From the Plaza Felix Saenz, at the southern end of Calle Nueva, turn onto Sagasta to reach the most colorful market in all of Andalusia. The typical 19th-century iron structure incorporates the original **Puerta de Atarazanas,** the exquisitely crafted 14th-century Moorish gate that once connected the city with the port.

❺ Museo Picasso. The city's most prestigious museum houses works that Pablo Picasso kept for himself or gave to his family. The holdings were largely donated by two family members—Christine and Bernard Ruiz-Picasso, the artist's daughter-in-law and grandson. The works are displayed in chronological order according to the periods that marked his development as an artist, from blue and rose to cubism, and beyond. ⊠*C. de San Agustín* ☎*952/602731* ⊠*Permanent exhibition €6, combined permanent and temporary exhibition €8, last Sun. of every month free* ⊗*Tues.–Thurs. 10–8, Fri. and Sat. 10–9.*

FodorsChoice
★

❹ Palacio Episcopa *(Bishop's Palace).* This building has one of the most stunning facades in the city. It's now a venue for temporary art exhibitions. ⊠*Pl. Obispo 6* ☎*952/602722* ⊠*Free* ⊗*Tues.–Sun. 10–2 and 6–9.*

❷ Pasaje Chinitas. Wander the warren of passageways and peep into the dark, vaulted bodegas, where old men down glasses of *seco añejo* or *Málaga Virgen,* local wines made from Málaga's muscatel grapes. Silversmiths and vendors of religious books and statues ply their trades in shops that have changed little since the early 1900s. Backtrack across Larios, and, in the streets leading to Calle Nueva, you can see shoeshine boys, lottery-ticket vendors, Gypsy guitarists, and tapas bars with wine served from huge barrels.

NERJA
★ *52 km (32 mi) east of Málaga.*

Nerja—the name comes from the Moorish word *narixa,* meaning "abundant springs." The old village is on a headland above small beaches and rocky coves. In high season, Nerja is packed with tourists, but the rest of the year it's a pleasure to wander the old town's narrow streets.

Nerja's highlight is the **Balcón de Europa,** a tree-lined promenade with magnificent views, on a promontory just off the central square.

⊙ The **Cuevas de Nerja** *(Nerja Caves)* lie between Almuñecar and Nerja on a road surrounded by giant cliffs and dramatic seascapes. The caves are floodlighted for better views of the spires and turrets created by millennia of dripping water. One suspended pinnacle, 200 feet long, is in fact the world's largest known stalactite. ☎*952/529520* ⊕*www.cuevanerja.com* ⊠*€6* ⊗*Oct.–Apr., daily 10–2 and 4–6:30; May–Sept., daily 10–2 and 4–8.*

MARBELLA
52 km (32 mi) west of Málaga.

Playground of the rich and home of movie stars, rock musicians, and dispossessed royal families, Marbella has attained the top rung on Europe's social ladder. Dip into any Spanish gossip magazine and chances are the glittering parties that fill its pages are set in Marbella. However, much of this action takes place on the fringes—grand hotels and luxury restaurants line the waterfront for 20 km (12 mi) on each side of the town center. In the town itself, you may well wonder how Marbella became so famous.

Marbella's appeal lies in the heart of the **old village**, which remains miraculously intact. Here, narrow alleys of whitewashed houses cluster around the central **Plaza de los Naranjos** (Orange square), where colorful, albeit pricey, restaurants vie for space under the orange trees. Climb onto what remains of the old fortifications and stroll along the Calle Virgen de los Dolores to the Plaza de Santo Cristo. Wander the maze of lanes and enjoy the geranium-speckled windows and splashing fountains.

Marbella's wealth glitters most brightly along the Golden Mile, stretching from Marbella to **Puerto Banús** (about 7 km [4½ mi] west of central Marbella). Here, a mosque, Arab banks, and the onetime residence of Saudi Arabia's King Fahd betray the influence of oil money in this wealthy enclave. Though now hemmed in by a belt of high-rises, Marbella's plush marina, with 915 berths, is a gem of ostentatious wealth, a Spanish answer to St. Tropez.

GRANADA
128 km (80 mi) northeast of Málaga.

Granada rises majestically from a plain onto three hills, dwarfed—on a clear day—by the Sierra Nevada. Atop one of these hills perches the pink-gold Alhambra palace. The stunning view from its mount takes in the sprawling medieval Moorish quarter, the caves of the Sacromonte, and, in the distance, the fertile *vega* (plain), rich in orchards, tobacco fields, and poplar groves. These days much of the Alhambra and Albaicín areas are closed to cars, because of the difficult access, but starting from the Plaza Nueva there are now minibuses—numbers 30, 31, 32, and 34—that run frequently to these areas.

Fodor's Choice ★ With around 2 million visitors a year, the **Alhambra** is Spain's most popular attraction. Simply take one of the minibuses, numbers 30 and 32, up from the Plaza Nueva. They run every few minutes; pay the fare of €0.90 on board. The Alhambra was begun in the 1240s by Ibn el-Ahmar, or Alhamar, the first king of the Nasrids. The great citadel once comprised a complex of houses, schools, baths, barracks, and gardens surrounded by defense towers and seemingly impregnable walls. Today, only the Alcazaba and the Palacios Nazaríes, built chiefly by Yusuf I (1334–54) and his son Mohammed V (1354–91), remain. The palace is an endless, intricate conglomeration of patios, arches, and cupolas made from wood, plaster, and tile; lavishly colored and adorned with marquetry and ceramics in geometric patterns; and topped by delicate, frothy profusions of lacelike stucco and *mocárabes* (ornamental stalactites).

Entrance to the Alhambra complex of the Alcazaba, Nasrid Palaces, Mosque Baths, and Generalife is strictly controlled by quotas. There are three types of timed tickets: morning, afternoon, and evening, but the evening ticket is valid only for the Nasrid Palaces. Because the number of tickets is limited and subject to availability, try to book your tickets in advance. You can do this in several ways: via the Web (www.alhambratickets.com), via phone (902/224460 in Spain, 34 91/5379178 outside Spain), and at any BBVA branch in Spain.

If you wait and take your chances at the ticket office, its hours are March to October, daily from 8 to 7 and 9:30 to 10:30, and November to February, daily from 8 to 5 and 7:30 to 8:30. ⊠ *Cuesta de Gomérez, Alhambra* ⊕ *www.alhambra-patronato.es* 🎫 *€12.*

SHOPPING

Málaga offers a full range of local specialties made throughout the region. Shoes and leather goods are of high quality. Handmade and mass-produced ceramics are produced in a range of colors and styles. Fans and silk shawls, along with other traditional Spanish dress, range in price, depending on quality. Olives and olive oil will make gourmets happy, and olive oil is also used for a range of hair and beauty products. Other edibles include dried serrano ham, Manchego cheese, and *turrón* (an almond and honey sweet). *Seco añejo* sweet wine is also produced in the region.

In Málaga the main shopping street is Marqués de Larios, known locally as Larios, a traffic free boulevard with excellent boutiques. The **Corte Inglés** department store offers one-stop shopping over its six vast floor. Head to the fifth floor for year-round sale items. ⊠ *Av. de Andalucía 4–6* 🕾 *952/300000* 🕙 *Mon.–Sat. 10–10.*

BEACHES

Lobster-pink sun worshippers from northern Europe pack these beaches in summer so heavily that there's little towel space on the sand. Beach chairs can be rented for around €4 a day. Beaches range from shingle and pebbles (Almuñecar, Nerja, Málaga) to fine, gritty sand (westward of Málaga). The best are those around Marbella. It's acceptable for women to go topless; if you want to take it *all* off, go to beaches designated *playa naturista.* The most popular nude beaches is Maro (near Nerja).

WHERE TO EAT

¢ ✕ **Logueno.** This traditional tapas bar has two dining spaces: the original

Fodor's Choice well-loved bar shoehorned into a deceptively small space on a side street

★ near Calle Larios and a more recent expansion across the street. Check out the original with its L-shape wooden bar crammed with a choice of more than 75 tantalizing tapas, including many Logueno originals, such as grilled oyster mushrooms with garlic, parsley, and goat cheese. There's an excellent selection of Rioja wines, and the service is fast and good, despite the lack of elbow room. ⊠ *Marin Garcia s/n* 🕾 *No phone* ▤ *No credit cards* 🕙 *Closed Sun.*

¢ ✕ **Pitta Bar.** Tables spill out onto the attractive pedestrian street fronting this bright pine-clad Middle Eastern restaurant. Falafel, kebabs, hummus, and tabbouleh salad are on the menu, along with a choice of 14 stuffed pita. ⊠ *Echegaray 8* 🕾 *952/608675* ▤ *No credit cards* 🕙 *Closed Sun.*

MALLORCA, SPAIN

More than five times the size of its fellow Balearic islands, Mallorca is shaped roughly like a saddle. The Sierra de Tramuntana, a dramatic mountain range soaring to nearly 5,000 feet, runs the length of its northwest coast, and a ridge of hills borders the southeast shores; between the two lies a great, flat plain that in early spring becomes a sea of almond blossoms, "the snow of Mallorca." The island draws more than 10 million visitors a year, many of them bound for summer vacation packages in the coastal resorts. The beaches are beautiful, but save time for the charms of the northwest and the interior: caves, bird sanctuaries, monasteries and medieval cities, local museums, outdoor cafés, and village markets.

4

ESSENTIALS

CURRENCY The euro (€1 to US$1.46 at this writing); U.S. currency is generally not accepted in Europe, but ATMs are common and credit cards are widely accepted.

HOURS Museums generally open 9 until 7 or 8, many are closed on Monday and some close in the afternoon. Most stores are open Monday through Saturday 9 to 1:30 and 5 to 8, but tourist shops may open in the afternoon and also on Sunday between May and September.

INTERNET **Cibertango.com** ✉ *Calle San Cristobal 20, Palma* ☏*971/442826.*

TELEPHONES Most tri-band or quad-band GSM phones will work in Spain, where services are 3G-compatible. Public kiosks accept phone cards that support international calls (cards sold in press shops, bars, and telecom shops). Major companies include Vodafone.

COMING ASHORE

Vessels dock at the port directly in front of the old town of Palma. There is no shuttle, so passengers docking at the farthest berth have a 15-minute walk to the terminal building and the port entrance. From the port entrance, you can walk into Palma town. There are few facilities at the cruise terminal or in the port.

If you only want to enjoy Palma, you won't need to worry about transportation; however, Mallorca is a small island, and you can see a great deal of it in a day with a vehicle or on public transportion. Regular and reliable bus services link the major towns, though services are fewer on Sunday. Car rentals cost around €87 per day for an economy manual vehicle, but it's much cheaper to explore by public transit.

EXPLORING MALLORCA

PALMA DE MALLORCA

If you look north of the cathedral (La Seu, or the "seat" of the Bishopric, to Mallorcans) on a map of the city of Palma, you can see the jumble of tiny streets around the Plaça Santa Eulalia that made up the early town. A stroll through these streets will bring you past many interesting neoclassical and modernist buildings.

Numbers in the margin correspond to points of interest on the Mallorca map.

5 Ajuntament *(Town Hall).* Carrer Colom brings you to the 17th-century; stop in to see the collection of *gigantes*—the huge painted and costumed mannequins paraded through the streets at festivals—on display in the lobby. The olive tree on the right side of the square is one of Mallorca's so-called *olivos milenarios*—thousand-year-old olives—and may be even older. ⊠*Plaça Cort.*

MALLORCA BEST BETS

The Cathedral. Palma's Cathedral has a unique circular design as well as decrations by Gaudí.

Museu d'Es Baluard. The museum of modern and contemporary art is an exciting convergence of old and new.

Sóller. One of the most beautiful towns on the island, with a large collection of moderniste buildings.

---

8 Castell de Bellver *(Bellver Castle).* Overlooking the city and the bay from a hillside above the Terreno nightlife area, this castle was built at the beginning the 14th century, in Gothic style but with a circular design—the only one of its kind in Spain. The fortress houses an archeological **museum** of the history of Mallorca, and a small collection of classical sculpture. ⊠*Camilo José Cela s/n* ☎971/730657 ⊞*€2, free Sun.* ☉*Oct.–Mar., Mon.–Sat. 8–8; Apr.–Sept., Mon.–Sat. 8–9; open Sun. year-round 10–5, when admission to castle is free, but museum is closed.*

2 Cathedral. Palma's cathedral is an architectural wonder that took almost 400 years to build (1230–1601). The extraordinarily wide (63-foot) expanse of the nave is supported on 14 extraordinarily slender 70-foot-tall columns, which fan out at the top like palm trees. The nave is dominated by an immense rose window, 40 feet in diameter, from 1370. Over the main altar (consecrated in 1346) is the almost surrealistic **baldoquí** by Antoni Gaudí: an enormous canopy, lamps suspended from it like elements of a mobile, rising to a Crucifixion scene at the top. This is Gaudí's most remarkable contribution to the remodeling of the Royal Chapel—a project he worked on for six years, and completed in 1912. To the right of it, in the Chapel of the Santísima, is an equally remarkable work, by the modern sculptor Miquel Barceló: a painted ceramic tableau that covers the walls of the chapel like a skin. Unveiled in 2007, the tableau is based on the New Testament account of the miracle of the loaves and fishes. ⊞*€4* ☉*Apr.–May, weekdays 10–5:15; June–Sept., weekdays 10–6:15; Nov.–Mar., weekdays 10–3:15; Sat. 10–2:15 year-round; Sun. for worship only, 8:30–1:45, 6:30–7:45 year-round.*

FodorśChoice
★

1 Llotja *(Exchange).* This commodities exchange was built in the 15th century. With its decorative turrets, battlements, fluted pillars, and Gothic stained-glass windows—part fortress, part church—it attests to the veneration of wealth Mallorca achieved in its heyday as a Mediterranean trading power. It can be visited inside only when there are special exhibitions in the Merchants Chamber. ⊠*Pl. de la Llotja 5, La Llotja* ☎971/711705 ☉*During exhibits, Tues.–Sat. 11–2 and 5–9, Sun. 11–2.*

4 Museu d'Art Espanyol Contemporani. This fine little museum was established by the Joan March Foundation in a sumptuous private home dating to the 18th century. The second and third floors were redesigned to accommodate a series of small galleries with works by Picasso, Miró, and Dalí. ⊠*C.*

★

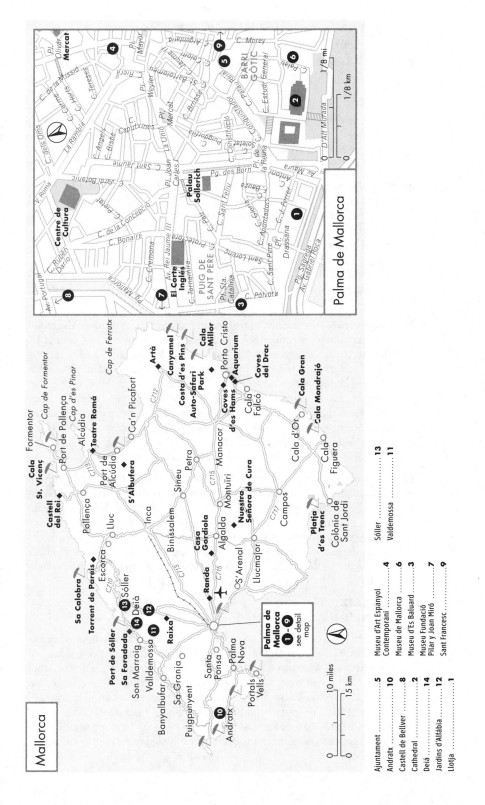

4

Mallorca

Palma de Mallorca

Sant Miguel 11 ☎*971/713515* ⊕*www.march.es/museupalma* 🎟*Free*
⊘ *Weekdays 10–6:30, Sat. 10:30–2.*

⑥ Museu de Mallorca. From the Plaça Sant Francesc, take Carrer Pere Nadal
south toward the bay; the street changes names as it descends. On the
left as it turns to Carrer de la Portella, is the 18th-century ducal palace of
the Condes de Ayamans. The museum housed here exhibits the findings
of all the major archeological research on Mallorca, from prehistory to
the Roman, Vandal, and Moorish occupations: pottery, bronzes, stone
burial chambers, tools, and ornaments. ⊠*Portella 5, Barrio Antiguo*
☎*971/717540* 🎟*€2.40* ⊘ *Tues.–Sat. 10–7, Sun. 10–2.*

③ Museu d'Es Baluard. Inaugurated in January 2004, the Museum of Modern
★ and Contemporary Art of Palma is an outstanding convergence of old
and new: the exhibition space uses and merges into the surviving 16th-
century perimeter walls of the fortified city, with a stone courtyard facing the sea and a promenade along the ramparts. The collection includes
work by Miró, Picasso, Magritte, Tapiès, Calder, and other major artists. ⊠*Plaça Porta de Santa Catalina s/n, Puig Sant Pere* ☎*971/908200*
⊕*www.esbaluard.org* 🎟*€6* ⊘ *Oct.–May, Tues.–Sun. 10–8; June–Sept.,*
Tues.–Sun. 10–10.

⑦ Museu Fundació Pilar y Joan Miró *(Pilar and Joan Miró Foundation Museum).*
The permanent collection includes a great many drawings and studies by
the Catalan artist, who spent his last years on Mallorca. The adjacent studio was built for Miró by his friend the architect Josep Lluis Sert; the artist
did most of his work here from 1957 on; the rooms are filled with paintings—on easels, stacked against walls—still in progress when he died.
The museum is 3 km (2 mi) west of the city center, off the Passeig Marítim. ⊠*Carrer Joan de Saridakis 29, Cala Major, Marivent* ☎*971/701420*
⊕*http://miro.palmademallorca.es* 🎟*€5* ⊘ *Sept. 16–May 15, Tues.–Sat.*
10–6, Sun. 10–3; May 16–Sept. 15, Tues.–Sat. 10–7, Sun. 10–3.

⑨ Sant Francesc. From the Plaça de Sant Eulalia, take the Carrer del Convent
de Sant Francesc to see the beautiful 13th-century monastery church established by Jaume II when his eldest son took monastic orders and gave up
rights to the throne. Fra Junípero Serra, the missionary who founded San
Francisco, California, was later educated here; his statue stands to the
left of the main entrance. The basilica houses the tomb of the eminent
13th-century scholar Ramón Llull. ⊠*Plaça Sant Francesc, Barrio Antiguo*
⊘ *Mon.–Sat. 9:30–1 and 3–6, Sun. 9:30–1* 🎟*€1.*

ANDRATX
⑩ *16 km (10 mi) west of Palma*

Andratx is a charming cluster of white and ocher hillside houses, rather
like cliff dwellings, with the 3,363-foot Mt. Galatzó behind it. Many of
the towns on Majorca are at some distance from their seafronts; from
Andratx you can take a 4-km (1½-mi) drive through S'Arracó to Sant
Elm and on to the rocky shore opposite Sa Dragonera—an island shaped
indeed like the long-armored back of a dragon. Local history has it that
the tiny island of Pantaleu, just to the west of it, was where Jaume I chose
to disembark in September 1200, on his campaign to retake Majorca from
the Moors.

VALLDEMOSSA

⑪ *18 km (11 mi) north of Palma.*

The **Reial Cartuja** *(Royal Carthusian Monastery)* was founded in 1339, but when the monks were expelled in 1835, it was privatized, and the cells became apartments for travelers. The most famous lodgers were Frédéric Chopin and his lover, the Baroness Amandine Dupin—better known by her nom de plume, George Sand—who spent three difficult months here in the winter of 1838–39. The tourist office, in the plaza next to the church, sells a ticket good for all of the monastery's attractions. ✉ *Pl. de la Cartuja s/n* ☎ *971/612106* 🖷 *971/612514* ⊕ *www.valldemossa.com* 🎫 *€8* ⊙ *Dec. and Jan., Mon.–Sat. 9:30–5; Feb., Mon.–Sat. 9:30–5, Sun. 10–1; Mar. and Oct., Mon.–Sat. 9:30–5:30, Sun. 10–1; Apr.–Sept., Mon.–Sat. 9:30–6:30, Sun. 10–1; Nov. 9:30–4:30, Sun. 10–1.*

JARDINS D'ALFÀBIA

⑫ *17 km (10½ mi) north of Palma.*

You don't often hear in the Majorcan interior what you hear in the Alfàbia Gardens: the sound of falling water. The Moorish viceroy of the island developed the springs and hidden irrigation systems here sometime in the 12th century, to create this remarkable oasis on the road to Sóller, with its 40-odd varieties of trees, climbers, and flowering shrubs. The 17th-century manor house has a collection of original documents that chronicle the history of the estate. ✉ *Ctra. Palma–Sóller, Km. 17* ☎ *971/613123* 🎫 *€4.50* ⊙ *Nov.–Mar., weekdays 9–5:30, Sat. 9–1; Apr.–Oct., Mon.–Sat. 9–6:30.*

SÓLLER

⑬ *13 km (8 ½ mi) north of Jardins d'Alfàbia, 30 km (19 mi) north of Palma.*

★ This is one of the most beautiful towns on the island, thick with palatial homes built in the 19th and early 20th centuries by the owners of agricultural estates in the Sierra de Tramuntana, and the merchants who thrived on the export of the region's oranges, lemons, and almonds. Many of the buildings here, like the **Church of Sant Bartomeu** and the **Bank of Sóller,** on the Plaça Constitució, and the nearby **Can Prunera,** are gems of the Moderniste style, designed by contemporaries of Antoni Gaudí. The tourist information office in the **Town Hall,** next to Sant Bartomeu, has a walking tour map of the important sites.

Travel retro to Sóller from Palma on one of the six daily trains (round-trip: €14) from Plaça d'Espanya: a string of wooden coaches with leather-covered seats, dating from 1912.

Sóller's **Station Building Galleries** (✉ *Pl. Espanya 6* ☎ *971/630301* 🎫 *Free* ⊙ *Daily 10:30–6:30)* have two small collections, one of engravings by Joan Miró, the other of ceramics by Picasso.

Visit the galleries before you set out on your exploration of the town—and if you're spending the night, book early: Sóller is not overly endowed with hotels.

Return to the station to catch the charming old blue-and-brass trolly (€3) that threads its way through town, down to Port de Sóller. Spend the day at the beach. Better yet: rent a car at the port for the spectacular drive over the Sierra de Tramontana to Deià and Son Marroig, or the Monestary of Lluc.

DEIÀ

⑭ *9 km (5½ mi) southwest of Sóller.*

★ Deià is perhaps best known as the adopted home of the English poet and writer Robert Graves, who lived here off and on from 1929 until his death in 1985. The village is still a favorite haunt of writers and artists, including Graves's son Tomás, author of *Pa amb oli (Bread and Olive Oil)*, a guide to Majorcan cooking, and British painter David Templeton. The setting is unbeatable; all around Deià rise the steep cliffs of the Sierra de Tramuntana. On warm afternoons, literati gather at the beach bar in the rocky cove at Cala de Deià, 2 km (1 mi) downhill from the village. Walk up the narrow street to the village church; the small **cemetery** behind it affords views of mountains terraced with olive trees and of the coves below. It's a fitting spot for Graves's final resting place, in a quiet corner beneath a simple slab.

In 2007, the Fundació Robert Graves opened a museum dedicated to Deià's most famous resident, in **Ca N'Alluny,** the house he built in 1932, overlooking the sea. (✉*Ctra. Deià-Sóller s/n* ☎*971/636185* ⊕*www.fundaciorobertgraves.com* 🎟*€5* ⊙*Tues.–Sat. 10–5, Sun. 10–3)*

SHOPPING

Mallorca's specialties are leather shoes and clothing, porcelain, souvenirs carved from olive wood, handblown glass, artificial pearls, and espadrilles. Top-name fashion boutiques line **Avinguda Jaume III** and the nearby Plaça Joan Carles I. You can find several antiques shops on Plaça Almoina. Less-expensive shopping strips are **Carrer Sindicat** and **Carrer Sant Miquel**—both pedestrian streets running north from the Plaça Major— and the small streets south of the Plaça Major. The **Plaça Major** itself has a modest crafts market Monday, Thursday, Friday, and Saturday 10 to 2. In summer the market is open daily 10 to 2; January and February, it's open weekends only.

Las Columnas (✉*C. Sant Domingo 24, Barrio Antiguo*) has ceramics from all over the Balearic Islands.

Visit **Gordiola** (✉*Carrer de la Victoria 8–12, Centro* ☎*971/711541*), glassmakers since 1719, for a variety of original bowls, bottles, plates, and decorative objects.

Leather is best in the high-end **Loewe** (✉*Av. Jaime III 1, Centro* ☎*971/715275*), a branch of the famed Spanish firm founded in 1846.

GOLF

Mallorca has more than a score of 18-hole golf courses, among them PGA championship venues of fiendish difficulty. **Son Vida Golf** (✉*Next to Castillo Son Vida hotel, 5 km [3 mi] from Palma, Son Vida* ☎*971/791210*) offers 18 holes.

BEACHES

The closer a beach is to Palma, the more crowded it's likely to be. West of the city is **Palma Nova**; behind the lovely, narrow beach rises one of the most densely developed resorts on the island. **Paguera,** with several small beaches, is the only sizable local resort not overshadowed by high-rises. **Camp de Mar,** with a good beach of fine white sand, is small and relatively undeveloped but is sometimes overrun with day-trippers from other resorts. **Sant Elm,** at the end of this coast, has a pretty little bay and a tree-shaded parking lot. East of Palma, a 5-km (3-mi) stretch of sand runs along the main coastal road from C'an Pastilla to Arenal, forming a package-tour nexus also known collectively as **Playa de Palma**; the crowded beach is long with fine white sand.

WHERE TO EAT

$ ✗**Café la Lonja.** Both the sunny terrace in front of the Llotja—a privileged dining spot—and the restaurant inside are excellent places for drinks, tapas, baguettes, sandwiches, and salads. The seasonal menu might include a salad of tomato, avocado, and manchego cheese; fluffy quiche; and tapas of squid or mushrooms. It's a good rendezvous point and watering hole. ✉*Carrer Lonja del Mar 2, La Llotja* ☎971/722799 🖃*AE, MC, V* ⊘*Closed Sun.*

¢–$ ✗**La Bóveda.** Within hailing distance of the Llotja, with a huge front window, this bustling, popular eatery serves tapas and inexpensive platters such *revuelto con setas y jamón* (scrambled eggs with mushrooms and ham). Tables are at a premium; there's additional seating at the counter, or on stools around upended wine barrels. Nothing fancy here: just ample portions of good food. ✉*Carrer de la Botería 3, La LlotjaPalma* ☎971/714863 🖃*AE, MC, V* ⊘*Closed Sun.*

MARSEILLE, FRANCE

Marseille may sometimes be given a wide berth by travelers in search of a Provençal idyll, but it's their loss. Miss it and you miss one of the vibrant, exciting cities in France. With its cubist jumbles of white stone rising up over a picture-book seaport, bathed in light of blinding clarity and crowned by larger-than-life neo-Byzantine churches, the city's neighborhoods teem with multiethnic life, its souklike African markets reek deliciously of spices and coffees, and its labyrinthine Vieille Ville is painted in broad strokes of saffron, cinnamon, and robin's-egg blue. Feisty and fond of broad gestures, Marseille is a dynamic city, as cosmopolitan now as when the Phoenicians first founded it, and with all the exoticism of the international shipping port it has been for 2,600 years. Vital to the Crusades in the Middle Ages and crucial to Louis XIV as a military port, Marseille flourished as France's market to the world—and still does today.

ESSENTIALS

CURRENCY The euro (€1 to US$1.46 at this writing); U.S. currency is generally not accepted in Europe, but ATMs are common.

HOURS Stores are open Monday through Saturday 9–7, but many close at lunchtime (usually noon–2 or 3) and some will open later and on Sunday during

July and August. Museums are open 10–5, but most are closed on either Monday or Tuesday.

INTERNET **Info Café** (✉*1 Quai de Rive Neuve* ☎*04–91–33–74–98*), at the southeast corner of the port, is convenient; it's open Monday–Saturday 9 AM–10 PM and Sunday 2:30–7:30, and charges about €4 per hour of access.

TELEPHONES Tri-band GSM phones work in France. You can buy prepaid phone cards at telecom shops, news-vendors, and tobacconists in all towns and cities. Phone cards can be used for local or international calls. France Telecom and Orange are leading telecom companies.

MARSEILLE BEST BETS

Order bouillabaise. This aromatic fish stew is one of the world's most famous dishes and originated here as a way for fishermen to use the leftover catch.

Stroll around Viuex Port and La Panier. The Vieux Port bustles with activity but especially during the morning fish market. Neighboring Le Panier is a maze of narrow streets and picturesque corners with pretty boutiques and good museums.

Centre de la Vieille Charite. The museums here have important collections and artifacts from civilizations and societies from around the world.

COMING ASHORE

The Marseille Cruise terminal is north of the Vieux Port historic area and has recently benefited from a €90 million redevelopment. It now offers three different docking areas depending on the size of the vessel and a state-of-the-art welcome center with an ATM, shops, bars, and restaurants. Aside from this, the terminal is in an industrial area and is too distant to allow you to walk into the city. Most cruise lines offer shuttle service into town, but you should spring for a taxi if you don't take the shuttle.

A taxi from cruise terminal into town is approximately €27 and takes around 20 minutes. Once in the Vieux Port area most of the major attractions are reachable on foot. Taxis are plentiful and can provide tourist itineraries. Single journeys begin at €2.30 and then €0.69 per km thereafter.

Although there is no reason to drive if you're just staying in Marseille, renting a vehicle is the ideal way to explore the beautiful Provençal towns and landscapes around the city. Expect to pay around €70 per day for an economy manual vehicle.

EXPLORING MARSEILLE

Numbers in the margin correspond to points of interest on the Marseille map.

6 **Cathédrale de la Nouvelle Major.** A gargantuan, neo-Byzantine 19th-century fantasy, the cathedral was built under Napoléon III—but not before he'd ordered the partial destruction of the lovely 11th-century original, once a perfect example of the Provençal Romanesque style. You can view the flashy decor—marble and rich red porphyry inlay—in the newer of the two churches; the medieval one is being restored. ✉*Pl. de la Major, Le Panier.*

⑤ **Centre de la Vieille Charité** *(Center of the Old Charity).* At the top of the Pan-
★ ier district, this superb ensemble of 17th- and 18th-century architecture
was designed as a hospice for the homeless by Marseillais artist-architects
Pierre and Jean Puget. Even if you don't enter the museums, walk around
the inner court, studying the retreating perspective of triple arcades and
admiring the baroque chapel with its novel egg-peaked dome. Of the complex's two museums, the larger is the **Musée d'Archéologie Méditerranée-
nne** (Museum of Mediterranean Archaeology), with a sizable collection
of pottery and statuary from classical Mediterranean civilization, elemen-
tally labeled (for example, "pot"). There's also a display on the mysterious Celt-like Ligurians who first peopled the coast, cryptically presented
with emphasis on the digs instead of the finds themselves. The best of the
lot is the evocatively mounted Egyptian collection, the second largest in
France after the Louvre's. There are mummies, hieroglyphs, and gorgeous
sarcophagi in a tomblike setting. Upstairs, the **Musée d'Arts Africains,
Océaniens, et Amérindiens** (Museum of African, Oceanic, and American
Indian Art) creates a theatrical foil for the works' intrinsic drama: the
spectacular masks and sculptures are mounted along a pure black wall,
lighted indirectly, with labels across the aisle. ⊠*2 rue de la Charité, Le
Panier* ☎*04–91–14–58–80* ⊟*€2 per museum* ☉*May–Sept., Tues.–Sun.
11–6; Oct.–Apr., Tues.–Sun. 10–5.*

⑫ **Château d'If.** François I, in the 16th century, recognized the strategic advan-
★ tage of an island fortress surveying the mouth of Marseille's vast harbor, so
he had one built. Its effect as a deterrent was so successful that it never saw
combat, and was eventually converted into a prison. It was here that Alexandre Dumas locked up his most famous character, the Count of Monte
Cristo. Though the count was fictional, the hole Dumas had him escape
through is real enough, and is visible in the cells today. Video monitors
playing relevant scenes from dozens of Monte Cristo films bring each tower
and cell to life. On the other hand, the real-life Man in the Iron Mask,
whose supposed cell is still being shown, was not actually imprisoned here.
You get here by boat, and the ride plus the views from the broad terrace
alone are worth the trip. ☎*04–91–59–02–30 château, 04–91–46–54–65
boat information* ⊟*Château €4.60, boat ride from Quai des Belges €10*
☉*Apr.–Sept., daily 9:30–6:30; Oct.–Mar., Tues.–Sun. 9:30–5.*

⑨ **Ferry Boat.** Departing from the quay below the Hôtel de Ville, the ferry is a
Marseille treasure. To hear the natives pronounce "fer-ry bo-at" (they've
Fodor's Choice adopted the English) is one of the joys of a visit here. For a pittance you
★ can file onto this little wooden barge and chug across the Vieux Port. ⊠*Pl.
des Huiles on Quai de Rive Neuve side and Hôtel de Ville on Quai du
Port, Vieux Port* ⊟*€1.*

④ **Jardin des Vestiges** *(Garden of Remains).* Just behind the Marseille History
Museum, this garden stands on the site of Marseille's classical waterfront
and includes remains of the Greek fortifications and loading docks. It was
discovered in 1967 when roadwork was being done next to the Bourse
(stock exchange). ⊠*Centre Bourse, Vieux Port* ☎*04–91–90–42–22*
⊟*€3, includes entry to Musée d'Histoire* ☉*Mon.–Sat. noon–7.*

⑧ **Musée des Docks Romains** *(Roman Docks Museum).* In 1943, Hitler destroyed
the neighborhood along the Quai du Port—some 2,000 houses—displac-

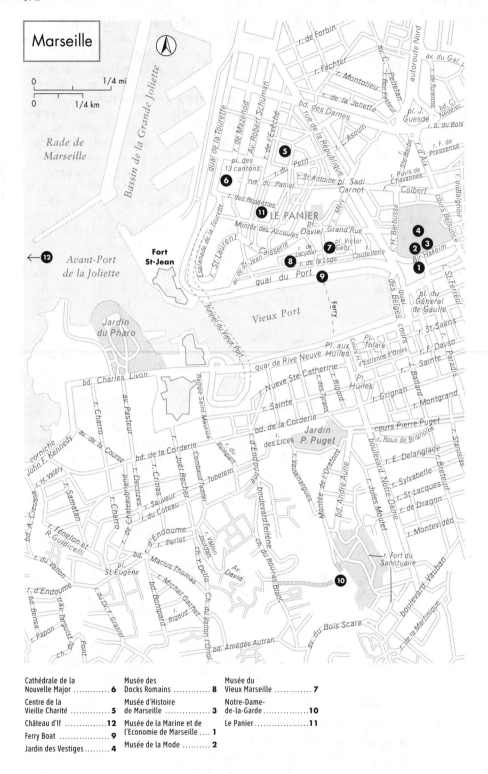

Marseille

0 — 1/4 mi
0 — 1/4 km

Rade de Marseille

Bassin de la Grande Joliette

Avant-Port de la Joliette

Fort St-Jean

Jardin du Pharo

Vieux Port

Jardin P. Puget

ing 20,000 citizens. This act of brutal urban renewal, ironically, laid the ground open for new discoveries. When the rebuilding of Marseille was begun in 1947, workers dug up remains of a Roman shipping warehouse full of the terra-cotta jars and amphorae that once lay in the bellies of low-slung ships. The museum created around it demonstrates the scale of Massalia's shipping prowess. ⊠2 pl. de Vivaux, Vieux Port 🕾04–91–91–24–62 ⊡€2 ⊙Oct.–May, Tues.–Sun. 10–5; June–mid-Sept., Tues.–Sun. 11–6.

❸ Musée d'Histoire de Marseille (Marseille History Museum). The modern, open
★ museum illuminates Massalia's history by mounting its treasure of archaeological finds in didactic displays and miniature models of the city as it appeared in various stages of history. There's a real Greek-era wooden boat in a hermetically sealed display case. ⊠Centre Bourse, entrance on Rue de Bir-Hakeim, Vieux Port 🕾04–91–90–42–22 ⊡€3, includes entry into Jardin des Vestiges ⊙June–Sept., Mon.–Sat. 10–7; Oct.–May, Tues.–Sun. 10–5.

❶ Musée de la Marine et de l'Economie de Marseille (Marine and Economy Museum). One of many museums devoted to Marseille's history as a shipping port was inaugurated by Napoléon III in 1860. The impressive building houses both the museum and the city's Chamber of Commerce. The front entrance and hallway are lined with medallions celebrating the ports of the world with which the city has traded, or trades still. The museum charts the maritime history of Marseille from the 17th century onward with paintings and engravings. It's a model-lover's dream with hundreds of steamboats and schooners, all in miniature. ⊠Palais de la Bourse, 7 La Canebière, La Canebière 🕾04–91–39–33–33 ⊡€2 ⊙Daily 10–6.

❷ Musée de la Mode de Marseille (Marseille Fashion Museum). With more than 3,000 outfits and accessories, these well-displayed and ever-changing exhibitions cover fashion from the 1920s to the present. Thematic shows also highlight new and cutting-edge designers like Fred Sathel. ⊠11 La Canebière, La Canebière 🕾04–96–17–06–00 ⊡€2 ⊙June–Sept., Tues.–Sun. 11–6; Oct.–May, Tues.–Sun. 10–5.

❼ Musée du Vieux Marseille (Museum of Old Marseille). In the 16th-century **Maison Diamantée** (diamond house)—so named for its diamond-faceted Renaissance facade—was built in 1570 by a rich merchant. Focusing on the history of Marseille, the newly reopened, painstakingly renovated museum features santons (figurines), crèches, and furniture offering a glimpse into 18th-century Marseille life. ⊠Rue de la Prison, Vieux Port 🕾04–91–55–28–69 ⊡€2 ⊙June–Sept., Tues.–Sun. 10–6; Oct.–May, Tues.–Sun. 10–5.

❿ Notre-Dame-de-la-Garde. Towering above the city and visible for miles around, the preposterously overscaled neo-Byzantine monument was erected in 1853 by the ever-tasteful Napoléon III. Its interior is a Technicolor bonanza of red-and-beige stripes and glittering mosaics. The gargantuan Madonna and Child on the steeple (almost 30 feet high) is covered in real gold leaf. The boggling panoply of naive ex-votos, mostly thanking the Virgin for death-bed interventions and shipwreck survivals, makes the pilgrimage worth it. ⚓On foot, climb up Cours Pierre Puget, cross Jardin Pierre Puget, cross bridge to Rue Vauvenargues, and hike up to Pl. Edon. Or catch Bus 60 from Cours Jean-Ballard ☏04–91–13–40–80 ☉May–Sept., daily 7 AM–8 PM; Oct.–Apr., daily 7–7.

⑪ Le Panier. The old heart of Marseille is a maze of high shuttered houses looming over narrow cobbled streets, *montées* (stone stairways), and tiny squares. Long decayed and neglected, it is the principal focus of the city's efforts at urban renewal. Wander this atmospheric neighborhood at will, making sure to stroll along Rue du Panier, the montée des Accoules, Rue du Petit-Puits, and Rue des Muettes.

SHOPPING

Marseille offers contrasting shopping opportunities. For lovers of French haute couture there are many boutiques in the new town stocking the major designer labels—Christian Lacroix is a local boy—plus a thriving new fashion scene of young designers selling their own ready-to-wear collections from stylish galleries. Cours Julien is lined with stores, while Rue de la Tour in the Opera district is a center of modern design, known locally as "Fashion Street."

By contrast, the city, particularly Le Panier and rue St-Ferréol, also has numerous shops selling regional crafts and delicacies including bright fabrics of blue and yellow, pottery, olive-wood items, plus delicious olives, olive oils, honey, tapenade (an olive paste), and dried herbs. **Savon de Marseille** (Marseille soap) is a household standard in France, often sold as a satisfyingly crude and hefty block in odorless olive-oil green. But its chi-chi offspring are dainty pastel guest soaps in almond, lemon, vanilla, and other scents.

The locally famous bakery **Four des Navettes** (⊠*136 rue Sainte, Garde Hill* ☏*04–91–33–32–12*), up the street from Notre-Dame-de-la-Garde, makes orange-spice, shuttle-shape *navettes*. These cookies are modeled on the little boat in which Mary Magdalene and Lazarus washed up onto Europe's shores and are a Marseille specialty.

La Compagnie de Provence (⊠*1 rue Caisserie, Le Panier* ☏*04–91–56–20–94*) is a major producer of savon de Marseille and has an excellent range to choose from. **Terre è Provence** (⊠*19 rue Montgrand, Le Panier* ☏*04–91–33–93–38*) has a copious display of colorful Provençal pottery.

WHERE TO EAT

$$$$ ✕**Chez Fonfon.** Tucked into the film-ready tiny fishing port Vallon des Auffes, this is a Marseillais landmark. Yes it's expensive, but try classic bouillabaisse served with all the bells and whistles—broth, hot-chili rouille, and flamboyant table-side filleting. ⊠*140 rue du Vallon des Auffes, Vallon des Auffes* ☏*04–91–52–14–38* ⊕*www.chez-fonfon.com* ⌂*Reservations essential* ═*AE, DC, MC, V* ☉*Closed Sun. and 1st 2 wks in Jan. No lunch Mon.*

¢–$$ ✕**Etienne.** This historic Le Panier hole-in-the-wall has more than just good fresh-anchovy pizza from a wood-burning oven. There are also fried squid, eggplant gratin, a slab of rare-grilled beef big enough for two, and the quintessential *pieds et paquets*, Marseille's earthy classic of sheeps' feet and stuffed tripe. Be warned: pizza is considered an appetizer here and main courses are huge. ✉*43 rue de la Lorette, Le Panier* ☎*No phone* ▭*No credit cards.*

MENORCA, SPAIN (MAHÓN)

Menorca, the northernmost Balearic island, is a knobby, cliff-bound plateau with a single central hill—El Toro—from whose 1,100-foot summit you can see the whole island. Prehistoric monuments—*taulas* (huge stone T-shapes), *talayots* (spiral stone cones), and *navetes* (stone structures shaped like overturned boats)—left by the first Neolithic settlers are everywhere on the island, rising up out of a landscape of small, tidy fields bounded by hedgerows and drystone walls. Tourism came late to Menorca, but having sat out the early Balearic boom, Menorca has avoided many of the other islands' industrialization troubles: there are no high-rise hotels, and the herringbone road system, with a single central highway, means that each resort is small and separate.

ESSENTIALS

CURRENCY The euro (€1 to US$1.46 at this writing); U.S. currency is generally not accepted in Europe, but ATMs are common and credit cards are widely accepted.

HOURS Museums generally open 9 until 7 or 8, many are closed on Mondays and some close in the afternoon. Most stores are open Monday through Saturday 9 to 1:30 and 5 to 8, but a few tourist shops may open in the afternoon and also on Sunday between May and September.

TELEPHONES Most tri-band or quad-band GSM phones will work in Spain, where services are 3G-compatible. Public kiosks accept phone cards that support international calls (cards sold in press shops, bars and telecom shops). Major companies include Vodafone.

COMING ASHORE

Vessels dock at the commercial port in Mahón, which sits directly below the old town. From here, it is a short but steep walk up to the heart of the old town. There are few facilities at the port itself, but a selection of shops and cafés line the shady street outside. Taxis wait outside the port, and drivers can be hired for the day to do tourist itineraries.

Menorca is a small island, and you can travel across it in 40 minutes by vehicle. Public bus services are modern and reliable, but services to the smaller towns may not be frequent. The bus station is at the far side of Mahón and involves a steep climb from the port area. It might be advisable to take a taxi to the station. The journey time from Mahón to Ciutadella is 1 hour. Renting a car is the ideal—but expensive—way to get around; expect to pay as much as €87 per day for an economy manual vehicle.

EXPLORING MENORCA

MAHÓN

Numbers in the margin correspond to points of interest on the Menorca map.

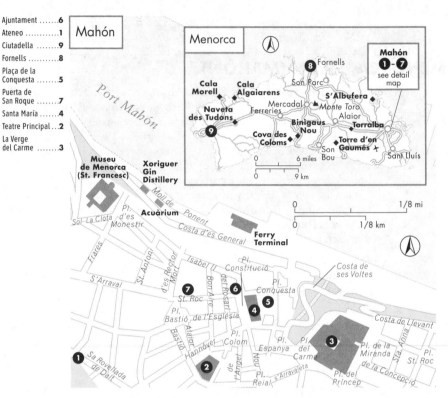

Established as the island's capital in 1722, when the British began their nearly 80-year occupation, Mahón stills bears the stamp of its former rulers. The streets nearest the port are lined with four-story Georgian town houses in various states of repair; the Mahónese still nurse a craving for Chippendale furniture, and drink gin.

6 Ajuntament. Mahón's city hall is a large Georgian building. Reach it by walking up Carrer Alfons III from the Plaça de la Conquesta. Nearby, on Carrer Isabel II, you'll find many of the more imposing Georgian homes in Menorca. ⊠*Pl. de la Constitució 1* ☎971/369800.

1 Ateneo. A good place to begin your tour of Mahón is at the northwest corner of the Plaça de S'Esplanada. Stop in at No. 25, the island's cultural and literary society has displays of wildlife, seashells, seaweed, minerals, and stuffed birds. Side rooms include paintings and mementos of Menorcan writers, poets, and musicians. ⊠*Rovellada de Dalt 25* ☎971/360553 ⊠*Free* ⊙*Weekdays 10–2 and 4–10, Sat. 5–9.*

5 Plaça de la Conquesta. Behind the church of Santa María is this plaza with a statue of Alfons III of Aragón, who wrested the island from the Moors in 1287.

7 Puerta de San Roque. At the far end of Carrer Rector Mort is the massive gate of the only surviving portion of the 14th-century city walls, rebuilt in 1587 to protect Mahón from the pirate Barbarossa (Redbeard). ⊠*Carrer Rector Mort.*

4 **Santa María.** A few steps north from the Cloister del Carme bring you to the church of St. Mary, which dates from the 13th century but was rebuilt during the British occupation and restored after being sacked during the civil war. The church's pride is its 3,200-pipe baroque organ, imported from Austria in 1810. There are concerts (€3) here weekdays 11:30–12:30. ✉*Pl. de la Constitució* ☎971/363949.

2 **Teatre Principal.** From Sa Rovellada de Dalt, turn left on Carrer de ses Moreres, then right on Carrer Bastió to where it becomes Carrer Costa d'en Deià, and—if it's open—have a look at Mahón's lovely theater. It was built in 1824 as an opera house, with five tiers of boxes, red plush seats, and gilded woodwork—a La Scala in miniature. Opera companies from Italy would make this their first port of call, en route to their mainland tours; anything that went down poorly with the critical audience in Mahón would get cut from the repertoire. Fully restored in 2005, the Principal still hosts a brief opera season; if you're visiting in the first week of December or June, get tickets at all costs. ✉*Carrer Costa d'en Deia s/n* ☎971/355776.

3 **La Verge del Carme.** Carrer Costa d'en Deaià descends to the Plaça Reial (a bit grandiosely named, for an unimposing little rectangle dominated by a café called the American Bar), where it becomes the Carrer sa Ravaleta. Ahead is this church, which has a fine painted and gilded altarpiece. Adjoining are the cloisters, now used as a **public market,** the intervals between the massive stone arches filled with stalls selling fresh produce and a variety of local specialties such as cheeses and sausages. ✉*Pl. del Carme* ☎971/362402.

FORNELLS

8 *35 km (21 mi) northwest of Mahón.*

The first fortifications built here to defend the Bay of Fornells from pirates date to 1625. A little village (full-time population: 500) of whitewashed houses with red tile roofs. The bay—Menorca's second-largest and its deepest—offers ideal conditions for windsurfing, sailing and scuba diving. The real draw of Fornells is its restaurants. This is the best place on the island to try Menorca's specialty, *Es Pla caldereta de langosta* (lobster stew).

CIUTADELLA

9 *44 km (27 mi) west of Mahón.*

Ciutadella was Menorca's capital before the British settled in Mahón, and its history is richer. As you arrive via the ME1, the main artery across the island from Mahón, turn left at the second roundabout and follow the ring road to the Passeig Maritim; at the end, near the **Castell de Sant Nicolau** watchtower (visits daily, June–October 10–1 and 5–10)

MENORCA BEST BETS

Explore the Gothic and Renaissance core of Ciutadella. The island's old capital was the religious and commercial heartbeat for several hundred years.

Tuck into a pot of *Es Pla caldereta de langosta.* This lobster stew is always the most expensive item on the menu, but it's Menorca's pièce de résistance.

Take to the water. The bay at Fornells is the perfect place to take up sailing or windsurfing.

4

is a **monument to David Glasgow Farragut,** the first admiral of the U.S. Navy, whose father emigrated from Ciutadella to the United States. From here, take Passeig de Sant Nicolau to the **Plaça de s'Esplanada,** and park near the Plaça d'es Born.

From a passage on the left side of Ciutadella's columned and crenelated **Ajuntament** (⊠ *Pl. d'es Born*), on the west side of the Born, steps lead up to the **Mirador d'es Port,** a lookout from which you can survey the harbor.

The local **Museu Municipal** houses artifacts of Menorca's prehistoric, Roman, and medieval past, including records of land grants made by Alfons III to the local nobility after defeating the Moors. It's in the Bastió de Sa Font (Bastion of the Fountain), an ancient defense tower at the east end of the harbor. ☎ *971/380297* ⊕ *www.ciutadella.org/museu* ⊠ *€2.20, free Wed.* ☺ *Nov.–Apr., Tues.–Sat. 10–2; May–Oct., Tues.–Sat. 10–2 and 6–9.*

The monument in the middle of the Plaça d'es Born commemorates the citizens' resistance of a Turkish invasion in 1588. South from the plaza along the east side of the Born is the block-long 19th-century **Palau Torresaura** (⊠ *Carrer Major del Born 8*), built by the Baron of Torresaura, one of the many noble families from Aragón and Catalonia that repopulated Menorca after it was captured from the Moors in the 13th century. The interesting facade faces the plaza, though the entrance is on the side street (it is not open to the public).

The **Palau Salort,** on the opposite side of the Carrer Major, is the only noble home regularly open to the public. The coats of arms on the ceiling are those of the families Salort (a salt pit and a garden: *sal* and *ort,* or *huerta*) and Martorell (a marten). ⊠ *Carrer Major des Born* ⊠ *€2* ☺ *May–Oct., Mon.–Sat. 10–2.*

The Carrer Major leads to the Gothic **Cathedral** (⊠ *Pl. de la Catedral at Plaça Píus XII*), which has some beautifully carved, intricate choir stalls. The side chapel has round Moorish arches, remnants of the mosque that once stood on this site; the bell tower is a converted minaret.

Follow the arcade of Carrer de Quadrado north from the cathedral and turn right on Carrer del Seminari, lined on the west side with some of the city's most impressive historic buildings. Among them is the **Seminari of the 17th-century Convent and Eglésia del Socors** (⊠ *Carrer del Seminari at Carrer Obispo Vila*), which hosts Ciutadella's summer festival of classical music.

Ciutadella's **port** is accessible from steps that lead down from Carrer Sant Sebastià. The waterfront here is lined with seafood restaurants, some of which burrow into caverns far under the Born.

SHOPPING

Menorca is known for shoes and leather, cheese, gin (introduced during British rule)—and recently, wine. The fine supple quality of the leather here serves high-class couturiers around the world with the surplus being sold in island factory shops. The streets of the compact center of Mahón are excellent for shopping.

In Mahón, buy leather goods at **Marks** (✉ *S'Arravaleta 18* ☎ *971/322660*). Visit the **Xoriguer distillery** (✉ *Anden de Poniente 91* ☎ *971/362197*), on Mahón's quayside, near the ferry terminal, and take a guided tour, sample various types of gin, and buy some to take home.

Inland, the showroom of **Pons Quintana** (✉ *Calle San Antonio 120, Alaior* ☎ *971/371050*) has a full-length window overlooking the factory where they make their ultrachic women's shoes. The company also has a shop in Mahón, at Sa Ravaleta 21. Both locations are closed weekends. The showroom of **Jaime Mascaro** (✉ *Poligon Industrial s/nFerreries* ☎ *971/373837*), on the main highway to Cuitadella, features not only shoes and bags but fine leather coats and belts for men and women. Mascaro also has a shop in Mahón, at Carrer ses Moreres.

SPORTS & ACTIVITIES

Several miles long and a mile wide, but with a narrow entrance to the sea and virtually no waves, the Bay of Fornells gives the windsurfing and sailing beginner a feeling of security and the expert plenty of excitement.

Wind Fornells (✉ *Ctra. Mercaval Fornells s/n, Es Mercadal* ☎ *971/188150 or 659/577760* ⊕ *www.windfornells.com*) rents boards, dinghies, and catamarans, and gives lessons in English or Spanish; they're open from May to October.

WHERE TO EAT

$–$$ ✗ **Pilar.** On a side street a few steps from the Plaça de l'Esplinada, in the center of Mahón, this pleasant little restaurant (eight tables) has a simple decor of white walls and beams, and antique sideboards. Under owners Jesus Saavedra and Fanny Mateu it offers a range of traditional Spanish dishes—including a hearty *sopa de ajo* (garlic soup) with cured ham, chorizo (spicy sausage), and whole cooked cloves of garlic. ✉ *Carrer des Forn 61* ☎ *971/366817* ▭ *AE, DC, MC, V* ⊙ *Closed Sun. and Jan. 1–15. No dinner Mon.–Thurs.*

¢–$ ✗ **Itake.** On the port since 1994, Itake is an amiable clutter of 12 tables, specials of the day on a chalkboard, ceiling fans, paper place mats, and frosted-glass lamps. This is arguably the best place in Mahón for an inexpensive, informal meal with a different touch. Where neighboring eateries pride themselves on fresh fish, Itake serves goat cheese and burgers, kangaroo steaks in mushroom sauce, and ostrich breast with strawberry coulis. That said, nothing here is made with any real elaboration: orders come out of the kitchen at nearly the rate of fast food. ✉ *Moll de Llevant 317* ☎ *971/354570* ▭ *AE, DC, MC, V* ⊙ *No dinner Sun. Sept.–June. Closed Mon.*

MESSINA, ITALY (FOR TAORMINA & MT. ETNA)

Sicily has beckoned seafaring wanderers since the trials of Odysseus were first sung in Homer's *Odyssey*. Strategically poised between Europe and Africa, this mystical volcanic land has been a melting pot of every great civilization on the Mediterranean: Greek and Roman; then Arab and Norman; and finally French, Spanish, and Italian. Today Sicily fuses the remains of sackings past: graceful Byzantine mosaics rubbing elbows with Greek temples, Roman amphitheaters, Romanesque cathedrals, and baroque flights of fancy. Messina's ancient history lists a series of disasters, but the city nevertheless managed to develop a fine university and a thriving cultural environment. On December 28, 1908, Messina changed from a flourishing metropolis of 120,000 to a heap of rubble, shaken to pieces by an earthquake that turned into a tidal wave and left 80,000 dead and the city almost completely leveled. For this reason there are few historical treasures but the town makes a good jumping off point for explorations of other treasures.

ESSENTIALS

CURRENCY   The euro (€1 to US$1.46 at this writing); U.S. currency is generally not accepted in Europe, but ATMs are common.

HOURS   Shops are generally open 9 to 1 and 3:30 to 7:30 and are closed Sunday and Monday morning most of the year. Summer (June to September) hours are usually 9 to 1 and 4 to 8.

INTERNET   **Fast Net Café** ✉ *Via Garibaldi 72* ☎*090662758.*

TELEPHONES   Tri-band GSM phones work in Italy. You can buy prepaid phone cards at telecom shops, news-vendors, and tobacconists in all towns and cities. Phone cards can be used for local or international calls.

COMING ASHORE

Ships dock in the main port of Messina. Passenger facilities cater to the many commercial ferry passengers who enter Sicily here, and though there are refreshment stands, they are often busy. There is no shuttle service, but it is possible to walk into Messina. Taxis wait at the port entrance, and it's a five-minute transfer to the train station.

It is possible to reach Taormina by train from Messina followed by the cable car from the town below up to Taormina proper. Most services take around 45 minutes and cost approximately €6 round-trip. Taxis charge approximately €2.33 initially, then €0.78 per km with an increment of €0.11 per 140m when the taxi travels at less than 20 kph (12 mph). Mt. Etna is not easy to reach by public transport.

Taormina makes a good departure point for excursions around—but not always to the top of—Mt. Etna, with private companies offering a guiding service. A rental car would allow you to explore much of northern Sicily during your day in port. Rental costs are approximately €45 per day for a compact manual vehicle.

EXPLORING NORTHEASTERN SICILY

MESSINA

❶ *Numbers in the margin correspond to points of interest on the Sicily and Taormina maps.*

The reconstruction of Messina's Norman and Romanesque **Duomo,** originally built by the Norman king Roger II in 1197, has retained much of the original plan, including a handsome crown of Norman battlements, an enormous apse, and a splendid wood-beamed ceiling. The adjoining **bell tower** contains one of the largest and most complex mechanical clocks

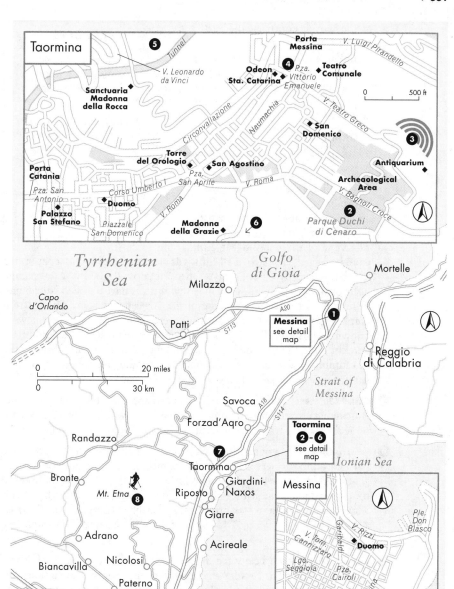

Taormina

Porta Messina
V. Luigi Prandello
Odeon
Sta. Catarina
Pza. Vittorio Emanuele
Teatro Comunale
V. Leonardo da Vinci
Sanctuaria Madonna della Rocca
V. Teatro Greco
San Domenico
Circonvallazione
Naumachia
Torre del Orologio
San Agostino
Antiquarium
Porta Catania
Pza. San Aprile
V. Roma
Archeaological Area
V. Bagnoli Croce
Pza. San Antonio
Corso Umberto I
Duomo
Palazzo San Stefano
Piazzale San Domenico
Madonna della Grazie
Parque Duchi di Cenaro

Tyrrhenian Sea
Golfo di Gioia
Mortelle
Capo d'Orlando
Milazzo
Patti
Messina see detail map
S113
A20
Reggio di Calabria
Strait of Messina
0 / 20 miles
0 / 30 km
Savoca
A18
S114
Forzad'Aqro
Taormina ❷-❻ see detail map
Ionian Sea
Randazzo
Taormina
Bronte
Mt. Etna
Giardini-Naxos
Messina
Riposto
Giarre
Ple, Don Blasco
V. Tom. Cannizzaro
Garibaldi
V. Rizzi
Duomo
Adrano
Acireale
Lgo. Seggiola
Pza. Cairoli
Biancavilla
Nicolosi
Vle. S. Marino
Vle. la Farina
Paterno
A19
S192
Catania
Golfo di Catania

Northeastern Sicily

in the world, constructed in 1933 with a host of gilded automatons, including a roaring lion, that spring into action every day at the stroke of noon. ⊠*Piazza del Duomo* ☏*090/675175* ⊙*Daily 8–12:30 and 4–7.*

TAORMINA
43 km (27 mi) southwest of Messina.

The medieval cliff-hanging town of Taormina is overrun with tourists and trinket shops, but its natural beauty is still hard to argue with. The view of the sea and Mt. Etna from its jagged cactus-covered cliffs is as close to perfection as a panorama can get, especially on clear days, when the snow-capped volcano's white puffs of smoke rise against the blue sky. Writers have extolled Taormina's beauty almost since its founding in the 6th century BC by Greeks from Naples; Goethe and D.H. Lawrence were among its more recent well-known enthusiasts. The town's boutique-lined main streets get old pretty quickly, but don't overlook the many hiking paths that wind through the beautiful hills surrounding Taormina. Nor should you miss the trip up to stunning Castelmola—whether by foot or by car.

⑤ Castello Saraceno. By footpath or car you can approach the medieval castle, enticingly perched on an adjoining cliff above town, but you cannot continue all the way to the castle itself. ⊠*Monte Tauro.*

④ Palazzo Corvaja. Many of Taormina's 14th- and 15th-century palaces have been carefully preserved. Especially beautiful, the Palazzo Corvaja has characteristic black-lava and white-limestone inlays. Today it houses the tourist office and the **Museo di Arte e Storia Popolare,** which has a collection of puppets and folk art, carts, and cribs. ⊠*Largo Santa Caterina* ☏*0942/610274 Palazzo* 🗪*Museum €2.50* ⊙*Museum Tues.–Sun. 9–1 and 4–8.*

⑥ Taormina Mare. Down below the main city of Taormina, at sea level, is this beach near Giardini Naxos, where beachgoers hang out in summer. It's accessible by a **funivia** (gondola) that glides past incredible views on its way down. 🗪*Funivia €1.80* ⊙*Apr.–Oct. daily, every 15 mins 8 AM–midnight; Nov.–Mar. daily, every 15 min 8–8.*

③ Teatro Greco. The Greeks put a premium on finding impressive locations to stage their dramas, and the site of Taormina's hillside theater is a fine one. Beyond the columns you can see the town's rooftops spilling down the hillside, the arc of the coastline, and Mt. Etna in the distance. The theater was built during the 3rd century BC and rebuilt by the Romans during the 2nd century AD. Its acoustics are exceptional: even today a stage whisper can be heard in the last rows. In summer Taormina hosts an arts festival of music and dance events and a film festival; many performances are held in the

Teatro Greco. ⊠ *Via Teatro Greco* ☎0942/23220 🎟️*€6, free in certain parts of winter* ⊙ *Daily 9–1 hr before sunset. Closed Mon. Oct.–Mar.*

② Villa Comunale. Stroll down Via Bagnoli Croce from the main Corso
★ Umberto to this oasis. Also known as the Parco Duca di Cesarò, the lovely public gardens were designed by Florence Trevelyan Cacciola, a Scottish lady "invited" to leave England following a romantic liaison with the future Edward VII (1841–1910). Arriving in Taormina in 1889, she married a local professor and devoted herself to the gardens, filling them with Mediterranean plants, ornamental pavilions (known as the beehives), and fountains. Stop by the panoramic bar, which has stunning views. ⊠ *Via Bagnoli Croce* ⊙ *May–Oct., daily 9–10; Nov.–Apr., daily 9–5.*

CASTELMOLA
❼ *5 km (3 mi) west of Taormina.*

You may think that Taormina has spectacular views, but tiny Castelmola, floating 1,800 feet above sea level, takes the word "scenic" to a whole new level. Along the cobblestone streets within the ancient walls, the 360-degree panoramas of mountain, sea, and sky are so ubiquitous that you almost get used to them (but not quite). Collect yourself with a sip of the sweet almond wine (best served cold) made in the local bars, or with lunch at one of the humble pizzerias or panino shops.

FodorsChoice The best place to take in Castelmola's views is from the old **Castello Nor-**
★ **manno** ruin, reached by a set of steep staircases rising out of the town center. In all Sicily, there may be no spot more scenic than atop the castle ruins, where you can gaze upon two coastlines, smoking Mt. Etna, and the town spilling down the mountainside. As the castle is completely open-air, you can visit at any time, but you should come to Castelmola during daylight hours for the view.

A 10-minute drive on a winding but well-paved road leads from Taormina to Castelmola; you must park in one of the public lots on the hillside below and climb a series of staircases to reach the center. On a nice day, hikers are in for a treat if they walk instead of driving. It's a serious uphill climb, but the 1½-km (¾-mi) path is extremely well maintained and not too challenging. You'll begin at Porta Catania in Taormina, with a walk along Via Apollo Arcageta past the Chiesa di San Francesco di Paolo on the left. The Strada Comunale della Chiusa then leads past Piazza Andromaco, revealing good views of the jagged promontory of Cocolanazzo di Mola to the north. Allow 45 minutes on the way up, a half-hour down. There's another, slightly longer—2-km (1-mi)—path that heads up from Porta Messina past the Roman aqueduct, Convento dei Cappuccini, and the northeastern side of Monte Tauro. You could take one path up and the other down.

MT. ETNA
❽ *64 km (40 mi) southwest of Taormina.*

FodorsChoice Mt. Etna is one of the world's major active volcanoes and is the largest and
★ highest in Europe—the cone of the crater rises to 10,902 feet above sea level. Plato sailed in just to catch a glimpse in 387 BC; in the 9th century AD, the oldest gelato of all was shaved off of its snowy slopes; and in the 21st century the volcano still claims annual headlines. Etna has erupted 12

times in the past 30 or so years, most spectacularly in 1971, 1983, 2001, and 2002; many of these eruptions wiped out cable-car stations. The most recent fiery display was a medium-size flank eruption in 2006. The refuge at Sapienza, however, is currently operational. Although each eruption is predictably declared a "tragedy" by the media, owing to the economic losses, Etna almost never threatens human life. Travel in the proximity of the crater depends on Mt. Etna's temperament, but you can walk up and down the enormous lava dunes and wander over its moonlike surface of dead craters. The rings of vegetation change markedly as you rise, with vineyards and pine trees gradually giving way to growths of broom and lichen. Taormina makes a good the departure points for excursions around—but not always to the top of—Mt. Etna.

Instead of going up Mt. Etna, you can circle it on the **Circumetnea railroad,** which runs near the volcano's base. The private railway almost circles the volcano, running 114 km (71 mi) between Catania and Riposto—the towns are 30 km (19 mi) apart by the coast road. The line is small, slow, and only single-track, but has some dramatic vistas of the volcano and goes through lava fields. The round trip takes about 5 hours, there are about 10 departures a day. ⊠ *Via Caronda 352, Catania* ☎*095/541250* ⊕*www.circumetnea.it* ✉*€11 round-trip* ⊗*Mon.–Sat.* 6 AM–9 PM.

SHOPPING

Taormina is the place in eastern Sicily for shopping, especially along Corso Umberto I and the surrounding alleyways where chic boutiques sell lace and linen, including placemats and napkins. The island as a whole is famed for its ceramics, particularly its practical folk pottery from Calta-girone, close by along the north coast. Marble and wrought iron are also fashioned into souvenir pieces and antique shops are numerous, though prices can be high.

A marzipan devotee should not leave Taormina without trying one of the almond-based sweets—maybe in the guise of the ubiquitous *fico d'India* (prickly pear), or in more unusual *frutta martorana* varieties. Locals also swear by the cannoli, and a block of almond paste makes a good souvenir—you can bring it home to make an almond latte or granita. Local wines and spirits, including limocello are worth seeking out.

Carlo Panarello (⊠*Corso Umberto 122, Taormina* ☎*0942/23910*) sells an excellent range of local handicrafts.

NEED A BREAK?   **Pasticceria Etna** (⊠*Corso Umberto 112, Taormina* ☎*0942/24735* 🖷*0942/21279*) is the place fwr marzipan.

SPORTS & ACTIVITIES

Mount Etna is a natural magnet for adventure-seekers, but because the volcano is active you should consult experts before tackling the peak. Hiking is certainly a popular choice on the lower slopes, while climbing Mt. Etna proves more challenging.

Club Alpino Italiano (⊠*Piazza Scammacca, Catania* ☎*095/7153515 or 347/4111632*) in Catania is a great resource for Mt. Etna climbing and hiking guides. If you have some experience and don't like a lot of hand-holding, these are the guides for you.

If you're a beginning climber, call the **Gruppo Guide Etna Nord** (⊠ *Via Roma 93, Linguaglossa* ☎*095/7774502 or 348/0125167* ⊕*www.guidetnanord. com*) to arrange for a guide. Their service is a little more personalized—and expensive—than others. Reserve ahead.

For a bird's-eye view of Mt. Etna, you can try paragliding or hang gliding; contact **No Limits Etna Center** (⊠*Hotel Lido Caparena, Via Nazionale 189, Taormina* ☎*0942/652033* 🖷*0942/36913* ⊕*www.etnacenter.net*), based at a hotel in Taormina Mare. The company also organizes climbing, caving, and diving expeditions.

WHERE TO EAT

$$$–$$$$ ✕ **L'Arco dei Cappuccini.** Just off the radar screen of the main tourist strip lies this clean, diminutive restaurant with white tablecloths. Outdoor seating and an upstairs kitchen help make room for a few extra tables—necessary because the locals are well aware that both the price and the quality cannot be beat elsewhere in town. Indulge in *sopressa di polipo* (steamed octopus carpaccio), gnocchi *con pistacchi* (with pistachio cream sauce), or the fresh catch of the day. ⊠*Via Cappuccini 7, off Via Costanino Patricio near Porta Messina, Taormina* ☎*0942/24893* ⌟*Reservations essential* 🝤*AE, DC, MC, V* ⊗*Closed Wed.*

$$–$$$ ✕ **Terrazza Auteri.** Just below Castelmola's center, on the road heading down to Taormina, stands this three-level, multiterraced restaurant and pizzeria. The food—seafood dishes like mixed shellfish risotto, grilled prawns or swordfish, along with pizzas from a wood-burning oven and a standard assortment of pastas—is eclipsed by the memorable views from almost every table on the terraces. ⊠*Via Madonna della Scala 1, Castelmola* ☎*0942/28603* ⊕*www.terrazza-auteri.com* 🝤*AE, DC, MC, V* ⊗*Closed Mon. Oct.–Apr.*

MONTE CARLO, MONACO

In 1297, the Grimaldi family seized this fortified town and, except for a short break under Napoléon, they have ruled here ever since. The Principality of Monaco covers 473 acres; it would fit comfortably inside New York's Central Park while its 5,000 citizens would fill only a small fraction of the seats in Yankee Stadium. The Grimaldis made money from gambling and attracted a well-heeled, monied crowd, but the whole world watched as Hollywood Princess Grace Kelly wed Prince Rainier ruler of Monaco to put this place on the map. It's the very favorable tax system, not the gambling, that makes Monaco one of the most sought-after addresses in the world, and the principality bristles with gleaming high-rise apartment complexes owned by tax-exiles. But at the town's great 1864 landmark Hôtel de Paris—still a veritable crossroads of the buffed and befurred Euro-gentry—at the Opéra, or the ballrooms of the Casino, you'll still be able to conjure up Monaco's belle epoque.

ESSENTIALS

CURRENCY The euro (€1 to US$1.46 at this writing); U.S. currency is generally not accepted in Europe, but ATMs are common and credit cards widely accepted.

HOURS Most stores open Monday through Saturday from 9 to 7, but many close at lunchtime (usually noon to 2 or 3), and some will open later and on Sunday during July and August. Museums are usually open 10 to 5, but most are closed on either Monday or Tuesday.

INTERNET **Stars n Bars** (⊠ *Quai Antoine 1, west side of harbor* ☎ *377/97–97–95–90* ⊕ *www.starsnbars.com*) is a great American-style fast food restaurant that sees its fair share of celebrities. It's open Monday–Saturday until midnight. It's closed Monday between October and April.

TELEPHONES Tri-band GSM phones work in Monte Carlo, as in France. You can buy prepaid phone cards at telecom shops, news-vendors and tobacconists in all towns and cities. Phone cards can be used for local or international calls. France Telecom and Orange are leading telecom companies.

COMING ASHORE

Cruise ships dock at Port Hercule, just below Monaco-Ville, at a state-of-the-art cruise port within a $200-million breakwater that can accommodate several ships at a time. Even still, on busy days you may be tendered to the landing dock. There are few facilities at the port itself. An elevator about 500 yards away leads up to the town, where the attractions of old Monaco are located. It is approximately one mile from the port to the Monte Carlo district, this is a 15- to 30-minute walk depending on your level of fitness. While the distance is not too great, there are a lot of hills.

If you intend to confine your explorations to the principality, there is no need to hire a car. All the attractions of the Old town are less than a 10-minute walk apart. Bus services 1 and 2 link Monaco-Ville with Monte Carlo; prices are €1 per journey. If you want to tour the stunning surrounding Provençal countryside, a vehicle would be useful. Expect to pay €70 for an economy manual vehicle for the day. Taxis wait outside the port gates and can provide tourist itineraries. For single journeys, tariffs are €2.30 initially, then €0.69 per km.

EXPLORING MONTE CARLO

Numbers in the margin correspond to points of interest on the Monte Carlo map.

Monte Carlo or Monaco? Many people use the names interchangeably but officially, the old town or Vieille Ville is officially **Monaco-Ville** (or Le Rocher because it sits on a rocky plateau). This is where the Grimaldis live and the business of government is done. The "new" town, built in the 18th and 19th centuries and expanding upward rapidly even today, is called **Monte Carlo**, while the harbor area, or **La Condamine**, connects the two.

❶ **Casino de Monte Carlo.** The Place du Casino is the center of Monte Carlo, and the Casino itself is a must-see, even if you don't bet a *sou*. Into the gold-leaf splendor of the Casino, the hopeful traipse from tour buses

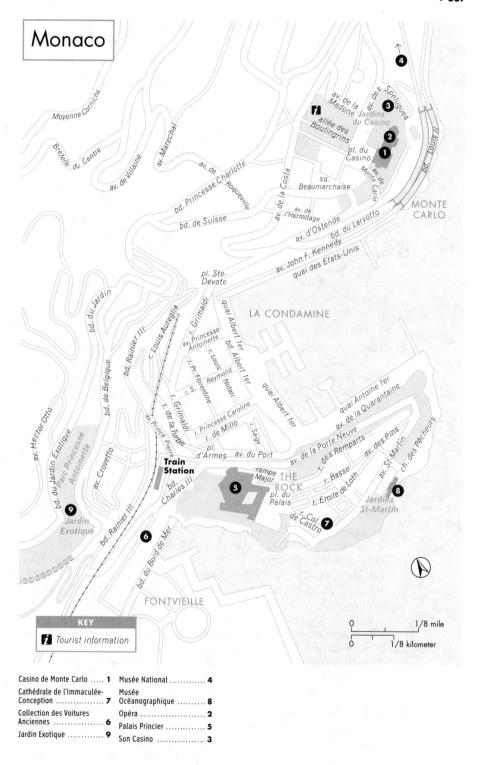

Monaco

MONTE CARLO

LA CONDAMINE

THE ROCK

FONTVIEILLE

Train Station

Parc Princesse Antoinette

Jardin Exotique

Jardins du Casino

Jardins St-Martin

Moyenne Corniche
Bretelle du Centre
av. de Villaine
av. Marechal
av. de Roqueville
bd. Princesse Charlotte
bd. de Suisse
av. de la Costa
av. de l'Hermitage
av. de l'Ostende
sq. Beaumarchaise
allée des Boulingrins
av. de la Madone
av. des Spelugues
pl. du Casino
bd. Louis II
av. de Monte Carlo
bd. du Larvotto
av. John F. Kennedy
quai des Etats-Unis
pl. Ste-Devote
bd. du Jardin
bd. Rainier III
r. Louis Aureglia
r. Grimaldi
av. Princesse Antoinette
r. Louis Notari
r. Princesse Caroline
r. de Millo
r. S. Florentine
r. Pr. Florentine
r. Reymond
bd. Albert 1er
quai Albert 1er
quai Antoine 1er
av. de la Quarantaine
av. de la Porte Neuve
r. des Remparts
r. Basse
r. Emile de Loth
r. Col. de Castro
av. St-Martin
av. des Pins
ch. des Pêcheurs
pl. d'Armes
av. du Port
rampe Major
pl. du Palais
bd. Charles III
bd. Rainier III
bd. du Bord de Mer
av. Hector Otto
av. Cravetta
av. Prince Pierre
bd. de Belgique
bd. du Jardin Exotique
r. Saige
r. de Millo
r. de Grimaldi
r. de la Turbie

0   1/8 mile
0   1/8 kilometer

to tempt fate beneath the gilt-edge rococo ceiling. (But do remember the fate of Sarah Bernhardt, who lost her last 100,000 francs here.) Jacket and tie are required in the back rooms, which open at 3 PM. Bring your passport (under-18 not admitted). Note that there are special admission fees to get into many of the period gaming rooms—only the Salle des Jeux Americains (where you'll find the slot machines) is free. ⊠ *Pl. du Casino* ☎ *377/92–16–20–00* ⊕ *www.sbm. mc* ⊗ *Daily noon–4* AM.

> ### MONTE CARLO BEST BETS
>
> **Watch the Changing of the Guard.** This short ceremony at exactly 11:55 AM in the palace square has been taking place for centuries.
>
> **Place your bets.** The Casino de Monte Carlo is surely the most beautiful place in the world to lose your shirt. If you don't want to bet, buy a chip as a souvenir.
>
> **Have an aperitif at the café in the place de Casino.** This is the place to watch the beautiful and megarich come and go and to enjoy the genteel atmosphere.

❼ Cathédrale de l'Immaculée-Conception. Follow the flow of crowds down the last remaining streets of medieval Monaco to the principality's cathederal, an uninspired 19th-century version of the Romanesque style. Nonetheless, it harbors a magnificent altarpiece, painted in 1500 by Bréa, and the tomb of Princess Grace. (⊠ *Av. St-Martin*)

❻ Collection des Voitures Anciennes. On the Terrasses de Fontvieille are two remarkable sights (opened in 2003): the vintage car collection and the **Jardin Animalier** (Animal Garden). The former is a collection of Prince Rainier's vintage vehicles from a De Dion Bouton to a Lamborghini Countach; the latter, a mini-zoo housing the Rainier family's animal collection, an astonishing array of wild beasts including monkeys and exotic birds. ⊠ *Terrasses de Fontvieille* ☎ *377/92–05–28–56 or 377/93–25–18–31* ⊠ *Collection des Voitures €6 Jardin Animalier €4* ⊗ *June–Sept., daily 10–6.*

❾ Jardin Exotique de Monaco. Carved out of the rock face—and one of Monte Carlo's most stunning escape hatches—the "exotic" garden is studded with thousands of succulents and cacti, all set along promenades and belvederes over the sea, and even framing faux boulders (actually hollow sculptures). There are rare plants from Mexico and Africa, and the hillside plot, threaded with bridges and grottoes, can't be beat for coastal splendor. Thanks go to Prince Albert I, who started it all. Also on the grounds, or actually under them, are the **Grottes de l'Observatoire**—spectacular grottoes and caves a-drip with stalagmites and spotlit with fairy lights. The largest cavern is called La Grande Salle (the big room) and looks like a Romanesque rock cathedral. Traces of Cro-Magnon civilization have been found here so the grottoes now bear the official name of the **Musée d'Anthropologie Préhistorique.** ⊠ *Bd. du Jardin Exotique* ☎ *377/93–15–29–80* ⊠ *€6.90* ⊗ *Mid-May–mid-Sept., daily 9–7; mid-Sept.–mid-May, daily 9–6* ⊗ *Closed mid-Nov.–mid-Dec.*

Fodor'sChoice
★

❹ Musée National Automates et Poupées. From Place des Moulins an elevator descends to the Larvotto Beach complex, artfully created with imported sand, and this museum housed in a Garnier villa within a rose garden. It has a beguiling collection of 18th- and 19th-century dolls and automatons. ⊠*17 av. Princesse Grace* ☎*377/93–30–91–26* ✉€6 ⊙*Easter–Aug., daily 10–6:30; Sept.–Easter, daily 10–12:15 and 2:30–6:30.*

❽ **Musée Océanographique.** At the prow of the Rock, the grand oceanography
🄲 museum perches dramatically on a cliff. It's a splendid Edwardian struc-
★ ture, built under Prince Albert I to house specimens collected on amateur
explorations. Jacques Cousteau (1910–97) led its missions from 1957
to 1988. The main floor displays skeletons and taxidermy of enormous
sea creatures; early submarines and diving gear dating from the Middle
Ages; and a few interactive science displays. The main draw is the famous
aquarium, a vast complex of backlighted tanks containing every imaginable species of fish, crab, and eel. ⊠*Av. St-Martin* ☎*377/93–15–36–00*
🌐*www.oceano.mc* ✉€11 ⊙*July and Aug., daily 9:30–7:30; Apr.–June,
daily 8:30–7; Sept., daily 9:30–7; Oct.–Mar., daily 10–6.*

The little **Azur Express Tourist Train** takes a tour around Monaco and Monte
Carlo, passing all the major sites and accompanying audio guide in English. The trip lasts 30 minutes, offers a useful overview of the principality,
and saves those tired feet. ⊠*Oceanographic Museum, av. Saint Martin* ☎*377/92–05–64–38* ✉€6 ⊙*Winter daily 10:30–5, summer daily
10–5.*

❷ **Opéra de Monte-Carlo.** In the true spirit of the town, it seems that the opera
house, with its 18-ton gilt-bronze chandelier and extravagant frescoes, is
part of the casino complex. The grand theater was designed by Charles
Garnier, who also built the Paris Opéra. Its main auditorium, the Salle
Garnier, was inaugurated by Sarah Bernhardt in 1879. (⊠*Pl. du Casino*
☎*377/98–06–28–28* 🌐*www.opera.mc*).

❺ **Palais Princier.** West of Monte Carlo stands the famous Rock, crowned by
the palace where the royal family resides. A 40-minute guided tour (summer only) of this sumptuous chunk of history, first built in the 13th century
and expanded and enhanced over the centuries, reveals an extravagance of
16th- and 17th-century frescoes, as well as tapestries, gilt furniture, and
paintings on a grand scale. Note that the **Relève de la Garde** (Changing
of the Guard) is held outside the front entrance of the palace most days
at 11:55 AM.

One wing of the Palais Princier, open throughout the year, is the **Musée
Napoléon** (☎*377/93–25–18–31*), filled with Napoleonic souvenirs—
including that hat and a tricolor scarf—and genealogical charts of France's
famous emperor. ⊠*Pl. du Palais* ☎*377/93–25–18–31* ✉*Palace €6,
museum €4, joint ticket €9* ⊙*Palace and museum Apr., daily 10:30–6:30;
May–Sept., daily 9:30–6:30; Oct., daily 10–5:30. Museum only Dec.,
daily 10:30–5.*

❸ **Sun Casino.** Some say the most serious gamblers play at in the Monte Carlo
Grand Hotel, which is near the vast convention center that juts over the
water. ⊠*12 av. des Spélugues* ☎*377/92–16–21–23* ⊙*Tables open weekdays at 5 PM and weekends at 4 PM; slot machines open daily at 11 AM.*

SHOPPING

The wealthy live in Monaco, and the wealthy visit Monaco, so it should not be a surprise that you can buy the finest designer clothing and accessories from very smart boutiques on the streets radiating out from the **place du Casino.** Monaco Ville, on the hill, has a range of souvenir emporia with a predominance of Princess Grace memorabilia, from the tacky to the tasteful. **La Condamine** has a range of shopping for those without sky-high credit card limits. Look out also for Formula 1 motor racing souvenirs; this race around the streets takes place in late May and is one of the highlights of the social season.

Bijoux Marlene (⊠ *Les Galereries du Métropole* ☎377/93–50–17–57) sells high-class costume jewelry based on Cartier and Van Arpels, usually made of silver. **Boutique du Rocher** (⊠ *1 av. de la Madone* ☎377/93–30–91–97) was set up by Princess Grace to promote Monagasque handicrafts. Everything here is locally made. **Formule 1** (⊠ *15 rue Grimaldi* ☎377/93–15–92–44) handles official race merchandise. **Jeunemaitre Haute Fourrures** (⊠ *2 rue des Iris* ☎377/93–30–00–87) supplies furs to the royal family and others. **Lanvin** (⊠ *pl. du Casino* ☎377/93–25–00–79 ⊕ *www.lanvin.com*) offers bespoke tailoring for men who want to look elegant at the casino or the opera. **Stock Griffe** (⊠ *5 bis av. St-Michel* ☎377/93–51–86–06), an upscale outlet, has up to 90% reductions on designer labels.

SPORTS & ACTIVITIES

Monte Carlo Golf Club has a highly rated course just outside the principality, and the Monte Carlo Country Club offers a range of provision but is most renowned for its tennis. This is the club that hosts the prestigious Monte Carlo Tennis Masters tournament. Admission to the clubs is €38 per day, plus greens fees for golf. Both clubs are run by the **Société des Bains de Mer** (⊠ *Pl. du Casino* ☎377/98–06–25–25 ⊕ *www. montecarloresort.com*).

BEACHES

Larvotto is the public beach of the principality, but many people choose to buy a temporary membership into a private beach club, which also has facilities such as changing cabins, showers, and restaurants. **Monte Carlo Beach Club** (⊠ *Larvotto, Monte Carlo* ☎377/98–06–52–46), where access is €40 per day weekdays, and €60 per day weekends.

WHERE TO EAT

$$–$$$$ ✕ **Castelroc.** With its tempting pine-shaded terrace just across from the entrance to the palace, this popular local lunch spot serves up specialties of cuisine Monegasque, ranging from *anchoïade* (a garlic and anchovy dip) to stockfish. The fixed-price menus are a bargain. ⊠ *Pl. du Palais* ☎377/93–30–36–68 ▤ *AE, MC, V* ⊘ *Closed weekends and Dec. and Jan.*

$$–$$$ ✕ **Café de Paris.** This landmark belle epoque brasserie, across from the casino, offers the usual classics (shellfish, steak tartare, matchstick frites, and fish boned table-side). Supercilious, super-pro waiters fawn gracefully

over titled preeners, gentlemen, jet-setters, and tourists alike. ✉*Pl. du Casino* ☎*377/92–16–20–20* ⊟*AE, DC, MC, V.*

NAPLES, ITALY (WITH HERCULANEUM, POMPEII & CAPRI)

Campania is a region of evocative names—Capri, Sorrento, Pompeii, Herculaneum—that conjure up visions of cliff-shaded coves, sun-dappled waters, and mighty ruins. The area's unique geology is responsible for its gorgeous landscape. A languid coastline stretches out along a deep blue sea, punctuated by rocky islands. Heading inland, the hills at first roll gently, then transform into mountains. Campania's complex identity is most intensely felt in its major city, Naples, which sprawls around its bay as though attempting to embrace the island of Capri, while behind it Mt. Vesuvius glowers. It's one of those few cities in the world that is instantly recognizable: lush, chaotic, scary, funny, confounding, intoxicating, and very beautiful. Few who visit remain ambivalent. You needn't participate in the mad whirl of the city, however. The best pastime in Campania is simply finding a spot with a stunning view and indulging in *il dolce far niente* (the sweetness of doing nothing).

ESSENTIALS

CURRENCY The euro (€1 to US$1.46 at this writing); U.S. currency is generally not accepted in Europe, but ATMs are common and credit cards are widely accepted.

HOURS Shops are open 9:30 until 1, then 4:30 until 8. Most are closed on Sunday and also on Monday morning.

INTERNET **Internet Bar by Tightrope Associazione Culturale** ✉*Piazza Bellini 74, Naples* ☎*081/295237.*

TELEPHONES Tri-band GSM phones work in Italy. You can buy prepaid phone cards at telecom shops, news-vendors, and tobacconists in all towns and cities. Phone cards can be used for local or international calls.

COMING ASHORE

The Stazione Maritima is located on the city's seafront; passenger facilities at the terminal were extended and refurbished in 2005, adding a tourist information office, shops, and cafés.

Buses 3S, 152, Sepsa, and CTP run to the train station along with tram routes 1 to 4. By the Circumvesuviana line from Piazza Garibaldi, you can reach Pompeii, Ercolano (Herculanium), and Castellammare (for the funicular to Mount Vesuvius). There are at least four hourly trains, and fares range from €0.70 to €2.30 to Pompeii (both one-way).

The hydrofoil to Capri departs from the same port where cruise ships disembark, and you can just walk to the vessel after buying a ticket. The funicular railway from the port up to Capri Town is (€1.60 round-trip).

Taxis charge approximately €2.33 initially, then €0.78 per km (½-mi) with an increment of €0.11 per 140 meters (260 feet) in slow traffic. A car rental could be useful if you want to explore the Amalfi coast, but it imperative that you return to Naples with time to spare because traffic

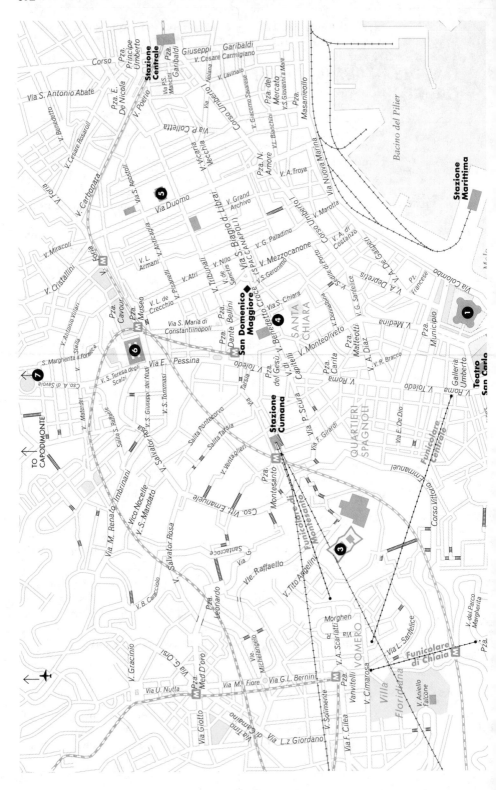

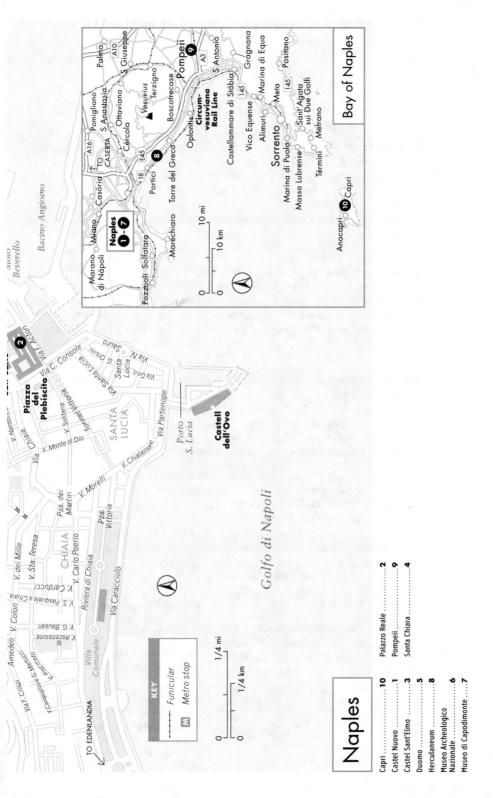

Bay of Naples

Naples

Capri	10
Castel Nuovo	1
Castel Sant'Elmo	3
Duomo	5
Herculaneum	8
Museo Archeologico Nazionale	6
Museo di Capodimonte	7
Palazzo Reale	2
Pompeii	9
Santa Chiara	4

KEY

Funicular

M Metro stop

along the coast can be very heavy and slow-moving. Expect to pay €45 per day for a compact manual vehicle.

EXPLORING NAPLES & VICINITY

NAPLES

Numbers in the margin correspond to points of interest on the Naples and region map.

❶ Castel Nuovo. Also known as the Maschio Angioino, this massive fortress was built by the Angevins in the 13th century and completely rebuilt by the Aragonese rulers who succeeded them. The decorative marble triumphal arch that forms the entrance was erected during the Renaissance in honor of King Alfonso V of Aragon (1396–1458). Within the castle is the city's **Museo Civico,** and the **Sala dell'Armeria,** the Armory with the remains of a Roman villa and a medieval necropolis. ✉*Piazza Municipio* ☎*081/7952003* 🎟️*€5* ☉*Mon.–Sat. 9–6; Sun. courtyard only 9–1.*

❸ Castel Sant'Elmo. Perched on Vomero hill, this castle was built by the Angevins in the 14th century to dominate the port and the old city and remodeled by the Spanish in 1537. The stout fortifications are still in use today by the military, and occasionally there are performances, exhibitions, and fairs. You get in free if you have a ticket to the adjoining Certosa di San Martino. ✉*Largo San Martino, Vomero* ☎*081/5784030* 🎟️*€3* ☉*Thurs.–Tues. 8:30–7:30.*

❺ Duomo. Though the Duomo was established in the 1200s, the building you see was erected a century later and has since undergone radical changes, especially during the baroque age. Inside the cathedral are 110 ancient columns salvaged from pagan buildings. Off the left aisle you step down into the 4th-century church of **Santa Restituta,** which was incorporated into the cathedral.

On the right aisle of the cathedral is the **Cappella di San Gennaro,** honoring St. Januarius, miracle-working patron saint of Naples. Three times a year—on September 19; on the Saturday preceding the first Sunday in May; and on December 16—his dried blood, contained in two sealed vials, is believed to liquefy during rites in his honor. The **Museo del tesoro di San Gennaro** houses a rich collection of treasures associated with the saint. ✉*Via Duomo 147, Spaccanapoli* ☎*081/449097 Duomo, 081/294764 museum* 🎟️*€7* ☉*Daily 8:30–12:30 and 4:30–7.*

Fodor's Choice
★

❻ Museo Archeologico Nazionale. The National Archaeological Museum holds one of the world's great collections of Greek and Roman antiquities, including such extraordinary sculptures as the *Hercules Farnese,* an exquisite Aphrodite attributed to the 4th-century BC Greek sculptor Praxiteles. Countless objects from Pompeii and Herculaneum

> ### NAPLES BEST BETS
>
> **Pompeii.** The finest and largest Roman site in the world is less than an hour from Naples.
>
> **Herculaneum.** Pompeii's smaller sibling is smaller, but it's more manageable and better preserved.
>
> **Museo Archeologico Nazionale.** The daily lives of Roman citizens at Pompeii and Herculaneum are brought to life with monumental statues and a wealth of personal and domestic items.

provide insight into life in ancient Rome. ⊠*Piazza Museo 19, Spaccanapoli* ☎*081/440166* ⊕*www.archeona.arti.beniculturali.it* ⊠*€6.50, €9 for special exhibits* ۞*Wed.–Mon. 9–7.*

➐ **Museo di Capodimonte.** The grandiose 18th-century neoclassical Bourbon
★ royal palace houses an impressive collection of fine and decorative art. Capodimonte's greatest treasure is the excellent collection of paintings well-displayed in the **Galleria Nazionale,** on the palace's first and second floors. Part of the **royal apartments** still has a complement of beautiful antique furniture. ⊠*Via Miano 2, Porta Piccola, Via Capodimonte* ☎*848/800288* ⊠*€7.50, €6.50 after 2* PM ۞*Daily 8:30–7:30; ticket office closes at 6:30.*

➋ **Palazzo Reale.** Dominating Piazza del Plebiscito, the huge palace dates from the early 1600s. It was renovated and redecorated by successive rulers, including Napoléon's sister Caroline and her husband, Joachim Murat (1767–1815), who reigned briefly in Naples. Don't miss seeing the **royal apartments,** sumptuously furnished and full of precious paintings, tapestries, porcelains, and other objets d'art. ⊠*Piazza del Plebiscito* ☎*081/400547* ⊠*€4* ۞*Thurs.–Tues. 9–7.*

➍ **Santa Chiara.** This monastery church is a Neapolitan landmark and the subject of a famous old song. It was built in the 1300s in Provençal Gothic style, and it's best known for the quiet charm of its cloister garden. ⊠*Piazza Gesù Nuovo, Spaccanapoli* ☎*081/5526209* ⊕*www.santachiara.info* ⊠*Museum and cloister €4* ۞*Church daily 7–noon and 4:30–6:30; museum and cloister Mon.–Sat. 9:30–7, Sun. 9:30–1.*

HERCULANEUM
➑ *10 km (6 mi) southeast of Naples.*

★ About 5,000 people lived in Herculaneum when it was destroyed. In AD 79 the gigantic eruption of Pompeii buried the town under a tide of volcanic mud. The semiliquid mass seeped into the crevices of every building, sealing all in a compact, airtight tomb.

Much excitement is presently focused on one excavation in a corner of the site, the Villa dei Papiri, built by Julius Caesar's father-in-law. The building is named for the 1,800 carbonized papyrus scrolls dug up here in the 18th century, leading scholars to believe that this may have been a study center or library.

Domestic, commercial, and civic buildings are accessible. Decorations are especially delicate in the **Casa del Nettuno ed Anfitrite** (House of Neptune and Amphitrite), and in the **Terme Femminili** (Women's Baths). On the other side of the house is the **Casa del Bel Cortile** (House of the Beautiful Courtyard). In one of its inner rooms is the temporary display of a cast taken of some skeletons found in the storerooms down at the old seafront, where almost 300 inhabitants were encapsulated for posterity. The sumptuously decorated **Terme Suburbane** (Suburban Baths)—open only mornings—and the **Casa dei Cervi** (House of the Stags), are all evocative relics of a lively and luxurious way of life.

⊠*Corso Ercolano, a 5-min walk downhill from Ercolano Circumvesuviana station* ☎*081/8575347* ⊕*www.pompeiisites.org* ⊠*€11; €20 includes Pompeii and 3 other sites for 3 days* ۞*Apr.–Oct., daily 8:30–*

7:30 (ticket office closes at 6); Nov.–Mar., daily 8:30–5 (ticket office closes at 3:30).

POMPEII

9 *11 km (7 mi) southeast of Herculaneum, 24 km (15 mi) southeast of Naples.*

Fodor'sChoice

★ The Scavi di Pompeii, petrified memorial to Vesuvius's eruption on the morning of August 23, AD 79, is the largest and most accessible of excavations anywhere. A busy commercial center with a population of 10,000 to 20,000, ancient Pompeii covered about 160 acres on the seaward end of the fertile Sarno Plain.

As you enter the ruins at Porta Marina, make your way to the **Foro** (Forum), which served as Pompeii's cultural, political, and religious center. The **Anfiteatro** (Amphitheater) was the ultimate in entertainment for local Pompeians, but quite small by Roman standards (seating 20,000). Built in about 80 BC, it was oval and divided into three seating areas like a theater. The **Terme Suburbane** (Suburban Baths) have eyebrowraising frescoes in the *apodyterium* (changing room). On the walls of **Lupanare** (brothel) are scenes of erotic games in which clients could engage.

Several homes were captured in various states by the eruption of Vesuvius. The **Casa del Poeta Tragico** (House of the Tragic Poet) is a typical middle-class house. On the floor is a mosaic of a chained dog and the inscription CAVE CANEM (beware of the dog). The **Casa degli Amorini Dorati** (House of the Gilded Cupids) is an elegant, well-preserved home with original marble decorations in the garden. Many paintings and mosaics were executed at **Casa del Menandro** (House of Menander), a patrician's villa named for a fresco of the Greek playwright.

The House of the Vettii is the best example of a house owned by wealthy *mercatores* (merchants). It contains vivid murals, but there also magnificently memorable frescoes on view at the **Villa dei Misteri** (Villa of the Mysteries). This villa had more than 60 rooms painted with frescoes; the finest are in the triclinium.

✉ *Porta marina, a 5-min walk from Pompeii-Villa dei Misteri station* ☎*081/8575347* ⊕*www.pompeiisites.org* 🎫*€11; €20 includes Herculaneum and 3 other sites for 3 days* ☉*Apr.–Oct., daily 8:30–7:30 (ticket office closes at 6); Nov.–Mar., daily 8:30–5 (ticket office closes at 3:30).*

CAPRI

10 *75 min by boat, 40 min by hydrofoil from Naples.*

Once a pleasure dome to Roman emperors and now Italy's most glamorous seaside getaway, Capri (pronounced with an accent on the first syllable) is a craggy island at the southern end to the bay of Naples.

Capri Town, is perched some 450 feet above the harbor. Piazza Umberto I, much better known as the Piazzetta, is the island's social hub.

You can window-shop along Via Vittorio Emanuele, which leads south toward the many-domed **Certosa di San Giacomo.** You can visit the church and cloister of this much-restored monastery and also pause long enough to enjoy the breathtaking view of Punta Tragara and the Faraglioni, three towering crags, from the viewing point at the edge of the cliff. ⌧ *Via Certosa* ☎*081/8376218* ⊙*Tues.–Sun. 9–2.*

From the terraces of the **Giardini di Augusto** *(Gardens of Augustus)*, a beautifully planted public garden with excellent views, you can see the village of Marina Piccola below and admire the steep and winding Via Krupp, actually a staircase cut into the rock. ⌧ *Via Matteotti, beyond monastery of San Giacomo* ⊙ *Daily dawn–dusk.*

A tortuous road leads up to **Anacapri**, the island's "second city," about 3 km (2 mi) from Capri Town. Crowds are thick down Via Capodimonte leading to Villa San Michele and around the square, Piazza Vittoria, which is the starting point of the chairlift to the top of Monte Solaro. Elsewhere, Anacapri is quietly appealing.

Only when the **Grotta Azzurra** was "discovered" in 1826 by the Polish poet August Kopisch and Swiss artist Ernest Fries, did Capri become a tourist haven. The water's extraordinary sapphire color is caused by a hidden opening in the rock that refracts the light. ⌧*Marina Grande* ⌧€16–€19, *depending on boat company, including admission to grotto* ⊙*Apr.–Sept., daily 9:30–2 hrs before sunset; Oct.–Mar., daily 10–noon.*

An impressive limestone formation and the highest point on Capri (1,932 feet), **Monte Solaro** affords gasp-inducing views toward the bays of both Naples and Salerno. A 12-minute chairlift ride will take you right to the top. ⌧*Piazza Vittoria, Anacapri* ☎*081/8371428* ⌧€4:50 one-way, €6 *round-trip* ⊙*Mar.–Oct., daily 9:30–6; Nov.–Feb., daily 10:30–3.*

In the heart of Anacapri, the octagonal baroque church of **San Michele**, finished in 1719, is best known for its exquisite majolica pavement designed by Solimena. ⌧*Piazza Nicola, Anacapri* ☎*081/8372396* ⌧€3 ⊙*Nov.–Mar., daily 9:30–5; Apr.–Oct., daily 9–7.*

SHOPPING

Leather goods, jewelry, and cameos are some of the best items to buy in Campania. In Naples you'll generally find good deals on handbags, shoes, and clothing. If you want the real thing, make your purchases in shops, but if you don't mind imitations, rummage around at the various street-vendor *bancherelle* (stalls).

In Naples, the immediate area around **Piazza dei Martiri**, in the center of Chiaia, has the densest concentration of luxury shopping, with perfume shops, fashion outlets, and antiques on display. **Via dei Mille** and **Via Filangieri**, which lead off Piazza dei Martiri, are home to Bulgari, Mont Blanc, and Hermes stores. The small, pedestrian-only **Via Calabritto**, which leads down from Piazza dei Martiri toward the sea, is where you'll find high-end retailers such as Prada, Gucci, Versace, Vuitton, Cacharel, Damiani, and Cartier. **Via Chiaia** and **Via Toledo** are the two busiest shopping streets for most Neapolitans; there you'll find reasonably priced clothes and shoes. The **Vomero** district yields more shops, especially along Via Scarlatti and Via Luca Giordano. **Via Santa Maria di Costantinopoli**, which runs from Piazza Bellini to the Archaeological Museum, is the street for antiques shops.

Melinoi (✉ *Via Benedetto Croce 34, Spaccanapoli, Naples* ☎ *081/5521204*) stands out from the many small boutiques in Naples for its originality; it stocks clothes and accessories by Romeo Gigli as well as a number of French designers. **Nel Regno di Pulcinella** (✉ *Vico San Domenico Maggiore 9, Spaccanapoli, Naples* ☎ *081/5514171*) is the workshop of Lello Esposito, renowned maker of Neapolitan puppets.

WHERE TO EAT

$$–$$$ ✕**Ristorante Pizzeria Aurora.** Though often frequented by celebrities—their photographs adorn the walls—this restaurant offers *simpatia* to all its patrons. The cognoscenti start off by sharing a pizza *all'acqua*, a thin pizza with mozzarella and a sprinkling of *peperoncino* (dried chili peppers). ✉ *Via Fuorlovado 18–20, Capri Town* ☎ *081/8370181* 🖃 *AE, DC, MC, V* ⊘ *Closed Jan. and Feb.*

$–$$$ ✕**Vecchia Cantina.** This place is well worth seeking out for its combination of old-style Neapolitan hospitality, high-quality food and wine, and excellent prices. ✉ *Via S. Nicola alla Carità 13–14, Spaccanapoli, Naples* ☎ *081/5520226* ⋈ *Reservations essential* 🖃 *AE, DC, MC, V* ⊘ *Closed Sun. June–Aug. and 2 wks in Aug. No dinner Tues. and Sun.*

NICE, FRANCE

The fifth-largest city in France, Nice is also one of the noblest. The city is capped by a dramatic hilltop château, at whose base a bewitching warren of ancient Mediterranean streets unfolds. Although now French to the core, the town was allied with a Latin Duchy until 1860, and this almost 500 years of history adds a rich Italian flavor to the city's culture, architecture, and dialect. In the late 19th century, Nice saw the birth of tourism as English and Russian aristocrats began to winter in the temperate climate along the famed waterfront, Promenade des Anglais, which is now lined with grand hotels, a part of their legacy. Nowadays, Nice strikes an engaging balance between historic Provençal grace, port-town exotica, urban energy, whimsy, and high culture. Its museums—particularly its art collections—are excellent, and the atmosphere is langourous yet urbain.

ESSENTIALS

CURRENCY The euro (€1 to US$1.46 at this writing); U.S. currency is generally not accepted in Europe, but ATMs are common.

HOURS Most stores open Monday through Saturday from 9 to 7, but many close at lunchtime (usually noon to 2 or 3), and some will open later and on Sunday during July and August. Museums are usually open 10 to 5, but most are closed on either Monday or Tuesday.

INTERNET **Cyberpoint**(✉ *10 av. Félix Faure* ☎ *04–93–92–70–63* ⊕ *www.cyberpoint-nice. com*) is open Monday–Saturday 10–8, Sunday 3–8.

TELEPHONES Tri-band GSM phones work in France. You can buy prepaid phone cards at telecom shops, news-vendors, and tobacconists in all towns and cities. Phone cards can be used for local or international calls. France Telecom and Orange are leading telecom companies.

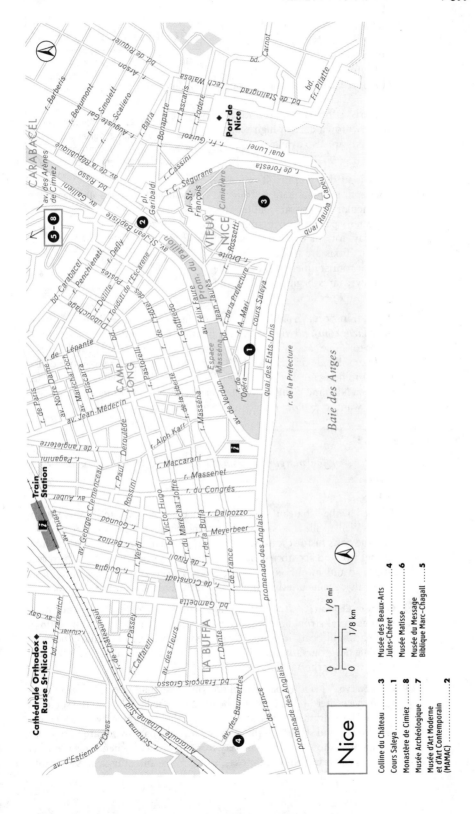

Nice

4

Cathédrale Orthodox♦ Russe St-Nicolas

CARABACEL

VIEUX NICE

CAMP LONG

LA BUFFA

Train Station

Port de Nice

Baie des Anges

av. des Arènes de Cimiez
av. Gallieni
bd. Risso
av. de la République
r. Barberis
r. Beaumont
r. Auguste Gal
r. Smolett
r. Scaliero
r. Barla
r. Arson
bd. de Riquier
bd. Carnot
bd. Pilatte
bd. Stalingrad
fr. Pilatte
Lech Walesa
r. Cassini
r. Fodere
r. Lascaris
r. Bonaparte
r. Fr. Guizol
quai Lunel
pl. Garibaldi
r. C. Ségurane
r. de la Foresta
r. St-Jean Baptiste
r. Defly
r. Penchienatti
bd. Carabacel
Debouchage
r. Delille
Postes
r. Tonduti de l'Escarène
r. Pertinax
r. Gioffredo
pl. St-François
r. Droite
r. Rossetti
Cimietière
quai Rauba Capeu
de Lépante
r. Biscarra
av. Maréchal Foch
Prom. du Paillon
av. Félix Faure
bd. Jean Jaurès
r. A. Mari
Cours Saleya
Espace Masséna
r. de la Préfecture
r. de Paris
r. Notre Dame
av. Jean-Médecin
r. Pastorelli
r. de la Liberté
r. Masséna
r. de Verdun
r. de l'Opéra
quai des États-Unis
r. Paganini
r. de l'Angleterre
r. Paul Déroulède
r. Alph Karr
r. Maccarani
r. Massenet
r. du Congrés
av. Georges Clemenceau
av. Auber
r. Rossini
r. Victor Hugo
bd. du Maréchal Joffre
r. de la Buffa
r. Dalpozzo
r. Meyerbeer
av. Thiers
r. Gounod
r. Berlioz
r. Verdi
r. de Rivoli
r. de France
r. Guigla
r. de Constadt
bd. Gambetta
r. Dante
r. F. Passey
r. de Châteauneuf
r. Caffarelli
av. des Fleurs
bd. François Grosso
r. cluvier
av. Gay
bd. du Tzarewitch
Autoroute Urbaine Sud
Schuman
av. d'Estienne d'Orves
av. des Baumettes
promenade des Anglais
r. de France

0   1/8 mi
0   1/8 km

Colline du Château 3
Cours Saleya 1
Monastère de Cimiez 8
Musée Archéologique 7
Musée d'Art Moderne
et d'Art Contemporain
(MAMAC) 2

Musée des Beaux-Arts
Jules-Chéret 4
Musée Matisse 6
Musée du Message
Biblique Marc–Chagall 5

COMING ASHORE

Ships dock at Nice Port, east of the city center and a 30- to 40-minute walk from the city's attractions. The port facilities include a tourist office and currency exchange desk. There is a free shuttle service into the downtown core in high season, and taxis are also available.

Don't rent a car if you intend to explore in the city, but it is a sensible option if you want to tour the spectacular Provencal countryside. Expect to pay approximately €70 per day for an economy manual vehicle. Taxis are plentiful and can provide tourist itineraries. For single journeys, fares begin at €2.30 and then €0.69 per km.

> ### NICE BEST BETS
>
> **Musée Matisse.** Nice, where the artist made his home from 1917 until his death in 1954, has the finest collection of his work.
>
> **Musée du Message Biblique Marc-Chagall.** Specially designed galleries house the 17 canvases making up "Biblical Message," one of the Postimpressionist's most charismatic works.
>
> **Strolling through the alleyways of Vieux Nice.** The pastel facades of the lively old town have inspired generations of artists. Enjoy the cafés, the quaint boutiques, and the flower market on Cours Saleya.

Public transport is reliable and comprehensive with Ligne d'Azur (⊕*www.lignedazur.com*), providing services within the city and suburbs. Route 15 heads to Cimiez and offers a free transfer between the Chagall and Matisse museums. Single tickets are €1.30 at this writing and allow you to ride for for 74 minutes. A day pass is €4. There is fast and reliable train service between Nice and Cannes, Monte Carlo, Antibes, and other coastal towns if you want to explore further afield without a car.

EXPLORING NICE

Numbers in the margin correspond to points of interest on the Nice map.

VIEUX NICE

Framed by the "château"—really a rocky promontory—and Cours Saleya, Nice's Vieille Ville is its strongest drawing point and the best place to capture the city's historic atmosphere. Its grid of narrow streets, darkened by houses five and six stories high with bright splashes of laundry fluttering overhead and jewel-box baroque churches on every other corner, creates a magic that seems utterly removed from the French Riviera fast lane.

❸ Colline de Château *(Château Hill).* Though nothing remains of the once-massive medieval stronghold but a few ruins left after its 1706 dismantling, this park still bears its name. From here take in extraordinary views of the Baie des Anges, the length of the Promenade des Anglais, and the red-ocher roofs of the Vieille Ville. ☉ *Daily 7–7.*

❶ Cours Saleya. This long pedestrian thoroughfare, half street, half square, is
★ the nerve center of Old Nice, the heart of the Vieille Ville and the stage-set for the daily dramas of marketplace and café life. Framed with 18th-century houses and shaded by plane trees, the long, narrow square bursts into a fireworks-show of color Tuesday through Sunday, when flower-market vendors roll armloads of mimosas, irises, roses, and orange blossoms into

cornets (paper cones) and thrust them into the arms of shoppers. Cafés and restaurants, all more or less touristy, fill outdoor tables with onlookers who bask in the sun. At the far-east end, antiques and *brocantes* (collectibles) draw avid junk-hounds every Monday morning.

② **Musée d'Art Moderne.** The assertive contemporary architecture of the Modern Art Museum makes a bold and emphatic statement regarding Nice's presence in the modern world. The art collection inside focuses intently and thoroughly on contemporary art from the late 1950s onward, but pride of place is given to sculptor Nikki de Saint Phalle's recent donation of over 170 exceptional pieces. ⊠*Promenade des Arts, Vieux Nice* ☎*04–97–13–42–01* ⊕*www.mamac-nice.org* 🖃*€4, free the 1st and 3rd Sun. of every month* ۞*Tues.–Sun. 10–6.*

④ **Musée des Beaux-Arts Jules-Chéret** *(Jules-Chéret Fine Arts Museum).* While the ★ collection here is impressive, it is the 19th-century Italianate mansion that houses it that remains the showstopper. Originally built for a member of Nice's Old Russian community, the Princess Kotschoubey, this was a belle epoque wedding cake, replete with one of the grandest staircases on the coast, salons decorated with Neo-Pompéienne frescoes, an English-style garden, and white columns and balustrades by the dozen. After the *richissime* American James Thompson took over and the last glittering ball was held here, the villa was bought by the municipality as a museum in the 1920s. Unfortunately, much of the period decor was sold but, in its place now hang paintings by Degas, Boudin, Monet, Sisley, Dufy, and Jules Chéret, whose posters of winking *damselles* distill all the *joie* of the belle époque. From the Negresco Hotel area the museum is about a 15-minute walk up a gentle hill. ⊠*33 av. des Baumettes, Centre Ville* ☎*04–92–15–28–25* ⊕*www.musee-beaux-arts-nice.org* 🖃*€4* ۞*Tues.–Sun. 10–6.*

CIMIEZ
Once the site of the powerful Roman settlement Cemenelum, the hilltop neighborhood of Cimiez—4 km (2½ mi) north of Cours Saleya—is Nice's most luxurious quarter (use Bus 15 from Place Masséna or Avenue Jean-Médecin to visit its sights).

⑧ **Monastère de Cimiez.** This fully functioning monastery is worth the pilgrimage. You'll find a lovely **garden,** replanted along the lines of the original 16th-century layout; the **Musée Franciscain,** a didactic museum tracing the history of the Franciscan order; and a 15th-century **church** containing three works of remarkable power and elegance by Bréa. ⊠*Pl. du Monastère, Cimiez* ☎*04–93–81–00–04* 🖃*Free* ۞*Mon.–Sat. 10–noon and 3–6.*

⑦ **Musée Archéologique** *(Archaeology Museum).* This museum, next to the Matisse Museum, has a dense and intriguing collection of objects extracted from the digs around the Roman city of Cemenelum, which flourished from the 1st to the 5th centuries. ⊠*160 av. des Arènes-de-Cimiez, Cimiez* ☎*04–93–81–59–57* 🖃*€4, guided tour (Thurs. at 3:30) €3* ۞*Wed.–Mon. 10–6.*

⑤ **Musée du Message Biblique Marc-Chagall** *(Marc Chagall Museum of Biblical Themes).* This museum has one of the finest permanent collections ★ of Chagall's (1887–1985) late works. Superbly displayed, 17 vast canvases depict biblical themes, each in emphatic, joyous colors. ⊠*Av. du Dr-Ménard, head up Av. Thiers, then take a left onto Av. Malausséna, cross railway tracks, and take first right up Av. de l'Olivetto, Cimiez* 🕾*04–93–53–87–20* 🎫*€6.70* 🕙*July–Sept., Wed.–Mon. 10–6; Oct–June, Wed.–Mon. 10–5.*

❻ Musée Matisse. In the '60s the city of Nice bought this lovely, light-bathed

Fodor's Choice
★

17th-century villa, surrounded by the ruins of Roman civilization, and restored it to house a large collection of Henri Matisse's works. Matisse settled in Nice in 1917, seeking a sun cure after a bout with pneumonia, and remained here until his death in 1954. During his years on the French Riviera, Matisse maintained intense friendships and artistic liaisons with Renoir, who lived in Cagnes, and with Picasso, who lived in Mougins and Antibes. Settling first along the waterfront, he eventually moved up to the rarefied isolation of Cimiez and took an apartment in the Hôtel Regina (now an apartment building), where he lived out the rest of his life. Matisse walked often in the parklands around the Roman remains and was buried in an olive grove outside the Cimiez cemetery. The collection of artworks includes several pieces the artist donated to the city before his death; the rest were donated by his family. In every medium and context—paintings, gouache cutouts, engravings, and book illustrations—it represents the evolution of his art, from Cézanne-like still lifes to exuberant dancing paper dolls. Even the furniture and accessories speak of Matisse, from the Chinese vases to the bold-printed fabrics with which he surrounded himself. A series of black-and-white photographs captures the artist at work, surrounded by personal—and telling—details. ⊠*164 av. des Arènes-de-Cimiez, Cimiez* 🕾*04–93–81–08–08* 🎫*€4* 🕙*Wed.–Mon. 10–6.*

SHOPPING

As the largest city in Provence, Nice is a treasure-trove of regional crafts and delicacies including basketware, bright fabrics, perfumes, lavender soaps, olive wood items, plus delicious olives, olive oils, honey, dried herbs, and quaffable local wines. The city is particularly renowned for its delicious crystallized fruit. The best place to find crafts is in the old town, while French couture can be found on the elegant boulevards of the new town.

Olive oil by the gallon in cans with colorful, old-fashioned labels is sold at tiny **Alziari** (⊠*14 rue St-François-de-Paule, Vieux Nice*). For fragrances, linens, and pickled-wood furniture, head to **Boutique 3** (⊠*3 rue Longchamp, Vieux Nice*). Good sources for crystallized fruit, is the **Confiserie du Vieux Nice** (⊠*14 quai Papacino, Vieux Nice*), on the west side of the port. or **Henri Auer** (⊠*7 rue St-François-de-Paule, Vieux Nice*) has been open since 1820.

BEACHES

Nice's pebble beaches extend all along the Baie des Anges, backed full-length by the Promenade des Anglais. Public stretches alternate with posh private beaches that have restaurants—and bar service, mattresses and parasols, waterskiing, parasailing, windsurfing, and jet-skiing. One of the handiest private beaches is the **Beau Rivage** (☎*04–92–47–82–82*), set across from the Opera. The sun can also be yours for the basking at **Ruhl** (☎*04–93–87–09–70*), across from the casino.

WHERE TO EAT

$-$$$$ ✕**Grand Café de Turin.** Whether you squeeze onto a banquette in the dark, low-ceiling bar or win a coveted table under the arcaded porticoes on place Garibaldi, this is *the* place to go for shellfish in Nice: sea snails, clams, plump *fines de claires* and salty *bleue* oysters, and urchins by the dozen. It's packed noon and night, so don't be too put off by the some-times brusque reception of the waiters. ✉*5 pl. Garibaldi, Vieux Nice* ☎*04–93–62–29–52* @*www.cafedeturin.com* ▭*AE, DC, MC, V.*

¢–$ ✕**Chez René/Socca.** This back-alley landmark is the most popular dive in town for *socca*, the chickpea-pancake snack food unique to Nice. Rustic olive-wood tables line the street, and curt waiters splash down your drink order. For the food, you get in line at the Socca, choose your €3 plate (or plates), and carry it steaming to the table yourself. It's off Place Garibaldi on the edge of the Vieille Ville, across from the *gare routière* (bus station). ✉*2 rue Miralheti, Vieux Nice* ☎*04–93–92–05–73* ▭*No credit cards* ⊘*Closed Mon.*

PALERMO, ITALY

Once the intellectual capital of southern Europe, Palermo has always been at the crossroads of civilization. Favorably situated on a crescent-shaped bay at the foot of Monte Pellegrino, it has attracted almost every culture touching the Mediterranean world. To Palermo's credit, it has absorbed these diverse cultures into a unique personality that is at once Arab and Christian, Byzantine and Roman, Norman and Italian. The city's heri-tage encompasses all of Sicily's varied ages, but its distinctive aspect is its Arab-Norman identity, an improbable marriage that, mixed in with Byzantine and Jewish elements, created some resplendent works of art. No less noteworthy than the architecture is Palermo's chaotic vitality, on display at some of Italy's most vibrant outdoor markets, public squares, street bazaars, and food vendors, and above all in its grand climax of Italy's most spectacular *passeggiata* (the leisurely social stroll along the principal thoroughfare).

ESSENTIALS

CURRENCY The euro (€1 to US$1.46 at this writing); U.S. currency is generally not accepted in Europe, but ATMs are common and credit cards are widely accepted.

HOURS Most shops are open 9 to 1 and 4 or 4:30 to 7:30 or 8 and closed Sun-day; in addition, most food shops close Wednesday afternoon, and other shops normally close Monday morning. Most museums/attractions open throughout the day, though some, particularly churches, close in the afternoon.

INTERNET There is Internet access in the port terminal building at the Western Union desk.

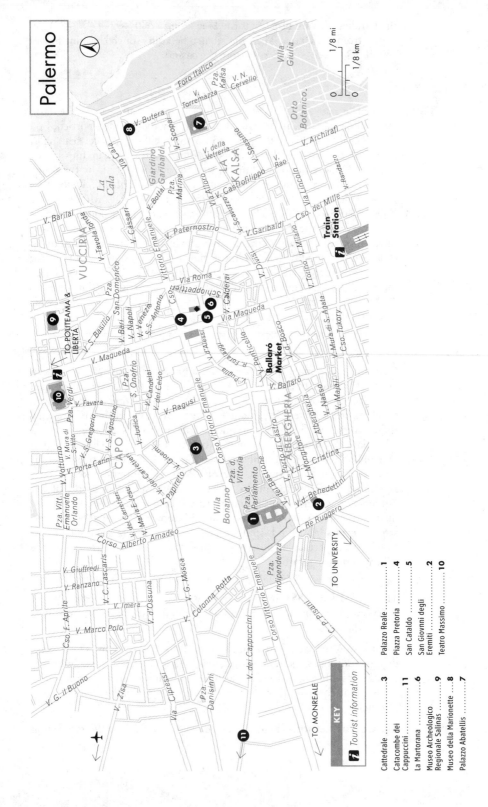

Palermo

1/8 mi

1/8 km

KEY

🛈 Tourist Information

Cattedrale	3	Palazzo Reale	1
Catacombe dei Cappuccini	11	Piazza Pretoria	4
La Martorana	6	San Cataldo	5
Museo Archeologico Regionale Salinas	9	San Giovnni degli Eremiti	2
Museo della Marionette	8	Teatro Massimo	10
Palazzo Abatellis	7		

TO MONREALE

TO UNIVERSITY

TELEPHONES Tri-band GSM phones work in Italy. You can buy prepaid phone cards at telecom shops, news-vendors, and tobacconists in all towns and cities. Phone cards can be used for local or international calls.

COMING ASHORE

At this writing, Palermo port is undergoing expansion and rede-velopment of the cruise terminal to accommodate larger vessels and more than one cruise ship at one time. The terminal building has a café and a shop. Just outside the gates are taxis and horse-drawn car-riages. It is possible to walk directly from the ship into the city; however, the port area has a reputation for pickpockets and scam artists, so be aware.

> **PALERMO BEST BETS**
>
> **Marvel at the Duomo in Monreale.** The finest example of Norman fusion architecture in Sicily blends Eastern and Western influences.
>
> **Take a peek at Palazzo Real.** Once home to Bourbon royalty and their particular taste in home decor it now houses the Sicilian parliament.
>
> **Stroll the old town.** A genuine slice of life southern Italian style will play out before your eyes as you kick the dust off your shoes by walking through these streets.

Three bus routes (Gialla, Rossa, and Verde) ply the streets of the old town, but none links with the port; tickets cost €1. Taxis charge approximately €2.33 initially, then €0.78 per km (½-mi) with an increment of €0.11 per 140 meters (260 feet) when traffic is slow. Renting a car would open up much of the island to you. Expect to pay about €45 per day for a compact manual vehicle.

EXPLORING PALERMO

Numbers in the margin correspond to points of interest on the Palermo map.

⓫ Catacombe dei Cappuccini. The spookiest sight in all of Sicily, this 16th-cen-tury catacomb houses more than 8,000 corpses of men, women, and young children, some in tombs but many mummified and preserved, hanging in rows on the walls. Many of the fully clothed corpses wear priests' smocks (most of the dead were Capuchin monks). The Capuchins were founders and proprietors of the bizarre establishment from 1559 to 1880. ⊠*Pi-azza Cappuccini off Via Cappuccini, near Palazzo Reale* ☏*091/212117* 🎫*€1.50* ⊘*Daily 9–noon and 3–5:30.*

❸ Cattedrale. This church is a lesson in Palermitan eclecticism—originally
★ Norman (1182), then Catalan Gothic (14th–15th century), then fitted out with a baroque and neoclassical interior (18th century). Its turrets, towers, dome, and arches come together in the kind of meeting of diverse elements that King Roger II (1095–1154), whose tomb is inside along with that of Frederick II, fostered during his reign. The back of the apse is gracefully decorated with interlacing Arab arches inlaid with limestone and black volcanic tufa. ⊠*Corso Vittorio Emanuele, Capo* ☏*091/334373* ⊕*www. cattedrale.palermo.it* 🎫*Church free, crypt €2.50* ⊘*Daily 9:30–5:30.*

❻ La Martorana. Distinguished by an elegant Norman campanile, this church was erected in 1143 but had its interior altered considerably during the baroque period. High along the western wall, however, is some of the oldest and best-preserved mosaic artwork of the Norman period. Near the entrance is an interesting mosaic of King Roger II being crowned by Christ. ⊠*Piazza Bellini 3, Kalsa* ☎*091/6161692* ⊙*Mon.–Sat. 8–1 and 3:30–5:30, Sun. 8:30–1.*

⑨ Museo Archeologico Regionale Salinas. Especially interesting pieces in this small but excellent collection are the examples of prehistoric cave drawings and a marvelously reconstructed Doric frieze from the Greek temple at Selinunte created some 2,500 years ago. ⊠*Piazza Olivella 24, Via Roma, Olivella* ☎*091/6116805* 🎫*€6* ⊙*Tues.–Fri. 8:30–2 and 2:30–6:45, Sat.–Mon. 8:30–1:45.*

⑧ Museo delle Marionette. The traditional Sicilian *pupi* (puppets), with their glittering armor and fierce expressions, have become a symbol of Norman Sicily. Plots of the weekly performances center on the chivalric legends of the troubadours, who, before the puppet theater, kept alive tales of Norman heroes in Sicily. ⊠*Piazzetta Niscemi 1, at Via Butera, Kalsa* ☎*091/328060* ⊕*www.museomarionettepalermo.it* 🎫*€5* ⊙*Weekdays 10–1 and 3:30–6:30.*

⑦ Palazzo Abatellis. Housed in this late-15th-century Catalan Gothic palace with Renaissance elements is the **Galleria Regionale.** Among its treasures are an *Annunciation* (1474) by Sicily's prominent Renaissance master Antonello da Messina (1430–79) and an arresting fresco by an unknown painter, titled *The Triumph of Death,* a macabre depiction of the plague years. ⊠*Via Alloro 4, Kalsa* ☎*091/6230011* ⊕*www.regione.sicilia.it/beniculturali/dirbenicult/palazzoabatellis/index.htm* 🎫*€6, guided tour an additional €3.50* ⊙*Tues.–Fri. 9–1 and 2:30–7, Sat.–Mon. 9–1.*

❶ Palazzo Reale. The historical royal palace, also called Palazzo dei Normanni (Norman Palace), was for centuries the seat of Sicily's semiautonomous rulers. The building is an interesting mesh of abutting 10th-century Norman and 17th-century Spanish structures. Because it now houses the Sicilian Parliament, little is accessible to the public. The **Cappella Palatina** (Palatine Chapel) remains open. Built by Roger II in 1132, it's a dazzling example of the harmony of artistic elements produced under the Normans. Here the skill of French and Sicilian masons was brought to bear on the decorative purity of Arab ornamentation and the splendor of 11th-century Greek Byzantine mosaics.

Upstairs are the royal apartments, including the **Sala di Re Ruggero** (King Roger's Hall), decorated with medieval murals of hunting scenes—an earlier (1120) secular counterpoint to the religious themes seen elsewhere. To see this area of the palace, ask one of the tour guides (free) to escort you around the halls once used by one of the most splendid courts in Europe. ⊠*Piazza Indipendenza, Albergheria* ☎*091/7051111* 🎫*€5* ⊙*Mon.–Tues. and Sat. 8:30–noon and 2–5, Sun. 8:30–2.*

❹ Piazza Pretoria. The square's centerpiece, a lavishly decorated fountain with 500 separate pieces of sculpture and an abundance of nude figures, so shocked some Palermitans when it was unveiled in 1575 that it got the nickname "Fountain of Shame."

❺ San Cataldo. Three striking Saracenic scarlet domes mark this church, built in 1154 during the Norman occupation of Palermo. The church now belongs to the Knights of the Holy Sepulchre, and the spare but intense stone interior is rarely open to the public. ⊠*Piazza Bellini 3, Kalsa* ☎*091/6375622* 🖂*€1* ⊙*By tour Sept.–May, Mon.–Sat. 9:30–12:30; June–Aug., weekdays 9:30–12:30 and 3:30–6:30, Sun. 9:30–12:30.*

② **San Giovanni degli Eremiti.** Distinguished by its five reddish-orange domes and stripped-clean interior, this 12th-century church was built by the Normans on the site of an earlier mosque—one of 200 that once stood in Palermo. The emirs ruled Palermo for nearly two centuries and brought to it their passion for lush gardens and fountains. One is reminded of this while sitting in San Giovanni's delightful cloister of twin half columns, surrounded by palm trees, jasmine, oleander, and citrus trees. The last tickets are sold a half hour before closing. At this writing, the cloister was under construction and half the church was not viewable. ⊠*Via dei Benedettini, Albergheria* ☎*091/6515019* 🖂*€3* ⊙*Daily 9–6:30.*

⑩ **Teatro Massimo.** Construction of this formidable neoclassical theater was started in 1875 by Giovanni Battista Basile and completed by his son Ernesto in 1897. A fire in 1974 rendered the theater inoperable but it reopened with great fanfare in 1997, its interior as glorious as ever. *The Godfather Part III* ended with a famous shooting scene on the theater's steps. Visits are by 25-minute guided tour only; English-speaking guides are available 10–2 and 3–4. ⊠*Piazza Verdi 9, at top of Via Maqueda, Olivella* ☎*091/322949 or 0800/655858* ⊕*www.teatromassimo.it* 🖂*€5* ⊙*Tues.–Sun. 10–2:30 for general (nonguided) visits, except during rehearsals.*

10 km (6 mi) southwest of Palermo.

★ Monreale's splendid **Duomo** is lavishly executed with mosaics depicting events from the Old and New Testaments. After the Norman conquest of Sicily the new princes showcased their ambitions through monumental building projects. William II (1154–89) built the church complex with a cloister and palace between 1174 and 1185, employing Byzantine craftsmen. The result was a glorious fusion of Eastern and Western influences, widely regarded as the finest example of Norman architecture in Sicily.

The major attraction is the 68,220 square feet of glittering gold mosaics decorating the cathedral interior. *Christ Pantocrator* dominates the apse area; the nave contains narratives of the Creation; and scenes from the life of Christ adorn the walls of the aisles and the transept. The painted wooden ceiling dates from 1816–37. The roof commands a great view (a reward for climbing 172 stairs).

Bonnano Pisano's **bronze doors,** completed in 1186, depict 42 biblical scenes and are considered among the most important of medieval artifacts. Barisano da Trani's 42 panels on the north door, dating from 1179, present saints and evangelists. ⊠*Piazza del Duomo* ☎*091/6404413* ⊙*Daily 8–6.*

The lovely **cloister** of the abbey adjacent to the Duomo was built at the same time as the church but enlarged in the 14th century. The beautiful enclosure is surrounded by 216 intricately carved double columns, every other one decorated in a unique glass mosaic pattern. Afterward, don't forget to walk behind the cloister to the **belvedere,** with stunning panoramic views over the Conca d'Oro (Golden Conch) valley toward Palermo. ⊠*Piazza del Duomo* 🕾*091/6404403* 🕾*€4.50* 🕘*Daily 9–7:30.*

SHOPPING

Sicilan specialties include lace and linen, including place mats and napkins, and ceramics, particularly its practical folk pottery from Caltagirone, on the north coast. Marble and wrought iron are also fashioned into souvenir pieces and antique shops are numerous, though prices can be high. Edibles include an excellent range of wines and olive oils, jams, and tasty sweets.

In Palermo, north of Piazza Castelnuovo, **Via della Libertà** and the streets around it represent the luxury end of the shopping scale, with some of Palermo's best-known stores. A second nerve center for shoppers is the pair of parallel streets connecting modern Palermo with the train station, **Via Roma,** and **Via Maqueda,** where boutiques and shoe shops become increasingly upmarket as you move from the Quattro Canti past Teatro Massimo to Via Ruggero Settimo, but are still a serious notch below their counterparts in the Libertà area.

If you're interested in truly connecting with local life while searching for souvenirs, a visit to one of Palermo's many bustling markets is essential. Between Via Roma and Via Maqueda the many **bancherelle** *(market stalls)* on Via Bandiera sell everything from socks to imitation designer handbags.

Enoteca Picone (⊠*Via Marconi 36, Libertà* 🕾*091/331300* ⊕*www.enotecapicone.it* ⊠*Viale Strasburgo 235Libertà*) is the best wine shop in town, with a fantastic selection of Sicilian and national wines. Seekers of fringes, tassels, and heavy fabrics stop at **Giuseppe Gramuglia** ⊠*Via Roma 412–414, at Via Principe di Belmonte, Vucciria* 🕾*091/583262.*

WHERE TO EAT

$$ ✕**Trattoria Altri Tempi.** The "olden days" restaurant is a favorite among locals
★ searching for the true rustic cooking of their Sicilian ancestors. Knickknacks fill the walls of the small friendly space. A meal begins with a carafe of the house red set down without asking and a superb spread of traditional antipasti. Dishes have old Palermitan names: *fave a cunigghiu* is fava beans prepared with olive oil, garlic, and remarkably flavorful oregano; and *vampaciucia c'anciova* is a lasagna-like pasta dish with a concentrated sauce of tomatoes, anchovies, and grapes. The meal ends well, too, with free house-made herb or fruit liquors and excellent cannoli. ⊠*Via Sammartino 65/67, Libertà* 🕾*091/323480* 🖃*MC, V* 🕘*Closed Aug. 15–Sept. 15. No dinner Sun.*

¢–$$ ✕**Pizzeria Ai Comparucci.** One of Palermo's best pizzerias doubles as an informal modern art gallery, with colorful modern paintings on the walls, giving it a fun, casual vibe that draws in local crowds on the spur of the moment. Better yet are the delicious Neapolitan pizzas coming out of the big oven in the open kitchen. The genius is in the crust, which is seared in the oven in a matter of seconds (so don't expect a long, leisurely meal). The place serves until 11 PM or midnight—later than almost any other restaurant in the neighborhood. ✉*Messina 36, between Yarzili and Libertà, Libertà* ☎*091/6090467* 🖃*AE, MC, V.*

POLTU QUATU, SARDINIA, ITALY

An uncut jewel of an island, Sardinia remains unique and enigmatic. Would-be conquerors have left their marks, but inland, a proud Sard culture and language flourish. Sardinia has some of Europe's most expensive resort destinations, but it's also home to areas as rugged and undeveloped as anywhere on the continent. Fine sand and clean waters draw sunseekers to beaches that are unquestionably among the best in the Mediterranean. Best known are those along the Costa Smeralda (Emerald Coast), where the superrich have anchored their yachts since the 1960s. But most of the coast is unsettled, a jagged series of wildly beautiful inlets accessible only by sea. And inland, Sardinia remains shepherd's country, silent and stark. Spaghetti Westerns were once filmed here, and it's not hard to imagine why: the desolate mountainous terrain seems the perfect frontier set. Against this landscape are the striking and mysterious stone *nuraghi* (ancient defensive structures), which provide clues to the lifestyles of the island's prehistoric peoples.

ESSENTIALS

CURRENCY The euro (€1 to US$1.46 at this writing); U.S. currency is generally not accepted in Europe, but ATMs are common and credit cards are widely accepted.

HOURS Stores are generally open from 9 or 9:30 to 1 and from 3:30 or 4 to 7 or 7:30. Many shops close Sunday. Many national museums are closed on Monday and may have shorter hours on Sunday.

INTERNET **Libreria Il Labirinto** (✉*Via Carlo Alberto 119, Alghero* ☎*079/237734)* is a well-stocked book and press store that has four Internet ports.

TELEPHONES Tri-band GSM phones work in Sardinia, which is a part of Italy. You can buy prepaid phone cards at telecom shops, news vendors, and tobacconists in all towns and cities. Phone cards can be used for local or international calls.

COMING ASHORE

Poltu Quatu means "hidden port" in the Sardinian dialect, and it is hidden at the head of a narrow inlet. Small cruise ships can dock at the port, but larger ships dock beyond the mouth of the inlet and tender passengers ashore. The port is one element in an extended tourist "village"; other facilities include a selection of cafés, sports outfitters, and shops. You can rent a boat for the day directly from the harbor to cruise the coast. There is no public transport to the port.

Although prices are steep, renting a car gives you a great opportunity to explore the northern half of the island and still have time to relax. Europcar has an office in the port. Other car rental companies will deliver to the port for an extra charge. Rental prices for a compact manual vehicle start at €90 per day. There is a taxi stand within the resort village. Taxis will meet boats at the port but must be prebooked. Taxi fares are €20 into Puerto Cervo, which is just around the headland.

EXPLORING NORTHERN SARDINIA

PORTO CERVO

1 *Numbers in the margin correspond to points of interest on the Sardinia map. 30 km (19 mi) north of Olbia.*
★

Sardinia's northeastern coast is fringed with low cliffs, inlets, and small bays. This has become an upscale vacationland, with glossy resorts such as Baia Sardinia and Porto Rotondo just outside the confines of the famed Costa Smeralda, developed by the Aga Khan (born 1936), who in 1965 accidentally discovered the coast's charms—and potential—when his yacht took shelter here from a storm. In the late 1960s and '70s, the Costa Smeralda, with its heart in Porto Cervo, was *the* place to summer. The attractions remain geared to those who can measure themselves by the yardstick of Khan's fabled riches. Italy's most expensive hotels are here, and the world's most magnificent yachts anchor in the waters of Porto Cervo.

All along the coast, carefully tended lush vegetation surrounds vacation villages and discreet villas that have sprung up over the past decade in spurious architectural styles best described as bogus Mediterranean. The trend has been to keep this an enclave of the very rich. Outside the peak season, however, prices plunge and the majesty of the natural surroundings shines through, justifying all the hype and the Emerald Coast's fame as one of the truly romantic corners of the Mediterranean.

LA MADDALENA

❷ *35 km (22 mi) northwest of Porto Cervo.*

From the port of Palau you can visit the archipelago of La Maddalena, seven granite islands embellished with lush green scrub and wind-bent pines. Car ferries make the 3-km (2-mi) trip about every half hour.

Pilgrims pay homage to national hero **Giuseppe Garibaldi's tomb** (1807–82) on the grounds of his hideaway. Take the ferry to Isola Maddalena and then the bridge to Isola Caprera. ✉ *7 km (4½ mi) east of Isola Maddalena* ☎ *0789/727162* 💶 *€2* 🕐 *Oct.–Apr., Tues.–Sun. 9–1:30; May–Sept., Tues.–Sun. 9–6:30.*

> ### SARDINIA BEST BETS
>
> **Take an espresso in the harbor at Porto Cervo.** Most of Europe's royalty spends at least some time here every summer, as does a sprinkling of celebrities. This is a prime place for people-watching.
>
> **Take a dip on the Costa Smeralda.** The setting of golden sand, russet rocks, and limpid waters is sublime.
>
> **Take a stroll around Alghero.** Built by the Spanish as their capital in medieval times, Alghero is still a little piece of Spain in modern Italy.

SANTA TERESA DI GALLURA

❸ *55 km(34 mi) west of Porto Cervo*

At the northern tip of Sardinia, Santa Teresa di Gallura retains the relaxed, carefree air of a former fishing village. Nearby beaches rival those farther down the coast but manage not to seem overtouristed.

GOLFO ARANCI

❹ *47 km (29 mi) southeast of Puerto Cervo*

At the mouth of the Gulf of Olbia, Golfo Aranci is a small-scale resort and major arrival point for ferries from the mainland. The craggy headland west of town has been left undeveloped as a nature reserve, and there are some inviting beaches within an easy drive.

OLBIA

❺ *30 km (19 mi) south of Porto Cervo, 19 km (12 mi) southwest of Golfo Aranci, 65 km (41 mi) southeast of Santa Teresa di Gallura*

Amid the resorts of Sardinia's northeastern coast, Olbia is a lively little seaport and port of call for mainland ferries at the head of a long, wide bay.

The little basilica of **San Simplicio,** a short walk behind the main Corso Umberto, is worth searching out if you have any spare time in Olbia. The simple granite structure dates from the 11th century, part of the great Pisan church-building program, using pillars and columns recycled from Roman buildings. ✉ *Via San Simplicio* ☎ *0789/23358* 🕐 *Daily 6:30–12:30 and 4–7.*

SASSARI

❻ *100 km (62 mi) southwest of Santa Teresa di Gallura*

Inland, Sassari is an important university town and administrative center, notable for its history of intellectualism and bohemian student culture, an ornate old cathedral, and a good archaeological museum. Look for downtown vendors of *fainè,* a pizzalike chickpea-flour pancake glistening with olive oil, which is a Genoese and Sassarese specialty. Sassari is the hub of several highways and secondary roads leading to various coastal resorts, among them Stintino and Castelsardo.

It took just under 600 years to build Sassari's **Duomo**, dedicated to Saint Nicolas of Bari. The foundations were laid in the 12th century and the facade, in Spanish colonial style, was finished in the 18th. Of particular interest in the interior are the ribbed Gothic vaults, the 14th-century painting of the Maddona del Bosco on the high alter, and the early-19th-century tomb of Placido Benedetto di Savoia, the uncle of united Italy's first king. ⊠*Piazza Duomo 3* ☏*079/233185* 🎟*Free* ☉*Apr.–Oct., daily 9–noon and 5–7; Nov.–Mar., daily 9–12:30 and 4–6.*

Sassari's excellent **Museo Sanna** has the best archaeological collection outside Cagliari, spanning nuraghic, Carthaginian, and Roman histories, including well-preserved bronze statues and household objects from the two millennia BC. Summer hours vary from one year to the next. ⊠*Via Roma 64* ☏*079/272203* 🎟*€2* ☉*Tues.–Sun. 9–8.*

ALGHERO

❼ *34 km (21 mi) southwest of Sassari, 137 km (85 mi) southwest of Olbia.*

A tourist-friendly town with a distinctly Spanish flavor, Alghero is also known as Barcelonetta (little Barcelona). Rich wrought-iron scrollwork decorates balconies and screened windows; a Spanish motif appears in stone portals and in bell towers. The town was built and inhabited in the 14th century by the Aragonese and Catalans, who constructed seaside ramparts and sturdy towers encompassing an inviting nucleus of narrow, winding streets with whitewashed palazzi. The native language spoken here is a version of Catalan, not Italian, although you probably have to attend one of the masses conducted in Algherese (or listen in on stories swapped by older fishermen) to hear it.

The **Torre San Giovanni**, an old tower fortress, can be climbed for good views from the terrace. Stop at the interesting city history display on the computer terminals inside the tower. There's also a rotating set of exhibits and a miniature model of Alghero's old town. ⊠*Via Mateotti 12* ☏*079/9734045* 🎟*€2.50* ☉*By appointment.*

The **Museo Diocesano d'Arte Sacra** is housed in a 13th-century church. The usual assortment of religious treasures—paintings, wooden sculptures, and bronzes—is on display; look for the masterful 16th-century Catalan silverware. ⊠*Via Maiorca 1* ☏*079/9733041* 🎟*€2.50* ☉*Jan.–Mar., Thurs.–Tues. by appointment; Apr., May, and Oct., Thurs.–Tues. 10–1 and 5–8; June and Sept., Thurs.–Tues. 10–1 and 5–9; July and Aug., Thurs.–Tues. 10–1 and 6–11; Dec., Thurs.–Tues. 10–1 by appointment and 4–7. Closed Nov.*

West of Alghero are broad sandy beaches and the spectacular heights of **Capo Caccia**, an imposing limestone headland.

☾ At the base of a sheer cliff the pounding sea has carved an entrance to
★ the vast **Grotta di Nettuno** *(Neptune's Caves)*, a fantastic cavern filled with water pools, stalactites, and stalagmites. You must visit with a guide; tours start on the hour. ⊠*13 km (8 mi) west of Alghero* ☏*079/946540* 🎟*€10* ☉*Apr.–Sept., daily 9–7; Oct., daily 9–5; Nov.–Mar., daily 9–4.*

CASTELSARDO

8 *32 km (20 mi) northeast of Sassari.*

The walled seaside citadel of Castelsardo is a delight for craft lovers, with tiny shops crammed with all kinds of souvenirs, particularly woven baskets. The appropriately shaped **Roccia dell'Elefante** *(Elephant Rock)* on the road into Castelsardo was hollowed out by primitive man to become a *domus de janas* (literally, "fairy house," in fact a Neolithic burial chamber).

SHOPPING

The Sard are very adept craftsmen and women. For many generations the people in the mountains had to be self-sufficient and worked with bone, wood, and clay to produce practical yet beautiful items, including fine knives, the must-have tool of the shepherd. The women were traditionally weavers—in wool and straw—or lace-makers. Red coral and filigree jewelry also have a long tradition here. If you are looking for some comestibles to take home, Sardinian wine and honey are highly prized. The narrow streets of Alghero and Castelsardo are the best places to shop for locally made crafts. Porto Cervo has fewer craft shops, but designer names line the shopping streets with top-quality haute couture and jewelry stores plus independent boutiques selling gifts and collectibles.

ISOLA is an organization set up to promote Sardinian crafts. Sassari has Sardinia's main **ISOLA** (✉ *Giardini Pubblici* ☎*079/230101*), a craft exhibition center in the public gardens next to Viale Mancini built specifically as a showcase for gifts and souvenirs.

The walled seaside citadel of **Castelsardo**, 32 km (20 mi) northeast of Sassari, is a delight for basket lovers. Roadside stands and shops in the old town sell woven baskets, as well as rugs and wrought iron.

SPORTS & ACTIVITIES

The Costa Smeralda has world-class water-sports facilities and boat rentals from the harbor.

The **Yacht Club Costa Smeralda** (✉ *Via della Marina* ☎*0789/902200* ⊕*www.yccs.it*) provides use of its pool, restaurant, bar, and guest rooms to those with memberships at other yacht clubs.

The world-class, 18-hole **Pevero Golf Course** (✉ *Bay of Pevero* ☎*0789/96210* ⊕*www.golfclubpevero.com*) was designed by Robert Trent Jones.

BEACHES

The beaches around the Costa Smeralda are some of the most exclusive in Europe, but they don't disappoint, with fine golden sand sheltered by red cliffs and fronting azure waters. Most can only be reached by boat and there are regular small ferries from Porto Cervo. Rental of sunbeds and towel are reassuringly expensive.

WHERE TO EAT

$$ ✕ **Da Pietro.** A menu that includes *bucatini all'algherese* (hollow, spaghetti-like pasta with a sauce of clams, capers, tomatoes, and olives) and baked fish with a white-wine sauce keeps this seafood restaurant bustling below its vaulted ceilings. Look for Da Pietro in the old town near Largo San Francesco. ⊠ *Via Ambrogio Machin 20, Alghero* ☎*079/979645* ⊟*AE, MC, V* ⊘*Closed Wed. and 2 wks in Dec.*

¢–$ ✕ **L'Assassino.** Get a true taste of great local Sassarese cooking—and many of the other obscure Sardinian specialties you might have been looking for but not yet found. Horse, donkey, and roast pig figure prominently on the menu, though there are lots of other choices; best of all is a *cena sarda*, a 10-dish tasting menu with *porcetto* (roast suckling pig), alternatively spelled porcheddu. The service is friendly, and the room is warm and cozy. Food is, unusually, served all afternoon long. ⊠ *Vicolo Ospizio Cappuccini 1, near Via Rosello, Sassari* ☎*079/235041* ⊟*AE, DC, MC, V* ⊘*Closed Sun.*

PORTOFINO, ITALY

Like the family jewels that bedeck its habitual visitors, the Italian Riviera is glamorous, but in an old-fashioned way. The rustic and elegant, the provincial and chic, the cosmopolitan and the small-town are blended together here in a sun-drenched pastiche that defines the Italian side of the Riviera. Although the region bearing the name Liguria extends inland, its greatest charms are found on the coast, which has inspired poets and artists for centuries. One of the most photographed villages along the Ligurian coast, with a decidedly romantic and affluent aura, Portofino has long been a popular destination for foreigners. Once an ancient Roman colony and taken by the Republic of Genoa in 1229, it has also been ruled by the French, English, Spanish, and Austrians, as well as by marauding bands of 16th-century pirates. Elite British tourists first flocked to the lush harbor in the mid-1800s and today, some of Europe's wealthiest lay anchor in Portofino in summer.

ESSENTIALS

CURRENCY   The euro (€1 to US$1.46 at this writing); U.S. currency is generally not accepted in Europe, but ATMs are common and credit cards are widely accepted.

HOURS   Stores are generally open from 9 or 9:30 to 1 and from 3:30 or 4 to 7 or 7:30. Many shops close Sunday. Many national museums are closed Monday and may have shorter hours on Sunday.

TELEPHONES   Tri-band GSM phones work in Italy. You can buy prepaid phone cards at telecom shops, news-vendors, and tobacconists in all towns and cities. Phone cards can be used for local or international calls.

COMING ASHORE

Ships must tender passengers ashore in the heart of the picturesque port. There is no train station in Portofino: you must take the bus to Santa Margherita (€1) and pick up train services from there. An alternative is to take a boat around the bay to Santa Margherita Ligure. The journey time to Genoa (⇨*above*) is between 40 and 60 minutes and costs €2.10.

4

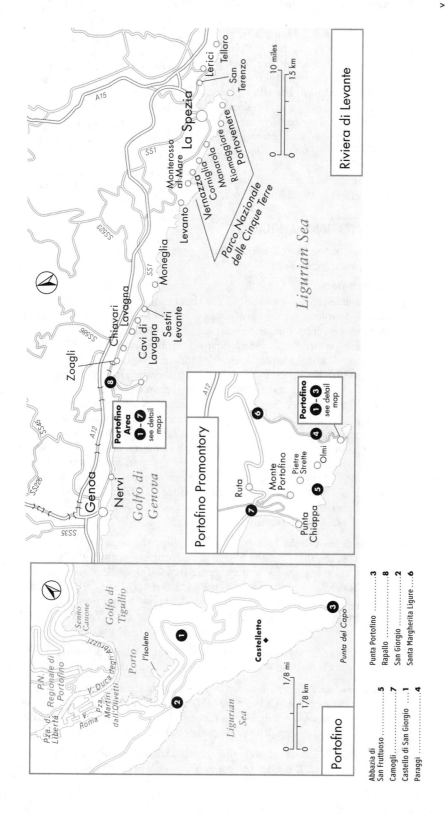

Riviera di Levante

Portofino Promontory

Portofino

Abbazia di
San Fruttuoso.........**5**
Camogli.................**7**
Castello di San Giorgio **1**
Paraggi **4**

Punta Portofino **3**
Rapallo.................**8**
San Giorgio **2**
Santa Margherita Ligure....**6**

Taxis charge €2.33 initially, then €0.78 per km (½-mi), €0.11 per 140 meters (260 feet) in slow traffic. A rental car is useful to explore the Ligurian coast, but allow plenty of time to return your rental car as roads become extremely busy during the summer, and journey times may be longer than the distance suggests. Expect to pay about €45 for a compact manual vehicle. Delivery to the portside is an additional cost.

> ### PORTOFINO BEST BETS
>
> **Linger over an espresso at a waterfront cafe.** Portofino is a place to see and be seen, so relax and survey your surroundings.
>
> **Walk the hillside paths above the town.** The views along the Riviera are delightful.
>
> **Visit Camogli.** You'll get a touch of gritty reality contrasting with the glitz of Portofino itself.

EXPLORING PORTOFINO & VICINITY

Numbers in the margin correspond to points of interest on the Portofino & Ligurian Riviera map.

PORTOFINO

❺ Abbazia di San Fruttuoso *(Abbey of San Fruttuoso).* On the sea at the foot of Monte Portofino, the medieval abbey—built by the Benedictines of Monte Cassino—protects a minuscule fishing village that can be reached only on foot or by water (a 20-minute boat ride from Portofino and also reachable from Camogli, Santa Margherita Ligure, and Rapallo). The restored abbey is now the property of a national conservation fund (FAI) and occasionally hosts temporary exhibitions. The church contains the tombs of some illustrious members of the Doria family, an influential dynasty during Liguria's medieval heyday. The old abbey and its grounds is a delightful place to spend a few hours, perhaps lunching at one of the modest beachfront trattorias nearby (open only in summer). Boatloads of visitors can make it very crowded very fast; you might appreciate it most off-season. The last entry is 30 minutes before closing time. ✉*15-min boat ride or 2-hr walk northwest of Portofino* ☎*0185/772703* 💶*€4, €6 during exhibitions* ☉*Mar., Apr., and Oct., Tues.–Sun. 10–4; May–Sept., daily 10–6; Dec.–Feb., weekends 10–4.*

❶ Castello di San Giorgio. From the harbor, follow the signs for the climb to the castle, the most worthwhile sight in Portofino, with its medieval relics, impeccable gardens, and sweeping views. The castle was founded in the Middle Ages but restored in the 16th through 18th century. In true Portofino form, it was owned by Genoa's English consul from 1870 until its opening to the public in 1961. ✉*Above harbor* ☎*0185/269046* 💶*€3* ☉*Apr.–Sept., Wed.–Mon. 10–6; Oct.–Mar., Wed.–Mon. 10–5.*

❹ Paraggi. The only sand beach near Portofino is at a cove on the road between Santa Margherita and Portofino. The bus will stop there on request.

❸ Punta Portofino. Pristine views can be had from the deteriorating *faro* (lighthouse) at this point, a 15-minute walk along the point that begins at the southern end of the port. Along the seaside path you can see numerous impressive, sprawling private residences behind high iron gates.

❷ San Giorgio. This small church, sitting on a ridge, was rebuilt four times during World War II. It is said to contain the relics of its namesake, brought back from the Holy Land by the Crusaders. Portofino enthusiastically celebrates St. George's Day every April 23. ⊠*Above harbor* ☎*0185/269337* ⊙*Daily 7–6.*

SANTA MARGHERITA LIGURE

6 *5 km (3 mi) from Portofino.*

A beautiful old resort town favored by well-to-do Italians, Santa Margherita Ligure has everything a Riviera playground should have—plenty of palm trees and attractive hotels, cafés, and a marina packed with yachts. Some of the older buildings here are still decorated on the outside with the trompe l'oeil frescoes typical of this part of the Riviera. This is a pleasant, convenient base, which for many represents a perfect balance on the Italian Riviera: bigger and less Americanized than the Cinque Terre; less glitzy than San Remo; more relaxing than Genoa and environs; and ideally situated for day trips, such as an excursion to Portofino.

CAMOGLI

7 *15 km (9 mi) northwest of Portofino, 20 km (12 mi) east of Genoa.*

★ Camogli, at the edge of the large promontory and nature reserve known as the Portofino Peninsula, has always been a town of sailors. By the 19th century it was leasing its ships throughout the continent. Today, multicolor houses, remarkably deceptive trompe l'oeil frescoes, and a massive 17th-century seawall mark this appealing harbor community, perhaps as beautiful as Portofino but without the glamour. When exploring on foot, don't miss the boat-filled second harbor, which is reached by ducking under a narrow archway at the northern end of the first one.

The Castello Dragone, built onto the sheer rock face near the harbor, is home to the **Acquario** *(Aquarium)*, which has tanks filled with local marine life built into the ramparts. ⊠*Via Isola* ☎*0185/773375* ⊠€*3* ⊙*May–Sept., daily 10–noon and 3–7; Oct.–Apr., Fri.–Sun. 10–noon and 2:30–6, Tues.–Thurs. 10–noon.*

RAPALLO

8 *8 km (5 mi) north of Portofino, 3 km (2 mi) north of Santa Margherita, 28 km (17 mi) east of Genoa.*

Rapallo was once one of Europe's most fashionable resorts, but it passed its heyday before World War II and has suffered from the building boom brought on by tourism. Ezra Pound and D.H. Lawrence lived here, and many other writers, poets, and artists have been drawn to it. Today, the town's harbor is filled with yachts. A single-span bridge on the eastern side of the bay is named after Hannibal, who is said to have passed through the area after crossing the Alps.

The highlight of the town center, the cathedral of **Santi Gervasio e Protasio**, at the western end of Via Mazzini, was founded in the 6th century. ⊠*Via Mazzini* ☎*0185/52375* ⊠*Free* ⊙*Daily 6:30–noon and 3–6:30.*

The **Museo del Pizzo a Tombolo**, in a 19th-century mansion, has a collection of antique lace, a dying art for which Rapallo was once renowned. ⊠*Villa Tigullio* ☎*0185/63305* ⊠*Free* ⊙*Oct.–Aug., Tues., Wed., Fri., and Sat. 3–6, Thurs. 10–11:30* AM.

SHOPPING

In addition to the Italian reputation for fine leather and haute couture, Liguria is famous for its fine laces, silver-and-gold filigree work, and ceramics. Look for bargains in velvet, macramé, olive wood, and marble. Don't forget the excellent wines, cheeses, dried meats, and olive oils.

Portofino is awash with small boutiques selling fashion and gift items, but it's also one of the most expensive places to shop along the coast, catering to the wealthy yacht owners who call in during the summer. However, all the coastal villages have pretty shops to explore.

Guido Porati's aromatic shop, **Bottega dei Sestieri** (⊠ *Via Mazzini 44, Rapello* ☎ *0185/230530*), sells Ligurian cheeses, wines, and other delicacies. For something truly regional, try the *trarcantu*, a cow's-milk cheese aged in grape skins. The store is on a narrow lane that runs parallel to Rapallo's waterfront.

The attractive coastal village of **Zoagli** (⊠ *On S1, 4 km [2½ mi] east of Rapallo*) has been famous for silk, velvet, and damask since the Middle Ages.

SPORTS & ACTIVITIES

If you have the stamina, you can hike to the **Abbazia di San Fruttuoso** from Portofino. It's a steep climb at first, and the walk takes about 2½ hours one way. If you're extremely ambitious and want to make a day of it, you can hike another 2½ hours all the way to Camogli. Much more modest hikes from Portofino include a 1-hour uphill walk to Cappella delle Gave, a bit inland in the hills, from where you can continue downhill to Santa Margherita Ligure (another 1½ hours) and a gently undulating paved trail leading to the beach at Paraggi (½ hour). Finally, there's a 2½-hour hike from Portofino that heads farther inland to Ruta, through Olmi and Pietre Strette. The trails are well marked and maps are available at the tourist information offices in Rapallo, Santa Margherita, Portofino, and Camogli.

BEACHES

The Ligurian coast is known for its rocky vistas but the Portofino promontory has one sandy beach, on the east side, at **Paraggi**.

WHERE TO EAT

¢–$ ✕ **Pizzeria Il Lido.** As the name suggests, this popular spot is right across from Camogli's narrow beach, and the outside tables have great views of the sea. If you don't fancy one of the many varieties of pizza, you can choose one of the pasta dishes. ⊠ *Via Garibaldi 133, Camogli* ☎ *0185/770141* ▤ *MC, V* ⊗ *Closed Tues.*

¢ ✕ **Canale.** If the staggering prices of virtually all of Portofino's restaurants put you off, the long line outside this family-run bakery indicates that you're not alone and that something special is in store. Here all the focaccia is baked on the spot and served fresh from the oven, along with all kinds of sandwiches, pastries, and other refreshments. The only problem is there's nowhere to sit—time for a picnic! ⊠ *Via Roma 30* ☎*0185/269248* ▭*No credit cards* ⊘*Closed Nov. and Dec. No lunch Jan.–Apr. and Oct.*

ST-TROPEZ, FRANCE

Brigitte Bardot kick-started the rush in the early 1960s, and she was followed by the likes of Liz Taylor and Sophia Loren. People still flock to St-Tropez for the sun, the sea, and, the celebrities. The new generation includes Elton, Barbra, Oprah, Jack, and Uma, though they stay hidden in villas, and the people you'll see on the streets are mere mortals, lots of them, many intent on displaying the best—and often the most—of their youth, beauty, and wealth. Still, if you take an early morning stroll around the pretty port or down the narrow medieval streets with their candied-almond hues, you'll see just how charming St-Tropez can be. There's a weekend's worth of boutiques to explore and many cute cafés where you can sit under colored awnings and watch the spectacle that is St-Trop (*trop* in French means "too much") saunter by. Or head to the beaches, which are some of the most fashionable in Europe.

ESSENTIALS

CURRENCY The euro (€1 to US$1.46 at this writing); U.S. currency is generally not accepted in Europe, but ATMs are common.

HOURS Most stores are open Monday–Saturday 9–7, but many close at lunchtime (usually from noon to 2 or 3), and some open on Sunday during July and August. Museums are generally open 10–5, but most are closed either Monday or Tuesday.

TELEPHONES Tri-band GSM phones work in France. You can buy prepaid phone cards at telecom shops, news-vendors, and tobacconists in all towns and cities. Phone cards can be used for local or international calls. France Telecom and Orange are leading telecom companies.

COMING ASHORE

The port at St-Tropez is too small to accept commercial cruise vessels, so passengers are tendered to a landing dock, which is about a five-minute walk from town. There are no passenger facilities portside. Taxis and tour buses are not allowed into the staging area, which means a walk from the landing stage to transport connections is unavoidable.

Car-rental offices can be found in the town; expect to pay about €70 for an economy manual vehicle. Taxis are available at the port entrance and can provide tourist itineraries or transfers to the beaches. For single journeys, prices are €2.30 then €0.69 per km (½-mi). Be aware that, especially during the summer, traffic heading into St-Tropez builds up, and you can spend more than an hour just traveling the last two or three miles to the port and town. Always allow plenty of time to return any rental car or make the return taxi journey.

EXPLORING ST-TROPEZ

Numbers in the margin correspond to points of interest on the St-Tropez map.

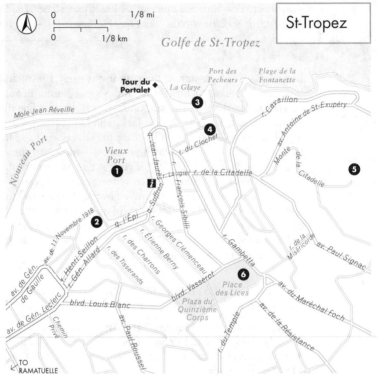

⑤ Citadelle. Head up Rue de la Citadelle to the 16th-century citadel, which stands in a lovely hilltop park; its ramparts offer a fantastic view of the town and the sea. Although it's hard to imagine St-Tropez as a military outpost amidst today's bikini-clad sun worshippers, inside the Citadelle's donjon the **Musée Naval** (Naval Museum) displays ship models, cannons, maps, and pictures of St-Tropez from its days as a naval port. At this writing, the museum is closed for renovations, expected to reopen in late 2008. It is likely that the theme of the museum will change, but until that decision is made you can still see some of the navy models in the Citadelle, as well as a series of temporary art exhibitions. ⊠*Rue de la Citadelle* ☎*04-94-97-59-43* 🖅 *€2.50* ☉*Oct.–Mar., daily 10–12:30 and 1:30–5:30; Apr.–Sept., daily 10–12:30 and 1–6:30.*

④ Église de St-Tropez. Head up rue Guichard to this baroque church to pay your respects to the bust and barque of St. Torpes every day but May 17, when they are carried aloft in the Bravade parade honoring the town's namesake saint. ⊠*Rue Guichard.*

② Musée de l'Annonciade. Just inland from the southwest corner of the Vieux Port stands the extraordinary Annunciation Museum, where the legacy of the artists who loved St-Tropez has been lovingly preserved. This 14th-century chapel, converted to an art museum, alone merits a visit to St-Tropez. Cutting-edge temporary exhibitions keep visitors on their toes while works stretching from pointillists to fauves to cubists line the walls of the permanent collection. Signac, Matisse, Signard, Braque, Dufy, Vuillard, Rouault: many of them painted in (and about) St-Tropez, tracing the evolution of painting from impressionism to expressionism. The museum also hosts temporary exhibitions every summer, from local talent to up-and-coming international artists. ✉ *Quai de l'Épi/Pl. Georges Grammont* ☎ *04-94-17-84-10* 🖃 *€5, €6 special exhibits* ⊗ *June–Sept., Wed.–Mon. 10–1 and 3–7; Oct.–May, Wed.–Mon. 10–noon and 1–6.*

❻ **Place des Lices.** This square, which is also called the Place Carnot, is the social center of the old town. Here, you'll hear *pétanque* balls clicking in the sand square. (Pétanque is a a southern version of *boules,* a French lawn-bowling game similar to boccie.) The square's symmetrical forest of plane trees (what's left of them) provides shade to rows of cafés and restaurants, skateboarders, children, and the grandfatherly pétanque players. Enjoy a time-out in the town "living room," Le Café (not to be confused with the nearby Café des Arts). The square becomes a moveable feast (for both eyes and palate) on market days—Tuesday and Saturday.

❸ **Quartier de la Ponche.** The old fisherman's quarter is just east of the Quai Jean-Jaurès. Complete with gulf-side harbor, this old-town maze of backstreets and old ramparts is daubed in shades of gold, pink, ocher, and sky-blue. Trellised jasmine and wrought-iron birdcages hang from the shuttered windows, and many of the tiny streets dead-end at the sea. Here you'll find the **Port des Pécheurs** (Fishermen's Port), on whose beach Bardot did a star-turn in *And God Created Woman*. Twisting, narrow streets, designed to break the impact of the mistral, open to tiny squares with fountains. The main drag here, Rue de la Ponche, leads into Place l'Hôtel de Ville, landmarked by a **mairie** (town hall) marked out in typical Tropezienne hues of pink and green.

❶ **Vieux Port.** Bordered by the Quai de l'Epi, the Quai Bouchard, the Quai Peri, the Quai Suffren, and the Quai Jean-Jaurès, Old Port is the nerve center of this famous yachting spot, a place for strolling and looking over the shoulders of artists daubing their versions of the view on easels set up along the water's edge, surreptitiously looking out for any off-duty celebs. For it is here, from folding director's chairs at the famous port-side cafés Le Gorille (named for its late exceptionally hirsute manager), Café de Paris, and Sénéquier's—which line Quai Suffren and Quai Jean-Jaurès—that the cast of St-Tropez's living theater plays out its colorful roles. Head beyond the 15th-century Tour du Portalet to the Mole Jean Réveille, the harbor wall, for a good view of Ste-Maxime across the sparkling bay, the hills of Estérel and, on a clear day, the distant Alps.

ST-TROPEZ BEST BETS

Stroll around the Port. This is the place to see and be seen; to dress and strut whether you are 17 or 70. Yes, the celebrities flock here but so do Europe's fashion peacocks.

Sip an aperitif in the Place des Lices. Sit in the shade of an ancient plane tree, soak in the Provencal atmosphere, and watch the southern French *joie-de-vivre.*

Browse the boutiques. This is stylish shopping at its best with myriad small and exclusive and upscale shops.

4

RAMATUELLE

12 km (7 mi) southwest of St-Tropez.

A typical hilltop whorl of red-clay roofs and dense inner streets topped with arches and lined with arcades, this ancient market town was destroyed in the Wars of Religion and rebuilt as a harmonious whole in 1620, complete with venerable archways and vaulted passages. Now its souvenir shops and galleries attract day-trippers out of St-Tropez, who enjoy the pretty drive through the vineyards as much as the village itself. At the top of the village you can visit the Moulin de Paillas, on Route du Moulin de Paillas, a windmill recently restored in the old style with a mechanism made entirely of wood; the site offers a panoramic view of the coastline. Free guided tours of the windmill are held every Tuesday from 10 to noon. Ramatuelle is also just a heartbeat away from the **Plage de Pamplonne**—a destination location amongst hippies and starlets alike.

The ever famous **Club 55** (⊠*Plage de Pamplonne* ☎*04–94–55–55–55* ⊕*www.leclub55.com*) is located in Ramatuelle; it's one of the places where the area's rich and famous are known to play.

SHOPPING

This high-fashion town abounds in boutiques full of the latest modes and chic accessories plus stylish items for the home you'll find in the pages of design magazines. The must-have souvenirs are the handmade strappy leather sandals, called Tropéziennes, or the delicious Tarte Tropézienne (a cream-filled cake) invented by a local confectioner and enjoyed by Brigitte Bardot during the filming of *And God Created Woman* in 1955.

Designer boutiques may be spreading like wild mushrooms all over St-Tropez, but the main fashionista-strutting runways are still along **Rue Gambetta** or **Rue Allard.Rue Sibilli**, behind the Quai Suffren, is lined with all kinds of trendy boutiques. The **Place des Lices** overflows with produce, regional foods, clothing, and *brocantes* (collectibles) on Tuesday and Saturday mornings. Don't miss the picturesque little fish market that fills up **Place aux Herbes** every morning.

Artists have long found the colors of the town inspirational, as witnessed at the Musée de l'Annonciade. Today, a new generation of artists crowds the port, setting up impromptu stalls around their easels. Simply choose a style you like.

For Tropéziennes head to **Rondini** (⊠*16 rue Clemenceau* ☎*04–94–97–19–55*), a family-run store where the owners have been hand-crafting sandals since 1927. **La Tarte Tropézienne** (⊠*36 rue Clemenceau* ☎*04–94–97–71–42*) is the place to buy your cakes.

BEACHES

The famous beaches of St-Tropez lie southeast of the town on a small peninsula. The long stretch of fine sand at **Pampelonne** (⊠*Along route des Plages, Ramatuelle Peninsula, 5 mi from St-Tropez*) is now divided into a number of sections, each served by a trendy restaurant and beach club, where the glitterati head to lunch and the paparazzi are kept at a discreet distance. Rent a beach bed and soak in the sun for a few hours. Be aware that topless sunbathing is accepted practice here, so there will be bare breasts on view.

WHERE TO EAT

$$–$$$$ ✕**Le Café.** The busy terrace here often doubles as a stadium for different factions cheering on favorite local pétanque players in the Place des Lices. You, too, can play—borrow some *boules* from the friendly bar staff (and get your pastis bottle at the ready: you'll need it to properly appreciate the full pétanque experience). This casual café is a great place to really sink into the local culture, it's an even bigger bonus that the food is as good as the setting. Try the beef carpaccio with olive tapenade or the large prawns flambéed with Pastis à la Provençal. ⊠*5 pl. des Lices* ☎*04–94–97–44–69* ▭*AE, MC, V.*

$$–$$$$ ✕**La Table du Marché.** With an afternoon tearoom and a summer deli/sushi bar, this charming bistro from celebrity chef Christophe Leroy offers up a mouthwatering spread of regional specialties in a surprisingly casual atmosphere. Sink into one of the overstuffed armchairs in the upstairs dining room, cozy with chic Provençal accents and antique bookshelves, and, for a light snack, try the tomato *pistou* tart. Hungry guests can happily dive into a nicely balanced €18 or €26 set lunch menu while perusing the good wine list. ⊠*38 rue Georges Clemanceau* ☎*04–94–97–85–20* ▭*AE, MC, V.*

VALENCIA, SPAIN

Despite its proximity to the Mediterranean, Valencia's history and geography have been defined most significantly by the River Turia and the fertile floodplain (*huerta*) that surrounds it. Modern Valencia was best known for its flooding disasters until the River Turia was diverted to the south in the late 1950s. Since then, the city has been on a steady course of urban beautification. The lovely *puentes* (bridges) that once spanned the Turia look equally graceful spanning a wandering municipal park, and the spectacular futuristic Ciudad de las Artes y de las Sciencias (City of Arts and Sciences), designed by Valencian-born architect Santaigo Clalatrava, has at long last created an exciting architectural link between this river town and the Mediterranean. Valencia's port, and parts of the city itself, underwent major structural refurbishment for the 2007 America's Cup sailing classic held here in June 2007.

ESSENTIALS

CURRENCY   The euro (€1 to US$1.46 at this writing); U.S. currency is generally not accepted in Europe, but ATMs are common and credit cards are widely accepted.

HOURS   Museums are generally open from 9 until 7 or 8, but many are closed on Monday and some close in the afternoon. Most stores are open Monday–Saturday 9–1:30 and 5–8, but tourist shops may open in the afternoon and also on Sunday between May and September.

INTERNET   **Cantonet** ⊠*Av. Vicente Blasco Ibánez.*

TELEPHONES   Most tri-band and quad-band GSM phones will work in Spain, where mobile services are 3G-compatible. Public kiosks accept phone cards that support international calls (cards sold in press shops, bars, and telecom shops). Major companies include Vodafone.

COMING ASHORE

Valencia's port area received a facelift to coincide with the arrival of the America's Cup competition in June 2007. Though the terminal itself has limited facilities, the public interface areas, where the port and waterfront meet the city, has lots of restaurants, cafés, and shops.

It is a long walk from the port to the historic downtown district, but the trip is enjoyable if you want to take the time. Two buses are useful for exploring the city. Route 5B plies a route through the old town, while route 19 leads past the port into the old town. The city has an excellent public transport system, so reaching all parts of the city by bus or metro is a cinch. A day ticket in €7.

Renting a car won't be an advantage when exploring the city, but it will allow you to head out along the coast or inland to explore the countryside. For an economy manual vehicle, expect to pay about €85 per day.

EXPLORING VALENCIA

Numbers in the margin correspond to points of interest on the Valencia map.

⓫ Casa Museo José Benlliure. The modern Valencian painter-sculptor Jose Benlliure is known for his portraits and large-scale historical and religious paintings, many of which hang in Valencia's Museo de Bellas Artes (Museum of Fine Arts). Here in his elegant house and studio are 50 of his works. On display are also works by his son, Pepino, and iconographic sculptures by Benlliure's brother, the well-known sculptor Mariano Benlliure. ⊠ *Calle Blanquerías 23* ☎ *963/919103* 🖃 *€2* ⊙ *Tues.–Sat. 10–2 and 4:30–8, Sun. 10–3.*

❶ Cathedral. Valencia's 13th- to 15th-century cathedral is the heart of the city. The building has three portals—Romanesque, Gothic, and rococo respectively. Inside, Renaissance and baroque marble were removed in a successful restoration of the original Gothic style, as is now the trend in Spanish churches. The Capilla del Santo Cáliz (Chapel of the Holy Chalice) displays a purple agate vessel once said to be the Holy Grail (Christ's cup at the Last Supper) and thought to have been brought to Spain in the 4th century. Behind the altar you can see the left arm of **St. Vincent,** who was martyred in Valencia in 304. Stars of the cathedral **museum** are Goya's two famous paintings of St. Francis de Borja, Duke of Gandia. To the left of the cathedral entrance is the octagonal tower **El Miguelete,** which you can climb: the roofs of the old town create a kaleidoscope of orange and brown terra-cotta, and the sea appears in the background. It's said that you can see 300 belfries from here, including bright-blue cupolas made of ceramic tiles from nearby Manises. The tower was built in 1381, and the final spire added in 1736. ⊠ *Pl. de la Reina* ☎ *963/918127* 🖃 *Cathedral free, museum €1.20, tower €1.20* ⊙ *Cathedral Mon.–Sat. 7:30–1 and 4:30–8:30, Sun. 7:30–1 and 5–8:30. Museum and chapel Dec.–Feb.,*

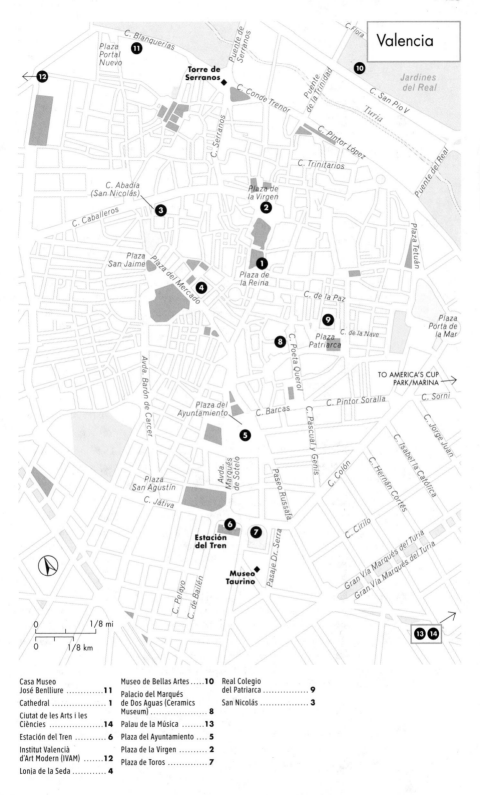

Valencia

4

Mon.–Sat. 10–1; Mar.–May, Oct., and Nov., Mon.–Sat. 10–1 and 4:30–6; June–Sept., Mon.–Sat. 10–1 and 4:30–7. Tower weekdays 10–12:30 and 4:30–6:30, weekends 10–1:30 and 5–6:30.

⑭ Ciutat de les Arts i les Ciències. Designed

Fodor'sChoice
★

by native son Santiago Calatrava, this sprawling futuristic complex is the home of Valencia's **Museu de les Ciències Príncipe Felipe** (Prince Philip Science Museum), **L'Hemisfèric** (Hemispheric Planetarium), **L'Oceanogràfic** (Oceanographic Park), and **Palau de les Arts** (Palace of the Arts). With resplendent buildings resembling combs and crustaceans, the Ciutat is a favorite of architecture buffs and curious kids. The Science Museum has soaring platforms filled with lasers, holograms, simulators, and hands-on lab experiments. The eye-shape planetarium projects 3-D virtual voyages on its huge IMAX screen. At the Oceanographic Park you can take a submarine ride through a coastal marine habitat. ⊠*Av. Autovía del Saler 7* ☎*902/100031* 📠*961/974505* ⊕*www.cac.es* 🎟*Museu de les Ciències €7.50, L'Hemisfèric €7.50, €11.20 for admission to both, L'Oceanogràfic €22, €30.50 for admission to all three* ☉*Mid-Sept.–June, daily 10–7; July–mid-Sept., daily 10–9. L'Oceanogràfic mid-Sept.–May, Sun.–Fri. 10–6, Sat. 10–8; June–mid-July and early Sept., daily 10–8; mid-July–late Aug. 10–midnight. L'Hemisfèric daily shows generally every hr on the hr 10–9 PM.*

VALENCIA BEST BETS

Go straight to the top. The view of Valencia from the Miguelete Tower is magnficient.

Cast an eye over Ciutat de les Arts i les Ciències. One of Spain's most imaginative Moderniste developments is in Valencia.

Leave the bull at home. Tread carefully in the Museo Nacional de Cerámica, which showcases porcelain, one of the city's most famous exports.

❻ Estación del Tren. Designed by Demetrio Ribes Mano in 1917, the train station is a splendid Moderniste pile replete with citrus motifs. ⊠*Down Av. Marqués de Sotelo from ayuntamiento.*

⑫ Institut Valencià d'Art Modern (IVAM). Dedicated to modern and contemporary pieces, the art institute has a permanent collection of 20th-century avant-garde works, European Informalism (including the Spanish artists Saura, Tàpies, and Chillida), pop art, and photography. ⊠*Guillem de Castro 118* ☎*963/863000* ⊕*www.ivam.es* 🎟*€2, free Sun.* ☉*June–Aug., Tues.–Sun. 10–10; Sept.–May, Tues.–Sun. 10–8.*

❹ Lonja de la Seda. The Silk Exchange is a product of Valencia's golden age, when the arts came under the patronage of Ferdinand I. Widely regarded as one of Spain's finest Gothic buildings, it has a perfect Gothic facade decorated with ghoulish gargoyles, complemented inside by high vaulting and twisted columns. Opposite the Lonja stands the **Iglesia de los Santos Juanes** (Church of the St. John), whose interior was destroyed during the civil war, and, next door, the Moderniste **Mercado Central** (Central Market), built entirely of iron and glass. ⊠*Plaza del Mercado* 🎟*Free* ☉*Tues.–Fri. 9:30–2 and 4:30–8, weekends 9:30–1:30.*

❿ Museo de Bellas Artes. Valencia was a thriving center of artistic activity in the 15th century, and the city's Museum of Fine Arts is one of the best in Spain. Many of the best paintings by Jacomart and Juan Reixach, two of several artists known as the Valencian Primitives, are here, as is work by Hieronymus Bosch—or El Bosco, as they call him here. The ground floor has and a room devoted to Goya. ⊠*C. San Pío V s/n* ☎*963/932046* ⊕*www.cult.gva.es/mbav* ⊠*Free* ⊙*Tues.–Sun. 10–8.*

⑧ Palacio del Marqués de Dos Aguas. This building has a fascinating baroque ★ alabaster facade. Embellished with fruits and vegetables, it centers on the figures of the *Dos Aguas (Two Waters)*, carved by Ignacio Vergara in the 18th century. The palace contains the **Museo Nacional de Cerámica,** with a magnificent collection of mostly local ceramics. ⊠*C. Poeta Querol 2* ☎*963/516392* ⊠*Palace and museum €2.40, free Sat. afternoon and Sun. morning* ⊙*Tues.–Sat. 10–2 and 4–8, Sun. 10–2.*

⑬ Palau de la Música. On one of the nicest stretches of the Turia riverbed, a pond is backed by a huge glass vault: Valencia's Palace of Music. Supported by 10 porticoed pillars, the dome gives the illusion of a greenhouse, both from the street and from within its sun-filled, tree-landscaped interior. Home of the Orquesta de Valencia, the main hall also hosts performers on tour from around the world, including chamber and youth orchestras, opera, and an excellent concert series featuring early, baroque, and classical music. To see the building without concert tickets, pop into the **art gallery,** which is host to free changing exhibits. ⊠*Paseo de la Alameda 30* ☎*963/375020* ⊕*www.palauvalencia.com* ⊙*Gallery daily 10:30–1:30 and 5:30–9.*

⑤ Plaza del Ayuntamiento. Down Avenida María Cristina from the market, this plaza is the hub of city life, a fact well conveyed by the massiveness of its baroque facades. The **ayuntamiento** itself contains the city tourist office and a museum on the history of Valencia. ⊙*Ayuntamiento weekdays 8:30–2:30.*

② Plaza de la Virgen. From the cathedral's Gothic Puerta de los Apóstoles (Apostle Door), emerge on this pedestrian plaza, a lovely place for a refreshing *horchata* (tiger-nut milk) in the late afternoon. Next to its portal, market gardeners from the huerta bring their irrigation disputes before the Water Tribunal, which has met every Thursday at noon since 1350. It is said that it is the oldest surviving legal system in the world. Verdicts are given on the spot, and sentences have ranged from fines to deprivation of water.

⑦ Plaza de Toros. This bullring is one of the oldest in Spain. Just beyond, down Pasaje Dr. Serra, the **Museo Taurino** *(Bullfighting Museum)* has bullfighting memorabilia, including bulls' heads and matadors' swords. ⊠*Free* ⊙*Bullring and museum Tues.–Sun. 10–2.*

⑨ Real Colegio del Patriarca. The Royal College of the Patriarch stands on the far side of Plaza Patriarca, toward the center of town. Founded by San Juan de Ribera in the 16th century, it has a lovely Renaissance patio and an ornate church, and its museum holds works by Juan de Juanes, Francisco Ribalta, and El Greco. ⊠*Entrance off C. de la Nave* ⊠*€1.20* ⊙*Daily 11–1:30.*

③ San Nicolás. A small plaza contains Valencia's oldest church, once the parish of the Borgia Pope Calixtus III. The first portal you come to, with a tacked-on, rococo bas-relief of the Virgin Mary with cherubs, hints well at what's inside: every inch of the originally Gothic church is covered with Churrigueresque embellishments. ⊠*C. Abadía San Nicolás* ✉*Free* ☉*Open for mass daily 8–9* AM *and 7–8* PM, *Sat. 6:30–8:30* PM, *Sun. various masses 8–1:15.*

SHOPPING

Shoes and leather goods are among Valencia's main products. Both handmade and mass-produced ceramics are created in a range of colors and styles. Fans and silk shawls, along with other traditional Spanish dress, are priced according to quality. Olives and olive oil will make gourmets happy, and olive oil is also used for a range of hair and beauty products.

The town of Manises, 9 km (5 ½ mi) west of Valencia, is a center for Valencian ceramics, known particularly for its azulejos. Porcelain-figure-maker **Lladró** (⊠*Ctra de Alboraya, Tavernes Blanqués* ☎*96/3187008*) has its world headquarters, including a factory shop and museum, on the city outskirts to the northeast. The retail outlet of **Lladró** (⊠*Poeta Querol 9, Valencia* ☎*96/3511625*) is in the center of the city. **Salvador Ribes** (⊠*Vilaragut 7, Valencia*) has top-quality antiques with correspondingly daunting price tags. For better deals, try stores on Calle Avellanas near the cathedral.

GOLF

Mild conditions year-round mean the countryside around Valencia is dotted with golf courses, and most don't need membership to play a round. **El Bosque** (⊠*Godelleta, Km 4.1, Chiva* ☎*96/1808009*) is a Robert Trent Jones–designed course. **El Saler** (⊠*Av. de los Pinares, El Saler* ☎*96/1611186*), the most famous course in the region, is well-regarded by both professionals and amateurs.

WHERE TO EAT

$-$$ ✕**La Riuà.** This local secret, which serves Valencian food, is decorated with beautiful ceramic tiles. House specialties include *anguilas* (eels) prepared with *all i pebre* (garlic and pepper), *pulpitos guisados* (stewed baby octopus), and traditional rice dishes. Wash it down with a cold bottle of *Llanos de Titaguas,* a dry yet snappy white Valencian table wine. The restaurant is just off Plaza de la Reina. ⊠*C. del Mar 27* ☎*963/914571* ▭*AE, DC, MC, V* ☉*Closed Sun., Easter wk, and Aug. No dinner Mon.*

¢-$ ✕**Patos.** Small, cozy, and very popular with locals, this restored 18th-century town house has an earthy look, thanks to the terra-cotta tiles, wood-panel walls, and overhead beams. On weekdays, the set lunch menu is a real bargain at €10 and usually includes *ternera* (veal) and *lomo* (pork loin). The set dinner (and weekend) menu is €18 and sometimes includes *cordero* (lamb) and *solomillo* (pork sirloin). Get here by 9:30 PM to snag a table; you can also dine outside in summer. The restaurant is just north of Calle de la Paz, in the old quarter. ⊠*C. del Mar 28* ☎*963/921522* ▭*MC, V* ☉*No dinner Sun. and Mon.*

VALLETTA, MALTA

Hulking megalithic temples, ornate baroque churches, narrow old-world streets, and hilltop citadels are Malta's human legacy. Dizzying limestone cliffs, sparkling seas, and charming rural landscapes make up its natural beauty. In its 7,000 years of human habitation, Malta has been overrun by every major Mediterranean power: Phoenicians, Carthaginians, Romans, Byzantines, and Arabs; Normans, Swabians, Angevins, Aragonese, and the Knights of the Order of St. John of Jerusalem; the French, the British, and now tourists. The Germans and Italians tried to take it in World War II—their air raids were devastating—but could not. The islands' history with the Knights of the Order of St. John has given them their lasting character. In 1565, when the forces of Süleyman the Magnificent laid siege here, it was the Knights' turn, with the faithful backing of the Maltese, to send the Turks packing. The handsome limestone buildings and fortifications that the wealthy Knights left behind are all around the islands.

ESSENTIALS

CURRENCY The Maltese lira (Lm1 is $3.16 or €2.33, €1 is $1.46). Prices in this section are given in Maltese lira, but at this writing Malta is expected to adopt the euro on January 1, 2008. As a very rough rule of thumb, subtract about 1/3 of the lira price to get the equivalent in euros. U.S. currency is generally not accepted in Europe, but ATMs are common and credit cards are widely accepted.

HOURS Government museums are open October–mid-June, Monday–Saturday 8:15–5, Sunday 8:15–4:15; mid-June–September, daily 7:45–2. Shops are open Monday–Saturday 9–1 and 4–7.

INTERNET **YMCA** (✉ *178 Merchant St.* ☎ *21/240–80*) has several Internet-connected computers.

TELEPHONES Malta's mobile services operate on a single GSM-band system. The system supports text and data but not 3G technology. Public phones operate by means of telecards with smartchip technology. They can be used to make international calls. Maltacom is the main provider.

COMING ASHORE

Cruise ships dock at the Valletta Waterfront Facility in the heart of the historic Grand Harbour. The facility is extensive and houses modern, high-quality shops, eight restaurants, and exhibition spaces. Taxi fare to the town of Valetta is Lm4 and takes only 5 minutes. It's a steep walk up to the Valletta citadel on foot, but it's an easy route.

Malta has a very well-organized public bus service. Most routes across the island start at Valletta Terminal just outside the entrance to the Citadel. Local fares are Lm0.20 for most trips, Lm0.25 for longer rides. Bus routes are marked on the maps distributed by the tourist office. Renting a car would allow you to visit many of Malta's attractions during a day. Prices for a compact manual vehicle are about Lm14 per day.

Taxis operate on a fixed-fee basis from the port. Sample fares are Lm6 (€14) to Marsaxlokk and Lm8 (€18.63) to Mdina. Taxi tours can be organized on a per-hour basis; for example, the fare for five hours is about Lm 69.88.

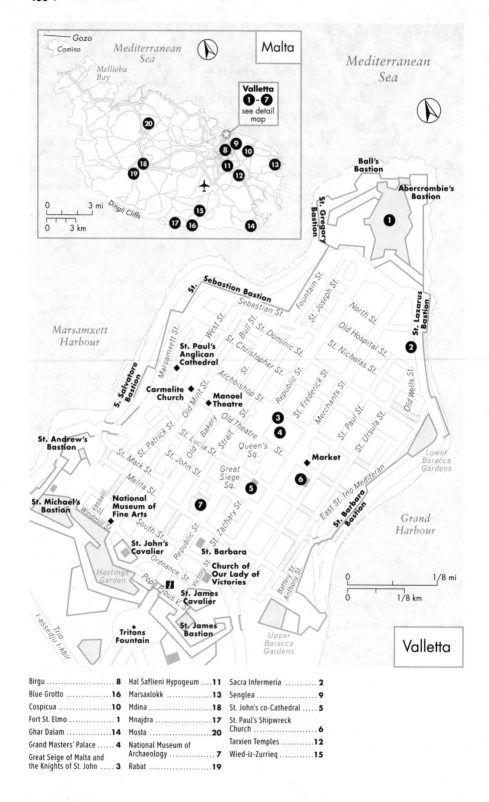

Malta

Mediterranean Sea

Valletta

EXPLORING MALTA

Numbers in the margin correspond to points of interest on the Malta map.

VALLETTA

Malta's capital, the minicity of Valletta, has ornate palaces and museums protected by massive fortifications of honey-color limestone. Houses along the narrow streets have overhanging wooden balconies for people-watching from indoors. The main entrance to town is through the City Gate (where all bus routes end), which leads onto Triq Repubblika (Republic Street), the spine of the grid-pattern city and the main shopping street. Triq Mercante (Merchant Street) parallels Repubblika to the east and is also good for strolling. From these two streets, cross streets descend toward the water; some are stepped. Valletta's compactness makes it ideal to explore on foot. Before setting out along Republic Street, stop at the tourist information office (just inside the city gate) for maps and brochures.

① **Fort St. Elmo.** Built in 1552 by the Knights to defend the harbor, the fort was completely destroyed during the siege of 1565 and rebuilt by succeeding military leaders. Today part of the fort houses the **War Museum** (☎222430), with its collection of military objects related to World War II, including the George Cross, a medal awarded to the people of Malta for bravery in 1942 by British King George VI. Also on display are an Italian E-boat and one of the three Gloster Gladiator biplanes that defended the island. ⊠*St. Elmo Pl.* ☎*226400* 🎟*Lm1* 🕐*Daily 9–5.*

④ ★ **Grand Masters' Palace.** The palace houses the president's office, and Malta's parliament meets here. Completed in 1574, the palace has a unique collection of Gobelin tapestries; the main hall is decorated with frescoes depicting the history of the Knights and the Great Siege. On view are works by Ribera, Van Loo, and Batoni. At the back of the building is the **Armoury of the Knights,** with exhibits of arms and armor through the ages. ⊠*Palace Sq., Triq Repubblika* ☎*221221* 🎟*Lm2* 🕐*Daily 9–5.*

③ ★ **Great Siege of Malta and the Knights of St. John.** A walk-through presentation traces the order's history from its founding in 1099 in the Holy Land and its journeys from Jerusalem to Cyprus, Rhodes, and Malta. Also depicted are epic scenes from the Great Siege of 1565, the naval Battle of Lepanto, and the order's eviction from Malta by the French. ⊠*Cafe Premier Complex, Treasury St.* ☎*21247300* ⊕*www. siegemalta.com* 🎟*Lm3.50* 🕐*Daily 10–4.*

⑦ ★ **National Museum of Archaeology.** Housed in the Auberge de Provence (the hostel of the Knights from Provence), the museum has an excellent collection of finds from Malta's many prehistoric sites—Tarxien, Hagar Qim, and the Hypogeum at Paola. ⊠*Triq Repubblika* ☎*233821* 🎟*Lm3* 🕐*Daily 9–5.*

② **Sacra Infermeria** *(Hospital of the Knights).* This gracious building near the seawall has been converted into the Mediterranean Conference Center. For an introduction to the island, see the *Malta Experience,* a multimedia presentation on the history of Malta that is given here daily on the hour. ⊠*Mediterranean St.* ☎*21224135* 🎟*Lm1.85* 🕐*Weekdays 11–4, weekends 11–1 (11–2 Oct.–June).*

⑤ St. John's co-Cathedral. Functional in
★ design but lavishly decorated, the
Order of St. John's own church
(1578) is Malta's most important
treasure. The Knights' colored-
marble tombstones on the floor are
gorgeous. Each of the side chapels
was decorated by a national hostel
of the Knights. Many of the paintings and the decoration scheme are
by the island's beloved 17th-cen-
tury painter Mattia Preti (b. 1613).
The artistic tour de force, however
is Caravaggio's *The Beheading
of St. John the Baptist,* commissioned by the Knights and the only
painting the artist ever signed. The
cathedral **museum** has illuminated
manuscripts and a rich collection of
Flemish tapestries. ⊠*Pjazza San Gwann* ⊙ *Weekdays 9:30–12:30 and
1:30–4:30, Sat. 9:30–12:30.*

⑥ St. Paul's Shipwreck Church. The importance of St. Paul to the Maltese explains
★ the work lavished on this baroque marvel—its raised central vault, oval
dome, and marble columns. The *os brachii* (arm bone) relic of the saint is
housed in a chapel on the right, a splendid gated chapel is on the left, and
a baptismal font stands by the entrance. ⊠*Triq San Pawl.*

THE THREE CITIES
Birgu is 8 km (5 mi) east of Valletta

⑧ East across the Grand Harbor from Valletta, the three cities of **Birgu** (aka
⑨ Vittoriosa), **Senglea,** and **Cospicua** are where the Knights of the Order of St.
John first settled—and where crucial fighting took place in the Great Siege
⑩ of the Turks in 1565. Vittoriosa is named for the victory over the Turks.
The 5 km (3 mi) of great walls around the cities are the Cottonera Lines,
built in the 1670s. On the narrow streets north of the main square you
can loop from the Triq La Vallette to the Triq Majjistral on the right. Triq
It-Tramuntana takes you past baroque doorways, the Knights' Auberge
d'Angleterre (Inn of England), and a Saracen-style house that is thought
to date from the 1200s.

Below Birgu's main square, the **Church of St. Lawrenz** is the city's finest church,
with the 17th-century painter Mattia Preti's *Martyrdom of San Lawrenz.*
⊠*Triq San Lawrenz, Birgu.*

The displays in Birgu's **Inquisitor's Palace** reveal less-discussed aspects of
less-tolerant times in Malta. ⊠*Triq Il-Mina Il-Kbira, Birgu* ▭*Lm2*
⊙*Daily 9–5.*

At the tip of Senglea, **Gardjola Garden,** once a guard post, has great views
and a turret carved with a vigilant eye and ear.

PAOLA & TARXIEN
Paola 4.8 km (3 mi) south of Valletta

⓫ The **Ħal Saflieni Hypogeum**, a massive labyrinth of underground chambers,
★ was used for burials more than 4,000 years ago. Many chambers are
decorated with red ocher or fine carvings. ✉*On road to Santa Lucija*
☎*233821* ⊗*By appointment.*

⓬ The three interconnecting **Tarxien Temples** have curious carvings, oracular
chambers, and altars, all dating from about 2800 BC. Nearby are remains
of an earlier temple from about 4000 BC. ✉*Behind Paola's Church of
Christ the King* 🎟*Lm1* ⊗*Daily 9–5.*

MARSAXLOKK
⓭ *8 km (5 mi) southast of Valletta*

At the pretty fishing and resort town Marsaxlokk, on the southeast coast,
you can see the *luzzu,* Malta's multicolor, traditional fishing boat, a symbol of the island. Its vertical prow has Phoenician ancestry.

GĦAR DALAM
⓮ *9 km (6 mi) southeast of Valletta*

The semifossilized remains of long-extinct species of dwarf elephants and
hippopotamuses that roamed the island some 125,000 years ago were
found in a cave in Għar Dalam. The fossils are now on display in the small
museum. ✉*Għar Dalam* 🎟*Lm1.50* ⊗*Daily 9–5.*

ZURRIEQ
11km (7 mi) south of Valletta

On the way to Zurrieq from Valletta you will pass limestone quarries,
where orchards are planted, protected from the wind, after the limestone
is exhausted.

⓯ On the far side of town, **Wied-iz-Zurrieq** *(Zurrieq Valley)* runs along the road
to a lookout over the towering walls of the Blue Grotto's bay.

⓰ The turnoff for the **Blue Grotto** (✉*Coast Rd.*) is 1 km (½-mi) beyond the
★ lookout. A steep road takes you to the rocky inlet where noisy boats leave
for the grottoes (there are many) and the stained-glass-blue waters that
splash their walls. Bring a bathing suit in case the water is calm enough
for swimming.

⓱ From the temple of **Mnajdra** *("mna-EE-dra"* ✉*Coast Rd.*), on the edge of a
★ hill by the sea, views are superb. The temple is encircled by hard coralline
limestone walls and has the typical, cloverlike trefoil plan.

MDINA
⓲ *12km (7 mi) southwest of Valletta*

★ In Mdina, Malta's ancient, walled capital—the longtime stronghold of
Malta's nobility—traffic is limited to residents' cars, and the noise of the
world outside doesn't penetrate the thick, golden walls. The quiet streets
are lined with sometimes block-long, still-occupied noble palaces.

★ The serene, baroque **Mdina Cathedral**, dedicated to St. Peter and St. Paul,
contains Mattia Preti's 17th-century painting *The Shipwreck of St. Paul.* In

the cathedral museum are Dürer woodcuts and illuminated manuscripts. ⊠*Archbishop Sq.* ☏*454679* ⊙*Mon.–Sat. 9–1 and 1:30–4.*

RABAT

⑲ *13km (8 mi) southwest of Valletta*

Rabat means "suburb"—in this case of Mdina.

The beautiful **St. Paul's Church** (⊠*Parish Sq.*) stands above a grotto where St. Paul reputedly took refuge after his shipwreck on Malta.

Catacombs run under much of Rabat. Up Triq Santa Agatha from Parish Square, the **Catacombs of St. Paul** are devoid of bones but full of carved-out burial troughs. Don't forget the way out when you set off to explore. **St. Agatha's Crypt and Catacombs,** farther up the street, were beautifully frescoed between 1200 and 1480, then defaced by Turks in 1551. ⊠*St. Agatha St.* ☏*Lm2* ⊙*Daily 9–5.*

MOSTA
10 km (6 mi) west of Valletta

⑳ The **Rotunda** *(Church of St. Mary)* has the third-largest unsupported dome in Europe, after St. Peter's in Rome and Hagia Sophia in Istanbul. A German bomb fell through the roof during World War II—without detonating. ⊠*Rotunda Sq.* ⊙*Daily 9–noon and 3–6.*

SHOPPING

Malta has several crafts that make excellent souvenirs. Mdina glass (there is a store in the cruise-terminal area) is a modern phenomenon but is now a signature gift of the island. More traditional are *bizzilla* (hand-woven lace), silver filigree, muslin fabrics, and wooden items. Valletta's main shopping street, **Triq Repubblika,** is lined with touristy shops—pick up postcards and film here, and then venture onto side streets for a look at everyday Maltese wares. The **Government Craft Center** (⊠*Pjazza San Gwann, Valletta*) has traditional handmade goods. At the **open-air market** *(Triq Mercante)* , in Valletta, with some haggling you may snap up a good bargain.

SPORTS & ACTIVITIES

Water sports are well-organized, and all the major beaches have water-sports centers offering windsurfing, wakeboarding, and paragliding. Scuba diving is particularly well organized with exciting wreck and cave dives.

Divewise (⊠*Westin Dragonara Hotel, St Julian's* ☏*21/356–441* ⊕*www.divewise.com.mt*) is one of the oldest dive schools on the island, with almost 30 years experience.

BEACHES

Malta has many lovely beaches, which range from small rock-flanked coves to vast strands. Many beaches see lots of European (mainly British) tourists during the summer season, so they may be busy.

Sandy **Ghajn Tuffieha Bay** on the northwestern coast is wonderful for an afternoon by the sea. The sometimes bumpy bus (Route 47) ride takes you through the rolling countryside, which is patchworked with ancient stone walls and occasional fields of root crops.

Mellieha Bay (✉ *Mellieha*) is the island's largest beach, with a range of water sports and eateries. It's popular with families.

Paradise Bay (✉ *Cirkewwa*) is the most attractive beach on the island, set in a natural cove.

WHERE TO EAT

$-$$ ✕ **Ix-Xlukkajr.** Seafood is the draw at this harborside restaurant. Octopus marinated in garlic sauce is a wonderful cold starter. Try the whole-fish specials and, for dessert, homemade prickly-pear and kiwi ice creams. ✉ *Village Sq., Valletta* ☎21612109 ▭*MC, V* ⊘*Closed Wed.*

¢ ✕ **Caffe Cordina.** On the ground floor of the original treasury of the Knights
★ is Valletta's oldest café. Since 1837, this ornate, vaulted confectionery has produced hot, savory breakfast pastries and *qaghaq ta' l-ghasel* (honey rings). ✉*244–45 Triq Repubblika, Valletta* ☎21234385 ▭*AE, DC, MC, V.*

VENICE, ITALY

It's called La Serenissima, "the most serene," a reference to the majesty, wisdom, and monstrous power of this city that was for centuries the unrivaled mistress of trade between Europe and the Orient and the bulwark of Christendom against the tides of Ottoman expansion. Built entirely on water by men who defied the sea, Venice is unlike any other town. No matter how many times you've seen it in movies or on TV, the real thing is more dreamlike than you could ever imagine. Its landmarks, the Basilica di San Marco and the Palazzo Ducale, are exotic mixes of Byzantine, Gothic, and Renaissance styles. Shimmering sunlight and silvery mist soften every perspective here, and you understand how the city became renowned in the Renaissance for its artists' rendering of color. It's full of secrets, inexpressibly romantic, and at times given over entirely to pleasure.

ESSENTIALS

CURRENCY The euro (€1 to US$1.46 at this writing); U.S. currency is generally not accepted in Europe, but ATMs are common.

HOURS Shops are generally open 9–1 and 3:30–7:30 and are closed Sunday and Monday morning most of the year, however tourist shops in the city will remain open throughout the day and into the evening.

INTERNET **Logic Internet Point** ✉*2799 Dorsoduro* ☎*041/0994555.*

TELEPHONES Tri-band GSM phones work in Italy. You can buy prepaid phone cards at telecom shops, news-vendors, and tobacconists in all towns and cities. Phone cards can be used for local or international calls.

COMING ASHORE

Venice is a huge port handling vast numbers of cruise ships and a lot of commercial traffic as well. The cruise terminal sits at the southeastern corner of city and has two main docking areas, the Marittima area for large ships and the San Basilio for smaller ones.

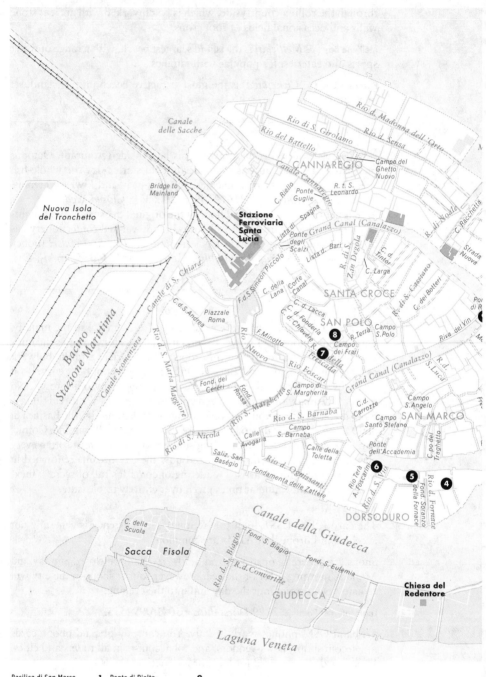

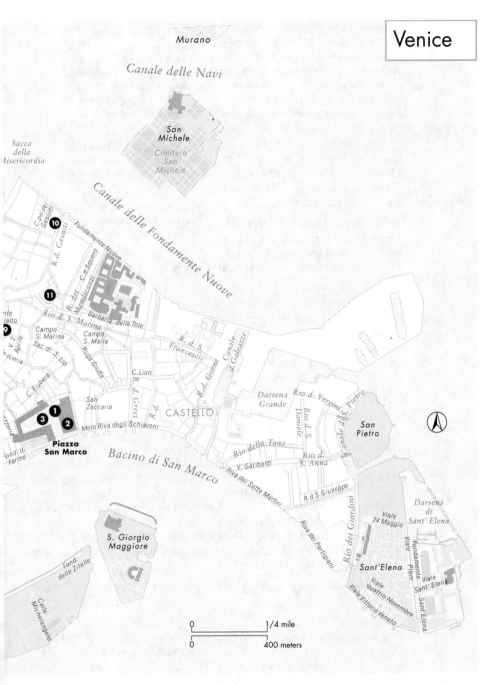

Murano

Canale delle Navi

San Michele

Cimitero San Michele

Sacca della Misericordia

4

Canale delle Fondamente Nuove

C.po dei Gesuiti

10

R. d. Gesuiti

Fondamenta Nuove

C. d. Squero

R. dei Mendicanti

11

Rio d. S. Marina

Barbaria delle Tole

nte alto

V. 2 Aprile

Sal. di S. Lio

erceria

C. Fiubera

Campo S. Marina

Campo S. Maria

Ruga Giuffa

R. d. S. Francesco

R. d. Gorne

Canale S. Galazza

C. Lion

R. d. Greci

R. d.

San Zaccaria

CASTELLO

Darsena Grande

Rio d. Vergini

Rio d. S. Daniele

Canale delle S. Pietro

San Pietro

1

3

2

Molo Riva degli Schiavoni

Piazza San Marco

fond. d. Farine

Bacino di San Marco

Rio della Tana

Riva dei Sette Martiri

V. Garibaldi

Rio d. S. Anna

R. d. S. Giuseppe

Rio dei Giardini

Riva dei Partigiani

Darsena di Sant' Elena

Viale 24 Maggio

Viale Piave

Fondamenta Plave

Viale Sant' Elena

Viale Sant' Elena

Sant'Elena

Viale quattro Novembre

Viale Vittoria Veneto

S. Giorgio Maggiore

CI

fond. delle Zitelle

Calle Michelangelo

0]/4 mile

0 400 meters

Venice

Marittima has duty-free shops and information desks but no refreshment facilities. From here, there is a shuttle bus to Piazza le Roma at the eastern edge of the city, just outside the port, or you can take Bus 6 from the port entrance. You can also take a boat. Among the seafaring options are the Alilaguna Blu Line boat from Marittima to Piazza San Marco as well as vaporetto sevices 41, 42, 51, 52, 61, 62. The journey takes around 20 minutes.

At San Basilio there are fewer passenger facilities, but the quay has a vaporetto stop, from which services 61, 62 and 82 take you into the heart of Venice. The current fare is €5.

VENICE BEST BETS

Take a gondola ride along the canals. Despite the high cost, the views are sublime, and the minor waterways take you to quiet backwaters that are little visited by the masses.

Explore Basilica San Marco. The mother lode of Byzantine treasure and art lies within the walls of this great church.

Sip an espresso in St Mark's Square. From here you can admire the architecture and watch the world go by.

Taxis charge approximately €2.33 initially, then €0.78 per km (½-mi) and €0.11 per 140 meters (460 feet) in slow traffic, but taxis can't take you into the heart of the city, just to its edge, so it seems a needless expense to us. Vaporetto services are much more useful once you reach the city since they can take you right to St. Mark's Square. Since cars aren't allowed into Venice proper, there is no point to renting a car unless you want to explore the Veneto region. Expect to pay about €45 for a compact manual vehicle.

EXPLORING VENICE

There's no better introduction to Venice than a trip down the Grand Canal, or as Venetians refer to it, Canalazzo. It is, without a doubt, one of the world's great "avenues." For 4 km (2½ mi) it winds its way in a backward "S," past 12th- to 18th-century palaces built by the city's richest families. There is a definite theatrical quality to the Grand Canal; it's as if each facade had been designed to steal your attention from its rival across the way. The most romantic—albeit expensive—way to see the canal is from a gondola. The next best thing—at a fraction of the cost—is to take in the view from vaporetto Line 1.

Numbers in the margin correspond to points of interest on the Venice map.

PIAZZA SAN MARCO

One of the world's most evocative squares, Piazza San Marco (St. Mark's Square) is the heart of Venice, a vast open space bordered by an orderly procession of arcades marching toward the fairy-tale cupolas and marble lacework of the Basilica di San Marco.

Piazzetta San Marco, the "little square" leading from Piazza San Marco to the waters of Bacino San Marco (St. Mark's Basin), is a *molo* (landing) that was once the grand entryway to the republic. It's distinguished by two columns towering above the waterfront. One is topped by the winged lion, a traditional emblem of St. Mark that became the symbol of Venice itself; the other supports St. Theodore, the city's first patron, along with his dragon.

❶ Basilica di San Marco. An opulent synthesis of Byzantine and Romanesque styles, Venice's gem didn't become the cathedral of Venice until 1807, but its role as the Chiesa Ducale (the duke's private chapel) gave it kudos. The original church was built in 828 to house the body of St. Mark the Evangelist, filched from Alexandria by the duke's agents.

Fodor's Choice
★

A 976 fire destroyed the original church. The replacement would serve as a symbol of Venetian wealth and power, endowed with all the riches of the Orient, to the point where it earned the nickname Chiesa d'Oro (golden church). The four bronze horses that prance over the doorway are copies of sculptures that victorious Venetians took from Constantinople in 1204 after the fourth crusade (the originals are in the Museo di San Marco).

The basilica is famous for its 43,055 square feet of mosaics, which run from floor to ceiling. The earliest mosaics are from the 11th and 12th centuries, and the last were added in the early 1700s. In the **Santuario** (sanctuary), the main altar is built over the tomb of St. Mark. Perhaps even more impressive is the **Pala d'Oro**, a dazzling gilt silver screen encrusted with 1,927 precious gems and 255 enameled panels. The **Tesoro** (treasury), entered from the right transept, contains many treasures carried home from conquests abroad.

Climb the steep stairway to the **Galleria** and the **Museo di San Marco** for the best overview of the basilica's interior. From here you can step outdoors for a sweeping panorama of Piazza San Marco and out over the lagoon to San Giorgio. The displays focus mainly on the types of mosaic and how they have been restored over the years. But the highlight is a close-up view of the original gilt bronze horses that were once on the outer gallery.

Be aware that guards at the basilica door turn away anyone with bare shoulders or knees; no shorts, short skirts, or tank tops are allowed. ⊠ *Piazza San Marco* ☎ *041/5225205 basilica, 041/2702421 for free tours Apr.–Oct. (call weekday mornings)* 🎫 *Basilica free, Tesoro €2, Santuario and Pala d'Oro €1.50, Galleria and Museo di San Marco €3* ⊙ *May–Sept., Mon.–Sat. 9:45–5:30, Sun. 2–4; Oct.–Apr., Mon.–Sat. 9:45–4:30, Sun. 2–4; last entry ½ hr before closing* Ⓜ *Vallaresso/San Zaccaria.*

❸ Campanile. Venice's famous brick bell tower (325 feet tall, plus the angel) had been standing nearly 1,000 years when in 1902, practically without warning, it collapsed. The new tower, rebuilt to the old plan, reopened in 1912. The stunning view from the tower on a clear day includes the Lido, the lagoon, and the mainland as far as the Alps but, strangely enough, none of the myriad Venetian canals. ⊠ *Piazza San Marco* ☎ *041/5224064* 🎫 *€6* ⊙ *Apr.–Sept., daily 9:30–5:30; Oct.–Mar., daily 9:30–4:30; last entry ½ hr before closing* Ⓜ *Vallaresso/San Zaccaria.*

❷ Palazzo Ducale *(Duke's Palace).* Rising above the Piazzetta San Marco, this Gothic-Renaissance fantasia of pink-and-white marble is a majestic expression of the prosperity and power attained during Venice's most glorious period. Always much more than a residence, the palace was Venice's White House, senate, torture chamber, and prison rolled into one. The palace's sumptuous chambers have walls and ceilings covered with works by Venice's greatest artists including Veronese and Tintoretto. The ceiling of the **Sala del Senato** (senate chamber), featuring *The Triumph of Venice* by Tintoretto, is magnificent, but it's dwarfed by his masterpiece *Paradise* in the **Sala del Maggiore Consiglio** (Great Council Hall). ⊠ *Piazzetta San Marco* ☎ *041/2715911* ✑ *Piazza San Marco museum card €12, Musei Civici museum pass €18* ⊙ *Apr.–Oct., daily 9–7; Nov.–Mar., daily 9–5; last tickets sold 1 hr before closing* Ⓜ *Vallaresso/San Zaccaria.*

ELSEWHERE IN VENICE

❻ **Gallerie dell'Accademia.** Napoléon founded these galleries in 1807 on the site of a religious complex he'd suppressed, and what he initiated now amounts to the world's most extraordinary collection of Venetian art, with works by father and son Jacopo and Giovanni Bellini, Cima da Conegliano (circa 1459–1517), Vittore Carpaccio (circa 1455–1525), Veronese and Titian amongst many others. ⊠ *Campo della Carità, Dorsoduro 1050* ☎ *041/5222247, 041/5200345 reservations* ⊕ *www.gallerieaccademia. org* ✑ *€6.50, €11 includes Ca' d'Oro and Museo Orientale* ⊙ *Tues.–Sun. 8:15–7:15, Mon. 8:15–2* Ⓜ *Accademia.*

❿ **Madonna dell'Orto.** From a campo elegantly parqueted in red brick and white Istrian stone rises an Oriental-style campanile complete with its own cupola. There, captured between earth and sky are the 12 apostles, hovering upon the facade of this 14th-century church. Madonna dell'Orto remains one of the most typical Gothic churches in Venice. Named for a miraculous state found in the nearby *orto* (garden) now displayed inside the **Cappella di San Mauro.**

Tintoretto lived nearby, and this, his parish church, contains some of his most powerful work. Lining the chancel are two huge (45 feet by 20 feet) canvases, *Adoration of the Golden Calf* and *Last Judgment,* in contrast to Tintoretto's *Presentation at the Temple* and the simple chapel where Tintoretto and his children, Marietta and Domenico, are buried. ⊠ *Campo della Madonna dell'Orto, Cannaregio* ☎ *041/2750462* ✑ *€2.50* ⊙ *Mon.–Sat. 10–5, Sun. 1–5* Ⓜ *Orto.*

❺ **Peggy Guggenheim Collection.** A small but choice selection of 20th-century painting and sculpture is on display at this gallery in the heiress Guggenheim's former Grand Canal home. Her collection here in Palazzo Venier dei Leoni includes works by Picasso, Kandinsky, Pollock, Motherwell, and Ernst (at one time her husband). ⊠ *Fondamenta Venier dei Leoni, Dorsoduro 701* ☎ *041/2405411* ⊕ *www.guggenheim-venice.it* ✑ *€10* ⊙ *Wed.–Mon. 10–6* Ⓜ *Accademia.*

❾ **Ponte di Rialto** *(Rialto Bridge).* One of Venice's most famous sights, the bridge was built in the late 16th century. Along the railing you'll enjoy one of the city's most famous views: the Grand Canal vibrant with boat traffic. Ⓜ *Rialto.*

❹ **Santa Maria della Salute.** Built to honor the Virgin Mary for saving Venice from a plague that killed 47,000 residents, this simple white octagon is adorned with a colossal cupola lined with snail-like buttresses and a Palladian-style facade. The Byzantine icon above the main altar has been venerated as the Madonna della Salute (of health) since 1670, when Francesco Morosini brought it here from Crete. The **Sacrestia Maggiore** contains a dozen works by Titian. You'll also see Tintoretto's *The Wedding at Canaan.* ⊠*Punta della Dogana, Dorsoduro* ☎*041/2743928* ⊠*Church free, sacristy €1.50* ☉*Apr.–Sept., daily 9–noon and 3–6:30; Oct.–Mar., daily 9–noon and 3–5:30* Ⓜ*Salute.*

❽ Santa Maria Gloriosa dei Frari. This immense Gothic church, completed in the 1400s, is deliberately austere, befitting the Franciscan brothers' insistence on spirituality and poverty. However, *I Frari* (as it's known locally) contains some of the most brilliant paintings in any Venetian church including works by Titian, Giovanni Bellini, and sculptures by Antonion Canova and Jacopo Sansovino. ⊠*Campo dei Frari, San Polo* ☎*041/2728618* ⊠*€2.50* ☉*Mon.–Sat. 9–6, Sun. 1–6* Ⓜ*San Tomà.*

Fodor'sChoice
★

❼ Scuola Grande di San Rocco. St. Rocco's popularity stemmed from his miraculous recovery from the plague and his care for fellow sufferers. Followers and donations abounded, including a series of more than 60 paintings by Tintoretto. ⊠*Campo San Rocco, San Polo 3052* ☎*041/5234864* ⊕*www.scuolagrandesanrocco.it* ⊠*€7* ☉*Apr.–Oct., daily 9–5:30; Nov.– Mar., daily 10–5; last entry ½ hr before closing* Ⓜ*San Tomà.*

⑪ Santa Maria dei Miracoli. Tiny yet perfectly proportioned, this early Renaissance gem is sheathed in marble and decorated inside with exquisite marble reliefs. The church was built in the 1480s to house *I Miracoli*, an image of the Virgin Mary that is said to perform miracles—look for it on the high altar. ⊠*Campo Santa Maria Nova, Cannaregio* ⊠*€2.50* ☉*Mon.–Sat. 10–5, Sun. 1–5* Ⓜ*Rialto.*

★

SHOPPING

Glass, most of it made on the separate island of Murano, is Venice's number one product, and you'll be confronted by mind-boggling displays of traditional and contemporary glassware, much of it kitsch. Carnival masks also make a unique souvenir. The finest ones are hand-crafted to fit the wearer, but inexpensive alternatives abound. The city also has a long history of supplying lace and luxury materials though many of the cheaper items on sale are now imported. Don't forget classic Italian design in clothing, shoes, and leather accessories such as purses and belts. All these can be found in the streets radiating out from St Mark's Square.

For chic, contemporary glassware, Carlo Moretti is a good choice; his designs are on display at **L'Isola** (⊠*Campo San Moisè, San Marco 1468* ☎*041/5231973* ⊕*www.carlomoretti.com*). **Il Merletto** (⊠*Sotoportego del Cavalletto, under the Procuratie Vecchie, Piazza San Marco 95* ☎*041/5208406*), sells the authentic, handmade lace kept in the drawers behind the counter. Guerrino Lovato, proprietor of **Mondonovo** (⊠*Rio Terà Canal, Dorsoduro 3063* ☎*041/5287344* ⊕*www.mondonovomaschere. it*) is one of the most respected mask-makers in town. Go to **Lorenzo Rubelli** (⊠*Palazzo Corner Spinelli, San Marco 3877* ☎*041/5236110* ⊕*www. rubelli.it*) for the same brocades, damasks, and cut velvets used by the world's most prestigious decorators.

WHERE TO EAT

$$–$$$ ✕**Alla Vedova.** This warm trattoria has a Venetian terrazzo floor, old
★ marble counter, and rustic furnishings lend a pleasant authenticity that's
matched by the food and service. ✉*Calle del Pistor, Cannaregio 3912*
☎*041/5285324* ▤*No credit cards* ☉*Closed Thurs. No lunch Sun.*
Ⓜ*Ca' d'Oro.*

$–$$$ ✕**Bancogiro.** Come to this casual spot in the heart of the Rialto market in
★ a 15th-century loggia for a change from standard Venetian food. There
are tables upstairs in a carefully restored room with a partial view of
the Grand Canal; when it's warm you can sit outdoors and get the full
canal view. ✉*Campo San Giacometto, Santa Croce 122 (under the porch)*
☎*041/5232061* ▤*No credit cards* ☉*Closed Mon.* Ⓜ*Rialto.*

VIGO, SPAIN (FOR SANTIAGO DE COMPOSTELA)

Spain's most Atlantic region is en route to nowhere, an end in itself. North-
western Spain is a series of rainy landscapes, stretching from your feet to
the horizon and the country's wildest mountains, the Picos de Europa.
Ancient granite buildings wear a blanket of moss, and even the stone
horreos (granaries) are built on stilts above the damp ground.

Santiago de Compostela, where a cathedral holds the remains of the apos-
tle James, has drawn pilgrims over the same roads for 900 years, leaving
northwestern Spain covered with churches, shrines, and former hospitals.
Asturias, north of the main pilgrim trail, has always maintained a separate
identity, isolated by the rocky Picos de Europa. This and the Basque Coun-
try are the only parts of Spain never conquered by the Moors, so regional
architecture shows little Moorish influence.

ESSENTIALS

CURRENCY The euro (€1 to US$1.46 at this writing); U.S. currency is generally not
accepted in Europe, but ATMs are common and credit cards are widely
accepted.

HOURS Museums generally open from 9 until 7 or 8, many are closed on Mondays
and some close in the afternoons. Most stores are open Monday–Saturday
9–1:30 and 5–8, but tourist shops may open in the afternoon and also on
Sunday between May and September.

INTERNET **Ciber Station Street** (✉*Principe 22, Vigo* ☎*No phone*). **Cibernova Street**
(✉*Rúa Nova 50, Santiago de Compostela* ☎*No phone*).

TELEPHONES Spain has good land and mobile services. Public kiosks accept phone cards
that support international calls (cards sold in press shops, bars, and tele-
com shops). Mobile services are 3G compatible. Major companies include
Vodafone.

COMING ASHORE

The cruise terminal sits on the waterfront directly off the old town. It's
possible to walk from the ship and explore on foot with shops and res-
taurants close by. Facilities are basic at the terminal but there are plans to
expand and add a hotel, spa, and leisure area.

In Vigo a tourist bus operates a continuous hop-on, hop-off service during the summer (April–September). Tickets cost €7.50. The bus passes the port when cruise ships are in dock.

There is at least one train per hour to Santiago de Compostela. Journey time is 1½ hours and tickets cost approximately €12 round-trip. It's a 30-minute walk from the port to the railway station or a 10-minute taxi trip.

Renting a vehicle would allow you to explore Santiago de Compostela and the rugged countryside of this wild corner of Spain. Rental price for an economy manual vehicle is approximately €93.

> **SANTIAGO DE CAMPOSTELA BEST BETS**
>
> **Take in the detail of Santiago's Cathedral.** One of the holiest places in Christendom; the quality of the Romanesque stonework is exquisite.
>
> **Visit the Museo de las Peregrinaciones.** Learn about the triumphs, trials, and tribulations of the Medieval pilgrims who journeyed across Europe to worship at the cathedral.
>
> **Soak in the atmosphere at Santiago's medieval quarter.** These narrow streets have been serving the needs of travelers since the Cathedral was completed in the 12th century.

EXPLORING VIGO & SANTIAGO DE COMPOSTELA

Numbers in the margin correspond to points of interest on the Santiago de Compostela map.

VIGO

Vigo's formidable port is choked with trawlers and fishing boats and lined with clanging shipbuilding yards. Its sights (or lack thereof) fall far short of its commercial swagger. The city's casual appeal lies a few blocks inland where the port commotion gives way to the narrow, dilapidated streets of the old town. From 8:30 to 3:30 daily on **Rúa Pescadería**, in the barrio called La Piedra, Vigo's famed *ostreras*—a group of rubber-glove fisherwomen who have been peddling fresh oysters to passersby for more than 50 years. South of Vigo's old town is the hilltop **Parque del Castro** (⊠ *Between Praza de España and Praza do Rei, beside Av. Marqués de Alcedo*), a quiet park with sandy paths, palm trees, mossy embankments, and stone benches. Atop a series of steps are the remains of an old fort and a *mirador* (lookout) with fetching views of Vigo's coastline and the Islas Cíes.

SANTIAGO DE COMPOSTELA
80 km (50 mi) north of Vigo, 77 km (48 mi) southwest of À Coruña.

A large, lively university makes Santiago one of the most exciting cities in Spain, but its cathedral makes it one of the most impressive. The building is opulent and awesome, yet its towers create a sense of harmony as a benign St. James, dressed in pilgrim's costume, looks down from his perch.

❻ **Casco Antiguo** *(Old Town)*. Walk around Santiago do Campostela's old quarter, losing yourself in its maze of stone-paved narrow streets and little plazas. The most beautiful pedestrian thoroughfares are Rúa do Vilar, Rúa do Franco, and Rúa Nova—portions of which are covered by arcaded walkways called *soportales,* designed to keep walkers out of the rain.

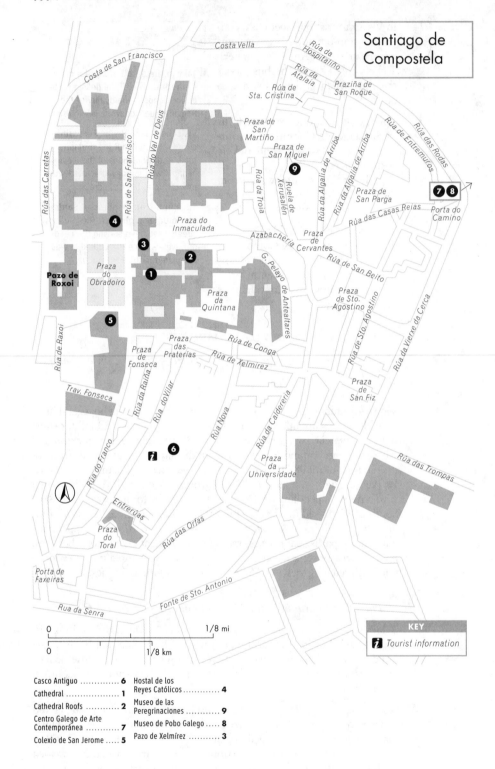

Santiago de Compostela

Costa Vella
Costa de San Francisco
Rúa da Hospitaliño
Rúa da Atalaia
Praziña de San Roque
Rúa de Sta. Cristina
Rúa do Val de Deus
Rúa de San Francisco
Rúa das Carretas
Praza de San Martiño
Praza de San Miguel
Rúa da Troia
Rúa de Entremuros
Rúa das Rodas
Rúa da Algalia de Arriba
Rúa da Algalia de Arriba
Ruela de Xerusalén
Praza de San Parga
Porta do Camino
Praza do Inmaculada
Azabachería
Praza de Cervantes
Rúa das Casas Reias
Rúa de San Beito
Pazo de Roxoi
Praza do Obradoiro
G. Pelayo de Antealtares
Praza da Quintana
Praza de Sto. Agostino
Rúa de Santo Agostino
Rúa de Raxoi
Praza das Praterías
Praza de Fonseca
Rúa de Conga
Rúa de Xelmírez
Praza de San Fiz
Trav. Fonseca
Rúa da Raiña
Rúa do Vilar
Rúa Nova
Rúa da Caldeirería
Rúa da Vierce da Cerca
Rúa das Trompas
Rúa do Franco
Praza da Universidade
Entrerrúas
Praza do Toral
Rúa das Orfas
Porta de Faxeiras
Fonte de Sto. Antonio
Rua da Senra

0   1/8 mi
0   1/8 km

KEY
🛈 Tourist information

Casco Antiguo 6
Cathedral 1
Cathedral Roofs 2
Centro Galego de Arte
Contemporánea 7
Colexio de San Jerome 5
Hostal de los
Reyes Católicos 4
Museo de las
Peregrinaciones 9
Museo de Pobo Galego 8
Pazo de Xelmírez 3

1 **Cathedral.** From the **Praza do Obradoiro,** climb the two flights of stairs to the main entrance to Santiago's Cathedral. Although the facade is baroque, the interior holds one of the finest Romanesque sculptures in the world, the **Pórtico de la Gloria.** Completed in 1188 by Maestro Mateo (Master Mateo), this is the cathedral's original entrance, its three arches carved with biblical figures from the Apocalypse, the Last Judgment, and purgatory. On the left are the prophets; in the center, Jesus is flanked by the four evangelists (Matthew, Mark, Luke, and John) and, above them, the 24 elders of the Apocalypse playing celestial instruments. Just below Jesus is a serene St. James, poised on a carved column. Look carefully and you can see five smooth grooves, formed by the millions of pilgrims who have placed their hands here over the centuries. St. James presides over the **high altar.** The stairs behind it are the cathedral's focal point, surrounded by dazzling baroque decoration, sculpture, and drapery. Here, as the grand finale of their spiritual journey, pilgrims embrace St. James and kiss his cloak. In the crypt beneath the altar lie the remains of St. James and his disciples, St. Theodore and St. Athenasius.

A huge *botafumeiro* (incense burner used since medieval times) and other cathedral treasures are on display in the **museums** downstairs and next door. On the right (south) side of the nave is the **Porta das Praterías** (Silversmiths' Door), the only purely Romanesque part of the cathedral's facade. The statues on the portal were cobbled together from parts of the cathedral. The double doorway opens onto the **Praza das Praterías,** named for the silversmiths' shops that used to line it. ⊠*Praza do Obradoiro* ☎*981/560527 museums, 981/583548 cathedral* ⊠*Cathedral free, combined museum ticket €5* ⊘*Cathedral daily 7* AM*–9* PM*; museums June–Oct., Mon.–Sat. 10–2 and 4–8, Sun. 10–2; Nov.–May, Mon.–Sat. 10–1:30 and 4–6:30, Sun. 10–1:30.*

2 **Cathedral Roofs.** For excellent views of the city and the plazas surrounding the cathedral, join a tour across the granite steps of cathedral roofs. Pilgrims made the same 100-foot climb in medieval times to burn their travel-worn clothes below the Cruz dos Farrapos (cross of rags). ⊠*Pazo de Xelmírez, Praza do Obradoiro* ☎*981/552985* ⊠*€10* ⊘*Tues.–Sun. 10–2 and 4–8.*

7 **Centro Galego de Arte Contemporánea** (*Galician Center for Contemporary Art*). On the north side of town off the Porta do Camino, the contemporary art center is a stark but elegant modern building that offsets Santiago's ancient feel. Portuguese designer Álvaro Siza built the museum of smooth, angled granite, which mirrors the medieval convent of San Domingos de Bonaval next door. The museum has a good permanent collection and even better changing exhibits. ⊠*Rúa de Valle Inclán s/n* ☎*981/546619* ⊕*www.cgac. org* ⊠*Free* ⊘*Tues.–Sun. 11–8.*

5 **Colexio de San Xerome.** The 16th-century offices of the rector of the University of Santiago is worth a stop to see the building's beautifully carved facade. Its 15th-century entrance was brought from another city college and includes virgins and saints with the Virgin and Child above the door. ⊠*Praza do Obradoiro* ☎*981/563100*

4 **Hostal de los Reyes Católicos** (*Hostel of the Catholic Monarchs*). Facing the cathedral from the left, this hostel was built in 1499 by Ferdinand and

Isabella to house the pilgrims who slept on Santiago's streets every night. Having lodged and revived travelers for nearly 500 years, it's the oldest refuge in the world and was converted from a hospital to a luxury parador in 1953. The facade bears a Castilian coat of arms along with Adam, Eve, and various saints. ⊠*Praza do Obradoiro 1* ☏*981/582200 hostel* ⊕*www.parador.es* ⊗*Daily 10–1 and 4–6.*

⑨ Museo de las Peregrinaciones *(Pilgrimage Museum).* North of Azabachería (follow Ruela de Xerusalén) is this museum, which contains Camino de Santiago iconography from sculptures and carvings to *azabache* (compact black coal, or jet) talismans. For an overview of the history of the pilgrimage and the role of the *camino* in the development of the city itself, this is a key visit. ⊠*Rúa de San Miguel 4* ☏*981/581558* 🎫*€2.40* ⊗*Tues.–Fri. 10–8, Sat. 10:30–1:30 and 5–8, Sun. 10:30–1:30.*

⑧ Museo do Pobo Galego *(Galician Folk Museum).* Next door to the Center for Contemporary Art is this museum, in the medieval convent of Santo Domingo de Bonaval. The star attraction is the 13th-century self-supporting spiral granite staircase that still connects three floors. ⊠*Rúa de Bonaval* ☏*981/583620* ⊕*www.museodopobo.es* 🎫*Free* ⊗*Tues.–Sat. 10–2 and 4–8, Sun. 11–2.*

③ Pazo de Xelmírez *(Palace of Archbishop Xelmírez).* On the wide Praza da Quintana, stop into this rich 12th-century palace, an unusual example of Romanesque civic architecture with a cool, clean, vaulted dining hall. ⊠*Praza do Obradoiro* 🎫*Included in combined museum* ⊗*Tues.–Sun. 10–2 and 4–8.*

SHOPPING

Galicia is known throughout Spain for its distinctive blue-and-white ceramics with bold modern designs, authentic Galician *zuecos* (hand-painted wooden clogs) still worn in some villages to navigate mud, jewelry and trinkets carved from azabache (jet, or compact black coal), ceramics, and excellent leather-wear of all kinds. Santiago has an excellent selection of religious items in all price ranges.

Look for beautifully crafted jewelry with the black stone azabache at **Antonio Uzal Vázquez** (⊠*Abril Ares 8, Santiago de Compostela* ☏*981/583483*). A boutique founded in 1906 and run by **Augusto Otero** (⊠*Casa de Cabildo, Praza de Praterías 5, Santiago de Compstela* ☏*981/581027*) has fine handcrafted silver.

WHERE TO EAT

$-$$$ ✕**A Barrola.** Polished wooden floors, a niche with wine and travel books, and a lively terrace make this tavern a favorite with university faculty. The house salads, mussels with *santiaguiños* (crabmeat), *arroz con bogavante* (rice with lobster), and seafood empanadas are superb. ⊠*Rúa do Franco 29* ☏*981/577999* ⊕*www.restaurantesgrupobarrola.com* ▭*AE, MC, V* ⊗*Closed Mon. and Jan.–Mar.*

$-$$ ✕**Carretas.** This casual spot for fresh Galician seafood is around the corner from the Hostal de los Reyes Católicos. Fish dishes abound, but the specialty here is shellfish. For the full experience, order the labor-intensive *variado de mariscos,* a comprehensive platter of langostinos, king prawns, crab, and goose barnacles that comes with a shell-cracker. *Salpicón de mariscos* presents the same creatures preshelled. ⊠*Rúa de Carretas 21* ☎*981/563111* ▭*AE, DC, MC, V* ⊘*Closed Sun.*

VILLEFRANCHE-SUR-MER

Nestled discreetly along the deep scoop of harbor between Nice and Cap Ferrat, this pretty watercolor of a fishing port is a stage-set of brightly colored houses—the sort of place where Pagnol's *Fanny* could have been filmed. Genuine fishermen actually skim up to the docks here in weathered blue *barques,* and the streets of the Vieille Ville flow directly to the waterfront, much as they did in the 13th century. The deep harbor, in the caldera of a volcano, was once preferred by the likes of Onassis and Niarchos and royals on their yachts. The character of Villefranche was subtly shaped by the artists and authors who gathered at the Hôtel Welcome, and above all, Jean Cocteau, who came here to recover from the excesses of Paris life. Villefranche is also the gateway to other treasures along this most select part of the Riviera.

ESSENTIALS

CURRENCY The euro (€1 to US$1.46 at this writing); U.S. currency is generally not accepted in Europe, but ATMs are common and credit cards are widely accepted.

HOURS Stores open Monday–Saturday 9–7 but many close at lunchtime (usually noon to 2 or 3) and some will open later and on Sunday during July and August. Museums open 10–5 but most are closed on either Monday or Tuesday.

INTERNET **Chez Net Australian Bar** (⊠*5 pl. de la Marché* ☎*04–93–01–83–06* ⊕*www.cheznet.fr*) is a stylish spot offering drinks and snacks as well as computer terminals and Wi-Fi.

TELEPHONES Tri-band GSM phones work in France. You can buy prepaid phone cards at telecom shops, news-vendors and tobacconists in all towns and cities. Phone cards can be used for local or international calls. France Telecom and Orange are leading telecom companies.

COMING ASHORE

Cruise ships dock offshore in the bay of Villefranche-sur-Mer and passengers are tendered to the quayside in the heart of the town. The terminal is small but has an information center, restrooms, and car-rental kiosks. You can tour Villefranche-sur-Mer itself on foot from here, but to visit surrounding attractions you'll need transport. The train station is a five-minute walk from the cruise port and the service along the coast to Beaulieu and Èze-sur-Mer is frequent (at least two trains per hour), fast (less than 10 minutes travel time), and reliable. Tickets cost around €2 for the short hop between Villefranche-sur-Mer and Beaulieu-sur-Mer. From the train station at Èze-sur-Mer there are frequent shuttle buses to Èze village (15 minutes, route 83). By train both Nice and Monte Carlo are also within 15-minutes journey time. Frequent bus services by Ligne d'Azur (⊕*www.lignedazur.com*) links Villefranche-sur-Mer with Beaulieu-sur-Mer, Cap Ferrat, Èze, Nice, and Monte Carlo. One ride is €1.30, 10 tickets is €10, and a day pass is €4. Route 81 links Villefranche-sur-Mer with Beaulieu-sur-Mer and St Jean Cap Ferrat (also with Nice). Line 100 links Villefranche-sur-Mer with Èze-sur-Mer (and on to Monte Carlo).

The cost of car rental is approximately €70 for an economy manual vehicle. However, there are no car-rental options in town so vehicles have to be prebooked and there are fees for delivery and return.

Taxis are plentiful and can provide tourist itineraries. For a single journeys, fares are €2.30 for pick-up followed by a day fare of €0.69 per km (1/2-mi) plus a fee for any waiting time. Taxis can be pre-booked for return journeys, making them a good option for transfer to local attractions.

> ### VILLEFRANCHE-SUR-MER BEST BETS
>
> **Èze.** One of the most charming of France's *villages perchés* or perched villages is built high on a rocky parapet. Views down the Riviera coast are spectacular.
>
> **Villa Kerylos.** The splendors of ancient Greek art and architecture are beautifully re-created here in the south of France at the home of a wealthy amateur archaeologist.
>
> **Villa Ephrussi de Rothschild.** This magnificent century-old mansion surrounded by glorious gardens is stuffed with the finest furniture and decoration its Baroness owner could afford.

EXPLORING VILLEFRANCHE-SUR-MER & VICINITY

VILLEFRANCHE-SUR-MER

Numbers in the margin correspond to points of interest on the Villefranche-sur-Mer map.

❶ So enamored was Jean Cocteau of this painterly fishing port that he decorated the 14th-century **Chapelle St-Pierre** with images from the life of St. Peter and dedicated it to the village's fishermen. ⊠*Pl. Pollanais* ☎*04–93–76–90–70* ⊡*€2* ⊗*Mid-June–mid-Sept., Tues.–Sun. 4–8:30; mid-Sept.–mid-Apr., Tues.–Sun. 10–noon and 2–6:30; mid-Apr.–mid-June, Tues.–Sun. 10–noon and 3–7.*

Running parallel to the waterfront, the extraordinary 13th-century **Rue Obscure** ("dark street") is entirely covered by vaulted arcades; it sheltered the people of Villefranche when the Germans fired their parting shots—an artillery bombardment—near the end of World War II.

The stalwart 16th-century **Citadelle St-Elme,** restored to perfect condition, anchors the harbor with its broad, sloping stone walls. Beyond its drawbridge lie the city's administrative offices and a group of minor gallery-museums, with a scattering of works by Picasso and Miró. Whether or not you stop into these private collections of local art (all free of charge), you are welcome to stroll around the inner grounds and to circle the imposing exterior.

BEAULIEU-SUR-MER

❷ *4 km (2½ mi) east of Villefranche.*

With its back pressed hard against the cliffs of the corniche and sheltered between the peninsulas of Cap Ferrat and Cap Roux, this once-grand resort basks in a tropical microclimate that earned its central neighbor-

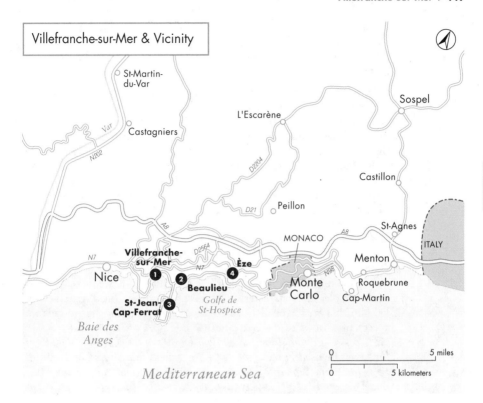

Villefranche-sur-Mer & Vicinity

hood the name *Petite Afrique* (little Africa). The town was the pet of 19th-century society, and its grand hotels welcomed Empress Eugénie, the Prince of Wales, and Russian nobility. Today it's still a posh address.

Fodor's Choice ★ One manifestation of Beaulieu's belle epoque excess is the eye-knocking **Villa Kerylos**, a mansion built in 1902 in the style of classical Greece (to be exact, of the villas that existed on the island of Delos in the 2nd century BC). It was the dream house of the amateur archaeologist Théodore Reinach, who originally hailed from a superrich family from Frankfurt, helped the French in their excavations at Delphi, and became an authority on ancient Greek music. He commissioned an Italian architect from Nice, Emmanuel Pontremoli, to surround him with Grecian delights: cool Carrara marble, rare fruitwoods, and a dining salon where guests reclined to eat *à la Greque*. Don't miss this—it's one of the most unusual houses in the south of France. ⊠ *Rue Gustave-Eiffel* ☎ *04–93–01–01–44* ⊕ *www. villa-kerylos.com* ☞ *€8, joint ticket with Villa Ephrussi de Rothschild (must be used in same wk) €14.50* ⊘ *Mid-Feb.–June and Sept.–mid-Nov., daily 10–6; July and Aug., daily 10–7; mid-Dec.–mid-Feb., weekdays 2–6, weekends 10–6.*

ST-JEAN-CAP-FERRAT

❸ *2 km (1 mi) south of Beaulieu on D25.*

This luxuriously sited pleasure port moors the peninsula of Cap Ferrat; from its port-side walkways and crescent of beach you can look over the sparkling blue harbor to the graceful green bulk of the corniches. Yachts purr in and out of port, and their passengers scuttle into cafés for take-out drinks to enjoy on their private decks. Unfortunately, Cap Ferrat is a vast peninsula and hides its secrets—except for the Villa Ephrussi, most fabled estates are hidden behind iron gates and towering hedges—particularly well.

★ Between the port and the mainland, the floridly beautiful **Villa Ephrussi de Rothschild** stands as witness to the wealth and worldly flair of the baroness who had it built. Constructed in 1905 in neo-Venetian style (its flamingo-pink facade was thought not to be in the best of taste by the local gentry), the house was baptized "Ile-de-France" in homage to the Baroness Bétrice de Rothschild's favorite ocean liner (her staff used to wear sailing costumes and her ship travel-kit is on view in her bedroom). Precious artworks, tapestries, and furniture adorn the salons—in typical Rothschildian fashion, each room is given over to a different 18th-century "époque." Upstairs are the private apartments of Madame la Baronne, which can only be seen on a guided tour offered around noon. The grounds are landscaped with no fewer than seven theme gardens and topped off with a Temple of Diana (no less); be sure to allow yourself time to wander here, as this is one of the few places on the coast where you'll be allowed to experience the lavish pleasures characteristic of the belle époque Côte d'Azur. Tea and light lunches are served in a glassed-in porch overlooking the grounds and spectacular views of the coastline. ⊠ *Av. Ephrussi* ☎ *04–93–01–33–09* 🖃 *Access to ground floor and gardens €9.50, joint ticket with Villa Kerylos (must be used in same wk) €14.50, guided tour upstairs €3* ☉ *Mid-Feb.–June and Sept.–mid-Nov., daily 10–6; July and Aug., daily 10–7; mid-Dec.–mid-Feb., weekdays 2–6, weekends 10–6.*

ÈZE

❹ *2 km (1 mi) east of Beaulieu.*

Fodor's Choice
★
Towering like an eagle's nest above the coast and crowned with ramparts and the ruins of a medieval château, preposterously beautiful Èze (pronounced *ehz*) is the most accessible of all the perched villages—this means crowds, many of whom head here to shop in the boutique-lined staircase-streets. (Happily most shops here are quite stylish, and there is a nice preponderance of bric-a-brac and vintage fabric dealers.) But most come here to drink in the views, for no one can deny that this is the most spectacularly sited of all coastal promontories; if you can manage to shake the crowds and duck off to a quiet overlook, the village commands splendid views up and down the coast, one of the draws that once lured fabled visitors—lots of crowned heads, Georges Sand, Friedrich Nietzsche—and residents: Consuelo Vanderbilt, when she was tired of being duchess of Marlborough, traded in Blenheim Palace for a custom-built house here.

From the crest-top **Jardin Exotique** *(Tropical Garden)*, full of rare succulents, you can pan your videocam all the way around the hills and waterfront. But if you want a prayer of a chance of enjoying the magnificence of the village's arched passages, stone alleyways, and ancient fountains, come at dawn or after sunset—or (if you have the means) stay the night—but spend the midday elsewhere to avoid the searing afternoon sun. ⊠ *Èze* ☎ *No phone* 🖃 *€5* ☉ *July and Aug., daily 9–8; Sept.–June, daily 9–5:30.*

The church of **Notre-Dame**, consecrated in 1772, glitters inside with baroque retables and altarpieces.

Èze's tourist office, on Place du Général-de-Gaulle, can direct you to the numerous footpaths—the most famous being the **Sentier Friedrich Nietzsche**— that thread Èze with the coast's three corniche highways. The views from the 1,001 switchbacks leading to and from the village are breathtaking.

SHOPPING

This part of the Riviera coastline has some of the smartest addresses, and thus some of the finest shopping, with excusive boutiques selling very high-class fashion and decorative goods. In the shops of the Cap Ferrat and Beaulieu you'll shop among France's more mature lunching ladies, while Villefranche-sur-Mer has a good selection of characterful boutiques with more down-to-earth prices. The streets of Èze are replete with artists studios selling excellent art and ceramics, plus cute collectibles. In every town you'll find local Provençal specialties such as excellent olive oil, soaps, dried herbs, colorful fabrics, pottery, and basketware.

Savonnerie de Villfranche (⊠*10 av. Sadi Carnot, Villefranche-sur-Mer* ☎*04–93–76–66–75*) sells a range of fragrant handmade soaps. **Art dessin JMB Studio** (⊠*8 rue de la Paix, Èze* ☎*04–92–10–83–17*), a gallery, is full of oil and watercolor images of wonderful Provençal landscapes in a variety of sizes. **Feaux et Flammes** (⊠*Av. du Jardin Exotique, Èze* ☎*04–93–41–06–33*) is a small shop with genuine local arts and handicrafts.

SPORTS & ACTIVITIES

While Cap Ferrat's villas are sequestered for the most part in the depths of tropical gardens, you can nonetheless walk its entire **coastline promenade** if you strike out from the port. From the restaurant Capitaine Cook, cut right up Avenue des Fossés, turn right on Avenue Vignon, and follow the Chemin de la Carrière. The 11-km (7-mi) walk passes through rich tropical flora and, on the west side, over white cliffs buffeted by waves. Wear comfortable footwear.

WHERE TO EAT

$ ✕**La Grignotière.** Tucked down a narrow side street just a few steps away from the marketplace, this small and friendly local restaurant offers up top-quality, inexpensive dishes. The homemade lasagna is excellent, as is the spaghetti pistou. ⊠*3 rue du PoiluVillefranche-sur-Mer* ☎*04–93–76–79–83* ▭*MC, V* ⊙*No lunch.*

¢–$ ✕**Loumiri.** Classic Provençal and regional seafood dishes are tastily prepared and married with decent, inexpensive wines at this cute little bistro near the entrance to the Vieille Ville. The best bet is to order *à l'ardoise*—that is, from the blackboard listing of daily specials. The lunch menu prix-fixe (€15) is the best deal in town. Prix-fixe dinner menus start at €23. ⊠*Av. Jardin Exotique, Èze* ☎*04–93–41–16–42* ▭*MC, V* ⊙*Closed Mon. and mid-Dec.–mid-Jan. No dinner Wed.*

Eastern Mediterranean & Aegean

Dubrovnik, Croatia

WORD OF MOUTH

"Ephesus is probably one of the most incredible sights you will ever see. Even better than Pompeii, IMHO! You will enjoy it more if you're not in a group of 50 or 100. If you stop in Istanbul, you're in for a treat. . . . There is no place like Istanbul."

—zwho

www.fodors.com/forums

Lindsay Bennett

MANY EASTERN MEDITERRANEAN ITINERARIES BEGIN in Pireaus, the seaport of Athens, or Istanbul, and visit ports in Greece and Turkey. Some may cross the Mediterranean to call in Alexandria or Port Said (for an exhausting, daylong visit to Cairo). Other cruises begin in Italy, often in Rome or Venice. These cruises may take in ports in Sicily and southern Italy (if they leave from Rome) or even Malta before heading toward Greece. Cruises beginning in Venice may call at one or more ports along Croatia's breathtaking Adriatic coast, and these port calls are highlights of any voyage. Eastern Mediterranean cruises are especially good for travelers who want to see the archaeological ruins of Europe's two great classical civilizations, Rome and Greece. These ports are rich in history, and some are even rich in natural beauty. There are few ports of call more breathtaking than Santorini or the island of Hvar.

ABOUT THE RESTAURANTS

All the restaurants we recommend serve lunch; they may also serve dinner if your cruise ship stays late in port and you choose to dine off the ship. Cuisine in Europe is varied, but Europeans tend to eat a leisurely meal at lunch, but in most ports there are quicker and simpler alternatives for those who just want to grab a quick bite before returning to the ship. Note that several Eastern Mediterranean countries do not use the euro, including Croatia, Cyprus, Egypt, and Turkey. Price categories in those countries are based on the euro-equivalent costs of eating in restaurants.

WHAT IT COSTS IN EUROS				
$$$$	$$$	$$	$	¢
RESTAURANTS	over €30	€23–€30	€17–€23	€11–€17	under €11

Restaurant prices are per person for a main course at dinner, including tax.

ALEXANDRIA, EGYPT

Ancient Egypt's gateway to the Mediterranean was founded by Alexander the Great in 331 BC, but its name is inextricably linked with Cleopatra. She inhabited vast palaces and worshipped at monumental temples. The city's great library was also under her control, and her city was protected by one of the Seven Wonders of the Ancient World, the great Pharos of Alexandria, a lighthouse. Sadly, all of these great treasures are lost or buried underneath the modernity. That doesn't mean Alexandria is bereft of history; in a second incarnation it became a decadent, early-20th-century mercantile and colonial enclave with a multicultural mix. It seduced novelist E. M. Forster during World War I and gave birth to Lawrence Durrell's *Alexandria Quartet,* which captivated a generation of American readers in the late 1950s. At the same time, its reputation as an Arabic seat of learning has stayed in the ascendant. With lively streets and graceful cafés, Alexandria is still a great city and remains an utterly charming place to visit.

ESSENTIALS

CURRENCY   The Egyptian pound (£e5.45 to US$1; £e7.75 to €1 at this writing). U.S. currency is accepted for high-value items but not in restaurants or markets. ATMs are not common.

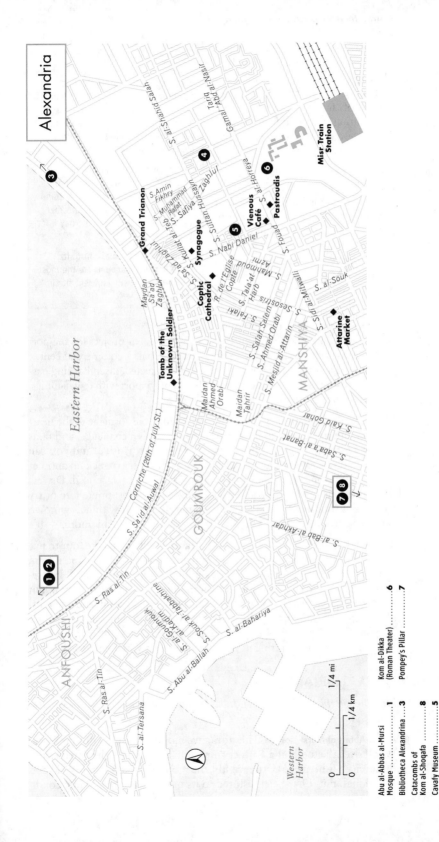

Alexandria

5

Eastern Harbor

Western Harbor

ANFOUSHI

GOUMROUK

MANSHIYA

Misr Train Station

Tomb of the Unknown Soldier

Grand Trianon

Coptic Cathedral

Synagogue

Vienous Café

Pastroudis

Attarine Market

Maydan Sa'ad Zaghlul

Maidan Ahmed Orabi

Maidan Tahrir

Corniche (26th of July St.)

S. Ras al-Tin
S. Ras al-Tin
S. al-Tersana
S. al-Gournouk
S. al-Kadim
S. Souk al-'Tabbakhine
S. Sa'id al-Auwal
S. Abu al-Ballah
S. al-Bahariya
S. Said al-Auwal
S. al-Akhdar
S. al-Bab al-Akhdar
S. Saba'a al-Banat
S. Kaid Gohar
S. Kaid Gohar

S. al-Shahid Salah
Tariq al-Nasir
Gamal 'Abd al-Nasir
S. Amin Fikhry
S. Muhammad Rafat
S. Safiya Hussayn
S. Sultan Hussayn
S. Sa'ad Zaghlul
S. Kuliat al-Teb
S. al-Horreya
S. Nabi Daniel
S. Fouad
S. Azmi
S. Mahmoud
S. Tala'at Harb
R. de l'Eglise Copte
S. Falaki
S. Salah Salem
S. Ahmed Orabi
S. Sesostris
S. Meslid al-Attarin
S. Sidi al-Mitwalli
S. al-Souk

Abu al-Abbas al-Mursi
Mosque **1**

Bibliotheca Alexandrina **3**

Catacombs of
Kom al-Shoqafa **8**

Cavafy Museum **5**

Fort Qayt Bay (Pharos) **2**

Greco-Roman Museum **4**

Kom al-Dikka
(Roman Theater) **6**

Pompey's Pillar **7**

1/4 mi

1/4 km

0

HOURS Museums are usually open from 9 to 5. Many museums are closed on Monday. Shops open from 8 until 7. During Ramadan (the Muslim month of fasting) opening times vary; during this period shops close during the day but stay open late into the evening.)

TELEPHONES GSM phones work in Egypt, where mobile systems are single-band and are not 3G-compatible. Telecom Egypt runs the fixed line system. Public phones accept calling cards available from retail outlets; however, connections are not always smooth. Major companies are MobiNil and Vodafone.

> ### ALEXANDRIA BEST BETS
>
> **Explore the Archaeological Museum.** A wealth of artifacts found under the modern city—and more recently under the shallow waters of Alexandria Bay—offers a tantalizing glimpse of Alexandria's greatness.
>
> **Fort in Quayt Bay.** The site of Alexandria's famous ancient *pharos* or lighthouse, the fort protected Alexandria harbor throughout the Crusader and colonial eras. Survey the bay from its walls.
>
> **Catacombs of Kom al-Shoqafa.** These Roman catacombs are the most completely excavated ancient site in the city.

COMING ASHORE

At the end of 2006, the Egyptian government announced an impressive redevelopment project for the port of Alexandria that is to include a modern terminal, a commercial center, marina, and a hotel. Until the devlopment is completed, disembarking passengers must pass through a decaying 19th-century port with few facilities. Passengers on larger ships must be tendered ashore.

From the port, it is an easy 20-minute walk along the corniche to the heart of town, but navigating to the various attractions is a challenge, and taxis are the best way to get around. They are very inexpensive, and you can flag them down almost anywhere. The driver might try to pick up another passenger en route—it's standard practice, so don't be surprised. Drivers don't use their meters, so you have to guess at the appropriate fare or try to negotiate one in advance. A ride from the cruise port within downtown should be around £e10. If you look rich, expect to pay a bit more.

Though they're picturesque and cheap, trams are likely to take four to five times longer to get where you're going than a taxi would. The main tram station is Raml, near Maydan Sa'd Zaghlul. Buy tickets on board. Horse-drawn *caleches* (carriages) offer an alternative way to tour the town, but agree on a price before you get aboard. We do not recommend car rentals in Egypt because of the difficulty of driving here, but **Avis** (⊠ *16 Sa'd Zaghlul Sq.* ☎ *03/485 7400* ⊕ *www.avis.com*) has an office at the Cecil Hotel and has prices staring at $45 for an economy manual vehicle.

EXPLORING ALEXANDRIA

Numbers in the margin correspond to points of interest on the Alexandria map.

❶ **Abu al-Abbas al-Mursi Mosque.** This attractive mosque was built during World War II over the tomb of a 13th-century holy man, who is the patron saint of the city's fishermen. Until recently, the mosque looked suitably old and traditional, but it has been restored to its original gleaming-white condition and is less charming for it—although a few details, such as the wood-and-metalwork doors, are still stunning. The area surrounding it has been turned into Egypt's largest and most bizarre religious/retail complex, with a cluster of mosques sharing a terrace that hides an underground shopping center. If you are dressed modestly and the mosque is open, you should be able to get inside. If you do, remove your shoes and refrain from taking photos. ✉ *Corniche, al-Anfushi.*

❸ **Bibliotheca Alexandrina.** This monumental, $190-million, UNESCO-sponsored project began with an instinctively appealing idea: to resurrect the Great Library of Alexandria, once one of the ancient world's major centers of learning. It was here, for example, that Eratosthenes measured the circumference of the Earth. And it was here that the conqueror Julius Caesar had a new, more accurate calendar drawn up—the Julian calendar—that became the framework for the measurement of time throughout the Western world. The modernist Norwegian-designed building is in the form of an enormous multitiered cylinder tilted to face the sea, with a roof of diamond-shape windows, which allow controlled light into the seven cascading interior floors. The most impressive feature, however, is the curving exterior wall covered in rough-hewn granite blocks from Aswan that have been engraved with letters from ancient languages. The Bibliotheca is the greatest intellectual resource in the country after the National Library in Cairo, and has resulted in a renaissance for the city. ✉ *63 Shar'a Soter, Chatby* ☎ *03/483–9999* ⊕ *www.bibalex.org.*

❽ **Catacombs of Kom al-Shoqafa.** This is the most impressive of Alexandria's
★ ancient remains, dating from the 2nd century AD. Excavation started in 1892, and the catacombs were discovered accidentally eight years later when a donkey fell through a chamber ceiling. A long spiral staircase leads to the main hall. The stairs run down the outside of a shaft, which excavators used to transport the bodies of the dead. The staircase leads to the rotunda, which, like all but the lowest chamber, is undecorated but striking for the sheer scale of the underground space, supported by giant columns carved out of the bedrock ✉ *Karmouz* ☎ *03/482–5800* 🎟 *£e25* ⏰ *Daily 9–4.*

❺ **Cavafy Museum.** Constantine Cavafy was born in Alexandria in 1863 and
★ began writing poetry at age 19. It wasn't until much later that he gained fame for his poetry, as a result of praise by the novelist E. M. Forster. His former flat is in a building that was once a cheap pension. The building is now a museum and library dedicated to his life and work. ✉ *4 Shar'a Sharm al-Sheikh* ☎ *03/482–5205* 🎟 *£e8* ⏰ *Tues.–Sun. 10–3.*

❷ **Fort Qayt Bay (Pharos).** This sandstone fort lies on the very tip of the Corniche, dominating the view of the Eastern Harbor. It was built on the site of the giant Pharos, one of the Seven Wonders of the Ancient World, and incorporates its remains, which are still visible, into the foundation. The lighthouse was constructed under the Ptolemies by a Greek named Sostratus in the 3rd century BC. Standing about 400 feet high and capable of projecting a light that could be seen 53 km (35 mi) out to sea, it was one of the most awesome structures created by ancients. In the centuries that followed, the Pharos was damaged and rebuilt several times, until it was finally destroyed in the great earthquake of 1307. It lay in ruins for two centuries until the Mamluk Sultan Qayt Bay had the current fortress constructed in 1479. Recently, a French team found what are thought to be parts of the Pharos in shallow waters just offshore, rekindling local interest in the ancient monument—there is even talk of an underwater museum, although that is unlikely to materialize any time soon. ⊠ *Corniche* ☎ *03/480–9144* ✉ *£e20* ⊙ *Daily 9–4.*

4 **Greco-Roman Museum.** This museum was founded in 1895 and contains the best of the pieces found at Pompey's Pillar—including a statue of the Apis Bull—and two statues from the catacombs at Kom al-Shoqafa. In spite of some uninteresting pieces, this is one of Egypt's finest museums covering the period of Egyptian history from Alexander the Great's conquest in 332 BC to the third Persian occupation in AD 619. There are a great many pharaonic pieces here as well—indeed, the most impressive thing about the museum is that it shows the scale of cross-fertilization between pharaonic culture and the Greek and Roman cultures that followed. Highlights of the collection include its early Christian mummies, remnants of a temple to the crocodile god Sobek, and a courtyard full of sun-drenched statuary. At this writing, the museum was closed for renovations until sometime in 2008; if it's open when your ship calls, this is a must-see. ⊠ *5 Shar'a al-Mathaf, Raml Station* ☎ *03/483–6434* ✉ *£e30* ⊙ *Daily 9–5, (the museum closes on Fri. 11:30–1:30. During Ramadan the museum closes at 4).*

6 **Kom al-Dikka (Roman Theater).** A Polish team has been excavating the site since 1960 (and work continues), and a recent sprucing-up makes this a quiet retreat in the middle of the city. The focal point is a well-preserved amphitheater—the only one of its kind in Egypt—originally constructed in the 4th century AD, then rebuilt in the 6th century, following an earthquake. The other half of the site is the ancient baths and living quarters, although this area is, in fact, best seen through the fence from the side near Pastroudis café, where the cisterns and walls are clearly visible. ⊠ *Downtown (opposite the Misr train station)* ☎ *03/490–2904* ✉ *£e15* ⊙ *Daily 9–4.*

7 **Pompey's Pillar** *(Serapium Oracle).* Despite being Alexandria's most famous tourist sight, Pompey's Pillar is a disappointment. After all it's just a granite pillar—albeit at 88 feet, a very tall one—placed on a hill surrounded by ruins. Known in Arabic as *al-'Amud al-Sawiri* (Column of the Horseman), the pillar was misnamed after Pompeius (106–48 BC) by the Crusaders. In fact it dates to the 3rd century AD, when it was erected in honor of the emperor Diocletian on the site of a Ptolemaic temple to Serapis. Late-model sphinxes lying around on pedestals add a little character. The most interesting element, ironically, is that from the hill you can get a glimpse inside the walled cemetery next door, as well as a view of a long and busy market street. ⊠ *Karmouz* ☎ *203/482–5800* ✉ *£e15* ⊙ *Daily 9–5.*

SHOPPING

Egyptians are shrewd businessmen and retailers, and Alexandria has long been a trading city. You'll find an amazing array of crafts, but quality varies from first-class to dreadful, so do check items carefully.

Egyptians specialize in worked brass and copper articles, wood inlay on jewelry boxes and chess sets, and leather. The hookah or hubble-bubble pipe is also an interesting remembrance of the country. Egyptian cotton is a byword for quality, and the shops of Alexandria are the place to buy items like bedding and towels. The long flowing *jellabas* worn by the men are cool and comfortable, and there's a neverending supply of cut-price T-shirts.

If you want to purchase genuine antiques and antiquities, you'll need to have a certificate of approval from the Egyptian authorities to export your purchase, but copies are on sale everywhere. These items needn't be expensive: you can buy a lucky alabaster scarab beetle for a few Egyptian pounds (it's almost a compulsory souvenir of your trip to Egypt).

Whatever you buy, you'll need to haggle. In Egypt very few items have a set price. Some visitors find this stressful, but try to remember that bartering isn't meant to be a argument; it's a discussion to reach a mutually suitable price. Start at around 40% of the first asking price and rise little by little, but walk away if the offer price seems too high. Once you've agreed a price, it's very bad form to walk away from a transaction.

For cottons visit the shops on the streets radiating from Sa'd Zaghlul Square. The new cruise terminal promises upmarket shopping opportunities just a short distance from the ship.

The Attarine Market is a fascinating place. Explore the tiny workshops where the reproduction French-style furniture so popular in Egypt originates. Almost all the workshops will be happy to sell direct if you find a piece that appeals to you, but consider the challenge of shipping it back before you give in to temptation. To find the market, walk a block west of the Attarine Mosque and cross Shar'a al-Horreya to the alley between the café and the ball-bearings store.

WHERE TO EAT

$ **Grand Trianon.** One of Alexandria's most stylish institutions since it opened
★ in the 1920s, the Grand Trianon remains a forum for courtship, gossip, and rediscovery. The most popular area is the café, which has a certain old-world grandeur, despite being the least decorated part of the place. The adjacent restaurant is an extravagant art nouveau jewel, with colorful murals on the wall and a spectacular stained-glass window over the entrance to the kitchen. But the pièce de résistance is in the patisserie around the corner. There, behind elaborately carved wooden cabinets, a series of Venetian wood-panel paintings of sensual water nymphs will take your breath away. ⊠*Maydan Sa'd Zaghlul* ☎*03/482–0986.*

CORFU, GREECE

Kerkyra (Corfu) is the greenest and, quite possibly, the prettiest of all Greek islands—emerald mountains, ocher and pink buildings, shimmering silver olive leaves. The turquoise waters lap rocky coves and bougainvillea, scarlet roses, and wisteria spread over cottages. This northernmost of the major Ionian islands has, through the centuries, inspired artists, conquerors, royalty, and, of course, tourists. Indeed, when you look at Corfu in total, it's hard to believe that any island so small could generate a history so large. Classical remains vie with architecture from the centuries of Venetian, French, and British rule, leaving Corfu with a pleasant combination of contrasting design elements. The town of Corfu remains one of the loveliest in all of Greece, every nook and cranny tells a story, every street meanders to a myth, even during the busiest summer day. Corfu today is a vivid tapestry of cultures; a sophisticated weave, where charm, history, and natural beauty blend.

ESSENTIALS

CURRENCY The euro (€1 to US$1.46 at this writing). U.S. currency is generally not accepted in Europe, but ATMs are common.

HOURS Store hours are typically 9 to 9 on weekdays and 9 to 6 on Saturday. Museums are generally from open 9 to 5, but many are closed on Monday. Some shops, restaurants, and museums close between October and April.

INTERNET Have a drink from the bar at **Internet Cafe Netoikos** (⊠ *Kalokeretou 12–14* ☎ *26610/47479*) while you do business online from 10 AM to midnight every day except Sunday, when the place opens at 6 PM.

TELEPHONES Tri-band GSM phones work in Greece. You can buy prepaid phone cards at telecom shops, news-vendors, and tobacconists in all towns and cities. Phone cards can be used for local or international calls. Vodafone is the leading mobile telecom company. OTE is the national domestic provider. Calls can be made at OTE offices and paid for after completion.

COMING ASHORE

Boats dock at Corfu's new cruise port, which has a welcome center with an information desk, car rental desks, and a taxi stand. It's a 10-minute ride into the old town cost around €15. Alternatively you can walk along the seafront in about 30 minutes.

You can explore the town on foot, but you need a car to get to some of the island's loveliest places. Prices can range from €25 a day for a Fiat 127 (where you pay an additional fee for each km driving) to €80 a day for a four-wheel-drive jeep with extras. Expect additional charges of around €15 for insurance, delivery, and so forth.

EXPLORING CORFU

Numbers in the margin correspond to points of interest on the Corfu map.

CORFU TOWN

8 **Archaeological Museum.** Examine finds from ongoing island excavations; most come from Kanoni, the site of Corfu's ancient capital. The star attraction is a giant relief of snake-coiffed Medusa, depicted as her head was cut off by the hero Perseus—at which moment her two sons, Pegasus and Chrysaor, emerged from her body. The 56-foot-long sculpture once adorned the pediment of the 6th-century BC Temple of Artemis at Kanoni and is one of the largest and best-preserved pieces of Archaic sculpture in Greece. ⊠ *Vraila 1, off Leoforos Dimokratias, past Corfu Palace hotel* ☎ *26610/30680* 🔲 *€3* 🕓 *Tues.–Sun. 8:30–3.*

Corfu

Corfu Town

4 Byzantine Museum. Panagia Antivouniotissa, an ornate church dating from the 16th century, houses an outstanding collection of Byzantine religious art. More than 85 icons from the 13th to the 17th century hang on the walls as the ethereal sounds of Byzantine chants are piped in overhead. Watch for works by the celebrated icon painters Tzanes and Damaskinos; they are perhaps the best-known artists of the Cretan style of icon painting. ⊠ *Arseniou Mourayio* ☎ *26610/38313* ✉ *€2* ☉ *Tues.–Sun. 8:30–3.*

2 Campiello. Narrow, winding streets and steep stairways make up the Campiello, the large, traffic-free medieval area of the town. Balconied Venetian buildings are mixed among multistory, neoclassical 19th-century, with laundry festooned between them. Small cobbled squares centered with wells, high-belfry churches, and alleyways that lead nowhere and back, with artisans' shops along the way, add to an utterly lovely urban space. ⊠ *West of the Esplanade, northeast of New Fortress.*

Fodor'sChoice
★

3 Church of St. Spyridon. Built in 1596, this church is the tallest on the island, thanks to its distinctive red-domed bell tower, and is filled with silver treasures. The patron saint's mummified body, which can be seen through a glass panel while his internal remains are contained in a silver reliquary. His miracles are said to have saved the island four times. ⊠ *Agiou Spyridon* ☎ *No phone.*

6 The Esplanade. Central to the life of the town, this huge, open parade ground on the land side of the canal is, many say, the most beautiful *spianada* (esplanade) in Greece. It is bordered on the west by a street lined with arcades and seven- and eight-story Venetian and English Georgian houses, called the **Liston**. Cafés spill out onto the passing scene and this is the place to watch the world go by. Sunday cricket matches, a holdover from British rule, are sometimes played on the northern half of the Esplanade. ⊠ *Between Old Fortress and old town.*

1 New Fortress. Built in 1577–78 by the Venetians, the New Fortress was constructed to strengthen town defenses only three decades after the "old" fortress was built. The French and the British subsequently expanded the complex to protect Corfu town from a possible Turkish invasion. You can wander through the maze of tunnels, moats, and fortifications. The moat (dry now) is the site of the town's marketplace. A classic British citadel stands at its heart. ⊠ *Solomou, on promontory northwest of Old Fortress* ☎ *26610/27370* ✉ *€2* ☉ *June–Oct., daily 9 AM–9:30 PM.*

7 Old Fortress. Corfu's entire population once lived within the walls of the Old
★ Fortress, or Citadel, built by the Venetians in 1546 on the site of a Byzantine castle. Separated from the rest of the town by a moat, the fort is on a promontory mentioned by Thucydides. Its twohills, or *korypha* (known

---

CORFU BEST BETS

Relax over a coffee at the Liston. This is a wonderful place to immerse yourself in modern Greek life.

Take pictures of Pontikonisi. Mouse Island, as this tiny islet is also known, is one of the iconic Greek landscape views. Shimmering waters and verdant foliage contrast dramatically with the modest whitewashed chapel.

Explore Paleokastritsa. A breathtaking landscape of tiny rocky coves, azure waters, and fragrant woodland offers exceptional vistas surrounded by the sound of buzzing cicadas.

as the "bosom"), gave the island its Western name. Inside the fortress, many Venetian fortifications were destroyed by the British, who replaced them with their own structures. The most notable of these is the quirky **Church of St. George**, built like an ancient Doric temple on the outside and set up like a Greek Orthodox church on the inside. ⊠*Northeastern point of Corfu town peninsula* ☎26610/48310 ⊡€4 ⊙*Weekdays 8–7, weekends 8:30–3.*

⑤ **Palace of St. Michael & St. George.** Admire Ming pottery in an ornate colonial palace as Homer's Ionian sea shimmers outside the windows. This elegant, colonnaded 19th-century Regency structure houses the **Museum of Asiatic Art**, a notable collection of Asian porcelains and Sino-Japanese art. ⊠*North end of the Esplanade* ☎26610/30443 *Museum of Asiatic Art* ⊡€3 ⊙*Tues.–Sun. 8:30–3.*

Fodor's Choice
★

KANONI
5 km (3 mi) southwest of Corfu town.

At Kanoni, 5 km (3 mi) south of Corfu town, the site of the ancient capital, you may behold Corfu's most famous view, which looks out over two beautiful islets.

⑩ The little island of **Moni Viahernes** is reached by causeway and has a tiny, pretty convent.

⑪ **Pontikonisi**, or Mouse Island, has tall cypresses guarding a 13th-century chapel. Legend has it that the island is really Odysseus's ship, which Poseidon turned to stone here: the reason why Homer's much-traveled hero was shipwrecked on Phaeacia (Corfu) in the *Odyssey*. June to August a little motorboat runs out to Pontikonisi every 20 minutes.

⑨ The royal palace of **Mon Repos** was built in 1831. After Greece won independence, it was used as a summer palace for the royal family of Greece. Prince Philip, the duke of Edinburgh, was born here. After touring the palace, wander around the extensive grounds, which include ruins of temples from the 7th and 6th centuries BC. Opposite Mon Repos are ruins of Ayia Kerkyra, the 5th-century church of the Old City. ⊠*1 km (½ mi) north of Kanoni, near Mon Repos beach* ☎26610/41369 ⊡€3 ⊙*Tues.–Sun. 8:30–7.*

GASTOURI
⑫ *19 km (12 mi) southwest of Corfu town.*

The village of Gastouri, still lovely despite the summer onrush of day-trippers, is the site of the **Achilleion**. Although in remarkably eclectic taste, the palace is redeemed by lovely gardens stretching to the sea. Built in the late 19th century by the Italian architect Rafael Carita for Empress Elizabeth of Austria, the palace was named by the empress after her favorite hero, Achilles. After Elizabeth was assassinated, Kaiser Wilhelm II bought it and lived here until the outbreak of World War I. After the armistice, the Greek government received it as a spoil of war.

The interior contains a pseudo-Byzantine chapel, a pseudo-Pompeian room, and a pseudo-Renaissance dining hall, culminating in a vulgar fresco called *Achilles in His Chariot*. One of the more interesting furnishings is Kaiser Wilhelm II's saddle seat, used at his desk. In 1962 the palace

5

was restored, leased as a gambling casino, and later was the set for the casino scene in the James Bond film *For Your Eyes Only.* The casino has since moved to the Corfu Holiday Palace. ⊠*Main St.* ☎*26610/56210* 🖃*€6* ⊙*June–Aug., daily 8–7; Sept.–May, daily 9–4.*

PALEOKASTRITSA

⑬ *25 km (16 mi) northwest of Corfu town.*

This spectacular territory of grottoes, cliffs, and turquoise waters is breathtaking.

Paleokastritsa Monastery, a 17th-century structure, is built on the site of an earlier monastery, among terraced gardens overlooking the Adriatic Sea. Its treasure is a 12th-century icon of the Virgin Mary, and there's a small museum with some other early icons. ⊠*Northern headland* 🕾*No phone* 🖃*Donations accepted* ⊙*Daily 7–1 and 3–8.*

The village of **Lakones** is on the steep mountain behind the Paleokastritsa Monastery. Most of the current town was constructed in modern times, but the ruins of the 13th-century **Angelokastro** also loom over the landscape. ⊠*5 km (3 mi) northeast of Paleokastritsa.*

SHOPPING

Corfu town has myriad tiny shops. For traditional goods head for the narrow streets of the Campiello where olive wood, ceramics, lace, jewelry, and wine shops abound. Kumquat liqueur is a specialty of the island.

Alexis Traditional Products (⊠*Solomou 10–12, Spilia* ☎*26610/21831*) sells locally made wines and spirits, including kumquat liqueur and marmalade, traditional sweets, local olive oil, olives, and olive oil soap—as well as honey, herbs, and spices. **Katafigio** (⊠*N. Theotoki 113* ☎*26610/43137*) sells replicas of favorite museum artifacts. There's also a display of chess sets, some of which have pieces depicting ancient Greek heroes. **Mironis Olive Wood** (⊠*Filarmonikis 27* ☎*26610/40621* ⊠*Agiou Spyridon 65* ☎*26610/40364*) deals in dowls, sculptures, wooden jewelry, and much more in its two tiny family-run shops. **Nikos Sculpture and Jewellery** (⊠*Paleologou 50* ☎*26610/31107* ⊠*N. Theotoki 54* ☎*26610/32009* ⊕*www. nikosjewellery.gr*) makes original gold and silver jewelry designs, and sculptures in cast bronze; they're expensive but worth it. **Rolandos** (⊠*N. Theotoki 99* ☎*26610/45004*), a talented artist, produces paintings and handmade pottery in his studio.

SPORTS & ACTIVITIES

Snorkeling and diving are best in the many rocky inlets and grottos on the northwest coast, and Paleokastritsa and Ermones have diving schools where you can take lessons and rent equipment. The winds on the west coast are best for windsurfing, although the water on the east coast is calmer. Sailboards are available, and paddleboats and rowboats can be rented at many beaches. Waterskiing, water polo, parasailing, jet skiing, and other water activities are sponsored by resorts throughout the island. Motorboats and sailboats can be rented at the old port in Corfu town; in Paleokastritsa, Kondokali, and Kassiopi; and on the northeast coast. To charter a yacht or sailboat without a crew, you need a proficiency certificate from a certified yacht club.

Archilleon Diving Center (✉*Ermones Bay* ☎*26610/95350* ⊕*www.achilleondivingcenter.gr*) offers dive tuition and equipment rental for qualified divers. **Pinnacle Yachts** (✉*Gouvia MarinaGouvia* ☎*26610/90411*) has yachts for rent and provides cruising flottilas.

BEACHES

The beach at **Pelekas** has soft, golden sand and clear water but is developed and tends to be crowded. Free minibuses regularly transport people to the beach from the village, which is a long and steep walk otherwise. The large, golden beaches at **Glyfada** (✉*2 km [1 mi] south of Pelekas*) are the most famous on the island and the sands are inevitably packed with sunbathers. Sun beds, umbrellas, and water sports equipment is available for rent and there are several tourist resorts.

The isolated **Myrtiotissa** (✉*3 km [2 mi] north of Pelekas*) beach, between sheer cliffs, is noted for its good snorkeling (and nude sunbathing). This sandy stretch was called by Lawrence Durrell in *Prospero's Cell* "perhaps the loveliest beach in the world," but summer crowds are the norm.

WHERE TO EAT

¢–$$ ✕**Gerekos.** One of the island's most famous seafood tavernas, Gerekos always has fresh fish. Opt for a table on the terrace and try the whitefish *me ladi* (cooked in olive oil, garlic, and pepper). ✉*Kondokali Bay, 6 km (4 mi) north of Corfu town* ☎*26610/91281* ⚑*Reservations essential* ▭*AE, V.*

¢–$$ ✕**Rex Restaurant.** A friendly Corfiot restaurant in a 19th-century town ★ house, Rex has been a favorite for nearly 100 years. Classic local specialties are reliably delicious. Dishes such as rabbit stewed with fresh figs and chicken with kumquats are successful twists on the regional fare. Outside tables are perfect for people-watching on the Liston. ✉*Kapodistriou 66, west of Liston* ☎*26610/39649* ⊕*www.restaurantrex.gr* ▭*AE, D, MC, V.*

DUBROVNIK, CROATIA

Commanding a splendid coastal location, Dubrovnik is one of the world's most beautiful fortified cities. Its massive stone ramparts and splendid fortress towers curve around a tiny harbor, enclosing graduated ridges of sun-bleached orange-tiled roofs, copper domes, and elegant bell towers. In the 7th century AD, residents of the Roman city Epidaurum (now Cavtat) fled the Avars and Slavs of the north and founded a new settlement on a small rocky island, which they named Laus, and later Ragusa. On the mainland hillside opposite the island, the Slav settlement called Dubrovnik grew up. In the 12th century, the narrow channel separating the two settlements was filled in, and Ragusa and Dubrovnik became one. The city was surrounded by defensive walls during the 13th century, and these were reinforced with towers and bastions during the late 15th century. The city became a UNESCO World Heritage Site in 1979. During the war for

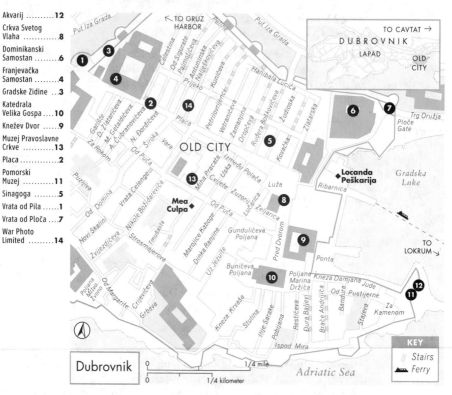

independence, it came under heavy siege, though thanks to careful restoration work, few traces of damage remain. Today Dubrovnik is once again a fashionable, high-class destination, with recent visitors including Tom Cruise, Sharon Stone, John Malkovich, and Sir Roger Moore.

ESSENTIALS

CURRENCY The Croatian kuna (5.3 Kn to US$1 at this writing). U.S. dollars are not generally accepted in Croatia, so you will need some local currency. ATMs are easy to find, and it is also possible to exchange currency in banks and also in most local travel agencies. Credit cards are accepted at many restaurants and shops.

HOURS Offices are open weekdays from 8:30 to 4. Shops often close for lunch around 1 and may close for as long as 3 hours; banks also sometimes close for lunch. Post offices are open on Saturday during the main summer season, from June through September.

INTERNET During the summer, small temporary Internet cafés spring up in the seaside resort towns, so even on the islands you will find somewhere to check e-mail. However, many are nothing more than a regular café with a PC in the corner. The one well-established, fully equipped Internet café of note is **Netcafe** (⌧*Prijeko 21, Stari Grad* ☎*020/321–025*).

TELEPHONES Most tri- and quad-band GSM phones will work in Croatia. Public phones use calling cards, which can be purchased at the post office, newsstands, and hotels. Major mobile phone companies include TMobile and VIPNet.

COMING ASHORE

In Dubrovnik, almost all ships dock at Gruz Harbor, which is 4 km (2½ mi) from Stari Grad (Old Town). Some ships will provide a free shuttle. The trip to Dubrovnik's Old Town takes about 10 minutes by taxi or 30 to 40 minutes by foot. You can also take a public bus. There's a taxi stand at the harbor.

A few smaller ships might still tender passengers ashore in the Old Town, where you're just steps from everything that Dubrovnik has to offer.

Since the Old Town is compact and pedestrian-friendly, we recommend that you not rent a car in Dubrovnik. It's easy to reach Cavtat by bus or ferry, and unless you want to explore the countryside away from Dubrovnik, a car will not help you. If you choose to rent, expect to pay about €55 for a manual compact vehicle, though you can rent a semiautomatic Smart car at some outlets for about €50.

> **DUBROVNIK BEST BETS**
>
> **Walk the city Walls.** The Old Town's massive Gradske Zidine were begun in the 13th century and reinforced over the years.
>
> **Strolling along the harborfront.** Dubrovnik's picturesque harbor has a promenade perfect for a stroll.
>
> **Relaxing in a café.** All summer long, Dubrovnik's many cafés and restaurants have tables outside (many on the waterfront), where you can sit under an umbrella and enjoy a seafood lunch or a drink.

5

EXPLORING DUBROVNIK

All of the main sites lie in Stari Grad (Old Town) within the city walls, an area that is compact and car-free.

⑫ Akvarij *(Aquarium).* This dark, cavernous space houses several small pools and 27 well-lighted tanks containing a variety of fish from rays to small sharks, as well as other underwater denizens such as sponges and sea urchins. Children will find the octopus, in his glass tank, either very amusing or horribly scary. ⊠*Damjana Jude 2, Stari Grad* ☎*020/323–978* ⊠*25 Kn* ☉*June–Sept., daily 9–8; Apr., May, Oct., and Nov., daily 9–6; Dec.–Mar., daily 9–1.*

❽ Crkva Svetog Vlaha *(Church of St. Blaise).* This 18th-century baroque church replaced an earlier one destroyed by fire. Of particular note is the silver statue on the high altar of St. Blaise holding a model of Dubrovnik, which is paraded around town each year on February 3, the Day of St. Blaise. ⊠*Luza, Stari Grad* ⊠*Free* ☉*Daily 8–noon and 4:30–7.*

❻ Dominikanski Samostan *(Dominican Monastery).* With a splendid, late-15th-century floral Gothic cloister as its centerpiece, the monastery is best known for its museum, which houses a rich collection of religious paintings by the so-called Dubrovnik School from the 15th and 16th centuries. Look out for works by Bozidarevic, Hamzic, and Dobričevic, as well as gold and silver ecclesiastical artifacts crafted by local goldsmiths. ⊠*Sv Domina 4, Stari Grad* ☎*020/321–423* ⊠*10 Kn* ☉*May–Oct., daily 9–6; Nov.–Apr., daily 9–5.*

❹ Franjevacka Samostan *(Franciscan Monastery).* The monastery's chief claim to fame is its pharmacy, which was founded in 1318 and is still in existence today; it's said to be the oldest in Europe. There's also a delightful cloistered garden, framed by Romanesque arcades supported by double columns, each crowned with a set of grotesque figures. In the Treasury a painting shows what Dubrovnik looked like before the disastrous earthquake of 1667. ⊠*Placa 2, Stari Grad* ☎*020/321–410* 🎫*15 Kn* ☉*May–Oct., daily 9–6; Nov.–Apr., daily 9–5.*

❸ Gradske Zidine *(City Walls).* Most of the original construction took place
★ during the 13th century, though the walls were further reinforced with towers and bastions during the following 400 years. On average they are 80 feet high and up to 10 feet thick on the seaward side, 20 feet on the inland side. ⊠*Placa, Stari Grad* ☎*020/324–641* 🎫*30 Kn* ☉*May–Sept., daily 8–7; Oct.–Apr., daily 9–3.*

⓭ Muzej Pravoslavne Crkve *(Orthodox Church Museum).* Next door to the Orthodox Church, this small museum displays religious icons from the Balkan region and Russia, as well as several portraits of eminent early-20th-century Dubrovnik personalities by local artist Vlaho Bukovac. ⊠*Od Puca 8, Stari Grad* ☎*020/323–823* 🎫*10 Kn* ☉*May–Oct., daily 9–2; Nov.–Apr., Mon.–Sat. 9–2.*

❿ Katedrala Velika Gospa *(Cathedral of Our Lady).* The present structure was built in baroque style after the original was destroyed in the 1667 earthquake. The interior contains a number of notable paintings, including a large polyptych above the main altar depicting the *Assumption of Our Lady,* attributed to Titian. The Treasury displays 138 gold and silver reliquaries, including the skull of St. Blaise in the form of a bejeweled Byzantine crown and also an arm and a leg of the saint, likewise encased in decorated golden plating. ⊠*Buniceva Poljana, Stari Grad* ☎*020/323–459* 🎫*Cathedral free, Treasury 7 Kn* ☉*Daily 8–7.*

❾ Knezev Dvor *(Bishop's Palace).* Originally created in the 15th century but reconstructed several times through the following years, this exquisite building with an arcaded loggia and an internal courtyard shows a combination of late-Gothic and early Renaissance styles. On the ground floor there are large rooms where, in the days of the Republic, the Great Council and Senate held their meetings. Over the entrance to the meeting halls a plaque reads: OBLITI PRIVATORUM PUBLICA CURATE (Forget private affairs, and get on with public matters). Upstairs, the rector's living quarters now accommodate the Gradski Muzej (City Museum), containing exhibits that give a picture of life in Dubrovnik from early days until the fall of the Republic. ⊠*Pred Dvorom 3, Stari Grad* ☎*020/321–497* 🎫*20 Kn* ☉*May–Oct., daily 9–6; Nov.–Apr., daily 9–2.*

❷ Placa. This was once the shallow sea channel separating the island of Laus from the mainland. Although it was filled in during the 12th century, it continued to divide the city socially for several centuries, with the nobility living in the area south of Placa and the commoners living on the hillside to the north. Today it forms the venue for the *korzo,* an evening promenade where locals meet to chat, maybe have a drink, and generally size one another up. ⊠*Stari Grad.*

⓫ Pomorski Muzej *(Maritime Museum).* Above the Aquarium, on the first floor of St. John's Fortress, this museum's exhibits illustrate how rich and powerful Dubrovnik became as one of the world's most important seafaring nations. On display are intricately detailed models of ships as well as engine-room equipment, sailors' uniforms, paintings, and maps. ⊠*Damjana Jude 2, Stari Grad* ☎*020/323–904* 💷*15 Kn* ⊙*May–Oct., daily 9–6; Nov.–Apr., Tues.–Sun. 9–2.*

⑤ Sinagoga *(Synagogue).* This tiny 15th-century synagogue, the second-oldest in Europe (after Prague's) bears testament to Dubrovnik's once thriving Jewish community, made up largely of Jews who were expelled from Spain and Italy during the medieval period. ⊠*Zudioska 5, Stari Grad* ☎*020/321–028* 💷*10 Kn* ⊙*Weekdays 10–8.*

❶ Vrata od Pila *(Pile Gate).* Built in 1537 and combining a Renaissance arch with a wooden drawbridge on chains, this has always been the main entrance to the city walls. A niche above the portal contains a statue of Sveti Vlah (St. Blaise), the city's patron saint, holding a replica of Dubrovnik in his left hand. From May to October, guards in deep-red period-costume uniforms stand vigilant by the gate through daylight hours, just as they would have done when the city was a republic. ⊠*Pile, Stari Grad.*

❼ Vrata od Ploca *(Ploče Gate).* One of two entrances into the town walls, Ploče comprises a stone bridge and wooden drawbridge plus a 15th-century stone arch bearing a statue of Sveti Vlah (St. Blaise). As at Pile Gate, guards in period costume stand vigilant here through the summer season. ⊠*Ploče, Stari Grad.*

⑭ War Photo Limited. Shocking but impressive, this modern gallery devotes two entire floors to war photojournalism. Past exhibitions include images from conflicts in Afghanistan, Iraq, former-Yugoslavia, Israel, and Palestine. Refreshingly impartial by Croatian standards, the message—that war is physically and emotionally destructive whichever side you are on—comes through loudly and clearly. You'll find it in a narrow side street running between Placa and Prijeko. ⊠*Antuninska 6, Stari Grad* ☎*020/322–166* ⊕*www.warphotoltd.com* 💷*25 Kn* ⊙*May–Oct., daily 9–9; Nov.–Apr., Tues.–Sat. 10–4, Sun. 10–2.*

Fodor'sChoice
★

CAVTAT
17 km (10½ mi) southeast of Dubrovnik.

Founded by the ancient Greeks, then taken by the Romans, the original settlement on the site of Cavtat, which is 17 km (10½ mi) southeast of Dubrovnik, was subsequently destroyed by tribes of Avars and Slavs in the early 7th century. Today's town, which developed during the 15th century under the Republic of Dubrovnik, is an easygoing fishing town and small-scale seaside resort. The medieval stone buildings of the Old Town occupy a small peninsula with a natural bay to each side. A palm-lined seaside promenade with open-air cafés and restaurants curves around the main bay. Cavtat can be visited easily as a half-day trip from Dubrovnik. If you're going on your own, the easiest way to get there is by bus or taxi-boat ride; the trip takes about an hour.

Galerija Vlaho Bukovac *(Vlaho Bukovac Gallery).* The former home of local artist Vlaho Bukovac (1855–1922) has been renovated to provide a gallery for contemporary exhibitions on the ground floor. Upstairs, around 30 of Bukovac's oil paintings, tracing the periods he spent in Paris, Prague, and Cavtat, are on display in his former studio, along with pieces of period furniture. ⊠*Bukovceva* ☎*020/478–646* 🎟*20 Kn* ⊗*Tues.–Sat. 10–1 and 4–8; Sun. 4–8.*

BEACHES

The more upmarket hotels, such as the Excelsior and Villa Dubrovnik, have their own beaches that are exclusively for the use of hotel guests. The most natural and peaceful beaches lie on the tiny island of **Lokrum**, a short distance south of the Old Town. Through high season boats leave from the Old Harbor, ferrying visitors back and forth from morning to early evening. Ferries run every half hour from 9 AM to 7:30 PM. Tickets cost 25 Kn.

The **Eastwest Beach Club** (⊠*Frana Supila, Banje Beach* ☎*020/412–220*), just a short distance from Ploče Gate, is a fashionable spot with a small pebble beach complete with chaise-longue and parasols, waterskiing and jet-skiing facilities, and a chic café.

SHOPPING

Despite its role as an important tourist destination, Dubrovnik offers little in the way of shopping or souvenir hunting. If you're in search of gifts, your best bet is a bottle of good Dalmatian wine or *rakija* (a fruit brandy popular throughout much of eastern Europe).

Croata (⊠*Put Frane Supila 12, Ploče* ☎*020/353–279*), a small boutique in the Hotel Excelsior, specializes in "original Croatian ties" in presentation boxes. **Djardin** (⊠*Miha Pracata 8, Stari Grad* ☎*No phone*) sells beautiful, funky modern jewelry made from colored stones: chunky necklaces, bracelets, and dangling earrings. Sophisticated and tasteful, with a touch of eccentricity, pieces are displayed in an old building with a courtyard garden. You'll find it in the Old Town, close to the Orthodox Church Museum. **Dubrovačka Kuca** (⊠*Svetog Dominika, Stari Grad* ☎*020/322–092*), a tastefully decorated wine shop, stocks a fine selection of regional Croatian wines, rakija, olive oil, and truffle products, plus works of art by contemporary artists on the upper two levels; it's close to Ploče Gate.

WHERE TO EAT

¢ ✕**Lokanda Peskarija.** Just outside the town walls, overlooking the old harbor
Fodor's Choice and next to the covered fish market, this seafood restaurant is a particu-
★ larly good value. It has a split-level interior with exposed stone walls and wooden beams, plus outdoor candlelighted tables by the water. Locals love it. ⊠*Na Ponti, Stari Grad* ☎*020/324–750* ☐*AE, DC, MC, V* ⊗*Closed Jan. and Feb.*

¢ ✕**Mea Culpa.** Within the city walls and open until midnight year-round, Mea Culpa is said to make the best pizza in town. The dining room is a bit cramped, and you may find the music unreasonably loud, but from spring to autumn there are large wooden tables outside on the cobbled street. ⊠*Za Rokom 3, Stari Grad* ☎*020/323–430* ☐*No credit cards.*

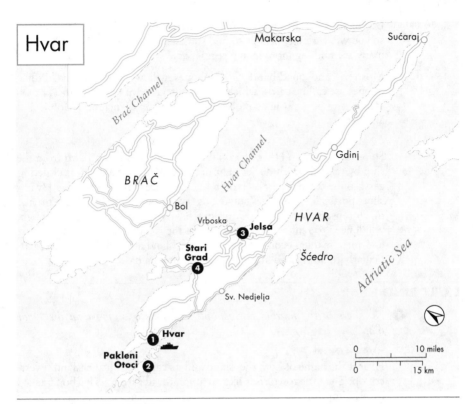

HVAR, CROATIA

The island of Hvar bills itself as the "sunniest island in the Adriatic." Not only does it have the figures to back up this claim—an annual average of 2,724 hours of sunshine with a maximum of two foggy days a year—but it also makes visitors a sporting proposition, offering them a money-back guarantee if there is ever a foggy day (which has been known to happen). While fog has been known to happen, hotels don't ordinarily have to give much of their income back. All this sun is good for the island's fields of lavender, rosemary, and grapes. Hvar is also probably Croatia's hippest island, attracting gossip column-worthy celebrities, would-be artists, politicians, and nudists. Visitors have included King Abdullah of Jordan and his wife, Queen Rania, Italian clothing entrepreneur Luciano Benetton, and local tennis champion Goran Ivanisevic.

ESSENTIALS

CURRENCY The Croatian kuna (5.3 Kn to US$1 at this writing). U.S. dollars are not generally accepted in Croatia, so you will need some local currency. ATMs are easy to find, and it is also possible to exchange currency in banks and also in most local travel agencies. Credit cards are accepted at many restaurants and shops.

HOURS Offices are open weekdays from 8:30 to 4. Shops often close for lunch around 1 and may close for as long as three hours; banks also sometimes close for lunch. Post offices are open on Saturday during the main summer season, from June through September.

INTERNET   During the summer, small temporary Internet cafés spring up in the islands, so you will certainly be able to find somewhere to check e-mail. However, many are nothing more than a regular café with a PC in the corner.

TELEPHONES   Most tri- and quad-band GSM phones will work in Croatia. Public phones use calling cards, which can be purchased at the post office, newsstands, and hotels. Major mobile phone companies include TMobile and VIPNet.

COMING ASHORE

Ships can't dock in Hvar, so you'll be brought into Hvar Town from the ship by tender, which docks right in town. Most of the town is closed to cars, so the town is best seen on foot, and since many ships make Hvar a short port call (sometimes staying as few as four hours), it doesn't make much sense to set out to do too much. If you are in port long enough, you'll need to rent a car to see more of the island. Expect to pay at least €55 for a manual economy vehicle. The island also has bus service, particularly to Stari Grad and Jelsa, several times a day.

EXPLORING HVAR

❶ *Numbers in the margin correspond to points of interest on the Hvar map.*

HVAR TOWN

Hvar is the name of both the island and its capital, near the island's western tip. The little town rises like an amphitheater from its harbor, backed by a hilltop fortress and protected from the open sea by a scattering of small islands known as Pakleni Otoci. Along the palm-lined quay, a string of cafés and restaurants is shaded by colorful awnings and umbrellas. Hvar town seems to have it all: beautifully preserved Venetian-style architecture, stylish modern hotels, classy seafood restaraunts, and a sophisticated nightlife. Much of the town was built during the Medieval period, so you'll find gothic palaces amid the twisting, narrow streets just away from the shoreline. And what a shoreline it is.

You can walk far along the seaside **promenade**, looking out over the Adriatic and the Pakleni Islands, the largest of which—Sveti Klementi—holds the island's yacht harbor. The town itself remains traffic-free because there are no through streets for driving.

A few steps away from the shorefront promenade, the magnificent main square, **Trg Sveti Stjepan**, the largest piazza in Dalmatia, is backed by the 16th-century **Katedrala Sveti Stjepanp** (Cathedral of St. Stephen). Other notable sights include the kazaliste (theater) and the Franjevački Samostan (Franciscan Monastery).

Commanding a prime site on the edge of the main square and overlooking the harbor, the **Hotel Palace** is the island's most atmospheric hotel. A former Venetian loggia is incorporated into the hotel and used as an elegant salon. Stop in for a drink at the bar or lunch at the hotel's open-air restaurant, which offers some of the finest views of the harbor. ✉ *Trg Sv Stjepana, Hvar Town* ☎ *021/741–966.*

Hotel Palace is the island's most atmospheric hotel. A former Venetian loggia is incorporated into the hotel and used as an elegant salon. Stop in for a drink at the bar or lunch at the hotel's open-air restaurant, which offers some of the finest views of the harbor. ⊠ *Trg Sv Stjepana, Hvar Town21450* ☎*021/741–966.*

East of town, along the quay past the Arsenal, lies the **Franjevacki Samostan** *(Franciscan Monastery).* Within its walls, a pretty 15th-century Renaissance cloister leads to the former refectory, now housing a small museum with several notable artworks. ⊠ *Obala Ivana Lučica Lavčevica, Hvar Town* 🎫*15 Kn* ◷*May–Oct., daily 10–noon and 5–7.*

> **HVAR BEST BETS**
>
> **See the Tvrdalj.** This oddly interesting house in Stari Grad is worth a trip.
>
> **Visit the Pakleni Otoci.** The small islands off Hvar's southwest coast have Hvar's best beaches and are scenic enough to be worth a trip in their own right.
>
> **Wander the Stari Grad.** If you have just a few hours in port, spend them wandering the car-free streets of Hvar's picturesque Old Town, stopping at a café or two.

On the upper floor of the Arsenal, the **Kazaliste** *(Theater)* opened in 1612, making it the oldest institution of its kind in Croatia and one of the first in Europe. The Arsenal building, where Venetian ships en route to the Orient once docked for repairs, dates back to the 13th century but was reconstructed after damage during a Turkish invasion in 1571. ⊠ *Trg Sv Stjepana, Hvar Town* 🎫*15 Kn* ◷*May–Oct., daily 9–1 and 5–9; Nov.–Apr., daily 10–noon.*

PAKLENI OTOCI

2 *Sveti Klement is approximately 20 minutes by boat from Hvar Town.*

The 20 small islets that make up the Pakleni Islands are directly southwest of Hvar Town's harbor. Their name derives from the Croatian word *paklina,* which is what melted pine resin is called (the resin from the island's many pine trees was melted down to make ships watertight). The largest of the islands, Sveti Klement, is where Hvar's main yacht harbor is located; a church here is dedicated to the saint. Summer homes and some small resorts are built on many of the islands, some of which have excellent beaches that are reachable only by boat. Jerolim, the closest of the islands to Hvar Town, has a famous nude beach.

JELSA

3 *10 km (6 mi) east of Stari Grad, 27 km (17 mi) east of Hvar Town.*

In this village on the northern coast of the island, you'll see many structures from the Renaissance and baroque periods, though St. Mary's Church dates back to the early 1300s. A tower built by the ancient Greeks overlooks the harbor; it dates to the 3rd or 4th century BC. About 1 km (½ mi) east of the modern town is the older Grad, the original fortified area that was protected by the fortress called Galesink, which now stands in ruins. The small town is an alternative to the busier Hvar Town and is surrounded by swimmable beaches—including the island's most popular nude beaches—and some resorts. It's surrounded by thick forests of pine trees.

STARI GRAD

4 *17 km (11 mi) east of Hvar Town.*

The site of the original Greek settlement on Hvar, called Pharos by the Greeks, Stari Grad is a conglomeration of smaller communities; it's also the entry point to the island for bus transportation from the mainland, as well as most passenger ferries.

The main sight in Stari Grad is **Tvrdalj**, the fortified Renaissance villa of the 16th-century poet Petar Hektorovic. The home has been renovated twice over the centuries, first in the 18th-century baroque style; a partial restoration was done in the 19th century. Hektorovic attempted to create a "model universe" to be embodied in his home. To that end, a large fish pond is stocked with gray mullet, as they were in the poet's own time, representing the sea; above the fish pond in a tower is a dovecote, representing the air. Ivy was allowed to cover the walls to tie the home to the land. Quotations from Hektorovic's poetry are inscribed on many walls. ⊠*Trg Tvrdalj* ☎*765–068* ⊡*10 Kn* ⊙*June–Sept. daily 8–1 and 5–9.*

SPORTS & ACTIVITIES

DIVING

Those with a taste for underwater adventure might have a go at scuba diving. The seabed is scattered with pieces of broken Greek amphorae, while the area's biggest underwater attraction is the Stambedar sea wall, home to red and violet gorgonians (a type of coral), which is close to the Pakleni Islands. For courses at all levels, try **Diving Center Viking** (⊠*Podstine, Hvar Town* ☎*021/742–529* ⊕*www.viking-diving.com*).

SAILING

Hvar Town is a popular port of call for those sailing on the Adriatic; the town harbor is packed out with flashy yachts through peak season. **ACI Marina** (⊠*Palmizana Bay, Sveti Klement* ☎*021/744–995* ⊕*www. aci-club.hr*) in Palmižana Bay on the island of Sveti Klement, one of the Pakleni Otoci, lies just 2.4 nautical mi from Hvar Town. This 160-berth marina is open from April through October and is served by regular taxi boats from Hvar Town through peak season.

BEACHES

Although there are several decent beaches within walking distance of town—the best-equipped being the Hotel Amfora's pebble beach, 10 minutes west of the main square—sun-worshippers in-the-know head for the nearby Pakleni Otoci (Pakleni Islands), which can be reached by taxi boats that depart regularly (in peak season, every hour, from 8 to 8) from in front of the Arsenal in the town harbor. The best known and best served are **Sveti Jerolim** (on the island of the same name, predominantly a nudist beach), **Stipanska** (on the island of Marinkovac, a clothing-optional beach), and **Palmizana** (on the island of Sveti Klement, also clothing-optional).

WHERE TO EAT

¢–$ ✕**Restoran Palmizana.** On the tiny island of Sveti Klement, a 20-minute taxi boat ride from Hvar Town, this restaurant is backed by a romantic wilderness of Mediterranean flora and offers stunning views over the open sea. The interior is decorated with modern Croatian art, and there are classical-music recitals on Sunday morning. Besides fresh seafood, goodies include *kozji sir sa rukolom* (goat cheese with arugula), and *pašticada* (beef stewed in sweet wine and prunes). Recent customers have included retired Croatian soccer player Davor Šuker and Formula One multimillionaire Bernie Ecclestone. ⊠*Vinogradišce Uvala, Sveti Klement* ☎*021/717–270* ⊟*AE, DC, MC, V* ⊗*Closed Nov.–Mar.*

¢ ✕**Bacchus.** With outdoor tables on the main square, this small and sometimes chaotic eatery is popular with locals for its *merenda* (inexpensive prix-fixe lunch), and is reputed to prepare the best *ramsteak* (rump steak) in town. It stays open year-round. ⊠*Trg Sv Stjepana, Hvar Town* ☎*021/742–698* ⊟*AE, DC, MC, V.*

ISTANBUL, TURKEY

Though it is often remarked that Turkey straddles Europe and Asia, it's really the city of Istanbul that does the straddling. European Istanbul is separated from its Asian suburbs by the Bosphorus, the narrow channel of water that connects the Black Sea, north of the city, to the Sea of Marmara in the south. What will strike you more than the meeting of East and West in Istanbul, though, is the juxtaposition of the old and the new, of tradition and modernity. Office towers creep up behind historic old palaces; women in jeans or elegant designer outfits pass others wearing long skirts and head coverings; donkey-drawn carts vie with shiny BMWs for dominance of the streets; and the Grand Bazaar competes with Western-style boutiques and shopping malls. At dawn, when the muezzin's call to prayer rebounds from ancient minarets, there are inevitably a few hearty revelers still making their way home from nightclubs while other residents kneel in prayer.

ESSENTIALS

CURRENCY The New Turkish Lira (YTL1.29 to US$1 and YTL 1.76 to €1 at this writing). U.S. dollars are accepted in shops and in some restaurants. ATMs and currency exchange kiosks are common.

HOURS Shops open daily from 9 to 9, though some will close for an hour or so on Friday lunchtime for prayers. Attractions are usually open daily from 8 until 5 or 6 pm, though some are closed on Monday.

INTERNET **Istanbul Cyber Café** (⊠*Balkan Carsisi 5/31, floor 1, Bayazit* ☎*212/516–5528*) has 18 computers.

TELEPHONES Most tri- and quad-band GSM phones will work in Turkey. The Turkish mobile system is not 3G-compatible, and handsets are single band. Public phones accept tokens or telephone cards (which can be purchased at newsstands and telecom shops); phones accepting cards will also accept credit cards in payment for calls. Turk Telekom, Turkcell, and Telcim are the major telecom companies.

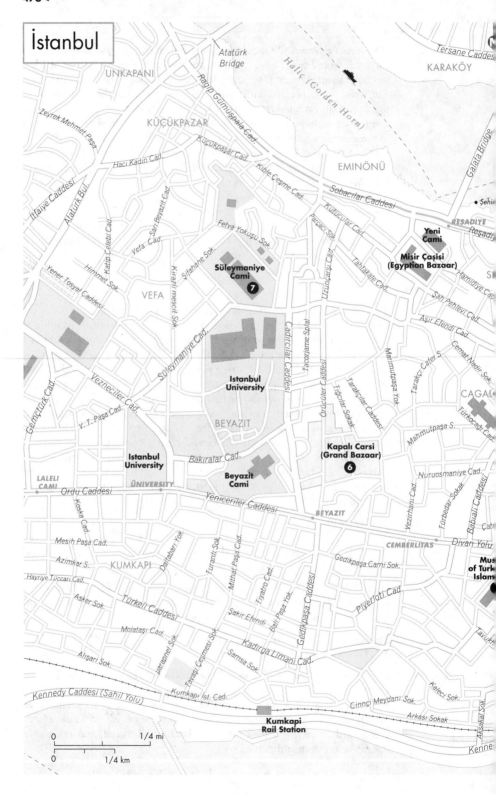

İstanbul

UNKAPANI

Atatürk
Bridge

KARAKÖY

Tersane Caddes

Haliç (Golden Horn)

KÜÇÜKPAZAR

Zeyrek Mehmet Paşa

Ragıp Gümüşpala Cad.

Küçükpaşar Cad.

Hacı Kadın Cad.

Kible Çeşme Cad.

EMİNÖNÜ

Sobacılar Caddesi

Galata Bridge

RESADİYE

Resadi

• Şehir

İtfaiye Caddesi

Atatürk Bul.

Sarı Beyazıt Cad.

Vefa Cad.

Katip Çelebi Cad.

Himmet Sok.

VEFA

Yener Tosyal Caddesi

Fetva Yokuşu Sok.

Kırazlı mescit Sok.

Şifahane Sok.

Süleymaniye Cami

Süleymaniye Cad.

Kutucular Cad.

Parçacı Sok.

Uzunçarşı Cad.

Tahtakale Cad.

Yeni
Cami

Misir Çasisi
(Egyptian Bazaar)

Şah Pehlevi Cad.

Hamidiye Cad.

Aşir Efendi Cad.

Cemat Nadir Cad.

S

⑦

Cadırcılar Caddesi

Taccarjame Splat.

Örducüler Caddesi

Tığcılar Sokak

Tarakçılar Caddesi

Mahmutpaşa Yok.

Tarakçı Cafer S.

CAGAL

Gerngtürk Cad.

Vezneciler Cad.

v. T. Paşa Cad.

Istanbul
University

BEYAZIT

Mahmutpaşa S.

Türkocağı Cad.

LALELİ
CAMİ

Istanbul
University

ÜNİVERSİTY

Bakıralar Cad.

Beyazıt
Cami

Yeniçeriler Caddesi

Kapalı Carsi
(Grand Bazaar)

⑥

BEYAZIT

Nuruosmaniye Cad.

Turbedar Sokak

Babıali Caddesi

Çate

Ordu Caddesi

Koska Cad.

CEMBERLITAS

Divan Yolu

Mus
of Turk
Islam

Mesih Paşa Cad.

Azimkar S.

Hayriye Tüccari Cad.

Asker Sok.

KUMKAPI

Dahbarı Yok.

Turantı Sok.

Mithat Paşa Cad.

Triyatro Cad.

Batı Paşa Yok.

Şakir Efendi

Gedikpaşa Cami Sok.

Gedikpaşa Caddesi

Piyerloti Cad.

Türkeli Caddesi

Molataşı Cad.

Jaralpel Sok.

Tavcısı Çeşmesi Sok.

Samsa Sok.

Kadırga Limani Cad.

Alışari Sok.

Tavcısı

Kaleci Sok.

Ahşakal Sok.

Kennedy Caddesi (Sahil Yolu)

Kumkapı Ist. Cad.

Cinnçi Meydanı Sok.

Arkası Sokak

Kenne

Kumkapi
Rail Station

0   1/4 mi

0   1/4 km

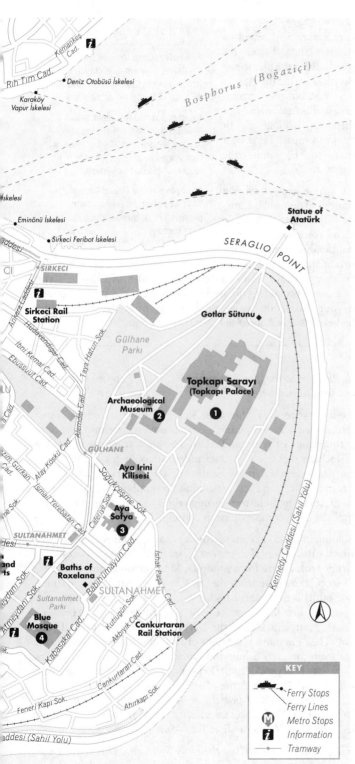

COMING ASHORE

Ships dock at Karakoy, in the shadow of the famous Galata Tower. It's possible to walk from the pier to the Sultanahmet (the historic quarter) in about 45 minutes, but the immediate and pervasive bustle of the city might be offputting (though it's not intrinsically dangerous). Taxis wait at the pier for the 10-minute ride into Sultanahmet.

We strongly advise against renting a car in Istanbul. The public transport system is also quite chaotic, so we recommend you take taxis. Once you reach Sultanahmet, many of the most important sights are all within walking distance of each other. Private tours with a guide are useful and popular. Guides will also help you shop at the Grand Bazaar. If you are looking to set up a private guided tour before your cruise, you can locate the names of licensed tour guides through the **Turkish Guides Association** (⊕*www.turkishguides.org*).

> **ISTANBUL BEST BETS**
>
> **Aya Sofya.** Once the epicenter of the Christian world, this church constructed in the 6th century is the tour de force of Byzantine architecture.
>
> **Topkapı Sarayı.** This giant palace provides a behind-the-scenes look at daily life, sultan-style, from how a concubine filled her day to where the ruler kept his stash of jewels.
>
> **Shopping at the Grand Bazaar.** Istanbul's giant bazaar has been providing retail therapy since the mid-15th century!

EXPLORING ISTANBUL

Numbers in the text correspond to numbers in the margin and on the Istanbul and Bosphorus maps.

❷ **Arkeoloji Müzesi** *(Archaeology Museum)*. Step into this vast repository of spectacular finds for a head-spinning look at the civilizations that have thrived for thousands of years in Turkey. The most stunning pieces are tombs that include the so-called Alexander Sarcophagus, carved with scenes from Alexander the Great's battles and once believed, wrongly, to be his final resting place. An excellent exhibit on Istanbul through the ages shows off artifacts from prehistory through the Byzantines and Ottomans and helps put the city's complex past in context.

Fodor'sChoice ★

Another building in the courtyard of Topkapı Sarayı houses the **Eski Şark Eserleri Müzesi** *(Museum of the Ancient Orient)*, where the mosaics, obelisks, and other artifacts are from Anatolia, Mesopotamia, and elsewhere in the Arab world, and date from the pre-Christian centuries. A particularly intricate tablet is the Treaty of Kadesh from the 13th century BC, perhaps the world's earliest known peace treaty, recording an accord between the Hittite king Hattusilis III and the Egyptian pharaoh Ramses II. The **Çinili Köşkü** *(Tiled Pavilion)* is a bright profusion of colored tiles. Inside are ceramics from the early Seljuk and Ottoman empires, as well as tiles from Iznik, the city that produced perhaps the finest ceramics in the world during the 17th and 18th centuries. ⊠ *Gülhane Park, next to Topkapı Sarayı* ☎ *212/520–7740* ✉ *$3 (total) for the 3 museums* ⊙ *Archaeology Museum Tues.–Sun. 9:30–5, ticket sales until 4:30; Museum of the Ancient Orient Tues.–Sun. 1–5; Tiled Pavilion Tues.–Sun. 9:30–noon.*

❸ **Aya Sofya** *(Hagia Sophia, Church of the Holy Wisdom)*. This soaring edifice is perhaps the greatest work of Byzantine architecture and for almost

Fodor'sChoice ★

a thousand years, starting from its completion in 537, was the world's largest and most important religious monument. Only Saint Peter's in Rome, not completed until the 17th century, surpassed Aya Sofya in size and grandeur. The Emperor Justinian commissioned the church and, in response to his dictum that Aya Sofya be the grandest place of worship ever built, craftsmen devised the magnificent dome.

Mehmet converted the church into a mosque when he took the city in 1453, and succeeding sultans added its four minarets. In the 16th century Süleyman the Magnificent ordered the church's Byzantine mosaics to be plastered over in accordance with the Islamic proscription against the portrayal of the human figure in a place of worship. The multicolor tiles that cover parts of the cavernous interior weren't rediscovered until after Atatürk made the Aya Sofya into a museum in 1936. Today, mosaics and frescoes of saints, emperors, and Christ enliven the vast space. ⊠ *Aya Sofya Sq.* ☎ *212/522–1750* ✉ *$6* ☉ *Tues.–Sun. 9–7, ticket sales until 6:30.*

❹ Blue Mosque *(Sultan Ahmet Cami).* Only after you enter the Blue Mosque do you understand why it is so named. Inside, 20,000 shimmering blue-green Iznik tiles are interspersed with 260 stained-glass windows; an airy arabesque pattern is painted on the ceiling. After the dark corners and somber faces of the Byzantine mosaics in Aya Sofya, this light-filled mosque is positively uplifting. Such a favorable comparison was the intention of architect Mehmet Aga, known as Sedefkar (Worker of Mother-of-Pearl), whose goal was to surpass Justinian's crowning achievement. At the bequest of Sultan Ahmet I (ruled 1603–17), he spent just eight years creating this masterpiece of Ottoman craftsmanship, beginning in 1609.

FodorsChoice
★

Within the mosque are the **Hünkar Kasrı** (Carpet and Kilim Museums), where rugs are treated as works of art and displayed in suitably grand settings. ⊠ *Sultanahmet Sq.* ☎ *212/518–1330 for museum information only* ✉ *Mosque free; museums $2* ☉ *Blue Mosque daily 9–5, access restricted during prayer times, particularly at midday on Fri.; museums weekdays 8:30–noon and 1–3:30.*

❻ Grand Bazaar *(Kapalı Çarşısı).* Take a deep breath and plunge into this maze of 65 winding, covered streets crammed with 4,000 tiny shops, cafés, restaurants, mosques, and courtyards. It's said that this early version of a shopping mall is the largest concentration of stores under one roof anywhere in the world, and that's easy to believe; it's also easy to believe that some of the most aggressive salesmanship in the world takes place here. Oddly enough, though, the sales pitches, the crowds, the sheer volumes of junky trinkets on offer can be hypnotizing. Originally built by Mehmet II (the Conqueror) in the 1450s, the Grand Bazaar was ravaged twice by fire in relatively recent years—once in 1954 and once in 1974. In both cases, the bazaar was quickly rebuilt into something resembling the original style, with its arched passageways and brass-and-tile fountains at regular intervals.

★

The amazingly polylingual sellers are all anxious to reassure you that you do not have to buy . . . just drink a glass of tea while you browse. A sizable share of the goods are trinkets tailored for the tourist trade, but a separate section for antiques at the very center of the bazaar, called the *bedestan,* always has some beautiful items on offer. ⊠ *Yeniçeriler Cad. and Fuatpaşa Cad.* ▣ *Free* ⊙ *Apr.–Oct., Mon.–Sat. 8:30–7; Nov.–Mar., Mon.–Sat. 8:30–6:30.*

❺ Ibrahim Paşa Sarayı *(Ibrahim Paşa Palace).* Süleyman the Magnificent commissioned the great architect Sinan to build this stone palace, the most grandiose residence in Istanbul. The palace now houses the **Türk Ve İslâm Eserleri Müzesi** (Museum of Turkish and Islamic Arts), where you can learn about the lifestyles of Turks at every level of society, from the 8th century to the present. ⊠ *Atmeydanı 46, Sultanahmet* ☎ *212/518–1385* ▣ *$2* ⊙ *Tues.–Sun. 9–4:30.*

❼ Süleymaniye Cami *(Mosque of Süleyman).* Perched on a hilltop near Istanbul
★ University, the largest mosque in Istanbul is a masterful achievement and a grand presence. This mosque houses Sinan's tomb, along with that of his patron, Süleyman the Magnificent, and the sultan's wife, Roxelana. The architectural thrill here is the enormous dome. The soaring space gives the impression that it's held up principally by divine cooperation. The complex still incorporates a hospital, a kervansaray (roadside inn), a kitchen, several schools, and other charitable institutions that mosques traditionally operate. ⊠ *Süleymaniye Cad., near Istanbul University's north gate* ⊙ *Daily dawn–dusk.*

❶ Topkapı Sarayı *(Topkapı Palace).* This vast palace on Seraglio Point, above
Fodor'sChoice the confluence of the Bosphorus and the Golden Horn, was the residence
★ of sultans as well as the seat of Ottoman rule from the 1450s until the middle of the 19th century. Few other royal residences can match this hilltop compound when it comes to the lavishly exotic intricacies of court life.

Sultan Mehmet II built the original Topkapı Palace in the 1450s, shortly after his conquest of Constantinople. Over the centuries sultan after sultan expanded the palace until some 5,000 full-time residents lived here, including slaves, concubines, and eunuchs. Topkapı was finally abandoned in 1853 when Sultan Abdül Mecit I moved his court to the palace at Dolmabahçe on the Bosphorus.

The main entrance, or Imperial Gate, leads to the **Court of the Janissaries,** also known as the First Courtyard, today converted into a parking lot. You will begin to experience the grandeur of the palace when you pass through **Bab-ı-Selam** (Gate of Salutation).

The **Second Courtyard** is filled with a series of ornate *köşks,* pavilions once used for the business of state. To one side are the palace's kitchens, where more than 1,000 cooks once toiled at the rows of immense ovens to feed the palace residents, whose numbers sometimes swelled to 15,000 during special occasions. The space now displays one of the world's best collections of porcelain, much of it amassed over years of Ottoman rule as powers from China, Persia, and Europe bestowed gifts on the sultans; the thousands of Ming blue-and-white pieces were made to order for the palace in the 18th century. Straight ahead is the **Divan-ı-Humayun** (Assembly Room of the Council of State), once presided over by the grand vizier. The sultan would sit behind a latticed window here, hidden by a curtain, so no one would know when he was listening.

The **Harem,** a maze of 400 halls, terraces, rooms, wings, and apartments grouped around the sultan's private quarters, evokes all the exoticism and mysterious ways of the Ottoman Empire. The first Harem compound housed about 200 lesser concubines and the palace eunuchs. As you move into the Harem, the rooms become larger and more opulent. The chief wives of the sultan lived in private apartments around a shared courtyard. Beyond are the lavish apartments of the *valide* sultan (queen mother), the absolute ruler of the Harem, and finally, the sultan's private rooms—a riot of brocades, murals, colored marble, wildly ornate furniture, gold leaf, and fine carving.

Beyond the Harem, access was restricted to the **Third Courtyard,** in part because it housed the **Treasury,** filled with imperial thrones, lavish gifts bestowed to sultans, and the spoils of war. Two uncut emeralds, each weighing about 8 pounds(!), once hung from the ceiling, but are now displayed behind glass. Other pavilions show off a curious assortment of treasures—Turkish and Persian miniatures; relics of the prophet Muhammad (including hair from his beard); and sultans' robes.

The **Fourth Courtyard** was the private realm of the sultan, and the small, elegant pavilions, mosques, fountains, and reflecting pools are scattered amid the gardens that overlook the Bosphorus and Golden Horn. In the **Iftariye** (Golden Cage), also known as the Sofa Köşkü, the closest relatives of the reigning sultan lived in strict confinement under what amounted to house arrest—superseding an older practice of murdering all possible rivals to the throne. ⊠ *Topkapı Sarayı, Gülhane Park, near Sultanahmet Sq.* ☎ *212/512–0480* ⊕ *www.topkapisarayi.gov.tr* ⊠ *$6 for the palace plus another $6 for the Harem tour* ☉ *Palace Wed.–Mon. 9–7 in summer and 9–5 in winter for the palace itself. Harem Wed.–Mon. 9:30–3:30 year-round.*

SHOPPING

Istanbul has been a shopper's town for, well, centuries—the sprawling Grand Bazaar could easily be called the world's oldest shopping mall—but this is not to say that the city is stuck in the past. Along with its colorful bazaars and outdoor markets, Istanbul also has a wide range of modern options. Whether you're looking for trinkets and souvenirs, kilims and carpets, brass and silverware, leather goods, old books, prints and maps, or furnishings and clothes (Turkish textiles are among the best in the world), you can find them here. **Nuruosmaniye Caddesi,** one of the major streets leading to the Grand Bazaar, is lined with some of Istanbul's most stylish shops, with an emphasis on fine carpets, jewelry, and antiques.

★ **The Arasta Bazaar** (⊠*Sultanahmet*) is one of few markets open on Sunday; you can get a lot of the same items here as at the Grand Bazaar, but the atmosphere is much calmer.

★ **The Egyptian Bazaar** (⊠*Eminönü*) is definitely worth seeing. Also known as the Spice Market, it has stall after enticing stall filled with mounds of exotic spices and dried fruits. **Sahaflar Çarşışı** (⊠*Grand Bazaar*), just outside the western end of the Grand Bazaar, is home to a bustling book market, with old and new editions; most are in Turkish, but English is represented, too. The market is open daily, though Sunday has the most vendors.

WHERE TO EAT

¢–$ ✕**Konuk Evi.** A little oasis near Aya Sofya, this restaurant has an outdoor patio with wicker chairs, all shaded by leafy trees. The small menu is comprised of pastas, salads, and grilled meats, as well as an assortment of cakes and Turkish milk puddings. ⊠*Sogukçeşme Sok., Sultanahmet* ☎*212/513–3660* ▭*AE, MC, V.*

¢ ✕**Doy-Doy.** Unlike many other spots in tourist-filled Sultanahmet, this is a place where locals come to fill up (*doy-doy* is a Turkish expression for "full"). The restaurant serves simple kebabs, chicken and lamb stews, and *pide* (Turkish pizza) baked in a wood-burning oven. A variety of mezes are also available. Service is friendly, and the prices are clearly stated in the menu. A pleasant rooftop terrace is open in the summer. ⊠*Şifa Hamamı Sok. 13, Sultanahmet* ☎*212/517–1588* ▭*V.*

KATAKOLON, GREECE (FOR OLYMPIA)

Katakolon could not seem less of a cruise port if it tried. A tiny enclave clinging to the western Peloponnese coast, it's a sleepy place except when ships dock. But it's a popular cruise destination because of its proximity to Olympia. Ancient Olympia was one of the most important cities in classical Greece. The Sanctuary of Zeus was the raison d'être of the city and attracted pilgrims from around the eastern Mediterranean, and later the city played host to Olympic Games, the original athletic games that were the inspiration for today's modern sporting pan-planetary meet. At the foot of the tree-covered Kronion hill, in a valley near two rivers, Katakolon is today one of the most popular ancient sites in Greece. If you don't want to make the trip to Olympia, then Katakolon is an ideal place for a leisurely Greek lunch while you watch the fishermen mend their nets, but there's just not much else to do there.

ESSENTIALS

CURRENCY The euro (€1 to US$1.46 at this writing). U.S. currency is generally not accepted in Europe, but ATMs are common.

HOURS Stores are generally open from 9 to 9 on weekdays and 9 to 6 on Saturday. Museums are generally open from 9 to 5, but many are closed on Monday.

TELEPHONES Tri-band GSM phones work in Greece. You can buy prepaid phone cards at telecom shops, news-vendors, and tobacconists in all towns and cities. Phone cards can be used for local or international calls. Vodafone is the leading mobile telecom company. OTE is the national domestic provider. Calls can be made at OTE offices and paid for after completion.

COMING ASHORE

Katakolon is a very small port. Ships dock at the jetty, from where it is a short walk (five minutes) into Katakolon town. It's a small Greek town with a lot of character; most residents still make their living from fishing; a few restaurants are along waterfront as well as shops selling souvenirs to cruise-ship passengers. There are no passenger facilities at the

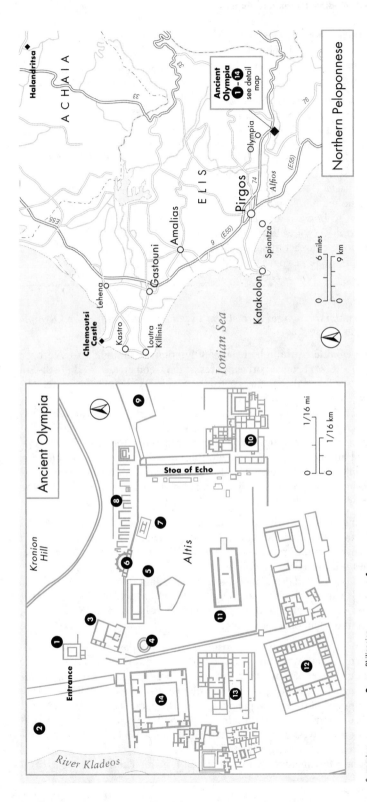

Northern Peloponnese

Ancient Olympia

Gymnasion	2
Heraion	5
House of Nero	10
Leonidaion	12
Metroon	7
Nymphaion	6
Palaestra	14
Pheidias's workshop	13
Philippeion	4
Prytaneion	3
Roman bath	1
Stadium	9
Temple of Zeus	11
Treasuries	8

5

jetty itself. Though there are refreshment stands, telephones, currency-exchange offices, and an ATM in the town.

Taxis are available at the dock to meet ships. However, cabs charge an overinflated fixed fare for the journey to Olympia, so it's often better to go on a ship-sponsored excursion. Displas Dionysios runs **Katakolon Car Rental** (☎*26210/41727*) but has a limited number of vehicles, so it's vital to book in advance if you want to drive yourself to Olympia. Prices for a compact manual vehicle are approx €50 per day.

> ### OLYMPIA BEST BETS
>
> **The Twelve Labors of Hercules.**
> This series now in the archaeological museum is regarded as a high point in classical Greek sculpture.
>
> **Statue of Hermes by Praxiteles.**
> Also in the museum, this is one of the most complete classical statues to have been unearthed.
>
> **Remains of the Temple of Zeus.**
> The abovementioned treasures once adorned this vast temple, which was one of the largest and finest in ancient Greece. Today only the platform remains.

EXPLORING OLYMPIA

Numbers in the margin correspond to points of interest on the Olympia map.

Ancient Olympia. Although the first Olympiad is thought to have been held in 776 BC, bronze votive figures of the Geometric period (10th–8th century BC) reveal that the sanctuary was in use before that date. The festival took place every four years over a five-day period in the late summer during a sacred truce, observed by all Greek cities. Initially only native speakers of Greek (excepting slaves) could compete, but Romans were later admitted. The events included the footrace, boxing, chariot and horse racing, the pentathlon (combining running, jumping, wrestling, and both javelin and discus throwing), and the *pankration* (a no-holds-barred style of wrestling in which competitors could break their opponent's fingers and other body parts).

The long decline of Olympia began after the reign of Hadrian. In AD 267, under threat of an invasion, many buildings were dismantled to construct a defensive wall; Christian decrees forbade the functioning of pagan sanctuaries and caused the demolition of the Altis. The Roman emperor Theodosius I, a Christian, banned the games, calling them "pagan rites," in AD 393. Earthquakes settled the fate of Olympia, and the flooding of the Alpheios and the Kladeos, together with landslides off the Kronion hill, buried the abandoned sanctuary.

Olympia's ruins are fairly compact, occupying a flat area at the base of the Kronion hill where the Kladeos and Alpheios rivers join. It's easy to get a quick overview and then investigate specific buildings or head to the museum. The site is very pleasant, with plenty of trees providing shade. It is comprised of the sacred precinct, or **Altis**, a large rectangular enclosure south of the Kronion, with **administrative buildings, baths, and workshops** on the west and south and the **Stadium** and **Hippodrome** on the east. In 1829, a French expedition investigated the Temple of Zeus and brought a few metope fragments to the Louvre. The systematic excavation begun by the German Archaeological Institute in 1875 has continued intermittently to this day.

1 South of the entrance are the remains of a small **Roman bath.**

2 The **Gymnasion,** essentially a large, open practice field surrounded by stoas.

3 The large complex opposite the Gymnasion was the **Prytaneion,** where the *prytaneis* (magistrates in charge of the games) feted the winners and where the Olympic flame burned on a sacred hearth. South is the gateway to the Altis, marked by two sets of four columns.

4 Beyond is the **Philippeion,** a circular shrine started by Philip II and completed after his death by Alexander the Great.

5 Directly in front of the Philippeion is the large Doric temple of Hera, the **Heraion** (circa 600 BC). It is well preserved, especially considering that it is constructed from the local coarse, porous shell limestone. At first it had wooden columns, which were replaced as needed, so although they are all Doric, the capitals don't exactly match. Three of the columns, which had fallen, have been set back up. A colossal head of a goddess, possibly from the statue of Hera, was found at the temple and is now in the site museum.

6 There is no doubt about the location of the **Nymphaion,** or Exedra, which brought water to Olympia from a spring to the east. A colonnade around the semicircular reservoir had statues of the family of Herodes Atticus and his imperial patrons.

7 The 4th-century **Metroon,** at the bottom of the Nymphaion terrace, was originally dedicated to Cybele, Mother of the Gods, and was taken over by the Roman imperial cult. Nearby, at the bottom of the steps leading to the Treasuries and outside the entrance of the Stadium, were **16 bronze statues of Zeus,** called the Zanes, bought with money from fines levied against those caught cheating at the games. Bribery seems to have been the most common offense (steroids not being available).

8 On the terrace itself are the city-state **Treasuries,** which look like small temples and were used to store valuables, such as equipment used in rituals.

9 Just off the northeast corner of the Altis is the **Stadium,** which at first ran along the terrace of the Treasuries and had no embankments for the spectators to sit on; embankments were added later but were never given seats, and 40,000–50,000 spectators could be accommodated. The starting and finishing lines are still in place, 600 Olympic feet (about 630 feet) apart.

10 The **House of Nero,** a 1st-century villa off the southeastern corner of the Altis, was hurriedly built for his visit.

11 In the southwestern corner of the Altis is the **Temple of Zeus.** Only a few column drums are in place, but the huge size of the temple platform is impressive. Designed by Libon, an Elean architect, it was built from about 470 to 456 BC. The magnificent sculptures from the pediments are on view in the site's museum. A gilded bronze statue of Nike (the winged goddess of Victory) stood above the east pediment, matching a marble Nike (in the site museum) that stood on a pedestal in front of the temple. Both

Eastern Mediterranean and Aegean

were the work of the sculptor Paionios. The cult statue inside the temple, made of gold and ivory, showed Zeus seated on a throne, holding a Nike in his open right hand and a scepter in his left. It was created in 430 BC by Pheidias, sculptor of the statue of Athena in the Parthenon, and was said to be seven times life size; the statue was one of the Seven Wonders of the Ancient World. It is said that Caligula wanted to move the statue to Rome in the 1st century AD and to replace the head with one of his own, but the statue laughed out loud when his men approached it. It was removed to Constantinople, where it was destroyed by fire in AD 475. Pausanias relates that behind the statue there was "a woolen curtain . . . decorated by Assyrian weavers and dyed with Phoenician crimson, dedicated by Antiochos." It is possible this was the veil of the Temple at Jerusalem (Antiochos IV Epiphanes forcibly converted the Temple to the worship of Zeus Olympias in the 2nd century BC).

(12) Outside the gate at the southwestern corner of the Altis stood the **Leonidaion,** at first a guesthouse for important visitors and later a residence of the Roman governor of the province of Achaea.

(13) Immediately north of the Leonidaion was **Pheidias's workshop,** where the cult statue of Zeus was constructed in a large hall of the same size and orientation as the interior of the temple. Tools, clay molds, and Pheidias's own cup (in the site museum) make the identification of this building certain. It was later used as a Byzantine church.

(14) North of Pheidas's workshop is the **Palaestra,** built in the 3rd century BC, for athletic training. The rooms around the square field were used for bathing and cleansing with oil, for teaching, and for socializing. ⊠ *Off Ethnikos Odos 74, ½ km (¼ mi) outside modern Olympia* ☎*26240/22517* ⊕*www.culture.gr* ✉*€6, combined ticket with Archaeological Museum €9* ⊗*May–Oct., daily 8–7; Nov.–Apr., daily 8:30–5.*

Archaeological Museum at Olympia. Located in a handsome glass and marble pavilion at the edge of the ancient site, this museum has in its magnificent collections the sculptures from the Temple of Zeus and the Hermes of Praxiteles, discovered in the Temple of Hera in the place noted by Pausanias. The central gallery of the museum holds one of the greatest sculptural achievements of classical antiquity: the pedimental sculptures and metopes from the Temple of Zeus, depicting Hercules's Twelve Labors. The Hermes was buried under the fallen clay of the temple's upper walls and is one of the best-preserved classical statues. Also on display is the famous Nike of Paionios. Other treasures include notable terra-cottas of Zeus and Ganymede; the head of the cult statue of Hera; sculptures of the family and imperial patrons of Herodes Atticus; and bronzes found at the site, including votive figurines, cauldrons, and armor. Of great historic interest are a helmet dedicated by Miltiades, the Athenian general who defeated the Persians at Marathon, and a cup owned by the sculptor Pheidias. ⊠*Off Ethnikos Odos 74, north of Ancient Olympia site* ☎*26240/22742* ⊕*www.culture.gr* ✉*€6, combined ticket with Ancient Olympia €9* ⊗*May–Oct., Mon. 11–7, Tues.–Sun. 8–7; Nov.–Apr., Mon. 10:30–5, Tues.–Sun. 8:30–3.*

Museum of the Olympic Games. This museum is just about the only tourist attraction in modern Olympia. The collection of medals and other memorabilia of the contemporary games is of some, if not great, interest. ✉*Spiliopoulou* ☎26240/22544 💶€2 ⊙ *Weekdays 8–3:30, weekends 9–2:30.*

SHOPPING

Lovers of handicrafts will really enjoy shopping in Greece. There's an abundance of ceramics, both traditional and modern, wooden bowls, reproductions of ancient statuary, woven rugs, jewelry, lace, and edibles such as delicious honey and olive oil. Cotton clothing is perfect for the summer temperatures along with strong handcrafted sandals and leather goods that have always been popular purchases here. Around Olympus another popular souvenir are reproductions of ancient artifacts found at the ancient site. Shop in modern Olympia or in Katakalon before reboarding your ship. There are just a few shops in Kalakon, but they sell a full range of souvenirs.

★ The **Archaeological Museum Shop** (✉*Off Ethnikos Odos 74, north of Ancient Olympia site* ☎26240/22742) carries an appealing line of figurines, bronzes, votives, and other replicas of objects found in the ruins.

★ At **Atelier Exekias** (✉*Kondoli, Olympia* ☎6936/314054) Sakis Doylas sells exquisite, handmade and hand-painted ceramic bowls and urns, fashioned after finds in Ancient Olympia; the glazes and colors are beautiful.

WHERE TO EAT

¢ ✕**Aegean.** Don't let the garish signs depicting menu offerings put you off: the far-ranging offerings are excellent. You can eat lightly on a gyro or pizza, but venture into some of the more serious fare, especially such local dishes as fish, oven-baked with onion, garlic, green peppers, and parsley. The house's barrel wine is a nice accompaniment to any meal. ✉*Douma, near Hotel New Olympia, Olympia* ☎26240/22540 ▭MC, V.

¢ ✕**Zeus.** A seat on the attractive terrace gives you a nice view of the comings and going through the center of town. Offerings are straightforward Greek fare, but nicely prepared. ✉*Praxitelous Kondili, near Commercial Bank, Olympia* ☎26240/23913 ▭MC, V ⊙*Closed Nov.–Mar.*

KORČULA, CROATIA

Southern Dalmatia's largest, most sophisticated, and most visited island, Korcula was known to the ancient Greeks, who named it *Kerkyra Melaina,* or "Black Corfu." Between the 10th and 18th centuries it spent several periods under Venetian rule. Today, most Croatians know it for its traditional sword dances and its excellent white wines. Korčula is also the name of the capital, which is near the island's eastern tip. Eight centuries under Venetian rule bequeathed the town a treasure trove of Gothic and Renaissance churches, palaces, and piazzas, all built from fine local stone. Korčula's main claim to fame, though one still disputed by historians, is that it was the birthplace of Marco Polo (1254–1324). The approach by sea is breathtaking; if the hour isn't too early, make sure you're on deck for this one.

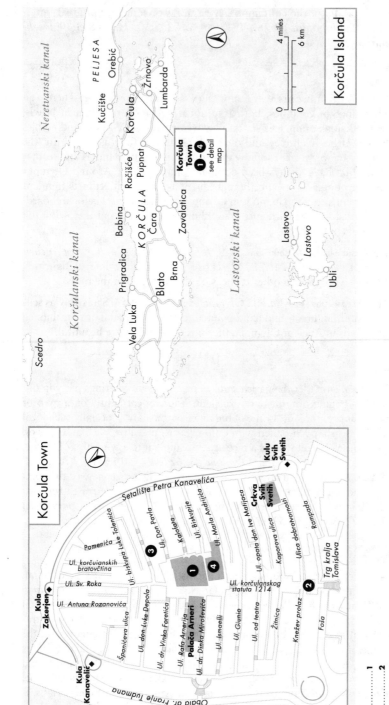

Korčula Island

PELJEŠA

Neretvanski kanal

Kučište
Orebić

Korčula
Žrnovo
Lumbarda

Račišće

Pupnat

KORČULA

Babina

Čara

Zavalatica

Korčula Town
❶–❹
see detail map

Korčulanski kanal

Prigradica

Blato

Brna

Vela Luka

Lastovski kanal

Lastovo

Lastovo

Ublí

Ščedro

0   4 miles
0   6 km

Korčula Town

Kula Zakerjan ◆

Kula Kanavelić ◆

Kulu Svih Svetih ◆

Šetalište Petra Kanavelića

Pomenića

Ul. biskupa Luke Tolenića

Ul. Don Pavla

Kaldala

Ul. Biskupije

Ul. korčuianskih bratovčtina

Ul. Marka Andrijića

❸

Crkva Svih Svetih

Ul. Sv. Roka

❶

❹

Ul. opata don Ive Matijaca

Ul. Antuna Rozanovića

Ul. korčulanskog statuta 1214

Kaporova ulica

Ulica dobrovornosti

Rampada

Španićeva ulica

Ul. don Luke Depola

Ul. dr. Vinka Foretića

Ul. Rafa Arnerii
Palača Arneri

Ul. dr. Dinka Miroševića

Ul. Ismaelli

Ul. Giunia

Ul. od teatra

Žitnica

Knežev prolaz

Foša

Trg kralja Tomislava

❷

Obala dr. Frane Tuđmana

Katedrala 1
Kopnena Vrata 2
Kuća Marca Pola 3
Opatska Riznica 4

ESSENTIALS

CURRENCY The Croatian kuna (5.3 Kn to US$1 at this writing). U.S. dollars are not generally accepted in Croatia, so you will need some local currency. ATMs are easy to find, and it is also possible to exchange currency in banks and also in most local travel agencies. Credit cards are accepted at many restaurants and shops.

HOURS Offices are open weekdays from 8:30 to 4. Shops often close for lunch around 1 and may close for as long as three hours; banks also sometimes close for lunch. Post offices are open on Saturday during the main summer season, from June through September.

INTERNET During the summer, small temporary Internet cafés spring up in all the seaside resort towns. However, many are nothing more than a regular café with a PC in the corner.

TELEPHONES Most tri- and quad-band GSM phones will work in Croatia. Public phones use calling cards, which can be purchased at the post office, newsstands, and hotels. Major mobile phone companies include TMobile and VIPNet.

COMING ASHORE

Smaller ships may be able to dock at two cruise-ship docks in Korcular Town, but larger vessels will have to anchor and tender passengers ashore at the same dock. The dock area is lined with stores, cafés, and tourism offices. If you are staying in town, then there's no advantage to having a car for your day in port. If you'd like to explore the island, then you can rent a car, scooter, or even bicycle. Expect to pay about €55 per day for a compact manual vehicle. Guided tours can also be arranged, including visits to local vineyards.

KORČULA BEST BETS

Search for Marco Polo. The explorer's purported birthplace is right in the Old Town.

Sip some wine. Korcula is a major wine-producing region in Dalmatia; have a glass or buy a bottle of one of the local vintages.

Watch the Dance of the Moors. If your ship remains in port on one of the nights the island's famous dance is offered, this is a must-do.

EXPLORING KORČULA TOWN

At first view, Korčula may seem like a much smaller version of Dubrovnik: the same high walls, the circular corner fortresses, and the church tower projecting from within an expanse of red roofs. The main difference lies in the town plan, as narrow side streets run off the main thoroughfare at odd angles to form a herring-bone pattern, preventing cold winter winds from whistling unimpeded through town. The center is small and compact and can be explored in an hour.

❶ **Katedrala** *(Cathedral)*. On the main square, the splendid Gothic-Renaissance cathedral is built from a wheat-color stone that turns pale gold in sunlight, amber at sunset. Enter through the beautifully carved Romanesque main portal, which is guarded by Adam and Eve standing upon twin lions. Inside, check out the elegant 15th-century ciborium; within, two paintings are attributed to the Venetian master Tintoretto. ⊠*Trg Sv Marka* 10 Kn ☉*May–Oct., daily 9–2 and 5–8; Nov.–Apr., by appointment.*

❷ **Kopnena Vrata** *(Land Gate).* The main entrance into the Old Town is topped by the 15th-century Revelin Tower, housing an exhibition connected with the *Moreska* sword dance, and offering panoramic views over the Old Town. ⊠*Kopnena Vrata* 🖾*10 Kn* ⊗*July and Aug., daily 9–9; May, June, Sept., and Oct., daily 9–7; Nov.–Apr., by appointment only.*

❸ **Kuca Marca Pola** *(Marco Polo House).* A couple of blocks east of the main square is the place where the legendary 13th-century discoverer is said to have been born, when Korčula was part of the Venetian Empire. At present only the tower is open, with a modest exhibition about Polo's life on the first floor, and a belvedere up top offering panoramic views. There were plans at this writing to restore the entire house and garden to form an educational museum before the end of 2007. ⊠*Ul Marka Pola* 🖾*10 Kn* ⊗*July and Aug., daily 9–9; May, June, Sept., and Oct., daily 9–7; Nov.–Apr., by appointment only.*

❹ **Opatska Riznica** *(Abbot's Treasury).* Next to the cathedral, the treasury museum occupies the 17th-century Renaissance Bishop's palace. This collection of sacral art includes Italian and Croatian Renaissance paintings, the most precious being a 15th-centruy triptych, *Our Lady with Saints,* by the Dalmatian master Blaz Jurjev Trogiranin, plus gold and silver ecclesiastical artifacts and ceremonial vestments. ⊠*Trg Sv Marka* 🖾*10 Kn* ⊗*May–Oct., daily 9–2 and 5–8; Nov.–Apr., by appointment only.*

SHOPPING

Cukarin (⊠*Hrvatska Bratske Zajednice* ☎*020/711–055*), is a family-run store renowned for its four different types of delicious handmade biscuits, as well as homemade *rakija* (fruit brandy) flavored with local herbs.

SPORTS & ACTIVITIES

DIVING

MM Sub (⊠*Lumbarda* ☎*020/712–288* ⊕*www.mm-sub.hr*) is a diving center based in Lumbarda offering diving instruction and trips for those with some experience. Nearby diving destinations include an underwater archaeological site, as well as several sea caves and shipwrecks.

MOREŠKA DANCES

The Moreška is a colorful sword dance originally performed each year on July 29 (the feast day of the town's protector, St. Theodore). Now it's performed at 9 PM each Monday and Thursday evening from May to October just outside the city walls, next to the Kopnena Vrata (Land Gate). The word *Moreška* means "Moorish." The dance is said to celebrate the victory of the Christians over the Moors in Spain, but the dance's real roots are conjecture. The dance itself is not native to Croatia and was performed in many different mediterranean countries, including Spain, Italy, and Malta. The story of the dance is a clash between the Black (Moorish) king and the White (Christian) king over a young maiden. The dance is done with real swords.

SAILING

The 159-berth **ACI marina** (⊠*Korcula* ☎*020/711–661*) remains open all year.

WINE TASTING

Atlas Travel Agency (✉ *Trg 19 Travanja* ☎ *020/711–060* ⊕ *www.atlas-croatia.com*) organizes one-day wine tours of either Korčula Island or the Pelješac Peninsula, combining visits to the vineyards, wine tasting, and lunch in a typical Dalmatian *konoba* (pub). Transfers to and from Korčula Town by bus is included.

BEACHES

The closest spot for a quick swim is Banje, a small pebble beach about 10 minutes by foot east of the town walls, close to Hotel Liburnija. For more leisurely bathing, the best beaches lie near the village of **Lumbarda**, which is 6 km (4 mi) southeast of Korčula Town. The most popular of these is the sandy south-facing Przina, 2 km (1 mi) south of Lumbarda, while the smooth-white-stoned Bili Žal lies a short distance east of Lumbarda. If you don't like the local beach options, rent a speed boat from **Rent-a-Djir** (✉ *Obala Hrvatskih Mornara* ☎ *020/715–120* ⊕ *www.korcula-rent.com*) and take to the open sea to explore the tiny scattered islets of the nearby Korčula archipelago, which has many secluded bays for swimming.

WHERE TO EAT

¢–$ ✗ **Adio Mare.** A longstanding favorite with locals and visitors alike, Adio Mare occupies a Gothic-Renaissance building in the Old Town, close to Kuca Marca Pola. There's a high-ceiling dining room as well as an open-plan kitchen so you can watch the cooks while they work. The menu has not changed since the restaurant opened in 1974: expect Dalmatian classics such as *pasta-fažol* (beans with pasta) and *pašticada* (beef stewed in wine and prunes), as well as fresh fish and seafood. The local wine, *pošip*, is excellent. ✉ *Ul Marka Pola* ☎ *020/711–253* ▭ *AE, DC, MC, V* ☾ *Closed Nov.–Mar. No lunch.*

Fodor'sChoice ★

¢ ✗ **Planjak.** This down-to-earth eatery harks back to the former Socialist era. Expect hearty Balkan home cooking such as *sarma* (cabbage leaves stuffed with rice and meat) and *gulas* (goulash). Locals tend to sit inside, while visitors eat out on the terrace. You'll find it on a small piazza, one block back from the ferry landing station. It's open year-round. ✉ *Plokata 19 Travanja 1914* ☎ *020/711–015* ▭ *AE, DC, MC, V.*

KUŞADASI, TURKEY (FOR EPHESUS)

The central and southern Aegean is probably the most developed area of Turkey, and the rolling hills, mountains surrounded by clear blue seas, and glorious white-sand beaches are just a few of the reasons why. Wandering through historic ruins, boating, scuba diving, basking in the Anatolian sun, and eating fresh fish are just some of the ways you can fill your day. Kuşadasi itself is the most developed resort along the coast. Surrounding the tiny, atmospheric Old Town, a brash, very touristy development replete with tacky pubs and fish-and-chips restaurants has mushroomed in the last 20 years. On a positive note, Kuşadası is the stepping stone to some of Turkey's most important ancient sites, including Ephesus and the early Christian site of Meryemana. Kuşadası also offers excellent shopping in high-class goods.

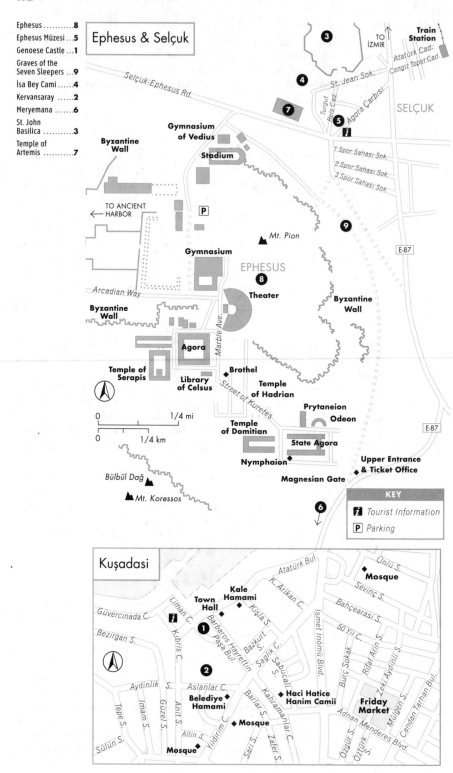

Ephesus & Selçuk

- Selçuk-Ephesus Rd.
- TO İZMIR
- Train Station
- Atatürk Cad.
- Cengiz Topel Cad.
- SELÇUK
- St. Jean Sok.
- Turgut Reis Cad.
- Agora Çarbısı
- i
- 1. Spor Sahası Sok.
- 2. Spor Sahası Sok.
- 3. Spor Sahası Sok.
- Byzantine Wall
- Gymnasium of Vedius
- Stadium
- TO ANCIENT HARBOR
- P
- Mt. Pion
- Gymnasium
- EPHESUS
- Theater
- Byzantine Wall
- E-87
- Arcadian Way
- Byzantine Wall
- Marble Ave.
- Agora
- Temple of Serapis
- Brothel
- Library of Celsus
- Temple of Hadrian
- Street of Kuretes
- Temple of Domitian
- Nymphaion
- Prytaneion
- Odeon
- State Agora
- Magnesian Gate
- Upper Entrance & Ticket Office
- E-87
- 0 ___ 1/4 mi
- 0 ___ 1/4 km
- Bülbül Dağ
- Mt. Koressos

KEY
- i Tourist Information
- P Parking

Kuşadasi

- Atatürk Bul.
- Ünlü S.
- Mosque
- Kale Hamami
- K. Arikan C.
- Sevinç S.
- Town Hall
- i
- Kişla S.
- Bahçearasi S.
- Güvercinada C.
- Liman C.
- Barbaros Hayrettin Paşa Bul.
- Bazkurt S.
- İsmet İnönü Blvd.
- 50 Yil C.
- Bezirgan S.
- Kibris C.
- Saglik C.
- Sabucali S.
- Burç Sokak
- Rifat Atin S.
- Zeki Aydinli S.
- Aydinlik S.
- Aslanlar C.
- Kahramanlar C.
- Friday Market
- Milgen S.
- Candan Tarhan Bul.
- Belediye Hamami
- Barlar S.
- Haci Hatice Hanim Camii
- Adnan Menderes Blvd.
- Tepe S.
- Imam S.
- Güzel S.
- Anit S.
- Yildirim C.
- Mosque
- Sari S.
- Zafer S.
- Özgür S.
- Öztürk S.
- Altin S.
- Sülün S.
- Mosque

ESSENTIALS

CURRENCY The New Turkish Lira (YTL1.29 to US$1; YTL1.76 to €1 at this writing). U.S. dollars are accepted in shops and in some restaurants. ATMs and currency exchange kiosks are common.

HOURS Most shops are open daily from 9 until 9. Attractions are open daily from 8 to 5 or 6, though some are closed on Mondays.

INTERNET You can check your email at the **Red and White Steak House** (✉ *Mumcu Sok 2, Kahramanlar Cad, Kuşadası* ☎ *256/612–1827*).

KUŞADASI BEST BETS

Kuretes Street, Ephesus. Follow in the footsteps of millions of Roman citizens and celebrity visitors including St. Paul of Tarsus.

The Terrace House, Ephesus. Venture inside this house to catch a glimpse of high-class interior design, circa the 2nd century AD.

Ephesus Museum, Selçuk. Monumental archaeological treasures vie with personal items for prize of best artifact.

TELEPHONES Most tri- and quad-band GSM phones will work in Turkey, but the Turkish mobile system is not 3G-compatible and handsets are single band. Public phones accept tokens or telephone cards, phones accepting cards will also accept credit cards in payment for calls. Tokens and cards can be purchased at newsstands and telepcom shops. Turk Telekom, Turkcell, and Telcim are the major telecom companies.

COMING ASHORE

Boats dock at the Ephesus town port. There is a new passenger cruise terminal, Scala Nuova, with international shops such as Body Shop, plus a Starbucks and a Burger King. There is also a duty-free shop for reboarding passengers. From the dock, it's a short walk of a few minutes to the port gate and into the town directly beyond, with immediate access to taxis, car rental offices, shops, and restaurants.

The public bus service from Kaşadasi to the site at Ephesus and into Selçuk (the town near to Ephesus) is cheap and quick. *Dolmuş* (15-seat minivans) are the bulk of the fleet, and they depart from the bus terminus at Süeyman Demirel Boulevard, a 20-minute walk from the port. There are several services every hour except in mid-afternoon when services drop to a couple per hour. Journey time is around 15 minutes. Most services stop at the end of the entry road to the archaeological site, leaving passengers with a 10-minute walk to the site entrance.

Taxis are plentiful, and they are metered with prices fixed by the municipality. Check that the meter is set to the day (lower) tariff. There are also numerous tour companies who can provide day tours to surrounding attractions. You can make these arrangements in travel agencies in Kuşadası.

Renting a car would allow you to have a full day of sightseeing and to tailor a schedule to your own desires. Car rental companies are plentiful. Car rental is approximately $67 per day for a compact manual vehicle. You will be quoted a rate in dollars and can pay in dollars.

EXPLORING KUŞADASI, SELÇUK & EPHESUS

KUŞADASI

Numbers in the margin correspond to points of interest on the Kuşadası map.

One of the most popular resort towns in the southern Aegean, Kuşadası is an ideal base, geographically, from which to explore the surrounding area. Unfortunately, being popular isn't always easy, and Kuşadası long ago lost its local charm. The huge yacht marina, the largest in the region, has only exacerbated the situation. What was a small fishing village up until the 1970s is now a sprawling, hyperactive town packed with curio shops and a year-round population of around 60,000, which swells several times over in summer with the influx of tourists and Turks with vacation homes.

❶ **Genoese Castle.** There aren't many sights in Kuşadası proper, but the causeway off Kadınlar Denizi, just south of the harbor, connects the town to an old on Güvercin Adası (Pigeon Island). Today the site of a popular disco and several teahouses with gardens and sea views, the fortress there was home to three Turkish brothers in the 16th century. These infamous pirates—Barbarossa, Oruc, and Hayrettin—pillaged the coasts of Spain and Italy and sold passengers and crews from captured ships into slavery in Algiers and Constantinople. Rather than fight them, Süleyman the Magnificent (ruled 1520–66) hired Hayrettin as his grand admiral and set him loose on enemies in the Mediterranean. The strategy worked: Hayrettin won victory after victory and was heaped with honors and riches.

❷ **Kervansaray.** Kuşadası's 300-year-old inn, now the Club Kervansaray, is loaded with Ottoman atmosphere. Its public areas are worth a look even if you're not staying here. And there's a good carpet shop here (⇨below). ⊠*Atatürk Bul. 1.*

SELÇUK

20 km (12 mi) northeast of Kuşadası on Rte. 515.

Selçuk, the closest city to the archaelogical site of Ephesus, lies beneath an ancient fortress and is, unfortunately, often overlooked. The former farming town has interesting sights of its own to offer—St. John the Evangelist was purportedly buried here, and the city has one of the oldest mosques in Turkey.

❺ **Ephesus Müzesi.** The small Ephesus Museum has one of the best collections ★ of Roman and Greek artifacts found anywhere in Turkey. Along with some fine frescoes and mosaics are two white statues of Artemis. In each she is portrayed with several rows of what are alternatively described as breasts or a belt of eggs; in either case, they symbolize fertility. ⊠*Agora Çarsısı, opposite visitor center* ☎232/892–6010 ⊠$2 ⊗*Daily 8:30– noon and 1–7.*

❹ **Isa Bey Cami.** One of the oldest mosques in Turkey dates from 1375. Its jumble of architectural styles suggests a transition between Seljuk and Ottoman design: Like later Ottoman mosques, this one has a courtyard, something not found in Seljuk mosques. The structure is built out of "borrowed" stone: marble blocks with Latin inscriptions, Corinthian columns, black-granite columns from the baths at Ephesus, and pieces from the altar of the Temple of Artemis. ⊠*St. Jean Sok.* ☉*Daily 9–6.*

6 **Meryemana.** The House of the Virgin Mary is becoming an increasingly popular pilgrimage for Catholics. The site received a papal visit in November 2006. A small church was built above a leafy gully on what had been the site of an ancient house believed by many to have been the place where St. John took the mother of Jesus after the crucifixion and from which she ascended to heaven. ⊠*Off Rte. E87, 5 km (3 mi) south of Ephesus* ☉*Daily 7:30–sunset.*

3 **St. John Basilica.** The emperor Justinian built this church over a 2nd-century tomb on Ayasoluk Hill, believed by many to have once held the body of St. John the Evangelist. Eleven domes formerly topped the basilica, which rivaled Istanbul's Aya Sofya in scale. The barrel-vaulted roof collapsed after a long-ago earthquake, but the church is still an incredible sight, with its labyrinth of halls and marble courtyards. ⊠*Entrance off St. Jean Sok., just east of Isa Bey Cami* ☎*No phone* 🎫*$2* ☉*Daily 8–5.*

7 **Temple of Artemis.** The fragments of the temple on display at the Isa Bey Mosque are about all you will see of the holy site that drew pilgrims from around the ancient world and was one of the Seven Wonders of the Ancient World. Begun in the 7th century BC, greatly expanded by the wealthy Lydian king Croesus, and redone in marble in the 6th century BC, the temple was burned down by a disgruntled worshiper in 356 BC. Rebuilt by Alexander the Great, it was sacked by Goths in AD 263 and later stripped for materials to build Istanbul's Aya Sofya and Selçuk's St. John Basilica. Today a lone column towering over a scattering of fallen stones in a green field on the Selçuk–Ephesus road is all that remains of a temple that was once four times larger than the Parthenon in Athens.

EPHESUS

8 *20 km (12 mi) north of Kuşadası.*

Ephesus (*Efes*, in Turkish), the showpiece of Aegean archaeology, is probably the most evocative ancient city in the eastern Mediterranean, and one of the grandest reconstructed ancient sites in the world. Ancient Ephesus grew from a seaside settlement to a powerful trading port and sacred center for the cult of Artemis. Like most Ionian cities in Asia Minor, Ephesus was conquered by the Romans, and eventually became Christian. St. Paul is believed to have written some of his Epistles here and was later driven out by the city's silversmiths for preaching that their models of Diana were not divine. In 431 Ephesus was the scene of the Third Ecumenical Council, during which Mary was proclaimed the Mother of God. Ephesus was doomed by the silting in its harbor. By the 6th century the port had become useless, and the population had shifted to what is now Selçuk.

The road leading to the parking lot passes a 1st-century AD **stadium**, where chariot and horse races were held on a track 712 feet long and where gladiators and wild beasts met in combat before 70,000 spectators. On your left after you enter the site is the 25,000-seat **theater,** still used for music and dance performances each May during the Selçuk Ephesus Festival of Culture and Art. Leading away from the theater toward the ancient port, now a marsh, is the **Arcadian Way.** This 1,710-foot-long street was once lined with shops and covered archways. Only a long line of slender marble columns remains.

In front of the theater is Marble Avenue. Follow it to the beautiful, two-story **Library of Celsus**. a much-photographed building. The library is near Marble Avenue's intersection with the **Street of Kuretes,** a still-impressive thoroughfare named for the college of priests once located there. At this corner is a large house believed to have been a **brothel.** To the right along the street are the multistoried houses of the nobility, with terraces and courtyards, one of which **Terrace House** has been renovated to display its large wall frescoes and mosaic floors in situ (separate fee). A block from the brothel is the facade of the **Temple of Hadrian,** with four Corinthian columns and a serpent-headed hydra above the door to keep out evil spirits. The street then forks and opens into a central square that once held the **Prytaneion,** or town hall; the **Nymphaion,** a small temple decked with fountains; and the **Temple of Domitian,** on the south side of the square, which was once a vast sanctuary with a colossal statue of the emperor for whom it was named. All are now a jumble of collapsed walls and columns.

Returning to the Street of Kuretes, turn right to reach the **odeon,** an intimate semicircle with just a few rows of seats, where spectators would listen to poetry readings and music. Columns mark the northern edge of the state **agora** (market). Beyond, the **Magnesian Gate** (also known as the Manisa Gate), at the end of the street, was the starting point for a caravan trail and a colonnaded road to the Temple of Artemis. ⊠*Site entry 4 km (2½ mi) west of Selçuk on Selçuk–Ephesus Rd.* ☎*232/892–6402 or 232/892–6940* ☒*$10* ⊙*Daily 8–5:30.*

❾ According to the legend attached to the **Graves of the Seven Sleepers,** seven young Christian men hid in a cave to avoid persecution by the Romans in the 3rd century AD. They fell into a sleep that lasted 200 years, waking only after the Byzantine Empire had made Christianity the official state religion. When they died, they were buried here, and the church that you see was built over them. The tombs in the large cemetery are largely from the Byzantine era. ⊠*South of Sor Sahasi Sok. 3* ☒*Free* ⊙*Dawn–dusk.*

SHOPPING

The downtown cores of Kuşadaş and Selçuk offer excellent shopping opportunities, though prices and quality vary enormously. Generally, Turkey offers an exceptional range of handicrafts in all price ranges but is most famed for its hand-woven carpets and kilims in a range of sizes and patterns. The finest are made of silk threads but more common is cotton or wool. Other traditional wares include items with worked brass and copper articles such as large pots and ornate tables, ceramics, marble items, inlaid wooden articles including jewelry boxes and chess sets, or leatherwear fashioned into bags, shoes, or clothing. For a truly exotic gift, take home a genuine *nargile* (hubble-bubble pipe), or a blue glass *boncuk,* talisman said to ward off the evil eye.

Kuşadaş also has several excellent jewelry shops selling gold, precious stones, and modern jewelry and designer watches at competitive prices.

Don't forget to haggle over the price of your souvenirs; never pay the first price asked, whatever you want to buy.

Caravanserail Carpets (✉*Okuz Mehmet Pasa Kervansarayi 2, Kuşadaş* ☎*256/614–3110*) offers a good range of high-quality carpets in all sizes. **Orient Bazaar** (✉*Dag Mh. Yali Cad. 9, Kuşadaş* ☎*256/612–8298*) offers high-class jewelry and carpets.

BEACHES

There are many fine beaches around Kuşadası, and these are also served by dolmuş buses. The closest beach to town is **Ladies Beach** (✉*2 mi north of the cruise port, Kuşadası*). It has sun beds and umbrellas to rent and a range of bars and restaurants, but it does get very busy.

If you head north from Kuşadası, **Pamucak** (✉*7 mi north of Kuşadası*) has a long, sandy stretch of beach backed by four- and five-star hotels with good watersports facilities.

WHERE TO EAT

$ ✗**Günhan Restaurant.** One of the few places to eat at the Ephesus ruins, this restaurant serves a variety of foods, from sandwiches to traditional stewed Turkish dishes, kebabs, and grilled lamb chops. Shaded by awnings, it's perfect for a rest and cool drink before or after a trip to the ruins. ✉*Ephesus Ruins, Selçuk* ☎*232/892–2291* ▭*MC, V* ☉*No dinner.*

¢ ✗**Özurfa.** The focus at this Turkish fast-food spot is kebabs. The Urfa kebab—spicy, grilled slices of lamb on pita bread—is the house specialty, and the fish kebabs are tasty, too. The location just off Barbaros Hayrettin Caddesi is convenient to the market and a step away from the crowds. ✉*Cephane Sok. No 9, Kuşadası* ☎*256/614–6070* ▭*AE, MC, V.*

LIMASSOL, CYPRUS

Cyprus, once a center for the cult of the Greek goddess Aphrodite, is a modern island nation that retains an essentially Mediterranean character. Its 3,572 square mi (about the size of Connecticut) encompass citrus and olive groves, pine-forested mountains, and some of Europe's cleanest beaches. Cyprus's strategic position as the easternmost island in the Mediterranean Sea has made it subject to regular invasions by powerful empires. Greeks, Phoenicians, Assyrians, Egyptians, Persians, Romans, Byzantines, the Knights Templar, Venetians, Ottomans and the British—all have either ruled or breezed through here. Vestiges of the diverse cultures that have ruled here dot the island, from remnants of Neolithic settlements and ancient Greek and Roman temple sites, to early Christian basilicas and painted Byzantine churches. But Cyprus isn't limited to its architecture and history; there's also a vibrant lifestyle to be explored.

ESSENTIALS

CURRENCY Cyprus adopted the euro as its official currency on January 1, 2008, but as of this writing the Cyprus pound is still in use, though the value of the pound is already tied to that of the euro (C£1 to US$2.35; C£1 to €1.71

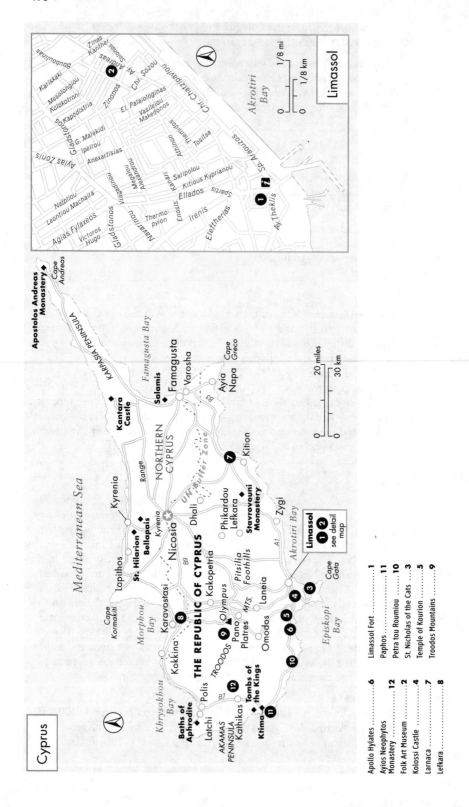

Limassol

Akrotiri Bay

Boubouljmas
Zinas Kanthet
Ay. Andreas
Ay. Sozous
Chr. Sozou
Chr. Chatzizavou
Kariskaki
Mesolongiou
Kolokotroni
El. Palaiologinas
Vasileiou Makedonos
S.Kapodistria
Zinonos
Ipeirou
G.G. Malekidi
Gladstonos
Tremmous
Tositsa
Anthinon
Ay. Zonis
Ayias Zonis
Anexartisias
Kenari
Saripolou
Kitious Kyprianou
Megalou Alexandrou
Vragadinou
Ellados
Sozous
Nafpliou
Leontiou Machaira
Navarinou
Thermo-pylon
Enosis
Spartis
Irenis
Ay. Theklis
Agias Fylaxeos
Gladstonos
Victoros Hugo
Eleftherias

1/8 mi
1/8 km
0

Cyprus

Mediterranean Sea

Apostolos Andreas Monastery◆
Cape Andreas

KARPASIA PENINSULA

Cape Kormakiti
Lapithos
Kyrenia
Kyrenia Range
Famagusta Bay
Kantara Castle
Salamis
Famagusta
Varosha
Cape Greco

Morphou Bay
Karavostasi
St. Hilarion◆
Bellapais◆
NORTHERN CYPRUS
Nicosia
Kyrenia
B9
Dhali
UN Buffer Zone
Ayia Napa
B3

Kokkina
THE REPUBLIC OF CYPRUS
Kakopetria
Phikardou
Lefkara◆
Stavrovouni Monastery◆
Kition
Zygi
A1
Kitima

Khrysokhou Bay
Polis
Latchi
Baths of Aphrodite
AKAMAS PENINSULA
Kathikas
TROODOS
Olympus
TROODOS MTS.
Pano Platres
Omodos
Laneia
Pitsilia Foothills
Akrotiri Bay
Cape Gata
Episkopi Bay

B7
Tombs of the Kings
Ktima

Limassol
see detail map

0   20 miles
0   30 km

at this writing). When you make port calls in 2008, you should expect to use euros for all purchases.

HOURS Museum hours vary; so it pays to check ahead. Generally, museums are closed for lunch and on Sunday. Most ancient monuments are open from dawn to dusk. During the summer—from about mid-June through August—many shops close for an afternoon break from 2 to 5. In tourist areas, shops may stay open late and on Sunday in the summer.

INTERNET **Netwave Internet Club** ✉ *Y Court, 153 Makarios III Ave., Limassol* ☎ *25730239* ⊕ *www.netwave.com.cy.*

TELEPHONES GSM phones work in Cyprus provided that they can operate at 900 or 1800mh. Public phones accept Telecards, which can be purchased at post offices, banks, souvenir shops, and kiosks.

COMING ASHORE

Vessels dock at the main port in Limassol. This is a vast commercial enterprise but has dedicated cruise berths and offers a shuttle to the passenger terminal. Here you'll find refreshments, tourist information, currency exchange, and a taxi station. Cruise ships also call at Larnaca, but at this writing Limassol is the major cruise port.

If you want to explore independently, take a taxi from the port into the downtown. Service taxis (4- to 8-seat minibuses) link all major towns for a fixed fee; urban taxis are generally very cheap for local travel but far more expensive than service taxis between towns. Urban taxis have an initial charge of C£1.25 (C£1.65 at night) and then 22¢ per km in the daytime, 26¢ at night. Drivers are bound by law to run their meter.

You can reach many interesting and ancient attractions in the surrounding Cypriot countryside if you hire a vehicle for the day. Car rentals are about C£20 for an economy manual vehicle. There will be an extra charge for delivery to the port or pick-up in central Limassol.

EXPLORING CYPRUS

Numbers in the margin correspond to points of interest on the Cyprus map.

LIMASSOL & VICINITY

A major commercial port, cruise-ship port of call, and wine-making center on the south coast, Limassol, 75 km (47 mi) from Nicosia, is a bustling, cosmopolitan town. Luxury hotels, apartments, and guest houses stretch along 12 km (7 mi) of seafront. In the center, the elegant, modern shops of Makarios Avenue contrast with those of the old part of town, where local handicrafts prevail.

CYPRUS BEST BETS

Visit the mosaics of Paphos. Some of the finest Roman workmanship yet uncovered, they are an awe-inspiring sight.

Enjoy the galleries at Larnaca Museum. The museum is stuffed with ancient Greek and Roman artifacts, from monumental statues to precious jewelry to mundane kitchen utensils.

Browse for souvenirs at Lefkara. This whitewashed village has a vibrant Greek heartbeat.

5

2 **Folk Art Museum.** For a glimpse of Cypriot folklore, the collection includes national costumes and fine examples of weaving and other crafts. ☒*Agiou Andreou 253* ☎*05/362303* ☉*Oct.–May, Mon.–Wed. and Fri. 8:30–1:30 and 3–5:30, Thurs. 8:30–1:30; June–Sept., Mon.–Wed. and Fri. 8:30–1:30 and 4–6:30, Thurs. 8:30–1:30.*

4 **Kolossi Castle.** This Crusader fortress of the Knights of St. John was constructed in the 13th century and rebuilt in the 15th. ☒*Road to Paphos* ★ ☉*June–Aug., daily 9–7:30; Apr., May, Sept., and Oct. 9–6; Nov.–Mar, daily 9–5.*

1 **Limassol Fort.** The 14th-century fort was built on the site of a Byzantine fortification. Richard the Lion-Hearted married Berengaria of Navarre ★ and crowned her Queen of England here in 1191. The **Cyprus Medieval Museum** in the castle displays medieval armor and relics. ☒*Near old port* ☎*25330419* ☉*Mon.–Sat. 9–5, Sun. 10–1.*

3 **St. Nicholas of the Cats.** This peaceful convent is seemingly occupied by cats instead of nuns. According to legend, the cats are descendants of the animals St. Helena imported in the 4th century AD to whittle down the area's snake population. Their feline forebears must have done a good job, because today the dozens of cats in residence seem more inclined to laze in the sun than anything else. The little peninsula past the Akrotiri military base is still called Cape Gata (She-Cat). ☒*Edge of Akrotiri village.*

5 **The Temple of Kourion.** The Curium, west of Limassol, has Greek and Roman ruins. Classical and Shakespearean plays are sometimes staged *Fodor's Choice* in the **amphitheater.** Next to the theater is the **Villa of Eustolios,** a sum- ★ mer house built by a wealthy Christian. Nearby is the partially rebuilt **Roman stadium.**

6 The **Apollo Hylates** (Sanctuary of Apollo of the Woodlands), an impressive archaeological site, stands 3 km (2 mi) farther on. ☒*Main Paphos Rd.* ☉*June–Aug., daily 9–7:30; Apr., May, Sept., and Oct. 9–6; Nov.–May, daily 9–5.*

LARNACA

7 *51 km (32 mi) southeast of Nicosia, 66 km (41 mi) east of Limassol.*

The seaside resort with its own airport has a flamboyant Whitsuntide celebration, called Cataklysmos, as well as fine beaches, a palm-fringed seaside promenade, and a modern harbor.

In the marina district, the **Larnaca Museum** displays treasures, including outstanding sculptures and Bronze Age seals. ☒*Kimon and Kilkis Sts.* ☎*24630169* ☉*Mon.–Wed. and Fri. 9–2:30, Thurs. 9–2:30 and (except July and Aug.) 3–5.*

Kition, the old Larnaca of Biblical times, was one of the most important ancient city-kingdoms. Architectural remains of temples date from the 13th century BC. ☒*Kyman St., north of Larnaca Museum* ☉*Weekdays 9–2:30, Sept.–June, Thurs. 3–5.*

The **Pierides Collection** is a private assemblage of more than 3,000 pieces distinguished by its Bronze Age terra-cotta figures. ☒*Paul Zenon Kitieos St. 4, near Lord Byron St.* ☎*24652495* ☉*Mid-June–Sept., Mon.–Sat. 9–1 and 4–7; Oct.–mid-June, weekdays 9–1 and 3–6, Sat. 9–1.*

The **Medieval Museum** is in a 17th-century Turkish fort and has finds from Hala Sultan Tekke and Kition. ✉*Within sight of marina on seafront* ⊙*Mon.–Sat. 9–1, Sun. 11–1.*

In the town center stands one of the island's more important churches, **Ayios Lazarus** (Church of Lazarus), resplendent with icons. It has a fascinating crypt containing Lazarus's sarcophagus. ✉*Plateia Agiou Lazarou* ⊙*Sept.–Mar., Mon.–Sat. 8–12:30 and 2:30–5; Apr.–Aug., Mon.–Sat. 8–12:30 and 3:30–6:30.*

South of Larnaca on the airport road is the 6½-square-km (2½-square-mi) **Salt Lake**. In winter it's a refuge for migrating birds.

★ On the lake's edge a mosque stands in an oasis of palm trees guarding the **Hala Sultan Tekke,** burial place of the prophet Muhammad's aunt Umm Haram; it's an important Muslim shrine. ✉*Salt Lake* ⊙*July and Aug. daily 7:30–7:30; Apr., May, Sept., and Oct., daily 9–6; Nov.–Mar., daily 9–5.*

The 11th-century **Panayia Angeloktistos** church, 11 km (7 mi) south of Larnaca, has extraordinary Byzantine wall mosaics that date from the 6th and 7th centuries. ✉*Rte. B4, Kiti* ⊙*Daily 8–noon and 2–4.*

On a mountain 40 km (25 mi) west of Larnaca stands the **Stavrovouni** (Mountain of the Cross) monastery. It was founded by St. Helena in AD 326; the present buildings date from the 19th century. The views from here are splendid. Ideally, you should visit the monastery in a spirit of pilgrimage rather than sightseeing, out of respect for the monks. Male visitors are allowed inside the monastery daily sunrise–sunset, except between noon and 3 (or between noon and 2, September–March).

LEFKARA
❽ *40 km (25 mi) northwest of Larnaca, 64 km (40 mi) north of Limassol.*

Some 40 km west of Larnaca, this picturesque village—one of the prettiest in Cyprus—is best known for its lace: Lefkaritika has been woven by hand here for centuries. Much of it is indeed beautiful, and most shopkeepers are willing to bargain. But considerably more evocative is the village itself, clustered on two hills and split between an upper portion, Kato Lefkara, and lower portion, Pano Lefkara. The tiny streets open up to a small plaza in front of the Church of the Holy Cross in Pano Lefkara, with a stupendous view of the surrounding sun-drenched hills.

TROODOS MOUNTAINS
❾ *20 km (25 mi) north of Limassol.*

These mountains, which rise to 6,500 feet, have shady cedar and pine forests and cool springs. Small, painted Byzantine churches in the Troodos and Pitsilia Foothills are rich examples of a rare indigenous art form. **Asinou Church,** near the village of Nikitari, and **Agios Nikolaos tis Stegis** (St. Nicholas of the Roof), south of Kakopetria, are especially noteworthy. In winter, skiers take over the mountains; **Platres,** in the foothills of Mt. Olympus, is the principal resort.

At the **Kykkos** monastery, founded in 1100, the prized icon of the Virgin is reputed to have been painted by St. Luke. On the southern slopes of the Troodos is the village of Omodos, one of the prettiest in Cyprus, with whitewashed villas, narrow streets, and a broad central square. Laneia is not as beautiful but its many artisans and craftspeople make it worth a detour.

PETRA TOU ROMIOU

❿ *20 km (12 mi) west of Limassol.*

The legendary **birthplace of Aphrodite**—Greek goddess of love and beauty—is just off the main road between Limassol and Petra. Signs in Greek and English identify the offshore rock that is viewed from the shoreline. Park in the lot and take the passageway under the highway to the large pebble beach.

PAPHOS

⓫ *68 km (42 mi) west of Limassol.*

In the west of the island Paphos combines a seaside with stellar archaeological sites and a buzzing nightlife. Since the late 1990s it has attracted some of the most lavish resorts on the island. The modern center has a pleasant leisure harbor anchored by a medieval fortress.

FodorśChoice Don't miss the elaborate **Roman mosaics** in the **Roman Villa of Theseus,**
★ the **House of Dionysos,** and the **House of Aion.** The impressive site is an easy walk from the harbor. ✉*Kato Paphos (New Paphos), near harbor* ☎26940217 ⊙*June–Aug., daily 8–7:30; Sept.–May, daily 8–5.*

The **Paphos District Archaeological Museum** displays pottery, jewelry, and statuettes from Cyprus's Roman villas. ✉*43 Grivas Dighenis Ave., Ktima* ☎26940215 ⊙*Weekdays 9–5, Sat. 9–1.*

★ There are notable 6th-century mosaics and icons in the **Byzantine Museum.** ✉*7 Andreas Ioannou St.* ☎26931393 ⊙*Weekdays 9–4, Sat. 9–1.*

The squat 16th-century **Paphos Fort** guards the entrance to the harbor; from the rooftop there's a lovely view. ✉*Paphos* ⊙*Daily 10–5, June–Aug., 10–6.*

★ The **Tombs of the Kings,** an early necropolis, date from 300 BC. The coffin niches are empty, but a powerful sense of mystery remains. ✉*Kato Paphos (New Paphos)* ☎26940295 ⊙*June–Aug., daily 8–7:30; Apr., May, Sept., and Oct., 8–6.*

⓬ **Ayios Neophytos Monastery.** The hermit and scholar Neophytos settled at the site of this monastery in 1159, carving a home for himself out of the rock. Known in his time as the leading critic of Richard the Lion-Hearted and the Byzantine tax collectors, today he is best known for what became a series of grottoes hewn from the hillside rock and the evocative religious frescoes—some actually painted by Neophytos—they contain. The monastery itself, with no more than a half-dozen or so monks, is situated below the grottoes. ✉*10 km (6 mi) north of Paphos.*

SHOPPING

Cyprus has a great range of handicrafts. Lace and embroidery from Lefkara are still handmade and are widely available. Other items to look for are basketware, ceramics, blown glass, carved wood (the best being olive wood), hand-tied cotton rugs, silverware, and copperware, including beautiful decorative urns. Leather and shoes are excellent value. Museums sell copies of ancient artifacts, and the Orthodox Monasteries offer Byzantine icons. Edibles include superb olive oil, honey, and delicious wine.

Shopping in the villages of Lefkara, Omodos, and Laneia is a pleasure, with numerous galleries and shops set along the whitewashed alleyways. In Limassol, the main shopping street, Makarios Avenue, has a range of modern boutiques.

The large **KEO Winery** (⊠ *Roosevelt Ave., toward the new port* ☎*25362053*), just west of Limassol, welcomes visitors and gives tours weekdays at 10. **Lemba Pottery** (⊠*Elefttherias St. 18, Paphos* ☎*2670822*) has handmade pottery with vibrant glazes.

BEACHES

Cyprus has numerous excellent beaches but they get very busy between June and September with vacationers from across Europe. The **Ladies Mile** (⊠*Near new port, Limassol*) is the closest beach to the cruise port.

WHERE TO EAT

¢–$$ ✕**Porta.** A varied menu of international and Cypriot dishes, such as *foukoudha* barbecue (grilled strips of steak) and trout baked in prawn and mushroom sauce, is served in this (completely) renovated donkey stable. On many nights you'll be entertained by soft live music. ⊠*17 Yenethliou Mitella, Old Castle, Limassol* ☎*25360339* ▤*MC, V.*

¢–$ ✕**Militzis.** This restaurant is popular with locals for its homemade *meze* (hot and cold small plates) and other Cypriot specialties. ⊠*42 Pigiale Pasa Ave., Larnaca* ☎*24655867* ▤*AE, DC, MC, V.*

MYKONOS, GREECE

Put firmly on the map by Jackie O, Mykonos has become one of the most popular of the Aegean islands. Although the dry, rugged island is one of the smallest of the Cyclades—16 km (10 mi) by 11 km (7 mi)—travelers from all over the world are drawn to sandy beaches, its thatched windmills, and its picturesque, whitewashed port town of Mykonos, whose cubical two-story houses and churches have been long celebrated as some of the best examples of classic Cycladic architecture. Here backpackers rub elbows with millionaires, and the atmosphere is decidedly cosmopolitan. Happily, the islanders seem to have been able to fit cosmopolitan New Yorkers or Londoners gracefully into their way of life. For almost 1,000 years neighboring Delos Island was the religious and political center of the Aegean and host every four years to the Delian games, the region's greatest festival. This is a must-visit site for anyone interested in ancient history.

ESSENTIALS

CURRENCY The euro (€1 to US$1.40 at this writing). U.S. currency is generally not accepted in Europe, but ATMs are common.

HOURS Museums are generally open from 9 to 5, but many are closed on Monday. Shops are open daily in the summer (9 to noon or 1, reopening at 4 or 5 until 9 on weekdays and 9 to 6 on Saturday).

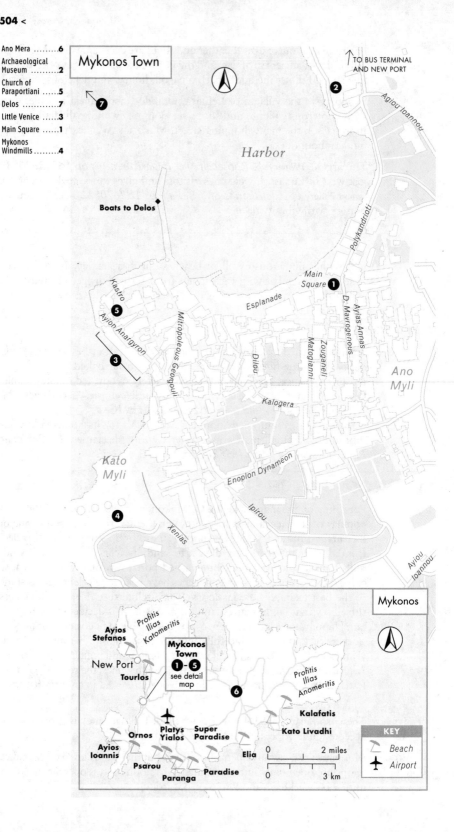

Mykonos Town

TO BUS TERMINAL
AND NEW PORT

Agiou Ioannou

Harbor

Boats to Delos

Polykandrioti

Main
Square ❶

Kastro

❺

Esplanade

Ayias Annas

D. Mavrogenous

Ayion Anargyron

❸

Mitropoleous Geogouli

Diiou

Zouganeli

Matogianni

Ano
Myli

Kalogera

Kato
Myli

Enoplon Dynameon

Ipirou

❹

Xenias

Ayiou
Ioannou

Mykonos

Ayios
Stefanos

Profitis
Ilias
Katomeritis

Mykonos
Town
❶-❺
see detail
map

New Port

Tourlos

❻

Profitis
Ilias
Anomeritis

Kalafatis

Kato Livadhi

Ornos

Platys
Yialos

Super
Paradise

Ayios
Ioannis

Elia

Psarou

Paranga

Paradise

0   2 miles

0   3 km

KEY
⚑ Beach
✈ Airport

INTERNET **Mykonos Cyber Cafe** (✉*26 M Axioti St.* ☎*22890/27–684*) is open daily from 9 AM to 10 PM and offers rates by the hour or per 15 minutes.

TELEPHONES Tri-band GSM phones work in Greece. You can buy prepaid phone cards at telecom shops, news-vendors, and tobacconists in all towns and cities for local or international calls. Vodafone is the leading mobile telecom company. OTE is the national domestic provider. Calls can be made at OTE offices and paid for after completion.

COMING ASHORE

The main cruise port is about a mile north of Mykonos Town (on the other side of a very steep hill). Shuttle buses transport passengers to town, where you can catch buses or take a taxi to the beaches. If you anchor offshore and are tendered to the island, you'll alight at the old port in the town itself.

Because the island is so small, journey times anywhere are short. There is a cheap (fares between €1.10 and €1.50) and reliable bus service from the town to all the main beaches, but services can get crowded in July and August. Small boats called *caïques* also act as taxis, taking people from the old port to the various beaches. These are reliable and popular services. Commercial taxis operate on fixed fare routes, but the taxi system is easily overburdened when a large ship is in port. These are posted at the taxi rank in Mavro Square, just inland from the old harbor.

Most travel offices in Mykonos town run guided tours to Delos that cost about €30, including boat transportation and entry fee. Alternatively, take one of the caïques that visit Delos daily from the old port: the round-trip costs about €9, and entry to the site (with no guide) is €6. They leave between 8:30 AM and 1 PM and return noon to 2 PM.

With reliable transport services, a car rental isn't absolutely necessary, but if you want to do some exploring on your own you can rent an ATV for two people in town for about €20. A rental car costs about €90 per day for a subcompact, though you may be able to rent a Smart car for much less.

MYKONOS BEST BETS

Explore Ancient Delos. Delos was the religious center of the Aegean. Large sections of the city have been excavated, revealing treasures magnificent and humble.

Stroll the streets of Mykonos Town. Cosmopolitan and bohemian, Mykonos is one of the most fashionable places to be during the European summer, yet the alluring narrow streets retain an vibrant Greek character.

Spend some time at the beach. The town sleeps during the heat of the afternoon, so choose one of the island's famous beaches—from fun to hedonism—there's something for every taste.

5

EXPLORING MYKONOS

Numbers in the margin correspond to points of interest on the Mykonos map.

MYKONOS TOWN

If your ship remains in port late (often the case in Myknos), the best time to visit the central harbor is in the cool of the evening, when the islanders promenade along the esplanade to meet friends and visit the numerous cafés. By the open-air fish market, Petros the Pelican preens and cadges eats. In the 1950s a group of migrating pelicans passed over Mykonos, leaving behind a single exhausted bird; Vassilis the fisherman nursed it back to health, and locals say that the pelican in the harbor is the original Petros, though you'll see several lurking around the fish tavernas right off the esplanade.

2 **Archaeological Museum.** The museum affords insight into the intriguing history of the Delos shrine. The museum houses Delian funerary sculptures discovered on the neighboring islet of Rhenea, many with scenes of mourning. The most significant work from Mykonos is a 7th-century BC *pithos* (storage jar), showing the Greeks in the Trojan horse and the sack of the city. ⊠ *Ayios Stefanos road, between boat dock and town* ☎ *22890/22325* 🖂 *€3* ☉ *Wed.–Mon. 8:30–2:30.*

5 **Church of Paraportiani.** Mykoniots claim that exactly 365 churches and chapels dot their landscape, one for each day of the year. The most famous
★ of these is Our Lady of the Postern Gate. The sloping, whitewashed conglomeration of four chapels, mixing Byzantine and vernacular idioms, has been described as "a confectioner's dream gone mad," and its position on a promontory facing the sea sets off the unique architecture. ⊠ *Ayion Anargyron, near folk museum.*

3 **Little Venice.** Many of the early ship's captains built distinguished houses directly on the sea here, with wooden balconies overlooking the water.
★ Today this neighborhood, at the southwest end of the port, is full of bars and shops. A few of the old houses have been turned into stylish bars, which are quite romantic at twilight (but disco-loud at night). A block inland are many of Mykonos's famous clubs. ⊠ *Mitropoleos Georgouli.*

1 **Main square.** A bust of Mando Mavroyennis, the island heroine, stands on a pedestal in the town's main square. In the 1821 War of Independence the Mykoniots, known for their seafaring skills, volunteered an armada of 24 ships, and in 1822, when the Ottomans later landed a force on the island, Mando and her soldiers forced them back to their ships. After independence, a scandalous love affair caused her exile to Paros, where she died.

4 **Mykonos windmills.** Overlooking the town from a high hill are the famous windmills, echoes of a time when wind power was used to grind the island's grain.

ANO MERA

6 *8 km (5 mi) east of Mykonos town.*

Interesting little tavernas line the central square of Ano Mera, which is the "second city" of Mykonos, in the hills near the center of the island.

Monastery buffs should head to Ano Mera, a village in the central part of the island, where the **Monastery of the Panayia Tourliani**, founded in 1580 and dedicated to the protectress of Mykonos, stands in the central square. Its massive baroque iconostasis (altar screen), made in 1775 by Florentine artists, has small icons carefully placed amid the wooden structure's painted green, red, and gold-leaf flowers. At the top are carved figures of the apostles and large icons depicting New Testament scenes. The hanging incense holders with silver molded dragons holding red eggs in their mouths show an Eastern influence. In the hall of the monastery, an interesting **museum** displays embroideries, liturgical vestments, and wood carvings. ⌂ *Central Square* ☎ *0289/71249* ⊘ *By appointment only; call in advance.*

DELOS

❼ *25-minute boat ride southwest from Mykonos Town.*

Fodor's Choice
★

Why did Delos become the religious and political center of the Aegean? One answer is that Delos provided the safest anchorage for vessels sailing between the mainland and the shores of Asia. But the myth that the Greek deities Artemis and Apollo were born here meant it had a powerful for the ancients. Later the island became the headquarters and bank for the Delian League but the island was sacked during Roman rule and never recovered.

On the left from the harbor is the **Agora of the Competialists** (circa 150 BC), members of Roman guilds, mostly freedmen and slaves from Sicily who worked for Italian traders. They worshipped the *Lares Competales,* the Roman "crossroads" gods; in Greek they were known as Hermaistai, after the god Hermes, protector of merchants and the crossroads. The **Sacred Way,** east of the agora, was the route, during the holy Delian festival, of the procession to the sanctuary of Apollo.

The **Propylaea,** at the end of the Sacred Way, were once a monumental white marble gateway with three portals framed by four Doric columns. Beyond the Propylaea is the **Sanctuary of Apollo.** Though little of it remains today, when the Propylaea were built in the mid-2nd century BC, the sanctuary was crowded with altars, statues, and temples—three of them to Apollo. Inside the sanctuary and to the right is the **House of the Naxians,** a 7th- to 6th-century BC structure with a central colonnade. Dedications to Apollo were stored in this shrine.

One of the most evocative sights of Delos is the 164-foot-long **Avenue of the Lions.** These are replicas; the originals are in the museum. The five Naxian marble beasts crouch on their haunches, their forelegs stiffly upright, vigilant guardians of the Sacred Lake. They are the survivors of a line of at least nine lions, erected in the second half of the 7th century BC by the Naxians. One, removed in the 17th century, now guards the Arsenal of Venice. The **Archaeological Museum** is also on the road south of the gymnasium; it contains most of the antiquities found in excavations on the island: monumental statues of young men and women, stelae, reliefs, masks, and ancient jewelry.

Immediately to the right of the museum is a small **Sanctuary of Dionysos,** erected about 300 BC; outside it is one of the more boggling sights of ancient Greece: several monuments dedicated to Apollo by the winners of the choral competitions of the Delian festivals, each decorated with a huge phallus, emblematic of the orgiastic rites that took place during the Dionysian festivals.

Beyond the path that leads to the southern part of the island is the **ancient theater,** built in the early 3rd century BC in the elegant residential quarter inhabited by Roman bankers and Egyptian and Phoenician merchants. Their one- and two-story houses were typically built around a central courtyard, sometimes with columns on all sides. Floor mosaics of snakes, panthers, birds, dolphins, and Dionysus channeled rainwater into cisterns below; the best-preserved can be seen in the **House of the Dolphins,** the **House of the Masks,** and the **House of the Trident.** A flight of steps goes up 368 feet to the summit of **Mt. Kynthos,** on whose slope Apollo was born. ☎22890/22259 ⊕*www.culture.gr* ◫€5 ⊘*Apr.–Oct., Tues.–Sun. 8:30–3.*

SHOPPING

Mykonos Town has excellent shopping, with many high-class boutiques aimed at the well-healed sitting side by side with moderately priced shops selling Greek crafts and fashionable clothing. It's a real pleasure for retail junkies, with a seemingly limitless array of choices. Almost every surface of the narrow alleyways is festooned with cotton clothing or cheerful ceramics, leather shoes, or bars of olive-oil soap. Artists are drawn here as much by the clientele as the beauty and light of the Aegean, so galleries are numerous. The town is especially famed for its jewelry, from simple strings of colourful beads to precious stones in designer settings. Upscale, duty-free jewelry shops also abound.

Ilias LALAoUNIS (⊠*Polykandrioti 14, near taxis* ☎22890/22444 🖷22890/24409 ⊕*www.lalaounismykonos.com*) is known internationally for jewelry based on classic ancient designs, especially Greek; the shop is as elegant as a museum.

Ioanna Zouganelli (☎22890/22309), makes mohair shawls and traditional Mykonian weavings in her tiny shop on the square in front of Paraportiani.

Loco (⊠*Kalogera 29 N.* ☎22890/23682) sells cotton and linen summer wear in lovely colors. The Marla knits are from the family factory in Athens.

Mykonos used to be a weaver's island with where 500 looms. Two shops remain. In **Nikoletta** (⊠*Little Venice*), Nikoletta Xidakis sells her skirts, shawls, and bedspreads made of local wool.

Precious Tree (⊠*Dilou 2* 🖷🖷2289024685) is a tiny shop aglitter in gems elegantly set at the workshop in Athens.

Soula Papadakou's **Venetia** (⊠*Ayion Anargyron 16, Little Venice* ☎22890/24464) carries authentic copies of traditional handmade embroideries in clothing, tablecloths, curtains, and such, all in white.

SPORTS & ACTIVITIES

There's a full range of watersports on offer, and many concessions operate directly on the beach (from May through September). Windsurfing is particularly popular because of the prevailing *meltemi* winds that blow across the island throughout the summer. The windy northern beaches on Ornos Bay are best for this.

Mykonos Diving Center (⊠*Psarou* ☎*22890/24808* ⊕*www.dive.gr*) has a variety of scuba courses and excursions at 30 locations.

Aphrodite Beach Hotel (⊠*Kalafati Beach* ☎*28890/71367* 🖶*22890/71525*) has water sports. The program at **Surfing Club Anna** (⊠*Agia Anna* ☎*22890/71205*) is well organized.

BEACHES

There is a beach for every taste in Mykonos. Beaches near Mykonos town, within walking distance, are **Tourlos** and **Ayios Ioannis.Ayios Stefanos**, about a 45-minute walk from Mykonos town, has a minigolf course, water sports, restaurants, and umbrellas and lounge chairs for rent. The south coast's **Psarou**, protected from wind by hills and surrounded by restaurants, offers a wide selection of water sports and is often called the finest beach. Nearby **Platys Yialos**, popular with families, is also lined with restaurants and dotted with umbrellas for rent. **Ornos** is also perfect for families.

Paranga, Paradise, Super Paradise, and **Elia** are all on the southern coast of the island, and are famously nude, though getting less so. **Super Paradise** is half-gay, half-straight, and swings at night. All have tavernas on the beach. At the easternmost end of the south shores is **Kalafatis**, known for package tours, and between Elia and Kalafatis there's a remote beach at **Kato Livadhi**, which can be reached by road.

WHERE TO EAT

¢–$$$ ✗**Sea Satin Market–Caprice.** On the far tip of land below the windmills, the restaurant, sprawls out onto a seaside terrace and even onto the sand. Prices vary according to weight. Shellfish is a specialty, and everything is beautifully presented. If the wind is up, the waves sing. Live music and dancing add to the liveliness in summer. ⊠*At seaside under windmills* ☎*22890/24676* ▤*AE, MC, V.*

¢–$ ✗**Lotus.** For over 30 years, Giorgos and Elsa Cambanis have lovingly run this tiny restaurant. The roast leg of lamb with oregano, lemon, and wine is succulent, and the moussaka is one of Greece's best. For dessert, have *pralina,* which resembles tiramisu. ⊠*Matoyanni 47* ☎*22890/22881* ▤*No credit cards.*

PIRAEUS, GREECE (FOR ATHENS)

If you come to Athens in search of gleaming white temples, you may be aghast to find that much of the city has melded into what appears to be a viscous concrete mass. Amid the sprawl and squalor, though, the ancient city gives up its treasures. Lift your eyes 200 feet above the city to the Parthenon, and you behold architectural perfection that has not been surpassed in 2,500 years. Today this shrine of classical form, this symbol of Western civilization and political thought, dominates a 21st-century boomtown. To experience Athens fully is to understand the essence of Greece: tradition juxtaposed with a modernity that the ancients would strain to recognize but would heartily endorse. Ancient Athens is certainly the lure for the millions of visitors to the city, but since the late 1990s, inspired by the 2004 Olympics, the people have gone far toward transforming

Athens

VATHI

❻

Tositsa

Paleologou

Liossion

Marni

Aharnon

Aristotelous

Stournara

Th. Diligianni

Chiou

Nikolaou-Iosif Maizonos

Mager

Vathis Square

Kapodistriou

Solomou

Favierou

Kapodistriou

Elefsinion

Victoros Ougo

Marni

Kaningos Square

Kerameon

Kodratou

Veranzerou

Sokratous

Triti Septemviou

Kaningos

Themiste

Em.

Lenorman

Karaïskaki Square

Karolou

Satovriandou

Omonia Square

28 Oktovriou (Patission)

Panepistimiou (Eleftheriou Venizelou)

Aka

Ahilleos

Ayiou Konstantinou

Menandrou

Athinas

Meg. Alexandrou

Deligiorgi

Zinonos

Kerameikou

P. Tsaldari (Pireos)

Sokratous

Kotzia Square

Stadiou

O
Univ
Com

Kolonou

Marathonos

Leonidou

Kolokynthou

Pireos

Sofokleous

Aristidou

Korai

Thermopilon

Kerameikou

Agisilaou

Epikourou

Menandrou

Armodiou

Aristogitonos

Dragatsaniou

Klafthmonos Sq.

Ayii Theodoroi

Ch. Lada

Natio
Histor
Muse

Eleutherias Square

KERAMEIKOS

Dipilou

Ay. Assomaton

Sarri

Leokoriou

Aristofanous

Ay. Anargiron Square

Evripidou

Iroon Square

PSIRRI

Aiolou

Miltiadou

Paparigopoulou

Praxitelous

Kolokotroni

Kerameikos Cemetery

Navarchou Apostoli

Taki

Miaouli

Perikleous

Karageo
Servias

Ermou

Thissiou

Monastiraki Square

Athinaïdos

Ermou

Poulopoulou

Hephaistion

Adrianou Ifestou

Areos

Mitropoleos

Pandrossou

Mit

Iraklidon

Stoa of Attalos

Dexippou

❺

Aeolos Hotel

Adrianou

Apollonos

Voulis

Pende

THISSION

Tholos

Fethiye Mosque

❹

Pelopida

PLAKA

Akamantos

Polignotou

Tower of the Winds

Kyrrestou

Navarhou Nikodimo

Panos

Tholou

Pritaniou

Lysiou

Flessa

Adrianou

Kodra

Observatory

Apostolou Pavlou

Areopagus

Theorias

Ayios Simeon

Epicharmou

ANAFIOTIKA

Tripodon

Kid

Pnyx

❶

Acropolis

Ayios Georgios tou Vrachou

Epimenidou

Lysikratous

Goura

Pittako

Vironos

❷

Dionyssiou Areopagitou

Temple of Olympian Zeus

0   1/8 mile

Rovertou Galli

Kallisperi

❸

0   200 meters

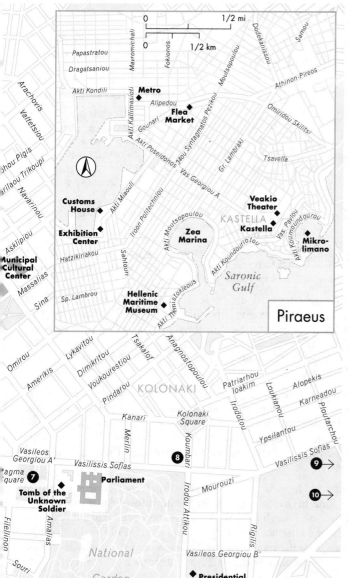

5

Athens into a sparkling modern metropolis.

ESSENTIALS

CURRENCY The euro (€1 to US$1.38 at this writing). U.S. currency is generally not accepted in Europe, but ATMs are common.

HOURS Most stores are open from 9 to 9 on weekdays, from 9 to 6 on Saturday. Museums are generally open from 9 to 5, but many are closed on Mondays.

INTERNET **Cafe 4U** (⊠*44 Ippokratous St.* ☎*210/361–1981* ⊕*www.cafe4u. gr*) is situated close to Syntagma Square. It is open 24 hours a day and serves drinks and snacks. You'll find both terminals and Wi-Fi service.

> ### ATHENS BEST BETS
>
> **The Parthenon.** Regarded as the pinnacle of ancient architectural achievement, this classical temple has inspired poets, artists, and architects. It is the epitome of Greek nationhood.
>
> **The National Archaeological Museum.** A wide-ranging collection covering all eras of Greece's ancient history, from the splendid finds Schliemann excavated at Mycenae to the monumental statues that graced the cities of Attica.
>
> **Changing of the Evzone guards.** With its colorful uniforms and footwear, plus the tendon-stretching step routine, this ceremony is unique and always undertaken with suitable pomp.

TELEPHONES Tri-band GSM phones work in Greece. You can buy prepaid phone cards at telecom shops, news vendors, and tobacconists in all towns and cities. Phone cards can be used for local or international calls. Vodafone is the leading mobile telecom company. OTE is the national domestic provider. Calls can be made at OTE offices and paid for after completion.

COMING ASHORE

Piraeus is the port of Athens, 11 km (7 mi) southwest of the city center, and is itself the third-largest city in Greece with a population of about 500,000. In anticipation of a flood of visitors during the 2004 Olympics, the harbor district was given a general sprucing up. The cruise port has 12 berths and the terminal has duty-free shops, information, and refreshments.

The fastest and cheapest way to get to Athens from Piraeus is to take the metro. Line 1 (Green Line) reaches the downtown Athens stops most handy to tourists, including Platia Victorias, near the National Archaeological Museum; Omonia Square; Monastiraki, in the old Turkish bazaar; and Thission, near the ancient Agora. The Piraeus metro station is off Akti Kallimasioti on the main harbor, a 20-minute walk from the cruise port.

For those who don't have much time, take Bus 904, 905, or 909 opposite the Piraeus station directly to the Archaeological Museum; get off at the Fillelinon stop.

Tickets are €0.80 per journey. A flat fare covering all forms of public transport and valid for 1 hour, 30 minutes is €1. A day pass valid on all buses, trams, metro, and suburban railway is €3. Passes should be validated when first used and are then valid for 24 hours from that time.

Taxis wait outside the terminal entrance. Taxis into the city are not necessarily quicker than public transport. Taxis rates are €1 flat rate, then €0.34 per km (½-mi). Athens taxi drivers have a reputation for overcharging passengers, so make sure the meter is switched on.

EXPLORING ATHENS

Numbers in the margin correspond to points of interest on the Athens map.

Fodor's Choice
★

❶ Acropolis. The massive Acropolis remains an emblem of the glories of classical Greek civilization. The great Panathenaic temple that crowns the rise has the power to stir the heart as few other ancient relics can. The term *akropolis* (to use the Greek spelling) refers to the ancient Athenian "upper city" that occupies the tablelike hill. The Akropolis has many structures, each an architectural gem.

The **Propylaea** is a typical ancient gate, an imposing structure designed to instill proper reverence in worshippers as they crossed from the temporal world into the spiritual world of the Acropolis sanctuary. The Propylaea was used as a garrison during the Turkish period; in 1656, a powder magazine there was struck by lightning, causing much damage; and the Propylaea was again damaged during the Venetian siege 1687. The view from the inner porch of the Propylaea is stunning: the Parthenon is suddenly revealed in its full glory, framed by the columns.

Designed by Kallikrates, the **Temple of Athena Nike,** or Wingless Victory, was built in 427–424 BC to celebrate peace with Persia. The best sections of the temple's frieze were whisked away to the British Museum two centuries ago and replaced with cement copies.

At the loftiest point of the Acropolis is the **Parthenon,** the architectural masterpiece conceived by Pericles and executed between 447 and 438 BC by the brilliant sculptor Pheidias. Although dedicated to the goddess Athena, the Parthenon was primarily the treasury of the Delian League, an ancient alliance of cities. For the populace the Parthenon remained Athena's holiest temple.

If the Parthenon is the masterpiece of Doric architecture, the **Erechtheion** is undoubtedly that of the more graceful Ionic order. Here it was that the contest between Poseidon and Athena took place for possession of the city. Athena was declared the winner, and the city was named after her. The Erechtheion was completed in 406 BC. ✉*Dionyssiou Areopagitou, Acropolis* ☎*210/321–4172 or 210/321–0219* ⊕*www.culture.gr* ⊠*Joint ticket for all Unification of Archaeological Sites €12* ⊙*Apr.–Oct., daily 8–sunset; Nov.–Mar., daily 8–2:30* Ⓜ*Acropolis.*

❷ Acropolis Museum. Full of fabled objects found on the Acropolis, the museum has, among its exhibits, legendary sculptures and votive offerings to Athena. Most notable are sculptures from the Archaic and classical periods, including the *Rampin Horseman* and the compelling *Hound,* both by the sculptor Phaidimos, showing the mastery of the human form that inspired the Neoclassicists. This small museum is scheduled to close once the New Acropolis Museum (expected to open in mid- to late 2008) is completed; the smaller museum's collection will be housed in the new structure. ✉*Dionyssiou Areopagitou, Acropolis* ☎*210/323–6665* ⊕*www.culture.gr* ⊠*Joint ticket for all Unification of Archaeological Sites €12* ⊙*Apr.–Oct., daily 8–7:30; Nov.–Mar., Mon. 10–3, Tues.–Sun. 8:30–3* Ⓜ*Acropolis.*

⑤ Ancient Agora. This marketplace was the hub of ancient Athenian life.
★ Besides administrative buildings, it was surrounded by the schools, theaters, workshops, houses, stores, and market stalls of a thriving town.
Look for markers indicating the circular Tholos, the seat of Athenian
government; the Mitroon, shrine to Rhea, the mother of gods, and the
state archives; the Bouleterion, where the Council met; the Monument of
Eponymous Heroes, the Agora's information center; and the Sanctuary
of the Twelve Gods, a shelter for refugees and the point from which all
distances were measured.

Prominent on the grounds is the **Stoa of Attalos II,** a two-story building
that holds the Museum of Agora Excavations. It was designed as a retail
complex and erected in the 2nd century BC by Attalos, a king of Pergamum.
The stoa was reconstructed in 1953–56. The most notable sculptures, of
historical and mythological figures from the 3rd and 4th centuries BC, are
at ground level outside the museum. In the exhibition hall, chronological
displays of pottery and objects from everyday life illustrate the settlement
of the area from Neolithic times. ⊠ *Three entrances: from Monastiraki*
on Adrianou; from Thission on Apostolou Pavlou; and descending from
Acropolis on Ayios Apostoloi, Monastiraki ☎ *210/321–0185* ⊕ *www.cul-*
ture.gr ⊠ *€4, joint ticket for all Unification of Archaeological Sites €12*
⊙ *May–Oct., daily 8–7; Nov.–Apr., daily 8–5; museum closes ½ hr before*
site Ⓜ *Thiseio.*

⑧ Benaki Museum. This immense collection moves chronologically from prehis-
Fodor's Choice tory to the formation of the modern Greek state. You might see anything
★ from a 5,000-year-old hammered gold bowl to an austere Byzantine icon
of the Virgin Mary. ⊠ *Koumbari 1, Kolonaki* ☎ *210/367–1000* ⊕ *www.*
benaki.gr ⊠ *€6, free Thurs.* ⊙ *Mon., Wed., Fri., and Sat. 9–5, Thurs. 9*
AM*–midnight, Sun. 9–3* Ⓜ *Syntagma.*

⑩ Byzantine and Christian Museum. One of the few museums in Europe concen-
★ trating exclusively on Byzantine art, this collection displays an outstanding collection of icons, mosaics, and tapestries. You can also explore the
on-site archaeological dig of Aristotle's Lyceum. ⊠ *Vasilissis Sofias 22,*
Kolonaki ☎ *210/721–1027, 210/723–2178, or 210/723–1570* ⊕ *www.*
culture.gr ⊠ *€4* ⊙ *Tues.–Sun. 8:30–3* Ⓜ *Evangelismos.*

⑨ Goulandris Cycladic and Greek Ancient Art Museum. This outstanding collection
Fodor's Choice of 350 Cycladic artifacts dating from the Bronze Age includes many of
★ the enigmatic marble figurines whose slender shapes fascinated such artists
as Picasso, Modigliani, and Brancusi. ⊠ *Neofitou Douka 4 or Irodotou*
1, Kolonaki ☎ *210/722–8321 through 210/722–8323* ⊕ *www.cycladic.gr*
⊠ *€3.50* ⊙ *Mon. and Wed.–Fri. 10–4, Sat. 10–3* Ⓜ *Evaneglismos.*

⑥ National Archaeological Museum. By far the most important museum in
Fodor's Choice Greece, this collection contains artistic highlights from every period of
★ ancient Greek civilization, from Neolithic to Roman times.

Holdings are grouped in five major collections: prehistoric artifacts (7th
millennium BC to 1050 BC), sculptures, bronzes, vases and minor arts, and
Egyptian artifacts. The museum's most celebrated display is the **Myce-**
naean Antiquities. Here are the stunning gold treasures from Heinrich
Schliemann's 1876 excavations of Mycenae's royal tombs: the funeral

mask of a bearded king, once thought to be the image of Agamemnon but now believed to be much older, from about the 15th century BC; a splendid silver bull's-head libation cup; and the 15th-century BC Vaphio Goblets, masterworks in embossed gold.

Other stars of the museum include the works of Geometric and Archaic art (10th–6th centuries BC), and kouroi and funerary stelae (8th–5th centuries BC), among them the stelae of the warrior Aristion signed by Aristokles, and the unusual *Running Hoplite* (a hoplite was a Greek infantry soldier). The collection of classical art (5th–3rd centuries BC) contains some of the most renowned surviving ancient statues: the bareback *Jockey of Artemision,* a 2nd-century BC Hellenistic bronze salvaged from the sea, and the *Varvakios Athena,* a half-size marble version of the gigantic gold-and-ivory cult statue that Pheidias erected in the Parthenon. ⊠*28 Oktovriou (Patission) 44, Exarchia* ☎*210/821–7717* ⊕*www.culture.gr* ⊠*€6* ⊙*Apr.–Oct. 15, Mon. 12:30–7, Tues.–Sun. 8:30–7; Oct. 16–Mar., Mon. 10:30–5, Tues.–Sun. 8:30–3.*

❸ **New Acropolis Museum.** Designed by renowned architect Bernard Tschumi, this museum, built specifically to house the treasures that once adorned the Acropolis site, is expected to open in mid- to late 2008. The Greek Government awaits the return of the Elgin Marbles (called the Parthenon marbles in Greece), parts of an immense ornate frieze that once adorned the Parthenon and now reside in the British Museum. The building's centerpiece is a glassed-in rooftop room, built with the exact proportions of the Parthenon, and with views of the temple itself. Contact Acropolis Museum *(⇨above)* for updates on opening. ⊠*Dionyssiou Areopagitou and Makriyianni, Acropolis* ⊕*www.culture.gr* Ⓜ*Acropolis.*

❹ **Roman Agora.** The city's commercial center from the 1st century BC to the
★ 4th century AD, this market's most notable remaining feature is the west entrance's Bazaar Gate, or **Gate of Athena Archegetis,** completed around AD 2. On the north side of the Roman Agora stands one of the few remains of the Turkish occupation, the **Fethiye (Victory) Mosque,** built in the late 15th century on the site of a Christian church to celebrate the Turkish conquest of Athens and to honor Mehmet II (the Conqueror). The octagonal **Tower of the Winds (Aerides)** is the most appealing and well-preserved of the Roman monuments of Athens, keeping time since the 1st century BC. It was originally a sundial, water clock, and weather vane topped by a bronze Triton with a metal rod in his hand, which followed the direction of the wind. ⊠*Pelopidas and Aiolou, Plaka* ☎*210/324–5220* ⊕*www. culture.gr* ⊠*€2, joint ticket for all Unification of Archaeological Sites €12* ⊙*May–Oct., daily 8–7; Nov.–Apr., daily 8–3* Ⓜ*Monastiraki.*

❼ **Syntagma (Constitution) Square.** At the top of the city's main square stands
★ **Parliament,** formerly the royal palace. Here you can watch the **changing of the Evzone guards at the Tomb of the Unknown Soldier**—in front of Parliament on a lower level—which takes place at intervals throughout the day. On Sunday, the honor guard of tall young men don dress costume—a short white *foustanella* (kilt) and red shoes with pompons, arriving in front of Parliament by 11:15 AM. ⊠*Vasilissis Amalias and Vasilissis Sofias, Syntagma Sq.* Ⓜ*Syntagma.*

SHOPPING

Athens has great gifts, particularly handmade crafts. Shops stock copies of traditional Greek jewelry, silver filigree, Skyrian pottery, onyx ashtrays and dishes, woven bags, attractive rugs (including *flokati*, or shaggy goat-wool rugs), wool sweaters, and little blue-and-white pendants designed as amulets to ward off the *mati* (evil eye). Greece is also known for its well-made shoes (most shops are clustered around the Ermou pedestrian zone and in Kolonaki), its furs (Mitropoleos near Syntagma), and its durable leather items (Pandrossou in Monastiraki).

Shops on Pandrossou sell small antiques and icons, but keep in mind that many of these are fakes. You must have government permission to export genuine objects from the ancient Greek, Roman, and Byzantine periods. Many museums sell good quality reproductions or miniatures of their best pieces.

★ **Goutis** (⊠ *Dimokritou 40, Kolonaki* ☎ *210/361–3557*) has an eclectic jumble of jewelry, costumes, embroidery, and old, handcrafted silver objects. At **Riza** (⊠ *Voukourestiou 35, at Skoufa, Kolonaki* ☎ *210/361–1157*) you can pick up wonderful lace, and decorative items such as hand-blown glass bowls and brass candlesticks. Iconographer Aristides Makos creates the beautiful hand-painted, gold-leaf icons on wood and stone that are sold at **Thiamis** (⊠ *Apollonos 12, Plaka* ☎ *210/331–0337*). The **Center of Hellenic Tradition** (⊠ *Mitropoleos 59 and Pandrossou 36, Monastiraki* ☎ *210/321–3023, 210/321–3842 café*) is an outlet for quality handicrafts—ceramics, weavings, sheep bells, and old paintings.

WHERE TO EAT

On Mitropoleos off Monastiraki Square are a handful of counter-front places selling souvlaki—grilled meat rolled in a pita with onions, *tzatziki* (yogurt-garlic dip), and tomatoes—the best bargain in Athens. Make sure you specify whether you want a souvlaki sandwich or a souvlaki plate, which is an entire meal. A contender for the best souvlaki in town is **Thanassis** (⊠ *Mitropoleos 69, Monastiraki* ☎ *210/324–4705*), which is always crowded.

Vyzantino (⊠ *Kidathineon 18, Plaka* ☎ *210/322–7368*) is directly on Plaka's main square—great for people-watching and a good, reasonably priced bite to eat. Try the fish soup, roast potatoes, or baked chicken.

RHODES, GREECE

The island of Rhodes (1,400 square km [540 square mi]) is one of the great islands of the Mediterranean. It was long considered a bridge between Europe and the East and has seen many waves of settlement throughout recorded history. Ancient Rhodes was a powerful city and its political organization became the model for the city of Alexandria in Egypt. When Rome took the city in 42 BC, it was fabled for its beauty and for the sanctuary of Lindos, which drew pilgrims from around the region. Rhodes was a crucial stop on the road to the Holy Land during the Crusades. It came briefly under Venetian influence, then Byzantine, then Genoese, but in

1309, when the Knights of St. John took the city from its Genoese masters, its most glorious modern era began. Today Rhodes is a popular holiday island for Europeans who come for the sun and the beaches.

ESSENTIALS

CURRENCY   The euro (€1 to US$1.46 at this writing). U.S. currency is generally not accepted in Europe, but ATMs are common.

HOURS   Shop are open from 9 to 9 on weekdays and from 9 to 6 on Saturday. Museums are generally open from 9 to 5, but many are closed on Monday.

INTERNET   **Galileo Internet** (✉*13 Iroon Politechniou St.* ☎*22410/20610*) has 25 machines and is open daily from 9 AM to 2 AM.

TELEPHONES   Tri-band GSM phones work in Greece. You can buy prepaid phone cards at telecom shops, news vendors, and tobacconists in all towns and cities. Phone cards can be used for local or international calls. Vodafone is the leading mobile telecom company. OTE is the national domestic provider. Calls can be made at OTE offices and paid for after completion.

COMING ASHORE

Ships dock at the commercial port directly outside the city walls of Rhodes Town. It is a very short walk from the port to all the attractions of the walled citadel. For this reason, there are few facilities in the port itself.

The bus station for services down the east coast is found by turning right outside the port and walking for 10 minutes to Rimini Square. There are several services to Lindos each day. Journey time is about one hour.

Taxis wait outside the port gates but can also be found at Rimini Square. For a journey to Lindos, prices are fixed at a fare of €35 one way. Journey time is approximately 30 minutes. You could enjoy a full day touring Rhodes island if you rent a car, though both Rhodes's old town and Lindos are pedestrian-only or have very limited vehicular access. Costs are €90 per day for a subcompact vehicle and the major companies can bring a car to the port for you.

EXPLORING RHODES

Numbers in the margin correspond to points of interest on the Rhodes map.

RHODES TOWN

Rhodes town is still a city of two parts: the old town, a UNESCO World Heritage site, contains exceptional medieval architecture, Orthodox and Catholic churches, and an alluring old Turkish quarter. Spreading away from the walls that encircle the old town is the modern metropolis, or new town. You can purchase a multisight ticket (€10), which gets you admission to the Palace of the Grand Masters, Archaeological Museum, Museum of Decorative Arts, and Byzantine Museum.

5 **Archaeological Museum.** The hospital was the largest of the Knights' public buildings, completed in 1489. The imposing facade opens into a courtyard, where cannonballs remain from the siege of 1522. Today it contains the Archaelogical Museum. On the main floor there's a collection of ancient pottery and sculpture, including two well-known representations of Aph-

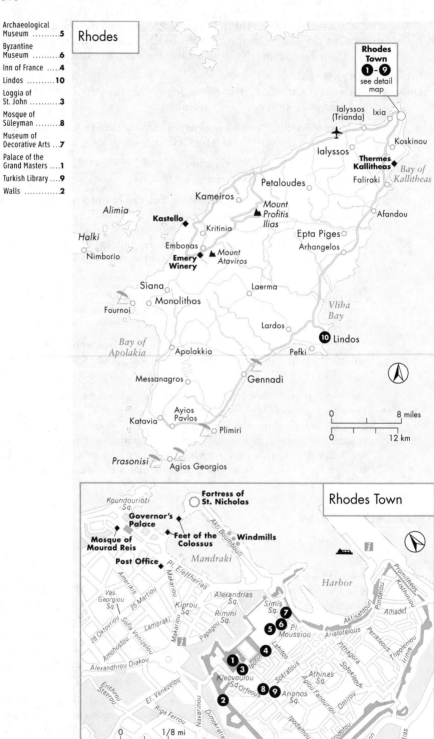

rodite: the *Aphrodite of Rhodes,* who, while bathing, pushes aside her hair as if she's listening; and a standing figure, known as *Aphrodite Thalassia,* or "of the sea," as she was discovered in the water off the northern city beach. Other important works include a 6th-century BC *kouros* (a statue of an idealized male youth, usually nude) that was found in Kameiros, and the beautiful 5th-century BC funerary stele of Timarista bidding farewell to her mother, Crito. ⊠*Pl. Moussiou* ☎*22410/25500* ⊕*www.culture.gr* ⊠*€3* ⊙*Tues.–Sun. 8:30–3.*

⑥ **Byzantine Museum.** This collection of icons is displayed within the 11th-century Lady of the Castle church. ⊠*Off Pl. Moussiou* ☎*22410/23359* ⊠*€2* ⊙*Tues.–Sun. 8:30–3.*

RHODES BEST BETS

Walk down the Street of the Knights. This medieval street is one of the most complete of its kind in the world. Imagine the crusader knights going about their business here in the 14th and 15th centuries.

Explore the Turkish Quarter. These narrow alleyways now play host to boutiques and cafés, but it's still a living district with real Aegean character.

Survey Lindos town from the Acropolis above. This height offers a splendid vista, from the tangle of narrow streets, whitewashed walls, and terra-cotta roofs down to the golden horseshoe bay with its azure waters.

④ The **Inn of France** was the largest of the Knights' gathering spots and is now the French Consulate. The facade is carved with flowers and heraldic patterns and bears an inscription that dates the building between 1492 and 1509. ⊠*About halfway down Str. of the Knights from Loggia of St. John.*

③ **Loggia of St. John.** In front of the court of Palace of the Grand Masters is the Loggia of St. John, on the site where the Knights of St. John were buried in an early church. From the Loggia, the **Street of the Knights** descends toward the **Commercial Port,** bordered on both sides by the **Inns of the Tongues,** where the Knights supped and held their meetings.

⑧ **Mosque of Süleyman.** This mosque at the top of Sokratous street was built circa 1522 and rebuilt in 1808. At this writing, the site was closed indefinitely for restoration work. ⊠*Sokratous St.*

⑦ **Museum of Decorative Arts.** This collection exhibits finely made ceramics, crafts, and artifacts from around the Dodecanese. ⊠*Pl. Argyrokastrou* ☎*22410/23359* ⊠*€2* ⊙*Tues.–Sun. 8:30–3.*

① **Palace of the Grand Masters.** In the castle area, a city within a city, the Knights of St. John built most of their monuments. The Palace of the Grand Masters, at the highest spot of the medieval city, is the best place to begin a tour of Rhodes; here you can get oriented before wandering through the labyrinthine old town. Of great help is the permanent exhibition downstairs, with extensive displays, maps, and plans showing the layout of the city. The palace building withstood the Turkish siege unscathed, but in 1856, an explosion of ammunition stored nearby in the cellars of the Church of St. John devastated it; the present structures are 20th-century Italian reconstructions. Note the Hellenistic and Roman mosaic floors throughout, which came from the Italian excavations in Kos. ⊠*Ippoton,* *old town* ☎*22410/23359* ⊕*www.culture.gr* 🎫*€6* ⊘*May–Oct., Mon. 12:30–7, Tues.–Sun. 8:30–7; Nov.–Apr., Tues.–Sun. 8.30–3.*

❾ The **Turkish Library** dates to the late 18th century. Striking reminders of the Ottoman presence, the library and the mosque opposite are still used by those members of Rhodes's Turkish community who stayed behind after the population exchange of 1922. ✉*Sokratous opposite the Mosque of Süleyman* ☎*22410/74090* 🎫*Free* ⊘*Mon.–Sat. 9:30–4.*

❷ The **walls** of Rhodes in themselves are one of the great medieval monuments in the Mediterranean. Wonderfully restored, they illustrate the engineering capabilities as well as the financial and human resources available to the Knights. Twentieth-century Italian rulers erased much of the Ottoman influence, preferring to emphasize the Knights's past when restoring architecture. For 200 years the Knights strengthened the walls by thickening them, up to 40 feet in places, and curving them so as to deflect cannonballs. The moat between the inner and outer walls never contained water; it was a device to prevent invaders from constructing siege towers. Part of the road that runs along the top for the entire 4 km (2½ mi) is accessible through municipal guided tours. ✉*Old town, tours depart from Palace of the Grand Masters entrance* ☎*22410/23359* 🎫*Tour €6* ⊘*Tours Tues. and Sat. at 2:45 (arrive at least 15 min early).*

LINDOS

❿ *19 km (12 mi) southwest of Epta Piges, 48 km (30 mi) southwest of Rhodes town.*

Lindos, cradled between two harbors, had a particular importance in antiquity. Lindos possessed a revered sanctuary, consecrated to Athena, whose cult probably succeeded that of a pre-Hellenic divinity named Lindia, and the sanctuary was dedicated to Athena Lindia. Lindos prospered during the Middle Ages, and under the Knights of St. John. Only at the beginning of the 19th century did the age-old shipping activity cease. The population decreased radically, reviving only with the 20th-century influx of foreigners.

Lindos is enchanting and remarkably well-preserved. Many 15th-century houses are still in use. Everywhere are examples of Crusader architecture: substantial houses of finely cut Lindos limestone, with windows crowned by elaborate arches. Intermixed with these Crusader buildings are whitewashed, geometric, Cycladic-style houses. Many floors are paved with black-and-white pebble mosaics. The narrow alleyways can get crowded in summer.

The **Church of the Panayia** (✉*Off main square*) is a graceful building with a beautiful bell tower. The body of the church probably antedates the Knights, although the bell tower bears their arms with the dates 1484–90. The interior has frescoes painted in 1779 by Gregory of Symi.

FodorśChoice For about €5, you can hire a donkey for the 15-minute climb from the
★ modern town up to the **Acropolis of Lindos.** The final approach ascends a steep flight of stairs, past a marvelous 2nd-century BC **relief** of the prow of a Lindian ship carved into the rock, and through the main gate.

The entrance to the Acropolis takes you through the **medieval castle,** with the Byzantine **Chapel of St. John** on the next level above. On the **upper terraces** are the remains of the elaborate **porticoes** and **stoas.** The site and temple command an immense sweep of sea; the lofty white columns on the summit must have presented a magnificent picture. The main portico had 42 Doric columns, at the center of which an opening led to the staircase up to the **propylaea.** The temple at the very top is surprisingly modest, given the drama of the approach. As was common in the 4th century BC, both the front and the rear are flanked by four Doric columns, like the Temple of Athena Nike on the Acropolis of Athens. Numerous inscribed statue bases were found all over the summit, attesting in many cases to the work of Lindian sculptors, who were clearly second to none. ⊠*Above new town* ☏*22410/22410* ⊕*www.culture.gr* ▣*€6* ☉*May–Oct., Mon. 1–7.30, Tues.–Sun. 8–7:30; Nov.–Apr., Tues.–Sun. 8–3.*

SHOPPING

Lovers of handicrafts will really enjoy shopping in Rhodes. There's an abundance of ceramics, both traditional and modern, wooden bowls, reproductions of ancient statuary, woven rugs, jewelry, lace, and edibles such as delicious honey, olive oil, and of course, olives themselves. Cotton clothing is perfect for the summer temperatures. Strong handcrafted sandals and leather goods are also excellent choices.

Souvenir shopping in Rhodes Town is concentrated on Sokratous Street and the labyrinth of narrow alleyways in the old Turkish Quarter. You'll find the same merchandise in the alleyways of Lindos, where every inch of wall space is used for display—sometimes to the detriment of pedestrian traffic flow. Rhodes town has a number of high-class jewelers and camera shops, whereas Lindos has more art galleries. The winding path that leads up to the citadel of Lindos is traditionally where Lindian women spread out their lace and embroidery over the rocks like fresh laundry.

The owner of **Astero Antiques** (⊠*Ayiou Fanouriou 4, at Sokratous* ☏*22410/34753*) travels throughout Greece each winter to fill his shop.

Famous Silver Jewellery (⊠*27 Papanikolaou St.* ☏*22410/70863*) has a huge range of silver items.

Tradition (⊠*8 Ippodamou St.* ☏*22410/24236*) sells delicious olive oil, herbs, olives, wine, and honey, plus some interesting ceramics.

SPORTS & ACTIVITIES

Faliraki Beach (⇨*below*) is the place for a whole range of water sports. You can also head to the southern island tip of **Prasonisi** (⊠*17 km [10½ mi] south of Plimiri*), around an hour and 15 minutes from Rhodes town, for some of Greece's best windsurfing. Boards and wet suits can be rented at the beach.

BEACHES

Rhodes is a very popular island with European vacationers and the beaches all around the island have well-developed facilities.

Faliraki Beach (✉ *16 km [10 mi] south of Rhodes town*), with its long stretch of sandy beach and water park, has a reputation for its twentysomething, boozing crowds.

Two quieter alternatives to Faliraki Beach are just south. Turn left at the sign to Ladico and you'll reach the twin bays of **Ladico Beach** and **Anthony Quinn Beach** (extolled for its beauty by the actor when he filmed *The Guns of Navarone* here). Both coves have deep, turquoise water, surrounded by high, tree-covered rocks.

Lindos has a lovely sandy crescent flanking the old town but it does get busy during the summer. The long **Lachania Beach** begins a mile before Gennadi and stretches south, uninterrupted for several miles; drive alongside until you come to a secluded spot.

WHERE TO EAT

¢–$$$$ ✕ **Mavrikos.** The secret of this longtime favorite is an elegant, perfect simplicity. Seemingly straightforward dishes, such as sea-urchin salad, fried *manouri* cheese with basil and pine nuts, swordfish in caper sauce, and lobster risotto, become transcendent with the magic touch of third-generation chef Dimitris Mavrikos. He combines the freshest ingredients with classical training and an abiding love for the best of Greek village cuisine. ✉ *Main square, Lindos* ☎ *22440/31232* ☐ *MC, V* ⊗ *Closed Nov.–Mar.*

¢–$$$ ✕ **Alexis.** Continuing the tradition begun by his father in 1957, Yiannis
★ Katsimprakis serves the very best seafood and speaks passionately of eating fish as though it were a lost art. Don't bother with the menu; just ask for suggestions and then savor every bite, whether you choose caviar, mussels in wine, smoked eel, or sea urchins. He even cooks up *porphyra*, the mollusk yielding the famous purple dye of the Byzantine emperors. A side dish might be sautéed squash with wild *glistrida* (purslane). ✉ *Sokratous 18, Rhodes Town* ☎ *22410/29347* ☐ *AE, MC, V* ⊗ *Closed Nov.–Apr. No lunch Sun. June–Aug.*

SANTORINI, GREECE

Undoubtedly the most extraordinary island in the Aegean, crescent-shape Santorini remains a mandatory stop on the Cycladic tourist route—even if it's necessary to enjoy the sensational sunsets from Ia, the fascinating excavations, and the dazzling white towns with a million other travelers. Arriving by boat, you are met by one of the world's truly breathtaking sights, the caldera: a crescent of cliffs, striated in black, pink, brown, white, and pale green, rising 1,100 feet, with the white clusters of the towns of Fira and Ia perched along the top. The encircling cliffs are the ancient rim of a still-active volcano, and you are sailing east across its flooded caldera. Victims of their own success, the main towns of Santorini can at peak times seem overburdened by an unrelenting mass of backpackers and tour groups. Even so, if you look beneath the layers of gimcrack tourism, you'll find that Santorini is still a beautiful place.

ESSENTIALS

CURRENCY   The euro (€1 to US$1.46 at this writing). U.S. currency is generally not accepted in Europe, but ATMs are common.

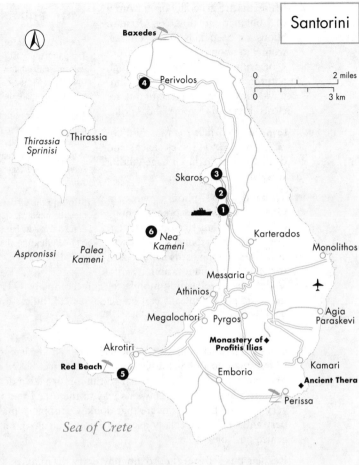

Santorini

Baxedes

Perivolos **4**

0   2 miles
0   3 km

Thirassia Sprinisi   Thirassia

Skaros **3**
2
1

6 *Nea Kameni*

Karterados

Monolithos

Aspronissi   *Palea Kameni*

Messaria

Athinios

Megalochori   Pyrgos

Akrotiri

Monastery of Profitis Ilias ◆

Agia Paraskevi

Red Beach   **5**

Emborio

Kamari

Ancient Thera ◆

Perissa

Sea of Crete

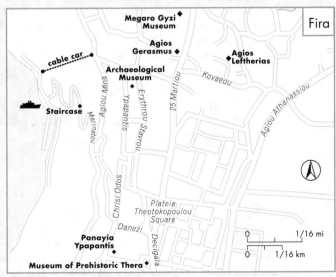

Fira

Megaro Gyzi Museum ◆

Agios Gerasmus ◆

cable car

Archaeological Museum

Agios Leftherias ◆

Kovaeou

Agiou Mina
Ypapantis
Erythrou Stavrou
25 Martiou

Agiou Athanassiou

Staircase

Marinatou

Chrisi Odos

Plateia Theotokopoulou Square

Danezi

Decigala

Panayia Ypapantis ◆

0   1/16 mi
0   1/16 km

Museum of Prehistoric Thera ◆

5

HOURS Museums are generally open from 9 to 5, but many are closed on Monday. Shops are open daily in the summer, from 9 to noon or 1, reopening from 4 or 5 until 9 on Monday through Saturday; and from 9 to 6 on Sunday. Many shops and restaurants are closed between October and April.

INTERNET **Lava Café** (✉ *Main road, at Fira Sq.* ☎ *22860/25291*) serves snacks and drinks and also has image-editing software.

TELEPHONES Tri-band GSM phones work in Greece. You can buy prepaid phone cards at telecom shops, news vendors, and tobacconists in all towns and cities. Phone cards can be used for local or international calls. Vodafone is the leading mobile telecom company. OTE is the national domestic provider. Calls can be made at OTE offices and paid for after completion.

> ### SANTORINI BEST BETS
>
> **The view of Santorini from the ship.** The panoramic vista of the immense volcano with whitewashed settlements tumbling over the caldera edge is unique and quite unforgettable.
>
> **The remains of ancient Akrotiri.** A city frozen in time by volcanic ash, ancient Akrotiri tells a fascinating story of a rich Aegean civilization that seems to have escaped before disaster struck.
>
> **Strolling the streets of Ia.** Santorini's most beautiful village has foliage-draped Cycladic houses, boutiques, and eateries. The views are best at sunset.

COMING ASHORE

Cruise ships anchor in the spectacular caldera and passengers are tendered to the small port of Skala Fira, a sheer 1,000 feet below the capital, Fira. You can either take the funicular to the top or take a donkey ride up the steep winding path that claws its way to the top. The donkey drivers are very persistent, but be aware that donkey droppings make the path slippery and smelly (especially relevant if you decide to go up by foot, which is also possible).

Regular bus services (approximately every 30 minutes in summer, dropping to every 1½ hours in winter with shoulder seasons) travel from Thira to Ia and Akrotiri. Schedules are posted in the station. Ticket prices range from €1.10 to €1.80. The main taxi stand sits next to the bus station in the main town square. Fares are reasonable, with a trip from Fira to Ia costing approximately €15.

If you rented a car for the day, you could probably see most of what Santorini has to offer. The island is compact and it's difficult to get lost. Prices are €90 per day for a subcompact manual vehicle, but you can get an ATV for around €25.

EXPLORING SANTORINI

Numbers in the margin correspond to points of interest on the Santorini map.

FIRA

❶ Tourism, the island's major industry, adds more than 1 million visitors per year to a population of 7,000. As a result, Fira, the capital, midway along the west coast of the east rim, is no longer only a picturesque village but a major tourist center, overflowing with discos, shops, and restaurants. It soon becomes clear what brings the tourist here: with its white, cubical white houses clinging to the cliff hundreds of feet above the caldera, Fira is a beautiful place. The blocked-off Ypapantis Street (west of Panayia Ypapantis cathedral) leads to Kato Fira (Lower Fira), built into the cliff side overlooking the caldera, where prices are higher and the vista wonderful. For centuries, the people of the island have been digging themselves rooms-with-a-view right in the cliff face. Along Eikostis Pemptis Martiou (25th March Street), you'll find inexpensive restaurants and accommodations—many bars and hotel rooms now occupy the caves. The farther away from the caldera you get, the cheaper the restaurants.

The **Archaeological Museum** displays pottery, statues, and grave artifacts found at excavations mostly from ancient Thira and Akrotiri, from the Minoan through the Byzantine periods. ⊠ *Stavrou and Nomikos* ☎ *22860/22217* ✉ *€5, including Museum of Prehistoric Thera* ⊙ *Tues.–Sun. 8:30–3.*

★ **The Museum of Prehistoric Thera** displays pots and frescoes from the famed excavations at Akrotiri. Note the fresco fragments with the painted swallows (who flocked here because they loved the cliffs) and the women in Minoan dresses. The fossilized olive leaves from 60,000 BC prove the olive to be indigenous. ⊠ *Mitropoleos, behind big church* ☎ *22860/23217* ⊕ *www.culture.gr* ✉ *€5 including Archaeological Museum, €8 including Archeological Museum and Akrotiri* ⊙ *Tues.–Sun. 8:30–3.*

Panayia Ypapantis, Fira's modern Greek Orthodox cathedral, is a major landmark; the local priests, with somber faces, long beards, and black robes, look strangely out of place in summertime Fira. ⊠ *Southern part of town.*

To experience life here as it was until only a couple of decades ago, walk down the much-photographed winding **Staircase** that descends from town to the water's edge—walk or take the cable car back up, avoiding the drivers who will try to plant you on the sagging back of one of their bedraggled donkeys. Note, however, that however you choose to return to the top, the price is the same (cable car or donkey). ⊠ *Marinatou*

FIROSTEFANI

❷ Firostefani used to be a separate village, but now it is an elegant suburb north of Fira. The 10-minute walk between it and Fira, along the caldera, is one of Santorini's highlights. From Firostefani's single white cliff-side street, walkways descend to traditional vaulted cave houses, which are fast becoming pensions. Though close to the action, Firostefani feels calm and quiet.

IMEROVIGLI

❸ Imerovigli, on the highest point of the caldera's rim, is what Firostefani was like a decade and a half ago. It is now being developed, and for good reasons: it is quiet, traditional, and less expensive. The 25-minute walk from Fira, with incredible views, should be on everyone's itinerary. The lodgments, some of them traditional cave houses, are mostly down stairways from the cliff-side walkway. The big rock backing the village was once crowned by Skaros castle, where Venetial the conqueror raised his flag in 1207; it housed the island's administrative offices. It collapsed in an earthquake, leaving only the rock.

IA

❹ At the tip of the northern horn of the island sits Ia (or Oia), Santorini's sec-
Fodor's Choice   ond-largest town and the Aegean's most photographed village. Ia is more
★   tasteful than Fira, and the town's cubical white houses stand out against
the green, brown, and rust-color layers of rock, earth, and solid volcanic
ash that rise from the sea. Every summer evening, travelers from all over
the world congregate at the caldera's rim—sitting on whitewashed fences,
staircases, beneath the town's windmill, on the old castle—each looking
out to sea in anticipation of the performance: the Ia sunset.

In the middle of the quiet caldera, the volcano smolders away eerily,
adding an air of suspense to an already awe-inspiring scene. The 1956
eruption caused tremendous earthquakes (7.8 on the Richter scale) that
left 48 people dead (thankfully, most residents were working outdoors
at the time), hundreds injured, and 2,000 houses toppled. The island's
west side—especially Ia, until then the largest town—was hard hit, and
many residents decided to emigrate to Athens, Australia, and America.
And although Fira, also damaged, rebuilt rapidly, Ia proceeded slowly,
sticking to the traditional architectural style.

Ia is set up like the other three towns—Fira, Firostefani, and Imerovigli—
that adorn the caldera's sinuous rim. There is a car road, which is new,
and a cliff-side walkway, which is old. Shops and restaurants are all on
the walkway, and hotel entrances mostly descend from it—something to
check carefully if you cannot negotiate stairs easily. In Ia there is a lower
cliff-side walkway writhing with stone steps, and a long stairway to the
tiny blue bay with its dock below. Short streets leading from the car road
to the walkway have cheaper eateries and shops. There is a parking lot at
either end; the northern one marks the end of the road and the rim. Nothing is very far from anything else. The three-hour rim-edge walk from Fira
to Ia, through Firostefani and Imerovigli, is unforgettable.

ANCIENT AKROTIRI

❺ The best archaeological site on Santorini is near the tip of the southern
★   horn of the island. Unfortunately, at this writing, the site is closed (and
has been for some time) for structural repairs. There was some hope that
it might reopen in 2008, but such hopes have become commonplace for
the past few years, so check ahead before you plan a visit.

In the 1860s, in the course of quarrying volcanic ash for use in the Suez
Canal, workmen discovered the remains of an ancient town. The town
was frozen in time by ash from an eruption 3,600 years ago, long before
Pompeii's disaster. In 1967 Spyridon Marinatos of the University of Athens began excavations. It is thought that the 40 buildings that have been
uncovered are only one-thirtieth of the huge site and that excavating the
rest will probably take a century.

Culturally an outpost of Minoan Crete, **Akrotiri** was settled as early as
3000 BC and reached its peak after 2000 BC, when it developed trade and
agriculture and settled the present town. The inhabitants cultivated olive
trees and grain, and their advanced architecture—three-story frescoed
houses faced with masonry (some with balconies) and public buildings of
sophisticated construction—is evidence of an elaborate lifestyle. Unlike at
Pompeii, no human remains, gold, silver, or weapons were found here—

probably tremors preceding the eruption warned the inhabitants to pack their valuables and flee. After the eruptions Santorini was uninhabited for about two centuries while the land cooled and plant and animal life regenerated. ✉*South of modern Akrotiri, near tip of southern horn, 13 km (8 mi) south of Fira* ☎*22860/81366* ⊕*www.culture.gr* 🎫*€5* 🕙*Tues.–Sun. 8:30–3.*

NEA KAMENI

6 To peer into a live, sometimes smoldering volcano, join one of the popular excursions to **Nea Kameni,** the larger of the two Burnt Isles at the center of the caldera. After disembarking, you hike 430 feet to the top and walk around the edge of the crater, wondering if the volcano is ready for its fifth eruption during the last hundred years—after all, the last was in 1956. Some tours continue on to Therasia, where there is a village. ✉*In the Caldera, 2 km (1 mi) west of* 🎫 *Fira*Tours (about €15) are scheduled regularly by **Bellonias Tours** (☎*22860/22469 Fira, 22860/31117 Kamari*) and **Nomikos Travel** (☎*22860/23660* 🖷*22860/23666* ⊕*www.nomikosvillas.gr*).

SHOPPING

The dramatic landscapes and light of Santorini are an inspiration to the creative—the archipelago is home to artists working in many genres. There are many galleries selling exquisite one-of-a-kind jewelry and hundreds of others selling artistic accessories for the home.

The locals say that in Santorini there is more wine than water, and it may be true: Santorini produces more wine than any two other Cyclades. Thirty-six varieties of grape thrive here. Farmers twist the vines into a basketlike shape, in which the grapes grow, protected from the wind.

Husband and wife artistic team Christoforos and Eleni Asimis sell their fine art, crafts, and jewelry at **Phenomenon** (✉*Ypapantis Walkway, Palia Fabrika, Fira* ☎*22860/23041* ⊕*www.santorini.info/paliafabrika/index.html*).

Costas Dimitrokalis (✉*1 block from cable car, Fira* 🖷*22860/22957*) and Matthew Dimitrokalis sell locally made embroideries of Greek linen and Egyptian cotton, rugs, and pillowcases in hand-crocheted wool with local designs.

The original pieces at **Kostas Antoniou Jewelry** (✉*Opposite cable car, Fira* 🖷*22860/22633*) are inspired by ancient Thera. The work is both classic and creative.

Art Gallery (✉*Main shopping St., Fira* 🖷*22860/71448*) sells large, three-dimensional representations of Santorini architecture by Bella Kokeenatou and Stavros Galanopoulos. **Caldera** (✉*Main shopping St. Fira* 🖷*22860/71363*), in a vaulted cliff-side room, shows paintings and sculptures by artists on Santorini, and also objects and rugs.

BEACHES

Santorini's volcanic rocks have produced unusual beaches of black and red sand that make for dramatic vistas. One thing to note is that this sand absorbs the suns rays and gets much hotter than golden sand. The black-sand beaches of **Kamari** (and of Perissa) are popular and consequently overdeveloped. Deck chairs and umbrellas can be rented, and tavernas and refreshment stands abound. **Red Beach** (⊠ *On southwest shore below Akrotiri*) is quiet and has a taverna.

WHERE TO EAT

¢–$ ✕**Nicholas.** This is Santorini's oldest taverna, where you'll find locals in winter. Island dishes are prepared well and served in a simple, attractive room. Try the local yellow lentils and the lamb fricassee with an egg-lemon sauce. ⊠*2 streets in from cliff side on Erythrou Stavrou* ☎*No phone* ⊟*No credit cards.*

¢–$ ✕**Skaros Fish Taverna.** This rustic open-air taverna, one of three restaurants in Imerovigli, has spectacular caldera views. It serves fresh fish and Santorini specialties, such as octopus in onion sauce, and mussels with rice and raisins. ⊠*On cliff-side walkway, Imerovigli* ☎*22860/23616* ⊟*AE, MC, V* ☉*Closed Nov.–Mar.*

The North Sea

Bruges, Belgium

6

WORD OF MOUTH

"Amsterdam is so walkable and safe, you can easily just 'follow your nose' without needing a walking plan. We loved wandering around that lovely city, at all hours of the day and night."

—MaureenB

"[In Edinburgh] we walked the Royal Mile (more than once), visited Holyrood Palace, the Britannia, Mary King's Close."

—d1carter

Lindsay Bennett **PORTS IN THE UNITED KINGDOM** have long been the starting points for many transatlantic crossings, but these days, your ship is more likely to begin its journey in Harwich as Southampton and may cruise around the North Sea and British Isles or continue to the Baltic or even around the Mediterranean. Royal Caribbean announced that the line's new ship, *Independence of the Seas,* would make its European home in Southampton and Harwich for the 2008 Mediterranean cruising season. These increasingly busy ports sometimes include more exotic destinations such as the Canary Islands on their itineraries.

ABOUT THE RESTAURANTS

All the restaurants we recommend serve lunch; they may also serve dinner if your cruise ship stays late in port and you choose to dine off the ship. Europeans tend to eat a leisurely meal at lunch, but in most ports there are quicker and simpler alternatives for those who just want to grab a quick bite before returning to the ship. You'll be able to pay in euros only in Belgium, Ireland, and the Netherlands; prices in England and Scotland are in British pounds. Price categories in those countries are based on the euro-equivalent costs of eating in restaurants.

WHAT IT COSTS IN EUROS & POUNDS					
	$$$$	$$$	$$	$	¢
RESTAURANTS in euros	over €30	€23–€30	€17–€23	€11–€17	under €11
RESTAURANTS in pounds	over £15	£12–£15	£8–£12	£5–£8	under £5

Restaurant prices are per person for a main course, including tax.

AMSTERDAM, NETHERLANDS

Amsterdam has as many facets as a 40-carat diamond polished by one of the city's gem cutters: the capital, and spiritual "downtown," of a nation ingrained with the principles of tolerance; a veritable Babylon of old-world charm; a font for homegrown geniuses such as Rembrandt and Van Gogh; a cornucopia bursting with parrot tulips and other greener—more potent—blooms; and a unified social zone that takes in cozy bars, archetypal "brown" cafés, and outdoor markets. While impressive gabled houses bear witness to the Golden Age of the 17th century, their upside-down images reflected in the waters of the city's canals symbolize and magnify the contradictions within the broader Dutch society. With a mere 730,000 friendly souls and with almost everything a scant 10-minute bike ride away, Amsterdam is actually like a village that happens to pack the cultural wallop of a megalopolis.

ESSENTIALS

CURRENCY The euro (€1 to US$1.46); exchange rates were accurate at this writing but are subject to change. U.S. currency is generally not accepted in Europe, but ATMs are common and credit cards are widely accepted.

HOURS Shops open Tuesday, Wednesday, Friday, and Saturday from 9 or 10 until 6; they are open later on Thursday. Most stores are closed on Sundays and some on Mondays. Museums open from 9 until 6 with one late-opening night during the week.

INTERNET   **Underworld Café** ✉*7-a Voetboogstraat* ☎*020/6381388.*

TELEPHONES   Most tri- and quad-band GSM mobile phones should work in the Netherlands, which operates a 3G mobile system with dual-band handsets. Public phones take phone cards (available at numerous shops) and credit cards and will connect international calls. Major telecom companies are Vodafone and Orange.

COMING ASHORE

Shops dock at the cruise terminal adjacent to the historic old town, a five-minute walk to the transport hub of the city. The terminal has tourist information, extensive shopping facilities, and a range of eateries. Passengers can walk directly from the terminal into the town or rent a bike and take to the cycle tracks that crisscross the city. The main train station and city bus station are adjacent for trips to other locations around the Netherlands.

The so-called "Canal Bus" (which is actually a boat) stops at 14 of Amsterdam's major museums, traveling around on the water. A day ticket for the Canal Bus is €18, plus discounts on some museum entrance fees. The bus makes a stop just outside the central train station. Public bus and tram services are also useful for visiting the attractions: tickets cost €1.60 for a one-zone journey.

EXPLORING AMSTERDAM

Numbers in the margin correspond to points of interest on the Amsterdam map.

❺ **Amsterdams Historisch Museum** *(Amsterdam Historical Museum).* Any city that began in the 13th century as a sinking bog of a fishing village and eventually became the 17th century's most powerful trading city has a fascinating story to tell, and this museum does it superbly. It's housed in a rambling amalgamation of buildings that were used as an orphanage in 1580 and then reopened as a museum in 1975. Although rich with art, models, and plain old treasures, the museum also employs a lot of state-of-the-art technologies: many will delight in the five different **speaking dollhouses** that tell of daily life through the centuries and a "white car" (a small car originally formulated to be a utopian form of urban transportation in the 1960s) in which you can cruise the city's streets. ✉*Kalverstraat 92 and Nieuwezijds Voorburgwal 357, Nieuwe Zijde* ☎*020/523–1822* ⊕*www.ahm.nl* ☞*€7* ☉*Weekdays 10–5, weekends 11–5.*

FodorsChoice
★

❷ **Anne Frankhuis** *(Anne Frank House).* In the precious pages of *The Diary of Anne Frank* (published in 1947 as *The Secret Annex* by her father after her death) the young Anne kept her sad record of two increasingly fraught years living in secret confinement from the Nazis. Along with the Van Pels family (called Van Daan in the book) family, the Frank family felt the noose tighten, so decided to move into a hidden warren of rooms at the back of this 1635-built canal house. Anne's diary has now sold over 30 million copies and been translated into more than 50 languages. The museum explores the wider issues of genocide and oppression but visitors flock to feel the reality of Anne's daily existence. ✉*Prinsengracht 263, Jordaan* ☎*020/556–*

FodorsChoice
★

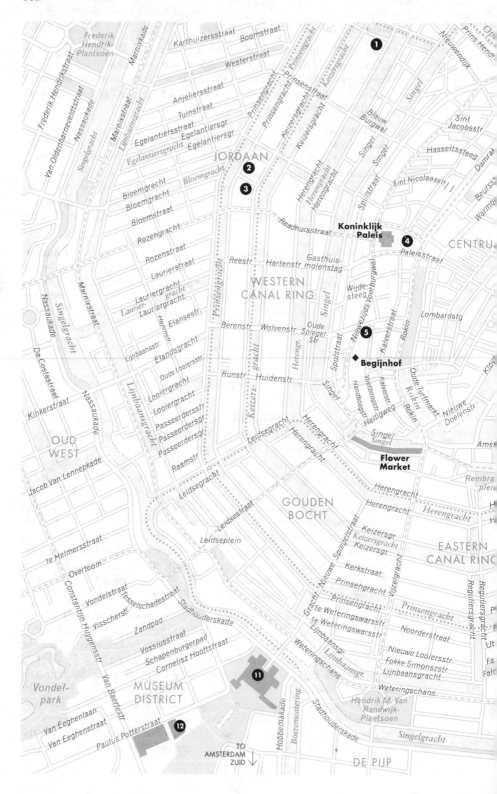

Centraal
Station

Het Ij

Stationsplein

Amsterdam

M

Centraal
Station

Warmoesstraat

Lange Korte   St Stormstg
Niezel Niezel

7

Molenstg

Gelderskade

Oosterdokskade

Oosterdok

Prins Hendrikkade

Oude Waal

Recht Boomssloot

Recht Boomssloot

Koningsstraat

6

Nieuwmarkt M

wal

◆ **Zuiderkerk**

NIEUWMARKT

Prins Hendrikkade

IJ-tunnel

Nieuwevaart

Hoogte Kadijk

Nieuwe Herengracht

Laagte Kadijk

Valkenbergerstr.

-bergerstr.

Nieuwe Herengr.

8

Waterlooplein

Rapen-

JEWISH QUARTER

Waterloopl. Jodenbreestr.

Plantage

Plantage-Parklaan

Doklaan

**Muziek-
theater**

M **Waterlooplein**

Muiderstr.

Kerklaan

Artis

Blauwbrug

Plantage

Plantage Plantage Middenlaan

10

gracht

Nieuwe Harengr

Nieuwe
Nieuwe
Nieuwe

Keizersgr
Keizersgr
Keizersgr

Plantage
Muidergracht

R0etersfr

PLANTAGE

gracht

Utrechtsestraat

Keizersgracht

Keizersgracht

Magere
Brug **9**

Nieuwe Kerkstr

Nieuwe Prinsengr

Nieuwe Prinsengr

straat

Nieuwe Prinsengr

Weesperstraat

Nieuwe Achtergracht

gracht

Prinsengracht
gracht

Amstel

Amstel

Nieuwe Achtergracht

en-
ën:

straat

Amstel

sedwars-

Achtergracht

Weesperplein M

raat
aat

*Frederiks-
plein*

Sarphatistraat

Westeinde

Stadhouderskade

KEY
+—+—+ *Rail lines*
▭▭▭ *Metro lines*
- - - *Tram lines*
······· *Canal bus*

0 _____ 1/4 mi

0 _____ 1/4 km

7100 ⊕*www.annefrank.nl* ✉*€7.50*
⊙*Sept. 15–Mar. 14, daily 9–7; Mar.
15–Sept. 14, daily 9–9.*

❶ **Brouwersgracht.** The Jordaan (pronounced Yoarh-*dahn*), now a wanderer's paradise lined with quirky boutiques, excellent restaurants, and galleries—has evolved into one of the city's most singular neighborhoods. One of the most photographed spots in town is Brouwersgracht, a pretty, tree-lined canal at the northern border of the Jordaan district, bordered by residences and historic warehouses of the brewers who traded here in the 17th century, when Amsterdam was the "warehouse of the world." ✉ *Western Canal Ring, Jordaan.*

*Fodor's*Choice
★

❹ **Dam** *(Dam Square).* Home to the Koninklijk Paleis and the Nieuwe Kerk, Amsterdam's official center of town is the Dam, which traces its roots to the 12th century, when wanderers from central Europe came floating in their canoes down the Amstel River and thought to stop to build a dam. The **National Monument,** a towering white obelisk in the center of the square, was erected in 1956 as a memorial to the Dutch victims of World War II. The urns embedded in the monument's rear contain earth from all the Dutch provinces and former colonies (Indonesia, Suriname, and the Antilles). ✉ *Nieuwe Zijde.*

❾ **Magere Brug** *(Skinny Bridge).* Of Amsterdam's 60-plus drawbridges, the Magere (which derives from "meager" in Dutch) is the most famous. It was purportedly built in 1672 by two sisters living on opposite sides of the Amstel, who wanted an efficient way of sharing that grandest of Dutch traditions: the *gezellig* (socially cozy) midmorning coffee break. Nowadays, it's spectacularly lighted with electric lights at night, and often drawn up to let boats pass by. ✉ *Between Kerkstraat and Nieuwe Kerkstraat, Eastern Canal Ring.*

*Fodor's*Choice
★

❼ **Museum Amstelkring** *(Our Lord in the Attic Museum).* With its elegant gray-and-white facade and spout gable, this appears to be just another canal house, and on the lower floors it is. The attic of this building, however, contains something unique: the only surviving *schuilkerken* (clandestine church) that dates from the Reformation in Amsterdam, when open worship by Catholics was outlawed. Since the Oude Kerk was then relieved of its original patron, St. Nicholas, when it was de-catholicized, this became the church dedicated to him until the Sint Nicolaaskerk was built. The chapel itself is a triumph of Dutch classicist taste, with magnificent marble columns, gilded capitals, a colored-marble altar, and the *Baptism of Christ* (1716) painting by Jacob de Wit presiding over all. Sunday services and weddings are still offered here. ✉ *Oudezijds Voorburgwal 40, Oude Zijde* ☎*020/624–6604* ⊕*www.museumamstelkring.nl* ✉*€7* ⊙*Mon.–Sat. 10–5, Sun. 1–5.*

*Fodor's*Choice
★

8 **Museum het Rembrandthuis** *(Rembrandt's House).* One of Amsterdam's more remarkable relics, this house was bought by Rembrandt, flush with success, for his family and is where he lived and worked between 1639 and 1658. Rembrandt chose this house on what was once the main street of the Jewish Quarter because he thought he could then experience daily and firsthand the faces he would use in his Old Testament religious paintings. Rembrandt later lost the house to bankruptcy: when he showed a quick recovery—and an open taste for servant girls—after his wife Saskia's death, his uncle-in-law, once his greatest champion, became his biggest detractor. Rembrandt's downfall was sealed. He came under attack by the Amsterdam burghers, who refused to accept his liaison with his amour, Hendrickje. Rembrandt's scandal notwithstanding, the family rooms and the artist's studio have been painstakingly restored. ⊠*Jodenbreestraat 4–6, Jewish Quarter and Plantage* ☎*020/520–0400* ⊕*www.rembrandthuis. nl* ⌨*€8* ⊙*Daily 10–5.*

Fodor'sChoice ★

6 **Oude Kerk** *(Old Church).* The Oude Kerk is indeed Amsterdam's oldest church and has been surrounded by all the trappings of humanity's oldest trade (i.e., prostitution) for the vast majority of its history—a history that has seen it chaotically evolve from single-nave chapel to hall church to a cross basilica. It began as a wooden chapel in 1306 but was built for the ages between 1366 and 1566 (and fully restored between 1955 and 1979), when the whole neighborhood was rife with monasteries and convents. It is now a wholly unique exhibition space for modern-art exhibitions and the annual World Press Photo competition. Its carillon gets played every Saturday between 4 and 5. ⊠*Oudekerksplein 23, Oude Zijde* ☎*020/625–8284* ⊕*www.oudekerk.nl* ⌨*€4.50* ⊙*Mon.–Sat. 11–5, Sun. 1–5.*

★

6

11 **Rijksmuseum** *(State Museum).* The Netherlands' greatest museum, the Rijksmuseum is home to Rembrandt's *Night Watch,* Vermeer's *The Kitchen Maid,* and a near infinite selection of world-famous masterpieces by the likes of Steen, Ruisdael, Brouwers, Hals, Hobbema, Cuyp, Van der Helst, and their Golden Age ilk. This national treasure, however, will be largely closed until 2010 for extensive renovation and rebuilding, following the plans of Seville's architect duo Antonio Cruz and Antonio Ortiz. Only the South Wing—which has now through corporate sponsorship been renamed the Philips Wing—will remain reliably open to house a "Best of" selection. ⊠*Stadhouderskade 42; Entrance during renovations: Jan Luijkenstraat 1, Museum District* ☎*020/674–7000* ⊕*www.rijksmuseum. nl* ⌨*€10* ⊙*Sat.–Thurs. 9–6, Fri. 9 AM–10 PM.*

Fodor'sChoice ★

12 **Rijksmuseum Vincent Van Gogh** *(Vincent Van Gogh Museum).* Opened in 1973, this remarkable light-infused building, based on a design by famed De Stijl architect Gerrit Rietveld, venerates the short, certainly not sweet, but highly productive career of everyone's favorite tortured 19th-century artist. Although some of the Van Gogh paintings that are scattered throughout the world's high-art temples are of dubious provenance, this collection's authenticity is indisputable: its roots trace directly back to brother Theo van Gogh, Vincent's artistic and financial supporter. ⊠*Paulus Potterstraat 7, Museum District* ☎*020/570–5200* ⊕*www.vangogh-museum.nl* ⌨*€10* ⊙*Sat.–Thurs. 10–6, Fri. 10–10.*

Fodor'sChoice ★

③ Westerkerk *(Western Church).* Built between 1602 and 1631 by the ubiq-
★ uitous Hendrick de Keyser and presumed the last resting place of Rembrandt, the Dutch Renaissance Westerkerk was the largest Protestant
church in the world until Christopher Wren came along with his St.
Paul's Cathedral in London. Its tower—endlessly mentioned in Jordaan
songs—is topped by a gaudy copy of the crown of the Habsburg emperor
Maximilian I. The crown's "XXX" marking was quickly exploited by
the city's merchants as a visiting card of quality. ⊠*Prinsengracht 281
(corner of Westermarkt), Jordaan* ☎*020/624–7766, 020/689–2565 for
tower appointments* ⊕*www.westerkerk.nl* ☉*Tower June–Sept., Tues.,
Wed., Fri., and Sat. 2–5; interior Apr.–Sept., weekdays 11–3; tower by
appointment* ⊠*€5.*

⑩ Willet-Holthuysen Museum. Few patrician houses are open to the public along
*Fodor's*Choice the Herengracht, so make a beeline to this mansion to see Grachten-
★ gordel (Canal Ring) luxury at its best. In 1895, the widow Sandrina Lou-
isa Willet-Holthuysen donated the house and contents—which included
her husband's extensive art collection—to the city of Amsterdam. You
can now wander through this 17th-century canal house, now under the
management of the Amsterdams Historisch Museum, and discover all its
original 18th-century interiors, complete with that era's mod-cons from
ballroom to *cabinet des merveilles* (rarities cabinet). You can air out the
aura of Dutch luxury by lounging in the French-style garden in the back.
⊠*Herengracht 605, Eastern Canal Ring* ☎*020/523–1822* ⊕*www.wil-
letholthuysen.nl* ⊠*€4* ☉*Weekdays 10–5, weekends 11–5.*

SHOPPING

Souvenir shops are filled with wooden clogs and ceramics bearing windmill or tulip motifs, but Amsterdam offers more than just cheap and cheerful items. There's a major market in diamonds and also in antiques. At the
lower end of the price scale, there's a market in collectibles and one-of-a-
kind items, plus cutting-edge design for the home.

Kalverstraat, the city's main pedestrians-only shopping street, is where much
of Amsterdam does its day-to-day shopping. Running parallel to Kalverstraat is the **Rokin,** a main tram route lined with shops offering high-priced
trendy fashion, jewelry, accessories, antiques, and even an old master
painting or two. Shoppers will love to explore the **Negen Straatjes** (Nine
Streets), nine charming, tiny streets that radiate from behind the Royal
Palace. Here, in a sector bordered by Raadhuisstraat and Leidsestraat,
specialty and fashion shops are delightfully one-of-a-kind. Heading even
farther to the west you enter the chic and funky sector of the **Jordaan,**
where generation after generation of experimental designers have set up
shop to show their imaginative creations. Though adventurous collectors
are increasingly looking to the Jordaan district for unique finds, the more
expensive **Spiegelkwartier** is the city's mainstay for high-end antiques. The
De Baarsjes neighborhood in the western part of the city is progressively
attracting small galleries that showcase exciting works of art.

★ Whether hunting for treasures or trash, you could get lucky at one of
Amsterdam's flea markets. The best is **Waterlooplein** flea market, which surrounds the perimeter of the Stopera (Muziektheater/Town Hall complex)

building. The **Bloemenmarkt** (along the Singel canal, between Koningsplein and Muntplein), is another of Amsterdam's must-see markets, where flowers and plants are sold from permanently moored barges.

WHERE TO EAT

¢–$ ✕**Bakkerswinkel.** This genteel yet unpretentious bakery/tearoom evokes an
Fodor'sChoice English country kitchen, one that lovingly prepares and serves breakfasts,
★ high tea, hearty-breaded sandwiches, soups, and divine (almost manly) slabs of quiche. This place is a true oasis if you want to indulge in a healthful breakfast or lunch. It opens at 8 AM daily, and there's a second location, complete with garden patio, in the Museum District. ✉*Warmoestraat 69, Oude Zijde* ☎*020/489–8000* ▭*No credit cards* ⊘*No dinner. Closed Mon.* ✉*Roelef Hartstraat 68* ☎*020/662–3594* ▭*No credit cards* ⊘*No dinner. Closed Mon.*

¢–$ ✕**Café Luxembourg.** One of the city's top grand cafés, Luxembourg has a
★ stately interior and a view of a bustling square, both of which are maximized for people watching. Famous for its brunch, its classic café menu includes a terrific goat cheese salad, dim sum, and excellent Holtkamp *krokets* (croquettes, these with a shrimp or meat and potato filling). The "reading table" is democratically packed with both Dutch and international newspapers and mags. ✉*Spuistraat 24, Nieuwe Zijde and Spui* ☎*020/620–6264* ⊕*www.luxembourg.nl* ▭*AE, DC, MC, V.*

ANTWERP, BELGIUM

In its heyday, Antwerp (Antwerpen in Flemish, Anvers in French) played second fiddle only to Paris. It became Europe's most important commercial center in the 16th century and this wealth funded many architectural and artistic projects. Masters such as Rubens and Van Dyck established the city as one of Europe's leading art centers and its innovative printing presses produced missals for the farthest reaches of the continent. It also became, and has remained, the diamond capital of the world. Antwerp today is Europe's second-largest port and has much of the zest often associated with a harbor town. The historic Oude Stad, the heart of the city, distils the essence of Antwerp. The narrow, winding streets, many of them restricted to pedestrian traffic, are wonderful for strolling, the squares are full of charm, and the museums and churches are the pride of the city.

ESSENTIALS

CURRENCY The euro (€1 to US$1.46); exchange rates were accurate at this writing but are subject to change. U.S. currency is generally not accepted in Europe, but ATMs are common.

HOURS Museums and attractions are usually open from 9:30 to 5; many are closed on Monday. Most shops are open Monday–Saturday 9–6.

INTERNET **2zones** ✉*Wolstraat 15, Oude Stad* ☎*03/232–2400.*

TELEPHONES Tri-band GSM phones work in Belgium. You can buy prepaid phone cards at telecom shops, news vendors and tobacconists in all towns and cities. Phone cards can be used for local or international calls. Proximus and Mobistar are the leading telecom companies.

COMING ASHORE

The cruise port couldn't be better placed for passengers, as vessels dock directly at the heart of the city. All the major attractions and museums of the historic center are within walking distance of the dock. The commercial port has no facilities for disembarking passengers, but a wealth of shopping options and restaurants lie just outside the gates.

Antwerp's tram and metro public transit system is extensive and reliable. A €1 ticket is good for one hour on all forms of public transport, including buses; a €3 pass buys unlimited travel for one day. Car rental offices are located in Antwerp (around €30 per day for a compact manual vehicle). Travel by taxi has a per-km charge of around €2.50, which makes it expensive for day tours but acceptable for short trips.

EXPLORING ANTWERP

Numbers in the margin correspond to points of interest on the Antwerp map.

⓯ Diamondland. A spectacular showroom, Diamondland was created to enable visitors to get a sense of the activity that goes on behind closed doors in the security-conscious Diamantwijk. All explanations are in English and you can watch several diamond cutters at work. ⊠*Appelmansstraat 33A, Diamantwijk* ☎*03/229–2990* ⊕*www.diamondland.be* ☉*Nov.–Mar., Mon.–Sat. 9:30–5:30; Apr.–Oct., Mon.–Sat. 9:30–5:30, Sun. 10–5.*

⓮ Diamantwijk. The diamond trade has its own quarter in Antwerp, bounded by De Keyserlei, Pelikaanstraat, Lange Herentalsestraat, and Lange Kievitstraat, where the skills of cutting and polishing the gems have been handed down for generations by a tightly knit community. A large part of the community is Jewish, so you'll see shop signs in Hebrew and Hasidic men with traditional dark clothing and side curls. Some 85% of the world's uncut diamonds pass through Antwerp. Twenty-five million carats are cut and traded here every year, more than anywhere else in the world. A long row of stalls and shops gleams with jewelry and gems.

❷ Etnografisch Museum. This fascinating ethnographic museum explores the art, myths, and rites of the native peoples of Africa, the Americas, Asia, and the South Seas. André Malraux described some of its thousands of masks, tools, weapons, sculptures, and other objects in his work *La Musée Imaginaire*, a compilation of the world's most important art and artifacts. Look for such rare pieces as a Wayard Aparai dance costume worn during a boy's initiation ceremony. A detailed pilgrimage painting on cloth entitled *Lhasa and surrounding* is one of only two such paintings known in the world. ⊠*Suikerrui 19, Oude Stad* ☎*03/220–8600* ⊕*museum.antwerpen.be* 🎟*€4, free on Fri.* ☉*Tues.–Sun. 10–5.*

❶ Grote Markt. The heart of the Oude Stad, the Grote Markt is dominated by a huge fountain splashing water onto the paving stones. Atop the fountain stands the figure of the legendary Silvius Brabo, who

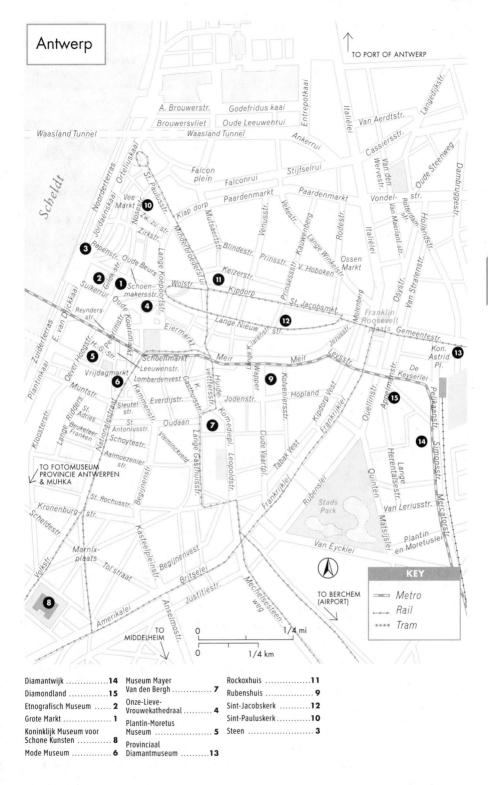

Antwerp

TO PORT OF ANTWERP

A. Brouwerstr.   Godefridus kaai

Brouwersvliet   Oude Leeuwenrui

Waasland Tunnel   Waasland Tunnel

Scheldt

Falcon plein   Falconrui   Stijfselrui

Paardenmarkt   Paardenmarkt   Vondel-str.

Vee Markt ⑩

Klap dorp

Blindestr.   Prinsstr.   Ossen Markt

Kelzerstr.

Wolstr. ⑪   Kipdorp   St. Jacobsmkt.

Lange Nieuw ⑫

Franklin Roosevelt plaats   Gemeentestr.

Eiermarkt   Meir   Meir   Kon. Astrid Pl. ⑬

Schoenmarkt   Leeuwenstr.

Vrijdagmarkt ⑥

Muntstr.   Lombardenvest   Jodenstr.   Hopland ⑮

Everdijstr.   Oudaan ⑦

De Keyserlei

⑨

⑭

Stads Park

Van Eycklei

Plantin en Moretuslei

TO FOTOMUSEUM PROVINCIE ANTWERPEN & MUHKA

Marnix-plaats

⑧

TO MIDDELHEIM

TO BERCHEM (AIRPORT)

0   1/4 mi
0   1/4 km

KEY
Metro
Rail
Tram

has been poised to fling the hand of the giant Druon Antigon into the river Scheldt since the 19th century. Another famous monster slayer, St. George, is perched on top of a 16th-century guild house at Grote Markt 5, while the dragon appears to be falling off the pediment.

The triangular square is lined on two sides by guild houses and on the third by the Renaissance **Stadhuis** (⊠*Grote Markt, Oude Stad* ☎*03/220–8020*). Antwerp's town hall was built in the 1560s during the city's Golden Age, when Paris and Antwerp were the only European cities with more than 100,000 inhabitants. In its facade, the fanciful fretwork of the late Gothic style has given way to the discipline and order of the Renaissance. Admission to the Stadhuis is €0.75

8 ★ **Koninklijk Museum voor Schone Kunsten.** The Royal Museum of Fine Arts collection is studded with masterworks of Flemish art. The collection of Flemish Primitives includes works by Rubens, Bruegel, Van Dyck, and Memling. There's also a representative survey of Belgian art of the past 150 years— Emile Claus, Rik Wouters, René Magritte, Paul Delvaux, and especially James Ensor. An English-language audioguide is available. ⊠*Leopold de Waelplaats 2, Het Zuid* ☎*03/238–7809* ⊕*museum.antwerpen.be/kmska* 💳€6 ۩*Tues.–Sat. 10–5, Sun. 10–6.*

6 **Mode Museum.** To get up to speed on the latest clothing designers, head to MoMu for a fashion crash course. Inside the early-20th-century building you'll find comprehensive exhibits, some highlighting the avant-garde work of contemporary Flemish designers. Also in the museum's complex are the Flanders Fashion Institute, the fashion academy of the Royal Academy of Fine Arts (the designer wellspring), a brasserie, and a boutique. You can pick up a brochure with information in English. ⊠*Nationalestraat 28, Sint-Andrieskwartier* ☎*03/470–2770* ⊕*www.momu.be* 💳€7 ۩*Tues.–Sun. 10–6, every first Thurs. of the month 10–9.*

7 Fodor's Choice ★ **Museum Mayer Van den Bergh.** Pieter Bruegel the Elder's arguably greatest and most enigmatic painting, *Dulle Griet,* is the showpiece here. Often referred to in English as "Mad Meg," it portrays an irate woman wearing helmet and breastplate—a sword in one hand, and food and cooking utensils in the other—striding across a field strewn with the ravages and insanity of war. In 1894, Mayer Van den Bergh bought *Dulle Griet* for 480 Belgian francs. Today it is priceless. ⊠*Lange Gasthuisstraat 19, Kruidtuin* ☎*03/232–4237* ⊕*museum.antwerpen.be/mayervandenbergh* 💳€4, €6 combination ticket with Rubenshuis ۩*Tues.–Sun. 10–5.*

4 Fodor's Choice ★ **Onze-Lieve-Vrouwekathedraal.** A miracle of soaring Gothic lightness, the Cathedral of Our Lady contains some of Rubens's greatest paintings, including four alterpieces, and is topped by a 404-foot-high north spire serving as a beacon that can be seen from far away. Work began in 1352 and continued in fits and starts until 1521. Despite this, it is a homogeneous monument, thanks to a succession of remarkable architects. ⊠ *Handschoenmarkt, Oude Stad* ☎ *03/213–9940* ⊕ *www.dekathedraal. be* ☒ *€2* ⊙ *Weekdays 10–5, Sat. 10–3, Sun. 1–4.*

5 Plantin-Moretus Museum. This was the home and printing plant of an extraordinary publishing dynasty. For three centuries, beginning in 1576, the
★ family printed innumerable Bibles, breviaries, and missals. The first three rooms were the family quarters, furnished in 16th-century luxury and containing several portraits by Rubens. Others remain as they were when occupied by accountants, editors, and proofreaders, while many contain Bibles and religious manuscripts dating back to the 9th century. There's a free information brochure available in English. ⊠ *Vrijdagmarkt 22–23, Sint-Andrieskwartier* ☎ *03/221–1450* ⊕ *museum.antwerpen.be/plantin_ Moretus* ☒ *€6, free last Wed. of month* ⊙ *Tues.–Sun. 10–5.*

13 Provinciaal Diamantmuseum. The high-tech interactive displays in this diamond museum illustrate the entire production process, from mining to
★ gem cutting. A free English-language audioguide explains the wonderful collections of jewelry. ⊠ *Koningin Astridplein 19–23, Centraal Station* ☎ *03/202–4890* ⊕ *www.diamantmuseum.be* ☒ *€6* ⊙ *May–Mar., Thurs.–Tues. 10–5:30.*

11 Rockoxhuis. This was the splendid Renaissance home of Rubens's friend and patron Nicolaas Rockox, seven times mayor of Antwerp. The art on display includes two Rubens pieces and works by Van Dyck, Frans Snyders, Joachim Patinir, Jacob Jordaens, and David Teniers the Younger. The setting makes visiting this collection an exceptional experience. Rather than being displayed on museum walls, the paintings are shown in the context of an upper-class baroque home, furnished in the style of the period (early 1600s). A documentary slide show in English describes Antwerp at that time. ⊠ *Keizerstraat 10–12, Stadswaag* ☎ *03/201–9250* ☒ *€2.50* ⊙ *Tues.–Sun. 10–5.*

9 Rubenshuis. A fabulous picture of Rubens as painter and patrician is presented here at his own house. Only the elaborate portico and temple,
★ designed by Rubens in Italian Baroque style, are original—most of what's here is a reconstruction (completed in 1946) from the master's own design. The most evocative room in Rubens House is the huge studio. In Rubens's day, visitors could view completed paintings and watch from the mezzanine while Rubens and his students worked. Rubens completed about 2,500 paintings. A few of his works hang in the house but unfortunately, his widow promptly sold off some 300 pieces after his death in 1640. ⊠ *Wapper 9, Meir* ☎ *03/201–1555* ⊕ *http://museum.antwerpen.be* ☒ *€6, free Fri.* ⊙ *Tues.–Sun. 10–5.*

12 Sint-Jacobskerk. Peter Paul Rubens is buried in the white sandstone St. Jacob's Church. A painting depicting him as St. George posed between his two wives, Isabella Brant and Helena Fourment, hangs above his tomb. The three-aisle church blends late-Gothic and Baroque styles; the tombs are practically a who's who of prominent 17th-century Antwerp families. ⊠ *Lange Nieuwstraat 73, Meir* ☎ *03/232–1032* ⊙ *Daily 2–5.*

⑩ Sint-Pauluskerk. The late-Gothic St. Paul's Church, built 1530–71, is a repository of more than 50 outstanding paintings. There are three by Rubens, as well as early works by Jordaens and Van Dyck. The church is further enriched by more than 200 17th- and 18th-century sculptures, including the confessionals attributed to Peeter Verbruggen the Elder. ⊠*Sint Paulusstraat 20, Oude Stad* ☏*03/232–3267* ⊙*May–Sept., daily 2–5.*

❸ Steen. The Steen is more than 1,000 years old and looks it. A 9th-century waterfront fortress, it was built to protect the western frontier of the Holy Roman Empire. It was partially rebuilt 700 years later by Emperor Charles V. The Steen was used as a prison for centuries. It now houses the **Nationaal Scheepvaartmuseum** (National Maritime Museum), with a large collection of models, figureheads, instruments, prints, and maps. ⊠*Steenplein, Oude Stad* ☏*03/201–9340* ⊕*museum.antwerpen.be/ scheepvaartmuseum* ⊠*€4* ⊙*Tues.–Sun. 10–4:45.*

SHOPPING

Antwerp has a reputation for edgy chic, due in large part to its clothing designers; followers of fashion consider the city in a league with Milan and Paris. Credit for this development goes to the so-called Antwerp Six (students of Linda Loppa from the class of 1981 at Antwerp's Fashion Academy) and in equal measure to the new wave of talent that has more recently stormed the catwalks. Ready-to-wear by stalwarts Ann Demeulemeester, Dirk Bikkembergs, Dries Van Noten, and relative newcomers Raf Simons, Véronique Branquinho, and Wim Neels command high prices. However, in the shopping area south of Groenplaats, prices are less astronomical. And, of course, the Diamantwijk is prime territory for glittering precious stones.

The elegant **Meir,** together with its extension to the east, **De Keyserlei,** and at the opposite end, **Huidevettersstraat,** is where you will find high-street standbys and long-established names. Shopping galleries branch off all three streets. The area in and around the glamorous **Horta Complex,** on Hopland is also a popular shopping hub. For avant-garde tastes, the best-known area is **De Wilde Zee,** which straddles the Meir and Oude Stad. The nearby Schuttershofstraat, Kammenstraat, and Nationalestraat are also fizzing with new spots. Another pedestrian area for general shopping is **Hoogstraat.**

Louis (⊠*Lombardenstraat 2, Sint-Andrieskwartier* ☏*03/232–9872*) was one of the first places to sell the work of Antwerp's top designers in the late 1980s. Today, it sells the collections of the city's more recent talent—Martin Margiela, Ann Demeulemeester, A.F. Vandervorst, and Raf Simons.

Ann Demeulemeester (⊠*Verlatstraat 38, Het Zuid* ☏*03/216–0133*) sells her clothes in an elegant corner store close to the Koninklijk Museum voor Schone Kunsten.

The work of Dries Van Noten is in the splendid renovated **Modepaleis** (⊠*Kammenstraat and Nationalestraat 16, Sint-Andrieskwartier* ☏*03/470–2510*), a men's and women's outfitter.

Owned by Walter Van Beirendonck and Dirk Van Saene, **Walter** (⊠ *Sint-Antoniustraat 12, Sint-Andrieskwartier* ☎*03/213–2644*) sells the best of their collections against a futuristic backdrop.

The largest diamond showroom is **Diamondland** (⊠ *Appelmansstraat 33a, Diamantwijk* ☎*03/229–2990* ⊕*www.diamondland.be*).

WHERE TO EAT

$–$$ ✕ **'t Hofke.** It's worth visiting here for the location alone: the Vlaeykensgang alley, where time seems to have stood still. The cozy dining room has the look and feel of a private home, and the menu includes a large selection of salads and omelets, as well as more substantial fare. Try for a table in the courtyard. ⊠ *Vlaeykensgang, Oude Koornmarkt 16, Oude Stad* ☎*03/233–8606* ▭*AE, MC, V.*

¢–$$ ✕ **'t Brantyser.** This old, two-level café with dark rafters, brick, and stucco, serves more than just drinks and the usual snacks: the tavern fare is supplemented by a range of meal-size salads and affordable specials. ⊠ *Hendrik Conscienceplein 7, Oude Stad* ☎*03/233–1833* ▭*AE, MC, V.*

COBH, IRELAND (FOR CORK)

The major metropolis of the South, Cork is Ireland's second-largest city—but it runs a distant second, with a population of 119,400, roughly a tenth the size of Dublin. Cork is a spirited place, with a formidable pub culture, a lively traditional music scene, a respected and progressive university, attractive art galleries, and offbeat cafés. The city received a major boost in 2005 when it was named a Capital of Culture by the EU—the smallest city ever to receive the designation. The result was a burst in development; one of the lasting legacies is a striking but controversial redesign of the city center (Patrick Street and Grand Parade) by Barcelona-based architect Beth Gali. Outside the city, the rolling countryside gives way to rugged coastline hosting tiny villages, each with their own piece of history. Many set sail for the New World from here; some were destined not to arrive.

ESSENTIALS

CURRENCY The euro (€1 to US$1.46 at this writing). U.S. currency is generally not accepted in Europe, but ATMs are common.

HOURS Shops and businesses are generally open Monday through Saturday from 9:30 to 5:30 or 6; some open later and some open on Sunday. Most museums are open Monday–Saturday 9–5 and may have shorter hours on Sunday.

INTERNET **Internet Exchange** (⊠ *5 Woods St., off Washington St.Cork* ☎*021/4254666*) is a centrally located Internet café.

TELEPHONES Most tri- and quad-band GSM phones will work in Ireland, and the country's mobile system is 3G-compatible with excellent coverage. Public phones accept prepaid call cards (available in shops and telecom offices) and credit cards. Eircom, BT Ireland, and Vodafone are the major telecom suppliers.

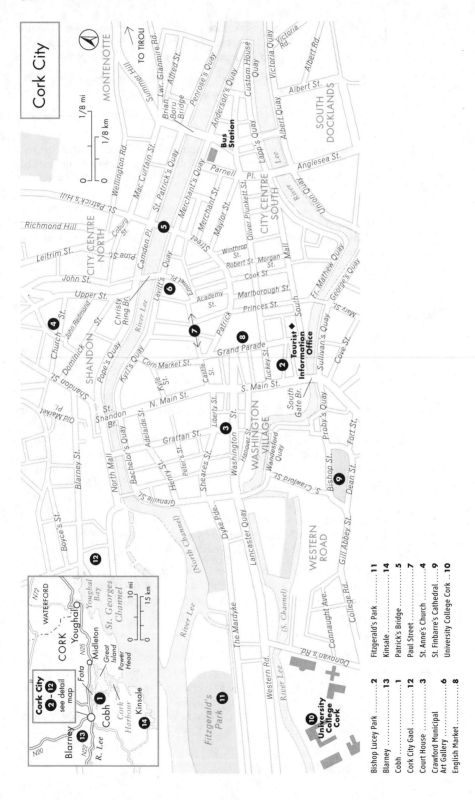

Cork City

MONTENOTTE

TO TIROLI

1/8 mi
1/8 km

SOUTH DOCKLANDS

CITY CENTRE NORTH

Richmond Hill

Leitrim St.

John St.

Upper St.

SHANDON

Old Market Pl.

Shandon St.

Blarney St.

Boyce's St.

Church St.

John Redmond St.

Dominick St.

Pope's Quay

Kyrl's Quay

Corn Market St.

Castle St.

Kyle St.

N. Main St.

St. Shandon Br.

Adelaide St.

Bachelor's Quay

North Mall

Grattan St.

Peter's St.

Sheares St.

Henry St.

Greville St.

Liberty St.

Hanover St.

Washington St.

Wandesford Quay

S. Main St.

South Gate Br.

WASHINGTON VILLAGE

Proby's Quay

S. Crawford St.

Bishop St.

Dean St.

Fort St.

Lancaster Quay

Dyke Pde.

The Mardyke

Western Rd.

River Lee (S. Channel)

River Lee (North Channel)

Fitzgerald's Park

WESTERN ROAD

College Rd.

Connaught Ave.

Donovan's Rd.

Gill Abbey St.

Mary St.

Cove St.

Sullivan's Quay

George's Quay

Ft. Mathew Quay

Union Quay

Tuckey St.

Grand Parade

Patrick St.

Princes St.

Marlborough St.

Cook St.

Morgan St.

Robert St.

Winthrop St.

Oliver Plunkett St.

Mall

CITY CENTRE SOUTH

South

Academy St.

Emmet Pl.

Lavitt's Quay

River Lee

Christy Ring Br.

Pine St.

Camden Pl.

Coburg St.

St. Patrick's Quay

Merchant's Quay

Parnell Pl.

Merchant St.

Maylor St.

Mac Curtain St.

Wellington Rd.

St. Patrick's Hill

Summer Hill

Lwr. Glanmire Rd.

Alfred St.

Brian Boru Bridge

Penrose's Quay

Anderson's Quay

Custom House Quay

Lapp's Quay

Albert Quay

Victoria Quay

Victoria Rd.

Albert Rd.

Albert St.

Anglesea St.

Lee

Bus Station

Tourist ◆ Information Office

2
3
4
5
6
7
8
9
10

Inset map (Cork City 2–12 see detail map)

WATERFORD
N72
N25
CORK
Midleton
Youghal
Youghal Bay
St. Georges Channel
Great Island
Fota
Power Head
N20
N22
Blarney
Cobh
Cork Harbour
Kinsale
R. Lee
St. Georges Channel
10 mi
15 km

Cork City 2–12 see detail map

1
12
13
14

Bishop Lucey Park **2**
Blarney **13**
Cobh **1**
Cork City Gaol **12**
Court House **3**
Crawford Municipal
Art Gallery **6**
English Market **8**

Fitzgerald's Park **11**
Kinsale **14**
Patrick's Bridge **5**
Paul Street **7**
St. Anne's Church **4**
St. Finbarre's Cathedral .. **9**
University College Cork .. **10**

University College Cork

COMING ASHORE

Large ships dock at Cobh's dedicated cruise terminal adjacent to the Cobh Heritage Centre (see below). There are basic facilities for passengers, including restrooms, taxis, and tourist information, but no cafés, restaurants, or shops.

There is a rail link between Cobh and Cork. It runs once or twice an hour throughout the day and costs €5.25, so it would be possible to explore Cork and Cobh in the same day by public transport. Smaller vessels dock at the City Quays in the heart of Cork City; from here, you can tour the town on foot.

> **CORK BEST BETS**
>
> **Strolling along Patrick Street.** The historic storefronts along this famous thoroughfare have graced a thousand tourist brochures—it's an atmospheric place to browse for a souvenir or two.
>
> **Kissing the Blarney Stone.** The "magic" stone at Blarney Castle is said to give you the gift of gab to get what you want.
>
> **Visiting the Queenstown Story at Cobh Heritage Center.** This site tells the story of the millions of emigrants who set sail to the United States, and of the tragic last voyage of the Lusitania.

Renting a car would be an advantage for touring the Kerry countryside around the town and the associated attractions. The cost for a compact manual vehicle is approx €26. Taxis can be engaged to run tour itineraries, although charges are complicated. Initial charges are a maximum of €3.80, then €0.95 per km for the first 14 km (9 mi), rising to €1.63 per km (½-mi) once the ride lasts longer than 30 km (19 mi). Drivers can choose to charge by the minute rather than per kilometer.

EXPLORING COUNTY CORK

Numbers in the margin correspond to points of interest on the Cork map.

COBH

1 *24 km (15 mi) southeast of Cork City.*

Many of the people who left Ireland on immigrant ships for the New World departed from Cobh, a pretty fishing port and seaside resort 24 km (15 mi) southeast of Cork City on R624.

The **Queenstown Story at Cobh Heritage Center,** in the old Cobh railway station, re-creates the experience of the million emigrants. It also tells the stories of great transatlantic liners, including the *Titanic,* whose last port of call was Cobh, and the *Lusitania,* which was sunk by a German submarine off this coast on May 7, 1915. Many of the *Lusitania's* 1,198 victims are buried in Cobh, which has a memorial to them on the local quay. ☎021/481-3591 ⊕*www.cobhheritage.com* €6.60 ⊙*Oct.–Apr., daily 9:30–5; May–Sept., daily 9:30–6.*

The best view of Cobh is from **St. Colman's Cathedral,** an exuberant neo-Gothic granite church designed by the eminent British architect E. W. Pugin in 1869, and completed in 1919. Inside, granite niches portray scenes of the Roman Catholic Church's history in Ireland, beginning with the arrival of St. Patrick. ☎021/481-3222 *Free.*

CORK CITY

2 **Bishop Lucey Park.** This tiny green park in the heart of the city opened in 1985 in celebration of the 800th anniversary of Cork's Norman charter. During its excavation, workers unearthed portions of the city's original fortified walls, now preserved just inside the arched entrance. Sculptures by contemporary Cork artists are found throughout the park. ⊠*Grand Parade, Washington Village* ⊠*Free.*

12 **Cork City Gaol.** This castlelike building contains an austere, 19th-century prison. Life-size figures occupy the cells, and sound effects illustrate the appalling conditions that prevailed here from the early 19th century through the founding of the Free State, after the 1916 Uprising. ⊠*Sunday's Well Rd., Sunday's Well* ☎*021/430–5022* ⊕*www.corkcitygaol.com* ⊠*€8* ☉*Nov.–Feb., daily 10–5; Mar.–Oct., daily 9:30–6.*

3 **Court House.** A landmark in the very center of Cork, this magnificent classical building (1835) has an imposing Corinthian portico and is still used as the district's main courthouse. ⊠*Washington St., Washington Village* ☎*021/427–2706* ☉*Weekdays 9–5.*

6 **Crawford Municipal Art Gallery.** The large redbrick building was built in 1724 as the customs house and is now home to Ireland's leading provincial art gallery. An imaginative expansion has added an extra 10,000 square feet of gallery space for visiting exhibitions and adventurous shows of modern Irish artists. The permanent collection includes landscape paintings depicting Cork in the 18th and 19th centuries. ⊠*Emmet Pl., City Center South* ☎*021/427–3377* ⊕*www.crawfordartgallery.com* ⊠*Free* ☉*Weekdays 9–5, Sat. 9–1.*

8 **English Market.** Food lovers: head for this brick-and-cast-iron Victorian building with the legendary fresh-fish alley, purveying local smoked salmon. O'Reilly's Tripe and Drisheen is the last existing retailer of a Cork specialty, tripe (cow's stomach) and *drisheen* (blood sausage). Upstairs is the Farmgate, an excellent café. ⊠*Entrances on Grand Parade and Princes St., City Center South* ☉*Mon.–Sat. 9–5:30.*

11 **Fitzgerald's Park.** This small, well-tended park is beside the River Lee's north channel in the west of the city. The park contains the **Cork Public Museum,** a Georgian mansion that houses a well-planned exhibit about Cork's history since ancient times, with a strong emphasis on the city's Republican history. ⊠*Western Rd., Western Road* ☎*021/427–0679* ⊠*Free* ☉*Museum weekdays 11–1 and 2:15–5, Sun. 3–5.*

5 **Patrick's Bridge.** From here you can look along the curve of Patrick Street and north across the River Lee to St. Patrick's Hill, with its tall Georgian houses. The hill is so steep that steps are cut into the pavement. Tall ships that served the butter trade used to load up beside the bridge at Merchant's Quay before heading downstream to the sea. The design of the large, redbrick shopping center on the site evokes the warehouses of old. ⊠*Patrick St., City Center South.*

7 **Paul Street.** A narrow street between the River Lee and Patrick Street and parallel to both, Paul Street is the backbone of the trendy shopping area that now occupies Cork's old French Quarter. The area was first settled by Huguenots fleeing religious persecution in France. Musicians and other street performers often entertain passersby in the Rory Gallagher Piazza, named for the rock guitarist (of the band Taste), whose family was from Cork. The shops here offer the best in modern Irish design—from local fashions to handblown glass—and antiques, particularly in the alley north of the piazza. ⊠ *City Center South.*

④ St. Anne's Church. The church's pepper-pot Shandon steeple is visible throughout the city and is the chief reason why St. Anne's is so frequently visited. The Bells of Shandon were immortalized in a 19th-century ballad of that name. Your reward for climbing the 120-foot-tall tower is the chance to ring the bells out over Cork. ⊠ *Church St., Shandon* 🖃 *€1.50 church, €2 church and bell tower* ⊙ *May–Oct., Mon.–Sat. 9:30–4:30; Nov.–Apr., Mon.–Sat. 10–3:30.*

⑨ St. Finbarre's Cathedral. This was once the entrance to medieval Cork. According to tradition, St. Finbarre established a monastery on this site around AD 650 and is credited as being the founder of Cork. The present, compact, three-spire Gothic cathedral, which was completed in 1879, belongs to the Church of Ireland and houses a 3,000-pipe organ. ⊠ *Bishop St., Washington Village* ☎ *021/496–3387* ⊕ *www.cathedral.cork.anglican.org* 🖃 *€3* ⊙ *Oct.–Mar., Mon.–Sat. 10–12:45 and 2–5, Sun. 12:30–5; Apr.–Sept., Mon.–Sat. 9:30–5:30, Sun. 12:30–5.*

⑩ University College Cork. ★ The porticoed gates of UCC stand about 2 km (1 mi) from the center of the city. The main quadrangle is a fine example of 19th-century university architecture in the Tudor-Gothic style, reminiscent of many Oxford and Cambridge colleges. The Honan Collegiate Chapel, east of the quadrangle, was built in 1916 and modeled on the 12th-century Hiberno-Romanesque style. The UCC chapel's stained-glass windows, as well as its collection of art and crafts, altar furnishings, and textiles in the Celtic Revival style, are noteworthy. The **Lewis Glucksman Gallery** opened in late 2004 in a striking new building in a wooded gully beside the college's entrance gates. Besides displaying works from the college's collection, it hosts cutting-edge contemporary art exhibits. ⊠ *Western Road* ☎ *021/490–1876* ⊕ *www.ucc.ie* 🖃 *Free. Guided tours €4* ⊙ *Weekdays 9–5, but call to confirm hrs Easter wk, July and Aug., and mid-Dec.–mid-Jan. Guided tours May–Oct., Mon., Wed., Fri., and Sat. at 3 PM.*

BLARNEY
⑬ *10 km (6 mi) northwest of Cork City.*

In the center of Blarney is **Blarney Castle,** or what remains of it: the ruined central keep is all that's left of this mid-15th-century stronghold. The castle contains the famed Blarney Stone; kissing the stone, it's said, endows the kisser with the fabled "gift of gab." It's 127 steep steps to the battlements. To kiss the stone, you must lie down on the battlements, hold on to a guardrail, and lean your head way back. It's good fun and not at all dangerous.

☎ *021/438–5252* ⊕ *www.blarneycastle.ie* 🖃 *€8* ⊙ *May and Sept., Mon.–Sat. 9–6:30, Sun. 9–5:30; June–Aug., Mon.–Sat. 9–7, Sun. 9–5:30; Oct.–Apr., Mon.–Sat. 9–sundown, Sun. 9–5:30.*

KINSALE

14 *29 km (18 mi) southwest of Cork City on R600.*

Foodies flock to Kinsale, a picturesque port that pioneered the Irish small-town tradition of fine dining in unbelievably small restaurants. In the town center, at the tip of the wide, fjordlike harbor that opens out from the River Bandon, upscale shops and eateries with brightly painted facades line small streets. Kinsale is also a center for sailing.

★ The British built **Charles Fort** on the east side of the Bandon River estuary in the late 17th century, after their defeat of the Spanish and Irish forces. One of Europe's best-preserved "star forts" encloses some 12 cliff-top acres and is similar to Fort Ticonderoga in New York State. If the sun is shining, take the footpath signposted SCILLY WALK; it winds along the harbor's edge under tall trees and then through the village of Summer Cove. ✉ *3 km (2 mi) east of town* ☎ *021/477–2263* ⊕ *www.heritageireland.ie* ✉ *€3.70* ⏱ *Mid-Mar.–Oct., daily 10–6; Nov.–mid-Mar., weekends 10–5.*

The **Desmond Castle and the International Museum of Wine** are in a 15th-century fortified town house—originally a custom house. Now it contains displays that tell the story of the wine trade and its importance to the Irish diaspora to France, America, Australia, and New Zealand. ✉ *Cork St.* ☎ *021/477–4855* ⊕ *www.winegeese.ie* ✉ *€2.90* ⏱ *Mid-Apr.–mid-June, Tues.–Sun. 10–6; mid-June–mid-Oct., daily 10–6.*

SHOPPING

Ireland is *the* place to buy linen and wool products, crystal by Waterford, ceramics and antiques. Celtic motifs are found on everything from jewelry to coffee cups. In Cork, Paul Street is the backbone of the trendy shopping scene while Patrick Street has high-end names mixed with antique and souvenir shops. Blarney and Kinsale both have a range of shops selling arts and crafts from around the country.

Blarney Woolen Mills (✉ *Blarney* ☎ *021/438–5280* ⊕ *www.blarney.ie*) has the largest stock of Irish crafts and quality items. It sells everything from Irish-made high fashion to Aran hand-knit items.

The best place for recordings of Irish music is **Living Tradition** (✉ *40 Mac-Curtain St., City Center North Cork* ☎ *021/450–2040*).

Quills (✉ *107 Patrick St., City Center South Cork* ☎ *021/427–1717*) has a good selection of Irish-made apparel for women and men.

Philip Gray served as a diver in the Irish navy, and left to paint, which he does extremely well. The sea in all its guises is his subject. **The Philip Gray Gallery of Fine Art** (✉ *Slipway Two, Cork Dockyard, Rushbrooke, Cobh* ☎ *021/481–4170* ⊕ *www.philipgray.com*) is on a slipway of a dockyard in Cork Harbour.

WHERE TO EAT

$–$$$ ✕ **Jim Edwards.** This is a Kinsale institution, known for its generous portions of local steak, lamb, duck, and fresh seafood, all prepared under the careful eye of the owner and his wife, Paula. Choose from the daily specials in the busy bar, or have a more relaxed meal in the attached restaurant. ⊠*Market Quay, Kinsale* ☎*021/477–2541* ⊟*AE, DC, MC, V.*

¢–$$ ✕**Farmgate Café.** One of the best—and busiest—informal lunch spots in town is on a terraced gallery above the fountain in the English Market. One side of the gallery opens onto the market and is self-service; the other side is glassed-in and has table service (reservations advised). Tripe and drisheen is one dish that is always on the menu; daily specials include similarly traditional dishes, such as corned beef with colcannon (potatoes and cabbage mashed with butter and seasonings) and loin of smoked bacon with *champ* (potatoes mashed with scallions or leeks). ⊠*English Market, City Center South* ☎*021/427–8134* ⊟*DC, MC, V* ⊗*Closed Sun. No dinner.*

DOVER, UNITED KINGDOM

In an era when everything small is fashionable, from cell phones to digital cameras, South East England will inevitably have great appeal. Here, the landscape ravishes the eye in spring with apple blossoms, and in the autumn with lush fields ready for harvest. It is a county of orchards, market gardens, and round oasthouses with their tilted, pointed roofs, once used for drying hops (many now converted into pricey homes). Gentle hills and woodlands are punctuated with farms and storybook villages rooted in history, while the region's cathedral cities, including noble Canterbury, wait patiently to be explored. Busy ports, the biggest of which is Dover, have served for centuries as gateways to continental Europe. Indeed, because the English Channel is at its narrowest here, a great deal of British history has been forged in the Southeast.

ESSENTIALS

CURRENCY The British pound sterling (£1 is $US2.07 at this writing). U.S. currency is generally not accepted in Europe. ATMs are common and credit cards are widely accepted.

HOURS Museums are open daily from 9 until 5, while shops usually open from 9 until 5:30 or 6. Some shops are open on Sunday.

INTERNET **Canterbury Library** ⊠*High St., Canterbury* ☎*01227/452747.*

TELEPHONES Tri-band GSM phones work in the UK. You can buy prepaid phone cards at telecom shops, news vendors and tobacconists in all towns and cities. Phone cards can be used for local or international calls. Vodafone and Orange are the leading telecom companies.

COMING ASHORE

Ships dock at the Western Docks in Dover. There are two passenger terminals. Terminal 1 is in a converted Victorian railway station while Terminal 2 is a purpose-built passenger facility opened in 2001. The terminals have money exchange facilities, car rental kiosks, and cafés, plus a taxi stand.

London can be reached in two hours by train. Take a taxi to the station in Dover. Ticket prices start at £16 round trip but vary depending on the time of the train. London can also be reached in 2½ hours by bus. There are bus departures from the Eastern Docks (a taxi ride or a 15-minute walk along the seafront) and, occasionally, directly from the cruise terminal. Prices start at £12.30 round-trip. Canterbury is a 30-minute ride

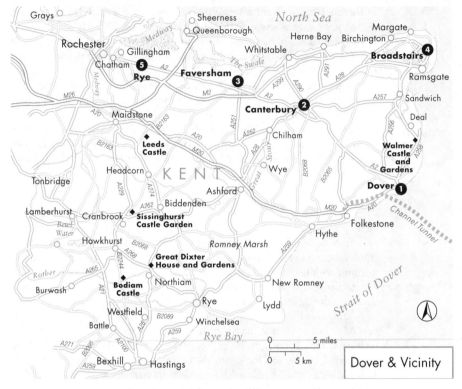

Dover & Vicinity

away, with prices starting at £5.60 round trip. Local buses 15 and 15X link Dover with Canterbury every hour.

A car rental is recommended for exploring the Kent countryside but not for a visit to London, where traffic, congestion charges, and parking difficulties abound. Rental rates are £30 per day for an economy manual vehicle. But given the distance, this is a good opportunity to see the beauty of Kent rather than trek all the way into Central London.

EXPLORING DOVER & VICINITY

Numbers in the margin correspond to points of interest on the Dover & Vicinity map.

DOVER

1 *122 km (76 mi) southeast of London.*

The busy passenger port of Dover has for centuries been Britain's gateway to Europe. Its chalk **White Cliffs** are a famous and inspirational sight, though you may find the town itself a bit disappointing; the savage bombardments of World War II and the shortsightedness of postwar developers left the city center an unattractive place. Roman legacies include a lighthouse, adjoining a stout Anglo-Saxon church.

The **Roman Painted House,** believed to have been a hotel, includes some wall paintings, along with the remnants of an ingenious heating system. ✉*New St.* ☎*01304/203279* 🎫*£3.80* 🕓*Apr.–Sept., Tues.–Sat. 10–5, Sun. 1–5.*

✪ Spectacular **Dover Castle**, tower-
★ ing high above the ramparts of the
White Cliffs, was a mighty medieval castle, and it has served as an
important strategic center over the
centuries, even in World War II.
Most of the castle, including the
keep, dates to Norman times. It
was begun by Henry II in 1181 but
incorporates additions from almost
every succeeding century. There's
a lot to see here besides the castle
rooms: exhibits, many of which will
appeal to kids, include the Siege of
1216, the Princess of Wales Regimental Museum, and Castle Fit for
a King. ■TIP➔ Take time to tour the
secret wartime tunnels, a medieval and
Napoleonic-era system that was used as
a World War II command center during the evacuation of Dunkirk in 1940. Note:
Some of the tunnels are expected to be closed in early 2008 for conservation work,
although some will be accessible at all times. ✉ *Castle Rd.* ☎ *01304/211067*
⊕ *www.english-heritage.org.uk/server/show/nav.14571* ✍ *£9.50* ✆ *Feb.
and Mar., daily 10–4; Apr.–Sept., daily 10–6; Oct., daily 10–5; Nov.–Jan.,
Thurs.–Mon. 10–4.*

> **DOVER BEST BETS**
>
> **Canterbury Cathedral.** One of
> Britain's greatest churches, this was
> an important place of pilgrimage and
> the scene of one of the country's
> darkest crimes.
>
> **The white cliffs of Dover.** Best seen
> from the water, these iconic cliffs are
> part of the national psyche and, on a
> sunny day, an exceptionally breathtak-
> ing vista.
>
> **Rye.** Though there are no attractions
> as such here, the sheer quaintness
> and "Englishness" of Rye makes it a
> great place to relax, soak in the atmo-
> sphere, and shop for souvenirs.

CANTERBURY

❷ *28 km (17 mi) northwest of Dover.*

The cathedral city of Canterbury is an ancient place that has attracted travelers since the 12th century. The city's magnificent cathedral, the Mother
Church of England, remains a powerful draw. The mere mention of Canterbury conjures images of Geoffrey Chaucer's *Canterbury Tales*, about
medieval pilgrims making their way to Canterbury Cathedral. Although
there is evidence of prosperous society in and around Canterbury as far
back as the Bronze Age (around 1000 BC), the height of Canterbury's popularity came in the 12th century, when thousands of pilgrims flocked here
to see the shrine of the murdered Archbishop St. Thomas à Becket, making
this southeastern town one of the most visited in England, if not Europe.
Buildings that served as pilgrims' inns (and which survived the World War
II bombing of the city) still dominate the streets of Canterbury's center.

Fodor's Choice **Canterbury Cathedral**, the nucleus of worldwide Anglicanism—formally the
★ Cathedral Church of Christ Canterbury—is a living textbook of medieval
architecture. The building was begun in 1070, demolished, begun anew
in 1096, and then systematically expanded over the next three centuries.
When the original choir section burned to the ground in 1174, another
replaced it, designed in the new Gothic style, with tall, pointed arches.
Don't miss the North Choir aisle, which holds two windows that show
Jesus in the Temple, the three kings asleep, and Lot's wife turned to a pillar of salt. The windows are among the earliest parts of the cathedral, but
only 33 of the original 208 survive.

6

The cathedral was only a century old, and still relatively small, when Thomas à Becket, the archbishop of Canterbury, was murdered here in 1170. Becket, a defender of ecclesiastical interests, had angered his friend Henry II, who was heard to exclaim, "Who will rid me of this troublesome priest?" Thinking they were carrying out the king's wishes, four knights burst in on Becket in one of the side chapels and killed him. Two years later Becket was canonized, and Henry II's subsequent submission to the authority of the Church helped establish the cathedral as the undisputed center of English Christianity. Becket's tomb, destroyed by Henry VIII in 1538 as part of his campaign to reduce the power of the Church and confiscate its treasures, was one of the most extravagant shrines in Christendom. In **Trinity Chapel**, which held the shrine, you can still see a series of 13th-century stained-glass windows illustrating Becket's miracles. The actual site of Becket's murder is down a flight of steps just to the left of the nave. In the corner, a second flight of steps leads down to the enormous Norman **undercroft,** or vaulted cellarage, built in the early 12th century. A row of squat pillars whose capitals dance with animals and monsters supports the roof.

If time permits, be sure to explore the **cloisters** and other small monastic buildings to the north of the cathedral. The 12th-century octagonal water tower is still part of the cathedral's water supply. The cathedral is very popular, so arrive early or late in the day to avoid the worst crowds. ■TIP➜ **You get a map and an overview of the building's history when you enter; audio guides have the most detail, or take a tour for the personal touch.** ⊠*Cathedral Precincts* ☎*01227/762862* ⊕*www.canterbury-cathedral.org* 🎫*£6.50, free for services and ½ hr before closing; £4 for tour, £3 for audio guide* ◷*Easter–Sept., Mon.–Sat. 9–6:30, Sun. 12:30–2:30 and 4:30–5:30; Oct.–Easter, Mon.–Sat. 9–5, Sun. 12:30–2:30 and 4:30–5:30. Restricted access during services.*

Below ground, at the level of the remnants of Roman Canterbury, the **Canterbury Roman Museum** features colorful mosaic Roman pavement and a hypocaust—the Roman version of central heating. Displays of excavated objects (some of which you can hold in the Touch the Past area) and computer-generated reconstructions of Roman buildings and the marketplace help re-create history. ⊠*Butchery La.* ☎*01227/785575* ⊕*www.canterbury-museums.co.uk* 🎫*£3* ◷*June–Oct., Mon.–Sat. 10–5, Sun. 1:30–5; Nov.–May, Mon.–Sat. 10–5; last admission at 4. Closed last wk in Dec.*

The Canterbury Tales is a kitschy audiovisual (and occasionally olfactory) dramatization of 14th-century English life—popular but touristy. You'll "meet" Chaucer's pilgrims at the Tabard Inn near London and view tableaus illustrating five tales. An actor in period costume often performs a charade as part of the scene. ⊠*St. Margaret's St.* ☎*01227/479227* ⊕*www.canterburytales.org.uk* 🎫*£7.25* ◷*Nov.–Feb., daily 10–4:30; Mar.–June, Sept., and Oct., daily 10–5; July and Aug., daily 9:30–5.*

For an essential Canterbury experience, follow the circuit of the 13th- and 14th-century **Medieval city walls,** built on the line of the Roman walls. Those to the east survive intact, towering some 20 feet high and offering a sweeping view of the town. You can access these from a number of places, including Castle Street and Broad Street.

FAVERSHAM

❸ *45 km (28 mi) northwest of Dover.*

In Roman times, Faversham was a thriving seaport. Today the port is hidden from sight, and you could pass through this market town without knowing it was there. Still, Faversham is a worthwhile stop for those in search of Ye Quaint Olde Englande: the town center, with its Tudor houses grouped around the 1574 guildhall and covered market, looks like a perfect stage set. There are no actual sights here, as such, but it's a lovely place to take a break and have a stroll.

BROADSTAIRS

❹ *36 km (22 mi) north of Dover.*

Like other Victorian seaside towns on this stretch of coast, Broadstairs was once the playground of vacationing Londoners. Charles Dickens spent many summers here between 1837 and 1851 and wrote glowingly of its bracing freshness. Today, grand 19th-century houses line the waterfront. In the off-season Broadstairs is a peaceful retreat, but day-trippers pack the town in July and August.

One of Dickens's favorite abodes was **Bleak House,** perched on a cliff overlooking Viking Bay, where he wrote much of *David Copperfield* and drafted the eponymous *Bleak House.* His study and other rooms have been preserved. Displays explore local history, including the wrecks at nearby Goodwin Sands, and the cellars have exhibits about smuggling, a longtime local activity. The house is currently being renovated, so it's possible some exhibits may be closed when you visit. ✉*Fort Rd.* ☏*01843/862224* 🎫*£3* ⏱*Late-Feb.–June and Sept.–mid-Dec., daily 10–6; July and Aug., daily 10–9.*

What is now the **Dickens House Museum** was originally the home of Mary Pearson Strong, on whom Dickens based the character of Betsey Trotwood, David Copperfield's aunt. There's a reconstruction of Miss Trotwood's room, a few objects that once belonged to the Dickens family, and prints and photographs commemorating Dickens's association with Broadstairs. ✉*2 Victoria Parade* ☏*01843/863453* ⊕*www.dickenshouse. co.uk* 🎫*£2.50* ⏱*Apr.–Oct., daily 2–5.*

RYE

❺ *64 km (40 mi) south of Dover.*

★ With cobbled streets and ancient timbered dwellings, Rye is an artist's dream. Once a port (the water retreated, and the harbor is now 2 mi away), the town starts where the sea once lapped at its ankles and then winds its way to the top of a low hill that overlooks the Romney Marshes. Virtually every building in the little town center is intriguingly old; some places were smugglers' retreats. This place can be easily walked without a map, but if you prefer guidance, the local tourist office has an interesting audio tour of the town, as well as maps.

SHOPPING

The little towns of Kent are great places to browse for collectibles, china, silver and second hand books. The streets of Canterbury have an excellent selection of souvenirs, some of it decidedly kitsch. Rye has great antique shops, perfect for an afternoon of rummaging, with the biggest cluster at the foot of the hill near the tourist information center. The English can find bargains; it's harder for Americans, given the exchange rate. The town still has a number of potteries. **Black Sheep Antiques** (⊠*72 The Mint, Rye* ☎*01797/224508*) has a superior selection of antique crystal and silver. Of Rye's working potteries, **Cinque Ports Pottery** (⊠*The Monastery, Conduit Hill, Rye* ☎*01797/222033*) is one of the best. **Collectors Corner** (⊠*2 Market Rd.Rye* ☎*01797/225796*) sells a good mix of furniture, art, and silver. **David Sharp Pottery** (⊠*55 The Mint, Rye* ☎*01797/222620*) specializes in the ceramic name plaques that are a feature of the town.

Hawkin's Bazaar (⊠*34 Burgate, Canterbury* ☎*01227/785809*) carries an exceptional selection of traditional and modern toys and games. The **National Trust Shop** (⊠*24 Burgate, Canterbury* ☎*01227/457120*) stocks the National Trust line of household items, ideal for gifts.

WHERE TO EAT

⊕ ✗**Landgate Bistro.** Although definitely a bistro, this restaurant in a small shop unit near one of the ancient gateways is serious about its food. Fish is always a good choice, or you can opt for the duck soaked in a tangy port sauce or griddle-cooked cutlets of venison with winter vegetables. A fixed-price menu (£18 for three courses) is available Tuesday through Thursday. ⊠*5–6 Landgate,Rye* ☎*01797/222829* ▭*DC, MC, V* ⊙*Closed Sun. and Mon., last wk in Dec., and 1st wk in Jan. No lunch.*

¢ ✗**City Fish Bar.** Long lines and lots of satisfied finger licking attest to the deserved popularity of this excellent fish-and-chips outlet in the center of town. Everything is freshly fried, the batter crisp and the fish tasty; the fried mushrooms are also surprisingly good. It closes at 7. ⊠*30 St. Margarets St.,Canterbury* ☎*01227/760873* ▭*No credit cards.*

DUBLIN, IRELAND

In his inimitable, irresistible way, James Joyce immortalized the city of Dublin in works like *Ulysses* and *Dubliners*. He claimed to have chosen Dublin as the setting for his work because it was a "center of paralysis" where nothing much ever changed. What would he make of Temple Bar—the city's erstwhile down-at-the-heels neighborhood, now crammed with restaurants and hotels? Or of the city's newfound status as a bustling hub of the European economy? Yet despite all these advances, traditional Dublin is far from buried. The fundamentals—the Georgian elegance of Merrion Square, the Norman drama of Christ Church Cathedral, the foamy pint at an atmospheric pub—are still on hand to gratify. Most of all, there are the locals themselves: the nod and grin when you catch their eye on the street, the eagerness to share a tale or two, and their paradoxically dark but warm sense of humor.

ESSENTIALS

CURRENCY The euro (€1 to US$1.46 at this writing). U.S. currency is generally not accepted in Europe, but ATMs are common.

HOURS Shops and businesses are generally open Monday through Saturday from 9:30 to 5:30 or 6; some open later and some open on Sunday. Most museums open daily Monday through Saturday from 9 until 5; museums may have shorter hours on Sunday.

INTERNET **Central Café** (⊠*6 Grafton St.* ☎*01/6778298*), above Bus Stop News, is a centrally located café.

TELEPHONES Most tri- and quad-band GSM phones will work in Ireland, and the country's mobile system is 3G compatible with excellent coverage. Public phones accept prepaid call cards (available in shops and telecom offices) and credit crads. Eircom, BT Ireland, and Vodafone are the major telecom suppliers.

COMING ASHORE

Small ships dock at the quayside of the River Liffey, close to the downtown area. Larger ships berth at Alexandra Quay, only 1.2 mi from downtown. Alexandra Quay is part of the great Dublin Port, with a range of visitor facilities including cafés, shops, information desks, and restrooms. Buses 53 and 53A run from the port into the city. Ticket prices are set according to the number of zones traveled, with a maximum fare of €1.90. Ticket machines on the bus only accept coins.

Taxis can be hired to run tour itineraries, although charges are complicated. Initial charges are a maximum of €3.80, then €0.95 per km (½-mi) for the first 14 km (9 mi), rising to €1.63 per km once the ride lasts longer than 30 km (19 mi). Drivers can choose to charge by the minute rather than per km, with the initial charge, plus €0.34 per minute for the first 40 minutes, climbing to €0.58 for journeys over 86 minutes. Don't rent a car if you are planning to tour Dublin, but a rental car does offer freedom to explore the countryside and coast around the city. The cost per day for a compact manual vehicle begins at €27.

EXPLORING DUBLIN

Numbers in the margin correspond to points of interest on the Dublin map.

8 **City Hall.** This grand Georgian municipal building (1769–79) once housed the Royal Exchange. Today it's the seat of the Dublin Corporation, the elected body that governs the city. The building houses a multimedia exhibition tracing the evolution of Ireland's 1,000-year-old capital. ⊠*Dame St., Dublin West* ☎*01/222–2204* ⊕*www.dublincity.ie* ☎*€4* ⊘*Mon.– Sat. 10–5:15, Sun. 2–5.*

10 **Custom House.** The Custom House is the city's most spectacular Georgian building. Note the exquisitely carved lions and unicorns supporting the arms of Ireland at the far ends of the facade. ⊠*Custom House Quay, Northside* ☎*01/888–2538* ☎*€1.30* ⊘*Mid-Mar.–Oct., weekdays 10– 12:30, weekends 2–5; Nov.–mid-Mar., Wed.–Fri. 10–12:30, Sun. 2–5.*

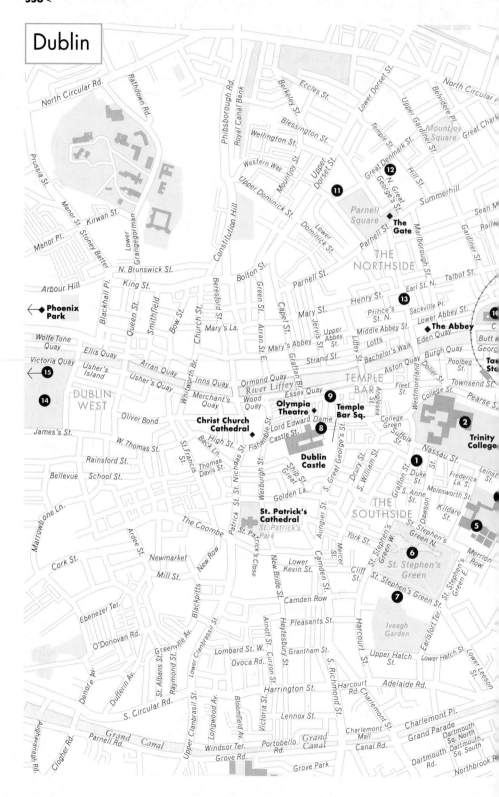

Dublin

6

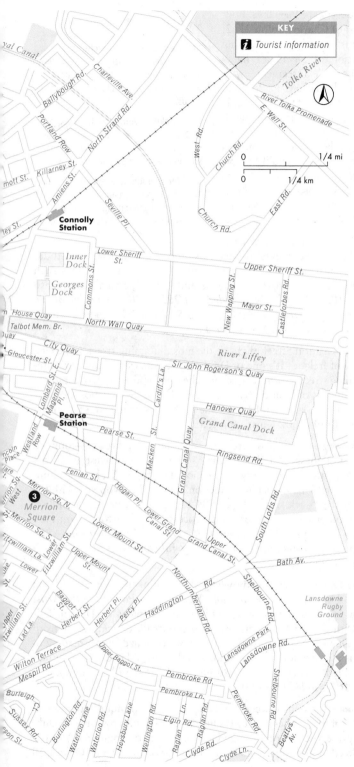

KEY

i Tourist information

11 **Dublin City Gallery, The Hugh Lane.** Built for the Earl of Charlemont in 1762, this home is now a gallery housing the collection of Sir Hugh Lane. A complicated agreement with the National Gallery in London (reached after heated diplomatic dispute) stipulates that a portion of the 39 French paintings amassed by Lane shuttle between London and here. If you're lucky, you'll be able to see Pissarro's *Printemps,* Manet's *Eva Gonzales,* Morisot's *Jour d'Été,* and, the jewel of the collection, Renoir's *Les Parapluies.*

The late Francis Bacon's partner donated the entire contents of Bacon's studio to the gallery. The studio has been reconstructed here as a permanent display and includes such masterpieces as *Study After Velázquez* and the tragic splash-and-crash *Triptych.* ⊠*Parnell Sq. N, Northside* ☎*01/222–5550* ⊕*www.hughlane.ie* ⊠*Gallery free; Bacon Studio €7.50, €3.50 Tues. 9:30–noon* ☉*Tues.–Thurs. 10–6, Fri. and Sat. 10–5, Sun. 11–5.*

1 **Grafton Street.** Grafton Street might be the most humming street in the city, if not in all of Ireland. It's one of Dublin's vital spines and the city's premier shopping street. Grafton Street and the smaller alleyways that radiate off it offer dozens of boutiques and some of the Southside's most popular watering holes. In summer, buskers line both sides of the street, pouring out the sounds of drum, whistle, pipe, and string.

14 **Guinness Brewery and Storehouse.** Ireland's all-dominating brewer—founded by Arthur Guinness in 1759—spans a 60-acre spread west of Christ Church Cathedral. The brewery itself is closed to the public, but the Guinness Storehouse is a spectacular attraction, designed to woo you with the wonders of the "dark stuff." In a 1904 cast-iron-and-brick warehouse, the exhibition elucidates the brewing process and its history—you even get to enjoy a free pint. ⊠*St. James' Gate, Dublin West* ☎*01/408–4800* ⊕*www.guinness-storehouse.com* ⊠*€14* ☉*July and Aug., daily 9:30–7; Sept.–June, daily 9:30–5.*

12 **James Joyce Centre.** Joyce is acknowledged as one of the greatest modern authors, and his *Dubliners, Finnegan's Wake,* and *A Portrait of the Artist as a Young Man* can even be read as quirky "travel guides" to Dublin. This restored 18th-century Georgian town house, once the dancing academy of Professor Denis J. Maginni (which many will recognize from a reading of *Ulysses*), is a center for Joycean studies and events related to the author. ⊠*35 N. Great George's St., Northside* ☎*01/878-8547* ⊕*www.james-joyce.ie* ⊠*€5, guided tour €10* ☉*Tues.–Sat. 10–5.*

3 **Merrion Square.** Created between 1762 and 1764, this tranquil square a few blocks east of St. Stephen's Green is lined on three sides by some of Dublin's best-preserved Georgian town houses. Several distinguished Dubliners have lived on the square, including Irish nationalist Daniel O'Connell and author W. B. Yeats. As you walk past the houses, read the plaques on the house facades, which identify former inhabitants. ⊠*Along Upper and Lower Mount Sts., Southside* ☉*Daily sunrise–sunset.*

4 **National Gallery of Ireland.** Featuring works by Caravaggio, Van Gogh, and Vermeer, the National Gallery of Ireland—the first in a series of major civic buildings on the west side of Merrion Square—is one of Europe's finer small art museums. The collection holds more than 2,500 paintings and some 10,000 other works. ⊠*Merrion Sq. W, Southside* ☎*01/661–5133* ⊕*www.nationalgallery.ie* ⊠*Free; special exhibits €10* ☉*Mon.–Wed., Fri., and Sat. 9:30–5:30, Thurs. 9:30–8:30, Sun. noon–5:30.*

Fodor'sChoice
★

5 **National Museum of Archaeology and History.** This museum houses a fabled collection of Irish artifacts dating from 7000 BC to the present. Organized around a grand rotunda, the museum is elaborately decorated, with mosaic floors, marble columns, balustrades, and fancy ironwork. It has the largest collection of Celtic antiquities in the world, including gold jewelry, carved stones, bronze tools, and weapons. The newest attraction is Kinship and Sacrifice, centering on a number of Iron Age "bog bodies" and other objects found in Ireland's peat bogs. The Annex is at 7–9 Merrion Row. ⊠*Kildare St.,Southside* ☎*01/677–7444* ⊕*www.museum.ie* ⊠*Free* ☉*Tues.–Sat. 10–5, Sun. 2–5.*
★

6

7 **Newman House.** One of the greatest glories of Georgian Dublin, Newman House is actually two imposing town houses joined together. The earlier of the two, No. 85 St. Stephen's Green (1738) was originally known as Clanwilliam House. Designed by Richard Castle, it has two landmarks of Irish Georgian style: the Apollo Room, decorated with stuccowork; and the magnificent Saloon. The Saloon is crowned with an exuberant ceiling aswirl with cupids and gods, created by the Brothers Lafranchini, the finest *stuccadores* (plaster-workers) of 18th-century Dublin. Next door at No. 86 (1765), the staircase, on pastel walls, is one of the city's most beautiful Rococo gems. To explore the houses you must join a guided tour. ⊠*85–86 St. Stephen's Green, Southside* ☎*01/716-7422* ⊠*House and garden €5* ☉*Tours June–Aug., Tues.–Fri. at 2, 3, and 4.*

13 **O'Connell Street.** Dublin's most famous thoroughfare was previously known as Sackville Street, but its name was changed in 1924, two years after the founding of the Irish Free State. A 395-foot-high Spire dominates the street. At the south end is a statue dedicated to Daniel O'Connell (1775–1847), "The Liberator," erected as a tribute to the orator's achievement in securing Catholic Emancipation in 1829.

15 **Royal Hospital Kilmainham.** This replica of Les Invalides in Paris is regarded as the most important 17th-century building in Ireland. The entire edifice has been restored to house the **Irish Museum of Modern Art**, which concentrates on the work of contemporary Irish artists. The museum also displays works by some non-Irish 20th-century greats, including Picasso and Miró. ⊠*Kilmainham La., Dublin West* ☎*01/612–9900* ⊕*www.modernart.ie* ⊠*Free* ☉*Royal Hospital Tues.–Sat. 10–5:30, Sun. noon–5:30; tours every ½ hr. Museum Tues. and Thurs.–Sat. 10–5:30, Wed. 10:30–5:30, Sun. noon–5:30; tours Wed. and Fri. at 2:30, Sat. at 11:30.*
★

6 **St. Stephen's Green.** Dubliners call it simply Stephen's Green—a verdant,
27-acre Southside square that was used for the public punishment of crim-

inals before it became a park. On the north side you'll find the legendary
Shelbourne Hotel where you can enjoy afternoon tea. On the south side
is the alluring Georgian Newman House. ⊠*Southside* ◻*Free* ☉*Daily
sunrise–sunset.*

9 **Temple Bar.** A visit to modern Dublin wouldn't be complete without spending some time in the city's most vibrant area. This is Dublin's version
of New York's SoHo, Paris's Bastille, London's Notting Hill—a thriving
mix of high and alternative culture distinct from what you'll find in any
other part of the city. Dotting the area's narrow cobblestone streets and
pedestrian alleyways are new apartment buildings, vintage clothing stores,
postage-stamp-size boutiques, art galleries, hip restaurants, pubs, clubs,
European-style cafés, and a smattering of cultural venues. ⊠*Bound by the
Liffey, Westmoreland St., Dame St.-College Green, and Fishamble St.*

2 **Trinity College.** Founded in 1592, Trinity is Ireland's oldest and most famous
college. The memorably atmospheric campus is a must; here you can track

the shadows of such noted alumni as Jonathan Swift (1667–1745), Oscar
Wilde (1854–1900), and Samuel Beckett (1906–89). Trinity's grounds
cover 40 acres. Most of its buildings were constructed in the 18th and
early 19th centuries and together comprise an exceptional collection of
neo-Classical architecture. The **Old Library** houses Ireland's largest collection of books and manuscripts; its principal treasure is the *Book of Kells,*
generally considered to be the most striking manuscript ever produced in
the Anglo-Saxon world and one of the great masterpieces of early Christian art. The book, which dates to the 9th century, is a splendidly illuminated version of the Gospels. The main library room, also known as the
Long Room, is one of Dublin's most staggering sights. At 213 feet long and
42 feet wide, it contains approximately 200,000 of the 3 million volumes
in Trinity's collection. ⊠*Front Sq., Southside* ☎*01/896-2320* ⊕*www.
tcd.ie* ◻*€8* ☉*May–Sept., Mon.–Sat. 9:30–5, Sun. 9:30–4:30; Oct.–Apr.,
Mon.–Sat. 9:30–5, Sun. noon–4:30.*

SHOPPING

There's a tremendous variety of stores in Dublin, many of which are quite
sophisticated. Department stores stock internationally known fashion
designer goods and housewares, and small boutiques sell Irish crafts and
other merchandise. If you're at all interested in modern and contemporary
literature, be sure to leave yourself time to browse through the bookstores.
Don't forget a bottle of Irish whisky or a bottle or two of Guinness.

Francis Street is the hub of Dublin's antiques trade. **Grafton Street** has mainly
chain stores. The smaller streets off Grafton Street have worthwhile crafts,
clothing, and designer houseware shops. **Nassau Street,** Dublin's main tour-
ist-oriented thoroughfare, has some of the best-known stores selling Irish
goods. **Temple Bar** is dotted with small boutiques—mainly intimate, quirky
shops that traffic in a selection of trendy goods, from vintage clothes to
some of the most avant-garde Irish garb anywhere in the city. Note that
many museums have excellent gift shops selling crafts, books, and prints,
among other items.

Blarney Woollen Mills (⊠*21–23 Nassau St., City Center* ☎*01/671–0068*) is one of the best places for Belleek china, Waterford and Galway crystal, and Irish linen. **Cathach Books** (⊠*10 Duke St., City Center* ☎*01/671–8676*) sells first editions of Irish literature and many other books of Irish interest, plus old maps of Dublin and Ireland.

WHERE TO EAT

¢–$ ✕**Bewley's Oriental Café**. This granddaddy of the capital's cafés has been serving coffee and sticky buns to Dubliners since its founding by the Quakers in 1842. Today it serves pizza and pasta as well. The place is worth a visit if only to sit over a cup of quality coffee and people-watch, just like Dubliners have for well over 150 years. ⊠*78 Grafton St., Southside* ☎*01/677–6761.*

¢–$ ✕**Irish Film Institute Café**. This trendy café is a pleasant place for a lunchtime break. Sandwiches are large and healthful, with plenty of vegetarian choices, and the people-watching is unmatched. ⊠*6 Eustace St., Temple Bar* ☎*01/679–5744.*

GREENOCK, SCOTLAND (FOR GLASGOW)

In the days when Britain still ruled over an empire, Glasgow pronounced itself the Second City of the Empire. The term "Clyde-built" (from Glasgow's River Clyde) became synonymous with good workmanship and lasting quality. Glasgow had fallen into a severely depressed state by the mid-20th century, but during the last two decades of the 20th century the city cleaned up and started looking forward. Modern Glasgow has undergone an urban renaissance: a booming cultural life, stylish restaurants, and an air of confidence make it Scotland's most exciting city. Glasgow is particularly remarkable for its architecture, from the unique Victorian cityscapes of Alexander "Greek" Thomson (1817–75) to the cutting-edge art nouveau vision of Charles Rennie Mackintosh (1868–1928). The city also has some of the most exciting museum collections outside London.

ESSENTIALS

CURRENCY The British pound sterling (£1 is $US2.07 at this writing). U.S. currency is generally not accepted in Europe. ATMs are common and credit cards are widely accepted.

HOURS Museums are open from 9 until 5, while shops usually open from 9 until 5:30 or 6. Some shops are open on Sunday.

INTERNET **Café.com** (⊠*8 Renfield St., City Center* ☎*0141/221–5042*).

TELEPHONES Tri-band GSM phones work in the U.K. You can buy prepaid phone cards at telecom shops, news vendors, and tobacconists in all towns and cities. Phone cards can be used for local or international calls. Vodafone and Orange are the leading telecom companies.

COMING ASHORE

Vessels dock at Greenock's Ocean Terminal in the main port. Passengers walk the few yards to the terminal building, which has tourist information, refreshments, currency exchange, car rental kiosks, and a taxi stand. A new waterfront walkway leads into the town of Greenock, where there

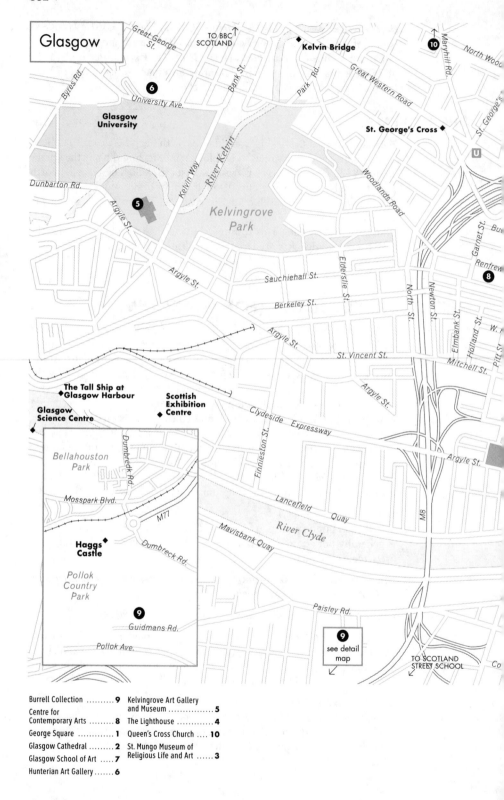

Glasgow

TO BBC
SCOTLAND

Great George St.

Kelvin Bridge ◆

Bank St.

Park Rd.

Maryhill Rd.

North Woo

10

Great Western Road

North St.

Byres Rd.

6
University Ave.

Glasgow
University

Kelvin Way

River Kelvin

St. George's Cross ◆

St. George's

U

Dunbarton Rd.

Argyle St.

5

Kelvingrove
Park

Woodlands Road

Garnet St.

Bue

Renfrew

8

Argyle St.

Sauchiehall St.

Elderslie St.

North St.

Newton St.

Elmbank St.

Holland St.

Pitt St

W.

Berkeley St.

Argyle St.

St. Vincent St.

Mitchell St.

Argyle St.

The Tall Ship at
◆Glasgow Harbour

Scottish
Exhibition
◆ Centre

Clydeside Expressway

Glasgow
Science Centre
◆

Finnieston St.

Argyle St.

M8

Bellahouston
Park

Dumbreck Rd.

Lancefield
Quay

River Clyde

Mosspark Blvd.

M77

Mavisbank Quay

Haggs ◆
Castle

Dumbreck Rd.

Pollok
Country
Park

9

Guidmans Rd.

Paisley Rd.

9
see detail
map

TO SCOTLAND
STREET SCHOOL

Co

Pollok Ave.

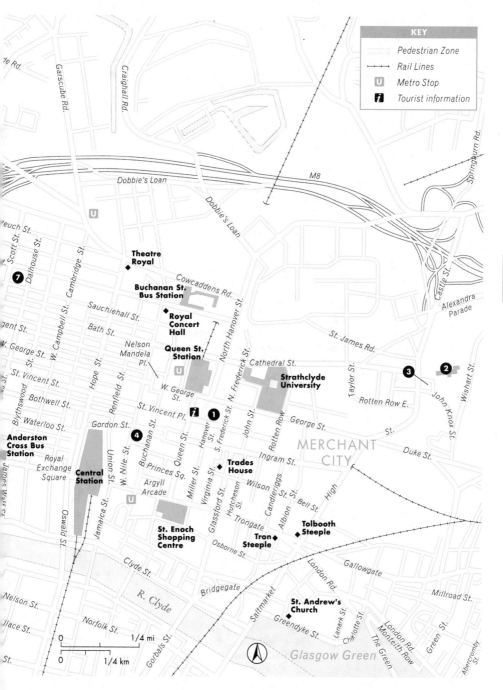

KEY

- ┈┈ Pedestrian Zone
- ┼┼┼ Rail Lines
- U Metro Stop
- ℹ Tourist information

te Rd.

Garscube Rd.

Craighall Rd.

Dobbie's Loan

M8

Springburn Rd.

Castle St.

Alexandra Parade

euch St.

Scott St.

Dalhouse St.

7

W. Campbell St.

Cambridge St.

Theatre Royal

Cowcaddens Rd.

St. James Rd.

6

Sauchiehall St.

Buchanan St. Bus Station

Royal Concert Hall

North Hanover St.

Cathedral St.

Taylor St.

Rotten Row E.

John Knox St.

Wishart St.

3

2

ent St.

Bath St.

Hope St.

Nelson Mandela Pl.

Queen St. Station

W. George St.

Frederick St.

N. Frederick St.

Strathclyde University

W. George St.

Renfield St.

St. Vincent St.

St. Vincent Pl.

ℹ 1

Hanover St.

John St.

George St.

Rotten Row

St.

Duke St.

Blythswood

Bothwell St.

Gordon St.

Buchanan St.

Queen St.

S. Frederick St.

MERCHANT CITY

Waterloo St.

Anderston Cross Bus Station

4

W. Nile St.

Princes Sq.

Miller St.

Virginia St.

Trades House

Hutcheson St.

Wilson

Ingram St.

Candleriggs

Albion St.

Bell St.

High

Royal Exchange Square

Central Station

Union St.

Jamaica St.

Argyll Arcade

Glassford St.

Trongate

James Watt St.

Oswald St.

U

St. Enoch Shopping Centre

Osborne St.

Tron Steeple

Tolbooth Steeple

London Rd.

Gallowgate

Millroad St.

Clyde St.

Bridgegate

Saltmarket

St. Andrew's Church

Greendyke St.

Lanark St.

Charlotte St.

London Rd.

Monteith Row

Green St.

Nelson St.

R. Clyde

Norfolk St.

Gorbals St.

Glasgow Green

The Green

Abercromby St.

llace St.

St.

0 ——— 1/4 mi

0 ——— 1/4 km

are shops, restaurants, and some fine Victorian architecture dating from the time when the town was an important transatlantic port. However, there's little to hold visitors here.

A taxi to downtown Glasgow is approximately £40 one way. From the station in Greenock, regular train services run into Glasgow city. The journey to Glasgow takes 30 to 40 minutes; trains run three or more times per hour and tickets start at £5.30 round trip. You can also take bus number 901 into Glasgow from the Greenock bus station.

Once in Glasgow, metro and bus services (tickets £0.90) can get you around easily. There are also numerous metered taxis. If you want to explore the majestic landscapes of southwestern Scotland independently, it pays to rent a vehicle (approximately £50 per day for a manual economy vehicle) or take a custom guided tour.

EXPLORING GLASGOW

Numbers in the margin correspond to points of interest on the Glasgow map.

⑨ Burrell Collection. An elegant, ultramodern building of pink sandstone and stainless steel houses thousands of items of all descriptions, from ancient Egyptian, Greek, and Roman artifacts to Chinese ceramics, bronzes, and jade. You'll also find medieval tapestries, stained-glass windows, Rodin sculptures, and exquisite French impressionist paintings—Degas's *The Rehearsal* and Sir Henry Raeburn's *Miss Macartney,* to name a few. Eccentric millionaire Sir William Burrell (1861–1958) donated the magpie collection to the city in 1944. You can get there via buses 45, 48, and 57 from Union Street. ⊠ *2060 Pollokshaws Rd., South Side* ☎ *0141/287–2550* ⌨ *Free* ⊙ *Mon.–Thurs. and Sat. 10–5, Fri. and Sun. 11–5.*

FodorsChoice ★

⑧ Centre for Contemporary Arts. This arts, cinema, and performance venue is in a post-industrial-revolution Alexander Thomson building. It has a reputation for unusual visual arts exhibitions, from paintings and sculpture to new media, and has championed a number of emerging artists, including Toby Paterson, winner of the Beck's Futures award in 2001. Simon Starling, the Scottish representative at the Venice Bienalle in 2003, has also exhibited work here. The vibrant Tempus Bar Café is designed by Los Angeles-based artist, Jorge Pardo. ⊠ *350 Sauchiehall St., City Center* ☎ *0141/352–4900* ⊕ *www.cca-glasgow.com* ⌨ *Free* ⊙ *Tues.–Fri. 11–6, Sat. 10–6.*

① George Square. The focal point of Glasgow's business district is lined with an impressive collection of statues of worthies: Queen Victoria; Scotland's national poet, Robert Burns (1759–96); the inventor and developer of the steam engine, James Watt (1736–1819); and towering above them all, Scotland's great historical novelist, Sir Walter Scott (1771–1832). On the square's east side stands the magnificent Italian Renaissance–style **City Chambers**; the handsome **Merchants' House** fills the corner of West George Street. Off and around George Square, several streets—Virginia Street, Miller Street, Glassford Street—recall the yesterdays of mercantile wealth. The French-style palaces, with their steep mansard roofs and cupolas, were once tobacco warehouses. Inside are shops and offices; here and there you may trace the elaborately carved mahogany galleries where auctions once took place. ✉ *Between St. Vincent and Argyle Sts., City Center.*

2 Glasgow Cathedral. The most complete of Scotland's cathedrals, this is an unusual double church, one above the other, dedicated to Glasgow's patron saint, St. Mungo. Consecrated in 1136 and completed about 300 years later, it was spared the ravages of the reformation—which destroyed so many of Scotland's medieval churches—mainly because Glasgow's trade guilds defended it. In the lower church is the splendid crypt of St. Mungo, who features prominently in local legends; Glasgow's coat of arms bears the various symbols of his famous deeds. ✉ *Cathedral St., City Center* ☎ *0141/552–6891* ⊕ *www.glasgow-cathedral.com* ✉ *Free* ⊙ *Apr.–Sept., Mon.–Sat. 9:30–6, Sun. 2–5; Oct.–Mar., Mon.–Sat. 9:30–4, Sun. 2–4.*

7 Glasgow School of Art. The exterior and interior, structure, furnishings, and ★ decoration of this art nouveau building, built between 1897 and 1909, form a unified whole—architect Charles Rennie Mackintosh was only 28 years old when he won a competition for its design. Guided tours are available; it's best to make reservations. You can always visit the four on-site galleries that host frequently changing exhibitions. A block away is Mackintosh's Willow Tearoom. ✉ *167 Renfrew St., City Center* ☎ *0141/353–4526* ⊕ *www.gsa.ac.uk* ✉ *£6.50* ⊙ *Tours Oct.–Mar., Mon.–Sat. 11 and 2; Apr.–Sept., daily 10:30, 11, 11:30, 1:30, 2, and 2:30.*

6 Hunterian Art Gallery. This Glasgow University gallery houses William Hunt- ★ er's (1718–83) collection of paintings (his antiquarian collection is housed in the nearby Hunterian Museum), together with prints and drawings by Tintoretto, Rembrandt, Sir Joshua Reynolds, and Auguste Rodin, as well as a major collection of paintings by James McNeill Whistler, who had a great affection for the city that bought one of his earliest paintings. Also in the gallery is a replica of **Charles Rennie Mackintosh's town house,** which once stood nearby. The rooms contain Mackintosh's distinctive art nouveau chairs, tables, beds, and cupboards, and the walls are decorated in the equally distinctive style devised by him and his artist wife, Margaret. ✉ *Hillhead St., West End* ☎ *0141/330–5431* ⊕ *www.hunterian.gla.ac.uk* ✉ *Free, Mackintosh house £3* ⊙ *Mon.–Sat. 9:30–5.*

5 Kelvingrove Art Gallery and Museum. This magnificent combination of cathe- ★ dral and castle was designed in the Renaissance style and built between 1891 and 1901. The stunning red-sandstone edifice is an appropriate home for an art collection—including works by Botticelli, Rembrandt, and Monet—hailed as one of the greatest civic collections in Europe. The Glasgow Room houses extraordinary works by local artists. The museum has a visitor center, a café, and a restaurant. ✉ *Argyle St., Kelvingrove*

GLASGOW BEST BETS

Kelvingrove Art Gallery and Museum. A fantastic collection of European art, featuring such luminaries as Rembrandt and Monet, set in a stunning neo-Renaissance edifice.

Glasgow School of Art. Designed by Charles Rennie Mackintosh, this building is a tour-de-force of British art nouveau and one of the finest architectural statements in a city full of fine civic buildings.

Hunterian Art Gallery. This gallery features works by Tintoretto, Sir Joshua Reynolds, and Auguste Rodin— all donated by a private collector.

6

Park, West End ☎ *0141/276–9599* ⊕ *www.glasgowmuseums.com* 🖭 *Free* ⊙ *Mon.–Thurs., Sat. 10–5, Fri.–Sun. 11–5.*

❹ The Lighthouse. Charles Rennie Mackintosh designed these former offices of the *Glasgow Herald* newspaper in 1893. Mackintosh's building now serves as a fitting setting for Scotland's **Centre for Architecture, Design and the City,** which celebrates all facets of the architectural profession. The **Mackintosh Interpretation Centre** is a great starting point for discovering more about his other buildings in the city. ⊠ *11 Mitchell La., City Center* ☎ *0141/225–8414* ⊕ *www.thelighthouse.co.uk* 🖭 *£3* ⊙ *Mon. and Wed.– Sat. 10:30–5, Tues. 11–5, Sun. noon–5.*

❿ Queen's Cross Church. The headquarters of the Charles Rennie Mackintosh Society, this is the only church to have been designed by the Glasgow-born architect and designer. Although one of the leading lights in the turn-of-the-20th-century art nouveau movement, Mackintosh died in 1928 with his name scarcely known. Today he's widely accepted as a brilliant innovator. The church has beautiful stained-glass windows and a light-enhancing, carved-wood interior. The center's library and shop provide further insight into Glasgow's other Mackintosh-designed buildings, which include Scotland Street School, the Martyrs Public School, and the Glasgow School of Art. A cab ride can get you here, or take a bus toward Queen's Cross from stops along Hope Street. ⊠ *870 Garscube Rd., West End* ☎ *0141/946– 6600* ⊕ *www.crmsociety.com* 🖭 *£2* ⊙ *Weekdays 10–5, Sun. 2–5.*

❸ St. Mungo Museum of Religious Life and Art. An outstanding collection of artifacts, including Celtic crosses and statuettes of Hindu gods, reflects the many religious groups that have settled throughout the centuries in Glasgow and the west of Scotland. This rich history is depicted in the stunning Sharing of Faiths Banner, which celebrates the city's many different creeds. A Zen Garden creates a peaceful setting for rest and contemplation, and elsewhere, stained-glass windows feature a depiction of St. Mungo himself. ⊠ *2 Castle St., City Center* ☎ *0141/553–2557* ⊕ *www.glasgowmuseums.com* 🖭 *Free* ⊙ *Mon.–Thurs. and Sat. 10–5, Fri. and Sun. 11–5.*

SHOPPING

Glasgow is a shopper's dream, with its large department stores, designer outlets, quirky boutiques, and unique markets. Choice items include such traditional Scottish crafts as tartans, kilts, knitwear, and of course, whiskey. Join the throngs of style-conscious and unseasonably tan locals along Argyle, Buchanan, and Sauchiehall streets. Should the weather turn *dreich,* you can avoid getting *drookit* by sheltering in one of the many covered arcades in the city center. For more unusual items, head to the West End's Byres Road and Great Western Road.

Many of Glasgow's young and upwardly mobile make their home in **Merchant City,** on the edge of the city center. Shopping here is expensive, but the area is worth visiting if you're seeking the youthful Glasgow style. If you're an antiques connoisseur and art lover, a walk along **West Regent Street,** particularly its **Victorian Village,** is highly recommended, as there are various galleries and shops, some specializing in Scottish antiques and paintings.

The **Glasgow School of Art** (⊠*167 Renfrew St., City Center* ☎*0141/353–4526*) sells books, cards, jewelry, and ceramics. Students often display their work in June.

Hector Russell Kiltmakers (⊠*110 Buchanan St., City Center* ☎*0141/221–0217*) specializes in Highland outfits, wool and cashmere clothing, and women's fashions.

At the shop for the **National Trust for Scotland** (⊠*Hutchesons' Hall, 158 Ingram St., Merchant City* ☎*0141/552–8391*) many of the items for sale, such as china, giftware, textiles, toiletries, and housewares, are designed exclusively for trust properties and are often handmade. Wander around **Stockwell Bazaar** (⊠*67–77 Glassford St., Merchant City* ☎*0141/552–5781*) to view a huge selection of fine china and earthenware, glass, and ornaments. Items can be packed and sent overseas.

By far the best shopping complex is the art nouveau **Princes Square** (⊠*48 Buchanan St., City Center* ☎*0141/204–1685*), with high-quality shops alongside pleasant cafés. Look particularly for the Scottish Craft Centre, which carries an outstanding collection of work created by some of the nation's best craftspeople.

SPORTS & ACTIVITIES

The **Royal Troon** (⊠*Craigend Rd.* ☎*01292/311555* ⊕*www.royaltroon. co.uk* ⌕*Old Course: 18 holes, 7,150 yds, SSS 74. Portland Course: 18 holes, 6,289 yds, SSS 70*) is a golf club founded in 1878 and has two 18-hole courses: the Old, or Championship, Course and the Portland Course. Access for nonmembers is limited between May and mid-October to Monday, Tuesday, and Thursday only; day tickets cost £200 and include two rounds, morning coffee, and a buffet lunch. The course is 45 km (28 mi) south of Glasgow.

WHERE TO EAT

$-$$$ ✕**Café Gandolfi.** Once the offices of a cheese market, this trendy café is now
★   popular with the style-conscious crowd. Wooden tables and chairs crafted by Scottish artist Tim Stead are so fluidly shaped it's hard to believe they're inanimate. The menu lists interesting soups, salads, and local specialties, all made with the finest regional produce. Don't miss the smoked venison or the finnan haddie (smoked haddock). ⊠*64 Albion St., Merchant City* ☎*0141/552–6813* ⊟*MC, V.*

$-$$ ✕**Willow Tearoom.** There are two branches of this restaurant, but the Sauchiehall Street location is the real deal. Conceived by the great Charles Rennie Mackintosh, the Room De Luxe (the original tearoom) is kitted out with his trademark furnishings, including high-back chairs with elegant lines and subtle curves. The St. Andrew's Platter is an exquisite selection of trout, salmon, and prawns. Scottish and continental breakfasts are available throughout the day, and the scrambled eggs with salmon is traditional Scots food at its finest. The in-house baker guarantees fresh scones, cakes, and pastries. ⊠*217 Sauchiehall St., City Center* ☎*0141/332–0521* ⊟*MC, V* ⊗*No dinner.*

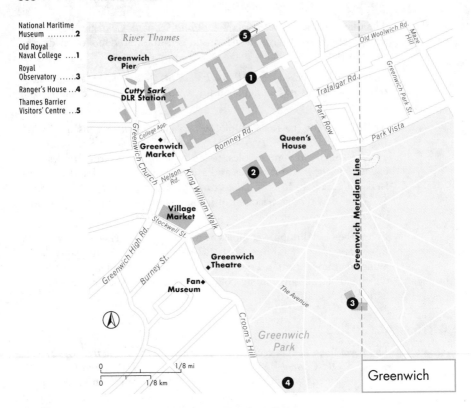

GREENWICH, UNITED KINGDOM

Visit Greenwich and you'll discover what makes Londoners tick. Situated
on the Greenwich Meridian Line at 0° longitude, this smart Thames-side
town literally marks the beginning of time. For an island nation whose
reputation was built on sea-faring adventure, Britain's centuries-old maritime tradition lays anchor here. Fans of elegant architecture will be in
heaven-on-sea, while landlubbers can wander acres of rolling parkland
and immaculately kept gardens. And while the world-famous *Cutty Sark*
may have long since unloaded its last tea chest, trading traditions live on
in Greenwich's maze of market stalls that sell a Davy Jones locker's worth
of bric-a-brac, antiques, and retro gear. Set apart from the rest of London,
Greenwich is worth a day to itself, to make the most of walks in the rolling parklands and to immerse yourself in its richness of maritime art and
entertainment.

ESSENTIALS

CURRENCY   The British pound sterling (£1 is $US2.07 at this writing). U.S. currency
is generally not accepted in Europe. ATMs are common and credit cards
are widely accepted.

HOURS   Museums are open from 9 until 5, while shops usually open from 9 until
5:30 or 6. Some shops are open on Sunday.

TELEPHONES   Tri-band GSM phones work in the U.K. You can buy prepaid phone cards
at telecom shops, news vendors, and tobacconists in all towns and cities.

Phone cards can be used for local or international calls. Vodafone and Orange are the leading telecom companies.

COMING ASHORE

Greenwich is the closest dock to Central London for vessels up to a maximum of 240 m (787 feet), but because most cruise ships are larger, you're more likely to dock in Harwich than Greenwich (*See "Harwich," below, for coverage of Central London.*) The dock at Greenwich Reach is a mooring point and has no passenger terminal. The attractions of Greenwich itself are all within walking distance of the mooring, but for central London attractions you'll need to take public transport.

A network of buses connects all the attractions of London, but journey times can be slow. A quicker option is to use a combination of the Underground and Docklands Light Railway (DLR) system. The Underground's Jubilee Line runs from north Greenwich's Millennium Dome to Canary Wharf in London. The zippy "driverless" Docklands Light Railway (DLR) runs from Cutty Sark station to Canary Wharf or Bank. Fares from Greenwich DLR to Kings Cross in central London are £4 one way. Services run every 10 minutes or so throughout the day. You can also take the DLR to Island Gardens and retrace the steps dockworkers used to take back and forth on the old Victorian Foot Tunnel under the river.

A river boat service is probably the most scenic way to get into central London. The fare from Greenwich to Tower in central London costs £6 one-way. Services run from 11:15 AM until 6:10 PM (last service from Tower back to Greenwich).

A rental car is both expensive and unadvisable if you are just touring Greenwich or central London. Rental costs approx £30 per day for an economy manual vehicle, and gasoline is very expensive. Taxis fares are regulated and determined by time of day, distance traveled, and taxi speed. Typical fares for a 6-mi journey are between £14 and £20 from 6 AM until 8 PM. A 1-mi journey (for transfers between attractions in central London) costs between £4.20 and £6.20 from 6 AM until 8 PM.

GREENWICH BEST BETS

Greenwich Meridian Line. Stand astride the line that marks the start of the international date.

National Maritime Museum. Relive the *Titanic's* last moments with rescued artifacts and underwater footage of the wreck.

Ranger's House. Marvel at the range of treasures in this gem of 18th-century Georgian architecture, including more than 650 works of art.

EXPLORING GREENWICH

Numbers in the margin correspond to points of interest on the Greenwich map.

2 **National Maritime Museum.** Following a millennial facelift, one of Greenwich's star attractions has been completely updated to make it one of London's most entertaining museums. Its glass-covered courtyard of grand stone, dominated by a huge revolving propeller from a powerful frigate, is reminiscent of the British Museum. The collection spans everything from seascape paintings to scientific instruments, interspersed with exhibitions on heroes of the waves. A permanent Horatio Nelson gallery contains the uniform he wore, complete with bloodstain, when he met his end at Trafalgar in 1805. Allow at least two hours in this absorbing, adventurous place; if you're in need of refreshment, the museum has a good café with views over Greenwich Park. The **Queen's House** is home to the largest collection of maritime art in the world, including works by William Hogarth, Canaletto, and Joshua Reynolds. Inside, the Tulip Stair, named for the fleur-de-lis–style pattern on the balustrade, is especially fine, spiraling up without a central support to the Great Hall. The Great Hall itself is a perfect cube, exactly 40 feet in all three dimensions, decorated with paintings of the Muses, the Virtues, and the Liberal Arts. ⊠*Romney Rd., Greenwich, SE10* ☎*020/8858–4422* ⊕*www.nmm.ac.uk* ✉*Free* ⊙*Apr.–Sept., daily 10–6; Oct.–Mar., daily 10–5; last admission 4:30* Ⓜ*DLR: Greenwich.*

❶ **Old Royal Naval College.** Begun by Christopher Wren in 1694 as a rest home,
★ or hospital for ancient mariners, this became instead a school for young ones in 1873. Today the University of Greenwich and Trinity College of Music have classes here. You'll notice how the structures part to reveal the Queen's House across the central lawns. Behind the college are two buildings you can visit. The **Painted Hall,** the college's dining hall, derives its name from the baroque murals of William and Mary (reigned 1689–95; William alone 1695–1702) and assorted allegorical figures. James Thornhill's frescoes, depicting scenes of naval grandeur with a suitably pro-British note of propaganda, were painstakingly done over installments in 1708–12 and 1718–26, and good enough to earn him a knighthood. The hall is still used for dinners, parties, schools, and weddings today. In the opposite building stands the **College Chapel,** which was rebuilt after a fire in 1779 and is altogether lighter, in a more restrained, neo-Grecian style.
■**TIP→** Trinity College of Music holds free classical music concerts in the chapel every Tuesday lunchtime. ⊠*Old Royal Naval College, King William Walk, Greenwich* ☎*020/8269–4747* ⊕*www.oldroyalnavalcollege.org* ✉*Free, guided tours £4* ⊙*Painted Hall and Chapel Mon.–Sat. 10–5, Sun. 12:30– 5, last admission 4:15; grounds 8–6* Ⓜ*DLR: Greenwich.*

❹ **Ranger's House.** This handsome, early-18th-century villa, which was the Greenwich Park Ranger's official residence during the 19th century, is hung with Stuart and Jacobean portraits. But the most interesting diversion is the Wernher Collection, more than 650 works of art with a north European flavor, amassed by diamond millionaire Julius Wernher at the turn of the 20th century. After making his money in diamond mining, he chose to buy eclectic objects, sometimes beautiful, often downright quirky, like the silver coconut cup. Sèvres porcelain and Limoges enamels, the largest jewelry collection in the country, and some particularly bizarre reliquaries form part of this fascinating collection. Wernher's American wife, Birdie, was a strong influence and personality during the belle epoque, which is easy to imagine from her striking portrait by Sargent. The house also makes a superb setting for concerts, which are regularly scheduled here. ⊠*Chesterfield Walk, Blackheath, Greenwich, SE10* ☎*020/8853– 0035* ⊕*www.english-heritage.org.uk* ✉*£5.50* ⊙*Apr.–Sept., Sun.–Wed. 10–5; Oct.–Mar., by appointment only. Closed Jan. and Feb.* Ⓜ*DLR: Greenwich; no direct bus access, only to Vanbrugh Hill (from east) and Blackheath Hill (from west).*

❸ Royal Observatory. Founded in 1675 by Charles II, this imposing institution was designed the same year by Christopher Wren for John Flamsteed, the first Royal Astronomer. The red ball you see on its roof has been there since 1833, and drops every day at 1 PM, although it started to malfunction in 2006. This Greenwich Timeball and the Gate Clock inside the observatory are the most visible manifestations of Greenwich Mean Time—since 1884, the ultimate standard for time around the world. Greenwich is on the **prime meridian** at 0° longitude. A brass line laid among the cobblestones here marks the meridian, one side being the eastern hemisphere, one the western.

In 1948 the Old Royal Observatory lost its official status: London's glow had grown too intense, and the astronomers moved to Sussex, while the Astronomer Royal decamped to Cambridge, leaving various telescopes, chronometers, and clocks for you to view. An excellent exhibition on the solution to the problem of measuring longitude includes John Harrison's famous clocks, H1–H4, now in working order. The museum recently unveiled "Time and Space," a major exhibit that added a planetarium and new galleries to the observatory. ⊠*Greenwich Park, Greenwich, SE10* ☎*020/8858–4422* ⊕*www.rog.nmm.ac.uk* ⊠*Free* ⊗*Apr.–Sept., daily 10–6; Oct.–Mar., daily 10–5; last admission 30 min before closure* Ⓜ*DLR: Greenwich.*

❺ Thames Barrier Visitors' Centre. Learn what comes between London and its famous river—a futuristic-looking metal barrier that has been described as the eighth wonder of the world. Multimedia presentations, a film on the Thames' history, working models, and views of the barrier itself put the importance of the relationship between London and its river in perspective. ⊠*Unity Way, Eastmoor St., Woolwich, SE18* ☎*020/8305–4188* ⊕*www.thamesbarrierpark.org.uk* ⊠*£1* ⊗*Apr.–Sept., daily 10:30–4:30; Oct.–Mar., daily 11–3:30* Ⓜ*National Rail: Charlton (from London Bridge), North Greenwich (Jubilee Line), then Bus 161 or 472.*

SHOPPING

Greenwich is a collector's paradise, offering everything from English china (manufacturers such as Royal Doulton) and glass to silver and art in the small emporia in the city streets. Don't forget mainstream souvenirs like T-shirts and mugs featuring London buses or the Houses of Parliament (Palace of Westminster). Royal memorabilia is also popular and widespread.

You'll find the Victorian-era **Greenwich Market** (⊠*College Approach, Greenwich, SE10* ☎*020/7515–7153* ⊕*www.greenwich-market.co.uk* Ⓜ*DLR: Cutty Sark*) on College Approach. Established as a fruit-and-vegetable market in 1700, and granted a royal charter in 1849, the glass-roof enclosure now offers arts and crafts Friday through Sunday, and antiques and collectibles on Thursday and Friday. Shopping for crafts is a pleasure, since in most cases you're buying directly from the artist.

If you're around Greenwich Market during the weekend, the nearby **Village Market** on Stockwell Street has bric-a-brac and books, and it's well known among the cognoscenti as a good source for vintage clothing.

On the opposite block to the Village Market, the weekend **Antiques Market** on Greenwich High Road, has more vintage shopping, and browsing among the "small collectibles" makes for a good half-hour diversion.

WHERE TO EAT

¢–$ **Trafalgar Tavern.** For the best pub in Greenwich, head to this local favorite, with excellent views of the Thames. It's a grand place to have a pint and some upscale grub. In warm weather, the terrace has outdoor seating overlooking the Millenium Dome. ⊠*Park Row, SE10* ☎*020/8858–2909* ⊕*www.trafalgartavern.co.uk.*

¢ **The Honest Sausage.** Up by the Royal Observatory, beside the Wolfe monument, this spot serves up delicious homemade organic sausages and huge jacket potatoes drenched in onion gravy. The views are great, too. ⊠*Greenwich Park, Greenwich, SE10* ☎*020/858–9695* ▤*No credit cards.*

HARWICH, UNITED KINGDOM (FOR LONDON)

London is an ancient city whose history greets you at every turn. If the city contained only its famous landmarks—the Tower of London or Big Ben—it would still rank as one of the world's top cities. But London is so much more. The foundations of London's character and tradition endure. The British bobby is alive and well. The tall, red, double-decker buses (in an updated model) still lumber from stop to stop. Then there's that greatest living link with the past—the Royal Family with all its attendant pageantry. To ice the cake, swinging-again London is today one of the coolest cities on the planet. The city's art, style, and fashion make headlines around the world, and London's chefs have become superstars. Plus, London's hosting of the 2012 Olympics means the city will be a hot spot for years to come. Harwich is now commonly used as the point of embarkation for many ships that use "London" as a base.

ESSENTIALS

CURRENCY   The British pound sterling (£1 is $US2.07 at this writing). U.S. currency is generally not accepted in Europe. ATMs are common and credit cards are widely accepted.

HOURS   Museums are open from 9 until 5, while shops usually open from 9 until 5:30 or 6. Some shops are open on Sunday.

INTERNET   **easyInternetcafé** (⊠*358 Oxford St., London* ☎*020/7241–9000*) is open 8 AM–midnight

TELEPHONES   Tri-band GSM phones work in the UK. You can buy prepaid phone cards at telecom shops, news vendors, and tobacconists in all towns and cities. Phone cards can be used for local or international calls. Vodafone and Orange are the leading telecom companies.

COMING ASHORE

Vessels dock in the commercial port at Harwich, which is small but busy, with commercial and ferry traffic. Port amenities include a mainline train station for transfers into London, a café, bar, ATMs, and an exchange bureau.

When larger cruise ships dock, the port schedules extra trains for the transfer into London. The journey time is 80 minutes. Normal rail services involve one change and take one hour 45 minutes. Taxi transfer to London is prohibitively expensive at around £125 or more.

EXPLORING LONDON

Numbers in the margin correspond to points of interest on the London map.

❸ British Airways London Eye. If you want a pigeon's-eye view of London, this is the place. The highest observation wheel in the world, at 500 feet, towers over the South Bank from the Jubilee Gardens. On a clear day you can take in a range of up to 25 mi, viewing London's most famous landmarks. ■TIP→ Buy your ticket online to avoid the long lines. ⌖*Jubilee Gardens, South Bank, SE1* ☎*0870/500–0600* ⊕*www.ba-londoneye.com* 🎫*£12.50* ⊙*June–Sept., daily 9:30 AM–10 PM; Oct.–May, daily 9:30–8* Ⓜ *Waterloo.*

❽ British Museum. This celebrated treasure house is filled with plunder of incalculable value and beauty from around the globe. If you want to navigate the highlights of the almost 100 galleries, join the free **Eyeopener** 50-minute tour by museum guides (details at the information desk).

Fodor'sChoice
★

Here follows a highly edited resume of the British Museum's greatest hits. The **Rosetta Stone,** carved in 196 BC. This inscription provided the French Egyptologist Jean-François Champollion with the key to deciphering hieroglyphics. The **Parthenon Marbles** include the spectacular remains of the Parthenon frieze carved around 440 BC. Close by is one of the Seven Wonders of the Ancient World—in fragment form: the **Mausoleum of Halikarnassos.** There are also galleries of **Egyptian mummies,** the splendid 8th-century Anglo-Saxon **Sutton Hoo Treasure,** and the remains of **Lindow Man,** retrieved from a Cheshire peat marsh, having been ritually slain in the 1st century, probably as a human sacrifice. The museum's **Great Court** is now roofed over and has a lovely, albeit expensive, ourdoor café. ⌖*Great Russell St., Bloomsbury, WC1* ☎*020/7636–1555* ⊕*www.thebritishmuseum.ac.uk* 🎫*Free, suggested donation £2* ⊙*Museum Sat.–Wed. 10–5:30, Thurs. and Fri. 10–8:30. Great Court Sun.–Wed. 9–6, Thurs.–Sat. 9 AM–11 PM* Ⓜ*Holborn, Russell Sq., Tottenham Court Rd.*

❻ Buckingham Palace. Buckingham Palace tops many must-see lists, although the building itself is no masterpiece. The palace contains some 600 rooms, including the Ballroom and the Throne Room. The state rooms are where much of the business of royalty is played out and these are open to the public while the Royal Family is away during the summer.

Fodor'sChoice
★

The **Changing of the Guard** culminates in front of the palace. ■TIP→ **Get there by 10:30 AM to grab a spot in the best viewing section at the gate facing the palace.** ⌖*Buckingham Palace Rd., St. James's, SW1* ☎*020/7766–7300* ⊕*www.royal.gov.uk* 🎫*£14, includes audio tour, credit-card reservations subject to booking charge; prebooking recommended* ⊙*Late July–late Sept., daily 9:45–6, last admission 3:45; confirm dates, which are subject to Queen's mandate. Changing of the Guard Apr.–July, daily 11:30 AM;*

6

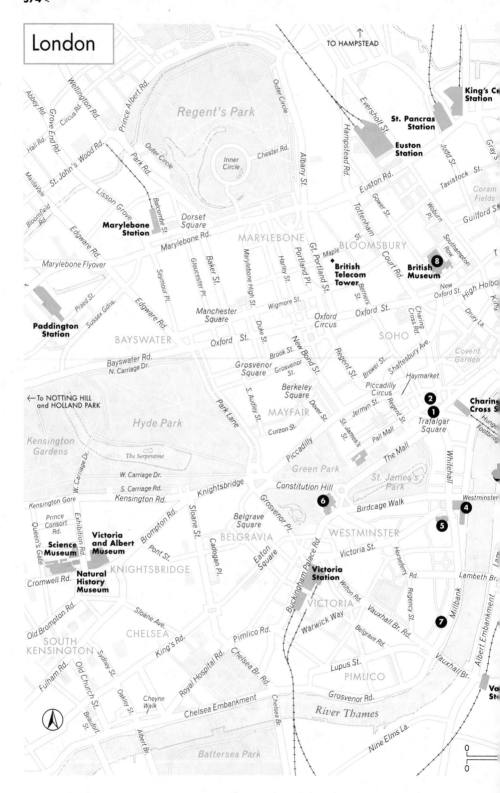

London

TO HAMPSTEAD

King's Cross Station

St. Pancras Station

Euston Station

Regent's Park

Inner Circle

Wellington Rd.

Prince Albert Rd.

Abbey Rd.

Grove End Rd.

Circus Rd.

Hall Rd.

Maida Vale

St. John's Wood Rd.

Park Rd.

Outer Circle

Chester Rd.

Albany St.

Eversholt St.

Hampstead Rd.

Euston Rd.

Gower St.

Judd St.

Tavistock St.

Gray's

Coram Fields

Guilford St.

Lisson Grove

Bloomfield Rd.

Edgware Rd.

Praed St.

Balcombe St.

Marylebone Station

Dorset Square

Marylebone Rd.

MARYLEBONE

BLOOMSBURY

Tottenham Court Rd.

Woburn Pl.

Southampton Row

Marylebone Flyover

Sussex Gdns.

Seymour Pl.

Gloucester Pl.

Baker St.

Marylebone High St.

Harley St.

Portland Pl.

Gt. Portland St.

Maple St.

Berners St.

British Telecom Tower

British Museum **8**

New Oxford St.

High Holbo

King

Paddington Station

Edgware Rd.

Manchester Square

Wigmore St.

Oxford Circus

Oxford St.

SOHO

Charing Cross Rd.

Drury La.

BAYSWATER

Oxford St.

Duke St.

Brook St.

New Bond St.

Regent St.

Brewer St.

Shaftesbury Ave.

Covent Garden

Bayswater Rd.

N. Carriage Dr.

Grosvenor Square

Grosvenor St.

Berkeley Square

Piccadilly Circus

Haymarket

To NOTTING HILL and HOLLAND PARK

Park Lane

S. Audley St.

MAYFAIR

Dover St.

Jermyn St.

Regent St.

Pall Mall

2

1

Trafalgar Square

Charing Cross S

Hunger Footbridge

Kensington Gardens

Hyde Park

The Serpentine

Curzon St.

Piccadilly

St. James's St.

The Mall

W. Carriage Dr.

S. Carriage Rd.

Green Park

St. James's Park

Whitehall

Kensington Rd.

Knightsbridge

Constitution Hill

Birdcage Walk

Westminster

Kensington Gore

Prince Consort Rd.

Queen's Gate

Exhibition Rd.

Science Museum

Victoria and Albert Museum

Brompton Rd.

Sloane St.

Belgrave Square

BELGRAVIA

Grosvenor Pl.

6

WESTMINSTER

4

5

Cromwell Rd.

KNIGHTSBRIDGE

Natural History Museum

Pont St.

Cadogan Pl.

Eaton Square

Buckingham Palace Rd.

Victoria St.

Horseferry Rd.

Millbank

Lambeth Br.

Old Brompton Rd.

Sydney St.

SOUTH KENSINGTON

Sloane Ave.

CHELSEA

King's Rd.

Pimlico Rd.

Victoria Station

Wilton Rd.

VICTORIA

Warwick Way

Belgrave Rd.

Vauxhall Br. Rd.

Regency St.

Va St.

Fulham Rd.

Old Church St.

Oakley St.

Cheyne Walk

Royal Hospital Rd.

Chelsea Br. Rd.

Lupus St.

PIMLICO

7

Vauxhall Br.

Albert Embankment

Beaufort St.

Albert Br.

Chelsea Embankment

Chelsea Br.

Grosvenor Rd.

River Thames

Nine Elms La.

Battersea Park

0

0

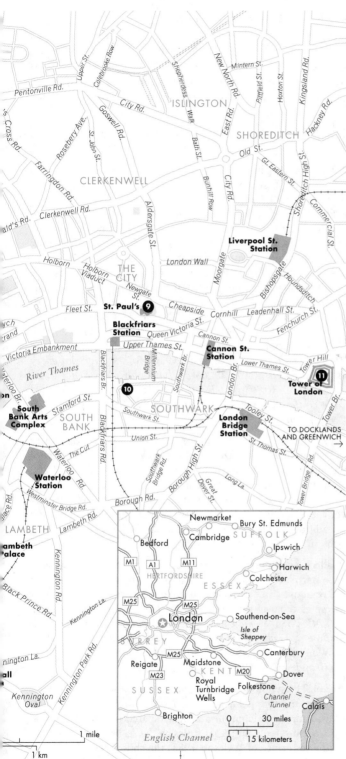

Aug.–Mar., alternating days only 11:30 AM ▭*AE, MC, V* Ⓜ*Victoria, St. James's Park.*

❹ **Houses of Parliament.** Seat of Great Britain's government, the Houses of Parliament are, arguably, the city's most famous and photogenic sights. Designed in glorious, mock-medieval style by two Victorian-era architects, Sir Charles Barry and Augustus Pugin in the 1830s, the Palace of Westminster, as the complex is still properly called, was first established by Edward the Confessor in the 11th century. It has served as the seat of English administrative power, on and off, ever since. Now virtually the symbol of London, the 1858 **Clock Tower** designed by Pugin contains the bell known as **Big Ben** that chimes the hour (and the quarters). Weighing a mighty 13 tons, the bell takes its name from Sir Benjamin Hall, the far-from-slim Westminster building works commissioner. ⊠*St. Stephen's Entrance, St. Margaret St., Westminster, SW1* ☎*020/7219–4272 Commons information, 020/7219–3107 Lords information* ⊕*www.parliament.uk* 🎟*Free, £7 summer tours* ⊘*Commons Mon. 2:30–10:30, Tues. and Wed. 11:30–7:30, Thurs. 11:30–6:30, Fri. 9:30–3 (although not every Fri.). Lords Mon.–Thurs. 2:30–10; Lord Chancellor's Residence Tues. and Thurs. 10:30–12:30. Closed Easter wk, late July–early Sept., 3 wks for party conference recess mid-Sept.–early Oct., and 3 wks at Christmas* Ⓜ*Westminster.*

FodorsChoice
★

❷ **National Gallery.** Jan Van Eyck's *Arnolfini Marriage*, Leonardo da Vinci's *Virgin and Child*, and Diego Velázquez's *Rokeby Venus* are only a few of the highlights in this priceless collection. There are approximately 2,200 paintings in the museum, many of them among the most treasured works of art anywhere. The National's collection includes paintings of the early Renaissance, the Flemish and Dutch masters, the Spanish school, and the English tradition (notably William Hogarth, Thomas Gainsborough, George Stubbs, and John Constable).

FodorsChoice
★

The **Micro Gallery,** a computer information center in the Sainsbury Wing, is a great place to start. You can access information on any work, choose your favorites, and print out a free personal tour map. There's another computer center in the espresso bar in the lower hall. ⊠*Trafalgar Sq., Westminster, WC2* ☎*020/7747–2885* ⊕*www.nationalgallery.org.uk* 🎟*Free, charge for special exhibitions* ⊘*Daily 10–6, Wed. until 9; 1-hr free guided tour starts at Sainsbury Wing daily at 11:30 and 2:30, and additionally Wed. 6 and 6:30, Sat. 12:30 and 3:30* Ⓜ*Charing Cross, Leicester Sq.*

❾ **St. Paul's Cathedral.** The symbolic heart of London, St. Paul's may take your breath away. The structure is Sir Christopher Wren's masterpiece, completed in 1710, and, much later, miraculously spared (mostly) by World War II bombs. Most famous in recent times as the scene of the marriage of Diana to Charles Prince of Wales in 1981, the church has played host

FodorsChoice
★

to the funerals of English heroes the Duke of Wellington and Admiral Lord Nelson, both of whom lie in the **Crypt.** Behind the high altar is the **American Memorial Chapel,** dedicated in 1958 to the 28,000 GIs stationed in the United Kingdom who lost their lives in World War II. ✉*St. Paul's Churchyard, The City, EC4* ☎*020/7236–4128* ⊕*www.stpauls. co.uk* ✉*£9, audio tour £3.50, guided tour £3* ⊘*Cathedral Mon.–Sat. 8:30–4, closed occasionally for special services. Ambulatory, Crypt, and galleries Mon.–Sat. 9–5:15. Shop and Crypt Café also open Sun. 10:30–* Ⓜ*St. Paul's.*

7 **Tate Britain.** This museum is a brilliant celebration of great British artists from the 16th century to the present day. The collection's crowning glory is the Turner Bequest, consisting of Romantic painter J.M.W. Turner's personal collection. ✉*Millbank, Westminster, SW1* ☎*020/7887–800, 020/7887–8008 recorded information* ⊕*www.tate.org.uk* ✉*Free, exhibitions £3–£10* ⊘*Daily 10–5:50* Ⓜ*Pimlico (signposted 5-min walk).*
★

10 **Tate Modern.** This former power station has undergone a dazzling renovation by Herzog de Meuron, to provide a grand space for a massive collection of international modern art. On permanent display are classic works from 1900 to the present day by Matisse, Picasso, Dalí, Francis Bacon, Warhol, and the most talked-about upstarts. ✉*Bankside, South Bank, SE1* ☎*020/7887–8888* ⊕*www.tate.org.uk* ✉*Free* ⊘*Sun.–Thurs. 10–6, Fri. and Sat. 10–10* Ⓜ*Blackfriars, Southwark.*

Fodor'sChoice
★

11 **Tower of London.** Nowhere else does London's history come to life so vividly as in this minicity of 20 towers filled with heraldry and treasure, the intimate details of lords and dukes and princes and sovereigns etched in the walls (literally, in some places), and quite a few pints of royal blood spilled on the stones. Yeoman Warders, better known as Beefeaters, have been guarding the Tower since Henry VII appointed them in 1485.
★

The Tower holds the royal gems because it's still one of the royal palaces, although no monarch since Henry VII has called it home. Its most well-known and titillating function has been as a jail and place of torture and execution.

The most famous exhibits are the **Crown Jewels,** in the Jewel House, Waterloo Block. Moving walkways on either side of the jewels hasten progress at the busiest times. Finest of all is the Royal Sceptre, containing the earth's largest cut diamond, the 530-carat Star of Africa.

✉*H.M. Tower of London, Tower Hill, The City, EC3N* ☎*0870/756–6060 recorded information and advance booking* ⊕*www.hrp.org.uk* ✉*£15* ⊘*Mar.–Oct., Tues.–Sat. 9–6, Sun. and Mon. 10–6; Nov.–Feb., Tues.–Sat. 9–5, Sun. and Mon. 10–5. Tower closes 1 hr after last admission time and all internal bldgs. close 30 min after last admission. Free guided tours leave daily from Middle Tower (subject to weather and availability) about every 30 min until 3:30 Mar.–Oct., 2:30 Nov.–Feb.* Ⓜ*Tower Hill.*

1 **Trafalgar Square.** This is the center of London, both geographically and symbolically. Great events, such as royal weddings, political protests, and sporting triumphs, always draw crowds to the city's most famous square. Trafalgar Square takes its name from the Battle of Trafalgar, Admiral Lord Horatio Nelson's great naval victory over the French, in 1805. Appropri-

6

ately, the dominant landmark here is **Nelson's Column,** a 145-foot-high granite perch from which a statue of Nelson keeps watch. ⊠*Trafalgar Sq., WestminsterSW1* Ⓜ*Charing Cross, Leicester Sq.*

❺ **Westminster Abbey.** A monument to the nation's rich—and often bloody and scandalous—history, this is one of London's most iconic sites. Nearly

Fodor's Choice
★

all of Britain's monarchs have been crowned here since the coronation of William the Conqueror on Christmas Day 1066—and most are buried here, too.

The current abbey is a largely 13th- and 14th-century rebuilding of the 11th-century church founded by Edward the Confessor, with one notable addition being the 18th-century twin towers over the west entrance, designed by Sir Christopher Wren and completed by Nicholas Hawksmoor. Highlights of the interior are the **Coronation Chair,** where monarchs are crowned, plus the tombs of Elizabeth I, buried with her half-sister, "Bloody" Mary I. The **Chapel of St. Edward** contains the tombs of more ancient Medieval monarchs while the **Henry VII Chapel** (also known as the Lady Chapel), offers magnificent sculptures and exquisite fan vaulting above. In 1400 Geoffrey Chaucer became the first poet to be buried in **Poets' Corner.** There are memorials to William Shakespeare and Charles Dickens (who is also buried here). ⊠*Broad Sanctuary, Westminster, SW1* ☎*020/7222–5152* ⊕*www.westminster-abbey.org* ✉*£10* ⊙*Abbey Mon., Tues., Thurs., and Fri. 9:30–3:45, Wed. 9:30–6, Sat. 9–1:45 (closes 1 hr after last admission). Museum daily 10:30–4. Cloisters daily 8–6. College Garden Tues.–Thurs. Apr.–Sept. 10–6, Oct.–Mar. 10–4. Separate admission for Chapter House daily 10–4. Abbey closed to visitors during weekday and Sun. services* Ⓜ*Westminster.*

SHOPPING

Napoléon was being scornful when he called Britain a nation of shopkeepers, but Londoners have had the last laugh. The finest emporiums are in London, still. You can shop like royalty at Her Majesty's glove-maker, discover an uncommon Toby jug in an antique shop, or find a leatherbound edition of *Wuthering Heights* on Charing Cross Road. If you have limited time, zoom in on one of the city's grand department stores, such as Harrods or Selfridges, where you can find enough booty for your entire gift list.

Chelsea centers on King's Road, once synonymous with ultra-high fashion; it still harbors some designer boutiques, plus antiques and home furnishings stores. **Covent Garden** has chain clothing stores and top designers, stalls selling crafts, and shops selling gifts of every type. Kensington's main drag, **Kensington High Street,** houses some small, classy shops, with a few larger stores at the eastern end. Try Kensington Church Street for expensive antiques, plus a little fashion.

Crafts Council Gallery Shop (⊠*44A Pentonville Rd., Islington, N1* ☎*020/7806– 2559* Ⓜ*Angel*) showcases a microcosm of British crafts.

Fodor's Choice
★

Fortnum & Mason (⊠*181 Piccadilly, St. James's, W1* ☎*020/7734–8040* Ⓜ*Piccadilly Circus*), the Queen's grocer, is paradoxically the most egalitarian of gift stores, with plenty of luxury foods, stamped with the gold By Appointment crest, for less than £5.

Fodor'sChoice **Harrods** (⊠*87 Brompton Rd., Knightsbridge, SW1* ☎*020/7730–1234*
★ Ⓜ*Knightsbridge*), one of the world's most famous department stores. The food halls are stunning—so are the crowds.

WHERE TO EAT

¢–$ ✕**The Pig's Ear.** This inventive gastro-pub is a Chelsea favorite. Elbow in
★ at the boisterous ground-floor pub area, or choose a restaurant vibe in the wood-panel salon upstairs. You'll find creative dishes on the short menu: shallot and cider soup, roast bone marrow, or skate wing and leeks are all typical, and executed . . . royally. ⊠*35 Old Church St., Chelsea, SW3* ☎*020/7352–2908* ≜*Reservations essential* ▤*AE, DC, MC, V* Ⓜ*Sloane Sq.*

¢–$ ✕**The Eagle.** *The* original 1990s gastro-pub serves good-value Portuguese–Spanish food. You'll find about nine dishes on the blackboard menu daily—a pasta, three vegetarian choices, and a risotto usually among them. ⊠*159 Farringdon Rd., The City, EC1* ☎*020/7837–1353* ≜*Reservations not accepted* ▤*MC, V* Ⓜ*Farringdon.*

INVERGORDON, SCOTLAND

The port of Invergordon is your gateway to the Great Glen, an area of Scotland that includes Loch Ness and the city of Inverness. Inverness, the capital of the Highlands, has the flavor of a Lowland town, its winds blowing in a sea-salt air from the Moray Firth. The Great Glen is also home to one of the world's most famous monster myths: in 1933, during a quiet news week, the editor of a local paper decided to run a story about a strange sighting of something splashing about in Loch Ness. But there's more to look for here besides Nessie, including inland lochs, craggy and steep-sided mountains, rugged promontories, deep inlets, brilliant purple and emerald moorland, and forests filled with astonishingly varied wildlife, including mountain hares, red deer, golden eagles, and ospreys.

ESSENTIALS

CURRENCY The British pound sterling (£1 is $US2.07 at this writing). U.S. currency is generally not accepted in Europe. ATMs are common and credit cards are widely accepted.

HOURS Museums are open from 9 until 5, while shops usually open from 9 until 5:30 or 6. Some shops are open on Sunday.

INTERNET **Invergordon Naval Museum and Heritage Centre** (⊠*High St., Invergordon* ☎*01349/8548911*) is a museum, archive, and library, and it also offers Internet access.

TELEPHONES Tri-band GSM phones work in the U.K. You can buy prepaid phone cards at telecom shops, news vendors, and tobacconists in all towns and cities. Phone cards can be used for local or international calls. Vodafone and Orange are the leading telecom companies.

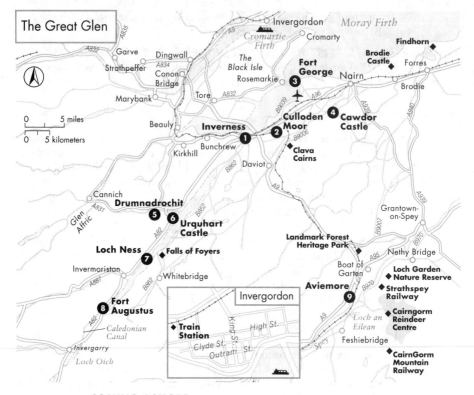

The Great Glen

COMING ASHORE

There is no dedicated cruise terminal at Invergordon. Ships dock at one of the town quays—usually Admiralty Quay, the closest to the town. At the pier, there is a tourist information kiosk manned only when ships are in dock.

Passengers can walk into the center of Invergordon for public transportation to surrounding sights. The Invergordon railway station is 1 km (½ mi) from the port and runs five round-trip trains south to Inverness per day, as well as trains north to Dornoch.

A car is a great asset for exploring the Great Glen, especially since the best of the area is away from the main roads. You can use the main A82 from Inverness to Fort William, or use the smaller B862/B852 roads (former military roads) to explore the much quieter east side of Loch Ness. **Ken's Garage** (☎014663/717606) will meet you at the docks with a car, but you must book in advance.

Taxis do not meet the ships as a matter of course. **Duncan Maclean** (☎01349/865955) can provide taxi services, but he must be prebooked.

EXPLORING INVERGORDON & THE GREAT GLEN

Numbers in the margin correspond to points of interest on the Great Glen map.

INVERNESS

1 Inverness seems designed for the tourist, with its banks, souvenirs, high-quality woolens, and well-equipped visitor center. Compared with other Scottish towns, however, Inverness has less to offer visitors who have a keen interest in Scottish history. Throughout its past, Inverness was burned and ravaged by the restive Highland clans competing for dominance in the region. Thus, a decorative wall panel here and a fragment of tower there are all that remain amid the modern shopping facilities and 19th-century downtown developments. The town does make a good base, however, for exploring the northern end of the Great Glen.

One of Inverness's few historic landmarks is the **castle** (the local Sheriff Court), nestled above the river. The current structure is Victorian, built after a former fort was blown up by the Jacobites in the 1745 campaign.

The excellent, although small, **Inverness Museum & Art Gallery** (⊠ *Castle Wynd* ☎ *01463/237114* ⊕ *www.invernessmuseum.com*) covers archaeology, art, local history, and the natural environment in its lively displays. The museum, which is free, is open Monday through Saturday, from 10 to 5.

CULLODEN MOOR

2 Culloden Moor was the scene of the last major battle fought on British soil—to this day considered one of the most infamous and tragic in all of warfare. Here, on a cold April day in 1746, the outnumbered Jacobite forces of Bonnie Prince Charlie were destroyed by the superior firepower of King George II's army. The victorious commander, the Duke of Cumberland (George II's son), earned the name of "Butcher" Cumberland for the bloody reprisals carried out by his men on Highland families—Jacobite or not—caught in the vicinity. In the battle itself, the duke's army—greatly outnumbering the Scots—killed more than 1,000 soldiers. The National Trust for Scotland has re-created a slightly eerie version of the battlefield as it looked in 1746. ⊠ *5 mi east of Inverness via B9006* ☎ *01463/790607* ⊕ *www.nts.org.uk* ☜ *£5* ☉ *Visitor center Feb., Nov., and Dec., daily 11–4; Mar., daily 10–4; Apr.–Oct., daily 9–6; last entry half hr before closing.*

FORT GEORGE

3 As a direct result of the battle at Culloden, the nervous government in London ordered the construction of a large fort on a promontory reaching into the Moray Firth: Fort George was started in 1748 and completed some 20 years later. It survives today as perhaps the best-preserved 18th-century military fortification in Europe. A visitor center and tableaux at

Fodor's Choice
★

the fort portray the 18th-century Scottish soldier's way of life, as does the **Regimental Museum of the Queen's Own Highlanders.** To get here take the B9092 north from A96 west of Nairn. ✉*Ardersier* ☎*01667/460232* ⊕*www.historic-scotland.gov.uk* 🎟*£6* ☉*Apr.–Sept., daily 9:30–6:30; Oct.–Mar., daily 9:30–4:30; last admission 45 min before closing.*

Fodor'sChoice
★

CAWDOR CASTLE

❹ Shakespeare's (1564–1616) Macbeth was Thane of Cawdor, but the sense of history that exists within the turreted walls of Cawdor Castle is more than fictional. Cawdor is a lived-in castle, not an abandoned, decaying structure. The earliest part of the castle is the 14th-century central tower; the rooms contain family portraits, tapestries, fine furniture, and paraphernalia reflecting 600 years of history. Outside the castle walls are sheltered gardens and woodland walks. Children will have a ball exploring the lush and mysterious Big Wood, with its wildflowers and varied wildlife. There are lots of creepy stories and fantastic tales amid the dank dungeons and drawbridges. The Cawdor estate has cottages to rent on the property. ✉*Off B9090, 5 mi southwest of Nairn, 24 km (15 mi) northeast of Inverness, Cawdor* ☎*01667/404401* ⊕*www.cawdorcastle.com* 🎟*Grounds £3.50; castle £7* ☉*May–mid-Oct., daily 10–5.*

LOCH NESS EXHIBITION CENTRE

❺ If you're in search of the infamous beast Nessie, head to Drumnadrochit: here you'll find the Loch Ness Monster Exhibition Centre, a visitor center that explores the facts and the fakes, the photographs, the unexplained sonar contacts, and the sincere testimony of eyewitnesses. You'll have to make up your own mind on Nessie. All that's really known is that Loch Ness's huge volume of water has a warming effect on the local weather, making the lake conducive to mirages in still, warm conditions. These are often the circumstances in which the "monster" appears. Whether or not the *bestia aquatilis* lurks in the depths—more than ever in doubt since 1994, when the man who took one of the most convincing photos of Nessie confessed on his deathbed that it was a fake—plenty of camera-toting, sonar-wielding, and submarine-traveling scientists and curiosity seekers haunt the lake. ✉*Off A82, 23 km (14 mi) southwest of Inverness* ☎*01456/450573 or 01456/450218* ⊕*www.loch-ness-scotland.com* 🎟*£5.95* ☉*Easter–May, daily 9:30–5; June and Sept., daily 9–6; July and Aug., daily 9–8; Oct., daily 9:30–5:30; Nov.–Easter, daily 10–3:30; last admission half hr before closing.*

URQUHART CASTLE

❻ Urquhart Castle, near Drumnadrochit, is a favorite Loch Ness monster–watching spot. This weary fortress stands on a promontory overlooking the loch, as it has since the Middle Ages. Because of its central and strategic position in the Great Glen line of communication, the castle has a complex history involving military offense and defense, as well as its own destruction and renovation. The castle was begun in the 13th century and was destroyed before the end of the 17th century to prevent its use by the Jacobites. The ruins of what was one of the largest castles in Scotland were then plundered for building material. A visitor center relates these events and gives an idea of what life was like here in medieval times. Today swarms of bus tours pass through after investigating the Loch Ness phenomenon. ✉*2 mi southeast of Drumnadrochit on A82* ☎*01456/450551*

⊕www.historic-scotland.gov.uk 📧*£6.50* ☉*Apr.–Sep., daily 9:30–5:30; Oct.–Mar., daily 9:30–4:30; last admission 45 min before closing.*

LOCH NESS

❼ **Loch Ness.** From the B862, just east of Fort Augustus, you'll get your first good long view of the formidable and famous Loch Ness, which has a greater volume of water than any other Scottish loch, a maximum depth of more than 800 feet, and its own monster—at least according to popular myth. Early travelers who passed this way included English lexicographer Dr. Samuel Johnson (1709–84) and his guide and biographer, James Boswell (1740–95), who were on their way to the Hebrides in 1783, and naturalist, Thomas Pennant (1726–98), who noted that the loch kept the locality frost-free in winter. None of these observant early travelers ever made mention of a monster. Clearly, they hadn't read the local guidebooks.

FORT AUGUSTUS

❽ Fort Augustus at the southern tip of Loch Ness is the best place to see the locks of the Caledonian Canal in action. The fort itself was captured by the Jacobite clans during the 1745 Rebellion. It was later rebuilt as a Benedictine abbey, but the monks no longer live here. The **Caledonian Canal Heritage Centre** (✉*Ardchattan House, Canalside, Fort Augustus* ☎*01320/366493*), in a converted lockkeeper's cottage, gives the history of the canal and its uses over the years.

AVIEMORE

❾ Once a quiet junction on the Highland Railway, Aviemore now has all the brashness and concrete boxiness of a year-round holiday resort. The Aviemore area is a versatile walking base, but you must be dressed properly and carry emergency safety gear for high-level excursions onto the near-arctic plateau.

★ For skiing and rugged hiking, follow the B970 to **Cairngorm National Park.** Past Loch Morlich at the high parking lots on the exposed shoulders of the Cairngorm Mountains are dozens of trails for hiking and cycling. The park is especially popular with birding enthusiasts, as it is the best place to see the Scottish Crossbill, the only bird unique to Britain. Cairngorm became Scotland's second national park in March 2003. ✉*Aviemore* ☎*01479/873535* ⊕*www.cairngorms.co.uk.*

The **CairnGorm Mountain Railway,** a funicular railway to the top of Cairn Gorm (the mountain that gives its name to the Cairngorms), operates year-round and affords extensive views of the broad valley of the Spey. At the top is a visitor center and restaurant. Be forewarned: it can get very cold above 3,000 feet, and weather conditions can change rapidly, even in the middle of summer. Prebooking is recommended. ✉*Off B9152* ☎*01479/861261* ⊕*www.cairngormmountain.com* 📧*£8.95* ☉*Daily 10–5.*

SHOPPING

All things "Highland" make the best souvenirs. Tartans and kilts, tweed clothing, and woolen and cashmere knits are made here in the glens. Modern breathable outdoor clothing is also in great abundance. The beauty of the landscape inspires artists and craftspeople, and you'll find their paintings, ceramics, and wooden carved items in markets and specialty shops. Foodies will love the natural smoked salmon.

★ **Hector Russell Kiltmakers** (⊠*Loch Ness Rd., Inverness* ☎*014563240189* ⊕*www.hectorrussell.com*) explains the history of the kilt, shows how they are made, and gives you the opportunity to buy from a huge selection or have a kilt made to measure. The firm offers overseas shipping. **James Pringle Ltd.** (⊠*Dores Rd., Inverness* ☎*01463/223311*) stocks a vast selection of cashmere, lamb's wool, and Shetland knitwear, tartans, and tweeds. There's a weaving exhibit, as well as an explanation of the history of tartan. The **Riverside Gallery** (⊠*11 Bank St., Inverness* ☎*01463/224781* ⊕*www.riverside-gallery.co.uk*) sells paintings, etchings, and prints of Highland landscapes, and contemporary work by Highland artists. Don't miss the atmospheric indoor **Victorian Market** (⊠*Academy St., Inverness*), built in 1870, which houses more than 40 privately owned specialty shops.

★ **Made in Scotland** (⊠*Station Rd., Beauly, IV4 7EH* ☎*01463/782821* ⊕*www.madeinscotland.co.uk*) is well worth a 23-km (14-mi) drive west from Inverness (on Route A862) to Beauly to see one of the biggest and best selections of Scottish-made gifts, textiles, and crafts. There's a restaurant here, too.

The **Scottish Crafts and Whisky Centre** (⊠*135–139 High St., Fort William* ☎*01397/704406*) has lots of crafts and souvenirs, as well as homemade chocolates and a vast range of malt whiskies, including miniatures and limited-edition bottlings.

WHERE TO EAT

$$$$ ✕**Abstract.** Chef Gordon Ramsey helped transform this restaurant into
★ one of the best in the region. Its French-influenced cuisine, which includes dishes such as roasted scallops on a pea puree and sea bream with an oyster-and-citrus tartar, has garnered numerous awards. The bar is arguably the most sophisticated-looking place in town to sample a malt or two—indeed there are nearly 200 to choose from and a decent cocktail list to boot. ⊠*Glenmoriston Town House Hotel, Ness Bank, InvernessIV2 4SF* ☎*01463/223777* ⊕*www.abstractrestaurant.com* ▭*AE, DC, MC, V.*

¢–$ ✕**Cas Bar.** This lounge bar at the Cairngorn Mountain Welcome Centre offers casual meals, including baked potatoes with fillings, and hot and cold sandwiches. The hot chocolate is a favorite with hikers. ⊠*Cairngorm Mountain Welcome Centre, Aviemore* ☎*01479/861261* ▭*MC, V.*

LEITH, SCOTLAND (FOR EDINBURGH)

One of the world's stateliest cities and proudest capitals, Edinburgh is built—like Rome—on seven hills, making it a striking backdrop for the ancient pageant of history. In a skyline of sheer drama, Edinburgh Castle watches over the capital city, frowning down on Princes Street as if disapproving of its modern razzmatazz. Nearly everywhere in Edinburgh (the "-burgh" is always pronounced *burra* in Scotland) there are spectacular buildings, whose Doric, Ionic, and Corinthian pillars add touches of neoclassical grandeur to the largely Presbyterian backdrop. The city is justly proud of its gardens, green lungs that bring a sense of release to frenetic modern life. Conspicuous from Princes Street is Arthur's Seat, a child-size mountain with steep slopes and little crags, like a miniature Highlands set down in the middle of the busy city. Appropriately, these theatrical elements match Edinburgh's character—after all, the city has been a stage that has seen its fair share of romance, violence, tragedy, and triumph.

ESSENTIALS

CURRENCY The British pound sterling (£1 is $US2.07 at this writing). U.S. currency is generally not accepted in Europe. ATMs are common and credit cards are widely accepted.

HOURS Museums are open from 9 until 5, while shops usually open from 9 until 5:30 or 6. Some shops are open on Sunday.

INTERNET **E Corner** (✉ *54 Blackfriars St., Edinburgh* ☎ *0131/5587858*) is an Internet café in the heart of the old town.

TELEPHONES Tri-band GSM phones work in the U.K. You can buy prepaid phone cards at telecom shops, news vendors, and tobacconists in all towns and cities. Phone cards can be used for local or international calls. Vodafone and Orange are the leading telecom companies.

COMING ASHORE

Currently ships larger than 55,000 tons must anchor offshore at Leith and passengers must be tendered ashore. Smaller ships can dock at the quay-side in Leith town. The whole waterfront area, named Ocean Terminal, has received a multimillion-pound redevelopment since the late 1990s, and significantly more is due to be invested in the years up to 2019; by 2009, larger ships should be able to dock, and a tram system to link the Leith waterfront to Central Edinburgh will open by 2010. There are few facilities at the passenger terminal itself, but a huge complex of shopping, eating, and entertainment venues sits right outside the door.

From Leith, buses 1, 11, 22, 34, 35 and 36 make the 15-minute trip to the Princes St stop in central Edinburgh; one-way fare is £1, and a day ticket £2.50. Taxis are plentiful and wait at the Ocean Terminal taxi line. Costs include an initial charge of £2.50, then £0.25 for every 225 meters (758 feet) until 2 km (1½ mi), after which charges climb to £0.25 per 260 meters (853 feet). Don't rent a car if you plan to spend your port day in Edinburgh, but a car will open up much of the surrounding countryside to exploration if you want to venture further. Rental rates for a compact manual vehicle are approximately £45 per day.

EXPLORING EDINBURGH

Numbers in the margin correspond to points of interest on the Edinburgh map.

⑤ Calton Hill. Robert Louis Stevenson's favorite view of his beloved city was from the top of this hill. Among the array of Gothic and neoclassical monuments here, the so-called **National Monument,** often referred to as "Edinburgh's (or Scotland's) Disgrace," commands the most attention. Intended to mimic Athens's Parthenon, this monument for the dead of the Napoleonic Wars was started in 1822 to the specifications of a design by William Playfair; in 1830, only 12 columns later, money ran out. The

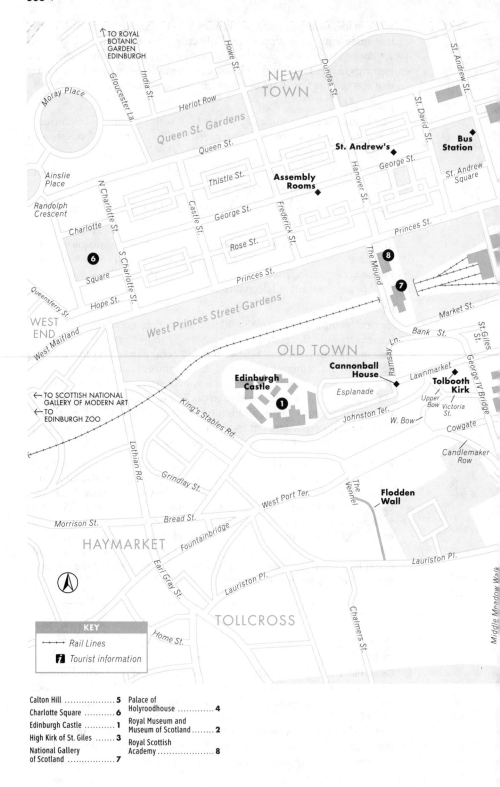

TO ROYAL
BOTANIC
GARDEN
EDINBURGH

NEW TOWN

Moray Place

Gloucester La.

India St.

Howe St.

Heriot Row

Dundas St.

St. Andrew St.

Queen St. Gardens

St. David St.

Bus Station ◆

Queen St.

St. Andrew's ◆

George St.

Ainslie Place

Thistle St.

Assembly Rooms ◆

Hanover St.

St. Andrew Square

Randolph Crescent

N Charlotte St.

George St.

Frederick St.

Charlotte

S Charlotte St.

Rose St.

Princes St.

The Mound

8

Square

6

Princes St.

7

Queensferry St.

Hope St.

West Princes Street Gardens

Market St.

WEST END

West Maitland

OLD TOWN

Bank St.

St. Giles St.

Ramsay Ln.

Cannonball House ◆

Lawnmarket

George IV Bridge

TO SCOTTISH NATIONAL
GALLERY OF MODERN ART

TO
EDINBURGH ZOO

Edinburgh Castle

1

Esplanade

Tolbooth Kirk ◆

Upper Bow

Victoria St.

King's Stables Rd.

Johnston Ter.

W. Bow

Cowgate

Candlemaker Row

Lothian Rd.

Grindlay St.

West Port Ter.

The Vennel

Flodden Wall

Morrison St.

Bread St.

HAYMARKET

Fountainbridge

Lauriston Pl.

Earl Gray St.

Lauriston Pl.

Chalmers St.

TOLLCROSS

Home St.

Middle Meadow Walk

KEY

┣━━━┫ Rail Lines

🛈 Tourist information

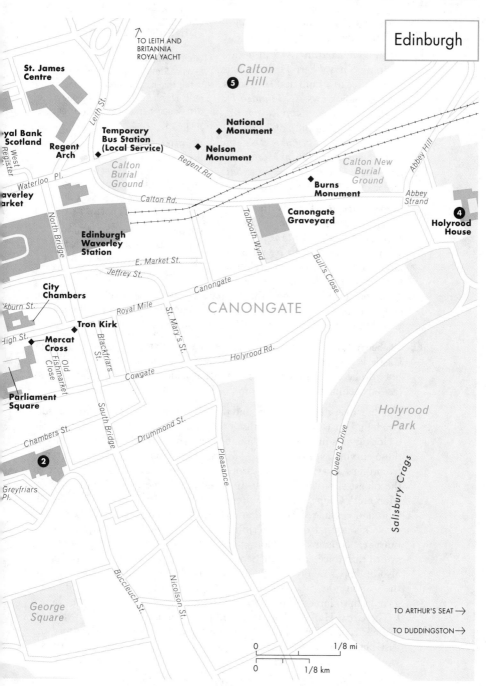

Edinburgh

TO LEITH AND
BRITANNIA
ROYAL YACHT

St. James Centre

Calton
5 *Hill*

Leith St.

National Monument ◆

yal Bank Scotland

Temporary Bus Station (Local Service) ◆

Nelson Monument ◆

Regent Arch ◆

Regent Rd.

Calton New Burial Ground

Abbey Hill

West Register

Calton Burial Ground

Burns Monument ◆

Abbey Strand

Waterloo Pl.

Calton Rd.

averley arket

Canongate Graveyard

4 **Holyrood House**

North Bridge

Edinburgh Waverley Station

E. Market St.

Tolbooth Wynd

Jeffrey St.

Canongate

Bull's Close

City Chambers

kburn St.

Royal Mile

CANONGATE

St. Mary's St.

High St.

Tron Kirk

Mercat Cross ◆

Blackfriars St.

Old Fishmarket Close

Holyrood Rd.

Holyrood Park

Cowgate

Parliament Square

South Bridge

Drummond St.

Queen's Drive

Salisbury Crags

Chambers St.

2

Pleasance

Greyfriars Pl.

Buccleuch St.

Nicolson St.

George Square

0   1/8 mi

0   1/8 km

TO ARTHUR'S SEAT →

TO DUDDINGSTON →

6

tallest monument on Calton Hill is the 100-foot-high **Nelson Monument,** completed in 1815 in honor of Briatin's naval hero Horatio Nelson; you can climb its 143 steps for sweeping views. ⊠*Bounded by Leith St. to the west and Regent Rd. to the south, Calton* ☎*0131/556–2716* ⊕*www.cac.org.uk* ✉*Nelson Monument £3* ☉*Nelson Monument Apr.–Sept., Mon. 1–6, Tues.–Sat. 10–6; Oct.–Mar., Mon.–Sat. 10–3.*

❻ **Charlotte Square.** This is the New Town's centerpiece—an 18th-century square with one of the proudest achievements of Robert Adam, Scotland's noted neoclassical architect. On the north side, Adam designed a palatial facade to unite three separate town houses of such sublime simplicity and perfect proportions that architects come from all over the world to study it. ⊠ *West end of George St., New Town.*

❶ **Edinburgh Castle.** The crowning glory of the Scottish capital, Edinburgh Castle is popular not only because it is the symbolic heart of Scotland but also because of the views from its battlements: on a clear day the vistas—stretching to the "kingdom" of Fife—are breathtaking.

Fodor'sChoice
★

Heading over the drawbridge and through the gatehouse, past the guards, you'll find the rough stone walls of the **Half-Moon Battery,** where the one-o'clock gun is fired every day in an impressively anachronistic ceremony; these curving ramparts give Edinburgh Castle its distinctive appearance from miles away. Climb up through a second gateway and you come to the oldest surviving building in the complex, the tiny 11th-century **St. Margaret's Chapel,** named in honor of Saxon queen Margaret (1046–93), who had persuaded her husband, King Malcolm III (circa 1031–93), to move his court from Dunfermline to Edinburgh. The **Crown Room,** a must-see, contains the "Honours of Scotland"—the crown, scepter, and sword that once graced the Scottish monarch. Upon the **Stone of Scone,** also in the Crown Room, Scottish monarchs once sat to be crowned. In the section now called **Queen Mary's Apartment,** Mary, Queen of Scots, gave birth to James VI of Scotland who was also to rule England as James I. The **Great Hall** displays arms and armor under an impressive vaulted, beamed ceiling. During the Napoleonic Wars in the early 19th century, the castle held French prisoners of war, whose carvings can still be seen on the vaults under the Great Hall.

⊠*Off Castle Esplanade and Castlehill, Old Town* ☎*0131/225–9846 Edinburgh Castle, 0131/226–7393 War Memorial* ⊕*www.historic-scotland.gov.uk* ✉*£9.80* ☉*Apr.–Oct., daily 9:30–6; Nov.–Mar., daily 9:30–5.*

❸ **High Kirk of St. Giles** *(St. Giles's Cathedral).* There has been a church here since AD 854, although most of the present structure dates from either

---

EDINBURGH BEST BETS

Edinburgh Castle. The twists and turns of Scottish history have unfolded in this true bastion atop a volcanic peak. Stay for the firing of the one o'clock gun, but remember to cover your ears!

The Palace of Holyroodhouse. Home to Scottish and English monarchs throughout the ages, Holyroodhouse has many stories to tell—including one of the most vile deeds in Edinburgh's history.

Calton Hill. The architectural panorama of Edinburgh plays out before your eyes from this height.

1120 or 1829, when the church was restored. The most elaborate feature is the **Chapel of the Order of the Thistle,** built in 1911 for the exclusive use of Scotland's only chivalric order, the Most Ancient and Noble Order of the Thistle. Inside the church stands a life-size statue of the Scot whose spirit still dominates the place—the great religious reformer and preacher John Knox, before whose zeal all of Scotland once trembled. ✉*High St., Old Town* ☎*0131/225–9442* ⊕*www.stgiles.net* ☞*£2 suggested donation* ⊗*May–Sept., weekdays 9–7, Sat. 9–5, Sun. 1–5; Oct.–Apr., Mon.– Sat. 9–5, Sun. 1–5.*

❼ National Gallery of Scotland. The National Gallery presents a wide selection of paintings from the Renaissance to the postimpressionist period within a grand neoclassical building designed by William Playfair. Most famous are the old-master paintings bequeathed by the Duke of Sutherland, including Titian's *Three Ages of Man.* All the great names are here; works by Velázquez, El Greco, Rembrandt, Goya, Poussin, Clouet, Turner, Degas, Monet, and Van Gogh, among others, complement a fine collection of Scottish art. ✉*The Mound, Old Town* ☎*0131/624–6200 general inquiries, 0131/332–2266 recorded information* ⊕*www.nationalgalleries.org* ☞*Free* ⊗*Fri.–Wed. 10–5, Thurs. 10–7.*

FodorsChoice ★

❹ Palace of Holyroodhouse. Once the haunt of Mary, Queen of Scots, and the setting for high drama—including at least one notorious murder—this is now Queen Elizabeth's official residence in Scotland. When the queen or royal family is not in residence, you can take a guided tour. Many monarchs, including Charles II, Queen Victoria, and George V, have left their mark on its rooms, but it is Mary, Queen of Scots, whose spirit looms largest. For some visitors the most memorable room here is the little chamber in which David Rizzio (1533–66), secretary to Mary, Queen of Scots, met an unhappy end in 1566. Mary's second husband, Lord Darnley (Henry Stewart, 1545–65), burst into the queen's rooms with his henchmen, dragged Rizzio into an antechamber, and stabbed him more than 50 times; a bronze plaque marks the spot. Darnley himself was murdered the next year to make way for the queen's marriage to her lover, Bothwell.

The **King James Tower** is the oldest surviving section, containing the rooms of Mary, Queen of Scots, on the second floor, and Lord Darnley's rooms below. At the south end of the palace front you'll find the **Royal Dining Room,** and along the south side are the **Throne Room** and other drawing rooms now used for social and ceremonial occasions.

At the back of the palace is the **King's Bedchamber.** The 150-foot-long **Great Picture Gallery,** on the north side, displays the portraits of 110 Scottish monarchs by Dutch artist Jacob De Witt. These were commissioned by Charles II—some of the royal figures here are fictional and the likenesses of others imaginary.

Queen's Gallery, in a former church and school at the entrance to the palace, holds rotating exhibits from the Royal Collection. ✉*Abbey Strand, Holyrood, Old Town* ☎*0131/556–1096* 🖷*0131/557–5256* ⊕*www.royal.gov.uk* ☞*£8.50* ⊗*Apr.–Oct., daily 9:30–5:15; Nov.–Mar., daily 9:30–3:45. Closed during royal visits.*

② Royal Museum and Museum of Scotland. In an imposing Victorian building, the

Fodor'sChoice Royal Museum houses an internationally renowned collection of art and

★ artifacts. Its treasures include the Lewis Chessmen, 11 intricately carved ivory chessmen found on one of the Western Isles in the 19th century. The museum's main hall, with its soaring roof and "birdcage" design, is architecturally interesting in its own right. Redevelopment, ongoing through 2011, is modernizing many displays. The striking, contemporary building next door houses the Museum of Scotland, with modern displays concentrating on Scotland's own heritage. This state-of-the-art, no-expense-spared museum is full of playful models, complex reconstructions, and paraphernalia ranging from ancient Pictish articles to 21st-century cultural artifacts. ⊠*Chambers St., Old Town* ☎*0131/225–7534* ⊕*www.nms.ac.uk* ☞*Free* ۞*Mon. and Wed.–Sat. 10–5, Tues. 10–8, Sun. noon–5.*

⑧ RoywScottish Academy. The William Playfair–designed Academy hosts temporary art exhibitions but is also worth visiting for a look at the imposing, neoclassic architecture. The underground Weston Link connects the museum to the National Gallery of Scotland. ⊠*The Mound, Old Town* ☎*0131/225–6671* ⊕*www.royalscottishacademy.org* ☞*Free* ۞*Mon.–Sat. 10–5, Sun. noon–5.*

SHOPPING

Despite its renown as a shopping street, **Princes Street** in the New Town disappoints some visitors with its dull, anonymous modern architecture, average chain stores, and fast-food outlets. It is, however, one of the best spots to shop for tartans, tweeds, and knitwear, especially if your time is limited. One block north of Princes Street, **Rose Street** has many smaller specialty shops; part of the street is a pedestrian zone, so it's a pleasant place to browse.

The streets crossing George Street—Hanover, Frederick, and Castle—are also worth exploring. **Dundas Street,** the northern extension of Hanover Street, beyond Queen Street Gardens, has several antiques shops. **Thistle Street,** originally George Street's "back lane," or service area, has several boutiques and more antiques shops. **Stafford and William streets** form a small, upscale shopping area in a Georgian setting.

As may be expected, many shops along the **Royal Mile** sell what may be politely or euphemistically described as tourist-ware—whiskies, tartans, and tweeds. Careful exploration, however, will reveal some worthwhile establishments. Shops here also cater to highly specialized interests and hobbies. Close to the castle end of the Royal Mile, just off George IV Bridge, is **Victoria Street,** with specialty shops grouped in a small area. Follow the tiny West Bow to **Grassmarket** for more specialty stores.

Edinburgh Crystal (⊠*Eastfield, Penicuik* ☎*01968/675128*), 10 mi south of the city center, is renowned the world over for its fine glass and crystal ware, but Jenners also stocks it.

At the **Edinburgh Old Town Weaving Company** (⊠*555 Castlehill, Old Town* ☎*0131/226–1555*), you can watch the cloth and tapestry weavers as they work, then buy the products. The company can also provide information on clan histories, and, if your name is a relatively common English or Scottish one, tell you which tartan you are entitled to wear.

Jenners. Edinburgh's equivalent of London's Harrods department store, Jenners is noteworthy not only for its high-quality wares and good restaurants but also because of the building's interesting architectural detail. ⊠*48 Princes St., New Town* ☎*0131/225–2442* ⊕*www.jenners.com* ⊙*Mon., Tues., Wed., Fri., and Sat. 9–6, Thurs. 9–8, Sun. 11–5.*

WHERE TO EAT

$$ ✕**David Bann.** In the heart of the Old Town, this ultrahip vegetarian and
★ vegan favorite attracts young locals with its light, airy, modern dining room and creative menu. The food is so flavorful that carnivores may forget they're eating vegetarian. ⊠*56–58 St. Mary's St., Old Town* ☎*0131/556–5888* ⊕*www.davidbann.com* ▭*AE, DC, MC, V.*

ROTTERDAM, NETHERLANDS

Rotterdam is the industrial center of Holland and the world's largest port. When Rotterdam's city center and harbor were completely destroyed in World War II, the authorities decided to start afresh rather than try to reconstruct its former maze of canals. The imposing, futuristic skyline along the banks of the Maas River has been developing since then, thanks in large part to the efforts of major figures such as Rem Koolhaas, Eric van Egeraat, and UN Studio. Elsewhere in the region, you can step back in time: wander through the ancient cobbled streets in Leiden and buy china in Delft that once colored the world with its unique blue. Many other colors are on view in Holland's fabled tulip fields. Every spring, green thumbs everywhere make a pilgrimage to Lisse to view the noted tulip gardens at Keukenhof and to drive the Bollenstreek Route, which takes them through miles of countryside glowing with gorgeous hues and blooms.

ESSENTIALS

CURRENCY The euro (€1 to US$1.46 at this writing). U.S. currency is generally not accepted in Europe, but ATMs are common and credit cards are widely accepted.

HOURS Shops open Tuesday, Wednesday, Friday, and Saturday from 9 or 10 until 6; they are open later on Thursday. Most stores are closed on Sunday and some on Monday. Museums open from 9 until 6 with one late opening night during the week.

INTERNET **Rotterdam Public Library** (⊠*110 Hoogstraat, Rotterdam 3011* ☎*010/2816100*) offers free Internet service, although the facilities here aren't the newest.

> ### ROTTERDAM BEST BETS
>
> **Modernist architecture.** Rotterdam eschewed rebuilding the city after the destruction of WWII and instead strode resolutely into modernism; the city now has some of the most cutting-edge architecture in the world.
>
> **The Kinderdijk Windmills.** This archetypal Dutch landscape isn't a theme park—the windmills were grouped to pump water into the polders. Today, the vista is picture perfect.
>
> **Old Delft.** This tangle of canals and medieval streets, with its array of ornate decoration and flower-bedecked windows, offers some of the prettiest views in Holland.

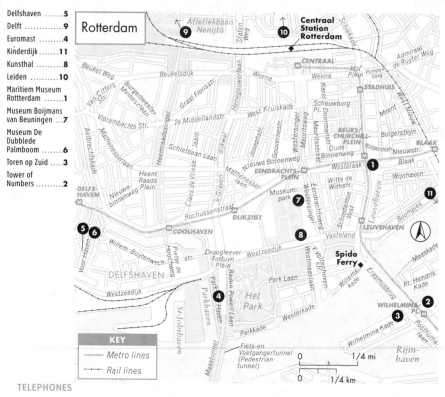

Most tri- and quad-band GSM mobile phones should work on the Netherlands, which operates a 3G mobile system with dual-band handsets. Public phones take phone cards (available at numerous shops) and credit cards and will connect international calls. Major telecom companies are Vodafone and Orange.

COMING ASHORE

Ships dock at the historic terminal building in the city dock, once the headquarters of the Holland America Line. The terminal offers handicraft displays, shopping facilities and an information desk. A shuttle service operates between the terminal and the town. Each bus has an English-speaking host who can answer any questions that you have. A water taxi service also operates from the port across the River Maas into the heart of the old town. A 15-minute round-trip costs approximately €28.

The terminal has a taxi service desk where you can arrange for trips at fixed prices. It is also possible to book journeys and trips ahead of time. All drivers speak English. Public transport is efficient and modern. A single journey costs €1.20, and a day card costs €6.40. Rotterdam is very bicycle friendly. Bikes can be rented at the Central train station at a cost of €6 per day.

The train journey from Rotterdam to Delft takes 15 minutes and there are several services per hour; ticket prices are €4.90 round-trip. The train journey from Rotterdam to Leiden takes 30 minutes with several services every hour; ticket prices are €11.90 round-trip. The journey to Amster-

dam (⇨*above*) takes one hour with several services every hour; round-trip
tickets are €22.90.

EXPLORING ROTTERDAM & VICINITY

*Numbers in the margin correspond to points of interest on the Rotterdam
map.*

ROTTERDAM

Cobbled streets, gabled houses, narrow canals overhung with lime trees,
and antiques shops give the historic center a tangible feeling of history, and
Leiden's university's academic buildings, the historic Waag (Weigh House)
and the Burcht fortress, the stately mansions lining the Rapenburg—the
most elegant canal in the town—and no fewer than 35 hofjes (groups
of houses surrounding little courtyards) make it a rewarding place for a
stroll. As you walk about, keep a watch for verses painted on lofty gables,
a project started some 10 years ago. The proverbs, sayings, and poems
now number more than 70, and are in a multitude of languages.

6

⑤ **Delfshaven.** The last remaining nook of old Rotterdam, an open-air museum
★ with rows of gabled houses lining the historic waterfront, Delfshaven is
now an area of trendy galleries, cafés, and restaurants. Walk along the
Voorhaven and marvel at the many historic buildings; most of the port
area has been reconstructed, with many of its 110 buildings now appearing just as they were when originally built.

For historic sights in Delfshaven's environs, check out the working mill of
Korenmolen de Distilleerketel (open Wednesday and Saturday only), the
fascinating **Museum de Dubbelde Palmboom** on Rotterdam city history,
and the **Oudekerk/Pilgrimvaders Kerk.** ⊠*Achterhaven and Voorhaven,
Delfshaven.*

④ **Euromast.** The Euromast provides a spectacular view of the city and harbor,
if you can handle the 600-foot-high vista. On a clear day, you can just
about see the coast from the top. And if you have the stomach for it, you
can rappel down the tower. ⊠*Parkhaven 20, Delfshaven* ☎*010/436–
4811* ⊕*www.euromast.com* ☞*€8, rappel €39.50* ☉*Apr.–Sept., daily
9:30 AM–11 PM; Oct.–Mar., daily 10 AM–11 PM.*

⑧ **Kunsthal.** The corrugated exterior of this "art house" sits at one end of
the visitor-friendly museum quarter and hosts major temporary exhibitions. Designed by architect-prophet Rem Koolhaas, some say the design
bridging the gap between the Museumpark and the dike is a clever spa-
tial creation; others consider it ugly. ⊠*Westzeedijk 341, Museumpark*
☎*010/440–0301* ⊕*www.kunsthal.nl* ☞*€8.50* ☉*Tues.–Sat. 10–5, Sun.
11–5.*

① **Maritiem Museum Rotterdam.** A sea-lover's delight, the Maritime Museum is
Rotterdam's noted nautical collection. The museum's prize exhibit is the
☺ warship *De Buffel,* moored in the harbor outside, dating back to 1868.
★ The ship has been perfectly restored and is fitted out sumptuously, as can
be seen in the mahogany-deck captain's cabin. ⊠*Leuvehaven 1, Witte
de With* ☎*010/413–2680* ⊕*www.maritiemmuseum.nl* ☞*€5* ☉*July*

and Aug., Mon.–Sat. 10–5, Sun. 11–5; Sept.–June, Tues.–Sat. 10–5, Sun. 11–5.

7 **Museum Boijmans van Beuningen.** Rotterdam's finest shrine to art, with treasures ranging from Pieter Bruegel the Elder's 16th-century *Tower of Babel* to Mondriaan's extraordinary *Composition in Yellow and Blue,* this museum ranks as one of the greatest painting collections in Europe. Created more than 150 years ago—when Otto Boijmans unloaded a motley collection of objects on the city, then greatly enhanced by the bequest of Daniel van Beuningen in 1955—it is housed in a stunning building ideally designed to hold the collections of painting, sculpture, ceramics, prints, and furnishings.

Fodor's Choice
★

Fifteenth- and 16th-century art from the northern and southern Netherlands and 17th-century Dutch works are particularly well represented, including painters such as Van Eyck, Rubens, and Rembrandt. Highlights include Bruegel's famous *Tower of Babel* (1563). Other notable artists include Peter Paul Rubens, Jan Van Eyck, Hieronymous Bosch, Claude Monet, René Magritte, Andy Warhol, and Salvador Dalí. ⊠ *Museumpark 18–20, Museumpark* ☎ *010/441–9475* ⊕ *www.boijmans.nl* ⊠ *€7* ⊗ *Tues.–Sat. 10–5, Sun. 11–5.*

6 **Museum de Dubbelde Palmboom.** Devoted to the history of Rotterdam and its role as an international nexus, this museum traces the city's history from prehistoric times to the current day. The special and very fascinating focus is on how exotic wares imported by the East India Company affected the city. The building itself is literally redolent of history: not only do its heavy beams and brick floors waft you back to yesteryear, but there even seems to be a faint smell of grains, recalling its many years spent as a warehouse. ⊠ *Voorhaven 12, Delfshaven* ☎ *010/476–1533* ⊕ *www. dedubbeldepalmboom.nl* ⊠ *€3* ⊗ *Tues.–Fri. 10–5, weekends 11–5.*

3 **Toren op Zuid.** An office complex by celebrated modern architect Renzo Piano, this structure houses the head offices of KPN Telecom. Its eye-catching billboard facade glitters with 1,000-odd green lamps flashing on and off, creating images provided by the city of Rotterdam, in addition to images provided by KPN and an art academy. The facade fronting the Erasmus Bridge leans forward by 6 degrees, which is the same as the angle of the bridge's pylon. It is also said that Piano could have been making a humorous reference to his homeland, as the Tower of Pisa leans at the same angle. ⊠ *Wilhelminakade 123, Kop van Zuid.*

2 **Tower of Numbers.** Near Piano's Toren op Zuid structure is this creation of Australian architect Peter Wilson. The tower is topped by five LED (light-emitting diodes) boxes, hung from a mast, with digital figures showing—among other things—the time and the world population. This "fluxus" is in contrast to the fixity of the **Garden of Lost Numbers,** found below the yellow bridge-watcher's house designed as a series of numbers set into the pavement. These numbers refer to the city's decommissioned harbors, all of which once were identified by numbers. As Rotterdam has such a heightened awareness of lost identity, these stainless-steel figures serve as a remembrance of things past. ⊠ *Wilhelminakade, Kop van Zuid.*

DELFT

9 *15 km (9 mi) northwest of Rotterdam.*

With time-burnished canals and streets, Delft possesses a peaceful calm that recalls the quieter pace of the Golden Age of the 17th century. Back then the town counted among its citizens the artist Johannes Vermeer, who decided one spring day to paint the city gates and landscape across the Kolk harbor from a house's window on the Schieweg (now the Hooi-kade). The result was the 1660 *View of Delft* (now the star of the Mau-ritshuis Museum in The Hague), famously called by Marcel Proust "the most beautiful painting in the world." Spending a few hours in certain parts of Delft, in fact, puts you in the company of Vermeer. Imagine a tiny Amsterdam, canals reduced to dollhouse proportions, narrower bridges, merchants' houses less grand, and you have the essence of Old Delft. But even though the city has one foot firmly planted in the past, another is planted in the present: Delft teems with hip cafés, jazz festivals, and revelers spilling out of bars.

KINDERDIJK

11 *32 km (20 mi) southeast of Rotterdam.*

★ The Kinderdijk Windmills are, arguably, the most famous tourist sight in Holland. The 19 mills line Het Nieuwe Waterschap in pairs, each facing another on opposite banks. In 1740, 19 mills were built in the meadows of Kinderdijk, to drain the excess water from the Alblasserwaard polders, which lie below sea level. Electrical pumping stations have now taken over water management, but the majority of mills operate at certain times for the delight of tourists. The mills are open in rotation, so there is always one interior to visit during opening hours. Looking around the inside of a mill provides a fascinating insight into how the millers and their families lived. Tours can be taken of the mechanical workings if you want to get a closer look. ⊠*Molenkade, Kinderdijk* ☎*078/691–5179* ✉*Interior of mill €1.50* ⊗*Interior Apr.–Sept., daily 9:30–5:30.*

LEIDEN

10 *37 km (23 mi) north of Rotterdam.*

The town of Leiden owes its first importance to its watery geography—it stands at the junction of two branches of the Rhine—the "Old" and the "New." But as birthplace of Rembrandt and site of the nation's oldest and most prestigious university, Leiden has long continued to play an important part in Dutch history. A place where windmills still rise over the cityscape, Leiden offers the charm of Amsterdam with little of the sleaze.

★ **Rijksmuseum van Oudheden** *(National Museum of Antiquities)*, Leiden's most notable museum, houses the largest archaeological collection in Holland. Collections include pieces from ancient Egypt, the classical world, the Near East, and the Netherlands, from prehistory to the Middle Ages. Among the 6,000 objects on display, exhibits to look out for include the chillingly ghoulish collection of 13 ancient Egyptian human mummies. ⊠*Rapenburg 28* ☎*071/516–3163* ⊕*www.rmo.nl* ✉*€7.50* ⊗*Tues.–Fri. 10–5, weekends noon–5.*

SHOPPING

Rotterdam is the number one shopping city in the south of Holland and it offers some excellent interior design galleries. Its famous **Lijnbaan** and **Beurstraverse** shopping centers, as well as the surrounding areas, offer a dazzling variety of shops. The archways and fountains of the Beurstraverse—at the bottom of the Coolsingel, near the Stadhuis—make this newer, pedestrianized area more pleasing to walk around. **Van Oldenbarneveldtstraat** and **Nieuwe Binnenweg** are the places to be if you want something different; there is a huge variety of alternative fashion to be found here. Exclusive shops and boutiques can be found in the Entrepotgebied, Delfshaven, Witte de Withstraat, Nieuwe and Oude Binnenweg, and Van Oldenbarneveldtstraat. **West Kruiskade** and its vicinity offers a wide assortment of multicultural products in the many Chinese, Suriname, Mediterranean, and Arabic shops. You should also walk through the **Entrepot Harbor design district,** alongside the city marina at Kop van Zuid, where there are several interior-design stores.

De Bijenkorf (⊠ *Coolsingel 105, Centrum* ☎0900/0919) is a favorite department store, designed by Marcel Breuer (the great Bauhaus architect) with an exterior that looks like its name, a beehive. **De Porceleyne Fles** (⊠ *Royal Delftware Factory, Rotterdamseweg 196Delft* ☎015/251–2030) is home to the popular blue-and-white Delft pottery. Regular demonstrations of molding and painting pottery are given by the artisans.

WHERE TO EAT

¢–$$ ✕ **Annie's Verjaardag.** A low-ceilinged, arched cellar, often full of chatty students, and a water-level canal-side terrace with great views guarantee a special atmosphere no matter where you sit in this popular eatery. During the day, there is a modest selection of salads and sandwiches on baguettes, and at least one offering that is more substantial. ⊠ *Hoogstraat 1a, Leiden* ☎071/512–5737 ⚓ *Reservations not accepted* ⊟MC, V.

¢–$ ✕ **Café Dudok.** Lofty ceilings, a cavernous former warehouse, long reading
★   tables stacked with international magazines and papers—little wonder this place attracts an artsy crowd. At its most mellow, this spot is perfect for a lazy afternoon treat of delicious homemade pastries, but you can come here for breakfast, lunch, high tea, dinner, or even a snack after midnight. They also offer a small selection for vegetarians. The brasserie, on a mezzanine above the open kitchen at the back, looks out over the Rotte River. Since it's terribly crowded at times, you should get here unfashionably early to avoid disappointment—there's nowhere else like it in Rotterdam. ⊠ *Meent 88, Centrum, Rotterdam* ☎010/433–3102 ⊟*AE, DC, MC, V.*

SOUTHAMPTON, UNITED KINGDOM

Southampton may not be in every tourist brochure, but this inland city and its environs hold all kinds of attractions—and not a few quiet pleasures. Two important cathedrals, Winchester and Salisbury (pronounced *sawls*-bree), are found in Hampshire, the county that contains Southampton, as are intriguing market towns, and hundreds of haunting prehistoric remains; Stonehenge, the most famous in nearby Wiltshire, should not

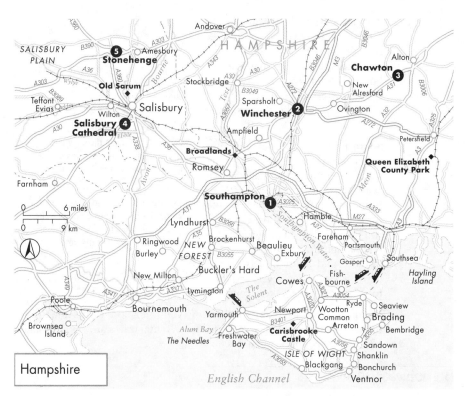

Hampshire

be missed. However, these are just the tourist brochure superlatives. Like those who migrate here from every corner of the country in search of upward mobility, anyone spending time in the South of England should rent a car and set out to discover the back-road villages not found in brochures. After a drink in the village pub and a look at the cricket game on the village green, stretch out in a field for a nap.

ESSENTIALS

CURRENCY   The British pound sterling (£1 is $US2.07 at this writing). U.S. currency is generally not accepted in Europe. ATMs are common and credit cards are widely accepted.

HOURS   Museums are open from 9 until 5, while shops usually open from 9 until 5:30 or 6. Some shops are open on Sunday.

INTERNET   Public libraries in all the cities and many of the smaller towns of the region offer free Internet access. **Salisbury Online** (⊠ *14 Endless St., above the Endless Life café, Salisbury* ☎ *01722/421328*) is a convenient Internet café.

TELEPHONES   Tri-band GSM phones work in the U.K. You can buy prepaid phone cards at telecom shops, news vendors, and tobacconists in all towns and cities. Phone cards can be used for local or international calls. Vodafone and Orange are the leading telecom companies.

COMING ASHORE

Ships to Southampton dock in three places, all within close proximity of major cruise terminals. Dock 10 is less than a mile from the terminal; both the railway station and coach station are half a mile away. Berth 101 is

430 yards from the terminal and 1 mi from the railway and coach station. Dock Gate 1 is 1 mi from the terminal; this terminal has a shuttle bus into Southampton city center. All three terminals have a bar or café for departing passengers, and a taxi stand.

Southampton is about 90 minutes from central London by train. There are four or five train services every hour, and fares start at £27.50 round-trip. By bus, the journey takes three hours; prices start at £14.50 round-trip. The rail journey from Southampton to Salisbury takes 30 minutes and starts at £10 round-trip; there are trains every half hour. The rail journey from Southampton to Winchester also takes around 30 minutes; fares start at £7 round-trip.

Renting a car for the day would allow you to explore towns and attractions in the surrounding area more easily. Rental prices are approximately £28 for an economy manual vehicle.

> ## HAMPSHIRE BEST BETS
>
> **Stonehenge.** This world-famous megalithic monument has captured the popular imagination. While we're sure of its age, its origins and exact purpose remain a mystery.
>
> **Winchester.** Once the capital of England, this diminutive city has many architectural treasures on show, including one of the finest cathedrals in Britain.
>
> **Chawton.** Jane Austen lived here for many years; devotees can be inspired by the atmosphere in the very room where she wrote her greatest works.

EXPLORING HAMPSHIRE

Numbers in the margin correspond to points of interest on the Hampshire map.

SOUTHAMPTON

❶ *Central Southampton is about 2 km (1 mi) from the cruise-ship docks.*

Seafaring Saxons and Romans used Southampton's harbor, Southampton Water, as a commercial trading port for centuries, and the city thrived, becoming one of England's wealthiest. But Plymouth eventually supplanted it, and Southampton has been going downhill ever since. Still, it remains England's leading passenger port, and as the home port of Henry V's fleet bound for Agincourt, the *Mayflower,* the *Queen Mary,* and the ill-fated *Titanic,* along with countless other great ocean liners of the 20th century, Southampton has one of the richest maritime traditions in England. Much of the city center is shoddy, having been hastily rebuilt after World War II bombing, but bits of the city's history peek out from between modern buildings. The Old Town retains its medieval air, and considerable parts of Southampton's castellated town walls remain. Other attractions include an art gallery, extensive parks, and a couple of good museums. The Southampton International Boat Show, a 10-day event in mid-September, draws huge crowds.

Incorporated in the town walls are a number of old buildings, including **God's House Tower,** originally a gunpowder factory and now an archaeology museum. Displays focus on the Roman, Saxon, and medieval periods of Southampton's history, and an interactive computer allows virtual access to the archaeological collections. ✉ *Winkle St.* ☎ *023/8063–5904*

⊕*www.southampton.gov.uk* ✉*Free* ☉*Apr.–Oct., Tues.–Fri. 10–noon and 1–5, Sat. 10–noon and 1–4, Sun. 2–5; Nov.–Mar., Tues.–Fri. 10–4, Sat. 10–noon and 1–4, Sun. 1–4.*

Mayflower Park and the Pilgrim Fathers' Memorial commemorate the departure of 102 passengers on the North America–bound *Mayflower* from Southampton on August 15, 1620. A plaque also honors the 2 million U.S. troops who left Southampton in World War II. ⊠ *Western Esplanade.*

The **Southampton Maritime Museum** brings together models, mementos, and items of furniture from the age of the great clippers and cruise ships, including a wealth of memorabilia relating to the *Titanic*—footage, photos, crew lists, etc. Boat buffs will relish plenty of vital statistics dealing with the history of commercial shipping. ⊠*Bugle St.* ☎*023/8022–3941* ⊕*www.southampton.gov.uk* ✉*Free* ☉*Apr.–Oct., Tues.–Fri. 10–1 and 2–5, Sat. 10–1 and 2–4, Sun. 2–5; Nov.–Mar., Tues.–Fri. 10–4, Sat. 10–1 and 2–4, Sun. 1–4.*

WINCHESTER

❷ *25 km (16 mi) northeast of Southampton.*

Winchester is among the most historic of English cities. Although it is now merely the county seat of Hampshire, for more than four centuries Winchester served as England's capital. Here, in AD 827, Egbert was crowned first king of England, and his successor, Alfred the Great, held court until his death in 899. After the Norman Conquest in 1066, William I ("the Conqueror") had himself crowned in London, but took the precaution of repeating the ceremony in Winchester.

★ **Winchester Cathedral.** The city's greatest monument, begun in 1079 and consecrated in 1093, presents a sturdy, chunky appearance in keeping with its Norman construction, so that the Gothic lightness within is even more breathtaking. Its tower, transepts, and crypt, and the inside core of the great Perpendicular nave, reveal some of the world's best surviving examples of Norman architecture. Other features, such as the arcades, the presbytery (behind the choir, holding the high altar), and the windows, are Gothic alterations carried out between the 12th and 14th centuries. Among the many well-known people buried in the cathedral is Jane Austen, whose grave lies in the north aisle of the nave. Special services or ceremonies may mean the cathedral is closed to visits, so telephone first to avoid disappointment. Tours of the bell tower are offered at least two times daily. ⊠*The Close, Cathedral Precincts* ☎*01962/857200* ⊕*www. winchester-cathedral.org.uk* ✉*£5, bell tower tour £5* ☉*Mon.–Sat. 8:30–6, Sun. 12:30–3:30, longer for services. Library and Triforium Gallery Easter–Oct., Mon.–Sat. 11–4; Nov.–Easter, Sat. 11–3.30. Free tours on the hr Mon.–Sat. 10–3. Bell tower tours June–Sept., weekdays 2:15, Sat. 11:30 and 2:15; Oct.–May, Wed. 2:15, Sat. 11:30 and 2:15.*

Great Hall. A few blocks west of the cathedral, this hall is all that remains of the city's Norman castle. Here the English Parliament met for the first time in 1246; Sir Walter Raleigh was tried for conspiracy against King James I and condemned to death here in 1603. The hall's greatest relic hangs on its west wall: King Arthur's Round Table has places for 24 knights and features a portrait of Arthur bearing a remarkable resemblance to King

Henry VIII. In fact, the table dates back no further than the 13th century and was repainted by order of Henry on the occasion of a visit by the Holy Roman Emperor Charles V. Take time to wander through Queen Eleanor's Medieval Garden—a re-creation of a noblewoman's shady retreat. ⊠*Castle Hill* ☎*01962/846476* ⊡*Free* ⊙*Mar.–Oct., daily 10–5; Nov.–Feb., daily 10–4.*

CHAWTON

❸ *49 km (30 mi) northeast of Southampton.*

Jane Austen (1775–1817) lived the last eight years of her life in the village of Chawton. The site has always drawn literary pilgrims, but with the ongoing release of successful films based on her novels, the popularity of the town among visitors has grown enormously.

★ Here, in an unassuming redbrick house, Austen wrote *Emma, Persuasion,* and *Mansfield Park,* and revised *Sense and Sensibility, Northanger Abbey,* and *Pride and Prejudice.* Now a museum, the rooms of **Jane Austen's House** retain the atmosphere of restricted gentility suitable to the unmarried daughter of a clergyman. Her mahogany writing desk still resides in the family sitting room. ⊠*Signed off A31/A32 roundabout* ☎*01420/83262* ⊕*www.janeaustenmuseum.org.uk* ⊡*£5* ⊙*Mar.–May and Sept.–Dec., daily 10:30–4:30; June–Aug., daily 10–5; Jan. and Feb., weekends 10:30–4:30; last admission 30 min before closing.*

SALISBURY CATHEDRAL

❹ *39 km (24 mi) northwest of Southampton.*

FodorsChoice Salisbury is dominated by the towering cathedral, a soaring hymn in stone.
★ It is unique among cathedrals in that it was conceived and built as a whole, in the amazingly short span of 38 years (1220–58). The spire, added in 1320, is the tallest in England and a miraculous feat of medieval engineering—even though the point, 404 feet above the ground, leans 2½ feet off vertical. ■TIP➡ You can join a free 45-minute tour of the church leaving two or more times a day, and there are tours to the roof and spire at least once a day. The **cloisters** are the largest in England, and the octagonal **Chapter House** contains a marvelous 13th-century frieze showing scenes from the Old Testament. In the Chapter House you can also see one of the four original copies of the **Magna Carta,** the charter of rights the English barons forced King John to accept in 1215; it was sent here for safekeeping in the 13th century. ⊠*Cathedral Close* ☎*01722/555120* ⊕*www.salisburycathedral.org.uk* ⊡*Cathedral £5 requested donation, roof tour £5.50, Chapter House free* ⊙*Cathedral mid-June–Aug., Mon.–Sat. 7:15–7:15, Sun. 7:15–6:15; Sept.–mid-June, daily 7:15–6:15. Chapter House mid-June–Aug., Mon.–Sat. 9:30–6:45, Sun. noon–5:30; Sept. and Oct. and Mar.–mid-June, Mon.–Sat. 9:30–5:30, Sun. noon–5:30; Nov.–Feb., Mon.–Sat. 10–4:30, Sun. noon–4:30. Access to cathedral restricted during services.*

STONEHENGE

❺ *76 km (47 mi) northwest of Southampton.*

FodorsChoice Mysterious and ancient, Stonehenge has baffled archaeologists for centu-
★ ries. One of England's most visited monuments, the circle of giant stones that sits in lonely isolation on the wide sweep of Salisbury Plain still has

the capacity to fascinate and move those who view it. Sadly, though, this World Heritage Site is now enclosed by barriers after incidents of vandalism and amid fears that its popularity could threaten its existence. Visitors can no longer walk among the giant stones or see up close the prehistoric carvings, some of which show axes and daggers.

Stonehenge was begun about 3000 BC, enlarged between 2100 and 1900 BC, and altered yet again by 150 BC. It has been excavated and rearranged several times over the centuries. The medieval term "stonehenge" means "hanging stones." Many of the huge stones that ringed the center were brought here from great distances, but it is not certain by what ancient form of transportation they were moved.

Although some of the mysteries concerning the site have been solved, the reason Stonehenge was built remains unknown. It is fairly certain that it was a religious site, and that worship here involved the cycles of the sun; the alignment of the stones to point to sunrise at midsummer and sunset in midwinter makes this clear. The druids certainly had nothing to do with the construction: the monument had already been in existence for nearly 2,000 years by the time they appeared. Excavations at Durrington Walls, another henge a couple of miles northeast (off A345), have unearthed a substantial settlement dating from around 2500 BC, probably built and occupied by those who constructed Stonehenge.

A paved path for visitors skirts the stones, ensuring that you don't get very close to the monoliths. Bring a pair of binoculars to help make out the details more clearly. Your ticket entitles you to an informative audio tour, but in general, visitor amenities at Stonehenge are limited, especially for such a major tourist attraction.

The monument stands near the junction with A344. ⊠*Junction of A303 and A344/A360, near Amesbury* ☎*0870/333–1181, 01722/343834 for information about private access outside regular hrs* ⊕*www.english-heritage.org.uk* ⊠*£6.30* ⊙*Mid-Mar.–May and Sept.–mid-Oct., daily 9:30–6; June–Aug., daily 9–7; mid-Oct.–mid-Mar., daily 9:30–4.*

SHOPPING

Almost every town in this part of England has a tempting array of shops selling antiques, collectibles, and one-of-a-kind items. English china makes a fitting souvenir, as do copies of the various Austen novels set in the region. For a post-tour pick-me-up, try English blended teas in presentation sets.

Watsons (⊠*8–9 Queen St., Salisbury* ☎*01722/320311*) specializes in Aynsley and Wedgwood bone china, Waterford and Dartington glass, Royal Doulton tableware and collectibles, and fine ornaments. The buildings, dating from 1306 and 1425, have their original windows and an oak mantelpiece.

King's Walk, off Friarsgate in Winchester, has a number of stalls selling antiques, crafts, gift items, and bric-a-brac. **The Jays' Nest** (⊠*King's Walk, Winchester* ☎*01962/865650*) specializes in silver and china.

WHERE TO EAT

$$-$$$ ✕**Après LXIX Bar and Bistro.** A stone's throw from the cathedral, this convivial and relaxed bistro has a cool, modern style, making it an ideal spot for a light lunch or dinner. The menu lists everything from fish cakes and pastas to sea bass and steaks, and there are good-value early-evening fixed-price deals. ⊠*69 New St., Salisbury* ☎*01722/340000* ▭*AE, DC, MC, V* ✆*Closed Sun. and last wk in Dec.*

$-$$ ✕**Cathedral Refectory.** The bold, modern style of this self-service eatery next to the cathedral helps make it a refreshing lunch or snack stop. The menu ranges from traditional soups to cottage pie and fish dishes, but do sample the local "trenchers." This thick bread was used in medieval times as a plate from which to eat meat; once soaked in the meat juices, the bread was passed down to the poor. Today the trenchers, soaked in toppings such as pesto or ham and goat's cheese, are grilled. ⊠*Inner Close, Winchester* ☎*01962/857200* ▭*MC, V* ✆*No dinner.*

ZEEBRUGGE, BELGIUM (FOR BRUGES)

Long thought of as a Sleeping Beauty reawakened, Bruges is an ancient town where the rhythm of medieval life resonates from every street corner. The city thrived during the 13th century as a member of the Hanseatic League, and an era of unprecedented wealth began under such Burgundian rulers as Philip the Good and Charles the Bold in the 15th century. At this time, Hans Memling and Jan van Eyck took art in a new direction with the famed Flemish Primitive style of painting, while fine civil and domestic buildings advertised the wealth generated by trade. When the city fell into poverty as its rivers silted in the 16th century, this architecture was preserved as if in aspic. Today, Bruges is a compact and atmospheric maze of tangled streets, narrow canals, handsome squares, and gabled buildings. The town has not only awakened from its slumbers, but is also bright-eyed with spruced-up shops, restaurants and cafés.

ESSENTIALS

CURRENCY   The euro (€1 to US$1.46 at this writing). U.S. currency is generally not accepted in Europe, but ATMs are common and credit cards are widely accepted.

HOURS   Shops open Tuesday, Wednesday, Friday, and Saturday from 9 or 10 until 6; they are open later on Thursday. Most stores are closed on Sunday and some on Monday. Museums open from 9 until 6 with one late opening night during the week.

INTERNET   **The Coffee Link** (⊠*Congresgebouw, Mariastraat 38* ☎*050/34–99–73* ⊕*www. thecoffeelink.com*) is a stylish spot offering a huge range of coffees, teas, and hot chocolates, as well as computer terminals. It's open Monday through Saturday until 9:30 PM.

TELEPHONES   Tri-band GSM phones work in Belgium. You can buy prepaid phone cards at telecom shops, news vendors, and tobacconists in all towns and cities. Phone cards can be used for local or international calls. Proximus and Mobistar are the leading telecom companies.

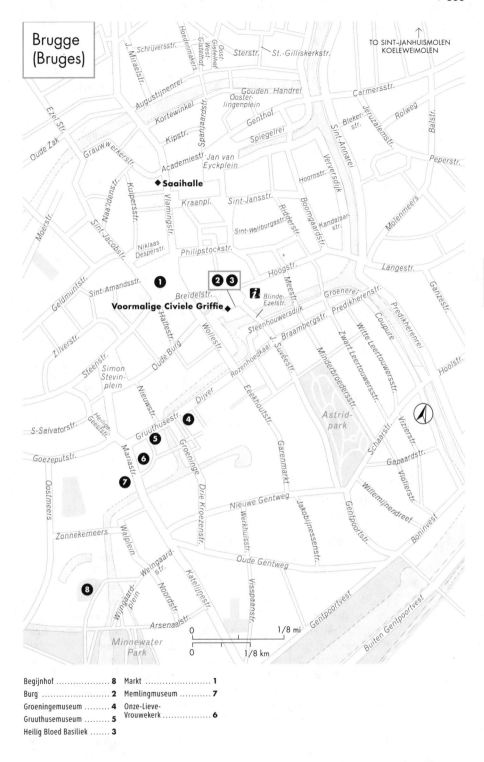

Brugge (Bruges)

TO SINT-JANHUISMOLEN
KOELEWEIMOLEN

◆ **Saaihalle**

Voormalige Civiele Griffie ◆

6

COMING ASHORE

Cruise ships dock at Zeebrugge—
14 km (9 mi) from the city of Bruges—at the King Leopold II dam
or in Albert II dock, both at the
western outer port. These locations are 2 km (1½ mi) from Zeebrugge train station. There are no
passenger facilities within the port
itself. The reliable and modern rail
system ensures swift and efficient
transfer from the station to a range
of Belgian cities, including Ghent,
Antwerp, and Brussels. The dock is
within walking distance of the seafront of Zeebrugge town, with its
seafront promenade, Russian submarine exhibit, and historic fishing district.

BRUGES BEST BETS

Boat trip on the canals. The life-
blood of medieval Bruges, the canals
now offer some of the finest views of
the city's delightful architecture and
distinctive streets and alleyways.

Belfort. Climb the medieval tower
for exceptional views across the tiled
rooftops and ornate gables of this
tiny enclave.

Groeningemusem. The art of the
Flemish Primitives and their successors form the core of this gallery, one
of the finest of its kind in the world.

Taxis wait at the dockside to transfer passengers not booked on organized
trips into Zeebrugge. By rail from the center of Zeebrugge, it is a 15-min-
ute journey to Bruges at a current cost of €2.50 one-way; the rail journey
to Antwerp takes one hour and 45 minutes, at a cost of €14.50 one way
(⇨Antewrp, *above*). It is 15 minutes by road from the Zeebrugge docks
to Bruges. Travel by taxi has a per-km (per-½-mi) charge of around €2.50,
which makes it expensive for day tours but acceptable for short trips.

Vehicle rental offices are located in Bruges (around €30 per day for a
compact manual shift vehicle), but rail transport is most practical for
independent travelers unless you really want to see more of the Belgian
countryside.

EXPLORING BRUGES

*Numbers in the margin correspond to points of interest on the Bruges
map.*

8 Begijnhof. The convent is a pretty and serene cluster of buildings surround-
★ ing a pleasant green at the edge of a canal. Founded in 1245 by Margaret,
Countess of Constantinople, the beguinage flourished for 600 years. The
last of the Beguines died about 50 years ago and today the site is occupied by the Benedictine nuns, who still wear the Beguine habit. Although
most of the present-day houses are from the 16th and 17th centuries, they
have maintained the architectural style of the houses that preceded them.
One house has been set aside as a small museum. The horse-and-carriage
rides around the town have a 10-minute stop outside the beguinage—long
enough for a quick look around. Visitors are asked to respect the silence.
⊠*Oude Begijnhof, off Wijngaardstraat* ☎*050/33–00–11* ✉*Free, house
visit €2* ⊙*Mar.–Nov., daily 10–noon and 1:45–5; Dec.–Feb., Mon., Tues.,
Fri. 10–noon, Wed. and Thurs. 2–4.*

2 Burg. A popular daytime meeting place and an enchanting, floodlighted
scene after dark, the Burg is flanked by striking civic buildings. Named for
Fodor'sChoice the fortress built by Baldwin of the Iron Arm, the Burg was also the former
★

site of the 10th-century Carolingian Cathedral of St. Donaas, which was destroyed by French Republicans in 1799. You can wander through the handsome, 18th-century law court, the Oude Gerechtshof, the Voormalige Civiele Griffie with its 15th-century front gable, the Stadhuis, and the Heilig Bloed Basiliek (⇨*below*). The Burg is not all historic splendor, though—in sharp contrast to these buildings stands a modern construction by Japanese

artist Toyo Ito, added in 2002. Public opinion is sharply divided over Ito's pavilion over a shallow pool; you'll either love it or hate it. ✉*Hoogstraat and Breidelstraat.*

4 **Groeningemusem.** The tremendous holdings of this gallery give you the makings for a crash course in the Flemish Primitives and their successors. Petrus Christus, Hugo van der Goes, Hieronymus Bosch, Rogier van der Weyden, Gerard David, Pieter Bruegel (both Elder and Younger), Pieter Pourbus—all are represented here. Jan van Eyck's wonderfully realistic *Madonna with Canon Van der Paele*, vies with Hans Memling's, the *Moreel Triptych* as best piece. Thoughtfully, there's a play area to keep antsy children busy. An audioguide is available in English. ✉*Dijver 12* ☎*050/44-87-11* ✉*€8, includes an audioguide* ☉*Tues.–Sun. 9:30–5.*

*Fodor's*Choice ★

5 **Gruuthusemuseum.** If you want to understand the daily life of 15th-century Bruges, visit this applied arts museum. The collection is housed in the Gothic former home of Lodewijk Van Gruuthuse, a prominent Dutch nobleman. The home features displays of furniture, tapestries, lace, ceramics, kitchen equipment, weaponry, and musical instruments. The audioguides are available in English. ✉*Dijver 17* ☎*050/44-87-11* ✉*€6, includes audioguide* ☉*Tues.–Sun. 9:30–5.*

3 **Heilig Bloed Basiliek.** The Basilica of the Holy Blood plays host to one of Europe's most precious relics. Architecturally bipolar, a 12th-century Lower Chapel retains a sober, Romanesque character while a lavish Gothic Upper Chapel sits above. The basilica's namesake treasure is a vial thought to contain a few drops of the blood of Christ, brought from Jerusalem to Bruges in 1149. It is exposed here every Friday in the Lower Chapel from 8:30 to 10 and in the Upper Chapel from 10 to 11 and from 3 to 4. On Ascension Day, it becomes the centerpiece of the magnificent *De Heilig Bloedprocessie* (Procession of the Holy Blood), a major medieval-style pageant in which it is carried through the streets of Bruges. The small **museum** next to the basilica contains the 17th-century reliquary. ✉*Burg* ☎*No phone* ⊕*www.holyblood.org* ✉*Basilica free, museum €1.25* ☉*Apr.–Sept., Thurs.–Tues. 9:30–11:50 and 2–5:50, Wed. 9:30–11:50; Oct.–Mar., daily 10–11:50 and 2–3:50.*

1 **Markt.** Used as a marketplace since 958, this square is still one of the liveliest places in Bruges. In the center stands a memorial to the city's medieval heroes, Jan Breydel and Pieter De Coninck, who led the commoners

*Fodor's*Choice ★

6

of Flanders to a short-lived victory over the aristocrats of France. Old guild houses line the west and north sides of the square, their step-gabled facades overlooking the cafés spilling out onto the sidewalk. These buildings aren't always as old as they seem, though—often they're 19th-century reconstructions. The medieval **Belfort** (Belfry) on the south side of the Markt, however, is the genuine article. The tower dates to the 13th century, its crowning octagonal lantern to the 15th century. Altogether, it rises to a height of 270 feet, commanding the city and the surrounding countryside with more presence than grace. The valuables of Bruges were once kept in the second floor treasury; now the Belfort's riches are in its remarkable 47-bell carillon. You can climb 366 winding steps to the clock mechanism, and from the carillon enjoy a gorgeous panoramic view. Back down in the square, you may be tempted by the **horse-drawn carriages** that congregate here; a half-hour ride for up to four people, with a short stop at the Begijnhof, costs €30, plus "something for the horse." ⊠*Intersection of Steenstraat, St-Amandstraat, Vlamingstraat, Philipstockstraat, Breidelstraat, and Wollestraat* ☎*050/44–87–11* 🏛*€5* ⊗*Tues.–Sun., 9:30–5. Carillon concerts Sun. 2:15–3; June 15–July 1 and Aug. 15–Sept., Mon., Wed., and Sat. 9* PM*–10* PM; *Oct.–June 14, Wed. and Sat. 2:15–3.*

❼ **Memlingmuseum.** This collection contains only six works, but they are of
★ breathtaking quality and among the greatest—and certainly the most spiritual—of the Flemish Primitive school. Hans Memling (1440–94) was born in Germany, but spent the greater part of his life in Bruges. In *The Altarpiece of St. John the Baptist and St. John the Evangelist,* two leading personages of the Burgundian court are believed to be portrayed: Mary of Burgundy as St. Catherine, and Margaret of York as St. Barbara. The Memling Museum is housed in **Oud Sint-Janshospitaal,** one of the oldest surviving medieval hospitals in Europe. It was founded in the 12th century and remained in use until the early 20th century. There is a short guide to the museum in English, and also an audioguide in English. ⊠*Mariastraat 38* ☎*050/44–87–11* 🏛*€8, includes audioguide* ⊗*Tues.–Sun. 9:30–5.*

❻ **Onze-Lieve-Vrouwekerk.** The towering spire of the plain, Gothic Church of Our Lady, begun about 1220, rivals the Belfry as Bruges's symbol. It is 381 feet high, the tallest brick construction in the world. Look for the small *Madonna and Child* statue, an early work by Michelangelo. The great sculptor sold it to a merchant from Bruges when the original client failed to pay and now the white-marble figure sits in a black-marble niche behind an altar at the end of the south aisle. The choir contains many 13th- and 14th-century polychrome tombs, as well as two mausoleums: that of Mary of Burgundy, who died in 1482; and that of her father, Charles the Bold, killed in 1477 while laying siege to Nancy in France. Mary was as well loved in Bruges as her husband, Maximilian of Austria, was loathed. Her finely chiseled effigy captures her beauty. ⊠*Dijver and Mariastraat* ☎*No phone* 🏛*€2.50* ⊗*Weekdays 9–12:30 and 1:30–5, Sat. 9–12:30 and 1:30–4, Sun. 2–5.*

SHOPPING

Bruges has many trendy boutiques and shops, especially along Nordzandstraat, as well as Steenstraat and Vlamingstraat, both of which branch off from the Markt. Ter Steeghere mall, which links the Burg with Wollestraat, deftly integrates a modern development into the historic center. The largest and most pleasant mall is the Zilverpand off Zilverstraat, where 30-odd shops cluster in Flemish gable houses. Souvenir shops crowd around the Markt, Wollestraat, Breidelstraat, and Minnewater. Bruges has been a center for lace-making since the 15th century. Handmade lace in intricate patterns, however, takes a very long time to produce, and this is reflected in the price. For work of this type, you should be prepared to part with €250 or more. Art and antiques abound, with furniture and decorative objects from the surrounding Flanders region. You also can't go far in the city center without seeing a tempting window display of handmade chocolates, truffles, and pralines. These are delicious to enjoy while you stroll.

A good shop for the serious lace lover is in the Sint-Anne quarter, behind the church: **'t Apostelientje** (⊠ *Balstraat 11* ☎ *050/33–78–60*).

One of the best chocolate shops is **The Chocolate Line** (⊠ *Simon Stevinplein 19* ☎ *050/34–10–90*); along with delicious handmade candy, it sells handy cases for packing your chocolates to take home. **Guyart** (⊠ *Fort Lapin 37* ☎ *050/33–21–59*) is both an art gallery and a tavern. **Papyrus** (⊠ *Walplein 41* ☎ *050/33–66–87*) specializes in antique silverware. **'t Leerhuis** (⊠ *Groeninge 35* ☎ *050/33–03–02*) deals in contemporary art. **Vincent Lebbe's Het Witte Huis** (⊠ *Gistelsesteenweg 30* ☎ *050/31–63–01*) offers furniture and decorative objects from the 18th and 19th centuries.

SPORTS & ACTIVITIES

CYCLING

The city is easy to explore on two wheels and many Bruges city dwellers use bicycles daily. Cyclists can go in both directions along more than 50 one-way streets, marked on the tarmac with an image of a bicycle circled in blue. The Bruges tourist office sells a cycling brochure outlining five different routes around the city. The city also offers one-day bike rental and entrance to three municipal museums for €15. You can rent bicycles at the following places: **Koffieboontje** (⊠ *Hallestraat 4* ☎ *050/33–80–27*); **Snuffel Backpacker Hostel** (⊠ *Recollettenlei 32* ☎ *050/33–31–33*).

WHERE TO EAT

¢–$$ ✕ **De Garre.** This tiny, two-tier, brick-and-beam coffeehouse and pub offers Mozart and magazines with your coffee or beer. You won't lack for a choice of brews; the menu lists 127 regional beers, four beers on tap, and five Trappist beers. A plate of cheese, such as Oude Bruges, is a good match with one of the heartier beers. ⊠ *De Garre 1* ☎ *050/34–10–29* 🖹 *No credit cards.*

¢–$$ ✕ **Eetcafé De Vuyst–Restaurant Bistrot De Serre.** The spires of Bruges are dramatically framed within the glass walls of the popular, light-filled Eetcafé. Go through to the back of the building and you'll come to a lovely garden restaurant. The café is ideal for a sandwich or light meal with the kids while the restaurant homes in on classic Belgian specialties such as waterzooi, mussels, and eel. ⊠*Simon Stevinplein 15* ☎*050/34–22–31* ⊟*AE, DC, MC, V* ⊗*Closed Tues., 1st 2 wks in Feb., and last 2 wks in Nov.*

The Baltic

PORTS IN DENMARK, ESTONIA, FINLAND, GERMANY, LATVIA, POLAND, RUSSIA & SWEDEN

Vegetable and flower vendor, Helsinki

WORD OF MOUTH

"We did the Baltic in June [,and] St. Pete[rsburg] was the highlight of the trip. . . . The sights are amazing . . . . For us, we disembarked [in] every port except St. Pete[rsburg] on our own, so we did not have to wait in lines for a tour to assemble and begin."

—jacketwatch

"We got our own visas for St. Pete[rsburg] and arranged our own car, driver, and guide. We saw twice as much as those on the ship's tour because we could move much faster. Our guide still got us to the head of the line, and we saw things we had read about in guidebooks that were not on the tours."

—kleroux

www.fodors.com/forums

Lindsay Bennett   **NORTHERN EUROPEAN ITINERARIES ARE INCREASINGLY** popular. You may depart from Stockholm or Copenhagen and visit several of the Baltic's top ports. A special treat for Baltic cruisers is often a stop in St. Petersburg, Russia, and this is why many people take these cruises. Some Baltic itineraries begin in a British port or even in Amsterdam (⇨ *Chapter 6 for more information about these ports*). Some may include stops in Norway (⇨ *Chapter 8 for Norwegian ports*). These cruises may be longer than the typical Mediterranean cruise and may cost more, which is one reason why they aren't as popular with first-timers to European cruising. But the number of ships doing Baltic itineraries continues to expand, and there are now some one-week cruises in these northern waters during the summer.

ABOUT THE RESTAURANTS

All the restaurants we recommend serve lunch; they may also serve dinner if your cruise ship stays late in port and you choose to dine off the ship. Cuisine in Europe is varied, but Europeans tend to eat a leisurely meal at lunch, but in most ports there are quicker and simpler alternatives for those who just want to grab a quick bite before returning to the ship. Note that several Baltic countries do not use the euro, including Denmark, Estonia, Finland, Latvia, Poland, Russia, and Sweden. Price categories in those countries are based on the euro-equivalent costs of eating in restaurants.

WHAT IT COSTS IN EUROS					
	$$$$	$$$	$$	$	¢
RESTAURANTS	over €30	€23–€30	€17–€23	€11–€17	under €11

Restaurant prices are per person for a main course, including tax.

ÅRHUS, DENMARK

Århus is Denmark's second-largest city, and, with its funky arts and college community, one of the country's most pleasant. The Vikings settled in Århus at the mouth of the river Aros. Traces of Viking life can still be found in Århus. Cutting through the center of town is a canal called the Århus Å (Århus Creek), once an underground aqueduct but now uncovered. An amalgam of bars, cafés, and restaurants has sprouted along its banks, creating one of Denmark's most lively thoroughfares. At all hours of the day and night this waterfront strip is abuzz with crowds that hang out on the outdoor terraces and steps that lead down to the creek.

ESSENTIALS

CURRENCY   Denmark is an EU country but has opted to keep its currency, the Danish *krone* or *kroner* (DKr 5.5 to US$1; DKr 7.44 to €1); exchange rates were accurate at this writing but are subject to change. ATMs are common, so it's easy to get local currency, but you can't generally use the euro or dollar here.

HOURS   Most shops are open from 9 or 10 to 5:30 or 6 weekdays, Saturday from 9 to 5, and are closed Sunday.

INTERNET   **Boom Town Netcafé** (⊠*Åboulevarden 21* ☎*89/41–39–30*). **Gate58 APS** (⊠*Vestergade 58 B* ☎*87/30–02–80*).

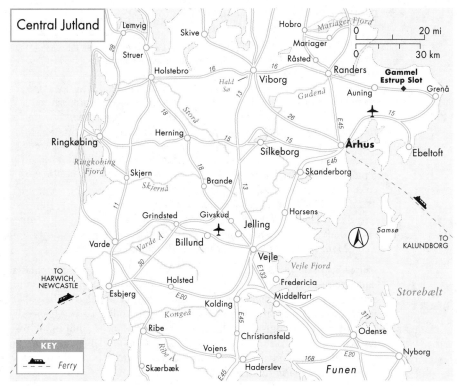

Central Jutland

TELEPHONES Most tri- and quad-band GSM phones will work in Denmark. If your service provider offers service in Europe, you will likely be able to use your mobile phone in Århus. Pay phones are increasingly rare in Europe, particularly in tech-savvy Scandinavia and Northern Europe.

COMING ASHORE

Cruise ships dock at Pier 2, only a 10-minute walk to the city center. If your ship calls during the summer, you may arrive in time for one of Århus' many festivals.

EXPLORING ÅRHUS

Århus Domkirke. Rising gracefully over the center of town, the Århus Cathedral was originally built in 1201 in a Romanesque style, but was later expanded and redesigned into a Gothic cathedral in the 15th century. Its soaring, whitewashed nave is one of the longest in Denmark. The cathedral's highlights include its chalk frescoes, in shades of lavender, yellow, red, and black that grace the high arches and towering walls. Dating from the Middle Ages, the frescoes depict biblical scenes and the valiant St. George slaying a dragon and saving a maiden princess in distress. Also illustrated is the poignant death of St. Clement, who drowned with an anchor tied around his neck; nonetheless, he became the patron saint of sailors. Climb the tower for bird's-eye views of the rooftops and thronged streets of Århus. ⊠*Bispetorv* ☎*86/20–54–00* ⊕*www.aarhus-domkirke. dk* ⊠*Tower DKr 10* ⊗*Jan.–Apr. and Oct.–Dec., Mon.–Sat. 10–3; May– Sept., Mon.–Sat. 9:30–4.*

★ **Den Gamle By.** Don't miss the town's open-air museum, the only three-star museum outside Copenhagen. Its 75 historic buildings, including 70 half-timber houses, a mill, and millstream, were carefully moved from locations throughout Denmark and meticulously re-created, inside and out. Actors portray people from times past. You can explore the extensive exhibits, and then have a pint in the beer cellar or coffee and cake in the garden. ✉ *Viborgvej 2* ☎ *86/12–31–88* ⊕ *www.dengam-leby.dk* 🎫 *DKr 50–DKr 90 depending on season and activities* ☉ *June–Aug., daily 9–6; Apr., May, Sept., and Oct., daily 10–5; Jan., daily 11–3; Feb., Mar., Nov., and Dec., daily 10–4. Grounds always open.*

Marselisborg Slot. Just south of the city is Marselisborg Castle, the palatial summer residence of the royal family. The changing of the guard takes place daily at noon when the queen is staying in the palace. The palace itself is not open for tours, but when the royal family is away (generally in winter and spring), the palace grounds, including a sumptuous rose garden, are open to the public. Take Bus 1, 8, or 19. ✉ *Kongevejen 100* ☎ *No phone* ⊕ *www.kongehuset.dk* 🎫 *Free* ☉ *Daily dawn–dusk, when Royal Family not in residence.*

Moesgård Forhistorisk Museum. In a 250-acre forest south of Århus, the Prehistoric Museum has exhibits on ethnography and archaeology, including the famed Grauballe Man, a 2,000-year-old corpse so well preserved in a bog that scientists could determine his last meal. In fact, when the discoverers of the Grauballe Man stumbled upon him in 1952, they thought he had recently been murdered and called the police. The Forhistorisk vej (Prehistoric Trail) through the forest leads past Stone- and Bronze Age displays to reconstructed houses from Viking times. ✉ *Moesgård Allé (Bus 6 from center of town)* ☎ *89/42–11–00* ⊕ *www.moesmus.dk* 🎫 *DKr 45* ☉ *Apr.–Sept., daily 10–5; Oct.–Mar., Tues.–Sun. 10–4.*

Rådhus. Århus's municipal building is probably the most unusual city hall in Denmark. Built in 1941 by noted architects Arne Jacobsen and Erik Møller, the pale Norwegian-marble block building is controversial, but cuts a startling figure when illuminated in the evening. Go to the Kommune Information booth next to the tower entrance to obtain multiride tickets and passport tourist tickets, and to get information on everything connected with traveling by bus in Århus. That office is open from 10 to 5:30. ✉ *Park Allé* ☎ *89/40–67–00* 🎫 *City hall DKr 10, tower DKr 5* ☉ *Guided tours (in Danish only) mid-June–early Sept., weekdays at 11; tower tours weekdays at noon and 2.*

☺ **Tivoli Friheden.** If you are in Århus with children, or simply wish to enjoy a young-at-heart activity, visit the provincial amusement park with more than 40 rides and activities, attractive gardens, and restaurants. Pierrot the Clown entertains, and concerts are given by contemporary artists.

✉*Skovbrynet* ☎*86/14–73–00* ⊕*www.friheden.dk* 🎫*DKr 60; rides cost extra* ⊙*Call or check Web site as opening times vary greatly throughout summer.*

SHOPPING

With more than 800 shops and many pedestrian streets (Strøget, Fredericksgade, Sct. Clemensgade, Store Torv, and Lille Torv), this city is a great place to play havoc with your credit cards. As befits a student town, Århus also has its "Latin Quarter," a jumble of cobbled streets around the cathedral, with boutiques, antiques shops, and glass and ceramic galleries that may be a little less expensive. In Vestergade street, you can turn on Grønnengade and stroll along Møllestien to see its charming old homes.

The Fredericksbjerg quarter, which includes the streets Bruunsgade, Jægergårdsgade, and Fredericks Allé, is called "the larder of the city" because there are so many specialty food shops here. There's also a shopping center, Bruun's Galleri.

At the **Bülow Duus Glassworks** (✉*Studsg. 14* ☎*86/12–72–86*) you can browse among delicate and colorful glassworks from fishbowls to candleholders. While there, visit Mette Bülow Duus's workshop and witness the creation of beautiful glassware. **Folmer Hansen** (✉*Sønderg. 43* ☎*86/12–49–00*) is packed with Danish tableware and porcelain, from sleek Arne Jacobsen-designed cheese cutters, ice buckets, and coffeepots to Royal Copenhagen porcelain plates. For the best selection of Georg Jensen designs, head to the official **Georg Jensen** (✉*Sønderg. 1* ☎*86/12–01–00* ⊕*www.georgjensen.com*) store. It stocks watches, jewelry, table settings, and art nouveau vases. The textile designs of Georg Jensen Damask, in a separate department, are truly beautiful.

SPORTS & ACTIVITIES

FISHING

For the past 24 years the same four friends from England have been fishing in the Silkeborg region on their vacation—surely an excellent endorsement for angling opportunities in the region. The Lake District is a great place for fishing—more than 15 popular species of fish can be found here. License requirements vary, and package tours are also available; contact the local tourist office for details.

WHERE TO EAT

$$–$$$ ✕**Bryggeriet Sct. Clemens.** At this popular pub you can sit among copper
★ kettles and quaff the local brew, which is unfiltered and without additives, just like in the old days. Between the spareribs and Australian steaks, you won't go hungry, either. ✉*Kannikeg. 10–12* ☎*86/13–80–00* ⊕*www.bryggeriet.dk* ☰*AE, DC, MC, V.*

$$ ✕**Prins Ferdinand.** Sitting on the edge of old town, and right next to the entrance of Den Gamle By, this premier Danish-French restaurant is named after the colorful Århus-based Prince Frederik (1792–1863), who was much loved despite his fondness for gambling and carousing about town. Here, elegant crystal chandeliers hang over large round tables with crisp linen tablecloths and ceramic plates created by a local artist. Vases of sunflowers brighten the front room. Grilled turbot is topped with a cold salsa of radishes, cucumber, and dill. Cabbage, foie gras, and new potatoes accompany a venison dish. A daily vegetarian option is offered, and might include grilled asparagus with potatoes, olives, and herbs. ✉ *Viborgvej 2* ☎ *86/12–52–05* ⊕ *www.prinsferdinand.dk* 🖃 *AE, DC, MC, V* ⊗ *Closed Sun. and Mon.*

COPENHAGEN, DENMARK

Copenhagen—"København" in Danish—has no glittering skylines, few killer views, and only a handful of meager skyscrapers. Bicycles glide alongside manageable traffic at a pace that's utterly human. The early-morning air in the pedestrian streets of the city's core, Strøget, is redolent of freshly baked bread and soap-scrubbed storefronts. If there's such a thing as a cozy city, this is it. Filled with museums, restaurants, cafés, and lively nightlife, the city has its greatest resource in its spirited inhabitants. The imaginative, unconventional, and affable Copenhageners exude an egalitarian philosophy that embraces nearly all lifestyles and leanings. Despite a tumultuous history, Copenhagen survives as the liveliest Scandinavian capital with some excellent galleries and museums. With its backdrop of copper towers and crooked rooftops, the venerable city is amused by playful street musicians and performers, soothed by one of the highest standards of living in the world, and spangled by the thousand lights and gardens of Tivoli.

ESSENTIALS

CURRENCY   The krone (DKr 5.54 to US$1; DKr 7.44 to €1); exchange rates were accurate at this writing but are subject to change. U.S. currency is accepted in some shops and restaurants. ATMs are common.

HOURS   Museum hours vary, though the major collections are open Tuesday through Sunday from 10 to 5. Stores are open Monday through Friday from 9:30 to 5:30 (or sometimes 7).

INTERNET   **Boomtown** (✉ *Axel Torv 1* ☎ *33/32–10–32* ⊕ *www.boomtown.net*) offers Internet access and gaming. It's open 24 hours a day.

TELEPHONES   Tri-band GSM phones work in Denmark. You can buy prepaid phone cards at telecom shops, news vendors, and tobacconists in all towns and cities. Phone cards can be used for local or international calls.

COMING ASHORE

The city's cruise port is one of the best in Europe. Although it's 10 minutes from the downtown core, it's within walking distance of the Little Mermaid and the attractions of the seafront. Taxis wait outside the cruise terminal. The on-site Copenhagen Cruise Information Center is run by the city tourist office and there is a selection of shops housed in the renovated old wharf warehouses selling typical souvenirs. There is a dedicated cruise lounge at Magasin at Kongens Nytorv in the city center where you can wait for transfers, leave purchases for later collection, or have a rest during your trip.

Taxis are expensive, but useful for short trips. A starting fee of DKr 19 (if hailed on the street) or DKr 22 (if booked by phone) is then supplemented by a charge of DKr 7 to 10 per half-mile (more after 4 PM and at night). Most taxis accept credit cards. Car rentals cost around DKr 185 per day for an economy manual vehicle; however, public transport is much more convenient for a short city visit. The metro and bus services are clean and efficient with tickets costing DKr 18 for a one-hour ticket, DKr 105 for a one-day pass.

EXPLORING COPENHAGEN

Numbers in the margin correspond to points of interest on the Copenhagen map.

④ **Amalienborg** *(Amalia's Castle)*. The four identical rococo buildings occupying this square have housed the royals since 1784. The Christian VIII palace across from the queen's residence houses the **Amalienborg Museum,** which displays part of the Royal Collection and chronicles royal lifestyles between 1863 and 1947.

In the square's center is a magnificent equestrian statue of King Frederik V by the French sculptor Jacques François Joseph Saly. Every day at noon, the Royal Guard and band march from Rosenborg Slot through the city for the changing of the guard. On Amalienborg's harbor side are the trees, gardens, and fountains of **Amalienhaven.** ⊠ *Christian VIII's Palace–Amalienborg Pl., Sankt Annæ Kvarter* ☎ *33/12–21–86* ⊠ *DKr 75* ☯ *May–Oct., daily 10–4; Nov.–Apr., Tues.–Sun. 11–4. Guided tours in English July–Sept., weekends at 1* PM.

⑩ **Carlsberg Bryggeri** *(Carlsberg Brewery)*. As you approach the world-famous Carlsberg Brewery, the unmistakable smell of fermenting hops greets you, a pungent reminder that this is beer territory. Nearby, on Gamle Carslbergvej, is the visitor center, in an old Carlsberg brewery. ⊠ *Gamle Carlsbergvej 11, Vesterbro* ☎ *33/27–13–14* ⊕ *www.carlsberg.com* ⊠ *Free* ☯ *Tues.–Sun. 10–4.*

③ **Christiansborg Slot** *(Christiansborg Castle)*. Surrounded by canals on three sides, the massive granite castle is where the queen officially receives guests. From 1441 until the fire of 1795, it was used as the royal residence. Even though the first two castles on the site were burned, Christiansborg remains an impressive baroque compound, even by European standards. The complex contains the Danish Parliament, the Supreme Court, and Royal Reception Chambers, as well as some ruins. Free tours of the **Folketinget** *(Parliament House* ☎ *33/37–55–00* ⊕ *www.folketinget.dk)* are given Monday through Saturday from June to mid-August, as well as on Sunday from July to mid-August; tours run Sunday to Friday from mid-August through September, and on weekdays from October through April. English-language groups begin at 2. At the **Kongelige Repræsantationlokaler** *(Royal Reception Chambers* ☎ *33/92–64–92)*, you're asked to don slippers to protect the floors. Tours are given daily May through September, and Tuesday, Thursday, and weekends from October through April; English-language tours are at 11, 1, and 3. The **Højesteret** *(Supreme Court)*, on the site of the city's first fortress, was built by Bishop Absalon in 1167. While the castle was being rebuilt around 1900, the Nationalmuseet excavated the **ruins** (☎ *33/92–64–92)* of one of the earlier structures beneath

Fodors Choice
★

7

Copenhagen

NØRREBRO

ØSTERBRO

TO ASSISTENS
KIERKEGÅRD

Tagensv.

Blegdamsv.

Dossering

Dag Hammarskjölds Al.

Fredensg.

Fredensbro.

Sortedam

Sø

Øster Søg.

Øster

Farimagsg.

Stockholmsg.

Øster
Anlæg

Blegdamsv.

Møller.

Nørre Al.

Elmeg.

Ravnborg

Fælledv.

Grüffenfeldsg.

Nørrebrog.

Sortedam

Sortedams

Øster Søg.

Sølvg.

Rigensg.

Blågårdsg.

Peblinge Dossering

Peblinge Sø

Dronning
Louises
Bro.

Øster Farimagsg.

Gothersg.

Botanisk
Have

Øster Voldg.

Kongens
Have

Sølvg.

Kronprincessestr.

Adelg.

Aboulevard

Nørre Søg.

Nansensg.

Frederiksborgg.

Åbenrå

Rosenørns A.

Gyldenløvesg.

Nørre Farimagsg.

Ørsteds
Parken

Nørreport
Station

Fiolstr.

Nørreg.

Krystalg.

Købmagerg.

Lande-
maerket

Pilestr.

Vognmagerg.

Gammelmønt.

Gothersg.

Ny Østerg.

Jørgens Sø

Vester Søg.

Kampmannsg.

Nørre Voldg.

DOWNTOWN

Kr.Berniko

Østerg.

Kr.Bernikg

Bremerhol

Skt.

Svineryggen

Nyropsg.

Vester Farimagsg.

Axeltorv.

H.C. Andersen Blvd.

Teglgaards
Str.

Vester
Voldg.

Vor Frue
Kirken

Larsbjørns
Str.

Gammel-
torv

Nyg.

Vimmelsk.

Amagertorv

Østergade

Læderstr.

Gammel Strand

Kompagnistr.

Vindelbr

Christiansbo
Slotsplads

Holm

Vodrolfsv.

Hammrichsg.

Frederiksbergg.

Kattesundet

Farverg.

Rådhus
Pl.

Rådhusstr.

Tøjhusg.

Frederiksholms
Kanal

Gammel Kongev.

TO ZOOLOGISKE
HAVE

Vesterport

Vesterbrog.

Vesterbrog.

Rådhus

Tivoli

Bernstorffsg.

Central
Railway
Station
(Hovedbanegården)

Dantes
Plads

Vester Voldg.

H.C. Andersen Blvd.

Christians Brygge

Langebro

Lar

VESTERBRO

Istedg.

Tietgensg.

Niels Brocks G.

Hambrosg.

TO ASSISTENS KIERKEGÅRD

① ② ③ ⑥ ⑦ ⑧ ⑨ ⑩ 🛈

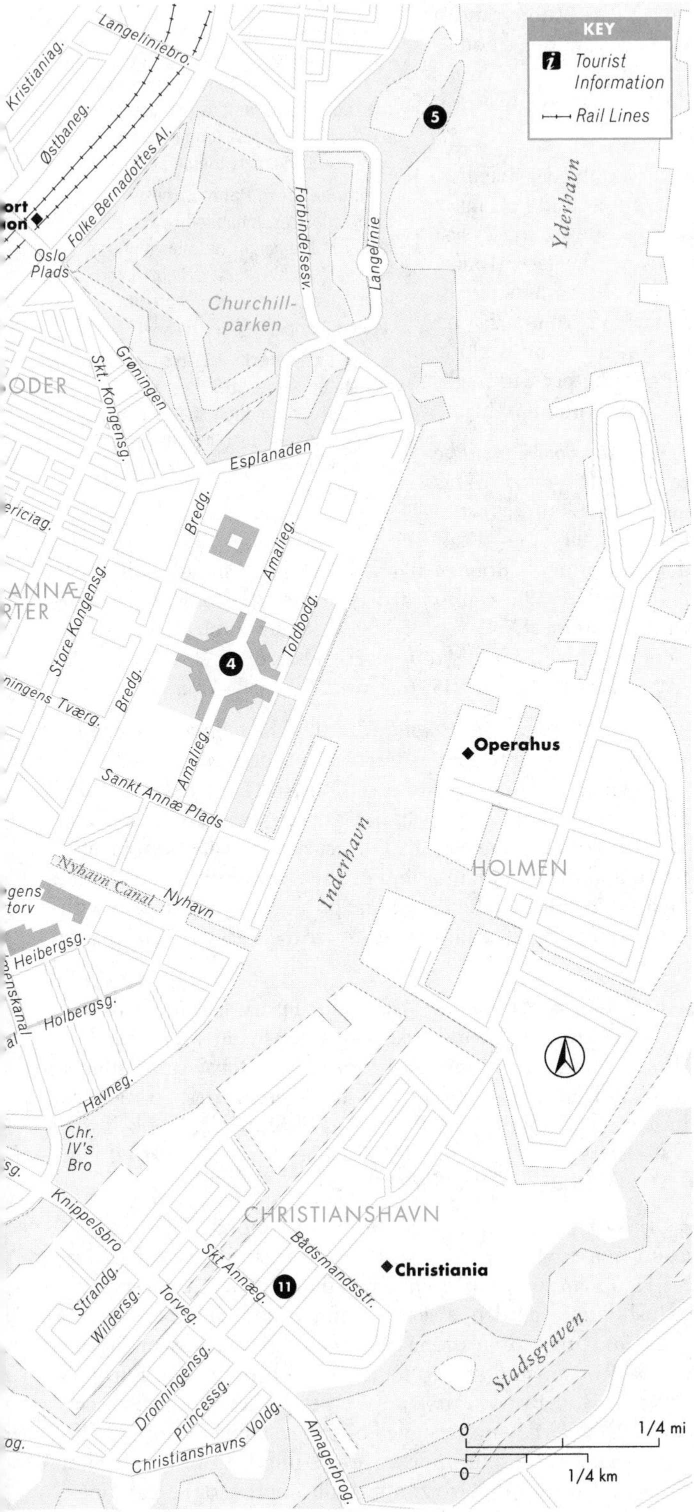

KEY

🛈 *Tourist Information*

⊢—⊣ *Rail Lines*

7

Langeliniebro.

Kristianiag.

Østbaneg.

Folke Bernadottes Al.

ort
on ◆

Oslo
Plads

Forbindelsesv.

Langelinie

Yderhavn

❺

Churchill-
parken

ODER

Grøningen

Skt. Kongensg.

Esplanaden

ericiag.

Bredg.

Amalieg.

ANNÆ
RTER

Store Kongensg.

Toldbodg.

ningens Tværg.

Bredg.

❹

Amalieg.

Sankt Annæ Plads

Operahus ◆

gens
torv

Nyhavn Canal

Nyhavn

Inderhavn

HOLMEN

Heibergsg.

Holbergsg.

al

Havneg.

Chr.
IV's
Bro

CHRISTIANSHAVN

Knippelsbro

Skt Annæg.

Bådsmandsstr.

◆ **Christiania**

Strandg.

Wildersg.

Torveg.

⓫

Dronningensg.

Princessg.

Christianshavns Voldg.

Amagerbrog.

Stadsgraven

0   1/4 mi

0   1/4 km

it. The resulting dark, subterranean maze contains fascinating models and architectural relics. The ruins are open October through April, daily 10–4.

⑪ **Christianshavn.** Cobbled avenues, antique street lamps, and Left Bank charm make up one of the oldest neighborhoods in the city. Today, the area harbors restaurants, cafés, and shops, and its ramparts are edged with green areas and walking paths, making it the perfect neighborhood for an afternoon amble.

⑦ **Den Hirschsprungske Samling** *(The Hirschsprung Collection).* This museum showcases paintings from the country's Golden Age—Denmark's mid-19th-century school of naturalism—as well as a collection of paintings by the late-19th-century artists of the Skagen School. Their luminous works capture the play of light and water so characteristic of the Danish countryside. ⊠*Stockholmsg. 20, Østerbro* ☎*35/42–03–36* ⊕*www.hirschsprung.dk* ⊠*DKr 35, free Wed.* ☉*Wed.–Mon. 11–4.*

⑤ *Den Lille Havfrue (The Little Mermaid).* On the Langelinie promenade, this 1913 statue commemorates Hans Christian Andersen's lovelorn creation, and is the subject of hundreds of travel posters. Donated to the city by Carl Jacobsen, the son of the founder of Carlsberg Breweries, the innocent waif has also been the subject of some cruel practical jokes, including decapitation and the loss of an arm, but she is currently in one piece. Especially on a sunny Sunday, the Langelinie promenade is thronged with Danes and visitors making their pilgrimage to see the statue. ⊠*Langelinie promenade, Østerbro.*

② **Nationalmuseet** *(National Museum).* An 18th-century royal residence, peaked by massive overhead windows, now hosts what is regarded as one of the best national museums in Europe. The extensive permanent exhibits chronicle Danish cultural history from prehistoric to modern times—including one of the largest collections of Stone Age tools in the world. ⊠*Ny Vesterg. 10, Downtown* ☎*33/13–44–11* ⊕*www.natmus. dk* ⊠*DKr 50, free Wed.* ☉*Tues.–Sun. 10–5.*

⑨ **Ny Carlsberg Glyptotek** *(New Carlsberg Museum).* Among Copenhagen's most important museums, the New Carlsberg Museum was donated in 1888 by Carl Jacobsen, son of the founder of the Carlsberg Brewery. Surrounding its lush indoor garden, a series of nooks and chambers houses works by Degas and other impressionists, plus an extensive assemblage of Egyptian, Greek, Roman, and French sculpture, not to mention Europe's finest collection of Roman portraits and the best collection of Etruscan art outside Italy. A modern wing, designed by the acclaimed Danish architect Henning Larsen, houses an impressive pre-impressionist collection that includes works from the Barbizon school; impressionist paintings,

Fodor's Choice
★

including works by Monet, Alfred Sisley, and Pissarro; and a postimpressionist section, with 50 Gauguin paintings and 12 of his very rare sculptures. ⊠ *Dantes Pl. 7, Vesterbro* ☎ *33/41–81–41* ⊕ *www.glyptoteket.dk* 🎫 *DKr 40, free Wed. and Sun.* ⊗ *Tues.–Sun. 10–4.*

6 **Statens Museum for Kunst** *(National Art Gallery).* Old-master paintings—including works by Rubens, Rembrandt, Titian, El Greco, and Fragonard—as well as a comprehensive array of antique and 20th-century Danish art make up the gallery collection. Also notable is the modern art, which includes pieces by Henri Matisse, Edvard Munch, Henri Laurens, Emil Nolde, and Georges Braque. ⊠ *Sølvg. 48–50, Sankt Annæ Kvarter* ☎ *33/74–84–94* ⊕ *www.smk.dk* 🎫 *DKr 50, free Wed.* ⊗ *Tues. and Thurs.–Sun. 10–5, Wed. 10–8.*

7 ★ **Strøget.** Though it is referred to by one name, the city's pedestrian spine, pronounced *Stroy*-et, is actually a series of five streets: Frederiksberggade, Nygade, Vimmelskaftet, Amagertorv, and Østergade. By mid-morning, particularly on Saturday, it is congested with people, baby strollers, and street performers. Past the swank and trendy—and sometimes flashy and trashy—boutiques of **Frederiksberggade** is the double square of **Gammeltorv** (Old Square) and **Nytorv** (New Square). In addition to shopping, you can enjoy Strøget for strolling, as hundreds do. In summer, the sidewalks have a festive street-fair atmosphere.

8 ☺ **Fodor's** Choice ★ **Tivoli.** Copenhagen's best-known attraction draws an astounding number of visitors: four million people from mid-April to mid-September and from late-November to Christmas. Tivoli is more sophisticated than a mere amusement park: among its attractions are a pantomime theater, an open-air stage, 38 restaurants (some of them very elegant), and frequent concerts. Fantastic flower exhibits color the lush gardens and float on the swan-filled ponds.

The park was established in the 1840s, when Danish architect George Carstensen persuaded a worried King Christian VIII to let him build an amusement park on the edge of the city's fortifications, rationalizing that "when people amuse themselves, they forget politics." On Wednesday and weekend nights, elaborate fireworks are set off, and every day the Tivoli Guard, a youth version of the Queen's Royal Guard, performs. Try to see Tivoli at least once by night, when 100,000 colored lanterns illuminate the Chinese pagoda and the main fountains. ⊠ *Vesterbrog. 3, Vesterbro* ☎ *33/15–10–01* ⊕ *www.tivoli.dk* 🎫 *Grounds DKr 68, ride pass DKr 195* ⊗ *Mid-Apr.–mid-Sept,, Sun.–Wed. 11–11, Thurs. 11* AM*–midnight, Fri. 11* AM*–1* AM*, Sat. 11* AM*–midnight; late Nov.–Dec. 23, Sun.–Wed. 11–9, Fri. and Sat. 11* AM*–10* PM.

OFF THE BEATEN PATH

Museet for Moderne Kunst (Arken). The museum, 20 km (12 mi) southwest of Copenhagen, also known as the Arken, opened in March 1996 to great acclaim, both for its architecture and its collection. The museum's massive sculpture room exhibits both modern Danish and international art, as well as experimental works. Dance, theater, film, and multimedia exhibits are additional attractions. To reach the museum, take the S-train in the direction of either Hundige, Solrød Strand, or Køge to Ishøj Station, then pick up Bus 128 to the museum). ⊠ *Skovvej 100, Ishøj* ☎ *43/54–02–22* ⊕ www.arken.dk 🎫 *DKr 60* ⊗ *Tues.–Sun. 10–5, Wed. 10–9.*

620 < The Baltic

SHOPPING

A showcase for world-famous Danish design and craftsmanship, Copenhagen seems to have been designed with shoppers in mind. The best buys are such luxury items as crystal, porcelain, silver, and furs. Although prices are inflated by a hefty 25% Value-Added Tax (Danes call it MOMS), non-European Union citizens can receive about an 18% refund. For more details and a list of all tax-free shops, ask at the tourist office for a copy of the *Tax-Free Shopping Guide.*

The pedestrian-only **Strøget** and adjacent Købmagergade are *the* shopping streets. The most exclusive shops are at the end of Strøget, around Kongens Nytorv, and on Ny Adelgade, Grønnegade, and Pistolstræde. **Kronprinsensgade** has become the in-vogue fashion strip. **Bredgade,** just off Kongens Nytorv, is lined with elegant antiques and silver shops, and furniture stores. A very popular mall in the city is the gleaming **Fisketorvet Shopping Center,** built in what was Copenhagen's old fish market. It includes 100 shops. It's near the canal, south of the city center, and within walking distance of Dybbølsbro Station.

The **Information Center for Danish Crafts and Design** (⊠*Amagertorv 1, Downtown* ☎*33/12–61–62* ⊕*www.danishcrafts.dk*) provides helpful information on the city's galleries, shops, and workshops specializing in Danish crafts and design, from jewelry to ceramics to wooden toys to furniture. Its Web site has listings and reviews of the city's best crafts shops.

Bodum Hus (⊠*Østerg. 10, on Strøget, Downtown* ☎*33/36–40–80* ⊕*www.bodum.com*) shows off a wide variety of reasonably priced Danish-designed functional, and especially kitchen-oriented, accoutrements.

Birger Christensen (⊠*Østerg. 38, Downtown* ☎*33/11–55–55*), is purveyor to the royal family and Copenhagen's finest furrier. Denmark, the world's biggest producer of ranched minks, is the place to go for quality furs.

Georg Jensen (⊠*Amagertorv 4, Downtown* ☎*33/11–40–80* ⊕*www. georgjensen.com*) is one of the most-recognized names in international silver, and his elegant, austere shop is aglitter with sterling.

Illums Bolighus (⊠*Amagertorv 10, Downtown* ☎*33/14–19–41*) is part gallery, part department store, showing off cutting-edge Danish and international design—art glass, porcelain, silverware, carpets, and loads of grown-up toys.

Royal Copenhagen (⊠*Amagertorv 6, Downtown* ☎*33/13–71–81* ⊕*www. royalcopenhagen.com*) sells firsts and seconds of its famous porcelain ware.

WHERE TO EAT

$$ ✕**Ida Davidsen.** Five generations old, this world-renowned lunch spot is
FodorsChoice synonymous with smørrebrød. Creative sandwiches include the H. C.
★ Andersen, with liver pâté, bacon, and tomatoes. The terrific smoked duck is smoked by the family, and served alongside a horseradish-spiked cabbage salad. ⊠*Store Kongensg. 70, Sankt Annæ Kvarter* ☎*33/91–36–55* ⊕*www.idadavidsen.dk* ⚁*Reservations essential* ⊟*AE, DC, MC, V* ☺*Closed weekends and Dec. 23– Jan 16. No dinner.*

¢–$$ ✕**Pasta Basta**. This bright, casual eatery just off the Strøget is always crammed with happy diners. Pasta Basta has all the ingredients for its well-deserved success: an all-you-can-eat fresh pasta and salad bar for a refreshingly low price. ⊠ *Valkendorfsg. 22, Downtown* ☎*33/11–21–31* ▱*DC, MC, V.*

GDAŃSK, POLAND

Gdańsk is special to Poles—and to Scandinavians and Germans, who visit the region in great numbers. From 1308 to 1945, Gdańsk was an independent city-state called Danzig. In 1997 Gdańsk celebrated its 1,000th year as a Baltic city. It remains well-known as the cradle of the anti-Communist workers' movement that came to be known as *Solidarność* (Solidarity)—after the collapse of the Soviet bloc in 1989, Solidarity leader Lech Wałęsa became president of Poland in the nation's first free elections since World War II. Although Gdańsk was almost entirely destroyed during World War II, the streets of its Główne Miasto (Main Town) have been lovingly restored and still retain their historical and cultural richness. The Stare Miasto (Old Town) contains several churches and the beautifully reconstructed Ratusz Główny (Old Town Hall). At the north end of the Old Town sit the shipyards which captivated world attention during the 1970s and '80s, but have since settled back into their daily grind.

ESSENTIALS

CURRENCY The Złoty (Zł 2.81 to US$1; Zł 3.84 to €1); exchange rates were accurate at this writing but are subject to change. U.S. currency is not accepted, and credit cards are not universally accepted, especially in smaller shops and eateries. ATMs are widespread.

HOURS Shopping hours are generally Monday through Friday from 6AM until 6 or 7PM, with shorter hours on the weekend. Museums are open Tuesday through Sunday from 10AM until 4PM.

INTERNET **Internet Café** ⊠*ul. Karmelicka 1* ☎*058/320–9230.*

TELEPHONES Most tri- and quad-band GSM mobile phones work in Poland, where the mobile system is not 3G-compatible. Hand sets are dual-band. Most public phones operate with phone cards, which can be bought at newsagents. Public phones support international calls. Major telecom companies are Polkmotel and Centertel.

COMING ASHORE

Vessels dock at two sites in the outer harbor of the city: Oliwskie Quay on the east bank and Westerplatte Quay on the west bank. Both lie 6 km (3.7 mi) from the downtown center. Facilities at Oliwskie Quay, the bigger of the two, include shops and taxi kiosks. It is 1 km (½ mi) to the city train station for the journey into downtown Gdańsk, or 300m to a tram stop (routes 2, 5, 10, 14, and 15 head into the city). Westerplatte Quay has almost no facilities, with only restrooms and a taxi kiosk. Bus route 106 travels into the city. The downtown core can be easily explored on foot.

Car rentals are not useful for exploring the city but would allow you to visit the surrounding Pomeranian region. An economy manual vehicle is approximately €63 per day. Companies will pick you up at the port but may add an extra charge. Taxis or limousines can be hired for touring.

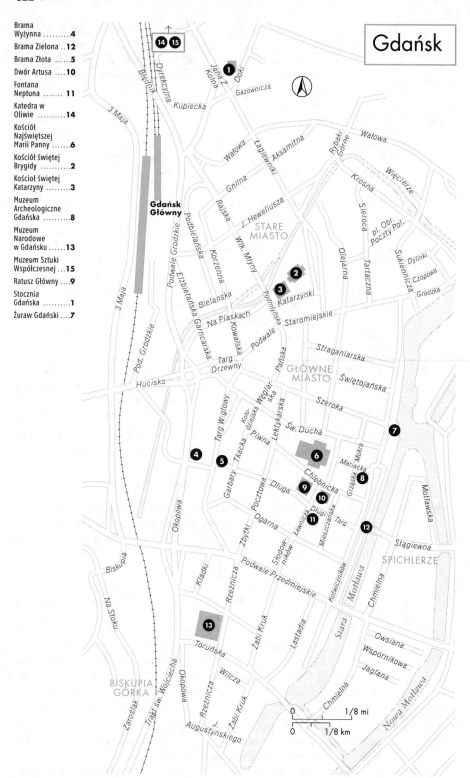

Gdańsk

Taxi rates are Zł 5 at pick up then Zł 3 per km.

Gdańsk forms part of the so-called Trójmiasto (Tri-City), together with the historic resort of Sopot, and the much newer town and port of Gdynia, which was created in the 1920s and '30s. They are conveniently joined together by a commuter train: the SKM (Szybka Kolej Miejska, or "Fast City Rail"). The Oliwa District of Gdańsk is best reached by train—get off at Gdańsk-Oliwa and walk west up ulica Piastowska to ulica Opacka—or take Tram 2 or 6 toward Sopot. Ticket prices on trams and buses are currently Zł 1.40 for a 10-minute period (short journey), Zł 2.80 for a 30-minute period, and Zł 4.20 for a 60-minute period. Drivers on buses only sell packs of three tickets.

> ## GDAŃSK BEST BETS
>
> **Stocznia Gdańska.** This shipyard was the seat of the social movement that began the downfall of Communism in Eastern Europe, so the site resonates with living history.
>
> **Stroll the lanes and alleyways of the old town.** This district is a triumph of Renaissance architecture and a riot of ornate gables, cornices and lintels.
>
> **Kościół Najświętszej Marii Panny.** This is the largest brick-built church in the world and the largest church of any kind in Poland.

EXPLORING GDAŃSK

Numbers in the margin correspond to points of interest on the Gdańsk map.

④ ★ **Brama Wyżynna** *(High Gate)*. The historic entrance to the old town of Gdańsk is marked by this magnificent Renaissance gate, which marks the beginning of the so-called "Royal Route," along which the king passed through the city on his annual visit. The gate is adorned with the flags of Poland, Gdańsk, and the Prussian kingdom. Its builder, Hans Kramer of Dresden, erected it as a link in the chain of modern fortifications put up to frame the western city borders between 1574 and 1576. The brick gate was renovated and decorated in 1588 by Flemish sculptor Willem van den Blocke, whose decorations you can still see today. ⊠ *Off Wały Jagiellońskie, at ul. Długa, Stare Miasto.*

⑫ **Brama Zielona** *(Green Gate)*. The eastern entrance to the medieval city of Gdańsk is at the water's edge. Construction, supervised by Regnier of Amsterdam and Hans Kramer of Dresden, lasted from 1568 to 1571. This 16th-century gate also doubled as a royal residence. Unfortunately, the name no longer fits: the gate is now painted brown. ⊠ *At eastern end of Długi Targ, Stare Miasto.*

⑤ **Brama Złota** *(Golden Gate)*. Just behind the Brama Wyżynna, the Golden Gate was the second through which the king passed on the Royal Route. This structure dates from 1614 and combines characteristics of both the Italian and Dutch Renaissance. It was built to the design of Abraham van den Blocke. The stone figures (by Pieter Ringering) along the parapet (on the Wały Jagiellońskie facade) represent allegories of the city's citizen's virtues: caution, justice, piety, and concord. On the Długa street facade, there are allegories of peace, freedom, wealth, and fame—the pursuits of

Gdańsk city over the centuries. Next to the Golden Gate squats the house of **St George's Brotherhood** that was erected by Glotau between 1487 and 1494 in the late-Gothic style. ⊠ *Off Wały Jagiellońskie, at western end of ul. Długa, Stare Miasto.*

⑩ **Dwór Artusa** *(Artus Mansion).* Behind the Fontanna Neptuna on Długi Targ, one of the more significant of the grand houses was constructed over a period from the 15th through the 17th centuries and is now a museum. The mansion was named for mythical English King Arthur, who otherwise has no affiliation with the place. This and the other stately mansions on the Długi Targ are reminders of the traders and aristocrats who once resided in this posh district. The court's elegant interior houses a huge, 40-foot-high Renaissance tiled stove, possibly the world's largest, a mid-16th-century masterpiece by George Stelzener. The mansion's collection also includes Renaissance furnishings, paintings, and holy figures. The building was the meeting place of the Gdańsk city nobles. ⊠ *Długi Targ 43, Stare Miasto* ☎ *058/346–33–58* ⊠ *Zł 5* ☉ *Tues.–Sat. 10–4, Sun. 11–4.*

⑪ **Fontanna Neptuna** *(Neptune Fountain).* One of the city's most distinctive landmarks is the elaborately gilded, 17th-century fountain at the western end of Długi Targ. The fountain itself is perhaps the best-known symbol of Gdańsk, emphasizing its bond with the sea. It was sculpted by Peter Husen and Johann Rogge. The general conceptual design was developed by Abraham van den Blocke. The magnificent surrounding fencing was added in 1634. Between 1757 and 1761 Johann Karl Stender remade the fountain chalice and plinth in the rococo style and added a whole array of sea creatures. ⊠ *ul. Długa, east of Wały Jagiellońskie, Stare Miasto.*

⑭ **Katedra w Oliwie** *(Oliwa Cathedral).* The district of Oliwa, northwest of the old town, is worth visiting if only for its magnificent cathedral complex. Originally part of a Cistercian monastery, the church was erected during the 13th century. Like most other structures in Poland, it has been rebuilt many times, resulting in a hodgepodge of styles from Gothic to Renaissance to rococo. The cathedral houses one of the most impressive rococo organs you're ever likely to hear—and see. It has more than 6,000 pipes, and when a special mechanism is activated, wooden angels ring bells and a wooden star climbs up a wooden sky. Demonstrations of the organ and a brief narrated church history are given almost hourly on weekdays in summer (May through September), less frequently on weekends and the rest of the year. ⊠ *ul. Cystersów 10, Oliwa.*

⑥ **Kościół Najświętszej Marii Panny** *(St. Mary's Church).* The largest brick church in the world—and the largest church of any kind in Poland—St. Mary's is on the north side of ulica Piwna. The sanctuary can accommodate 25,000 people. This enormous 14th-century church underwent major restoration after World War II. Although it originally held 22 altars, 15 of them have been relocated to museums in Gdańsk and Warsaw. The highlight of a visit is the climb up the hundreds of steps to the top of the church tower. The church also contains a 500-year-old, 25-foot-high astronomical clock that has only recently been restored to working order after years of neglect. It keeps track of solar and lunar progressions, and it displays the signs of the zodiac, something of an anomaly in a Catholic church. ⊠ *Podkramarska 5, at ul. Piwna, Stare Miasto* ⊠ *Tower Zł 3* ☉ *Daily 9–5.*

Fodor's Choice ★

Fodor's Choice ★

Fodor's Choice ★

2 **Kosciół swietej Brygidy** *(St. Brigitte's Church)*. This church, a few blocks north of the shipyards, is a prime example of the fundamental link in the Polish consciousness between Catholicism and political dissent. After the Communist government declared martial law in 1981 in an attempt to force Solidarity to disband, the union's members began meeting here secretly during celebrations of mass. A statue of Pope John Paul II can be seen in front of the church. ✉*ul. Profesorska 17, near Ratusz Główny (Old Town Hall), Stare Miasto.*

3 **Kościół świętej Katarzyny** *(St. Catherine's Church)*. The former parish church in Gdańsk's Old Town is supposedly the oldest church in the city: its construction was begun in the 1220s; the tower was constructed in the 1480s; the carillon of 37 bells was added in 1634. The 17th-century astronomer Jan Hevelius is buried in the presbytery of the church, below which lies what's left of the town's oldest Christian cemetery (which dates from the 10th century). ✉ *Wielki Młyn, Stare Miasto* ☎*058/301–15–95.*

8 **Muzeum Archeologiczne Gdańska** *(Gdańsk Archaeological Museum)*. Gdańsk's small archaeological museum displays Slavic tribal artifacts, including jewelry, pottery, boats, and bones. ✉*ul. Mariacka 25–26, Stare Miasto* ☎*058/301–50–31* 💰*Zł 3* ☉*Tues.–Sun. 10–4.*

13 **Muzeum Narodowe w Gdańsku** *(National Museum in Gdańsk)*. The former Franciscan monastery, just south of the old walls of the Main Town, exhibits 14th- to 20th-century art and ethnographic collections. Hans Memling's triptych *Last Judgment* is the jewel of the collection. ✉*ul. Toruńska 1, off ul. Okopowa, Stare Miasto* ☎*058/301–70–61* 💰*Zł 5, free Sun.* ☉*Daily 10–3.*

15 **Muzeum Sztuki Współczesnej** *(Modern Art Museum)*. Two museums can be found in a beautiful park surrounding the cathedral in Oliwa in the former Abbots' Palace. The Modern Art Museum has a large collection of works by Polish artists from the inter-war period onward. Connected to the Modern Art Museum, administratively and physically, is the **Muzeum Etnograficzne** *(Ethnographic Museum)* (✉*ul. Opacka 12, Oliwa* ☎*058/552–12–71*), in the former Abbots' Granary. The museum display has fine examples of local crafts from the 19th century and also has an interesting display of amber folk jewelry. It has a separate entrance from the Modern Art Museum and a separate admission fee (Zł 9), but the hours and other contact information are the same for both museums. ✉*Pałac Opatów, Cystersów 15A, Oliwa* ☎*058/552–12–71* ⊕*www.muzeum.narodowe. gda.pl* 💰*Zł 8* ☉*Tues.–Sun. 9–4.*

9 **Ratusz Główny** *(Old Town Hall)*. Although Gdańsk's original town hall was completely destroyed during World War II, a careful reconstruction of the exterior and interior now re-creates the glory of Gdańsk's medieval past. Inside, the **Muzeum Historii Miasta Gdańska** *(Gdańsk Historical Museum)* covers more than five centuries of Gdańsk's history in exhibits that include paintings, sculptures, and weapons. ✉*ul. Długa 47, Stare Miasto* ☎*058/301–48–72* 🏛*Museum Zł 4* ☉*Tues.–Sun. 11–4.*

1 **Stocznia Gdanńska** *(Gdańsk Shipyard)*. Three huge and somber crosses perpetually draped with flowers stand outside the gates of the former Lenin Shipyards, which gave birth to the Solidarity movement. The crosses out-

626 <   The Baltic

side the entrance to the shipyards are the **Pomnik Poległych Stocznio-wców** *(Monument to Fallen Shipyard Workers)*. There are also plaques that commemorate the struggle, and a quotation by Pope John Paul II inspired by his visit to the monument in 1987: "The Grace of God could not have created anything better; in this place, silence is a scream." Formerly inside the shipyard gates (and now a bit further away), the **Roads to Freedom** exhibition once consisted of a number of symbolic gates, which until recently led to a multimedia exhibition in the historic BPH room on Plac Solidarności, where the Gdańsk Agreements were signed. The BPH room, which has been renovated, reopened in 2007 in a new location at Wały Piastowskie Street (a short walk from the shipyard itself, half way between the shipyards and the Main Railway Station). The exhibition traces the beginning and development of the Solidarity movement, taking you on a virtual tour through 1980s Poland. ⊠ *Wały Piastowskie 24, Stare Miasto* ☎*058/308–47–12* ⊕*www.fcs.org.pl* ⊠*Zł 6* ☾*Oct.–Apr., Tues.–Sun. 10–4; May–Sept., Tues.–Sun. 10–5.*

❼ Żuraw Gdański *(Harbor Crane)*. Built in 1444, Gdańsk's crane was medieval Europe's largest—and today it's also Europe's oldest. It used to play the double role of a port crane and city gate. The structure was given its present shape between 1442 and 1444. Today, it houses the **Muzeum Morskie** *(Maritime Museum)*, with a collection of models of the ships constructed in the Gdańsk Shipyards since 1945. At the museum ticket office, inquire about tickets for tours of the *Sołdek,* a World War II battleship moored nearby on the canal. ⊠*Ołowianka 9–13, Stare Miasto* ☎*058/301–86–11* ⊠*Zł 8* ☾*Oct.–June, Tues.–Sun. 10–4; July–Sept., daily 10–4.*

SHOPPING

Gdańsk's main souvenir product is amber, sold carved or made into jewelry.

Wielki Młyn *(Great Mill)*. On a small island in the canal just north of St. Catherine's Church, the largest mill in medieval Europe operated from the time of its completion in 1350 until 1945. Today, it's filled with shops and boutiques, which are open weekdays from 11 to 7, Saturday from 11 to 3. ⊠*Intersection of Podmłyńska and Na Piaskach, Stare Miasto.*

WHERE TO EAT

¢–$ ✕**Czerwone Drzwi.** Behind the red door (that's what "Czerwone Drzwi" means in Polish) is a very elegant café-cum-restaurant, a favorite with Gdańsk's fashionable people (with well-stocked wallets). The menu changes with the seasons. ⊠*ul. Piwna 52/53, Stare Miasto* ☎*058/301–57–64* ⊟*AE, DC, MC, V.*

¢–$ ✕**Barracuda.** Although the interior may be rather simple, most people agree
★ that this is one of the best restaurants in Gdańsk. The menu offers a tempting array of seafood dishes, which are the specialties of the house. No matter which you choose, you won't go wrong. ⊠*ul. Piwna 61/63, Stare Miasto* ☎*058/301–49–62* ⊟*AE, DC, MC, V.*

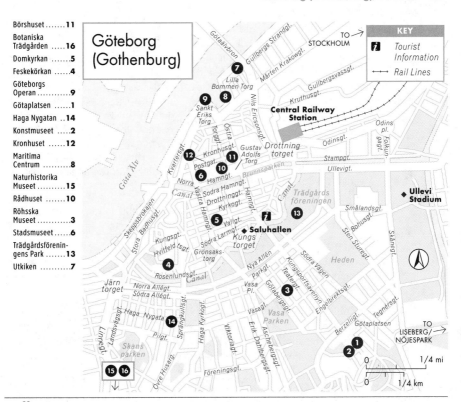

GÖTEBORG (GOTHENBURG), SWEDEN

Historically, Göteborg owes its existence to the sea. Tenth-century Vikings sailed from its shores, and a settlement was founded here in the 11th century. Not until 1621, however, did King Gustavus Adolphus grant Göteborg a charter to establish a free-trade port. Home to Scandinavia's largest port and largest corporation (Volvo Cars), the city is a thriving commercial success. You'll find it's easier to ask what Göteborg hasn't got to offer rather than what it has. Culturally it boasts a fine opera house and theater, one of the country's best art museums, and a fantastic applied-arts museum. There's plenty of history to soak up, from the ancient port that gave the city its start to the 19th-century factory buildings and workers' houses that helped put it on the commercial map. And don't forget the food—from 1995 to 2005, 8 of the 10 "Swedish Chef of the Year" winners were cooking in Göteborg.

ESSENTIALS

CURRENCY The Swedish krona (SKr 6.87 to US$1; SKr 9.37 to €1); exchange rates were accurate at this writing but are subject to change. U.S. currency is not generally accepted in Europe. ATMs are common and credit cards are widely accepted.

HOURS General shopping hours are weekdays from 10 to 6, Saturday from 10 to 5, and Sunday from noon until 3. Museums open at 10 or 11 in the morning, closing at 5 or 6 in the evenings, with most open on Sunday.

INTERNET   **Palatset** (✉ *Ekelundsgatan 9–11* ☎ *031/132480*) stays open late into the night (it's a bar, restaurant, and billiards hall) but doesn't open until 2 PM during the week and noon on weekends.

TELEPHONES   Most tri- or quad-band GSM phones work in Sweden, though handsets are single-band, where the system is 3G-compatible. Public phones in Sweden take phone cards or credit cards. Phone cards can be bought at telecom shops, newsstands, and tobacconists. Public phones support international calls. Main providers include Telia, Vodafone and T-Mobile.

COMING ASHORE

Cruise ships dock in the inner harbor of the vast port. There are no passenger facilities at the docking site. It's a 1-km (½-mi) walk to the downtown area but only a couple of minutes by taxi.

The public transport network in the city is excellent, but Göteborg is a small, neat package of a city that begs to be explored by foot. A single ticket for public transportation costs SKr 20 (valid for 90 minutes on all services). A day card costs SKr 50. Taxis cost SKr 31 plus SKr 10.30 per km.

EXPLORING GÖTEBORG

Numbers in the margin correspond to points of interest on the Göteborg map.

⓫ **Börshuset** *(Stock Exchange).* Completed in 1849, the former stock exchange building houses city administrative offices. The building is not open to the public. ✉ *Gustav Adolfs torg 5, Nordstan.*

⓰ **Botaniska Trädgården** *(Botanical Gardens).* With 1,200 plant species, this is Sweden's largest botanical garden. Herb gardens, bamboo groves, a Japanese valley, forest plants, and tropical greenhouses are all on display. ✉ *Carl Skottsbergsg. 22A, Slottsskogen* ☎ *031/7411101* 💲 *Park free, greenhouses SKr 20* 🕐 *Park daily 9–sunset; greenhouses May–Aug., daily 10–5; Sept.–Apr., daily 10–4.*

❺ **Domkyrkan** *(Göteborg Cathedral).* The cathedral, in neoclassic yellow brick, dates from 1802, the two previous cathedrals on this spot having been destroyed by fire. Though disappointingly plain on the outside, the interior is impressive. Two glassed-in verandas originally used for the bishop's private conversations run the length of each side of the cathedral. The altar is impressively ornate and gilt. Next to it stands a post-Resurrection cross, the figure of Jesus notably absent, his gilded burial garments strewn on the floor. ✉ *Kyrkog. 28, Centrum* ☎ *031/7316130* 💲 *Free* 🕐 *Weekdays 8–6, Sat. 9–4, Sun. 10–3.*

❹ **Feskekörkan** *(Fish Church).* Built in 1872, this fish market gets its nickname from its Gothic-style architectural details. The beautiful arched and vaulted wooden ceiling covers rows and rows of stalls, each offering silvery, slippery goods to the shoppers who congregate in this vast hall. ⊠ *Fisktorget, Rosenlundsg, Centrum.*

❾ Göteborgs Operan *(Göteborg's Opera).* A statement in steel and glass, the opera house opened in 1994, immediately dominating this section of the waterfront with its bold lines and shape. Set against a backdrop of the old docks, it makes for a striking image. ⊠ *Christina Nilssonsg., Nordstan* ☎ *031/108000 for bookings.*

❶ Götaplatsen *(Göta Place).* This square was built in 1923 in celebration of the city's 300th anniversary. In the center is the Swedish-American sculptor Carl Milles's fountain statue of Poseidon choking a codfish. Behind the statue stands the Konstmuseet (Art Museum), flanked by the **Konserthuset** *(Concert Hall)* and the **Stadsteatern** *(Municipal Theater)* , contemporary buildings in which the city celebrates its important contribution to Swedish cultural life.

Fodor's Choice
★

⓮ Haga Nygatan. The redbrick buildings that line this street were originally poorhouses donated by the Dickson family, the city's British industrialist forefathers. ROBERT DICKSON can still be seen carved into the facades of these buildings. Like most buildings in Haga, the buildings' ground floors were made of stone in order to prevent the spread of fire (the upper floors are wood). ⊠ *Haga Nyg. Haga.*

❷ Konstmuseet *(Art Museum).* This impressive collection of the works of leading Scandinavian painters and sculptors encapsulates some of the moody introspection of the artistic community in this part of the world. The museum's Hasselblad Center devotes itself to showing progress in the art of photography. The Konstmuseet's holdings include works by Swedes such as Carl Milles, Johan Tobias Sergel, Impressionist Anders Zorn, Victorian idealist Carl Larsson, and Prince Eugen. The 19th- and 20th-century French art collection is the best in Sweden, and there's also a small collection of old masters. ⊠ *Götaplatsen/Avenyn* ☎ *031/612980* ⊕ *www. konstmuseum.goteborg.se* ⊠ *SKr 40* ☉ *Tues. and Thurs. 11–6, Wed. 11– 9, Fri.–Sun. 11–5.*

⓬ Kronhuset *(Crown House).* Göteborg's oldest secular building, dating from 1643, was originally the city's armory. In 1660 Sweden's Parliament met here to decide who would succeed King Karl X Gustav, who died suddenly while visiting the city. The building is now used for classical concerts and the City Museum's annual Christmas market. ⊠ *Postg. 68, Nordstan* ☎ *031/710832.*

❽ Maritima Centrum *(Marine Center).* In the world's largest floating maritime museum you'll find modern naval vessels, including submarines, a lightship, cargo vessel, and various tugboats, providing insight into Göteborg's historic role as a major port. The main attraction is a huge naval destroyer, complete with a medical room in which a leg amputation operation is graphically re-created with mannequins. ⊠ *Packhuskajen 8, Nordstan* ☎ *031/105950* ⊠ *SKr 60* ☉ *May–July, daily 10–6; Aug.–Apr., daily 10–4.*

⓯ Naturhistorika Museet. Although the Natural History Museum has a collection containing more than 10 million preserved animals, you may be disappointed to discover that the majority are tiny insects that sit unnoticed

7

in rows of drawers. It's worth a visit to see the world's only stuffed blue whale, harpooned in 1865. ✉*Slottskogen and Linnéplatsen Slottsskogen* ☎*031/7752400* ⊕*www.gnm.se* ✈*SKr 60* ⊙*Sept.–Apr., Tues.–Fri. 9–4, weekends 11–5; May–Aug., daily 11–5.*

⑩ Rådhuset. Though the town hall dates from 1672, when it was designed by Nicodemus Tessin the Elder, its controversial modern extension by Swedish architect Gunnar Asplund is from 1937. The building therefore offers two architectural extremes. One section has the original grand chandeliers and trompe-l'oeil ceilings; the other has glass elevators, mussel-shape drinking fountains, and vast expanses of laminated aspen wood. Together they make a fascinating mix. ✉*Gustav Adolfs torg 1, Nordstan.*

❸ Röhsska Museet *(Museum of Arts and Crafts).* This museum's fine collection of furniture, books, manuscripts, tapestries, and pottery are on view. Artifacts date back as far as 1,000 years, but it's the 20th-century gallery, with its collection of many familiar household objects, that seems to provide the most enjoyment. ✉*Vasag. 37–39, Vasastan* ☎*031/613850* ⊕*www.designmuseum.se* ✈*SKr 40* ⊙*Tues. noon–8, Wed.–Fri. noon–5, weekends 10–5.*

❻ Stadsmuseet *(City Museum).* Once the warehouse and auction rooms of the Swedish East India Company, a major trading firm founded in 1731, this palatial structure dates from 1750. Today it contains exhibits on the Swedish west coast, with a focus on Göteborg's nautical and trading past. One interesting exhibit deals with the East India Company and its ship called the *Göteborg.* On its 1745 return from China, she sank just outside the city, while crowds there to greet the returning ship watched from shore in horror. ✉*Norra Hamng. 12, Centrum* ☎*031/612770* ✈*SKr 40* ⊙*Daily 10–5.*

⑬ Trädgårdsföreningens Park *(Horticultural Society Park).* Beautiful open green spaces, manicured gardens, and tree-lined paths are the perfect place to escape for some peace and rest. Rose fanciers can head for the magnificent rose garden with 5,000 roses of 2,500 varieties. Also worth a visit is the Palm House, whose late-19th-century design echoes that of London's Crystal Palace. ✉*Just off Kungsportsavenyn, Centrum* ☎*031/3655858* ✈*Park SKr 15, Palm House SKr 20* ⊙*Park May–Aug., daily 7 AM–9 PM; Sept.–Apr., daily 7 AM–7:30 PM. Palm House May–Aug., daily 10–5; Sept.–Apr., daily 10–4.*

Fodor'sChoice
★

❼ Utkiken *(Lookout Tower).* This red-and-white-stripe skyscraper towers 282 feet above the waterfront, offering an unparalleled view of the city, its green spaces, and the contrasting industrial landscape of the port—so don't miss out on a visit to the viewing platform at the top. ✉*Lilla Bommen 1, Lilla Bommen* ☎*031/3655858.*

FARTHER AFIELD

Liseberg Nöjespark. Göteborg proudly claims Scandinavia's largest amusement park. Liseberg is one of the best-run, most efficient parks in the world. In addition to a wide selection of carnival rides, nostalgists will love the huge wooden roller coaster here. It's the largest in Scandinavia and, just to add to the thrill, it creaks throughout the ride. ✉*Örgrytev. 5, Liseberg* ☎*031/400100* ⊕*www.liseberg.se* ✈*SKr 60* ⊙*Mid-Apr.–mid-May,*

Sat. noon–9, Sun. noon–8; mid-May–July, weekdays 3–10, Sat. noon–11, Sun. noon–8; Aug., Mon.–Thurs. and Sun. 11–11, Fri. and Sat. 11 AM–midnight; Sept., Thurs. and Fri. 4 PM–10 PM, Sat. noon–10, Sun. noon–8.

Världskulturmuseet. Next door to the amusement park Liseberg, World Culture Museum, Göteborg's newest museum, addresses the many issues facing various global cultures. By using art and photography exhibitions and by running workshops, discussion forums, and lectures, the museum manages to alert the conscience and keep visitors interested at the same time. ✉ *Söderv. 54, Liseberg* ☎ *031/632730* ⊕ *www.varldskulturmuseet. se* 🎟 *Free* ⊙ *Tues. noon–5, Wed.–Fri. noon–9, weekends noon–5.*

Volvo Museum. In Arendal, 8 km (5 mi) west of the city center, the Volvo Museum pays homage to the car company that in one way or another helps support 25% of Göteborg's population. Not surprisingly, exhibits include most of Volvo's cars over the years as well as some prototypes, the first electric car, and an early jet engine, the first one used by the Swedish Air Force. A 20-minute film helps to put the whole history into perspective at this well-put-together museum. ✉ *Avd. 1670 ARU (off Rd. 155 toward Öckerö/Torslanda), Arendal* ☎ *031/664814* ⊕ *www.volvo.com* 🎟 *SKr 40* ⊙ *June–Aug., Tues.–Fri. 10–5, weekends 11–4; Sept.–May, Tues.–Fri. noon–5, weekends 11–4.*

SHOPPING

The city has several shopping malls, including **Nordstan**, the largest mall in Sweden. Other shopping areas are Kungsgaten/Fredsgaten, Kungsportsavenyn (known as Avenyn), and Arkaden. The district including Vallgatan and Larmgatan is up-and-coming for young designers and couturiers. The clean lines of Scandinavian design have long been admired, and the trend is also expanded into clothing, seen most inexpensively in stores like H&M. Look for home accessory items for your most portable 'designed in Sweden' souvenirs.

Antikhallarna (*Antiques Halls* ✉ *Västra Hamng. 6, Centrum* ☎ *031/7741525*) has one of Scandinavia's largest antiques selections.

Excellent examples of local arts and crafts can be bought at **Bohusslöjden** (✉ *Kungsportsavenyn 25, Centrum* ☎ *031/160072*).

If you are looking to buy Swedish arts, crafts and glassware, visit the various shops in **Kronhusbodarna** (✉ *Kronhusg. 1D, Nordstan* ☎ *031/7110832*). They have been selling traditional handcrafted quality goods, including silver and gold jewelry, watches, and handblown glass, since the 18th century.

★ If you love the cool, sleek Scandinavian interiors you see on your travels, head to **Room** (✉ *Magasing. 3, Centrum* ☎ *031/606630*), a shop that is tastefully stuffed with furniture, fabrics, soft furnishings, ornaments, and kitchen gadgets—all of it divine.

WHERE TO EAT

$-$$$ ✗ **Cyrano.** A little piece of southern France in Sweden, this superb, authenti-
Fodor's Choice cally Provençal bistro is an absolute must. Inside, the tables are crammed
★ close together, art hangs on the walls, and French touches extend through-
out. Cyrano continues to draw in the trendier citizens of Göteborg.
⊠*Prinsg. 7, Linnéstaden* ☎*031/143110* ▭*AE, DC, MC, V.*

¢-$$ ✗ **Joe Farelli's.** Dimly lighted, with booths along the walls and black-and-
white photographs of the Big Apple, Joe Farelli's is as close to a New York
restaurant as you'll get in Göteborg. It's a good place to stop for a dish
of pasta or a burger between sights. ⊠*Kungsportsavenyn 12, Centrum*
☎*031/105826* ▭*AE, MC, V.*

HAMBURG, GERMANY

Water—in the form of the Alster Lakes and the Elbe River—is Hamburg's
defining feature and the key to the city's success. A harbor city with an
international past, Hamburg is the most tolerant and open-minded of
German cities. The media have made Hamburg their capital. Add to that
the slick world of advertising and you have a populace of worldly and
fashionable professionals. Not surprisingly, the city of movers and shakers
is also the city with most of Germany's millionaires. Hamburg has been a
major port for more than 1,000 years but it reached the crest of its power
during the 19th century. What you see today is the "new" Hamburg.
World War II bombing raids destroyed more than half of the city. In spite
of the 1940–44 raids, Hamburg now stands as a remarkably faithful replica of that glittering prewar city—a place of enormous style, verve, and
elegance, with considerable architectural diversity, including turn-of-the-
20th-century art nouveau buildings.

ESSENTIALS

CURRENCY The Euro (€1 to US$1.46 at this writing); U.S. currency is generally not
accepted in Europe, but ATMs are common.

HOURS Stores are open Monday through Saturday from 8 am until 8 pm. Museums hours vary but core hours are 10 am until 5 pm with shorter opening
on Sundays. Some state museums are closed on Monday.

INTERNET **Global Callshop and Internet Café** ⊠*210 Wandsbecker Chausee* ☎*040/2392–*
4040 ⊕*www.global-callshop.de)* is open Monday through Saturday from
9 AM until 11 PM, Sunday from 10 AM until 11 PM.

TELEPHONES Tri- and quad-band GSM phones should work in Germany, where the
mobile system supports 3G technology. Phone cards for public phones are
available at newsagents and will allow international calls. Major companies include Vodafone, T2, and T-Mobile.

COMING ASHORE

Hamburg is constructing a state-of-the-art cruise port and terminal as
part of the regeneration of the Überseequartier district and surrounding
HafenCity (a totally new city district). This is due to be completed in 2011.
The current terminal is a modern but temporary structure that provides
facilities including shops and an information desk, but at present there are
no cafés or restaurants. Although city attractions are not far from the ter-

minal, it would be sensible to take transportation to the attractions rather than walking, due to the heavy construction going on in the area.

Passengers exploring the city will find no benefit in renting a car; in fact, many major attractions are within walking distance of each other. But if you want to explore the area by car, a car rental costs €51 for a compact manual vehicle. Taxi meters start at €2.20, and the fare is €1.67 per km (½ mi) for the first 12 km and then 1.28 € for each km thereafter. You can hail taxis on the street or at stands, or order one by phone.

The HVV, Hamburg's public transportation system, includes the U-bahn (subway), the S-bahn (suburban train), and buses. The ticketing and fare system is likely to be completely changed in 2008. At this writing, a one-way fare starts at €1.05; €1.40–€1.95 covers *one* unlimited ride in the Hamburg city area. Tickets are available on all buses and at automatic machines in all stations and at most bus stops. A *Ganztageskarte* (all-day ticket), valid until 6 AM the next day, costs €5.50. A *9 Uhr-Tageskarte* costs €4.65 and is valid between 9 AM on the day of purchase and 6 AM the next morning. If you're traveling with family or friends, a *Gruppen-* or *Familienkarte* (group or family ticket) is a good value—a group of up to five can travel for the entire day for only €7.75–€18.60 (depending on the number of fare zones the ticket covers).

EXPLORING HAMBURG

Numbers in the margin correspond to points of interest on the Hamburg map.

❷ **Alster** *(Alster Lakes)*. These twin lakes provide downtown Hamburg with one of its most memorable vistas. The two lakes meet at the Lombard and Kennedy bridges. In summer, the boat landing at the Jungfernstieg, below the Alsterpavillion, is the starting point for the *Alsterdampfer,* the flat-bottom passenger boats that traverse the lakes. Small sailboats and rowboats, hired from yards on the shores of the Alster, are very much a part of the summer scene.

From April through October, Alster Touristik operates boat trips around the Alster Lakes and through the canals. There are two tour options; both leave from the Jungfernstieg promenade in the city center. The Aussenalster 50-minute lake tour (Alster-Rundfahrt) costs €9.50 to €10 (depending on the season) and leaves every half hour, April through October 3, daily from 10 to 6. A two-hour-long *Fleet-Fahrt* costs €14 and explores the canals of the historic Speicherstadt (late March through November, daily at 10:45, 1:45, and 4:45). From May through September there's also the romantic twilight tour, called Dämmertour, every evening (Wednesday through Saturday in September) at 8 (€15). Ⓜ *Jungfernstieg (U-bahn).*

❼ **Deichstrasse.** The oldest residential area in the old town of Hamburg, which
★ dates from the 14th century, now consists of lavishly restored houses from the 17th through the 19th centuries. Many of the original houses on Deichstrasse were destroyed in the Great Fire of 1842, which broke out in No. 42 and left approximately 20,000 people homeless; only a few of the early dwellings escaped its ravages. Today Deichstrasse and neighboring **Peterstrasse** (just south of Ost-West-Strasse) are of great historical interest.

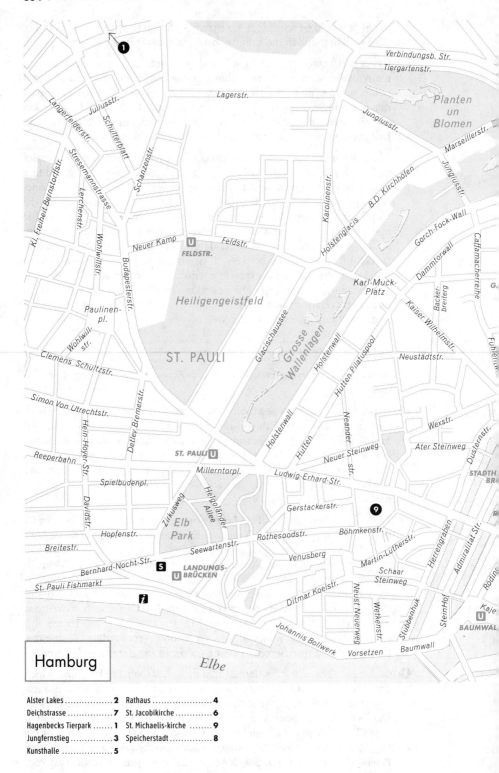

Hamburg

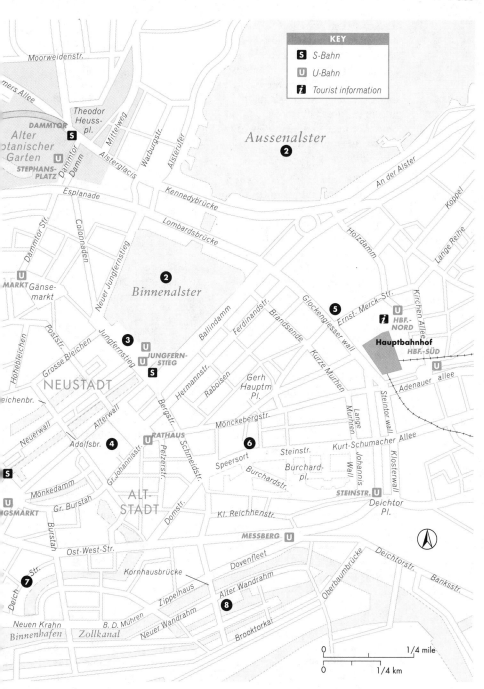

KEY

S S-Bahn

U U-Bahn

i Tourist information

Moorweidenstr.

mers Allee

DAMMTOR

Theodor
Heuss-
pl.

Alter
otanischer
Garten

STEPHANS-
PLATZ

Dammtor
Damm

Mittelweg

Warburgstr.

Alsterglacis

Alsterufer

Aussenalster
2

An der Alster

Koppel

Lange Reihe

Esplanade

Kennedybrücke

Dammtor Str.

Colonnaden

Neuer Jungfernstieg

Lombardsbrücke

Holzdamm

MARKT
Gänse-
markt

Binnenalster

Ballindamm

Ferdinandstr.

Brandsende

Glockengiesser wall

Ernst-Merck-Str.

5

Kirchen Allee

HBF.-
NORD

Hauptbahnhof

HBF.-SÜD

Postr.

Grosse Bleichen

Jungfernstieg

3

JUNGFERN-
STIEG

Kurze Mühren

Höhebleichen

NEUSTADT

Hermannstr.

Raboisen

Gerh
Hauptm
Pl.

Lange
Mühren

Adenauer allee

Steintor wall

eichenbr.

Bergstr.

Mönckebergstr.

Klosterwall

Neuerwall

Alterwall

Adolfsbr.
4

Gr. Johannisstr.

Pelzerstr.

Schneidstr.

RATHAUS

Speersort

Burchardstr.

6

Steinstr.

Burchard-
pl.

Kurt-Schumacher Allee

Lange
Johannis
Wall

STEINSTR.

S

Mönkedamm

IGSMARKT

Gr. Burstah

ALT-
STADT

Domstr.

Kl. Reichenstr.

Deichtor
Pl.

Burstah

Ost-West-Str.

MESSBERG

Kornhausbrücke

Dovenfleet

Deichtorstr.

Bankstr.

Oberbaumbrücke

Deich Str.

7

Zippelhaus

Alter Wandrahm

8

Neuen Krahn

Binnenhafen

B. D. Mühren

Zollkanal

Neuer Wandrahm

Brooktorkai

0   1/4 mile

0   1/4 km

7

At No. 39 Peterstrasse, for example, is the baroque facade of the Beyling-stift complex, built in 1700. Farther along, No. 27, constructed as a warehouse in 1780, is the oldest of its kind in Hamburg. All the buildings in the area have been painstakingly restored, thanks largely to the efforts of individuals. ⊠ *Altstadt* Ⓜ *Rödingsmarkt (U-bahn).*

> **HAMBURG BEST BETS**
>
> ■ **Enjoy the art in the Kunsthalle.** With works ranging from the Renaissance to the modern era, the gallery offers a visual timeline of European art.
>
> ■ **Tour the Rathaus.** The sumptuous décor of the Town Hall epitomizes the power and confidence of the 19th-century city.
>
> ■ **Tour the Alster Lakes.** Wonderful vistas of the city pass by at a genteel pace when you take a boat cruise here.

❶ Hagenbecks Tierpark *(Hagenbecks Zoo).* One of the country's oldest and most popular zoos is family owned. Founded in 1848, it was the world's first city park to let wild animals such as lions, elephants, chimpanzees, and others roam freely in vast, open-air corrals. Weather permitting, you can ride one of the elephants. In the Troparium, an artificial habitat creates a rain forest, an African desert, and a tropical sea. ⊠ *Lokstedter Str. at Hamburg-Stellingen, Niendorf* ☎ *040/540–0010* ⊕ *www.hagenbeck.de* 💶 *€15* 🕐 *Mid-Mar.–June, daily 9–6; July–Aug., daily 9–7; Sept.–Oct., daily 9–6; Nov.–Feb., daily 9–4:30* Ⓜ *Hagenbecks Tierpark (U-bahn).*

❸ Jungfernstieg. This wide promenade looking out over the Alster Lakes is the city's premier shopping boulevard. Laid out in 1665, it used to be part of a muddy millrace that channeled water into the Elbe. Hidden from view behind the sedate facade of Jungfernstieg is a network of nine covered arcades that together account for almost a mile of shops selling everything from souvenirs to haute couture. Many of these air-conditioned passages have sprung up in the past two decades, but some have been here since the 19th century; the first glass-covered arcade, called Sillem's Bazaar, was built in 1845. ⊠ *Neustadt* Ⓜ *Jungfernstieg (U-bahn).*

❺ Kunsthalle *(Art Gallery).* One of the most important art museums in Germany, the Kunsthalle has 3,000 paintings, 400 sculptures, and a coin and medal collection that dates from the 14th century. In the postmodern, cube-shape building designed by Berlin architect O. M. Ungers, the **Galerie der Gegenwart** has housed a collection of international modern art since 1960, including works by Andy Warhol, Joseph Beuys, Georg Baselitz, and David Hockney. Graphic art is well-represented, with a special collection of works by Pablo Picasso and the late Hamburg artist Horst Janssen, famous for his satirical worldview. In the old wing, you can view works by local artists dating from the 16th century. The outstanding collection of German Romantic paintings includes works by Runge, Friedrich, and Spitzweg. Paintings by Holbein, Rembrandt, Van Dyck, Tiepolo, and Canaletto are also on view, while late-19th-century impressionism is represented in works by Leibl, Liebermann, Manet, Monet, and Renoir. ⊠ *Glockengiesserwall, Altstadt* ☎ *040/4281–31200* ⊕ *www.hamburger-kunsthalle.de* 💶 *Permanent and special exhibits €8.50, permanent exhibit only €6, children under 18 free* 🕐 *Tues., Wed., and Fri.–Sun., 10–6, Thurs. 10–9* Ⓜ *Hauptbahnhof (U-bahn).*

④ Rathaus *(Town Hall).* To most Hamburgers this large building is the symbolic heart of the city. As a city-state—an independent city and simultaneously one of the 16 federal states of Germany—Hamburg has a city council and a state government, both of which have their administrative headquarters in the Rathaus. A pompous neo-Renaissance affair, the building dictates political decorum in the city. To this day, the mayor of Hamburg never welcomes VIPs at the foot of its staircase but always awaits them at the very top—whether it's a president or the queen of England.

FodorśChoice
★

The immense building, with its 647 rooms (6 more than Buckingham Palace) and imposing central clock tower, is not the most graceful structure in the city, but the sheer opulence of its interior is astonishing. A 45-minute tour begins in the ground-floor Rathausdiele, a vast pillared hall. Although you can only view the state rooms, their tapestries, huge staircases, glittering chandeliers, coffered ceilings, and grand portraits give you a sense of the city's great wealth in the 19th century and its understandable civic pride. ⊠*Rathausmarkt, Altstadt* ☎*040/428–310* ⊕*www.hamburg.de* ⌨*English-language tour €3* ☉*Tours Mon.–Thurs. hourly 10:15–3:15, Fri.–Sun. hourly 10:15–1:15* Ⓜ*Mönckebergstr. (U-bahn).*

❻ St. Jacobikirche *(St. James's Church).* This 13th-century church was almost completely destroyed during World War II. Only the furnishings survived, and reconstruction was completed in 1962. The interior is not to be missed—it houses such treasures as the vast baroque organ on which Bach played in 1720 and three Gothic altars from the 15th and 16th centuries. ⊠*Jacobikirchhof 22, at Steinstr., Altstadt* ☎*040/303–7370* ☉*Apr.–Sept., Mon.–Sat. 10–5, Sun.10 AM–11 AM; Oct.–Mar., Mon.–Sat. 11–5; tour of organ Thurs. at noon* Ⓜ*Mönckebergstr. (U-bahn).*

★

❾ St. Michaeliskirche *(St. Michael's Church).* The Michael, as it's called locally, is Hamburg's principal church and northern Germany's finest baroque-style ecclesiastical building. Constructed between 1649 and 1661 (the tower followed in 1669), it was razed after lightning struck almost a century later. It was rebuilt between 1750 and 1786 in the decorative Nordic baroque style but was gutted by a terrible fire in 1906. The replica, completed in 1912, was demolished during World War II. The present church is a reconstruction.

FodorśChoice
★

The distinctive 433-foot brick-and-iron tower bears the largest tower clock in Germany, 26 feet in diameter. Just above the clock is a viewing platform (accessible by elevator or stairs) that affords a magnificent panorama of the city, the Elbe River, and the Alster Lakes. ■ TIP→ Twice a day, at 10 AM and 9 PM (Sunday at noon), a watchman plays a trumpet solo from the tower platform, and during festivals an entire wind ensemble crowds onto the platform to perform. The **Multivisionsshow** (slide and audio show), one floor beneath the viewing platform, recounts Hamburg's history on a 16-foot screen. ⊠*St. Michaeliskirche, Altstadt* ☎*040/376–780* ⊕*www.st-michaelis.de* ⌨*Tower €2.50; crypt €1.25; tower and show €4; crypt and show €2.75; show, tower, and crypt €4.50* ☉*May–Oct., Mon.–Sat. 9–6, Sun. 11:30–5:30; Nov.–Apr., Mon.–Sat. 10–5, Sun. 11:30–4:30; multimedia screening Thurs. and weekends on the half hr, 12:30–3:30* Ⓜ*Landungsbrücken, Rödingsmarkt (U-bahn).*

7

8 **Speicherstadt** *(Warehouse District)*. These imposing warehouses in the Freihafen Hamburg reveal yet another aspect of Hamburg's extraordinary architectural diversity. A Gothic influence is apparent here, with a rich overlay of gables, turrets, and decorative outlines. These massive rust-brown buildings are still used to store and process every conceivable commodity, from coffee and spices to raw silks and handwoven Oriental carpets.

Although you won't be able to enter the buildings, the nonstop comings and goings will give you a good sense of a port at work. If you want to learn about the history and architecture of the old warehouses, detour to the **Speicherstadtmuseum.** ⊠*St. Annenufer 2, Block R, Speicherstadt* ☎*040/321–191* ⊕*www.speicherstadtmuseum.de* ✉*€3* ☉*Tues.–Fri. 10–5, weekends 10–6* Ⓜ*Messberg (U-bahn)*.

SHOPPING

Hamburg's shopping districts are among the most elegant on the continent, and the city has Europe's largest expanse of covered shopping arcades, most of them packed with small, exclusive boutiques. The streets **Grosse Bleichen** and **Neuer Wall**, which lead off Jungfernstieg, are a high-price-tag zone. The Grosse Bleichen leads to six of the city's most important covered (or indoor) malls, many of which are connected. The marble-clad **Galleria** is modeled after London's Burlington Arcade. Daylight streams through the immense glass ceilings of the **Hanse-Viertel**, an otherwise ordinary reddish-brown brick building. The **Kaufmannshaus**, also known as the Commercie, and the upscale (and former first-class hotel) **Hamburger Hof** are two of the oldest and most fashionable indoor malls. There are also the **Alte Post** and the **Bleichenhof**, while over-the-top, stunningly designed **Europa Passage** is the city's latest arrival on the luxury shopping mall scene.

Some of the country's premier designers, such as Karl Lagerfeld, Jil Sander, and Wolfgang Joop, are native Hamburgers, or at least worked here for quite some time, so high-class fashion is well in evidence. For souvenirs, the most famous must-buys are *Buddelschiffe* (ships in bottles) and other maritime memorabilia.

Hamburg's premier shopping street, **Jungfernstieg**, is just about the most expensive in the country. It's lined with jewelers' shops—Wempe, Brahmfeld & Guttruf, and Hintze are the top names—and chic clothing boutiques such as Linette, Ursula Aust, Selbach, Windmöller, and Jäger & Koch. In the fashionable **Pöseldorf** district north of downtown, take a look at Milch-strasse and Mittelweg. Both are filled with small boutiques, restaurants, and cafés. Running from the main train station to Gerhard-Hauptmann-Platz, the boulevard **Spitalerstrasse** is a pedestrian-only street lined with stores. ■TIP➔ Prices here are noticeably lower than those on Jungfernstieg.

The **Antik-Center** (⊠*Klosterwall 9–21, Altstadt* ☎*040/359–010*) is an assortment of 39 shops in the old market hall, close to the main train station. It features a wide variety of antiques from all periods. **Binikowski** (⊠*Lokstedter Weg 68, Eppendorf* ☎*040/462–852 or 040/4607–1848*) sells *Buddelschiffe*. There are few better places to shop for one, or for a blue-and-white-stripe sailor's shirt, a sea captain's hat, ship models, or even ships' charts.

WHERE TO EAT

$–$$ ✕ **Nil.** The intellectual and cultural elite of Hamburg gather at this trendy venue for business dinners and prepartying on weekends. Nil is worth a visit for its interior alone: it's in an old 1950s-style, three-floor shoe shop. The kitchen serves seafood and modern German cuisine, including four different three- to six-course menus, offering fare such as *Enten-keule Hamburger Art* (roasted duck joint in spicy sauce) in winter and lighter, Italian-oriented fare in summer. ⊠*Neuer Pferdemarkt 5, St. Pauli* ☎*040/439–7823* ♨*Reservations essential* ⊟*No credit cards* ☉*Closed Tues. No lunch* Ⓜ*Feldstr. (U-bahn).*

$–$$ ✕ **Rive.** This harborside oyster bar is a Hamburg establishment, known for both its German nouvelle cuisine and its classic local fare. Choose among dishes such as hearty *Matjes mit drei Saucen* (herring with three sauces) or *Dorade in der Salzkruste* (dorado fried in salt crust). Media types come to this shiplike building for the fresh oysters, clams, and spectacular view. ⊠*Van der Smissen Str. 1, Kreuzfahrt-Center, Altona* ☎*040/380–5919* ♨*Reservations essential* ⊟*AE* Ⓜ*Königstr. (S-bahn).*

HELSINKI, FINLAND

A city of the sea, Helsinki was built along a series of oddly shaped peninsulas and islands jutting into the Baltic coast along the Gulf of Finland. Nature dictates life in this Nordic land, where winter brings perpetual darkness, and summer, perpetual light. A disastrous fire in the early 1800s destroyed many of Helsinki's traditional wooden structures, and as a result, Helsinki has some of the purest neoclassical architecture in the world. Add to this foundation the influence of Stockholm and St. Petersburg sprinkled with the local inspiration of 20th-century Finnish design, and the result is a European capital city that is as architecturally eye-catching as it is distinct. Today, Helsinki is still a meeting point of eastern and western Europe, a fact reflected in its cosmopolitan image, its influx of Russians and Estonians, and its generally multilingual population. Outdoor summer bars (*terrassit,* as the locals call them) and cafés in the city center are perfect for people-watching on a summer afternoon.

ESSENTIALS

CURRENCY The euro (€1 is US$1.46); exchange rates were accurate at this writing but are subject to change. ATMs are common and credit cards are widely accepted.

HOURS Smaller stores are generally open weekdays from 9 to 6 and Saturday from 9 to 1; larger department stores are open until 9 weekdays and until 6 on Saturday. Stores are often open on Sunday from June through August and during December. The majority of museums are closed on Monday.

INTERNET **Robert's Coffee** (⊠*Aleksanterinkatu 21, Kaytava* ☎*09/6228–1960*) is a stylish spot offering a huge range of coffees, teas, and hot chocolates, as well as computer terminals.

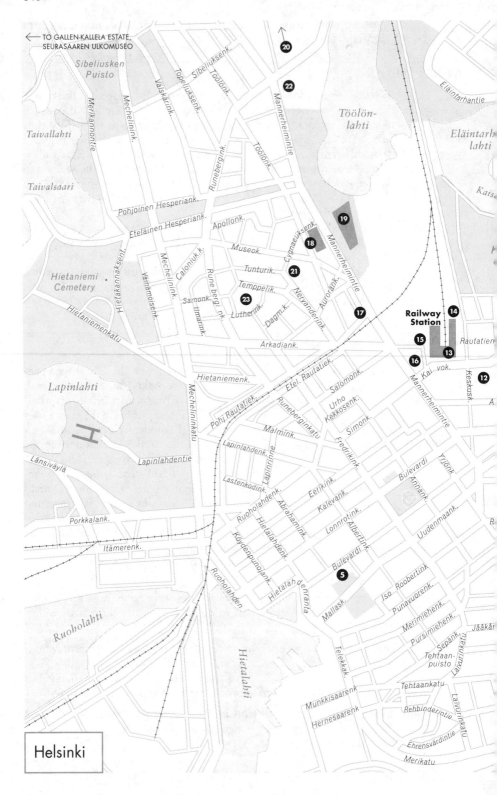

Helsinki

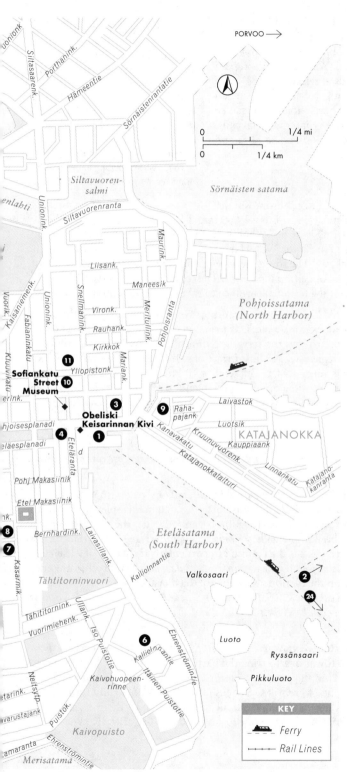

PORVOO ⟶

Sörnäisten satama

Pohjoissatama
(North Harbor)

Etelasatama
(South Harbor)

KATAJANOKKA

7

KEY

🚢 Ferry

⊢⊢⊢⊢ Rail Lines

TELEPHONES   Most tri-band and quad-band GSM phones work in Finland, but the Finnish mobile system is not 3G-compatible. You can buy prepaid phone cards at telecom shops, news vendors and tobacconists in all towns and cities. Phone cards can be used for local or international calls. Major companies include Elisa and Finnish 2G.

COMING ASHORE

Ships dock at one of two terminals in the South Harbor. From Kataja-nokka Terminal, local Bus 13 or Tram T4 will take you to Helsinki city center, but this is also reachable on foot. Larger ships dock at the city commercial port in the West Harbor, which is 15 minutes by car from the downtown area. The shuttle service provided by the ship is the most cost-effective way of getting into town. The terminal is also served by Bus 15. Taxis wait at the terminal entrance to take visitors downtown.

Tickets for the Helsinki public transport system cost €2.20 from the driver, or €2 from a ticket machine. Day tickets are €6—these are valid on trams, buses, the metro and the ferry to Soumenlinna. Taxis are plentiful and make a convenient way to link attractions. Taxis take credit cards. A 5-km (3-mi) trip is currently €10.30, while a 10-km (6-mi) trip is €16.10. A car rental is not a sensible option if you intend to explore the city, as parking is difficult. Expect to pay €76 per day for a compact manual vehicle.

> **HELSINKI BEST BETS**
>
> ■ **Temppeliaukio Kirkko.** This church, seemingly rising out of living rock, pushes the boundaries of architecture.
>
> ■ **Senaatintori.** The symmetry of this neoclassical city square is a joy to the eye.
>
> ■ **Kauppatori.** Enjoy a steaming cup of coffee while browsing in the market or immersing yourself in daily life.

EXPLORING HELSINKI

Numbers in the margin correspond to points of interest on the Helsinki map.

⑫ **Ateneumin Taidemuseo** *(Atheneum Art Museum of the Finnish National Gallery).* The best traditional Finnish art is housed in this splendid neoclassical complex, one of three museums organized under the Finnish National Gallery umbrella. The gallery holds major European works, but the outstanding attraction is the Finnish art, particularly the works of Akseli Gallen-Kallela, inspired by the national epic *Kalevala*. The two other museums that make up the National Gallery are **Kiasma** and **Synebrychoff.** ✉ *Kaivok. 2–4, Keskusta* ☎ *09/1733–6401* ⊕ *www.fng.fi* ✆ *€5.50, additional charge for special exhibits* ⊙ *Tues. and Fri. 9–6, Wed. and Thurs. 9–8, weekends 11–5.*

❻ **Cygnaeuksen Galleria** *(Cygnaeus Gallery).* This diminutive gallery, in a cottage with a tower overlooking the harbor, is the perfect setting for works by various Finnish painters, sculptors, and folk artists. This was once the summer home of Fredrik Cygnaeus (1807–81), a poet and historian who generously left his cottage and all the art inside to the Finnish public. ✉ *Kalliolinnantie 8, Kaivopuisto* ☎ *09/4050–9628* ✆ *€3* ⊙ *Wed. 11–7, Thurs.–Sun. 11–4.*

8 **Designmuseo** *(Design Museum)*. The best of Finnish design can be seen here in displays of furnishings, jewelry, ceramics, and more. ⊠*Korkeavuorenk. 23, Keskusta* ☎*09/622–0540* ⊕*www.designmuseum.fi* ⌨*€7* ⊙*Sept.– May, Tues. 11–8, Wed.–Sun. 11–6; June–Aug., daily 11–6.*

17 **Eduskuntatalo** *(Parliament House)*. The imposing, colonnaded Eduskuntatalo stands on Mannerheimintie. The legislature has one of the world's highest proportions of women. ⊠*Mannerheimintie 30, Keskusta* ☎*09/432–2027* ⊕*www.eduskunta.fi.*

19 **Finlandiatalo** *(Finlandia Hall)*. This white, winged concert hall was one of Alvar Aalto's last creations. If you can't make it to a concert here, try to take a guided tour. ⊠*Karamzininkatu 4, Keskusta* ☎*09/402–41* ⊕*www. finlandia.fi* ⊙*Symphony concerts usually held Wed. and Thurs. nights.*

4 **Havis Amanda.** This fountain's brass centerpiece, a young woman perched on rocks surrounded by dolphins, was commissioned by the city fathers to embody Helsinki. Sculptor Ville Vallgren completed her in 1908. Partying university students annually crown the Havis Amanda with their white caps on the eve of Vappu, the May 1 holiday. ⊠*Eteläespl. and Eteläranta, Keskusta/Kauppatori.*

21 **Helsingin Taidehalli** *(Helsinki Art Gallery)*. Here you'll see the best of contemporary Finnish art, including painting, sculpture, architecture, and industrial art and design. ⊠*Nervanderink. 3, Keskusta* ☎*09/454–2060* ⌨*€7, can vary for special exhibitions* ⊙*Tues., Thurs., and Fri. 11–6; Wed. 11–8; weekends noon–5.*

1 **Kauppatori** *(Market Square)*. At this Helsinki institution, open year-round, wooden stands with orange and gold awnings bustle in the mornings when everyone comes to browse. You can buy a bouquet of bright flowers for a friend, or a fur pelt or hat. ⊠*Eteläranta and Pohjoisespl., Keskusta/ Kauppatori* ⊙*Sept.–May, weekdays 6:30–2, Sat. 6:30–3; June–Aug., weekdays 6:30–2 and 3:30–8, Sat. 6:30–3, Sun. 10–4; hrs can vary.*

2 **Korkeasaari Eläintarha** *(Helsinki Zoo)*. Snow leopards and reindeer like the cold climate at one of the world's most northern zoos set entirely within the limits of this small island. ⊠*Korkeasaari (Korkea Island), Korkeasaari* ☎*09/169–5969* ⊕*www.korkeasaari.fi* ⌨*€5* ⊙*Mar. and Apr., daily 10–6; May–Sept., daily 10–8; Oct.–Feb., daily 10–4.*

16 **Mannerheimin Patsas** *(Statue of national hero Marshal Karl Gustaf Mannerheim)*. The equestrian gazes down Mannerheimintie, the major thoroughfare named in his honor. ⊠*Mannerheimintie, in front of main post office and Museum of Contemporary Art, west of main train station, Keskusta/Pääposti.*

15 ★ **Nykytaiteenmuseo (Kiasma)** *(Museum of Contemporary Art)*. Praised for the boldness of its curved steel shell, this striking museum displays a wealth of Finnish and foreign art from the 1960s to the present. ⊠*Mannerheiminaukio 2, Keskusta/Pääposti* ☎*09/1733–6501* ⊕*www.kiasma.fi* ⌨*€5.50* ⊙*Tues. 9–5, Wed.–Sun. 10–8:30.*

20 **Olympiastadion** *(Olympic Stadium)*. At this stadium built for the 1952 Games, take a lift to the top of the tower for sprawling city views. ⊠*East* of Mannerheim, Olympiastadion ⊕www.stadion.fi ⊠€2 ⊗Weekdays 9–8, weekends 9–6.

③ Presidentinlinna (President's Palace). The long history of this edifice mirrors the history of Finland itself: built between 1813 and 1820 as a private residence for a German businessman, it was redesigned in 1843 as a palace for the czars; then it served as the official residence of Finland's presidents from 1919 to 1993. Today it houses the offices of Finland's first female president, Tarja Halonen. ⊠Pohjoisespl. 1, Keskusta/Kauppatori ☎09/2288–1222.

⑬ Rautatieasema (train station). The station's huge granite figures are by Emil Wikström; the solid building they adorn was designed by Eliel Saarinen, one of the founders of the early-20th-century National Romantic style. ⊠Kaivok., Rautatientori, Keskusta ☎0600/41–902 for information in English (a €1 charge applies), 0307/23703 international fares ⊕www.vr.fi.

⑩ Senaatintori (Senate Square). You've hit the heart of neoclassical Helsinki.
★ The harmony of the three buildings flanking Senaatintori exemplifies one of the purest styles of European architecture, as envisioned and designed by German architect Carl Ludvig Engel. On the square's west side is one of the main buildings of **Helsingin Yliopisto** (Helsinki University) , and up the hill is the university library. On the east side is the pale yellow **Valtionneuvosto** (Council of State), completed in 1822 and once the seat of the Autonomous Grand Duchy of Finland's Imperial Senate. At the lower end of the square, stores and restaurants now occupy former merchants' homes. ⊠Bounded by Aleksanterink. to south and Yliopistonk. to north, Senaatintori.

⑤ Sinebrychoffin Taidemuseo (Sinebrychoff Museum of Foreign Art). The wealthy Russian Sinebrychoffs lived in this splendid yellow-and-white 1840 neo-Renaissance mansion, which is now a public museum filled with their art and furniture. ⊠Bulevardi 40, Hietalahti ☎09/1733–6460 ⊕www.sinebrychoffintaidemuseo.fi ⊠€7 ⊗Tues. and Fri. 10–6, Wed. and Thurs. 10–8, weekends 11–5.

⑱ Suomen Kansallismuseo (National Museum of Finland). Architect Eliel Saarinen and his partners combined the language of Finnish medieval church architecture with elements of art nouveau to create this vintage example of the National Romantic style. The museum's collection of archaeological, cultural, and ethnological artifacts gives insight into Finland's past. ⊠Mannerheimintie 34, Keskusta ☎09/40–501 ⊕www.nba.fi ⊠€5.50 ⊗Tues. and Wed. 11–8, Thurs.–Sun. 11–6.

㉒ Suomen Kansallisooppera (Finnish National Opera). Helsinki's splendid opera house is a striking example of modern Scandinavian architecture. ⊠Helsinginkatu 58, Keskusta ☎09/4030–2210 house tours, 09/4030–2211 box office ⊕www.operafin.fi ⊗Tues.–Fri. 10–5; house tours, in English, in summer Tues. and Thurs. at 3, also by appointment.

⑭ Suomen Kansallisteatteri (National Theater). The elegant granite facade overlooking the railway station square is decorated with quirky relief typical of the Finnish National Romantic style. In front is a statue of writer Aleksis

Kivi. ⊠*Läntinen Teatterikuja 1, Keskusta/Rautatieasema* ☎*09/1733– 1331* ⊕*www.nationaltheatre.fi.*

㉔ Suomenlinna *(Finland's Castle).* A former island fortress is now a perenni-
Fodor'sChoice
★
ally popular collection of museums, parks, and gardens, which has been designated a UNESCO World Heritage Site. In 1748, the Finnish army helped build the impregnable fortress. Since then, it has expanded into a series of interlinked islands. Although Suomenlinna has never been taken by assault, its occupants surrendered once to the Russians in 1808 and came under fire from British ships in 1855 during the Crimean War.

Suomenlinna Visitor Centre (⊠*Suomenlinna* ☎*09/684–1880, 09/684–1850 tours* ⊕*www.suomenlinna.fi*)

❼ Suomen Rakennustaiteen Museo *(Museum of Finnish Architecture).* Stop in to buy an architectural map of Helsinki that includes the locations of several buildings by Alvar Aalto, the most famous being Finlandiatalo in Töölö. ⊠*Kasarmik. 24, Keskusta* ☎*09/8567–5100* ⊕*www.mfa.fi* ⛱*€3.50* ⊙*Tues. and Thurs.–Sun. 10–4, Wed. 10–8.*

㉓ Temppeliaukio Kirkko *(Temple Square Church).* Topped with a copper dome,
★
the church looks like a half-buried spaceship from the outside. In truth, it's really a modern Lutheran church carved into the rock outcrops below. ⊠*Lutherinkatu 3, Töölö* ☎*09/494–698* ⊙*Weekdays 10–7:45, Sat. 10– 6, Sun. noon–1:45 and 3:15–5:45; closed Tues. 1–2, and during weddings, concerts, and services.*

⓫ Tuomiokirkko *(Lutheran Cathedral of Finland).* The steep steps and green domes of the church dominate Senaatintori. Completed in 1852, it houses statues of German reformers Martin Luther and Philipp Melancthon, as well as the famous Finnish bishop Mikael Agricola. ⊠*Yliopistonk. 7, Senaatintori* ☎*09/709–2455* ⊙*June–Aug., Mon.–Sat. 9–midnight, Sun. noon–midnight; Sept.–May, Mon.–Sat. 9–6, Sun. noon–6.*

❾ Uspenskin Katedraali *(Uspenski Cathedral).* The biggest Orthodox church
★
in Scandinavia is the main cathedral of the Orthodox community in Finland. Its brilliant gold onion domes are its hallmark. ⊠*Kanavak. 1, Katajanokka* ☎*09/634–267* ⊙*May–Sept., Mon. and Wed.–Fri. 9:30–4, Tues. 9:30–6, Sat. 9:30–3, Sun. noon–3; Oct.–Apr., Tues.–Fri. 9:30–4, Sat. 9:30–3, Sun. noon–3; closed for weddings and other special events.*

OFF THE
BEATEN
PATH
Seurasaaren Ulkomeseo. On an island about 3 km (2 mi) northwest of the city center, the Seurasaari Outdoor Museum was founded in 1909 to preserve rural Finnish architecture. The old farmhouses and barns dating from the 17th century were of primary inspiration to the late 19th-century architects of the national revivalist movement in Finland. Guided tours in English available mid-June through mid-August, at 3, starting at ticket kiosk. ⊠ Seurasaari ☎ 09/4050–9660 in summer, 09/4050–9574 in winter ⊕ www.nba.fi ⛱€5 ⊙ Mid-May–late-May and early- Sept.–mid-Sept., weekdays 9–3, weekends 11–5; June–Aug., Thurs.–Tues. 11–5, Wed. 11–7; closed mid-Sept.–mid-May.

SHOPPING

Finnish handicrafts and 21st-century design staples for the home are the must-have souvenirs of your trip. Handicrafts take the form of handwoven woolen rugs, knitted sweaters, glass, ceramics and porcelain, and textiles. There is also a thriving modern jewelry industry with many young designers. For antiques hunters, Helsinki is an excellent city for tracking down old Russian *objets*.

The southern part of **Senaatintori** has a host of souvenir and crafts stores, with several antiques shops and secondhand bookstores on the adjoining streets. You'll find many smaller boutiques in the streets **west of Mannerheimintie**, Fredrikinkatu and Annankatu, for example. There is one pedestrian shopping street a few blocks south of the Esplanade, on **Iso Roobertinkatu**; stores here are conventional, and are more relaxed than around Mannerheimintie and the Esplanade. **Pohjoisesplanadi**, on the north side of the Esplanade, packs in most of Helsinki's trademark design stores.

Hietalahden Tori (✉ *Bulevardi and Hietalahdenk., Hietalahti*) is a famed market and flea market.

Arabian Tehtaanmyymälä (*Arabia Factory Shop* ✉ *Hämeentie 135, Arabia* ☎ *0204/393–507*) has Arabia, Hackman, Iittala, and Rörstrand tableware, glassware, cutlery, and cookware for outlet prices. Next to Senaatintori is the **Kiseleff Bazaar Hall** (✉ *Aleksanterinkatu 22–28*), an attractive shopping gallery. **Union Design** (✉ *Eteläranta 14, inner courtyard Kauppatori* ☎ *09/6220–0333*) is an atelier of jewelers displaying top-notch talent in Finnish design.

SPORTS & ACTIVITIES

Taking a sauna is the big Finnish pastime. It's a place to get cleansed and do some socializing. The oldest and one of the most famous saunas in Helsinki is **Yrjönkatu Uimahalli** (✉ *Yrjönk. 21B, Keskusta* ☎ *09/3108–7400*), which allows swimming and taking saunas in the nude. It's not compulsory to be nude, but the local people will be. The hall periodically closes during the summer months.

WHERE TO EAT

¢–$$ ✕ **Maxill.** Helsinki's café boom and an increasing demand for Continental-style bars have inspired this hybrid on a lively street just south of the city center. The trendy menu includes salad with goat-cheese croutons. ✉ *Korkeavuorenkatu. 4, Keskusta* ☎ *09/638–873* ⊕ *www.maxill. fi* ▭ *AE, DC, MC, V.*

¢–$ ✕ **Zucchini.** For a vegetarian lunch or just coffee and dessert, Zucchini is a cozy hideaway with quiet music, magazines, and a few sidewalk tables. Pizzas, soups, and salads are all tasty here. ✉ *Fabianinkatu 4, Keskusta* ☎ *09/622–2907* ▭ *DC, MC, V* ☺ *Closed weekends. No dinner.*

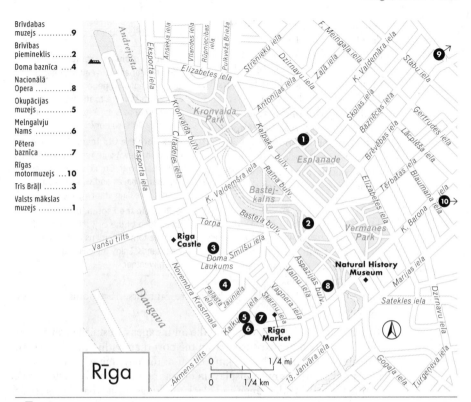

RĪGA, LATVIA

Rīga has an upscale, big-city feel unmatched in the Eastern Baltic region. The capital is almost as large as Tallinn and Vilnius combined and is the business center of the area. Original, high-quality restaurants and hotels have given Rīga something to brag about. The city has many faces and is a delight for lovers of both architecture and history, having thrived as a Hanseatic port in the Late Middle Ages. A Baltic trading center in the early 20th century, Rīga eventually re-created itself as the city of art nouveau. This style dominates the city center and long avenues of complex and sometimes whimsical Jugendstil facades hint at Rīga's grand past. Many were designed by Mikhail Eisenstein, the father of Soviet director Sergei.

ESSENTIALS

CURRENCY The Lat (Ls 1 to US$1.95; Ls 1 to €1.42); exchange rates were accurate at this writing but are subject to change. Lats are made up of 100 santimi. U.S. currency generally is not accepted in payment. There are ATMs and exchange kiosks in the passenger terminal of the cruise port. ATMs are widely available in town.

HOURS Shops are open weekdays from 10 AM until 7 PM and 10 AM until 5 PM on Saturday; most close on Sunday. Museums are generally open from 10 AM until 5 PM; many close on Monday.

INTERNET There are facilities for checking e-mail and surfing the Internet at the passenger welcome center within the cruise port.

TELEPHONES Wireless telecommunication is developing in Latvia, with Lattelekom being the main provider, but most tri- and quad-band GSM phones should work in Rīga itself. The Latvian mobile phone system is dual-band. It supports texts but not data and is not yet 3G-compatible. Public phones support international calls. Some kiosks accept credit cards. Phone cards are available at tobacconists/newspaper shops.

COMING ASHORE

The cruise port is in the main port, close to the historic downtown core. The walk from port to the downtown core is 15 minutes along the waterfront. The passenger welcome center has good facilities, including restaurants, restrooms, currency exchange facilities, and ATMs.

> ### RĪGA BEST BETS
>
> ■ **Stroll around Elizabetes Street.** The heart of art nouveau Rīga has some exceptional period architecture and is a testament to the wealth generated here by shipping and trade in the early 20th century.
>
> ■ **Explore the Old Town.** The fabric of this medieval core remains remarkably intact, with Gothic spires sheltering church naves and winding cobbled streets revealing sturdy gables.
>
> ■ **Relax in the Esplanāde.** The green lung of the city, this huge park has fine formal gardens and planned woodlands. Enjoy a picnic here in warm weather.

To reach the Old Town you can take an inexpensive shuttle transfer or taxi. Taxis are more expensive from the port than within the city center. The official rate is 50 Ls per km 1/2 mi in the daytime with an Ls 1.50 pick-up fee. Drivers must display an operating license and a meter. Stick to the state cabs with orange and black markings. Insist that the meter be turned on; if there is no meter, choose another taxi or decide on a price beforehand. Public transportation costs 20 Ls and runs from 5:30 AM to midnight. Some routes have 24-hour service. Trams 6 and 11 connect the Old Town with the Esplanāde area and run regularly throughout the day. Buy tickets at numerous outlets and validate them in the machine on board.

EXPLORING RĪGA

Numbers in the margin correspond to points of interest on the Rīga map.

In many ways, the wonder of Rīga resides less in its individual attractions and more in the fabric of the town itself. In the medieval **Old Town**, an ornate gable or architrave catches the eye at every turn. The somber and the flamboyant are both represented in this quarter's 1,000 years of architectural history. Don't hesitate to just follow where your desire leads—the Old Town is compact and bounded by canals, so it's difficult to get totally lost.

When the Old Town eventually became too crowded, the city burst out into the newer inner suburbs. The rich could afford to leave and build themselves fine fashionable mansions in the style of the day; consequently, city planners created a whole new Rīga. Across the narrow canal, you'll find the **Esplanāde,** a vast expanse of parkland with formal gardens and period mansions where the well-heeled stroll and play. Surrounding this is the **art nouveau district.** Encompassing avenues of splendid family homes (now spruced up in the postcommunist era), the collection has been praised by UNESCO as Europe's finest in the art nouveau style. The best examples are at Alberta 2, 2a, 4, 6, 8, and 13; Elizabetes 10b; and Strēlnieku 4a.

If the weather permits, eschew public transport and stroll between the two districts, taking in the varied skylines and multifaceted facades, and perhaps stopping at a café or two as you go. The city has churches in five Christian denominations and more than 50 museums, many of which cater to eclectic or specialist tastes.

❾ Brīvdabas muzejs. The Open-Air Ethnographic Museum is well worth the 9-km (5-mi) trek from downtown. At this countryside living museum, farmsteads and villages have been crafted to look like those in 18th- and 19th-century Latvia, and costumed workers engage in traditional activities (beekeeping, smithing, and so on). ⊠ *Brīvības 440* ☎ *799–4515* ☉ *Daily 10–5.*

❻ Melngalvju Nams. The fiercely Gothic Blackheads House was built in 1344 as a hotel for wayfaring merchants (who wore black hats). Partially destroyed during World War II and leveled by the Soviets in 1948, the extravagant, ornate building was renovated and reopened in 2000 for Rīga's 800th anniversary. The facade is a treasured example of Dutch Renaissance work. ⊠ *Strēlnieku laukums* ☎ *704–4300* ☉ *Tues.–Sun. 10–5.*

❷ Brīvības piemineklis. The central Freedom Monument, a 1935 statue whose upheld stars represent Latvia's united peoples (the Kurzeme, Vidzeme, and Latgale), was the rallying point for many nationalist protests during the late 1980s and early 1990s. Watch the changing of the guard every hour on the hour between 9 and 6. ⊠ *Brīvības and Raina.*

❹ Doma baznīca *(Dome Cathedral).* In Doma laukums (Dome Square), the nerve center of the Old Town, the stately 1210 cathedral dominates. Reconstructed over the years with Romanesque, Gothic, and baroque elements, this place of worship is astounding as much for its architecture as for its size. The massive 6,768-pipe organ is among the largest in Europe, and it is played nearly every evening at 7 PM. Check at the cathedral for schedules and tickets. ⊠ *Doma laukums* ☎ *721–3498* ☉ *Tues.–Fri. 1–5, Sat. 10–2.*

❺ Okupācijas muzejs. The Latvian Occupation Museum details the devastation of Latvia at the hands of the Nazis and Soviets during World War II as well as the Latvians' struggle for independence in September 1991. In front of the museum is a monument to the Latvian sharpshooters who protected Lenin during the 1917 revolution. ⊠ *Strēlnieku laukums 1* ☎ *721–2715* ☉ *Tues.–Sun. 11–5.*

❿ Rīgas motormuzejs. At the Motor Museum, the Western cars on display can impress, but the Soviet models—including Stalin's iron-plated limo and a Rolls-Royce totaled by Brezhnev himself—are the most fun. ⊠ *Eizensteina 6* ☎ *709–7170* ☉ *Mon. 10–3, Tues.–Sun. 10–6.*

❽ Nacionālā Opera. Latvia's restored 18th-century National Opera House, where Richard Wagner once conducted, is worthy of a night out. ⊠ *Aspazijas 3* ☎ *707–3777* ☉ *Daily 10–7.*

7

❼ Pētera baznīca. Towering St. Peter's Church, originally built in 1209, had a long history of annihilation and conflagration before being destroyed most recently in 1941. Rebuilt by the Soviets, it lacks authenticity but has a good observation deck on the 200-foot spire. ⊠ *Skārnu 19* ☎ *722–9426* ⊗ *Tues.–Sun. 10–7.*

❸ Trīs Brāli. The Three Brothers—a trio of houses on Mazā Pils—show what the city looked like before the 20th century. The three oldest stone houses in the capital (No. 17 is the oldest, dating from the 15th century) span several styles, from the medieval to the baroque. The building at No. 19 is the city's **architecture museum.** ⊠ *Mazā Pils 17, 19, 21* ☎ *722–0779* ⊗ *Weekdays 9–5, Sat. noon–4.*

❶ Valsts mākslas muzejs. The National Art Museum has a gorgeous interior with imposing marble staircases linking several large halls of 19th- and 20th-century Latvian paintings. ⊠ *K. Valdemāra 10a* ☎ *732–4461* ⊗ *Wed.–Mon. 11–5.*

SHOPPING

You'll find many souvenir and gift shops in the streets of the Old Town, many of which specifically cater to visitors. Latvia is famed for its linen, which is fashioned into clothes and household items such as tea towels and table runners. Woolen sweaters, mittens and socks with traditional patterns have been worn by generations of locals during the winter. Amber items are everywhere, although their quality can vary, so shop around. Also popular are jewelry, carved ornaments, and Rīga Black Balsam, a liqueur made from an ancient recipe incorporating herbs and medicinal roots.

Galerija Tornis (⊠ *Grēcinieku 11–12* ☎ *722–0270*) sells a range of jewelry and gift items featuring amber and other semi-precious stones, along with pretty linen items. **Souvenirs Klota** (⊠ *3 Town Hall Square* ☎ *714–4308*), as its name suggests, is a good general souvenir store. **Ti nes** (⊠ *Amatu 5* ☎ *6721–1009*) sells an excellent range of linen and woolen clothes and household items.

WHERE TO EAT

$ ✗ **A. Suns.** "Andalusian Dog" has long been an expat hangout in Rīga— and why not? With an art-house cinema upstairs, a breezy restaurant downstairs, and a wall of windows perfect for people-watching, the restaurant is decidedly hip, with a tasty Tex-Mex menu. ⊠ *Elizabetes 83–85* ☎ *728–8418* ▭ *MC, V.*

¢ ✗ **Staburags.** Located in an art nouveau building in downtown Rīga, this may be the capital's best place to sample Latvian national cuisine, with such offerings as roast leg of pork, sauerkraut, an assortment of potato dishes, and smoked chicken. ⊠ *Caka 55* ☎ *729–9787* ▭ *No credit cards.*

ST. PETERSBURG, RUSSIA

Commissioned by Peter the Great as "a window looking into Europe," St. Petersburg is a planned city built on more than one-hundred islands in the Neva Delta linked by canals and arched bridges. It was first called the "Venice of the North" by Goethe. Little wonder it's the darling of today's fashion photographers. With its strict geometric lines and perfectly planned architecture, so unlike the Russian cities that came before it, St. Petersburg is almost too European to be Russian. And yet it's too Russian to be European. Memories of revolutionary zeal and one of the worst ordeals of World War II, when the city—then known as Leningrad—withstood a 900-day siege and blockade by Nazi forces, are still fresh in the minds of citizens. Nevertheless, St. Petersburg is filled with pleasures and tantalizing treasures, from golden spires and gilded domes to pastel palaces and candlelit cathedrals.

ESSENTIALS

CURRENCY The ruble (25.68R to US$1; 35.12R to €1); exchange rates were accurate at this writing but are subject to change. There are ATMs in the city, but exchange bureaus are more plentiful. Credit cards are increasingly accepted, but ask first to be sure.

HOURS Stores have recently extended their opening hours considerably—many stay open until 8 or 9 PM, or on Sunday.

INTERNET Check your e-mail at **Quo Vadis** ✉ *76 Nevsky Propsekt* ☎*812/3330708.*

TELEPHONES Some tri- and quad-band mobile phones may work in St. Petersburg, but mobile service on the whole is patchy. The network does not yet support 3G services, and handsets are single-band. Public phones take phone cards, which can be bought at newsstands. Note that public phones in Metro stations work on a different system and require a different card. Russia has 15 major mobile service providers.

COMING ASHORE

Independent travel is not as easy in St. Petersburg as in other destinations, as you need to obtain a tourist visa prior to the cruise departure to explore without a certified guide. Also, independent travelers need to line up for tickets at museums and attractions, while guided groups do not. This can cut down your sightseeing time considerably.

If you prebook an independent tour with a certified guide company (so that you aren't with a large group) you don't need a tourist visa. **Explorer-Tour** (✉*50 ul. Marata, Vladimirskaya* ☎*812/320–0954* 🖷*812/712–1967* Ⓜ*Mayakovskaya*) operates city tours for individuals. This is certainly the safest and most productive way to tour St. Petersburg without being part of a large group. Whether you travel independently or with an accredited small tour company, it is approximately 20 minutes by foot to the port entrance, from where you will be able to take a taxi.

EXPLORING ST. PETERSBURG

Numbers in the margin correspond to points of interest on the St. Petersburg map.

St. Petersburg

0   1/2 mi
0   1/2 km

PETROGRAD SIDE

Kamennostrovsky pr.

Skorochodova ul.

Mira ul.

Bolshoy Sampsonievsky

Pirogovskaya nab.

Vyborgskaya

Smirnov

Bolshaya Nevka

Petrogradskaya nab.

Kronverksky pr.

Kuybysheva ul.

Svobody most

Lebe

Krasnogo kursanta ul.

Bolshoy pr.

Maly pr.

Dobrolubova

Kronverk Canal

Troitskaya Pl.

Petrovskaya nab.

Litei
mos

5

Peter and Paul Fortress

Troitsky most

Malaya Neva

Makarova

Birzhevoy most

Marble Palace

VASILIEVSKY ISLAND

nab.

Stock Exchange

Dvortsovy most

Dvortsovaya nab.

Sadovaya ul.

Engineer's Castle

Mokhovaya ul.

Liteiny pr.

Svezdovskaya l.

4-5 Liniya

Bolshoy pr.

Mend. l.

3

2

1

Ethnography Museum

Ne

Universitetskaya nab.

Neva

Armiralteistvo

Nevsky pr.

Admiralteysky pr.

Gorokhovaya ul.

7

Zf

most Leytenanta Shmidta

4

Pl. Iskusstv

Anglijskaya nab.

Konnogvardeyskiy bulvar

Truda ul.

Moika

reka

Kazanskaya ul.

6

Griboyedov Canal

Sadovaya ul.

Lomonosova

Z. Rossi

Lomonosov Pl.

ul.

Pisareva ul.

Voznesensky pr.

Dostoyevs Litera Muse

Dekabristov ul.

reka Fontanka

Zagorodny pr.

Zvenigorodskaya ul.

Maklina

Rimskogo-Korsakova

St. Nicholas Cathedral

Turgenyeva ploshchad

Vitebsky Station

7

❶ Dvortsovaya Ploshchad *(Palace Square).*
One of the world's most magnifi-
cent plazas, the square is a stunning
ensemble of buildings and open space,
a combination of several seemingly
incongruous architectural styles in
perfect harmony. It's where the city's
imperial past has been preserved in
all its glory, but it also resonates with
the history of the revolution that followed. Here, on Bloody Sunday
in 1905, palace troops opened fire
on peaceful demonstrators, killing
scores of women and children, kin-
dling the revolutionary movement. It
was across Palace Square in October
1917 that Bolshevik revolutionaries
stormed the Winter Palace, an event
that led to the birth of the Soviet
Union. Almost 75 years later, huge
crowds rallied on Palace Square in support of perestroika and democracy.
Today, the beautiful square is a bustling hubbub of tourist and marketing
activity. Horseback and carriage rides are available for hire here. ⊠*City
Center* Ⓜ*Nevsky prospekt.*

> ## ST. PETERSBURG BEST BETS
>
> ■ **Try not to be overwhelmed by the State Hermitage Museum.** This immense and ornate royal palace is one of the finest art repositories in the world.
>
> ■ **Soak in the atmosphere at Dvortsovaya Ploshchad.** The seeds of the revolution were sown in this historic and architecturally stunning square.
>
> ■ **Appreciate the architectural symmetry of the downtown core.** Known by the epithet "Venice of the North," St. Petersburg offers marvelous vistas at every turn.

❷ Winter Palace *(Zimny Dvorets).* With its 1,001 rooms swathed in malachite, jasper, agate, and gilded mirrors, this famous palace—the residence of Russia's rulers from Catherine the Great (1762) to Nicholas II
(1917)—is the focal point of Palace Square. The palace, now the site of
the State Hermitage Museum, is the grandest monument of that strange
hybrid: the Russian rococo, in itself an eye-popping mix of the old-fashioned 17th-century baroque, and the newfangled 18th-century neoclassical style. Now "Russianized," the palace's neoclassic ornament lost its
early gracefulness and Greek sense of proportion and evolved toward the
heavier, more monumental, imperial style. Still, the exterior is particularly
successful and pleasing.

The palace, which was created by the Italian architect Bartolomeo Francesco Rastrelli, stretches from Palace Square to the Neva River embankment. It was the fourth royal residence on this site, commissioned in 1754
by Peter the Great's daughter Elizabeth. By the time it was completed, in
1762, Elizabeth had died and the craze for the Russian rococo style had
waned. Catherine the Great left the exterior unaltered but had the interiors
redesigned in the neoclassical style of her day. In 1837, after the palace
was gutted by fire, the interiors were revamped once again. Three of the
palace's most celebrated rooms are the **Gallery of the 1812 War,** where
portraits of Russian commanders who served against Napoléon are on
display; the **Great Throne Room,** richly decorated in marble and bronze;
and the **Malachite Room,** designed by the architect Alexander Bryullov.
⊠*Dvortsovaya Pl., City Center* ⊕*www.hermitagemuseum.org* Ⓜ*Nevsky
Prospekt.*

❸ State Hermitage Museum (*Gosudarstvenny Ermitazh Muzey*). Leonardo's *Benois Madonna* ... Rembrandt's *Danaë* ... Matisse's *The Dance* ... you get the picture. As the former private art collection of the tsars, this is one of the world's most famous museums, virtually wallpapered with celebrated paintings. In addition, the walls are works of art themselves, for this collection is housed in the lavish Winter Palace, one of the most outstanding examples of Russian baroque magnificence. The museum takes its name from Catherine the Great (1729–96), who used it for her private apartments. Between 1764 and 1775, the empress undertook to acquire some of the world's finest works of art.

Fodor'sChoice
★

A wealth of Russian and European art is on show: Florentine, Venetian, and other Italian art through the 18th century, including Leonardos and Michelangelos, two Raphaels, eight Titians, and works by Tintoretto, Lippi, Caravaggio, and Canaletto. The Hermitage also houses a superb collection of Spanish art, of which works by El Greco, Velázquez, Murillo, and Goya are on display. Its spectacular presentation of Flemish and Dutch art contains roomfuls of Van Dycks. Also here are more than 40 canvasses by Rubens and an equally impressive number of Rembrandts. There is a smattering of excellent British paintings includes works by Joshua Reynolds, Thomas Gainsborough, and George Morland.

Reflecting the Francophilia of the Empresses Elizabeth and Catherine, the museum is second only to the Louvre in its assortment of French art. Along with earlier masterpieces by Lorrain, Watteau, and Poussin, the collection runs the whole gamut of 19th-century genius, with Delacroix, Ingres, Corot, and Courbet. There is also a stunning collection of impressionists and postimpressionists, including works by Monet, Degas, Sisley, Pissarro, and Renoir. Sculptures by Auguste Rodin and a host of pictures by Cézanne, Gauguin, and van Gogh are followed by Picasso and a lovely room of Matisse.

Possibly the most-prized section of the Hermitage is the first-floor's **Treasure Gallery**, also referred to as the *Zolotaya Kladovaya* (Golden Room). This spectacular collection of gold, silver, and royal jewels includes ancient Scythian gold and silver treasures, plus precious stones, jewelry, and jewel-encrusted items from the 16th through the 20th centuries. ✉*2 Dvortsovaya Pl., City Center* ☎*812/710–9625, 812/571–3420, 812/571–8446 tours* ⊕*www.hermitagemuseum.org* ✉*State Hermitage Museum 350R (free 1st Thurs. of month); multi-access ticket 700R; Treasure Gallery 300R, plus 160R for daily English-language tour, which takes place around noon* ⊗*Tues.–Sat. 10:30–6, Sun. 10:30–5* Ⓜ*Nevsky prospekt.*

❹ St. Isaac's Cathedral (*Isaakievsky Sobor*). St. Isaac's is the world's third-largest domed cathedral and the first monument you see of the city if you arrive by ship. Tsar Alexander I commissioned the construction of the cathedral in 1818 to celebrate his victory over Napoléon.

Fodor'sChoice
★

The interior of the cathedral is lavishly decorated with malachite, lazulite, marble, and other precious stones and minerals. Gilding the dome required 220 pounds of gold. When the city was blockaded during World War II, the gilded dome was painted black to avoid its being targeted by enemy fire. Despite efforts to protect it, the cathedral nevertheless suffered heavy damage, as bullet holes on the columns on the south side attest. ✉*1*

Isaakievskaya Pl., Admiralteisky ☎*812/315–9732* ✉*Cathedral 270R, colonade 120R* ⊙*Cathedral: May–Sept., Thurs.–Tues. 11–6, kassa closes at 6. Colonnade 11–10* PM*, kassa closes at 10; Oct.–Apr., Thurs.–Tues. 11–6, kassa closes at 5* Ⓜ*Sennaya Ploshchad.*

⑤ **Peter and Paul Fortress** *(Petropavlovskaya Krepost).* The first building in Sankt-Piter-Burkh, as the city was then called, the fortress was erected in just one year, between 1703 and 1704. The date on which construction began on the fortress is celebrated as the birth of St. Petersburg.

Fodor's Choice
★

The fortifications display several gates, along with arsenal buildings and the **Engineer's House** (*Inzhenerny Dom*), which is now a branch of the Museum of the History of St. Petersburg (as are all exhibits in the fortress) and presents displays about the city's pre-revolutionary history.

The main attraction of the fortress, however, is the **Cathedral of Sts. Peter and Paul** *(Petropavlovsky Sobor).* Constructed between 1712 and 1733 on the site of an earlier wooden church, it's highly unusual for a Russian Orthodox church. Instead of the characteristic bulbous domes, it's adorned by a single, slender, gilded spire whose height (400 feet) made the church the city's tallest building for more than two centuries. Starting with Peter the Great, the cathedral served as the burial place of the tsars.

Several of the fortress's bastions were put to use over the years mainly as political prisons. One of them, **Trubetskoi Bastion,** is open to the public as a museum. Famous prisoners include some of the People's Will terrorists, who killed Alexander II in 1881; plus revolutionaries Leon Trotsky and Maxim Gorky. ✉*3 Petropavlovskaya Krepost, Petrograd Side* ☎*812/238–4511* ✉*120R* ⊙*Thurs.–Tues. 11–6, kassa open until 5 Thurs.–Mon., until 4 on Tues.; Cathedral of Sts. Peter and Paul closed Wed.; fortress closed last Tues. of month* Ⓜ*Gorkovskaya.*

⑥ **Kazan Cathedral** *(Kazansky Sobor).* After a visit to Rome, Tsar Paul I (1754–1801) commissioned this magnificent cathedral, wishing to copy—and perhaps present the Orthodox rival to—that city's St. Peter's. It was erected between 1801 and 1811 from a design by Andrei Voronikhin. Inside and out, the church abounds with sculpture and decoration. On the prospect side the frontage holds statues of St. John the Baptist and the apostle Andrew as well as such sanctified Russian heroes as Grand Prince Vladimir (who advanced the Christianization of Russia) and Alexander Nevsky. Note the enormous bronze front doors—exact copies of Ghiberti's Gates of Heaven at Florence's Baptistery. ✉*2 Kazanskaya Pl., City Center* ☎*812/314–4663* ⊙*Open daily 8:30–8; services weekdays at 10* AM *and 6* PM*, weekends at 7 and 10* AM *and 6* PM Ⓜ*Nevsky prospekt.*

⑦ **State Museum of Russian Art** *(Gosudarstvenny Russky Muzey).* In 1898 Nicholas II turned the stupendously majestic neoclassical **Mikhailovsky Palace** (*Mikhailovsky Dvorets*) into a museum that has become one of the country's most important art galleries. The collection at the museum, which is sometimes just referred to as the Russian Museum, has scores of masterpieces on display, from outstanding icons to mainstream art of all eras. For many years much of this work was unknown in the West, and it's fascinating to see the stylistic parallels and the incorporation of outside influences into a Russian framework. Painters of the World of Art

Fodor's Choice
★

movement—Bakst, Benois, and Somov—are also here. There are several examples of 20th-century art, with works by Kandinsky and Kazimir Malevich. ⊠*4–2 Inzhenernaya ul., City Center* ☎*812/595–4248* ⊕*www.rusmuseum.ru* ⊠*300R* ☽*Mon. 10–5, Wed.–Sun. 10–6, kassa open until 1 hr before closing* Ⓜ*Nevsky prospekt.*

SHOPPING

Pick up a copy of Russian *Vogue* and you may be surprised to see that it nearly outdoes its Parisian and American counterparts for sheer glitz and trendy garb. And all those nifty threads that the models are wearing are fully stocked in the international boutiques around the city.

A two-tiered system of stores exists in St. Petersburg. "Western-style" shops taking credit-card payment have replaced the old *Beriozkas* (Birch Trees) emporiums, which were stocked only for foreigners. State-run shops are also better stocked now than before. Only rubles (as opposed to credit cards) are accepted here, however, and you'll have a tough time maneuvering through the cashiers if you don't speak some Russian.

The central shopping district is Nevsky prospekt and the streets running off it. Don't expect too many bargains beyond the bootlegged CDs and videos (which could be confiscated at customs in the United States), however, because prices for items such as clothes and electronic goods are just as high as in the West, and in the chic stores in hotels they are even higher.

For true souvenirs of the city, think quality crafts just like the tsars did. Ceramic painted eggs, á la Fabergé, and almost anything ornate and gilded are typical of the 'imperial' style. Look also for good quality linens. Furs may not be to everybody's taste but wealthy locals still prefer them during the freezing winters. For kitsch, what better than a set of Russian dolls? These vary in quality and in price.

Guild of Masters. Jewelry, ceramics, and other types of Russian traditional art, all made by members of the Russian Union of Artists, are sold here. ⊠*82 Nevsky pr., City Center* ☎*812/279–0979* Ⓜ*Mayakovskaya.*

Lena. A wide selection of furs is sold at this store. Note that some furs from protected species, such as seals, cannot be brought into the United States. ⊠*50 Nevsky pr., at Malaya Sadovaya, City Center* ☎*812/312–3234* Ⓜ*Gostinny Dvor.*

WHERE TO EAT

¢–$$ ✕**Tinkoff.** The crowded, loftlike Tinkoff is St. Petersburg's first microbrewery. People come to enjoy good beer and tasty comfort food in a relaxed, almost clublike dining room. There's a sushi bar, too, but you're better off sticking with the beer and burgers. ⊠*7 Kazanskaya ul., City Center* ☎*812/718–5566* ⊟*AE, DC, MC, V* Ⓜ*Nevsky prospekt.*

¢–$ ✕**James Cook.** Upon entering James Cook you have a choice: turn right for the pub with a decent menu, or left for one of the finest coffee shops in town. Choose from 40 kinds of coffee, elite teas, various coffee cocktails, and desserts. ⊠*2 Svedsky per., City Center* ☎*812/312–3200* ▤*DC, MC, V* Ⓜ*Nevsky prospekt.*

STOCKHOLM, SWEDEN

Stockholm is a city in the flush of its second youth. In the last 10 years Sweden's capital has emerged from its cold, Nordic shadow to take the stage as a truly international city. The streets are flowing with a young and confident population keen to drink in everything the city has to offer. The glittering feeling of optimism, success, and living in the "here and now" is rampant in Stockholm. Of course, not everyone is looking to live so much in the present; luckily, Stockholm also has plenty of history. Stockholm boasts a glorious medieval old town, grand palaces, ancient churches, sturdy edifices, public parks, and 19th-century museums—its history is soaked into the very fabric of its airy boulevards, built as a public display of the city's trading glory.

ESSENTIALS

CURRENCY The krona (SKr 6.84 to US$ 1; SKr 9.37 to €1); exchange rates were accurate at this writing but are subject to change. U.S. currency is not generally accepted in Europe, but ATMs are common and credit cards are widely accepted.

HOURS General shopping hours are weekdays 10 to 6, Saturday from 10 to 5, Sunday from noon until 3. Museums open at 10 or 11 in the morning, closing at 5 or 6 in the evenings, with most open on Sunday.

INTERNET **Stockholms Stadsbiblioteket** *(Stockholm City Library)* (⊠*Sveav. 73, Vasastan* ☎*08/50831100* ⊕*www.ssb.stockholm.se* ⊙*Mon.–Thurs. 9–9, Fri. 9–7, weekends noon–4)*

TELEPHONES Most tri- and quad-band GSM phones will work in Sweden, where the mobile phone system is up-to-date, with a 3G system and network compatibility. Public phones in Sweden take phone cards or credit cards. Phone cards can be bought at telecom shops, newsstands, and tobacconists. Public phones support international calls. Handsets are single band. Main providers include Telia, Vodafone, and T-Mobile.

COMING ASHORE

Most vessels dock at various quays in the heart of the Gamla Stan (Old Town). How far you have to walk to the attractions depends on at which quay you are moored. This is one port where you'll want to be out on deck as the ship arrives and the city comes within camera distance. If all berths are full (eight of them) there is a mooring buoy in the harbor, and passengers will be tendered ashore. You can reach everything in the city (museums, shops, restaurants, and cafés) from the quays on foot.

Alternatively, some vessels dock at Nynasham outside the city. It is a 15-minute walk from the port at Nynasham to the railway station for the one-hour journey into central Stockholm. A one-day travel card covers this journey and all other public transport trips within the city. SL (Stockholm Transport) runs a modern and reliable public transit system. Tickets are valid for one hour from validation and cost SKr 20–SKr 26 per journey within Zone 1 (central Stockholm). A one-day card is SKr 90.

Taxis are plentiful but expensive, and most drivers speak some English. Current rates are SKr 45 for pick up, then SKr 8.40 per km.

EXPLORING STOCKHOLM

Numbers in the margin correspond to points of interest on the Stockholm map.

⑰ Historiska Museet *(Museum of National Antiquities).* Viking treasures and the Gold Room are the main draw, but well-presented temporary exhibitions also cover various periods of Swedish history. The gift shop here is excellent. ⊠*Narvav. 13–17, Östermalm* ☎*08/51955600* ⊕*www. historiska.se* ⊠*Free* ⊙*May–Sept., daily 10–5; Oct.–Apr., Tues., Wed., and Fri.–Sun. 11–5, Thurs. 11–8.*

❸ Kulturhuset. Stockholm's controversial cultural center is a glass-and-stone monolith on the south side of Sergels Torg. The restaurant Panorama, at the top, has great views and traditional Swedish cuisine. ⊠*Sergelstorg 3, Noormalm* ☎*08/50831508.*

❺ Kungliga Slottet *(Royal Palace).* Designed by Nicodemus Tessin, the Royal Palace was completed in 1760 and replaced the previous palace that had burned here in 1697. Watch the changing of the guard in the curved terrace entrance, and view the palace's fine furnishings and Gobelin tapestries on a tour of the **Representationsvän** (State Apartments). To survey the crown jewels, which are no longer used in this self-consciously egalitarian country, head to the **Skattkammaren** (Treasury). The **Livrustkammaren** (Royal Armory) has an outstanding collection of weaponry, coaches, and royal regalia. Entrances to the Treasury and Armory are on the Slottsbacken side of the palace. ⊠*Gamla Stan* ☎*08/4026130* ⊕*www. royalcourt.se* ⊠*State Apartments SKr 80, Treasury SKr 80, Royal Armory SKr 90, combined ticket for all areas SKr 130* ⊙*State Apartments and Treasury May 15–31, daily 10–4; June–Aug, daily 10–5; Sept. 1–Sept. 14, daily 10–4; Sept. 15–May 14, Tues.–Sun. noon–3. Armory May–Aug., daily 11–4; Sept.–Apr., Tues.–Sun. 11–4.*

❾ Kungsträdgården *(King's Garden).* This is one of Stockholm's smallest and most central parks. Once the royal kitchen garden, it now hosts a large number of festivals and events each season. The park has numerous cafés and restaurants, a playground, and, in winter, an ice-skating rink. ⊠*Between Hamng. and the Operan, Norrmalm.*

⑫ Moderna Museet *(Museum of Modern Art).* This excellent collection includes works by Picasso, Kandinsky, Dalí, Brancusi, and other international artists. You can also view examples of significant Swedish painters and sculptors and an extensive section on photography. The building itself is striking. Designed by the well-regarded Spanish architect Rafael Moneo, it has seemingly endless hallways of blond wood and walls of glass. ⊠*Skeppsholmen, Lower Norrmalm* ☎*08/51955200* ⊕*www.modernamuseet.se* ⊠*SKr 80* ⊙*Tues. 10–8, Wed.–Sun. 10–6.*

⑩ Nationalmuseum. The museum's collection of paintings and sculptures is made up of about 12,500 works. The emphasis is on Swedish and Nordic art, but other areas are well represented. Look especially for some fine works by Rembrandt. The print and drawing department is also impres-

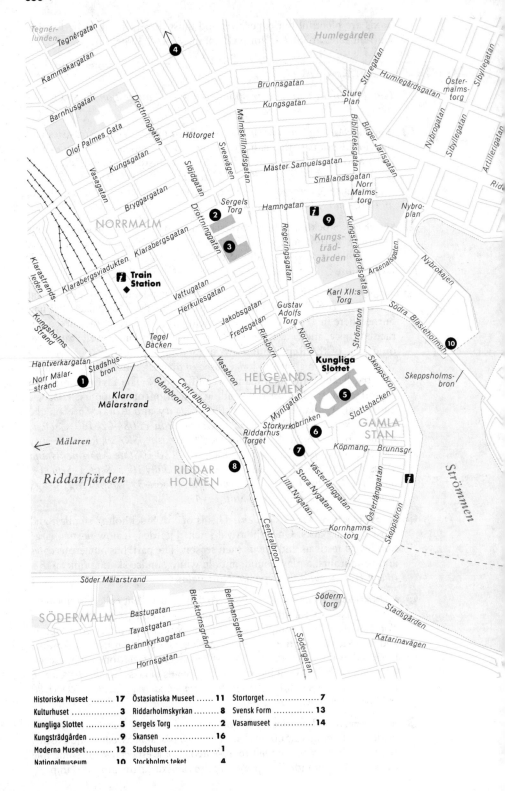

Stockholm

Karlaplan

Kommendörsgatan

ÖSTERMALM

Narvavägen

Banérgatan

Karlavägen

Oxenstiernsgatan

LADUGÅRDSGÄRDET

Linnégatan

Gärdesgatan

Skarpögatan

Greugatan

Styrmangatan

Storgatan

Linnégatan

Strandvägen

17

Strandvägen

Djurgårdsbron

Djurgårdsbrunnsviken

15

Rosendalsvägen

14

12

SKEPPSHOLMEN

Alkärret

16

DJURGÅRDEN

Sirishovsvägen

Svensksundsvägen

Falkenbergsg.

Djurgårdsvägen

Djurgårds
Slätten

Sollidsbacken

Singelbacken

Allmänna Gränd

KASTELL-
HOLMEN

Baltic →

BECKHOLMEN

Saltsjön

0 ——— 1/4 mi

0 ——— 1/4 km

KEY	
🚢	Ferry
+—+	Rail Lines
🛈	Tourist information

7

sive, with a nearly complete collection of Edouard Manet prints.
⊠*Södra   Blasieholmshamnen,
Lower Norrmalm* ☎*08/51954428*
⊕*www.nationalmuseum.se* ☒*SKr
80* ⊗*Jan.–Aug., Tues. 11–8, Wed.–
Sun. 11–5; Sept.–Dec., Tues. and
Thurs. 11–8, Wed., Fri., and weekends 11–5.*

🟤 **Nordiska Museet** *(Nordic Museum).*
An imposing late-Victorian structure housing peasant costumes from
every region of the country and
exhibits on the Sámi (pronounced
sah-mee), or Lapps—the formerly
seminomadic reindeer herders who inhabit the far north—and many other
aspects of Swedish life. ⊠*Djurgårdsv. 6–16, Djurgården* ☎*08/51954600*
⊕*www.nordiskamuseet.se* ☒*SKr 60* ⊗*June–Aug., daily 10–5, Sept.–
May, Mon., Tues., Thurs., and Fri. 10–4, Wed. 10–8, weekend 11–5.*

🟤 **Östasiatiska Museet** *(Museum of Far Eastern Antiquities).* If you have an
affinity for Asian art and culture, don't miss this impressive collection of
Chinese and Japanese Buddhist sculptures and artifacts. ⊠*Skeppsholmen,
Lower Norrmalm* ☎*08/51955750* ⊕*www.mfea.se* ☒*SKr 60* ⊗*Tues.
11–8, Wed.–Sun. 11–5.*

🟤 **Riddarholmskyrkan** *(Riddarholm Church).* Dating from 1270, the Grey Fri-
ars monastery is the second-oldest structure in Stockholm, and has been
the burial place for Swedish kings for more than 400 years. The redbrick structure, distinguished by its delicate iron-fretwork spire, is rarely
used for services: it's more like a museum now. The most famous figures
interred within are King Gustavus Adolphus, hero of the Thirty Years'
War, and the warrior King Karl XII, renowned for his daring invasion of
Russia, who died in Norway in 1718. The most recent of the 17 Swedish kings to be put to rest here was Gustav V, in 1950. ⊠*Riddarholmen*
☎*08/59059009* ☒*SKr 20* ⊗*June–Aug., daily 10–5; late May and early
Sept., daily 10–4.*

🟤 **Sergels Torg.** Named after Johan Tobias Sergel (1740–1814), one of Sweden's greatest sculptors, this busy junction in Stockholm's center is dominated by modern, functional buildings and a sunken pedestrian square
with subterranean connections to the rest of the neighborhood. Visitors
are often put off by its darkened, covered walkways and youths in hooded
tops, but it is relatively safe and a great place to witness some real Stockholm street life. ⊠*Norrmalm.*

🟤 **Skansen.** The world's first open-air museum, Skansen was founded in 1891
by philologist and ethnographer Artur Hazelius, who is buried here. He
preserved examples of traditional Swedish architecture brought from all
parts of the country, including farmhouses, windmills, barns, a working
glassblower's hut, and churches. Not only is Skansen a delightful trip
out of time in the center of a modern city, but it also provides insight
into the life and culture of Sweden's various regions. ⊠*Djurgårdsslätten*

4951, Djurgården ☎08/4428000 ⊕www.skansen.se ▤Park and zoo: Sept.–Apr. SKr 50; May–Aug. SKr 70. Aquarium SKr 60 ⊙Jan. and Feb., weekdays 10–3, weekends 10–4; Mar. and Apr., daily 10–4; May, daily 10–8; June–Aug., daily 10–10; Sept., daily 10–5; Oct., daily 10–4; Nov., weekdays 10–4, weekends 10–5; Dec. weekdays 11–5, certain days in Dec. longer hrs.

❶ Stadshuset *(City Hall).* The architect Ragnar Östberg, one of the founders of the National Romantic movement, completed Stockholm's city hall in 1923. Headquarters of the city council, the building is functional but ornate: its immense **Blå Hallen** (Blue Hall) is the venue for the annual Nobel Prize dinner, Stockholm's principal social event. Take a trip to the top of the 348-foot tower, most of which can be achieved by elevator, to enjoy a breathtaking panorama of the city and Riddarfjärden. ⊠*Hantverkarg. 1, Kungsholmen* ☎08/50829058 ⊕*www.stockholm.se* ▤*SKr 60, tower SKr 20* ⊙*Guided tours only. Hourly tours in English, June–Aug., daily 10–4; Sept., daily 10, noon, and 2; Oct.–May, daily 10 and noon. Tower open May–Sept., daily 10–4:30.*

FodorśChoice
★

❹ Stockholms Stadsbiblioteket *(Stockholm City Library).* Libraries aren't always a top sightseeing priority, but the Stockholm City Library is among the most captivating buildings in town. Designed by the famous Swedish architect E. G. Asplund and completed in 1928, the building's cylindrical, galleried main hall gives it the appearance of a large birthday cake. ⊠*Sveav. 73, Vasastan* ☎08/50831100 ⊕*www.ssb.stockholm.se* ⊙*Mon.–Thurs. 9–9, Fri. 9–7, weekends noon–4.*

❻ Storkyrkan. Swedish kings were crowned in the 15th-century Great Church as late as 1907. Today its main attractions are a dramatic wooden statue of St. George slaying the dragon, carved by Bernt Notke of Lübeck in 1489, and the *Parhelion* (1520), the oldest-known painting of Stockholm. ⊠*Trångsund 1, Gamla Stan* ☎08/7233016 ⊙*Sept.–Apr., daily 9–4; May–Aug., daily 9–6.*

❼ Stortorget *(Great Square).* Here in 1520 the Danish king Christian II ordered a massacre of Swedish noblemen. The slaughter paved the way for a national revolt against foreign rule and the founding of Sweden as a sovereign state. ⊠*Near Kungliga Slottet, Gamla Stan.*

⓭ Svensk Form *(Swedish Form).* This museum emphasizes the importance of Swedish form and design, although international works and trends are also covered. Exhibits include everything from chairs to light fixtures to cups, bowls, and silverware. Find out why Sweden is considered a world leader in industrial design. ⊠*Holmamiralens väg 2, Skeppsholmen, Lower Norrmalm* ☎08/4633130 ⊕*www.svenskform.se* ▤*SKr 20* ⊙*Wed. 5–8, Thurs.–Fri. noon–5, weekends noon–4.*

⓮ Vasamuseet *(Vasa Museum).* The warship *Vasa* sank 10 minutes into its maiden voyage in 1628, consigned to a watery grave until it was raised from the seabed in 1961. Its hull was preserved by the Baltic mud, free of the worms that can eat through ships' timbers. Now largely restored to her former glory (however short-lived it may have been), the man-of-war resides in a handsome museum. The political history of the world may have been different had she made it out of harbor. Daily tours are available
★

7

year-round. ⊠*Galärvarsv., Djurgården* ☎*08/51954800* ⊕*www.vasamu-seet.se* ⊠*SKr 80* ⊙*June–Aug., daily 8.30–8; Sept.–May, Thurs.–Tues. 10–5, Wed. 10–8.*

SHOPPING

Sweden is recognized globally for its unique design sense and has contributed significantly to what is commonly referred to as Scandinavian design. **Kosta Boda and Orrefors** produce the most popular and well-regarded lines of glassware. All of this makes Stockholm one of the best cities in the world for shopping for furniture and home and office accessories. If you like to shop, charge on down to any one of the three main department stores in the central city area, all of which carry top-name Swedish brands for both men and women. For souvenirs and crafts peruse the boutiques and galleries in Västerlånggatan, the main street of Gamla Stan. For jewelry, crafts, and fine art, hit the shops that line the raised sidewalk at the start of Hornsgatan on Södermalm. Drottninggatan, Birger Jarlsgatan, Biblioteksgatan, Götgatan, and Hamngatan also offer some of the city's best shopping.

On the corner of Östermalmstorg, in the same building as the marketplace, is **Bruka** (⊠*Humlegårdsg. 1, Östermalm* ☎*08/6601480*), which has a wide selection of creative kitchen items, as well as wicker baskets and chairs. The **Crystal Art Center** (⊠*Tegelbacken 4, Lower Norrmalm* ☎*08/217169*), near the central station, has a great selection of smaller glass items. Though prices are high at **Iris Hantverk** (⊠*Kungsg. 55, Lower Norrmalm* ☎*08/214726*), so is the quality of gift items and souvenirs. Swedish pottery, jewelry, kitchen items, wooden toys, linens, and cookbooks from all over the country are available at **Svensk Hemslöjd** (⊠*Sveav. 44, Lower Norrmalm* ☎*08/232115*).

WHERE TO EAT

¢–$$$$ ✕**Tranan.** There's something about Tranan that makes you want to go back. The food is Swedish with a touch of French and is consistently very good. The stark walls covered with old movie posters and the red-and-white-checked tablecloths are reminders of the days when it was a workingman's beer parlor. Try the *biff rydberg,* a fillet of beef, fried potatoes, horseradish, and egg yolk—it's a Swedish classic. ⊠*Karlbergsv. 14, Vasastan* ☎*08/52728100* ⊟*AE, DC, MC, V* ⊙*No lunch weekends.*

¢–$$$ ✕**Pelican.** Beer is the order of the day at Pelican, a traditional working-class Fodor'sChoice drinking hall. The food here is some of the best traditional Swedish fare ★ in the city. The herring, meatballs, and salted bacon with onion sauce are not to be missed. ⊠*Blekingeg. 40, Södermalm* ☎*08/55609090* ⚐*Reservations not accepted* ⊟*MC, V* ⊙*Closed Sun.*

TALLINN, ESTONIA

Tallinn's tiny gem of an Old Town, the most impressive in the region, is an ideal cruise destination. It has romantic towers, ankle-wrenching cobblestone streets, cozy nooks, city-wall cafés, and a dozen other attractions—all within 1 square km. In many ways still the same town as during the medieval era, it is compact enough to reveal itself on a short visit.

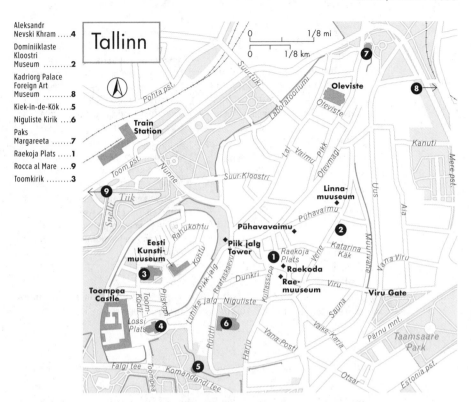

In this eminently walkable city, it is possible to see the main sights and venture into intimate corners during your trip and feel that you've found your own personal Tallinn. The city has blossomed in the post-Communist era and revels in its resurgent popularity, but it hasn't forgotten its roots. It's still charming and distinctive despite having strode headlong into the 21st century.

ESSENTIALS

CURRENCY The Estonian kroon (11.44EEK to US$1; 15.66EEK to €1); exchange rates were accurate at this writing but are subject to change. U.S. dollars are not accepted in Estonia. Credit cards are widely accepted, and ATMs are common in Tallinn.

HOURS Shops are open from 10 AM until 7 PM, though some close early on Saturday. Museums are open Wednesday through Sunday from 10 AM or 11 AM until 5 PM or 6 PM.

INTERNET Post offices in Tallinn have Internet access. **Toompea Post Office** (⊠ *Lossi plats 4*) is the post office for the Old Town; it's open weekdays 9 AM–5 PM. There are more than 100 free Wi-Fi spots in the city, including one at the town hall.

TELEPHONES Most tri- and quad-band mobile phones should work in Estonia. The mobile service is dual-band and supports text and data services. Pay phones take phone cards worth 30EEK, 50EEK, or 100EEK. Buy cards at any kiosk. You can use these to make international calls.

COMING ASHORE

The Old City Harbor Port sits in the very heart of modern Tallinn and is only half a mile from the city center. Terminal facilities are comprehensive and include a restaurant, bank/exchange facilities, tourist information shops, and restrooms. Taxis wait outside the terminal building for journeys into the Old Town; otherwise, it's only a short walk from the port.

Taxi fares generally start at between 35EEK and 70EEK with an additional charge of 7EEK per km in the daytime, more at night or in bad weather. Drivers are bound by law to display an operating license and a meter. There is no need to rent a car while in Tallinn, as all the major attractions are in the Old Town, which is very close to the dock.

TALINN BEST BETS

■ **Shopping in Vanalinn.** These alleyways have been a bustling commercial center for more than 500 years. History practically oozes from every stone and the galleries are a shopper's delight.

■ **Raekoja Plats.** One of the finest city squares in the Baltic, Raekoja Plats is the social center of the city, hosting markets, concerts and parades.

■ **Aleksandr Nevski Khram.** This Orthodox church is a wonderfully ornate example of its type, with onion domes and an interior full of votives and icons.

EXPLORING TALLINN

Numbers in the margin correspond to points of interest on the Tallinn map.

Tallinn's historic Old Town retains almost 80% of its medieval buildings—impressive enough to gain UNESCO World Heritage status. The city is made up of two parts. Vanalinn (Lower Old Town) was historically the domain of traders, artisans, and ordinary citizens—a workaday commercial hub whose streets were always noisy and busy. The stately, sedate Toompea (Upper Town), a hillock that was the site of the original Estonian settlement, is on the burial mound of Kalev, the epic hero of Estonia. Toompea Castle, crowning the hill, is now the seat of the country's parliament and, sadly, is not open to visitors. As you wander the cobbled alleyways even with crowds of fellow visitors, it's easy to feel the atmosphere of the Tallinn of old. The commerce of the streets in Vanalinn may disappoint some, but the ancestors of today's gallery and restaurant owners would surely be pleased to see the bustling streets of their city today.

4 **Aleksandr Nevski Khram.** The19th-century Russian Orthodox Alexander Nevsky Cathedral, with the country's largest bell, is a symbol of the centuries of Russification endured by Estonia. ⊠ *Lossi pl. 10, Toompea* ☎ *644–3484* ☼ *Daily 8–7.*

2 **Dominiiklaste Kloostri Muuseum.** Wander through the ages in the ancient stone galleries and narrow hallways of the Dominican Monastery Museum, founded in 1246 and now displaying 15th- and 16th-century stone carvings. At 5 PM enjoy a half-hour baroque music concert. ⊠ *Vene 16, Vanalinn* ☎ *644–4606* ⊕ *kloostri.ee* ☼ *Daily 10–6.*

8 **Kadriorg Palace Foreign Art Museum.** The baroque palace, built for Catherine I by her husband Peter the Great in 1721, merits a visit not just for its impressive and thorough exhibition of 16th- to 20th-century art, but also for the palace's architectural beauty and manicured gardens. Kadriorg Palace offers a glimpse into history, from Russian imperial splendor to Soviet Socialist realist art, with Estonian and European masterpieces along the way. ⌧ *Weizenbergi 37* ☎ *602–6001* ⊕ *www.ekm.ee* ⊙ *May–Sept., Tues.–Sun. 10–5; Oct.–Apr., Wed.–Sun. 10–5.*

❺ Kiek-in-de-Kök. At the southern end of the Old Town looms this magnifi-
★ cent, six-story tower church (the name is Low German for "peep in the kitchen"), so called because during the 15th century one could peer into the kitchens of lower town houses from here. The tower has a museum of contemporary art and ancient maps and weapons. ⌧ *Komandandi 2Vanalinn* ☎ *644–6686* ⊙ *Mar.–Oct., Tues.–Sun. 10:30–6; Nov.–Feb., Tues.–Sun. 10:30–5.*

❻ Niguliste Kirik. The 15th-century Church of St. Nicholas, part of the Estonian Art Museum, is famed for its fragment of a treasured frieze, Bernt Notke's (1440–1509) *Danse Macabre,* a haunting depiction of death. ⌧ *Niguliste 3, Vanalinn* ☎ *602–6001* ⊕ *www.ekm.ee* ⊙ *Wed.–Sun. 10–5.*

❼ Paks Margareeta. The stocky guardian of the northernmost point of the Old Town, Fat Margaret, is a 16th-century fortification named for a par-ticularly hefty cannon it contained. Now it houses a Maritime Museum and a roof with a view of Old Town. ⌧ *Pikk 70, Vanalinn* ☎ *641–1408* ⊙ *Wed.–Sun. 10–6.*

❶ Raekoja Plats. Tallinn's town hall square has a long history of intrigue, exe-cutions, and salt (Tallinn's main export in the Middle Ages). Take a guided
Fodor'sChoice tour of the only surviving original Gothic **town hall** (☎ *645–7900*) in north-
★ ern Europe. Old Thomas, its weather vane, has been atop the town hall since 1530. Near the center of the square, an L-shape stone marks the site of a 17th-century execution, where a priest was beheaded for killing a waitress who had offered him a rock-hard omelet. Across the square stands the town **apothecary,** which dates from 1422. ⌧ *Raekoja plats 11* ☎ *631–4860* ⊙ *Weekdays 9–7, Sat. 9–5, Sun. 9–4.*

❾ Rocca al Mare. Just a 15-minute taxi ride from the center, the 207-acre Open-
♺ Air Ethnographic Museum provides a breath of fresh air and an informa-tive look into Estonia's past, from farm architecture to World War II–era deportations. ⌧ *Vabaõhumuuseumi 12* ☎ *654–9117* ⊙ *Daily 10–6.*

❸ Toomkirik. The Lutheran Dome Church, the oldest church in the country, was founded by the occupying Danes in the 13th century and rebuilt in 1686. ⌧ *Toom-kooli 6, Toompea* ☎ *644–4140* ⊙ *Tues.–Sun. 9–5.*

SHOPPING

Travelers from outside the European Union can buy goods from tax free shops and will receive a tax exemption on purchases over 2500EEK (price of the item includes tax). The shop will provide you with the paperwork and this must be presented to the customs officials at the port. Purchases must not be unwrapped before you leave the country.

Tallinn has a wide range of crafts on sale. Fragrant juniper wood is carved into bowls and dolomite stone is fashioned into candlesticks and coasters.

A whole range of handblown glass, ceramics, delicate wrought iron, and art is sold in tiny galleries. Hand-knitted sweaters, gloves and socks keep the locals snug in winter and are signature souvenirs here. Warming quilts are also available, as well as a good range of leather goods. Sweet tooths will love the chocolates made by Kalev and the hand-painted marzipan that's sold in presentation boxes. The Old Town is the place to browse, with some excellent shops around Katerina kälk (Catherine Passage).

At **Bogapott.** (⊠*Pikk-jalg 9* ☎*372 631 3181* ⊕*www.bogapott.ee*) a husband and wife team of artists offer a wide range of Estonian-produced crafts. There's a pretty café on-site. **Galerii Kaks** (⊠*Lühike jalg 1* ☎*372 641 8308*) stocks locally produced jewelry, glass textiles ceramics and leatherwork. **Saaremaa Sepad** (⊠*Nunne tn 7* ☎*372 64 6 4315*) has wrought-iron workshops with a huge selection of objects large and small, ranging from practical to decorative.

WHERE TO EAT

$ ✕**Café Anglais.** With an excellent view of Old Town Square, this second-floor café attracts a steady clientele with its nightly live jazz and refreshingly light menu of sandwiches, soups, and salads. ⊠*Raekoja plats 14* ☎*644–2160* ▭*No credit cards.*

$ ✕**Tristan ja Isolde.** Possibly the most sedate café in Tallinn, Tristan and Isolde is inside the medieval stone walls of the town hall. With a dozen varieties of fresh-roasted coffee and soothing jazzy tunes on the sound system, this is a great place to relax morning, noon, or night. ⊠*Town Hall, Raekoja Plats 1* ☎*644–8759* ▭*MC, V.*

VISBY, SWEDEN

Gotland is Sweden's main holiday island, a place of ancient history with a relaxed summer-party vibe, wide sandy beaches, and wild cliff formations called *raukar.* Measuring 125 km (78 mi) long and 52 km (32 mi) at its widest point, Gotland is where Swedish sheep farming has its home. In its charming glades, 35 varieties of wild orchids thrive, attracting botanists from all over the world. The first record of people living on Gotland dates from around 5000 BC. By the Iron Age it had become a leading Baltic trading center. When German marauders arrived in the 13th century, they built most of its churches and established close trading ties with the Hanseatic League in Lübeck. They were followed by the Danes, and Gotland finally became part of Sweden in 1645. Gotland's capital, Visby, reflects this full and fascinating history, and the architecture of its downtown core is classified as a World Heritage Site.

ESSENTIALS

CURRENCY   The Swedish krona (SKr 6.75 to US$1; SKr 9.21 to €1); exchange rates were accurate at this writing but are subject to change. U.S. currency is not generally accepted in Europe. ATMs are common and credit cards are widely accepted.

HOURS   General shopping hours are weekdays from 10 to 6, Saturday from 10 to 5, and Sunday from noon until 3. Museums open at 10 or 11 in the morning, closing at 5 or 6 in the evenings, with most open on Sunday.

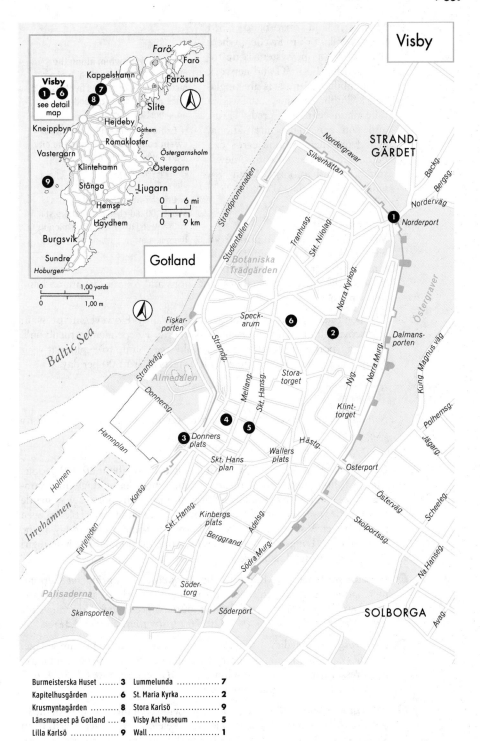

Visby

Gotland

TELEPHONES Most tri- and quad-band GSM phones will work in Sweden, where the mobile phone system is up-to-date and has both 3G and network compatibility. Hand sets are single-band. Public phones in Sweden take phone cards or credit cards, and you can make international calls from them; phone cards can be bought at telecom shops, news-stands and tobacconists. Main providers include Telia, Vodafone, and T-Mobile.

COMING ASHORE

Vessels dock in the town port; from here, it is a 5- to 10-minute walk into the center of town. The port has only the most basic facilities, but shops and restaurants are on hand in town.

> **VISBY BEST BETS**
>
> ■ **Follow your whim along the streets of Visby.** The wealth of architectural splendor funded by Hanseatic trade means there's a wonderful vista on almost every corner.
>
> ■ **Explore the dramatic and windswept countryside beyond the city walls.** Wild orchids, rocky coastal precipices, and grassy meadows abound.
>
> ■ **Church-hopping.** Gotland has about 100 old churches that are still in use (Visby itself has 13); exploring them is a major pastime.

You don't need public transport to explore Visby. However, if you want to discover all that Gotland island has to offer independently, then you'll need transportation. Renting a car would free you up to explore at your own pace. An economy manual vehicle starts at SKr 600 per day.

EXPLORING GOTLAND

Numbers in the margin correspond to points of interest on the Visby map.

VISBY

Gotland's capital, Visby, is a delightful hilly town of about 20,000 people. Medieval houses, ruined fortifications, churches, and cottage-lined cobbled lanes make Visby look like a fairy-tale place. Thanks to a very gentle climate, the roses that grow along many of the town's facades bloom even in November. Visby might be better known to some people today as the home of Pippi Longstocking. Movies featuring the popular red-haired girl with pigtails were filmed here.

❸ **Burmeisterska Huset.** The home of the *Burmeister*—or principal German merchant—organizes exhibitions displaying the works of artists from the island and the rest of Sweden. Call the tourist office in Visby to arrange for a viewing. ⊠*Strandg. 9* ☎*0498/201700 Visby tourist office* ✆*Free.*

❻ **Kapitelhusgården.** Medieval activities are re-created at this museum village. Families can watch and take part in metal- and woodworking, coin making, dressmaking, archery, and hunting. ⊠*Drottensg. 8* ☎*0498/247637* ✆*Free* ⊙*June–Aug., daily noon–6.*

❹ **Länsmuseet på Gotland.** Gotland's county museum contains examples of medieval artwork, prehistoric gravestones and skeletons, and silver hoards from Viking times. Be sure to also check out the ornate "picture stones" from AD 400–600, which depict ships, people, houses, and animals. ⊠*Strandg. 14*

Gotland's Churches

The island has about 100 old churches dating from Gotland's great commercial era that are still in use today. **Barlingbo,** from the 13th century, has vaulted paintings, stained-glass windows, and a remarkable 12th-century font. The exquisite **Dalhem** was constructed around 1200. **Gothem,** built during the 13th century, has a notable series of paintings of that period. **Grötlingbo** is a 14th-century church with stone sculptures and stained glass (note the 12th-century reliefs on the

facade). **Öja,** a medieval church decorated with paintings, houses a famous holy rood from the late-13th century. The massive ruins of a Cistercian monastery founded in 1164 are now called the **Roma Kloster Kyrka** (Roma Cloister Church). **Tingstäde** is a mix of six buildings dating from 1169 to 1300.

☎*0498/292700* ⊕*www.lansmuseetgotland.se* ✉*SKr 40* ⊗*Mid-June–mid-Sept., daily 10–6; Mid-Sept.–mid-June, Tues.–Sun. noon–4.*

② **St. Maria Kyrka.** Visby's cathedral is the only one of the town's 13 medieval churches that is still intact and in use. Built between 1190 and 1225 as a place of worship for the town's German parishioners, the church has few of its original fittings because of the extensive and sometimes clumsy restoration work done over the years. That said, the sandstone font and the unusually ugly angels decorating the pulpit are both original features worth a look. ✉*Västra Kyrkogatan 5* ☎*0498/206800* ⊗*Daily 8–5.*

⑤ **Visby Art Museum.** The town's primary art museum has some innovative exhibitions of contemporary painting and sculpture. On the first floor is the permanent display, which is mostly uninspiring, save for a beautiful 1917 watercolor by local artist Axel Lindman showing Visby from the beach in all its splendid medieval glory. ✉*St. Hansg. 21* ☎*0498/292775* ✉*SKr 75* ⊗*June–Sept., daily 11–5.*

① **Wall.** In its heyday Visby was protected by a wall, of which 3 km (2 mi) survive today, along with 44 towers and numerous gateways. It is considered the best-preserved medieval city wall in Europe after that of Carcassonne, in southern France. Take a stroll to the north gate for an unsurpassed view of the wall.

GOTLAND

There's a lot to see out on the island, so if you want to spend the day exploring, you can see a fair amount in your day in port. Definitely get out of Visby itself if you want to see some of the island's churches.

⑦ **Lummelunda.** The 4 km (2½ mi) of stalactite caves, about 18 km (11 mi) north of Visby on the coastal road, are unique in this part of the world and are worth visiting. The largest was discovered in 1950 by three boys out playing. ✉*Lummelunds Bruk* ☎*0498/273050* ⊕*www.lummelundagrottan.se* ✉*SKr 90* ⊗ *May–Sept., daily 10–2, but hrs are sometimes extended to 3 or 4.*

⑧ A pleasant stop along the way to Lummelunda is the **Krusmyntagården** (✉*Brissand, Väskinde* ☎*0498/296900*), a garden with more than 200 herbs, 8 km (5 mi) north of Visby. It's open daily from 10 to 4.

⑨ Curious rock formations dot the coasts of Gotland, remnants of reefs formed more than 400 million years ago, and two **bird sanctuaries,Stora** and **Lilla Karlsö,** stand off the coast south of Visby. The bird population consists mainly of guillemots, which look like penguins. Visits to these sanctuaries are permitted only in the company of a recognized guide. ☎*0498/240500 for Stora, 0498/485248 for Lilla* 🎫*SKr 225 for Stora, SKr 200 for Lilla* ⊙*May–Aug., daily.*

SHOPPING

Gotlanders are self-sufficient and resourceful people and have developed many handicrafts, so there is a range of handcrafted souvenirs to choose from, including blown glass, metal objects, sculptures, woven items, and ceramics. Sheepskin and wool items are a particular specialty. **Barbro Sandell** (✉*Kustv. 146Norrlanda* ☎*0498/39075*) is a bright shop with one of the island's best selections of fabrics, textiles, and paper printed with patterns inspired by original designs from the 1700s.

G.A.D (*Good Art and Design* ✉*Södra Kyrkog. 16, Visby* ☎*0498/249410*) sells stunningly simple modern furniture that has been designed and made on Gotland.

SPORTS & ACTIVITIES

The unspoiled countryside and onshore waters are a perfect playground if you want to get active. Many visitors simply rent a bike and take to the safe open roads, or try kayaking or windsurfing on the water. Bicycles can be rented from **Gotlands Cykeluthyrning** (✉*Skeppsbron 2* ☎*0498/214133* ⊕*www.gotlandscykeluthyrning.com*).

For an aquatic adventure, **Gotlands Upplevelser** (☎*0730/751678*) will rent you a canoe and a life jacket or windsurfing equipment. Call for prices and locations.

BEACHES

If you do nothing else on Gotland, go for a swim. The island has miles and miles of beautiful golden beaches and unusually warm water for this part of the world. The best and least-crowded beaches are at **Fårö** and **Själsö** in the north of the island.

WHERE TO EAT

$–$$$ ✕**Clematis.** This campy restaurant is one of the most popular in Visby—guests are thrown back a few centuries to the Middle Ages for an authentic night of food, song, and dance. You get a flat slab of bread instead of a plate, and your only utensil is a knife. The staff dons period attire and is known to break into a tune while delivering food to tables. Traditional Swedish fare is served, with a focus on meats and island ingredients. Drinks are served in stone goblets. ✉*Strandg. 20* ☎*0498/292727* ▭*AE, DC, MC, V* ⊙*No lunch.*

$–$$$ ✕**Krusmyntagården.** This marvelous little garden café opened in the late '70s and has been passed down through several owners. The garden now has more than 200 organic herbs and plants, many of which are used in the evening BBQ feasts. ⊠*Brissund* ☏*0498/296900* ▭*AE, DC, MC, V.*

WARNEMÜNDE, GERMANY (FOR BERLIN)

Since the fall of the Iron Curtain, no city in Europe has seen more development and change. Two Berlins that had been separated for 40 years struggled to meld into one, and in the scar of barren borderland between them sprang government and commercial centers that have become the glossy spreads of travel guides and architecture journals. But even as the capital moves forward, history is always tugging at its sleeve. Between the wealth of neoclassical and 21st-century buildings, there are constant reminders, both subtle and stark, of the events of the 20th century. For every relocated corporate headquarters, a church stands half-ruined, a synagogue is under 24-hour guard, and an empty lot remains where a building either crumbled in World War II or went up in dynamite as East Germany cleared a path for its Wall. There are few other cities where the past and the present collide with such energy.

ESSENTIALS

CURRENCY The euro (€1 to US$1.46 at this writing); U.S. currency is generally not accepted in Europe, but ATMs are common and credit cards are widely accepted.

HOURS Stores are open Monday through Saturday from 8 AM to 8PM. Museums hours vary but core hours are from 10 AM to 5 PM with shorter opening on Sunday. Some state museums are closed on Monday.

INTERNET **Sinn E.V.** (⊠*Zum Lebensbaum 16 Rostock* ☏*0381/6867843* ⊕*www.sinnev. de*) is closest to the port.

TELEPHONES Most tri- and quad-band GSM phones will work in Germany, where the mobile system supports 3G technology. Phonecards for public phones are available at newsagents and will allow international calls. Major companies include Vodafone, T2, and T-Mobile.

COMING ASHORE

A state-of-the-art Warnemünde cruise terminal opened in 2005, but this has limited passenger facilities. However, the terminal is within 300 yards of a railway station for easy onward connection to the German railway system through the town of Rostock. Travel time into Rostock is 20 minutes, with train journeys to Berlin taking 2 hours 45 minutes. Prices to Berlin are €33 round-trip. Trains from Rostock to Berlin run approximately three times per hour depending on time of day.

Berlin has an integrated network of subway (U-bahn) and suburban (S-bahn) train lines, buses, and trams (in eastern Berlin only). Most visitor destinations are in the broad reach of the fare zones A and B. At this writing, both the €2.10 ticket (fare zones A and B) and the €2.60 ticket (fare zones A, B, and C) allow you to make a one-way trip with an unlimited number of changes between trains, buses, and trams. There are reduced rates for children ages 6–13. Rates are likely to be higher in the near future.

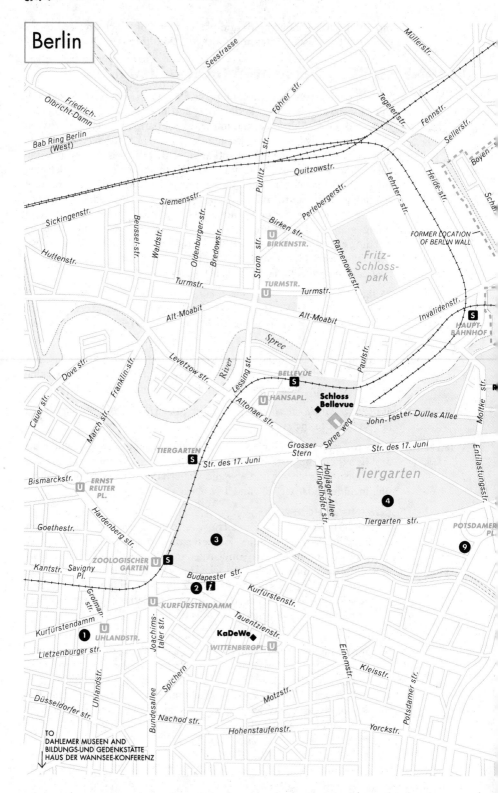

Berlin

Müllerstr.

Seestrasse

Föhrer str.

Friedrich-Olbricht-Damm

Bab Ring Berlin (West)

Tegeler str.

Fennstr.

Sellerstr.

Boyen

Scha

Quitzowstr.

Putlitz str.

Lehrter str.

Heide-str.

Siemensstr.

Perlebergerstr.

FORMER LOCATION OF BERLIN WALL

Sickingenstr.

Birken str.

Strom str.

U BIRKENSTR.

Fritz-Schloss-park

Beussel-str.

Oldenburger-str.

Bredowstr.

Waldstr.

Ratenowerstr.

Huttenstr.

Turmstr.

U TURMSTR.

Turmstr.

Invalidenstr.

S HAUPT-BAHNHOF

Alt-Moabit

Alt-Moabit

Spree

Paulstr.

Levetzow str.

River

Lessing str.

Dove str.

Franklin-str.

BELLEVUE

S

Schloss Bellevue ◆

Moltke str.

R

Altonaer str.

U HANSAPL.

Cauer str.

March str.

John- Foster- Dulles Allee

Grosser Stern

Spree weg

TIERGARTEN

S

Str. des 17. Juni

Str. des 17. Juni

Bismarckstr.

U ERNST REUTER PL.

Tiergarten

Hofjäger-Allee

Klingelhöfer str.

Entlastungsstr.

Goethestr.

Hardenberg str.

④

Tiergarten str.

POTSDAMER PL.

Kantstr.

Savigny Pl.

ZOOLOGISCHER GARTEN **U** **S**

③

⑨

Groman str.

Budapester str.

②⑦

Kurfürstenstr.

Kurfürstendamm

U

U KURFÜRSTENDAMM

Tauentzienstr.

① UHLANDSTR.

Joachims-taler str.

KaDeWe ◆

Einemstr.

Lietzenburger str.

WITTENBERGPL. **U**

Uhlandstr.

Spichern

Bundesallee

Motzstr.

Kleisstr.

Potsdamer str.

Düsseldorfer str.

Nachod str.

Hohenstaufenstr.

Yorckstr.

↙ TO
DAHLEMER MUSEEN AND
BILDUNGS-UND GEDENKSTÄTTE
HAUS DER WANNSEE-KONFERENZ

Buy a Kurzstreckentarif ticket (€1.20) for short rides of up to six bus or tram stops or three U-bahn or S-bahn stops. The best deal if you plan to travel around the city extensively is the Tageskarte (day card for zones A and B), for €5.80, good on all transportation. (It's €6 for A, B, C zones.) A 7-Tage-Karte (seven-day ticket) costs €25.40 and allows unlimited travel for fare zones A and B; €31.30 buys all three fare zones.

There are no car rental offices at the port, so you will need to arrange to have a car waiting when the ship docks (extra charges may apply). Alternatively, you can easily travel by train into nearby Rostock and pick up a vehicle there. If you want to visit Berlin, public transport is more practical than car rental. However, renting a vehicle would allow you to explore the other towns along the Baltic coastline and enjoy the countryside and beaches. The cost for a compact manual vehicle is approximately €51 per day.

EXPLORING BERLIN

Numbers in the margin correspond to points of interest on the Berlin map.

⑭ **Berliner Fernsehturm** *(Berlin TV Tower)*. Finding Alexanderplatz is no problem: just head toward the 1,198-foot-high tower piercing the sky. You can get the best view of Berlin from within the tower's disco ball-like observation level; on a clear day you can see for 40 km (25 mi).

⌂*Panoramastr. 1a, Mitte* ☎*030/242–3333* ⊕*www.berlinerfernsehturm. de* ⌨*€8.50* ⊘*Nov.–Feb., daily 10* AM*–midnight; Mar.–Oct., daily 9* AM*–midnight; last admission ½ hr before closing* Ⓜ*Alexanderpl. (S-bahn and U-bahn).*

❻ **Brandenburger Tor** *(Brandenburg Gate)*. Once the pride of Prussian Berlin and the city's premier landmark, the Brandenburger Tor was left in a desolate no-man's-land when the Wall was built. Since the Wall's dismantling, the sandstone gateway has become the scene of the city's Unification Day and New Year's Eve parties. This is the sole remaining gate of 14 built by Carl Langhans in 1788–91, designed as a triumphal arch for King Frederick Wilhelm II. Its virile classical style pays tribute to Athens's Acropolis. On the southern side, Berlin's sleek Academy of Arts and the DZ Bank, designed by star architect Frank Gehry, are cheek-by-jowl with the new American embassy built on its prewar location. ⌂*Pariser Pl., Mitte* Ⓜ *Unter den Linden (S-bahn).*

Fodor'sChoice
★

❼ **Denkmal für die Ermordeten Juden Europas** *(Memorial to the Murdered Jews of Europe)*. An expansive and unusual memorial dedicated to the 6 million Jews who were killed in the Holocaust, the monument was designed by American architect Peter Eisenman. The stunning place of remembrance consists of a grid of more than 2,700 concrete stelae, planted into undulating ground. An information center that goes into specifics about the Holocaust lies underground at the southeast corner. ⌂*Cora-Berliner-Str. 1, Mitte* ☎*030/2639–4336* ⊕*www.holocaust-mahnmal.de* ⌨*Free* ⊘*Daily 24 hrs; information center: Nov.–Feb., Tues.–Sun. 10–7; Mar.–Oct., Tues.–Sun. 10–8* Ⓜ *Unter den Linden (S-bahn).*

⑫ Deutsches Historisches Museum *(German History Museum)*. The museum is composed of two buildings. The magnificent pink, baroque Prussian arsenal (Zeughaus) was constructed between 1695 and 1730 and is the oldest building on Unter den Linden. The permanent exhibits offer a modern and fascinating view of German history since the early Middle Ages. Behind the arsenal, the granite-and-glass Pei-Bau building by I.M. Pei holds changing exhibits. ⊠ *Unter den Linden 2, Mitte* ☎ *030/203–040* ⊕ *www.dhm.de* ⛶ *€4, free Mon.; visitors under 18 free* ☉ *Daily 10–6.*

⑪ Jüdisches Museum *(Jewish Museum)*. The history of Germany's Jews from the Middle Ages through today is chronicled here, from prominent historical figures to the evolution of laws regarding Jews' participation in civil society. An attraction in itself is the highly conceptual building, which was designed by Daniel Libeskind. ⊠ *Lindenstr. 9–14, Kreuzberg* ☎ *030/2599–3300* ⊕ *www.jmberlin.de* ⛶ *€5* ☉ *Mon. 10–10, Tues.–Sun. 10–8* Ⓜ *Hallesches Tor (U-bahn).*

② Kaiser-Wilhelm-Gedächtnis-Kirche *(Kaiser Wilhelm Memorial Church)*. A dramatic reminder of World War II's destruction, the ruined bell tower is all that remains of the once massive church, which was dedicated to the emperor Kaiser Wilhelm I. The exhibition revisits World War II's devastation throughout Europe. In stark contrast to the old bell tower (dubbed the Hollow Tooth), are the adjoining Memorial Church and Tower, designed by the noted German architect Egon Eiermann in 1959–61. Brilliant blue stained glass from Chartres dominates the interiors. ⊠ *Breitscheidpl., Western Downtown* ☎ *030/218–5023* ⛶ *Free* ☉ *Old Tower, Mon.–Sat. 10–6:30; Memorial Church, daily 9–7* Ⓜ *Zoologischer Garten (U-bahn and S-bahn).*

⑨ Kulturforum *(Cultural Forum)*. This unique ensemble of museums, galleries, and the Philharmonic Hall was long in the making. The first designs were submitted in the 1960s and the last building completed in 1998. The **Gemäldegalerie** *(Picture Gallery)* reunites formerly separated collections from East and West Berlin. Seven rooms are reserved for paintings by German masters, among them Dürer, Cranach the Elder, and Holbein. A special collection has works of the Italian masters—Botticelli, Titian, Giotto, Lippi, and Raphael—as well as paintings by Dutch and Flemish masters of the 15th and 16th centuries: Van Eyck, Bosch, Brueghel the Elder, and van der Weyden. The museum also holds the world's second-largest Rembrandt collection. ⊠ *Matthäikirchpl. 4, Tiergarten* ☎ *030/266–2951* ⊕ *www.smb.museum* ⛶ *€8* ☉ *Tues., Wed., and Fri.–Sun. 10–6, Thurs. 10–10* Ⓜ *Potsdamer Pl. (U-bahn and S-bahn).*

⑩ Mauermuseum-Museum Haus am Checkpoint Charlie. Just steps from the famous
★ crossing point between the two Berlins, the Wall Museum—House at
Checkpoint Charlie tells the story of the Wall and, even more riveting,
the stories of those who escaped through, under, and over it. ⊠ *Friedrichstr. 43–45, Kreuzberg* ☎ *030/253-7250* ⊕ *www.mauermuseum.com*
☒ *€9.50* ⊗ *Daily 9 AM–10 PM* Ⓜ *Kochstr. (U-bahn).*

⑬ Museumsinsel *(Museum Island).* On the site of one of Berlin's two original settlements, this unique complex of four state museums is an abso-
★ lute must. The **Alte Nationalgalerie** (Old National Gallery, entrance on
Bodestrasse) houses an outstanding collection of 18th-, 19th-, and early-
20th-century paintings and sculptures. The **Altes Museum** (Old Museum),
a red marble, neoclassical building abutting the green Lustgarten, was
Prussia's first building purpose-built to serve as a museum. Designed by
Karl Friedrich Schinkel, it was completed in 1830. Until 2009, when the
collection will relocate to the Neues Museum, it serves as temporary home
to the **Egyptian collection,** whose prize piece is the exquisite 3,300-year-
old bust of Queen Nefertiti. At the northern tip of Museum Island is the
Bode-Museum, a somber-looking gray edifice graced with elegant columns. Reopened in 2006, it now presents the state museum's stunning
collection of German and Italian sculptures since the Middle Ages, the
Museum of Byzantine Art, and a huge coin collection. Even if you think
you aren't interested in the ancient world, make an exception for the **Pergamonmuseum** (entrance on Am Kupfergraben), one of the world's greatest museums. The museum's name is derived from its principal display, the
Pergamon Altar, a monumental Greek temple discovered in what is now
Turkey and dating from 180 BC. ⊠ *Entrance to Museumsinsel: Am Kupfergraben, Mitte* ☎ *030/2090-5577* ⊕ *www.smb.museum* ☒ *All Museum
Island museums €8* ⊗ *Pergamonmuseum and Altes Museum Fri.–Wed.
10–6, Thurs. 10–10. Alte Nationalgalerie Tues., Wed., and Fri.–Sun. 10–6,
Thurs. 10–10. Bode-Museum Fri.–Wed. 10–6, Thurs. 10–10* Ⓜ *Hackescher Markt. (S-bahn).*

❺ Reichstag *(Parliament Building).* After last meeting here in 1933, the Bundestag, Germany's federal parliament, returned to its traditional seat in the
★ spring of 1999. British architect Sir Norman Foster lightened up the gray
monolith with a glass dome, which quickly became one of the city's main
attractions: you can circle up a gently rising ramp while taking in the
rooftops of Berlin and the parliamentary chamber below. At the base of
the dome is an exhibit on the Reichstag's history, in German and English.
⊠ *Pl. der Republik 1, Tiergarten* ☎ *030/2273-2152* ☒ *030/2273-0027*
⊕ *www.bundestag.de* ☒ *Free* ⊗ *Daily 8 AM–midnight; last admission 10
PM. Reichstag dome closes for one week four times a year* Ⓜ *Unter den
Linden (S-bahn).*

❶ The Story of Berlin. Eight hundred years of the city's history, from the first settlers casting their fishing poles to Berliners heaving sledgehammers at the
Wall, are conveyed through hands-on exhibits, film footage, and multimedia devices in this unusual venue. ⊠ *Ku'damm Karree, Kurfürstendamm
207–208, Western Downtown* ☎ *030/8872-0100* ⊕ *www.story-of-berlin.de* ☒ *€9.80* ⊗ *Daily 10–8; last entry at 6* Ⓜ *Uhlandstr. (U-bahn).*

4 **Tiergarten** *(Animal Garden).* The quiet greenery of the 630-acre Tiergarten is a beloved oasis, with some 23 km (14 mi) of footpaths, meadows, and two beer gardens. The inner park's 6½ acres of lakes and ponds were landscaped by garden architect Joseph Peter Lenné in the mid-1800s. On the shores of the lake in the southwest part, you can relax at the **Café am Neuen See** (✉ *Lichtensteinallee*), a café and beer garden. Off the Spree River and bordering the Kanzleramt (Chancellory) is the **Haus der Kulturen der Welt** (✉ *House of the World Cultures, John-Foster-Dulles Allee 10* ☎ *030/397– 870* ⊕ *www.hkw.de*), referred to as the "pregnant oyster" for its design. Thematic exhibits and festivals take place here, and it's also a boarding point for Spree River cruises.

8 **Unter den Linden.** The name of this historic Berlin thoroughfare, between the Brandenburg Gate and Schlossplatz, means "under the linden trees"—and as Marlene Dietrich once sang, "As long as the old linden trees still bloom, Berlin is still Berlin." Imagine Berliners' shock when Hitler decided to fell the trees in order to make Unter den Linden more parade-friendly. The grand boulevard began as a riding path that the royals used to get from their palace to their hunting grounds (now Tiergarten). Lining it now are linden trees planted after World War II.

3 **Zoologischer Garten** *(Zoological Gardens).* Germany's oldest zoo opened in 1844 and today holds more species than any other zoo in Europe, among them stars like the little polar bear Knut, one of the world's few endangered species to be born in captivity. Home to more than 14,000 animals belonging to 1,500 different species, the zoo has been successful at breeding rare and endangered species. The animals' enclosures are designed to resemble their natural habitats, though some structures are ornate, such as the 1910 Arabian-style Zebra house. ✉ *Hardenbergpl. 8 and Budapester Str. 34, Western Downtown* ☎ *030/254–010* ⊕ *www.zoo-berlin. de* 🗺 *Zoo or aquarium €11, combined ticket €16.50* ☉ *Zoo, Nov.–mid-Mar., daily 9–5; mid-Mar.–mid-Oct., daily 9–6:30. Aquarium, daily 9–6* Ⓜ *Zoologischer Garten (U-bahn and S-bahn).*

SHOPPING

Although Ku'damm is still touted as the shopping mile of Berlin, many shops are ho-hum retailers. The best stretch for exclusive fashions are the three blocks between Leibnizstrasse and Bleibtreustrasse. For gift items and unusual clothing boutiques, follow this route off Ku'damm: Leibnizstrasse to Mommsenstrasse to Bleibtreustrasse, then on to the ring around Savignyplatz. Fasanenstrasse, Knesebeckstrasse, Schlüterstrasse, and Uhlandstrasse are also fun places to browse.

The finest shops in Mitte (historic Berlin) are along Friedrichstrass. Nearby, Unter den Linden has just a few souvenir shops and a Meissen ceramic showroom. Smaller clothing and specialty stores populate the Scheunenviertel. The area between Hackescher Markt, Weinmeister Strasse, and Rosa-Luxemburg-Platz alternates pricey independent designers with groovy secondhand shops. Neue Schönhauser Strasse curves into Alte Schönhauser Strasse, and both streets are full of stylish casual wear. Galleries along Gipsstrasse and Sophienstrasse round out the mix.

The largest department store in continental Europe, classy **Kaufhaus des Westens** (*KaDeWe* ✉*Tauentzienstr. 21, Western Downtown* ☎*030/21210* ⊕*www.kadewe.de*) surpasses even London's Harrods and turned 100 in 2007. It has a grand selection of goods on seven floors, as well as food and deli counters, champagne bars, beer bars, and a winter garden on its two upper floors.

Fine porcelain is still produced by **Königliche Porzellan Manufaktur** the former Royal Prussian Porcelain Factory, also called KPM. They have a shop at (✉*Unter den Linden 35, Mitte* ☎*030/206–4150*)

Puppenstube im Nikolaiviertel (✉*Propststr. 4, Mitte* ☎*030/242–3967*) is the ultimate shop for any kind of (mostly handmade) dolls, including designer models as well as old-fashioned German dolls. It's for collectors, not kids.

WHERE TO EAT

$-$$ ✕**Café Einstein.** The Einstein is a Berlin landmark and one of the leading
★ coffeehouses in town serving some of Germany's best coffee (the Einstein has its very own roasting facility) and some great cakes. In summer, the fresh strawberry cake is a treat. The Einstein also excels in preparing solid Austrian fare such as schnitzel or goulash for an artsy, highbrow clientele. ✉*Kurfürstenstr. 58, Tiergarten* ☎*030/261–5096* ⊟*AE, DC, MC, V* Ⓜ*Kurfürstenstrasse (U-bahn).*

$-$$ ✕**Florian.** The handwritten menu is just one page, but there's always a changing variety of fish, fowl, and meat dishes in this well-established restaurant. *Steinbeisser,* a white, flaky fish, might be served with an exciting salsa of rhubarb, chili, coriander, and ginger. Or you can opt for some Franconian comfort cuisine such as *Kirchweihbraten* (marinated pork with baked apples and plums), or the *Nürnberger Rostbratwurst* (small pork sausages) served as late-night snacks. ✉*Grolmanstr. 52, Western Downtown* ☎*030/313–9184* ⊟*MC, V* ⊘*No lunch* Ⓜ*Savignypl. (S-bahn).*

Norway

ÅLESUND, BERGEN, HAMMERFEST, HONNINGSVAG, OSLO, TROMSØ, TRONDHEIM

Bergen harbour, Norway

WORD OF MOUTH

"We sailed from Bergen to Kirkenes in late July. It never did get dark, just a very long twilight. By October, say, the days would be quite short. Some ports—Aalesund, for example—were visited for several hours. Others, only minutes. It's a wonderful, scenic voyage, so free of hassles."

—USNR

Ralph Grizzle   **NORWAY'S MOST RENOWNED CRUISE ITINERARY** is the *Hurtigruten,* which literally means "Rapid Route." Boats that follow this route, which were historically known as coastal steamers, depart from Bergen and stop at 36 ports along the coast in a week, ending in Kirkenes, near the Russian border, before turning back. The ships may stop in one port for just a few minutes to load and unload passengers, who use the scenic route for transportation, so these steamers are more than just pleasure cruises for the people who choose to live in the isolated coastal villages in Norway's northern reaches. But many passengers on these routes are Americans here to enjoy the dramatically beautiful Norwegian scenery. Many of these ships, which are operated primarily by Hurtigruten (which was formerly known in the U.S. as Norwegian Coastal Voyage), are more than just ferries and have some cruise-ship-style amenities, though not "big-ship" amenities. Norway is also a popular destination among major cruise lines, and many northern European cruises in the summer include some ports in Norway, though they may also include Århus or Copenhagen in Denmark or stops in Sweden, which are covered in the "The Baltic" chapter.

ABOUT THE RESTAURANTS

All the restaurants we recommend serve lunch; they may also serve dinner if your cruise ship stays late in port and you choose to dine off the ship. Cuisine in Europe is varied, but Europeans tend to eat a leisurely meal at lunch, but in most ports there are quicker and simpler alternatives for those who just want to grab a quick bite before returning to the ship. The currency of Norway is the Norwegian krone, and equivalent kroner prices to our regular euro price categories are given below.

WHAT IT COSTS IN EUROS AND KRONE				
$$$$	$$$	$$	$	¢
RESTAURANTS in euros	over €30	€23–€30	€17–€23	€11–€17	under €11
RESTAURANTS in kroner	over Nkr 240	Nkr 185–Nkr 240	Nkr 135–Nkr 185	Nkr 85–Nkr 135	under Nkr 85

Restaurant prices are per person for a main course, including tax.

ÅLESUND, NORWAY

On three islands and between two bright blue fjords is Ålesund, home to 38,000 inhabitants and one of Norway's largest harbors for exporting dried and fresh fish. About two-thirds of its 1,040 wooden houses were destroyed by a fire in 1904. In the rush to shelter the 10,000 homeless victims, Germany's Kaiser Wilhelm II, who often vacationed here, led a swift rebuilding that married German art nouveau (*Jugendstil*) with Viking flourishes. Winding streets are crammed with buildings topped with turrets, spires, gables, dragon heads, and curlicues. Today, it is considered one of the few art nouveau cities in the world. Inquire at the tourism office for one of the insightful guided walking tours.

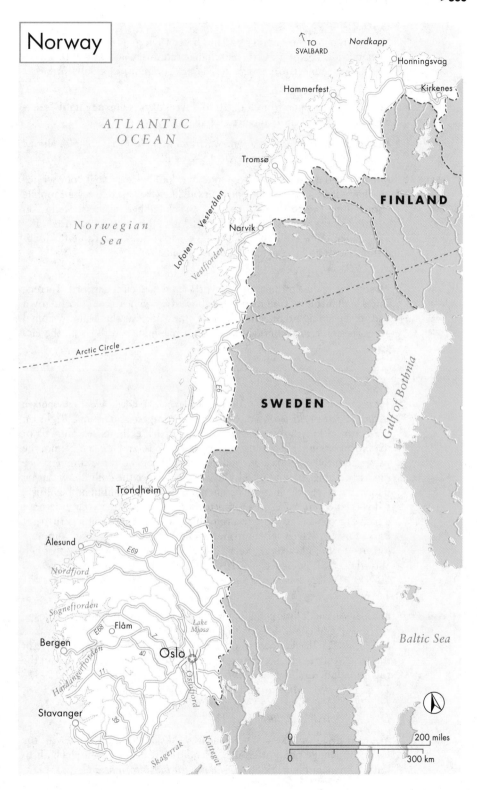

Norway

TO
SVALBARD

Nordkapp

Honningsvag

Hammerfest

Kirkenes

ATLANTIC
OCEAN

Tromsø

FINLAND

*Norwegian
Sea*

Vesterålen

Lofoten

Narvik

Vestfjorden

Arctic Circle

E6

SWEDEN

Gulf of Bothnia

Trondheim

70

Ålesund

E69

Nordfjord

Sognefjorden

*Lake
Mjøsa*

Baltic Sea

Flåm

E68

Bergen

40

Oslo

Hardangerfjorden

11

Oslofjord

Stavanger

39

Skagerrak

Kattegat

8

0 | 200 miles
0 | 300 km

ESSENTIALS

CURRENCY   Norway is a non-EU country and has opted to keep its currency, the Norwegian *krone* (Nkr 6 to US$1); exchange rates were accurate at this writing but are subject to change. ATMs are common, especially in larger cities.

HOURS   Most shops are open from 9 or 10 to 5 weekdays, Thursday until 7, Saturday from 9 to 2 or 4, and are closed Sunday.

INTERNET   **Ålesund Folkebibliotek** (*Public Library* ⊠*Rådhuset* ☎*70–16–22–50*). **Ålesund Tourist Office** (⊠*Skateflukaia* ☎*70–15–76–00*).

TELEPHONES   Most tri- and quad-band GSM phones work in Norway, so if your service provider offers service in Europe, you will likely be able to use your mobile phone along the Norwegian coast, even while hugging the shoreline on ship. Public telephones take Nkr 1, 5, 10, and 20 coins, and you need HKr 5 at a minimum. International phone cards are the best value for long-distance calls and are available at newsstands.

COMING ASHORE

Ålesund is at the entrance to the world-famous Geirangerfjord. Turrets, spires, and medieval ornaments rise above the skyline of the colorful town and its charming architecture. Cruise ships dock at the cruise terminal at Stornespiren/Prestebrygga, less than a five-minute walk from the city center.

EXPLORING ÅLESUND

☺ Teeming with aquatic life, Ålesund's **Ålesund Akvarium Atlanterhavsparken** *(Atlantic Sea Park)* is one of Scandinavia's largest aquariums. Right on the ocean, 3 km (2 mi) west of town, the park exhibits sea animals of the North Atlantic, including anglerfish, octopus, and lobster. Nemo, the park's adorable seal mascot, waddles freely throughout the complex. See the daily diving show at which the fish are fed. See the daily show during which divers feed the huge and sometimes aggressive halibut and wolffish, who become frenzied as they compete for their meals. After your visit, have a picnic, go on a hike, or take a refreshing swim at the adjoining Tueneset Park. Bus 18, which leaves from St. Olavs Plass, makes the 15-minute journey to the park once every hour during the day, Monday through Saturday. ⊠*Tueneset* ☎*70–10–70–60* ⊕*www.atlanterhavsparken.no* ▧*Nkr 100* ⊙*June–Aug., Sun.–Fri. 10–7, Sat. 10–4; Sept.–May, daily 11–4.*

Fodor'sChoice   **Ålesunds Museum**, a little gem, highlights the city's past, including the escape
★   route to the Shetland Islands that the Norwegian Resistance established in World War II. Handicrafts on display are done in the folk-art style of the area. You can also see the art nouveau room and learn more about the town's unique architecture. ⊠*Rasmus Rønnebergsgt. 16* ☎*70–12–31–70* ▧*Nkr 40* ⊙*Mid-June and mid-Aug., Mon.–Sat. 11–4, Sun. noon–4; mid-Aug., Oct., Jan., and Apr.–June, Mon.–Sat. 11–3, Sun. noon–3; Nov., Dec., Feb., and Mar., weekdays 11–3.*

You can drive or take a bus up nearby Aksla Mountain to **Kniven** (*the knife*), a vantage point offering a splendid view of the city—which absolutely glitters at night. ☎*70–13–68–00 for bus information.*

SHOPPING

The first Saturday of each month is known as "Town Saturday," when shops in the city center are open later than usual. Visit **Husfliden** (⊠*Parkgt. 1* ☎*70–12–16–68*) for collections of beautiful Norwegian and Nordic arts and crafts. **Ingrids Glassverksted** (⊠*Moloveien 15* ☎*70–12–53–77*) has a fine selection of glassware and decorative art glass. For leather clothing, handbags, knitwear and souvenirs, drop into **Skinncompagniet** (⊠*Kongensgt. 14* ☎*70–12–77–77*) on Ålesund's main pedestrian street.

SPORTS & ACTIVITIES

BICYCLING

Fjellstova Ørskogfjellet (⊠*Ørskog 6240* ☎*70–27–03–03*) rents mountain bikes for riding five well-marked routes.

FISHING

Maud af Ålesund (⊠*Ålesund 6001* ☎*95–14–53–85*) is one of several boat companies that take anglers out to sea to cast their hooks. Board the renovated 53-foot-long fishing boat, dating from 1917, for sightseeing, fishing, and sailing along the coast of Sunnmøre.

GOLF

Only 30 minutes from Ålesund is **Solnør Gaard Golfbane** (⊠*Skodje 6260, Solnør* ☎*70–27–42–00*), an 18-hole course with driving range and pro shop.

HIKING

You can trek up the 418 steps to Fjellstua for a panoramic view of the town and the Sunnmøre Alps. A restaurant is at the top.

WHERE TO EAT

$–$$ ✗**Cavatelli Mat og Vinhus.** The Food and Wine House is in a beautiful art nouveau building in the heart of Brosundet and aims to satisfy sophisticated palates in a wonderfully aesthetic setting overlooking the harbor. ⊠*Apotekergata 9B* ☎*70–11–77–00* ⊕*www.cavatelli.no.*

$–$$ ✗**Let's Eat Deli.** An American-inspired café offers a wide selection of hot and cold international dishes as well as delicious cakes and made-to-order sandwiches. ⊠*Keiser Wilhelmsgt. 39* ☎*70–15–11–92.*

BERGEN, NORWAY

A place of enchantment, Bergen's epithets include "Trebyen" (Wooden City), for its many wooden houses, "Fjordbyen" (Gateway to the Fjords), for obvious reasons, and "Regnbyen" (Rainy City), for its 200 days of rain a year. Most visitors quickly learn the necessity of rain jackets and umbrellas, and Bergen has even handily provided the world's first umbrella vending machine. Norway's second-largest city was founded in 1070 by Olav Kyrre as a commercial center. The surviving Hanseatic wooden buildings on Bryggen (the quay) are topped with triangular gingerbread roofs and painted in red, blue, yellow, and green. Monuments in themselves (they are on the UNESCO World Heritage List), the buildings tempt travelers and locals to the shops, restaurants, and museums inside. Evenings, when Bryggen is illuminated, these modest buildings, together with the stocky Rosenkrantz Tower, the Fløyen, and the yachts lining the pier, are reflected in the water and combine to create one of the loveliest cityscapes in northern Europe.

ESSENTIALS

CURRENCY Norway is a non-EU country and has opted to keep its currency, the Norwegian *krone* (Nkr 6 to US$1); exchange rates were accurate at this writing but are subject to change. ATMs are common, especially in larger cities.

HOURS Most shops are open from 9 or 10 to 5 weekdays, Thursday until 7, Saturday from 9 to 2 or 4, and are closed Sunday.

INTERNET **Accezzo** (⊠*Galleriet Torgallm. 8* ☎*55–31–11–60*). **Cyberhouse** (⊠*Hollendergt. 3* ☎*55–36–66–16*).

TELEPHONES Most tri- and quad-band GSM phones work in Norway, so if your service provider offers service in Europe, you will likely be able to use your mobile phone along the Norwegian coast, even while hugging the shoreline on ship. Public telephones take Nkr 1, 5, 10, and 20 coins, and you need NKr 5 at a minimum. International phone cards are the best value for long-distance calls and are available at newsstands.

COMING ASHORE

Cruise ships dock at Skoltegrunnskaien and Jekteviken/Dokkeskjærskaien. Both are situated within a 15-minute walk to the city center, and shuttle buses are available from Jekteviken/Dokkeskjærskaien. From Skoltegrunnskaien, buses stop near the docks. The trip to the city center costs NKr 12. Once in the city center nearly all of the attractions are within walking distance.

EXPLORING BERGEN

Numbers in the text correspond to numbers in the margin and on the Bergen map.

4 **Bergenhus Festning** *(Bergenhus Fortress).* The buildings here date from the mid-13th century. Håkonshallen, a royal ceremonial hall erected during the reign of Håkon Håkonsson, between 1247 and 1261, was badly damaged by the explosion of a German ammunition ship in 1944, but was restored by 1961. Erected in the 1560s by the governor of Bergen Castle (Bergenhus), Erik Rosenkrantz, Rosenkrantztårnet (Rosenkrantz Tower) served as a combined residence and fortified tower. ⊠*Bergenhus, Bryggen* ☎*55–58–80–10* ⊡*Nkr 25* ☉*Mid-May–mid-Aug., daily 10–4; mid-Aug.–mid-May, Sun. noon–3. Closed during Bergen International Music Festival.*

2 **Bryggen** *(The Quay).* A trip to Bergen is incomplete without a trip to Bryggen. A row of mostly reconstructed 14th-century wooden buildings that face the harbor makes this one of the most charming walkways in Europe, especially on a sunny day. The original structures were built by Hansa merchants, while the first reconstruction dates from 1702. Several fires, the latest in 1955, destroyed the original structures.

Fodor'sChoice
★

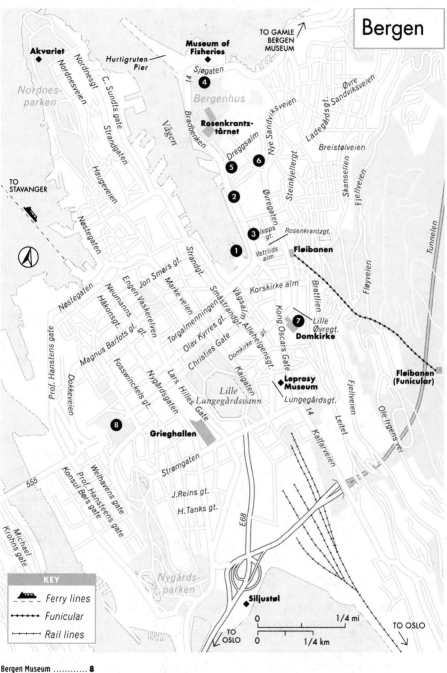

Bergen

KEY

🛥 *Ferry lines*

•••••• *Funicular*

╫╫╫ *Rail lines*

5 Bryggens Museum. This museum contains archaeological finds from the Middle Ages. An exhibit on Bergen circa 1300 shows the town at the zenith of its importance, and has reconstructed living quarters as well as artifacts such as old tools and shoes. Back then, Bergen was the largest town in Norway, a cosmopolitan trading center and the national capital. ⊠ *Dreggsalmenning 3* ☎ *55–58–80–10* ⊕ *www.uib.no/bmu* 🎟 *Nkr 40* ⊙ *May–Aug., daily 10–5; Sept.–Apr., weekdays 11–3, Sat. noon–3, Sun. noon–4.*

7 Domkirke *(Bergen Cathedral).* The cathedral's long, turbulent history has shaped the eclectic architecture of the current structure. The Gothic-style choir and the lower towers are the oldest sections, dating from the 13th century. Note the cannonball lodged in the tower wall—it dates from a battle between English and Dutch ships in Bergen harbor in 1665. From June through August, a Sunday service is held in English at 9:30 AM in the Chapter House, an organ recital is held Thursday at noon, and there is a concert in the church every Sunday at 7:30 PM. September through May the Sunday concerts are held at 6 PM. ⊠ *Kong Oscars gt. and Domkirke gt.* ☎ *55–59–32–73* ⊙ *June–Aug., Mon.–Sat. 11–4; Sept.–May, Tues.–Fri. 11–12:30.*

1 Fisketorget *(Fish Market).* Turn-of-the-20th-century photographs of this pungent square show fishermen in Wellington boots and raincoats and women in long aprons. Now the fishmongers wear bright-orange rubber overalls as they look over the catches of the day. In summer the selection is mostly limited to shrimp, salmon, and monkfish. There is much greater variety and more locals shop here the rest of the year. There are also fruit, vegetable, and flower stalls, as well as some handicrafts and souvenir vendors at this lively market. You'll also find the world's first umbrella vending machine. Have a classic lunch of smoked shrimp or salmon on a baguette with mayonnaise and cucumber. ⊠ *Zachariasbryggen* ☎ *55–31–56–17* ⊕ *www.torgetibergen.no* ⊙ *June–Aug., daily 7–7; Sept.–May, Mon.–Sat. 7–4.*

3 Hanseatisk Museum. ★ One of the best-preserved buildings in Bergen, the Hanseatic Museum was the 16th-century office and home of an affluent German merchant. The apprentices lived upstairs, where they slept in boxed-in beds, and windows were cut into the wall. Although claustrophobic, the snug rooms had the benefit of being relatively warm—a blessing in the unheated building. ⊠ *Finnegårdsgaten 1A* ☎ *55–54–46–90* ⊕ *www.hanseatisk.museum.no* 🎟 *Nkr 45, off-season Nkr 25* ⊙ *May, daily 11–2; June–Aug., daily 9–5; early–mid-Sept., daily 10–3; late Sept. daily 11–2; Oct.–Apr., Tues.–Sat. 11–2, Sun. noon–5.*

6 **Mariakirken** *(St. Mary's Church).* Considered one of the most outstanding

Romanesque churches in Norway, this is the oldest building in Bergen still used for its original purpose. It was built in the 12th century and eventually gained a Gothic choir, richly decorated portals, and a splendid baroque pulpit—much of which was added by the Hanseatic merchants who owned it from 1408 to 1766. See the gilded triptych at the high altar that dates from the late Middle Ages. Organ recitals are held every Tuesday at 7:30 PM from late June through August. ⊠*Dreggen, Bryggen* ☎*55–59–32–73* ⊡*Nkr 20* ☉*Late June–Aug., weekdays 9:30–11:30 and 1–4; Sept.–early June, Tues.–Fri. 11–12:30.*

8 **Bergen Museum.** Part of the University of Bergen, this museum has two collections. The Cultural History Department has a fascinating collection of archaeological artifacts and furniture and folk art from western Norway. Some of the titles of the displays are "Inherited from Europe," "Viking Times," "Village Life in the Solomon Islands," and "Ibsen in Bergen," which focuses on the famous playwright's six years in Bergen working with the local theater. The Natural History Department is perfect for lovers of the outdoors, since it includes botanical gardens. Exhibits include "The Ice Age," "Oil Geology," "Fossils," "Mineral Collections," and "The Evolution of Man." ⊠*Haakon Sheteligs pl. 10 and Musépl. 3, City Center* ☎*55–58–81–72 or 55–58–29–05* ⊕*www.museum.uib.no* ⊡*Nkr 40* ☉*June–Aug., Tues.–Fri. 10–4, weekends 11–4; Sept.–May, Tues.–Fri. 10–2, weekends 11–3.*

NIGHTLIFE

Bergen is a university town, and the thousands of students who live and study here year-round contribute to making the city's nightlife livelier than you might expect in a small town. Most nightspots center around Ole Bulls *plass,* the plaza at one end of Torgallmenningen. Within a stone's throw of the plaza you can find dozens of relaxing bars, bustling pubs, dancing, live music, and trendy cafés.

If you prefer a quiet glass of wine in peaceful historic surroundings, try **Altona** (⊠*Strandgaten 81* ☎*55–30–40–72*), a bar in a 400-year-old wine cellar neighboring the Augustin Hotel. **Café Opera** (⊠*Engen 18* ☎*55–23–03–15*) is a classic, both sumptuous and stylish. It's often crowded on Friday and Saturday nights. **Jonsvoll** (⊠*Engen 10* ☎*55–90–03–84*), just across the street from Café Opera, is another popular hangout, both for the sensible food served during the day and for the hip crowd sipping cocktails and beer at night. If you prefer conversation over dancing, try **Logen Bar** (⊠*Øvre Ole Bulls pl. 6* ☎*55–23–20–15*), a popular meeting place with live acoustic music every Sunday.

SHOPPING

Bergen has several cobblestoned pedestrian shopping streets, including Gamle Strandgaten, (Gågaten), Torgallmenningen, Hollendergaten, and Marken. Stores selling Norwegian handicrafts are concentrated along Bryggen boardwalk. Near the cathedral, tiny Skostredet has become popular with young shoppers. The small, independent specialty stores here sell everything from army surplus gear to tailored suits and designer trinkets.

Kløverhuset (⊠*Strandkaien 10*), between Strandgaten and the fish market, has 40 shops under one roof, including a shop for the ever-so-popular Dale knitwear, as well as shops selling souvenirs, leathers, and fur. **Galleriet** on Torgallmenningen, is the best of the downtown shopping malls. Here you will find GlasMagasinet and more exclusive small shops along with all the chains, including H & M (Hennes & Mauritz). **Bergen Storsenter,** by the bus terminal near the train station, is a newer shopping center. **Sundt** (⊠*Torgallmenningen 14*) is the closest thing Norway has to a traditional department store, with everything from fashion to interior furnishings. But you can get better value for your kroner if you shop around for souvenirs and sweaters.

SPORTS & ACTIVITIES

Bergen is literally wedged between the mountains and the sea, and there are plenty of opportunities to enjoy the outdoors. Bergensers are quick to do so on sunny days. In summer, don't be surprised to see many Bergensers leaving work early to enjoy sports and other outdoor activities, or to just relax in the parks.

FISHING

With so much water around, it's no wonder sport fishing is a popular pastime in Bergen. Angling along the coast around Bergen is possible all year, although it is unquestionably more pleasant in summer. In late summer many prefer to fish the area rivers to catch spawning salmon and trout. Whether you prefer fishing in streams, fjords, or the open sea, there are several charter services and fishing tours available. Most can also provide all the fishing gear you need, but be sure to bring warm and waterproof clothes, even in summer.

GOLF

Near Flesland Airport and Siljustøl, **Fana Golf Club** (⊠*Rådal* ☎*55–29–41–40* ⊕*www.melandgolf.no*) is an 18-hole course that opened in 2004. North of Bergen at Fløksand, the **Meland Golf Club** (⊠*Frekhaug* ☎*56–17–46–00* ⊕*www.melandgolf.no*) has an 18-hole championship course with high-quality golf clubs and carts for rent.

HIKING

Like most Norwegians, Bergensers love to go hiking, especially on one or more of the seven mountains that surround the city. Take the funicular up **Mt. Fløyen** (⊠*Vetrlidsallmenningen 21, 5014* ☎*55–33–68–00* ⊕*www.floibanen.no*), and minutes later you'll be in the midst of a forest. From the nearby gift shop and restaurant, well-marked paths fan out over the mountains. Follow Fløysvingene Road down for an easy stroll with great views of the city and harbor.

WHERE TO EAT

$$$$ ✕**Bryggen Tracteursted.** In the heart of Bergen's Bryggen Wharf at the picturesque Bryggestredet, dating back to 1708, this restaurant has a menu of contemporary cuisine, based on local and Hanseatic culinary traditions. ⊠*Bryggestredet 2* ☎*55–31–40–46* ⊕*www.bryggen-tracteursted.no* ⊟*AE, MC, V.*

$$$–$$$$ ✕**Bryggeloftet & Stuene.** Dining here on lutefisk in fall and at Christmastime is a time-honored tradition for many Bergensers. Beautiful views of the bay at Vågen Harbor complement a wide-ranging menu that features specialty dishes prepared in traditional Bergen style. Consider the *pinnekjøtt* (lumpfish) or the reindeer fillets. The hearty Norwegian country fare suits the somber, wooden dining room, with its fireplace and old oil paintings on the walls. ⊠*Bryggen 11* ☎*55–31–06–30* ⊕*www.bryggeloftet. no* ⊟*AE, MC, V.*

HAMMERFEST, NORWAY

More than 600 miles north of the Arctic Circle, the world's northernmost town is also one of the most widely visited and oldest places in northern Norway. "Hammerfest" means "mooring place" and refers to the natural harbor (remarkably ice-free year-round thanks to the Gulf Stream) formed by the crags in the mountain. Hammerfest is the gateway to the Barents Sea and the Arctic Ocean, a jumping-off point for Arctic expeditions. Once a hunting town, Hammerfest's town emblem features the polar bear. In 1891, the residents of Hammerfest, tired of the months of darkness that winter always brought, decided to brighten their nights: they purchased a generator from Thomas Edison, and Hammerfest thus became the first city in Europe to have electric street lamps.

ESSENTIALS

CURRENCY Norway is a non-EU country and has opted to keep its currency, the Norwegian *krone* (Nkr 6 to US$1); exchange rates were accurate at this writing but are subject to change. ATMs are common, especially in larger cities.

HOURS Most shops are open from 9 or 10 to 5 weekdays, Thursday until 7, Saturday from 9 to 2 or 4, and are closed Sunday.

INTERNET Within walking distance of the cruise-ship piers, Internet access can be found at **Hotel Rica** (⊠*Sørøygata 15*). If you buy something, you can use the Internet at **Redrum Café** (⊠*Storgata 23*).

TELEPHONES Most tri- and quad-band GSM phones work in Norway, so if your service provider offers service in Europe, you will likely be able to use your mobile phone along the Norwegian coast, even while hugging the shoreline on ship. Public telephones take Nkr 1, 5, 10, and 20 coins, and you need Nkr 5 at a minimum. International phone cards are the best value for long-distance calls and are available at newsstands.

COMING ASHORE

Ships dock either at a pier that is within walking distance of the town center or at Fugienes, about a mile away. Be prepared to pay about Nkr 84 (US$15) for taxi transfer from Fugienes to the town center. Rather than tie up at Fugienes, ships sometimes anchor and tender passengers ashore to the dock in the town center. There is no terminal in the port area and only limited facilities, but the town center is only a few steps away and has everything you might need.

8

EXPLORING HAMMERFEST

In addition to two museums, there are several shops within Hammerfest's small city center. There is also a market selling souvenirs and other goods outside the town hall. You'll do better if you go back to your ship for lunch

Although it covers the county of Finnmark's history since the Stone Age, the **Museum of Post-War Reconstruction** mainly focuses on World War II, when the German army forced Finnmark's population to evacuate, and the county was burned to the ground as part of a scorched-earth policy. Through photographs, videos, and sound effects, the museum recounts the residents' struggle to rebuild their lives. The exhibition includes authentic rooms that were built in caves after the evacuation, as well as huts and postwar homes. ⊠*Kirkegt. 21* ☏*78-42-26-30* ⊕*www.museumsnett.no/ gjenreisningsmuseet* ▣*Nkr 50* ☉*Jan.–mid-June, daily 11–2; mid-June– late Aug., daily 9–4; late Aug.–Dec., daily 11–2.*

The **Royal and Ancient Polar Bear Society** was founded by two businessmen whose goal was to share the town's history as a center for hunting and commerce. Exhibits depict aspects of arctic hunts, including preserved and stuffed polar bears, seals, lynx, puffins, and wolves. ⊠*Town Hall basement* ☏*78-41-31-00* ▣*Nkr 40* ☉*Call for hrs.*

ACTIVITIES

If you stop into the office of **Hammerfest Turist Informasjon** (⊠*Havnegt. 3* ☏*78-41-31-00* ⊕*www.hammerfest-turist.no*), you can find out about activities in the region that include golf, walking tours, bird-watching trips, and boating.

HONNINGSVÅG, NORWAY

Searching in 1553 for a northeast passage to India, British navigator Richard Chancellor came upon a crag 307 meters above the Barents Sea. He named the jut of rock North Cape, or *Nordkapp*. Today, Europe's northernmost point is a rite-of-passage journey for nearly all Scandinavians. And much of the world has followed. Most cruise passengers visit Nordkapp from Honningsvåg, a fishing village situated on Magerøya Island. The journey from Honningsvåg to Nordkapp covers about 35 km (22 mi) across a landscape characterized by rocky tundra and grazing reindeer, which are rounded up each spring by Sami herdsmen in boats. The herdsmen force the reindeer to swim across a mile-wide channel from their winter home on the mainland. Honningvåg's northerly location makes for long, dark winter nights and perpetually sun-filled summer days. The village serves as the gateway to Arctic exploration and the beautiful Nordkapp Plateau, a destination that calls to all visitors of this region.

ESSENTIALS

CURRENCY Norway is a non-EU country and has opted to keep its currency, the Norwegian *krone* (Nkr 6 to US$1); exchange rates were accurate at this writing but are subject to change. ATMs are common, especially in larger cities.

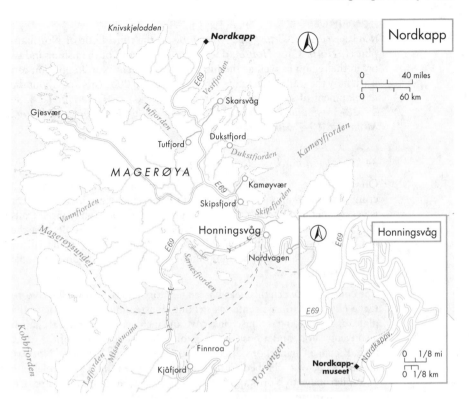

HOURS   Most shops are open from 9 or 10 to 5 weekdays, Thursday until 7, Saturday from 9 to 2 or 4, and are closed Sunday.

INTERNET   Internet access can be found within walking distance of the five cruise-ship piers. **Nordkapp Mikrobryggeri AS** (⊠ *Bryggerie Nordkappgata 1* ☎78–47–26–00), a café and pub, sells its own locally made beer and also offers Internet access. You can check your e-mail at the **Tourist Information/Nordkapp Reiseliv AS.** (⊠*Fiskeriveien 4D* ☎78–47–70–3).

TELEPHONES   Most tri- and quad-band GSM phones work in Norway, so if your service provider offers service in Europe, you will likely be able to use your mobile phone along the Norwegian coast, even while hugging the shoreline on ship. Public telephones take Nkr 1, 5, 10, and 20 coins, and you need Nkr 5 at a minimum. International phone cards are the best value for long-distance calls and are available at newsstands.

COMING ASHORE

Northern Norway's largest port welcomes about 100 cruise ships annually during the summer season. Ships dock at one of five piers, all within walking distance of the city center. The piers themselves have no services, but within 100 meters are shops, museums, tourist information, post office, banks, restaurants, and an ice bar.

EXPLORING HONNINGSVÅG & NORDKAPP

Numbers in the margin correspond to points of interest on the Nordkapp map.

HONNINGSVÅG

Nordkappmuseet *(North Cape Museum)*, on the third floor of Nordkapphuset *(North Cape House)*, documents the history of the fishing industry in the region as well as the history of tourism at Nordkapp. You can learn how the trail of humanity stretches back 10,000 years and about the development of society and culture in this region. ⊠*Fiskerivn. 4* ☎*78–47–28–33* ⊕*www.nordkappmuseet.no* ⊴*Nkr 30* ⊙*June–mid-Aug., Mon.–Sat. 10–7, Sun. noon–7.*

NORDKAPP

34 km (21 mi) north of Honningsvåg.

On your journey to Nordkapp, you'll see an incredible treeless tundra, with crumbling mountains and sparse dwarf plants. The subarctic environment is very vulnerable so don't disturb the plants. Walk only on marked trails and don't remove stones, leave car marks, or make campfires. Because the roads are closed in winter, the only access is from the tiny fishing village of Skarsvåg via Sno-Cat, a thump-and-bump ride that's as unforgettable as the desolate view.

The contrast between this near-barren territory and **Nordkapphallen** *(North Cape Hall)*, the tourist center, is striking. Blasted into the interior of the plateau, the building is housed in a cave and includes an ecumenical chapel, a souvenir shop, and a post office. Exhibits trace the history of the cape, from Richard Chancellor's discover in 1533, to Oscar II, king of Norway and Sweden, who climbed to the top of the plateau in 1873. Celebrate your pilgrimage to Nordkapp at Café Kompasset, Restaurant Kompasset, or at the Grotten Bar coffee shop. ⊠*Nordkapplatået* ☎*78–47–68–60* 🖷*78–47–68–61* ⊕*www.visitnorthcape.com* ⊴*Nkr 190* ⊙*Call for hrs.*

SHOPPING

The small village of Honningsvåg doesn't exactly qualify as a shopper's paradise, but there are shops that sell Norwegian souvenirs and handicrafts. **Arctic Souvenir** (⊠*Fiskeriveien 4* ☎*78–47–37–12*) is in the same building as the Nordkappmuseet and the tourist information center, staying open until very late at night when cruise ships call. The shop features a range of Norwegian souvenirs, T-shirts, books, knitting products, pewter and international calling cards—all tax-free. The shop can also mail purchased goods. Accepts all major credit cards and foreign currency.

SPORTS & ACTIVITIES

BIRD-WATCHING

Gjesvær Turistsenter (☎*78–47–57–73* ⊕*www.birdsafari.com*) organizes bird safaris and deep-sea fishing. **Nordkapp Reiseliv** (☎*78–47–70–30* ⊕*www. visitnorthcape.com*) books adventures and activities including bird safaris, deep-sea fishing, boat excursions, and winter expeditions.

RAFTING

Deep-sea rafting is as exhilarating as it is beautiful. After getting a flotation suit to protect against the subarctic wind, board a rubber dinghy at the North Cape Adventure Center and speed toward Nordfågen, an uninhabited fishing hamlet. Continue on to see the Helnes Lighthouse, which was built in 1908 for trading vessels coming from northern Russia and the East. **Nordkapp Safari** (☎*78–47–52–33*) organizes three-hour trips to Nordkapp.

WHERE TO EAT

$–$$$ ✕**Corner AS.** Local fish dishes and a daily chef's special are always on the menu, not to mention the best pizza in town. ✉*Fiskeriveien 2A* ☎*78–47–63–40* ⊕*www.corner.no* ▭*AE, MC, V.*

OSLO, NORWAY

What sets Oslo apart from other European cities is not so much its cultural traditions or its internationally renowned museums as its simply stunning natural beauty. How many world capitals have subway service to the forest, or lakes and hiking trails within the city limits? But Norwegians will be quick to remind you that Oslo is a cosmopolitan metropolis with prosperous businesses and a thriving nightlife. During the mid-19th century, Norway and Sweden were ruled as one kingdom, under King Karl Johan. It was then that the grand main street that is his namesake was built, and Karl Johans Gate has been at the center of city life ever since. In 1905 the country separated from Sweden, and in 1925 an act of Parliament finally changed the city's name back to Oslo from Kristiania, its Swedish name. Today, Oslo is Norway's political, economic, industrial, and cultural capital. The Norwegian royal family lives in Oslo, and it is also where the Nobel peace prize is awarded.

ESSENTIALS

CURRENCY Norway is a non-EU country and has opted to keep its currency, the Norwegian *krone* (Nkr 6 to US$1); exchange rates were accurate at this writing but are subject to change. ATMs are common.

HOURS Most shops are open from 9 or 10 to 5 weekdays, Thursday until 7, Saturday from 9 to 2 or 4, and are closed Sunday.

INTERNET **Arctic Internet** (✉*Oslo S Station, Sentrum* ☎*22–17–19–40*). **Studenten Nett-Café** (✉*Karl Johans gt. 45Sentrum* ☎*22–42–56–80*).

TELEPHONES Most tri- and quad-band GSM phones work in Norway, so if your service provider offers service in Europe, you will likely be able to use your mobile phone along the Norwegian coast, even while hugging the shoreline on ship. Public telephones take Nkr 1, 5, 10, and 20 coins, and you need Nkr 5 at a minimum. International phone cards are the best value for long-distance calls and are available at newsstands.

COMING ASHORE

Cruise ships navigate beautiful Oslofjord en route to Oslo and dock in the compact city center. Many of Oslo's attractions can be explored on foot from the docks, but Olso has a good subway system, as well as plentiful buses and taxis.

Taxis are radio dispatched from a central office, and it can take up to 30 minutes to get one during peak hours. Taxi stands are located all over town. It is possible to hail a cab on the street, but cabs are not allowed to pick up passengers within 100 yards of a stand. Never take pirate taxis;

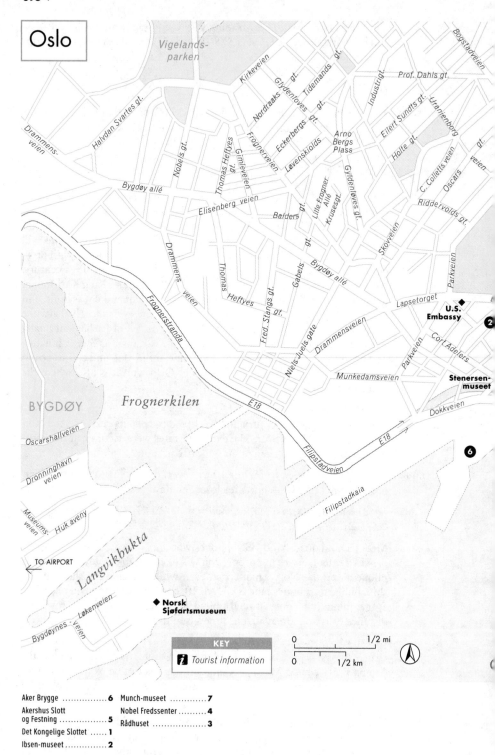

Oslo

KEY
ℹ️ Tourist information

0 ———— 1/2 mi
0 ———— 1/2 km

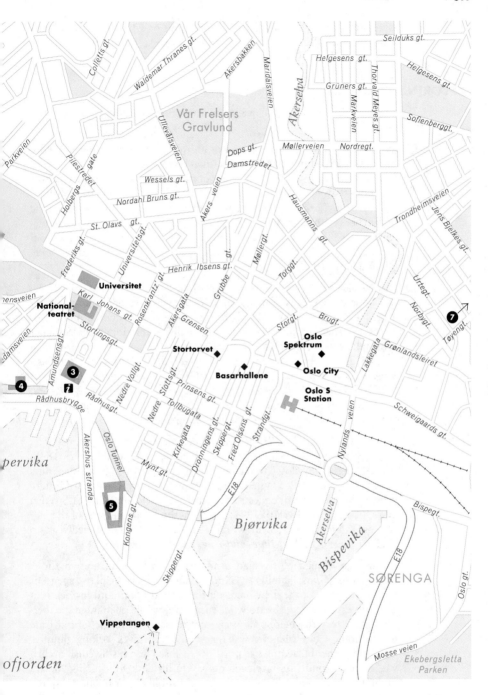

8

all registered taxis should have their roof lights on when they're available. Rates start at Nkr 30 for hailed or rank cabs, and Nkr 49 for ordered taxis, depending on the time of day.

EXPLORING OSLO

Numbers in the margin correspond to points of interest on the Oslo map.

6 **Aker Brygge.** This area was the site of a disused shipyard until redevelopment saw the addition of residential town houses and a commercial sector. Postmodern steel and glass buildings dominate the skyline now. The area has more than 40 restaurants and 60 shops, including upmarket fashion boutiques, as well as pubs, cinemas, theaters, and an indoor shopping mall. There is outdoor dining capacity for 2,500 as well as an open boulevard for strolling. Service facilities include banks, drugstores, and a parking lot for 1,600. ⊠*Aker Brygge* ☎*22–83–26–80* ⊠*Free* ⊙*Shopping hrs weekdays 10–8, Sat. 10–6.*

Fodor's Choice
★

5 **Akershus Slott og Festning** *(Akershus Castle and Fortress).* Dating from 1299, this stone medieval castle and royal residence was developed into a fortress armed with cannons by 1592. After that time, it withstood a number of sieges and then fell into decay. It was finally restored in 1899. Summer tours take guests through its magnificent halls, the castle church, the royal mausoleum, reception rooms, and banquet halls. ⊠*Akershus Slott, Festningspl., Sentrum* ☎*22–41–25–21* ⊠*Grounds and concerts free, castle Nkr 40* ⊙*Grounds: daily 6 AM–9 PM. Castle: May–mid-Sept., Mon.–Sat. 10–6, Sun. 12:30–4; mid-Sept.–Apr., Thurs. tours at 1. Guided tours: May–mid-Sept., daily at 11, 1, and 3; mid-Sept.–Apr., Thurs. at 1.*

1 **Det Kongelige Slottet** *(The Royal Palace).* At one end of Karl Johans Gate, the vanilla- and cream-color neoclassical palace was completed in 1848. Although generally closed to the public, the palace is open for guided tours in summer at 2 and 2:20 PM. The rest of the time, you can simply admire it from the outside. An equestrian statue of Karl Johan, King of Sweden and Norway from 1818 to 1844, stands in the square in front of the palace. ⊠*Drammensvn. 1, Sentrum* ☎*81–53–21–33* ⊕*www.kongehuset.no* ⊠*Tour Nkr 95* ⊙*Mid-June–mid-Aug. (guided tours only).*

2 **Ibsen-museet.** Famed Norwegian dramatist Henrik Ibsen, known for *A Doll's House, Ghosts,* and *Peer Gynt,* among other classic plays, spent his final years here, in the apartment on the second floor, until his death in 1906. Every morning, Ibsen's wife, Suzannah, would encourage the literary legend to write before allowing him to head off to the Grand Café for his brandy and foreign newspapers. His study gives striking glimpses into his psyche. Huge, intense portraits of Ibsen and his Swedish archrival, August Strindberg, face each other. On his desk still sits his "devil's orchestra," a playful collection of frog and troll-like figurines that inspired him. Take a guided tour by well-versed and entertaining Ibsen scholars. Afterward, visit the museum's exhibition of Ibsen's drawings and paintings and first magazine writings. ⊠*Arbiensgt. 1, across Drammensvn. from Royal Palace, Sentrum* ☎*22–12–35–50* ⊕*www.ibsenmuseet.no* ⊠*Nkr*

70 🕐 *Tues.–Sun., guided tours at noon, 1, and 2; June–Aug., additional guided tours at 11 and 3.*

❼ Munch-museet. *(Munch Museum).* Edvard Munch, Norway's most famous artist, bequeathed his enormous collection of works (about 1,100 paintings, 3,000 drawings, and 18,000 graphic works) to the city when he died in 1944. The museum is a monument to his artistic genius, housing the largest collection of his works as well as changing exhibitions. Munch actually painted several different versions of *The Scream,* the image for which he is known best. An important one of his Scream paintings, as well as

Fodor'sChoice
★

another painting, *The Madonna,* were stolen from the Munch-museet in an armed robbery in 2004. After two years of intense investigation the paintings were recovered by the police on August 31, 2006. While most of the Munch legend focuses on the artist as a troubled, angst-ridden man, he moved away from that pessimistic and dark approach to more optimistic themes later in his career. ✉ *Tøyengt. 53, Tøyen* 📞 *23–49–35–00* 🌐 *www.munch.museum.no* 💶 *Nkr 65* 🕐 *June–mid-Sept., daily 10–6; mid-Sept.–May, weekdays 10–6, weekends 11–5.*

❹ Nobel Fredssenter *(Nobel Peace Center).* Situated near the **Rådhuset** *(City Hall)* in a converted historic train station, the Nobel Peace Center was opened by King Harald on June 11, 2005. With changing exhibits, intriguing digital presentations, and inspiring films and lectures, the Center reflects on the men and women who have been honored over the years. ✉ *Rådhusplassen, Sentrum* 📞 *48–30–10–00* 🌐 *www.nobelpeacecenter.org* 💶 *Tour Nkr 160* 🕐 *Tues., Wed., Fri. 10–4, Thurs. 10–6, weekends 11–5.*

❸ Rådhuset *(City Hall).* This redbrick building is best known today for the awarding of the Nobel peace prize, which takes place here every December. In 1915, the mayor of Oslo made plans for a new city hall and ordered the clearing of slums that stood on the site. The building was finally completed in 1950. Inside, many museum-quality masterpieces hang on the walls. After viewing the frescoes in the main hall, walk upstairs to the banquet hall to see the royal portraits. In the east gallery, Per Krogh's mosaic of a pastoral scene covers all four walls, making you feel like you're part of the painting. On festive occasions, the central hall is illuminated from outside by 60 large spotlights that simulate daylight. ✉ *Rådhuspl., Sentrum* 📞 *23–46–16–00* 🌐 *www.rft.oslo.kommune.no* 💶 *Nkr 40* 🕐 *May–Aug., daily 9–5; Sept.–Apr., daily 9–4.*

Fodor'sChoice
★

SHOPPING

Oslo is the best place in the country for buying anything Norwegian. Popular souvenirs include knitwear, wood and ceramic trolls, wood spoons, rosemaling boxes, gold and silver jewelry, pewter, smoked salmon, caviar, *akvavit* (a caraway seed-flavored liquor), chocolate, and goat cheese.

Established Norwegian brands include Porsgrund porcelain, Hadeland and Magnor glass, David Andersen jewelry, and Husfliden handicrafts. You may also want to look for popular, classical, or folk music CDs; English translations of Norwegian books; or clothing by Norwegian designers.

Prices in Norway, as in all of Scandinavia, are generally much higher than in other European countries. The cost of handmade articles such as knitwear is controlled, making comparison shopping useless. Otherwise, shops have both sales and specials—look for the words *salg* and *tilbud*.

Near the cruise ship docks is **Aker Brygge** (⊠ *Vestbanen*), Norway's first major shopping center. It's right on the water across from the tourist information center. Shops are open until 8 most days, and some open on Sunday.

SPORTS & ACTIVITIES

Oslo's natural surroundings and climate make it ideally suited to outdoor pursuits. The Oslofjord and its islands, the forested woodlands called the *marka,* and as many as 18 hours of daylight in summer all make the Norwegian capital an irresistible place for outdoor activities.

BICYCLING

Oslo is a great biking city. One scenic ride starts at Aker Brygge and takes you along the harbor to the Bygdøy peninsula, where you can visit the museums or cut across the fields next to the royal family's summer house. **Syklistenes Landsforening** (*National Organization of Cyclists* ⊠ *Storgata 23D, Sentrum* ☎ *22–47–30–30*) sells books and maps for cycling holidays in Norway and abroad and the staff gives friendly, free advice.

CANOEING

Villmarkshuset (⊠ *Christian Krohgs gt. 16, Sentrum* ☎ *22–05–05–22*) is an equipment, activities, and excursion center specializing in hiking, climbing, hunting, fishing, cycling, and canoeing. You can rent a canoe from here, drop it into the Akers River at the rear of the store, and paddle out into the Oslofjord. There is also an indoor climbing wall, a pistol range, and a diving center and swimming pool. Books and maps are available. The **Oslo Archipelago** is a favorite destination for sunbathing urbanites, who hop ferries to their favorite isles. A ferry to Hovedya and other islands in the harbor basin leaves from Aker Brygge (take Bus 60 from Jernbanetorget).

FISHING

A national fishing license and a local fee are required to fish in the Oslofjord and the surrounding lakes. For information on fishing areas and on where to buy a license, contact **Oslomarkas Fiskeadministrasjon** (⊠ *Sørkedalen 914, Holmenkollen* ☎ *40–00–67–68*). You can fish throughout the Nordmarka woods area in a canoe rented from **Tomm Murstad** (⊠*Tryvannsvn. 2, Holmenkollen* ☎22–13–95–00).

GOLF

Golfsenteret (⊠*Sandakerveien 24C, Torshov* ☎23–22–65–65), five minutes outside the city center, has a driving range, putting green, simulator, and pro shop. Oslo's international-level golf course, **Oslo Golfklubb** (⊠*Bogstad, Bogstad0740* ☎22–51–05–60) is private and heavily booked. However, it admits members of other golf clubs weekdays before 2 and weekends after 2 if space is available. Visitors must have a handicap certificate of 20 or lower for men, 28 or lower for women. Fees range from Nkr 250 to Nkr 500.

NIGHTLIFE

More than ever, the Oslo nightlife scene is vibrant and varied. Cafés, restaurant-bars, and jazz clubs are laid-back and mellow. But if you're ready to party, there are many pulsating, live-rock and dance clubs to choose from. Day or night, people are usually out on Karl Johans Gate, and many clubs and restaurants in the central area stay open until the early hours. Aker Brygge, the wharf area, has many bars and some nightclubs, attracting mostly tourists, couples on first dates, and other people willing to spend extra for the waterfront location. Grünerløkka and Grønland have even more bars, pubs, and cafés catering to a younger crowd. A more mature, upmarket crowd ventures out to the less busy west side of Oslo, to Frogner and Bygdøy.

Drinking out is very expensive in Oslo, starting at around Nkr 50 for a beer or a mixed drink. Many Norwegians save money by having drinks at friends' houses—called a *forschpiel*—before heading out on the town. Some bars in town remain quiet until 11 PM or midnight when the first groups of forschpiel partyers arrive.

WHERE TO EAT

$$$–$$$$ ✕**Lofoten Fiskerestaurant.** Named for the Lofoten Islands off the northwest
★ coast, this Aker Brygge restaurant is considered one of Oslo's best for fish, from salmon to cod to monkfish. It has a bright, fresh, minimalist interior with harbor views and a summertime patio. Call ahead, since sometimes only large groups are served. ⊠*Stranden 75, Aker Brygge* ☎22–83–08–08 ⊟*AE, DC, MC, V.*

$$–$$$$ ✕**Det Gamle Rådhus.** Inside Oslo's City Hall, built in 1641, this is the city's oldest restaurant. Its reputation is based mostly on traditional fish and game dishes. The backyard has a charming outdoor area for dining in summer. ⊠*Nedre Slottsgt. 1, Sentrum* ☎22–42–01–07 ⊟*AE, DC, MC, V* ☺*Closed Sun.*

TROMSØ, NORWAY

Tromsø surprised visitors in the 1800s: they thought it very sophisticated and cultured for being so close to the North Pole. It looks the way a polar town should, with ice-capped mountain ridges and jagged architecture that is an echo of the peaks. The midnight sun shines from May 21 to

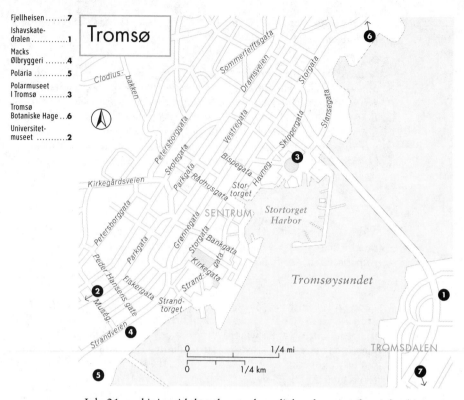

July 21, and it is said that the northern lights decorate the night skies over Tromsø more than any other city in Norway. The so-called "Capital of the North" (the city was once the capital of Norway—though for only 38 days) is about the same size as Luxembourg, but home to only 58,000 people. The city's total area—2,558 square km (987 square mi)—is actually the most expansive in Norway. The downtown area is on a small, hilly island connected to the mainland by a slender bridge. The 13,000 students at the world's northernmost university are one reason the nightlife here is uncommonly lively for a northern city.

ESSENTIALS

CURRENCY Norway is a non-EU country and has opted to keep its currency, the Norwegian *krone* (Nkr 6 to US$1); exchange rates were accurate at this writing but are subject to change. ATMs are common.

HOURS Most shops are open from 9 or 10 to 5 weekdays, Thursday until 6 or 7, Saturday from 9 to 2 or 4, and are closed Sunday.

INTERNET For passengers docking in Breivika, Internet service is available at the public library, **Tromsø Bibliotek** (⊠ *Grønnegt*). The **Meieriet Café** (⊠ *og Storpub, Grønnegt. 37–39*) offers Internet service if you need to check your e-mail.

Passengers disembarking in the city center can check their e-mail at the **Universitetsmuseet** (⊠ *Universitetet, Lars Thørings v. 10*).

TELEPHONES If your service provider offers service in Europe, you will likely be able to use your mobile phone along the Norwegian coast, even while hugging the shoreline on ship. Before leaving home, however, be sure to check international roaming rates for phone service and data transfer if you plan to check e-mail or browse the Web using your mobile phone. Public telephones take Nkr 1, 5, 10, and 20 coins, and you need Nkr 5 to get through. International phone cards are the best value for long-distance calls. Phone cards typically are available at newsstands. The international prefix for dialing out of Norway is 00.

COMING ASHORE

Cruise ships dock either in the city center at Prostneset or 4 km (2.5 mi) north of the city center at Breivika. Step off the ship in Prostneset, and you're in the city center, but there are no facilites at either pier.

EXPLORING TROMSØ

Numbers in the margin correspond to points of interest on the Tromsø map.

7 Fjellheisen. To get a sense of Tromsø's immensity and solitude, take the cable car from behind Tromsø Cathedral up to the mountains, just a few minutes out of the city center. **Storsteinen** *(Big Rock)*, 1,386 feet above sea level, has a great city view. In summer a restaurant is open at the top of the lift. ⊠*Sollivn. 12* ☎*77–63–87–37* *Nkr 85* ☉*Apr.–Aug., daily 10–5; Sept.–Mar., weekends 10–5.*

1 Ishavskatedralen. The Arctic Cathedral is the city's signature structure. Designed by Jan Inge Hovig, it's meant to evoke the shape of a Sámi tent as well as the iciness of a glacier. Opened in 1964, it represents northern Norwegian nature, culture, and faith. The immense stained-glass window depicts the Second Coming. ⊠*Tromsdalen* ☎*77–75–34–40* ⊕*www.ishavskatedralen. no* *Nkr 25* ☉*June–mid-Aug., Mon.–Sat. 9–7, Sun. 1–7.*

4 Macks Ølbryggeri. Ludvik Mack founded Mack's Brewery in 1877 and it is still family-owned. Take a guided tour and afterward receive a beer stein, pin, and a pint of your choice in the Ølhallen pub. Call ahead to reserve a place on the tour. ⊠*Storgt. 5–13* ☎*77–62–45–00* ⊕*www.mack.no* *Nkr 110* ☉*Guided tours June–Aug., Mon.–Thurs. at 1 and 3:30.*

5 Polaria. The adventure center examines life in and around the polar and Barents regions with exhibits on polar travel and arctic research, and a panoramic film from Svalbard. The aquarium has sea mammals, including seals. ⊠*Hjarmar Johansens gt. 12* ☎*77–75–01–00* ⊕*www.polaria.no* *Nkr 90* ☉*Mid-May–mid-Aug., daily 10–7; mid-Aug.–mid-May, daily noon–5.*

3 Polarmuseet i Tromsø. In an 1830s former customs warehouse, the Polar Museum documents the history of the polar region, focusing on Norway's explorers and hunters. ⊠*Søndre Tollbugt. 11B* ☎*77–68–43–73* ⊕*www.polarmuseum.no* *Nkr 50* ☉*Mar.–mid-June, daily 11–5; mid-June–mid-Aug., daily 10–7; mid-Aug.–Sept., daily 11–5.*

6 Tromsø Botaniske Hage. Tromsø's Botanic Garden has plants from the Antarctic and Arctic as well as mountain plants from all over the world. Encompassing 4 acres, the garden has been designed as a natural landscape with terraces, slopes, a stream, and a pond. Guides are available by advance arrangement. ⊠*Tromsø University, Breivika* ☎*77–64–50–78* ⊕*www. uit.no/botanisk* ⊠*Free* ⊘*Daily 24 hrs.*

❷ Tromsø Museum, Universitetsmuseet. Northern Norway's largest museum is dedicated to the nature and culture of the region. Learn about the northern lights, wildlife, fossils and dinosaurs, minerals and rocks, and church art from 1300 to 1800. Outdoors you can visit a Sámi *gamme* (turf hut), and a replica of a Viking longhouse. ⊠*Universitetet, Lars Thørings v. 10* ☎*77–64–50–00* ⊕*www.imv.uit.no* ⊠*Nkr 30* ⊘*June 1–Aug. 31, daily 9–6.*

SPORTS & ACTIVITIES

HIKING & WALKING
With wilderness at its doorstep, Tromsø has more than 100 km (62 mi) of walking and hiking trails in the mountains above the city. They're reachable by funicular. **TROMSØ Troms Turlag-DNT** (☎*77–68–51–75* ⊕*www.turistforeningen.no*) organizes tours and courses.

HORSEBACK RIDING
Holmeslet Gård (☎*77–61–9974*) offers horseback riding, carriage tours, and wildlife-viewing adventures.

SHOPPING

One of Norway's leading regions for handmade arts and crafts, Tromsø is a treasure trove of shops, particularly along the main pedestrian street Storgata, where a market sells regional and international products. Pick up art from the city's many galleries or craft shops (such as glass-blowing and candle-making studios), or score such Arctic delicacies as reindeer sausages.

Arppa Sami Duodje Gallery (⊠*Fredrik Langes Gate 13* ☎*41–57–51–31*) sells gifts based on traditional Sami culture, including works in leather, wood, silver, and pewter, as well as arts and handicrafts from Sami artisans. **Husfliden** (⊠*Sjørgata 4* ☎*77–75-88-70*) carries traditional handicrafts and souvenirs as well as traditional folk dress, called bunads.

WHERE TO EAT

$$$$ ✕**Skarven.** A Tromsø institution, Skarven features several restaurants that share the same building. Specialties range from seafood (including whale and seal) to Arctic cuisine to meats such as steak, lamb, goat, and chicken. ⊠*Strandtorget 1* ☎*77–60–07–20* ⊕*www.skarven.no.*

$ ✕**Kaffe à Lars.** Opposite the town cathedral and on the ground floor of Emma's Drømmekjøkken (Kitchen of Dreams), Kaffe å Lars is an intimate coffee shop that serves breakfast and lunch as well as locally brewed beers. ⊠*Kirkegt 8* ☎*77–63–77–30* ⊕*www.emmaoglars.no.*

TRONDHEIM, NORWAY

One of Scandinavia's oldest cities, Trondheim is Norway's third largest, with a population of 150,000. Founded in AD 997 by Viking king Olav Tryggvason, it was first named Nidaros (still the name of the cathedral), a composite word referring to the city's location at the mouth of the Nid River. The city was also the first capital of Norway, from 997 to 1380. Trondheim became a pilgrimage center because the popularity of King Olaf II Haraldsson (later St. Olaf), who was buried here after being killed in a battle in 1030. Today Trondheim is a university town as well as a center for maritime and medical research, but the wide streets of the historic city center are still lined with brightly painted wood houses and striking warehouses.

ESSENTIALS

CURRENCY Norway is a non-EU country and has opted to keep its currency, the Norwegian *krone* (Nkr 6 to US$1); exchange rates were accurate at this writing but are subject to change. ATMs are common.

HOURS Most shops are open from 9 or 10 to 5 weekdays, Thursday until 7, Saturday from 9 to 2 or 4, and are closed Sunday.

INTERNET **Library** (⊠*Petter Eggens plass 1*). **Space Bar** (⊠*Kongens gt. 19*).

TELEPHONES If your service provider offers service in Europe, you will likely be able to use your mobile phone along the Norwegian coast, even while hugging the shoreline on ship. Before leaving home, however, be sure to check international roaming rates for phone service and data transfer if you plan to check e-mail or browse the Web using your mobile phone. Public telephones take Nkr 1, 5, 10, and 20 coins, and you need Nkr 5 to get through. International phone cards are the best value for long-distance calls. Phone cards typically are available at newsstands. The international prefix for dialing out of Norway is 00.

COMING ASHORE

Cruise ships dock at one of two piers. Both of these are within easy walking distance of the city center. There are no facilities at the piers, but you'll find everything you need—from banks to tourist offices—in the city.

EXPLORING TRONDHEIM

The **Erkebispegården** *(Archbishop's Palace)* is the oldest secular building in Scandinavia, dating from around 1160. It was the residence of the archbishop until the Reformation in 1537; after that it was a residence for Danish governors, and later a military headquarters. The oldest parts of the palace, which face the cathedral, are used for government functions. A **museum** has original sculptures from Nidaros Cathedral and architectural pieces from throughout the palace's history. ⊠*Kongsgårdsgt.* ☎*73–53–91–60 museum* ⊕*www.nidarosdomen.no* ✉*Nkr 35* ☺*May–mid-Sept., weekdays 10–3, Sat. 10–4, Sun. noon–4; mid-Sept.–Apr., Wed.–Fri., 11–2, Sat. 11–3, Sun. noon–4.*

Built after the great fire of 1681, the **Kristiansten Festning** *(Kristiansten Fort)* saved the city from conquest by Sweden in 1718. During Norway's occupation by Germany, from 1940 to 1945, members of the Norwegian Resistance were executed here; there's a plaque in their honor. The fort has a spectacular view of the city, the fjord, and the mountains. ☎73–99–52–80 📠Free ⊙June–Aug., weekdays 10–3, weekends 11–4.

King Olav formulated a Christian religious code for Norway in 1024, during his reign. It was on his grave that **Nidaros Domkirke** *(Nidaros Cathedral)* was built. The town became a pilgrimage site for the Christians of northern Europe, and Olav was canonized in 1164.

Although construction began in 1070, the oldest existing parts of the cathedral date from around 1150. It has been ravaged by fire on several occasions and rebuilt each time, generally in a Gothic style. Since the Middle Ages, Norway's kings have been crowned and blessed in the cathedral. The crown jewels are on display here. Forty-five minute guided tours are offered in English from mid-June to mid-August, weekdays at 11 and 4. ⊠*Kongsgårdsgt. 2* ☎*73–53–91–60* ⊕*www.nidarosdomen.no* 📠*Nkr 50* ⊙*May–mid-Sept., weekdays 9–3, Sat. 9–2, Sun. 1–4; mid-Sept.–Apr., weekdays, noon–2:30, Sat. 11:30–2, Sun. 1–3.*

The **Ringve Museum,** Norway's national museum of music and musical instruments, is on a country estate outside Trondheim. The **Museum in the Manor House,** the oldest section, focuses on instruments in the European musical tradition. Guides demonstrate their use. The Museum in the Barn features modern sound-and-light technology as well as Norwegian folk instruments. ⊠*Lade Allé 60* ☎*73–92–24–11* ⊕*www.ringve.com* 📠*Nkr 75* ⊙*July–mid-Aug., daily 11–5; mid-Aug.–mid-Sept., daily 11–3; mid-Sept.–mid-Dec., Sun. 11–4.*

Fodor's Choice
★
The**Stiftsgården,** Scandinavia's largest wooden palace, was built between 1774 and 1778 as the home of a prominent widow. Sold to the state in 1800, it's now the official royal residence in Trondheim. The architecture and interior are late baroque and highly representative of 18th-century high society's taste. Tours offer insight into the festivities marking the coronations of the kings in Nidaros Domkirke. ⊠*Munkegt. 23* ☎*73–80–89–50* 📠*Nkr 60* ⊙*June 1–19, Mon.–Sat. 10–3, Sun. noon–5; June 20–Aug. 20, Mon.–Sat. 10–5, Sun. noon–5. Tours on the hr.*

Near the ruins of King Sverre's medieval castle is the **Sverresborg Trøndelag Folkemuseum,** which has re-creations of coastal, inland, and mountain-village buildings that depict life in Trøndelag during the 18th and 19th centuries. The **Haltdalen stave church,** built in 1170, is the northernmost preserved stave church in Norway. In the Old Town you can visit a 1900 dentist's office and an old-fashioned grocery that sells sweets. A special exhibit examines how the stages of life—childhood, youth, adulthood, and old age—have changed over the past 150 years. The audiovisual **Trønderbua** depicts traditional regional wedding ceremonies with artifacts and a 360-degree film. ⊠*Sverresborg Allé* ☎*73–89–01–00* ⊕*www.sverresborg.no* 📠*Nkr 80* ⊙*June–Sept., daily 11–6; Oct.–May, weekdays 11–3, weekends noon–4.*

SHOPPING

Trondheim's **Mercur Centre** and **Trondheim Torg** shopping centers have helpful staffs and interesting shops.

Arne Ronning (⊠*Nordregt. 10* ☎*73–53–13–30*) carries fine sweaters by Dale of Norway. Trondheim has a branch of the handicraft store **Husfli-**

den (⊠*Olav Tryggvasongt. 18* ☎*73–83–32–30)*. For knitted sweaters by such makers as Oleana and Oda, try **Jens Hoff Garn & Ide** (⊠*Olav Tryg-gvasongt. 20* ☎*73–53–15–27)*. Founded in 1770 and Norway's oldest extant goldsmith, **Møllers Gullsmedforretning** (⊠*Munkegt. 3*) sells versions of the Trondheim Rose, the city symbol since the 1700s.

ACTIVITIES

BICYCLING

Some 300 **Trondheim Bysykkel City Bikes** can be borrowed in the city center. Parked in easy-to-see stands at central locations, the distinctive green bikes have shopping baskets. You'll need a 20-kroner piece to release the bike (your money's refunded when you return the bike to a parking rack). The Trampe elevator ascends the steep Brubakken Hill near Gamle Bybro and takes cyclists nearly to Kristiansten Festning (Kristiansten Fort). Contact the tourist office to get the card you need in order to use the Trampe.

FISHING

The Nid River is one of Norway's best salmon and trout rivers, famous for its large salmon (the record is 70 pounds). You can fish right in the city, but you need a license. For further information and fishing licenses, contact **TOFA (Trondheim og Omland Jakt- og Fiskeadministrasjon)** (⊠*Leirfossvn. 76* ☎*73–96–55–80* ⊕*www.tofa.org)*.

HIKING & WALKING

Bymarka, a wooded area on Trondheim's outskirts, has a varied and well-developed network of trails—60 km (37 mi) of gravel paths, 80 km (50 mi) of dirtpaths, and 250 km (155 mi) of ski tracks. **Ladestien** *(Lade Trail)* is a 14-km (9-mi) trail that goes along the edge of the Lade Peninsula and offers great views of Trondheimsfjord. **Nidelvstien** *(Nidelv Trail)* runs along the river from Tempe to the Leirfossene waterfalls.

SWIMMING

Trondheim Pirbadet (⊠*Havnegt. 12* ☎*73–83–18–00* ⊕*www.pirbadet.no)* is Norway's largest indoor swimming center. There's a wave pool, a sauna, and a Jacuzzi, as well as a gym here.

WHERE TO EAT

Trondheim is known for the traditional dish *surlaks* (marinated salmon served with sour cream). A sweet specialty is *tekake* (tea cake), which looks like a thick-crust pizza topped with a lattice pattern of cinnamon and sugar. The city's restaurant scene is vibrant and evolving, with more and more international restaurants serving Continental food, and bars and cafés where the city's considerable student population gathers.

$$-$$$ ✕**Egon Tårnet.** An attractive rotating restaurant situated 74 meters over the city. ⊠*Otto Nielsens vei 4* ☎*73–87–35–00* ⊕*www.egon.no* ⊟*AE, MC, V.*

$-$$ ✕**Vertshuset Grenaderen.** Dine in a 17th-century blacksmith's house on traditional Norwegian food such as reindeer and fish. Boasts one of the city's most attractive terraces for summer outdoor dining. ⊠*Kongsgårdsgt. 1* ☎*73–51–66–80* ⊕*www.grenaderen.no* ⊟*AE, MC, V.*

INDEX

PHOTO CREDITS

NOTES

NOTES

NOTES

NOTES

NOTES

NOTES

ABOUT OUR WRITERS

Linda Coffman is a freelance travel writer and the originator of CruiseDiva.com, her Web site, which has been dishing out cruise-travel advice and information since 2000. Before that, she was the cruise guide for About.com. Her columns and articles have appeared in *Cruise Travel, Porthole, Consumers Digest,* and other regional and national magazines; the *Chicago Sun-Times, Denver Post*; and on numerous Web sites, including those for *USA Today,* Fodors.com, and the Travel Channel. She's an avid cruiser, who enjoys sailing on ships of every size to any port worldwide but spends most of her time cruising the Caribbean. Linda thinks cruising is in her Norwegian blood and credits her heritage for a love of all things nautical. When not at sea, she makes her home in Augusta, Georgia, with her husband, Mel, and two very finicky teenage cats.

Lindsay Bennett discovered a love of travel while backpacking around the globe between studies that led to a degree in politics. Today, she's written over 40 travel guides for leading international publishers on destinations worldwide, from little explored wilderness to the latest fashionable urban metropolis, and her passion for exploring far horizons is as fresh as ever. She divides her time between France and the U.K.

Ralph Grizzle began his journalistic career at the age of 32, following the conclusion of his "sabbatical decade." From 1980 through 1990, he bicycled across America, island-hopped the South Pacific, traveled by train across India, and pedaled through Europe. A journalism graduate of the University of North Carolina at Chapel Hill, Ralph is editor of *The Avid Cruiser.* His award-winning work appears frequently in *Hemispheres*, United Airlines' in-flight magazine. Ralph splits his time between Asheville, North Carolina, and Copenhagen, Denmark, as well as cruise ships and port destinations worldwide.